THE
ADVENTURE
OF THE
AMERICAN PEOPLE

HENRY F. GRAFF · JOHN A. KROUT

TEACHER EDITION ANNOTATED

ARTHUR W. SPRAGUE, JR.
Chairman, Social Studies Department
Lyons Township High School
La Grange, Illinois

INTRODUCTION TO THE TEACHER EDITION

The history of a nation has a timeless fascination. This is because it is the chief source for understanding a people's ideals, hopes, successes, and even "tragic lessons." Students ought reasonably to expect that a textbook on the history of their own nation will be not only replete with excitement and color but also believable—faithful to the canons of good scholarship as well as to the narrative art. We have written *The Adventure of the American People* with an awareness that these standards of scholarship and narrative are constantly being changed.

The interests of young people are steadily broadening, and the questions they address to historical materials seem constantly more incisive. Young people, moreover, determinedly testing the ground rules of our culture, are invoking precepts of the social sciences. Having ourselves profited from the writings of fellow social scientists working in disciplines other than our own, we have included in our book those social-science conclusions that seem to be appropriate.

Young people, in particular, want history to be not only readable but also unvarnished—as we have aimed to write it. They know from observation—and they will find compelling new evidence in these pages—that "little people" as well as "big people" have shaped the American way of life.

Young people expect more than a one-track interpretation of history, for they know that "history" is only rarely a single theme of human experience. They realize that it is sometimes an account of the world of politics, sometimes of the world of fine art, and at other times of the world of advancing technology. It may focus on public entertainment or social change or urban and suburban problems or developments in sports or in agriculture—or on one of a myriad of other subjects.

Young people today know better than those of any previous generation that American history is inseparably tied, as this book shows in fresh fashion, to the history of mankind, and that what once were called "strange cultures" are today only "other cultures," with which Americans are daily involved. Finally, young people today have a remarkably well-developed sense of justice, which makes them measure the past more acutely, and often more harshly, than their parents did. They will find much to ponder in our book.

Particularly because we have written for young Americans who will shortly exercise the ballot, we have dealt with the nation's past without special pleading. We have been cognizant always that people from every section of the country and from many lands, diverse races, and various religious traditions have built the edifice of our republic. We hope that the students who read *The Adventure of the American People* and the teachers who teach from it will find satisfaction both in the peerless story it presents and in the presentation itself.

H. F. G.
J. A. K.

PART ONE (Chapters 1, 2, 3, 4, 5)

The transit of western European culture to the New World, a decisive event in history, is the great theme of this part. The explorations that led to new knowledge of the world are treated as outgrowths of European national and international needs, expressed through the achievements of individual men.

The enormous efforts of the Spanish to impress their culture on the New World during their quest for glory and gold, the French attempts to master the American wilderness, and the Dutch and Swedish labors are presented. But the origins of the English footholds in America are examined in great detail, since these were the enterprises that largely determined the nature of American culture.

The coming of the first English settlers to the eastern coast of the present-day United States was a political, religious, and social event. It was also a drama without precedent, and as such it supplied a tradition in the shaping of the new society that soon emerged: how a resistant land, under-used or badly used by the Indians, was transformed by determination and hard work into a land of abundance. The step-by-step establishment of the English settlements under a variety of circumstances is traced through a period of 130 years.

The relationship between the settlers' hopes and qualifications and the geographical environments they encountered is discussed in order to help explain the variety as well as the common characteristics in societies that developed. A leading purpose of the material on colonial history is to show how a new way of life arose in each colony out of disparate elements that included luck, moral and physical strength, and a worthy inheritance from the "old country."

The English colonial thrust westward and the French colonial thrust southward are described and analyzed in order to give the background of the French and Indian War. England's gigantic victory was felt throughout the world, but nowhere with more force than within the British Empire itself. Britain's efforts to "reorganize" the governing of its American colonies are described in relation to the diverse economies being formed in the New World.

Particular attention is paid to the growth of a mercantile economy in the northern colonies as compared with the plantation economy developing in the southern colonies. These differing economies and their accompanying styles of life are shown to be related to the total economy of the British Empire, then reaching the zenith of its power.

Britain's failure to retain the affection of many of the most influential citizens in America is treated as a result of shortsightedness, ignorance, and plain incompetence on the British side. On the American side, it is shown as the consequence of careful organizing, of economic fears and dislocations, and, above all, of the colonists' yearning to be as free as Englishmen at home. The break between the colonies and the mother country is examined not only as a military adventure on the part of Americans and their faithful foreign allies but also as an occasion for expressing and giving substance to the highest aspirations of free men. The Declaration of Independence is viewed as a document—penned in the heat of conflict—that became in time a beacon for free men everywhere.

The War for Independence is studied as an internationally significant occurrence, important both as a catalyst of world politics and as an episode that created the first *American* heroes. Also examined is the war's role in helping produce a new American society that achieved a wider distribution of land, an extended suffrage, the ending of vestiges of European feudalism, the beginnings of abolition, and the development of American nationalism.

PART TWO (Chapters 6, 7, 8, 9)

The dominating themes are the firm establishment of a national government under a written constitution and the creation of national strength. The background is laid in an examination of the Articles of Confederation and the government they set in motion. An analysis of its achievements and shortcomings reveals that a new frame of government was required.

The Constitution is also seen as the work of

3

remarkably able and purposeful men. Their characters and contributions and the nation's needs are discussed as interacting elements in the great work at Philadelphia.

The political triumph in obtaining the Constitution's ratification and the virtuosity of Washington's first administration are explored in detail. The combination of events—including emerging sectional differences—that produced first factions and then the forerunners of modern political parties is elaborated. The emphasis is on the contributions of Jefferson and Hamilton.

Jefferson's election and ensuing administration are treated as the logical culmination of the Federalist era rather than as sharp departures from the national policy of Washington and Hamilton. The opening decade of the 1800's witnessed continued territorial expansion and population growth as well as persistent involvement in Europe. The purchase of Louisiana and the Lewis and Clark expedition are key episodes for understanding the era.

Although the new country was already playing a large role in international politics, it was also looking inward—upon its strengths and weaknesses, its needs and expectations, and its internal rivalries and rapid changes. These facets are examined as elements helping to regularize the party and presidential systems and to stimulate the growth of nationalism.

The pressures of European politics, the increasing self-confidence and growth of the United States, and the growing requirements of American trade are viewed as helping to cause the War of 1812. The war itself is presented as an evil that Jefferson and Madison tried valiantly but ineffectively to avoid. Yet the war was less disastrous than people expected.

The Americans thought of the conflict as a second war of independence. In the years afterward they fashioned a new national outlook, found new symbols, and fostered economic growth to enable them to take advantage of the fortunate treaty of peace.

These events are discussed against a backdrop of party politics and new international problems. The steps leading to the Missouri Compromise are presented as further examples of sectional differences and as the curtain-

raisers on grimmer events. The historical perspective of the Monroe Doctrine is explained carefully. The purpose is to help students see the Doctrine as a declaration to the world of proud principles well rooted and universally accepted in the United States.

PART THREE (Chapters 10, 11, 12, 13)

The unifying theme is the burgeoning sectionalism in the face of national needs. Chapter 10 opens with an examination of Jackson's time, introducing the leading personalities and explaining how they interacted with each other. The chief issues of the day are seen as arising from the personal animosities of the leaders as well as from the conflicting needs of the various sections and groups of people.

The bank question is interpreted in the most up-to-date way. Included is the idea that the bank did not victimize American businessmen as much as it was itself a victim of political intrigue. The controversy is viewed as an aspect of the growth of free enterprise. The nullification controversy is also a subject of continuing interest to professional historians. The discussion shows it as having an effect on the enlargement of the presidency and also as being a reflection of the fears of the South.

Jackson's reelection is regarded as evidence that his policies satisfied large numbers of people, even though these policies outraged a significant portion of them, too. The election and administration of Martin Van Buren showed the extent to which national and sectional politics and economics had become intertwined, leading to the election of Harrison, the first Whig President. The unexpected elevation of Tyler to the White House shortly afterward pitted a strong-willed chief executive against a no-less-determined Congress.

The meaning of Jacksonian democracy is examined in the light of the searching scholarly work done in the last twenty years. The blindness of the Jacksonians on the matters of Negro slavery and of the rights of freedmen points up further the inheritance from the epoch.

The chronological thread of the book is broken at this point, and what follows is an analysis of the main sections of the country—North, South, and West. This is no mere recital of "the facts." It is, rather, an effort to present the salient features of life in each section to aid in understanding the significance the Union had in the mid-nineteenth century.

The North is divided into three "sub-Norths": New England, the middle Atlantic states, and the old Northwest. Each region is dissected to show its dominant economic, social, and, to a lesser extent, political features. Due attention is paid to the elements that gave the North a distinctive tone: manufacturing, increased immigration, the movement for reform (including abolition), the growth of cities, the development of a grain trade, and the construction of a transportation system.

The South is also analyzed to clarify especially its economic and social order. The development of the Cotton Kingdom is traced, along with its accompanying form of labor, Negro slavery. Slavery is looked at closely both as a means of producing the cash crop of the region and as an affront to the nation. The leading arguments in favor of the "peculiar institution" are set down, as well as the opposing arguments. A discussion of "The South's Predicament" places the South's dilemma in the perspective that the passage of time now permits.

The West is examined as being the forward edge of America's thrust to the Pacific. The centers of this expansionist activity are considered one by one: Oregon (with a full account of its early links to the fur trade), Utah (with a discussion of the emergence of Mormonism), and Texas (including the history of the state under the Mexican flag).

In looking at the Mexican War, "manifest destiny" is explained as an ingredient—along with baser ones. The military events are narrated dramatically to help students comprehend the results of the acquisition of new territory at the end of the war. Accounts of the gold rush and of the Gadsden Purchase end the part.

PART FOUR (Chapters 14, 15, 16)

The many-sided theme—the most tragic and heroic in nineteenth-century United States his-

tory—is the failure of the Union to solve its sectional rift peacefully. How the rift led to civil war, how the war was fought, and how the Union was re-created when the bloodshed was over are part of it.

The part opens with the aftermath of the Mexican War. The insistent issue of how to dispose of the newly acquired territories is treated in its intricacy in order to lay the groundwork for examining the complexities Congress faced.

The election of 1848, which brought Taylor, a war hero, to the presidency, is offered as an indispensable element in the unfolding drama. The ensuing crisis, which brought the country to the edge of disaster, is examined, with a spotlight on the principal senatorial figures—Clay, Calhoun, and Webster—now engaged in the last encounter of their careers. Their labors, their political positions, and the events (the deaths of Calhoun and President Taylor) involved in producing the Compromise of 1850 are presented.

Douglas and Seward, two important new decision-makers, are introduced. Douglas' motives in reopening the slavery question, by proposing the Kansas-Nebraska Bill, are looked at closely. The effects on party politics of the terrible struggle over Kansas are weighed carefully. Among them were the disappearance of the Whig party, the split-up of the Democrats, and the formation of the Republican party. Due attention is also paid to the publication of *Uncle Tom's Cabin,* the violent raids led by John Brown, and the depression of 1857.

Lincoln's rise to national stature is followed attentively. The Supreme Court's decision in the Dred Scott case—a major factor in the crisis of 1860—is juxtaposed to Lincoln's stand on the extension of slavery. The nomination and election of Lincoln are shown as decisive factors in the secession movement.

The conduct of the war is traced with emphasis on the intertwining of military and political history. The Confederacy is studied as both a constitutional and a political experiment. Its leaders are described and assessed as civil and military officers.

The strategy and tactics of the opposing armies are fascinating to Americans for their own sake and because they shed light on many of the nation's subsequent problems. They are set forth in some detail, along with close-ups of many of the field commanders. Lincoln's gradual mastery of his great burdens, including especially the discovery in Grant of a general equal to the Union's needs, is an important feature of the military discussion. The home fronts, North and South, are analyzed.

Lincoln's assassination is regarded by the authors as a telling but not determining event in the tortuous road to reunion. Johnson's troubles as President are described not only as by-products of the nation's new problems but as, in part, difficulties of his own making. The leading Radical Republicans are looked at closely, to understand the positions they took and to understand them as men with deeply-felt motives. The steps in reconstruction are traced with an emphasis on its history in the South, where the role of Negroes and poorer white people in politics was a significant factor.

The effort to uplift the freedmen through legislation and constitutional amendments is presented as an enterprise that unfortunately remained important unfinished business when the era formally ended. The history of the Grant administration is seen as it was: an unsavory interlude in the reconstruction of the Union. The period was completed when Hayes became President by the Compromise of 1877.

PART FIVE (Chapters 17, 18, 19, 20, 21)

The underlying theme is the process by which the United States developed its industrial strength and transformed itself into a nation with an urban rather than a rural outlook. The sectional, economic, and political aspects of the process are seen.

The growth of the factory system is shown to be a result of changes in production methods that were years in the making. The sources of capital and the economic impact of the Civil War are discussed, including favorable laws passed while southerners were absent from Congress.

The immediate results of industrialization are measured: its effect on small businessmen

and its influence on urbanization. The building of a railroad network is seen as fascinating in itself and as basic to industrialization. Particular emphasis is laid on the construction of the great trunk lines and the transcontinentals.

Industrial development and railroad expansion are viewed against a background of rising oil, coal, and steel businesses. The appearance of the giant businesses is studied, and their formation is followed through a close review of the careers of Rockefeller, Carnegie, and Morgan.

The "conquest" of the "last West," a phenomenon occurring simultaneously with the growth of industry, is treated in segments. Attention is paid to the Indian and his helplessness before the tidal waves of American settlers. The history of the cattle kingdom is presented both as a drama that embraces the cowboy as a new type of frontiersman and as a step in the development of the beef industry. The mining frontier is discussed as replete with enduring interest—and with consequences that included the making of new states.

Finally, the farmer of the "last West" is introduced, a beneficiary of the northern factories that helped meet the peculiar needs that the Great Plains environment imposed. They included fencing materials, access to water supplies, and methods of farming with scanty rain.

These far-reaching social and economic developments—in the East and in the West—were accompanied by a tendency for the nation to want its politics "as usual." The parade of Presidents from Hayes to Cleveland is watched with an awareness that politicians were finding it increasingly difficult to mask with platitudes the rumblings of discontent.

At this point the position of the laboring man is looked at closely. A new type of American, he is unable to escape the factory and is gradually becoming convinced that he will never be self-employed. The course of union-organizing is traced from the eighteenth century on, the discussion being reserved for this place in the book because it is not meaningful to talk of a working *class* of Americans before the Civil War era.

The line of labor leaders—from Sylvis to Gompers—is presented, along with their successes and tribulations. The vicissitudes of the labor movement are seen through the history of the Knights of Labor, the American Federation of Labor, and the labor struggles of the 1890's. The attitudes of the rest of society toward the needs of the laboring man are discussed, with particular stress on the role of the courts. Consideration of the "new" immigration as an additional factor in labor's plight ends this discussion.

The readjustment of society to industrialization concludes the part. The significance of cities as an inescapable factor of national life is shown—including the effect of urbanization on the individual person. The numerous urban and suburban issues are introduced.

The response of the farmer to the economic dislocations he faced is described. The slow decline of the farmer's prestige and wealth, relative to the rest of the population, is remarked upon; the start of the Granger movement and the creating of the Populist party are treated as efforts to escape the unbending harshness of the industrial world. The election of 1896 brings the discussion to a close. Both the farmers and the industrial workers were still searching for answers to their difficulties.

PART SIX (Chapters 22, 23, 24)

The widening reach of the United States as a power and its management of some attendant problems in international politics make up the theme of the part. But, throughout, the concurrent domestic developments are treated.

As the part opens, the interest of the United States in acquiring colonies is explored. The interest is seen as a combination of novel intellectual currents, enthusiasm aroused by young, dynamic leaders, and national security needs. The intricacies of United States relations with the slowly-boiling Cuban revolution—ending with the clash with Spain—are followed closely. The Spanish-American War is treated as an adventurist undertaking and as an outlet for humanitarian feelings. Since the performance of Theodore Roosevelt is of enduring consequence, it is studied in perspective.

The altered relationship of the United States to the other nations of the world is examined.

The special relationship the United States claimed with Asia, and, in particular, with China, is discussed through a full account of the significant "open-door" notes.

A developing tension between the republican ideals of the nation and the idea of owning colonies is dealt with in a presentation of the work of the United States in leading its overseas holdings toward self-government. This presentation provides a basis for weighing the record of America in regard to imperialism.

The era of progressivism is treated as a time in which Americans created new standards for improving government and for meeting the needs of an urban society. The political history of this period was dominated by Roosevelt, and he is treated as an exuberant and responsive figure who was appreciated by the people.

Although other powerful political figures on the scene are not neglected, the emphasis remains on the defiant social problems that greeted the new century. The evils that drew the attention of the "muckrackers" and the attempt to confront these evils through legislation are examined.

The events leading to the three-cornered presidential election of 1912 are examined in detail. The difficulties of the Taft administration are shown to be a result of historical circumstances that helped pave the way for the election of Wilson and the enactment of the last "progressive" laws.

A matching chapter follows that surveys the international currents playing upon the United States in the time of the progressives. Special attention is devoted to the circumstances surrounding the building of the Panama Canal. The actions of "T.R.," which many people regarded as regrettably high-handed, are described in detail to help students understand the continuing difficulties of satisfying diverse groups and needs. The further involvement of the United States in Latin American affairs is traced. Included is an account of the various crises that produced United States intervention and the willingness to support the ideas of the Roosevelt corollary to the Monroe Doctrine.

The entire presentation is related to the policy of "dollar diplomacy," a concept underlying the diplomacy of the era. The keenness of the conflict between asserted national requirements and the ideals of the Declaration of Independence is shown in Wilson's experience in United States–Mexican relations.

The policies of the United States toward Asia, and especially toward China and Japan, are treated as part of the widening involvement in world politics. The importance of the Russo-Japanese War is shown. The issues in United States–Asian affairs arising subsequently are studied with an eye to their significance for the United States.

A section on the participation of the United States—and of many private citizens—in the organized peace movement touches on the movement's place in trying to provide a cushion between the technologically-advanced nations of Europe. The part ends on the eve of the First World War, with the United States uncommitted by treaties but involved in potentially dangerous affairs almost everywhere.

PART SEVEN (Chapters 25, 26, 27, 28, 29, 30)

The requirement that the country defend itself against dire external threats is the overriding theme of this part. The chief subtheme is the vast change created by the new conception of government's role: to protect the individual from the vagaries of the business cycle. The role is taken to include opening political, economic, and social opportunity to everybody.

Chapter 25 wrestles with the problems of the First World War—what caused it, what effects it had on the neutral countries, what kind of leadership President Wilson offered, and how, in the end, the making of the peace proved to be a failure. The European background of the war is described briefly in order to establish America's links to the conflict.

The United States' efforts to remain neutral are recounted step-by-step. The alternatives open to Americans seemed to that generation to be comparably viable options, and they are presented as such. Wilson's transformation from being "too proud to fight" to being a vigorous war leader is traced.

The entrance of the United States into the war is described with an appreciation of the effectiveness of the A.E.F. as a fighting force and of the decisive role it had in the victorious outcome. The contribution of the home front is discussed, suggesting that the nation had mastered ways of mobilizing the war effort.

Wilson's efforts to help write a lasting peace are presented in detail, beginning with announcement of the Fourteen Points and ending with the deeply disappointing experience of being frustrated by the Senate. The personalities of Wilson and his chief opponents are seen as vital elements in the debacle. Wilson's stroke at the height of the crisis is discussed as an important factor but not the determining one in the outcome.

The postwar era is treated as a time when Americans both played and worked hard, almost desperately trying to avoid facing the economic difficulties bubbling beneath the surface of American life. President Harding is presented as he saw himself, as a man occupying a position that was too big for him. His death and the elevation of Coolidge are treated with an awareness that most Americans had less interest in politics than in "having a fling."

Some of the diversions that Americans turned to are discussed. Some of the larger issues of the day are also described in order to show significant contrasts: the closing off of immigration, the fear of radicals, the prohibition experiment, the spread of the automobile and its influence, and the growth of leisure-time activities. The arrival of the "air age" is written about at some length.

The opening of Hoover's administration on a high note of optimism and the quick plunge into an abyss of unparalleled national suffering is described with a sense of the complexity of the contributing elements. Hoover is seen to be a victim of conditions he did not make and could not control. The emergence of Franklin D. Roosevelt is analyzed as a major historical event. The New Deal is examined closely both to aid students in understanding its main elements and to help them see its significance in the course of the nation's development.

The sequel to the momentous happenings on the home front was the apparently unavoidable involvement of the United States in the world's international crises despite the formal avowal of isolation. The account begins in the days after the First World War and goes to the terrifying acceleration of first fascist and then Nazi aggression. The response of the United States from the time of the Washington Arms Conference and the Pact of Paris through the period of neutrality legislation is studied. The clear recognition by Roosevelt that the fate of the United States was bound up with that of the beleaguered democracies of western Europe is emphasized.

Despite the most ardent hopes, the United States entered the Second World War. The process by which the involvement occurred is followed closely, as is the course of the terrible fighting itself. Due attention is devoted to the intricate diplomacy of the war and of its relationship to the problems of the postwar era.

The final chapter, the longest in the book, opens with Truman's accession to the presidency. It details the background of the cold war and the shift of attention from one world crisis to another. The frustrating Korean War is treated as being a part of and as revealing many of the remarkable historical components through which it is now possible to comprehend the 1950's.

The burdens of the cold war carried over from one President's administration to another are studied as they pass from Truman's hands to Eisenhower's and then to Kennedy's and Johnson's. Although the presidential policies were similar, the differences that gave each administration its own character are seen.

In the background of stunning world events —including the creation of the atomic and hydrogen bombs—were, as always, almost equally startling domestic changes. These included the extension of some of the New Deal measures and attacks on the vast array of insistent urban problems. The pollution of the natural environment, persistent unemployment, and the rebuilding of the cores of the older cities are discussed. The rise of the civil rights movement is traced.

The continuing obligations of the United States to other nations are examined, and the dilemmas posed by the war in Vietnam are analyzed. A host of other public matters—including the new role of the Supreme Court—are looked at in expectation that they will take new and influential forms in the next few years.

TESTS

The following tests may be reproduced by the teacher for class use. The correct or best answer for each question is shown in boldface type preceding the question or by underlining, in the case of sentence-completion tests. Instructions for students taking each kind of test are as follows:

Multiple-Choice
In each blank fill in the letter that precedes the best choice.

Matching
Write before each item in Column A the letter that identifies the matching option from Column B.

Completion
Write the correct answers in the blanks.

CHAPTER 1
Multiple-Choice

B   1. The Crusades resulted in: *A*. recovery of the Holy Land from the Turks; *B*. development of trade with the East; *C*. the Renaissance; *D*. European nationalism.

C   2. The chief reason for the search for a new trade route to the East was the desire of western European countries to: *A*. acquire new possessions; *B*. spread their cultures; *C*. share more directly in Asian trade; *D*. learn more about the world.

D   3. A geographical advantage the western countries had in finding a new route to the East was: *A*. the knowledge that the earth is round; *B*. Prince Henry's observatory; *C*. their skilled navigators; *D*. their locations along the Atlantic Ocean.

C 4. The Treaty of Tordesillas: *A.* led to the discovery of Brazil; *B.* gave people a new idea of the world; *C.* set up the Line of Demarcation dividing between Spain and Portugal the land taken from the heathen; *D.* recognized Viking voyages to America.

A 5. The chief aims of the Spanish in America were to: *A.* find gold and save souls; *B.* acquire more land than the Portuguese; *C.* carry on a fur trade and encourage industry at home; *D.* occupy all of North and South America and spread Spanish culture there.

B 6. The Spanish left their culture in: *A.* the West Indies; *B.* the present-day Southwest and much of Latin America; *C.* the area explored by De Soto; *D.* what became Texas.

C 7. French exploration and colonization were centered in: *A.* regions along the Atlantic coast; *B.* the Mississippi Valley; *C.* the St. Lawrence Valley and Great Lakes area; *D.* Greenland.

D 8. French colonization failed because: *A.* it centered on gaining wealth; *B.* France had no colonial policy; *C.* the French made too few contacts with the Indians; *D.* Frenchmen did not approve of it.

C 9. "Culture" refers to a people's: *A.* refinement; *B.* civilization; *C.* customs, language, and religion; *D.* educational system.

A 10. Two American products that changed the lives of Europeans were: *A.* furs and gold; *B.* fish and lumber; *C.* wheat and barley; *D.* spices and horses.

Matching

Column A

i 1. Cortés
b 2. De Soto
h 3. Magellan
d 4. Pizarro
i 5. Cartier
c 6. Ponce de León
k 7. Coronado

c 8. Estavanico
a 9. Balboa
g 10. Verrazano

Column B

a. Pacific Ocean
b. Mississippi River
c. Florida
d. Inca Indians
e. Negro explorer
f. Watling Island
g. American coastline
h. *Victoria*
i. Mexico
j. Gulf of St. Lawrence
k. Southwest

Completion

1. The country that took the lead in the Age of Exploration was <u>Portugal.</u>

2. <u>Vasco da Gama</u> reached India by way of the Cape of Good Hope.

3. The land called America was named for <u>Amerigo Vespucci.</u>

4. Magellan proved that one could reach the East Indies by sailing <u>west.</u>

5. <u>Cabeza de Vaca</u> looked for the "Seven Cities of Cibola."

6. Spanish colonies were divided into two <u>viceroyalties.</u>

7. The Frenchmen who introduced European culture to Indians were <u>friars.</u>

8. <u>Jean Nicolet,</u> an associate of Champlain's, explored as far west as Green Bay and the Fox River.

9. Samuel de Champlain established a French settlement at <u>Quebec.</u>

10. Another name for a French fur trader is <u>voyageur.</u>

CHAPTER 2

Multiple-Choice

C 1. Arguments for establishing English colonies in America were that the colonies would: *A.* produce much gold and silver; *B.* provide new opportunities for poor Englishmen; *C.* be markets for English goods and sources of raw materials for manufacturing; *D.* trade with the Spanish.

A 2. The Virginia Company was formed because: *A*. colonization required the money of more than one man; *B*. Raleigh's expeditions had failed; *C*. the colony it formed was in Virginia; *D*. its members expected profits.

D 3. Virginia was divided into large plantations because: *A*. the planters had been farmers in England; *B*. land in America was plentiful; *C*. few Englishmen settled in it; *D*. the cultivation of tobacco required immense acreage.

B 4. Feudal customs disappeared in Maryland, since: *A*. the Calverts were democratic; *B*. land and opportunity were abundant in America; *C*. prices for land were high; *D*. settlers kept pushing west.

A 5. The Act of Toleration provided that: *A*. religious toleration would be granted to Christians; *B*. all settlers would enjoy religious toleration; *C*. only Catholics would be permitted to live in Maryland; *D*. Protestants would have religious freedom.

C 6. Offshoots of Massachusetts Bay Colony were established largely because: *A*. Massachusetts was too heavily populated; *B*. the town system of government was unsatisfactory; *C*. there were religious restrictions in Massachusetts and economic opportunities elsewhere; *D*. Massachusetts was a royal colony.

D 7. Slavery developed from the indenture system in Virginia because: *A*. the planters needed workers; *B*. the headright system failed; *C*. Indians could not be enslaved; *D*. Negroes were unable to escape to freedom.

B 8. The government of Massachusetts Bay Colony: *A*. was a democracy; *B*. was a government by church members; *C*. was controlled by men of differing religious views; *D*. was in the hands of separatists.

A 9. The town system: *A*. helped settle New England on a planned basis; *B*. was created by the General Court; *C*. provided religious and political freedom; *D*. provided proprietary government.

C 10. The first colonists were able to endure the difficulties they met in the new land because they: *A*. established representative government; *B*. received help from the Indians; *C*. were convinced that they were under divine protection; *D*. brought supplies with them.

Matching

Column A

f 1. John Cabot
i 2. Anne Hutchinson
h 3. John Smith
k 4. Calverts
a 5. Roger Williams
b 6. Thomas Hooker
j 7. Francis Drake
d 8. Sir Ferdinando Gorges
c 9. Sir Walter Raleigh
e 10. William Bradford

Column B

a. Providence, Rhode Island
b. Connecticut Valley
c. Roanoke Island
d. Council for New England
e. Plymouth Colony
f. first English claim in America
g. town meetings
h. Virginia
i. Portsmouth, Rhode Island
j. *Golden Hind*
k. Maryland

Completion

1. The English geographer who advocated establishing English colonies in America was Richard Hakluyt.

2. The first English child born in America was Virginia Dare.

3. The first representative assembly in American history was the House of Burgesses.

4. A colony dominated by one man with privileges from the king was a proprietary colony.

5. The first written constitution creating a government in North America was the Funda-

mental Orders.

6. The only Constitution the Plymouth Colony had was the Mayflower Compact.

7. Members of the Church of England who wished to form their own religious units were called separatists.

8. In 1630 many Puritans left England in what is called the great migration.

9. Members of the Church of England who wanted to remove from it all Catholic practices were called Puritans.

10. A food brought from South America for slaves in the English colonies was the peanut.

CHAPTER 3
Multiple-Choice

B 1. The story of New Netherland: *A.* shows that the Dutch were successful colonizers; *B.* reflects the rivalries of the chief European countries; *C.* illustrates the Dutch talent for self-government; *D.* indicates that the Dutch were friendly to their neighbors in the new land.

C 2. Americans resented the Navigation Acts because they: *A.* remained in force for years; *B.* interfered with Dutch trade; *C.* hurt their pride and their pocketbooks; *D.* bound the British Empire together.

B 3. Georgia was founded to: *A.* supply products for England; *B.* provide protection from the Spanish and homes for poor Englishmen; *C.* trade with the Spanish; *D.* extend the frontier.

A 4. City people in the colonies: *A.* knew about new ideas and developments in Europe; *B.* attended college more than farmers did; *C.* included many merchants; *D.* carried on the triangular trade.

D 5. English colonists in the 1760's: *A.* lived chiefly in cities; *B.* enjoyed economic freedom; *C.* were situated between the French and the Dutch; *D.* had a sense of community and felt their own economic strength.

C 6. Some advantages the colonists gained from the Navigation Acts were: *A.* England depended upon colonial products, and its navy was strengthened; *B.* colonial products were sold in Europe, and the colonists profited; *C.* England paid a bounty on certain products, and the only tar and tobacco sold in England were from the colonies; *D.* colonial trade was strengthened, and merchants profited.

B 7. North Carolina was separated from the rest of Carolina because it: *A.* received a separate governor; *B.* was settled by "rebels" who did not cooperate with English officials sent to Carolina; *C.* was a frontier community; *D.* wanted to form a feudal society.

A 8. Quakerism promoted democracy in Pennsylvania because: *A.* it led to a belief in social equality; *B.* Quakers arrived in America with their own wealth; *C.* Quakers were chiefly separatists; *D.* Penn obtained a democratic charter.

D 9. The Dutch profited from the English Civil War because: *A.* Cromwell decided to crush Spain; *B.* the Dutch manufactured military supplies for the war; *C.* the Dutch seized English ships; *D.* the Dutch enjoyed trade that was formerly England's.

C 10. In 1750 the American frontier extended farthest inland: *A.* along the Carolina borders; *B.* in Pennsylvania; *C.* in New York; *D.* in the Potomac River Valley.

Matching
Column A

g	1.	Peter Minuit
k	2.	John Lord Berkeley
h	3.	John Locke
i	4.	James Oglethorpe
j	5.	George Fox
f	6.	Oliver Cromwell
a	7.	Peter Stuyvesant
c	8.	Henry Hudson
e	9.	Josiah Child
d	10.	Kiliaen Van Rensselaer

Column B

a. conqueror of New Sweden
b. founder of Charleston
c. *Half Moon*
d. successful patroon
e. *A New Discourse of Trade*
f. Lord Protector of England
g. third director of New Netherland
h. English social philosopher
i. founded Georgia
j. founder of Quakerism
k. proprietor of New Jersey, Carolina

Completion

1. The chief Swedish contribution to frontier life was the <u>log cabin.</u>

2. Colonists in Carolina found conditions ideal for growing <u>rice.</u>

3. In the New England colonies, the chief occupation was <u>farming.</u>

4. The leading port in the South was <u>Charleston.</u>

5. Pitch, tar, and turpentine are called <u>naval stores.</u>

6. The first two schools for advanced learning in the colonies were <u>Harvard and Yale.</u>

7. The Navigation Act of 1651 resulted from English trade rivalry with the <u>Dutch.</u>

8. The middle colonies are often called the "bread colonies."

9. Virginia, Maryland, the Carolinas, and Georgia were known as the <u>staple</u> colonies.

10. Sweden established a colony in America along <u>Delaware Bay.</u>

CHAPTER 4

Multiple-Choice

B 1. Conflict developed between the French and the English in America because: *A.* both wished to control the St. Lawrence Valley; *B.* the English push west took them to the area claimed by the French; *C.* New Englanders smuggled sugar from the French West Indies; *D.* the English feared the Indians' support of the French.

D 2. The Treaty of Paris in 1763 provided that: *A.* Britain would receive the West Indies and the territory east of the Mississippi; *B.* France would give England all of Louisiana and Canada; *C.* Spain would give Florida to England and France would give Martinique and Guadeloupe to England; *D.* England would gain Florida and most of the French land east of the Mississippi, and Spain would get the rest of Louisiana.

A 3. The colonists hesitated to declare their independence because: *A.* loyalty to the king was ingrained, and a premature declaration might backfire; *B.* they disagreed about the reasons for a declaration; *C.* they feared French reaction; *D.* they knew war would follow.

B 4. The colonists believed that England had a right to: *A.* levy taxes on the colonies; *B.* regulate colonial trade but not tax the colonies; *C.* tax them only to help pay for the French and Indian War; *D.* control colonial trade.

C. 5. The Quebec Act disturbed the colonists because: *A.* it established the Roman Catholic religion in Massachusetts; *B.* it robbed them of land claimed by various colonies; *C.* it extended Quebec to lands claimed by colonies and recognized Roman Catholicism in the whole province; *D.* it helped to bind the province to England.

D 6. The colonists brought about repeal of the Stamp Act through: *A.* smuggling; *B.* physical violence; *C.* the Townshend Act; *D.* a boycott of English goods.

A 7. The Tea Act aroused the colonists because: *A.* it was a threat to free enterprise in the colonies; *B.* it favored one English company; *C.* it caused high prices for tea; *D.* it injured smugglers.

C 8. Steps the First Continental Congress took against England included: *A.* the organization of Committees of

Correspondence; *B.* the burning of the *Gaspee; C.* an agreement to not import British and West Indian goods and to encourage colonial manufacturing; *D.* a complete break with the mother country.

B 9. The Proclamation of 1763 angered the colonists because: *A.* fur traders could no longer make a living; *B.* colonists, including land speculators, had been expecting to use the land west of the Appalachians; *C.* it stirred up the Indians; *D.* England intended to raise revenue through its various provisions.

B 10. After 1763 the British Empire required: *A.* a strong king; *B.* a thoroughgoing reorganization; *C.* a stronger colonial policy; *D.* an increase in revenue.

Matching

Column A

f   1. Jacques Marquette
h   2. William Pitt
i   3. George Grenville
a   4. Samuel Adams
k   5. Thomas Paine
j   6. Crispus Attucks
c   7. Pontiac
d   8. Edward Braddock
g   9. James Wolfe
b   10. Thomas Jefferson

Column B

a. leader of patriots
b. wrote Declaration of Independence
c. Ottawa leader of conspiracy
d. leader of attack on Fort Duquesne
e. wrote Treaty of Paris
f. explored Mississippi River to Arkansas River
g. captured Quebec
h. English prime minister
i. sponsor of Sugar Act
j. American Negro who was killed at "Boston Massacre"
k. wrote *Common Sense*

Completion

1. The man who claimed the Mississippi Valley for France was <u>Robert Cavelier, Sieur de La Salle.</u>

2. The center of French settlement in America was <u>Quebec.</u>

3. Benjamin Franklin's plan to unite the colonies was <u>the Albany Plan of Union.</u>

4. The people affected most by the Stamp Act were <u>lawyers and newspaper editors.</u>

5. Two patriot organizations were the <u>Sons of Liberty</u> and <u>Committees of Correspondence.</u>

6. Representatives from twelve colonies met in September, 1774, in <u>the First Continental Congress.</u>

7. England's plan to allow the direct sale of taxed tea in the colonies led to the <u>Boston Tea Party.</u>

8. The opening battles of the American Revolution were at <u>Concord</u> and <u>Lexington.</u>

9. The Declaration of Independence is divided into <u>two</u> parts.

10. The "Intolerable Acts" were Parliament's punishment of the city of <u>Boston.</u>

CHAPTER 5

Multiple-Choice

C 1. Problems arose during the Revolution involving: *A.* supplies, health, and treason; *B.* leadership, morale, and health; *C.* health, discipline, and supplies; *D.* English strategy, morale, and the Continental Congress.

A 2. The Continental Congress spent much of its time: *A.* trying to influence the states to contribute more to the conduct of the Revolution; *B.* planning military campaigns; *C.* dealing with the Indians; *D.* raising money.

D 3. Three important foundation stones of American democracy were: *A.* a lift for the underdog, creation of a social revolution, and acceptance of government by committees; *B.* the expansion of enterprise, new state constitutions, and the regulation of trade; *C.* the Treaty of Alliance in 1778, the establishment of new standards, and the abolition of slavery; *D.* the liberalization of land ownership, separation of church and state, and abolition of slavery in northern states.

B 4. England agreed to the generous terms of the Treaty of Paris (of 1783) because: *A.* it was defeated; *B.* it believed that an independent United States would be economically dependent on the mother country; *C.* Americans were clever negotiators; *D.* the United States agreed to pay the Loyalists for any losses they had suffered.

A 5. After the Revolution, Americans had to deal with problems about: *A.* regulation of trade, Indian relations, and the power of weakness of government; *B.* relations with the French, the dissatisfactions of Negro slaves, and the breakup of families; *C.* paying the war veterans, the use of the Newfoundland fisheries, and settling the West; *D.* veterans, debts, and the Indians.

C 6. Ideas that the American Revolution established were that: *A.* enterprising men had to depend upon their own resources, the United States would become mechanized, and millions of people would migrate to America; *B.* Americans would progress, Negroes would be freed, and the French could not be trusted; *C.* just government derives its power from the consent of the governed, all men are created equal, and every human being has a right to life, liberty, and the pursuit of happiness; *D.* the death rate should be lowered, leisure time increased, and scientific progress quickened.

D 7. Paper money issued by the Continental Congress fell in value because: *A.* people would not accept it; *B.* imports decreased; *C.* wages lagged; *D.* it was not backed by hard money.

B. 8. As prices rose out of control during the Revolution: *A.* trade was reduced; *B.* groups of people turned against each other; *C.* speculators were encouraged; *D.* smuggling first developed.

D 9. Americans in the late 1700's were suspicious of governors and judges because: *A.* these officials were often men born in England; *B.* these officials were often wealthy; *C.* these officials were pro-English; *D.* English rule had made them afraid of government they could not control.

A 10. The conservatives believed in strong property qualifications for voters because they: *A.* had no faith in the people's ability to rule themselves; *B.* were themselves wealthy; *C.* did not want western frontiersmen to vote; *D.* wanted protection against poorer Americans.

Matching

   Column A
b 1. John Burgoyne
h 2. Benedict Arnold
i 3. Robert Morris
a 4. Benjamin Rush
k 5. Ethan Allen
c 6. John Paul Jones
f 7. Charles Cornwallis
j 8. Benjamin Franklin
e 9. Nathanael Greene
d 10. George Rogers Clark
   Column B
a. Physician General in the Revolution
b. English general at Saratoga
c. American naval hero in Revolution
d. American leader of a military expedition to old Northwest
e. American leader of southern campaigns
f. British general who surrendered to Americans at Yorktown
g. British leader who attacked New York
h. traitor to Americans in Revolution
i. manager of finances in Revolution
j. negotiator of Treaty of Paris in 1783
k. leader of Green Mountain Boys

Completion

   1. The condition in which money is more plentiful than goods and in which prices rise is <u>inflation.</u>

   2. The turning point in the American Revolution was the <u>Battle of Saratoga.</u>

3. At Yorktown American forces were joined by <u>De Grasse and his fleet.</u>

4. Most new state constitutions did not provide a system of <u>checks and balances.</u>

5. Two feudal laws that were abolished in the Revolutionary era were the laws of <u>entail</u> and <u>primogeniture.</u>

6. In the Treaty of Paris in 1783, Florida was turned over to <u>Spain.</u>

7. Colonists who remained loyal to the king were called <u>Loyalists.</u>

8. A one-house legislature is called a <u>unicameral</u> legislature.

9. Separation of church and state was accomplished by cutting off state support for <u>established churches.</u>

10. The author of *Letters from an American Farmer* was <u>Michel de Crèvecoeur.</u>

CHAPTER 6

Multiple-Choice

A   1. England aroused resentment among Americans after the Revolution by: *A.* refusing to turn over the trading posts located between Lakes Champlain and Superior; *B.* carrying on intrigues with western frontiersmen; *C.* not trading with them; *D.* refusing to let them navigate the Mississippi.

C   2. The creation of a strong national government was the result of: *A.* the Mount Vernon Conference; *B.* Shays' Rebellion; *C.* the attempt to improve relations between and among the states; *D.* the government under the Articles of Confederation.

B   3. The chief difficulty farmers had after the Revolution was that: *A.* there was too much paper money; *B.* they could earn very little hard money; *C.* their mortgages were foreclosed; *D.* they were debtors.

D   4. The Connecticut compromise provided that: *A.* the slave trade be abolished; *B.* the President be chosen by an electoral college; *C.* the Virginia plan be adopted; *D.* there would be a two-house legislature, with representation in the lower house based on population and with equal representation of all the states in an upper house.

B   5. A federal union is one in which: *A.* there is a separation of powers; *B.* self-governing states are joined under a central government that handles common problems while the states retain sole power over local matters; *C.* there is a strong executive department; *D.* the Constitution is the supreme law of the land.

A   6. Under the Constitution the states: *A.* keep all powers not expressly delegated to Congress; *B.* levy taxes; *C.* elect the President; *D.* can issue paper money.

C   7. After 1783 Spain tried to: *A.* win back Florida; *B.* develop trade with the United States; *C.* acquire the land bounded by the Ohio River, the Mississippi, and the Appalachians; *D.* get New Orleans.

D   8. The Constitutional Convention was called to: *A.* discuss improving the navigation of the Potomac River; *B.* discard the Articles of Confederation; *C.* establish a new relationship between the states and the nation; *D.* revise the Articles.

B   9. A guarantee against infringement of civil liberties is found in: *A.* Article 1 of the Constitution; *B.* the first ten amendments; *C.* the federal principle; *D.* the Preamble to the Constitution.

A   10. The Constitution's system of checks and balances means that: *A.* one branch of the government may counter but not paralyze the actions of another; *B.* Congress can check the President; *C.* the Supreme Court was created by the President; *D.* Congress chooses judges for the Court.

Matching

Column A

i   1. Manasseh Cutler

j   2. Noah Webster

k   3. Daniel Shays

h   4. Alexander Hamilton

a   5. James Madison
g   6. George Clinton
b   7. William Paterson
c   8. Richard Henry Lee
d   9. Thomas Jefferson
e   10. Edmund Randolph
     Column B
a. "Father of the Constitution"
b. proposed the small-state plan
c. Virginia Antifederalist
d. father of American land policy
e. introduced large-state plan
f. planned the electoral college
g. Antifederalist from New York
h. helped write *The Federalist*
i. negotiated with Congress for land in Northwest Territory
j. known for dictionaries and spellers
k. leader of rebellion against issuing of judgments against debtors

Completion

1. Leaders in the early days of the United States considered personal integrity a prime qualification for office.

2. The plan of government adopted in 1777 was the Articles of Confederation.

3. Powers exercised by both the national and the state governments are called concurrent powers.

4. The first ten amendments to the Constitution are called the Bill of Rights.

5. The clause in the Constitution authorizing Congress to make all laws necessary and proper for executing its enumerated powers is called the elastic clause.

6. A person to whom money is owed is called a creditor.

7. The method of organizing the Northwest Territory was described in the provisions of the Northwest Ordinance.

8. The provision that Section 16 in every township should be set aside for the support of public schools was a part of the Land Ordinance of 1785.

9. The most difficult problems the new government faced in 1781 were related to the western lands.

10. The delegates to the Constitutional Convention are called the "Founding Fathers."

CHAPTER 7

Multiple-Choice

C   1. Jay's treaty angered Americans because it: *A.* stopped trade with England; *B.* violated American neutrality; *C.* did not settle the problems affecting English-American relations; *D.* ignored frontiersmen.

A   2. The X Y Z affair involved: *A.* a French demand for a bribe and a loan; *B.* a declaration of war; *C.* a change in Adams' Cabinet; *D.* James Monroe.

B   3. Jefferson held the belief that: *A.* men are by nature weak; *B.* people have the ability to solve their own problems; *C.* executive leadership should be strong; *D.* a government should be strong.

D   4. Hamilton believed that the national debt was: *A.* a public burden; *B.* a cause for alarm; *C.* the responsibility of the states; *D.* a "public blessing."

C   5. Through his economic program, Hamilton: *A.* made the United States powerful; *B.* applied strict construction of the Constitution; *C.* established the credit of the United States; *D.* authorized a bank.

A   6. The handling of the Whisky Rebellion showed: *A.* the power of the federal government; *B.* resistance to the federal government; *C.* the poor transportation of the day; *D.* opposition to internal taxes on certain products.

B   7. Political parties arose in the United States on account of: *A.* anti-English feelings; *B.* the differences over Hamilton's financial policy; *C.* the French Revolution; *D.* the Virginia and Kentucky resolutions.

D   8. Washington's decision in 1793 to keep the United States neutral was based on the fact that: *A.* Talleyrand was making trouble; *B.* the French revolutionists were going to extremes; *C.* England and France were at war; *D.* American prosperity depended on good American-English relations.

B 9. By the Treaty of Greenville, Indian chiefs: *A.* surrendered to Americans; *B.* gave up their rights to most of what is now Ohio; *C.* compromised with Americans; *D.* formed an alliance with the English.

A 10. Hamilton's Report on Manufactures was the most farseeing because: *A.* it spoke of the development of American industry; *B.* it recommended protective tariffs; *C.* it encouraged immigration; *D.* it said the United States would prosper.

Matching

Column A

i 1. Edmond Genêt
f 2. John Jay
g 3. John Adams
h 4. Aaron Burr
k 5. Charles C. Pinckney
a 6. Anthony Wayne
j 7. Alexander Hamilton
c 8. James Monroe
b 9. Edmund Randolph
e 10. Robert R. Livingston

Column B

a. defeated Indians at Fallen Timbers
b. Washington's attorney general
c. American minister to France
d. wrote Virginia and Kentucky resolutions
e. administered oath of office to President Washington
f. first Chief Justice
g. second President
h. Republican presidential candidate in 1800
i. French minister to United States
j. first Secretary of the Treasury
k. Federalist presidential candidate in 1800

Completion

1. The national debt was of two kinds— foreign and domestic.

2. Internal taxes on the sale of certain goods are called excise taxes.

3. Duties that raise the prices on manufactured goods imported from abroad are called protective tariffs.

4. In the Virginia and Kentucky resolutions, Jefferson and Madison expressed the principle of states' rights.

5. The idea that the powers of Congress are specifically named in the Constitution is called strict construction.

6. Three laws passed by the Federalist Congress in 1798 to check the growing power of the Republicans were the Naturalization Act and the Alien and Sedition Acts.

7. The charter of the first Bank of the United States ran for twenty years.

8. The location of the boundary of Florida along the 31st parallel was provided for in Pinckney's Treaty.

9. In his last year in office, Washington delivered a farewell address.

CHAPTER 8

Multiple-Choice

D 1. Macon's Bill No. 2 provided that: *A.* troops be sent to overcome the Indians of the Northwest Territory; *B.* the Nonintercourse Act be repealed; *C.* western farmers could not sell products to England; *D.* Americans could trade with every country.

A 2. At the Hartford Convention Federalists: *A.* proposed amendments to the Constitution; *B.* demanded that the War of 1812 be ended; *C.* protested the burning of Washington; *D.* planned a defense of New England.

C 3. A serious disadvantage that Americans had in the War of 1812 was that: *A.* they had to capture Canada; *B.* Indians were on the warpath; *C.* the country was not united; *D.* the President favored peace.

C 4. Judicial review: *A.* was created by the Judiciary Act of 1801; *B.* was established by the Constitution; *C.* is the power of the Supreme Court to declare a law of Congress unconstitutional; *D.* is a power of Congress.

B 5. Jefferson believed that errors in judgment on the part of the people could be prevented by: *A.* the use of arms; *B.* giving them full information about their affairs; *C.* their leaders; *D.* their good sense.

D 6. The case of *Marbury* v. *Madison* was a result of: *A.* the political activity of federal judges; *B.* the Judiciary Act of 1789; *C.* a writ of mandamus; *D.* the Republicans' refusal to issue commissions of office to Adams' "midnight judges."

A 7. Jefferson wanted to buy Louisiana because: *A.* the French had acquired it from Spain; *B.* the people of Santo Domingo had rebelled; *C.* Napoleon wanted to conquer Canada; *D.* Americans thought Florida was transferred to France.

C 8. Federalists objected to the Louisiana Purchase because: *A.* it cost much money; *B.* it depended upon loose construction of the Constitution; *C.* they thought it might lead to a loss in the influence of trade and business; *D.* Jefferson was a Republican.

D 9. Although the War of 1812 was a military failure, Americans had learned that: *A.* they could obtain an honorable peace; *B.* the Treaty of Ghent solved the problems that had led to war; *C.* both sides were ready for peace; *D.* they needed greater national unity.

B 10. American strategy in the War of 1812 was to win Canada, because: *A.* Canada belonged to England; *B.* it was impossible to defeat the British on the sea; *C.* the War Hawks favored taking Canada; *D.* New England wanted Canadian trade.

Matching

Column A

f 1. James Bridger
h 2. Thomas Jefferson
i 3. Francis Scott Key
k 4. Henry Clay
b 5. Lord Nelson
j 6. James P. Beckwourth
a 7. William Clark
c 8. Toussaint L'Ouverture
d 9. John Marshall
e 10. Zebulon Pike

Column B

a. took part in Lewis and Clark expedition
b. English admiral
c. led rebellion in Santo Domingo
d. established judicial review
e. explored southwestern Louisiana
f. "Mountain Man"
g. first Secretary of War
h. first Secretary of State
i. wrote the national anthem
j. Negro explorer of the West
k. War Hawk

Completion

1. In 1801 the United States went to war with the Barbary pirates.

2. Jefferson belonged to the Republican party.

3. Louisiana was purchased for the sum of $15,000,000.

4. The American frigate that won a battle with the *Java* is called "Old Ironsides."

5. An American victory after the War of 1812 had been ended involved the British attempt to capture New Orleans.

6. The peace treaty that ended the War of 1812 was the Treaty of Ghent.

7. The hero of the most important naval battle on the Great Lakes was Oliver Hazard Perry.

8. The law that provided that all trade between the United States and foreign countries would stop was the Embargo Act.

9. The law that reopened trade with all countries except Britain and France was the Nonintercourse Act.

10. The Vice-President who stood trial for treason in 1807 was Aaron Burr.

CHAPTER 9

Multiple-Choice

C 1. Southerners opposed high tariff rates because: *A.* they preferred the "American system"; *B.* high tariff rates enriched manufacturers; *C.* there was little manufacturing in the South; *D.* they favored states' rights.

D 2. The great importance of the decision in the case of *Fletcher* v. *Peck* is that:

A. Georgia could not break a contract; B. it paid respect to the states' independence; C. it forbade the sale of western land to land companies; D. it established that the Supreme Court has the right to declare a state law unconstitutional.

B 3. John C. Calhoun supported internal improvements in 1817 because he: A. thought the South would benefit from them; B. believed they would help unite the country; C. disapproved of sectionalism; D. was a nationalist all his life.

A 4. The importance of the Monroe Doctrine is that it: A. became a keystone of American foreign policy; B. contributed to American nationalism; C. showed American independence of Britain; D. kept European countries from colonizing in America.

A 5. The case of *Gibbons* v. *Ogden* became famous because: A. in his decision the Chief Justice declared that Congress alone could control interstate and foreign commerce; B. steamboats and railroads were important; C. states were seeking to control certain waters; D. monopolies were wrong.

C 6. The election of 1824 was thrown into the House of Representatives because: A. the Constitution was followed; B. there were too many candidates; C. no candidate had a majority; D. Jackson had 99 electoral votes.

A 7. The Missouri Compromise helped postpone a serious sectional disagreement by: A. maintaining the political balance in the Senate; B. forbidding slavery north of 36° 30′ in the Louisiana Purchase; C. giving the South a slave state; D. affirming that Congress could prohibit slavery in a state.

D 8. John Quincy Adams was attacked by westerners and southerners because: A. he was a Republican; B. Jackson disliked him; C. he appointed Clay as Secretary of State; D. they believed that he planned mainly to aid eastern

businessmen.

C 9. The Republicans had "outfederalized the Federalists," it was said, since: A. the Federalists had died out; B. everybody was Republican; C. the Republicans supported the Bank of the United States, a tariff, and manufacturing; D. the Republicans favored New England.

B 10. John Marshall spoke for nationalism at a time when: A. there was an "Era of Good Feelings"; B. states' rights feeling was strong; C. he was Chief Justice; D. he had no opposition.

Matching

Column A

f   1. John Quincy Adams
k   2. John Marshall
i   3. Henry Clay
a   4. Jesse P. Thomas
j   5. Andrew Jackson
e   6. Luis de Onís
b   7. Aaron Ogden
c   8. William H. Crawford
g   9. William Thornton
d   10. George Canning

Column B

a. proposed the Missouri Compromise
b. held a steamboat monopoly
c. presidential candidate in 1824
d. British foreign secretary
e. Spanish minister to the United States
f. Secretary of State for Monroe
g. provided design for the national Capitol
h. supported second United States bank
i. proposed the "American system"
j. captured West Florida
k. made Supreme Court strongly national

Completion

1. Two states that entered the Union by the terms of the Missouri Compromise were <u>Maine</u> and <u>Missouri.</u>

2. After 1815 the powers of Europe formed a league that is wrongly called <u>the "Holy Alliance."</u>

3. A book that helped create a distinctively American language was <u>Webster's dictionary.</u>

4. Five symbols of growing national unity

after the War of 1812 were <u>Old Glory, the Fourth of July, the bald eagle, the Liberty Bell, and Uncle Sam.</u>

5. The steamboat that set a speed record in navigating the Ohio and Mississippi rivers was <u>the *Vesuvius.*</u>

6. In 1818 the border between the United States and British North America between the Rockies and the Lake of the Woods was fixed <u>at the 49th parallel.</u>

7. The tariff law enacted in 1828 was called <u>the "Tariff of Abominations."</u>

8. In 1828 Jackson defeated <u>John Quincy Adams</u> in the presidential election.

9. The population of the United States by the end of the 1820's was nearing <u>13,000,000.</u>

10. Marshall declared that a state may not tax an agency of the federal government in his decision about the case called <u>*McCulloch* v. *Maryland.*</u>

CHAPTER 10
Multiple-Choice

B   1. Jackson's Indian policy was: *A.* military conquest; *B.* removal to western lands; *C.* to place them on reservations in desirable areas; *D.* coöperation with them.

A   2. In the Webster-Hayne debate, the issue was: *A.* the nature of the Union; *B.* southern views; *C.* strict-construction arguments; *D.* loose construction of the Constitution.

D   3. The doctrine of nullification was that: *A.* the tariff was unjust; *B.* the states had created the national government; *C.* a state could withdraw from the Union; *D.* a state could declare a congressional law unconstitutional and refuse to obey it.

C   4. Jackson has been called the "maker of the modern presidency" because he: *A.* developed the national nominating convention; *B.* accepted majority rule; *C.* showed what enormous power a President can use; *D.* attracted much attention.

A   5. Jacksonian democracy means: *A.* the changes in the people's ideas of democracy between 1820 and 1840; *B.* belief in an active government; *C.* close touch with the presidency; *D.* faith in the good sense of the people.

C   6. The weakness of the Age of Jackson was that: *A.* professional politicians appeared; *B.* rabble-rousers might influence the people; *C.* conditions of important minorities were ignored; *D.* banking laws were lax.

B   7. A side of Jacksonian democracy that Jefferson would have particularly approved was: *A.* poetry; *B.* the growth of free public schools and cheap newspapers; *C.* the spoils system; *D.* the passing of "King Caucus."

D   8. An aspect of Jacksonian democracy that Hamilton would have rejoiced in was: *A.* the acceptance of rule by the majority; *B.* the extension of the right to vote; *C.* more liberal state constitutions; *D.* the development of free enterprise.

A   9. Jackson lost southern support because: *A.* he sternly opposed South Carolina's nullification of tariffs; *B.* the Maysville veto disturbed southerners; *C.* he was an enemy of Henry Clay; *D.* he removed the Eastern Indians to western lands.

C   10. Jackson encouraged the growth of business by: *A.* heeding city needs; *B.* showing the advantages of a free society; *C.* easing credit and removing government monopolies; *D.* killing the Bank of the United States.

Matching
Column A

g   1. John C. Calhoun
k   2. Nicholas Biddle
j   3. Martin Van Buren
h   4. Walt Whitman
a   5. Daniel Webster
b   6. John H. Eaton
d   7. Robert Y. Hayne
e   8. Black Hawk
i   9. Henry Clay
c   10. William Henry Harrison

Column B

a. Secretary of State for Harrison and Tyler
b. Jackson's Secretary of War
c. "Tippecanoe"
d. defended the states' right to oppose federal interference in sale of public land
e. led war on the upper Mississippi
f. nullified the Force Bill
g. wrote *Exposition and Protest*
h. poet of democracy
i. Whig who sought the presidency
j. succeeded Jackson as President
k. president of Bank of the United States

Completion

1. The Erie Canal linked the Hudson River with the Great Lakes.

2. The chief issue of the election of 1832 concerned the second Bank of the United States.

3. In 1834 members of a new political party adopted the name "Whig."

4. Jackson's method of filling government jobs is called the spoils system.

5. Jeffersonian democracy was concerned mainly with people who were farmers, but Jacksonian democracy included city dwellers.

6. A source of trouble in Jackson's Cabinet was the Eaton affair.

7. The Maine boundary dispute was settled by the Webster-Ashburton Treaty.

8. State banks that issued paper money without proper backing were called "wildcat banks."

9. The Independent Treasury Act provided that federal money be placed in subtreasuries.

10. The withdrawal of a state from the Union is called secession.

CHAPTER 11

Multiple-Choice

D 1. Free public schools are necessary in a democracy because: *A.* they open the door to opportunity; *B.* life becomes increasingly complicated; *C.* people support them through taxes; *D.* self-governing people must be well informed.

C 2. A democratic belief held by northerners was that: *A.* there was no need to fear the future; *B.* discrimination against Negroes was wrong; *C.* free men could improve their own situations; *D.* everyone should be allowed to vote.

B 3. By 1840 most northerners made their living through: *A.* farming; *B.* trade and manufacturing; *C.* child labor; *D.* the growth of cities.

C 4. Technological changes that encouraged urban growth were: *A.* garbage removal and sewer lines; *B.* company stores and improved ships; *C.* machine-made nails, standard sizes of sawn lumber, and macadam; *D.* piped-in water and public policing.

A 5. The contributions of immigrants were: *A.* money, minds, and muscles; *B.* an increase in population and public schools; *C.* the growth of heavy industry and the development of mining; *D.* settlement of the West and an interest in schools.

B 6. The reform movement was encouraged by: *A.* free public education; *B.* leisure time and ideas of reform from abroad; *C.* slavery; *D.* technological advances.

D 7. New Englanders strongly supported the Union because: *A.* Daniel Webster was a New Englander; *B.* they started public education; *C.* they traded with the West; *D.* the "Yankee exodus" gave them strong ties with all parts of the country.

A 8. Free Negroes were unhappy because: *A.* they suffered discrimination; *B.* abolitionists ignored them; *C.* they lived in cities; *D.* they could not own property.

C 9. The Waltham system meant that: *A.* strikes were forbidden; *B.* wages were low and the workday was long; *C.* women employees lived in dormitories and were closely supervised; *D.* families worked together.

B 10. In the first half of the 1800's factory workers lived near the factories because: *A.* factories were located in cities; *B.* transportation was poor and the workday was long; *C.* young workers had a 10 P.M. curfew; *D.* the workers signed yellow-dog contracts.

Matching

Column A

i   1. Henry David Thoreau
k   2. Dorothea L. Dix
h   3. James G. Birney
a   4. Elizabeth Cady Stanton
j   5. William Lloyd Garrison
c   6. Horace Mann
f   7. Theodore Weld
e   8. Robert Rantoul
d   9. Angelina Grimké
g   10. De Witt Clinton

Column B

a. worked for woman's rights
b. established steamboat lines
c. worked to establish public schools
d. most important woman abolitionist
e. advocated the 10-hour day
f. made a career of abolition
g. governor who backed the Erie Canal
h. Alabama abolitionist
i. wrote *Walden*
j. published *The Liberator*
k. improved the lot of the insane

Completion

1. The first city in the old Northwest to become one of the nation's ten largest cities was <u>Cincinnati.</u>

2. In 1810 the National Road extended from <u>Cumberland,</u> Maryland, to <u>Wheeling,</u> on the <u>Ohio</u> River.

3. Two kinds of early roads were <u>turnpikes</u> and <u>plank roads.</u>

4. The most important cause of economic change in the 1800's was <u>the railroad.</u>

5. Most reformers lived in <u>the North.</u>

6. The largest numbers of immigrants settled in <u>the middle Atlantic states.</u>

7. The railroad center of the West was <u>Chicago.</u>

8. The success of <u>the Erie Canal</u> caused the "canal craze."

9. Most railroad lines linked the Northeast to <u>the old Northwest.</u>

10. The school that started coeducation was Oberlin College.

CHAPTER 12

Multiple-Choice

B   1. By the 1850's voices of reformers were scarcely heard in the South because: *A.* southerners depended on slavery; *B.* southerners associated reform with abolition, and few immigrants went to the South; *C.* most reformers lived in the North; *D.* southerners resented interference from northerners.

D   2. Two effects of the cotton gin were to: *A.* allow farmers to grow short-staple cotton and to remove its seeds easily; *B.* reduce the number of slaves and to relieve them of hard work; *C.* revive the declining seaboard and make it prosperous; *D.* permit cotton-raising on a large scale and to strengthen slavery.

A   3. Immigrant workers seldom settled in the South because: *A.* it offered little factory work and there was competition from slave labor; *B.* they generally entered at New York City and had little money to travel farther; *C.* southerners accepted them less readily than northerners did; *D.* southern states passed laws against collective bargaining for higher wages.

B   4. The South failed to industrialize chiefly because: *A.* southerners had no mineral resources; *B.* southerners did not invest money in industry; *C.* it had poor transportation; *D.* slavery was a way of life.

C   5. The differences between the North and the South between 1830 and 1860 were caused by: *A.* geography; *B.* the separation of northerners from southerners; *C.* history; *D.* censorship of mail entering the South.

D   6. The reason few railroads were built between the Gulf states and the rest of the South was that: *A.* there was no money for them; *B.* river transportation was adequate; *C*. the terrain made building railroads difficult; *D*. the light freight such railroads carried from the ports to the interior made profits small.

A   7. The South had less foreign trade than the North because: *A*. southerners imported little and did not spend money on merchandising and banking; *B*. there were few good harbors in the South; *C*. cotton planters owed money to northerners; *D*. southerners had few factories.

B   8. It was a mistake for southerners to fail to build a railroad between Charleston and Cincinnati because: *A*. Charleston did not receive cotton from interior plantations; *B*. the railroad would have helped to link the South with the old Northwest; *C*. Cincinnati was a center of pork-packing plants; *D*. both the South and the old Northwest were farming areas.

D   9. In 1860 the Cotton Kingdom extended from South Carolina westward to: *A*. Louisiana; *B*. Missouri; *C*. Arkansas; *D*. central Texas.

B   10. The South's predicament by the 1850's was that: *A*. the North refused to reopen the slave trade; *B*. it staked everything on continuing prosperity based on cotton-growing; *C*. it had few railroads; *D*. it had refused to try reform.

Matching

Column A

f   1. John Chavis
j   2. Thomas Dew
i   3. Harriet Tubman
a   4. George Fitzhugh
b   5. Hinton Rowan Helper
g   6. James H. Hammond
k   7. Eli Whitney
d   8. William Harper
e   9. Nat Turner
h   10. James De Bow

Column B

a. favored adopting slavery in the North
b. said slavery was making the South poor

c. wanted the slave trade reopened
d. wrote *Memoir on Slavery*
e. leader of a slave insurrection
f. free Negro who operated a school in North Carolina
g. governor of South Carolina
h. best-known southern editor
i. former slave who helped slaves escape
j. southern advocate of slavery
k. invented the cotton gin

Completion

1. "Manumit" means <u>to free from slavery.</u>
2. The southerners who occupied the highest social and political position were <u>the cotton planters.</u>
3. Many slaves escaped to Canada and freedom by means of <u>the underground railroad.</u>
4. The two highest-ranking southern ports were <u>New Orleans</u> and <u>Mobile.</u>
5. Before 1830 the great majority of abolitionists lived in <u>the South.</u>
6. The largest iron company in the South was the <u>Tredegar Iron Works,</u> in <u>Virginia.</u>
7. Southerners referred to slavery as <u>the "peculiar institution."</u>
8. Southerners who owned no slaves made up <u>three-fourths</u> of the population.
9. A country in Africa originally established as a home for freed American slaves is named <u>Liberia.</u>
10. The chief market for southern cotton was in <u>England.</u>

CHAPTER 13 (Covers "The Long View")

Multiple-Choice

B   1. The annexation of Texas was delayed for a time because: *A*. Americans feared Mexico's reaction; *B*. Americans feared to reopen the issue about the extension of slavery; *C*. Texans opposed it; *D*. the South opposed it.

D   2. "Manifest destiny" means: *A*. confidence in the future of one's country; *B*. a right to independence; *C*. adding new states to the Union; *D*. the expansion of the United States to the limits fixed by nature.

C   3. By the 1830's Americans were taking

a greater interest in the problems of their country as a result of: *A.* their technological advances; *B.* their strong leaders; *C.* public schools, newspapers, and the telegraph; *D.* immigration.

A   4. Utah was admitted to the Union after: *A.* polygamy was declared illegal; *B.* community living was abandoned; *C.* its boundaries were changed; *D.* the population was large enough.

B   5. Opposition to the Mexican War developed: *A.* throughout Congress; *B.* among the Whigs and antislavery men; *C.* in the South; *D.* in the White House.

A   6. By the Treaty of Guadalupe Hidalgo, the United States acquired: *A.* California; *B.* Florida; *C.* the Oregon Country; *D.* Texas.

C   7. The California gold rush indirectly led to the opening of the issue of the extension of slavery because: *A.* slaves had joined the gold rush; *B.* southerners had taken their slaves to California; *C.* the increase in its population justified California's desire to form a state; *D.* miners could afford to buy slaves.

D   8. The United States moved ahead of European countries in: *A.* making life pleasant; *B.* providing opportunities for everybody; *C.* technology; *D.* establishing free public schools, extending the vote, and organizing voters into political parties.

A   9. Most of the Americans who moved to the West were looking for: *A.* good farmland; *B.* religious freedom; *C.* gold; *D.* fame.

C   10. Polk's attitude toward western expansion was: *A.* unknown; *B.* unfavorable to it; *C.* extremely favorable; *D.* undecided.

Matching

Column A

i   1. Sam Houston
f   2. John C. Frémont
j   3. John A. Sutter
a   4. Brigham Young
k   5. John Jacob Astor
b   6. Zachary Taylor
c   7. Nicholas B. Trist
d   8. John L. O'Sullivan
e   9. Marcus Whitman
h   10. Matthew C. Perry

Column B

a. led Mormons west
b. "Old Rough and Ready"
c. negotiated the treaty ending the Mexican War
d. coined the expression "manifest destiny"
e. missionary in Oregon Country
f. inspired the Bear Flag revolt
g. President during Mexican War
h. won American access to Japanese ports
i. leader of Texan revolt in 1835
j. owned land where California gold was found
k. early fur trader in Oregon Country

Completion

1. Miners who rushed to California to find gold were called <u>forty-niners.</u>

2. The United States' southern boundary was completed by the <u>Gadsden Purchase.</u>

3. The area disputed over by Mexico and the United States lies between <u>the Nueces</u> and <u>the Rio Grande</u> rivers.

4. In 1849 the Mormons formed a government called the <u>State of Deseret.</u>

5. For a long time the Great Plains were wrongly called <u>the "Great American Desert."</u>

6. The Oregon Trail started at <u>Independence, Missouri.</u>

7. The first dark-horse presidential candidate in American history was <u>James K. Polk.</u>

8. In 1846 the northern boundary of the Oregon Territory was fixed at <u>the 49th parallel of north latitude.</u>

9. Independent Texas was called <u>the Lone Star Republic.</u>

10. The negotiations of Caleb Cushing opened to Americans certain ports in <u>China.</u>

CHAPTER 14 (Covers Part Introduction)

Multiple-Choice

A   1. The significance of the Dred Scott decision was that: *A.* slaves could be taken anywhere; *B*. Dred Scott was not a free man; *C*. Dred Scott was not a citizen; *D*. it badly hurt the Democrats.

C 2. Judging from history, Andrew Jackson would have met the secession of a state by: *A*. first seeking a compromise; *B*. adopting a policy like Buchanan's; *C*. using force against the seceded state; *D*. consenting to the secession.

D 3. According to the Freeport doctrine: *A*. Congress could keep slavery out of a territory; *B*. squatter sovereignty was null and void; *C*. the Missouri Compromise was unconstitutional; *D*. squatter sovereignty was possible in spite of what the Supreme Court said.

A 4. The struggle over slavery in Kansas showed that: *A*. the doctrine of squatter sovereignty was meaningless; *B*. the Missouri Compromise was repealed; *C*. the Compromise of 1850 was unsatisfactory; *D*. Douglas favored the South.

B 5. Southerners refused to support Douglas as a candidate for the presidency in 1860 because: *A*. he was a northerner; *B*. he ignored the Dred Scott decision; *C*. he was a Republican; *D*. they wanted slavery in the territories to be protected.

B 6. Americans were divided after the Mexican War more than they were before because: *A*. congressional leaders took extreme positions; *B*. they could not agree on what to do with the lands they had gained; *C*. the President was weak; *D*. they disliked the peace treaty.

C 7. The part of the Compromise of 1850 that aroused most conflict was: *A*. the provision about the loss of Texas territory; *B*. the assuming of Texas debts; *C*. the Fugitive Slave Law; *D*. slavery in the new territory.

D 8. The Whig party split apart because: *A*. it lost its leaders; *B*. members left it; *C*. it became pro-southern; *D*. it failed to take a position on the lead-

ing issue of the time that could attract large numbers of people.

C 9. The election of Lincoln as President in 1860 caused concern in the South since: *A*. he was from Illinois; *B*. he was a Republican; *C*. southerners thought his election meant abolition of slavery; *D*. the Democratic party had split.

A 10. The Civil War has been called a breakdown in democracy in the United States because: *A*. Americans failed to solve a serious problem through discussion and give-and-take; *B*. leaders became emotional; *C*. leaders were unimaginative; *D*. the country grew too fast.

Matching

Column A

f 1. John Brown

c 2. Dred Scott

h 3. Stephen A. Douglas

k 4. David Wilmot

a 5. William H. Seward

i 6. James Buchanan

j 7. Abraham Lincoln

b 8. Harriet Beecher Stowe

d 9. Charles Sumner

g 10. Henry Clay

Column B

a. coined "irrepressible conflict"

b. wrote *Uncle Tom's Cabin*

c. Negro slave who sued in court for freedom

d. antislavery Senator attacked in the Senate

e. organized the Emigrant Aid Society

f. organized raid on Harpers Ferry

g. proposed Compromise of 1850

h. proposed Kansas-Nebraska Bill

i. Democrat elected President in 1856

j. Republican elected President in 1860

k. proposed a ban on slavery in territory acquired from Mexico

Completion

1. The first southern state to secede was <u>South Carolina.</u>

2. The Republican party was formed on the basis of <u>the nonextension of slavery.</u>

3. Henry Clay's fame rests on his role as <u>a</u>

compromiser.

4. The Compromise of 1850 ended the slave trade in <u>Washington, D.C.</u>

5. The Shawnee Mission government in Kansas became proslavery with the help of <u>"Border Ruffians."</u>

6. The Know-Nothing party was made up of people who opposed <u>immigrants.</u>

7. Rifles sent to free-state supporters in Kansas were called <u>"Beecher's Bibles."</u>

8. The Ostend Manifesto called for seizing <u>Cuba</u> from the <u>Spanish.</u>

9. A war between the people of the same country is called <u>a civil war.</u>

10. A private citizen carrying on an unauthorized war with a country at peace with his own country is said to be <u>filibustering.</u>

CHAPTER 15
Multiple-Choice

A 1. Since southern congressmen were absent from Congress during the Civil War, members were able to: *A.* raise tariffs and create a national-banking system; *B.* control wages and issue paper money; *C.* favor northern farming and industry; *D.* make northerners rich and pass conscription laws.

C 2. Lincoln's chief purpose in 1861 was to: *A.* free the slaves; *B.* keep slavery out of the territories; *C.* save the Union; *D.* defend the North.

B 3. The principle of government that weakened the Confederacy was: *A.* that slaves were property; *B.* states' rights; *C.* that slaves could not be used to help win the war; *D.* inflation.

C 4. Britain deeply angered northerners during the Civil War because: *A.* it recognized the Confederacy; *B.* the *Trent* was carrying Confederates to Europe; *C.* British shipyards built cruisers for the Confederacy; *D.* British goods aided the Confederacy.

D 5. Confederate and Union strategy were similar in two respects, since both included: *A.* winning British support and defending the arsenals; *B.* winning the border states and defending home territory; *C.* invading enemy

territory and capturing important cities; *D.* capturing the capital of the enemy and cutting the enemy territory in two.

A 6. The Union campaigns in the West were designed to: *A.* cut the Confederacy in two; *B.* capture important rivers; *C.* seal off Vicksburg; *D.* cut off Confederate supplies.

B 7. The Battle of Antietam was a turning point in the war because: *A.* Union forces stopped the Confederate advance north; *B.* England and France decided as a result of it that the North could win the war and that they should stay out of it; *C.* more men were killed in a single day than on any other one day of the war; *D.* afterward Lincoln freed the slaves.

C 8. Two important reasons why the Confederacy lost the war were: *A.* the high tariffs and the shortage of supplies; *B.* the failure to tax the people and a poor banking system; *C.* the shortage of manufacturing and the lack of sufficient railroad lines; *D.* the lack of a strong executive and the shortage of medicine.

A 9. The Emancipation Proclamation was a military measure that freed: *A.* slaves in states at war with the United States; *B.* slaves in the District of Columbia; *C.* all slaves; *D.* slaves in the border states.

D 10. The chief result of the Civil War was that: *A.* slavery was ended; *B.* the North became more prosperous than before; *C.* much southern wealth was gone; *D.* the Union was saved.

Matching

Column A

f 1. Maximilian
i 2. Frederick Douglass
d 3. Thomas J. Jackson
k 4. Jefferson Davis
a 5. John J. Crittenden
b 6. Albert Sidney Johnston
e 7. David G. Farragut
h 8. George E. Pickett
g 9. William T. Sherman

c 10. Clara Barton

Column B

a. proposed a compromise after the secession of South Carolina
b. led Confederate forces at Shiloh
c. cared for wounded soldiers in the Civil War
d. Confederate general who lost his life at Chancellorsville
e. helped capture New Orleans
f. tried to set up French rule in Mexico
g. led Union forces through the Southeast
h. led a Confederate charge at Gettysburg
i. leading Negro abolitionist
j. led Union forces at Gettysburg
k. president of the Confederacy

Completion

1. Northern Democrats who favored ending the war in 1864 were called Copperheads.

2. The greatest battle of the Civil War was at Gettysburg.

3. The Confederate firing on Fort Sumter led to fighting in the Civil War.

4. The greatest southern general was Robert E. Lee; the greatest northern one, Ulysses S. Grant.

5. The Confederate capital was Richmond, Virginia.

6. The Homestead Act provided free land to Americans meeting certain requirements who would live on it five years.

7. The Union plan to join its forces in the East and West and destroy the Confederacy has been called the "anaconda policy."

8. The border states were Delaware, Maryland, Kentucky, and Missouri.

9. The developing shortage of food and clothing in the Confederacy was caused in part by the Union blockade.

10. During the war, a northerner could escape military service by hiring a substitute.

CHAPTER 16 (Covers "A Long View")
Multiple-Choice

D 1. Johnson was impeached because he: A. was against Negroes; B. did not know how to deal with the Radicals; C. advised southern states not to ratify the Fourteenth Amendment; D. ignored the Tenure of Office Act.

A 2. Lincoln probably would have opposed the Radicals' plan for reconstruction, for: A. he had planned a generous policy toward the South; B. he believed a state could not secede; C. the Radicals had criticized him severely; D. he had resisted control by the Radicals.

C 3. A series of laws, or codes, were enacted in the southern states to: A. prevent the education of Negroes; B. support the Freedmen's Bureau; C. restrict the rights of Negroes and keep them in an inferior position; D. resist the reconstruction governments.

B 4. The Fourteenth Amendment not only made former slaves citizens but also: A. outlawed the Ku Klux Klan; B. provided a barrier against the invasion of an individual's rights by a state government; C. forbade a state to deny the vote to anyone because of his race or color; D. abolished slavery.

C 5. Northerners generally did not oppose the policies of the Radicals because: A. they did not know what was going on; B. they trusted Grant; C. the South was blamed for over half a million casualties, the national debt, and higher taxes; D. they were prosperous.

D 6. The misdeeds of the Radical state governments in the South are explained in part by the fact that: A. conditions of life differed from those before the war; B. northerners interfered with the governments; C. not all southerners could vote; D. the work of rebuilding the South physically called for spending much money and corruption in postwar government existed on a nationwide basis.

B 7. The Civil Rights Act of 1875 sought to end racial discrimination by states and private businesses serving the public but did not mention: A. jury duty; B. public schools; C. theaters; D. inns.

A 8. Serious barriers to complete reconstruction after 1877 were: *A*. the position of the Negro, the existence of the solid South, and unequal living conditions in the North and South; *B*. ill feelings caused by the Radicals; *C*. the poverty of Negroes and the denial of their civil rights; *D*. the failure to provide internal improvements and democratic governments for the South.

C 9. The former slaves became less and less a concern for northerners in the 1870's because: *A*. Democratic voters were driving out the Republicans in many southern states; *B*. a long depression followed the panic of 1873; *C*. northerners had labor problems and also wished to invest in the South; *D*. the Civil Rights Act of 1875 protected former slaves.

B 10. The Fifteenth Amendment to the Constitution provides that: *A*. all the laws in a state must apply in the same way to everybody; *B*. neither the United States nor any state may keep a citizen from voting because of his race or color or because he was once a slave; *C*. the federal government must repay the money it borrowed for expenses in the Civil War; *D*. Negroes are to be counted in determining what a state's representation in Congress is to be.

Matching

Column A

i   1. Thaddeus Stevens
j   2. Salmon P. Chase
e   3. Blanche K. Bruce
b   4. Rutherford B. Hayes
a   5. William Marcy Tweed
k   6. Andrew Johnson
c   7. Oliver O. Howard
d   8. Samuel J. Tilden
f   9. Jay Gould
h   10. Carl Schurz

Column B

a. leader of grafters in New York City
b. became President in 1877
c. supervised Freedmen's Bureau
d. Democratic candidate for the presidency in

1876
e. Negro Senator from Mississippi
f. helped cause Black Friday
g. leader of the Ku Klux Klan
h. German immigrant who reported on conditions in the South
i. prominent leader of Radicals in the House of Representatives
j. presided at Johnson's impeachment trial
k. Vice-President who succeeded Lincoln

Completion

1. Republican orators who blamed the Democrats for the Civil War were said to be "waving the bloody shirt."

2. Radicals agreed on what they wanted to do but disagreed over the means of doing it.

3. In accordance with the Constitution the power to impeach belongs to the House of Representatives.

4. The dispute over the election of 1876 was settled by the Compromise of 1877.

5. Southerners who joined the freedmen in reconstruction governments were often called "scalawags."

6. A scandal involving a corporation and federal officials was the Crédit Mobilier affair.

7. Politicians who thought that public offices should be conducted for their own gain were called spoilsmen.

8. The Radicals' plans for reconstruction called for dividing the South into five military districts.

9. Northerners who went south to help form Radical governments were spoken of as "carpetbaggers."

10. The abolition of slavery in the United States was accomplished by the Thirteenth Amendment.

CHAPTER 17
(Includes the Part Introduction)

Multiple-Choice

B 1. Big businessmen became young men's models because: *A*. politicians had a bad name; *B*. they had power and money; *C*. Charles Darwin wrote about them; *D*. they provided jobs.

D 2. Carnegie defended industrialists by

saying that: *A*. rich men should help the poor; *B*. long hours and child labor had existed for many years; *C*. they had helped develop railroads; *D*. industrialization had made goods less expensive for everybody.

A 3. The increase in railroad mileage encouraged industrialization because: *A*. manufacturers could reach markets and acquire raw materials more easily; *B*. competition was increased; *C*. workers could travel to factories more easily; *D*. people built factories near railroads.

A 4. The effect of the Civil War on American industrialization was to: *A*. slow it down first and then speed it up; *B*. cause concentration on railroads; *C*. cripple it because of lack of workers; *D*. shift it to the West.

C 5. Two requirements for the growth of industry are: *A*. protective tariffs and a growing market; *B*. advanced technology and shrewd businessmen; *C*. technical skills and funds for investment; *D*. help from the government and good working conditions.

B 6. The combination of firms into a single company is called a: *A*. pool; *B*. merger; *C*. holding company; *D*. interlocking directorate.

D 7. An important result of the building of the transcontinentals was that: *A*. immigration was encouraged because of the labor demands; *B*. trunk lines were formed; *C*. the government started to give subsidies to businesses; *D*. they contributed greatly to the settlement of the West.

C 8. The unifying of the country by the railroads helped create: *A*. general prosperity; *B*. western cities; *C*. a national culture; *D*. better feeling between the North and the South.

A 9. The secret of Rockefeller's and Carnegie's success was that each man gained control of: *A*. businesses relating to their industries or on which their industries depended; *B*. transportation; *C*. natural resources; *D*. the

majority in the Senate.

B 10. The development of big businesses in the United States led to this problem: *A*. how could life in the crowded cities be improved? *B*. how could one small group of men be prevented from using their economic power to destroy democracy? *C*. how could the poor be helped? *D*. how could the need for workers be satisfied?

Matching
Column A
d   1. James J. Hill
i   2. Cornelius Vanderbilt
k   3. William Kelly
j   4. John D. Rockefeller
a   5. J. Pierpont Morgan
e   6. Thomas A. Edison
c   7. Andrew Carnegie
f   8. George Westinghouse
h   9. Henry Clay Frick
b   10. Samuel Slater
Column B
a. powerful American financier
b. established first American cotton factory
c. developed large-scale steel industry
d. built the Great Northern Railroad
e. invented the electric-light bulb
f. invented an air brake used by trains
g. developed the flour-milling industry
h. partner of Carnegie
i. developed the New York Central Railroad
j. gained control of the oil-refining industry
k. American developer of the Bessemer process of steel manufacturing

Completion
1. Horatio Alger was the author of popular books for boys in the late 1800's.

2. Andrew Carnegie wrote an essay about his success called "The Gospel of Wealth."

3. Placing control of competing corporations in the hands of a single group of stockholders creates a trust.

4. Three mineral resources on which American industrial development depended were iron, coal, and oil.

5. The "American method" of manufacturing meant the use of interchangeable parts.

6. By passing the Contract Labor Law,

Congress allowed employers to engage workers abroad to work out their passage to America.

7. The first transcontinental railroad resulted from joining the <u>Union Pacific</u> and <u>the Central Pacific railroads</u> in the year <u>1869.</u>

8. A new phrase that was used to justify the growth of big businesses was "<u>the survival of the fittest.</u>"

9. The business formed by Rockefeller was called <u>the Standard Oil Trust.</u>

10. The exclusive control or possession of something is called a <u>monopoly.</u>

CHAPTER 18

Multiple-Choice

D 1. In the 1860's serious trouble broke out with the Plains Indians because: *A.* the Indians were skilled with the short bow; *B.* these Indians were not farmers; *C.* federal officials treated the Indians harshly; *D.* miners had been attracted to the Indians' lands.

A 2. Since 1948 Congress has developed a policy of: *A.* withdrawing federal supervision of Indians; *B.* making Indians citizens; *C.* encouraging tribal organization; *D.* purchasing land for Indians.

C 3. Two reasons for the ending of the long drive and the open range were: *A.* people built ranches and used fences; *B.* cowboys clashed with Indians, and refused to go on the drives; *C.* farmers resented both, and the long drive was expensive; *D.* the price of beef dropped, and cattlemen lost money.

C 4. Farmers on the Great Plains were handicapped by: *A.* dry farming and the lack of vegetation; *B.* loneliness and a lack of workers; *C.* the lack of timber and water; *D.* poor transportation and communication.

B 5. People farmed successfully on the Great Plains because: *A.* they were hard workers; *B.* American industries aided them by providing needed machinery; *C.* railroads brought supplies; *D.* barbed-wire fencing was invented.

A 6. Settlers in Oklahoma moved in large numbers onto land that: *A.* had originally been set aside for Indians; *B.* had been opened up by railroads; *C.* was part of the Oklahoma District; *D.* was useless to Indians.

D 7. The Sioux Indians went to war in 1876 because: *A.* they did not want to sell their land to the United States; *B.* they refused to live on reservations; *C.* they feared the new rapid-fire Hotchkiss guns; *D.* miners prospected and made claims on Indian land.

B 8. Cattlemen and sheepmen were at odds for years because: *A.* sheepherders took cattlemen's land; *B.* cattlemen said that sheep ruined the land for cattle; *C.* neither wanted to build fences; *D.* both competed for markets in the East.

C 9. The invention of the reaper was a blessing to farmers because they: *A.* no longer had to work so hard; *B.* did not depend on the weather as completely as before; *C.* could harvest before weather turned bad and needed fewer workers; *D.* could have big farms.

A 10. The chief attraction that drew settlers to the Great Plains was: *A.* the railroad; *B.* good land; *C.* farm machinery; *D.* peace with the Indians.

Matching

Column A

h 1. Joseph F. Glidden
k 2. William F. Cody
f 3. Joseph J. McCoy
i 4. Henry Comstock
a 5. J. M. Chivington
j 6. Richard King
d 7. George A. Custer
e 8. Bill Pickett
g 9. Cyrus Hall McCormick
b 10. Helen Hunt Jackson

Column B

a. massacred 500 sleeping Indians located on a reservation

b. wrote books about the plight of Indians

c. led the run on Oklahoma

d. led army at Battle of Little Big Horn

e. Negro rodeo star
f. stockman who founded Abilene, Kansas
g. developed a mechanical reaper
h. inventor of barbed wire
i. struck world's richest silver deposit
j. rich Texan rancher
k. Buffalo Bill

Completion

1. The cattle trail from San Antonio, Texas, to Abilene, Kansas, was the Chisholm Trail.

2. The "last West" extended from the 100th meridian to the Pacific coast.

3. The law that dissolved the Plains Indians tribes and divided their lands among the members was the Dawes Act.

4. Law and order on the mining frontier were often maintained by the mass meeting and the vigilance committee.

5. Earliest settlers on the Great Plains lived in sod houses.

6. Huge farms in the Red River Valley were called "bonanza farms."

7. People who made a run on the Oklahoma District in 1889 were called "boomers."

8. Two states that entered the Union in 1912 were New Mexico and Arizona.

9. When the Plains Indians were finally overcome, they were placed on reservations.

10. In 1889 four states entered the Union: North Dakota, South Dakota, Montana, and Washington.

CHAPTER 19
Multiple-Choice

C 1. The enactment of a federal income tax required an amendment to the Constitution, since: *A.* income taxes are not named in the Constitution; *B.* income taxes vary from place to place; *C.* it is a direct tax not based on population; *D.* income taxes were unpopular.

A 2. The years from 1868 to 1896 made up a period of "slack-water politics" because: *A.* politicians acted in accordance with their own self-interest; *B.* "Grantism" affected everything; *C.* good men avoided politics; *D.* in-dustrialists dominated politics.

D 3. Reformers favored the election of Cleveland in 1884, since: *A.* he was known for his interest in social justice; *B.* Congressman Blaine had done favors for a railroad; *C.* Cleveland was courageous; *D.* Cleveland had fought Tammany Hall.

B 4. Cleveland's position on the tariff was that: *A.* there was a surplus in the federal treasury; *B.* he wanted it lowered; *C.* he attacked it; *D.* he favored the McKinley Tariff.

C 5. Many Americans objected to acquiring overseas possessions because: *A.* they required expensive defense; *B.* they wanted no entanglement in foreign affairs; *C.* it did not seem right to deny to other peoples the right to independence; *D.* manifest destiny did not apply to overseas areas.

C 6. The settlement of a difficulty by arbitration means: *A.* negotiation; *B.* compromise; *C.* submission of the issue to a neutral umpire or umpires; *D.* settlement by voting.

A 7. A bad result of the Olney doctrine was that: *A.* it aroused Latin American suspicions; *B.* Britain was angry; *C.* the Monroe Doctrine was weakened; *D.* Cleveland backed down.

D 8. Cleveland angered workingmen by: *A.* his attitude toward the tariff; *B.* his friendship with the British minister Sir Lionel Sackville-West; *C.* repealing the Sherman Silver Purchase Act; *D.* his handling of a railway strike and of Coxey.

C 9. Hawaii was long important to the United States because: *A.* sugar was produced there; *B.* Americans had moved there; *C.* it was a convenient place of call for American ships in the Pacific; *D.* it was very prosperous.

B 10. In the depression of 1893, Cleveland thought he should move first to: *A.* aid the working people who had lost their jobs; *B.* stop the flow of gold from the treasury; *C.* halt imports; *D.* spend heavily.

Matching

Column A

e   1. Chester A. Arthur
f   2. Grover Cleveland
i   3. William McKinley
a   4. Benjamin Harrison
j   5. Jacob S. Coxey
c   6. James G. Blaine
b   7. Richard Olney
k   8. James A. Garfield
d   9. Thomas B. Reed
h   10. Roscoe Conkling

Column B

a. Republican elected President in 1888
b. Secretary of State at time of Venezuela boundary dispute
c. Secretary of State who encouraged pan-Americanism
d. Speaker of House in the first "billion-dollar Congress"
e. Vice-President who became President in 1881
f. Democrat elected President in 1884 and 1892
g. arranged the purchase of Alaska
h. New York Senator who battled with Hayes and Garfield over appointments to jobs in New York
i. congressman responsible for high tariff in 1890
j. led a group of unemployed men to Washington, D.C.
k. President assassinated in 1881

Completion

1. The law that established the merit system in the federal civil service was the Pendleton Act of 1883.

2. The United States purchased the Virgin Islands from Denmark in the year 1917.

3. The period when a country's prestige in international politics was measured by the number and size of its subject possessions is called the age of imperialism.

4. American Samoa consists of all Samoan islands east of 171° W.

5. Union war veterans formed an organization called by the initials GAR, standing for Grand Army of the Republic.

6. Republicans after 1877 were divided into two separate groups, the Half-Breeds and the Stalwarts.

7. Today the word mugwump is generally used to mean a person who adopts a neutral or independent position.

8. Cleveland angered Civil War veterans by vetoing pension bills and ordering captured Confederate flags to be returned to southern states.

9. The law requiring the treasury to double the amount of silver bullion it bought each month was called the Sherman Silver Purchase Act.

10. The financial arrangement that Cleveland made with J. P. Morgan was called the "Morgan bond deal."

CHAPTER 20

Multiple-Choice

B   1. After 1880, immigrants to the United States differed from earlier ones because: *A.* labor leaders opposed them; *B.* they came from southern and eastern Europe; *C.* they spoke no English; *D.* they were likely to live in cities.

D   2. One reason for the establishment of utopian communities was to: *A.* provide vacation spots; *B.* offer writers a chance to think; *C.* help factory workers to become farmers; *D.* restore simple living to avoid the evils of industrialization.

A   3. Working people were more interested in joining unions after the Civil War because: *A.* working conditions in factories were poor and the number of immigrants was increasing; *B.* prices went up but wages did not; *C.* they disliked individual bargaining; *D.* the American Emigrant Company threatened them.

C   4. As a means of achieving their goals, the Knights of Labor depended on: *A.* strikes; *B.* including all workers in one union; *C.* legislation and arbitration; *D.* government ownership of the railroads.

B   5. The chief contribution the AFL made to the labor movement was: *A.* representation of workers in legislative matters; *B*. the practice of drawing up a contract; *C*. acceptance of Negroes as members; *D*. higher wages.

B 6. Attempts of employers to deal with unionization of workers included: *A*. the 8-hour day and equal pay for equal work; *B*. spying and use of injunctions; *C*. hiring scabs; *D*. establishing company stores.

A 7. Early unionization was slow because: *A*. workers feared the loss of their jobs and they believed in individual enterprise; *B*. workers could not save money for strikes and they suffered from layoffs; *C*. workers did not trust each other; *D*. good leaders were scarce.

D 8. Workingmen's parties disappeared by the mid-1830's because: *A*. Jackson left the White House; *B*. they were local parties; *C*. workingmen were not elected to offices; *D*. in general, the two main parties took over their ideas.

C 9. The case of *Commonwealth* v. *Hunt* is called a landmark in labor history, since: *A*. it affected all labor unions; *B*. it resulted from the decision of a union's members not to work for anyone who fired a journeyman belonging to their union; *C*. it said that the union's policy was not a conspiracy; *D*. it hindered the union movement.

B 10. Immigrants after 1880 often lived more cheaply than people born in the United States because they: *A*. were not used to the American standard of living; *B*. often had to save to bring other members of their families to America; *C*. required less; *D*. could live in cities more cheaply than on farms.

Matching

Column A
e 1. William Silvis
i 2. Samuel Gompers
k 3. Eugene V. Debs
j 4. Oliver Wendell Holmes
b 5. Allan Pinkerton
h 6. John Mitchell
f 7. Terence V. Powderly

a 8. John P. Altgeld
c 9. Uriah S. Stephens
d 10. George Ripley

Column B
a. Illinois governor and a friend of labor
b. detective who provided strikebreakers
c. led the organization of the Knights of Labor
d. leader of Brook Farm
e. first president of the National Labor Union
f. second president of Knights of Labor
g. organized the I.W.W.
h. wrote *Organized Labor*
i. long-time leader of the AFL
j. "The Great Dissenter"
k. head of the American Railway Union

Completion

1. Two attempts to restrict the immigration of Asians were the Chinese Exclusion Act and the gentleman's agreement with Japan.

2. A secret society of miners that planned to frighten mineowners was called the Molly Maguires.

3. The first American unions were formed during the eighteenth century.

4. In the 1830's the chief demand of strikers was for a 10-hour day.

5. A person who believes that all government is evil and that he should demonstrate against it by violence and terror is called an anarchist.

6. An event that was used as an excuse to attack labor organizations was the Haymarket affair.

7. The AFL was an organization of craft unions.

8. A refusal to deal with an individual or firm in order to punish it or to make it change its policies is called a boycott.

9. Two famous strikes in the 1890's were the one at Homestead and the one at Pullman.

10. Generally, the courts made decisions about important laws in a way that was favorable to employers.

CHAPTER 21 (Includes "A Long View" and "The Quality of Life")

Multiple-Choice
A 1. The problems of cities in the late

1800's were not easily solved because: *A.* Americans did not accept the idea that the government should be concerned with the personal welfare of people; *B.* urban population grew too fast; *C.* citizens disliked paying taxes; *D.* immigrants were inclined to be clannish.

C 2. The Grangers made their chief contributions to American life by: *A.* making Americans aware of the problems of farmers; *B.* providing social activities for farm communities; *C.* pushing for laws regulating railroads and warehouses; *D.* forming and operating coöperatives.

D 3. Farmers were slow to organize a political party of their own because they: *A.* could not agree on a program for such a party; *B.* were not used to politics; *C.* would not join with people who had hired workers; *D.* were loyal to old party ties.

C 4. Two reasons the Republicans won in the election of 1896 were: *A.* McKinley campaigned throughout the country and Bryan appeared to be dangerous; *B.* Bryan adopted the Populist program and lost Democratic support; *C.* the price of wheat started to go up and workers were generally Republicans; *D.* the Republicans spent a great deal of money in the election and they stood for high tariffs.

B 5. William A. Peffer in *The Kansas Farmer* argued that: *A.* farmers were benefiting from technological advances; *B.* farmers needed money and had to borrow it from easterners; *C.* farm work had remained unchanged over the years; *D.* farmers had become more self-reliant.

A 6. City people often supported "bosses" and city machines since: *A.* they helped newly arrived immigrants; *B.* immigrants could not speak English; *C.* the growing urban population caused numerous problems; *D.* city government was weak.

B 7. By the late 1880's, farmers believed that farm prices would rise if: *A.* they had a Greenback President; *B.* the amount of money in circulation was increased; *C.* the amount of money in circulation was decreased; *D.* there was a graduated income tax.

C 8. Cleveland and other Americans opposed free silver because: *A.* the supply of silver was limited; *B.* they thought it would lead to a depression; *C.* they believed it would cause inflation; *D.* it could not solve farmers' problems.

D 9. Reasons for the discontent of farmers after the Civil War were: *A.* farm life was harsh and medical care was lacking; *B.* people no longer respected farmers and they were even ridiculed; *C.* industrialization had changed their way of living and they were in debt; *D.* the abuses practiced by railroads and the dependence of farmers on middlemen.

B 10. Farmers learned in the post-Civil War years: *A.* to vote Republican; *B.* to organize and to accept big business; *C.* that the silver dollar was unpredictable; *D.* that the problems of cities were not easily solved.

Matching

Column A

d 1. Marcus A. Hanna
i 2. Cyrus W. Field
k 3. Mary E. Lease
a 4. James B. Weaver
j 5. Oliver H. Kelley
c 6. William Jennings Bryan
h 7. Hamlin Garland
b 8. George Eastman
g 9. Charles Darwin
e 10. Jerry Simpson

Column B

a. Populist candidate for President in 1892

b. invented a simple camera

c. Democratic candidate for the presidency in 1896

d. tycoon who dominated the Republicans in 1896

e. leader from Kansas who ran for Congress in 1888

f. a prominent city "boss"

g. developed a theory of evolution

h. wrote books about farm life

i. laid the first cable linking Europe and North America

j. founder of the Grange

k. helped organize the Kansas farm vote

Completion

1. Two laws passed by Congress to increase the amount of silver money were the Bland-Allison Act of 1878 and the Sherman Silver Purchase Act.

2. In 1873, when Congress dropped the silver dollar from the list of coins to be struck, it was said to demonetize silver.

3. The most vigorous supporters of the Grange lived in the Middle West and the South.

4. After the Civil War the plantation system in the South was replaced by the sharecropping system.

5. The goal of the Greenback party was to increase the amount of paper money in circulation without backing.

6. A country that makes all its currency convertible only into gold is said to be on the gold standard.

7. The first law giving the federal government control over large-scale private enterprise in the interest of the public good was the Interstate Commerce Act.

8. Currency that a creditor is required by law to accept in payment for a debt is called legal tender.

9. The struggle between the Democratic and the Republican candidates in the election of 1896 is called the "battle of the standards."

10. Two major problems of cities were finding a way to provide pure water and a method of disposing of sewage.

CHAPTER 22 (Includes the Part Introduction)

Multiple-Choice

C 1. The Senate did not readily ratify the Treaty of Paris in 1900 because: *A.* members thought the terms were not generous enough; *B.* McKinley was unpopular: *C.* Americans felt that acquiring colonies strained their tradition of liberty and self-government; *D.* neither party had a majority.

B 2. The open-door policy in China meant that: *A.* all foreigners must leave the country; *B.* all countries would be treated equally in regard to trade and navigation; *C.* no country would take Chinese territory; *D.* Chinese ports would be open to Westerners.

A 3. The Republican victory in the presidential election of 1900 showed that: *A.* Americans disliked Bryan's ideas and wished to keep a President whom they connected with their prosperity; *B.* Americans favored imperialism; *C.* acquiring colonies was unpopular; *D.* Bryan favored free silver.

B 4. After the Spanish-American War, the United States: *A.* adopted a policy of further expansion; *B.* turned to encouraging peace and fostering self-government among other peoples; *C.* freed its newly acquired lands; *D.* was undecided about what to do.

D 5. Newspapers played a part in stirring up Americans in 1898 by: *A.* attacking McKinley; *B.* influencing Spain to remove its prime minister; *C.* encouraging Roosevelt; *D.* blaming Spain for the *Maine* disaster and publicizing Spanish criticism of the President.

C 6. American strategy in the war with Spain was to: *A.* capture the Philippines and seize Puerto Rico; *B.* free the rebels and turn the Cuban government over to the Cuban people; *C.* blockade Cuba, take important Cuban points, and destroy the Spanic; *D.* the Chinese themselves were not considered.

B 7. A weakness of the Chinese policy developed by the United States was: *A.* other countries did not approve it: *B.* no military means of defending it were arranged; *C.* it was too idealistic; *D.* the Chinese were not themselves considered.

A 8. The route to statehood taken by Hawaii shows that: *A.* the provisions of the Northwest Ordinance remain valid; *B*. Hawaii was a valuable possession; *C*. adding new states is a continuing policy of the United States; *D*. Hawaiians were united in desiring statehood.

C 9. An argument for the independence of the Philippine Islands was that: *A*. freedom would help make the Filipinos prosperous; *B*. freedom would bring a reduction in the tariff paid to ship goods to Americans; *C*. Filipinos had a stable government; *D*. other former Spanish possessions were already independent.

D 10. As the Commonwealth of Puerto Rico, Puerto Rico possesses: *A*. complete independence; *B*. colonial status; *C*. freedom from taxation; *D*. a large measure of independence with economic advantages.

Matching

Column A

e 1. John Hay
k 2. Pascual Cervera
i 3. George Dewey
f 4. Dupuy deLôme
g 5. Theodore Roosevelt
a 6. John Fiske
d 7. William Randolph Hearst
b 8. William T. Sampson
h 9. William Shafter
c 10. William Howard Taft

Column B

a. a historian and an expansionist
b. American naval leader who blockaded Cuba
c. first governor of the Philippine Islands
d. owner of a very sensational New York newspaper
e. Secretary of State who expressed the open-door policy
f. Spanish minister to Washington who wrote an indiscreet letter
g. leader of Rough Riders
h. American general who led invasion of Cuba
i. American naval leader who took Manila Bay
j. negotiator of peace treaty after Spanish-American War
k. commander of the Spanish fleet at Cuba

Completion

1. Cuban rebels in 1895 were known as insurrectos.

2. General Weyler's policy of dealing with the rebels was reconcentration.

3. Trouble caused by an anti-Western organization in China in 1900 is called the Boxer Rebellion.

4. Advocates of an aggressive foreign policy are called jingoes.

5. The Spanish-American War was fought chiefly in Cuba and the Philippines.

6. The citizens of Puerto Rico became American citizens through the Jones Act of 1917.

7. To abrogate means to cancel.

8. Filipinos, led by Emilio Aguinaldo, waged a guerrilla war with Americans.

9. In the Teller Amendment, Cuba was given independence.

10. In the peace treaty ending the Spanish-American War, Spain gave Cuba its independence and ceded the Philippines, Guam, and Puerto Rico to the United States.

CHAPTER 23

Multiple-Choice

B 1. The progressive movement was an attack on: *A*. businessmen; *B*. abuses that industrialization had caused or made worse; *C*. corrupt politics; *D*. the trusts.

D 2. The progressive movement ending in 1916 had: *A*. destroyed child labor; *B*. reformed elections; *C*. corrected poor housing conditions; *D*. extended democratic reforms and led big business to take public responsibility.

C 3. Both Roosevelt and Wilson believed that: *A*. a man in politics should unite his party; *B*. a social revolution would occur in the nation; *C*. a President should be a strong leader; *D*. traditions should be preserved.

A 4. The main purpose of the Federal Reserve Act was to: *A*. control the volume of currency and credit as needed; *B*. provide sound money; *C*. please farmers; *D*. regulate member banks.

B 5. Roosevelt acquired a reputation as a

"trust-buster" in part from: *A.* the Volstead Act; *B.* the Northern Securities Case; *C.* the Elkins Act; *D.* his reduction of the power of the United States Steel Corporation.

D 6. Congress was able to pass the Hepburn Act as a result of: *A.* Roosevelt's leadership; *B.* the new nationalism; *C.* the temperance movement; *D.* the power it had to regulate interstate commerce.

C 7. Muckraking lost its vigor by 1914 because: *A.* evils muckrakers attacked were corrected; *B.* muckrakers were radicals and had lost public esteem; *C.* large corporations had begun to think more of their public relations and muckraking magazines became more cautious; *D.* people grew tired of it.

A 8. Taft's chief difficulty was that: *A.* he lacked political skill; *B.* the insurgents made trouble for him; *C.* Roosevelt opposed him; *D.* he identified himself with Joe Cannon.

B 9. The Democrats won the presidential election in 1912 because: *A.* people were disgusted with the Payne-Aldrich Tariff; *B.* the Bull Moose party split the Republicans; *C.* the Republican candidate was unknown; *D.* they called for federal aid to farmers.

C 10. Two laws in Wilson's administration that affected workers favorably were: *A.* the Underwood-Simmons Act and the Newlands Act; *B.* the Federal Farm Loan Act and the Meat Inspection Act; *C.* the Adamson Act and the La Follette Seamen's Act; *D.* the Keating-Owen Act and the Pure Food and Drug Act.

Matching
Column A
h 1. Henry George
g 2. Robert La Follette
e 3. Jane Addams
b 4. Jacob Riis
i 5. William E. B. Du Bois
c 6. William Howard Taft
k 7. Gifford Pinchot
f 8. Woodrow Wilson
d 9. Carrie Chapman Catt
j 10. Henry Demarest Lloyd

Column B
a. established Tuskegee Institute
b. crusaded for slum clearance
c. Republican elected President in 1908
d. leader in struggle for woman suffrage
e. leader in settlement-house movement
f. Democrat elected President in 1912
g. a Wisconsin progressive
h. advocated the single tax
i. advocate of a policy of full equality for Negroes
j. muckraker who attacked the growth of monopoly
k. chief of the Division of Forestry and an important conservationist

Completion
1. The Sixteenth Amendment to the Constitution gave Congress the power to <u>tax income directly.</u>

2. An act passed in 1914 to strengthen the Sherman Antitrust Act was called <u>the Clayton Antitrust Act.</u>

3. Roosevelt's help in the settlement of a strike of <u>coal workers in 1902</u> won him the regard of many Americans.

4. The model American girl in the progressive years was <u>the Gibson girl.</u>

5. Legislation in the South enacted from the 1890's on established <u>Jim Crow regulations</u> against Negroes.

6. A special election held before a regular election for the purpose of electing party candidates is called <u>the direct primary.</u>

7. Two other ways in which the progressives increased the people's control over legislators and state legislation were <u>the initiative</u> and <u>the referendum.</u>

8. The progressive movement appealed especially to two groups of Americans making up <u>the middle class.</u>

9. The amenament to the Constitution that said a woman citizen could not be prevented from voting by either the federal or state governments was <u>the Nineteenth.</u>

10. Although Wilson and other progressives

were concerned with social justice, they ignored the condition of <u>Negroes.</u>

CHAPTER 24 (Includes "The Long View")
Multiple-Choice

B   1. In the trouble between Japan and Russia beginning in 1904, Roosevelt helped Japan but kept it from crushing Russia since: *A.* Russia had attacked Manchuria; *B.* he did not want either to become strong enough to close the open door in China; *C.* he wanted the Nobel Prize for Peace; *D.* he had trouble with the Japanese at home.

D   2. The Taft-Katsura Agreement was injurious to the American policy of preventing loss of Chinese territory, since: *A.* Japan wanted Manchuria; *B.* it gave Japan control over a Russian leasehold in China; *C.* Korea was involved; *D.* China claimed Korea.

C   3. The Root-Takahira Agreement was supposed to strengthen the open-door policy, but it weakened it because: *A.* Japan favored imperialism; *B.* Japan was angry over the school question in San Francisco; *C.* it recognized the position of Japan in Manchuria; *D.* Britain opposed it.

B   4. By the Hay-Bunau-Varilla Treaty, the United States: *A.* obtained the exclusive right to build, own, and fortify a canal across the Isthmus of Panama; *B.* leased a canal zone 10 miles wide for $10,000,000 and an annual rent of $250,000; *C.* settled difficulties in Cuba; *D.* made loans of money to Nicaragua.

A   5. Two reasons political upheavals have occurred often in Latin America are that: *A.* most Latin Americans have had no experience in self-government and that they lack the education for it; *B.* the United States has interfered in Latin American affairs and that Latin Americans have resented it; *C.* these countries have been independent a short time and that they have

poor leaders; *D.* dictators have seized control and that the people cannot oust them. '

B   6. Both Roosevelt and Wilson agreed on: *A.* the canal-tolls controversy; *B.* defending the Panama Canal region; *C.* the overthrow of the Manchus; *D.* their Mexican policy.

D   7. In his Mobile speech, Wilson promised that the United States would not use the Monroe Doctrine to: *A.* interfere in the settlement of Latin American debts; *B.* disapprove of Latin American governments; *C.* build bases in Latin America; *D.* seek territory by conquest.

C   8. The United States weakened China by withdrawing from the consortium because: *A.* the consortium was going to provide money for railroad construction in China; *B.* the consortium was going to help China buy the railroads of Manchuria; *C.* Asia was left open to Japanese aggression; *D.* Japan had made up its mind to stay in Manchuria.

B   9. The Alaskan-boundary dispute was settled by: *A.* the Carnegie Endowment for International Peace; *B.* a board of jurists influenced by Roosevelt; *C.* the Second Hague Peace Conference; *D.* a special treaty.

A   10. Changes in the United States during the progressive era included: *A.* the paying of closer attention to everyday needs of the people; *B.* the rise of spectator sports; *C.* the modifying of laws; *D.* a change in methods of teaching.

Matching
Column A

d   1. Victoriana Huerta
f   2. John J. Pershing
j   3. Taro Katsura
a   4. John Dewey
e   5. William C. Gorgas
k   6. Philippe Bunau-Varilla
i   7. Pancho Villa
b   8. Elihu Root
c   9. George W. Goethals

g   10. William Allen White

    Column B

a. educator and advocate of what is called "progressive education"
b. Secretary of State for Roosevelt
c. chief engineer of the Panama Canal
d. Mexican dictator that Wilson refused to recognize
e. rid the Canal Zone of yellow fever
f. general who led American forces in Mexico
g. Kansas newspaper editor
h. sponsored the Algeciras Conference
i. ambitious Mexican who tried to oust the president of Mexico
j. Japanese prime minister
k. the chief spokesman for the French Canal Company

Completion

1. The chief result of the first Hague Conference was <u>the Permanent Court of International Arbitration.</u>

2. The ABC powers are <u>Argentina, Brazil,</u> and <u>Chile.</u>

3. The principle that the United States might act as an international policeman in Latin American affairs is called the <u>Roosevelt corollary</u> to <u>the Monroe Doctrine.</u>

4. The United States could build a canal across the Isthmus of Panama through either <u>Panama</u> or <u>Nicaragua,</u> but it chose to build it through <u>Panama.</u>

5. Before the United States could start the actual work of building the canal, it had to obtain the consent of <u>Colombia.</u>

6. The United States gained the perpetual right to build a canal through Nicaragua, a 99-year lease on the Corn Islands, and a 99-year right to build a naval base in Nicaragua through <u>the Bryan-Chamorro</u> Treaty.

7. In 1907 Roosevelt demonstrated to Japan the extent of American power by <u>sending the United States fleet around the world.</u>

8. The diplomacy favored by Taft is called <u>dollar diplomacy.</u>

9. Secretary of State William Jennings Bryan was responsible for a means of keeping peace called <u>the "cooling-off" treaty.</u>

10. In his dealings with foreign countries, Roosevelt's policy was to rely on <u>the big stick.</u>

CHAPTER 25
(Includes "The Quality of Life" and the Part Introduction)

Multiple-Choice

B   1. In his war message to Congress in 1917, Wilson said that Americans would be fighting for: *A.* the rights of neutrals and the freedom of the seas; *B.* democracy and the rights of small nations; *C.* peace and security; *D.* the ending of secret diplomacy and the reduction of arms.

D   2. Under the mandate system, a former colony of a defeated country was: *A.* prepared for independence by the League of Nations; *B.* supervised by the League and accountable to it; *C.* made independent; *D.* assigned by the League to an Allied power and administered under the supervision of the League.

A   3. The Germans' advance in France was halted in: *A.* the second Battle of the Marne; *B.* the Meuse-Argonne offensive; *C.* the Battle of Château-Thierry; *D.* Cantigny.

B   4. The First World War was not ended quickly because: *A.* it was fought over a wide front; *B.* new weapons and new methods of fighting were used on both sides; *C.* the Germans could not break British control of the seas; *D.* the United States was slow to enter the war.

C   5. Article 10 of the League of Nations provided that: *A.* there should be a Permanent Court of International Justice; *B.* Germany should pay reparations for damages and losses in the war; *C.* members of the League would preserve against external aggression the territory and political independence of its members; *D.* the League would have an international labor office.

B   6. Henry Cabot Lodge of Massachusetts favored participating in the League of Nations if: *A.* Germany was kept outside it; *B.* fourteen reservations were agreed to; *C.* League headquarters were located in America; *D.* Article 10 was dropped.

A   7. Arguments against the League of Nations included: *A.* the Monroe Doctrine would be destroyed and the United States would be fighting to save the British Empire; *B.* the Germans were receiving all the blame for the war and Germany would not be a member of the Council; *C.* Italians had been unfairly treated and Italy was to be excluded from the League; *D.* Washington had advised keeping out of entangling alliances.

C   8. New countries formed after the First World War consisted of: *A.* Poland, Hungary, Serbia, Austria, Yugoslavia; *B.* Czechoslovakia, Austria, Romania, Poland, Hungary; *C.* Yugoslavia, Austria, Poland, Czechoslovakia, Hungary; *D.* Turkey, the Soviet Union, Czechoslovakia.

D   9. The year 1917 was decisive in the First World War because: *A.* the Germans overran Belgium and threatened France; *B.* the Germans were within 50 miles of Paris; *C.* Wilson wrote peace terms; *D.* Russia threatened to withdraw from the war and it seemed as if Britain was about to defeat Turkey.

B   10. Americans lost interest in the League of Nations because: *A.* Germany had lost the war; *B.* domestic problems and events occupied their attention; *C.* Warren G. Harding became President; *D.* the Treaty of Versailles was not ratified.

Matching
Column A

c   1. Edward M. House
k   2. J. H. von Bernstorff
f   3. Arthur Zimmermann
i   4. Charles Evans Hughes
j   5. Bernard M. Baruch
g   6. David Lloyd George
b   7. Franz Ferdinand
a   8. Warren G. Harding
e   9. Ferdinand Foch

d   10. Henry Cabot Lodge
Column B

a. Republican elected President in 1920
b. Austrian archduke whose murder led to the First World War
c. personal adviser to Wilson
d. a reservationist from Massachusetts
e. supreme commander of the Allied forces
f. German foreign minister who invited Mexico to join Germany in the war
g. English prime minister and member of the Big Four
h. the "Tiger"
i. Republican presidential candidate in 1916
j. chairman of the War Industries Board
k. German ambassador and deliverer of notice on unrestricted submarine warfare

Completion

1. Americans coined the expression "<u>to Hooverize,</u>" meaning <u>to save food.</u>

2. The first distinctively American offensive was intended to drive the Germans out of <u>the St. Mihiel area.</u>

3. The American troops sent to France made up the <u>American Expeditionary Force.</u>

4. Goods necessary to warfare—guns and ammunition—are called <u>contraband of war.</u>

5. Before the First World War, two alliances existed in Europe—<u>the Triple Alliance</u> and the <u>Triple Entente.</u>

6. Americans on the British liner *Lusitania* were drowned after an attack by a <u>German submarine.</u>

7. During the First World War, the final judge in labor disputes was <u>the National War Labor Board.</u>

8. Wilson's statement of war aims was known as <u>the "Fourteen Points."</u>

9. Firing in the First World War stopped on <u>November 11, 1918.</u>

10. The treaty ending the First World War was <u>the Treaty of Versailles.</u>

CHAPTER 26
Multiple-Choice

C   1. In 1924 the year 1890 was chosen as the base year for determining the quota of immigrants a foreign country could send to the United States because: *A.* there were too many immigrants; *B.* some countries sent numbers of immigrants out of all proportion to their sizes; *C.* it was in the period before large numbers of eastern Europeans had arrived; *D.* few immigrants had come in 1890.

B 2. Some reasons for the nature of the 1920's included: *A.* the progressive era had changed the American outlook and the war was over; *B.* young people were disappointed in the results of the war and leisure time became a goal of millions; *C.* the Presidents were poor leaders and made no plans; *D.* "normalcy" had returned and people were prosperous.

A 3. Reformers were silent in the 1920's because: *A.* of the wave of fear in the United States; *B.* the Ku Klux Klan was formed; *C.* there was a conflict over religion; *D.* the "noble experiment" failed.

D 4. The purpose of advertising may be said to be to: *A.* encourage selling; *B.* start installment buying; *C.* create jobs; *D.* create new needs and tastes.

B 5. Radio helped encourage: *A.* an interest in sports; *B.* the standardizing of American tastes in the performing arts; *C.* the appearance of new styles; *D.* motion pictures.

C 6. The fever for stock speculation in the 1920's was based on: *A.* general prosperity; *B.* a rising gross national product; *C.* expansion and consolidation of business; *D.* confidence in businessmen.

A 7. The chief American contribution to the automobile was: *A.* the system for producing cars on a mass scale; *B.* the engine; *C.* the use of gasoline as fuel; *D.* the steering wheel.

C 8. In a campaign speech made in 1928, Hoover said that American prosperity was based in part on: *A.* manufacturing; *B.* Republican leadership; *C.* decentralized self-government; *D.* the workers.

B 9. Restriction on immigration became popular in the 1920's because: *A.* people sensed that dark times lay ahead; *B.* many people were unemployed and many Americans feared radicals; *C.* strikes were occurring; *D.* the Ku Klux Klan stirred up hatred.

C 10. The biggest farm problem in the 1920's was: *A.* how to keep farmers from going into debt; *B.* how to raise farm prices; *C.* what to do with the farm surpluses; *D.* how to form a farm bloc.

Matching

Column A

f   1. John L. Lewis
g   2. Charles A. Lindbergh
i   3. John Thomas Scopes
b   4. Herbert Hoover
a   5. Calvin Coolidge
k   6. Albert B. Fall
d   7. Henry Ford
j   8. Lee De Forest
c   9. Alfred E. Smith
e   10. Marcus Garvey

Column B

a. Vice-President who succeeded Harding
b. Republican elected President in 1928
c. Catholic Democratic presidential candidate in 1928
d. originated the assembly-line system of automobile manufacturing
e. Negro leader of "back to Africa" movement in early 1920's
f. head of the United Mine Workers
g. flew nonstop from New York to Paris
h. gangster of the prohibition era
i. biology teacher who was arrested for teaching the theory of evolution
j. laid the groundwork for the radio tube
k. Secretary of the Interior involved in an oil scandal

Completion

1. The period of extraordinary creativity for Negro artists and musicians in the early 1920's is called the Negro Renaissance.

2. In 1926 control over commercial aviation was made the responsibility of the Department of Commerce.

3. A famous legal battle of the 1920's occurred in the case of <u>Sacco</u> and <u>Vanzetti.</u>

4. In 1927 all immigration was cut to <u>150.000</u> annually.

5. In the 1920's Congress revised the tariff rates, making them <u>higher</u>.

6. Calvin Coolidge became a public hero because he sent the National Guard in response to the <u>Boston police strike.</u>

7. The increase in violence in the 1920's was chiefly the result of "<u>bootlegging.</u>"

8. The new car that Ford produced in great numbers and with low costs was the "<u>Model T.</u>"

9. The first commercial radio station was <u>KDKA</u> in <u>Pittsburgh.</u>

10. Hoover was elected President in 1928 in part because people associated him with <u>prosperity.</u>

CHAPTER 27

Multiple-Choice

C   1. The first stage of the Great Depression was: *A.* growing unemployment; *B.* a run on banks; *C.* the collapse of the stock market; *D.* low farm prices.

A   2. Hoover stuck to the idea that: *A.* the federal government had no direct responsibility for curing the evils of economic depression; *B.* prosperity was just around the corner; *C.* the federal government should borrow no money; *D.* there had been several other depressions.

B   3. Franklin D. Roosevelt attacked the Supreme Court because: *A.* he thought Justices were paid too much; *B.* he wanted favorable Supreme Court decisions; *C.* there were too many judges; *D.* he approved of the checks-and-balances system.

C   4. The CCC was organized to: *A.* build hydroelectric dams on rivers and provide revenue; *B.* provide electricity for farms and for outlying districts; *C.* conserve the nation's land and forests and its human resources; *D.* ask employers to help prepare codes of "fair competition."

A   5. Permanent improvements in American life resulted from: *A.* the Glass-Steagall Banking Act and the Federal Securities Act; *B.* the NRA and the first AAA; *C.* the Guffey-Snyder Act and the Fair Labor Standards Act; *D.* the "sick-chicken case" and the fireside chats.

B   6. The purpose of the WPA was to: *A.* raise wages; *B.* give men work that would restore their self-respect; *C.* builds towns near places of employment; *D.* eliminate strikes.

D   7. The purpose of the second AAA was to: *A.* pay for crop reduction by means of a processing tax; *B.* encourage farmers to produce more than before; *C.* help tenant farmers; *D.* reduce the production of crops through benefit payments from the federal treasury.

C   8. Franklin D. Roosevelt affected democracy in the United States by: *A.* using it and holding its ideals before the people; *B.* giving it new meaning and greater influence; *C.* renewing the people's faith in it and adding to their idea of it the belief that human resources should be conserved; *D.* showing its strength and usefulness.

A   9. The Roosevelt program was: *A.* in keeping with the American past; *B.* radical; *C.* completely new; *D.* devoted to helping business.

B   10. The New Deal has been called the Roosevelt Revolution because Franklin D. Roosevelt: *A.* revolutionized American life; *B.* gave the economic life of the country centralized direction and gave workers new self-respect; *C.* believed in social security; *D.* changed the face of the land.

Matching

    Column A

c   1. Cordell Hull

g   2. Huey Long

h   3. John Nance Garner

b   4. Adolf Hitler

f   5. Frances Perkins

k 6. Harry Hopkins
j 7. Harlan F. Stone
a 8. Alfred M. Landon
i 9. Benito Mussolini
e 10. James A. Farley
    Column B
a. Republican presidential candidate in 1936
b. Nazi dictator of Germany
c. appointed Secretary of State by Franklin D. Roosevelt
d. sponsored the Social Security Act
e. the chairman of the Democratic National Committee
f. Franklin D. Roosevelt's Secretary of Labor
g. Louisiana Senator and sponsor of the "share-our-wealth" movement
h. elected Vice-President in 1932
i. dictator of Italy
j. a dissenting Justice in the case about a minimum-wage law for women and children
k. administrator of the WPA

Completion

1. In the summer of 1932 a group of unemployed veterans called the "Bonus Army" marched to Washington.

2. A group of intimate advisers to Franklin D. Roosevelt was called the "brain trust."

3. The legislation Franklin D. Roosevelt proposed very early in 1933 can be divided into three classifications: relief measures, recovery measures, and reform measures.

4. A New Deal law that enforced the right of employees to bargain collectively with their employers is called the Wagner Act.

5. A congressman who serves the last part of his term after he has been defeated at the polls or has not run again is called a lame duck.

6. The CIO organized industrial unions that included skilled and unskilled workers.

7. The initials WPA stood for Works Progress Administration.

8. The first important step Franklin D. Roosevelt took as President was declaring a bank holiday.

9. The Twenty-first Amendment repealed the Eighteenth Amendment.

10. The TVA built dams in the Tennessee Valley.

CHAPTER 28

Multiple-Choice

D 1. Roosevelt was elected for a third term because: *A.* the United States was at war; *B.* he had led the country out of the Great Depression; *C.* his opponent was quite weak; *D.* there was a crisis abroad and prosperity was returning.

A 2. Many Americans opposed steps that might lead to their involvement in the Second World War, since: *A.* they were disillusioned with the results of the First World War and they had a horror of modern warfare; *B.* they had no money for arming and they did not wish to go into debt; *C.* they thought bankers helped cause wars and they thought the United States was not threatened; *D.* they were not members of the League of Nations and had no interest in the war.

C 3. In his "quarantine speech," Roosevelt said: *A.* Japan should be quarantined; *B.* China was a victim of aggression; *C.* peace-loving countries should unite for collective security; *D.* trade and travel of Americans would be restricted.

B 4. The purpose of the Hull Reciprocal Trade Program was to: *A.* help the Latin American countries; *B.* reduce barriers to international trade; *C.* extend the Monroe Doctrine; *D.* raise tariffs.

C 5. Many Americans believed that if the United States was drawn into the Second World War it would be because: *A.* it feared a German attack on the Panama Canal; *B.* most people sympathized with Britain; *C.* of its trade in arms and private loans to the western countries; *D.* of Roosevelt's attitude and sympathies.

D 6. In the conquest of Poland, Germany was aided by: *A.* the antiwar sentiment in the United States; *B.* Mussolini's troops; *C.* a change in feeling in the United States; *D.* its ally, the Soviet Union.

B 7. The Lend-Lease Bill provided that: *A.* the United States would lease military bases abroad; *B.* the President might lease, sell, transfer, or rent certain goods to any nation whose defense was considered necessary to the defense of the United States; *C.* the United States would give foreign aid to the western democracies; *D.* the nation would support the war.

A 8. In his speech called "Fundamentals of American Foreign Policy," Cordell Hull argued that: *A.* the United States should unite with other nations in maintaining morality in international relations; *B.* isolationism was dead; *C.* the interest and concern of the United States in foreign countries was determined by the amount of investment and trade there; *D.* Germany was an aggressor.

C 9. The neutrality laws were chiefly designed to: *A.* keep the United States neutral; *B.* aid Britain; *C.* prevent the sale of munitions and the making of loans to countries at war; *D.* increase American trade.

D 10. Between 1938 and 1941 Americans became convinced that: *A.* the neutrality laws were useless; *B.* they should provide a two-ocean navy; *C.* their nation might have to face the enemy alone; *D.* national security itself was at stake.

Matching

Column A

c   1. Aristide Briand

e   2. Dwight Morrow

h   3. Henry L. Stimson

i   4. Chiang Kai-shek

k   5. Neville Chamberlain

a   6. Wendell Willkie

f   7. William E. Borah

b   8. Winston S. Churchill

g   9. J. Reuben Clark

d   10. Charles Evans Hughes

Column B

a. Republican candidate for the presidency in 1940

b. prime minister of England in the Second World War

c. Frenchmen who helped arrange the Pact of Paris

d. Secretary of State who proposed naval disarmament

e. able United States ambassador to Mexico

f. Senator who worked for naval disarmament

g. Undersecretary of State who announced that Americans had rejected the Roosevelt corollary

h. Secretary of State who said the nation would recognize no territorial change resulting from aggression.

i. Chinese leader who led defense of China against Japan

j. ended the Tacna-Arica dispute

k. British prime minister who entered into the Munich agreement

Completion

1. The chief reason for the United States' recognition of the Soviet Union was Japanese aggression.

2. The Second World War began in 1939 after German troops invaded Poland.

3. The First World War changed the United States from being a debtor nation to being a creditor nation.

4. The policy Franklin D. Roosevelt adopted toward Latin America is called the Good Neighbor policy.

5. In 1931 Japan invaded and took the Chinese province named Manchuria.

6. Mussolini's first act of aggression was against Ethiopia.

7. The belief that a country can be self-sustaining is called economic nationalism.

8. The policy that Britain and France adopted toward Germany in 1938 was one of appeasement.

9. The British heroically rescued their forces from France after they had been defeated at the Battle of Dunkerque.

10. In order to help Britain, Roosevelt arranged in September, 1940, to give that country fifty overage destroyers.

CHAPTER 29

Multiple-Choice

C 1. The forcible removal of Americans of Japanese ancestry to relocation centers was a lasting blot on the nation's record because: *A.* many *nisei* served their country well in the war; *B.* no Japanese-American was guilty of espionage; *C.* their civil liberties were violated; *D.* it caused a wave of fear.

B 2. The decision to attack Europe first in the war was based on: *A.* the facts that Japan was farther away and war preparations were more difficult there; *B.* the beliefs that Germany was stronger than Japan and had to be defeated first; *C.* the influence of Churchill and De Gaulle; *D.* Eisenhower's opinion.

A 3. Some of the bloodiest fighting occurred in Italy because: *A.* Hitler sent some of his best troops to help Italy; *B.* Mussolini defended his country until his death; *C.* Italy is a mountainous country; *D.* the Allies were determined to take Italy.

C 4. The people of the world saw the extent of Nazi barbarity when: *A.* Paris was liberated; *B.* the Allied troops moved through Belgium; *C.* Allied soldiers found concentration camps where the Nazis had killed millions of Jews; *D.* the Germans surrendered.

D 5. A grave mistake Hitler made in 1941 was to: *A.* ally himself with Japan; *B.* allow his submarines to operate off Nova Scotia; *C.* occupy Denmark; *D.* attack the Soviet Union.

B 6. In September, 1941, Japan demanded that the United States and Britain: *A.* give it Lend-Lease supplies and recognize Japanese conquests; *B.* help it acquire raw materials and stop aiding China; *C.* give up their bases in East Asia and not build new ones; *D.* withdraw ships from the Pacific Ocean and leave Pearl Harbor.

A 7. The United States declared in the fall of 1941 that peace between Japan and the United States would be achieved only if: *A.* Japan withdrew from China and Indochina and recognized the Chinese Nationalist government; *B.* Japan would stop threatening the Philippines, Guam, and Wake Island; *C.* Japan restored Manchuria; *D.* Japan gave up its plans for the Greater East Asia Co-prosperity Sphere.

C 8. The United States declared war on Japan because: *A.* Japan threatened American possessions in the Pacific; *B.* of the Kurusu mission; *C.* of the bombing of Pearl Harbor; *D.* of the Japanese seizure of China.

B 9. The Battles of the Coral Sea and of Midway: *A.* helped the Americans capture the Solomons and kept the Japanese out of the Aleutians; *B.* stopped the Japanese advance on Australia and ended the threat to Hawaii; *C.* enabled the Americans to bomb Japan itself and helped them capture Saipan; *D.* showed that the Americans would be able to regain the Philippines.

C 10. At the Yalta Conference the Big Three promised: *A.* to form the UN and preserve world peace; *B.* that Japan would be stripped of all its gains and that Germany would be divided; *C.* that they would accept unconditional surrender only and that reparations would be demanded; *D.* that Poland would have a freely elected representative government and that other liberated countries of eastern Europe would have governments the people wanted.

Matching

Column A

e 1. George S. Patton, Jr.

g 2. Anthony C. McAuliffe

b 3. Hideki Tojo

f 4. Douglas MacArthur

h 5. Dwight D. Eisenhower

j 6. Chester W. Nimitz

d 7. Omar N. Bradley

k   8. Lewis B. Hershey
a   9. Thomas E. Dewey
c   10. Mao Tse-tung

Column B

a. Republican presidential candidate in 1944
b. the prime minister of Japan
c. Chinese Communist who fought a civil war for control of China
d. commander of the American ground forces in the invasion of western Europe
e. American general who joined with the British in invading Sicily
f. general who directed the Allied campaigns against the Japanese in the Pacific
g. American general in the Battle of the Bulge who refused to surrender
h. American general who led combined Allied forces in Europe
i. general who captured the Solomon Islands
j. commander of the United States naval forces in the Pacific
k. the supervisor of the draft

Completion

1. The day the Allies landed in northern France is called <u>D day,</u> and the day of victory in Europe is known as <u>V-E Day.</u>

2. Roosevelt and Churchill issued a joint declaration in 1941 called <u>the Atlantic Charter.</u>

3. The code name for the invasion of western Europe was <u>OVERLORD.</u>

4. The Germans' last effort to defend their country was in <u>the Battle of the Bulge.</u>

5. The Axis aim in North Africa was to <u>capture Egypt</u> and <u>seize the Suez Canal.</u>

6. Americans crossed the Rhine River into Germany by way of a bridge at <u>Remagen.</u>

7. Japanese suicide planes were called <u>kamikazes.</u>

8. Roosevelt, Churchill, and Stalin first met together at <u>the Tehran Conference.</u>

9. Atomic bombs were dropped on the Japanese cities of <u>Hiroshima</u> and <u>Nagasaki.</u>

10. The purpose of the OPA was to <u>hold prices in check.</u>

CHAPTER 30

Multiple-Choice

B 1. In 1967 many civil rights leaders worked to obtain open-housing laws, since such laws would: *A.* allow Negroes to live where they chose; *B.* end "ghettos" and their bad effects; *C.* end riots; *D.* provide jobs.

D 2. Americans have resisted the spread of communism because: *A.* they dislike communism; *B.* Communists use any or all means of spreading it; *C.* Communists seized control of eastern Europe; *D.* Communists aim to dominate the world and set up their system, which denies people their individual freedoms.

C 3. In order to force the Western powers out of Germany, the Soviets established in 1948: *A.* the atomic-arms race; *B.* a Communist government in Czechoslovakia; *C.* the Berlin blockade; *D.* the explosion of the hydrogen bomb.

B 4. In the Korean War the UN forces achieved: *A.* the disarmament of North Korea; *B.* the stopping of aggression and the restoring of the dividing line near the 38th parallel in Korea; *C.* coöperation among UN nations; *D.* victory.

A 5. The Peace Corps has worked mainly in: *A.* the fields of education, agriculture, and urban renewal; *B.* expanding its program; *C.* aiding young people; *D.* helping Asian countries.

C 6. The Vietcong attacks on South Vietnam were hard to resist because: *A.* the terrain handicapped Americans; *B.* the Vietcong used guerrilla methods; *C.* North Vietnam was the base for attacks supported by some Laotians, by some South Vietnamese, and by China and the Soviet Union; *D.* the South Vietnamese were divided.

D 7. Among the influences in the Middle East are: *A.* the UN and the United States; *B.* the Eisenhower doctrine and Britain; *C.* the Truman doctrine and Turkey; *D.* Arab nationalism, oil supplies, and Soviet interest.

B 8. Two threats to the health of Americans living in cities are: *A.* riots and housing problems; *B.* air and water pollution; *C.* labor and transportation problems; *D.* poor medical care and "dropouts."

A 9. The main feature of the Civil Rights Act of 1964 was: *A.* the prohibiting of racial discrimination in most public accommodations; *B.* the cutting of funds to federally assisted programs where racial discrimination existed; *C.* the forbidding of injuring or intimidating anyone engaged in certain protected activities; *D.* the closing of the last loopholes by which Negroes could be kept from voting.

C 10. In 1967 the administration faced a dilemma because: *A.* there was sluggish economic growth; *B.* automation had reduced the number of jobs; *C.* the needs of foreign policy threatened the domestic program; *D.* people were divided concerning the foreign policy.

Matching

Column A

i 1. Martin Luther King, Jr.
d 2. Earl Warren
k 3. Alexei N. Kosygin
h 4. Thurgood Marshall
a 5. Harry S Truman
j 6. John Foster Dulles
e 7. Gamal Abdel Nasser
c 8. Adlai E. Stevenson
b 9. Ho Chi Minh
f 10. William C. Westmoreland

Column B

a. President from 1945 to 1953
b. North Vietnamese leader
c. Democratic candidate for the presidency in 1952 and 1956

d. Chief Justice of the United States
e. Egyptian prime minister
f. commander of American forces in South Vietnam
g. organized the Common Market
h. first Negro Justice on the Supreme Court
i. leader of civil rights movement
j. Secretary of State for Eisenhower
k. Soviet Premier

Completion

1. The Marshall Plan provided massive aid to the countries of Europe with the exception of <u>the Soviet Union</u> and <u>its satellites.</u>

2. A word that Americans have adopted as an expression to refer to reckless name-calling is "<u>McCarthyism.</u>"

3. In 1958 six European countries formed an organization called <u>the Common Market</u> for buying and selling goods.

4. An organization to give aid to Latin America under certain conditions is called <u>the Alliance for Progress.</u>

5. The first two Americans in space were <u>Alan B. Shepard, Jr.,</u> and <u>John H. Glenn, Jr.</u>

6. Two new departments Congress created in 1965 and 1966 were <u>the Department of Transportation</u> and <u>the Department of Housing and Urban Development.</u>

7. The Supreme Court decision calling for the desegregation of public schools was *<u>Brown v. Board of Education of Topeka.</u>*

8. Poll taxes in national elections are outlawed by <u>the Twenty-fourth Amendment.</u>

9. The advance in civil rights owed much to three organizations called, in short, the <u>NAACP, CORE, and SNCC.</u>

10. Negotiations to achieve tariff cuts among the United States and certain European nations in 1967 were called <u>the Kennedy Round.</u>

THE
ADVENTURE
OF THE
AMERICAN PEOPLE

A HISTORY OF THE UNITED STATES

Second Edition

John Allen Krout is a distinguished American historian whose special field is social history. He taught at Columbia University and at Arizona State University. Among the books he has written are: The Origins of Prohibition; Annals of American Sport; An Outline History of the United · States; Approaches to American Social History; The Completion of Independence (with D. R. Fox); Great Expressions of Human Rights. He is a frequent contributor to professional journals.

Henry Franklin Graff is also an outstanding historian. His special field is the diplomatic history of the United States. He has taught at Columbia University since 1946 and has been a lecturer at Vassar College since 1953. He has written: Bluejackets with Perry in Japan; The Modern Researcher (with Jacques Barzun). He was Consulting Editor for Life's History of the United States, and he is a frequent contributor to professional journals and to the New York Times Magazine.

THE
ADVENTURE
OF THE
AMERICAN PEOPLE

HENRY F. GRAFF
Professor of History
Columbia University

JOHN A. KROUT
Professor Emeritus of History
Columbia University

RAND McNALLY & COMPANY | *Chicago*

Printed in U.S.A.

ACKNOWLEDGMENTS

"What's Ahead for International Science?" (pages 738–740), by Glenn T. Seaborg, is reprinted with permission from the January, 1967, issue of the *Bulletin of the Atomic Scientists*. Copyright 1967 by the Educational Foundation for Nuclear Science.

THIS BOOK IS SET IN TIMES ROMAN
COMPOSITION, PRINTING, AND BINDING BY RAND McNALLY & COMPANY
BOOK DESIGN BY GORDON HARTSHORNE AND VITO DE PINTO
COVER DESIGN BY GORDON HARTSHORNE

This book is dedicated to

IRIS AND ELLEN GRAFF

and

MARION AND STEPHEN BACHE

and to their generation,

which will write new chapters

in the continuing

"ADVENTURE OF THE AMERICAN PEOPLE"

Examine the list (below) of major themes the authors have used in this book. In addition, an important one is the development of American democracy from colonial times to the present. The authors have shown that democracy has developed steadily from the time when the first representative assembly was established in Virginia. Democratic advances are continuing, since the goals of American democracy have not yet been achieved.

PREFACE

The Adventure of the American People is a modern history of the United States. Because it is also a textbook, we have aimed to inspire our readers as well as to instruct them. We hope to arouse in them an enthusiasm for the possibilities that tomorrow always offers to men and women who are free.

As historians, we know that an understanding of the past can help make the present intelligible. Mankind, therefore, needs constantly to read stories of every place and period. And in all historical literature there is no more fascinating story than our own country's. We think we have told it in a manner that we ourselves would enjoy if we were high school students today—sympathetically and truthfully.

As teachers, we are aware that young Americans are more worldly, more critical, and better informed than ever before. And since they look forward to living an important portion of their lives in the twenty-first century, they will seek in a history of their country the background of matters newly of concern and relevance to Americans as a whole. Some of these elements constitute major themes of this book.

One is the powerful role of the United States as a nation among other nations in a competitive and threatening world. A second is the process by which the country's social, economic, and political institutions are continually being adapted to changing conditions. A third is the burgeoning of cities and suburbs, creating serious attendant problems. A fourth is the growing role of art and technology in shaping the character of national life. A fifth is the contribution of history's sister disciplines—anthropology, economics, geography, political science, and sociology—in illuminating American culture and society. A sixth is the rediscovery that the American people are of various races, national origins, religions, and viewpoints and that their separate identities together constitute a precious collective inheritance for the nation.

We take this opportunity to express our debt of gratitude to a number of friends and colleagues who have willingly allowed us to enlist their advice and help. Jacques Barzun, University Professor, and Richard B. Morris, Gouverneur Morris Professor of History—both of Columbia University—read an early version of our book and gave us the benefit of their wide-ranging criticism. Professor Edgar A. Toppin of Virginia State College provided a searching review of the entire book in its present form. Professors Alden T. Vaughan, John A. Garraty, and William E. Leuchtenburg of Columbia commented in close detail on chapters dealing with their specialties. The reference librarians of the Columbia University Libraries undertook to answer many difficult questions that arose.

We also thank cordially our devoted editor, Eileen Gibbons, for her tireless labors. Her keen judgment and high standards are reflected throughout the book. We value, too, the services of Nora O'Brien, our copy editor. Finally, we take note appreciatively of the research assistance of Patrick J. Abbazia and the critical and secretarial assistance of Edith Graff and Iris Graff.

H.F.G.
J.A.K.

The Adventure of the American People is divided into seven major parts. There are thirty chapters in all. In addition there are three sections called "The Quality of Life," which are pictorial essays on life in the late 1700's, the late 1800's, and the present. At the close of each of the seven parts is a one-page discussion of the whole period treated, providing a summary of what it was like to be an American in the years covered.

CONTENTS

PART ONE

EUROPE TRANSPLANTED

1

CHAPTER	1	THE OPENING OF A NEW WORLD	4
	2	THE ARRIVAL OF THE ENGLISH	22
	3	OLD RIVALRIES AND NEW COLONIES	42
	4	ENGLAND'S TRIUMPHS AND TROUBLES	58
	5	AMERICA'S SUCCESSFUL REVOLT	80
		A LONG VIEW	99
		THE QUALITY OF LIFE	102

PART TWO

MAKING A NEW NATION

105

CHAPTER	6	ERECTING THE FRAME OF GOVERNMENT	108
	7	THE DAY OF THE FEDERALISTS	126
	8	THE REPUBLICANS IN PEACE AND WAR	144
	9	STRENGTHENING THE NATIONAL SPIRIT	162
		A LONG VIEW	178

PART THREE

THE CHALLENGE OF SECTIONALISM

181

CHAPTER	10	THE AGE OF ANDREW JACKSON	184
	11	THE NORTH: DIVERSE INTERESTS	200
	12	THE SOUTH: THE COTTON KINGDOM	216
	13	THE WEST: MANIFEST DESTINY	230
		A LONG VIEW	246

PART FOUR

TESTING THE FEDERAL UNION

249

CHAPTER	14	THE UNITED STATES DIVIDED	252
	15	THE WAR BETWEEN THE SECTIONS	270
	16	REESTABLISHING NATIONAL UNITY	290
		A LONG VIEW	308

Call attention to the contents of the Appendix. Students should familiarize themselves with the kind of information given there and should have occasion to refer to it frequently. The list of dates and events is actually an outline of American history.

PART FIVE

CREATING INDUSTRIAL STRENGTH
311

CHAPTER 17 CONSOLIDATING THE FACTORY SYSTEM 314
18 SUBDUING THE "LAST WEST" 340
19 PARTISANSHIP AND STATESMANSHIP 370
20 ORGANIZING THE FORCES OF LABOR 398
21 THE READJUSTING OF SOCIETY 426
A LONG VIEW 457
THE QUALITY OF LIFE 460

PART SIX

REACHING INTO THE WORLD
463

CHAPTER 22 CARRYING THE FLAG OVERSEAS 466
23 THE TIME OF THE PROGRESSIVES 496
24 NEW INTERNATIONAL RESPONSIBILITIES 530
A LONG VIEW 555
THE QUALITY OF LIFE 558

PART SEVEN

THE QUEST FOR SECURITY
561

CHAPTER 25 INVOLVEMENT IN EUROPE 564
26 PROSPERITY'S PROMISE 598
27 CRASH, CRISIS, AND THE NEW DEAL 628
28 THE END TO ISOLATION 666
29 THE GLOBAL WAR 696
30 IN AN UNEASY WORLD 738
A LONG VIEW 786

APPENDIX

The Declaration of Independence 789
The Constitution of the United States and What It Means Today 791
Dates and Events in American History 810
Presidents, Vice-Presidents, and Secretaries of State 814
Facts About the States 816
Estimated Colonial Population: 1610 to 1780 817
Area—Territorial Expansion 817
Population, Decennial Summary 818
Area and Population 819
Continents and Metropolitan Centers 820
Exports and Imports of Merchandise by the United States,
with Trade Balances 821
Index 822

CHAPTER 1 From a letter from Columbus to Luis de Santangel on February 15, 1493   4–5

2 From *A Discourse on Western Planting* (1584), by Richard Hakluyt   22–23

3 From *A New Discourse of Trade* (1693), by Sir Josiah Child   42–43

4 From *Common Sense* (1776), by Thomas Paine   58–59

5 From *Letters from an American Farmer*, by Michel Guillaume Jean de Crèvecoeur   80–81

6 From "The Devil Is in You," an essay written by Noah Webster in 1786   108–109

7 From a letter written by Alexander Hamilton to Robert Morris on April 30, 1781   126–127

8 From a letter written by Thomas Jefferson to a friend in Virginia on January 16, 1787   144–145

9 From a speech by John C. Calhoun, delivered in the House of Representatives on February 4, 1817   162–163

10 From the farewell address of Andrew Jackson on March 4, 1837   184–185

11 From *Walden* (1854), by Henry David Thoreau   200–201

12 From *Memoir on Slavery* (1837), by William Harper   216–217

13 From an article written by John L. O'Sullivan in 1845   230–231

14 From a speech by William H. Seward, delivered at Rochester, New York, on October 25, 1858   252–253

15 From Abraham Lincoln's second inaugural address, March 4, 1865   270–271

16 From a report written by Carl Schurz in 1865   290–291

17 From "Popular Illusions About Trusts," an article by Andrew Carnegie published in 1900   314–315

18 From *The American Commonwealth* (1888), by James Bryce   340–341

19 From *Political Recollections: 1840–1872* (1884), by George Washington Julian   370–371

20 From *Organized Labor* (1903), by John Mitchell   398–399

21 From *The Farmer's Side* (1891), by William A. Peffer   426–427

22 From a speech entitled "The March of the Flag," delivered by Albert J. Beveridge on September 16, 1898   466–467

23 From a speech by Theodore Roosevelt, delivered in Providence, Rhode Island, on August 23, 1902   496–497

24 From President William Howard Taft's annual message to Congress, on December 3, 1912   530–531

25 From Woodrow Wilson's war message to Congress on April 2, 1917   564–565

26 From a campaign speech by Herbert Hoover, delivered in Madison Square Garden in New York City on October 22, 1928   598–599

27 From Franklin D. Roosevelt's first inaugural address, March 4, 1933   628–629

28 From a speech entitled "Fundamentals of American Foreign Policy," delivered by Cordell Hull in Washington, D.C., on March 17, 1938   666–667

29 General Dwight D. Eisenhower's "Order of the Day" to his troops on June 6, 1944   696–697

30 From an article written by Glenn T. Seaborg in 1967   738–740

Thirty primary sources are given in this book, as the list above indicates. Observe the wide variety--letters, books, speeches, reports, and documents. Students should appreciate the use of primary sources: they reveal details and aspects of the past which no secondary source can provide, and they help people realize what they sometimes forget--that history has been made by human beings, with all the strengths and weaknesses that people exhibit today. The authors of this text have given special attention to the human side of American history, and they have used numerous quotations from individuals in various situations as well as the primary sources listed here. In addition, they frequently take time to discuss possible reasons why people acted as they did in specific instances or to interpret historical movements in terms of their effects on human beings.

This list of graphic illustrations in the book shows the breadth of content covered and enables a student to locate quickly any one of them. The maps could make up a historical atlas.

MAPS, TABLES, GRAPHS, AND DIAGRAMS

PART ONE EUROPE TRANSPLANTED

Early Routes to the East   6
The Search for a New Route to the East   10
The Spanish in the New World   17
The Early French in the New World   18
Land Grants of the Virginia Company   27
Virginia and Maryland   31
Early Settlements in New England   35
A New England Town   36
Offshoots of Massachusetts Bay Colony   38
Dutch and Swedish Settlements   45
The Carolinas   51
Pennsylvania and New Jersey   53
The Thirteen Original Colonies in 1750   54
The French Hold on the Interior   61
British Strategy in the French and Indian War   65
North America, 1763   66
The War in New England, 1775–1776   89
The Retreat from New York, 1776–1777   90
Northern Campaigns, 1777   91
Clark's Route, 1778–1779   93
The War in the South, 1780–1781   94
The Final Campaign, 1781   94
North America, 1783   96

PART TWO MAKING A NEW NATION

Western Land Claims and Cessions   111
The Northwest Territory   112
The Controversial Posts   137
The Barbary Coast of Africa   147
Louisiana Purchase and Its Exploration   150
Campaigns in the War of 1812   158
Ten Largest Cities in the United States, 1790, 1800, 1810, 1820   165
The United States in 1819   166
The Slave-Free Balance, 1821   172

PART THREE THE CHALLENGE OF SECTIONALISM

The Removal of the Eastern Indians   189
Settlement of the Maine Boundary, 1842   196
Ten Largest Cities in the United States, 1830, 1840, 1850, 1860   205
National Road and Canals, 1840–1850   210
Railroads, 1860   212
The Cotton Kingdom   220
Slaves in 1850   226
Frontiers, 1750, 1850   232
The Advance to the Pacific   235
The Mexican War   239
Territorial Growth of the United States, 1853   242

PART FOUR   TESTING THE FEDERAL UNION
             The Compromise of 1850   256
             Kansas, Nebraska, 1854   260
             The War in the East, 1861–1863   276
             The War in the West, 1861–1863   277
             Campaigns of 1864–1865   282

PART FIVE   CREATING INDUSTRIAL STRENGTH
             Ten Largest Cities in the United States, 1870, 1880, 1890, 1900   319
             Main Eastern Railroads, 1875   322
             The Pacific Railroads, 1893   326
             Coal Production in the United States   330
             Petroleum Production in the United States   333
             Production of Steel Ingots and Castings in the United States   335
             The "Last West," 1860   344
             Miners and Cattlemen in the "Last West"   354
             United States of America   360–361
             Indian Reservations, 1900   366
             Samoa   392
             Hawaii   393
             Floor Plan of a Dumbbell Tenement   435
             The Presidential Election of 1896   453

PART SIX   REACHING INTO THE WORLD
             War in the Philippines, 1898   476
             War in Cuba, 1898   478
             Expansion Overseas   483
             Middle America   540
             The Settlement of the Alaskan Boundary, 1903   552

PART SEVEN   THE QUEST FOR SECURITY
             Europe in 1914   567
             The Western Front in the First World War   580
             Ten Largest Cities in the United States, 1910, 1920, 1930, 1940   604
             Unionization in the United States   654
             The Pacific Before the Second World War   681
             Aggressions in Europe, 1936–1940   688
             Second World War: The Height of Nazi Expansion, 1942   710–711
             The War in Korea   750
             The World   758–759
             Southeast Asia   760
             Southwest Asia and North Africa   765
             Israel   765
             Ten Largest Cities in the United States, 1950, 1960, 1970   776
             Rising World Trade   780

#Western culture is predominantly Christian. Christianity bears a close relationship to Judaism, and teachings of both have become part of Westerners' ways of living.

Each of the seven parts of this text begins with a discussion of some of the major ideas students should consider before beginning Chapter 1. The emphasis here is on aspects of the culture the European settlers brought to the Americas. This culture is called "Western," since it developed in the western part of the known world over a period of many centuries before Europeans began their explorations leading to the discovery of the New World. It is tremendously important to every American that Western culture was the one that became established in North America, because it is the one he learns. American culture is a branch of Western, although it has elements of other cultures, since people from many parts of the world have made contributions to it.

EUROPE TRANSPLANTED

A second start! Can you imagine beginning all over again and having the chance to repair the mistakes that mankind has made during the centuries? This is the incredible opportunity that was given to Europeans five hundred years ago. The occasion: the "discovery" of a new world.

It was an astonishing and unprecedented event. The door of history, without advance warning, had sprung wide open to reveal a vast and glorious vista on which men might rebuild their hopes and remake their lives. Europeans faced this awesome good fortune without maps or previous examples or "how-to-do-it" books. They stood on the threshold of a new epoch that was as trackless and as treacherous and potentially as wonderful as the Atlantic Ocean, which became their first pathway.

These men and women were the inheritors of an extraordinary tradition: it included the rich teachings of Judaism and Christianity and #
the magnificent culture of ancient Greece. They were well provided with ##
artistic and technical skills: their ancestors had produced the paintings and sculptures of the Renaissance, built the pyramids of Egypt, and laid the roads of the Roman Empire.

Some were accomplished in the craft of self-government: their forebears had begun to bring kings and queens under control by means of an institution called Parliament. They were the vigorous and ambitious people who had woven splendid patterns of law, of literature, and of learning in the chief countries of western Europe.

To think of the European, then, as really "starting from scratch" is to have a wrong impression. He carried on his lonely ocean journey not only home-style clothing with which to keep warm; he transported also

##Western Europeans had accomplished extraordinary achievements in art and architecture. They had an advanced technology. See "Sifting the Sources," question 2, p. 21.

#The English settlers especially brought ideas of self-government to the New World. They were accustomed to the idea of choosing men who would represent them as members of a legislative body to make laws in their behalf and otherwise protect their interests.

home-style ideas about religion, politics, economics, science—about everything. These were the furnishings of his mind.

Much of what he brought with him—both the physical and the mental —quickly proved either useless or needless; and in time the former European reequipped himself in American style to meet his unexpected requirements. Soon joined by the African, he gradually fashioned a new and remarkable civilization.

The full meaning of what was being achieved was not immediately apparent. But as the years passed, it struck forcibly those who chanced to revisit Europe—as it struck Thomas Jefferson in Paris in 1785. "My God!" he wrote to a friend, "how little do my countrymen know what precious blessings they are in possession of, and which no other people on earth enjoy!"

A map of Virginia drawn in 1608 by Captain John Smith, an early colonist whose bold explorations of the coastal areas provided first-hand information.

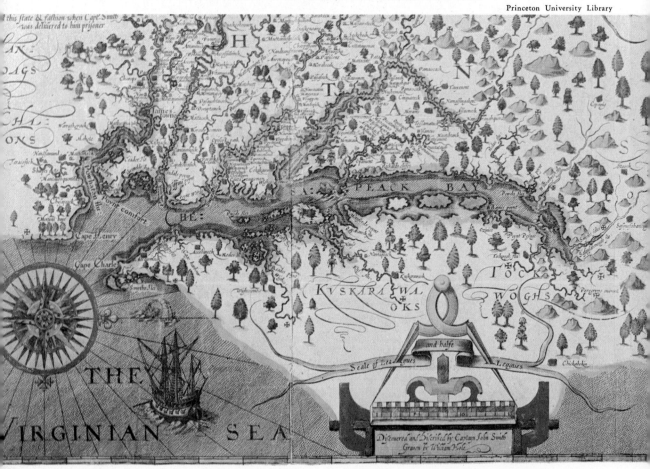

2 This map shows Jamestown, the site of the first permanent English colony in America. The original map was hand-colored. Ask which way is north. (Upper Chesapeake Bay points north.)

A page of contents showing the main heads in each of the chapters making up the section appears at the beginning of each part. Part One encompasses about three hundred twenty-five years--from the time of the first European explorations to the year when the United States became independent. The

PART ONE

EUROPE TRANSPLANTED

author telescoped the early portion of this period in order to emphasize purely American history.

| CHAPTER 1 | THE OPENING OF A NEW WORLD | 4 |

The Lure of Asia Proves Irresistible — 6

Modern Nations Rise Along the Atlantic Seaboard — 7

An Age of Exploration Stirs Western Europe — 12

CHAPTER 2 — THE ARRIVAL OF THE ENGLISH — 22

England Enters the European Contest for Power — 24

Ambitious Merchants Plant the Virginia Colony — 26

The Calverts Draw Catholics to Maryland — 31

Religious Dissenters Settle New England — 32

Emigrants from Europe and Africa Adjust to the New World — 40

CHAPTER 3 — OLD RIVALRIES AND NEW COLONIES — 42

America Mirrors the Conflicts of Europe — 44

Britain Sows a Second Crop of Colonies — 50

CHAPTER 4 — ENGLAND'S TRIUMPH AND TROUBLES — 58

Britain Emerges as the Greatest of Colonial Powers — 60

The Mother Country Arouses the American Colonists — 67

A Declaration of Independence Defies the Empire — 74

CHAPTER 5 — AMERICA'S SUCCESSFUL REVOLT — 80

The Era of Liberty Opens for Americans — 82

The Americans Fight Under George Washington — 87

England Recognizes Its Colonies' Independence — 95

A LONG VIEW — 99

Every chapter opens with a quotation from a significant primary source--a letter, speech, article, book--one that is closely related to one or more major aspects of the content that follows. Frequently the quotations are subjects of study suggested in the Workshops. (For example, see p. 21, "Understanding Documents." The fourth question is the type used to institute inquiry. It is a fruitful way of introducing students to new material since it generates interest and demands involvement. Any other unidentified document can be used.)

1

THE OPENING OF A NEW WORLD

#Sant Salvador--San Salvador--is now called Watling Island (see p. 17).

. . . I believe that I have discovered . . .

SIR: As I know that you will have pleasure from the great victory which our Lord hath given me in my voyage, I write you this, by which you shall know that in thirty-three days I passed over to the Indies with the fleet which the most illustrious King and Queen, our Lords, gave me; where I found very many islands peopled with inhabitants beyond number. And, of them all, I have taken possession for their Highnesses, with proclamation and the royal standard displayed; and I was not gainsaid. To the first which I found, I gave the name Sant Salvador, in commemoration of His High Majesty. . . .   #

The lands thereof are high, and in it are very many ranges of hills, and most lofty mountains incomparably beyond the island of Tenerife, all most beautiful in a thousand shapes, and all ac-   ##

##Tenerife is the largest of the Canary Islands, a mountainous group off northwestern Africa.

AMERICÆ PARS QVINTA.

The picture on this two-page spread is contemporary, like most of the illustrations in this book. Since it belongs to the period discussed in the chapter, it carries a special authenticity, of a kind impossible in an illustration created by an artist today, even with the most careful research.

cessible, and full of trees of a thousand kinds, so lofty that they seem to reach the sky. And I am assured that they never lose their foliage, as may be imagined, since I saw them as green and as beautiful as they are in Spain during May. And some of them were in flower, some in fruit, some in another stage. . . . And the nightingale was singing, and other birds of a thousand sorts, in the month of November. . . .

They [the people] have no iron or steel, nor any weapons; nor are they fit thereunto; not because they be not a well-formed people and of fair stature, but that they are most wondrously timorous. They have no other weapons than the stems of reeds in their seeding state, on the end of which they fix little sharpened stakes. Even these, they dare not use; for many times has it

happened that I sent two or three men ashore to some village to parley, and countless numbers of them sallied forth, but as soon as they saw those approach, they fled away in such wise that even a father would not wait for his son. And this was not because any hurt had ever been done to any of them. . . .

And in conclusion, to speak only of what has been done in this voyage, which has been so hastily performed, their Highnesses may see that I shall give them as much gold as they may need; . . . spices and cotton at once, as much as their Highnesses will order to be shipped . . . and aloe-wood as much as they shall order to be shipped; and slaves as many as they shall order to be shipped—and these shall be from idolators. And I believe that I have discovered rhubarb and cinnamon. . . .

This is enough; and [thanks to] Eternal God our Lord who gives to all those who walk His way, victory over things which seem impossible; and this was signally one such, for although men have talked or written of those lands, it was all by conjecture, without confirmation from eyesight. . . . Dated, on the caravel, off the Canary Islands, the 15 February of the year 1493.

At your command,

THE ADMIRAL.

This is Columbus' first report of his discovery of the islands he called the Indies. It was written as a letter to Luis de Santangel, keeper of King Ferdinand's purse, who had persuaded Queen Isabella to send Columbus on his famous voyage. The letter was written aboard the Niña when it was off the Azores, not the Canary Islands, probably incorrectly named here through an early printing error. It may properly be considered the first American document.

Ask which of the activities suggests the Spanish interest in American mines. Call attention to the Western weapons (examples of superior European technology).

An artist's idea of the heroic wave of exploration and settlement that followed the discovery of America: the Spanish, struggling over difficult terrain and relying on Indians for help, plant a cross—a symbol of Western culture—on a rugged height. This illustration is from a book published in Europe about a century after Columbus' great voyage.

The Latin words mean, "Part Five of America."

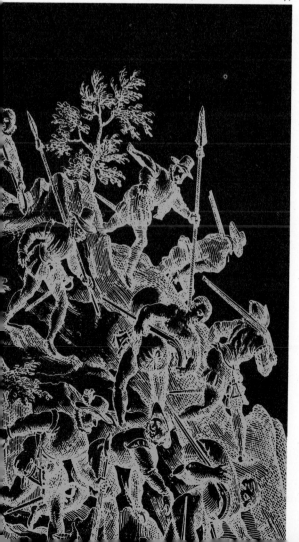

Theodore DeBry, *America*, 1590 (New York Public Library)

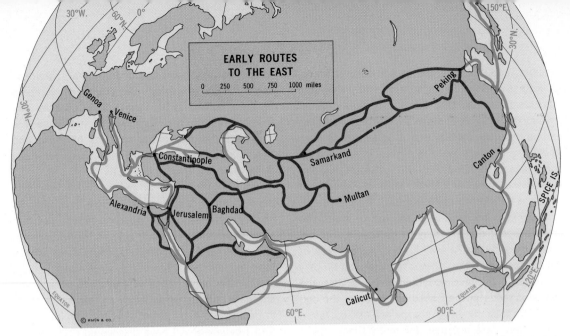

EARLY ROUTES TO THE EAST

0   250   500   750   1000 miles

People in Southwest Asia were strategically located for obtaining eastern goods, and Italians were well situated for reselling them. Western Europeans had no part in the profitable trade but envied those who did.

The point of the map is to show the centers of trade and also the distances men had to travel to bring back Eastern goods.

THE LURE OF ASIA PROVES IRRESISTIBLE

Like a magnet that draws iron filings to it, eastern Asia has long held a remarkable attraction for people in the Western world. The man who helped most to arouse this great interest was a Venetian, Marco Polo. Polo spent seventeen years in China, India, and Malaya in the thirteenth century. Europeans were fascinated by the tales he told of the riches, luxuries, and splendors of the East. He reported that daily a thousand wagonloads of silk came to Peking; that he had seen the rubies of Ceylon, the pearls and diamonds of India, and all manner of spices on the islands in the eastern sea.

But there was good reason why people in general were not eager to undertake a similar journey to Asia. The magnificent roads that the ancient Romans had built had fallen into disuse and decay, and the means of travel by sea were hardly better than they had been in the days of Julius Caesar, over 1200 years before. It was a brave man or a foolish one who ventured far from home—by water or by land.

THE IMPACT OF THE CRUSADES

The roads and commerce of Europe, however, were destined to be rebuilt as a result of the Crusades, those religious-military expeditions which had first stirred the imagination of Marco Polo. By the end of the thirteenth century, when Polo returned from his memorable trip, nine Crusades had been undertaken. Like the first, which was preached by Pope Urban II in 1095, they were designed to recover the Holy Land from the Turks, who had won it in 1071. From a military point of view the Crusades were a failure because in 1291 the last Christian stronghold, the city of Acre, fell to the Moslems. #

Trade with the East. The two centuries of peace that followed were extremely significant. The Italian cities that had grown wealthy by outfitting those who bore the cross now became channels through which passed the commerce between Europe and Southwest Asia. The trade increased year by year. Europeans had developed tastes for the goods from the East that they had discovered on their journeys to Jerusalem—spices, brocades, and fine ivories. These tastes would never die out; in fact, they would grow steadily. ##

Europeans, however, produced nothing that the people of the East wanted in return for

#Acre is a seaport on the Mediterranean Sea. It is now a city in northwestern Israel.

##The Crusades led to cultural diffusion (transmission of elements from one culture to another).

6

#Another reference to cultural diffusion. The Europeans particularly benefited from their contacts with the Moslems' knowledge of the sciences of medicine, mathematics, and astronomy.
##The high costs of the Crusades in both lives and money weakened the feudal nobility.

their goods. As a result, the Europeans had to pay in gold and silver. Obviously, they could not do this indefinitely. In time they would have to find new sources of precious metals— or give up the trade that had become so important to them.

As the Italian cities grew rich, they became the masters of Europe's commerce with Asia. Through the cities of Venice and Genoa poured silks, cottons, and cashmeres from India, rugs from Persia, spices from the East Indies, sugar from Arabia, porcelain from China, lacquer ware from Japan, and fine cutlery and glassware from Damascus. Everything the Italian merchants imported from Asia and then resold helped set the style for a new European way of life.

The Renaissance. The Crusaders had returned not only with tastes for eastern goods but also # with a knowledge of Moslem culture that played a large part in the European revival of learning in the twelfth and thirteenth centuries. Moreover, the holy wars had killed off many of the powerful feudal lords of Europe. The

absence of these men made it possible in some places for ruling families to increase their ## power with much less opposition than they might otherwise have met.

The combination of accumulated wealth, new ideas, and more stable governments stimulated a "rebirth" of interest in the arts and literature which is often called the Renaissance. In southern Europe we associate with this remarkable era the sonnets of Petrarch, the paintings of Leonardo da Vinci, and the sculpture of Michelangelo. In northern Europe, where the Renaissance also was felt, we think of the work of Flemish painters like the Van Eyck brothers and of the scholarly writing of the Dutchman Erasmus.

Sum and Substance

1. What products did Columbus offer the king and queen of Spain? 2. What were the principal effects of the Crusades on western Europe? What effect did they have on the Italian cities? 3. List some of Europe's eastern imports at that time. 4. What was the Renaissance?

This section gives an account of Portuguese and Spanish explorations of the world.

MODERN NATIONS RISE ALONG THE ATLANTIC SEABOARD

The day of Italian leadership in Europe was soon cut short. The Renaissance in northern Europe strengthened the feelings of kinship among people who had a common language and similar customs and traditions. Feudal principalities came to be united under one king as many Europeans began to feel greater devotion to a nation-state than they did to a local noble.

The spirit of nationalism that developed not only strengthened the power of various kings but also stimulated their territorial ambitions. The expanding western countries, such as Spain, Portugal, France, England, and the Netherlands, were not content to rely upon the Italian merchants. They wanted a more direct part in the Asian trade, and they were favorably situated geographically to challenge the older trade routes.

If the westerners could discover a way of

bypassing the Mediterranean, they could avoid having to purchase goods from the Italian merchants and the traders of Southwest Asia. If, in the bargain, they could find heathens to convert, they could at one and the same time do their own work and the Lord's also.

A WIDER RANGE FOR PORTUGAL

The task of discovery and exploration became an important interest of several monarchs in western Europe. Prince Henry the Navigator (1394–1460), a son of King John of Portugal, set in motion a chain of events that led to one discovery after another.

Acquiring lands overseas. Henry was a scholar, and he was fascinated by the possibilities of unveiling the unknown world. Pursuing this interest, he established in 1416 an observatory for studies in geography, navigation, and mathematics. Mariners came there to learn, and many

Nationalism is the devotion to or the promotion of national interest or unity. It has long been a force in international politics. Ask how nationalism shows itself in world affairs today.

The account of explorations offers a fine opportunity to review latitude, longitude, directions, locations, and facts of world geography in general. Use the map on p. 10 and a globe.

#Ask what large parts of Africa are still Portuguese.(Angola, Mozambique)

of them afterward set forth on voyages that advanced man's knowledge of his planet. They rediscovered the Azores and the Madeiras between 1420 and 1431; they reached out along the northwestern coast of Africa to about 5° north latitude; then they became familiar with the Guinea coast of the continent.

Access to the Guinea coast led the Portuguese to start a trade in Negro slaves, beginning in 1441. Henry approved only in order to convert the captured Negroes to Christianity. When abuses developed, he forbade the hideous commerce.

Finding the sea route to India. Henry died in 1460, but Portuguese navigators continued his work. Shortly they had reached the equator and then the Congo River. In 1488 Bartholomeu Dias became the first to round what was named, for good reason, the Cape of Good Hope. Now the road to India by sea lay open at last.

In 1497–1498 Vasco da Gama went beyond Dias' route and sailed across the Indian Ocean to Calicut in India. He returned to Lisbon in 1499 with a valuable cargo of gold and precious stones. From this voyage one may date the creation of the Portuguese empire. It had taken almost a century to reach by sea the great goal: fabulous eastern Asia.

UNDER THE SPANISH FLAG

Mariners from other lands were already following in the footsteps of the courageous Portuguese. The most famous and ultimately the most successful was Christopher Columbus. Born in 1451 in Genoa, Columbus spent his early years as a weaver—his father's trade— and as a seaman. He visited the eastern Mediterranean in 1475, and he was probably in England the next year. In 1477 he went to Lisbon, where he married the daughter of a Portuguese navigator. In that city at the time was Columbus' younger brother, Bartholomew, an expert chart-maker who, it is believed, later accompanied Dias to the Cape of Good Hope.

Persuading Ferdinand and Isabella. As a sugar buyer in the Portuguese possessions—the Azores, the Madeiras, and the Cape Verde Islands—Columbus met navigators who probably tempted him with suggestions that there were other islands farther to the west. When he could not get the Portuguese king, John II, to sponsor a voyage to Japan by a western route, he went to Spain. There, after years of frustration, he finally persuaded the monarchs, Ferdinand and Isabella, and some private investors to outfit an expedition and give him command of it.

The great landing. Ferdinand and Isabella bestowed on Columbus the title of "Admiral of the Ocean Sea" and promised him one-tenth of all the treasure he might find. In August, 1492, ready at last, he departed from the port of Palos in command of three vessels, the *Niña,* the *Pinta,* and the *Santa Maria,* and a crew of ninety men. Sailing by dead reckoning, Columbus led the vessels to the Canary Islands and then into the unknown.

Unfavorable winds and low morale had the men near mutiny just two days before Columbus saw a light which he said "was like a little wax candle rising and falling." What made this light we do not know, but on the twelfth day of October the Admiral landed on Watling Island in the Bahamas. Taking possession in the name of the Spanish crown, Columbus sailed on to explore the islands now called Cuba and Hispaniola. Thinking that he was near Asia, he called these islands the "Indies."

The Admiral's disappointment. But Columbus was not satisfied. These surely could not be the islands he had read and dreamed about. His own copy of Marco Polo said: "The king of Japan hath a mighty palace all roofed with finest gold, just as our churches are roofed with lead. The windows of that place are all decorated with gold; the floors of the halls and of many chambers are paved with golden plates, each plate a good two fingers thick. There are pearls in the greatest abundance." Disappointed, Columbus returned to Barcelona, where, as his son wrote, "All the court and the city came out to greet him."

Before he died in 1506, Columbus made three more voyages to the New World. On the last one he touched on the Honduran coast, exploring as far southward as central Panama.

#In 1961 Norwegian archeologists found the remains of a Viking settlement in Newfoundland. In 1963 Yale University made public the Vinland Map, said to be a Viking representation of Greenland and the surrounding area. Some doubt remains about it.

Imagined discovery and real achievement. Because Columbus mistakenly thought he had reached the East Indies, he called the people he saw Indians. Nevertheless, he also believed that he had found a new world. Learned men of the fifteenth century referred commonly to the outlying portions of Asia as a new world. Columbus probably thought, therefore, that these Asian islands were what he had found. We can never be sure exactly what he had in mind. But we do know that after the voyages of Columbus, the world was never the same again.

Viking voyages. It would be inconceivable to think that Europeans before Columbus had made no attempt to cross the Atlantic. It now seems clear that in the tenth and eleventh centuries the Vikings made significant voyages reaching to the North American continent, although the details remain shrouded in alluring uncertainties. Since the Vikings made no claims to discovering a new land and their settlements were not permanent, other peoples have received the credit and, in time, the rich rewards.

DIVIDING THE EARTH

The first international result of Columbus' explorations came in 1493. Spain sought the Pope's approval for the claims to territory that Columbus had made for his adopted country. By tradition, the Pope assigned rights to any lands that might be rescued from the heathen.

The Spanish, who dominated Pope Alexander VI, got him to draw a line of demarcation running north and south through a point 100 leagues west of the Cape Verde Islands, a Portuguese possession in the Atlantic. (One league was equal to about 4 miles.) From this line westward to the Indies, Spain would have exclusive rights to the commerce and use of lands it might discover. This meant that the Portuguese were barred from a tremendous area, now made Spain's exclusive preserve.

Treaty of Tordesillas. Understandably, Portugal raised objections to this division of the world and entered into direct negotiations with Spain. An agreement between the two nations in

As Columbus leaves, cashiers--behind the royal couple--presumably count their remaining money.

No artist—and almost certainly neither the king nor the queen of Spain—was at the waterfront of Palos, Spain, on August 3, 1492, to witness or depict the departure of Columbus. In this sixteenth-century conception, two men behind Columbus hold long-handled swords like those the Spanish would use so devastatingly in America.

Theodore DeBry, *Voyages*, 1594 (New York Public Library)

MAGELLAN 1521

EQUATOR

PACIFIC OCEAN

180°

MACTAN

Peking •

BLOCKED

BY

LAND

BLOCKED

NORTH POLE

90°W.

90°E.

Calicut •

INDIAN OCEAN

DA GAMA 1498

THE VICTORIA 1522

BY LAND

ATLANTIC

0°

DIAS

EQUATOR

MAGELLAN 1519

OCEAN

1488

Statute Miles

0   200   400   60°

Equator

Pole

CAPE OF
GOOD HOPE

WEST LONGITUDE   0°   EAST LONGITUDE

© RMCN & CO.

Western Europeans were at a geographical disadvantage in participating in trade along old routes to the East, but their situation on the Atlantic made up for the handicap. Aided by technological advances and spurred by a desire for economic gains, they broke new paths despite immense danger, even encircling the globe.

The map shows graphically why Da Gama, but not Columbus, was able to reach the East.

1494, known as the Treaty of Tordesillas, resulted in moving the line so that it ran through a point 370 leagues to the west of the Cape Verde Islands. Each country would keep out of the domain set aside for the other. When a Portuguese expedition commanded by Pedro Cabral touched the coast of Brazil in 1500, the Portuguese took control of the land because it fell on their side of the Line of Demarcation.

Amerigo Vespucci's voyages. One Portuguese expedition was, from the American point of view today, the most interesting of all. It sailed along the South American coast with an Italian pilot aboard named Amerigo Vespucci. The German geographer Martin Waldseemüller published a letter of Vespucci in 1507 in which the Italian talked of a "new world." Waldseemüller suggested that this new world be named America

#The map on p. 17 shows the Line of Demarcation established by the treaty. Ask the class what language is spoken in Brazil today. (Mainly Portuguese)

after Amerigo. The suggestion was popular throughout Europe and the name has stuck.

Magellan's trip around the world. All good navigators were convinced that the world was round. But Ferdinand Magellan was the first to make a round-the-world voyage and prove the fact. A Portuguese sailor of noble birth, he had served in Portuguese India and then in Morocco, where he got into trouble over financial matters. This affair cost him the favor of the king of Portugal. For that reason he could get no support from the Portuguese for his project of trying to reach the Spice Islands—now the Moluccas—by sailing to the west.

Magellan was not easily put off. He went to Spain in 1517 where, in the following year, he persuaded the king that he could find a passageway through America leading to Asia. This would be a direct route through the Spanish part of the world as fixed by the Treaty of Tordesillas.

In September, 1519, Magellan sailed from Spain with 5 vessels and 270 men and began the search for the passage he was sure existed. Though his sailors mutinied, he finally brought his ships through the strait to which he gave his name and reached the calm western ocean which he gratefully called the Pacific.

The long voyage across the Pacific was unbelievably terrible. For almost two months the mariners saw no land. Hunger was ever-present: rats and leather rigging finally served as food.

With three of his vessels and the dejected and bedraggled survivors of his crew, Magellan reached the Philippines on March 16, 1521. Before the next month was over, however, tribesmen on the island of Mactan had killed Magellan. One of his vessels, aptly named the *Victoria*, continued the trip across the Indian Ocean, around the Cape of Good Hope, and back to Spain. It had completed the first circumnavigation of the world. The commercial importance of the accomplishment is shown by the fact that the spices brought back by the *Victoria* more than paid the cost of the whole expedition!

Magellan's voyage in many respects was the high point of the Age of Discovery. For the first time it had been proved that the earth is round. For the first time the Indies had in fact been reached by traveling west. For the first time the enormous surface of the earth covered by water was revealed. For the first time it was shown that the "new world" which Amerigo Vespucci had talked about might turn out to be a continent of vast size.

Man's new conception of the world. It is impossible now to appreciate how these discoveries altered man's conception of the world. Europeans of the late fifteenth and early sixteenth centuries were overwhelmed by the continual reports mariners brought back of new places and things.

Imagine a young boy learning in school in 1480 that Europe was the center of the world —which was said to be round but certainly *looked* flat—and that it was surrounded by seas impossible to cross because of unknown dangers and uncharted waters. Imagine that same boy in 1525, grown up and become a grandfather, telling his grandson that there was an inhabited continent across the Atlantic many times the size of Europe, and that on the other side of that continent lay a Pacific Ocean twice the size of the Atlantic.

The grandson might be unimpressed, because he was already used to the fact that this was a far bigger world than before. But the grandfather very likely would never grow accustomed to thinking of these discoveries as real. He would reflect in his old age, though, that he had lived through probably the most thrilling, most breathtaking generation in man's history on Earth.

Sum and Substance

1. What were the three principal forces in western Europe which led to the Age of Discovery? 2. What were Prince Henry the Navigator's motives for exploration? What did he and other Portuguese captains achieve by 1500? 3. Contrast Columbus' actual achievements with what he thought he had achieved. 4. What was the Treaty of Tordesillas? How did it affect Portugal's role in the New World? 5. How did the New World acquire the name "America"? 6. What did Magellan's voyage accomplish?

The head "Sum and Substance" appears after every major division of a chapter. The questions test knowledge of basic facts only. The Workshops contain other kinds of questions.

AN AGE OF EXPLORATION STIRS WESTERN EUROPE

But the best was yet to be. What lay on the little-known oceans and continents of the world? Man has not even yet been able to examine them in all their intricate detail. Much remains to be learned about the interior of Africa. The upper reaches of many South American rivers are still poorly mapped. Antarctica is largely # unknown. The mineral and protein riches of the ocean depths remain uncharted and untapped. Surely, as we reach farther and farther into outer space, we are still living in the wonderful Age of Exploration. It well may be that the age will never end.

The exploration of the newly found lands attracted adventurers, brave soldiers and sailors, humanitarians, and fakers. In time they spent their strength seeking the "Fountain of Perpetual Youth" and the legendary Seven Cities. As late as the eighteenth century they were still searching doggedly for an all-water route, called the Straits of Anian, which was supposed to cut through North America and link the Atlantic and Pacific.

What dreams they dreamed! What energies they lavished on their projects! Think of the mountains they had to climb and the rivers they had to ford. Think of the trees they had to uproot and the animals in their path that had to be destroyed. And, if this is not enough, think, above all, of the thousands of men whose names will never be known—who perished in their search for gold, or for that trail that was supposed to be only a hundred miles to the north, or for that shelter from the sun or frost that would keep a man alive.

In the history of exploration only the successful men are remembered. Bearing in mind that scores failed for every one who triumphed, we turn to those who earned immortal fame because they had superior skill, stronger will, or merely better luck than their fellows.

AT WORK FOR KING AND GOD

The Spanish adventurers, or conquistadors, conducted their affairs in the New World as private enterprise. Yet each had to obtain a royal license which permitted him to recruit men and to purchase equipment and provisions.

On every expedition missionaries went along, ## for it was the sworn obligation of the conquistador to bring to the conquered land not only the king's law but also the Christian's gospel. Though the crown did not ordinarily subsidize expeditions, it assisted occasionally if the possibilities of success were attractive. It aided in such cases because the king acquired the title to all conquered lands. He also received one-fifth of any gold and silver that might be found.

The conquistador was a monarch in miniature: he was given the privilege of owning a private estate, and in turn he could grant land to his friends and followers. His power was absolute: he might build forts and, for the first year at least, appoint officers. He could force the Indians to work for him.

Balboa and the Pacific. Most of the Spanish expeditions were launched from the West Indies. It was from Hispaniola in 1511 that a bankrupt planter named Vasco Núñez de Balboa fled from his creditors to the Isthmus of Panama, then called the Isthmus of Darien. There he learned from an Indian leader that beyond the mountains lay an immense ocean.

On September 25, 1513, Balboa reached a mountain summit from which he and his band of followers, including thirty Negroes, became the first people from the Old World to behold "the great South Sea." (That name did not stick, for later generations preferred to call it the "Pacific," as Magellan saw it on his famous voyage.) Balboa claimed in the name of Spain the ocean and all the shores it washed.

Ponce de León and Florida. In the same year, Juan Ponce de León became the first of the conquistadors to set foot in what is now the United States. The governor of Puerto Rico, he had been inspired to sail northward by some tales he had heard from slave traders. They had told him about the mysterious land of Bimini on which there was a fountain of youth—the waters of which kept a man forever ageless. Landing on Easter Sunday, 1513, he named the land

#Relate technological advances to explorations. See question 2 under "Sifting the Sources," p. 21.
##The two main interests the Spanish had in America are discussed here. Emphasize both.

onto which he stepped "Florida" (from the Spanish *Pascua florida*) meaning "Easter."

Ponce de León never found what he was after, but he liked what he saw. Eight years later, in 1521, he returned with settlers and livestock and tried to colonize at or near what is now called Tampa Bay. The hostility of the Indians made permanent settlement impossible, and far from finding everlasting youth, Ponce de León was killed by the Indians.

Florida contained no gold—only people who seemed unfriendly. It was therefore never attractive to the Spanish conquistadors and empire-builders. In fact, the Spanish held a foothold in Florida only in order to control the Straits of Florida, through which their vessels plied the way from Mexico to Spain. In 1565, St. Augustine was built in Florida as a base.

Cortés and Mexico. Six years after Ponce de León's first visit to Florida and in the very year that Magellan began his epoch-making journey, Hernando Cortés marched against the Aztecs in Mexico. With an army of 500 men, he posed in the beginning as the friend and defender of these terribly oppressed people. Then he became their conqueror.

The Mexican emperor, Montezuma, had at first welcomed the Spanish as descendants of the god Quetzalcoatl. But Montezuma's reward was imprisonment by Cortés. The gold and silver Cortés sent home from Mexico was treasure far more valuable than anything that would come out of Asia. The possibility of matching Cortés' achievement was ever in the minds of later adventurers.

Pizarro and Peru. Finding precious metals became the goal of life of the conquistador, but only one other succeeded in reaching it. He was Francisco Pizarro, who conquered Peru between 1532 and 1536. Pizarro looted the Inca people brazenly. His most arrogant act was the slaying of Atahualpa, the Inca ruler, after enticing him with sugary words, arresting him, and exacting from him as ransom a room filled with gold.

De Soto and the Mississippi. A lieutenant of Pizarro was Hernando de Soto, who wanted to

Right: This woodcut shows the five bridges by which the Spanish entered the Aztec castle.

John Carter Brown Library, Brown University

Europeans saw this picture of the Christianizing of the Inca king in a book on the conquest of Peru written by Pizarro's secretary and published in 1534.

Above: Observe the Roman Catholic priest and the king carried on a litter.

Mexico City—which lay on an island in Lake Texcoco—is shown here as it appeared in a German account of the capture of Mexico, printed in 1522.

John Carter Brown Library, Brown University

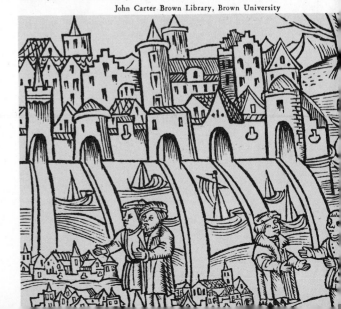

make himself as famous and as powerful as his commander. De Soto had heard from a fellow Spaniard, Alvar Cabeza de Vaca, a fascinating account of seven cities to the north of Mexico. Presumably they were waiting to be looted by the Spanish.

De Soto organized an elaborate expedition that landed in Tampa Bay in 1539, bent upon conquering as it moved westward. He cruelly mistreated the Indians he captured, using iron collars to keep them prisoners.

The fact that his westward march brought him to the Mississippi and that he was the first European to see and cross the Father of Waters hardly tickled De Soto's imagination at all. His mind was on finding gold and silver. He drove on and on furiously, following the Arkansas River and going as far as present-day Oklahoma. Still finding no treasure cities, he returned to the Mississippi, where he died. His followers secretly dropped his weighted body

Men of two differing cultures face each other.

De Soto encounters for the first time a group of Florida Indians, whose simple dress and mode of travel contrast sharply with the Europeans'.

New York Public Library

into the river, lest the Indians he had abused find out about his death and rejoice.

Coronado and the American Southwest. Cabeza de Vaca's vivid tales of the "Seven Cities of Cibola" and of the "hunchbacked cows"—buffaloes—he had seen, came to the attention of Antonio de Mendoza, the viceroy, or governor, of New Spain at Mexico City. Mendoza determined to make himself the master of this "empire." To head an exploring expedition he chose Francisco Coronado, one of the provincial governors of Mexico.

Coronado set forth in 1540 to become, if he could, another Cortés or Pizarro. But although he pushed from Mexico to the plains of what became Texas and into the middle of what is now Kansas, he found no spired cities of Cibola. He saw much awesome beauty, including huge buffalo herds and endless grassland. One of his men came upon the Grand Canyon; he and his companions gazed at it in stunned wonder. Yet, finding no gold, their leader, Coronado, considered himself cursed. History recalls him, however, as the most accomplished explorer of the American Southwest.

Coronado's guide—slain by Indians on the journey—was Estevanico, or Little Stephen, one of the greatest of Negro explorers. Negroes had accompanied many of the conquistadors on their expeditions. The first crop of wheat ever raised in the New World was planted and harvested in Mexico by a Negro traveling with Cortés.

ORGANIZING THE SPANISH EMPIRE

Spain was not primarily interested in establishing colonies in the New World. But the Spaniards who settled here had to be brought under a system of government that would assure protection for them and profits to Spain.

At home: Council and Board. Spanish colonial government was conducted through the Council of the Indies, organized in 1524 to make the major policies for the conduct of the Spanish empire. In addition, a board of trade (the *Casa de Contratación*) dealt with the various questions that arose concerning commerce. It also operated a warehouse in Seville through

##(in other words, bringing the large areas and scattered people under a Spanish system)

Josef Muench

The cities Cabeza de Vaca so glowingly described and Coronado so vainly sought doubtless were villages made up of cliff dwellings of the Pueblo Indians, like this ancient village in what is today the state of Arizona.

#An important idea: The Spaniards had not developed a tradition of self-government.

which passed all Spanish-American imports and exports.

In the colonies: viceroyalties. The Spanish colonies never were privileged to govern themselves. They were divided at the Isthmus of Panama into two domains or viceroyalties—New Spain and Peru. Each was ruled by a viceroy appointed by the king and responsible only to him. The viceroys chose their subordinates without consulting the wishes of the people. The towns had councils that could deal with local matters of limited importance, but in 1530 Emperor Charles V forbade these councils to meet without his specific approval.

The flow of wealth. Taxes made the mother country wealthy. They went almost directly to the king's purse, which was actually the national treasury. The monarch not only received one-fifth of the gold and silver from the New World mines but also sold government jobs in the colonies to the highest bidders. He sold for large sums the exclusive rights to sell certain commodities, such as gunpowder, salt, tobacco, and slaves. The contractor who had the slave-trade monopoly (*asiento*) paid a fee to the king for every Negro he brought into the colonies.

The royal grants. The Spanish colonies were sustained by agriculture organized on extensive grants, or *encomiendas,* made to royal favorites called *encomenderos.* Indians did the work, and they were kept in a servile condition. Cut off from their former tribal associations, they lost their skill as hunters and craftsmen, becoming completely dependent upon the Europeans.

By 1575, it is estimated, 5,000,000 Indians were living in encomiendas. In the approximately 200 towns of the sprawling Spanish empire there lived about 160,000 European heads of families. Of these, about 4000 were encomenderos. The huge Indian population resisted giving up its culture, but the small body of determined Spaniards fastened their language, laws, and customs on a huge area. The area ranged from the present-day Southwest southward through Mexico and Central America—eventually as far south as what is now Argentina.

Missions. The work of teaching the Indians the ways of the Spanish, including especially Catholic worship, was taken on by the dedicated friars. They organized *missions,* which served both as schools and as religious centers.

##Students may have visited some of the surviving buildings in California or elsewhere. The friars were chiefly responsible for the spread of Spanish culture in the New World.

Immediate gains. The Spaniards brought to their possessions a great many new food crops, such as wheat, barley, rye, chick-peas, and lentils. They introduced to America almonds, mulberries, cherries, walnuts, chestnuts, quinces, apples, apricots, all of the citrus fruits, and a host of Old World flowers. From Africa they brought sugar cane and varieties of bananas; and from Asia, the mango. The list is impressive as well as inviting.

Equally valuable were the European animals and animal products the Spanish introduced into the New World. It is said that the increasing number of beef cattle in the Spanish settlements put an end to cannibalism among some of the Caribbean tribes. But most important in revolutionizing the American way of life was the arrival of horses and mules. Truly, said a sixteenth-century writer, the Indians "blessed the beasts which relieved them from burden-bearing."

Lost opportunities. Although we can see after four hundred years what things were of enduring significance in the Spanish settlements, at the time only gold seemed worthwhile. In fact, the Spanish conquerors never took on the tasks of taming the forests and rivers of America and colonizing the land.

Finding gold so easily and so early drove them madly on to look for more. They never found it, but the search left its mark on Spanish culture in the New World, and in its turn it also affected the mother country. The conquistador considered manual labor something to be avoided, development of manufacturing something to be discouraged, and commercial activity something too far beneath the dignity of aristocrats to be engaged in.

At home, the Spaniards failed to reinvest the gold and silver drawn from the mines of the New World. When they had used it up, Spain lived only on memories of its past. Gambling always on "hitting the jackpot," it left to others the richest prize of all—what later became the United States. How different our history might have been if our own abundant gold and silver deposits had been found first by the Spaniards!

FRANCE'S CLAIMS IN AMERICA

By the time Spain had conquered Mexico, France was also developing into a strong country. Under Francis I, who became king in 1515, it gave clear indication that it would not sit idly by while Spain and Portugal divided the world between them.

France's interest first rested on the activities of French fishermen, who probably were dragging nets off Newfoundland as early as 1497 and by 1510 were regularly supplying northern France with cod. Fishing was scarcely as dramatic and exciting—or even as rewarding—as finding gold, but it was a good start in the New World. Later the Grand Banks were known as the "silver mines of the Atlantic" because the sleek and shiny fish caught there found a ready market.

Verrazano and the Atlantic coastline. But fish seemed unimportant to Francis I, who was a militant ruler. Eager for a source of quick wealth to pay for his wars against Charles V of Spain, his chief rival, he commenced French efforts to find a route to China. A Florentine sailor, Giovanni da Verrazano, who was living in France, came to the attention of Francis, and the King commissioned him to undertake an expedition to the New World. ##

Reaching the American coast at about the 34th parallel of latitude, Verrazano explored the shore from what became North Carolina to present-day Maine and Newfoundland. He was the first European known to enter what is now New York Bay. In July, 1524, Verrazano returned home, and on the basis of his voyages France laid its earliest claim to the New World. On a later trip to the West Indies, Verrazano was slain by Indians.

Cartier and the St. Lawrence. By Verrazano's death France lost a great pioneer of the sea. Yet Francis I persisted, sending Jacques Cartier, a pilot in the harbor of St. Malo, on three expeditions to North America. The first—in 1534—was organized to find a route to the East. It took Cartier to the Gulf of St. Lawrence, where he claimed the land for his king.

Cartier made other explorations along the

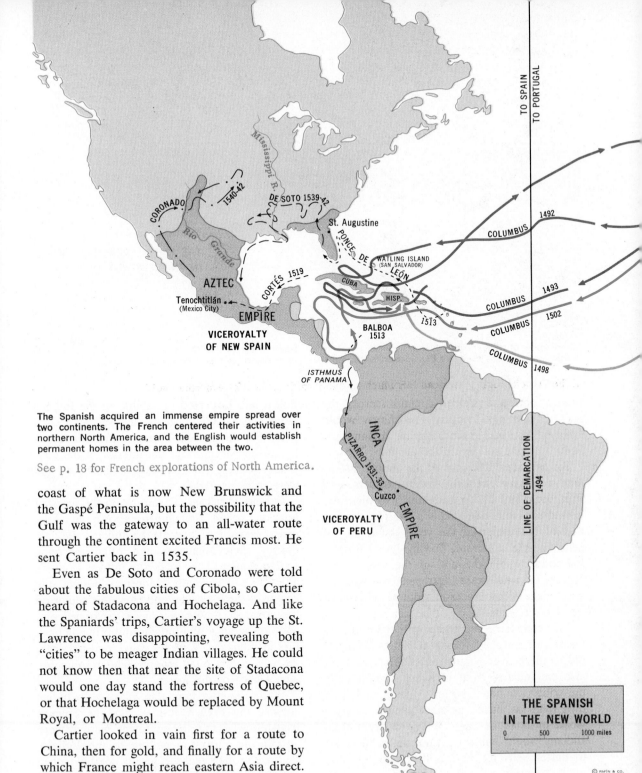

The Spanish acquired an immense empire spread over two continents. The French centered their activities in northern North America, and the English would establish permanent homes in the area between the two.

See p. 18 for French explorations of North America.

coast of what is now New Brunswick and the Gaspé Peninsula, but the possibility that the Gulf was the gateway to an all-water route through the continent excited Francis most. He sent Cartier back in 1535.

Even as De Soto and Coronado were told about the fabulous cities of Cibola, so Cartier heard of Stadacona and Hochelaga. And like the Spaniards' trips, Cartier's voyage up the St. Lawrence was disappointing, revealing both "cities" to be meager Indian villages. He could not know then that near the site of Stadacona would one day stand the fortress of Quebec, or that Hochelaga would be replaced by Mount Royal, or Montreal.

Cartier looked in vain first for a route to China, then for gold, and finally for a route by which France might reach eastern Asia direct. The rivers and forests and paths of the New World were still uncharted and unknown, but the extent of the American continents was suspected, at least, if not altogether appreciated.

Studying this map, students should be able to see (1) the advantage the Spanish enjoyed because of arriving in the New World first,

and (2) why the English and French concentrated on the places where they settled.

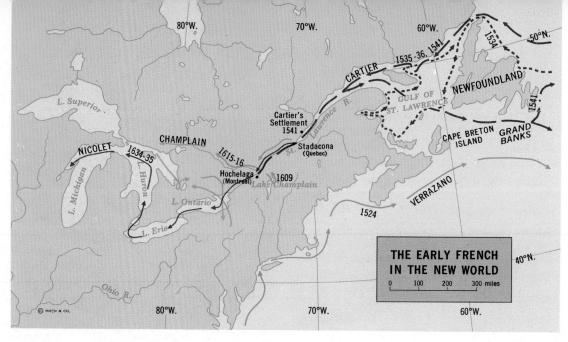

The voyages of Cartier gave France definite claim to North America as far south as the Spanish settlements.

Nevertheless, it was Champlain, the colonizer, who came to be known as the "Father of New France."

#The French sought American furs much as the Spanish looked for American gold.

France now had staked a claim across the seas. In the next century Frenchmen would learn to trap and trade with the Indians and build a unique society on the profits.

The fur traders. The first of the French fishermen were very likely the first fur traders, too. Furs could not have meant much to them except as souvenirs obtained in a swap for an iron tool or pot. But over the years the trickle of pelts became a torrent, flowing into Europe's hat industry. By the end of the seventeenth century the well-dressed European was wearing a hat made of felt processed from North American beaver skins.

This commerce altered not only the millinery fashion of Europe—to say nothing of what it did to the beaver population of America—but also the Indians' mode of living. Traditionally the tribesmen had laboriously fashioned their own weapons, beads, or other handiwork from wood or bone or bark. Within a generation, Indians would willingly travel miles in order to barter pelts for objects they had formerly made themselves.

The steadily growing trade in furs flourished more or less haphazardly until near the close of the seventeenth century. By then the demand for furs, especially beaver, had become so great

that it had surpassed the ability of the Indians along the St. Lawrence to supply the needed pelts. For this reason, French traders in America pushed deeper into the interior of the continent, looking for Indians who had furs and were willing to trade.

Exchange of cultures. To survive in the forested interior, young Frenchmen, known as *voyageurs,* learned to live as the Indians did, acquiring their languages and often marrying Indian women. They made the Indians France's allies and dependents. Montreal became the center of the fur trade, and from this center on the great St. Lawrence voyageurs fanned out, carrying goods to the Indians and bringing back furs in exchange. With his canoe and his pack, the voyageur was an independent, resourceful, lonely hero of the forest.

While the voyageurs were picking up Indian culture, the French Jesuits, like the Spanish friars elsewhere on the continent, were at work introducing European culture to the Indians. Because of their zeal the Jesuits notably helped enlarge French influence. Along with the voyageurs, they were the advance guard for the future French empire in America.

Samuel de Champlain and Quebec. Furs had attracted the greatest of all French explorers to

18 ##In this discussion the emphasis is on what the Indians and the French learned from each other. France was (and is) chiefly Roman Catholic, like Spain.

#Today the province of Quebec, of which the city of Quebec is the capital, is French-speaking, and other elements of French culture remain there.
##Self-government was not established--there was none in France, as there was none in Spain.

the New World. He was Samuel de Champlain, who between 1604 and 1607 traveled and mapped as far south as what became New England. He served under the Sieur de Monts, who had received a royal monopoly to trade in furs between the 40th and 46th parallels—a promising region called Acadia. But it proved to be unsuited to the fur trade, and Champlain advised the Sieur de Monts that they ought to make a settlement on the St. Lawrence River instead. There Champlain founded Quebec in 1608.

\# Though Quebec grew slowly, it gave the French a base in the St. Lawrence Valley. From this base Champlain conducted expeditions westward to Lakes Huron and Ontario and southward to Lake Champlain. Jean Nicolet, one of his trusted lieutenants, explored the Straits of Mackinac, Green Bay, and the Fox River. From the Winnebago tribe, Nicolet heard stories of a broad river that linked up with a "great water" (which probably was taken to be the Pacific). Champlain never found the link between the two, but he and other Frenchmen long continued to believe that the Northwest Passage was there and that they would find it eventually.

Richelieu and the Company of One Hundred Associates. The trading posts near Quebec limped along until the incomparable Cardinal Richelieu began to formulate French policy. In 1628 Richelieu founded the Company of One Hundred Associates, whose members pooled their capital and received a perpetual monopoly of the fur trade. The plan called for the Company to ship to New France 300 colonists annually, support each one for three years, and provide three priests in each new community. ##

Davis Strait is west of Greenland; Hudson Strait opens into Hudson Bay and Davis Strait.

Two of New France's most valuable natural resources are shown in this illustration from a book published in Amsterdam in the early 1700's, when France was still trying to attract settlers to the New World.

Rare Book Division, New York Public Library

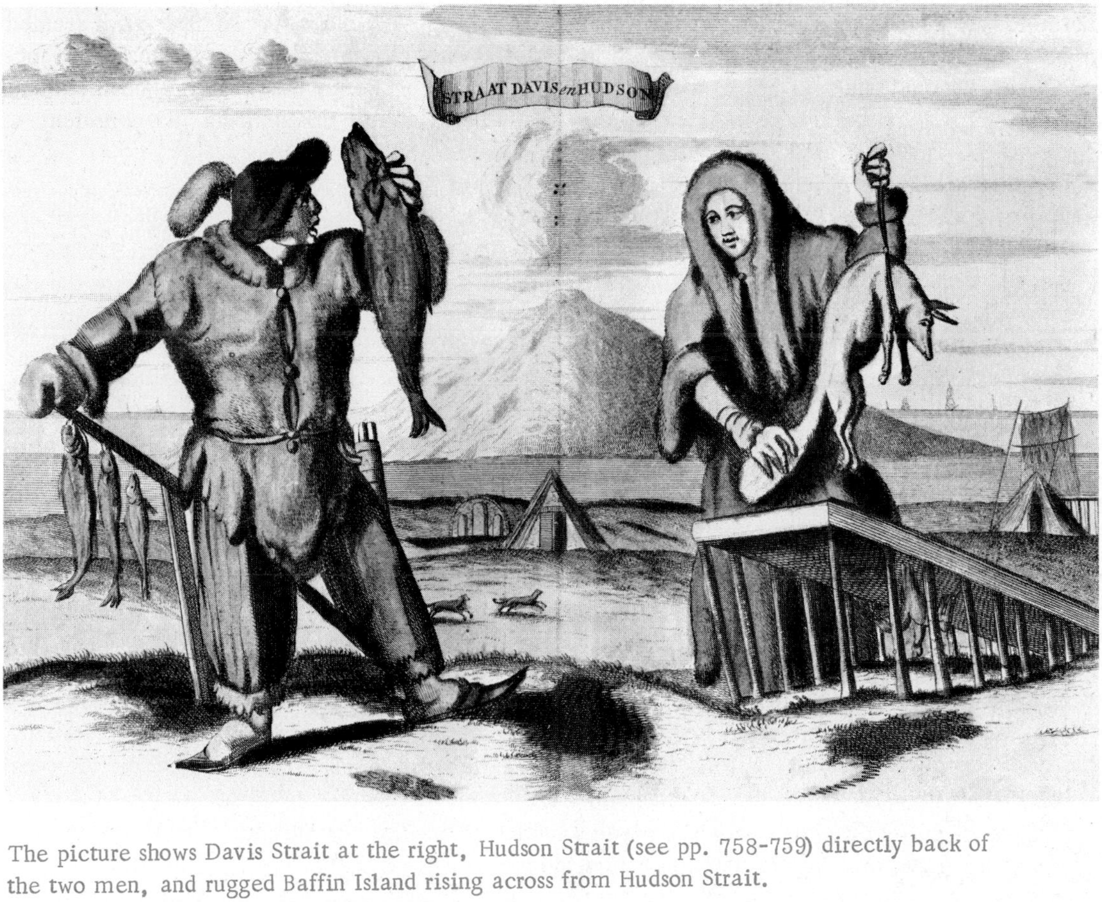

The picture shows Davis Strait at the right, Hudson Strait (see pp. 758-759) directly back of the two men, and rugged Baffin Island rising across from Hudson Strait.

The French zeal for Christianizing the Indians—work done chiefly by the Jesuits—is depicted in this drawing that appeared as a decoration on a map made especially for the French king.

The stream shown at the left (Le Sagnay) is the "Saguenay River," its name in present-day Canada.

The arrangement failed: the fur-trade profits were not great enough to sustain the immigration, non-Catholics were excluded, and the Company lacked capital for expansion. Furthermore, the French as a whole did not seem to have approved of colonization. In fact, it had to be decreed that no noble would lose caste or status by becoming a member of the Company of One Hundred Associates! How differently the Spanish conquistadors viewed their service in America.

We see that conditions in each European country markedly affected the impact each had on the colonial settlements it made. For the Frenchman, France was—and still is—the most beautiful land in the world: could anything be gained by migrating to an unknown one? For the Spaniard, there was no nobler purpose than serving the king and the church by finding gold and saving souls. For both, the mother country was the place to which one hoped and expected ultimately to return—rich and famous, of course.

In 1610, then, the French held the tiny town of Quebec on the banks of the St. Lawrence— a town based on the profits from furs. Far to the south lay St. Augustine, a fort that protected the northern flank of the Spanish em- pire, which had been built out of the golden riches of its miners. Between these two outposts lay millions of square miles largely unoccupied. Here England would make its bid for empire. In this unlikely place—or so, at least, it seemed to the explorers—English colonization succeeded so brilliantly that both France and Spain were in the end driven from the continent.

Sum and Substance

1. Describe the partnership arrangement of the Spanish conquistadors and the king. 2. What did Balboa achieve for Spain? 3. What were the two main purposes of Ponce de León's expedition to Florida? How successful was he? 4. How did Cortés conquer the Aztecs? 5. What was accomplished by each of the following: De Soto, Cabeza de Vaca, Coronado? 6. Explain the Spanish system of colonial government. 7. Who did the work for the encomenderos? 8. List some agricultural and social benefits which the Spanish gave to the New World. 9. What was the first economic activity which Frenchmen carried on in North America? 10. How did Verrazano and Cartier each contribute to knowledge of the New World? To the territory claimed by France? 11. Name the important effects of Champlain's explorations. 12. What system of colonization did Cardinal Richelieu set up?

A test for this chapter appears in the opening section of the Teacher Edition. The Workshop contains other means of evaluation, written and oral.

THE WORKSHOP

OF LASTING SIGNIFICANCE

Explain how each of the following was important in opening the New World.

the Crusades	Treaty of Tordesillas
Bartholomeu Dias	Amerigo Vespucci
conquistador	Ferdinand Magellan
Hernando Cortés	Núñez de Balboa
Hernando de Soto	Ponce de León
Giovanni	Francisco Coronado
da Verrazano	Jacques Cartier
Northwest Passage	voyageur
Vasco da Gama	Samuel de Champlain

UNRAVELING PUBLIC PROBLEMS

By understanding the problems of Americans of the past and by thinking critically of solutions they tried, we may learn to handle more competently the problems of our time.

1. What major problem faced the countries of western Europe in their competition with the Italian cities? What solution did Portugal try? Spain and France? How successful were the efforts of each country?

2. What obstacles did Columbus overcome in order to test his belief that the East could be reached by sailing westward? How well did he prove his point?

3. Name two problems the Spanish faced in establishing their colonies. How did they solve them? Were the solutions good or bad?

DOCUMENTS IN HISTORY

A document is an original paper, written or printed, furnishing information or evidence.

1. Why may the Columbus letter, pages 4–5, be called the first *American* document?

2. What special value does the letter have which no account of Columbus' expedition written later by a historian can have?

3. What was Columbus clearly trying to do in the letter? What method did he use?

4. If you did not know which group of islands Columbus visited, what clues would help you identify it?

INFORMED OPINION

To be respected, opinion must be informed, that is, based on facts or experience.

1. For each of the following pairs of explorers, answer these two questions and support your answers with facts.

A. Which explorer was more successful in achieving his purpose?

B. Which explorer probably had more influence on future developments?

(1) Columbus, Magellan

(2) Cortés, Coronado

(3) Prince Henry, Amerigo Vespucci

(4) Cartier, Champlain

2. What furnishings of the mind would an American today take to a new, unsettled part of the world or universe? #

SIFTING THE SOURCES

A source may be an original document, a reference book, or an eye-witness report. Each should be read critically.

1. Make a list of nations, cities, or natural features which are named for Columbus, Ponce de León, De Soto, and Champlain. Use the index of a recent atlas, such as *Goode's World Atlas* (12th ed.; Chicago: Rand McNally & Co., 1964). In Spanish, Columbus' name is "Colón"; in Italian, "Colombo."

2. One or more students should prepare oral reports on aids to navigation used by early explorers—such as the compass, the astrolabe, and square rigging. Some students should report on later improvements, such as the sextant, the chronometer, and the Mercator map, and on recent ones, such as radio, radar, and sonar.

A LOOK AT THE GLOBE

A degree of longitude at the equator covers about 70 statute miles. The equatorial circumference of the earth is about how many miles? Columbus believed that a degree covered only about 50 miles, underestimating the size of the earth by about what percent?

#This would be a good question for discussion after the study of Spanish and French explorations.

This chapter describes the establishment of the first English colonies in North America. One historian has called the document quoted the most important single paper for understanding the beginning of English colonization. The spelling and capitalization are archaic. Ask what passages show the sentiments named in the commentary on p. 23. At the time Hakluyt was writing, Britain's feeling against Spain was at a height. Queen Elizabeth, a Protestant, was unwilling to respect the Line of Demarcation, dividing newly discovered parts of the world between two Catholic countries. Sir Francis Drake had recently attacked Spanish ships and even Spanish settlements in America.

2

THE ARRIVAL OF THE ENGLISH

. . . to receave people from all partes of the worlde . . .

A brefe Collection of certaine reasons to induce her Majestie [Elizabeth I of England; reigned, 1558–1603] and the state to take in hande the westerne voyadge and the plantinge there.

1. The soyle yeldeth and may be made to yelde all the severall commodities of Europe, and of all kingdomes domynions and territories that England tradeth withe, that by trade of marchandize cometh into this realme.

2. The passage thither and home is neither to longe nor to shorte, but easie and to be made twise in the yere.

3. The passage cutteth not nere the trade of any Prince, nor nere any of their countries or ter-

English ships bear flags showing the cross of St. George, used before the Union Jack was adopted.

ritories and is a safe passage. . . .

6. This enterprise may staye the Spanishe Kinge from flowinge over all the face . . . of America, yf wee seate and plante there in time. . . .

11. At the first traficque with the people of these partes, the subjectes of this realme for many yeres shall chaunge many cheape commodities of these partes, for thinges of highe valor [value] there not estemed, and this to the greate inrichinge of the realme. . . .

12. By the greate plentie of those Regions the marchantes and their factors shall lye there cheape, buye and repaire their shippes cheape, and shall returne at pleasure. . . .

"Fry" (here "frye") means young fishes or young creatures--children.

16. Wee shall by plantinge there inlarge the ## glory of the gospell and from England plante sincere religion, and provide a safe and sure place to receave people from all partes of the worlde that are forced to flee for the truthe of Gods worde. . . .

20. Many men of excellent wittes and of divers singuler giftes overthrowen by suertishippe [becoming liable or surety for the debt of another] by sea or by some folly of youthe, that are not able to live in England, may there be raised againe, and doe their contrie goodd service. . . .

21. Many souldiers and servitors, in the ende of the warres, that mighte be hurtfull to this realme, may there be unladen, to the common profite and quiet of this realme, and to our forreine benefite there as they may be employed.

22. The frye of the wandringe beggars [orphaned and destitute children] of England that growe upp ydly, and hurtfull and burdenous to this realme, may there be unladen, better bredd upp. . . .

Richard Hakluyt (pronounced Hackloot), a famous English geographer, prepared a persuasive pamphlet in 1584 for his friend Sir Walter Raleigh, who was about to sponsor a colonizing expedition to Virginia. Called A Discourse on Western Planting, its arguments were effective because they conformed with the commercial, religious, and anti-Spanish sentiments of Elizabethan England. Hakluyt did not live to see his prophecies fulfilled. Observe how he predicted that the outcast and downtrodden might be rehabilitated in America.

Ask which of Hakluyt's statements proved to be untrue. (1, 2, and 3. Concerning 1: Englishmen tried to establish olive culture in Virginia, but it was impossible anywhere on the Atlantic seaboard.)

The English defeat in 1588 of the Spanish Armada in a battle in the English Channel gave Britain the freedom to sail its ships anywhere it chose and encouraged its colonization of North America.

Ask students to look back to p. 17 to see who was supposed to possess North America.

ENGLAND ENTERS THE EUROPEAN CONTEST FOR POWER

England's keen interest in exploration, like the rest of Europe's, arose primarily from the hope of finding a shorter route to eastern Asia. The first English claim in the New World was laid by John Cabot, a naturalized Venetian who had been born in Genoa. Convinced that Columbus had not located the rich parts of Asia, Cabot in 1496 obtained the authorization of King Henry VII to venture westward in search of them. The next year Cabot sailed from England and reached Cape Breton Island, on the North American coast. But he never found the lands he sought.

In 1553 Sir Hugh Willoughby and Richard Chancellor bravely tried to find a north*east* passage by sailing around northern Europe. Willoughby perished en route, but Chancellor pushed on and arrived in Moscow, where the czar, Ivan IV, made a trade agreement which led to the forming of the Muscovy Company.

These failures to find the East by sailing either northwest or northeast were discouraging. But events shortly opened exciting ways of achieving wealth. The commanding figure of this new era was the British queen, Elizabeth I.

AN AMBITIOUS QUEEN

Elizabeth, who came to England's throne in 1558, was a Protestant. Mary, her predecessor, had been a devout Catholic and a good friend of Spain. She had respected the Spanish and Portuguese claims in the New World because they had been based on a papal decision. But, being a Protestant, Elizabeth did not feel bound by the old ties of religion and tradition, and she made Spain her enemy. (She even abruptly turned down an offer of marriage made by the Spanish king, Philip II.) Soon riches came to England as Elizabeth's sailors plundered the homeward-bound Spanish treasure ships and raided the Spanish towns in Central and South America.

Drake's triumphs. The most famous of the English freebooters was Francis Drake, who later was knighted by Elizabeth for his services to her and to the country. In 1577 he received permission from the Queen to attack Spanish holdings along the Pacific coast of South America.

In this venture Drake was unbelievably lucky. Driven southward by a storm, he sailed through the Strait of Magellan in his little ship the *Golden Hind,* raiding the seaboard as he sailed north. Afraid to return the way he had come, he looked for a passageway to the Atlantic through the continent. Finding none, he sailed southward again and put in for repairs, probably just north of what is now San Francisco Bay. From there he sailed west, touching the Philippines and other islands, rounding the Cape of Good Hope, and arriving at Plymouth, England, at last in 1580.

Drake had become the first Englishman to circumnavigate the world. But even more important: the treasure he brought back is estimated to have been worth well over half a million pounds. Although the Queen received part of this sum, the sponsors of the expedition realized a profit of 4600 percent on their investment. It is no wonder that Drake's success caused Englishmen's thoughts to turn to the possibility that England's destiny lay on the sea.

THE SPIRIT OF EXPANSION

Elizabeth's time became a glorious period for the British crown. Shakespeare, the greatest poet and playwright of the day, expressed the ambition of many Englishmen when he made one of his characters boast, "The world's mine oyster, which I with sword will open."

Another popular spokesman for England was Richard Hakluyt, who published proudly in 1589 his collection of *Principal Voyages of the English Nation*—accounts of the travels and exploits of his countrymen on the oceans of the world. Hakluyt's book drew its readers' attention to the alluring economic opportunities being opened overseas by daring British sailors.

Even earlier, Hakluyt had advocated the establishment of English colonies in North America. He maintained that they would be not only markets for English goods and sources of raw material for English manufacturing but also bases from which the Spanish empire might be raided.

Sir Humphrey Gilbert's bold failure. A like-minded contemporary of Hakluyt was Sir Humphrey Gilbert. From the Queen, Gilbert received authority in 1578 to possess such lands as he should select that were not already the property of any other Christian prince. One-fifth of all the gold he might find was to be earmarked for the crown.

After one unsuccessful voyage, Sir Humphrey set sail in 1583 with a doomed band of followers. They reached Newfoundland and tried to make a settlement there, but they quickly decided that it was too dismal a spot for a colony. On his return voyage to England, Gilbert was lost at sea.

Sir Walter Raleigh's experiment. After Gilbert's death his rights in the New World were taken over by his half-brother, Sir Walter Raleigh.

We do not know for sure if Sir Walter ever laid his coat in the mud so that Elizabeth might walk on it, but certainly he was one of the Queen's favorites. He was also a close associate of Hakluyt's.

Hating the Spanish, longing to be rich, and encouraged by Hakluyt's writings, Raleigh decided to establish an English colony in America. A superb organizer, he carefully planned a settlement for a warmer part of the Atlantic coast than the region where Gilbert had failed.

In 1584 Raleigh equipped an expedition to reconnoiter Spanish defenses in the Caribbean and to find a suitable site for a colony. His men explored in Albemarle Sound and landed on Roanoke Island before returning to England. Raleigh was delighted with their report of the new land, which he named Virginia.

The next year a colonizing expedition, consisting mainly of gold seekers, arrived at the chosen place. From the outset the tiny settlement was troubled by Indians and Spaniards.

Indian villages shown are surrounded by palisades.   Notice the Indians' trap for fish near Roanoke I.

The artist John White, who landed at Roanoke Island in 1585, painted numerous pictures of American animals, birds, and scenes. This engraving was made from his drawing of the arrival of the English at the wooded island off a coast now a part of North Carolina. A number of Indian villages may be seen.

\# It disbanded in 1586 when Drake, fresh from a foray against the Spanish in the West Indies, offered the settlers a ride home.

In 1587 another expedition arrived there, bringing the first English women and children to America. The colony these brave souls planted could not survive, though, without a steady stream of supplies from the mother country. Unhappily these were cut off by the outbreak of war between Spain and England.

The leader of this forlorn band of settlers, John White, departed almost immediately after dropping off his passengers in America, and he did not return until 1590. When he did, he found not a trace of the settlers, who had included his own granddaughter, Virginia Dare— the first English child born in America. The only permanent legacy of Raleigh's "planting" was the potato he took to his estate in Ireland and the tobacco he popularized at court. \#\#

Sum and Substance

1. Tell what was achieved for English exploration by each of the following: John Cabot, Francis Drake, Richard Hakluyt, and Sir Humphrey Gilbert. What were their chief aims? 2. What was the outcome of Sir Walter Raleigh's attempts to colonize in Virginia?

\#\#Other examples of cultural diffusion. The Spanish had already taken the "Irish potato" to Spain.

AMBITIOUS MERCHANTS PLANT THE VIRGINIA COLONY

Raleigh had learned that successful colonization would require a larger amount of money than any one man possessed. With this in mind, he organized a number of London merchants into a company for the purpose of establishing a colony. The men would have trading privileges in the colony in return for helping to finance it. Raleigh, unfortunately for himself, was imprisoned for treason and lost his rights in America before he could carry out his plans. In 1606 the men he had organized received from King James I their own charter to exploit the New World.

This charter of 1606 was issued to the Virginia Company, made up of the London and Plymouth companies—two groups of adventurers. The London Company obtained land between the 34th and 41st parallels of latitude, and the Plymouth Company received an area of the same size, between the 38th and 45th parallels. The Plymouth people were more interested in finding good fishing and fur-trading sites than the London men, who were primarily looking for gold and silver. Both groups, like the explorers who had come before them, expected to profit greatly. They sought wealth

One of the first needs of Jamestown was defense. These illustrations from a book by John Smith probably exaggerate its security measures, but they show the influence of English culture on America.

Radio Times Hulton Picture Library

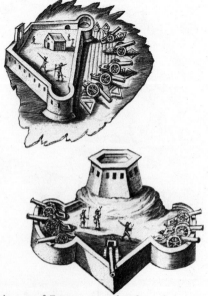

26

Smith's book is <u>Generall Historie of Virginia</u> (1624). The evidence of European technology is seen here. Note the house (modeled after an English house--not a log cabin) at the upper left.

rather than a place in which to make permanent homes.

A TOWN ON THE JAMES

The London Company sent out its first expedition just before Christmas in 1606. Three ships were provided—the *Susan Constant,* the *Goodspeed,* and the *Discovery*—carrying a party of 105 colonists. At the end of April, 1607, the expedition sailed gallantly into Chesapeake Bay and shortly afterward founded a settlement on the James River named in honor of the King.

But Jamestown was poorly located, malaria struck it, and bad blood among the men resulted in endless quarreling. And instead of getting to the business of earning a livelihood from the soil, the colonists spent—and wasted—their time looking for gold.

John Smith's contribution. John Smith was the dominant character among Virginia's leaders. He mapped the region and established trade relations with the Indians. As president of the colony's council, he tried to pull the tiny settlement through its early days of desperation.

Smith was sometimes an insufferable braggart, but he was also an able leader of men. He recognized that if the colony was to survive, its inhabitants would have to postpone for a time living the lives of gentlemen and start instead to raise food. He made the "gentlemen" work; and when they swore as they sweat at their tasks, he decreed that cold water be poured into their coat sleeves.

Adapting to the new environment. It was not easy for Europeans to adapt themselves to this new environment, but it was their first necessity. To their embarrassment, the settlers found they had much to learn from the Indians. For example, the tribesmen taught them to plant corn for several years in order to get the soil ready for a crop of wheat. Although the new land teemed with deer and bears and wild turkeys, and with ducks that flew in flocks large enough to blot out the sun, this abundance meant little. The settlers soon discovered that it was possible to die quickly even in a land where nature was so bountiful. By the spring of 1608, dis-

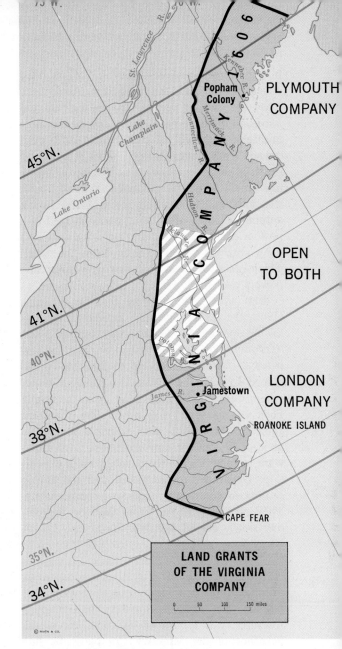

The area originally granted reached inland only 100 miles. In 1609 it was extended "from sea to sea."
Use the scale to find the north-south extent.

ease and accidents had taken the lives of all but 38 of the 105 people who had come to Jamestown so full of hope the year before.

The "starving time." Shortly 400 colonists arrived to bolster the original band. But the newcomers did not bring enough food for themselves, and the earlier settlers could not make up the supplies that were short. Afraid to go into the forests because of hostile Indians, they caught no game and gathered little wood.

By deep winter people were eating rats and mice and dried-up roots, and a few of the most miserable engaged in cannibalism and even opened fresh graves for food. This grim period has ever since been known as Virginia's "starving time." The firm guidance of John Smith was missing. He had left for England in the autumn of 1609, after being badly injured in a powder explosion. That year the Virginia Company obtained a new charter from the King, which placed a royal governor with autocratic powers over the colony.

Relief arrives. By the time that Sir Thomas Gates, the acting governor, arrived in the following spring, only about sixty emaciated settlers remained alive. Horrified by what he saw when at last he sailed up to Jamestown, he agreed to take the settlers to Newfoundland, where they might seek help from a fishing fleet. As his vessel was proceeding down the James River with the Virginia survivors aboard, he met the new governor, Lord Delaware, coming up the river with a relief expedition. Delaware ordered Gates and the fleeing settlers to return to Jamestown immediately. They obeyed him, and from then on the colony slowly gained strength.

A NEW WAY OF LIFE

The members of the Virginia Company were, as a rule, prominent merchants or wealthy landholders. Sir Thomas Smythe, the company treasurer, was typical of the rest. He was a governor of the Muscovy Company; he had helped in establishing the Levant Company for trade in Southwest Asia; and he had served as the first governor of the East India Company. He was much like a modern businessman who sits on the boards of directors of a number of corporations watching with an eagle eye over the affairs of each.

Another director of the Virginia Company was Robert Rich, the second Earl of Warwick. He was a member of the Bermuda and East India companies as well as of the Guinea Company, which traded primarily in African slaves.

A crop for profit. Men of affairs like Smythe and Rich were insistent that Virginia waste no time in becoming productive. But what could the settlers make or grow? The Virginia Company shareholders were repeatedly disappointed when vessels returning from their American "plantation" carried no precious stones, no precious metals, and no spices—for that matter, nothing that could be sold at a profit.

Some of the shareholders believed that the colonists ought to be making clapboards and spars, pitch, and soap ashes; others thought that they should be raising silkworms. Still others maintained that with so many trees to provide an inexhaustible supply of fuel, the colonists should be operating iron furnaces or producing glass.

A tobacco society. The Indians living near the colonists raised tobacco, but its taste did not appeal to Europeans. In 1612 a tropical variety, probably from Trinidad, was introduced experimentally into Virginia by Captain John Rolfe—who, by the way, later married the Indian princess Pocahontas. By 1614 the first Virginia tobacco had been sold in London, and within five years tobacco leaf was a leading export of the colony.

The cultivation of tobacco required vast acreage because the "weed" quickly wore out the soil. The major landholdings were scattered along the banks of the Potomac, the James, and the Rappahannock rivers, which provided the easiest and most natural avenues of transportation. On the river nearest their land planters constructed wharves to which small oceangoing vessels could navigate, enabling them to take the tobacco directly to Europe.

Virginia developed no large towns as centers of commerce and politics. But to the capital, first at Jamestown and later at Williamsburg, the important men came for the discussion of governmental and other public matters. Mostly they talked about land and tobacco—and of their greatest need: cheap labor to work the land.

The beginnings of self-government. At the same time that economic foundations were being laid, the Company granted Virginia a legislature.

On July 30, 1619, the first representative assembly in American history met in the little church in Jamestown. The House of Burgesses, as it was called, consisted of twenty-two members—two from each of the eleven settled communities in the colony. It was organized to make laws in coöperation with the governor of the colony and his council.

This event justified the colonists' firm belief that they did indeed possess all of the legal rights which Englishmen at home enjoyed. When King James took over the Company's charter in 1624 and made Virginia a royal colony, he did not interfere with the House of Burgesses. The right of colonists to govern themselves in local matters was recognized, and every English colony established thereafter assumed this right as a matter of course.

Indentured servants. Virginians at first found a partial solution to the labor problem in the unemployed of the mother country. These poor wretches had been driven off the land by what is known as the enclosure movement. Thousands of English farms were fenced, or "enclosed," and turned into sheep runs when the market for wool products expanded greatly in the sixteenth and seventeenth centuries.

Although many of the dispossessed farmers found work in the growing cities of England, where the wool was woven into cloth, untold numbers lived on the edge of starvation. With urban jobs scarce, the market for farm products dropped sharply, leading to more suffering.

The depressed town and farm dwellers could come to America and start over if they could get the money to pay for their transportation. The cost of the Atlantic crossing, however, was far beyond the means of poor Englishmen. Out of this difficulty the indenture system was invented. A planter in America would agree to pay the passage of an immigrant, who in turn would agree to work for a specified number of years—varying from four to seven.

As an "indentured servant" a worker was "bound" to his master. After his period of indenture was over, he became a free man again

Slaves proved to be the cheap labor planters looked for.   Notice the evidence of English technology.

After tobacco had made Virginia a success, English readers learned from a London magazine how the product was processed. *Background:* Slaves dry and roll leaves from an oversized plant (2). *Foreground:* Workers in England prepare leaves (3) for a pressing machine (4) and for slicing (5).

Universal Magazine, 1750 (Henry E. Huntington Library)

and might take up a farm for himself. But the system never worked satisfactorily. Indentured servants, being impatient to be free, were not usually willing hands. The chances to escape were many and were often eagerly taken.

The emergence of slavery. Among the indentured servants there early were Negroes. Twenty of them—the first—landed at Jamestown in 1619, from a Dutch vessel. For the next thirty years, Africans were treated, in general, like other servants, who were European. As late as 1651 some Negroes received land after their terms of indenture had been completed.

By then only 300 Negroes lived in Virginia, but it was apparent that Negroes—unlike Indians who could escape into the forest—could be advantageously made "servants for life." In # this way, slavery began in America—a desperate answer to the nagging problem of how to find labor. Furthermore, Englishmen became increasingly interested in the profits of the slave trade, hitherto a monopoly of Spain.

The headright system. For a long time, the old European notion persisted that land should not be sold but should only be granted for meritorious service to the ruler. This idea broke down quickly in the competition to get settlers. "Meritorious service" came to mean little more than transporting a servant to America. For each such servant brought to the tobacco colonies, the person responsible—a ship's crewman or planter or mere traveler—received a headright of 50 acres.

From the beginning of this system, a lively trade in the headrights developed. Frequently speculators bought headright warrants from people receiving them and then tried to dispose of them at good profits to later arrivals. Since the prices asked were usually high, an important effect was to force newcomers to seek the less desirable lands farther to the west. This in turn led to increased pressure upon the Indians, whose anger rose as they were pushed deeper and deeper into the interior.

Hostile Indians. On Good Friday, 1622, the Indians in their fury attacked the settlements along the James River, slaying over 300 men, women, and children. Again, in 1644 the In-

dians of Virginia massacred over 500 persons in the back country. Both times the English retaliated severely. The problem of defense against understandably wrathful Indians remained a leading one in the area until the eve of the American Revolution.

Sum and Substance

1. Why was the Jamestown colony not very successful during its first year? How did Captain John Smith attempt to improve it? 2. How did Lord Delaware save the Jamestown colony from abandonment? 3. What was the London Company's chief interest in Jamestown? How did tobacco serve that interest? 4. What was the significance of the House of Burgesses? 5. How did the indenture system solve both the unemployment problem in England and the need for laborers in Virginia? How successful was this system? 6. Why did slavery develop in the English colonies? 7. Explain the headright system. What two effects did it have?

A picture published in England, showing colonial life.

Slaves at work, seen in a woodcut of 1700.

Granger Collection

LONDON'S VIRGINIA.

##Try to influence students to see the Indian side of the trouble. The absence of the concept of private ownership of land was important--Europeans, of course, possessed this concept.

Important ideas in this section: (1) Maryland was established for religious and economic reasons (Lord Baltimore wanted to become a landholder). (2) Feudalism was attempted but failed. (3) Maryland formally granted religious freedom to people of either Catholic or Protestant faith.

THE CALVERTS DRAW CATHOLICS TO MARYLAND

Maryland, the neighbor of Virginia, was founded by Sir George Calvert, later Lord Baltimore—a good friend of King James I's, who made him a knight. This kind of colony, dominated by one man—known as the lord proprietor—with privileges from the king, was called a *proprietary* colony.

Hungry for the power and prestige of a landholder, Baltimore was fascinated by the prospects of starting a colony. In 1623 he re-

The Church of England became established there. The typical location of the English colonies—on navigable rivers between the mountains and the sea.

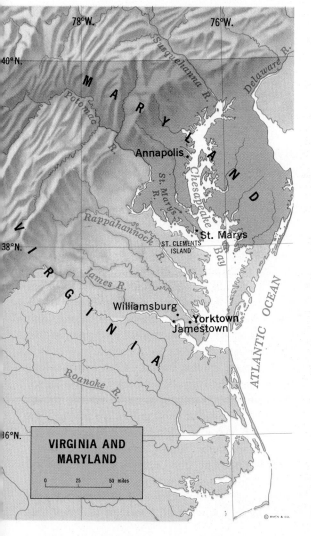

VIRGINIA AND
MARYLAND

0   25   50 miles

ceived a royal grant to establish a colony in Newfoundland, where he and his family lived for a couple of years. Finding the climate disagreeable, they moved to Virginia. Since life in this Anglican colony was uncomfortable for Baltimore, who was a Catholic, he returned to England. Shortly afterward, he obtained from King Charles I a grant to settle between the 40th parallel and the Potomac River—on land earlier granted to Virginia. The grateful Baltimore named his domain Maryland after Queen Henrietta Maria.

A PROMISING HAVEN

Before his colony was established, Baltimore died. His rights, privileges, and title passed to his son Cecilius. Cecilius chose his brother, Leonard, to be governor of the colony. When over 200 prospective settlers had been recruited, they departed for America aboard the *Ark* and the *Dove*. In 1634 they landed on an inlet of the Potomac, where their Jesuit priest celebrated what may have been the first Mass offered in English America.

Two communities. Maryland was originally conceived of as a refuge for Catholics. But Protestants as well as Catholics were welcomed, and any settler who caused dissension was subject to punishment.

Conflicts developed, nevertheless. The Virginians charged that Marylanders were poaching on their land. Catholics, who gathered near the town of St. Marys, had many disagreements with Protestants, who preferred Annapolis.

Manorial landholding. The soil of Maryland was fertile and the colony grew and prospered. But in theory, the colony was completely under one man's control. The royal charter had bestowed on Lord Baltimore powers which were second only to those of the king himself.

Subdivisions of the land—10,000,000 acres! —could be made by the Calverts. They bestowed enormous manors on their friends, who held them under old feudal custom. These manor lords engaged in the raising of tobacco with the help of indentured servants—as their

Points to emphasize on the map: The English settlements were located on a narrow strip of land between the Appalachians and the sea; these two colonies centered on Chesapeake Bay.

Since Catholics were unpopular and scarce in England, most prospective settlers of Maryland would be English Protestants. If the colony was to succeed, the Act of Toleration was necessary. It was a great step toward religious freedom in America, even though it granted tolerance to <u>Christians</u> only.

Virginia neighbors did. They also leased holdings to farmers who worked without any servants.

An independent legislature. The feudal arrangements did not last long, though, amid such abundance of land and opportunity. From the start the lord proprietor "permitted" a popular assembly. And from the beginning, this legislature refused to be a "rubber stamp" for the Calverts. It insisted on initiating legislation, refusing to wait for the proprietor to announce what laws he wanted passed. The name "manor" survived for a long time in Maryland, but the colony in fact had a plantation system. Within fifteen years after its establishment, Maryland ceased to be feudal.

The westward push. As the Virginians had, Marylanders discovered that steady immigration tended to keep high the prices for land along the seacoast. Consequently, the later arrivals pushed farther and farther into the wilderness to avoid having to purchase from speculators. But most important, as in Virginia,

tobacco culture exhausted the soil rapidly, making westward movement a necessity.

Religious toleration. The fear that the colony might be accused of being anti-Protestant, which would frighten many immigrants away, led to the passage in 1649 of the so-called Act of Toleration. This act provided that no one who was a Christian should "from henceforth bee any waies troubled, Molested or discountenanced for . . . his or her religion nor in the free exercise thereof within this Province or the Islands thereunto belonging. . . ." So the plentiful land of the frontier, with its constant demand for more hands, helped to break down Old World restraints on personal freedom.

Sum and Substance

1. What were George Calvert's motives and methods in founding the colony of Maryland? 2. Describe the original system of landholding in Maryland. What caused the system to be changed? 3. What powers did the Maryland legislature exercise? Why did it pass the Act of Toleration?

Plymouth and Massachusetts are grouped because of both location and reason for settlement.

RELIGIOUS DISSENTERS SETTLE NEW ENGLAND

Meanwhile, the Plymouth group of the Virginia Company was trying its luck in New England. For reasons that are not clear, the Plymouth Company's investors had convinced themselves that all the fruits and spices of the Garden of Eden could be grown in the vicinity of Maine. Here, they thought, would be the ideal place for a settlement within the limits set up by the Virginia Company charter (see page 27).

The guiding spirits of the new project were Sir Ferdinando Gorges, governor of the port of Plymouth, and Sir John Popham, England's lord chief justice. They fitted out an expedition of two ships and sent it forth in 1607. It was under the leadership of Sir John's brother, George Popham, who was fat and seventy, and Raleigh Gilbert, the scheming son of Sir Humphrey Gilbert. Their little settlement—on the Kennebec River in Maine—lasted one bleak winter; then the quarreling colonists returned to England.

THE PLYMOUTH PEOPLE

In 1620 the Plymouth Company was reorganized and received a royal charter establishing the Council for New England. Consisting of forty aristocrats, who had the power to grant land to actual settlers, its leaders were Gorges and Robert Rich. The Council was empowered to make land grants, create plantations, and write laws. It even controlled the right to fish in the waters adjacent to its territory.

The Council for New England. As an active colonizing force the Council for New England failed. Nevertheless, before it came to an end it had provided the initial land grants for all the New England colonies—Plymouth, Massachusetts, New Hampshire, Maine, and Connecticut.

Separatists. The first permanent New England settlement was not made up of men of substance and power. Rather, it consisted of people whom John Smith described as "men that

Discuss the meaning of dissent--religious and political. By examples, introduce the idea that a free society accepts dissent. Ask why dissent is desirable in any society but is forbidden in some.

have great spirits but small means." They were a band of humble folk, who were members of the Scrooby congregation in Nottinghamshire, England.

\# Dissatisfied with the established Church of England, members of the congregation refused to be governed by its hierarchy. They wanted instead to be a separate and self-governing religious unit. For this reason they were known \#\# as separatists or Congregationalists. Their leaders were William Brewster, the bailiff of Scrooby Manor; William Bradford, a well-to-do farmer's son who walked 10 miles regularly to participate in the congregation's meetings; and John Robinson, the minister.

Sojourn in the Netherlands. The congregation, which had been harried by church authorities because of its views, fled England between 1607 and 1608 and went to the Netherlands. In 1609 the members settled in the city of Leiden, where they found hospitality and tolerance. They prospered there for eleven years.

But many of them were not satisfied or happy. They were Englishmen who longed to live under their own flag. Even more important, their children were, as Bradford later wrote, "getting the reins from their necks, and departing from their parents. Some became soldiers, others embarked on far voyages by sea, and others on some worse courses . . . to the great grief of their parents and dishonour of God."

Toward America. Yet when the question of packing up and leaving the Netherlands was put to the congregation, the majority voted to remain. A minority, determined to depart, sent representatives to London, who obtained the permission of the Virginia Company to settle on its lands in America. James I is said to have been unwilling to grant the separatists religious toleration, but he promised to allow them to live in peace.

A London promoter named Thomas Weston arranged for a group of London merchants to give financial backing to the colony. Shares in the enterprise were sold in England at £10 each.

In all, thirty-five Pilgrims dared the venture

Gordon Tenney from Black Star

A replica of the *Mayflower*, built by English craftsmen working from all available information and using the implements of three centuries ago. A crew sailed it from England to Plymouth, Massachusetts, to commemorate the voyage of 1620.

The Mayflower II completed the trip to America in 54 days, 11 less than the one the Mayflower I made in 1620. The replica, which may be seen at Plymouth today, measures 90 feet in length. Americans who make tours of the little ship marvel that over 100 persons--with animals and supplies--were contained in it during the long trip across the ocean. John Carver (who later became the first governor of the colony) and two doctors were among those making the journey to Plymouth. Emphasize the courage and hardiness of the voyagers.

on a rotting, leaking ship, misnamed the *Speedwell,* which headed for Southampton. There they expected to fall in with a larger ship, the *Mayflower.* Many of the *Mayflower's* sixty-seven passengers were not separatists. They were chiefly employees of Weston, who had no interest in the religious side of the voyage. Among them, for example, was Miles Standish, the celebrated captain of the guard. The *Speedwell* turned out to be unseaworthy, and all its passengers were transferred to the *Mayflower.*

The Mayflower Compact. Late in November, 1620, the *Mayflower* arrived at Cape Cod, within the grant of the Council for New England, but not where the Pilgrims were supposed to settle according to their patent. Some of the nonseparatists announced they would leave the colony at the first opportunity, be-
cause the territory was not under the Virginia Company's jurisdiction.

To prevent such a mutiny, forty-one of the forty-four men aboard the ship signed what has come to be known as the Mayflower Compact. In it the colonists pledged to "covenant and combine ourselves together into a civil body politick, for our better ordering and preservation and furtherance of ye Ends aforesaid; and by vertue hereof to enacte, constitute, and frame, such just and equall lawes, ordinances, acts, constitutions, and offices, from 'time to time, as shall be thought most meete and convenient for ye generall good of ye colony."

This agreement was not intended to serve as a constitution. But because the settlers never were able to obtain a charter, it was the only constitution Plymouth ever had.

Help from Indians. The Pilgrims and their associates finally decided to settle in an abandoned Indian cornfield. On December 21 they went ashore to prepare for the first winter in their new land. They had arrived at the wrong time of year. Before spring came, disease and intense cold had reduced their number by one-half.

Fortunately, the Indians were not hostile. They had recently been decimated by a terrible plague, which left the survivors frightened and docile. One of the most friendly was Squanto, who helped the Pilgrims establish cordial relations with their neighbors. When the *Mayflower* sailed back to England in April, not a single settler was willing to leave Plymouth.

Throughout the spring and summer the colonists worked like Trojans, gathering wood and furs and tending their ground. By fall they reaped abundantly. To celebrate, they held a thanksgiving feast consisting of roast venison, wild fowl, deer, clams, puddings, and domestic wine. The local Indians shared in the festivities.

One bountiful harvest did not, of course, solve the persistent problem of food supply. But after 1623, when the land formerly held in common was divided among the settlers, agricultural production began to increase. Each man was now individually responsible for feeding his family. The colony never again faced starvation.

The London merchants, however, were irritated and disappointed over the return they received on their investment. In 1626 they sold their interest to the colonists themselves for £800, a debt which the Pilgrims paid off systematically.

The colony's fame does not rest on its size or its wealth or its power. It rests instead on the determination, the hard work, and the indomitable faith of the Pilgrim Fathers—as the Plymouth settlers are known in history. Their virtues set an example for all the pioneers who would follow them into the American wilderness.

A REFUGE FOR PURITANS

The Massachusetts Bay Colony was actually much more important than Plymouth, its struggling neighbor, which it finally absorbed in 1691. Massachusetts was granted a royal charter in 1629. The map opposite shows that this grant was within the holdings of the Council for New England. Despite court action, Sir Ferdinando Gorges of the Council was never able to get the Massachusetts charter annulled.

At odds with the Established Church. The settlement of Massachusetts was the work of a group of Puritans. The Puritans were members

The Mayflower Compact was an agreement to form a government--the first such written agreement in America, as far as we know. The king of England (James I) never recognized it.

Granger Collection

New England colonists uncover a supply of Indian corn that had been stored for the winter.

Another chance to review latitude and longitude.

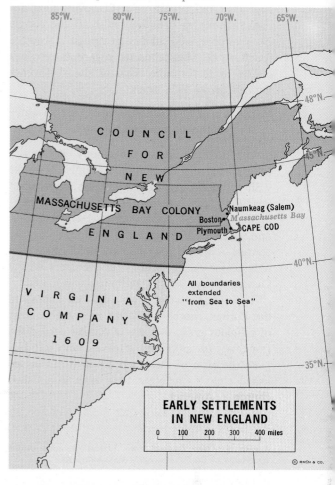

EARLY SETTLEMENTS IN NEW ENGLAND

0   100   200   300   400 miles

The Bay Colony was generously treated, receiving a domain that extended through 8 degrees of latitude.

of the Established Church who wanted to "purify" it of its remaining Catholic practices # —the organization of its clergy, the use of holy water, and the making of the sign of the cross. They made the literal interpretation of the Bible their guide. They disciplined themselves according to a strict moral code and opposed frivolity and gaiety. In America they hoped to find a place where they could worship freely without being pestered constantly by other Anglicans, who considered them to be heretics.

Although the Massachusetts Bay Company included in its membership men of various religious opinions, the Puritans got control of it. In order to make sure that this control would be permanent, they insisted upon taking their charter to America with them. Massachusetts Bay therefore became the first completely self-governing colony in the New World—subject only to royal wish.

The great migration. Unlike the Pilgrims, who were in meager circumstances, the Puritans included well-to-do men who had been made to feel insecure because of their religious views. The most prominent was John Winthrop, the manor lord at Groton, a village in eastern England. As a skillful lawyer he had gained a wide reputation, but he was heavily in debt and was finding it increasingly difficult to maintain his standard of living. Legal business that had formerly come his way was denied him because he was a Puritan.

In March, 1630, Winthrop and his three sons emigrated to the New World. This was the beginning of the first *large-scale* colonization in the history of America. By the end of the year, about 2000 colonists had arrived in Massachusetts Bay, and by the end of the decade almost 20,000 people were settled there. This vast transplantation of men, women, and children, known as "the great migration," was part of a larger movement which brought Englishmen to Virginia and Maryland and to England's possessions in the West Indies.

A government by church members. The government of Massachusetts was no democracy. John Cotton, one of the colony's foremost ministers, declared: "Democracy, I do not conceive that ever God did ordain as a fit government for either church or commonwealth. If the people be governors, who shall be governed?" And the founders of Massachusetts regarded religious liberty as undesirable. One of them, Thomas Dudley, wrote in a poem:

Let men of God in courts and churches watch
O'er such as do a toleration hatch.

The political life of the colony was inseparable from the religious life. Ministers spoke with authority, and their word was enforced as law. Only the "freemen"—at first the stockholders of the Massachusetts Bay Company and later only those who belonged to the church—enjoyed the right to hold office and to vote for the governor and members of the General Court, as the legislature was called.

Those in the colony who did not belong to the Puritan church—and this meant a number of religious groups—were of course denied the franchise. In short, the Puritans who left England because of their opposition to an established church organized their own established church in America.

"Common" marks land owned or used in common.

A plan of a New England town, typical of those settled by groups of Puritans in early Massachusetts.

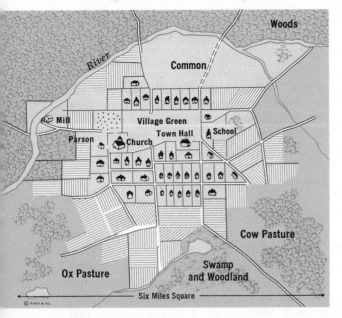

The town system. Although Massachusetts displayed many autocratic characteristics, the creation there of the town, or township, system was a notable contribution to the development of more democracy in government. Towns were created by grants from the General Court, which in the beginning was the board of directors of the Massachusetts Bay Company. As such, it controlled all the land within the boundaries of the colony.

A group of freemen designated by the General Court would become the proprietors of a town 6 miles square. In each town a village center was laid out, where 2 or 3 acres was set aside as the village common—pastureland for the village livestock. A suitable place was also chosen for the village school and for the church. The remaining land was divided into lots and distributed, one to each freeman of the town. Unassigned lots were available for those who came later. In addition, each freeman received a strip of land on the edge of the town for cultivation. Finally, there was usually a common woodlot, open to all.

The town meeting. The original freemen conducted the town's affairs in the "town meeting." Here the problems of the community were discussed. Here the selectmen, who supervised everything from health protection to road repair, were "selected." Here the town delegate to the General Court was chosen. Newcomers to the town could not vote at the town meeting, although they could speak at it and sometimes, in fact, were required to attend.

The town proprietors held power tightly in their hands and were unwilling to share it. But the free discussion of public issues at the town meeting, which they permitted, was a remarkable innovation in government.

The town system was not an unmixed blessing. It helped to settle Massachusetts—and, ultimately, all of New England—on a planned basis, and it spared the new arrivals the loneliness and some of the terrors of pioneer life. But many, thoroughly dissatisfied with the limits it put upon religious or political freedom, plunged farther into the wilderness.

These freedom-seeking farmers were respon-

##The point is discussed in the next to last paragraph. Town meetings were held as often as once a week. Local laws were passed and local officials chosen. Not everyone could vote.

Pioneers' Village, Salem, Mass.

Various kinds of Puritan buildings—sod-roofed dugouts, bark-covered wigwams, and thatched cottages—have been reproduced at Salem, Massachusetts. At the right is a pit for ripping logs into boards. Two sod-covered dugouts appear at the left, then a thatched cottage, and then a wigwam.

sible for pushing the line of settlement westward so rapidly in Massachusetts. We see, then, that the headright system of settlement in Virginia and the township system in Massachusetts both speeded, in their own ways, the filling up of the back country.

IN QUEST OF RELIGIOUS LIBERTY

The Puritans' restrictions on the individual were often most oppressive when they were religious. Because this was so, some men of independent spirit broke away and established colonies in other parts of New England. The most famous of these was Roger Williams.

Roger Williams' rebellion. Roger Williams had arrived in Massachusetts Bay in 1631. From the outset this minister was marked as a troublemaker by the leaders of the Puritan church.

From his pulpit in Salem, Williams preached that clerical interference in politics was limiting the freedom of the congregations to deal with local matters as they saw fit. He also argued against the continued tie between the Massachusetts church and the Church of England. Furthermore, he charged that the settlers had no right to take the land away from the Indians.

The more Williams preached, the greater became the distance between his religious ideas and those of his Puritan associates. His position gradually became that of the separatists, which placed him in open rebellion.

Williams' support of the Indians was the chief cause of the opposition to him. But he also aroused hostility when he stubbornly op-posed a Bay Colony law requiring an oath of allegiance from every citizen. Williams charged that an oath was a religious act and could not be demanded by the government. He asked, moreover, why a person who was not a freeman should take an oath to support a government in which he could not participate. This kind of argument made Williams a popular man with the unrepresented citizens. For this very reason, he was considered dangerous to the established authority of the commonwealth.

Out into the cold. In 1635 Massachusetts passed laws requiring church attendance and the payment of taxes to support the church. Williams, continuing to speak for freedom of the soul, maintained that the laws resulted in unwarranted interference with religious freedom. This stand led to an open break between him and the magistrates. Brought to trial, he was found guilty of attacking the colony's charter, of talking against compulsory church attendance and the oath of allegiance, and of attempting to incite other religious groups to insubordination.

Williams was finally banished from the colony in the fall of 1635, but he was to be allowed to remain until spring if he would keep silent. This he refused to do, and his arrest was ordered by the magistrates. At the last minute, lightly clad, he fled through snow to Narragansett Bay, where his friends, the Narraganset Indians, gave him help.

The founding of Providence. Other outcasts soon joined Williams and, although he originally had had no intention of becoming a colonizer, he

#The class should recognize Williams as a religious and political dissenter. Discuss (1) his views and those of the Puritans with whom he differed, and (2) treatment of dissenters in a democracy.

37

was inspired to found Providence Plantation in Rhode Island in 1636. Providence was organized on the township basis, and it arranged its affairs in a town meeting. But, most important, there was no religious requirement for voting, and the church and the government were to be forever separated. Beckoning to refugees of every faith, this colony was fostering an idea that has become one of the principal glories of the United States: each man's religion is a matter for his own conscience.

The banishment of Anne Hutchinson. A woman also offered thorny problems to the Puritans. She was Mrs. Anne Hutchinson, a colonist who in 1634 was deeply involved in religious controversies. She boldly held regular meetings in her house, where she passed judgment on the min-

Call attention to the English names.

The stern Puritan religious views and the lure of new land account for the large number of offshoots.

isters whose sermons she had heard.

Mrs. Hutchinson had come to believe that to be filled with the holy spirit was more important for salvation than to perform good works without actually being in "a covenant of grace." After a "trial" filled with the religious argument in which Puritans delighted, Anne Hutchinson was found guilty of "slandering the ministers" and was banished from Massachusetts. With friends she established Portsmouth, Rhode Island, in 1638.

Portsmouth and other settlements in Rhode Island that were organized by people fleeing for freedom were joined under a charter granted by Parliament in 1644. Although its wealth was always modest, Rhode Island prospered as a settlement of farmers who never forgot the vital matter of freedom which had first brought them there.

IN THE CONNECTICUT VALLEY

Some Massachusetts settlers who were restless under restrictions on their religious ideas also desired to improve their economic position. These men gave Connecticut its start. There were at least two valuable stakes in the land that became Connecticut: the fertile Connecticut Valley and the profitable fur trade.

Thomas Hooker's congregation. By 1635 a number of settlements had been made in the Connecticut Valley. In that year John Winthrop, Jr., was sent there by Massachusetts to serve as governor and to protect the land from the reach of the Dutch, who were in New Amsterdam. Winthrop was joined in his enterprise by the Reverend Thomas Hooker of Newtown, Massachusetts.

Hooker's congregation in Newtown had felt that it was being crowded by the continued influx of new settlers arriving through the growing port of Boston. Hooker was able to obtain permission from the Massachusetts General Court to move into the Connecticut River Valley with most of his congregation. Not only were the settlers eyeing the rich soil there, but also Hooker, who had taken a stand much like Williams', would have an opportunity to try out his ideas.

Thomas Hooker and his congregation with their livestock and other possessions—including iron kettles—trek through the New England forest in the direction of the broad Connecticut River Valley.

The colonists had settled in an area of broad-leaved forest that insured plentiful supplies of wood.

The Fundamental Orders. Representatives of the settlers in 1639 formally organized Connecticut when they drew up the Fundamental Orders, which provided for a frame of government. # This was the first written constitution creating a government on this continent. Among its provisions was the important one that new freemen were to be admitted in the towns by the vote of the majority of the "admitted inhabitants" already there. Church membership was not a requirement for voting as it was in Massachusetts. It is clear that the kind of restrictions that Massachusetts had imposed could not last in an atmosphere where land was so easily obtained.

In 1662 Charles II, then on the throne of England, granted Connecticut a royal charter. This charter established the boundaries of Connecticut and made legal its claim to self-government.

NEW HAMPSHIRE AND MAINE

New Hampshire also sprouted from Massachusetts. Commenced by the Council for New England, it struggled for years, absorbing an overflow of population from Massachusetts. By the 1640's it was imploring Massachusetts for help, and after 1644 it was practically a part of the older colony. It was separated again in 1679, when it got a royal charter from Charles II. Maine's history was much the same. Maine was absorbed by Massachusetts in 1658—not to be separated until 1820.

Sum and Substance
1. What caused the first attempt to found a colony on the Kennebec River to fail? 2. Why did the separatists leave England and, later, the Netherlands? How was their colony in the New World financed? 3. Describe the two groups that sailed on the *Mayflower*. Why did they adopt the Mayflower Compact? What was its significance? 4. Contrast the Puritans with the Pilgrims in religious beliefs, social position, and size of their migration to the New World. 5. Describe the township system of the Massachusetts Bay Colony. 6. Why did Roger Williams found a new settlement? 7. What part did Anne Hutchinson play in the founding of a colony in Rhode Island? 8. Explain why settlers moved into the Connecticut Valley. 9. How did the Massachusetts Bay Colony help to establish two additional colonies?

#Review other colonial firsts, such as: the first representative assembly, the first agreement to form a government, the first Thanksgiving, the first separation of church and state.

EMIGRANTS FROM EUROPE AND AFRICA ADJUST TO THE NEW WORLD

It is hard to appreciate today how inadequately prepared for America the first settlers were. Much of what they found in the new land differed from what they had left behind in Europe and Africa—the climate, the vegetation, and the animal life.

How to get used to this environment? Consider how many Old World ideas—like the layers of an onion—had to be peeled off. Most of the English settlers, for instance, came here believing that wheat would be their chief food. In Virginia, Massachusetts, and elsewhere, one wheat crop after another failed before the colonists were convinced they could not make their fields look like those of England. Virginia settlers also expected to build brick houses. They soon were adjusting to the fact that brick was not available.

Settlers from Africa also had many disappointments. They had to grow used to colder weather than they had ever experienced. They would long for foods they had known at home and that were not native to America—like rice and fruits that grow in tropical climates. (One inexpensive food imported from South America to feed the slaves was the ground nut, or peanut—called goober by the Africans.)

Yet the new environment was not only frustrating; it was also exhilarating. In eating habits it wrought a revolution. Delectable new varieties of foods known in Europe were found here: grapes, blackberries, blueberries, raspberries, gooseberries, cranberries, crab apples, plums. Still other foods were entirely new: the Jerusalem artichoke, kidney beans, the squash, and the pumpkin. From the Indians came tasty dishes they had long ago named, like pone, succotash, and hominy.

For the products of Indian craftsmanship, the colonists' debt was also immense. A New Englander unwittingly expressed his thanks when he said: "A moccasin's the best cover a man ever had for his feet in the woods, the easiest to get stuff for, the easiest to make, the easiest to wear. And a birch-bark canoe's the best boat a man can have on the river. It's the easiest to get stuff for, easiest to carry, the fastest to paddle. And a snowshoe's the best help a man can have in the winter. It's the easiest to get stuff for, the easiest to walk on, the easiest to carry."

What sustained the first colonists during their terrible trials and sore disappointments was their conviction that they were under divine protection. Cotton Mather spoke for his compatriots in Massachusetts when he said: "The ministers and Christians, by whom New England was first planted, were a chosen company of men picked out of, perhaps, all the counties in England, and this by no human contrivance, but by a strange work of God upon the spirits of men." Another divine put it this way, "God hath sifted a nation, that he might send choice grain into this wilderness."

Later colonists were no less self-assured— but the mystery and wonder of the new land were gone. When other colonies were formed, in the years that followed, the forest wilderness was still forbidding. But its ways were known. Moreover, the establishment of English rule and customs on this continent was well under way.

More successfully than either the Spanish or the French, English colonists demonstrated that America could be *home* to Europeans. The Englishman, unlike the Spaniard or the Frenchman, brought to the New World the organizing principle of representative government, which he had come to practice in his mother country. This was the principle on which he was able to build in later generations a democratic way of life.

Sum and Substance

1. Explain how Europeans and Africans had to adapt their ways to the new environment in America—for instance, in meeting the Indians, raising crops, eating new foods, and using new implements. 2. What conviction helped sustain most of the settlers? 3. What general advantage in settling in America did the English colonists have over the French and Spanish?

##A large number of Africans had come from the west-central areas of Africa, having a humid low-latitude climate, where the weather in the lowlands is both hot and wet.

40

THE WORKSHOP

OF LASTING SIGNIFICANCE

What was the role of each of the following in the early English colonies?

John Cabot	Ferdinando Gorges
Francis Drake	separatist
Richard Hakluyt	William Bradford
Humphrey Gilbert	Mayflower Compact
Walter Raleigh	Puritans
George Popham	John Winthrop
London Company	General Court
Plymouth Company	town, or township
John Smith	Roger Williams
enclosure movement	Anne Hutchinson
Robert Rich	indentured servant
John Rolfe	headright
House of Burgesses	Thomas Hooker
Act of Toleration	Fundamental Orders of
George and Cecilius	Connecticut
Calvert	

INFORMED OPINION

1. Two attempts to colonize Virginia failed before the settlement at Jamestown survived. Explain these differing results.

2. If you had been living in the Massachusetts Bay Colony, would you have favored the expulsion of Roger Williams? Of Anne Hutchinson? Why?

3. If there had been no Indians living east of the Appalachian Mountains in the seventeenth century, in what respects might English colonial settlement in America have been different?

4. In which English colony would you have been most at home? Why?

5. What group of people in the English colonies doubtless had to make the most adjustments? Explain.

UNRAVELING PUBLIC PROBLEMS

1. Of the three chief colonies treated in this chapter, which one do you think was most successful in (a) obtaining a livelihood, (b) dealing with the Indians, (c) regulating religious life? Give your reasons in each case.

2. How did the people in each colony solve the problem of governing themselves? Which plan do you regard as the best? Why?

3. In what two ways did the Virginians fill their need for a supply of cheap labor? Which of the ways was less objectionable? Why?

HISTORICAL REASONING

1. Why did England and Spain become rivals in the sixteenth century? How did the rivalry show itself?

2. Explain how the abundance of land in America (a) destroyed feudalism in Maryland, and (b) eliminated the restrictions on settlers imposed by Massachusetts.

3. Name the institutions established by the early English colonists which survive today, and account for their survival. #

PREPARING A TIME LINE

In order to see the time relationship of events, it is helpful to list them along a line which denotes time intervals. For this purpose, take a sheet of ruled note paper and write on the top line the title of this chapter.

Allowing each line to represent five years, write "1575" in the margin at the left of the first line, "1600" on the fifth line below, "1625" on the fifth line below that, and so on to the bottom of the page.

Then, to the right of the marginal line, list all the important events discussed in the chapter, placing each correctly. For instance, opposite "1575" write "Drake begins voyage around world (1577–80)." Your last event will probably be "Connecticut receives royal charter (1662)." Do not be disturbed by the empty lines—they are like the blank spaces on a map, which may be just as significant as the crowded spots.

This time line, and similar ones for other chapters, can be used as a handy reference on the chronology of events. To make the time line more valuable, the key entries may be underlined with a red pencil.

##Obviously, the slaves. The Africans had lost their personal freedom and had been forced from their homes and made to work for the benefit of others in an alien culture and land.

41

This chapter shows how European politics--particularly rivalry between countries of northwestern Europe --affected colonies in America. It also completes the account of English colonization. The quotation (see p. 57) gives the viewpoint of Child and of all other Englishmen who believed in mercantilism, the

policy carried out by all the colonial powers. Its purpose was to enrich the mother country. England expected its colonies to provide raw materials for its industries, and, in turn, to buy the products of those industries. Thus the colonies would help build up the home industries and at the same time increase English trade. Unlike Spain, England had no rich sources of gold. Its wealth had to come from trade.

3

OLD RIVALRIES AND NEW COLONIES

. . . we are very great gainers . . .

All colonies and foreign plantations injure their mother kingdoms if the trade of those plantations is not confined to their mother kingdoms by good laws and severe enforcement of those laws.

The practice of all the governments of Europe # bears out the truth of this proposition. The Danes keep the trade of Iceland to themselves; the Dutch, Surinam, and all their settlements in East India; the French, St. Christopher, and their other plantations in the West Indies; the Portuguese, Brazil and all the coasts thereof; the Spaniards, all their vast territories upon the Main [the route sailed by Spanish vessels from Europe to America] in the West Indies, and many islands

#Observe how Child bolsters his argument by saying in effect, "Everyone else is doing it."

The flourishing Dutch settlement at the mouth of the Hudson River. An old European rivalry between Britain and the Netherlands flared up in America when the Dutch planted a colony near English territory.

42 The sharp, gabled roofs of buildings seen here and on p. 47 were characteristic of Dutch architecture. The Dutch were chiefly interested in trade. Notice the wharves and the piers.

there; and our own laws seem to envision the same for all our plantations in New England, Virginia, Barbados, etc. . . .

All our American plantations, except that of New England, produce commodities of different natures from those of this kingdom, such as sugar, tobacco, cocoa, wool, ginger, sundry sorts of dyeing woods, etc. Whereas New England produces generally the same as we have here: corn [in England this means grain] and cattle. Some quantity of fish they do likewise kill, . . . which injures our Newfoundland trade. . . .

The other commodities we have from New England are some few great masts, furs, and train oil [whale or cod oil] of which the yearly value amounts to very little. Of much greater value from them are sugar, cotton, wool, tobacco, and such like commodities, which they first receive from some other of his Majesty's plantations, in barter for dry cod-fish, salt mackerel, beef, pork, bread, beer, flour, peas, etc. . . .

Of all the American plantations, his Majesty hath none so apt for the building of shipping as New England, nor none comparably so qualified for training seamen. This is not only because of the natural industry of that people, but, more important, by reason of their cod and mackerel fisheries. And in my poor opinion there is nothing more injurious and in prospect more dangerous to any mother kingdom, than the increase of shipping in its colonies, plantations, or provinces. . . .

Yet, to do right to that most industrious English colony, I must confess that though we lose by their unlimited trade with our foreign plantations, we are very great gainers by their direct trade to and from Old England. Our yearly exportations of English manufactures, malt, and other goods from hence thither, amounting in my opinion to ten times the value of what is imported from thence . . . and therefore, whenever a reformation of our trade relationship with that people shall be thought on, it will in my poor judgment require great tenderness and very serious circumspection.

This settlement was named for the home port.

H. Dunscombe Colt (Metropolitan Museum of Art)

In the seventeenth century, trade with colonies was expected to be a monopoly of the mother country. The overseas possessions were valued principally as sources for raw materials that were not produced at home. One can see in this statement by an Englishman that the New England settlements were considered the least desirable of the New World communities because they competed with "Old England." Nevertheless, they were beginning to be appreciated as a market for Britain's manufactured goods. This selection, adapted and modernized, is from A New Discourse of Trade, *by Sir Josiah Child (1630–1699), who once was a director and virtual ruler of the English East India Company. Written in 1665, it was published for the first time in 1693.* ##

##The English East India Company was founded in 1600. It competed with the Dutch East India Company for trade in the East Indies, East Asia, and India. It soon left the first to the Dutch.

43

AMERICA MIRRORS THE CONFLICTS OF EUROPE

Settlers who believed that by traveling across the Atlantic they could escape the military strife of the Old World were badly mistaken. The colonies, as outposts of their mother countries, represented their sovereigns' strength and prestige. The rivalries of the chief European countries—France, Spain, England, and even the Netherlands—were reflected in the history of their overseas possessions. Nothing illustrates this better than the story of the Netherlands' settlement in North America.

THE DILIGENT DUTCH

The Netherlands has never been a large country, but it is located at the mouth of the Rhine. Like a watchdog, it has sat astride the trade routes leading from and to western and central Europe. The Dutch, most of whom were Protestant, had won their independence from Catholic Spain in 1581 and immediately began to make themselves prosperous.

A commercial people. Becoming a great manufacturing and commercial center at a time when other nations concentrated on colonies and explorations, the Netherlands drew its prosperity from international trade. Dutch merchants set up trading posts as far away as the East Indies, but the Netherlands established only one colony in North America—that an accident of exploration.

Henry Hudson's exploit. The Dutch East India Company, which had been organized to obtain for the Netherlands a share of the trade of Asia, sought its own route to the East. Its officers hired an English navigator named Henry Hudson to find a northeast passage. He failed in that goal. But then, sailing across the Atlantic in 1609 in the *Half Moon,* he came upon Delaware Bay.

Next traveling northward, Hudson reached the magnificent river which bears his name. He thought he had found the Northwest Passage—which almost all the explorers before him had looked for in vain—and he followed the river to the present site of Albany, New York. What he had located was nothing less than the most

important river on the Atlantic seacoast, but because it was nothing more he went home disappointed. Stopping in England on his return across the Atlantic, he was arrested for having sailed as a British subject under a foreign flag. Yet his report reached his Dutch employers anyway. It told of a country rich in furs and peopled by seemingly friendly Indians.

New Netherland. The Dutch wasted no time in claiming the land. By 1614 their trading establishments were located on Manhattan Island, and Dutchmen had explored the surrounding area. Government officials in the Netherlands, intensely hostile to Spain, were determined to set up more trading posts in America from which the Spanish could be harassed. In this way, they hoped to create markets there for Dutch manufacturers and to win converts to Protestantism. In 1621 they granted a charter to a new organization—the Dutch West India Company—giving it a monopoly of trade on the eastern coast of America and the western coast of Africa.

Scattered settlements. Although the new company was mainly concerned with undermining the Spanish, Dutch settlers began to arrive at Manhattan Island in 1624. This was the beginning of the Dutch colony of New Netherland. Since the settlers were under company orders to engage in the fur trade, they immediately established trading posts. Some colonists went up the Hudson and founded Fort Orange at the site of Albany; others located on the Delaware River, building Fort Nassau opposite the present site of Philadelphia. But gradually New Amsterdam, on the southern tip of Manhattan Island, became the most important settlement.

The chief difficulty of the Dutch West India Company lay in getting settlers to migrate to the New World. The Dutch at home were satisfied with life. Commerce, manufacturing, and a wide-ranging merchant fleet absorbed their energies and interest. Their businessmen were prosperous, and so was the population as a whole. Moreover, the Dutch nation at the mid-

ENGLISH TERRITORY

CATSKILL MTS.

Mohawk R.

RENSSELAERSWYCK

Ft. Orange
(Albany)
(1623)

Hudson River

Long Island Sound

MANHATTAN ISLAND

New Amsterdam
(New York)
(1624)

Susquehanna R.

Schuylkill R.

Delaware R.

Ft. Nassau
(Dutch) (1623)

Ft. Christina
(Wilmington)
(1638)

New Gothenburg
(1643)

Ft. Casimir
(Dutch)

Delaware Bay

Swaanendael
(Lewes)
(1631)

ENGLISH TERRITORY

ATLANTIC OCEAN

Chesapeake Bay

Hackensack R.

Hudson River

East R.

New Amsterdam

MANHATTAN I.

Breuckelen

STATEN I.

New Utrecht

DUTCH AND SWEDISH SETTLEMENTS

0   25   50   75 miles

□ • Dutch   □ ○ Swedish

Along this part of the Atlantic coast, three European countries took up positions. The Dutch accused the Swedes of trespassing (compare the dates of the establishment of Forts Nassau and Christina). The English observed resentfully that their colonies were separated by New Netherland.

dle of the seventeenth century consisted of only two million people. Of these, many were already spread over four continents.

The policies of the Dutch West India Company, besides, were strict and unattractive to Dutchmen. All settlers were employees of the Company and had to agree to live for six years on land the Company parceled out to them. They were expected to grow the crops designated by the Company's representatives. The Dutch West India Company also made a formal requirement—not always enforced—that prospective settlers had to be members of the Dutch Reformed church.

The patroon system. In order to stimulate migration from the homeland to the colony, the Dutch West India Company as early as 1629 devised what was called the patroon system. A man was designated a *patroon* if he could persuade fifty adults to settle upon his land in New Netherland. The patroon's land, or patroonship, extended approximately 16 miles along one bank or 8 miles along each bank of a navigable stream and as far inland as its owner might want to go. The settlers were expected to pay feudal dues to their patroon and to use his mill for grinding their flour; in return he would supply necessary tools, buildings, and animals.

These terms attracted few people. In fact, only five patroonships were ever established. Of these, one was successful. It was that of Kiliaen Van Rensselaer, an energetic merchant who was himself a member of the Dutch West India Company. His estate, called Rensselaerswyck, occupied both sides of the Hudson near Albany. Extended by purchases from the Indians, this holding eventually measured 28 miles by 44.

Rensselaer conducted the affairs of his patroonship through an agent. He controlled his land like an absolute monarch, even making the Company ships pay a tariff and insisting that they salute his personal flag! By 1640 the patroon system had been modified to permit the creation of smaller estates—but even this was not effective in encouraging settlement. By 1664 the Dutch West India Company had been forced to buy back all but two patroonships.

##Students should recall that the effort to establish feudal practices in Maryland failed.
The map: Call attention to the survival of Dutch names in the Hudson Valley today.

45

The picture: By holding a mirror before it, one can see it as the artist intended it--with the settlement on the west shore of Manhattan Island and the Indians headed up the East River. A part of Long Island may be seen at the right. Observe the large fort and the typically Dutch windmill.

I. N. Phelps Stokes Collection, New York Public Library

A seventeenth-century engraver reversed this early sketch of New Amsterdam. Hold a mirror before it.

A choice deal. As if these arrangements were not sufficiently uninviting, the Dutch colony was mismanaged, too. Its second director was so unsatisfactory that he was quickly dismissed. The next one, Peter Minuit, is remembered best for protecting the colonists from the frequent Indian raids by "purchasing" Manhattan Island from the tribesmen for about twenty-four dollars' worth of trinkets—no doubt the best real-estate bargain in history!

When one gazes today at Manhattan's skyline, it is hard to think of the island as once having been an agricultural community. Yet when the Dutch were in charge there, they found the soil fertile and raised both wheat and rye. Their most important product was fur, although they made profits in shipbuilding and forestry, too.

Peter Stuyvesant's harsh rule. The last and best known of the Company agents who served as governor was Peter Stuyvesant, a soldier with a quick temper. He ruled with an iron fist and was so oppressive that in 1653 the leading citizens demanded the right to participate in choosing officials. This insistence on political liberty, characteristic of the English colonies in America, may have been stimulated by Englishmen living in New Netherland who were familiar with government in New England. But Stuyvesant refused to budge an inch.

New Sweden. Meanwhile, the government of Sweden, eager to get into the race for colonies, challenged the Dutch claims in America. In 1637 Sweden chartered the South Company to establish a colony on Delaware Bay—a region the Dutch had not fully exploited despite their claims there.

An expedition sent out by the South Company built Fort Christina in 1638, at the site of what became Wilmington, Delaware. (Its head was none other than Peter Minuit.) A short distance away, five years later, the Swedes built New Gothenburg. But the Swedish colonizing never came to much. Hardly 400 people made up New Sweden, and never did the settlements reach beyond 35 miles up the Delaware.* The aggressive Dutch leader Peter Stuyvesant conquered New Sweden in 1655, making it part of New Netherland.

The first Jews. In September, 1654, New Amsterdam was the scene of the arrival of twenty-three Jews from Brazil. Already tragic wanderers looking for a permanent home, they had originally come from Portugal. Received in New Netherland with only a lukewarm welcome, they gradually found acceptance. They had no idea that they were founding what would become the largest, most influential Jewish community in the world. #

ENGLAND AGAINST THE NETHERLANDS

In Europe the conflict between the Dutch and the English had been developing for years. By 1650, the Netherlands, although cramped into a small area in Europe, was carrying on a wider trade than even England.

Trade in tobacco. The Dutch, who had made New Amsterdam a bustling trading center in the New World, imported European wares and

*Although Swedish colonizing was not a success, the Swedish settlers left their mark. The log cabin which they contributed to American life furnished the ideal frontier-type home. By 1750 it was in general use in the hinterland of America. It originated in northern Europe, where it had long been known in the forested areas. Its special advantage was that it was easy to construct with merely an ax and an auger, and chinked with mud it protected sufficiently against ## the wind. When, well into the nineteenth century, Daniel Webster, the great Massachusetts Senator, apologized to an audience for not having been born in a log cabin, he was demonstrating how important it had become as a symbol of American life.

46 #Nearly half of all Jews in the United States, or about three million, live in New York City.
##Logs had to be nearly the same size, and they were notched so that they would fit together.

Friendly relations with the Indians were important to the Dutch, since the tribesmen supplied them with furs.

A nineteenth-century magazine

Here Peter Stuyvesant, standing in the center, meets with Indian visitors in New Amsterdam.

On each of the three houses is a little porch--stoop--from which the English got the idea of porches.

took them to Virginia in exchange for tobacco. They then freighted the tobacco to Europe, where they sold it in a waiting market. This irritated the English, who maintained that the Dutch were growing rich on English produce.

Before 1615 England had imported great quantities of tobacco from Spain and paid for it in gold and silver. When its own plantations began producing the "filthy weed," England determined to use its own ships and seamen to transport the tobacco home. In this way Englishmen would earn the fees and commissions that this commerce yielded.

Furthermore, by a series of regulations beginning in the 1620's the English government gave the American tobacco planters a virtual monopoly of the English market. In return the Virginia Company promised not to sell tobacco outside the mother country.

The English Civil War. The outbreak of civil war in England in 1642 disrupted this mutually advantageous relationship. King Charles I was beheaded, his family fled to France, and Oliver Cromwell became Lord Protector of England. The fighting between the armies of the two sides kept merchants and manufacturers busy furnishing military supplies. The opposing forces seized each other's vessels, forcing up the price of any cargo that by luck got inside a blockaded port.

#The production of tobacco in Virginia enabled England to avoid importing Spanish tobacco, a fact that fitted in perfectly with the English policy of mercantilism.

The Dutch jumped at their chance to profit from England's family quarrel. They entered English colonial shipping centers and sold hardware, dry goods, and spirits cheaply. Once again they received American tobacco in return. The Netherlands experienced a prosperity it had never known before.

Cromwell, whose followers were usually anti-Catholic, decided to try to crush Spain by forming a Protestant coalition. For this he needed the Dutch. As their price for joining the English, the Dutch shrewdly insisted upon the right to trade freely with the English colonies on the Atlantic and in the Caribbean. But the English were determined at all costs to keep their tight monopoly on the trade with their colonies. Negotiations with the Dutch fell through. The English turned now to a vigorous anti-Dutch policy. Their commercial competition grew more heated; it led Parliament to pass the Navigation Act of 1651.

Restrictions on Dutch shipping. The Act of 1651 was designed to drive the Dutch out of the carrying trade between England and other countries. It provided that goods from Asia, Africa, or America might enter English, Irish, or colonial ports only if they were shipped in English, Irish, or colonial vessels. Products from Europe might enter England, Ireland, or the colonies in foreign ships only if the vessels bore the flags of the countries in which the goods were made or grown.

This arrangement permitted the Portuguese to bring in their wines and the Spanish their olives, but it shut out the Dutch ships that almost invariably carried these products. Because the Spanish and the Portuguese had no merchant fleets, they were now forced to depend upon British vessels. It was expected, therefore, that the profits that formerly went to the Dutch would flow to Englishmen.

The trade rivalry between England and the Netherlands grew more fierce, and they went to war against each other in 1652. When the war ended, the English, although victorious, wrote a generous peace only because they still wanted Dutch help against the Spanish.

Enumeration of goods. When Charles II—called the "Merry Monarch"—was "restored" to the English throne in 1660, he curried the favor of the Puritan businessmen by regulating trade for their protection. One of his first steps was to approve the Navigation Act of 1660.

This act provided that certain goods En-

The men in this English shop of about 1750 are making beaver hats: using steaming felt made from cleaned American fur, the workers knead, cut, and mold it on wooden hat blocks, where it is then dyed and dried. In the back (right) piles of hair were cleaned, treated with hot water, and pressed into felt.

Universal Magazine, 1750 (William L. Clements Library)

gland and Europe needed be shipped direct to the mother country from the colonies. These "enumerated articles"—as they were called—were sugar, cotton, tobacco, indigo, ginger, and dyewoods. Subsequent acts added to the list of enumerated articles. Naval stores, rice, beaver and other skins, iron, lumber, and potash were included. Since the colonies were meant, above all else, to serve the mother country, it seemed perfectly right that they should first meet its needs before attempting to fill those of other countries.

Obligations of the colonies. The mother country learned to depend on the products of the New World. Ships' masts and naval stores from the American forests helped sustain its merchant marine and navy. Indigo and other plants provided indispensable dyes for its textile industry. The abundant foodstuffs aided in improving the diet of Englishmen. Moreover, the processing of hides, furs, tobacco, sugar, and rice from the colonies created jobs for thousands.

Disadvantages to the colonies. But the restrictions on trade hurt badly the colonists' pride and pocketbooks. "Enumeration," for example, prevented the colonists from selling their products direct to the markets of Europe. Adam Smith, the British political philosopher, writing in 1776 explained: "To prohibit a great people from making all that they can of every part of their own produce, or from employing their stock and their industry in the way that they judge most advantageous to themselves, is a manifest violation of the most sacred rights of mankind." Americans came to resent the system deeply.

Benefits to the colonies. For the colonial producers, though, there were some advantages in the Navigation Acts that made them bearable. First, England paid a bounty for certain products, such as indigo, which could not have been grown profitably without aid. Second, producers of tar and tobacco had a near monopoly of the English market. Third, the colonists, who had to buy most of what they used direct from England, rather than in the cheaper continental market, sometimes were given lower prices than consumers living in the mother country. Fourth, colonial shippers were pleased

to be protected by the British navy against the pirates, who took a heavy toll of shipping.

Finally, even if there had been no Navigation Acts, the American colonies would have bought and sold much through English middlemen anyway. England had become a kind of warehouse for the world, and a vessel could obtain there products from almost everywhere without having to seek them in the countries of their origin.

Binders of the Empire. The Navigation Acts stayed in force long after the late 1660's, when the Netherlands ceased to be a commercial threat. The Navigation Acts automatically applied to every colony; they helped bind the British Empire together under the crown.

A change of flags. Charles II, hoping to be popular as king, made the most of a gradual weakening of the Dutch hold in America. When a report reached him that New Netherland was seriously encroaching on English territory and that its inhabitants were discontented under Stuyvesant's rule, he decided to kill two birds with one stone. He offered to make his brother, the Duke of York, the proprietor of the land if he would conquer it.

A deputy of the Duke went to the harbor of New Amsterdam and demanded surrender. Stuyvesant fumed and stormed and made a show of resistance, but in vain—as he knew—because the colony was poorly defended. It surrendered on September 8, 1664, and as the British flag went up, New Netherland became New York in honor of its new proprietor.

Sum and Substance
1. Explain why Sir Josiah Child regarded the New England colonies as positively dangerous. What direct benefit did they provide? 2. What service did Henry Hudson render the Netherlands? 3. What product of New Netherland was most profitable? What hampered the colony's growth? 4. Why did the patroon system fail? 5. Explain how Dutch traders operated in the English colonies. 6. What was the purpose of the Navigation Acts? 7. What advantages and disadvantages did the Acts have for the colonies? 8. Why and how did the English take over New Netherland?

##Having considered Britain's point of view concerning the Navigation Acts, students should assess the colonists' situation. What was the most serious disadvantage for the colonists?

49

Charles II became king in 1660, ruling until 1685. He was succeeded by the Duke of York, who became James II of England. The establishment of Carolina and Pennsylvania illustrates again how politics in Europe affected America. The founders of both had earned special favors from the English king.

BRITAIN SOWS A SECOND CROP OF COLONIES

Charles and the Duke of York were eager to show their appreciation to friends who had stuck faithfully by them through the dark days of exile. In addition to bestowing on their supporters titles and high-rank commissions in the army and navy, the royal brothers rewarded special favorites with grants of territory in America.

NEW JERSEY AND CAROLINA

The Duke of York turned over to two courtiers, John Lord Berkeley and Sir George Carteret, the land lying between the Hudson and

Sierra Leone is on the northwestern African coast.

By displaying this sign as a broadside—a kind of poster—David and John Deas advertised their sale in Charles Town in 1769. Notice the source of the slaves.

American Antiquarian Society

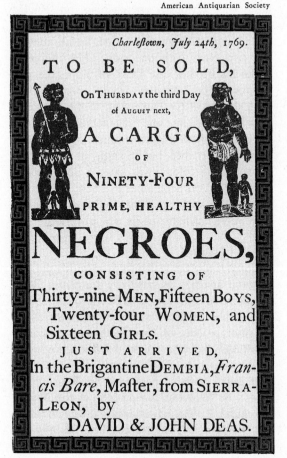

Charlestown, July 24th, 1769.

TO BE SOLD,

On THURSDAY the third Day of AUGUST next,

A CARGO

OF

NINETY-FOUR

PRIME, HEALTHY

NEGROES,

CONSISTING OF

Thirty-nine MEN, Fifteen BOYS, Twenty-four WOMEN, and Sixteen GIRLS.

JUST ARRIVED,

In the Brigantine DEMBIA, *Francis Bare*, Master, from SIERRA-LEON, by

DAVID & JOHN DEAS.

the Delaware. During the Civil War Carteret had fought bravely for the King on the island of Jersey, off the coast of France. In honor of his service, the grant in America was named New Jersey.

Royal designs. Charles II was determined to found a new colony in the part of America called Carolina. Charles I, for whom the land was named (Carolus is "Charles" in Latin), had originally granted a charter for its settlement, but nothing came of the elaborate plans. In 1663 Charles II granted a charter to eight aristocratic supporters by which they received a regal gift: the territory from sea to sea between # the 31st and 36th parallels. Among the eight were Berkeley and Carteret, proprietors of New Jersey, and Sir John Colleton, who had considerable holdings in the West Indies. This grant was enlarged in 1665 (see map opposite).

Useful products. The eight men thought they could govern the colony much as Lord Baltimore had attempted to run Maryland. They hoped to produce silk, wine, raisins, currants, almonds, and similar commodities, which could not be obtained from other British possessions. These bold hopes were never fulfilled. Many kinds of crops were tried, including pomegranates, figs, oranges, lemons, and bananas, but it was the production of naval stores that finally sustained the northern part of the colony. Pine, oak, cypress, and cedar trees grow plentifully almost to the Carolina coastline. Their trunks and the pitch, tar, and turpentine made from pine resins provided important supplies for the English navy.

Profitable plantations. Cutting down trees and boiling tar demanded an army of workers. Some planters who had come to Carolina from the West Indies were well acquainted with Negro slavery there. Shortly, through the port of Charles Town—later Charleston—slaves entered in a steady stream. The colony's proprietors had a financial interest in the slave trade and were pleased that such a ready market existed in Carolina.

After 1696 the growing of rice brought great

#As the map on p. 27 shows, much of the land assigned to Carolina had been granted to the Virginia Company, but no settlements had been made south of 36° and the king owned the land.

changes to Carolina. Introduced into the colony by a New England sea captain who transported the seed from Madagascar, rice was soon much in demand.

The humid climate in Carolina proved ideal for rice-growing. In addition, the rich soil could be flooded by means of a system of canals fed by the numerous creeks and streams. The same wet fields proved to be lively breeding places for mosquitoes, some of which carried malaria.

A try at feudalism. The Englishmen made Charles Town their gathering place, creating there an aristocratic society that tried to imitate the ways of European court life. This fact caused the leaders of the Carolina colony to form a tightly knit little group, whose members almost invariably intermarried.

The Carolina frame of government, called the Fundamental Constitutions, was probably drawn up by John Locke, the eminent English social philosopher. Locke's plan was a blueprint for an elaborate feudal society. But colonists could no more re-create the European patterns of behavior in Carolina than in Virginia or Maryland or New Netherland.

North Carolina's independence. We have been using the word *Carolina* for the whole tract of land that in time became North and South Carolina. Though North and South Carolina adjoined each other, the climates and physical features differed. These natural differences early produced not only differences in economic development but also in general outlook. Whereas South Carolina became an aristocratic planter province, North Carolina became an individualistic frontier community.

North Carolina was the only southern colony settled initially by people from other colonies instead of from Europe. Many of its early settlers were discontented Virginians. They had little respect for English law, and from the beginning they openly defied authority. The eight proprietors paid scant attention to the northern settlement, and their agents had very little success in securing obedience to the laws. In 1677, when customs officials tried to enforce English trade regulations there, the colonists threw the officials into jail.

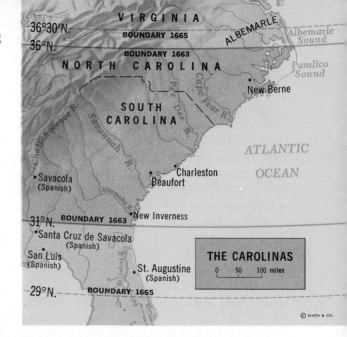

The southern boundary of Carolina was moved into Spanish territory by the terms of the charter of 1665. The Spanish and English claimed the same territory.

For almost a year the "rebels" ran the government before they finally yielded to the proprietors' representatives. In 1712 a separate governor was appointed for the northern region, and Carolina was divided in two.

PENNSYLVANIA

Pennsylvania, the last colony to be founded in the seventeenth century, benefited from all the experience that had accumulated since the first was established. Its guiding genius was William Penn, who wanted to establish a refuge in the New World for Quakers.

William Penn's religious views. Penn's father, a sea hero, had extracted from both King Charles II and the Duke of York the promise that after he was gone they would look after his unpredictable son. Young Penn was unpredictable, however, only to those who could not understand the intricacies of his sensitive mind. Educated at Oxford, he was expelled in 1662 for religious heresy. He spent much of his time reading religious writings. When he announced his conversion to Quakerism, his enraged father threw him out of the house.

But Penn was persistent. After 1667 he was in direct contact with George Fox, the founder of Quakerism. Fox preached that every man

51

may be enlightened by Christ's divine light. This "inward light" supplies all that is necessary for the soul to commune with God. Each individual becomes self-governing in religious matters. This idea was a step beyond the position of the separatists, who had argued that each congregation was self-governing. The Quakers were recruited largely from the ranks of the separatists.

A king's debt. Quaker religious teaching led logically to a belief in social equality. So, even though Penn was an aristocrat, he came more and more to accept the idea of the dignity of all human beings. How could he put this idea into practice? He found the answer in the debt the crown owed his father at his death—the sum of £16,000. Penn went to King Charles and persuaded him to pay this huge obligation in land.

The territory on the west bank of the Delaware River which Penn received was named at the King's insistence for Penn's father, the admiral. It was by far the richest domain ever given to a single individual. A little later the Duke of York turned over to Penn the region on the west shore of Delaware Bay. (This territory—now Delaware—was a part of Pennsylvania until 1776.)

The royal charter. Under Penn's charter, the laws of Pennsylvania had to conform to the laws of England. The charter also provided that the king would not tax the inhabitants of the colony except with the consent of their assembly or the proprietor or by act of Parliament. Finally, the charter allowed citizens to appeal direct to London authorities from any decisions rendered by Pennsylvania courts.

All these provisions appear to indicate that the English were tightening their control over the colonies. The English had learned that America seemed to stimulate a spirit of freedom in settlers, and no longer would the mother country give its possessions free rein to govern themselves. They might turn into runaways!

Liberal legislation. With the single exception of Rhode Island, Pennsylvania had the most liberal voting laws of any colony. A freeman

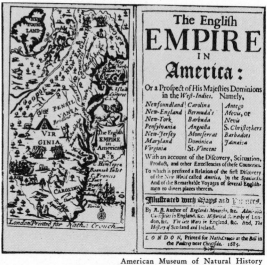

American Museum of Natural History

A page from a book printed in London in 1685, revealing British ideas about American geography.

Ask students to explain what is wrong on the map.

there did not have to be a Quaker or even a church member. And there were other liberal laws: Any trial was to be conducted before a jury. No persons who worshiped God were ever to be "molested or prejudiced for their religious persuasion, or practice" nor could they be "compelled at any time, to frequent or maintain any religious worship." All people, then, except atheists were to have freedom of conscience.

A city of brotherly love. The first Pennsylvania colonists arrived in 1681 and proceeded immediately to lay out Philadelphia, the "city of brotherly love." In September, 1682, Penn himself came to the New World. Almost the first place he visited was the new city, brilliantly situated between the Schuylkill and Delaware rivers. Its city hall was placed at its geographical center. The location of the avenues was carefully planned. This kind of city design reflected the keen interest in improving urban living which had been developing in England.

Pennsylvania prospered from the very beginning as a result of great success in the fur trade. The majority of its inhabitants were Quakers, who, arriving with their own wealth, were able to get off to a good start. Because

##How was the Pennsylvania law concerning religious freedom more liberal than the Act of Toleration? (The Act of Toleration had granted religious freedom to Christians only.)

#By 1700 Germans--called Pennsylvania Dutch--had begin to enter the colony.

they could obtain food and other supplies from their Dutch and Swedish neighbors, Pennsylvanians never had to endure a "starving time."

GEORGIA

During the early years of Pennsylvania's history, England was plagued in the New World by the threat of Spain on the southern and southwestern flanks of its American colonies. At home it was harassed by the presence of impoverished and unemployed people. The creation of a colony that could be both a fortress and a haven offered the possibility of solving both problems.

In June, 1732, a group with the engaging name of "The Associates of the late Dr. Bray" received a charter. This charter granted to twenty-one trustees a vast area—Georgia—extending between the Altamaha and the Savannah rivers and from the Atlantic all the way to the Pacific Ocean. There was to be no governor: a small committee of the trustees would manage the affairs of Georgia. The charter was to run twenty-one years, after which the crown would take over the government of the colony.

Humanitarian work. The enthusiasm for this experiment was widespread. Ministers praised it from the pulpit; thousands of pamphlets were distributed proclaiming Georgia's humanitarian purpose; contributions flowed in from every quarter. Parliament itself gave £10,000 for the venture—the first time the English government had ever made an outright gift for the establishment of a colony.

James Oglethorpe in charge. James Oglethorpe, a member of Parliament and one of the Associates, was in personal charge of the emigrants, numbering more than 100, who sailed for Georgia late in 1732. In January, 1733, the hopeful party arrived at Charles Town, where it was warmly welcomed by the Carolinians before heading for the new land. The next month the passengers landed along the Savannah River and there built their first settlement— Savannah.

Georgia benefited enormously from the wise leadership of Oglethorpe. His military training proved to be invaluable in dealing with the In-

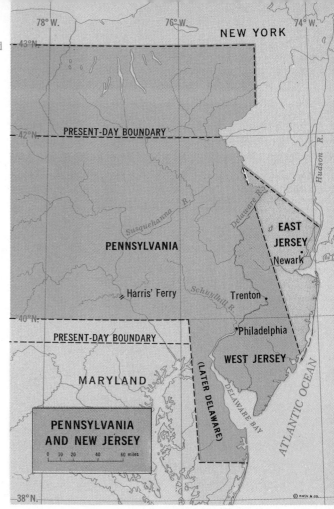

When Pennsylvania was established, New Jersey was divided as shown here. It remained so until 1702.

Indefinite provisions in the charter led to disputes.

dians. But in keeping with the lofty purposes of the Bray Associates, Oglethorpe's methods were peaceful. He made friends with the Creeks by treaty and by just dealings. From them he purchased land for Georgia's settlers as it was needed.

Economic expectations. The English sponsors of Georgia had convinced themselves that economic support for the colony should come from the silkworm. England had up to then depended upon eastern Asia and the continent of Europe for silk. Since the silkworm feeds upon the leaves of the mulberry tree, the trustees required that 1000 such trees be planted in Georgia for every 100 acres of land granted. Wine was another product which the English had been purchasing at high cost from outside

##The silkworm feeds on the leaves of the white mulberry tree, never successfully grown in the area now making up the United States. Again, emphasize the mercantile policy.

53

#Another reason why silk culture failed.
Call attention to the reason for the
demand for slaves.

their empire. This, too, the trustees said, would
now be produced on Georgian soil.

Disappointments. Despite sufficient fertile land,
a carefully thought-out economic plan, and its
high-minded trustees, Georgia failed to carry
out its stated aims. Why?

The answer is that, for one thing, the care
of silkworms and the culture of grapevines required a larger number of laborers than Geor- #
gia attracted at first. The colonists' demand for
slaves was checked for a time by the decision
of the humanitarian trustees to forbid Negro
bondage. Many settlers, objecting to the hard
work in the humid, exhausting climate, made
their way to South Carolina, where slavery was
already being practiced.

Newcomers. Meanwhile, however, other people
were being attracted to Georgia. Lutherans
from Salzburg in Austria established them- ##
selves at Red Bluff on the Savannah River in
1736. The following year Moravians, also Ger-
man-speaking, arrived in the colony. Since the
Moravians were pacifists, they found distasteful the constant preparations for war against
the Spanish; shortly they migrated to North
Carolina and Pennsylvania.

A defended frontier. The trustees needed fighting
men. From 1735 on, Scottish Highlanders were
encouraged to migrate to the colony. Over 100
of them settled on the Altamaha at New Inverness. On the map on this page, you see
that this put them in the forefront of the colony's defense line, directly facing the enemy.
A number of other forts were also built, and
none irritated the Spanish more than Fort St.
George, off the St. Johns River, only about 100
miles from St. Augustine, Spain's proud bastion
in Florida.

By 1751, although 5000 settlers had come to
the colony, only 2000 remained. Militarily the
colony had succeeded; financially it was a failure. In 1752 the trustees, distressed at the
thought that Georgia might be annexed by
South Carolina, surrendered their charter, and
Georgia became a royal colony.

THE THIRTEEN ORIGINAL COLONIES IN 1750

0   50   100   150 miles

▨ Settled Areas
— Frontier

Having made permanent settlements on the coastal
lowland bordering the Atlantic, the English colonists by
1750 were steadily pushing the frontier westward.

##These Lutherans were attracted to Georgia in part because slavery and the drinking of rum were
forbidden there. Non-English immigrants entered other English colonies in large numbers.

THE COLONIAL COMMUNITY

By the middle of the eighteenth century, England's colonies in America were firmly rooted. Each, to be sure, retained a distinctive atmosphere of its own, the product of a unique origin and development. Yet, without plan or intention, the colonies were growing dependent on one another. Already they fell into three groups, each identified by a distinct pattern of economic life.

Through the port of Boston. In the New England colonies—Massachusetts, Rhode Island, Connecticut, and New Hampshire—farming was the main enterprise. Sea-borne commerce, however, was truly enriching the section. The largest city, Boston, boasted 160 warehouses. It had become a clearing station for goods from England bound for the colonies and for exports from the colonies headed for England. From the mother country came hardware, cloth, furniture, and products from eastern Asia. From Virginia came tobacco; from the Carolinas, rice, tar, and turpentine; from the West Indies, sugar, molasses, and mahogany. And from Boston's offshore waters came catch after catch of fish.

Trading in a triangle. The West Indian molasses and sugar were indispensable in a pattern of commerce known as the *triangular trade.* Out of them New Englanders made rum, which slave traders carried to the western coast of Africa. There they bartered it for Negro slaves. Then they transported the slaves to the West Indies, where they sold them to sugar planters, usually at a handsome profit. Finally, loading up with more sugar and molasses for New England, the traders completed the third leg of the voyage—and the cycle began again.

An intellectual side. The prosperity that resulted created a well-developed intellectual life centered around Harvard College, founded at Cambridge, Massachusetts, in 1636, and Yale, established at New Haven, Connecticut, in 1701. The harshness of frontier days had in less than a century given way to a serener and more secure life.

Activity at New York and Philadelphia. The middle colonies—New York, New Jersey, Pennsyl-

Massachusetts Magazine, 1793 (William L. Clements Library)
Boston's Old State House, built in 1713, not only was the seat of government but also significantly influenced the architecture of the time.

The Old State House was the colonial capitol.

vania, and Delaware—shipped lumber, wheat, flour, and loaves of bread in enormous quantities to New England, the southern colonies, the West Indies, and Europe. The lines of commerce of these "bread colonies," as they were sometimes called, led to Philadelphia and New York. Vigorous and growing rapidly, these cities differed from Boston chiefly in that the exports they handled were produced in the section itself. The founding of the College of New Jersey (now Princeton University) in 1746, of the Philadelphia Academy (later the University of Pennsylvania) in 1751, and of New York City's King's College (now Columbia University) in 1754 was evidence that here, too, general economic well-being was producing the means and the need for formal intellectual training.

The staple producers. The southern colonies—Virginia, Maryland, the Carolinas, and Georgia—were known in the mid-eighteenth century as the "staple colonies." They raised tobacco, rice,

Charleston, the leading southern port, as it looked before 1739. Just as cities today are often photographed from the air, so colonial cities were frequently sketched as seen by people aboard ships.

By 1754 the number of barrels of rice shipped annually from Charleston was more than 100,000.

and indigo on large plantations run with slave labor. The most important city, Charleston, set the pattern of life for the planter "aristocracy," although the College of William and Mary, founded in 1693, gave Virginia an important advantage in the training of public leaders.

"Cities in the wilderness." Most colonial Americans, in the North as well as in the South, lived on farms or plantations. But villages and cities were indispensable to the life of the people as centers of economic and intellectual activity.

\# Urban dwellers early faced the problems which the people who lived in the cities of Europe had long had to deal with: filthy thoroughfares, persistent pockets of poverty, devastating fires, frequent crimes of violence, gambling, chronic drunkenness, epidemics of disease, and inadequate water supplies. The urban settlers quickly learned that coöperation rather than individual effort could reduce the size of these problems even if nothing could eliminate them entirely.

City people in the colonies were in closer touch with the Old World than most farming people could be, for they saw the latest books and newspapers from Europe and could observe and talk to newcomers when they arrived. This contact kept them up to date on new ideas and developments in European cities. City dwellers here, like city dwellers abroad, were more urbane and sophisticated than farm folk

and more interested in fashion and change.

The colonies were maturing and feeling a sense of community within themselves and with each other. They were beginning to recognize their economic strength, too. Benjamin Franklin expressed the opinion in 1760 that "the foundations of the future grandeur and stability of the British empire lie in America." Colonists everywhere must have shared this belief. ##

Situated between French possessions on the north and Spanish possessions on the south, the colonies would continue to feel keenly the influence of European international politics. Nevertheless, they had already discovered that they themselves could play more than a passive role in world affairs.

Sum and Substance

1. Explain the origin of New Jersey and Delaware. 2. What plans did the proprietors of Carolina originally have for the colony? How did these plans change? 3. How did North Carolina and South Carolina differ? 4. What restrictions did the King put upon Pennsylvania? What liberal laws were adopted there? 5. What two major purposes did the King have in founding Georgia? 6. What contributions did Oglethorpe make? 7. Why did Georgia generally fail to achieve its aims? How was it successful? 8. Describe the patterns of economic life in the three groups of colonies.

THE WORKSHOP

OF LASTING SIGNIFICANCE

Be sure you know the significance of each of the following:

Henry Hudson	naval stores
Dutch West India Company	Duke of York
	John Lord Berkeley
patroon	Sir George Carteret
Kiliaen Van Rensselaer	Sir John Colleton
	Fundamental Constitutions
New Amsterdam	
Fort Orange	William Penn
Peter Minuit	Quakers
Fort Christina	"inward light"
Peter Stuyvesant	George Fox
Oliver Cromwell	Philadelphia
Navigation Acts	James Oglethorpe
Charles II	Fort St. George
enumerated articles	triangular trade

GEOGRAPHY AND HISTORY

1. Englishmen tried and failed to establish grape and olive culture in Virginia. What crops did they try to produce in Carolina? With what success? On the world map in Chapter 30, locate the countries of Europe where such crops # grow. What mistake did Englishmen evidently make?

2. The colonists usually settled along rivers, because ships were the chief means of transportation and also because the best farmland lay in river valleys. On an outline map of the eastern coast of North America, name the waterways which attracted settlers. Also identify the groups that started the settlements—for instance, the Swedes along Delaware Bay and the Delaware River.

3. International trade has long linked nations of the world. What geographical advantages in carrying on such trade has the Netherlands enjoyed? Britain?

INFORMED OPINION

1. To which colony would you probably have preferred to migrate if you had been (a) an English Quaker in 1700, (b) a Dutch merchant in 1650, (c) a Barbados rice planter in 1665, (d) a German farmer in 1690, (e) a Portuguese Jew?

2. Compare the success of the Dutch and English colonizers in America, using New Netherland and Pennsylvania as your illustrations.

3. If Adam Smith's ideas (see page 49) had been followed by the English government, what important changes would probably have been made in its handling of the colonies? Defend your answer.

4. How might the settlement of the colonies have been affected if there had been no serious unemployment in England during the seventeenth and eighteenth centuries?

HISTORICAL REASONING

1. What development in international politics in the 1600's was reflected in the English colonies in America? How were the colonies affected?

2. In what ways did the Quaker religion encourage the development of democracy in Pennsylvania?

3. How was the kind of economic life that developed in each of the three groups of colonies related to the early history of the colonies in each group?

4. Boston and New York were both trading centers. What atmosphere would you ex- ## pect to find in Puritan Boston which would probably be lacking in a city established by Dutch traders?

DOCUMENTS IN HISTORY

1. What point of view about colonial trade did Josiah Child give in *A New Discourse of Trade*? How did he support his view?

2. What kind of colonies were most pleasing to Child? Why?

3. Which colonies were thought to have both a good and a bad side? Why?

4. What policy did Child recommend that England use in future handling of its trade relationship with its American colonies?

##One in which religion and church attendance were emphasized, where socializing was less frequent than in New York, and where laws rather strictly controlled human behavior.

57

This chapter gives an account of the French and Indian War and the events leading up to the adoption of the Declaration of Independence by the colonists. The quotation is from a pamphlet called <u>Common Sense</u>, appearing in 1776. It was the first frank demand for American independence. Ask what argu-ments used by Paine were most likely to appeal strongly to the colonists. How does Paine show himself to be a master of propaganda? (One way was by giving argu-ments opposing his views and answering them.)

4

ENGLAND'S TRIUMPH AND TROUBLES

Discuss the meaning of the words quoted below.

. . . her motive was *interest* not *attachment* . . .

I have heard it asserted by some that, as America hath flourished under her former con-nection with Great Britain, the same connec-tion is necessary toward her future happiness, and will always have the same effect. Nothing can be more fallacious than this kind of argu-ment. We may as well assert that, because a child has thrived upon milk, it is never to have meat, or that the first twenty years of our lives is to become a precedent for the next twenty. But even this is admitting more than is true; for I answer roundly that America would have flour-ished as much, and probably much more, had no European power taken any notice of her. The commerce by which she hath enriched herself

La Salle established the French claim to the heart of America, a claim contested by Britain.

#"Viz.," the abbreviation of "videlicet," is no longer as common as it once was. Latin students enjoy seeing that "videlicet" comes from <u>videre licet</u>--"it is permitted to see," or, as we say, "namely."
##Paine regularly speaks of "Great Britain," although that is the name of the island, not the country.

are the necessaries of life and will always have a market while eating is the custom of Europe.

But she has protected us, say some. That she hath engrossed us is true, and defended the continent at our expense as well as her own, is admitted; and she would have defended Turkey # from the same motive, viz., for the sake of trade and dominion.

Alas! we have been long led away by ancient prejudices and made large sacrifices to super-## stition. We have boasted the protection of Great Britain without considering that her motive was *interest* not *attachment* and that she did not protect us from *our enemies* on *our account,* but from her enemies on her own account, from those who had no quarrel with us on any *other account,* and who will always be our enemies on the *same account.* . . .

But Britain is the parent-country, say some. Then the more shame upon her conduct. Even brutes do not devour their young, nor savages make war upon their families. . . . Europe and not England, is the parent-country of America. This New World hath been the asylum for the persecuted lovers of civil and religious liberty from *every part* of Europe. Hither have they fled, not from the tender embraces of the mother, but from the cruelty of the monster; . . . the same tyranny which drove the first emigrants from home pursues their descendants. . . .

American Museum of Natural History

After two centuries under British rule, America's ties with the mother country were strong. English law, language, and tradition had been stamped permanently on the colonies. By 1775 many colonists had reached the point where they favored severing the political bonds. But this was not a matter to be taken lightly, and it required an irresistible appeal based on reason to overwhelm the good arguments based on sentiment. In this selection from Thomas Paine's Common Sense, *published in 1776, you see how brilliantly revolution could be justified even in the face of the widely held belief that conciliation with England was both possible and desirable.* Common Sense *was one of the most influential pamphlets ever written.*

Common Sense was printed in Philadelphia, in January, 1776. It is said that by late spring about 100,000 copies were sold, a staggering number. It may have had special appeal for the non-English colonists. Observe how Paine referred to them in the last paragraph quoted above.

Waving the insignia of the king of France, French explorer Robert Cavelier, Sieur de La Salle, with a fleet of bark canoes enters the Mississippi from the Illinois River. Hoping to win control of America from the British by staking out a hold on the interior of the continent, he heads here for the mouth of the Mississippi. There he grandly laid claim to the whole of the great river valley.

Ask what point Paine made about America which is related to Hakluyt's idea (p. 23) that it was a place of rehabilitation.

BRITAIN EMERGES AS THE GREATEST OF COLONIAL POWERS

At the beginning of the eighteenth century there were few Englishmen who doubted that England had become the master organizer and administrator of New World settlements. Indeed, its commerce even penetrated the colonies of its rivals—the Netherlands, France, and Spain. Its principal allies were the birthrate of the Americans and the increasing immigration to America.

In 1700 the area that subsequently became the United States contained about 275,000 people. It is convenient to consider them divided into three roughly equal groups: the people of the New England colonies—about 105,000; those of the middle colonies—about 85,000; and those of the southern colonies— about 85,000. By 1760 the colonists numbered 1,385,000.

EXPANSION OVER THE MOUNTAINS

The pressure of this increasing population intensified annually. The best land along the coast had already been taken up, and Englishmen, hungry for new and broader opportunities, were beginning to peer westward over the crests of the Appalachian Mountains. After 1716 a steady stream of settlers moved confidently across the mountains and began to fill up the river valleys. Englishmen, however, could not range unhindered in the West: the French were also making a bid to dominate it.

France's domain. French settlement in Canada, of which Quebec became the center, had grown slowly but steadily in the twenty-five years after the organization of the Company of One Hundred Associates (see page 19). Montreal, founded in 1642, quickly became an outpost for a brisk trade in the furs and skins which the Indians brought by canoe from the west, down the St. Lawrence and Ottawa rivers. By the 1650's, Frenchmen had discovered the rich fur-bearing region around the Great Lakes and were exploiting it vigorously. Moreover, French Jesuits built important missions there in a staunch attempt to convert the Indians.

French authorities at Quebec yearned to possess this western land. In 1673 they sent Father Jacques Marquette and Louis Joliet to find the great river that was supposed to flow westward from it. The two explorers traveled from Green Bay to the Wisconsin River and thence to the Mississippi, on which they sailed as far as the Arkansas River. Finding that the Mississippi flowed not west but south into the Gulf of Mexico, they turned back—not wishing to fall into the hands of their Spanish rivals.

A few years later another explorer, Robert Cavelier, Sieur de La Salle, followed this path in the search for the western river. He had built a fort at the entrance of Lake Ontario and had named it for Governor Frontenac of New France. From Fort Frontenac he conducted his explorations into the West. In 1680–1682 he traversed the Mississippi to its mouth and claimed in the name of France the entire valley it washed, calling it Louisiana in honor of his king, Louis XIV.

By the end of the seventeenth century, the French flag waved over a vast arc, one arm of which rested on the St. Lawrence and the other on the Mississippi. And, as time passed, the French built a string of posts along the line of their domain: Detroit, Forts Frontenac, Niagara, and Michilimackinac in the Great Lakes region; Kaskaskia and Natchez on the Mississippi; Biloxi and the southernmost one, New Orleans, on the Gulf of Mexico.

Points of friction. The continued westward push of Englishmen brought them more and more frequently into conflict with the French. By the beginning of the eighteenth century British crown officials favored the building of settlements beyond the mountains and the construction of forts along the Great Lakes. Pick out on the map opposite the forts that Britain established. You see that each was built in a strategic location to protect against what Englishmen called "the insults of the French."

As the two great powers of that era, England and France knew they might one day go to war against each other. They competed in many places on the globe in a rivalry that had at stake world supremacy on land and on sea.

#The arc and its arms are clearly seen with the aid of the map, p. 61. Discuss the strategic locations of Forts Oswego, Prince George, and Loudon. How was the location of Fort Niagara strategic?

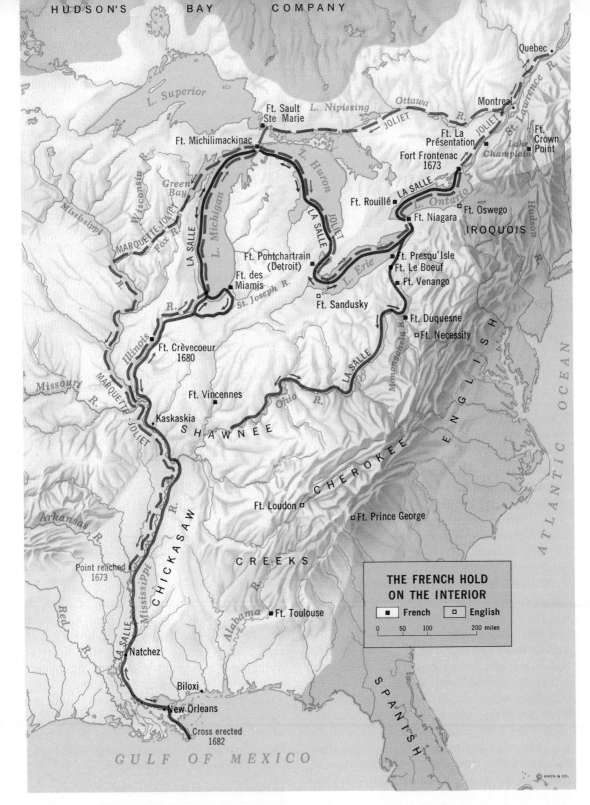

The setting of the developing struggle between the British and the French: as Englishmen moved west, they were on a collision course with the French, who were moving into the sparsely-settled Ohio Valley.

Review the chief handicap France had in its attempts to hold the large area it claimed: the lack of sufficient numbers of colonists to build settlements that would reinforce claims.

Drawing by Frederic Remington

A fur trader respected neither boundaries nor international claims. He traveled where the furs were.

Discuss the fur trader's equipment.

In America, the competition took various forms. For example, by 1715 English colonists on the New England frontier were encroaching upon Indians' hunting grounds. The French allied themselves with the infuriated Indians and armed them to help fight the advancing Englishmen.

The contest for furs. In the Hudson Bay region and elsewhere the struggle between the English and the French over the valuable traffic in furs # was also intense. The center of the French fur trade was Montreal. From there two principal routes led into Indian country. One followed a line to the northern tip of Lake Huron, branching there into two forks—one going to Sault Ste Marie and Lake Superior, and the other going to Michilimackinac and Lake Michigan. The other and more profitable trade route followed a line from Montreal along the St. Lawrence River, past Lake Ontario to the western part of Lake Erie.

The English, long dependent on the Iroquois for pelts, had made Albany a fur-trading cen-

#The two routes can be visualized by locating on the map on p. 61 the places named here.

ter. But by 1725 this mart was beginning to decline as increasing population pressure pushed the fur-bearing animals farther to the west. Consequently, New Yorkers were also beginning to reach into the Great Lakes country. They built Fort Oswego on Lake Ontario in 1725. The French answered them by strengthening Fort Niagara, first built in 1720.

The French were also feeling the presence of the English fur trappers and frontiersmen on the eastern frontier of Louisiana. On the Alabama River, therefore, the French had built Fort Toulouse in 1714. In 1731, to counter the threat of the population that flowed out of the Connecticut and Hudson river valleys, they constructed a fort at Crown Point on Lake Champlain. In the West Indies, as on the mainland, fear of the English was keeping the French busy with defense measures.

Smuggling by New Englanders. New Englanders ## had grown accustomed to smuggling molasses and sugar from the French West Indian islands into their own ports. This illicit traffic violated both French and English laws. The English authorities, however, ignored it since they were not enforcing the Navigation Acts rigidly. The French colonial officials also overlooked it, because it provided the French islands with foodstuffs more cheaply than was possible in any other way. Plainly, though, the illegal trade was another source of English-French antagonism.

The role of Spain. English and Spanish commercial relations in the New World also caused uneasiness. Under a treaty made in 1713, the English compelled Spain to grant them a monopoly of the slave trade in the Spanish colonies. The English shamefully violated the treaty by brazenly smuggling goods into the Spanish possessions in America. The Spanish coast-guard vessels seized guilty ships when they could—and sometimes innocent ones, too, which increased the bad feelings. France and Spain, having a common enemy—England—came together in virtual alliance.

FROM RIVALRY TO HOSTILITY

The friction between France and England led to the outbreak in 1745 of a war known in

##Discuss the object of smuggling. The Staple Act of 1663 forbade the colonies to import foreign products directly. Such goods were to go to England, then to the colonies.

In the expedition against Louisbourg, English colonists leave British ships off the coast of Cape Breton, climb into boats, and row toward shore. New Englanders held a grudge

Mabel Brady Garvan Collection, Yale University Art Gallery

against the French city, because it was a base of raids against their shipping. When the British sought men, the Americans joined the forces that launched the attack.

In 1701 by the Act of Union England, Ireland, and Scotland were joined. The Union flag seen here combines the symbols of the three.

the New World as King George's War. The French seized the prosperous sugar island of St. Lucia in the West Indies; and the British, with the help of their colonies, captured Louisbourg, on Cape Breton Island. (Find Louisbourg on the map on page 65.)

The war ended in a draw in 1748, and the treaty provided that the places captured by both sides during the fighting had to be restored to their original owners. The English withdrew from Cape Breton, but the French remained in St. Lucia. This failure to live up to the treaty became one more bone of contention in the struggle between the English and the French in the New World and the Old.

Fort-building. England tried to negotiate a settlement of the St. Lucia question. The French responded by complaining angrily about England's aggression in other places. They charged,

for example, that the Hudson's Bay Company was encroaching on France's land. When the English built a bastion in Nova Scotia (see the map on page 65), the French argued that this move was a challenge to their stronghold of Louisbourg.

Slowly the French had been winning important Indian tribes over to their side. They had given guarantees that they would protect the tribes from the English. To show their good intentions, they built new forts at the points of possible conflict. In each area the English replied by building forts of their own. In 1749 they made Halifax a strong naval base in Nova Scotia and constructed Fort Lawrence to guard the approach to the peninsula opposite.

In the south the French were also active. They were smoking the peace pipe with the Chickasaw and sending out feelers to the Creeks

#Students should realize that the French were more successful than the English in establishing friendly relations with the Indians. French missionaries were partly responsible.

63

and Cherokee. The prospect of losing Cherokee friendship and support induced the South Carolinians to construct Fort Prince George as a defense against the French.

Face to face in the Ohio Valley. Both sides considered the Ohio Valley to be the most valuable stake of all. Here events were taking place that would make it the arena of open conflict between the French and English.

In 1749 Virginia promoters had organized the Ohio Company to encourage settlers to go into the Ohio River Valley. They had obtained from the English king a grant of thousands of acres of land for their new venture. Before long a stream of frontiersmen from Virginia was flowing steadily into the Ohio Valley. The Marquis Duquesne, who had recently become governor of New France, decided to dam up the flow. He constructed forts from Lake Erie to the Ohio. Two of them were Forts Le Boeuf and Venango, on the upper Allegheny River.

George Washington's mission. The concern felt in Virginia was immediate. The brilliant Scottish lieutenant governor, Robert Dinwiddie, who was himself financially interested in the Ohio Company, did not hesitate long. In 1753 he sent a young man named George Washington to Fort Venango to try to persuade the French to leave English, that is, Virginian, soil. Washington was received cordially. Wine flowed freely and "soon banished the Restraint," but it availed little. The French were determined to have the Ohio Valley as their own.

THE SHOWDOWN

Dinwiddie arranged to build a fort at the Forks of the Ohio. Early in 1754 a small army led by George Washington set out to occupy it. En route the group heard that the French were constructing a great fort at the Forks to be known as Fort Duquesne.

Imprudently, Washington decided to go against the French with his pitifully small band of 150 men. He encountered a small reconnoitering party, which he fell upon and defeated. Knowing that the main French force would soon be after him, he ordered his men to establish a strong point immediately. Appro-

priately, he named it Fort Necessity. As Washington had feared, the French found his party of men. Decisively defeating it, they sent it reeling out of the Ohio country back to Virginia. This was the opening skirmish of the French and Indian War.

The Albany Plan of Union. English officials, knowing that the defense against the French would be greatly strengthened by a union of the colonies, called a meeting at Albany to bring this about. Seven colonies sent representatives to the gathering, which adopted a plan devised by Benjamin Franklin, a leading citizen of Philadelphia. In its final form it called for a president general, to be appointed by the king, and a council, whose members would be chosen by the colonial legislatures. The council would have power over Indian affairs and control over mutual problems of defense—subject to the approval of the president general and the crown.

The colonies never accepted the Albany Plan ## of Union. They refused to give up what they thought was too much power to a central authority. The English, for their part, were also dissatisfied with the plan. They believed it left too much control of affairs in the hands of the colonies. Franklin himself was incensed at the outcome. "Everybody cries, a union is absolutely necessary," he complained, "but when they come to the manner and form of the union, their weak noddles are perfectly distracted." Thirteen separate colonies, then, faced a common enemy without a common plan.

Braddock's brave effort. In later times the myth arose that no English army of redcoats could fight as well as the American colonists, who knew the lore of the forest and the ways of the Indian. But the fact is that the colonists welcomed with open arms the British regulars who arrived in 1755.

The two regiments the mother country sent were commanded by General Edward Braddock, a veteran of European campaigns, who brought the right spirit but the wrong strategy —and far too much personal baggage. Braddock himself led the troops that attacked Fort Duquesne. With 300 axmen preceding him in

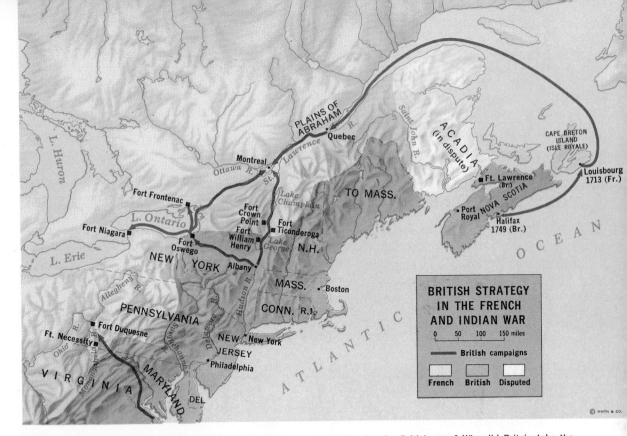

What were Pitt's objectives in each of the land campaigns shown here? In each step of the ambitious expedition undertaken by the British navy? Why did Britain take the offensive?

The English wished to win French territory or the right to the interior. Hence their offensive.

order to hack a way through the forest, the General pushed forward, accompanied by 1400 of his English regulars and 450 Virginia militiamen under Washington.

Brilliantly attired, their flags proudly flying, their bagpipes shrilly playing, they met an advance force of the enemy on July 9, 1755. They were decisively defeated and put to rout. Braddock fought bravely, but after four horses had been killed under him, he received a fatal wound.

Worldwide struggle. The fighting in America was only a part of a larger worldwide conflict known in Europe as the Seven Years' War. On three continents—here, in Europe, and in Asia—the French and English were locked in deadly embrace.

For almost two years the British suffered one reverse after another. In America Fort Oswego was captured by the French, and in Europe England's ally, Frederick II of Prussia, was menaced by the armies of Russia, Austria,

Sweden, and France. It was a dark hour for England—one of the darkest it has ever known.

Pitt to the rescue. At this low point, William Pitt, a leader in the House of Commons, became England's prime minister. Patriotic and proud, Pitt boasted, "I know I can save this country and that no one else can." He roused the country with flaming oratory and promises of ultimate success. "I want," he said, "to call England out of that enervated state into which twenty thousand men from France can shake her."

The tide turns. Pitt laid his plans. They called for a reorganized army and navy. They also provided for subsidies and for other assistance to Frederick of Prussia, who would then be able to keep French troops tied down on the European continent. Pitt reasoned, "We shall win Canada on the banks of the Elbe."

Pitt selected the military commanders for the New World operations. Two of the most important were Jeffrey Amherst and James

#France--instead of Spain--had become Britain's chief rival. The contest was for control of colonies in India and America, for control of the sea, and for first place in the world.

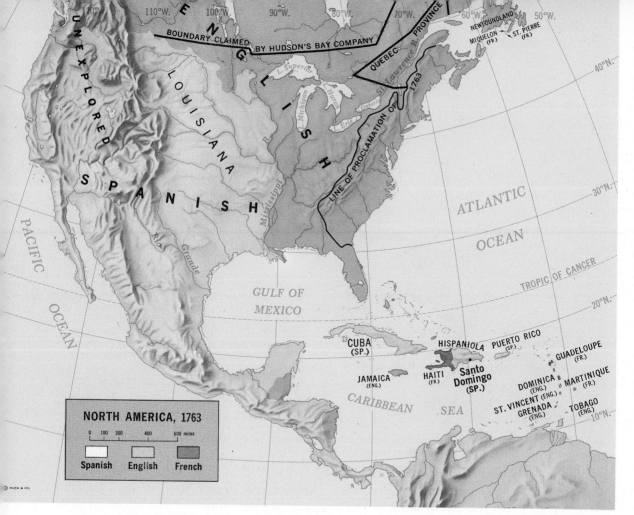

La Salle did not live to see the fate of the land he had named: in 1763, Britain and Spain divided it between them. "Louisiana" refers to Spain's part. France was left with only island possessions.

The fact that Canada became British is unpleasing to French Canadians to this day. Discuss this.

Wolfe, both accomplished officers. On July 26, 1758, a highly trained and well-equipped army of 12,000 under Amherst and Wolfe captured the French fortress of Louisbourg. English regulars wearing red coats, Scotsmen wearing kilts, and Americans wearing leather stockings now combined their efforts, swept across the Mohawk Valley, and captured Forts Oswego and Frontenac on Lake Ontario. You can see from the map on page 65 that this move cut New France in half.

By the time a force under the British general John Forbes had cut its way across Pennsylvania to Fort Duquesne, the French, seeing that the fort was indefensible, had blown it up. On its site the English erected Fort Pitt; later the city of Pittsburgh rose there—a mighty tribute to the English leader who had taken a dying cause and turned it into a winning one.

The fall of Quebec and Montreal. But a greater triumph was in store for Britain. Before the cliffs that guarded the mighty French fortress of Quebec, General Wolfe, with ships carrying 16,000 men, dropped anchor in June, 1759. The French general Louis Montcalm was sure Wolfe could not scale the rock barriers guarding the northern entrances to the city.

By deception, however, on the night of September 12 a British landing party went ashore 2 miles above Quebec and overcame the guards. Before morning 4500 soldiers had clambered up the cliff to an area of level land called the

#Louisbourg was an important naval base designed to control the entrance to the St. Lawrence.

##The capture of Louisbourg led to the fall of Quebec, center of the French population.

Plains of Abraham and were drawn up in battle formation.

Montcalm's troops were inexperienced and untrained. They fought gallantly, but they were outgunned, outnumbered, and outclassed by the British regulars.

A sensitive young man of thirty-two, Wolfe recited Gray's "Elegy Written in a Country Churchyard" as he approached the battle, and he said to his fellow soldiers, "Gentlemen, I had rather be the author of that poem than take Quebec."

Whether Wolfe pondered Gray's line "The paths of glory lead but to the grave," we do not know. His own path to the grave had only a little further to run. On the morning of the thirteenth he perished in battle; within a few hours Montcalm lay dead, too. Four days later the British flag was run up over the former stronghold of the French New World empire. In 1760 the city of Montreal also surrendered to the three British armies that converged upon it. The war in America was over.

Victories everywhere. British triumphs seemed to tumble one upon the other in unbroken succession. Horace Walpole, the author, and a son of England's first prime minister, declared with swagger, "It is necessary to inquire every morning what victory there is, for fear of missing one." On the sea, France's Atlantic and Mediterranean fleets were destroyed. In Africa, British success closed the French traffic in slaves. And in India, English victories ended French influence.

In 1762, attempting to stem the tide, Spain came into the war, but the British captured Spanish islands in the West Indies—including Cuba—one after another. In October the Philippines yielded to a British force from India. On the continent of Europe, meanwhile, Pitt continued to aid Frederick the Great until Prussia had disposed of all its enemies.

The Treaty of Paris, 1763. The peace that ended this world war is known as the Treaty of Paris of 1763. It reflected the complete triumph that England enjoyed throughout the world. France lost at a stroke almost all of its possessions and foreign trade, and New France became merely a memory.

In America, Britain acquired Canada and France's territory east of the Mississippi except New Orleans. Martinique and Guadeloupe, important sugar-producing islands in the West Indies, and Haiti—half of Hispaniola—were returned to France. The British gave back Cuba and the Philippines to Spain and received Florida in exchange.

France, having persuaded Spain to enter the war in what turned out to be a hopeless cause, gave it New Orleans and the land west of the Mississippi—the remains of Louisiana. France received fishing privileges off Newfoundland, and the islands of St. Pierre and Miquelon—useless except for drying fish.

No nation had ever known such a moment of glory as England experienced in 1763, when France and Spain lay prostrate at its feet. One can feel the vanity and scorn of the Britons of that time in Horace Walpole's boastful words: "I shall burn my Greek and Latin books. They are the histories of little people."

Sum and Substance
1. Explain Tom Paine's justification for a break between the colonies and England. 2. How did France gain and maintain its hold on the interior of North America? 3. Name the sources of English-French antagonism in the New World. 4. Where did Spanish sympathies lie? Why? 5. Where did conflict break out first? Why? 6. Describe British strategy in the French and Indian War. 7. What were the results of the war?

This section describes events leading up to the adoption of the Declaration of Independence.

THE MOTHER COUNTRY AROUSES THE AMERICAN COLONISTS

After 1763 the British Empire, spread out over the entire globe, required thoroughgoing military, economic, and political reorganization.

The task called for the wisdom of a Solomon. Unhappily, Britain's ministers were no Solomons. George II, who died in 1760, had al-

Ohio Historical Society Library

Pontiac, who organized his fellow Indians in an unsuccessful crusade to expel the English intruders.

Stress the difficulties of organizing the Indians.

lowed his ministers to run affairs, chiefly because, being German, he was uncomfortable with the English language and unfamiliar with the details of colonial problems. His grandson and successor, George III, was of a different stripe. He hoped to follow his mother's advice: "George, be a King." From the time of his accession to the throne, ministers catering to his wishes held office. Their policies cost him the American colonies.

THE NEW SCENE

At the end of the French and Indian War, the colonists could breathe a sigh of relief. France, the common enemy that had forced the Atlantic settlements to coöperate with one another, was gone. Henceforth they could go their separate ways, sometimes even as rivals and often with little concern for the mother country's wishes.

Besides, a new American-born generation was being reared that had never been in the old country. Even ties of sentiment were therefore stretched thinner each year. Moreover, thousands of Scotch-Irish and Germans, far from feeling a kinship with England, were in fact keenly anti-British.

Pontiac's resistance. A particularly baffling problem was what to do about the hostility of the Indians. Land speculators and frontiersmen were eager to get ahead with their plans for settlement beyond the Appalachians. But rumors of the plans understandably alarmed and frightened the tribesmen, who, in addition, believed that Englishmen cheated them in the fur trade.

In this inflammable atmosphere French traders succeeded in creating an explosion. They whispered that a French army was on its way to recover the Ohio Valley for France and the Indians. The Indians, under the inspired leadership of an Ottawa chieftain named Pontiac, formed a confederation to drive the English settlers back eastward across the mountains.

In 1763–1764 the entire western frontier was aflame with war. When Pontiac's conspiracy—as the English called the confederation—was broken, hundreds of settlers lay dead, and the Indians had captured all but three of the western outposts—Forts Pitt and Niagara, and Detroit. British redcoats finally forced Pontiac to withdraw, and in 1765 peace came again on the frontier.

The Proclamation Line. During the war with Pontiac the colonists had relied on the mother country because they had made no plan to defend themselves. In 1763 the British authorities, eager to be rid of responsibility for defending the colonists against the Indians, provided what seemed to be a way of avoiding the need for defense. They drew a line—the Proclamation Line of 1763—along the crest of the Appalachians and forbade settlement west of it. People already there were expected to leave. At a future time the English would open the land to settlement after first purchasing it through negotiations with the Indians.

An outcry. This arrangement stirred up a hornet's nest. Fur traders, to be sure, were delighted, because fur-bearing animals and their hunters would not be driven out by frontiersmen. But the Proclamation was denounced in the colonies that had charter claims extending into the forbidden area. Land speculators in both England and America who had already been busy organizing trans-Appalachian companies to exploit this choice domain were furious. These included some of the leading citizens in the colonies—men like George Washington and Benjamin Franklin. Frontiersmen were exasperated because they could not move freely westward to take up new land.

Putting on the pressure. Relations between the colonies and mother country were further strained by important financial matters. The English, stumbling under a crushing weight of debt incurred largely in protecting the colonies against the French, saw that the colonies were a source of needed revenue. As one Londoner explained: "The colonies are in a flourishing condition, increasing every day in riches, people, and territory. Britain is exhausted—she is manifestly sinking under oppressive and insupportable burdens."

The Sugar Act. The remedy appeared to be obvious: make the colonies pay a greater share of the cost of defending and administering them. This was the thought in the mind of George Grenville, who sponsored the Sugar Act in Parliament in 1764. Under this law the duty on foreign molasses (that is, molasses from the French, Dutch, or Spanish plantations in the West Indies) was reduced from six- to three-pence a gallon. (The old law—the Molasses Act of 1733—under which the duty had been set at six-pence, had never been enforced.) Molasses from the British West Indies would continue to come in free.

The colonists saw three objectionable things in the new Sugar Act. The first was the clear # indication that England intended to enforce this law strictly. The second was a duty that, in spite of the reduction, they still considered too high; the third was the attempt to discourage trade between English colonies and the foreign West Indies—a trade on which New England depended heavily.

Shortly the worry of the colonists seemed to be justified. The prices that they received in the British West Indies for their fish, flour, and lumber dropped because they no longer had the alternative of selling in the non-English islands. Rum, formerly made from the cheaper foreign molasses, now rose in price in the colonies. Besides, the amount of money the colonists normally got from the foreign West Indies declined markedly, making it difficult for the Americans to purchase manufactured goods from England. In short, the Sugar Act put a brake on the ## wheels of colonial trade. The colonists attacked the act as a monstrous tax law masquerading as an attempt to regulate trade. They granted that such *regulation* was the business of Parliament, but they considered *taxation* exclusively their own affair.

Troops to America. Grenville, who was an obstinate man, remained unmoved by colonial criticism of the Sugar Act. In fact, he went ahead with a plan to station 10,000 British troops in North America to protect the frontier and enforce the Proclamation of 1763. Then if the need should arise, the soldiers would be on hand to assist the officials attempting to end smuggling.

The Stamp Act. In order to raise the rest of the revenue Grenville anticipated, Parliament in 1765 passed another unpopular measure—the Stamp Act. By its terms revenue stamps would be applied to all newspapers and official documents circulated in the colonies. The law was difficult to ignore because no court action could take place without stamps on the legal papers involved. Further, no man could take a bride without having a stamp affixed to the marriage license; and no newspaper or pamphlet could even circulate its complaint about the law unless it bore a stamp!

ACTING AND REACTING

Grenville apparently had not foreseen that the law would hit hardest the most vocal people in America—lawyers and newspaper editors. They lost no time pointing out in the press and in public address that under the Stamp Act, Parliament was taxing the colonies directly, although this right had previously been reserved

##The main basis of colonial resentment, then, was economic. Observe that all the objectionable things the colonists saw in the Sugar Act were economic. What taxation was involved?

69

Library of Congress

In Boston indignant colonists, including a Negro, burn the hated British stamps and stamped paper.

Mobs formed also in New York City and other cities.

to the colonial legislatures. In Virginia's House of Burgesses Patrick Henry was exclaiming, "Caesar had his Brutus; Charles the First his Cromwell; and George the Third——" At this point voices interrupted to accuse him of treason. Henry continued unruffled, "may profit by their example! If this be treason, make the most of it."

\# **Violence.** The opposition to the Stamp Act was unexpectedly violent. A riot led by the Sons of Liberty, an organization of patriots, took place in Boston, and Andrew Oliver, the Massachusetts stamp distributor, was threatened with his life. A mob smashed in the front gates of Lieutenant Governor Thomas Hutchinson's beautiful house and destroyed most of those belongings—including his magnificent library—that they could not carry away.

Americans who had applied for positions as stamp agents quickly changed their minds. The agent in New Hampshire wrote as he resigned his post: "I did not know whether I should have escaped from this mob with my life, as some were for Cutting off my head, others for Cutting off my Ears and sending them home with my Commission."

Discuss the difference between the stamp tax-- a direct tax--and the duty on sugar, an indirect tax.

The Stamp Act Congress. James Otis, of Massachusetts, proposed that the colonies act together. Accordingly, what came to be known as the Stamp Act Congress met in New York in October, 1765. It sent an address to the King, and it petitioned Parliament to repeal the Stamp Act, which, it said, provided for taxation without representation. The members also resolved that the colonies would import nothing from England until the law was repealed. The Congress served the valuable purpose of bringing together for consultation the leading colonial figures.

Repeal. The boycott of British goods had the desired effect. English merchants begged Parliament to repeal the Stamp Act and so reestablish their trade with the colonists. The Marquis of Rockingham, who had replaced Grenville as prime minister, decided to satisfy the English businessmen as well as the Americans by obtaining the repeal of the Stamp Act. Though the repeal was a wise decision for the new prime minister, it was accompanied by the Declaratory Act, which asserted that Parliament could tax the colonies if it wanted to.

The Townshend Act. Because the need for revenue continued, the British government followed the recommendation of Charles Townshend, the new finance minister, levying import duties on certain products shipped from England into the colonies. These were glass, paper, lead, tea, and paint. The British reasoned that the colonists had objected to the Sugar Act as taxation that regulated trade; then they had opposed the Stamp Act as "internal taxation," because it was applied inside the colonies. Now they would get "external taxation"; that is, the new duties would be applied outside the colonies before the goods entered them. The truth of the matter was that the colonists did not want to be taxed internally *or* externally.

"Champagne Charley" Townshend, whose wit and gaiety made him a sought-after dinner guest and who was a brilliant orator when under the influence of liquor, found he required more substantial talents to quiet the colonists. He spurned the advice of the Earl of Chatham—we met him earlier as William Pitt— \#\#

\#\#Pitt had been made a peer and he became a member of the House of Lords, where friends of the colonies were in a minority. Observe that the British were trying various kinds of taxes.

who, sympathetic to the Americans, had advised against taxing them. "America is obstinate!" Pitt declared in Parliament.

New physical violence. Unfortunately, it was the undiplomatic Townshend, not the conciliatory Pitt, who determined British policy. Townshend only managed to arouse more opposition to the mother country. Outbreaks of physical violence against the customs commissioners in Boston brought the man-of-war *Romney* to ride at anchor in the harbor. Even so, rioting broke out when officials seized as a smuggler the sloop *Liberty,* which belonged to John Hancock, one of the leading merchants in Boston. The war of words grew fiercer.

John Dickinson's position. The best remembered of the American arguments were contained in *Letters from a Farmer in Pennsylvania,* written by a well-to-do lawyer named John Dickinson. In these essays Dickinson presented what was probably the position of most Americans: Parliament might regulate the commerce of the empire, and for this purpose duties might be imposed. But duties principally designed to

bring in revenue were a form of taxation and therefore were not acceptable.

Nonimportation. Action quickly followed argument. The colonists revived the method they had used in their opposition to the Stamp Act: nonimportation from England. The pressure again scared the British merchants who were engaged in American trade. They helped produce the repeal of the Townshend duties, which Parliament voted in 1770, keeping only the tax on tea.

The alarm of the merchants. The colonial merchants now began to reflect on the impact at home of the nonimportation agreements. They observed that these agreements had encouraged many people to believe that opposition to *all* public authority was a good thing. They suspected that they had unwittingly undermined their own authority at home.

After the repeal of the Townshend duties, the merchants were determined to dissolve the nonimportation associations and end agitation in the colonies. As one New Yorker said: "All men of property are so sensible of their danger, from Riots and tumults, that they will not rashly be induced to enter into combinations, which may promote disorder for the future, but will endeavor to promote due subordination to legal authority." Moreover, after a business depression in 1769, prosperity returned in 1770; and no man in business wanted to cause trouble that might interfere with trade.

FATEFUL BLUNDERS

Some popular leaders, however, wanted to keep alive the embers of discord. They feared that unless they did, what they called "the spirit of patriotism" would disappear forever. And the British inadvertently helped keep the embers glowing. The blunders of Frederick, Lord North, the King's newest and most favored prime minister, were the bellows that fanned the flame. He often slumbered in his seat in the House of Commons, and at least one fellow member wished North had "some one at his elbow, to pull him every now and then by the ear . . . to keep him awake to the affairs of America."

Call attention to the evidence of wealth.

John Hancock, the wealthiest New England patriot, posed with his wife for the American painter Edward Savage.

Bequest of Mr. Woodbury Blair, Corcoran Gallery of Art

#John Adams, a Massachusetts lawyer, helped defend the British soldiers who were brought to trial as a result of the "Boston Massacre." All but two were acquitted, and they received little punishment. ##The Gaspee in particular was looking for smugglers of tea, who were defying the last Townshend Act.

"Boston Massacre." English military men, believing that a show of force would revive American respect for them, persuaded the British government to station more troops in the colonies. The townspeople of Boston especially, led by such "radical" colonial leaders as Samuel Adams, were aroused to high pitch over the presence of these soldiers. The breaking point came on March 5, 1770. A mob of ruffians heckled soldiers at the customhouse with such taunts as, "Come on you Rascals, you bloody-backs, you lobster scoundrels, fire if you dare!" Tempers flared, a clash occurred, the crowd hurled snowballs at the English, and the soldiers fired upon the citizens. In the melee five Bostonians were killed, and others were wounded. One of the victims was Crispus Attucks, a runaway slave, who was the leader of the mob. Many people must have wondered at the irony of a Negro who was less than free becoming a martyr to the cause of freedom for the colonists.

The patriots began to refer to the shooting incident as the "Boston Massacre." Joseph Warren and Sam Adams, shouting loudly in protest, organized committees in the towns to keep high the flames of discontent. The British did little to extinguish them.

Vandalism at sea. On June 9, 1772, the schooner *Gaspee,* a revenue cutter looking for smugglers, ran aground near Providence. During the night a band of citizens boarded it, sent the crew ashore, and put a torch to the vessel. Although the enraged English sent a board of inquiry to investigate, they never caught the culprits. A result of the *Gaspee* incident was that the American patriots organized the intercolonial Committees of Correspondence to exchange ideas and information. At last the Sam Adamses of Massachusetts were linked with the Patrick Henrys and the Richard Henry Lees of Virginia—a potent combination that soon included in its network spokesmen from all the colonies.

Tea at a bargain. England's next step gave these colonists something exciting to write to one another about. In 1773 the English East India Company, heavily in debt, had in its

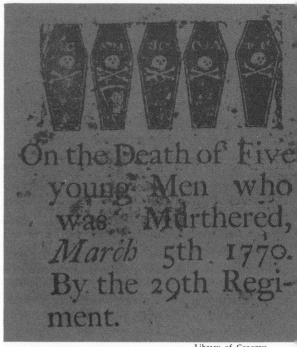

On the Death of Five young Men who was Murthered, March 5th 1770. By the 29th Regiment.

Broadsides like this publicized the loss of life in the "Boston Massacre" and stirred up the colonists.

Sam Adams was a second cousin of John Adams.

Samuel Adams was said to have one occupation—public business. Adept in politics and skilled as a writer, he was the father of the American Revolution.

72   Sam Adams was responsible for the idea of forming Committees of Correspondence.

warehouses a mountain of unsold tea. If it could sell the tea, its problems would be solved. Parliament obliged the Company by passing the Tea Act. It provided for the direct sale of tea by the East India Company to its agents in America, so bypassing the American merchants engaged in the tea business and eliminating their profits as middlemen. The Company was to be permitted to ship the tea to America from the mother country without first paying the regular duty for bringing it into England. Only the three-pence duty would be laid on the tea sold in the colonies.

Parliament hoped that by making tea cheaper in America than in England the whole arrangement would be acceptable to the colonists. But Parliament failed to reckon with the indignation of the American merchants. Their shelves were stocked with tea which they could not price nearly as low as the East India Company's tea. Fair traders as well as smugglers were going to be injured by this latest British action.

Not only were the tea merchants enraged. Almost all other merchants were stirred up, too. They were aware that if England could give a single company a monopoly on one item like tea, it could do the same thing with rum or grain or hardware or silks or iron—or anything else. This was a situation far more serious than the simple matter of taxes. This latest British act seemed to threaten all free enterprise in the colonies.

In these circumstances, many of the merchants were willing to join forces with the radicals whom they had previously shunned. They knew that the radicals had an effective intercolonial organization in the Committees of Correspondence. They did not anticipate that, once having encouraged the more extreme leaders, they themselves would never get control of things again.

A tea party in Boston. The American patriots knew that if the East India Company's tea was once landed, it would be sold and drunk. If that happened, Americans would, in effect, be admitting that England had the right to establish the kind of monopoly it had given to the East India Company. So the radicals spread propaganda among the colonists, saying that the East India tea was not good; that it had been sweating for several years in a warehouse; that, in fact, tea was bad for one's health, anyway! What they meant, of course, was expressed well by the colonist who exclaimed: "Do not suffer yourself to sip the acursed, dirtied stuff. For if you do, the devil will immediately enter into you, and you will instantly become a traitor to your country!"

Opposition to the Tea Act reached its peak in Boston. There a band of men disguised as Mohawk Indians went aboard the tea ships in the harbor on the night of December 16, 1773. They proceeded to dump into the water chests of tea valued at about £15,000. John Hancock and Sam Adams, it was alleged, were two of the "Indians." England's response to the news about the Boston Tea Party was instantaneous and severe. Not only was the tea in the sea; the fat was in the fire.

The "Intolerable Acts." Parliament decided to punish Massachusetts with a series of laws that Americans called the "Intolerable Acts." First, the port of Boston was to be closed until Boston paid for the tea dumped there. Second, any British official accused of committing an offense in enforcing laws was to be tried only in England. Third, soldiers would be quartered in the colonies whenever they were needed to suppress disorder. Other severe restrictions were placed upon the freedom of the colonists in Massachusetts, and Boston was forbidden to hold its town meeting.

Sum and Substance

1. Explain the British and the American points of view on the Proclamation of 1763. 2. What was the purpose of the Sugar Act? The Stamp Act? 3. Describe the colonists' specific objections to these two acts. 4. What action did they take? 5. How did the Townshend Act differ from the two earlier acts? 6. How did the colonists react to it? 7. What led to the Boston Massacre? The *Gaspee* incident? The Boston Tea Party? 8. How did each affect the colonists? British-American relations?

##Sam Adams had called together Committees of Correspondence in and near Boston, and they had decided that the tea was not to be landed. About fifteen men took part in the tea party.

73

A DECLARATION OF INDEPENDENCE DEFIES THE EMPIRE

Boston's economic life ground to a halt. It was said that "nine tenths of the inhabitants were render'd wretchedly miserable." In this critical hour the Committees of Correspondence in the various colonies went into action, spurring help. New York promised to supply Boston with enough food to withstand a ten years' siege. Other neighbors were equally helpful, and Virginia, in sympathy, set a day of fasting. As a result, Bostonians jeered at England and boasted "that their Sheep and their Flour, their Fish and their Rice came faster than they could use them."

THE CONTINENTAL CONGRESS

The exasperated royal governor of Virginia dissolved the House of Burgesses, which promptly was reassembled in the Raleigh Tavern, from which it defiantly sent out a call for a Continental Congress. The Virginians passed resolutions to cease the importation of British tea and to stop exporting tobacco. But they hoped still for a compromise with England that would save the empire.

A new grievance. Virginia's leaders warmly supported Boston's cause, but they also had their own grievances against the mother country. The chief one revolved around the fate of the province of Quebec. The French Canadians there, under English rule since 1763, had begun to show discontent which, if not checked, might merge with that which the seaboard colonies were showing.

To forestall more trouble, therefore, Parliament passed in 1774 a law recognizing French civil law and the Roman Catholic religion within the boundaries of Quebec. Moreover, it extended the boundaries northward to Hudson Bay, westward to the Mississippi, and southward to the Ohio. This law, called the Quebec Act, was from Quebec's point of view a most generous measure, and it undoubtedly cemented that colony to Britain.

American colonists were greatly distressed by the Act. In Massachusetts the patriots charged that the next step after this recognition of the Roman Catholic religion would be the establishment of a state church in Massachusetts to serve as another agency of English tyranny. Virginia was particularly indignant, because it held that its charter rights—giving it territory extending from "sea-to-sea"—were now arbitrarily canceled. West of the Appalachians, important Virginians, as you know, had already begun ambitious ventures in land speculation. The Quebec Act closed to them the site of their operations.

The passage of the Quebec Act, therefore, tied together Virginia patriots and Massachusetts patriots in a common hostility to England. The British had clumsily stepped hard on the toes of both the merchants of Boston and the planter-speculators of the Old Dominion—the two most powerful classes in the colonies.

Determined delegates. One can understand the sense of purpose felt by the delegates who came to Philadelphia from twelve of the thirteen colonies for the First Continental Congress, which met on September 5, 1774. Supporters of the mother country called the delegates such names as "zealots of anarchy" and "croakers of calamity."

Styling themselves "moderates," certain delegates, like John Jay of New York, Joseph Galloway of Pennsylvania, and Edward Rutledge of South Carolina, argued hard against separation from England. They said it would destroy law and order in the colonies and usher in "democracy"—by which they meant "mob rule." Galloway devised a compromise plan calling for an American parliament, similar to the British Parliament, to serve under the crown. This proposal failed of adoption by only one vote.

Thereafter, the radicals, that is, those advocating practically a complete break with England, took control of the Congress. The leaders—Sam Adams and John Hancock of Massachusetts, Charles Thomson of Pennsylvania, Richard Henry Lee and Patrick Henry of Virginia, and Christopher Gadsden of South Carolina—were less worried about the effects of "democracy" than they were about the "tyranny" of the British Parliament. They maintained that their natural rights had been infringed by Parliament, and they were determined to be entirely free of its control.

The Association. After long deliberation the First Continental Congress adopted an intercolonial agreement known as "The Association." It provided for reviving nonimportation against Britain and for commencing it against the British West Indies. It also provided for the encouragement of manufacturing, especially of wool, and the discouragement of every type of extravagance, such as horse-racing and "all kinds of gaming, cockfighting, exhibition of shows, plays, and other expensive diversions and entertainments." Clearly its framers saw the possibility of war and were preparing the way for a program of self-denial.

Watchdog committees were created in the colonies to spy out violators of The Association. They watched businessmen like hawks, inquiring into the whys and wherefores of transactions they suspected. In some instances they terrorized businessmen who would not join The Association. Letters from The Association's committee made more than one British

sympathizer turn "as pale as his shirt." The "community of merchants" must often have wondered whether it had protested against British tyranny only to fall victim to the tyranny of fellow citizens.

Radicals in the saddle. British merchants, meanwhile, were finding new markets in Europe and were far less inclined to yield to economic boycott than they had been in the 1760's. John Adams drew the logical conclusion. He wrote to Patrick Henry: "I expect no redress, but, on the contrary, increased resentment and double vengeance. We must fight." And Henry replied, "By God, I am of your opinion." The radicals were drawing the colonies into a position from which there could be no retreat.

Refusal to conciliate. The First Continental Congress sent to George III a conciliatory petition, but the King ignored it. In November, 1774, the King wrote to Lord North: "The New England governments are in a state of rebellion," and "blows must decide whether they are to be subject to this country or independent."

On February 9, 1775, Parliament declared Massachusetts to be in open rebellion. The New England colonies were forbidden to trade anywhere in the world except with Britain and

This picture was made from an on-the-spot sketch. North Bridge can be seen in the center.

Fight the colonists did: on April 19, 1775, the British regulars drew up at the right of the bridge, the American militia at the left of it in the Battle of Concord, painted here by a contemporary artist.

the British West Indies. This restriction was extended to five other colonies in April. Lord North pledged that the ban would be lifted on any colony which arranged satisfactorily to pay the salaries of its crown officials and the cost of its own defense.

"The shot heard round the world." Fundamentally, England never believed that the colonies would fight. It had guessed that a little force patiently applied would break the opposition.

The radicals, working through the Committees, however, had been busily collecting and storing arms and ammunition. In Massachusetts, where this seditious activity was concentrated, the British general Thomas Gage had orders to arrest Sam Adams and John Hancock and send them to England to stand trial.

The village of Concord had become a military depot, and in April Gage moved on it to seize the powder, muskets, and other stores hidden there. Warned by Paul Revere and William Dawes, the colonists were ready. On the way, the English soldiers fired at the seventy minutemen lined up on the village green at nearby Lexington. These men were a special force authorized by the Continental Congress to be ready to spring to arms on a moment's notice. The minutemen returned a few shots and then gathered up their dead and wounded. The British re-formed and swept on to Concord, where they were met by a larger force of American militiamen, who gave an excellent account of themselves. This brief engagement was immortalized about a half century later by Ralph Waldo Emerson, who wrote:

> Here once the embattled farmers stood
> And fired the shot heard round the world.

The redcoats were saved from disaster only by the prompt arrival of reinforcements. The raw Yankee farmers had shown they were able to stand up against the trained English regulars. At the Battle of Bunker Hill in June (actually fought on Breed's Hill nearby) the Americans, trying to hold heights to bombard Gage's troops in Boston, again acquitted themselves well. The British drove them off, but the Americans had many heroes, including particularly Peter Sa-

lem, recently a slave, whose shot killed one of the ranking British officers.

#

HESITATION AND RESOLVE

On May 10, 1775, the Second Continental Congress met in Philadelphia. The mother country had instructed the royal governors to forbid and prevent the naming of delegates by the colonial legislatures. Consequently, special conventions were called to choose them. This time all thirteen colonies sent delegates. More radical in outlook than the first one, the Second Continental Congress included Benjamin Franklin in addition to other heroes, like Sam Adams and John Hancock of Massachusetts and George Washington and Thomas Jefferson of Virginia.

While continuing to agree that the colonies' rights had been trampled upon, members of the Congress made a last conciliatory gesture in offering what is known as the "Olive Branch Petition." Written by John Dickinson of Pennsylvania, it reasserted the colonists' loyalty to the crown and asked only that the king protect them from Parliament. George III refused to receive the petition.

Some brakes. For fourteen months the Continental Congress hesitated to declare America independent. Americans of that generation have very aptly been called the "reluctant rebels." First of all, loyalty to the king was so deeply ingrained that it could be undermined only gradually. As late as 1774 John Adams was writing that independence was "a Hobgoblin of so frightful Mien, that it would throw a delicate person into fits to look it in the face."

##

Second, the Americans knew that if they struck for independence prematurely, they would be crushed. Much important groundwork would have to be laid before the thirteen colonies could become a unit. The radicals appreciated well the sense of Benjamin Franklin's warning, "We must all hang together, or we shall hang separately." Some parts of colonial America were, moreover, less hot for independence than others. They must be given the opportunity to catch up to the rest. Even such an enthusiast as Sam Adams was warning of

Congress votes independence: July, 1776. Samuel Adams sits at the far left; John Adams, in the foreground, faces

Benjamin Franklin, seated; Thomas Jefferson hands a paper to John Hancock, sitting at the desk.

The man with the cane is Robert Morris. Robert Edge Pine started this painting in 1788.

the necessity to "wait till the Fruit is ripe before we gather it."

The ripening occurred shortly. In October, 1775, George III announced his intention to fight the rebels with mercenary troops, and the Americans knew they were enemies in British eyes and no longer Englishmen.

Hard questions. By the beginning of 1776, colonial leaders in the Continental Congress were asking sticky questions: How do we govern ourselves now that royal authority has collapsed here? Is the Continental Congress to be permanent? How can the colonies obtain foreign coöperation and assistance in this struggle? A declaration of independence held the promise of answers to these questions, since such a declaration might open the way to aid from France. The American leaders knew that France would do anything it could to cut the ties between England and America.

Paine's mighty pamphlet. Thomas Paine gave the Americans the arguments for independence they needed to hear, and his logic made them glad to break with England. Paine, the son of an English corset maker, had come to America in 1774. In the past a failure at every-

thing to which he had turned his hand, he here became a skillful propagandist for the patriots. His pamphlet *Common Sense,* which appeared in January of 1776, enjoyed a phenomenal reception. It seemed to say the right things better and more bravely than they had ever before been said. Paine sneered at the monarchy and, in particular, George III, "the Royal Brute, a hardened, sullen-tempered Pharaoh." And Paine cautioned against accepting concessions from him. "Nothing but independence," he insisted, could save America from ruin.

Cutting the tie. The die was being cast for revolution. On June 7, 1776, Richard Henry Lee introduced three resolutions in the Continental Congress. The first announced that "these United Colonies are, and of right ought to be, free and independent states . . . and that all political connection between them and the state of Great Britain is, and ought to be, totally dissolved." The second urged that the colonies seek to make arrangements for foreign alliances. The third proposed that the colonies form themselves into a confederation under a constitution which each would separately approve. The moderates, like John Dickinson, #

#John Adams seconded the motion by Lee. The next day debate on the resolution began. On June 10 the group decided to postpone decision for three weeks. Debate started again July 11.

John Hancock declared that he would so sign his name to the Declaration of Independence that the king of England could not fail to read it. Other signers and their signatures are also shown.

All the signers are shown. Hancock, in profile, is seated at the right.

could now only delay, no longer stop, the movement for independence.

The immortal statement. Congress appointed a committee of five to draft a declaration of independence. The members included Thomas Jefferson, Benjamin Franklin, and John Adams. Jefferson drew up the document, and the others made minor changes in it as they saw fit. Lee's first resolution was debated briefly and approved on July 2. On July 4 Jefferson's handiwork was adopted. On August 2 a parchment copy of it, which survives to this day, was signed.

The Declaration of Independence is divided into two parts. The first is a general statement of principles. The second is a list of specific grievances against the King. These quickly became of historical interest only. As you read them, see how many you can connect with what we have been discussing in these pages.

The first section of the Declaration has endured. It offers the reasons, which remain valid today, for the grave act of separation from the mother country. "We hold these truths to be self-evident," it avowed, "that all men are created equal; that they are endowed by their Creator with certain unalienable rights; that among these are life, liberty, and the pursuit of happiness. That, to secure these rights, governments are instituted among men, deriving their just powers from the consent of the governed. . . ."

Jefferson was doing more than trying to justify "to a candid world" the awesome step the Americans were taking. He was also offering mankind a vision of a kind of government more responsive to its people than any had been before. But it could not be made real by words alone. It would have to be won on the battlefield at a high cost in blood and money—the first installment in a long series that Americans have paid for their republic.

Sum and Substance

1. How did the Quebec Act help to unite the colonies? 2. What measures were taken by the First Continental Congress? 3. Account for the outbreak of fighting at Concord and Lexington. 4. What finally led the colonists to declare their independence? Why had they hesitated at first? 5. Which is the more significant part of the Declaration of Independence? Why?

#Students should familiarize themselves with the Declaration of Independence, which begins on p. 789. Because some delegates were absent on August 2, they signed the document later.

THE WORKSHOP

OF LASTING SIGNIFICANCE

How was each of the following involved in England's triumphs and troubles in America in the 1700's?

Sieur de La Salle
Father Marquette
Louis Joliet
King George's War
Ohio Company
Robert Dinwiddie
George Washington
Fort Duquesne
Fort Necessity
Albany Plan of
    Union
Edward Braddock
William Pitt
Fort Pitt
James Wolfe
Louis Montcalm
Treaty of Paris,
    1763
Pontiac's Conspiracy
Proclamation Line of
    1763
Sugar Act of 1764
Stamp Act
Sons of Liberty

Stamp Act Congress
Townshend Act
John Dickinson
Nonimportation
    agreements
Samuel Adams
"Boston Massacre"
Gaspee incident
Committees of
    Correspondence
Boston Tea Party
"Intolerable Acts"
First Continental
    Congress
Quebec Act
minutemen
Lexington and
    Concord
Second Continental
    Congress
Common Sense
Declaration of
    Independence

PUTTING HISTORY ON THE MAP

1. On an outline map of North America, show Montreal, center of the French fur trade. Indicate by arrows the French fur-trading routes described on page 62, and name the waterways involved. Show Albany, fur-trading center of the English colonists, and indicate the land occupied by these colonists and that claimed by the Hudson's Bay Company. From your map explain (*a*) why the French went into the Mississippi Valley; (*b*) why fighting between the French and the English broke out in the Ohio Valley.

2. Using information from a recent atlas, name on an outline map the principal islands of the West Indies. Indicate the independent ones and the names of the countries which control the others. (*a*) How many of the islands have become independent since 1763? (*b*) Which remain in the same hands as in 1763? (*c*) Compare the colonists' interests in the West Indies in the eighteenth century with American interest in them today.

INFORMED OPINION

1. In colonial America, why did the Indians generally side with the French instead of the British? How do you think the British might have changed this situation?

2. Benjamin Franklin disapproved of the Boston Tea Party and thought that the East India Company should be paid for its loss of the tea. Do you agree? What other methods might the patriots have used to oppose the Tea Act?

3. The Declaration of Independence states that "all men are created equal." What do you think Jefferson meant by this statement? Some of the signers owned slaves. How do you think they probably reconciled this fact with these glowing words? Would you say that America today has fully achieved the "equality" of the Declaration?

4. Today a number of former British dependencies, like Canada and India, have been granted self-government within the Commonwealth of Nations. Find out what the Commonwealth is. Do you think that Britain and the thirteen colonies could have agreed to a similar arrangement in the years after 1763? Give your reasons.

UNRAVELING PUBLIC PROBLEMS

1. In what important ways did the patriots oppose British policies between 1763 and 1776? Which of these ways were most effective? The least damaging to the colonists themselves?

2. The rebel leaders had to find means of building up and maintaining a spirit of resistance to the British policies. What methods did they use? How successful were their efforts?

Excellent tests may be devised with the use of outline maps. For example, students might be asked to show on an outline map of North America the results of the French and Indian War.

79

How Americans won the independence they had declared is the subject of this chapter. The quotation used is, appropriately, a famous eighteenth-century description of what it meant to be an American. The class should analyze it, identifying the main points: the great change in the settlers, how it was accomplished, the characteristics of the new Americans. Observe that what is said applied only to the Europeans. Contrast their situation with that of the Africans. Notice also that "American" is used to refer to people in the United States, although the name properly applies to anyone in either North or South America.

5

AMERICA'S SUCCESSFUL REVOLT

What then is the American, this new man?

In this great American asylum [the English colonies], the poor of Europe have by some means met together, and in consequence of various causes. . . . Urged by a variety of motives, here they came. Everything has tended to regenerate them: new laws, a new mode of living, a new social system. Here they are become men: in Europe they were as so many useless plants, wanting vegetative mould and refreshing showers; they withered; and were mowed down by want, hunger, and war. But now, by the power of transplantation, like all other plants, they have taken root and flourished! . . .

Exuberant Americans in 1776 pull down a statue of George III to celebrate the overthrowing of British authority in the Declaration of Independence. The bystanders join in hailing the King's downfall.

More than one symbol of British authority was destroyed after the Declaration of Independence.

#Discuss the meaning of "a new social system." Although some attempts were made to establish in America social distinctions like those in England, they did not succeed.

By what invisible power has this surprising metamorphosis been performed? By that of the laws and that of their industry. The laws, the indulgent laws, protect them as they arrive, stamping on them the symbol of adoption. They # receive ample rewards for their labors; these accumulated rewards procure them lands; those lands confer on them the title of freemen, and to that title every benefit is affixed which men can possibly require. This is the great operation daily performed by our laws. . . .

What then is the American, this new man? . . . *He* is an American, who, leaving behind him all his ancient prejudices and manners, receives new ones from the new mode of life he has embraced, the new government he obeys, and the new rank he holds. He becomes an American by being received in the broad lap of our great *Alma Mater*.

Here individuals of all nations are melted into a new race of men, whose labours and posterity will one day cause great changes in the world. Americans are the western pilgrims who are carrying along with them that great mass of arts, sciences, vigour, and industry which began long since in the east. They will finish the great circle.

The Americans were once scattered. . . . Here they are incorporated into one of the finest systems of population which has ever appeared, and which will hereafter become distinct by the power of the different climates they inhabit. . . . The American is a new man, who acts upon new principles; he must therefore entertain new ideas, and form new opinions. From involuntary idleness, servile dependence, penury, and useless labour, he has passed to toils of a very different nature, rewarded by ample subsistence —This is an American.

Even before their break with England, Americans were aware of the effect that living in the New World was having on them. The traditional frustrations of the European seemed to vanish in America, and a "new man," freer than any in the past, was developing. (On the other hand, the difficulties of the transplanted Africans were multiplied.)

The mixing together of nationalities was al- ## *ready apparent as a characteristic of life here. Besides, Americans were ceasing to regard themselves as merely colonists. The author, Michel Guillaume Jean de Crèvecoeur (pronounced Krevker), was a naturalized American of French birth who lived in upstate New York on the eve of the American Revolution. This selection is out of* Letters from an American Farmer, *first published in 1782, although probably written between 1770 and 1775.*

New York Public Library

This section deals with internal social and political effects of the American Revolution and with economic aspects of the war. People in the former colonies wrote new state constitutions and otherwise prepared to live separate from Britain. They laid certain foundations of modern democracy.

THE ERA OF LIBERTY OPENS FOR AMERICANS

The signing of the Declaration of Independence ended America's hesitation. Now there could be no turning back on the road. Wrote John Adams, "It compleats a Revolution, which will make as good a figure in the History of Nations, as any that has preceded it."

BREAKING THE BONDS

But the rebels knew that only a triumph on the battlefield would induce the English and the rest of the world to accept the fact of American independence. The patriots also knew they required popular approval at home for the break with the mother country.

At the outset probably as many as one-third of the colonists were out of sympathy with the War for Independence. This is easy to understand: the habit of allegiance to the crown was firmly rooted. In 1776 the American ties with England were 169 years old. Think for a second how long that was. Not until 1945 were Americans able to say that they had lived free and independent as many years as they had lived as colonials. Revolution meant that the traditional bonds would be broken, and many colonists regarded this as unthinkable.

The Loyalists. The Americans who would not give up their loyalty to the king became known as "Loyalists" or "Tories." They were often people whose social and business connections made them directly dependent upon the crown. They included, for example, appointees of the royal governors, lawyers whose work was principally in behalf of the king's interests, military men whose advancement depended upon the mother country, nonsmuggling merchants, and Anglican clergymen, who recognized the king as the head of their church. In the back country of Virginia and the Carolinas, Scotch-Irish frontiersmen were also usually Loyalists because they were often in conflict with the planters. They sided with their enemies' enemy —England.

Loyalists were probably in the majority in three states—New York, Pennsylvania, and South Carolina. They were unorganized and therefore unable to defend themselves against the militant rebels, who were often more fiercely hostile toward them than toward the English.

The issue of loyalism sometimes split families, brother against brother, father against son. A brother of the William Hooper of North Carolina who signed the Declaration of Independence, for example, was a Loyalist; so, also, was Benjamin Franklin's son, William Franklin, royal governor of New Jersey.

There was no single nationwide policy for dealing with loyalism because there was still no truly national government, and because loyalism came in a confusing variety of shades and intensities. Many Loyalists fled to Halifax or to England, leaving their property claims to be settled later. Others were abused physically, even tarred and feathered. Some were left alone, especially in communities where Loyalists were numerous.

The rebels. The Continental Congress, which was dominated by rebels, contained some of the ablest men in America. Among them were George Washington of Virginia, a leading planter and veteran soldier; Charles Carroll of Maryland, perhaps the richest American of his day; Roger Sherman of Connecticut, who had started life as a shoemaker and had become a prosperous businessman; and Francis Hopkinson of New Jersey, a person of many talents, who wrote "My Days Have Been So Wondrous Free," the first nonreligious song by a native American. The Adamses were there from Massachusetts; so was John Hancock, who is alleged to have said that he wrote his signature on the Declaration of Independence so large that George III could read it without his spectacles.

Government by committees. Despite their great abilities, these delegates lacked the experience # to deal with the problems of government. They set up committees to carry on the war, to create and manage the treasury, to raise equipment for the army, and to obtain foreign aid. This was government by committee—at best, slow and clumsy.

#That is, with any problems but those of local governments. The war presented special problems. Discuss the last idea. Why is committee government slow? Why was it best under the circumstances?

As if this were not enough, the Continental Congress was forced to rely entirely on the newly independent colonies, or states, for money, troops, supplies, and goodwill. The states, therefore, made the important decisions. Congress became occupied mostly with attempts to persuade the states that they must increase their contributions to the common cause.

CONFLICT AT HOME

The conflict in America was not only between the states and the mother country. A struggle went on also inside the states themselves, where movements were afoot to write state constitutions, which eventually provided legal foundations for the independent states.

\# In every state there were radical and conservative factions, each striving to gain control of affairs. The conservatives, in general, lacked \#\# faith in the people's capacity to rule themselves. Frequently men of wealth, they believed they needed protection from their poorer neighbors. They insisted that "a Legislature of Beggars will be Thieves." They strongly favored high property qualifications for voters and officeholders and other curbs on popular rule.

The radicals' demands seemed strikingly bold, though today they might seem almost commonplace. Among them were easier access to officeholding, annual elections, and greater representation in the legislatures for the western parts of the states. From early colonial days the people living in the western communities had considered themselves to be at the mercy of the easterners.

Radicals and conservatives often agreed that a powerful state legislature could adequately take care of all the needs of the people. Both factions believed the executive ought to be weak and the courts subject to domination by the legislature. Americans of that generation were suspicious of governors and judges: their experience under English rule had made them afraid of any kind of government they could not control directly.

Pennsylvania's constitution. The case of Pennsylvania shows best the work of the radicals. There in 1776 they created a state constitution

##Since people in a democracy must have such faith, the conservatives were undemocratic.

which provided for a *unicameral,* or one-house, legislature elected by almost universal manhood suffrage, with no provision for a veto on legislation by the executive. Western frontiersmen controlled the legislature.

Men of position, both in Pennsylvania and elsewhere, who had pledged their lives, their fortunes, and their sacred honor to break with England, were disturbed. They wondered as they read this "leveling" constitution whether they had not delivered themselves to a worse evil, "the mob." They dreaded the thought that in the new scheme of things "good" men would be replaced by impoverished men.

South Carolina's constitution. The radicals, however, were not strong everywhere. In South Carolina the conservatives had the upper hand. There, under the constitution adopted in 1778, property qualifications for the top officeholders discriminated against the majority of people: to be governor, a man was required to own at least £10,000 worth of property; to be a member of the state senate, £2000; to be a member of the house of representatives or to vote, 50 acres of land or a town lot. (Actually, this 50-acre requirement was very easy to meet.)

Another contemporary illustration.

A recruiting poster calling for the enrolling of American youths in the Continental Army. Notice how George Washington's name as well as the war's purpose is used to attract volunteers.

Historical Society of Pennsylvania

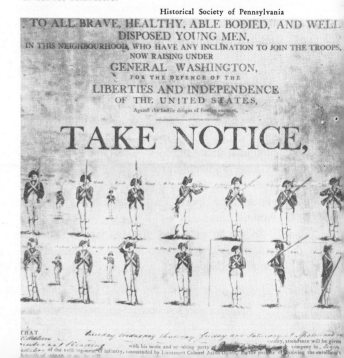

TO ALL BRAVE, HEALTHY, ABLE BODIED, AND WELL DISPOSED YOUNG MEN, IN THIS NEIGHBOURHOOD, WHO HAVE ANY INCLINATION TO JOIN THE TROOPS, NOW RAISING UNDER GENERAL WASHINGTON, FOR THE DEFENCE OF THE LIBERTIES AND INDEPENDENCE OF THE UNITED STATES,

TAKE NOTICE,

But here, as elsewhere, the fear of a strong executive was great. The governor was to be chosen by the legislature, and, like Pennsylvania's executive, he was not even given the power to veto legislation.

A system of checks and balances. Most of the new state constitutions failed to provide a system of *checks and balances*. Such a system would have made it possible for the power of each branch of the government—the legislative, executive, and judicial—to be checked or balanced by the power of another branch.

In American minds, checks and balances in government—like the strong executive—were associated with the British administration of the colonies. The people later found, though, that any legislature, whether radical or conservative, requires checks against the passage of ill-considered laws. In time they learned to appreciate the idea of keeping the separate branches of government equal in power and constantly watchful of each other.

FOUNDATIONS OF MODERN DEMOCRACY

While they were learning the difficult art of forging a government, Americans of the late 1700's made a number of changes which permanently affected their lives and ours. These changes may be considered foundation stones of American democracy.

Liberalization of landownership. One change was an increase in the number of people owning land. Lands belonging to the Loyalists and ungranted crown lands were seized by the states. They divided these properties into smaller parcels, which they either sold to help pay their share of the war's cost or distributed to soldiers in payment for military service.

The land was sometimes sold to small farmers direct. More often, though, speculators bought it in large blocks and later sold it piece by piece at sizable profit. An effect, either way, was to increase the number of small landholders and to speed up settlement west of the Appalachians.

An end to entail and primogeniture. Besides the general upheaval in landholding, feudal laws—long in effect—were abolished. One of them,

the law of *entail,* had forbidden the division of large estates, so that they would be passed intact from generation to generation. The related law of *primogeniture* was also discarded. By this law an eldest son had inherited all his father's real estate when the father died without making a will. Some of the states had already been abolishing these laws before the Revolution. The Revolution had the result of completing the process.

Separation of church and government. The Revolution brought a notable change to a number of churches, too. When the war began, there were "established churches"—those officially supported by the colonial governments—in nine of the thirteen colonies. By the end of the Revolutionary era in 1787, this support was cut off in all states but Massachusetts and Connecticut; that is, church and government, or, as we say, church and state, were *separated*. Religious groups henceforth would have to rely upon the voluntary contributions of their members.

In states where the established church happened to be on the Revolutionary side of the conflict with the mother country, the rebels were inclined to leave it undisturbed. The Congregational church, for example, to which Sam Adams and many other New England patriots belonged, remained established in Massachusetts and Connecticut.

In the southern states, where the Anglican church, or Church of England, was established, it seemed natural to separate church and state. Cutting off public support of the Anglican church amounted to punishing it for its political allegiance.

In Virginia the advocates of separation of church and state were led by Thomas Jefferson. He was the author of the Statute of Religious Freedom, which the Virginia legislature adopted in 1785. This act declared that no man could be forced to attend or support any church, or to suffer in any way for his religious beliefs. The statute was especially pleasing to the people in the southern interior who had been forced to contribute to the Anglican church even though they did not attend it. Jefferson always believed that, among the achievements of his life, only the writing of the Declaration of Independence was more important than his drafting of this law.

Although religious qualifications continued to bar Catholics from holding office in five states and Jews in nine, restrictions gradually # were abolished. In time, religious freedom became one of the glories of the new republic.

Criticism of slavery. The Revolution had affected slavery, too. The phrase in the Declaration which reads "all men are created equal" became a constant rebuke not only to slaveowners and defenders of slavery but also to all Americans. Jefferson's Declaration at first blamed George III for the cruel slave trade, but this charge was omitted from the final draft when some delegations objected. Many people everywhere must have shared the belief of John Jay of New York that as long as there was slavery on these shores, the people's "prayers to Heaven for liberty will be impious."

Some leading southerners long had considered human bondage to be a cursed evil and looked forward to its end. Henry Laurens, a patriot from Charleston, in a touching letter to his son included the sentence, "You know, my dear Sir, I abhor slavery." Thomas Jefferson with characteristic optimism wrote in 1782: "The spirit of the master is abating, that of the slave rising from the dust . . . the way I hope preparing, under the auspices of heaven, for a total emancipation. . . ."

In the North, Benjamin Franklin and the saintly Quaker John Woolman of New Jersey had long been crying out against slavery. In 1774 Rhode Island provided by law that any slave brought within its borders automatically became free. Other northern states went further and abolished the institution entirely. In Massachusetts, where the state constitution specifically stated "all men are created equal," slavery was declared unconstitutional.

A lift for the underdog.
Many Americans became aware that the war could widen the opportunities even for the least privileged. Slaves who at first were denied the chance to enlist in the army were later welcomed into the ranks, especially after the British began enlisting them

Bowdoin College Museum of Art

Thomas Jefferson, the versatile Virginian whose skilled pen told the world of America's independence. This portrait is by Gilbert Stuart.

Gilbert Stuart, American artist born in Rhode Island, is best known for painting Washington.

with the promise of emancipation. In most states they were promised their freedom at the end of their service. In this way, 5000 Negroes fought for their country's freedom as well as their own.

Members of the tiny Jewish community also understood instinctively the significance of the fight for independence. Haym Salomon, for instance, a recently-arrived Polish Jew, out of his own pocket and at enormous personal sacrifice, helped save the government at Philadelphia from bankruptcy.

The thought of creating a thoroughgoing social and political revolution was farthest from the minds of the Founding Fathers. Faced by a struggle against the most formidable power in the world, they made only those changes that seemed absolutely necessary at the moment. But those who looked closely could see that the sky was brightening for the underdog. And later generations would recognize that the patriots had planted the seeds of liberty better than they knew.

85

Examples of Revolutionary paper money. *Left and middle:* notes issued by Connecticut and South Carolina. *Right:* a Continental $40 bill (real worth by 1790, less than 80¢).

FINANCIAL PRESSURES

There was no national government, and states issued money.

The running of the war itself was often cause for discouragement. It called for large sums of money, which the states were reluctant to supply. Lacking the power to tax, the Continental Congress resorted to the printing of paper money. Before the end of 1779, there were over forty separate issues of it, which totaled $241,552,780. The states (especially Virginia and the Carolinas) also printed bank notes—in the amount of $209,524,776.

Inflation. This paper money amounted to little more than promissory notes which the issuing government hoped to make good sometime. Neither the Continental Congress nor the states made adequate provision to redeem it in coin, and its value fell rapidly. This cheapening, or *depreciation,* of the money almost brought disaster. Moreover, the supply of goods could not meet demand because there was far more money in circulation than there were goods to buy. Such a condition, called *inflation,* sent prices skyrocketing: by 1781 a pair of shoes cost $100; a bushel of corn, $40; and a barrel of flour, $1575.

Prosperity for some. Men engaged in trade or in contracting to supply the army were steadily expanding their activities and helped boost prices, too. A Bostonian groaned, "It is incredi-

ble what a profit the merchants take on their wares—double is the very least." Farmers also benefited. After the outbreak of the Revolution, farmers commanded prices twice as high as the highest on record in the ten years preceding.

Speculators were very busy, too. They often bought up necessities in order to make a killing when they resold them. In 1777, some Maryland merchants purchased the entire shoe supply in North Carolina, forcing the government and individuals to pay excessively for footwear.

Further, imports were reduced to a mere trickle by the devastating raids on American commerce by British naval and merchant vessels. Businessmen felt justified in charging very high prices for goods that got through the blockade. How difficult it was, reflected Henry Laurens, for a "covetous man to enter heartily into the kingdom of Patriotism"!

The high cost of living divided Americans at a time when they required unity. Attempts to fix prices failed. In time all restrictions on them were removed except those on salt. As prices rose out of control, parts of the populace were set one against another—merchants against customers, city dwellers against farmers, planters against shippers. A typical towns-

#Ask why our federal government proposes new taxes when inflation becomes a serious threat.
##Who suffered most? Who profited most? Why could prices not be fixed?

man said angrily: "Our Farmers are as cruel as Death. They don't consider the suffering seaports. I believe in General they have no feeling for us, but want all our money, goods, houses & then ourselves to be their servants."

Lagging wages. Among some people inflation took a heavy toll. The clergy, officeholders, town laborers, and army officers and men, being woefully underpaid to begin with, felt its effects keenly. As the war progressed wages rose, but never enough to keep pace with rising prices. In Massachusetts, wages doubled while prices tripled or quadrupled—a typical situation. More than once workers marched on the homes of merchants to protest prices.

Expanding enterprise. The war created a new group of rich men, among them the owners of privateers—vessels commissioned by the Congress to prey upon England's merchant fleet. The profits from the capture and sale of British ships were so high that they alone could have paid for the first two years of the war.

Some of the early great American fortunes came out of these successes at sea. John and Andrew Cabot of Beverly, Massachusetts, and Richard and Elias Hasket Derby of Salem were the leading owners of privateers in New England. Other venturesome men operated ships out of Newport (Rhode Island), Egg Harbor (New Jersey), Philadelphia, and Baltimore.

New kinds of commercial opportunities also appeared. A leader of the business interests was Robert Morris of Philadelphia. As Superintendent of Finance, Morris managed government finances with uncommon skill. His personal enterprises were also spectacular. His ships were privateers; his investments were in land and mines to the west; and his trading activities reached to Europe, Africa, and eastern Asia.

Morris' speculations finally got out of hand, and in 1798 he landed in a debtors' prison. But he had created the model of the "new businessman" who emerged from the Revolutionary era—more willing to take risks and readier to invest in varied undertakings, not only in land. Shortly men with foresight, like Morris, would be building turnpikes and canals and bridges, putting capital into factories, and establishing banks. They would pave the way for America's industrial growth. #

Sum and Substance

1. How did Crèvecoeur explain the development of "the American"? 2. What groups of Americans became Loyalists? 3. What difficulties did the Continental Congress have? 4. Explain how the conservatives and the radicals differed. 5. How did the Revolution affect landownership? Entail and primogeniture? Relations between church and state? Slavery? 6. Explain why inflation started. What were its effects?

This section describes the military course of the American Revolution.

THE AMERICANS FIGHT UNDER GEORGE WASHINGTON

For the command of the Continental Army, the choice had been obvious: Colonel George Washington. Quiet, determined, confident, he cut an impressive figure in the blue-and-buff uniform of a Virginia militia officer. A few Americans may have believed that the task Washington faced would be simple and short, but he knew better. Shortly after his appointment by Congress, he wrote that he had "imbarked on a tempestuous Ocean."

A man of iron will, Washington supplied the patience, virtue, and courage that made independence possible. Despite disappointments that would have overwhelmed a weaker leader, his sustaining spirit strengthened the American cause at every critical moment. Again and again he said that "the long and great suffering of the Army is unexampled in History," but he never lost his faith that in the end victory would come. He managed to convey this faith to his troops.

THE ARMY OF A FREE PEOPLE

The American soldiers were scornfully called by one of the British generals a "rabble in arms." Unjust though this sally was, the Con-

##Discuss the qualities a good leader must possess. The ability to inspire followers is perhaps the most significant one. Encourage students to read the biography of Washington listed on p. 101.

87

#The work of Benjamin Rush in medicine is described in the paperback <u>American Medicine, 1607-</u><u>1900</u>, by Ilza Veith and Leo M. Zimmerman, published in 1967 by Rand McNally & Company.

Metropolitan Museum of Art

The suffering of American soldiers in wintertime. Conditions like these—often the result of poor supply systems —contrasted sharply with the rosy pictures of army life presented in recruiting posters.

Conditions like this tested to the limit Washington's skillful leadership.

tinentals were often a ragged lot—and pitiful. They were paid in Continental paper money, which meant that they were hurt twice: once by their low wages and again by the rapid depreciation of the paper money. Besides, payment was often in arrears. No formal provision was made to maintain their families while they were away at war. Officers in a way fared even worse than their men: they had to pay for their own food and uniforms.

Morale. The soldiers believed that an ungrateful public ignored their plight. In a moment of despair one of them declared: "I despise my countrymen; I wish I could say I was not born in America. I once gloried in it but am now ashamed of it." Another asked, "What encouragement is there to the soldier to risque his life, by braving death in defence of his country, when, after the war is over he will be obliged to support a miserable existence on the crumbs that fall from the table of those who have created fortunes from the distresses of the army."

Health problems. Disease probably killed ten times more men than did the enemy's bullets. Medical facilities were few and badly run. The American army in 1777 had three to five times as many sick and wounded in hospitals as the British. Benjamin Rush, the Physician General, complained to Washington in 1777 that he had seen twenty feverish men confined to rooms too small for six or eight healthy ones. Moreover, he regretted, "Nothing but a miracle can save the life of a soldier who lies in a shirt and blanket which he has worn for four or five months before he came into the hospital." #

Discipline. Controlling the soldiers was a vexing problem. Since most of the officers were elected by their men, commissioned rank was better proof of popularity than of military skill. Maintaining respect for one's superiors was therefore somewhat difficult. In 1776 a Connecticut cavalry captain was caught shaving one of his men! Washington worked hard on the ##

##Compare the situation described here with the one in the American army today. How do its officers receive commissions? Why are "sharp distinctions in rank" observed?

problem of "fraternizing," for he knew well that a successful army observes sharp distinctions in rank.

Supplies. Among all the army's problems, the chief one was how to obtain adequate supplies. Ammunition and weapons, which were obtained from the French, were usually available in sufficient quantity. But the hunger of the American army in the early stages of the war reflected little credit upon the home front.

Uniforms, often promised to the soldiers, were seldom delivered. The men were too long garbed in tattered clothing. A smartly dressed army generally has high morale and fights accordingly. As the American general Anthony Wayne stated it, "I would soon[er] risque my Life, Reputation and the fate of America at the Head of five thousand troops neatly uniformed than double that number equally armed & disciplined, covered with rags and Vermin." Not until 1781 was the army properly clothed —although even then the men were poorly fed.

Prospects. Despite the formidable British strength, Americans did not consider their own position hopeless. They would be fighting on their own soil; they had become expert marksmen in the forest and on the frontier; and they # found out quickly that the American rifle was superior to the smoothbore musket used by the British. The Americans lacked an experienced corps of officers like that of the mother country, but their ranks included veterans of the French and Indian War, who could train others.

THE ENEMY'S FORCES

When the War for Independence opened, the immediate advantage seemed to lie with the British. They had on their side well-equipped and trained naval forces. Having the advantages of control of the sea and the money to pay for hired foreign troops to supplement their own, they were confident of victory.

British generals. A fatal weakness of the British, however, was that the senior officers lacked energy and the capacity to inspire their men. When William Pitt heard the names of the generals going to America, he is said to have moaned, "I do not know what effect these

names have on the enemy, but I confess they make me tremble."

The British navy was in no more competent hands. Its chief, the Earl of Sandwich, was, in addition, unpopular and dishonest. Sandwich is remembered today chiefly for the food novelty he created—two slices of bread with filling—which he munched at the gaming table.

English strategy. When the war opened, the ## British made the grave mistake of not concentrating the bulk of their army at any given point. A main objective, though, was the capture of New York because the seizure of this colony would separate New England from the southern colonies and set up the remaining colonies to be picked off one by one.

THE COURSE OF THE STRUGGLE

The British planned an attack on New York from Canada, but the plan was frustrated by an American expedition *against* Canada. After Discuss the strategy represented on this map.

The War for Independence broke out in New England, and the earliest campaigns were launched there.

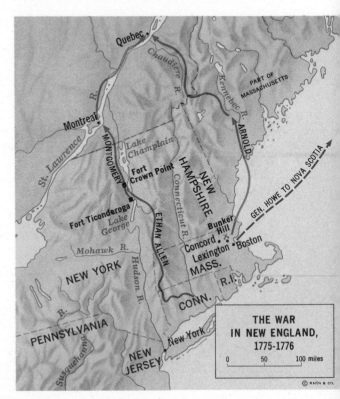

THE WAR IN NEW ENGLAND, 1775-1776

0   50   100 miles

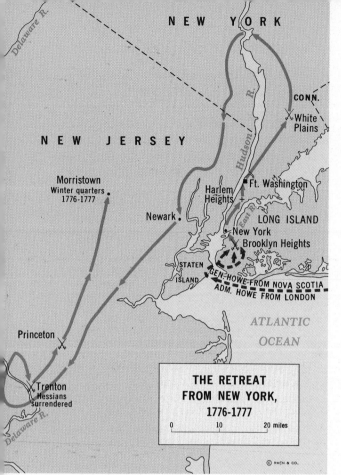

The evacuation of Boston. Meanwhile, militiamen and "embattled farmers" of New England, hammered into an effective army by Washington, were besieging the British under General William Howe in Boston. During the spring of 1776, the British finally evacuated Boston and went to Nova Scotia.

Early in 1776, Washington moved his forces from Boston to New York in anticipation of a new attempt on that colony. Unhappily, Washington had fewer than half of the 20,000 men he had hoped to have. Even the generous bounty being offered—a volunteer received £20 and 100 acres of land—failed to attract the necessary manpower.

Fighting in New York. In Nova Scotia Howe strengthened his army for the attack on New York. In the summer of 1776, he moved toward New York City under the protection of a powerful fleet commanded by his brother, Admiral Richard Howe. Anticipating the Howes' strategy, Washington had moved his soldiers to Brooklyn Heights, on the western end of Long Island. General Howe first took Staten Island and then went across to Long Island, defeating the Americans at the Battle of Brooklyn Heights on August 27. Fearing that his army might be cut in two, Washington retreated across the East River and took up a position on Manhattan Island at Harlem Heights, near Fort Washington.

The Howes did not give chase because they thought they could end the war by negotiation. Responding to their request, Congress appointed a committee of three, consisting of John Adams, Benjamin Franklin, and Edward Rutledge, to begin truce talks. At a meeting on Staten Island, however, Admiral Howe revealed that while his terms would be generous, he was not authorized to deal until the Declaration of Independence had been revoked. But the Americans would negotiate only on the basis of complete independence. Since compromise was impossible, the war continued. ##

A sample of the feelings on both sides was provided by the arrest of Captain Nathan Hale, of Connecticut, who had been spying on the British on Long Island. General Howe unhesi-

The map caption:

Washington had to rescue his men from Brooklyn Heights lest the British cut them off by way of the East River.
Use the scale to see how far Americans retreated.

THE RETREAT FROM NEW YORK, 1776-1777

0   10   20 miles

© RM̃N & CO.

Ethan Allen and his Green Mountain boys took Fort Ticonderoga and Crown Point early in 1775, the Continental Congress authorized a march northward. One force under General Richard Montgomery followed the Hudson River–Lake Champlain route, capturing Montreal in November. Another force of about 1100, under Benedict Arnold, slogged through Maine to the St. Lawrence at Quebec.

The two armies converged on Quebec, and on December 31, 1775, they opened a joint attack. Montgomery was killed and Arnold was wounded. The expedition, however, failed to break the British defenses. In the spring of 1776, when British reinforcements arrived, the Americans gave up their flimsy offensive, and # their hopes for the conquest of Canada were dashed.

##The condition for British negotiation and the American position should be emphasized. The Americans were unwilling to give up their independence and the British refused to recognize it.

#Washington was able to turn a dismal defeat and retreat into a triumph in New Jersey. However, the British held New York City.

tatingly had him executed by hanging. As Hale stood on the scaffold, his last words are said to have been, "I only regret I have but one life to lose for my country."

Washington's retreat. In September, 1776, as General Howe slowly occupied New York City, Washington withdrew northward. After checking the British at the indecisive Battle of White Plains, he crossed the Hudson River into New Jersey. The retreat across New Jersey was one of the low points of the war for the rebels. Tom Paine wrote in discouragement, "These are the times that try men's souls."

Late in 1776 Washington found the chance he had been looking for. Safely crossing the ice-filled Delaware River on December 26, near Trenton, he fell upon and defeated a thousand Hessians—mercenaries employed by the British and sent by Howe to hold Trenton. The Hessians were "sleeping off" the effects of their Christmas celebrating. Washington then swept on to Princeton, where he won an even more stunning victory on January 3, 1777. He now established winter quarters at Morristown, New Jersey, and the English troops returned to New York. Out of defeat Washington had succeeded in fashioning new hope.

New British plans. The British had not given up their plan to capture the state of New York. Their new effort called for three British forces to meet in the neighborhood of Albany: one, under General John Burgoyne, would march southward from Canada; another, under Lieutenant Colonel Barry St. Leger, would proceed through the Mohawk Valley; the third—a detachment of Howe's soldiers—would move up the Hudson from New York.

The whole complicated operation of 1777 was botched incredibly from the beginning, enabling the Americans to win the most significant campaign of the war. Howe failed to help Burgoyne, having decided instead to capture Philadelphia, which he took without much difficulty. Washington's men put up stubborn resistance in battles at Brandywine and Germantown but failed first to stop Howe and then to dislodge him. Following these defeats the Americans went into winter quarters at

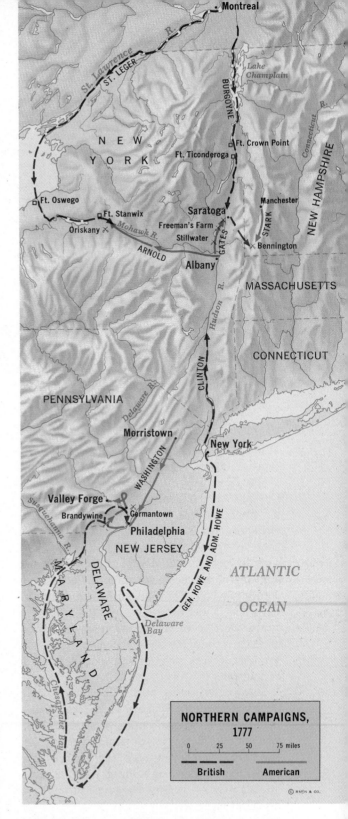

General Howe's move helped cripple Britain's neat plan to seize control of the pivotal state of New York.

##Call attention to the neatness of the British plan to surround New York State. Howe's change of plan left the eastern side of the triangle to Burgoyne, who met disaster.

The horse—America—throws its rider, in a cartoon from a British magazine of the year 1779.

The figure (background) suggests that the French had a hand in it (note the fleur-de-lis).

Valley Forge, while Howe's men lived in comparative luxury in nearby Philadelphia.

Their failure. Howe's move against the Quaker City had been foolhardy, for it had scrambled the English plans. St. Leger was defeated at Oriskany, New York, in August, 1777, and fell back to Canada. Of the three forces which were to have met in Albany, only Burgoyne's remained in the field. It captured Fort Ticonderoga July 6, 1777, and pushed steadily forward, but it was slowed by too much baggage and a shortage of supplies. On top of everything, a strong British detachment sent into Vermont to seek supplies was overwhelmed at Bennington.

Saratoga: the turning point. When Burgoyne's troops reached the vicinity of Saratoga, they found themselves confronting more than 7000 men under General Horatio Gates. On October 17, 1777, after having been engaged in fierce encounters at Freeman's Farm and Stillwater (Bemis Heights) nearby, Burgoyne surrendered his 5700 men.

The victory at Saratoga had worldwide consequences. In England Lord North, the prime minister, faced demands that he resign and turn his office over to Pitt. In France the foreign office, which had been secretly aiding the Americans with money and supplies, decided that the moment had come to help dismember the British Empire by openly entering the war on the rebels' side.

Alliance with France. The treaty of alliance between the United States and France which followed in 1778 was largely the work of Benjamin Franklin. As American representative in Paris, he had charmed the French with his wit and conversation. Under the terms of the treaty, the French agreed to fight at the side of the Americans until independence was achieved. In 1779 Spain entered the war as France's ally, but without committing itself to fighting for American independence.

Winter at Valley Forge. Meanwhile, however, Americans were their own worst enemies. The weather was no more severe than usual in the winter of 1777/1778, but Washington's troops at Valley Forge suffered unbelievable hardships. The soldiers, still licking their wounds after the defeats at Germantown and Brandy-

#Call attention to the role European politics had in the winning of French aid: it took the victory at Saratoga, the services of Franklin, and French-British enmity to gain it.

wine, had to endure a shocking shortage of clothing, meat, and soap. In addition, the Congress kept up a running criticism of the army. And to add to Washington's woes, a group of military and political leaders were conspiring —in vain it turned out—to replace him with General Gates.

One ray of light that entered the scene was the arrival from Prussia of Baron Friedrich von Steuben, magnificently dressed in scarlet and accompanied by his huge Italian greyhound, Azor. Steuben's prodigious and successful efforts to teach military drills and discipline in his mixed German, French, and English vocabulary helped to mold a more confident army even in those dark days at Valley Forge.

Valued assistance was rendered by other foreign officers, too. Notable among them were Thaddeus Kosciusko from Poland, who designed the defenses of West Point, and the youthful Marquis de Lafayette from France, who volunteered to serve in the American army without pay. The Pole Casimir Pulaski and the Baron de Kalb, a German, both gave their lives in the American cause.

The revived rebel army soon was proving itself. At the Battle of Monmouth in late June, 1778, it mauled the British army as it was being evacuated from Philadelphia to New York. These redcoats were now under the command of Sir Henry Clinton.

An emerging navy. Occasionally good news came from the high seas, where John Paul Jones and John Barry were helping to create a tradition of valor for the United States Navy. For example, in 1779 in English waters, Jones, aboard the *Bon Homme Richard,* attacked the British ship *Serapis* and captured it after one of the most savage naval duels ever fought. At its height, Jones, asked about surrender, replied, "I have not yet begun to fight!"

But disappointment and uncertainty still lay ahead. In 1780 Americans were shocked to discover that Benedict Arnold—after Washington himself the Americans' most talented general— had gone over to the enemy for a money bribe and been only narrowly prevented from handing West Point over to the British.

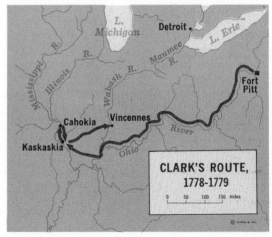

Clark's expedition was intended to check the Indian raids for which he blamed the British in Detroit.

The area north of the Ohio became the old Northwest.

The war in the West. Beyond the Appalachians, frontiersmen were also engaged with the British. In 1778 George Rogers Clark captured Kaskaskia and Cahokia, in what is now Illinois, and later Vincennes, in what is now Indiana. Clark's efforts won many of the Indians to the American side, but by the time the war ended the lack of troops and money had caused Clark to lose much of what he had gained.

The war in the South. In the South the British tried to use the Loyalist supporters to conquer areas in which sympathy with the mother country was strong. By the summer of 1780, redcoats held all of Georgia and South Carolina. The British general Cornwallis, in charge of the war in the South, had disastrously defeated the Americans in August, 1780, at Camden, South Carolina. This opened the way for a British invasion of North Carolina, but the tide was about to turn.

In October American patriots smashed a largely Tory force at Kings Mountain, a ridge extending across the border between North and South Carolina. At the same time, Gates, the general defeated at Camden, was replaced by General Nathanael Greene. Greene brought to these patriots the competent leadership they required. Early the next year, back-country troops under one of his generals, Daniel Morgan, destroyed part of the British forces at

##Charleston fell to the British in the spring of 1780. Clinton, who had led the attack, returned to New York, leaving Cornwallis in charge. Stress the significance of Kings Mountain.

93

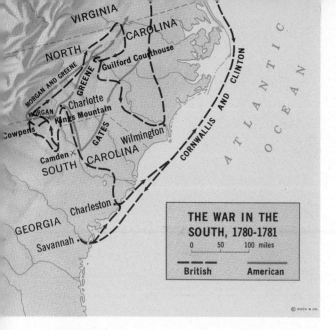

The map (left) shows the return to New York by Clinton; Cornwallis then proceeded inland.

American strategy, which succeeded magnificently, was to weaken Cornwallis by leading him on a fruitless chase through the Carolinas.

Marching from New York, Washington and his French allies bottled up and defeated the British general who had forced Washington to retreat from Long Island.

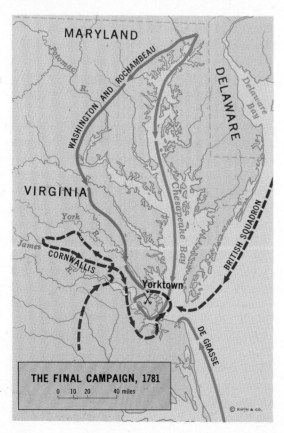

THE WAR IN THE SOUTH, 1780-1781

0   50   100 miles

British   American

THE FINAL CAMPAIGN, 1781

0   10   20   40 miles

Cowpens, South Carolina. Even though this weakened the British, Cornwallis was able to inflict defeat on Greene's army in March, 1781. Cornwallis' losses were so heavy, however, that he withdrew his forces to Wilmington, North Carolina.

THE FRENCH INTERVENTION

Cornwallis did not remain there long. He moved northward to Yorktown, Virginia, where he was joined by some of Sir Henry Clinton's troops sent south from New York. At this critical point in the war, France's intervention began to be felt on land and sea.

Naval support. The French had answered Washington's pleas for help by sending a first-rate fleet under Count François de Grasse. In August, 1781, word reached Washington that, as he had requested, the fleet would head for the Chesapeake by the middle of the month and coöperate in an attack on Yorktown.

Washington and Count de Rochambeau, who commanded the French forces in America, were overjoyed. They knew they could not risk an attack on New York, where Clinton was firmly dug in, and they feared being cut off from their supplies by Clinton's forces. The French fleet's presence assured that supplies could come in by sea. With that comfort, Washington in September stole secretly across New Jersey and Pennsylvania to join the French.

Battle of Yorktown. The French admiral, moving north swiftly, gained control of the waters of Chesapeake Bay. He accomplished this before the British could reinforce their naval squadron, which lay offshore at Yorktown, ready to assist Cornwallis.

Cornwallis was now in a trap, cut off from supplies and reinforcements and surrounded by American forces on three sides. He could escape only on the fourth—the north bank of the York River. After a siege of almost three weeks, he determined to cross the river, break out of the trap, and head for Philadelphia. He was too late—a storm roared in over the river. Nature had closed the quadrangle.

Cornwallis' surrender. On October 19, 1781, Cornwallis surrendered in the most significant

Washington marched his and Rochambeau's troops toward Yorktown. De Grasse sent ships up Chesapeake Bay to transport most of the American troops. The siege of Yorktown then began.

Commander in chief George Washington served from June, 1775, to the end of the war. He offered to serve without pay.

defeat in the history of the British Empire. The British band understandably played "The World Turned Upside Down." The redcoats would have preferred to surrender to the French, whom they considered gentlemen, rather than to the despised rebels. But Washington would not give them this satisfaction. To add to their humiliation, Lafayette ordered the band to play "Yankee Doodle," which reminded the Englishmen that their American cousins had won independence.

The war was over; Saratoga and Yorktown had destroyed the British plans. Benjamin Franklin observed that it is "a rare Circumstance, and scarce to be met with in History, that in one War two Armies should be taken Prisoners completely, not a Man in either escaping."

Sum and Substance
1. What problems did Washington face as commander in chief of the American army? 2. What advantages and disadvantages did the British have at the beginning of the war? The Americans? 3. Account for (a) the American expedition against Canada; (b) Washington's move to New York City; (c) his retreat from there; (d) the American victory at Saratoga; (e) French intervention in the war; (f) British defeat at Yorktown.

This section describes the results of the American Revolution.

Henry Francis du Pont Winterthur Museum
Washington reviews the French troops after the victory.

ENGLAND RECOGNIZES ITS COLONIES' INDEPENDENCE

In England, the news of Cornwallis' surrender was overwhelming. The King's ministers promptly agreed "it would be madness not to conclude Peace on the best possible Terms we can obtain." Lord North resigned as prime minister, and in March, 1782, the Marquis of Rockingham succeeded him. When Rockingham died in July, a friend of America, Lord Shelburne, became prime minister and guided peace negotiations.

\# **WRITING TERMS OF PEACE**

Shelburne sent a retired Scottish trader named Richard Oswald to Paris to negotiate there with Benjamin Franklin. Oswald had once lived in Virginia, and while he had been there he had come to know and like Americans.

The American negotiators. Franklin, as brilliant as ever but old and infirm, had urged John Jay, America's unacknowledged minister in Spain, to join him. Enduring "bad roads, fleas and bugs," Jay arrived in Paris in June, 1782. He would attend to most of the technical details of drafting the treaty.

John Adams, fresh from the Netherlands, where he had concluded a treaty recognizing American independence and had obtained a sizable loan for the United States, joined Jay and Franklin in October. Adams often was lacking in tact, but his aggressiveness served

#Here is an excellent opportunity to emphasize the importance of diplomacy in international affairs. The skills of the negotiators and elements in world affairs played a part.

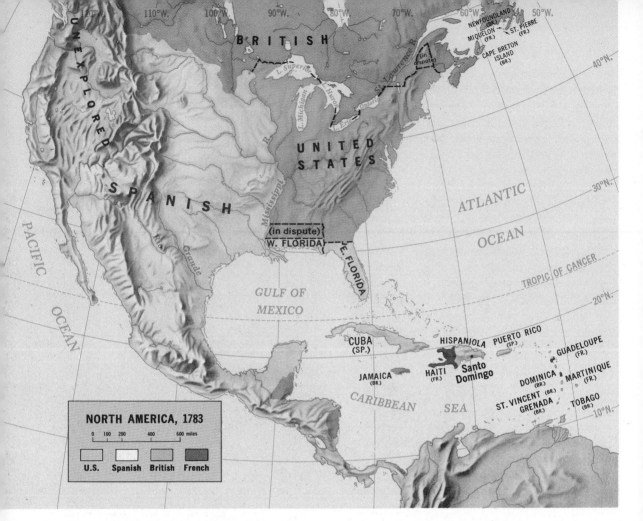

NORTH AMERICA, 1783

0 100 200   400   600 miles

U.S. Spanish British French

Military victories in the Revolution won American independence, but a diplomatic victory in France won the generous boundary settlements shown here. Much credit goes to the astute American negotiators.

Call attention to the large area Americans received. Compare this map with the one on page 66.

America. The three negotiators were reinforced by a fourth, Henry Laurens. Laurens had been captured in 1780, while en route to the Netherlands as minister, and had spent the rest of the war in the Tower of London.

Fear of French duplicity. Franklin had trouble handling his immensely competent colleagues. More than he, they suspected that the French foreign minister, Count de Vergennes, wished to confine the independent United States to the Atlantic seaboard, so that the new country could not grow too strong. The American commissioners had been clearly instructed by Congress to make no separate peace with England, for that would violate the Treaty of Alliance of 1778 with France. They hoped to follow orders.

The Treaty of Paris, 1783. But when Jay was able to confirm that the French were working hard # for a peace that would restrict America's westward movement, the commissioners signed a separate preliminary treaty. The French were furious. Vergennes rebuked the Americans in a note to Franklin: "I am at a loss, sir, to explain your conduct and that of your colleagues on this occasion." Actually, he understood it very well, and Franklin understood that Vergennes understood. Franklin, who wanted to retain France's friendship, replied shrewdly: "The English, I just now learn, flatter themselves they have already divided us. I hope this little misunderstanding will . . . be kept a secret, and that they will find themselves . . . mistaken."

#An example of an element in world affairs that had a bearing on the outcome of the negotiations. Another was the British aim of separating Americans from the French (see next page).

#Ask why this provision was important. (It especially benefited New Englanders, who based part of their trade on fish.)

The French were helpless to prevent the Americans from signing, in September, 1783, a treaty with England recognizing the independence of the United States. By the treaty's remarkably liberal terms the American boundaries were to extend to the Mississippi River on the west. To the north the line was fixed at approximately where it is today. To the south the limits would be the northern frontier of East and West Florida. Spain received Florida. As the map opposite shows, the location of two boundaries remained in dispute with England and Spain, respectively.

A provision in the treaty that permitted Americans to continue using the Newfoundland fisheries was as important as the land settlement. The British at first were reluctant to grant this privilege, but Adams was eloquently persuasive and won the argument.

Another thorny question was that of what to do about the debts owed by Americans to Englishmen. After extensive wrangling the negotiators agreed that the British merchants should be enabled to recover legitimate debts. The treatment of the Loyalists also presented difficulties that led to long and often sharp disputes among the commissioners. The English sought reimbursement for losses the Loyalists had sustained as a result of supporting the king in 1776. But the words of the treaty merely pledged Congress to recommend to the states that any properties they had confiscated during the war should be returned to the owners.

England's outlook. England agreed to the generous treaty because, being at war with three countries at that moment, it decided to end the American drain on its military strength. It felt it necessary to separate the United States from France, the ancient enemy of England. Finally, it surmised that even a politically independent United States would still be economically dependent upon the mother country.

UNFINISHED BUSINESS

A war cannot, by itself, solve all the issues that bring it on. It only settles which side has won the opportunity to attempt new solutions. In 1783 the American people had such an

Bequest of Charles Allen Munn, 1924, Metropolitan Museum of Art
Benjamin Franklin: printer, scientist, and ambassador.

Upper right: relates to work with lightning.

opportunity. The problems they faced, among others, revolved about land distribution, Indian relations, dealings between debtors and creditors, the regulation of trade, and the power or weakness of government. Some of these problems had been partly solved by the British during the colonial period, but completing the solutions would now become the responsibility of Americans.

Unquestionably, the most important problem of the British Empire in the years 1763 to 1776 had been how to establish a satisfactory relationship between its parts—particularly the American part—and the whole. The failure to find the right formula had led to the American Revolution. After 1783 this problem took a new form: what is the proper connection between each state and the union of all of them that will produce prosperity and happiness? The attempt to find the answer occupied Americans more and more in the decade after Yorktown.

Sum and Substance
1. State the terms of the peace treaty with England. 2. Why was England so generous? 3. What American problems remained unsolved? Which was most important? What form did it take after 1783?

##Discuss this statement. How did the situation in the United States after the war prove its truth? What problem was most important? Why? Has it been permanently solved?

THE WORKSHOP

OF LASTING SIGNIFICANCE

Tell how each of the following was involved in the Revolutionary period.

Michel de Crèvecoeur   George Rogers Clark
Loyalists   Nathanael Greene
unicameral   John Paul Jones
checks and balances   Robert Morris
entail   Ethan Allen
primogeniture   Richard Howe
separation of church   William Howe
  and state   Horatio Gates
Haym Salomon   Valley Forge
inflation   John Burgoyne
depreciation   Kings Mountain
Nathan Hale   François de Grasse
Saratoga   Yorktown
Baron von Steuben   Benjamin Franklin

IN YOUR EXPERIENCE

1. Find out when your state adopted its first constitution. When was the present one adopted? What type of legislature does it provide for? Can the governor veto legislation? What are the qualifications for voting? How does your state constitution compare with the one adopted in Pennsylvania in 1776?

2. If you live in an area which was in some way connected with the Revolution, find out what has been done to preserve or honor historic spots. Make a report on your state's or your community's part in the Revolution.

3. If you have ancestors who had a part in the Revolution, try to find out what they did, and write a report about it.

4. What countries in the world have very recently become independent? How did their method of achieving independence compare with that of the United States?

THE INTERNATIONAL SCENE

1. Explain how the Americans profited from European politics in the American Revolution in (a) winning allies, (b) obtaining generous peace terms.

2. What political effects did the peace treaty have?

3. A wartime alliance sometimes raises problems of coöperation between allies. In the Revolution, what problems of this nature did France and the United States have? How did they handle them?

AMERICAN DEMOCRACY

1. Name three changes in American life dating from the Revolutionary period which are called foundation stones of American democracy. Explain the name.

2. In what respect was slavery an affront to the Declaration of Independence in the late 1700's? To American democracy?

3. How did the Revolution benefit slaves?

HISTORY AND GEOGRAPHY

1. What problem in planning military strategy in the Revolution did the British have as a result of the geography of the colonies?   #

2. What strategy did the British adopt? How was American geography involved?   ##

3. What geographical advantages did the Americans employ in the final campaign?

BEING A SOCIAL SCIENTIST

1. At the Palace of Versailles in France, a huge painting of the British surrender at Yorktown is included among pictures of French victories. Is the French interpretation correct? Explain your answer.

2. In 1776 the odds seemed to favor the British in the war. How do you explain the American victory, rating in the order of importance such factors as British mistakes, Washington's leadership, French aid, American morale?

3. Investigate and evaluate the part played in the Revolution by one or more of the following and report your information either orally or in writing: Marquis de Lafayette, Count de Rochambeau, Baron von Steuben, Baron de Kalb, Casimir Pulaski, Thaddeus Kosciusko, John Paul Jones, Francis Marion, Betsy Ross, Molly Pitcher (Mary McCauley), John Stark.

#The British found it hard to plan a war over such a long expanse of coast.

##Seizing strategic spots--New York State and ports; they could not capture the whole coast.

This section sums up the characteristics of Americans on the eve of independence: their political ideas, their ideas about religion, the kind of work they did, their family life, their attitude toward their future in America. It also describes the far-reaching influence of the American Revolution upon world history. Discuss these influences.

A LONG VIEW

Europe Transplanted

WHEN the colonial period ended in 1776, American institutions and outlooks were well on their way to being formed. The people had developed political customs based on a passionate affection for self-government. They were a deeply religious people, increasingly aware of the moral and practical reasons for supporting religious toleration. As enterprising men and women they had learned how to depend on their own resourcefulness. Distinctive developments in technology, like the establishment of the first power saw—in New England in 1633—already foretold a country mechanized for people's comfort.

Since the colonies were still rural, a colonist probably died within 50 miles of the place where he had been born. Yet colonists were sailing their ships on every ocean, giving them an interest and an involvement in all mankind. As a whole they were proud of the cultural inheritances from their motherlands and eager to build upon those foundations. Only the Negroes—whose links with Africa had been forcibly broken—were unable to maintain contact with the "old country."

Most colonists worked with their hands either as farmers or as craftsmen, and they depended almost entirely upon man and woman power, child power, and the power of work animals. Except for the tiny percentage of people who lived in urban communities, the colonists were used to providing their own food supply. As a necessity for hunting, they developed remarkable skill with guns. Often living in isolation from others, they were almost completely at the mercy of natural disasters, such as blizzards, floods, and epidemics.

Families were closely knit and often large. Amusements were scarce and leisure time rare. Because the death rate of women and young children was high, the churchyards near every settled community were quickly crowded. And because medical and dental services were crude and primitive, older people especially, to a much greater extent than today, tended to ail without hope of effective relief.

In spite of the personal and communal dangers which held people together, forces were pulling them apart, too. Individuals of little means were envious of their wealthier townsmen and sometimes downright hostile to them. As a result, men of property often felt that they must be on guard against the "rabble."

Rich or poor, however, most people had felt the lift of American life and had sensed the sure progress of the inhabitants as a whole. Proud of their achievements in the years since the settlement at Jamestown and optimistic about their prospects, they lacked only the dignity of being completely self-governing. Consequently, they did not regard themselves as free men in the fullest sense of the term. This condition in time became intolerable and finally led them to fight for independence.

The successful American revolt at first was just a single episode in the history of Britain. Today we recognize that it belongs among the handful of events which changed world history significantly.

Most important, the existence of an independent land of opportunity attracted millions of men and women throughout the world and exerted pressure for reform in foreign countries practically everywhere. Yet the American Revolution did more than set people and governments into motion. It established new standards and principles for mankind which have never been erased, or for that matter, fully achieved. These include the ideas that all men are created equal, that just government derives its power from the consent of the governed, and that every human being is entitled to life, liberty, and the pursuit of happiness. Finally, whenever and wherever people talk of the dignity of man or of human rights, they unwittingly echo and salute the colonial Americans, who first gave life and meaning to those words. ★ ★ ★ ★ ★ ★ ★ ★ ★ ★ ★ ★

#A significant point. Pride in their cultural inheritances characterized most Americans. Negroes, denied such pride, suffered from a loss of self-identity and self-esteem.

The ability to think in terms of periods of history encompassing particular years and events is a goal of the study of history. The exercises under "Time and Change" help students develop this ability. Those under "Old Problems Become New" help them see the continuity of history.

PART ONE WORKSHOP

TIME AND CHANGE

In forming your own view of American history, the concept of time is indispensable. If you have not already completed a time line which records the significant dates and events in Part One, make one now.

1. Part One covers what space of time? How many centuries? Years?

2. Find the dates of the related events which may be grouped and spoken of as the Age of Discovery. As the Period of Colonization. The former was in what centuries? The latter?

3. Using your time line as a reference, list the major changes which took place in the period covered by Part One. Remember that an event is not necessarily a change, but that one or more events may bring about a change. For example, the Crusades were events. What changes did they bring to Europe? One change that you will certainly list is that America became a home for Europeans and Africans. What events led to that change?

4. Discuss (a) the part *people* played in bringing about the changes, (b) the effect the changes had *on* people.

5. Why, in your opinion, did the authors of this book decide to group the first five chapters in a single part?

AMERICA IN THE WORLD

1. Today North and South America, including the West Indies, are separated into two divisions—Latin America and Anglo-America. If you are uncertain about what each includes, consult a reference book. Using information given in Part One, account for the names of the two divisions and the inclusion of the countries or areas making up each. Find out what languages are established in each division and account for their wide use.

Using a globe, measure the distance between New York City and (a) any large city in Europe, (b) Rio de Janeiro, (c) Buenos Aires. In the past, which ties have been stronger, those between Anglo-America and Europe or those between Anglo-America and Latin America? Can your answer be explained by geography, history, or both? Explain.

2. In what various ways did the discovery and colonization of the New World affect life in Europe?

3. The cultures, or ways of living, that Europeans and Africans transplanted to America resulted in *Western* culture in the United States. What characteristics of this culture can you identify from your study of Part One? #

4. How do you account for the fact that the English—not the Spanish or Portuguese—colonies achieved independence first?

5. In what ways did the American Revolution change world history?

OLD PROBLEMS BECOME NEW

Because history is continuous, certain fundamental problems faced by people of one generation often recur in changed forms with the passing years.

1. Look for newspaper and magazine articles about American Indians today. A committee might find out the size of their present population, where and how most Indians live, the Indian policy of the federal government, and the fundamental problems connected with the Indians.

During this year's work observe how problems connected with Indians appeared at different times and what was done about them. Observe the continuity in the problems. As a start, identify the Indian problem the early settlers faced. How did they solve it?

2. What important problem connected with the British Empire did the British fail to solve between 1763 and 1776? State it in the form it took when Americans inherited it in 1783.

3. The belief of John Jay stated on page 85 helps explain why the problem of what to do about slavery early perplexed Americans. What do Jay's words mean? How and why did slavery become established in the colonies? How did some states seek to rid themselves of the slavery problem?

#Students should be able to name an advanced technology, the Christian religion, belief in self-government. Western culture is predominantly Christian--both Catholic and Protestant.

The heads indicate the nature of the books listed. An attempt was made to include at least one woman under the third head, but it was not always successful. Only books in print are named. Eyewitness accounts are particularly valuable as a means of giving insight into the era.

THE BOOKSHELF

Standard Reference Works

Dictionary of American Biography. Vols. 1–20, Allen Johnson and Dumas Malone (eds.). New York: Charles Scribner's Sons, 1928–1937. Supplement One, Harris E. Starr (ed.), 1944. Supplement Two, Robert L. Schuyler and Edward T. James (eds.), 1958.

Espenshade, Jr., Edward B. (ed.). *Goode's World Atlas.* 12th ed. Chicago: Rand McNally & Co., 1964.

Morris, Richard B. (ed.). *Encyclopedia of American History.* Rev. ed. New York: Harper & Row, Publishers, 1965.

Eyewitness Accounts

Chidsey, D. B. *The Siege of Boston: An On-the-Scene Account of the American Revolution.* New York: Crown Publishers, Inc., 1966.

Crèvecoeur, J. Hector St. John de. *Letters from an American Farmer* [Paperback—many editions].

Martin, Joseph P. *Private Yankee Doodle.* George F. Scheer (ed.). Boston: Little, Brown & Co., 1962.

Giant Men and Women

Barbour, Philip L. *The Three Worlds of Captain John Smith.* Boston: Houghton Mifflin Co., 1964.

Cunliffe, Marcus. *George Washington, Man and Monument.* Boston: Little, Brown & Co., 1958 [Paperback—reprinted as *George Washington.* New York: New American Library, Inc.].

Morison, Samuel Eliot. *John Paul Jones: A Sailor's Biography.* Boston: Little, Brown & Co., 1959 [Paperback—Boston: Little, Brown & Co.].

Peare, Catherine O. *William Penn* [Paperback—Ann Arbor: The University of Michigan Press, 1966].

Wendell, Barrett. *Cotton Mather: The Puritan Priest* [Paperback—New York: Harcourt, Brace & World, Inc., 1963].

Living and Making a Living

Bridenbaugh, Carl. *Cities in the Wilderness: Urban Life in America, 1625–1742.* New York: Alfred A. Knopf, Inc., 1955 [Paperback—New York: G. P. Putnam's Sons].

———. *Cities in Revolt: Urban Life in America, 1743–1776.* New York: Alfred A. Knopf, Inc., 1955 [Paperback—New York: G. P. Putnam's Sons].

Crane, Verner W. *The Southern Frontier, 1670–1732* [Paperback—Ann Arbor: The University of Michigan Press, 1956].

Horgan, Paul. *Conquistadors in North American History.* New York: Farrar, Straus & Giroux, Inc., 1963 [Paperback—New York: Fawcett World Library].

Knollenberg, Bernhard. *Origins of the American Revolution: 1759–1766* [Paperback—Rev. ed.; New York: The Free Press, Division of The Macmillan Co., 1961].

Nettels, Curtis. *The Roots of American Civilization.* 2nd ed. New York: Appleton-Century-Crofts, 1963.

Starkey, Marion L. *The Devil in Massachusetts: A Modern Enquiry into the Salem Witch Trials.* Gloucester, Mass.: Peter Smith, 1962 [Paperback—New York: Doubleday & Co., Inc., 1961].

Sydnor, Charles S. *American Revolutionaries in the Making* [Paperback—New York: The Free Press, Division of The Macmillan Co., 1965].

Van Every, Dale. *The Disinherited: The Lost Birthright of the American Indian.* New York: William Morrow and Co., 1966.

———. *A Company of Heroes: The American Frontier, 1775–1783.* New York: William Morrow and Co., 1962 [Paperback—New York: New American Library, Inc.].

Ver Steeg, Clarence L. *The Formative Years: 1607–1763.* New York: Hill & Wang, Inc., 1964.

Wallace, W. M. *Appeal to Arms: A Military History of the American Revolution.* Gloucester, Mass.: Peter Smith [Paperback—Chicago: Quadrangle Books, Inc., 1964].

Confronting the World

Jones, Howard Mumford. *O Strange New World: American Culture: The Formative Years.* New York: The Viking Press, Inc., 1964.

Kraus, Michael. *The Atlantic Civilization: Eighteenth Century Origins.* New York: Russell & Russell Publishers, Division of Atheneum Publishers, 1961.

Morris, Richard B. *The Peacemakers: The Great Powers and American Independence.* New York: Harper & Row, Publishers, 1965.

Price, Christine. *Cities of Gold and Isles of Spice: Travel to the East in the Middle Ages.* New York: David McKay Co., Inc., 1965.

Van Alstyne, Richard. *Empire and Independence.* New York: John Wiley & Sons, Inc., 1965 [Paperback—New York: John Wiley & Sons, Inc.].

Art, Science, and the Life of the Mind

Rossiter, Clinton. *Seedtime of the Republic.* New York: Harcourt, Brace & World, Inc., 1953 [Paperback—reprinted as *The Political Thought of the American Revolution.* New York: Harcourt, Brace & World, Inc.].

Wright, L. B., and Others. *The Arts in America: The Colonial Period.* New York: Charles Scribner's Sons, 1966.

Historical Fiction

Alderman, Clifford L. *Stormy Knight: The Life of William Phips.* Philadelphia: Chilton Books, 1964. (About a colonial governor of Massachusetts.)

Roberts, Kenneth. *Rabble in Arms.* New York: Doubleday & Co., Inc., 1947 [Paperback—New York: Fawcett World Library]. (Sequel to *Arundel,* dealing with Benedict Arnold against Burgoyne.)

———. *Arundel.* New York: Doubleday & Co., Inc., 1944 [Paperback—New York: Fawcett World Library]. (A young soldier from Maine goes with Benedict Arnold against Quebec.)

#Every student should have access to <u>Dictionary of American Biography</u> as well as to the other two volumes named. <u>Encyclopedia of American History</u> summarizes American history by year.

101

Point out the close cultural ties between America and Britain. (The evidence is the clothing, the ship--right--and the books, doubtless published abroad.)

A pert young miss is wearing an outfit made of imported cloth and ribbon. Her forest friends as well as the plumes adorning her hat are doubtless American.

Dressed in stylish knee breeches, a well-to-do man shows off his library and its rich furnishings.

The saltbox house, which originated in New England, seemed the ideal type of farm dwelling in the North. Having two stories in the front and one in the back, it was compact. It had single-size windows and one large central chimney.

Other industries already beginning to turn the colonists into a manufacturing people were iron, candle, brick-and-tile, paper, and furniture making and beer-and-whisky distilling.

Glassmaking, long performed by German-born craftsmen, met the endless demand for bottles and windowpanes.

THE QUALITY OF LIFE

The Revolutionary generation lived close to nature and aspired to acquire comforts like those the gentry in the "old country" enjoyed. Still, the society the people were building was based on a growing mastery of their own physical environment. Bountifully supplied with food, they were also able to enjoy the advantages the urban communities could offer.

The buildings of Boston seem haphazardly placed. This is because the first Bostonians tried to follow topography--an early instance of urban planning.

Boston in the 1760's—2 miles long and ¾ mile wide—had 3500 houses. During Sunday church services, no persons other than doctors were allowed on the streets.

In touch with scientific developments abroad, Americans followed with fascination in the 1780's the balloon ascents taking place in France. Shortly these experiments in flying were duplicated here.

103

Discuss why scientists have always considered themselves part of an international community (see p. 739).

Discuss the religious objections to horse-racing and public entertainment. (They were frivolity that turned man from God and work.)

THE QUALITY OF LIFE *continued*

Increasing wealth was weakening the devotion of most Americans to the simple life. But attending amusements or having one's portrait painted were activities usually limited to "aristocrats."

Columbian Magazine, April, 1787

Besides being used for transportation, horses were raced for sport. Here along the Delaware wild horses were hunted with dogs.

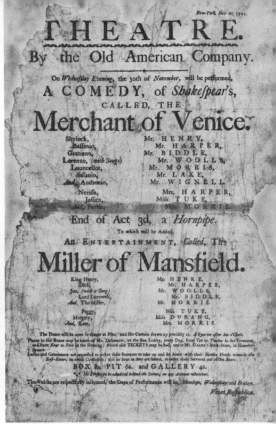

The first plays produced were old English favorites.

Ask how life was different when all pictures were scarce and required much training to make.

Some American artists studied in London for careers at home.

Metropolitan Museum of Art, Gift of Samuel P. Avery, 1897

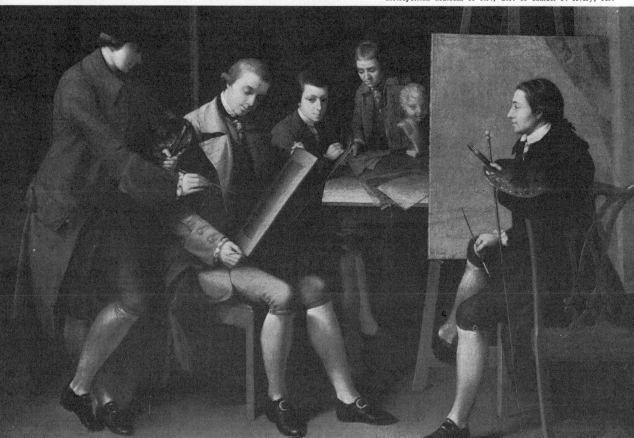

The requirements of fighting a war against England caused the colonists to unite to achieve victory, but after it was won, their differences came to the fore. Nevertheless, outstanding leaders could see beyond the concerns of any one section: they envisaged a united group of Americans--a nation. Part Two tells how their vision was realized--through the adoption of the Constitution, the efforts of giant leaders (including John Marshall), and the solidifying of a national spirit. Discuss: What is meant by personal integrity? The early national leaders valued it as the chief qualification for holding office. Is it so valued today? Explain your answer. What probably helped account for their belief that they should be responsible and humane in carrying out their duties?

MAKING
A
NEW
NATION

How do separate *peoples* become a unified *people*—a nation? Americans were arriving at an answer in the late eighteenth century.

The dividing lines between the various settlements had long since been blurred. The change from being "plural" to being "singular" was under way from the beginning. The people had in common the English language and the intellectual heritage of western Europe. In the passage of time, they had surmounted together numerous haunting perils—political, military, and natural. By 1776 they shared a strong and lively suspicion of Europe.

Now independent, Americans were developing forceful leaders who inspired attention and admiration throughout the country. They came out of every section. But whether they were men like the Adamses from Massachusetts or the Pinckneys from South Carolina, or like Benjamin Franklin from Pennsylvania, they all were able to think and talk from an American, not just from a local, point of view.

These extraordinary figures were "gentlemen" who saw a clear distinction between themselves and humbler folk. To their credit they considered personal integrity a prime qualification for holding office. Above all, they wisely understood that in exercising power they must be humane and responsible.

The greatest of these giants was George Washington of Virginia.
Repeatedly he pulled himself away from the Potomac's shores, and the land and house he dearly loved, to devote himself to public service. Soundly judging the future in the light of the past, he had a sure sense of the republic's limitless possibilities.

#The occasions were: as Commander in Chief of the American Revolution, to attend the Annapolis Convention, to preside over the Constitutional Convention, to become President. **105**

#Washington was, of course, a farmer. In a time when most Americans lived on farms, many words and expressions from farmers' vocabularies were in use. Some continue to be used today, long after their original meaning has lost its force.

\#   In farmer's words, Washington once observed, "Liberty, when it begins to take root, is a plant of rapid growth." The soil in which it could thrive was prepared with rare talent and vigor by him and the other patriots of his generation. Mingling their lives unsparingly with their country's life, they launched the United States of America.

The portraits of only two Americans are used in the part openings in this text: Washington and Lincoln. No other men so profoundly influenced the whole era in which they lived as these two did. Ask what is meant by "balanced leadership."

George Washington, first president of the United States, who gave the American people the balanced leadership they needed to establish a lasting republic.

106 This portrait of Washington was painted by Joseph Wright at the end of the war (1783). It is considered the General's favorite and the one most like him.

This section details the transition of Americans from being a disunited group to being a united one--a nation. A newly independent people may form a country, but it does not immediately become a nation. Nationhood results from the feeling of oneness a people develops.

PART TWO

MAKING A NEW NATION

CHAPTER 6   ERECTING THE FRAME OF GOVERNMENT   108

The United States Stand United, but Only in Name   110

The Need Grows for a Stronger National Government   115

The Philadelphia Convention Plans a New Regime   118

CHAPTER 7   THE DAY OF THE FEDERALISTS   126

Washington Takes the Wheel of Government   128

The Federalists Rally Round Hamilton's Plan   131

Political Parties Make Their First Appearance   135

CHAPTER 8   THE REPUBLICANS IN PEACE AND WAR   144

Jefferson and His Colleagues Come Into Power   146

The War Against Napoleon Involves America   153

James Madison Puts on the Mantle of the Presidency   155

CHAPTER 9   STRENGTHENING THE NATIONAL SPIRIT   162

Pride of Country Captivates the People   164

Andrew Jackson Reveals America's Military Strength   166

The United States Confronts the Monarchs of Europe   168

Marshall's Court Strengthens the Constitution   169

Politicians Embark on an "Era of Good Feelings"   170

A LONG VIEW   178

Part Two covers the years from about 1781 to 1828--the years often called the early national period. In these years the Constitution was written and adopted; the government it established was set in motion by Washington, Hamilton, Jefferson, and Madison; the War of 1812 was fought; the Monroe Doctrine was announced; and the federal government was strengthened by the Marshall Court. As the country gained in strength and prestige, the people began to develop the national spirit that signified they were becoming a nation.

The quotation given here is another primary source. It shows how one large group of people felt in 1786 about participation in public affairs by "the people." What arguments does Webster use to make his case? Does anyone today hold Webster's views?

6

ERECTING THE FRAME OF GOVERNMENT

#The reference, of course, is to the Articles of Confederation, discussed on page 110. Discuss the meaning of "requisite," spelled here in Webster's own way.

Believe me, my friends, for I am serious . . .

My countrymen, it is a common saying now that the devil is in you. . . . he is *in* you and *among* you, in a variety of shapes. #

In the first place, the weakness of our federal government is the devil. It prevents the adoption of any measures that are requisit for us, as a nation; it keeps us from paying our honest debts; it also throws out of our power all the profits of commerce, and this drains us of cash. Is not this the devil? Yes, my countrymen, an empty purse is the devil.

You say you are jealous of your rights, and dare not trust Congress. Well, that jealousy is an evil spirit, and all evil spirits are devils. So far the devil is in you. You act, in this particular, just like the crew of a ship, who would not trust the helm with one of their number, because he might

While the Constitution was being written, sentries were posted outside the delegates' room.

Ask the class what clues to the origin of this quotation they could have got from it if they had not been told who wrote it. (The quotation could have been dated by the first sentence in the first paragraph; "Congress" and "America" give clues; the sentiment is early American.)

possibly run her ashore, when by leaving her without a pilot, they were *certain* of shipwreck. You act just like men, who in raising a building, would not have a master workman, because he *might* give out wrong orders. You will be masters yourselves; and as you are not all ready to lift at the same time, one labors at a stick of timber, then another, then a third; you are then vexed that it is not raised; why let a master order thirteen of you to take hold together, and you will lift it at once.

Every family has a master (or a mistress—I beg the ladies' pardon). When a ship or a house is to be built, there is a master; when highways are repairing, there is a master; every little school has a master; the continent is a great school; the boys are numerous, and full of roguish tricks, and there is no master. The boys in this great school play truant, and there is no person to chastise them. Do you think, my countrymen, that America is more easily governed than a school?

You do very well in small matters; extend your reason to great ones. . . . You think a master necessary to govern a few harmless children in a school or family; yet leave thousands of great rogues to be governed by good advice. Believe me, my friends, for I am serious; you lose rights, because you will not giv your magistrates authority to protect them. Your liberty is despotism, because it has no control; your power is nothing, because it is not united.

Noah Webster (1758–1843), who is known best for his dictionaries and spellers, was also a journalist and pamphleteer of note. He repeatedly urged his fellow Americans to discover the outstanding qualities of their country and, especially, its distinctiveness from Europe. In this selection from an essay entitled "The Devil Is in You," which he wrote in 1786, he is tormented by the thought that unless the nation is ruled firmly it will lose its liberty. Like many other men of the 1780's, Webster was afraid that wide public participation in political affairs would easily become mob rule. (The words "requisit" and "giv" are not printer's errors. They represent Webster's experiment with a revised and, he thought, improved spelling. This effort was part of his lifelong labor to establish a uniquely American branch of the English language. See page 164.)

Webster was once a teacher. While he was teaching, he wrote his Spelling Book. However, his main work was An American Dictionary of the English Language. The latest edition of this work is Webster's Third New International Dictionary.

Historical Society of Pennsylvania

The State House at Philadelphia, where Washington took formal command of the Continental Army, the Declaration of Independence was adopted, and the United States Constitution was written. Now called Independence Hall, it preserves the setting of significant events of the American past and the treasured relics of the Revolutionary and early national periods.

THE UNITED STATES STAND UNITED, BUT ONLY IN NAME

At the time the Revolution ended, the idea of loyalty to the nation was only beginning to be accepted. Most Americans still felt that their first duty should be to their states or their particular sections of the country. One New Englander put it this way: "My affections still flow in what you will deem their natural order—toward Salem—Massachusetts—New England—the Union at large." Moreover, the force that had held the colonies together—opposition to British policies—had been removed by the ending of the war. Now old disputes began to reappear among Americans who only recently had worked together in harmony.

CREATING A PROPER GOVERNMENT

People were divided especially over the question of how they should govern themselves as an independent nation. This subject had been debated heatedly during the Revolution itself.

Proposing the Articles of Confederation. Lee's resolution urging independence (page 77) had been accompanied by another proposing that "a plan of confederation be prepared and transmitted to the respective Colonies for their consideration and approbation." The members of the Continental Congress had managed to hammer out a charter for a national government, called the Articles of Confederation. After months of intense debate, the Articles had been sent to the states for ratification, or formal acceptance, in November, 1777.

Reliance on the states. The new government would be a loose confederation, or league, of states. According to the Articles, the powers of the central government would be strictly limited: all powers not expressly granted to it would be left to the states. Congress might wage war and make peace, send diplomatic representatives and conclude treaties, but it must rely on the states for men and money. It would have the power to borrow money, but it could not tax.

The Articles made no provision for a national executive or a national judiciary—only for a legislative department. The new govern-ment would have no power over interstate commerce, but it might regulate trade with the Indians; it might regulate the value of money, but it would have no control over the issuing of paper money by the states.

Moreover, the Articles could not easily be changed. Amendments would need the approval of the Congress and then ratification by *each* of the thirteen states. The Articles also provided that almost every important measure enacted by Congress had to be approved by the representatives of at least nine states. Each state was to have one vote in the Congress, even though the number of its delegates could vary from as few as two men to as many as seven. But Congress was so weak that it could only urge—not force—the states to obey its laws. Remembering too well their recent dissatisfaction with centralized authority, Americans had made the mistake of creating under the Articles a government without the strength to compel devotion to itself.

"A firm league of friendship." Nevertheless, when Maryland formally approved the Articles of Confederation on March 1, 1781—the last state to do so—hope ran high that the new government would meet the needs of the country. A Pennsylvania newspaper reported: "This great event, which will confound our enemies and frustrate their plans of division, was announced to the public at twelve o'clock under the discharge of the artillery on the land, and the cannon of the shipping in the Delaware. The bells were rung, and every manifestation of joy shown. . . ." The new nation, the newspaper stated, had been "indissolubly cemented."

But after 1781, the "cement" proved to be only an illusion. The Confederation was merely what it called itself, "a firm league of friendship"; it was clearly not adequate to governing a nation.

DISPOSING OF THE WESTERN LANDS

The pre-Revolutionary problems reappeared in one form or another at the end of the war and were laid at the doorstep of the new govern-

#In what form had the problem appeared when the colonies were dependent on England? (How to deal with Indians there.)

ment.
The most difficult continued to be those connected with the western lands—the inviting area between the Appalachians and the Mississippi River. The chief question was, How could the government acquire control of these lands, which belonged to several of the states?

Acquiring a national domain. Connecticut, Georgia, Massachusetts, North and South Carolina, New York, and Virginia all had claims to vast stretches of land in the West that they had acquired in the colonial period. These claims caused serious arguments.

By 1779 twelve states had ratified the Articles of Confederation, but Maryland had refused to go along with the rest. It had insisted that the western lands, which "had been secured by the blood and treasure of all, ought . . . to be considered a common stock, to be parcelled out by Congress into free, convenient, and independent Governments." In other words, the western lands should become a national domain and eventually be carved into new states.

After much haggling, Virginia, early in 1781, agreed to yield its title to lands lying north of the Ohio River. Virginia's land cession was not completed until 1784, but immediately after the intention was announced, Maryland ratified the Articles and they went into effect. In the following years, New York and then Massachusetts and the southern states also gave up to the central government their claims to land in the West.

Jefferson's plan. Meanwhile, Congress had begun to lay plans for organizing the vast area. Thomas Jefferson, their chief architect, may be considered the father of America's land policy. Under it, new states would be brought into the Union on the basis of complete equality with the original thirteen.

Adopted by Congress in 1784, Jefferson's plan provided that the western domain be divided into ten districts; that these districts govern themselves under constitutions modeled after those of the original states; that each district, or territory, be organized permanently when its population should reach 20,000; and that each be admitted as a state whenever the

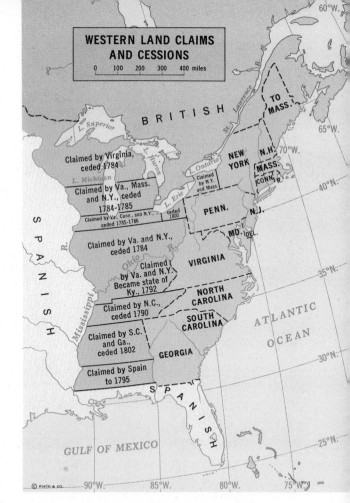

WESTERN LAND CLAIMS AND CESSIONS

0   100   200   300   400 miles

Most of the ambitious land claims shown were based on the "sea-to-sea" charters granted in colonial days.

For example, see the map on p. 35.

number of its free inhabitants should equal the number of free inhabitants in the smallest of the thirteen original states. Congress turned down Jefferson's proposal to prohibit slavery in all the lands after 1800. It also refused to approve the names that Jefferson supplied for the new states—names like Assenisipia, Pelisipia, Cherronesus, Metropotamia, and Polypotamia.

The Land Ordinance of 1785. The following year, 1785, Congress provided for the distribution of the land. It passed an ordinance dividing the area north of the Ohio River—called the Northwest Territory—into townships 6 miles square. Each township would be divided into thirty-six consecutively numbered sections, each of them 1 mile square, or 640 acres, in size. Section 16 in every township was to be set

##Although Jefferson's first land ordinance actually never went into effect, it became the basis for the Northwest Ordinance (p. 113), the greatest achievement under the Articles.

In United States public-land surveys, a range is one of a series of divisions numbered east or west from the principal meridian of the survey. It consists of a row of townships, each 6 miles square, which are numbered north or south of a base line.

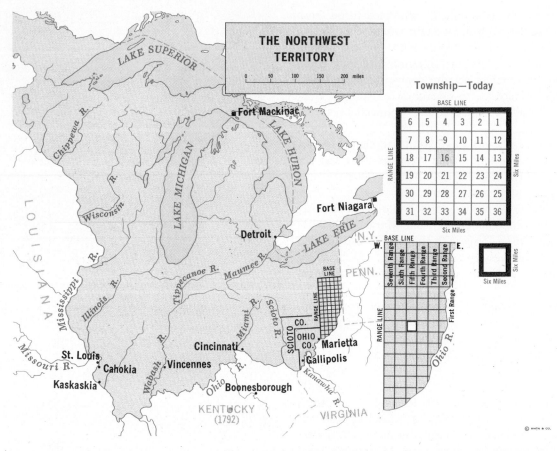

THE NORTHWEST TERRITORY

Township—Today

The area of the "Seven Ranges" was surveyed and opened to settlement first. The First Range was in Pennsylvania; the others in Ohio. The system of numbering townships shown here was adopted in 1796. Earlier, Section 36 had been Section 1, and the sections were numbered from south to north.

aside for the support of the public schools.

Four sections in each township were to be reserved for the national government, as was one-third of the wealth from any gold, silver, and copper mines discovered. The rest of the land was to be auctioned off at a minimum price of one dollar an acre.

The land companies. In practice the Land Ordinance of 1785 was ignored. Actual settlers remained few because Indians still ranged over the Northwest Territory. Needing large sums of money, Congress became susceptible to the pressure of land companies.

The Ohio Company of Associates, organized in Boston in 1786 by a group of former army officers, was such a company. Its leaders hoped that the Congress would exchange for an immense land grant the worthless paper money with which they had been paid for their military services. The negotiations with Congress were carried on by Manasseh Cutler, a Massachusetts clergyman and able businessman.

Since Congress would not be partial to Massachusetts men, Cutler agreed to include in the deal a second land company, the Scioto Company of New York. The Ohio Associates received 5,000,000 acres at approximately nine cents an acre, and the Scioto group received the right to 3,500,000 acres, although it never exercised its privilege. Through such arrangements, land speculators helped to provide the Confederation with money it needed badly. Later they would reap profits by selling their holdings in small tracts to eager settlers.

The significance of the Northwest Ordinance is that the method of organizing territories into states it set up has been followed ever since. The forbidding of slavery was also important.

112

The Northwest Ordinance. Congress also determined how the settlers would be governed. On July 13, 1787, even before the negotiations with Cutler were completed, it adopted the Northwest Ordinance. This law established for the Northwest Territory a plan of government which, in the years that followed, would be applied to all the lands included in the national domain. Its passage was forced upon the weak Congress by the land companies in order to get the western land organized for the benefit of their expected customers.

Under the Northwest Ordinance, not fewer than three nor more than five states would be carved out of the Northwest Territory. The area would at first be administered by a governor, three judges, and a secretary—all chosen by Congress. When 5000 free adult males had settled in any part of the Northwest Territory, that part could be organized as a separate "territory" and would have a representative assembly to make laws. No law could go into effect, however, unless the governor approved of it.

When there were 60,000 free inhabitants in one of these territories, they could petition the Congress for statehood in the Union. The Ordinance guaranteed to the inhabitants personal and religious freedom and the introduction of a system of free public education; it also forbade slavery.

FACING THE POWERS OF EUROPE

The problems involved in America's relations with Europe proved to be more difficult to solve than those of the West. Most Europeans either were ignorant of the new American country or held it in contempt. The early diplomats of the United States even had to explain sometimes that their countrymen did not live like savages in the forest. It required immense patience and tact to build goodwill and respect in such a hostile atmosphere.

England's continued hostility. The experience of John Adams, first minister to England, is illustrative. Though he was received by George III, his three years as minister were fruitless for his country and unrewarding to him personally. He

New York Public Library

Settlers build a log cabin in the lush forest that covered the wilderness of the Northwest Territory.
Review the origin of the log cabin (p. 46).

repeatedly complained about the way he was ignored. Moreover, the British showed their scorn for the United States by refusing to send any diplomatic representatives here.

The British also were hostile in matters of trade. Lord Sheffield, in an influential pamphlet, *Observations on the Commerce of the American States,* published in 1783, maintained that England could now seize the trade of America without having to bear the burden of governing Americans. "America," he insisted, "cannot retaliate. It will not be an easy matter to bring the American States to act as a nation. They are not to be feared as such by us." Acting upon this theory, England in 1783 closed the West Indies and Canada to American vessels with the avowed purpose of "strangling in the birth" American sea-borne shipping.

Because the Articles of Confederation did not give the Congress control over commerce, there could be no united national action against England. When the states acted separately, their efforts came to nothing. New York or Massachusetts might prohibit importations from England, but if neither could win the coöperation of all the other states, British products would enter from Canada or through Baltimore or Charleston.

New York Public Library

Detroit was one of the posts the British would not surrender to the Americans. Seen here as it looked during the controversy, it was the center of a rich fur trade and of British intrigue among the Indians.

George Rogers Clark undertook his western campaign to curb raiders directed from Detroit.

The British refusal to compensate the Americans for some 3000 Negro slaves, carried to other British territory during the Revolution, aroused the deep resentment of southern planters against the mother country. But even more important in poisoning Anglo-American relations was the continued British refusal to hand over to the United States the line of trading posts running from Lake Champlain to Lake Superior—all located south of the United States–Canadian border.

According to the treaty of 1783, these posts were to be turned over by the British "with all convenient speed." Canada, however, was putting pressure on England to hold the posts until it could capture the profitable fur trade conducted from them. Accordingly, the British found an excuse when Americans violated the treaty also by refusing to pay debts owed to Englishmen and by failing to restore property taken from Loyalists. The American secretary of foreign affairs predicted gloomily: "They [the English] may hold the posts, but they will hold them as pledges of enmity; and the time must and will come when the seeds of discontent, resentment, and hatred, which such measures always sow, will produce very bitter fruit."

Spain's intrigues. Relations with Spain were equally difficult. Spain held the key to the life-

line of many American settlers in the West: the freedom to navigate the Mississippi. These settlers depended on the river for transporting their exports and imports. In particular, they wanted to be able to ship goods through New Orleans duty-free.

Spain long had had an envious eye on these western settlers and the land they occupied. During the American Revolution, it had offered America an alliance in exchange for the territory lying south of the Ohio between the Appalachians and the Mississippi River. Spain's intention was to seal off the flood of American settlers before it overran the Spanish possessions of Texas and Mexico. Although Congress turned down this offer, Spain entered the Revolution anyway—as an ally of France.

In the peace treaty of 1783 at the end of the war, Spain, you recall, had exacted East and West Florida from England—gaining control of the mouth of the Mississippi River. From the Floridas the Spanish carried on a vast intrigue among western frontiersmen, whom they were eager to bring under their own flag.

Possibly the Spanish would have been more successful than they were if they had not incited the Creek, Choctaw, and Chickasaw Indians to harass Americans in Georgia and along the Cumberland and Tennessee rivers.

##Students should compare the maps on pp. 66 and 86. Florida--or the Floridas--had been taken by Britain in 1763, but Spain gained possession of the Floridas in 1783.

The fighting in those areas was fierce and bloody in the late 1780's. Furthermore, Spain insisted upon holding the post of Natchez on the Mississippi, which was well within the limits of the territory ceded to the United States by England.

Americans were not yet strong enough to seize from the English and the Spanish what they believed was theirs. If they could be patient, though, Europe's internal quarrels might provide them with valuable opportunities. Jefferson, minister to France from 1785 to 1789, understanding this, advised from Paris: "Those . . . who have influence in the new country would act wisely to endeavor to keep things quiet till the western parts of Europe shall be engaged in war."

Widening horizons of trade. In international commerce America fared considerably better than in international politics. Despite frustration over trade with the British West Indies, Americans saw their trade with England grow each year—and remain much more important than that with any other nation. France hospitably opened its West Indian ports to American vessels. The Netherlands also permitted trade in its chief ports, and Spain opened the Cuban ports of Havana and Santiago de Cuba, although somewhat reluctantly. In Europe four powers, including Prussia, concluded trade treaties with the United States.

Sum and Substance

1. Explain how the Articles of Confederation (*a*) kept the states powerful, (*b*) restricted the central government. 2. What three questions connected with western lands faced the new government? 3. How was each one finally answered or settled? 4. Why is Jefferson called the father of the land policy of the United States? 5. What difficulties did the United States have with England? With Spain?

The inadequacy of the government under the Articles, already seen, is demonstrated further.

THE NEED GROWS FOR A STRONGER NATIONAL GOVERNMENT

The attempt to establish relations between and among the states gave Americans another kind of problem to wrestle with. Finding a way to solve it ultimately led to the creation of a strong national government which could cope with international matters, too.

ECONOMIC DEVELOPMENTS

At the end of the Revolution, American business began to develop so fast that by 1790 it had far exceeded the dreams of the merchants and manufacturers of 1775. The war had removed the restrictions on the manufacture of certain important goods like hats, woolens, and iron. By the middle of the 1780's, Stephen Higginson, a well-to-do New Englander, said that "to increase our manufactures has become the rage of the day." A New Hampshire factory was making buttons, thread, and cloth; and plants in Pennsylvania, Rhode Island, and Connecticut were producing tenpenny nails and finished woolen and linen goods. Immigrants were arriving from Europe, lured not only by the considerable freedom of opportunity but also by good wages and a promising future.

The establishment of banks. To help oil the wheels of commerce, the Bank of North America was founded in Philadelphia in 1781. Presently there were a Bank of Massachusetts and a Bank of New York, and banks were being planned for other leading cities. These banks were helping to open a new era in which many new industrial activities would be undertaken.

Farm conditions. The farmer's fate was somewhat less happy than the businessman's. In the South after 1781, there was overproduction of tobacco. Wealthier planters moved to more fertile land farther west, leaving those who remained in the coastal areas to face bankruptcy.

In New England, although the townspeople often accused farmers of having profiteered during the war, the rural communities were actually impoverished. Farmers of the middle states were somewhat better off, but they were far from being as prosperous as the merchants.

The farmer's difficulty everywhere was that he could earn very little hard money, that is, gold and silver. Often paid in goods for his produce, he was nevertheless expected to pay his taxes and his mortgage obligations in hard money. Lacking it, he demanded that his state either issue paper notes, which he might find easier to come by, or pass stay laws, which were laws to postpone debt payments.

Creditors against debtors. Creditors—people to whom debts were owed—naturally opposed the issuance of paper money and the passage of stay laws. Meanwhile, debtors—those who owed money—became more insistent in de-

manding help. Men of large property in the 1780's daily grew more concerned. Harrison Gray Otis of Massachusetts told an old friend, "You and I did not imagine when the first war with Britain was over, that revolution was just begun."

What had developed was a struggle between men of large property—the creditors, themselves often under pressure from foreign creditors—and the men of small property—the debtors. In Rhode Island the debtor group got control of the state government, passed the laws it wanted, and made creditors accept depreciated paper currency in payment of debts. Many a merchant there closed his establishment and fled the state in order to prevent a gleeful debtor from discharging an obligation by forcing on him the near worthless currency.

Shays' Rebellion. Conditions in New England were worse than those elsewhere: the distilling industry had collapsed because of the closing of the West Indies trade, and there was widespread unemployment along the coast. In the interior, especially in Massachusetts, the number of foreclosures on mortgages began to rise, judgments against debtors increased, and the wages of farm laborers fell sharply—to forty cents a day by 1787.

To prevent further judgments for debt, a mob of infuriated farmers in Massachusetts in the fall of 1786 attempted to keep the courts from sitting. The leader was Daniel Shays—a Revolutionary War veteran who had been promoted for bravery at Bunker Hill.

This action, the beginning of Shays' Rebellion, showed the pent-up anger of farmers. They were demanding, in addition to stay laws, the issuance of additional paper money and the ending of what they thought was unequal taxation. The farmers were not wicked men or radical men. But they wanted to be secure in their own small holdings and in their persons—for the prisons were overflowing with debtors.

After Shays and his band had forced an adjournment of the court at Springfield, Massachusetts, Governor James Bowdoin sent troops to put down the rebellion, a mission accomplished with dispatch. Many frightened

Knee breeches were standard in men's dress.

A fight breaks out as a mob of irate farmers approaches the State Supreme Court Building in Springfield. It was the lawlessness of Shays' Rebellion that brought George Washington out of retirement.

Picture Collection, New York Public Library

Raise the question: Who was right in the events known as Shays' Rebellion? The farmers? Governor Bowdoin? Why cannot any government tolerate violence?

citizens wanted to see the rebels severely punished in order to restrain the spread of "democracy"—by which they meant "the rule of the mob." Good sense prevailed, however, and all of them were pardoned, including Shays.

SEEING THE ARTICLES' WEAKNESSES

Some serious questions had been raised by these events. Was the national government capable of preventing civil violence? Of providing equal justice for all? Of protecting creditors against the onslaughts of debtors? George Washington wrote from Mount Vernon in 1786:

> I am mortified beyond expression that in the moment of our acknowledged independence we should by our conduct verify the predictions of our trans-Atlantic foe, and render ourselves ridiculous and contemptible in the eyes of all Europe.

By 1786 there was much evidence that the government of the Confederation no longer was worthy of respect. It could neither thwart such episodes as Shays' Rebellion nor resolve the nagging difficulties with England and Spain.

Many thoughtful Americans believed that a central government able to make its power felt and respected in the states was sorely needed. This government, they hoped, would be able to issue currency and keep it sound, control and distribute the western lands, wage war when required, regulate commerce, and preserve order at home.

The Mount Vernon Conference. In 1784 the Virginia legislature opened negotiations with Maryland aimed at improving navigation on the Potomac River. The river, a boundary between the two states, was also a water route leading to the western lands. George Washington, who was personally interested in bettering communication with the West because he owned considerable land there, invited the representatives of the two states to Mount Vernon in 1785. At Washington's estate, plans were laid for the future use of the Potomac. Moreover, the representatives agreed that a conference should be held the following year—to include Maryland, Virginia, and Pennsylvania—to discuss still other mutual problems of commerce.

The Virginia legislature went even further. It

Mount Vernon, Washington's home, set on a height overlooking the Potomac River. The concern of two states about traffic on the waterway led to taking the first steps toward creating a stronger national government.

Rare Book Division, New York Public Library

sent out a call to *all* the states for a meeting to be held at Annapolis, Maryland, the following September. The purpose was to enable the states to "consider how a uniform system in their commercial regulations may be necessary to their common interests and their permanent harmony."

The Annapolis Convention. Nine states appointed representatives to the Annapolis conference, although only five actually sent them—Delaware, New Jersey, New York, Pennsylvania, and Virginia. The conference went beyond its original purpose and adopted a proposal of Alexander Hamilton of New York to hold a convention of all the states, in Philadelphia in May, 1787. Its business would be to discuss amendments to the Articles of Confederation that could strengthen the central government.

The call for revision. Congress approved this report and called the May meeting "for the sole and express purpose of revising the Arti-

cles of Confederation and reporting to Congress and the several legislatures such alterations and provisions therein as shall, when agreed to in Congress and confirmed by the states, render the federal constitution adequate to the exigencies of government and the preservation of the Union." In short, Congress emphasized that this latest conference was intended to *revise,* not *discard,* the Articles. Men who favored strong states would not have supported a move to write an entirely new constitution.

Sum and Substance

1. Compare the businessman's condition with that of the farmer after the Revolution. 2. How did the struggle between creditors and debtors develop? 3. What caused Shays' Rebellion? What was its outcome? 4. How did the Mount Vernon and Annapolis conventions lead to the Philadelphia Convention? 5. What was the sole purpose of the Philadelphia Convention? Why?

This important section describes the work of the Constitutional Convention.

THE PHILADELPHIA CONVENTION PLANS A NEW REGIME

Although Philadelphia had only about 40,000 inhabitants in 1787, it was the largest city in the United States. Its people were justly proud that it had become the political center of the young country. As the month of May approached, the city grew tense with anticipation. Gathering now for the momentous convention was what one of the local newspapers called "the collective Wisdom of the Continent."

ORGANIZING THE TASK

The delegates themselves sensed that their labors that spring and summer would not be forgotten, that this meeting would live in history. James Wilson, one of the brilliant Pennsylvania representatives, declared, "We should consider that we are providing a Constitution for future generations and not merely for the peculiar circumstances of the moment." And Elbridge Gerry, a delegate from Massachusetts, wrote: "Something must be done, or we shall disappoint not only America but the whole world."

Washington in the chair. Not until the twenty-fifth of May were delegates from seven states—the required number—present. Only then could the meetings begin. The scene of the deliberations was Philadelphia's impressive Independence Hall, where the Declaration of Independence had been signed eleven years earlier.

George Washington, the towering figure at the Convention, was chosen chairman unanimously. Having earned in the Revolution imperishable prestige, he had hoped that his country would make no further demands upon him. In fact, he almost declined to serve as a member of the Virginia delegation. A rheumatic shoulder kept him in almost constant pain; his brother had just died; his mother and sister were both seriously ill. Nevertheless, he had a keen sense of public duty and a feeling that this was the moment to complete the task of nation-building.

The members. Jefferson, who was in France at the time, later referred to the delegates as

#The names of the delegates are given on page 803 (not everybody signed). Twenty-nine had college training, more than half of them were lawyers, and the rest were chiefly planters and merchants, though a few doctors and college professors were members of the group.

"demi-gods." Even if we accept a lesser rank for them, it was a remarkable group of men. Of the fifty-five who attended, eight had signed the Declaration of Independence, two the Articles of Confederation. All were important public figures, the majority being lawyers. Many were college graduates in an era when higher education was very unusual. Madison, for example, was a Princeton man, and Gouverneur Morris and Alexander Hamilton alumni of King's College. Jonathan Dayton of New Jersey, at the age of twenty-seven, was the youngest delegate; and the irrepressible Benjamin Franklin of Pennsylvania, at eighty-one, the oldest.

The delegates, as a group, are often called the "Founding Fathers," because they were servants of the nation in its formative hours. Among them sixteen had been, or were later to be, governors. Fourteen would be Representatives and nineteen would be Senators. One would be a territorial governor; four would be Cabinet officers. Two would be presidents of the United States, and one would be a Vice-President. Two would be candidates for the presidency, and these and one other would be candidates for the vice-presidency. Among these many talented men, the most influential were Franklin and Washington. Both of them helped to furnish the experience and generosity by which conflicting interests were harmonized.

In session. From May 25 to September 17, 1787, the delegates held regular sessions. Secrecy was rigidly enforced so that persons outside the Convention would not be able to affect the discussions. Washington was so careful that even in his own diary he gave no hint of the nature of the debates. Today we know what went on from the notes that James Madison of Virginia kept. But because they were not published until 1840, the contemporary public remained in the dark concerning the details of the proceedings.

COMPETING PROPOSALS

Soon after the Convention was organized, the delegates reached a decision to revise the Articles so drastically as to necessitate drawing up a new Constitution. The meeting, there-

Washington presides at the Constitutional Convention in Philadelphia, as shown in an illustration from an American history of the early 1800's. Madison is the man at the table taking notes.

fore, is known as the Constitutional Convention. The result was the Constitution of the United States (see the Appendix of this book).

The large-state, or Virginia, plan. The opening move in the deliberations was made by Governor Edmund Randolph of Virginia. He introduced proposals that became known as the large-state, or Virginia, plan. This plan provided in the first place that the powers of government be separated into three branches— a legislative, an executive, and a judicial. Second, that there be a two-house legislature, the members of the upper house to be chosen by the lower. The number of members in both houses would be determined on the basis of population. Third, that the executive officer be chosen by the legislature and be ineligible for a second term. The executive, as well as the judiciary department, would be empowered to veto legislation, although subsequent votes by both houses of Congress could override such vetoes. Fourth, that a national judiciary, consisting of a supreme and inferior courts, be chosen by the legislature. The members of the judiciary would "hold their offices during good behavior." The Virginia plan provided also that amendments to the constitution might be made without the approval of the national legislature.

The small-state, or New Jersey, plan. Debate on the Virginia plan revealed the opposition of the small states—like Delaware, Connecticut, New Hampshire, and New Jersey*—which feared being devoured by the larger ones. On June 15 William Paterson of New Jersey put before the delegates what came to be known as the small-state, or New Jersey, plan.

The New Jersey plan continued to urge the revision rather than the abandonment of the Articles of Confederation. It provided for a one-house Congress, a plural executive—that is, one consisting of more than one person—to be chosen by Congress, and a national judiciary. The plan aimed to strengthen the government by designating as "the supreme law of the

respective States" all laws passed by Congress and all treaties made with foreign powers. The New Jersey plan also provided that each state would have one vote in Congress, its delegation to be chosen by its state legislature.

The Connecticut compromise. The disagreements between the large and small states over these two plans came close to breaking up the Convention. Good sense won out, however, and there emerged on July 16 what is called the Connecticut, or great, compromise, proposed by Connecticut's delegates. Eventually adopted, it provided for a two-house legislature. The House of Representatives, or lower house, with representation based on population, was to be elected every two years and was to have the sole right to originate money bills. The Senate, or upper house, whose members would be chosen by the respective state legislatures, would have equal representation for each state. Senators would vote individually, rather than by state, and serve for six years. #

When the matter of basing representation in the lower house on population was discussed, the delegates raised the question of how slaves would be counted. Were they to be counted in the same manner as the rest of the population, even though they were not expected to vote or hold office? The Connecticut compromise took care of this question. It included a provision that three-fifths of the slaves should be counted. Direct taxes would be levied on the same basis.

Argument on the slave trade. The slave trade was another vexing matter for the delegates. Northerners maintained that Congress should be able to pass navigation laws, levy taxes on imports or exports, and regulate the foreign slave trade. Southerners, as producers of commodities for foreign markets—tobacco, rice, cotton —wanted no export tax. Further, the South Carolina and Georgia delegations threatened to bolt the Convention if Congress was given the authority to control the slave trade. In the end, a bargain was made: Congress was given the power to regulate interstate and foreign commerce but not to levy an export tax. And Congress was not to interfere with the foreign slave trade before 1808.

---

* Rhode Island—the smallest state—did not send delegates to the Convention.

120 #After the small states gained equal representation in the Senate, their delegates were more willing to strengthen the national government. Those from large states accepted their situation.

Relationship between nation and states. Fundamental to the success of the new frame of government was the adoption of a new relationship between national (or federal) and state power. The Constitution and all the laws made in accordance with it were declared to be "the supreme Law of the Land."† Historians frequently have called this phrase the heart of the Constitution. First, it links the various parts of the Union together by making legislation apply everywhere; second, it gives the Supreme Court the basis for its power to declare laws, state or national, unconstitutional; third, it is the means by which the national government may act directly upon the people without necessarily having to work through the states.

The executive. One of the knottiest problems was creating the proper type of executive. The memory of an English king alleged to have been too powerful persuaded many delegates that the executive's term ought to be short. Others argued for a strong executive, drawing on the unhappy experience under the Confederation, when the nation had no chief executive. Alexander Hamilton, for example, at first declared that the President ought to be chosen for life. The term of office was finally fixed at four years.

The electoral college. Disagreement also developed between conservatives who thought the President should be selected by Congress and more radical delegates who thought he should be elected by the people direct. The Convention solved the problem by creating an electoral college to choose the President. Each state would have as many electors as the number of its Representatives and Senators in Congress.

Since a majority of the electoral votes was required for election, it was provided that in case no candidate received a majority, the House of Representatives, with each state having one vote, would select the President. It was expected that the House would frequently make the choice, but only two such occasions have arisen (see pages 142 and 175).

---

† Note the difference in meaning between this phrase and the one in the New Jersey plan, from which it was adapted, "supreme law of the . . . States."

A federal judiciary. There was almost no disagreement in Philadelphia concerning the establishment of a federal judiciary. The Virginia and New Jersey plans both recognized its necessity. The Convention provided for the creation of a Supreme Court, to be appointed by the President with the advice and consent of the Senate. It also authorized the organization of such lower courts as might be required.

COMPLETING THE INSTRUMENT

At last the almost completed document was turned over to committees of detail and of style to be put into final form. Its vigorous and precise phrasing is largely the work of Gouverneur Morris.

The signing. On September 17, 1787, the draft was formally presented to the delegates. Thirty-nine of those present affixed their names to it. In his notes Madison recorded: "Whilst the last members were signing it, Doctor Franklin, looking toward the President's chair, at the back of which a rising sun happened to be painted, observed to a few members near him, that painters had found it difficult to distinguish in their art a rising from a setting sun. 'I have,' said he, 'often and often in the course of the Session, and the vicissitudes of my hopes and fears as to its issue, looked at that [sun] behind the President without being able to tell whether it was rising or setting; but now at length I have the happiness to know that it is a rising and not a setting Sun.' " Their business having been concluded, the delegates took dinner together, bade one another farewell, and departed for their homes.

The grounds for opposition. Not many of the delegates were certain that the Constitution would ever go into effect. The assent of nine of the thirteen states—whose decisions would be made in specially chosen ratifying conventions —was required for adoption. Heated opposition in the states was expected because approval of the new instrument would be regarded as a reduction in the power of the states. Furthermore, the failure to include a bill of rights guaranteeing the basic English liberties of petition, assembly, speech, press, and jury trial was already arousing much anger and suspicion.

The range of agreement. It is important to be aware, however, that there had been full agreement at Philadelphia on fundamental issues. # These included the necessity to strengthen the national government, to prevent the irresponsible issuing of paper money, and to provide for national regulation of interstate commerce.

Those who might have been in disagreement simply had not been present in Philadelphia. Patrick Henry, for instance, had been asked to serve on the Virginia delegation but, guessing the kind of strong government the Convention would create, had refused. Later he explained, "I smelt a Rat."

The burning question now was, Would the state conventions ratify the Constitution?

STRUGGLE OVER RATIFICATION

The supporters of the Constitution, called Federalists, were in a favored position over those who opposed it—called Antifederalists. First, they included in their ranks a large number of Revolutionary War veterans, highly esteemed members of the clergy, and men of commerce and means. Madison's observation was correct: "The weight of abilities and of property is on the side of the Constitution." Second, the Federalists stood for something positive, whereas their opponents, who also recognized the need for change, had no alternative proposal to offer.

Persuasive essays. The remainder of 1787 and most of 1788 were months of argument and counterargument. Pamphlets, handbills, and papers were issued by both sides. The most famous document was a series of eighty-five essays called *The Federalist,* written by Hamilton, Madison, and Jay in support of ratification. First published in newspapers, these essays remain today the best commentary ever written on the Constitution. Yet the most compelling argument for ratification proved to be the general awareness that without the new Constitution the Union would probably fall apart.

First acceptances. As the state ratifying conventions began their work, Delaware led off with a unanimous acceptance of the Constitu-

tion on December 7, 1787. Five days later the Pennsylvania convention ratified it by a two-to-one majority—despite the fierce resentment of the Antifederalists. (They were angry because the convention had been called hastily; they charged that this had been done to prevent Antifederalist rural communities from being fully represented.) Shortly after Pennsylvania's action, New Jersey approved, followed by Georgia and Connecticut.

The battle in Massachusetts. Massachusetts gave the Federalists cause for worry. The memory of Shays' Rebellion was still green there, and the warm support the Constitution had among merchants in Boston made many people suspicious. Besides, two of the popular heroes of the Revolutionary era, Sam Adams and John Hancock, appeared to be opposed to ratification. In the end, although Adams was not won over to the Federalists, he was at least kept from open hostility.

Hancock was silenced when he was made chairman of the state ratifying convention and was whispered to about the possibility of becoming the vice-president of the United States! By a close vote Massachusetts ratified the Constitution in February, 1788, satisfying most Antifederalists by recommending amendments to it.

Triumphs in Virginia and New York. Maryland ratified the Constitution in April, and South Carolina in May. In June New Hampshire, by a narrow margin, became the ninth state to accept it. Although in fact the Constitution was now in operation, it could not really function until Virginia and New York ratified it. In Virginia the battle was sharp, with eminent men like Patrick Henry, Richard Henry Lee, and George Mason on the Antifederalist side against Federalists like Madison, young John Marshall, and George Washington. After recommending amendments to the Constitution, as Massachusetts had done, the Virginia convention ratified it by a hair's breadth.

New York was the only big state that now remained out of the fold. Governor George Clinton was a hot foe of ratification, but the Federalists had Alexander Hamilton on their side. By three votes the ratification resolution squeaked through late in July. Rhode Island and North Carolina—dominated by Antifederalists—did not come into the Union until well after its establishment; yet the new government could be launched without them.

The Bill of Rights. Many delegates to the ratifying conventions finally voted for the Constitution only because they had been given to understand that a bill of rights would be added to it. Such a guarantee against infringement of civil liberties by the federal government had not been included originally. The Convention had assumed that these rights already belonged to the people and had not been turned over to the central government.

When the first Congress met in 1789, it put among its most important duties the prepara-

tion of appropriate constitutional amendments that would guarantee certain civil liberties. Largely the work of James Madison, the first ten amendments to the Constitution, usually called the Bill of Rights, were ratified in 1791. Among the strongest bulwarks of the nation's freedom today, they will always be a tribute to the vigilance and foresight of eighteenth-century Americans.

Adoption. The Fourth of July, 1788, was a proud day in Philadelphia, where Francis Hopkinson, a signer of the Declaration, organized a "federal procession" to celebrate the adoption of the Constitution. Benjamin Rush, another patriot of the Revolution, in a letter to a friend described the spectacle—probably the greatest parade eighteenth-century America had ever witnessed:

Call attention to the information about Americans in the late 1700's this picture reveals.

A parade in New York City celebrating the adoption of the Constitution features a float in honor of the man whose arguments for ratification helped insure the establishment of the new national government.

New-York Historical Society

Men wore tricorn hats over their beribboned wigs. Every man is in knee breeches, and most of them wear long jackets over their waistcoats. Observe the spectacles at the far right.

The first thing that struck me in viewing the procession was the occasion of it. It was not to celebrate a victory obtained in blood over any part of our fellow creatures. No city reduced to ashes—no army conquered by capitulation—no news of slaughtered thousands brought the citizens of Philadelphia together. It was to celebrate a triumph of knowledge over ignorance, of virtue over vice, and of liberty over slavery. It was to celebrate the birth of a free government . . . and to establish and extend the blessings of peace. . . .

The achievement. The Constitution, sometimes called a "bundle of compromises" because it reconciled so many conflicting ideas, showed off the best eighteenth-century thinking on the nature of good government. It contained first of all the principle of the *separation of powers.* In accordance with this principle, the new government was divided into three theoretically separate and independent branches—executive, legislative, and judicial.

Second, the Constitution provided for a system of *checks and balances*‡ so that one branch could counter but not paralyze the actions of another. For instance, the President may veto a bill passed by Congress; Congress may check the President's action with a two-thirds vote in favor of the bill; the Supreme Court may check Congress by declaring the law unconstitutional. The President, with the approval of the Senate, makes appointments to the Supreme Court; by amendments proposed by Congress and approved by the people, even the Supreme Court can be checked.

Third, the Constitution contributed to the art of self-government a working formula for a *federal* union. Under the federal principle, the self-governing states are joined firmly under a central government capable of exercising power over common problems, while the states retain exclusive power over local matters.

One can easily see in Section 8 of Article 1 of the Constitution that Congress' power over war and peace, post roads, and coinage affects all of the states. The states keep all powers not expressly delegated to Congress. The federal government, however, is not handicapped by a lack of strength to deal with urgent questions. The last clause in Section 8 of Article 1—sometimes called the "elastic clause"—authorizes Congress "to make all laws which shall be necessary and proper for carrying into execution the foregoing powers." Of course some powers, like the power to levy taxes, are exercised by both the federal *and* the state governments. They are called *concurrent* powers.

The adoption of the Constitution completed the work of the Revolutionary generation. In the eleven years between 1776 and 1787 Americans had begun to learn how thirteen separate communities might live together harmoniously. It is illuminating that almost to a man the signers of the Declaration who were living in 1787 were on the side of the Federalists during the ratification controversy. The Declaration and the Constitution, far from being unrelated, are, in fact, two sides of the same shield. The Declaration announced the reasons which caused the American states to seek independence; the Constitution is the blueprint by which "the people of the United States" might, as its preamble says, "form a more perfect Union, establish justice, insure domestic tranquility, provide for the common defense, promote the general welfare, and secure the blessings of liberty. . . ."

Sum and Substance

1. Why were the proceedings at Philadelphia kept secret? How do we know what took place? 2. Compare the large-state and small-state plans. 3. Describe (*a*) the Connecticut compromise, (*b*) the compromise between the North and the South. 4. Explain the significance of the phrase "supreme Law of the Land," found in the Constitution. 5. What decisions were made concerning an executive? A federal judiciary? 6. What arguments were used for and against the Constitution? 7. What is the Bill of Rights? Account for its significance. 8. Explain the three basic principles of the Constitution.

‡ The man chiefly responsible for planning the system was James Madison, who, because of his magnificent contributions to the work of the Convention, is called the "Father of the Constitution."

##Students should find examples of the powers of Congress to take care of common problems. What actions are forbidden to the states? What powers do states have? Read Article 6.

#The questions here would make excellent test questions, perhaps combined with one asking for the identifications of certain names or terms under "Of Lasting Significance."

##This question introduces students to the complexity of making foreign policy.

THE WORKSHOP

OF LASTING SIGNIFICANCE

Identify or explain each of the following:

John Dickinson
Articles of
    Confederation
national domain
Thomas Jefferson
Land Ordinance of
    1785
Ohio Company of
    Associates
Scioto Company
Northwest Ordinance
stay laws
concurrent powers
Shays' Rebellion

Mount Vernon
    Conference
Annapolis Convention
Virginia plan
New Jersey plan
Connecticut
    compromise
electoral college
The Federalist
Antifederalists
Bill of Rights
federal union
"elastic clause"

INFORMED OPINION

1. The Constitution has been called "a bundle of compromises." Do you agree with this statement? Give your reasons.

2. Would you probably have favored or opposed the new Constitution—and why—if you had been (*a*) a banker in Rhode Island; (*b*) a farmer who was in debt; (*c*) a New York importer and exporter; (*d*) an owner of national bonds; (*e*) a Boston moneylender; (*f*) a southern shipper to the British West Indies?

3. Referring to the Constitution, which is printed in the Appendix, list in your own words the civil liberties guaranteed by the Bill of Rights. (The First Amendment alone includes four.) Give your ideas concerning (*a*) the reason for each guarantee; (*b*) the importance of each in a democracy; (*c*) a dictator's view of the guarantees.

UNRAVELING PUBLIC PROBLEMS

1. As the Articles of Confederation proved to be increasingly inadequate for the needs of the new country, the question arose, Should the Articles be revised, retaining such provisions as the equality of the states in Congress, or should they be replaced by a radically different constitution? Would you say that the Constitutional Convention answered this question wisely? Explain.

2. After the French and Indian War, the British tried to *eliminate* all problems connected with the land west of the Appalachians by issuing the Proclamation of 1763 (see page 68). Compare their way of handling the problems with the Congress' way at the close of the Revolution.

3. In dealing with England and Spain, the United States tolerated unfriendly actions—such as Britain's retention of the northwest forts and Spain's occupation of the southwest border. Was this policy wiser than one of insistence upon American rights, by arms if necessary? Give your reasons.

THE CONSTITUTION TODAY

In order to see the Constitution at work from day to day, bring in news clippings concerning the federal government's activities. Include decisions made by the Supreme Court (which are announced on Mondays when the Court is in session) and activities of the lower courts, Congress, and the executive departments. Presidential press conferences are important sources of news. Also, newsmagazines and weekend newspapers specialize in full reports of events, including cartoons, photographs, maps, diagrams, and news summaries.

To each clipping brought in should be added a brief explanation of its constitutional significance. This material might be arranged in a bulletin-board display, under such headings as "The Courts," "Congress," and "The President and Executive Departments" or under other headings. Later, individuals might use their clippings to add to scrapbooks of such material, which might be of lasting interest.

Periodically, students might make oral reports on the clippings they bring in, so that the class can ask questions and discuss issues involved. Questions relating to the Constitution should be settled by reference to appropriate sections of the document itself.

By giving attention to the Constitution throughout the year's work, students can see its relationship to federal and state activities and its influence on their own lives.

125

For inquiry: Ask students to look for evidence in this letter that would enable a person to identify the country that is referred to. (Evidence includes the references to carrying on a war in the first and fourth paragraphs, the reference to paper money in the third paragraph, the reference to emigrants in the sixth paragraph, and a clear statement to the effect that the nation being discussed is not in Europe--in the last paragraph.) Finding such evidence stimulates thinking and sharpens perception.

7

THE DAY OF THE FEDERALISTS

. . . order into our finances . . .

APRIL 30, 1781

. . . 'Tis by introducing order into our finances—by restoring public credit—not by gaining battles, that we are finally to gain our object. . . .

In the present system of things, the health of a State, particularly a commercial one, depends on a due quantity and regular circulation of cash, as much as the health of an animal body depends upon the due quantity and regular circulation of the blood. . . .

No paper credit [issue of paper money] can be substantial, or durable, [however] which has not funds [that is, backing in gold and silver], and which does not unite, immediately, the interest and influence of the moneyed men, in its

We would not regard the people shown here as a crowd, but in 1789 towns were not populous.

establishment and preservation. A credit begun on this basis, will, in process of time, greatly exceed its funds: but this requires time and a well-settled opinion in its favor. 'Tis in a national bank, alone, that we can find the ingredients to constitute a wholesome, solid, and beneficial credit. . . .

I see nothing to prevent the practicability of a plan of this kind, but a distrust of the final success of the war, which may make men afraid to risk any considerable part of their fortunes in the public funds; but, without being an enthusiast, I will venture to assert, that, with such a resource as is here proposed, the loss of our independence is impossible. All we have to fear is, that the want of money may disband the army, or . . . create in the people a general disgust and alarm, which may make them clamor for peace on any terms. . . .

Never did a nation unite more circumstances in its favor than we do; we have nothing against us but our own misconduct. . . .

Speaking within moderate bounds, our population will be doubled in thirty years; there will be a confluence of emigrants from all parts of the world, our commerce will have a proportionable progress, and of course our wealth and capacity for revenue. It will be a matter of choice if we are not out of debt in twenty years, without at all encumbering the people.

A national debt, if it is not excessive, will be to us a national blessing. It will be a powerful cement of our Union. It will also create a necessity for keeping up taxation to a degree which, without being oppressive, will be a spur to industry [that is, hard work], remote as we are from Europe. . . . We labor less now than any civilized nation of Europe; and a habit of labor in the people is as essential to the health and vigor of their minds and bodies, as it is to the welfare of the state. . . .

Alexander Hamilton wrote this perceptive letter to Robert Morris, the financier, just as the War for Independence was drawing to a close. Only twenty-six at the time, Hamilton already reveals his good grasp of the financial principles that, as Secretary of the Treasury a few years later, he made the basis of George Washington's program as President.

Like other Federalists, whose leading spokesman he was, Hamilton did not aspire to be a "man of the people." Conscious of the citizens' responsibilities—as well as rights—Hamilton was often on the unpopular side of public questions.

Ask why it is a citizen's responsibility to take at times the unpopular sides of questions.

The journey of General George Washington from his home at Mount Vernon to New York City for the first inauguration of a president of the United States ushered in the day of the Federalists. Sitting erect on horseback, the hero of the American Revolution rides toward a triumphal arch built and decorated by the people of Trenton, New Jersey. For them, the name Washington would always have a special association.

How does a President-elect today travel?

Columbian Magazine, 1789 (New-York Historical Society)

##Students should be able to recall what the special association was.

127

WASHINGTON TAKES THE WHEEL OF GOVERNMENT

The adoption of the Constitution was no doubt hastened by the general expectation that George Washington would be the first President. His talent, his experience, and his past service combined to make him an outstanding figure among his fellow Americans.

Not a sparkling personality like Franklin or a scholarly man like John Adams, Washington, nevertheless, could bring sound judgment # and integrity of character to the new country. Although he was a seaboard planter, he recognized that the future of American agriculture lay in the West; although his ties with Europe were many, he understood the importance of political isolation from Europe; although he owned slaves, he knew that slavery was a menace to a free people.

CREATING A NEW REGIME

The electors met in February, 1789, to cast their ballots for a President and Vice-President. Each was to vote for two men, and the man receiving the highest number of votes was to be President. The results would not be known until the new Congress met, at which time the votes would be counted.

The old Congress of the Confederation set March 4, 1789, as the date for the new Congress to convene. But when that day arrived, only eight Senators and thirteen Representatives had arrived in New York City, which had become the capital. Not until April 6 had enough Senators shown up to elect a tempo-## rary presiding officer, whose sole duty was to open and tally the electoral votes. When the ballots were counted, George Washington, to no one's surprise, was found to be the unanimous choice of the electors. He would be the President. John Adams, who had the second highest number of votes, was declared to be elected Vice-President.

Public acclaim. Duly notified of his election, Washington left his beloved Mount Vernon on April 16. He wrote to his former Chief of Artillery, Henry Knox, that "[m]y movements . . . will be accompanied by feel-ings not unlike those of a culprit who is going to the place of his execution, so unwilling am I, in the evening of a life nearly consumed in public cares, to quit a peaceful abode for an ocean of difficulties."

Revolutionary War veterans turned out everywhere to see their revered general once again and to pay homage to him. By the time Washington reached New York, people were in a state of excitement. Many had come great distances to witness the inauguration, and the inns and rooming houses of the city were filled to overflowing.

Breaking new ground. Probably that generation of Americans sensed that one era had ended and another had begun. They knew that almost every act Washington performed as President might set a precedent for the future. There was no model for him to copy, for as we must remember, he was the first President to be elected anywhere in the world.

There was not even agreement on how to address him! Roger Sherman, of Connecticut—

Federal Hall was planned to house Congress.

Washington takes the presidential oath of office at Federal Hall in New York City. The splendid building on Wall Street had just been completed.

Library of Congress

##Ask who presides over the Senate today (an opportunity to discuss the vice-presidency).

who, like Robert Morris, had signed all three of the first great national documents, the Declaration, the Articles, and the Constitution—was trying to find a more dignified and distinctive word than "Excellency." James Madison's idea that the simple title "President" was a suitable style of address finally won out, after the matter had even been heatedly discussed in the newspapers.

The first inauguration. Shortly after noon on April 30 Washington and his official associates made their way to Federal Hall, the new national Capitol in Wall Street. The President-elect stepped out onto the balcony, which was covered by a red-and-white-striped canopy, and there the chancellor of New York State, Robert R. Livingston, administered to him the oath of office.

Livingston then turned to the crowd below and shouted, "Long live George Washington, President of the United States"—a cry taken up by the people in the street. Moments later Washington began his inaugural address. Senator William Maclay of Pennsylvania, who was present, described the chief executive: "This great man was agitated and embarrassed more than ever he was by the leveled cannon or pointed musket."

Cabinet choices. Washington picked his Cabinet* tactfully. He selected Thomas Jefferson, a fellow Virginian, to be Secretary of State. This appointment pleased those who—like Jefferson himself—were not yet convinced that the new Constitution had been necessary or that it properly safeguarded the people's liberties.

Jefferson was minister to France at the time of his appointment, and six months passed before he assumed the new office. He would bring to the post not only broad experience but also a sure knowledge and appreciation of revolutionary forces then stirring in Europe. He had been an eyewitness in Paris to the beginnings of the French Revolution.

Washington chose Alexander Hamilton of New York to be Secretary of the Treasury. A hero of the Revolution, Hamilton was still in his mid-thirties. During the years of the Confederation he had devoted his considerable energy to establishing a powerful national government. Businessmen, rather than farmers, made him their champion. When New York ratified the Constitution, the merchants of New York City organized a gigantic procession which included a replica of a thirty-two-gun frigate flatteringly named the *Hamilton*. You saw a picture of it on page 123.

The forming of a lasting government had to be painstaking. The machinery for collecting taxes—which had been under state control—had to be created anew under federal law; federal courts had to be established to enforce and interpret the laws that Congress might pass. And the tough question of where the govern-

---

* The word *Cabinet* to describe the heads of the executive departments is not found in the Constitution and does not seem to have been used until about 1793. Yet the practice developed early of considering the men in the Cabinet personal advisers of Presidents in making policies. Cabinet officers, therefore, are sometimes called the President's "official family." In Washington's first administration Congress provided for three departments, State, Treasury, and War, and the office of the Attorney General.

How many have been added since Washington's first administration? (There are twelve now.)

Fire has always been a great threat to cities.

In private life Alexander Hamilton was a successful lawyer in New York City. He was also a director of one of the earliest fire insurance companies in America, whose purpose is dramatically portrayed here.

I. N. Phelps Stokes Collection, New York Public Library

THE
DEED OF SETTLEMENT
OF THE
Mutual Assurance Company,
FOR INSURING HOUSES FROM LOSS BY FIRE IN NEW YORK.

#Faith in the ability of people to solve their own problems is essential to democracy. See Question 5, col. 1, p. 143. Many of the problems must be solved through government, as Jefferson knew. Do students think Jefferson's point of view is practical? In what situation?

ment should be located permanently had to be answered.

Putting the Constitution into gear. Because there were no political parties, Washington depended heavily on the men who had been active in securing ratification of the Constitution. The most important were Hamilton, John Jay, James Wilson, and Robert Morris.

SEEDS OF DISCORD

Despite Washington's hope for harmony, two rival groups quickly developed in the administration, with Jefferson and Hamilton as the respective leaders. Each in his own way was a spokesman for new ideas which had become current in America in the thirteen years since the Declaration of Independence.

Jefferson's point of view. Jefferson conceived as his ideal an agricultural nation in which all men might be property owners. He believed that by nature men are good and that the purpose of government is to maintain an atmosphere in which the individual can pursue his own interests and goals without hindrance. Only in this way, he held, can good men likewise become happy men.

Jefferson had unbounded faith in the ability of people to solve their problems with a bare minimum of governmental action. He insisted passionately that every generation must make its own decisions about its destiny and never attempt to bind succeeding generations. Government, he said, must merit the continued approval of its citizens.

Hamilton's point of view. Hamilton, on the other hand, felt that since men are by nature weak, it is the task of government to control them. He was himself scrupulously honest, yet he doubted that others had equally high standards. Whether he ever really said "the people, Sir,

The artist lacked perspective, but his drawing shows a typical farm location along a stream.

This drawing of a newly cleared farm suggests the way of life Jefferson considered ideal. It illustrated a book a

Scotsman wrote about his travels in the interior of America. Observe the Indians in the foreground.

Rare Book Division, New York Public Library

is a great beast" is open to dispute, but the words adequately state his opposition to government by the people. The liberal ideas heard in America and in France at the end of the eighteenth century, which Jefferson so eloquently expressed, were alien to Hamilton.

Effects. The contrasting viewpoints of the two men resulted in clashing policies within Washington's administration. Jefferson wished to leave governing chiefly to the state and local governments, though he would limit all government as much as possible. Hamilton would attempt to make government a powerful national instrument for the advancement of the public interest. Jefferson would put his trust in the legislatures, whose members were elected by the people. Hamilton favored instead a strong executive leadership. Such differences made it impossible for these two men to work together smoothly.

It is wrong, however, to believe that Jefferson and Hamilton were at each other's throats from the outset. First of all, Hamilton took the oath of office in September, 1789, and it was not until the following March that Jefferson returned from Paris. Second, although Jefferson at first had been only lukewarm in his support of the Constitution, he had come to accept it.

He sincerely hoped that the new government would succeed, and in order to do his part, he expected to be on good terms with the Secretary of the Treasury.

Third, Jefferson and Hamilton had never met before they became associates in 1790. Twelve years older than the Secretary of the Treasury, Jefferson was better known, and Hamilton respected the achievements of his senior colleague.

It is doubtful that either man had at first a clear idea of the views of the other. Yet by August, 1792, President Washington was writing to both of them that each must be tolerant of the other lest their differences "tare the Machine asunder" and destroy the Union. What had happened?

Sum and Substance

1. In his letter to Morris, what arguments did Hamilton use for (*a*) restoring public credit; (*b*) establishing a national bank; (*c*) having a reasonable national debt? 2. Why was Washington the logical choice to be the first President? 3. Explain the slowness in putting the Constitution into effect. 4. Contrast the views of Jefferson and Hamilton. What government office did each hold?

This section deals with the measures Congress enacted to carry out Hamilton's plan.

THE FEDERALISTS RALLY ROUND HAMILTON'S PLAN

Hamilton was determined to establish the credit of the young country. He was concerned, but not actually alarmed, because the new government was already in debt.

FOUNDING PUBLIC CREDIT

Hamilton believed that the national debt, properly handled, could be one means of promoting the success of the young union of states. He insisted that businessmen and any others who held United States bonds—in other words, the creditors of the national government—would naturally want the nation to succeed and would support it staunchly. The national debt, therefore, far from being a public burden, could be turned into a "public blessing."

The national debt was of two kinds—foreign and domestic. The foreign debt had been incurred chiefly during the Revolution, when the Continental Congress had been forced to borrow money from foreign countries. The Confederation had also borrowed some money abroad. The domestic debt was owed to private citizens within the country, many of whom had loaned money to the Continental Congress by purchasing bonds.

Hamilton proposed also paying off the debts owed by various states. These had accumulated when the states sold bonds to meet their expenses in the Revolution.

Combining the debt. In January, 1790, Hamilton submitted to Congress his first Report on the Public Credit. In it he proposed that the national debt—both foreign and domestic—and the state debts should be combined and that the total (about $77,000,000) should be paid by the federal government. People who held government bonds would receive payments equal to their face value. Hamilton did not doubt that this sum could be met in gradual and regular installments and that the merchants would approve of the arrangement. He was not prepared for the storm of opposition that descended upon him from various parts of the country.

Resentful opposition. Of the plan to pay approximately $12,000,000 owed to foreign countries, there was almost universal approval. But the idea that the national government should be responsible for paying the state debts and the domestic debt in the manner proposed aroused severe criticism.

If the states had all been in debt, the story might have been different. But some had already taxed their citizens in order to wipe out their debts. Virginia, for example, had paid most of its obligations. Now, if Hamilton's plan went through, the new national government would tax the people of Virginia equally with those of Massachusetts and Connecticut—states that had left most of their debts unpaid.

Southerners were angry, too, because some of the bonds—both state and domestic—had been bought by speculators at very low prices from the original purchasers. Many speculators lived in such northern commercial centers as New York, Boston, and Philadelphia. Since these men stood to make a handsome profit on their meager investments, southerners directed their anger and resentment against the North, which was pictured as the stronghold of Hamilton's supporters.

James Madison was one of the most outspoken critics of Hamilton's plan, and, as he was considered "Father of the Constitution," his words were listened to. He did not favor refusing to pay the public debt, or even scaling it down; but he wanted justice for the *original* holders of the bonds. He advocated redeeming the bonds at the current market value and pay-

Art Commission of the City of New York

Hamilton was a short man, but his erect carriage, serious deep-blue eyes, and dignified manner—combined with his skill as a speaker—made him a convincing figure. Fond of luxury, he was always elegantly dressed.

ing to the original purchasers—many of whom had been Revolutionary soldiers—the difference between that value and the face value.

A bargain. Hamilton had a hard fight getting his plan through Congress, especially the part which provided for the paying of the state debts. He might have failed if he had not persuaded the Secretary of State to help him.

Jefferson agreed to obtain southern votes for the bill in return for Hamilton's pledge to support the situating of the national capital in a federal district between Virginia and Maryland. Later Jefferson said, "Of all the errors of my political life, this [bargain] has occasioned me the deepest regret." He came to believe he had been "duped" by Hamilton and "made a tool for forwarding his schemes."

##Madison's idea was turned down. There was no record showing who were the original holders, fo one thing. The capital was to be at Philadelphia for ten years and on the Potomac thereafter.

132

AUTHORIZING A BANK

Hamilton's program was still incomplete. In December, 1790, the Secretary submitted to Congress his second Report on the Public Credit. This provided for creating a Bank of the United States, under a charter from Congress to run for a period of twenty years.

The government would be authorized to buy 20 percent of the Bank's capital stock of $10,000,000. The remaining 80 percent of the capital stock was to be sold to private citizens, who might pay for it with specie (gold and silver coin) and new United States bonds. The Bank would have the power to issue bank notes, that is, paper money, in order to meet the monetary needs of the country.

Washington's hesitation. Fearing the power of the merchants and bankers, many opponents of the Bank bill were so outraged that Washington hesitated to sign it after Congress passed it in February, 1791. Particularly, he was afraid that the Constitution did not allow for such a bill—in other words, that it was unconstitutional. When his Attorney General, Edmund Randolph, pronounced the bill unconstitutional, Washington turned to Jefferson for an opinion.

"Strict construction." Jefferson responded by stating that Congress' powers were specifically named, or enumerated, in the Constitution and that the power to establish a bank was clearly not among them. He said it was a mistake to think that the Bank could be chartered under the elastic clause, which says that Congress may "make all laws which shall be necessary and proper" for implementing its powers (see page 124). The enumerated powers of Congress, he said, "can all be carried into execution without a bank. A bank therefore is not *necessary,* and consequently not authorized by this phrase." Jefferson's position, which was to interpret narrowly the powers of Congress, is known as *strict construction* of the Constitution.

"Loose construction." With two opinions before him opposing the Bank, Washington now asked Hamilton to state his views. Hamilton quickly swept aside Jefferson's statement that the Bank was "not necessary." He argued that the Bank was needed in raising and collecting taxes, because its issuing of bank notes would provide a stable currency (that is, sound paper money) with which people could pay the taxes. Hamilton favored what is known as *loose construction* of the Constitution—allowing the central government to exercise all powers not expressly forbidden to it. Washington felt convinced by Hamilton's argument and signed the Bank bill into law.

LAYING TAXES AND DUTIES

Hamilton's financial structure for the nation was almost finished, but taxes were necessary to support it. These would come from import duties and from *excise taxes*—internal taxes on the sale of certain commodities.

Angry farmers. There was little disagreement concerning the import duties. The opposition to excise taxes, however, was fierce, because one tax Hamilton proposed was to be on whisky. This aroused the western farmers who turned their grain into whisky—the most convenient form for transporting it eastward. Nevertheless, the Act of 1791 was passed, putting an excise tax of between nine and twenty-five cents on every gallon of whisky.

Whisky Rebellion. Defying the tax collectors in 1794, farmers of western Pennsylvania refused to pay the tax. This "Whisky Rebellion" was the first show of resistance to the new federal government, and Washington agreed to Hamilton's suggestion that soldiers be called out to enforce the law. The President himself led the troops into Pennsylvania before the resisting taxpayers gave up the struggle.

Unintended results. The military expedition had shown the power of the national government. It also had turned the frontiersmen into strong supporters of Jefferson. Carefully encouraged by him, they became the core of his political strength.

Toward an industrial nation. Hamilton's third and final report to Congress—the Report on Manufactures of 1791—was the most farseeing. In it Hamilton talked of the development of American industry. He called for government bounties to encourage manufacturers, exemp-

##Ask students to name some excise taxes today. Why do people especially dislike them? (They are conscious of paying any direct tax.) Why did the frontiersmen come to support Jefferson?

133

Philadelphia was the largest city in the United States in 1795, when this drawing of the Delaware waterfront was made. Hamilton looked beyond his era to a time when this city of 44,000 people would become a leading manufacturing center and a flourishing port that would rank among the busiest anywhere in the world.

#How did Hamilton justify the costs to taxpayers of the four measures he proposed?

tion from import duties on vital raw materials from abroad, roads and canals to facilitate the movement of goods, and *protective tariffs.* These tariffs would be import duties on goods manufactured abroad and would raise the price of those goods here and in this way "protect" American manufacturers producing similar goods. Hamilton thought that factory owners could add to the labor supply—as in England—by hiring women and children.

In an agricultural country this report was well ahead of its day, and Congress took no action on it. Jefferson, writing earlier, expressed the feeling of the times: "While we have land to labor then, let us never wish to see our citizens occupied at a workbench. . . . for the general operations of manufacture, let our workshops remain in Europe. . . . The mobs of great cities add just so much to the support of pure government, as sores do to the strength of the human body."

Taken as a whole. Hamilton's economic program established the credit of the United States, putting the young country on a sound financial footing. No one has ever paid him more deserved tribute than did Daniel Webster, who wrote years later: "He smote the rock of the national resources and abundant streams of revenue gushed forth. He touched the dead corpse of Public Credit, and it sprang upon its feet." Within a few years a nearly bankrupt nation basked in increasing prosperity.

Foreseeing the power and wealth that an industrial America could amass, Hamilton hoped to hasten their attainment. Jefferson had a vision of an agricultural country which would make its chief task the welfare of the individual. Hamilton and Jefferson seemed to be poles apart in their own day. But the ideas and ideals of both are woven into the American tradition. In fact, a persistently perplexing problem of the last hundred years has been how to preserve the individual's liberties and happiness in the face of demands made by industry—steadily growing larger. Hamilton's dream has been realized, but Jefferson's vision of a nation with a humanitarian purpose has never died.

Sum and Substance

1. Describe the nature of the national debt. How did Hamilton wish to deal with it? 2. What part of his proposal met criticism? Why? 3. How did he secure congressional approval? 4. How was the Bank bill involved in the controversy over strict and loose construction of the Constitution? Explain "strict construction" and "loose construction." 5. What was the Whisky Rebellion? 6. What were Hamilton's ideas for helping American industry?

##What in recent history shows that Jefferson's vision of a humanitarian national purpose has not died? How does the United States rank among nations today in industrial development?

POLITICAL PARTIES MAKE THEIR FIRST APPEARANCE

By 1792 the strife over Hamilton's financial policy had brought about the rise of political parties. In general, the Jeffersonians, led by Jefferson and Madison, were located in the rural sections of the North and South and in the frontier regions of the South and West. People called them Democratic-Republicans at first and later Republicans. In general, the supporters of Hamilton, who became known as Federalists, were found in the commercial centers of the East, where merchants and manufacturers were located.

Although Washington was reluctant to admit that political parties were appearing, the truth could not be denied. Jefferson, who hated controversy as much as Washington did, had become the leader of opposition to the policies of the administration. Nevertheless, at the request of his chief, Jefferson stayed as Secretary of State until the last day of 1793, when he resigned.

With party lines fast forming, the Federalists relied more heavily than ever on Washington's leadership. In 1792, although he yearned to retire to Mount Vernon, Washington was re-elected President. John Adams was again elected Vice-President.

THE IMPACT OF EUROPE

By the beginning of Washington's second term, events occurring thousands of miles from home were having a remarkable influence on American politics. Domestic and foreign policy became intertwined.

The French Revolution. When the French Revolution broke out in 1789, Americans almost everywhere had rejoiced. The French people, it seemed, were following the American example in revolting against a tyrannical king. Moreover, Americans had not forgotten the aid that France had extended during the Revolution; they were rejoicing over the success of a friend.

As news came from France, discontented people here reflected once more on their own freedom and on "dangers" to it. By 1793 Jefferson was telling the young Senator from Virginia, James Monroe, "All the old spirit of 1776 is rekindling."

Anti-English feeling. American feelings were greatly influenced by continued fear and distrust of England. The British still refused to leave the posts they occupied along the United States–Canadian border, as they had promised to do in the Treaty of Paris in 1783. They also continued to forbid American ships to carry on trade with the West Indies, and they attempted to collect long-standing debts in the southern states.

In 1793 England went to war against France. When this news reached the United States, many Americans saw no reason why the United States should not aid France by sending "riflemen and hardy woodmen." As a prominent westerner put it, "If Kings combine to support Kings, why not republics to support republics?"

The hostility toward England was strongest among people who thought they had been hurt by Hamilton's program. For this reason, the followers of Jefferson were pro-French in sympathy. It was the best way, it seemed to them, to look out for their own interests as farmers and planters.

The storming of a Paris prison—the Bastille—on July 14, 1789, marked the beginning of the French Revolution.
Research Libraries, New York Public Library

Reliance on Britain. Federalists, on the other hand, kept in mind that the prosperity of the country rested upon good relations between England and the United States. The British were America's best customers, and Americans theirs. Anything that interfered with British-American trade invited economic ruin.

Federalists warned that Britain's navy and privateers would paralyze or destroy America's overseas trade if the United States aided France. They even insisted that the United States ought to join England in the war against France. Consequently, Americans became pro-French or pro-English depending upon how they were affected by the domestic policies of the new federal government.

Neutrality Proclamation. In this crisis Washington consulted with his Cabinet. The Cabinet favored neutrality, and after lengthy discussion it was agreed to make this the country's policy. The announcement on April 22, 1793, has become known as Washington's Neutrality Proclamation. In it Washington pointed out that war with either France *or* England would be disastrous. He declared it was the country's "duty and interest" to be "friendly and impartial toward the belligerent powers."

The engaging Citizen Genêt. The resolve to remain neutral was soon tested by the arrival of Citizen Edmond Genêt. He was the first minister sent here by the new French republic established during the French Revolution. Instead of going straight to Philadelphia, then the seat of the federal government, he landed early in 1793 in Charleston, South Carolina. Slowly he made his way to the capital by way of the back country, where the supporters of Jefferson were most numerous.

The receptions that greeted Genêt as he proceeded northward were wild frenzies. Just turned thirty, witty in conversation and polished in manners, he was a public hero. John Adams declared afterward that if a yellow-fever epidemic had not occurred in Philadelphia, nothing could have saved the United States from yielding to the clamor "to declare war in favor of the French Revolution and against England." President Washington received Genêt coolly.

Despite much public enthusiasm for the Frenchman personally, the government's neutrality policy was unshakable. When Genêt defiantly fitted out a privateer to be sent against the English from an American port and threatened to appeal to the American people over the head of the President, his recall was demanded.†

Jefferson breathed a sigh of relief. He was aware, as he wrote to Madison, that Genêt's activities, if continued, would surely "sink the Republican interest." Everywhere the followers of Jefferson were embarrassed by Genet's behavior. Then news began to arrive of the terrible excesses of some French revolutionists, and Republicans as well as Federalists were horrified by the accounts. The wisdom of Washington's Neutrality Proclamation became clear even to those who had disputed it.

SETTLING DISAGREEMENTS

American relations with the British were stormy, too. But the Federalists were sympathetic to England, and they therefore kept trying to settle problems in British-American relations by negotiation.

The trading posts. The most serious American complaint was that ten years after the Treaty of Paris had ended the American Revolution, the English had still not withdrawn their soldiers and their flag from the trading posts in the North. Because the fur trade was profitable, the British seemed to have no intention of giving up the forts and getting off American soil.

In order to maintain themselves in the posts (see the map opposite), the British wooed the Indians, persuading them that American possession of the territory west of the Appalachians was only temporary. The redcoats, they said, would soon be back in full charge. The British also kept the Indians supplied with liquor, trinkets, and arms. Consequently, from 1783 on, the Indians, egged on by their English friends, often attacked the frontiersmen.

At Fallen Timbers. The Indians were convinced of British sincerity, especially when the British

---

† Genêt did not go home. He settled in New York, where shortly he married a daughter of Governor George Clinton, a Democratic-Republican who later served as Vice-President.

##Call attention to the fact that political leaders in a democracy are subjected to much criticism for their stands. A strong leader maintains his position in spite of criticism.

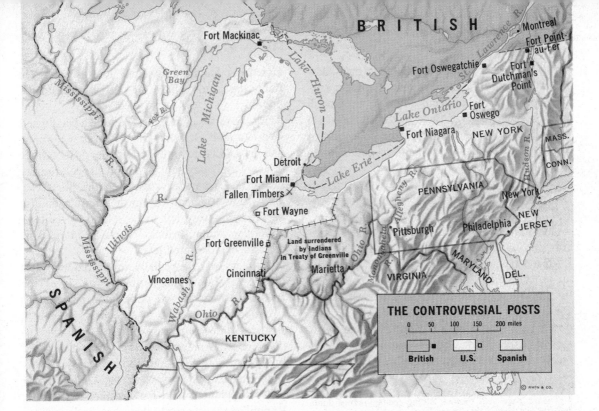

Trouble with the Indians on the western frontier, encouraged by the British in posts plainly on American land, led Washington to send General Wayne to the Northwest Territory. Settlers began to stream into the area outlined here as soon as they learned that the Treaty of Greenville had removed the hostile tribesmen.

This map clearly shows why the United States was irritated at the British over the trading posts.

built Fort Miami on the Maumee River—clearly on American soil—in order to protect Detroit. Word went through the forest in 1794 that the tribesmen should gather at the new fort by early summer to wage war against the Americans. To their dismay, on August 20, 1794, the American general "Mad Anthony" Wayne fell upon and defeated them at Fallen Timbers on the Maumee, near what is now Toledo.

Since the English commander at Detroit dared not attempt to aid the Indians with his mere handful of troops, the Indians were convinced that the English had betrayed them. The Indians had lost only fifty men in the battle but they knew that resistance was hopeless and that they would have to move westward again to lands that settlers did not yet want.‡

---

‡ Wayne assembled the Indian chiefs at Fort Greenville in 1795, and there they agreed to the Treaty of Greenville, under which they surrendered their rights to most of what is now Ohio.

Although the Indian threat was now broken, the British were still in the posts. How could the young government get them out?

Violations of neutrality. British activities elsewhere raised other questions. At war with France in 1793, England had ordered the seizure of any neutral vessel carrying foodstuffs to France or to ports under French control. It also ordered the detaining of neutral vessels engaged in trade with the French West Indies. Because the United States was the principal neutral concerned, the British shortly were seizing American ships and imprisoning the crews.

On the ocean as well as on the northern border of the United States, therefore, the English were scornful of American rights. Federalists in the shipping communities of the New England and middle states were as angry as the Republican frontiersmen. Once again hostility to England was uniting the country.

The Federalists, nevertheless, wishing to

#Genêt's activities and British violations of neutrality--not to mention the British refusal to leave the trading posts--all showed the lack of respect Europeans had for Americans.

avoid war with Britain at all costs, tried desperately to get the British seizure orders suspended. The Republicans wanted to punish England by stopping trade with it. Hamilton opposed such action, because the collecting of import duties—mainly on English goods—was helping his financial program to succeed. The Federalists temporarily quieted the Republicans by agreeing to send a special representative to England to discuss terms of a settlement.

Jay's treaty. But the choosing of Chief Justice John Jay as the representative brought protests from the Republican side because he was such an ardent Federalist. Being quickly confirmed by the Senate, however, he sailed for London. The protest against Jay's appointment was nothing compared with the outcry when word arrived in the United States that Jay had been received by the queen of England and had

kissed her hand. Roared one Republican, "He richly deserved to have his lips blistered to the bone!"

By the terms of Jay's treaty, which was signed in 1794, the British agreed—as they already had in 1783—to pull out of the posts. Other issues—the payment of pre-Revolutionary debts, the seizure of vessels on the high seas, and the settlement of northeastern-boundary differences—were left to be settled by British-American commissions. These commissions were to be appointed later.

Planters were especially infuriated by Jay's failure to obtain compensation for slaves the British had carried off during the Revolution. Frontiersmen resented that he had not won a British promise to cease plotting with the Indians in the American forest. Though Jay had probably obtained as favorable a treaty as possible, considering how weak the United States still was, planters and frontiersmen—generally Republicans—charged that he had ignored their interests.

In the South and the West, where the Republicans were already strong, John Jay was now burned in effigy, called traitor, and condemned at public meetings. Hamilton valiantly defended the treaty, insisting it was the best that America could hope for at that time. Again, # it was the firmness of George Washington that carried the day. Determined that there be no war, he urged the Senate to ratify the treaty, and the Senate obliged him after a tense debate. The Republicans outspokenly denounced Washington. Jefferson, for example, wrote of the President to a Virginia friend: "Curse on his virtues, they have undone the country."§

Pinckney's treaty. Both parties, however, were enthusiastic over the treaty with Spain that Thomas Pinckney negotiated and that the Senate ratified in 1796. It provided that the United States might freely navigate the Mississippi and deposit goods at New Orleans in warehouses (for later reshipment); that Spain's Florida

Americans gave vent to their strong feelings about John Jay and his treaty by hanging him in effigy.

Drawing by F. O. C. Darley, Library of Congress

Drawing by F. O. C. Darley, Courtesy Library of Congress

---

§ This remark should not be considered characteristic of Jefferson's judgment of Washington. In a calmer moment Jefferson once wrote: "He errs as other men do but he errs with ## integrity."

boundary be located along the 31st parallel; and that Indians living on Spanish territory be kept from raiding American settlements. Frontiersmen were delighted with Pinckney's treaty, and in a way this compensated them for the despised Jay Treaty.

ADAMS' LONELY ROAD

Washington now longed for retirement. During his first administration he had told Jefferson that he "really felt himself growing old, his bodily health less firm, his memory always bad, becoming worse." He had stood for reelection in 1792 because of the serious problems of foreign affairs. Now in 1796 he could go.

A nation well begun. Not all the outstanding questions had been settled, but the nation was improving its position and benefiting from Europe's distresses. If the British had not been at war with the French, they would not have agreed to Jay's treaty, inadequate as it was; if the Spanish had not feared the British, they would not have agreed to Pinckney's treaty. Yet even without these bits of luck, it was clear that by the close of Washington's administration the national government had been firmly established.

Washington's retirement. In his last year in office Washington delivered a farewell address to his countrymen. In it he warned against allowing political parties to weaken the national unity which many had worked so hard to achieve and upon which liberty itself depended. He emphasized the importance of religion, both to the nation and to the individual, in maintaining a high standard of morality. He declared that "it is our true policy to steer clear of permanent alliances with any portion of the foreign world." Only in this way, he said, could the United States "observe good faith and justice toward all nations."

Transfer of power. John Adams, who had been the Vice-President during Washington's two administrations, was elected President in 1796. Thomas Jefferson was chosen as the Vice-President.

Adams took over the presidency in an orderly fashion on March 4, 1797. The event demonstrated to the world that free men could, without upsetting their affairs, change the heads of their government.

Adams, deeply moved, wrote to his wife, Abigail, who could not be present for his inauguration: "A solemn scene it was, indeed; and it was made more affecting to me by the presence of the General, whose countenance was as serene and unclouded as the day. . . . In the Chamber of the House of Representatives was a multitude as great as the space could contain, and I believe scarcely a dry eye but Washington's. . . . All agree that taken altogether, it was the sublimest thing ever exhibited in America."

The new chief. Adams, a New England lawyer, had been a leader of the Revolution. Known as the "Atlas of Independence" because he bore so much of the burden of the Revolution on his own shoulders, he slaved in the public service and expected others to do the same. It was the purpose of government, he thought, to control unruly mankind—not, as Jefferson believed, to give mankind an opportunity to grow and flourish. Adams' fascinating diary and the revealing letters he wrote to his wife, one of the most accomplished women in North America, show the second President to have been as demanding of himself as of others.

Adams was a man of high principle, and he would never alter his views merely for party purposes. He once confided to his diary, "Vanity, I am sensible, is my cardinal vice and cardinal folly." But he worked to keep it suppressed, and he never allowed the possibility of public popularity to sway him from a position he had decided was right.

Without Washington, political bickering became even more intense. Not only was there the division between Republicans and Federalists, but also there was a split between Adams men and Hamilton men within the Federalists' ranks. The Hamiltonians believed—wrongly—that Adams was little interested in the continuing success of Hamilton's financial program. They also thought that the President was weakening Federalist support among the voters by refusing to coöperate with other party leaders.

Washington, D.C., as it looked in the administration of John Adams. The "President's House," which the Adams family was the first to occupy, is in the background. The building at the far right is the capital's new post office.

The "President's House" is the large white building at the far left in the background.

Foolishly keeping Washington's Cabinet practically unchanged, Adams soon found that he was surrounded by followers of Hamilton, who himself had retired to New York to practice law. These men betrayed Cabinet secrets and often appeared to be taking orders from Hamilton rather than from the President.

THE RECALL OF MONROE

Foreign affairs once again caused domestic rifts to show themselves. Just before Washington's administration ended, the American minister to France, James Monroe, was called home. Although popular in France, he was too Republican for the Federalists. To replace him, the United States sent General Charles C. Pinckney, a South Carolina Federalist. Angered because its friend and supporter, Monroe, had been recalled, the French government refused to accept Pinckney.

The X Y Z affair. Since every country judges for itself whether a minister or ambassador is acceptable to it and France had said Pinckney was not, the next move was Adams'. He appointed three men, Pinckney, Elbridge Gerry, of Massachusetts, and John Marshall, of Virginia, to discuss with the French the possibility of repairing diplomatic relations.

Shortly after the Americans arrived in Paris in October, 1797, they were approached by three go-betweens representing Talleyrand, the French foreign minister. These emissaries informed the Americans that for a price they could obtain what they wanted. The price: a bribe of $240,000 and a loan to France. This encounter became known as the X Y Z affair after Adams in reporting it to Congress referred to the three mysterious French personages as X, Y, and Z.

Although bribes were commonplace in diplomacy, Americans felt gravely offended when they heard the facts in the spring of 1798. People talked heatedly of war. The cry went up, "Millions for defense but not one cent for tribute." One of the country's earliest patriotic songs, "Hail, Columbia," was written during this crisis.

A decision for peace. Had Adams been a different kind of man, he could have become a hero overnight by taking the country into war. Many Federalists were, in fact, calling for such a course. Adams had decided, however, to throw away the possibility of a war President's popularity for himself by negotiating peace with France. If he had taken the easy road to war, many Republicans would have supported

#Again an emphasis on the integrity of the early American leaders. Adams in a sense had a more difficult situation than Washington had had, since both parties favored war in 1798.

him, since anti-French feeling ran high among them, too. Besides, war might have insured victory for the Federalists at the polls in 1800.

The negotiations with France proved successful, and in pressing them Adams sacrificed the people's acclaim and a second term as President. Years later he wrote: "I will defend my missions to France, as long as I have an eye to direct my hand, or a finger to hold my pen. . . . I desire. no other inscription over my gravestone than: 'Here lies John Adams, who took upon himself the responsibility of peace with France in the year 1800.' " For his brave and selfless act Adams earned only the contempt of his fellow Federalists.

NAME-CALLING AT HOME

The Republicans, appreciative of Adams' peaceful foreign policy, should have felt kindly toward him. But they did not. At the height of the war frenzy in 1798, the Federalist Congress had passed some laws aimed directly at the growing power of the Republican party. Having signed them, Adams was blamed for them.

The laws had grown out of the bad blood between the two parties. The Federalists had become used to picturing the Republicans as friends of democracy and as traitors taking orders from France. The Federalists feared democracy as "a government by the passions of the multitude, or . . . according to the vices and ambition of their leaders." They shuddered at the ideas behind the slogan of the French Revolution—"Liberty, Equality, Fraternity." As one of them said, "We do not wish to divide our property with idlers, nor daily tremble at the guillotine." Federalists believed that a Republican triumph in the next national election would be a victory of evil over good. How could they prevent it?

The Naturalization Act. The first step was the Naturalization Act of 1798, which would increase from five to fourteen years the time required for an immigrant to become an American citizen. Because immigrants were inclined to support the Republicans, this measure would make it harder for the Republicans

to recruit new members and votes.

The Alien and Sedition Acts. The second step followed from the first. A number of immigrants were leaders in the Republican party—men like Albert Gallatin, of Pennsylvania, who had been born in Switzerland, and Jefferson's friend, from France, E. I. du Pont de Nemours. In June, 1798, Congress passed the Alien Act, which authorized the President to expel from the United States all foreigners regarded as dangerous to the public peace and safety or suspected of "treasonable or secret" intentions. With this powerful law, the Federalists could strike at key Republicans on a moment's notice.

The most controversial step, though, was the passage of the Sedition Act in July. It made it a high misdemeanor, punishable by severe fine and imprisonment, for citizens or aliens to combine unlawfully to oppose the execution of laws, or to aid or attempt "any insurrection, riot, unlawful assembly, or combination." This act also provided for the punishment of persons convicted of publishing "any false, scandalous and malicious writing" discrediting the President, Congress, or the national government.

The Sedition Act was carefully designed to ## stifle anyone who said the Republicans could direct the federal government better than the Federalists. Said one Republican, "What an excellent harmonizer of parties the sedition bill will be; they must all sing to the same tune."

The irony was that this act, which protected President Adams and other federal officeholders from the criticism of the Republicans, was not used to protect Jefferson, the Republican Vice-President, from the Federalists! They slandered Jefferson mercilessly, picturing him as seeking "the utter subversion of our Government, the introduction of French *fraternity,* and the Slavery of the American people." It is to Adams' great credit that, although he supported the passage of these laws, he never approved the use of them for party purposes. Jefferson remained patient, convinced that "the reign of Witches" would soon come to an end.

Sharp reaction. Jefferson feared, though, that if the Federalists succeeded in smashing the Republicans, the United States government would

##Washington himself deplored newspaper criticism. Under the Sedition Law, a man was fined $100 for saying he wished that a cannon fired in salute had hit the President.

141

become a tyranny in which the Senate and President would be elected for life. He and Madison concluded that the states should have the right to decide whether or not laws were constitutional. The two men believed that the Sedition Act was clearly unconstitutional, because it violated the First Amendment, which protects freedom of speech, press, assembly, and petition. They thought that to leave the law unchallenged would be, in effect, to say the Constitution was a dead letter.

Virginia and Kentucky resolutions. Stirred to wrath, Madison and Jefferson wrote resolutions late in 1798 which were adopted by the legislatures of Virginia and Kentucky. These Virginia and Kentucky resolutions pronounced the Alien and Sedition Acts unconstitutional. Jefferson declared that liberty would end if no protection existed "against the passions and the powers of a majority of Congress." The need was plain: states must have the right to declare null and void any federal law which they thought violated the Constitution. The states, Madison maintained, "have the right and are in duty bound to interpose [step in] for arresting the progress of the evil."

In later years, the champions of *states' rights* accepted the principle set down by Jefferson and Madison in their resolutions. This was that the states had the right to decide whether an act of Congress violated the Constitution.

The election of 1800. A result of the Alien and Sedition Acts was to make Jefferson more popular than ever with farmers and frontiersmen, who by 1800 had many reasons for being Republican anyway. The Federalists that year nominated John Adams and C. C. Pinckney, of South Carolina, and the Republicans selected Jefferson and Aaron Burr, a New York politician. The presidential campaign was furiously fought, Jefferson being pilloried as "mad Tom" and as an "apostle of the race-track and the cockpit."

All the arguments used by both sides against each other for a decade boiled to the surface again. Supporters of Jefferson insisted that the nation's liberties would be endangered if the Federalists should win again; Adams' friends were equally convinced that Jefferson's election would doom the republic.

Tie vote untied. The election returns showed how the political outlook of the country was changing. The Federalists, as expected, carried New England, but New York and most of the South went Republican. Jefferson and Burr were tied for the presidency with seventy-three votes each. The Constitution had not provided for separate voting for the President and the Vice-President, ‖ and the election had to be thrown into the House of Representatives. Judging Jefferson less dangerous than Burr, Hamilton urged the Federalists to support his old rival.

Jefferson's election ended the Federalist era. The Republicans, who had been political "outs," had discovered that by organizing on a national scale they could capture the presidency. Jefferson called his triumph a "pacific revolution." Late in life he said: "The revolution of 1800 was as real a revolution in the principles of our government as that of 1776 . . . not effected, indeed by the sword, as that, but by the national and peaceable instrument of reform, the suffrage of the people." Jefferson and his followers would now have their turn in power.

Sum and Substance

1. Why did political parties appear? Who were their leaders? 2. How did the parties differ in their attitudes toward England and France? 3. Why did Washington favor neutrality? 4. Explain the recall of Genêt. 5. How was the controversy over the trading posts settled? 6. Explain the varying reactions to the Jay Treaty. 7. Whom did Pinckney's treaty please, and why? 8. What trouble rose among Federalists in Adams' term? 9. Describe the X Y Z affair. 10. Name and describe the controversial acts of 1798, and account for them. How did Madison and Jefferson respond? 11. What principle was accepted by the champions of states' rights? 12. Account for the Twelfth Amendment. 13. In what way was Jefferson's election a "revolution"?

‖ This defect was remedied in 1804, when the Twelfth Amendment was adopted.

##The class should read the Twelfth Amendment (p. 805) and particularly the commentary on it, which gives details about presidential elections today.

THE WORKSHOP

OF LASTING SIGNIFICANCE

Explain the importance of each of the following in the day of the Federalists.

Alexander Hamilton
Cabinet
Thomas Jefferson
domestic debt
Reports on the Public
   Credit
Bank of the
   United States
strict construction
loose construction
excise taxes
Whisky Rebellion
protective tariff
Republicans
Federalists
French Revolution

Neutrality
   Proclamation
Citizen Genêt
Battle of Fallen
   Timbers
Anthony Wayne
Jay Treaty
Pinckney Treaty
John Adams
X Y Z affair
Naturalization Act
Alien and Sedition
   Acts
Kentucky and Virginia
   resolutions
Twelfth Amendment

AMERICAN DEMOCRACY

1. What caused the appearance of the first political parties? To what extent were they formed on geographic lines? On economic lines?

2. In the election of 1796, a Federalist was chosen as President and a Republican as Vice-President. How was this possible? Could this happen today? Explain.

3. Look up the trial of Peter Zenger, the colonial printer who got into trouble in 1734. What principle did the verdict strengthen? How did the Sedition Act violate this principle?

4. Why do political parties always develop in a democracy? Why does a democracy have two or more, and a dictatorship only one?

5. Today faith in the ability of people to solve their own problems is recognized as a fundamental principle of democracy. Why *is* this principle fundamental to democracy?

6. In what respect was the American Revolution a victory for this principle?

7. In what ways can young people today strengthen the democratic principle which is stated above? How can they weaken it?

8. How is education related to the principle? What evidence is there that Jefferson believed in such a relationship?

9. Contrast Jefferson's point of view concerning people with that of Hamilton. How was each man's attitude toward government related to his viewpoint on people?

INTERNATIONAL POLITICS

1. There is a close relationship between the domestic and international politics of any country. How did domestic politics affect Americans' viewpoints regarding the situation in Europe between 1789 and 1793?

2. The President with the help of advisers makes foreign policy. What policy did Washington formulate in 1793? What consideration doubtless influenced him and his Cabinet?

3. How was Washington's handling of Citizen Genêt true to his policy?

4. In what ways did Britain embarrass Washington and his administration? How did Washington seek to solve problems the British raised? With what results?

5. How do the Jay and Pinckney treaties illustrate that the United States early profited from European troubles?

6. What advice about American foreign policy did Washington give his countrymen when he left the presidency? What reasons did he give for the various points he made? Do you think his advice applies today? Explain.

7. What crisis in American domestic politics did the X Y Z affair cause? What courses were open to Adams? Which did he choose? What were the results for him? For the country?

BEING A SOCIAL SCIENTIST

1. Compare the visions of the future United States Hamilton and Jefferson each had. How have the hopes of each man been realized?

2. How many members of the President's "official family" are there today? Which have been added since Washington's presidency? How do you account for the additions?

This chapter covers the period from 1800 through 1815. Jefferson's two terms are discussed in some detail, since they had tremendous influence on the country. The quotation used here beautifully expresses his trust in the ability of the people to solve their own problems. Observe Jefferson's use of "interposition" (lines 6-7). "Interpose" was used in the Kentucky and Virginia Resolutions (see p. 142). How did Jefferson believe "irregular interpositions" could be prevented? Ask: How does Jefferson show his faith in education? How does he exhibit his distrust of government? See "Documents in History," p. 161.

8

THE REPUBLICANS IN PEACE AND WAR

Cherish therefore
the spirit of our people . . .

The tumults in America [Shays' Rebellion], I expected would have produced in Europe an unfavorable opinion of our political state. But it has not. On the contrary, the small effect of those tumults seems to have given more confidence in the firmness of our governments. The interposition of the people themselves on the side of government has had a great effect on the opinion here. I am persuaded myself that the good sense of the people will always be found to be the best army. They may be led astray for a moment, but will soon correct themselves. The people are the only censors of their governors: and even their errors will tend to keep these to the true principles of their institution.

To punish these errors too severely would be to suppress the only safeguard of the public

The Stars and Stripes--already a national symbol--waves in a number of places.

#In 1782 the Continental Congress had guaranteed that mail would be private (before that, letters were commonly opened), but evidently there was no privacy in France, or at least on the packet (ship) that carried mail across the Atlantic.

liberty. The way to prevent these irregular interpositions of the people is to give them full information of their affairs thro' the channel of the public papers, and to contrive that those papers should penetrate the whole mass of the people. The basis of our governments being the opinion of the people, the very first object should be to keep that right; and were it left to me to decide whether we should have a government without newspapers, or newspapers without a government, I should not hesitate a moment to prefer the latter. But I should mean that every man should receive those papers, and be capable of reading them. . . .

Cherish therefore the spirit of our people, and keep alive their attention. Do not be too severe upon their errors, but reclaim them by enlightening them. If once they become inattentive to the public affairs, you and I, and Congress, and Assemblies, judges and governors, shall all become wolves. It seems to be the law of our general nature, in spite of individual exceptions; and experience declares that man is the only animal which devours his own kind, for I can apply no milder term to the governments of Europe, and to the general prey of the rich on the poor. . . .

I shall be happy to hear from you some times, only observing that whatever passes thro' the post is read, and that when you write what should be read only by myself only, you must be so good as to confine your letter to some passenger or # officer of the packet.

From France, where he was United States minister, Thomas Jefferson wrote this letter to a friend in Virginia on January 16, 1787. Jefferson had only recently learned of Shays' Rebellion in Massachusetts. Although he deplored this outbreak of violence against law and order, he remained trustful of the great mass of people. Jefferson's optimistic view of mankind contrasted sharply with the Federalists' philosophy (see again pages 130–131).

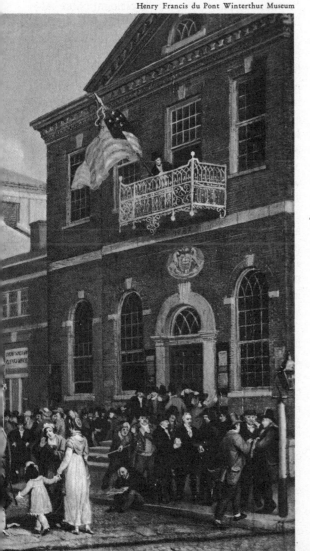

The polls are evidently at the far left, where placards announce the election. A man sitting on the curb at the right is reading a newspaper. Observe the lampposts. At the time, possibly 75,000 people lived in Philadelphia.

The spirit of Americans in the early 1800's—a rollicking crowd in Philadelphia on Election Day, which was an occasion calling for a turnout of the whole family. Electioneering—carried on just outside the polls—vending at the curbside, children playing, and dogs romping add to the festive atmosphere in a time when people generally were becoming increasingly attentive to public affairs.

145

JEFFERSON AND HIS COLLEAGUES COME INTO POWER

When Jefferson became President in 1801, the republic was well begun but still crude. Nothing was more symbolic of its condition than the recently built house* of the President in the new capital, Washington, D.C. John and Abigail Adams were the first to occupy it after the city of Washington became the seat of government in 1800.

Even by the time Jefferson moved in, the slate roof still leaked a little, and it continued to leak for some years. Furnishings were sparse, being mainly pieces that Washington and Adams had used. Jefferson set about completing both the government and the President's House. He was to find what all the chief executives have learned: neither job is ever wholly done.

THE MAN AND THE TASK

Jefferson brought to the presidency vast legislative, diplomatic, and executive experience. A shy person and a poor public speaker, he possessed nevertheless a pleasing way and disposition. Jefferson, a fifty-eight-year-old widower, relied on Dolley Madison to be his hostess when he entertained in Washington.

An observant British diplomat described the President's appearance in 1804: "He was a tall man, with a very red freckled face, and gray neglected hair; his manner good-natured, frank, and rather friendly, though he had somewhat of a cynical expression of countenance. He wore a blue coat, a thick gray-colored hairy waistcoat, with a red under-waistcoat lapped over it, green velveteen breeches with pearl buttons, yarn stockings, and slippers down at the heels—his appearance being very much like that of a tall, large-boned farmer."

Jefferson's most important task, as he himself saw it, was to gain the goodwill of the Federalists without at the same time forsaking his own supporters. As he took office, he delivered in his inaugural address a memorable appeal for political peace. ". . . every difference of opinion," he said, "is not a difference of principle. We have called by different names brethren of the same principle. We are all republicans, we are all federalists." He was President of the whole American people, and he pledged himself to the "encouragement of agriculture, and of commerce as its handmaid." (The Federalists were pleasantly surprised that the mischief they expected was not being planned.)

A harmonious Cabinet. Jefferson selected James Madison, an old friend and co-worker, as Secretary of State. "Little Jemmy," only slightly over 5 feet tall, was one of the principal architects of the Constitution and organizers of the Republican party. The new President chose Albert Gallatin to be Secretary of the Treasury.

The Cabinet as a whole was talented and harmonious. Jefferson named no Federalists—he was determined to have no bickering in his midst or leaking of secrets to his political enemies. When he appointed new federal jobholders, Jefferson almost without exception picked Republicans. He had resolved to inaugurate *Republican* policies.

Party program. One of Jefferson's first steps was to obtain the repeal of the Judiciary Act of 1801, passed by Congress shortly before the end of Adams' administration. This act had created sixteen circuit courts and provided for a judge in each one—arrangements which the Jeffersonians believed unnecessarily expanded the federal court system. A new Judiciary Act in 1802, more acceptable to Republicans, provided for only six circuit courts.

Also, Jefferson pardoned those who had been imprisoned under the Alien and Sedition Acts—many were his own friends—and he persuaded Congress to repeal the Naturalization Act. Moreover, Jefferson lowered taxes and reduced the national debt—from $83,038,000 in 1801 to $57,023,000 in 1809.

Jefferson and Gallatin practiced economy in government wherever they could. They cut support to the navy because they believed that a

---

* It became known popularly as the "White House" after 1814 when it was painted white in order to conceal the charring caused by the fire British soldiers set (see page 159). Theodore Roosevelt made the name official at the beginning of the twentieth century when he had it engraved on the presidential stationery.

navy was useful only to get the country into wars for the benefit of businessmen. To protect coastal shipping, the President authorized the construction of small gunboats that could be hauled ashore when not required at sea. This scheme turned out to be notably unsuccessful. After one of the vessels was washed inland during a heavy storm, a critic of Jefferson jeered, "If our gunboats are of no use upon the water, may they at least be useful upon the land."

The Barbary pirates. Despite his policy of reducing the navy and the cost of government, Jefferson felt forced to fight an expensive war. The enemy was the Barbary pirates, who preyed upon American trade in the Mediterranean Sea. Operating out of bases along the Barbary coast—the shores of Morocco, Algeria, Tunis, and Tripoli in North Africa—these corsairs raided or seized American vessels. The pirates often imprisoned the crews and passengers and held them for ransom. Some nations, including the United States, had avoided such attacks on their ships by paying tribute to their tormentors. This the President refused to do, sending ships of war instead to defend the interests of the

United States in the Mediterranean.

Although Jefferson tried to avoid open hostilities by negotiating, Tripoli commenced war against the United States in May, 1801. The Tripolitan War lasted until the pasha of Tripoli signed a peace treaty in 1805. Yet it was 1816 before the United States could force Algeria to make treaty terms ending the pirates' raids.

How strange it must have seemed to a Virginia planter like Jefferson to be defending American honor and liberty in a place as remote as North Africa then was. From the earliest days, however, American Presidents have had to think beyond domestic politics and party principles to the defense of the nation's place in the world.

FRUSTRATION: THE JUDICIARY

At home there were hostilities of a different sort: Jefferson was increasingly annoyed by the political bias of the courts. Although the legislative and executive branches of the government were now Republican, the judiciary remained solidly Federalist. In fact, in the closing minutes of his administration, Adams had named

Well situated for keeping tab on ships entering the Mediterranean, the Barbary pirates were brigands of the sea.

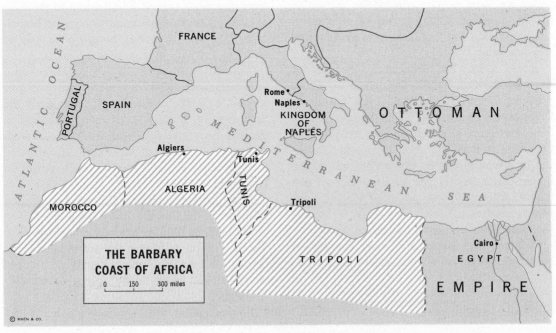

THE BARBARY
COAST OF AFRICA

0   150   300 miles

The Mediterranean coast of North Africa is still sometimes spoken of as the Barbary coast.
Ask what countries share this coast today. (Morocco, Algeria, Tunisia, Libya, Egypt.)

Federalists to the new court posts created by the Judiciary Act of 1801. These judges, many of whom were kept on under the Judiciary Act of 1802, ordinarily did not hesitate in the least to make partisan speeches to grand and trial juries. The courts, therefore, were strongholds for the opponents of the administration.

Mr. Marbury's case. Jefferson had refused to issue commissions of office to those of Adams' last-minute judicial appointees—the "midnight judges"—who had not already received them. One of the frustrated appointees was William Marbury, named to be justice of the peace in the District of Columbia. In 1803 he took his case—the case of *Marbury* v. *Madison*—to the Supreme Court to secure a writ of mandamus† forcing Secretary of State James Madison to issue him his commission.

The Chief Justice of the United States, John Marshall, a staunch Federalist himself, knew that if the Court issued the writ Marbury sought, Madison would ignore it. But if the Court did not issue it, the Republicans would appear to have won a victory. Marshall found a way out by referring to the Judiciary Act of 1789, which had created the federal court system. He declared that according to the Act Marbury was entitled to the writ, but the Court could not issue it. The reason: the section of the Act authorizing the issuance of such a writ conflicted with the Constitution and therefore was not valid.

Judicial review. The decision in the case of *Marbury* v. *Madison* was the first in which the Supreme Court had declared a law passed by Congress unconstitutional. This function of the Supreme Court is called *judicial review*. The Constitution does not directly provide for it, but its establishment by Marshall is one of the major landmarks in the development of the nation. After 1803 the power of the judiciary was as great as that of the legislative or executive branches—in fact as well as in theory.

Jefferson was discovering that changes in governmental policy are not easily made. The

Bank of the United States and the rest of Hamilton's financial program—all of which seemed to be working well—he left untouched. His policy of scrapping the navy had had to yield to the needs of foreign affairs. The Federalists remained in control of the judiciary. The Jeffersonians would have had little to show for their first administration had it not been for an exceptional stroke of luck in foreign affairs—the purchase of Louisiana in 1803.

TRIUMPH: LOUISIANA

The history of Louisiana (see page 67) was interwoven with the struggle for power in Europe. In 1762, just as the French and Indian War was ending, the French had transferred Louisiana—their land west of the Mississippi—to Spain, lest, like Canada, it fall to the victorious British. But the French had never lost hope that one day it would be theirs again.

Napoleon's New World scheme. In 1799 Napoleon Bonaparte became the powerful ruler of France. Having already gained control of much of continental Europe through military victories, he had hoped to defeat England also by seizing first Egypt and then India. The British navy ended this dream with a great victory over the French on the Nile River in 1798. Napoleon thereupon turned his attention to the New World, making up his mind to recover Louisiana. If he was successful, he might be able to strike at England by conquering Canada.

Through maneuvering begun in 1800, Napoleon persuaded Spain in a secret treaty to give Louisiana back to France. He convinced the Spanish that Spain was not strong enough to prevent aggressive American frontiersmen from entering its colonies of Mexico, California, and the Floridas. It would need French power in Louisiana.

In return for Louisiana (the Spanish refused to throw in the Floridas, too) Napoleon agreed to establish in Italy an independent kingdom—Tuscany. Because France delayed in keeping its part of the bargain, it was not until the autumn of 1802 that Spain finally agreed to transfer Louisiana.

In their plans for a revived empire in the

---

† This is a court order compelling a public officer to perform a particular act required by his office.

New Orleans, the strategically placed port on the Mississippi River, about the time of the Louisiana Purchase.

Sailing ships and boats are shown here on the river. Observe the church--the tallest building.

New World, the French considered Louisiana and the Caribbean islands a unit. Louisiana would supply the foodstuffs and timber that the tropical islands required. Santo Domingo, the chief French possession in the West Indies, would become a naval base from which Louisiana would be defended.

The President's alarm. When news of the transfer of Louisiana to France reached Jefferson's ears—it did not remain secret for long—the President was alarmed. In a telling phrase he declared that from the moment France establishes itself at New Orleans, "we must marry ourselves to the British fleet and nation." One wonders if he ever reflected that his country would not have been in such a predicament if it had built up its fleet, as Hamilton had urged.

At first Jefferson considered the possibility of entering into an Anglo-American alliance in order to frighten Napoleon. But instead, he instructed Madison, his Secretary of State, to find out from the United States minister to France, Robert R. Livingston, what price France wanted for New Orleans and the Floridas. (In Washington officials believed that the French had acquired these Spanish possessions.)

Meanwhile, in 1802, the Spanish had suspended shipping privileges of Americans at New Orleans. When some aroused westerners talked of marching on New Orleans and capturing it, Federalist leaders egged them on, hoping to embarrass the Republicans. Jefferson wanted to do something dramatic to reassure and quiet the West, where he had so many supporters. Accordingly, early in 1803 he sent to Paris James Monroe, a friend of the frontiersmen and an old friend of France, to help Livingston in the negotiations. Monroe and Livingston were instructed to buy New Orleans and the Floridas for $2,000,000 but were told that they could go as high as $10,000,000.

Disaster for the French. In France, news of disaster had reached Napoleon. The people of Santo Domingo under the flaming Negro leader Pierre Toussaint L'Ouverture had risen against the French. Although the rebellion was quickly put down, the bloodshed was incredibly heavy; then yellow fever came to the aid of the rebels, wiping out thousands of French soldiers.

Disturbed by the revolt and by difficulties in Europe, Napoleon lost his appetite for an empire in the New World. "Damn sugar, damn coffee, damn colonies!" he exclaimed. He announced he would sell Louisiana—all of it!

A glorious windfall. One can imagine the surprise of the American negotiators. Their wildest dreams had not included the *whole* of Louisiana. In accepting, they exceeded their instructions, yet they had obtained not only the city they had sought but also about 900,000 square miles of wilderness. They agreed to pay approximately $15,000,000.

It was a magnificent bargain. No one can calculate meaningfully the total value today of the land once known as the Louisiana Purchase.

In 1803 the most important fact was that the country had acquired the Mississippi River. As Livingston signed the treaty, he prophesied, "From this day the United States take their place among the powers of the first rank." The French foreign minister, Talleyrand, who had himself spent some years in America, commented, "You have made a noble bargain for yourselves, and I suppose you will make the

#Students can see the enormity of the task by naming the states formed from land in the purchase (see the corrected boundaries on the map on p. 166).

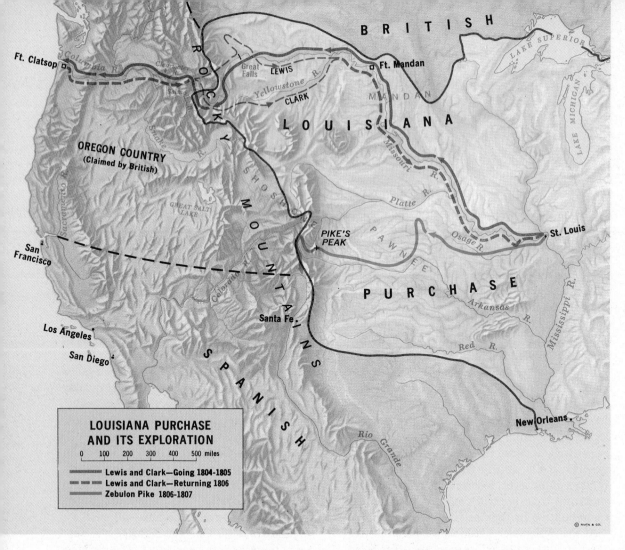

LOUISIANA PURCHASE AND ITS EXPLORATION

0	100	200	300	400	500 miles

Lewis and Clark—Going 1804-1805
Lewis and Clark—Returning 1806
Zebulon Pike 1806-1807

Since the boundaries of the Louisiana Purchase were not defined exactly in 1803, conflicting claims arose.

Where would conflicting claims arise? Compare this map with the one on p. 166.

most of it." Yet here at home some intense opposition to the deal developed.

A leading argument against the Purchase was that it was unconstitutional. Jefferson now found himself in the position of having to defend a loose Hamiltonian interpretation of the Constitution. The Federalists, on their side, were stating the arguments for strict construction that Jefferson had used in fighting the Bank in 1791! Underlying the Federalists' resistance was a fear that new agricultural states might be carved out of the Purchase. These, they thought, would reduce the influence of trade and business.

Moreover, the Federalists maintained that

Jefferson, despite his pledge of economy in government, had squandered $15,000,000 on land which France did not even have sure title to. "Suppose France had ceded to us the Island of Great Britain," said a Federalist congressman from Connecticut. "Would the mere cession give us the right to the soil and jurisdiction of that country?"

A Federalist from Delaware predicted pessimistically: "I believe it will be the greatest curse that could ever befall us. Citizens will be removed to the immense distance of two or three thousand miles from the Capital, where they will scarcely ever feel the rays of the Central Government. . . . they will gradually begin

#Students should understand exactly why and how Jefferson's and the Federalists' positions were switched on the interpretation of the Constitution.

to view us as strangers." It was hard to believe that only the year before the Federalists had wanted the frontiersmen to go to war to acquire merely the city of New Orleans.

Defending the bargain. Jefferson was sure he had strengthened the country by the Purchase and that in time his judgment would be vindicated. "It is the case," he wrote, "of a guardian investing the money of his ward in purchasing an important adjacent territory; and saying to him when he came of age, 'I did this for your good; I pretend to no right to bind you; you may disavow me, and I must get out of the scrape as I can; I thought it my duty to risk myself for you.'" Congress finally agreed to the Purchase. Jefferson had had to follow Federalist principles in order to further his ideal of an America composed of free farmers settled upon their own land.

FACING TO THE WEST

Whereas the Federalists had directed American attention toward English trade as a source of prosperity, the Jeffersonians maintained that the country's future greatness depended upon expansion westward. Jefferson had long been interested in finding out what lay on the other side of the Mississippi. He had been planning to send a scientific expedition to that region when news of the Louisiana Purchase arrived. Now he could justify a journey of discovery on the grounds that the new territory had to be explored in the national interest.

Lewis and Clark. To head the expedition Jefferson chose his private secretary, a twenty-nine-year-old fellow Virginian, Meriwether Lewis. Lewis, in turn, selected William Clark, a thirty-three-year-old younger brother of George Rogers Clark, also from Virginia, to accompany him. Wise in the ways of the frontier, they made a perfect pair, and the names Lewis and Clark are inseparably linked in history. They were commissioned to trace the Missouri River to its source and to find a water route to the Pacific. In addition, they were to make notes about the plant and animal life of the area they explored and record information concerning the geography.

Epic journeys. Starting from the East on July 5, 1803, they established winter quarters in late autumn near St. Louis. There they drilled and trained their forty-eight men. When spring came, they set out to follow the Missouri River. Late that year they reached the Mandan Indian villages in what is now North Dakota, where they built Fort Mandan. Wintering there, they also refitted themselves. From the fort Lewis wrote letters to his family and to Jefferson—the last news from him for a year and a half.

In April, 1805, the expedition started off again, this time with a remarkable Indian woman guide and interpreter, Sacajawea, who promised to lead it across the Rockies. A picturesque figure with her two-month-old papoose strapped to her back, this young squaw made an indispensable contribution to the success of the venture.

By July, 1805, the party reached the Great Falls of the Missouri. Near the headwaters of the Salmon River lived Sacajawea's own people—the Shoshone Indians. They supplied provisions and horses and also gave directions for journeying to the Columbia River.

In November, after canoeing over treacherous rapids, Lewis and Clark reached the Pacific, "the object of all our labours, the reward of all our anxieties." There they established a fort—Fort Clatsop. The continent had been crossed by means of two great rivers; the "Westward Passage" had at last been found. Lewis and Clark returned to St. Louis in 1806 to learn that the country had given them up for lost.

Even before the exploits of Lewis and Clark became known, other adventurers were also probing the secrets of the trans-Mississippi West. One of the most venturesome was a young army lieutenant, Zebulon Montgomery Pike. In 1806 he led an expedition into the southwestern part of the Louisiana Purchase, as the map opposite shows. During a side trip to the Colorado country, Pike unsuccessfully attempted to scale the mountain peak which today bears his name.

The exploring of the northern and central Rocky Mountains was largely the work of fur

A Mandan Indian village, like those Lewis and Clark found in the area of the upper Missouri River. In the center of a group of earth-covered lodges, tribesmen perform a religious rite, perhaps to insure good crops. The staffs shown are symbolically decorated.

Smithsonian Institution

The Mandans were an advanced tribe of Indians.

traders and trappers in search of beavers. Before the War of 1812 these men had found the South Pass in Wyoming—the only uninterrupted path from the Great Plains through the mountains.

William H. Ashley, of Missouri, and his followers conducted wide-ranging expeditions in the Rockies and surrounding country in the early 1820's. One of his most celebrated scouts was James Bridger, who later earned renown as the "Mountain Man." Another of Ashley's # pathbreaking frontiersmen was a Negro, James P. Beckwourth, whose craft and strength became a legend. Still another was Jedediah Smith, a native of New Hampshire, who was the first American to enter California from the east and leave it from the west.

The interest of the country in these exploits was heightened by the hope that a route through the heart of the continent would be found that could bring Americans closer to the potential wealth of Asia. Many great empires of the past had grown rich on trade with the East: the Byzantine, Portuguese, Spanish, Dutch, and British. Why should Americans not also prosper from such trade? Other problems required attention before the United States could extend its stake in the Pacific regions, but the outline of the future was already clear.

Burr's conspiracy. The West with its untold wealth promised in time to be a treasure house for the country—a guarantee of material greatness. But Jefferson now had to face the unpleasant fact that the Vice-President, Aaron Burr, was engaging in intrigue in the West. Jefferson had for some time been distrustful of Burr—even before Burr killed Hamilton with a pistol shot in a "duel of honor" in 1804. What the Vice-President was scheming is not clear. It may have been a plot to separate the West from the United States, or it may have been a plan to lead an expedition against the Spanish possessions to the south.

Whatever it was, Burr was up to no good. He appears to have been in close touch with that rascal James Wilkinson, a United States Army commander in Louisiana who was always ready to sell his services to the highest bidder. Burr, a charming man accompanied frequently by his exquisitely beautiful and accomplished daughter, Theodosia, made friends everywhere. In the winter of 1805/1806, it was widely rumored in the West that Burr was plotting treason. Wilkinson, turning on Burr, wrote an account of his activities to Jefferson. The President ordered Burr's arrest in November, 1806.

Presiding over the court where Burr stood trial for treason in 1807 was Chief Justice John

#Another opportunity to emphasize the contributions of American Negroes to American history.

Marshall. Marshall's rulings made it impossible for the jury to do otherwise than to acquit the prisoner. Marshall had insisted that under the Constitution no individual can be accused of # treason "unless on the testimony of two witnesses to the same overt act, or on confession in open court." However much his conduct of the case may have angered Republican politicians, Marshall won fresh respect for the authority of the Constitution.

Sum and Substance

1. How did Jefferson express his faith in people in his letter to a Virginia friend? 2. Describe his special qualifications for the presidency. 3. What was his policy concerning Cabinet appointments? The national debt? The navy? The Barbary pirates? The judiciary? 4. Why was the *Marbury* v. *Madison* decision important? 5. What circumstances led to the purchase of Louisiana? 6. What did Lewis and Clark accomplish?

This section deals with Jefferson's efforts to remain neutral in the war between England and France.

THE WAR AGAINST NAPOLEON INVOLVES AMERICA

Despite his keen interest in the West, Jefferson had to spend the greater part of his second administration, which began in 1805, in dealing with events on the high seas. Once more, war in Europe was affecting America's destinies.

THE FATE OF A NEUTRAL

Scarcely a month after Napoleon sold Louisiana to the United States, he declared war against England. For American merchants and shippers, this was a golden opportunity. ## As ships of a neutral country, their vessels sailed everywhere for the next two years, frequently entering ports that ordinarily would have been closed to them. Gradually the irritation of British shippers over this American commercial growth neared the breaking point.

The Rule of 1756. Britain had driven French merchant ships off the ocean, but American vessels were taking their places, nullifying in a way the overwhelming power of the British navy. One abuse of neutrality distressed Britain most. This was the Americans' practice of bringing sugar from the French Caribbean islands to the United States, paying a duty on it, and reshipping it (after the duty had been refunded by France) as American sugar entitled to protection as a neutral cargo.

The British insisted on applying the Rule of 1756, established by their courts during the French and Indian War. This rule stated that trade closed in peacetime might not be opened in wartime. This meant that since the French West Indies trade was not open to American vessels normally, France could not open it to them during hostilities. British naval units, under orders to enforce the Rule of 1756, seized United States vessels that violated it. American shippers were infuriated.

Impressment. Americans were aroused, too, by the British practice of impressing, or drafting by force, able-bodied men from American ships for service in the Royal Navy. Since American merchant seamen were paid higher wages than British sailors, desertions from His Majesty's service were common. The British impressed men, from ships anchored in British ports or ones they stopped at sea, without inquiring too closely whether they were Englishmen or not. Britain, engaged in a life-and-death struggle with Napoleon, was not inclined to draw a clear distinction between a man claiming American citizenship and one absent without leave from the Royal Navy.

The British rarely listened to the protests of the unfortunates they illegally seized. Their navy's main object in the crisis was to man ships. If Americans were abused in the circumstances, the British argued only that the fight against Napoleon was an American fight, too. When Americans protested against the boarding of ships on the high seas as a violation of the rights of neutrals and, in fact, of their territory, the British brushed the protests aside as impertinence.

American shipowners regarded impressment as only one of many risks in carrying on neutral trade in a war. Seamen saw it differently,

##The right of a neutral country to sail on the high seas is protected by international law. According to this law, ships of a neutral cannot be attacked unless a blockade has been declared. **153**

and it was for them that Jefferson took up the cudgels. In 1806 the United States and England undertook very promising negotiations with a view to settling their differences. But although the British were agreeable in other matters, they would not give up the practice of impressment, a point Americans refused to compromise on. The war was entering a new, more violent stage, and England needed every man it could lay its hands on.

The battle of the blockades. In October, 1805, the English admiral Lord Nelson won a smashing victory over the French and Spanish fleets at Trafalgar, off the coast of Spain. But Napoleon was still invincible on land. The war settled down to a duel of blockades between the British and the French.

The British issued commands called **Orders in Council.** These authorized the seizure of any vessel that attempted to trade on the continent of Europe unless it first had obtained British permission.

The French, on the other hand, declared in a number of decrees that they would seize neutral ships trading with the British or allowing themselves to be searched by them. This was only a "paper blockade" of England, because, although the French expected neutrals to observe it, they could not enforce it.

American ship captains were in a quandary. Outside any continental port, they were subject to seizure by the British if they *had not* stopped first in England; inside, they were subject to seizure by the French if they *had*.

A provocation and insult. It was becoming impossible for America to maintain its neutral position without loss of national dignity. The limit appeared to have been reached on June 22, 1807. The United States frigate *Chesapeake*, 10 miles out of Norfolk, Virginia, was hailed by the British frigate *Leopard*. Declaring that four of the *Chesapeake*'s crew were British deserters, the British commander demanded the right to search the vessel. When the American commander refused, the *Leopard* opened fire on the unprepared *Chesapeake*, killing three sailors and wounding eighteen. A boarding party then removed the four alleged deserters.

When the battered American ship limped back to Norfolk, the crew told its story; cries of indignation went up everywhere as news of the *Chesapeake-Leopard* affair spread like wildfire.

WHAT PRICE PEACE?

The country became alive with talk of war. One toast of the day went: "The President of the United States—The hand that drafted the Declaration of Independence will maintain, inviolate, the principles it recognizes."

Although Jefferson was irate that such a wanton attack had been made upon a United States naval vessel close to American shores, he counseled peace at all costs, just as Federalist Presidents had done. Somewhat later, he wrote that twenty years without war was the most precious gift the young United States could have. "At the end of that period," he said, "we shall be twenty millions in numbers, and forty in energy, when encountering the starved and rickety paupers and dwarfs of English workshops."

Nonimportation Act. But, if not war, what was the solution? Congress in 1806 had passed a Nonimportation Act prohibiting the importation from England of certain stated articles. But this act had failed to achieve its purpose. England continued its high-handed behavior.

The embargo and its consequences. Jefferson now turned to a more drastic economic measure: the Embargo Act, of 1807. This act, supported principally by southerners and westerners, was intended to stop *all* trade between the United States and foreign countries. American vessels would stay at home, safe from seizure.

In practice the embargo hurt many merchants —who were usually Federalists. Despite widespread evasion of the law by smugglers, business ground to a halt in some maritime communities. Ships lay idle in every port.

Although the Federalists insisted that the embargo showed Jefferson to be incompetent and under "French influence," the President steadfastly held his ground. Foreseeing that an unanticipated benefit would result from the law, he wrote to his old friend Lafayette: "Our Embargo . . . has set us all on domestic man-

##Compare the criticism of Jefferson with the attacks on Washington and Adams. The right to criticize openly their elected leaders has always been exercised by Americans.

Peabody Museum of Salem

No longer immoblized by the Nonintercourse Act, the *Hercules* arrives at Naples, Italy, from Salem, Massachusetts. Salem was a center of trade and shipbuilding. Its ships sailed throughout the world.

ufactures, and will I verily believe, reduce our future demands on England fully one half."

Yet across the Atlantic the embargo was not having the desired effect. British shippers gained, because their American competition was now removed by act of Congress. The French gained, because they seized American vessels coming into their ports. They argued that since American ships were not supposed to be at sea, these must be British vessels under false colors! Truly, American fortunes were at low ebb. Year after year the country was being humiliated by France and England, and it often seemed that the only way to defend the nation's honor would be by going to war against *both*.

Nonintercourse Act. Just before Jefferson's second term expired on March 4, 1809, the Presi-

dent signed the Nonintercourse Act. It repealed the embargo and reopened trade with all nations *except* England and France. The President was empowered to resume trade with England or France if either should lift its restrictions on neutral commerce. This was Jefferson's final act. As Jefferson prepared to retire to Monticello, his beautiful house in Virginia, he wrote that "never did a prisoner released from his chains feel such relief as I shall on shaking off the shackles of power. . . ."

Sum and Substance

1. Why did trouble develop with both England and France in Jefferson's second administration? 2. Describe the *Chesapeake-Leopard* affair. 3. What measures did Jefferson try in handling interference with American trade?

This last section of the chapter deals with the War of 1812--its course and outcome.

JAMES MADISON PUTS ON THE MANTLE OF THE PRESIDENCY

Jefferson's Secretary of State, friend, and Virginia neighbor, James Madison, was his successor. Madison and Jefferson had worked together closely to form the Republican party and to give it strength and direction. Yet political differences had appeared within the party. One group with its leadership in Virginia was opposed to anything appearing to be a compromise with Federalists.

By now, also, the Revolutionary generation was passing. Many of the new leaders were westerners. It may not seem logical, but Ameri-

ca's struggle for the rights of neutrals on the high seas would bring these men from the other side of the Appalachians to national prominence.

INHERITED AND ACQUIRED PROBLEMS

Shortly after Madison took office in 1809, Robert Smith, of Maryland, his Secretary of State, concluded a trade agreement with the British minister to the United States. By its terms, the American restrictions on trade with England were lifted. Scores of ships put to sea

#Students should recall the case of <u>Marbury</u> v. <u>Madison,</u> which arose because Jefferson ordered his Secretary of State not to deliver the commission of Marbury to be justice of the peace.

laden with goods that Britain desperately needed.

The British foreign minister, George Canning, refused to approve the agreement. Furthermore, Canning removed the British minister in the United States for having gone beyond his instructions from London in negotiating it.

The administration in Washington was greatly embarrassed, and in August the United States stopped trading with England again. To add insult to injury, Canning now sent to Washington as minister an insufferable anti-American, Francis James Jackson. He arrived with his own coach-and-four and soon had the effrontery to refer to Dolley Madison, the first lady, as "fat and forty, but not fair." When negotiations with him became impossible, the Department of State demanded his recall.

Meanwhile Napoleon's attitude and behavior also continued to irritate Americans. A new decree in 1810, which Bonaparte issued in answer to the Nonintercourse Act, allowed him to seize many American ships at anchor in French ports. Clearly, in allowing themselves to be scorned by England one day and abused by France the next, Americans were gradually frittering away their prestige as an independent nation.

Macon's Bill No. 2. The Republicans still believed that economic pressure could be used successfully against England and France. In 1810 they thought of an ingenious arrangement which was put into effect by a law known as Macon's Bill No. 2. It sanctioned American commerce with every nation in the world. But if either England or France changed its policy so as to favor commerce of the United States, then nonintercourse would be revived against the other.

Like its predecessors, the measure failed. In order to entrap the United States into acting against England, Napoleon pretended to repeal his decrees. Madison in consequence was tricked into again imposing the Nonintercourse Act against England.

Call for arms. In a message to Congress in November, 1811, Madison declared that American independence itself was at stake. Referring to England's "hostile inflexibility in trampling on rights which no independent nation can relinquish," he requested that Congress place the country "into an armor and an attitude demanded by the crisis." Even as Congress met, disturbing events were occurring elsewhere.

Indians on the warpath. On November 7, 1811, Americans under William Henry Harrison fought and defeated a band of Indians at Tippecanoe River near the Wabash River, in what is now Indiana. The Indians, organized by the chief Tecumseh, were trying to halt the loss of their lands to the increasing number of new settlers in the Northwest Territory.

The arms the defeated tribesmen left behind obviously had been recently received from the British. The Americans drew the conclusion that the English were up to their old tricks: plotting with the Indians against the frontiersmen. How easy it now was for westerners and easterners to be linked by their common hostility to the British. The cry spread: "Look at the Wabash, look at the impressed seaman!"

THE WAR HAWKS

The Twelfth Congress, which met in 1811, was led by a group of young men who counseled war. Known as the "War Hawks," they included from Kentucky, Henry Clay; from South Carolina, John C. Calhoun; from Tennessee, Felix Grundy. Clay, only thirty-four

Madison in his mid-fifties.

James Madison, shortly before he became President.

years old, was elected Speaker of the House.

Clay represented the "new West." Already well known throughout Kentucky, he owned 18 slaves and 600 acres of good land near Lexington, where he kept 65 horses. He was the new type of American politician, combining the roughness of the frontier with its directness and simplicity. A persuasive speaker, he won friends easily by his gracious manner and his vivacious conversation. It is striking that this man, whose later fame rested on his ability to make the North and South work together, should have started his career as an advocate of war.

Eyes on Canada. To westerners like Clay and Grundy, it seemed clear that England had too long tried American patience. In order to defeat England, they reasoned, Canada would have to be conquered. Victory would not only provide more land for frontiersmen but would also end the use of Canada as a base from which the Indians could be armed to attack Americans.

Demand for Florida. Where westerners desired Canada, southerners demanded Florida. East and West Florida, as Spanish possessions, were not only refuges for runaway slaves but also springboards for Indian attacks on Americans. Madison in 1810 had declared that the Louisiana Purchase included West Florida; now frontiersmen of the South were demanding East Florida, too. Since Spain happened to be an ally of England, the expansionist aims of southerners and westerners were easily linked.

Although the War Hawks were expansionists, they were also hostile to England because the British blockade had cut off the European market for their farm products. The War Hawks could combine their anti-British feeling with their ardent patriotism. They believed that love of country called for a strong stand against the oppressors of Americans. Despite # the opposition of New England to hostilities with Britain, these congressmen were ready to go to war in defense of the nation's position as a neutral. Andrew Jackson of Tennessee, rising to leadership in the army, wrote in March, 1812, ". . . we are going to fight

for the reestablishment of our national character, misunderstood and vilified at home and abroad. . . ."

New England's opposition. New Englanders opposed war, in part because they feared that their port cities would be attacked by the British fleet. In part, they resented the growing strength of the westerners—"foresters," they called them—who were continually adding new states to the list of those supporting the Republican party. In part, too, they considered war against England to be madness, because it would disrupt their overseas trade. Despite the losses New Englanders had suffered, this overseas trade continued to flourish.

THE WAR OF 1812

Although devoted to peace, Madison was unable to resist the pressure of the War Hawks. In June, 1812, he asked Congress to declare war on England. Unknown to Americans, England had repealed the offensive Orders in Council.

It is idle to speculate whether there would have been war if there had been an Atlantic cable. The issue of impressment still remained; also, the War Hawks were still determined to defend the country's good name. Wrote a Kentucky newspaper in urging Congress to declare war: "The wrath of Western America is in flame. You must breath our spirit and speak our sentiment." Taking this step, the newspaper insisted, would be a "Second Declaration of Independence." On June 18 Congress obliged, and hostilities formally began.

In the presidential election of 1812, Madison was reelected over DeWitt Clinton, a peace candidate. Madison's support came principally from the South and West, the sections that had favored war. The President was now completely in the hands of the War Hawks. The Federalists snarled that this was "Mr. Madison's War," but it was just as surely "Mr. Clay's."

Strategy. Since the United States knew it ## could not defeat England at sea, the American plan had to be to conquer Canada. A captive Canada could be used as a hostage to force

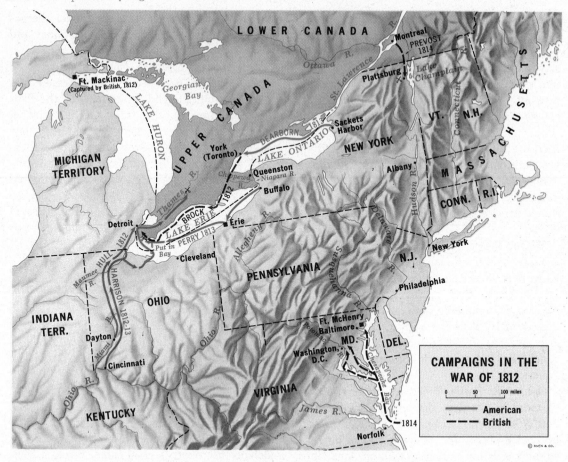

CAMPAIGNS IN THE
WAR OF 1812

0   50   100 miles

———— American
- - - - British

The several fronts on which the War of 1812 was fought. Washington was burned in retaliation for an attack on York.

Though Canada had a small population, its southern boundary is a long one.

Britain to recognize American rights or as an exchange for any American territory that might be won by England.

Self-made handicaps. At the beginning the Americans had the advantage and the initiative in the land fighting. Tied down by war with France, England had only 5000 men in Canada, with little hope of reinforcing them. The United States had a population of about 8,000,000, compared with Canada's 500,000. But Americans threw away their opportunity.

First of all, despite the brave talk, recruiting was slow. Congress had authorized a regular army of 35,000 men, but barely 10,000 were raised. Second, the military leadership was notably incompetent. The senior major general was Henry Dearborn. He had shown skill in

the Revolution, but his military talent had disappeared. Now old and rheumatic, he was so fat that a vehicle had to be especially designed to carry him around. The Secretary of War, William Eustis, was so inept he had to be removed almost immediately.

Third, the country was not united. The Federalists never reconciled themselves to the decision of Congress to declare war. New England bankers tried to prevent the sale of government bonds, and elsewhere also there was a lack of enthusiasm for the fighting. The British commander in chief was happy to report home that two-thirds of his troops "were eating beef provided by American contractors."

Fourth, Congress would not impose taxes to finance the war. It authorized borrowing

$11,000,000 through a bond issue, but not over $6,000,000 worth of the securities were sold. Finally, southern and western War Hawks fell out over aims and strategy. Each group opposed the territorial ambitions of the other.

Faced by these handicaps, the United States fought the only kind of war possible. Instead of driving hard against the strongholds of British power at Quebec or Montreal, Americans attacked on the fringes in the West. The capture of Montreal, for instance, would have given the United States the key to the provinces of Upper and Lower Canada.‡ Americans relied instead on the mistaken idea that Canadians in what is now Ontario would welcome the invaders as an army of liberation.

Failure at Detroit. In July General William Hull boldly started to march northward from Detroit to invade Upper Canada. Within a few days, however, he was in retreat, and almost immediately a British army under General Isaac Brock was able to surround Detroit.

Hull surrendered the city on August 16. Brock then went over to the Niagara River, where at Queenston he defeated Americans under Stephen Van Rensselaer, a Federalist who had recently been against the war. In northern New York General Dearborn, meanwhile, was timidly preparing to march against Montreal, but the attempt came to nothing.

‡ Upper Canada was the part of Canada now known as the province of Ontario; Lower Canada was what is now the province of Quebec. "Upper Canada" was so called because the land there is higher than that in the area farther east, which was therefore named "Lower Canada."

The naval war. England's mastery of the sea was complete, although in single-ship engagements early in the war Americans had some stunning triumphs. A stellar performer was the frigate *Constitution.* Off Nova Scotia in August, 1812, this brave ship outdueled and sank the *Guerrière* in one of the fiercest naval battles ever fought. In December, this time off the coast of Brazil, it destroyed the British frigate *Java,* earning the nickname "Old Ironsides."

The second year of the war, 1813, brought the most important naval engagement on the Great Lakes. Oliver Hazard Perry, a handsome, twenty-eight-year-old naval lieutenant, who at fifteen had fought against the Barbary pirates, defeated an English force at Put in Bay on Lake Erie. He was able to send to his superior a hastily scrawled note that became immortal: "We have met the enemy and they are ours; two ships, two brigs, one schooner and one sloop."

In the fall of 1813, General William Henry Harrison succeeded in recovering Detroit. But important forts like Michilimackinac and Dearborn (now Chicago) remained in British hands, and an invasion of Canada seemed out of the question. The year 1814 saw the end of the war in Europe, and it appeared that America was soon to feel the full force of British might.

The burning of Washington. In August, British forces landed on the Atlantic coast, burning many of the public buildings in the city of Washington, including the Executive Mansion. The President and the first lady were forced to flee ingloriously.

Perry's task was to destroy British naval power on Lake Erie. He was twenty-eight.

On Lake Erie, Perry—standing in the small boat—is transferred from one ship to another as he continues the fight.

Henry Francis du Pont Winterthur Museum

In spite of their dramatic success, the English were unable to hold the city. Furthermore, they were repulsed when they attempted to raid Baltimore. It was this battle that inspired Francis Scott Key to write the song that later became the national anthem. He has conveyed to generations of Americans his satisfaction that during the attack "the rockets' red glare, the bombs bursting in air, gave proof through the night that our flag was still there."

Jackson at New Orleans. A British attempt to capture New Orleans early in 1815 in order to close that port also failed. Here Andrew Jackson and his militiamen—including two battalions of Negroes—humbled English troops under Sir Edward Pakenham, an outstanding hero in the war against Napoleon. Seven hundred English soldiers were killed (among them Sir Edward himself), as compared with eight American fatalities. Unknown to Americans, a treaty of peace had already been signed in Europe. But that fact could not detract from the glory Jackson earned on that January day.

The Hartford Convention. When the British succeeded in occupying a part of Maine in September, 1814, the reaction in the rest of New England was immediate. Massachusetts called upon its neighbors to meet in a convention at Hartford, Connecticut, in December "to secure such amendments and explanations of the Constitution as will secure them from further evils."

Although a few of the delegates to the Convention called for outright secession from the Union, moderates won out. In the end the report suggested certain amendments to the Constitution. It proposed (1) to end the counting of slaves in determining representation in Congress; (2) to admit new states only by a two-thirds vote of Congress; (3) to limit embargoes to sixty days; (4) to require a two-thirds vote on nonintercourse acts; (5) to bar all naturalized Americans from holding office in the national government; (6) to require a two-thirds vote for a declaration of war; (7) to limit a President to one term and bar a state from providing a President twice in succession.

The stored-up anger of years under the Virginia Republicans was showing itself. But by the time the Convention's "ambassadors" to Washington arrived there, the news of New Orleans had been received. Still better, on February 14 came word that a treaty ending the war had been signed some two months earlier at Ghent in Belgium. The humiliated Federalists as a party never recovered from the political effects of their foolish behavior.

The Treaty of Ghent. The Treaty of Ghent was the result of the work of five American peace commissioners, John Quincy Adams, James A. Bayard, Albert Gallatin, Henry Clay, and Jonathan Russell. These men often disagreed with one another as much as they disagreed with the British. But they obtained an honorable peace for their country.

The treaty provided for a halt to hostilities, the release of prisoners, the mutual restoration of conquests, and an end to Indian border raids. It made no mention of what was to be done about impressment and the rights of neutrals; time would have to take care of those problems. Both sides were ready for peace. After a generation of fighting in Europe, the English wanted to turn to domestic development. The Americans were exhausted, torn by dissension, and discouraged.

Who in 1801 could have predicted this outcome for the Republican era? States' righters when they took power, the Jeffersonians became fervid nationalists, fighting in defense of the country's integrity and using the Federalist idea of a strong central government.

Militarily, the War of 1812 was a failure. The American people came so close to disaster that they learned the need for greater national unity. For a generation afterward, they were able to keep their sectional differences in check while they concentrated on the possibilities of territorial expansion and economic growth.

Sum and Substance

1. What events finally led to the American declaration of war? 2. What viewpoint on the war did the West have? The South? New England? 3. Account for the conduct of the war and tell where important fighting took place. 4. Give the provisions of the Treaty of Ghent.

THE WORKSHOP

OF LASTING SIGNIFICANCE

Tell how each of the following was involved in the Jefferson and Madison administrations.

Albert Gallatin	Barbary pirates
Marbury v. *Madison*	Sacajawea
John Marshall	Zebulon Pike
judicial review	Aaron Burr
Louisiana Purchase	Rule of 1756
Lewis and Clark	impressment
Toussaint	Orders in Council
L'Ouverture	*Chesapeake-Leopard*
Nonimportation Act	affair
Embargo Act	Henry Clay
Nonintercourse Act	William Hull
Macon Bill No. 2	Francis Scott Key
War Hawks	Hartford Convention
Judiciary Act of 1801	Treaty of Ghent

GEOGRAPHY AND HISTORY

1. To get a better idea of the size of the Louisiana Purchase, mark its boundaries on an outline map of the United States. The map on page 150 will be helpful, as will the one on page 166. Referring to the map on pages 360–361, show and name on the outline map the states which have been formed wholly or in part from land included in the Purchase.

2. On the map on pages 360–361, identify the chief waterways used by pioneers either to penetrate or to explore North America.

3. Mark in color on a road map of the United States or of the western states alone the routes followed by Lewis and Clark and by Pike. What large cities lie along the routes today? What highways?

DOCUMENTS IN HISTORY

1. What opinion of Shays' Rebellion did Jefferson express in the letter on pages 144–145? What accounted for his viewpoint? How did he think such events should be prevented?

2. Identify the democratic principles Jefferson expressed in the letter. How did they contrast with Hamilton's beliefs?

3. What part of the letter shows Jefferson's distrust of government? What did he consider the best safeguard against government trespassing on the rights of the people?

4. The French government in 1787 was a monarchy. What clue does the letter give about its methods of maintaining itself?

INFORMED OPINION

1. In his decision in the case of *Marbury* v. *Madison,* Chief Justice Marshall implied that only the Supreme Court has the power to judge whether legislative or executive acts are constitutional. Do you believe that *some* government agency must have this power? Why? If so, should it be the Court?

2. Explain these apparent contradictions: (*a*) Jefferson, although he disliked a national debt, greatly increased it during his term in office. (*b*) Jefferson had always been a friend of France; yet in 1803 he favored an alliance with England against France.

SIFTING THE SOURCES

1. Use the *Dictionary of American Biography* or other reference books to learn more about the personalities and activities of Dolley Madison, Albert Gallatin, Meriwether Lewis, William Clark, Zebulon Pike, John Marshall, Aaron Burr, Pierre Toussaint L'Ouverture, Tecumseh, and Oliver Hazard Perry. Report your findings to the class.

2. Using reference books, find the detailed history of the national anthem and present it to the class. Is "The Star-Spangled Banner" a better choice than "My Country, 'Tis of Thee" or "God Bless America"? Why?

3. The planning of the new capital city, Washington, D.C., was entrusted to a French friend of Lafayette's—Major Pierre L'Enfant—who was aided by two American surveyors, Andrew Elliott, a Quaker, and Benjamin Banneker, a Negro. Investigate this example of early city-planning and report on it. Use the *Readers' Guide to Periodical Literature* to find material in current magazines.

##Students will have varied opinions. "The Star-Spangled Banner" is associated with American history as the others are not. "My Country, 'Tis of Thee" is based on "God Save the King."

161

9

STRENGTHENING THE NATIONAL SPIRIT

Let us, then, bind the republic together . . .

In many respects, no country, of equal population and wealth, possesses equal materials of power with ours. The people, in muscular power, in hardy and enterprising habits, and in lofty and gallant courage, are surpassed by none. In one respect, and, in my opinion, in one only, are we materially weak. We occupy a surface prodigiously great in proportion to our numbers. The common strength is brought to bear with great difficulty on the point that may be menaced by an enemy. It is our duty, then, as far as in the nature of things it can be effected, to counteract this weakness. Good roads and canals, judiciously laid out, are the proper remedy. . . .

Those who understand the human heart best

The United States was chiefly rural in the early 1800's. How does this picture bear out this fact?

Ask how Calhoun thought of the United States government on the evidence presented here. How did
he plead for national unity? What idealism did he express? Students should observe that he specifically
rejected sectionalism in order to place "the common good" first.

know how powerfully distance tends to break the sympathies of our nature. Nothing—not even dissimilarity of language—tends more to estrange man from man. Let us, then, bind the republic together with a perfect system of roads and canals. Let us conquer space. It is thus the most distant parts of the republic will be brought within a few days' travel of the centre; it is thus that a citizen of the West will read the news of Boston still moist from the press. The mail and the press are the nerves of the body politic. By them, the slightest impression made on the most remote parts, is communicated to the whole system; and the more perfect the means of transportation, the more rapid and true the vibration.

Maryland Historical Society

To aid us in this great work—to maintain the integrity of this republic, we inhabit a country presenting the most admirable advantages. Belted around, as it is, by lakes and oceans—intersected in every direction by bays and rivers, the hand of industry and art is tempted to improvement. So situated, blessed with a form of government at once combining liberty and strength, we may reasonably raise our eyes to a most splendid future, if we only act in a manner worthy of our advantages. If, however, neglecting them, we permit a low, sordid, selfish and sectional spirit to take possession of this House, this happy scene will vanish. We will divide;—and in its consequences will follow, misery and despotism.

To legislate for our country, requires not only the most enlarged views, but a species of self-devotion not exacted in any other. In a country so extensive, and so various in its interests, what is necessary for the common good may apparently be opposed to the interest of particular sections. It must be submitted to as the condition of our greatness. . . .

By 1815 internal improvements—that is, roads and canals—were recognized as indispensable to knitting the sections of the country closely together. In this speech, delivered in the House of Representatives on February 4, 1817, John C. Calhoun of South Carolina argues their importance. Shortly many people, including Calhoun, would become sectionalist rather than nationalist in outlook. Nevertheless, this speech reflects the mood most Americans shared immediately after the War of 1812 was ended.

The main vehicles seen here are Conestoga wagons. Observe the man pitching hay from the barn to feed the horses German farmers in Pennsylvania first made the wagons

Traffic moves east and west along a road to and from the city of Baltimore, Maryland. Some families, migrating westward in Conestoga wagons creaking with loads of bulky household possessions, are stopping at the inn to eat and to feed and water their hard-working teams. A coach drawn by three horses and filled with curious passengers approaches on its way eastward, easily outstripping a procession of reluctant sheep and cattle being driven to markets in the East. A goat—right— pauses near a road marker.

The shouts of people and the noise of animals were probably much evident.

PRIDE OF COUNTRY CAPTIVATES THE PEOPLE

The United States that emerged from the War of 1812 was still an infant. But already it inspired affection and devotion—the kind that brings people to their feet when they hear the national anthem and makes patriots willing to die in battle for their country.

SYMBOLS OF THE NATION'S GLORY

Americans were acquiring a sense of national unity and common purpose. Schoolbooks, especially geographies and histories, emphasized the superiority of America, contrasting it with worn-out Europe. Noah Webster's texts were particularly influential. His spellers and readers, which began to appear in the 1780's, earnestly # preached patriotism.

Just as important was Webster's dictionary, first published in 1806. This book helped to create a distinctively *American* language, somewhat different in spelling, usage, and pronunciation from the tongue of the mother country. The language was the strongest bond of union Americans had. But the symbols of nationhood, honored and cherished everywhere, were signs of a deeply felt pride and love of country.

Old Glory. The most important of these symbols was the flag. Created during the Revolution, it had become a measure of the country's growth because a star was being added for every new state. Already in 1812 a prominent Bostonian was observing that Old Glory was "talked about as though there were something mystical in its very nature, as though a rag, with certain stripes and stars upon it, tied to a stick and called a flag, was a wizard's wand."

The Fourth of July. "The glorious Fourth" was another significant symbol. It called up the heroic deeds of the Revolutionary generation and the memory of self-sacrificing people who served the republic well. Americans everywhere marked the Fourth of July with feasting, parades, and firecrackers. Even amid the dangers of the unknown West, Lewis and Clark celebrated the day, they recorded, with "a sumptuous dinner of fat saddles of venison."

The bald eagle. The eagle became a widely used symbol of the nation from the time it appeared in 1782 on the seal of the United States. Congress had specified that it be not just any eagle but that true native of the United States, the American bald eagle! After the War of 1812 the eagle came into use as a decoration for magazines, chinaware, furniture, watch fobs—for almost everything. It was also stamped on the country's coins "to encourage a national spirit, and to foster national pride."

The Liberty Bell. First rung in 1776 to announce the Declaration of Independence, the Liberty Bell also became a hallowed emblem of the nation. Its peal was reserved for occasions of patriotic significance. It was tolled in 1832 when Charles Carroll, the last surviving signer of the Declaration, died; two years later for Lafayette's death; and in 1835 when Chief Justice John Marshall passed on.

Uncle Sam. Americans early made a character called "Brother Jonathan" a symbolic representation of themselves—a shrewd, hospitable, hard-working, bumptious fellow who was incredibly strong. We are not sure how, but by 1812 "Brother Jonathan" had become "Uncle Sam."* Although the earliest known cartoon of Uncle Sam did not appear until 1853, the words "Uncle Sam" long before had been

_____

* The first reference to "Uncle Sam" in print appeared in the Troy (N.Y.) *Post* on September 7, 1813. It is accepted that Samuel Wilson, a Troy meat-packer, was the original. He was called "Uncle Sam" by the soldiers stationed nearby to whom he supplied beef.

An eagle perched on a "rock" is a feature of the design of this carved headboard from a bed of the 1800's.

National Gallery of Art

Do students think that the symbols named on this page are meaningful today? Why?

commonly used as a synonym for "the United States."

SIGNS OF THE NATION'S GROWTH

The country's rapid growth was a source of pride for its people. The census report of 1810 listed a population of 7,239,881; in 1820 the total stood at 9,638,453. The eastern cities of Boston and New York doubled in size between 1800 and 1820, while western towns such as Pittsburgh, Cincinnati, Louisville, and New Orleans grew even more rapidly. These facts foretold great changes, although it is important to remember that in 1820 only four cities could boast more than 30,000 inhabitants.

The role of the steamboat. New improvements were linking the various parts of America and creating a firm basis for national unity. The steamboat made its successful debut when Robert Fulton's *Clermont* chugged up the Hudson in 1807. Now it became possible to go from New York City to Philadelphia in only 13 hours and from New York to Albany in 24. During the War of 1812 the *Vesuvius* made the trip from Pittsburgh to New Orleans in nine and a half days. This was a remarkable improvement over previous records and a promising omen for the future.

Post offices and post roads. The expanding postal service was helping Americans—frequently on the move—to keep in touch with one another. In 1801 the United States had 957 post offices; by 1817 there were 3459. In 1801 there were 25,000 miles of post road; by 1817

TEN LARGEST CITIES IN THE UNITED STATES*

	1790	1800	1810	1820
1	Philadelphia, Pa. 44,092	Philadelphia, Pa. 61,559	New York, N.Y. 100,775	New York, N.Y. 130,881
2	New York, N.Y. 33,131	New York, N.Y. 60,515	Philadelphia, Pa. 87,303	Philadelphia, Pa. 108,809
3	Boston, Mass. 18,320	Baltimore, Md. 26,514	Baltimore, Md. 46,555	Baltimore, Md. 62,738
4	Charleston, S.C. 16,359	Boston, Mass. 24,937	Boston, Mass. 38,746	Boston, Mass. 54,024
5	Baltimore, Md. 13,503	Charleston, S.C. 18,824	Charleston, S.C. 24,711	New Orleans, La. 27,176
6	Salem, Mass. 7,921	Salem, Mass. 9,457	New Orleans, La.†‡ 17,242	Charleston, S.C. 24,780
7	Newport, R.I. 6,716	Providence, R.I. 7,614	Salem, Mass. 17,221	Washington, D.C. 20,607
8	Providence, R.I. 6,380	Norfolk, Va.† 6,926	Washington, D.C. 13,156	Salem, Mass. 17,014
9	Marblehead, Mass. 5,661	Newport, R.I. 6,739	Albany, N.Y.† 10,762	Albany, N.Y. 12,630
10	Gloucester, Mass. 5,317	Washington, D.C.† 6,203	Providence, R.I. 10,071	Richmond, Va.† 12,067

* Population figures include immediate suburbs.   † New addition to list.   (Continued on page 205)
‡ New Orleans was part of the United States only after 1803.

What western city first appeared on the list? When? Ask how New Orleans became part of the United States. (Louisiana Purchase.) The westward movement can be traced on later charts.

165

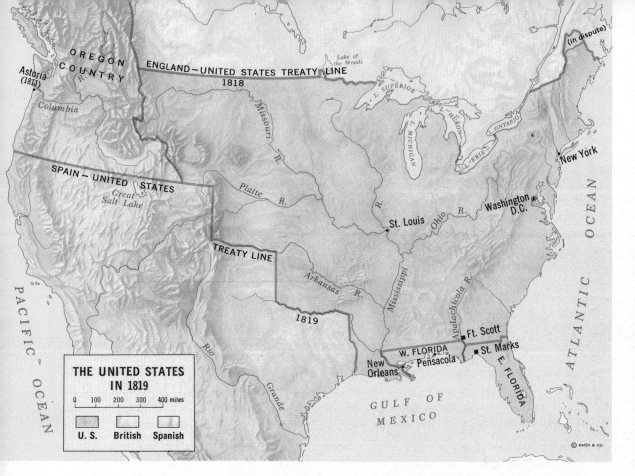

In 1819, except for one area (see page 196), the eastern United States occupied the area it does today. To see how the western boundary was changed by the Adams-Onís Treaty, compare this map with the one on page 150.

The area unoccupied in the East was the northern part of Maine. Observe how much land Spain held.

the mileage had doubled. By 1815 post roads already were being laid on the western side of the Mississippi.

Great expectations. Many powerful influences were at work to make a unique nation to which Americans might joyfully give loyalty and allegiance. These included, first, the continual entrance of more states into the Union;† second, expanding business opportunity throughout the country; third, the prospect of unbroken

peace; fourth, the existence of a vast, rich continent to bring under control. The nation seemed to have been born under a lucky star.

Sum and Substance

1. Name some national symbols cherished by Americans of the early nineteenth century. 2. By 1820 what advances had been made in water transportation? Road-building? 3. What change took place in the size of the population?

Jackson was made a major general before the Battle of New Orleans.

ANDREW JACKSON REVEALS AMERICA'S MILITARY STRENGTH

Americans made use of a bold military adventure to lift national spirit to a high pitch. Long-standing irritations over Florida set the stage.

Spain's ability to maintain order in Florida appeared to decline after the War of 1812. The Seminole Indians living there ignored the international boundary line between East Florida and Georgia and raided American settlements at will. The Indians were in an angry mood

_____
† Ohio joined in 1803, Louisiana in 1812, Indiana in 1816, Mississippi in 1817, Illinois in 1818, Alabama in 1819.

#The joining of Ohio, Indiana, and Illinois can be linked to what other events? (The passage of the Land Ordinance of 1785 and the Northwest Ordinance, the Battle of Fallen Timbers.)

For a detailed discussion of the diplomacy of John Quincy Adams, see American Foreign Policy to 1880, by Russell H. Bastert, a paperback in the Rand McNally Classroom Library. Spain had seized American ships without paying for them and did not prevent Indian raids from Florida.

after 1814 because the Creeks, who had been driven out of Georgia, had been forced to find refuge in Florida with the Seminoles, Creek kinfolk.

TROUBLES OVER FLORIDA

In Florida a British colonel took up the cause of the Indians, persuading them that they were entitled to recover their lands. Trouble was in the making. As soon as the United States began to survey the recently evacuated Indian lands in Georgia, preparatory to receiving American settlers there, clashes occurred. In November, 1817, fighting broke out when American soldiers burned an Indian village in southern Georgia. The Indians repaid them with a murderous assault on a group of Americans, including women and children, who were traveling on a nearby river.

The General's opportunity. Orders now went to General Andrew Jackson, the hero of the Battle of New Orleans, to proceed to Fort Scott on the Apalachicola River and take such measures as might be required to end hostilities. The orders permitted him to pursue the Indians into Florida if necessary.

Jackson prepared also to drive the Spanish out of East Florida. He wrote to James Monroe, who had succeeded Madison as President in March: "Let it be signified to me . . . that the possession of the Floridas would be desirable to the United States and in sixty days it will be accomplished." Although the administration never officially approved of Jackson's aggressiveness, it appears to have winked at it.

On the march. In April, 1818, Jackson swept into Florida, taking over the fort of St. Marks from the Spanish garrison there. Learning that the Spanish were harboring hostile Indians in Pensacola, Jackson marched his soldiers there, seized the town, and removed the governor. Jackson then placed one of his subordinates in charge as governor of West Florida.

Jackson had spent less than two months chastising the Indians and making West Florida American. He returned to Tennessee and a hero's welcome. The following toast to him expressed southern feelings: "The Floridas—

Ours without 16 years of negotiations."‡

Spain's ire. Spain raised a storm over Jackson's campaign. The Spanish minister, Luis de Onís, demanded indemnity for Spain's injuries and punishment for Jackson.

Secretary of State John Quincy Adams informed the Spanish government firmly that Jackson's actions had been necessary in order to defend the United States. He also told Spain that it must prepare to either maintain order in Florida or cede it to the United States. For the time the learned New Englander, Adams, and the unbridled Indian fighter, Jackson, agreed.

Adams-Onís Treaty. Spain yielded because it had no choice. After extended negotiations, the Adams-Onís Treaty was signed on Washington's birthday, 1819. Under its terms Spain gave up all claim to West Florida and turned over East Florida to the United States. The *western* limits of the Louisiana Purchase were defined, as the map opposite shows; and the United States agreed to pay the claims of its citizens against Spain (about $5,000,000). In effect, the United States yielded its claim to what is now Texas, but it acquired Spain's claim to the Oregon Country—the land north of the 42nd parallel.

This settlement took on added importance because in 1818 Americans had made an agreement with the British—who had disputed the United States' claim to the Oregon Country—to occupy it jointly with them. At the same time, the border between this country and British North America had been fixed along the 49th parallel from the Lake of the Woods to the Rockies. In this way the *northern* boundary of the Louisiana Purchase was established.

Sum and Substance

1. What events led to Jackson's invasion of Florida in 1818? 2. How did England and Spain react? 3. Give the terms of the agreement of the United States with Spain in 1819 and with Britain in 1818.

---

‡ Many Americans had insisted that the United States really had acquired West Florida in the Louisiana Purchase of 1803 and that officials had been vainly negotiating with France and Spain to make good the United States' title to it.

THE UNITED STATES CONFRONTS THE MONARCHS OF EUROPE

Spain's sale of Florida was another step in the shrinking of the Spanish empire in the New World. During the wars of Napoleon, independence movements had been launched in most of Spain's South and Central American colonies. When peace was restored in Europe, it seemed possible that Spain would try to recover control over its former possessions. Rumors were circulating that France, or perhaps even Russia, would assist Spain in such an undertaking.

Moreover, after 1815 the powers of Europe were banded together to preserve the peace and resist popular uprisings. Their mutual agreement, often erroneously called the "Holy Alliance" (in confusion with another pact so named), aroused in America deep suspicions of its intentions.

A FLATTERING PROPOSAL

In August, 1823, George Canning, the British foreign secretary, made a remarkable proposal to Richard Rush, the United States minister at London. He suggested that the United States join Britain in a warning to the powers of Europe that any attempt to help Spain recover its New World colonies would be opposed by force. This was a flattering and tempting offer from mighty Britain to the struggling young republic. Rush sent the startling invitation home and awaited instructions.

Advice from the elders. Upon receiving it, President Monroe immediately sought the counsel of the Virginia ex-Presidents, Jefferson and Madison. They both advised accepting Canning's offer.

Adams' stand. But when the Cabinet met in November, Adams' view prevailed over the ex-Presidents'. The Secretary insisted that the United States must not only reject the British offer but also make its own declaration—alone. Adams maintained that "it would be more candid as well as more dignified to avow our principles explicitly to Russia and France, than to come in as a cockboat in the wake of the British man-of-war."

Besides, Canning's proposed declaration would have included a statement that neither England nor the United States had any intention itself of taking over the former Spanish colonies. Adams feared that such a statement might one day prevent the United States from acquiring Cuba, on which many had already set their eyes.

The Monroe Doctrine. Following the counsel of his Secretary of State, the President in his annual message, of December 2, 1823, included a statement of policy that has since become known as the Monroe Doctrine. He made four main points: (1) "that the American continents . . . are henceforth not to be considered as subjects for future colonization by any European powers"; (2) that the United States would take the gravest view of any attempt to extend the European system of monarchy to the Americas; (3) that the United States would not interfere with existing European colonies here; and (4) that the United States would not meddle in the internal affairs of European countries.

The message itself contained nothing new, but it skillfully summed up American experiences and hopes in international affairs. Its boldness appealed enormously to Americans, who were acquiring national self-esteem and increasing strength. A Boston newspaper swelled with pride as it declared, "If the Holy Alliance attempt to control the destinies of South America they will find not only a lion, but an eagle in the way."

Of course, to many Europeans, this country looked less like a screaming eagle than like a freshly hatched chicken. But Lafayette in France, then sixty-six, wrote to congratulate Monroe. Sensing what the Monroe Doctrine could mean, Lafayette called it "the best little bit of paper that God ever permitted any man to give to the world."

The Doctrine's significance. In time the Monroe Doctrine became respected as the keystone of United States foreign policy. It may even have been partly responsible for keeping to a mini- #

In preparation for the study of the section on the nationalism of John Marshall, review the case of Marbury v. Madison, pp. 147-148, and particularly again review judicial review. In 1810 he established the power of the Supreme Court to declare a state law unconstitutional.

mum the interference of European countries in New World affairs. To Americans living in 1823, it was a new Declaration of Independence; the original had applied only to England—this one applied to all of Europe and included all the Americas.

Sum and Substance

1. What was the Holy Alliance? 2. What proposal did England make to the United States in 1823? 3. Why did John Quincy Adams oppose it? 4. Give the four main points of the Monroe Doctrine. What is the Doctrine's significance?

This section describes some decisions of Marshall's that contributed to nationalism.

MARSHALL'S COURT STRENGTHENS THE CONSTITUTION

While John Quincy Adams and James Monroe were delivering the American blast to the world, Chief Justice John Marshall was issuing Supreme Court rulings of no less importance. His far-reaching decisions, which provided arguments for the supremacy of the national government, helped strengthen the Constitution—the cornerstone of the nation.

THE VOICE OF NATIONALISM

Marshall, who had been appointed Chief Justice by John Adams, served from 1801 until his death in 1835 in his eightieth year. In that time he dominated the Court and made it strongly national—as opposed to states' rights —in its viewpoint.

Marshall had the ability to pierce to the heart of an issue and express his decision on it in forceful, crystal-clear language. His decisions were often criticized, but their logic defied the critics. A fellow-Virginian said of one of them, "All wrong, all wrong, but no man in the United States can tell why or wherein."

The power to declare a state law unconstitutional. In 1810 in the case of *Fletcher* v. *Peck,* Marshall and the Court were presented with the following facts: in 1795 Georgia's legislature had passed an act providing for the sale of the state's western land to land companies. A year later, finding that fraud had been involved in the passage of the act, the legislature annulled it. Could Georgia break a contract in this way?

Marshall unhesitatingly answered no. The act of annulment, he declared, was unconstitutional because it sanctioned the breaking of a contract. Marshall sidestepped the matter of the fraud involved, asserting that "it would be indecent in the extreme . . . to enter into an

#Today the Supreme Court very likely would not take jurisdiction of a case like this.

inquiry respecting the corruption of the sovereign power of a state."

At one stroke Marshall had protected the sanctity of contract—without which the conduct of business would be impossible—paid respect to the independence of the states, and established that the Supreme Court may declare a *state* law unconstitutional (see page 148). In 1816, in another case, in which Marshall did not participate because he was personally involved, the Supreme Court affirmed the power to overturn a decision that had been rendered by a state court.

The scope of Congress' power. In 1819 Marshall and his court handed down an opinion placing beyond question the power of Congress to legislate on any subject it considered necessary. The state of Maryland in 1818 had passed an act requiring each bank engaged in business

Marshall had a firm mouth and a kind expression.

John Marshall, who was Chief Justice of the United States for thirty-four years.

Equal Justice Under Law, Federal Bar Association

within its borders, but not chartered by it, to pay an annual tax of $15,000. Two years earlier, Congress had chartered the second Bank of the United States, of which a branch was opened in Baltimore. James McCulloch, its cashier, refused to pay the required tax, and Maryland sued him to collect it.

In this case, *McCulloch* v. *Maryland,* two questions had to be decided: (1) Did Congress have the power to incorporate a bank? (2) Was a state tax upon the bank incorporated by Congress constitutional?

To the first question Marshall replied that the establishment of the bank was "necessary and proper" for the exercise of Congress' stated powers. To the second question Marshall replied that a state might not tax an agency of the federal government. He said, ". . . the power to tax involves the power to destroy . . . the power to destroy may defeat and render useless the power to create. . . ."

Marshall had accepted, in effect, the opinion on the bank that Hamilton had written in 1791 (see page 133). Marshall declared that *any* measures Congress might choose to adopt in carrying out its powers were appropriate, provided the end in view was "legitimate" and consistent with the Constitution.

The control of interstate commerce. In 1824, the Marshall Court settled a different kind of issue. Robert Fulton and Robert Livingston, having developed a practical steamboat, had obtained in 1808 from the legislature of New York State the exclusive right to operate their vessels on the waters of New York. Accordingly, the two men granted to one Aaron Ogden sole permission to run steamboats between New York and New Jersey. Refusing to accept Ogden's monopoly, a man named Thomas Gibbons pro-

ceeded to operate competing boats.

When the resulting case of *Gibbons* v. *Ogden* reached the Supreme Court, John Marshall decided that the monopoly granted by New York was illegal. The Chief Justice declared that Congress alone could regulate interstate and foreign commerce. He insisted that to argue for a narrower interpretation of the powers of the national legislature would be to "explain away the Constitution of our country and leave it a magnificent structure indeed to look at, but totally unfit for use."

It is hard to exaggerate the importance of this decision. Within a few years steamboat navigation and railroad transportation revolutionized the nation's economic life. Both were able to grow and flourish without fear of old-fashioned monopolies created by the states.

The lasting effect. Some of Marshall's opinions have been modified or discarded, but their effect has been lasting. In his own day Marshall was a spokesman for nationalism at a time when states' rights sentiment was strong. He argued convincingly that the Constitution was a permanent agreement of the American *people* and not a mere compact among the # states to be broken when convenient.

Sum and Substance

1. What influence did Marshall have on the Constitution? On the Supreme Court? 2. Give the background of the *McCulloch* v. *Maryland* case. What two main points did Marshall make in his decision? 3. Describe the issues in the cases of *Gibbons* v. *Ogden* and *Flecher* v. *Peck*. What did Marshall decide? What principles did he uphold? 4. Name Marshall's chief contribution to the national development. 5. What doctrine did he oppose?

The administrations of Monroe and John Adams are discussed in this section.

POLITICIANS EMBARK ON AN "ERA OF GOOD FEELINGS"

Still flushed with what was called its victory in the War of 1812, the Republican party in 1816 had been able to elect to the presidency another Virginian, James Monroe. The Boston *Columbian Centinel* had referred to the "good feelings" which seemed to fill the air when the President visited the city of Boston after his inauguration. The phrase was taken up, and in time the name "Era of Good Feelings" was used as a description of Monroe's presidency. ##

##Monroe's administrations were part of the Republican era, too, but the Republicans had begun to disagree strongly among themselves and were preparing to split into two parties.

#The New Englander was John Quincy Adams. Obviously, he was pleased that the Republicans had adopted Federalist ideas. Review the establishment of the first Bank of the United States, p. 133. Jefferson opposed it. Review also the first discussion of tariffs, pp. 133-134.

Actually it was a poor name: there was just as much bad feeling as good feeling in this period. Nevertheless, on the surface there was an *appearance* of national political calm.

THE PASSING OF THE FEDERALISTS

As a force in national politics, the Federalist party disappeared following the defeat of its candidate, Rufus King, of New York, in the election of 1816. The groups the party had served—merchants, manufacturers, and bankers, especially—discovered that their needs were being met by Republicans. The measures Alexander Hamilton had advocated were now pet projects of the followers of Jefferson—a bank, the encouragement of manufacturing, a tariff, an army and navy. The Republicans, a # caustic New Englander observed, had "out-federalized Federalism."

The Republicans' bank. In 1816 the Republicans enthusiastically chartered the second Bank of the United States. All government funds would be deposited in it for safekeeping. Its operations would be subject to the scrutiny of Congress, which had the power to revoke its charter. In return for the charter, the Bank would pay a bonus of $1,500,000 into the United States treasury.

The Republicans' tariff. Like the bill to re-establish the Bank, the Tariff of 1816 also grew out of the nationalistic enthusiasm that followed the War of 1812. Wouldn't Hamilton have chuckled to know that Madison himself had recommended the bill to Congress! ## Congressmen from every part of the country voted for the tariff. They had become convinced that England was trying to stunt the growth of manufacturing in the United States by swamping American markets with low-priced goods. Calhoun supported the bill because he believed that with the help of a protective tariff, the South might become an important manufacturing section. Many westerners were agreeable to the bill because they thought the cost of transporting goods into the interior of the United States would always be prohibitively expensive. They considered that a tariff would enable them to establish

their own industries inland. Furthermore, they held that as domestic industry grew, the domestic market for farm products would also expand. The extent to which Americans were accepting the advent of industry is no better expressed than by the unaccustomed words Jefferson—of all people—wrote in 1816. Said he, "We must now place the manufacturer by the side of the agriculturist. . . ."

A CRACK IN REPUBLICAN RANKS

After 1816 the Republicans were the only national political party. Yet even then they were beginning to divide into two factions that actually were the beginnings of two new parties.

The old-school faction. One faction consisted of the old-school Republicans—those faithful to the views of the early Republicans. Its adherents argued for strict construction of the Constitution and for the economic principles fashionable among Jeffersonians twenty-five years earlier. These Republicans were convinced that their party had forsaken the farmers and had accepted far too much of the Hamiltonian program.

Clay's followers. The other faction was made up of the young Republicans. They took over the Federalists' idea of a strong national government, although they expressed greater respect for the people than Hamilton's party ever had. They thought that the federal government should help wherever possible in fostering economic improvement. Such aid, they believed, would contribute not only to national prosperity but also to national unity.

Henry Clay, who emerged early as the leader of this faction, had a picture in his mind of a gigantic nation bound together by both sentimental and economic ties. Unlike the old-school Republicans, Clay's followers looked to the future—and to the West. In Clay's own words: "We are not legislating for this moment only, or for the present generation, or for the present populated limits of these states. Our acts must embrace wider scope, reaching northwestwardly to the Pacific, and more southwardly to the River Del Norte [the Rio Grande]. Imagine this extent of territory covered with sixty, sev-

##Observe that in approving of the Tariff of 1816 both southern and western congressmen believed that their own sections of the country were going to benefit.

THE SLAVE-FREE BALANCE, 1821

0   100   200   300   400 miles

Free States | Free Terr. | Slave States | Slave Terr.

(in dispute)

BRITISH

UNORGANIZED TERRITORY
Closed to Slavery by Missouri Compromise

MICHIGAN TERRITORY
Free by Ordinance of 1787

MAINE 1820

VT. 1791

N.H.

MASS.

CONN. R.I.

NEW YORK

PENN.

N.J.

MD. DEL.

ILL. 1818 | IND. 1816 | OHIO 1803

MO. 1821

VIRGINIA

KENTUCKY 1792

NORTH CAROLINA

36°30'

TENN. 1796

ARKANSAS TERRITORY

S.C.

MISS. 1817 | ALA. 1819

GEORGIA

SPANISH

LA. 1812

THE FLORIDAS

How many Senators spoke for slave states in 1820? In 1821? For free states? Why was a balance urgent?

enty, or an hundred millions of people!"

The illusion of unity. Although the two groups in the Republican party differed significantly from each other in political ideas, until about 1823 both continued to call themselves Republicans. This fact, of course, led to a false sense of harmony in the country.

Moreover, after 1816 there was no longer a predictable lineup of the sections against each other, as there had been in the early days of the Federalists and Jeffersonians. Some questions produced East-West splits, some divided the country on North-South lines, and some produced crisscrossing patterns of disagreement and agreement. The lack of clearly drawn political battle lines also helped to foster the idea that this was an "Era of Good Feelings."

The Bank and depression. The second United States Bank was shortly under attack in the

This map shows the situation in the country after the Missouri Compromise.

South and West as a device that enriched a privileged few at the expense of the majority. In 1819, when a depression struck the country, the Bank—now sometimes called "The Monster"—was blamed for the disaster. Eastern businessmen, however, defended keenly the usefulness of the Bank.

Internal improvements. The question of federal support for internal improvements was raised in 1816. This issue, too, revealed clashing sectional interests. Calhoun had suggested (see pages 162–163) the building of a network of roads and canals financed out of a fund to be established with the bonus that the Bank had paid. Calhoun proposed also that all future dividends on Bank stock owned by the United States government be added to the fund.

This proposal, the "Bonus Bill," squeaked through Congress early in 1817. The western and middle states believed it would be a good thing because they could expect to gain from internal improvements. The South was divided about the bill. Many New Englanders opposed it because they could not benefit from its provisions. In addition, they were convinced it would drain away their section's labor supply by hastening the movement of people westward. Just before his term expired, Madison vetoed the bill, because he doubted that Congress had the power under the Constitution to authorize the building of roads and canals in the various states.

The Missouri question. A sharper disagreement #
arose in 1818. Missouri had applied for admission to the Union. Early in 1819, when a bill to admit Missouri was before the House, James Tallmadge, a New York Representative, suggested amending the bill to prohibit the further introduction of slavery into Missouri. He also wanted to free at the age of twenty-five all slaves born in Missouri after its admission. Tallmadge hated slavery, and in raising the slavery issue he was appealing to the East and Northwest to prevent the system from crossing the Mississippi.

Although the bill to admit Missouri passed the House, it was defeated in the Senate. The issue came up again at the close of 1819, when

#The necessity for a compromise in 1820 shows how jealously the North and the South were guarding their political power in Congress, particularly in the Senate.

a new Congress met. The fierce argument between northerners and southerners hinged now on whether Congress had the right to prohibit slavery in a new state.

The jam was broken when Maine applied for admission to statehood. The Maine bill was combined with the Missouri bill; and under a compromise proposed by Senator Jesse B. Thomas of Illinois, both states would be admitted without restriction on slavery. Slavery, however, was to be forever barred from the remainder of the Louisiana Purchase north of the parallel 36°30′. Maine, it was understood, would be free; and Missouri, slave. In this way, the political balance in the Senate between the North and the South would be retained—twelve free states and twelve slave states.

The Missouri Compromise, as Thomas' arrangement was called, was passed finally in 1820. One southern Senator expressed the relief that was felt all over the country: "It was a wise and necessary measure—and has saved the Republic."§

But there was no question about it: Tall- # madge had opened Pandora's box. Jefferson likened the debate on the proposed compromise to a fire bell sounding in the night. A Georgia congressman exclaimed prophetically, "You have kindled a fire which all the waters of the ocean cannot put out, which seas of blood can only extinguish!"

DAYS OF TRANSITION

Because these new public questions were only beginning to make themselves felt, politics tended for some time to revolve around personalities rather than issues. The dominant figure of the transition period was James Monroe. One of the youngest of Virginia's Revolutionary heroes,‖ he had been a Senator and served as governor before becoming the fourth President from Virginia.

An English visitor called Monroe "a plain quiet man with a deeply reflective face." Not imposing in appearance, he lacked the intellectual gifts, for example, of Jefferson and Madison; but he applied himself diligently and perseveringly to the problems of the day.

No President could reconcile the differences that divided America; he could only stand above them. This was the role that Monroe played. In 1820 he was reelected with all but one vote in the electoral college. Nobody opposed him because there was no other candidate of national standing upon whom the sections could agree.

Clay's American system. During Monroe's sec- ## ond term the sectional differences in the country sharpened. By 1820 the South had decided at last that its interests were being damaged

These men are burning fallen trees in a clearing.

Westerners like these frontiersmen needed roads: they favored tariff revenues as a means of paying for them.

Brooklyn Museum

---

§ The bill could not have passed without the support of northerners who accepted it at the last minute. John Randolph, of Virginia, called these men "doughfaces." Maybe he considered their ideas to be half-baked. Perhaps the name should have been spelled *doe faces* to refer to the female deer, timid and easily scared. At any rate, the word *doughface* was thereafter used to refer to northern men with southern principles.

‖ It seems fitting that Monroe, like John Adams and Jefferson before him, should die on a Fourth of July!

##Review the situation shortly before 1820, when all the sections agreed on having a protective tariff. Also review Calhoun's ideas, pp. 162-163. Now views had changed.

Charleston, the chief port of South Carolina, which shipped large quantities of cotton and rice abroad. Charlestonians and other southerners thought a protective tariff only a temporary requirement for northern industry.

Charleston was the place where South Carolina planters spent their money on large, cool homes.

by the tariff, and its congressmen helped defeat a new one. But western farmers and eastern manufacturers kept up the pressure on Congress for a higher tariff. Henry Clay, his heart set on winning the presidency, tried to bring these two groups together in a permanent political alliance and become its leader.

\# Clay called his formula for achieving these results the "American system." Manufacturers would get a protective tariff; westerners would support it because they would receive internal improvements paid for in part out of the increased customs receipts. Clay believed that the crying need was to shut out European manufactured goods in order to strengthen home manufacturing and the home market. Despite southern opposition, Congress passed a new protective tariff in 1824, because the American system appealed irresistibly to western farmers and eastern factory owners.

Southern misgivings. The South's irritation was intensified when the growing group of manufacturers kept demanding higher tariff rates year after year. Southerners, not having become manufacturers themselves, balked at paying high prices for manufactured goods that made northerners rich.

A college president in South Carolina asked: "Is it worth our while to continue this union of states, where the North demand to be our masters, and we are required to be their tributaries? Who with the most insulting mockery call the yoke they put upon our necks the American system! The question . . . is fast approaching to the alternative, of submission or separation."

The campaign of 1824. By 1824 the sectional disagreements on national questions had become so pronounced that each section had at least one candidate for the presidency. Three of the hopeful men were members of Monroe's Cabinet: John Quincy Adams, Secretary of State; William H. Crawford, of Georgia, Secretary of the Treasury; and John C. Calhoun, of South Carolina, Secretary of War. In addition, the hero of New Orleans, Andrew Jackson, of Tennessee, was available, as was Henry Clay, of Kentucky.

None of these men appeared to have strength outside his own locality. Crawford may well

\#Compare Clay's proposals with Calhoun's, pp. 162-163. (Both proposed internal improvements; Calhoun was idealistic, Clay politically oriented; Calhoun appealed to all sections.)

have been the most acceptable of them all, because he managed to support the American system while retaining the friendship of old Republicans. But before the election he suffered a stroke that affected his gait and eyesight, virtually eliminating him from the race.

Clay hoped that the American system would lure New England away from its favorite son, Adams. He took a chance and lost. Calhoun was willing to settle—at least for the time being—for the vice-presidency, to which he was elected.

Adams, despite his talent, never stood high in public favor. Intrepid and frank, he wrote of himself: "I am a man of reserved, cold, austere, and forbidding manners."

The outcome. Andrew Jackson proved to be the one man among the candidates who could arouse enthusiasm among people in all sections. The election returns gave Jackson 99 electoral votes, Adams 84, Crawford 41, and Clay 37. Because no candidate had a majority, the election, under the constitutional provision for such a case, was thrown into the House of Representatives. There in February, 1825, Clay gave his support to Adams, who was declared elected.

Immediately a clamor was raised: it had been generally expected that Jackson, who led in the number of electoral votes, would win. The Washington *Gazette* complained: "The Warrior, the Hero, the Statesman, and Republican was discarded for the cold-blooded calculator, the heavy diplomatist, the reviler of Jefferson . . . the haughty, unrelenting aristocrat."

When Adams appointed Clay Secretary of State, it was charged that he had made a "corrupt bargain" in return for the Kentuckian's support in the House contest. The accusation was never proved, but the Jackson men repeated it over and over again in order to destroy Adams' reputation.

Party labels again. The administration's supporters were soon known as the National Republicans. The friends of Jackson, considering themselves to be the true heirs of Jefferson, took the name Democratic-Republicans, which they later shortened to Democrats.

THE SECOND PRESIDENT ADAMS

No more learned or experienced man has ever come to the presidency than John Quincy Adams. At fourteen he had been secretary to the United States minister to Russia. He had served as Senator from Massachusetts and had shown the courage and conviction to switch from the Federalist party of his father to the Republican side. We have already seen the decisive part he played in shaping the Monroe Doctrine.

Under attack. In his first annual message to Congress, Adams advocated a great expansion of road- and canal-building with federal aid, a protective tariff, and a generally strengthened national government. This program, which appealed to the Northeast and to the West, alienated southerners and many westerners, who believed that it had been designed principally to aid eastern businessmen.

Adams was quickly under more savage attack than his father had ever been. His opponents sneered, "The cub is a greater bear than the old one." The President confidently wrote in his diary that his policies would "outlive the blast of faction and abide the test of time." The anger on both sides became keener as 1828 drew near.

"Tariff of Abominations." The Democrats made a new tariff bill which came before Congress in 1828 their chief interest. Their strategy was to propose so high a tariff—on raw materials as well as on manufactured goods—that all sections of the country, even New England, would be against it. Adams, as a supporter of the American system, would be discredited.

To the surprise and embarrassment of many, however, Congress passed this "Tariff of Abominations," and Adams signed the bill. The South, outraged that tariff duties had been pushed so high, pledged revenge.

The first "President of the people." In the election of 1828 Jackson, "the people's choice," easily emerged victorious over Adams. He won the South because he was anti-Adams, and the West because, as an Indian fighter, he seemed to be a friend of the frontiersmen. In the mid-

##The class should note the appeal of Jackson to each of the sections. Note the shift in party labels. Review the split in the Republicans. Jackson considered himself an old-school Republican.

175

dle states, he had the support particularly of the smaller businessmen, who considered him to be antiaristocratic.

No presidential inauguration has ever surpassed Jackson's in excitement. Wrote one eyewitness: "Orange punch by barrels full was made, but as waiters opened the door to bring it out, a rush would be made, the glasses broken, the pails of liquor upset, and the most painful confusion prevailed . . . it was certainly difficult to keep anything like order, and it was mortifying to see men, with boots heavy with mud, standing on the damask satin chairs, from their eagerness to get a sight of the President."

Adams, out of step with the times, was never reconciled to Jackson's victory. When Harvard College decided to confer an honorary Doctor of Laws degree on Jackson in 1837, Adams was incensed at this act of his alma mater. He indignantly wrote that he would not "be present to witness [Harvard's] disgrace in conferring its highest literary honors upon a barbarian who could not write a sentence of grammar and

hardly could spell his own name."

"Aristocrats" everywhere, however, were becoming accustomed to the changes afoot in America. The president of Harvard College might have been speaking in their behalf when he declared, "As the people have . . . decided that this man knows law enough to be their ruler, it is not for Harvard College to maintain that they are mistaken."

Sum and Substance

1. Why did the Federalist party disappear? 2. Give the terms of the charter of the second Bank. 3. Why did the country as a whole support the Tariff of 1816? 4. What helped to give Monroe's administration the name "Era of Good Feelings"? 5. Why did the Bank cause sectional clashes in 1819? 6. How did the nation react to Calhoun's "Bonus Bill"? 7. Describe the background and terms of the Missouri Compromise. 8. What was Clay's American system? 9. How did the election of 1824 produce a new party? 10. In what way did the "Tariff of Abominations" help elect Jackson?

Dr. Thornton's prize was $500 and a city lot. He became an architect in the construction.

The Capitol of the United States, as it appeared in 1826, during John Quincy Adams' time as President. Using a modification of a design by the physician-architect William Thornton, skilled workers began the building in 1793, when President Washington laid the cornerstone. The Capitol was rebuilt after it was burned in 1814.

Library of Congress

176 The cornerstone of the old capitol was laid in 1793 by Washington. The first wing completed was just right of the center wing, housing the Senate, House, and Supreme Court.

THE WORKSHOP

OF LASTING SIGNIFICANCE

How was each of the following related to the strengthening of the national spirit?

sectionalism
internal improvements
Noah Webster
Clermont
Adams-Onís Treaty
Holy Alliance
George Canning
John Quincy Adams
Monroe Doctrine
McCulloch v.
  Maryland
Gibbons v. *Ogden*

Fletcher v. *Peck*
"Era of Good
  Feelings"
John C. Calhoun
"Bonus Bill"
James Tallmadge
Missouri Compromise
American system
"Tariff of
  Abominations"
second Bank of the
  United States

DOCUMENTS IN HISTORY

1. In what respect did Representative John C. Calhoun consider his country weak?

2. What two purposes did Calhoun think a system of roads and canals could serve?

3. Name the American advantages that Calhoun believed could contribute to the "splendid future" of the United States? In his view, what could darken the future?

4. What mood of Americans shortly after the War of 1812 did Calhoun's speech (pages 162–163) reflect?

BEING A SOCIAL SCIENTIST

1. Public leaders, songs, ships, slogans, pictures, and expressions have become national symbols. Make a list of as many symbols as you can, including both early ones and some of recent origin. What good purposes do such symbols serve? How can they be abused? Give examples of their misuse.

2. Name the issues shortly after the War of 1812 on which the sections of the country took sides. In each case, state the viewpoints and account for them.

3. How did Henry Clay, John Quincy Adams, and John Marshall each contribute to American nationalism?

INTERNATIONAL POLITICS

1. Review the history of Florida: its ownership before 1763, between 1763 and 1783, and between 1783 and 1819. How did international politics affect the area in 1763? In 1783? In 1819?

What events led to the Adams-Onís Treaty? What prevented war with Britain and Spain before the treaty was made? How did the events preceding the treaty and the treaty itself strengthen the development of nationalism in the United States?

2. What international crises did the United States face between 1815 and 1823? What steps did President Monroe take to handle them? How successful was he?

In what sense did the Monroe Doctrine "sum #
up" American experiences and hopes in international affairs? How did it influence American foreign policy?

HISTORY AND GEOGRAPHY

1. According to the table on page 165, how many of the largest cities in 1790 were in New England? In the middle states? How do you account for this distribution? Explain the inclusion of Washington in the list for 1800. Compare the list of 1820 with that of 1790 and try to explain the changes.

2. Referring to the maps on pages 150 and 172, explain just how the purchase of the Louisiana territory later led to the controversy over Missouri.

3. Missouri and Illinois lie side by side, on opposite sides of the Mississippi. Why was there no slave-free issue when Illinois entered the Union in 1818? Why did the Missouri controversy begin in the *Senate*? How did the debate over the admission of Missouri strengthen sectionalism in the United States?

4. Study the map of the United States on ##
pages 360–361. How were geographical features related to the different ways in which the sections responded to the idea of building internal improvements? Be specific.

##For example, the West (old Northwest) was far from eastern markets and had to depend on the Mississippi or on roads. The South had access to the sea but wanted roads in the interior.

177

A LONG VIEW

Making a New Nation

BY the end of the 1820's the population of the United States was nearing 13,000,000. As thousands of Americans swarmed westward, they already had confidence that they would have the numerical strength to conquer the western lands. Being a people on the move, they gave an impression of possessing unlimited energy and of being always in a hurry.

One effect of the westward push was to scatter families over very great distances. Another was to stimulate improvements in land and water transportation. But the chief result of the movement west was that Americans turned their backs on Europe, concentrating on their labors at home.

An overwhelming majority of Americans were still engaged in agriculture, which at that time meant raising crops for a local market. Few young people grew up not knowing how to milk a cow, raise vegetables, or identify the various kinds of trees.

Most people regarded the land as a vast "Garden of Eden" in which to invest their toil happily. Out of that land would come a full storehouse of food to guard against hard times. Even for people in the cities the soil provided reassurance in the face of the uncertainty about the future which had always plagued mankind.

The value—and profitableness—of manufacturing was already apparent. The use of steam power in factories and on inland waterways was by now "old hat." Nevertheless, in the home the day's routine—which usually fell most heavily on the women—was still largely backbreaking drudgery. Moreover, the multitude of goods that delight today's shopper had not yet made their appearance. Money was comparatively scarce, and from year to year prices remained about the same.

But daily life was gradually becoming different from what it had been in the colonial period. People saw the need for education as an aid in the producing of technological improvements—as well as in the making of good citizens. (Most teaching in the grades and on the secondary level, however, was unprofessional, something a young man might do while waiting for an opportunity in business or in law.)

Another new characteristic of life in the early national years was its emphasis on simplicity—which was considered appropriate for a republic. For the first time in the history of Western civilization, people were running a country without the trappings of nobility or the authority of an established church. That is, they were building a society that did not rest on inherited position. To be sure, distinctions between people existed that were based on the amount of property they had. And there was discrimination based on religion or skin color. But property was easier to acquire than it had ever been, and to a greater degree than anywhere else an individual was respected on the basis of what he himself could achieve.

The type of dress Americans adopted seemed suited to citizens of a republic. No longer wearing knee breeches, which were "court wear" in Europe, men were attired instead in trousers. The wig had ceased to be fashionable even for important public men. Some women still carried parasols to prevent freckles and sunburn, but most of them could not pamper themselves in this way. In the "best of circles" women wore their hair tightly pulled back. They arranged it in ringlets only for a dress-up occasion.

These years, so full of optimistic feeling, are remembered with satisfaction today. They proved that a country could get along without a king—and prosper in the bargain. They taught that enlightened human beings could be trusted to rule themselves and be masters of their fate.

Even today, though most Americans are city-dwellers, the lessons from the early days of the republic remain valid. In addition, they show the peoples of new countries everywhere that the United States, only recently a "new nation" itself, developed from a modest and uncertain beginning through the efforts and self-discipline of resolute men and women. ★ ★ ★ ★ ★ ★ ★ ★ ★

#The lessons are listed in the paragraph above. People today can also learn the quality of optimism from the Americans of the early 1800's. Self-discipline was another quality of theirs.

PART TWO WORKSHOP

AMERICA IN THE WORLD

Almost from the beginning of Washington's administration, the United States found it necessary to determine the policy it would adopt toward foreign countries—its foreign policy.

1. Sum up the situations which demanded the formulation of foreign policy in the presidencies of Washington, John Adams, and Jefferson.

2. Describe the policies carried out by the Federalist administrations and by Jefferson. What single consideration influenced most strongly the foreign policy of each of the first three Presidents? What considerations had to be pushed aside? What made it difficult for each man to carry out his foreign policy?

3. What events in the first thirty years of the republic strengthened the position of the United States in world affairs? How?

4. Who was chiefly responsible for deciding what foreign policy the young United States would adopt? What assistance was available?

5. What policy adopted in the early years is still a basis of American foreign policy? Why?

6. What evidence from the events of the first years under the Constitution clearly shows that domestic and foreign affairs are closely related?

THE FEDERAL GOVERNMENT

The national, or central, government of the United States is called federal because it shares authority with the states.

1. How does the Constitution make plain the division of powers between the states and the federal government? What is a concurrent power? Name as many as you can.

2. Generally speaking, the federal government has power to handle what kind of problems? The powers of the states are limited to what problems?

3. Why is Article 1, Section 8 of the Constitution considered fundamental in making the federal government strong?

4. Explain how the system of checks and balances in the Constitution worked in the years 1789–1803, giving examples to show how the branches of the federal government checked and balanced each other.

5. What check not provided by the Constitution was proposed by Jefferson and Madison in the Virginia and Kentucky resolutions? Does this check conflict with the Preamble of the Constitution? Explain.

TIME AND CHANGE

Continue the time line you began earlier. Include the significant dates and events of Part Two.

1. The period covered in Part Two begins when? Ends when? The period includes what parts of what centuries?

2. Designate the dates and related events which, taken together, may be spoken of as the (*a*) Federalist era, (*b*) Age of Jefferson.

3. List the major changes that took place in the period shown on your time line (the class should agree on them). Keep the list.

4. Answer these questions about each change: (*a*) What caused it? (*b*) Was it opposed? Why?

OLD PROBLEMS BECOME NEW

1. Restate the problem about government which Americans inherited from Britain (see page 97). What solution did they agree on in 1781? In 1788? How did the Virginia and Kentucky resolutions, the Hartford Convention, and the arguments over strict and loose construction of the Constitution show that the problem had not disappeared?

2. Identify examples of other fundamental problems in the years covered in Part Two. Among them are: What policy should be adopted about the public land? Should the country acquire new territory? Should a protective tariff be enacted? What should be done when the interests of the various sections conflict (the problem of sectionalism)? What foreign policy should the country follow?

Begin to keep track of these problems. What was done to solve each during the period discussed in Part Two?

Observe the emphasis on foreign affairs of the United States in "Confronting the World," and notice the stress on technology and intellectual life in "Art, Science, and the Life of the Mind." Students should be encouraged to own some books they have especially enjoyed.

THE BOOKSHELF

Eyewitness Accounts

Butterfield, L. H., and Others (eds.). *John Adams, Diary and Autobiography*, Vols. 1–4. *Adams Family Correspondence*, Vols. 5–6. Cambridge, Mass.: Harvard University Press, 1961–1966 [Paperback—New York: Atheneum Publishers, 1964, 1965].

Commager, H. S. (ed.). *America in Perspective* [Paperback—New York: New American Library, Inc.].

Lewis, Meriwether, and William Clark. *Journals of the Lewis and Clark Expeditions to the Pacific* [Paperback—many editions].

Madison, James. *Notes on Debates in the Federal Convention of 1787.* Athens: Ohio University Press, 1966.

Giant Men and Women

Bakeless, John. *Lewis and Clark, Partners in Discovery.* Gloucester, Mass.: Peter Smith [Paperback—New York: Apollo Editions, Inc.].

Bemis, Samuel F. *John Quincy Adams and the Union.* New York: Alfred A. Knopf, Inc., 1956.

Brant, Irving. *Commander-in-Chief* (Vol. 6 of "James Madison"). Indianapolis: Bobbs-Merrill Co., Inc., 1961.

———. *The President* (Vol. 5 of "James Madison"). Indianapolis: Bobbs-Merrill Co., Inc., 1956.

Hebard, Grace R. *Sacajawea.* Woodland Hills, Calif.: Robert Clark, Publisher, 1957.

Malone, Dumas. *Jefferson and the Ordeal of Liberty.* Boston: Little, Brown & Co., 1962.

Tucker, Caroline. *John Marshall: The Great Chief Justice.* New York: Farrar, Straus & Giroux, Inc., 1962.

Living and Making a Living

Baldwin, Leland D. *The Keelboat Age on Western Waters.* Pittsburgh: University of Pittsburgh Press, 1960.

Coles, Harry L. *The War of 1812.* Chicago: University of Chicago Press, 1965 [Paperback—Chicago: University of Chicago Press].

Dangerfield, George. *The Awakening of American Nationalism, 1815–1828.* New York: Harper & Row, Publishers, 1965 [Paperback—New York: Harper & Row, Publishers].

———. *The Era of Good Feelings.* Gloucester, Mass.: Peter Smith [Paperback—Harcourt, Brace & World, Inc., 1963].

Horsman, Reginald. *The Causes of the War of 1812* [Paperback—Cranbury, N.J.: A. S. Barnes & Co., Inc.].

Miller, John C. *The Federalist Era, 1789–1801.* New York: Harper & Row, Publishers, 1960 [Paperback—New York: Harper & Row, Publishers].

Risjord, N. K. *The Old Republicans: Conservatism in the Age of Jefferson.* New York: Columbia University Press, 1965.

Rossiter, Clinton L. *The Grand Convention.* New York: The Macmillan Co., 1966.

Schachner, Nathan. *The Founding Fathers* [Paperback—New York: G. P. Putnam's Sons, 1961].

Tucker, Glenn. *Dawn like Thunder.* Indianapolis: Bobbs-Merrill Co., Inc., 1963.

Van Every, Dale. *Ark of Empire: The American Frontier, 1784–1803.* New York: William Morrow & Co., Inc., 1963 [Paperback—New York: New American Library, Inc.].

Wilkinson, Norman B. *Explosives in History: The Story of Black Powder.* Chicago: Rand McNally & Co., 1967.

Confronting the World

Bastert, Russell H. *American Foreign Policy to 1880* [Paperback—Chicago: Rand McNally & Co., 1967].

Engleman, Fred L. *The Peace of Christmas Eve.* New York: Harcourt, Brace & World, Inc., 1962.

Long, David F. *The Outward View: An Illustrated History of United States Foreign Relations.* Chicago: Rand McNally & Co., 1963.

Perkins, Bradford. *Prologue to War: England and the United States, 1805–1812.* Berkeley: University of California Press, 1961.

Varg, Paul A. *The Foreign Policies of the Founding Fathers.* East Lansing: Michigan State University Press, 1963.

White, Patrick C. T. *A Nation on Trial.* New York: John Wiley & Sons, Inc., 1965 [Paperback—New York: John Wiley & Sons, Inc.].

Art, Science, and the Life of the Mind

Green, Constance M. *Eli Whitney and the Birth of American Technology.* Boston: Little, Brown & Co., 1956 [Paperback—Boston: Little, Brown & Co.].

Hindle, Brooke. *The Pursuit of Science in Revolutionary America, 1735–1789.* Chapel Hill: University of North Carolina Press, 1959.

Nye, Russell B. *The Cultural Life of the New Nation: 1776–1830.* New York: Harper & Row, Publishers, 1960 [Paperback—New York: Harper & Row, Publishers].

Spiller, Robert E., and Others. *A Literary History of the United States.* New York: The Macmillan Co., 1963.

Historical Fiction

Forester, C. S. *The Captain from Connecticut.* Boston: Little, Brown & Co., 1941. (A Yankee naval commander in the War of 1812.)

Roberts, Kenneth. *Lydia Bailey.* New York: Doubleday & Co., Inc., 1947. [Paperback—New York: Fawcett World Library]. (An account of the war against Tripoli and of events in Haiti.)

———. *Captain Caution.* New York: Doubleday & Co., Inc., 1934. (Naval action and romance in the War of 1812.)

Seton, Anya. *My Theodosia.* Boston: Houghton Mifflin Co., 1941. (Aaron Burr and his daughter.)

This part of the book describes the rise of the sectionalism that was just beginning to show itself in the first years of the republic. It opens with the account of the Age of Jackson, and then it gives a detailed analysis of each of the three main sections of the country--the North, the South, and the West. The characteristics of each are emphasized to give students a better understanding of events that led to the Civil War (treated in Part Four). In the introduction to Part Three, given below, the authors stress Americans' great interest in politics and their beliefs that the governing of the country deserved their best thought and that democracy is an obligation. Ask if Americans today have this feeling.

THE CHALLENGE OF SECTIONALISM

Discuss the meaning of this sentence. What are our ideals? Are we being judged by them?

PART THREE

#
A people is judged by the ideals that guide it. Before the 1820's were over, American ideals were known throughout the world. The chief one of these was political liberty.

Political liberty implied the freedom to choose leaders by means of popular elections. People in this country believed that the business of government in a democracy was the obligation of every citizen. Having already made the ballot box a sacred thing, they were admitting new thousands each year to its privileges. Americans had discovered the value ## of informed discussion in the management of civic affairs—and were practicing it.

By the 1830's the rollicking election campaigns of determined candidates had become a trademark of politics in the United States. Office seekers in every part of the country seemed resolved to prove President Martin Van Buren's maxim: "One man with courage makes a majority."

The task of governing for the whole nation was recognized as worthy of enlisting the best minds of that generation. Since the interests of the sections then, as now, were varied and sometimes conflicting, the North, the South, and the West had exceptional needs for talented representatives.

The federal government had become an arena in which an intense war of words and ideas was being waged by men who never despaired of persuading their opponents. Yet despite the fierce conviction the sectional spokesmen poured into their arguments, they hoped to arrive at decisions peacefully. For they had this in common: they were the servants of the people who had elected them, and the people wanted a harmonious Union.

##Ask if Americans today carry on informed discussion in the management of civic affairs. If so, how have they becomed informed? If not, account for the change.

181

Observe that the three horses on the far bank of the canal are pulling the canal boat (center.) The other boat is carrying farm produce. This is a scene that shows a rural region that was typical of the United States in general. Observe the rough road in the foreground.

Boats on the Erie Canal, the man-made waterway across upper New York State that linked the Hudson River with the Great Lakes. The movements of people and goods along this and other canals and over the National Road helped marry the East and the old Northwest, despite their differing economic interests and requirements.

The Erie Canal influenced people to settle in northern New York, as well as in Michigan and other western areas. Towns sprang up along the canal's route as goods and people passed through the new waterway. One of the most important effects of the canal was to encourage the building of other canals. (For a detailed treatment of the Erie Canal and the canal era, see John F. Stover's paperback in the Rand McNally Classroom Library Series, Turnpikes, Canals, and Steamships.)

Students should acquire the habit of reading the contents page preceding each part as a means of getting a bird's eye view of each chapter and of the whole part. The main ideas in each chapter appear in the heads under the chapter titles.

PART THREE

THE CHALLENGE OF SECTIONALISM

Before beginning Chapter 10, review the election of 1824.

CHAPTER 10	THE AGE OF ANDREW JACKSON	184
	The People's President Occupies the White House	186
	Death Snatches Away the Whigs' Hard-earned Victory	194
CHAPTER 11	THE NORTH: DIVERSE INTERESTS	200
	New England Is Transformed by the Factory System	202
	The Middle Atlantic States Cultivate Crops and Trade	204
	The Old Northwest Relies on Grains and the Union	208
	Northerners Build Strong Internal Ties	209
CHAPTER 12	THE SOUTH: THE COTTON KINGDOM	216
	Slavery Takes Hold of Southern Agriculture	218
	The "Peculiar Institution" Is Weighed in the Balance	223
CHAPTER 13	THE WEST: MANIFEST DESTINY	230
	Frontiersmen Push Relentlessly Toward the Pacific	232
	The Annexation of Texas Opens the Door to War	236
	Diplomacy and a Gold Rush Net America the Far West	243
A LONG VIEW		246

The chapter titles (11, 12, and 13) show what the chief influence on each section of the country was. The North was considered to be made up of three regions--the Northeast, the middle Atlantic states, and the old Northwest, which were united by internal improvements.

Jackson was the first President to recognize that corporations were growing more numerous in the United States and to deal with the situation. Corporations were building bridges, constructing canals and turnpikes, carrying on manufacturing, and engaging in banking and insurance. Relationships between employers and employees became more and more impersonal. Jackson felt that he should fight to keep one group of people from acquiring most of the wealth of the country. He believed that banks helped take money from the workers and gave it to the wealthy. In this address he aired his views on banking.

10

THE AGE OF ANDREW JACKSON

. . . nothing but equal rights and equal laws . . .

It is one of the serious evils of our present system of banking that it enables one class of society—and that by no means a numerous one —by its control over the currency, to act injuriously upon the interests of all the others and to exercise more than its just proportion of influence in political affairs. The agricultural, the mechanical, and the laboring classes have little or no share in the direction of the great moneyed corporations, and from their habits and the nature of their pursuits they are incapable of forming extensive combinations to act together with united force. . . .

The planter, the farmer, the mechanic, and the laborer all know that their success depends upon their own industry and economy, and that they must not expect to become suddenly rich by the

Students should notice the evidence in this picture that business organizations were growing.

fruits of their toil. Yet these classes of society form the great body of the people of the United States; they are the bone and sinew of the country—men who love liberty and desire nothing but equal rights and equal laws, and who, moreover, hold the great mass of our national wealth, although it is distributed in moderate amounts among the millions of freemen who possess it. But with overwhelming numbers and wealth on their side they are in constant danger of losing their fair influence in the Government, and with difficulty maintain their just rights. . . .

The mischief springs from the power which the moneyed interest derives from a paper currency which they are able to control, from the multitude of corporations with exclusive privileges which they have succeeded in obtaining in the different States, and which are employed altogether for their benefit; and unless you become more watchful . . . and check this spirit of monopoly and thirst for exclusive privileges you will in the end find that the most important powers of Government have been given or bartered away, and the control over your dearest interests has passed into the hands of these corporations. . . .

In your hands is rightfully placed the sovereignty of the country, and to you every one placed in authority is ultimately responsible. It is always in your power to see that the wishes of the people are carried into faithful execution, and their will . . . must sooner or later be obeyed; and while the people remain, as I trust they ever will, uncorrupted and incorruptible, and continue watchful and jealous of their rights, the Government is safe, and the cause of freedom will continue to triumph over all its enemies. . . .

This is part of the farewell address that Andrew Jackson delivered to the country when he left the presidency in 1837. Here Jackson was providing a voice for the large numbers of rural and city people in moderate circumstances, citizens whose interests he thought government had neglected.

Jackson sensed that as the population grew and expanded westward, opportunity, particularly economic opportunity, would have to become freer. Easier credit and more generous laws under which a man could incorporate his own business were especially important to Jacksonians. The "laboring class" that Jackson talks about is not the same as the "working people" to which Americans refer today. Jackson's term meant the growing group of self-employed craftsmen in the cities and towns.

More generous corporation laws would let people incorporate their own businesses without depending on state legislatures.

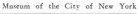

COLLEGE of HEALTH
WRIGHT

Looking north on Broadway in New York City, in 1836. Pedestrians and horse-drawn wagons and carriages cross the intersection at Canal Street without benefit of traffic signs. The rows of business houses and the merchants— outside and in—show how lively were the mercantile activities that helped make the city the nation's largest.

Goods are being displayed and sold on both sides of the street.

THE PEOPLE'S PRESIDENT OCCUPIES THE WHITE HOUSE

Andrew Jackson had for years been a fascinating national hero when his presidency began in 1829. In appearance he was thin, almost emaciated-looking; he spoke quickly and vigorously, his shock of bristling hair shaking. Frances Trollope, the English authoress, thought that Jackson "wore his hair carelessly but not ungracefully arranged, and in spite of his harsh, gaunt features looked like a gentleman and soldier."

Jackson had many apparent contradictions in his makeup. His principal achievements had been in military life, where his behavior had often been high-handed. Yet he became both the people's idol and a strong spokesman for democracy.

He was nearly sixty-two years of age when he was inaugurated, and by the standards of his day, an old man, set in his ways. Yet he became then the beloved and fiery leader of a new political movement. He was a southerner, reared in the Carolinas, who made his home in Tennessee. Yet he became the voice of northern politicians from the East. He was one of the large landholders of his section and a favorite of the planters. Yet he remained a frontiersman in spirit, with many antiaristocratic prejudices. Jackson had once said: "I know what I am fit for. I can command a body of men in a rough way: but I am not fit to be President." Yet "Old Hickory" is regarded as one of the great Presidents.

Jackson's early years in the Carolina back country were spent in poverty. But he studied law, and, moving to Tennessee, he became in time a member of the state supreme court and then of the· United States Senate. His military service was extensive and distinguished. When he was only a youngster, he fought in the Revolution; at later times he battled Englishmen at New Orleans (see page 160) and Indians on the southeastern border (see pages 166–167).

SUPPORTERS AND ADVERSARIES

When Jackson came into office, he had no well-defined program of action. His election had been made possible by support from all # sections of the country, and now each of them expected to dominate the new administration. His Cabinet contained representatives of the principal factions that had contributed to his victory. The only superior man in it was Martin Van Buren of New York, the Secretary of State.

Van Buren was a gifted politician who hid his aims so well it was said he "rowed to his object with muffled oars." The nicknames that he wore suggest the popular conception of him: "The Little Magician," "The Red Fox" (he was a redhead), and "The American Talleyrand."* His usefulness was appreciated by Jackson, and Van Buren quickly had easy access to the President's ear.

The "kitchen cabinet." Although he leaned on Van Buren, Jackson did not usually depend on other members of his Cabinet for advice. He relied instead on a group of newspaper editors and northern politicians who had worked for his election and who came to be labeled the "kitchen cabinet." The most important member was Amos Kendall, of Kentucky, once a tutor to Henry Clay's children. He was now described as "the moving spring of the Administration; the thinker, the planner, the doer." Because of their craft in finding out and exploiting public sentiment, members of the "kitchen cabinet" have been called "the first of America's great practical politicians."

The Eaton affair. It was the *official* Cabinet ## that raised a storm which came close to tearing the administration apart at its very start. Jackson had appointed his old friend John H. Eaton to be Secretary of War. Eaton had taken as his bride Peggy O'Neale, a tavern keeper's daughter and the widow of a sailor.

Immediately after the inauguration the other Cabinet wives, led by Mrs. John Calhoun, refused to have anything to do socially with

---

* Charles Maurice de Talleyrand-Périgord (1754–1838) was the foreign minister of France in the days of the French Revolution and Napoleon. He was a cunning diplomat known for his wit and cynicism.

##Jackson's attitude in the Eaton affair was related directly to the experience his wife had with gossipers. Ask a student to find out what the experience was.

Peggy Eaton. She was, they gossiped, a person of low moral character. Jackson, believing none of the rumors, championed her cause. In this he was supported by Van Buren. But Vice-President Calhoun accepted Mrs. Calhoun's judgment of Peggy Eaton.

The "Eaton trouble" might have been insignificant in itself. But it symbolized the serious antagonism between the President and the southerners who had so recently supported him in the election. Southerners complained that although they had worked hard to elect him, he was now forsaking their interests and selling out to the northern politicians. Actually # Jackson held strongly national views, while southerners—and especially Calhoun, their leading spokesman—had become sectionalist, standing firmly for states' rights.

SECTIONAL ANTAGONISMS

A dramatic example of the rising sectional feeling was a debate held in the Senate in January, 1830. Beginning as a discussion of public land policy, it shortly turned into an argument over the nature of the Union itself.

The Webster-Hayne debate. At a critical point Senator Robert Y. Hayne, of South Carolina, a close associate of Calhoun's and one of the debaters, spoke deeply-felt thoughts. Using strict-construction arguments he defended the right of states to oppose federal interference in the sale of public land. He insisted that "the very life of our system is the independence of the states. . . ."

Now Daniel Webster of Massachusetts, the finest orator of his time, rose. It was said "no man was as great as Webster looked." Once his piercing black eyes, shielded by his craggy brow, were fixed upon an audience, no one escaped the magic of his presentation or the musical quality of his language.

Pointing out that the states were sovereign only where their power had not been limited by the Constitution, Webster asserted that the federal government had supreme authority over the people. He condemned the southern sentiments being expressed, like "Liberty first and Union afterwards," as "words of delusion and

Corcoran Gallery of Art

Andrew Jackson, as he looked shortly after the Battle of New Orleans. His military victory there first gave some Americans the idea that the tall, slim Tennessean might someday become the president of the United States.

Jackson never lost his military bearing, either on foot or on horseback.

##Review Article 6, Clause 2 and Article 1, Section 10 of the Constitution. Of course, the granting of specific powers to Congress affects the states (see Section 8, Clause 17).

187

Illinois State Historical Library

Black Hawk, a victim of the relentless westward movement.

Black Hawk tried to regain land east of the Mississippi.

folly." He concluded, "Liberty *and* Union, now and forever, one and inseparable!"

Jackson's stand. To celebrate Jefferson Day on April 13, 1830, the Democratic party arranged a banquet at a Washington hotel. During the meal several leading men offered toasts showing marked agreement with the views expressed by Hayne in the Senate a few weeks earlier.

When Jackson's turn to lift his glass came, he stood up and, looking straight at Calhoun, said, "Our Union: it must be preserved." Calhoun, his hand trembling with emotion, causing the wine to run down the side of his glass, responded, "The Union: next to our liberty, the most dear." The distance between the President and his Vice-President now daily widened.†

† Fuel was added to the fire when Jackson discovered that Calhoun in 1818, as Secretary of War in Monroe's Cabinet, had favored punishing "Old Hickory" for his conduct in Florida (see page 167). The President demanded an explanation, which proved unsatisfactory to him. The split between the men could not be healed, and Calhoun resigned the vice-presidency in 1832.

#Ask how this supports the authors' summary of Jackson's views, line 15, p. 187.

The Maysville veto. The following month Jackson vetoed a bill authorizing the construction with federal money of a road in Kentucky—the Maysville Road. In a message accompanying the veto, the President seemed to accept the states' rights argument by declaring that a purely local road did not come under national jurisdiction. But the South was fooled only for an instant. A closer look showed the real purpose of the veto: to strike at Henry Clay, an enemy of long standing, by denying him this road in his own state. (Northeasterners and westerners were soon to be delighted with the President's enthusiasm for roads and canals built with federal funds.)

Relations with the West. Jackson reorganized his Cabinet after the Eaton affair and in his appointments included Lewis Cass, of Michigan. The President in this way showed his appreciation of the support the West was giving him.

Westerners applauded especially Jackson's Indian policy. During his presidency, ninety-four separate treaties were concluded with the Indians, resettling them across the Mississippi. Westerners knew that Jackson strongly supported their fights with the Indians—the Black Hawk War of 1832, for instance. In that war on the upper Mississippi, a raw-boned young westerner, Abraham Lincoln from Illinois, was a captain.

Northeasterners spoke approvingly of Jackson's stand in support of the Union. The Maysville veto, moreover, reassured them that he would not do *everything* the West wanted. The West and the Northeast had become the strongholds of Jackson's strength. The gradual loss of southern support was completed as a result of the intense struggle over the Tariff of 1832.

In 1828 Calhoun had written a pamphlet, *Exposition and Protest,* issued by South Carolina's legislature. In it he had called the tariff "unconstitutional, oppressive and unjust." He had maintained that the states had created the national government and therefore had the power to resist oppression by it. Consequently, he had argued, if a state considered a law passed by Congress to be unconstitutional, it could refuse to enforce it within the state's

##The situation can be dramatized for students by listing the names of the three sections and by writing under each name the event, law, or activity that affected each section.

borders. If three-fourths of the states believed a law was unconstitutional, he had argued further, such a law was *null and void*. This was Calhoun's statement of the doctrine of nullification.

Nullification by South Carolina. In the annual message to Congress in 1830, Jackson supported the principle of protection contained in the Tariff Act of 1828. A tariff subsequently enacted in 1832 was milder than the one of 1828; it was, however, still a protective tariff. As a result, in South Carolina the views advanced by Calhoun in *Exposition and Protest* grew in popularity.

South Carolinians seem to have concluded that if the Union could impose a tariff on them, it could also emancipate the slaves. Fear of a slave rebellion and guilt over slavery may also have aroused them to guard their institutions by the means they considered best: a defense of states' rights.

In 1832, the legislature of South Carolina, responding to the public anger, called a convention, which passed an ordinance nullifying the Tariffs of 1828 and 1832. The ordinance forbade the collection of duties in South Carolina after February 1, 1833. It also declared that any attempt by the federal government to use force would result in *secession*—the withdrawal of the state from the Union.

Jackson's answer was almost instantaneous. Nullification, the President announced, was "incompatible with the existence of the Union." Furthermore, he said to the citizens of South Carolina (where he himself had been born): "The Constitution . . . forms a *government* not a league. . . . To say that any state may secede is to say that the United States are not a nation. . . . Disunion by armed force is *treason*."

A South Carolinian predicted there would be no fighting "unless the driveling old dotard" in the White House wanted it. Jackson *hoped* there would be no fighting, but he intended to keep his presidential oath to defend the Constitution. He prepared to send soldiers to South Carolina. Earlier he had written intemperately to Van Buren that Calhoun "ought to be hung."

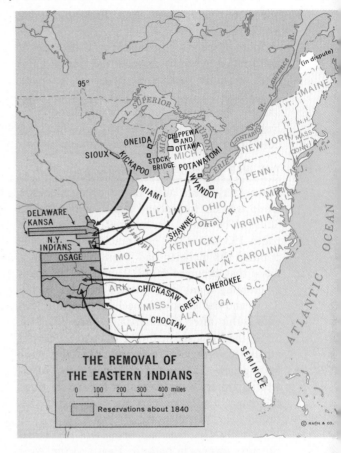

THE REMOVAL OF THE EASTERN INDIANS

0   100   200   300   400 miles

Reservations about 1840

Most of the Eastern Indians—themselves farmers—were moved to areas white farmers thought too arid. White men later took some of the new land (see p. 367).

Jackson quickly obtained from Congress a Force Bill, authorizing him to use troops if necessary to collect import duties. In the end, however, the moderates won out.

Compromise through Clay. The movement to settle the dispute without resort to arms was led by Henry Clay. He proposed a new tariff—known as the Compromise Tariff of 1833—providing for the immediate removal of duties on some goods. It also called for a gradual lowering of the duty rates on other items until, in 1842, the rates should reach the levels of 1816.

The Jacksonians at first were suspicious of Clay's motives. But his bill was a genuine compromise: the South won its argument in part, and the North was to have a protective tariff

#Have students read the oath (page 799). Why would any President have to oppose secession? Nullification? Discuss the meaning of "incompatible" and "treason."

189

almost ten years more. And, Jackson got his Force Bill.

South Carolina suspended its ordinance of nullification when it learned the compromise tariff was in the making. To save face, however, it nullified the Force Bill. Both South Carolina and the President claimed victory. Wrote Calhoun soon afterward: "The struggle, far from being over, has only just commenced."

THE WAR AGAINST THE BANK

Another storm was raised when Jackson made war on the second Bank of the United States. The Bank, rechartered in 1816 (see pages 133 and 171), had quickly become unpopular. Its policies had been blamed for a panic that occurred in 1819, and its strictness in granting loans had irritated farmers in the South and the West and mechanics in northern cities. But after *McCulloch* v. *Maryland* in 1819, the Bank seemed to be beyond successful attack. Nevertheless, Jackson's supporters were finding new reasons for criticizing "the Monster." Farmers were blaming it for the shortage of money, and easterners were saying it was responsible for inflation!

Actually what was happening was that small property owners in both the East and the West were becoming resentful of monopolies which their state legislatures granted to a few wealthy and influential merchants. A Jacksonian in New York State, for example, asserted, "Not a road can be opened, not a bridge can be built, not a canal can be dug, but a charter of exclusive privileges must be granted for the purpose. . . ." To thousands and thousands of Americans, the symbol of this evil was the biggest monopoly of them all: the Bank of the United States.

Well-run and profitable, the Bank was a powerful institution. Its policies affected credit throughout the country and it deserved praise for helping significantly to regulate the growing American businesses. Its strength was felt especially in the West. There its notes—the paper money it issued—tended to drive out of circulation the notes of the less secure state banks. Nevertheless, as one of the most influential newspaper editors in the country, Hezekiah

Niles, said, the Bank had "more power than we would grant to any set of men unless responsible to the people."

Nicholas Biddle, the president of the Bank, regarded himself as possessing influence equal to that of the president of the United States himself. This incensed Jackson. Besides, Jackson considered the Bank a personal enemy. He believed that in granting credit the Bank discriminated against his backers of 1828. It was obvious he would not consent to recharter the Bank when its charter expired in 1836. "The Bank," he said to Van Buren, "is trying to kill me, *but I will kill it.*"

The recharter issue. Biddle wanted to avoid raising the question of the rechartering until after the 1832 election, but, under Clay's leadership, the Republicans were impatient. They persuaded Biddle to apply immediately for a new charter and make the Bank an issue in the presidential campaign.

The bill granting the new charter passed the Senate and House. Jackson promptly vetoed it with a message that a Clay newspaper called "a mixture of the Demagogue and the Despot, of depravity, desperation and feelings of malice and vengeance. . . ." A newspaper supporting Jackson declared jubilantly that "in this act the glories of the battle-field are eclipsed—it is the crowning chaplet of an immortal fame."

Presidential veto. Jackson's veto message was planned to appeal not only to the farmer but also to the artisan, who might one day want to start his own business and would require easy bank credit. The President not only stated that the Bank was unconstitutional, but he also described it as an example of how "the rich and powerful too often bend the acts of government to their selfish purposes."

On the floor of the Senate, Webster denounced the message as inflammatory and aimed at setting the poor against the rich. The President's friends praised it as a forceful statement of Jackson's belief that the small businessman—on the farm or in the city—should have greater economic opportunity.

The election of 1832. The presidential campaign of 1832 had one issue: the Bank. The

#Discuss what the changes were and why people fear and resist change. What changes today are feared and resisted?

Democrats, of course, named Jackson again, although he was now ailing and aging. As their vice-presidential candidate they chose Martin Van Buren. The Republicans hopefully nominated Henry Clay, who received financial help from the Bank.

Many people, scared of the changes in American life that Jackson represented, turned their fears into an intense personal hatred of Jackson. An editorial in a Boston newspaper denounced him this way: "There is one comfort left: God has promised that the days of the wicked shall be short; the wicked is old and feeble, and he may die before he can be elected. It is the duty of every good Christian to pray to his maker to have pity on us."

Not in touch with popular sentiment, the Clay supporters did not appreciate how accurately the Jacksonians—rather than they themselves—had gauged what the majority of people wanted. Jackson's victory was overwhelming. Despite the prayers of his enemies, he won a second term.

Removal of deposits. Jackson believed that in reelecting him the people had authorized him to continue his war against the Bank. He made up his mind to destroy this "hydra of corruption" even before its charter would expire in 1836. He would withdraw the government's deposits from it, he decided, so that it could not at will tamper with the nation's prosperity —perhaps even causing a panic in order to embarrass the administration. Although Jackson had to remove Secretary of the Treasury William Duane because he refused to carry out his plan, Duane's successor, Roger B. Taney (pronounced *Taw*ney), of Maryland, coöperated.

Jackson deposited the federal funds in state banks. These "pet banks," as they were called, were considered the favorites of the government. The foes of the President were again enraged. One New Yorker declared, "I look upon Jackson as a detestable, ignorant, reckless, vain and malignant tyrant."

Wildcat banks. After the Bank of the United States had been destroyed, state banks sprang up throughout the country like mushrooms.

Library of Congress

A cartoonist of Jackson's day saw him as "King Andrew I" because of his vetoes and his strong stand on public issues.

Do students think the cartoonist was fair?

Known as "wildcat banks" because they were not secure, they issued paper money without sufficient restraint. The inflation caused by ## putting so much money into circulation obviously could be just as disastrous as the policies of the Bank.

For a time the plentiful money seemed to create prosperity. Land prices in the West rose to dizzy heights, and extensive internal improvements were built there. Moreover, revenues poured into the federal treasury. Not only was there enough revenue to wipe out the national debt, but also a surplus began to grow. Consequently, Congress passed a distribution bill in 1836 to divide the surplus among the states.

The Specie Circular. Since a brake on this inflation was needed, Jackson did what he could in the circumstances. He issued the Specie Circular in July, 1836, although he lost some western friends because of it. The Circular provided that public lands could henceforth be paid for only in specie, that is, gold or sil-

##Review p. 87, making sure that students understand what inflation is and what causes it. Does a condition of inflation exist today? What people suffer most from inflation?

ver, or in the notes of banks that paid specie.

The effects of the Specie Circular were quickly evident. Land speculation in the West began to slow down. This seemed like a good sign that the administration's policy was sound. But the demand for gold and silver put a heavy burden on the state banks everywhere, and large numbers of them drifted toward bankruptcy. Specie was drained from the East, and in many places it was hoarded.

Jackson went out of office on March 4, 1837. In his farewell address (see pages 184–185), he once again called for loyalty to the Union and urged continued attacks on monopolies, paper money, and speculation. A hostile New York newspaper referred to it as the President's "last humbug."

To the end, Jackson was both venerated and hated. An elderly New England minister stated that he knew "of nothing that a people may reasonably expect from good government, but that the United States have enjoyed under his administration." On the other hand, a New Yorker called Jackson's presidency "the most disastrous in the annals of the country."

THE OPPOSITION ORGANIZED

The Democratic party expected to stay in power, even though its greatest hero had retired from public life. Jackson's choice as his successor was Van Buren. The Republicans, who long before had dubbed Van Buren the "crown prince," looked forward to defeating him. They had been vastly strengthened in 1833 when the Calhoun men joined them. The three great Senate leaders—Clay, Webster, and Calhoun—were now linked in a new political party. In 1834 it adopted the name "Whig."

Whenever a new party has been formed in the United States, it has usually been because its members were *opposed* to something, not because they had a well-thought-out program of their own. The Whigs, like the Jacksonians in 1828, were a party of "antis." The only plank on which all of them could stand was a hatred of Andrew Jackson.

The Whig party. What groups were represented in the new party? First, the old Adams-Clay men who had supported the American system; second, southerners who believed in states' rights and who were angered by Jackson's stand on nullification; third, other former supporters of Jackson who disapproved of his Bank and money policies; fourth, cotton planters and northern businessmen who were critical of his democratic views; fifth, the Antimasonic party‡—which supplied an experienced leader in Thurlow Weed, of New York.

Too many candidates. Because the Whigs could not agree upon a national candidate in 1836, the sections named favorite sons. It was expected that—as had happened twelve years before—the election would have to be decided by the House of Representatives. New England chose Daniel Webster; the Southwest, Hugh White, of Tennessee; and the Northwest, William Henry Harrison, of Ohio, the elderly hero of the Battle of Tippecanoe.

Van Buren elected. Insisting that the issue was one of aristocracy against democracy, the Democrats nominated Van Buren. A campaign filled with abuse followed. The words of Davy Crockett are a sample: "When [Van Buren] enters the senate chamber in the morning, he struts and swaggers like a crow in a gutter. He is laced up in corsets such as women in a town wear. . . . It would be difficult to say, from his personal appearance whether he was a man or woman, but for his large *red* and *gray* whiskers."

Van Buren never lost confidence in the result. When the electoral votes were being counted, Henry Clay remarked to him, "It is a cloudy day, sir." The "Little Magician" replied pleasantly, "The sun will shine on the 4th of March, sir." So it did. Van Buren won more electoral votes than all of his opponents combined, a thumping endorsement of Jackson's policies.

A DEPRESSION

Almost before Van Buren was settled in the Executive Mansion, though, the country

‡ The Antimasons, organized in opposition to the Democrats in western New York, made hostility to Freemasonry the main plank of their platform. Its secrecy was their target.

#Crops failed in 1835. People on farms could not pay for goods they bought, and the merchants could not pay the banks the money they owed them. Though cotton fell in price, the prices of food doubled in some cases. Flour selling at $5.62 a barrel in 1835 sold for $12.00 in 1837.

fell into the grip of a serious depression, which appeared to be the result of Jackson's financial policies. Unemployment rose, and suffering became common in the cities. In New York the police had to be called to quell a flour riot. People protested furiously against increases in rent and fuel prices.

In New Orleans the price of cotton fell almost 50 percent in a month. Banks failed throughout the country. The number of bankrupt businesses mounted rapidly and by September, 1837, it was estimated that nine-tenths of the nation's factories had closed their doors. As early as May New York banks found it necessary to suspend specie payment; and the banks in Baltimore, Philadelphia, and Boston followed suit shortly afterward.

Fixing the blame. The Whigs lost no time blaming the administration for the depression, and Van Buren bore the brunt of the Whig attack. In one campaign of slander, people sent him make-believe bank notes bearing the message, "This is what you have brought the country to."

The Independent Treasury Act. The President decided that in order to get the country out of the doldrums he would take more drastic measures than Jackson ever had—he would attack *all* banks. He would protect federal funds by taking them out of the "pet banks" and putting them in subtreasuries, that is, vaults, for safekeeping. He anticipated that this would enable the federal government to limit the issue of paper money and in that way prevent inflation in the future.

The business groups and their party, the Whigs, considered the subtreasury policy an outrage. The policy of separating banking from the government seemed like the first step toward national disaster. Hamilton's arguments of almost fifty years earlier were heard again: the national government and the interests of business ought rightfully to be tied together.

Ignoring the attacks, Van Buren stuck to his guns. Democrats believed that the subtreasury system, in freeing the government from banks, would usher in true liberty at last. They thought it appropriate that the bill creating the subtreasuries—the Independent Treasury Act—became law in 1840 on the Fourth of July. But the reign of the Jackson-

Jackson had destroyed the Bank of the United States, which could have put a brake on inflation.

A Whig cartoon blames Jackson for the depression of 1837. His white hat and spectacles glisten above jobless men, a begging mother and child, the advertisements of "loan sharks," and reminders of the Specie Circular.

New-York Historical Society

#The Independent Treasury Act had also made enemies. It had removed money from "pet banks" and so had put them in the position of having less specie on which to issue paper money. In effect, it was a continuation of the "hard-money" policy Jackson had started.

ians was ending. The depression had killed Van
Buren's chances for reelection.

Sum and Substance

1. What advice did Jackson give about preserving American freedom? 2. What were the high points of his career before 1828? 3. What was the "kitchen cabinet"? 4. Explain the significance of the "Eaton trouble." 5. Why did Calhoun favor nullification? 6. What views were expressed in the Webster-Hayne debate? At the Jefferson Day dinner? 7. What steps did South Carolina take in 1832? With what results? 8. How did Jackson win support in the West and East? 9. Why did Jackson oppose the Bank of the United States? 10. Explain the origin of the wildcat banks. 11. What was the aim of the Specie Circular? 12. Who made up the Whig party? 13. What disaster befell Van Buren? 14. Explain the Independent Treasury Act.

Mention the order Van Buren issued in 1840 establishing a 10-hour day for government workers (p. 403).

DEATH SNATCHES AWAY THE WHIGS' HARD-EARNED VICTORY

By 1840 the Whigs recognized that the presidency would be theirs if they could only agree on a candidate. Henry Clay was eager to be that man. Upon hearing that the nominating convention had rejected him, he exclaimed angrily: "My friends are not worth the powder and shot it would take to kill them! . . . I am the most unfortunate man in the history of parties; always run by my friends when sure to be defeated, and now betrayed for a nomination when I, or anyone, would be sure of an election." William Henry Harrison, who had no program but no enemies, either, was nominated.

HARRISON THE MAN

Harrison had the qualifications the Whigs needed: like Jackson, he came from the West; like Jackson, he was a military hero. As consolation to the Clay men, the Whigs picked John Tyler—who had expected to be Clay's running mate—to be the vice-presidential nominee. Tyler was a states' rights Democrat from Virginia who had broken with the Jacksonians over nullification and had joined the Whig party.

A rollicking campaign. The Whigs took advantage of a Democratic taunt that Harrison would be happy in a log cabin with a pension and a barrel of hard cider. They made their symbols a log cabin and hard cider, and their slogan "Tippecanoe and Tyler, too." One of the jingles they created demonstrated a new tone in politics:

> Farewell, dear Van,
> You're not our man;
> To guide the Ship,
> We'll try old Tip.

At parades the Whigs used log-cabin floats; they held huge rallies, wore campaign emblems and ribbons, and handed out hard cider at many a gathering. These techniques, not widely used previously, became an enduring part of American political behavior.

The Whigs clearly had learned from the Jacksonians that a political party could no longer win an election by snubbing the people —as the Federalists and later the Republicans had done. Like the Democrats, the Whigs turned their candidate into a "man of the people."

Democrats at low ebb. Because of the Whigs' superior organization and the recent depression for which the Democratic party had been blamed, the Democrats were helpless. "Van, Van is a used-up man" was heard on all sides.

The vote. Harrison won by an electoral vote of 234 to 60, although the popular vote was much closer—1,275,017 to 1,128,702. The Liberty party, advocating abolition of slavery, entered a candidate for the first time—James G. Birney, of Kentucky. But support for him was insignificant.

President with "feet of Clay." Harrison seemed completely in the hands of the Whig leaders, Webster and Clay. John Quincy Adams shortly after the election wrote in his diary an opinion of "Old Tippecanoe" that was widely held:

194 ##It was the liberal Whigs who had passed over Clay. What lesson had they learned from the Democrats? (Harrison was as close to Jackson in appeal as possible; the log-cabin idea helped.)

#Ask what this sentence means. (He was a states' rights man; he opposed the Bank of the United States and a protective tariff.)

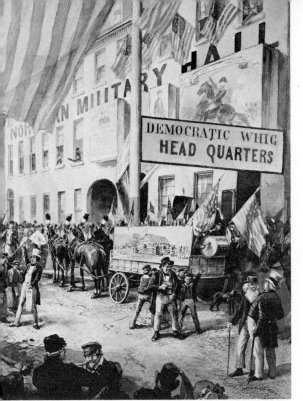

Old Print Shop

A rally for "Old Tip" in 1840, when the Whigs outdid the Democrats in appealing to the "common people." The figure on horseback may represent Harrison at the Battle of Tippecanoe in 1811.

"His present popularity is all artificial. There is little confidence in his talents or his firmness." Webster became the Secretary of State after Clay had declined the post. Clay preferred to be the power behind Harrison. In fact, so hard did "Harry of the West," as Clay was often called, press his opinions that on one occasion Harrison exclaimed to him, "Mr. Clay, you forget that I am the President."

Harrison, past sixty-eight (and the last President born a British subject), tried to do everything that was asked of him by his political advisers—and more. He was overwhelmed by office seekers and the endless round of social activities. Careless of his health, he would not wear an overcoat. He contracted a cold and died—probably of pneumonia—exactly a month after his inauguration.

THE UNCALLED-FOR TYLER

John Tyler, a Democrat at heart who differed with the Whigs on constitutional principles, on the bank issue, and on the tariff, was now President. He was the first Vice-President to be elevated by the death of a chief executive. The Whigs were dismayed—their plans had suddenly been destroyed. The question now was, Would *Tyler* knuckle under to Clay?

The fate of Whig proposals. On June 7, 1841, Clay introduced in Congress resolutions that represented Whig policy: the repeal of the Independent Treasury Act, the creation of a new Bank of the United States, the raising of the tariff.

The Independent Treasury Act was repealed, and the government once again began depositing its funds in state banks. But the Bank bill that Congress passed was vetoed by Tyler. Clay vainly pleaded with the President, who remained true to his "old-Republican" heritage by steadfastly refusing to sign it. Tyler, it is said, pointed his finger at "Harry of the West" and said sharply: "Go you now, then, Mr. Clay, to your end of the avenue, where stands the Capitol, and there perform your duty to the country as you shall think proper. So help me God, I shall do mine as I shall think proper." ##

The only other Whig measure Tyler signed was the Tariff of 1842. Faced by a shortage of revenue, the President agreed to raise the rates to the level of the Tariff of 1832 (see pages 188–189).

"The corporal's guard." The Whigs were beside themselves with anger when Tyler vetoed the Bank bill. Harrison's whole Cabinet, which Tyler had kept intact, resigned—with the exception of Secretary of State Webster. Tyler was abused in print across the country and barely escaped injury when an angry mob invaded the White House grounds. He was a President without a party.

A Whig leader in New York, Philip Hone, told his diary: "Poor Tippecanoe! It was an evil hour that 'Tyler too' was added to make out the line. There was rhyme but no reason in it." The small group of Whig friends and advisers in and out of Congress who stuck by the beleaguered President were referred to with contempt as "the corporal's guard."

##What was this heritage? (If students don't know, they should review Jefferson's view on the Bank of the United States, p. 133. Jefferson and his followers were Republicans.)

195

#Some of the Canadian rebels had taken up a position on Navy Island on the Canadian side of the Niagara River. The Caroline had been taking arms and supplies there. To attack the ship, the Canadian militiamen crossed to the American side. Ask how each country could be criticized.

Political frustration. Tyler was unable to build a significant following of his own. Democrats would not become attached to him because he had gone over to the Whigs in 1840. Besides, northern Democrats preferred Van Buren, and southern Democrats leaned toward Calhoun, their former leader—who favored states' rights. Clay resolutely resigned from the Senate and returned to his home "Ashland," near Lexington, Kentucky, fully trusting that in 1844 he would be elected President at last.

SUCCESS IN TRANSATLANTIC DIPLOMACY

Despite the confusion of party struggles at home, in international relations the country enjoyed some notable successes. These were a new gauge of the nation's growth.

By the 1840's two problems in relations with Britain especially required solution. Hap-

Better known as a Senator, Webster, as Secretary of State, achieved this settlement of a boundary dispute.

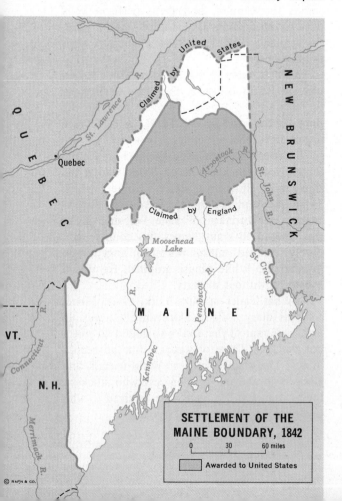

SETTLEMENT OF THE MAINE BOUNDARY, 1842

0   30   60 miles

Awarded to United States

© RMCN & CO.

pily, Daniel Webster was sympathetic to England. When he had visited there in 1840, he had been enthusiastically received (probably because many people confused him with the "dictionary Webster," Noah). England had sent a special representative, Lord Ashburton, to the United States in 1842 to settle difficulties between the two countries. His earlier marriage into a wealthy Philadelphia family helped seal his affection for the United States. Webster and Ashburton were an ideal pair to try to reduce the transatlantic tension.

An unfortunate incident. The first issue was the #
Caroline incident. In 1837–1838 a group of Canadians staged an unsuccessful revolt against British rule of Canada, and a small number of Americans supported them. In December, 1837, a unit of Canadian militiamen crossed the Niagara River at what is now Niagara Falls, New York, and burned the steamboat Caroline, which had been running arms to the rebels. The militiamen also killed an American aboard the ship.

The United States demanded reparations for the invasion of its territorial waters. The British replied that the Caroline was a pirate ship subject to destruction wherever found.

The issue remained unsettled until 1840. At that time a Canadian—Alexander McLeod—was arrested in New York for taking part in the Caroline affair and charged with murder and arson. The British declared that if McLeod were hanged there would be war. He was acquitted, because he had an acceptable alibi, but the United States and Britain had come dangerously close to hostilities.

Ashburton, who had recently arrived here, brought a new policy of conciliation. Soon afterward, Webster accepted a British apology for the Caroline affair, and Ashburton expressed regret that one had not been offered sooner.

The Webster-Ashburton Treaty. In the same spirit of friendliness, a second and more difficult issue was resolved. It concerned the establishment of the boundary line between Maine and ##
Canada. For more than fifty years this matter had troubled United States' relations with England. In 1832 America refused to accept a line

##Refer to the map on p. 96. The matter rested until Maine became a state in 1820.

#Discuss the meaning of "arbitrate." Britain was ready to accept the king's decision, but the
United States was not. Emphasize the importance of having an able Secretary of State who is
a skillful negotiator. (Incidents that can lead to war may be settled through negotiation.)

drawn by the King of the Netherlands, who
attempted to arbitrate the question. In 1838
when Canadians entered the Aroostook Valley
in Maine to cut timber, Maine men called out
the state militia.

Congress appropriated $1,000,000 for de-
fense. President Van Buren dispatched to the
scene General Winfield Scott, who arranged a
truce in this so-called "Aroostook War." In
1842 Webster and Ashburton reached a compromise. Of approximately 12,000 square miles
in the disputed region, the United States received about 7000.

To make the settlement acceptable to the
United States, the British conceded 200 miles
at the head of the Connecticut River and
adjusted in America's favor a boundary line
in the vicinity of Lake Champlain. Each side
received less than it desired in the Webster-
Ashburton Treaty, but both ratified it. Each
thought it was getting more than it deserved.

The subject of the slave trade almost broke
up the Webster-Ashburton negotiations. Having
abolished slavery in 1833 throughout its colonies, England now wanted to end the commerce
in slaves. American slave traders refused to
permit the search of their vessels by the British,
insisting that the right of search was illegal in
peacetime. Webster and Ashburton were able
to agree that their countries would each maintain a squadron to patrol the African coast in
order to control the awful traffic in humans.

The Webster-Ashburton Treaty, on the
American side, was essentially the work of
Webster, the Whig. Ironically, it was the single
outstanding triumph of the administration of
Tyler, really a Democrat.

JACKSONIAN DEMOCRACY

Between 1820 and 1840 profound changes
permanently altered the nation's ideas of democracy. Although Jackson was not personally
responsible for them, he was the first national
leader to understand and use them in managing
the country's affairs. Taken together, these
changes are called Jacksonian democracy.

Acceptance of majority rule. Foremost was the
increased participation of ordinary citizens in
the politics of the country. The growth of free
public schools and cheap newspapers helped
make people better aware of and better informed about public issues than ever before.

New western states refused to establish property qualifications limiting the ballot. Their
constitutions, therefore, usually provided that
all males were entitled to the suffrage upon
reaching the age of twenty-one. The older states
were forced to write more liberal constitutions
with respect to the vote in order to match those
of the newer states.

Just as important as the extension of the
suffrage itself was the remarkable increase in
its exercise. In the twenty years between 1828
and 1848, the number of people who voted
almost trebled.

Political job-holding, moreover, was no longer restricted to the few. It became a commonplace that any man could hold any public office
without special training. Jackson, more than
any previous President, used the *spoils system*
—the practice of making party loyalty and
service the chief basis for political appointment.

Finally, the belief spread that the people as
a whole can never be wrong. Calhoun might
insist that "the will of a majority is the will
of a rabble," but never again could the majority be ignored. This period of American history
is said to have witnessed "the rise of the common man." And, for the first time, it became
the business of government to provide for "the
greatest good of the greatest number."

Growth of free enterprise. On the economic side, ##
the most important change was the freeing of
the middle class of people to engage in businesses of their own choice without having to
compete with monopolies protected by government. The easier credit made possible by laxer
banking laws was an important stimulus to up-
and-coming businessmen.

Even risky enterprises were not discouraged.
State bankruptcy laws were passed which enabled any unsuccessful businessman to settle
his debts with his creditors as best he could,
without being sent to debtors' jail. By the beginning of the 1840's, most states no longer
imprisoned debtors.

Contrast Jeffersonian and Jacksonian democracy (see p. 130, 134).
##Free enterprise: the practice of a minimum amount of government control of industry.

A new view of the presidency. Jackson has justly been called the "maker of the modern presidency." Differing from his predecessors in the conduct of his lofty office, Old Hickory demonstrated for the first time the enormous power the President can and, in crises, must wield.

The President and the people, furthermore, were in much closer touch with each other than ever before. Jackson's messages were intended for the great mass of Americans as much as for Congress, to which they were officially addressed. The members of the electoral college ceased to be chosen by the state legislatures and by 1828 were in almost every state elected by the people.

The national nominating convention made its appearance as one of the most exciting features of political life.§ The Republicans in 1831 became the first major party to hold one, and the Jacksonian Democrats followed this lead the next year. The presidency was now becoming the center of the public's attention.

City needs. Where Jeffersonian democracy had been concerned mainly with the welfare of farmers, Jacksonian democracy embraced also the city dweller. Where Jeffersonian democracy had envisioned a government conducted *for* the people, Jacksonian democracy conceived of it also as government *by* the people. Where Jeffersonian democracy had made passive government its ideal, Jacksonian democracy considered government an instrument through which the will of the majority could be constantly expressed.

These extensions of democracy were not without dangers. There always would be the possibility that the people, instead of ruling themselves well, would act on impulse rather than on careful thought—or fall into the hands of rabble-rousers. The appearance in these years of the first modern-type professional politicians raised serious fears of evil results.

But the Jacksonians had faith in the good sense of the people. Ponder the reassuring

§ Presidential candidates formerly had been chosen by party caucuses of political leaders in Congress. "King Caucus," however, was discredited as "undemocratic" in the campaign of 1824. The first convention ever held was that of the Antimasonic party in 1831.

words of the greatest poet of democracy, Walt Whitman, who grew to manhood in Jackson's time. (He probably acquired his love for democracy from his father, who had named one son "Thomas Jefferson" and another "Andrew Jackson.")

Whitman wrote: "To attack the turbulence and destructiveness of the democratic spirit, is an old story. . . . But with the noble democratic spirit—even accompanied by its freaks and its excesses—no people can ever become enslaved; and to us all the noisy tempestuous scenes of politics witnessed in this country—all the excitement and strife, even—are *good* to behold. They evidence that *the people act.* . . ."

The seamy side. Despite Whitman's enthusiasm, the achievements of the Jacksonian era did not apply to all Americans. Women still played no role in politics and were not expected to. Negro slaves became more numerous than ever. Free Negroes who could vote in many states after the Revolution were gradually disfranchised directly or indirectly. After 1830, Negro voters were not significant anywhere.

The shameless abuse of Indians continued. Jackson's policy was to remove them forcibly to lands west of the Mississippi. The Cherokee in Georgia took to the courts to fight their evictions, and although they won a favorable decision from John Marshall, President Jackson callously refused to carry it out.

But if much of the work of extending democracy remained undone, the Jacksonians left an enduring legacy of the *possibilities* for personal liberty a free society can offer. The democratic spirit that his age discovered has survived and has been enlarged steadily.

Sum and Substance

1. What advantage did the Whigs have in the campaign of 1840? What campaign tactics did they use? 2. What were the Whig party's policies? 3. How did Tyler's policies compare with them? 4. Describe the *Caroline* affair. 5. What agreements were made in the Webster-Ashburton Treaty? 6. Name and explain the extensions of democracy in the Age of Jackson.

##Students should realize that democracy in the United States did not develop all at once. Democratic advances were made from time to time, but much remained to do. (Much still remains.)

THE WORKSHOP

OF LASTING SIGNIFICANCE

What role did each of the following play in the Age of Jackson?

Old Hickory
Martin Van Buren
"kitchen cabinet"
Peggy Eaton
Webster-Hayne
  debate
Daniel Webster
Maysville veto
Exposition and
  Protest
secession
Tariff of 1832
Compromise Tariff
  of 1833
Roger B. Taney
Specie Circular

Whigs
William Henry
  Harrison
Independent
  Treasury Act
"Tippecanoe and
  Tyler, too"
John Tyler
Caroline incident
Webster-Ashburton
  Treaty
spoils system
free enterprise
national nominating
  convention

AMERICAN DEMOCRACY

1. Using the Index, find and quote the passage in this book which best expresses Jefferson's concern with the welfare of farmers. Find and quote the one that best describes his ideal government.

Cite an event or act showing that Jackson was interested also in the welfare of city people and small businessmen. What act of his proves that he thought government should be active in carrying out the will of the majority? How do you account for the differences between # Jeffersonian and Jacksonian democracy?

2. A basic premise of democracy is a strong faith in *people*—in their ability to solve their own problems. Use the Index to find passages quoted from both Jefferson and Jackson which best express each man's view on this premise.

Quote words from the two men which voice Walt Whitman's idea that ". . . with the noble democratic spirit . . . no people can ever become enslaved. . . ."

3. Explain how the increase in the number of free public schools and cheap newspapers in Jackson's time contributed to the development of democracy.

4. How is it that limited suffrage always acts as a brake on the development of democracy?

THE PRESIDENCY

1. Every President takes the presidential oath of office (see the Constitution, Article 2, Section 1, Clause 8). *How* he carries out his oath depends on each President.

Describe the situation which tested Jackson's idea of a President's responsibility under the oath. How did he react? How far did he have to go? With what success?

2. Washington vetoed two congressional bills; Monroe, one; Jackson, twelve. What does this large increase in the number of vetoes reveal about Jackson's idea of the presidency? Describe the circumstances of one of his vetoes. How did he justify it?

3. Explain exactly how each of the following helped bring the presidency into closer touch with the people in Jackson's time: (*a*) the change in the method of nominating presidential candidates; (*b*) the change in the method of electing members of the electoral college; (*c*) Jackson's use of presidential messages to Congress.

4. Harrison was the first President to die in office. Find the part of the Constitution that provided for his successor. What provision is made if a President is disabled? Does the original Constitution say how a disability is to be determined? What does the Twenty-fifth Amendment provide?

PUTTING HISTORY ON THE MAP

1. Compare the maps on pages 189 and 360–361. In what present-day states were the reservations for the Eastern Indians established? Why were the reservations located in those areas?

2. The Maine boundary had been in dispute since what event? Look at the northern Maine boundary on the map on pages 360–361. What explanation of its location does the map on page 196 give?

The development of industry, new means of transportation, and trade are key ideas in this chapter. Although farming was highly significant in the North, it was not the only northern interest. This diversity is another key idea. The quotation on this page and the picture suggest the first three ideas. For inquiry: In the quotation from Thoreau, where can one find evidence that the railroads were encouraging trade? What suggests the identity of the fuel the trains used? What new personal traits of Americans does Thoreau attribute to the coming of the railroad?

11

THE NORTH: DIVERSE INTERESTS

. . . when I hear the iron horse . . .

The whistle of the locomotive penetrates my woods summer and winter, sounding like the scream of a hawk sailing over some farmer's yard, informing me that many restless city merchants are arriving within the circle of the town, or adventurous country traders from the other side. As they come under one horizon, they shout their warning to get off the track to the other, heard sometimes through the circles of two towns. Here come your groceries, country; your rations, countrymen! . . .

When I meet the engine with its train of cars moving off with planetary motion . . . with its

In the furnaces of the company whose buildings are seen here, metal is being heated and shaped into parts of steamships and locomotives, called forgings. Observe the air pollution.

A church may be seen in the background (left). Its spire dominates the skyline. Coal may be seen in railroad cars at the far left. Raw materials are brought in by rail (center, right).

Words to know: planetary (wandering or erratic); fodder (coarse roughages like cornstalks, used to feed livestock); superfluous (extra); wrought (worked); conveyance (a vehicle or carriage). Walden, or Life in the Woods, was a book written in 1854.

steam cloud like a banner streaming behind in golden and silver wreaths, like many a downy cloud which I have seen, . . . when I hear the iron horse make the hills echo with his snort like thunder, shaking the earth with his feet, and breathing fire and smoke from his nostrils . . . it seems as if the earth had got a race now worthy to inhabit it. . . .

The stabler of the iron horse was up early this winter morning by the light of the stars amid the mountains, to fodder and harness his steed. Fire, too, was awakened thus early to put the vital heat in him and get him off. . . . If the snow lies deep, they strap on his snowshoes, and, with the giant plow, plow a furrow from the mountains to the seaboard. . . . All day the fire-steed flies over the country, stopping only that his master may rest, and I am awakened by his tramp and defiant snort at midnight . . . and he will reach his stall only with the morning star, to start once more on his travels without rest or slumber. Or perchance, at evening, I hear him in his stable blowing off the superfluous energy of the day, that he may calm his nerves and cool his liver and brain for a few hours of iron slumber. . . .

Have not men improved somewhat in punctuality since the railroad was invented? Do they not talk and think faster in the depot than they did in the stage-office? There is something electrifying in the atmosphere of the former place. I have been astonished at the miracles it has wrought; that some of my neighbors, who, I should have prophesied, once for all, would never get to Boston by so prompt a conveyance, are on hand when the bell rings. To do things "railroad fashion" is now the byword. . . .

The coming of the railroad rudely shattered the calm of the American countryside and within a few years had reshaped American life. But would the mighty iron horse, ushering in an age of the machine, become a tyrant over those it served so faithfully? The poet and essayist Henry David Thoreau (1817–1862) was deeply troubled by this question as he watched industrialization come to his native New England. In this famous passage from his Walden, *published in 1854, Thoreau describes the disturbing beauty of the iron horse and the effect it is having on the people—in this case, of Concord, Massachusetts.*

Students should distinguish between light and heavy industry. Heavy industry produces materials that enable other industries to function.

Mary E. Maxwell Fund, Corcoran Gallery of Art

Black smoke curls from the smokestacks of furnaces of Lazell, Perkins & Company, a manufacturer of forgings for steamships and railroads in Bridgewater, Massachusetts, about 1850. Billows of smoke pour also from the locomotive pulling the train in the foreground, which, like the factory, symbolizes the growth of heavy industry and rail transportation that was remaking the North.

The Rand McNally Classroom Library contains a booklet called The Rise of Heavy Industry, by Robert L. Daniel, which describes the development of this kind of industry.

NEW ENGLAND IS TRANSFORMED BY THE FACTORY SYSTEM

By 1840 the ways of living in the northern part of the United States had become significantly different from those in the South and West. The symbol and lifeblood of the North was a free-flowing commerce increasingly based on manufacturing. It connected the distinctive parts of the section—New England, the middle Atlantic states, and the old Northwest.

New England, the segment of the North that was settled first, is upland, nestled between Canada and the Atlantic Ocean. Its people were prevented from moving directly westward by the Appalachian Mountains and the Canadian border. From the beginning, New Englanders found it easy to turn to the sea, on which they conducted a flourishing trade. But mainly they engaged in farming to supply their own needs.

THE ORIGINAL YANKEES

The physical environment of New England was demanding, for the winters were long and the soil was stubborn. New Englanders were thrifty, hardworking people who drove themselves mercilessly. An English traveler described them as "a cold, shrewd, calculating, and ingenious people, of phlegmatic temperament, with less of the stuff of which enthusiasts are made, than any other in the world."

Yet they could also display a crusading enthusiasm for a good cause or ideal. An example was public education, first introduced in Massachusetts in 1647, in which Yankees ardently believed. Unswervingly devoted to their township organization and their churches—as well as to their schools—New Englanders took their traditions with them everywhere they migrated.

Their exodus. Between 1790 and 1820 about 800,000 New Englanders left their section for other parts of the country. In 1850 there were 450,000 people who had been born in New England but were living elsewhere. This migration, which has been called the "Yankee exodus," was expensive to New England. Each emigrant represented an investment in upbringing and education that yielded its return to another part of the country. Moreover, the resulting shortage of young men in New England kept the cost of labor high there.

Their strongly national outlook. The steady outflow of population from New England had an interesting effect on the people who were left behind. Because their children and other kinsmen lived everywhere in the length and breadth of the land, New Englanders maintained strong ties with all sections of the country. This fact made them staunch supporters of the Union.

This may help to explain why some of the most familiar patriotic tributes, like "Old Ironsides," the "Battle Hymn of the Republic," and "Barbara Frietchie," were written by New Englanders—Oliver Wendell Holmes, Julia Ward Howe, and John Greenleaf Whittier. It is not merely chance that the greatest political spokesman of New England during the nineteenth century—Daniel Webster—was also the most eloquent defender of the Union.

The powerful role of New Englanders in the making of the nation is illustrated by the history of the name "Yankee" itself. Once used by the British as a term of contempt for New England soldiers, in time it came to describe the New Englanders and then northerners in general. Today it is a designation heard throughout the world for all Americans.

A CHANGED SCENE

The principal activity of New England in 1830 was still farming. But momentous changes were in the making. The Erie Canal, connecting Lake Erie with the Hudson River, had been completed in 1825. In the 1830's steamboat lines were established on the Great Lakes. In the following decade the East and West were being linked by railroads. A result was that New England farmers were overwhelmed by the wool, pork, and wheat pouring in from the more fertile West.

Decline of the farmers. Discouraged, many farmers left their plows altogether. Others went into specialized production, like dairy farming or

Words students should understand: phlegmatic (not easily excited); exodus (departure, usually of a large number of people); eloquent (having fluent speech); designation (name).

market gardening, in order to supply the needs of factory towns now springing up. By 1850 New England had become a food-importing section, dependent upon the West for most of its provisions.

Before the 1830's were over, farm families no longer produced in their own households the clothing and other everyday items they required. Instead, they used goods made in factories, which were cheaper, and maybe even better, than those they—especially the womenfolk—could make. As an observant minister of the time wrote, there was occurring "a transition from mother-and-daughter-power to water-and-steam-power." Shortly the daughters, no longer needed at home, headed for work in the factories. Jobs awaited them in the manufacturing of things they had formerly made at their mother's sides—cotton and wool cloth, in particular.

The Waltham system. Young women were first brought from villages and farms to Waltham, Massachusetts. In that town during the War of 1812 a textile factory had been established capable of performing every operation required to convert raw cotton into finished cloth.

The first factory like it in the world, its female employees were housed in dormitories run much as those in a boarding school were—except that there were no studies. The girls' health and morals were carefully supervised and guarded—the young workers had a strict 10 P.M. curfew. Although they rarely were paid more than two dollars a week each, they were not physically oppressed. The Waltham system, as these arrangements were called, was widely admired and copied.

The worker's lot. Such agreeable conditions did not last long. Manufacturers were increasingly in competition with each other; and in order to cut prices, they lowered wages and imposed long hours. The amount of production expected of an employee rose noticeably.

Although a 10-hour day had gone into effect for federal government workers in 1840, there was little national or state control over hours in private employment until after 1865. By the end of the 1840's, a woman was paid her board

and $1.50 for a 75-hour week. Family mills, where the father, mother, and children could all work together, paid even lower wages.

Moreover, workers were generally paid only four times a year, and then in company-store coupons rather than in cash. The company stores—owned by the employers—often charged excessively high prices, and the workers usually had no choice but to trade there because they could not get credit elsewhere. Besides, other stores would not honor the coupons.

Factory life. Factories were usually poorly heated, poorly lighted, and poorly ventilated, constantly menacing the health and safety of the employees. Periodic unemployment added to the uncertainty of life. Strikes were forbidden, and sometimes a yellow-dog contract was demanded of an employee—a contract in which he or she agreed, when hired, not to join a union. A close personal relationship between worker and employer became a thing of the past. One factory manager declared: "I regard my work-people just as I regard my machinery. So long as they can do my work for what I choose to pay them, I keep them, getting out of them all I can."

Factory workers in Lowell, Massachusetts, at the end of a long workday. In an era before the time of the company cafeteria, men, women, and children carried their own lunch.

Drawing by Winslow Homer in *Harper's Weekly* (1868), Library of Congress

Students may ask why the workers did not form unions (see pp. 402-403).

In Holyoke, Massachusetts, large-scale textile manufacturing had appeared by the middle of the century. Holyoke and other factory towns now drew their working force largely from the ranks of immigrants arriving in America from Ireland.

Since transportation was scarce and since workers usually labored from sunup to sundown, they were forced to live close to the factories. As families crowded into dwellings that were conveniently located, their living conditions became more and more wretched. A visitor to one of them reported in 1854: "I stopped at one of the shanties to sell some sugar. First, the man and woman came out of the door, then six children came out, then six boarders came out, then a cow came out, and then a sow and ten pigs came out, all from the same door."

The manufacturers felt helpless to remedy the evils because they were engaged in fierce "dog-eat-dog" competition with rival businessmen. And it had not yet become the business # of government to take an active hand in the personal welfare of the people.

Child labor. The factory was "home" to thousands of pasty-faced, undernourished, rickety children, few of whom would live to see their fortieth birthdays. Many worked from the time they were very young. Often a child was carried to his machine in the morning fast asleep in the arms of his father or his mother. Unwashed and badly fed and clothed, he knew no school and little carefree laughter.

In the 1840's and 1850's, the New England states began to require that children attend school at least three months out of every year. In 1842 Massachusetts limited to 10 hours a day the working time for children under twelve. But since an inspector relied on the word of the parent as to the age of the child, even this mild law was usually broken.

The smoke of manufacturing. Despite serious problems, industrialization in New England increased each year. More and more capital was being invested in manufacturing; more and more people depended on it for their living. Factories were scarring the green countryside and making it black and smoky, but their spokesmen—often scorned and hated—were becoming the voice of New England.

Sum and Substance

1. What effects of the railroad did Thoreau observe? 2. Name the parts of the North, the states in each, and tell what ties bound them. 3. Account for the strongly national viewpoint of New Englanders. 4. When and why did New England farming decline? 5. Describe the working conditions which developed in New England factories. 6. What steps did Massachusetts take to limit child labor? When were they taken?

This section helps develop the authors' theme of the developing urbanization of the nation.

THE MIDDLE ATLANTIC STATES CULTIVATE CROPS AND TRADE

The middle Atlantic states, like New England, presented distinguishing characteristics. Whereas New England was "off in a corner," the middle Atlantic states were at "the center of things." Consisting of New York, New Jersey, and Pennsylvania, this region bordered on the Atlantic Ocean, the St. Lawrence River, the Great Lakes, and the Ohio Valley.

THE SWELLING CITIES

In several ways, the middle Atlantic states ## were favored by nature. The land is more fertile than New England's, and mineral deposits are far more abundant. Mountains and rivers are more advantageously situated for carrying on internal commerce. Access to the West is easier.

Urban growth. Between 1830 and 1850 the population of the middle states grew from 3,500,000 to almost 6,000,000. Nearly a million people were of foreign birth. The increasing population enlarged the cities of the section, which became the nerve centers of trade and transportation. Whereas New York had about 215,000 people in 1830, twenty years later it had nearly 620,000; the populations of Philadelphia and Baltimore more than doubled.

##Ask how each advantage favored the growth of cities. (Farmers' crops support city people; minerals are raw products industries use, either in manufacturing or as a source of power, etc.)

For inquiry: Compare this chart with the one on p. 165. What city displaced Richmond? Observe the place of Salem before 1830. What happened to it by 1840? What does its displacement tell you? What cities are added in 1830 and after? What do these additions tell you?

TEN LARGEST CITIES IN THE UNITED STATES*

	1830	1840	1850	1860
1	New York, N.Y. 214,995	New York, N.Y. 352,015	New York, N.Y. 619,241	New York, N.Y. 1,126,447
2	Philadelphia, Pa. 161,271	Philadelphia, Pa. 226,690	Philadelphia, Pa. 361,304	Philadelphia, Pa. 579,887
3	Boston, Mass. 85,568	Boston, Mass. 127,240	Boston, Mass. 202,166	Boston, Mass. 311,012
4	Baltimore, Md. 80,620	New Orleans, La. 105,400	Baltimore, Md. 169,054	Baltimore, Md. 212,418
5	New Orleans, La. 46,082	Baltimore, Md. 102,313	Cincinnati, Ohio 130,738	Cincinnati, Ohio 187,561
6	Charleston, S.C. 30,289	Cincinnati, Ohio 46,338	New Orleans, La. 130,565	New Orleans, La. 179,598
7	Washington, D.C. 27,267	Albany, N.Y. 33,721	St. Louis, Mo.† 77,860	St. Louis, Mo. 164,766
8	Cincinnati, Ohio† 24,831	Pittsburgh, Pa.† 31,204	Pittsburgh, Pa. 71,595	Chicago, Ill.† 112,172
9	Albany, N.Y. 24,209	Washington, D.C. 30,676	Louisville, Ky.† 51,375	Pittsburgh, Pa. 93,359
10	Salem, Mass. 22,196	Charleston, S.C. 29,261	Albany, N.Y. 50,763	Louisville, Ky. 84,700

*Population figures include immediate suburbs.   † New addition to list.   (Continued on page 319)

The spur of technology. Several technological changes helped hurry the building of the urban communities. One was the appearance of cheap machine-made nails and standard sizes of sawn lumber, making possible the construction of inexpensive frame houses. Another was macadam—a type of road surface able to withstand heavy traffic—introduced from England after 1815.

A number of social and mechanical inventions enabled cities to grow without experiencing periodically civil commotion—widespread fires and raging epidemics—traditional curses for large concentrations of population. Among the contrivances were public policing, fire fighting, and garbage removal, piped-in water, mass transport, and supervised sewer lines and disposal systems.

The emerging modern cities also gained from the fact that family living was being transformed. Once a place where almost everything consumed was made or grown on the premises, "home" was becoming one in which everything consumed was brought in from outside. The release of energy and time this development brought about gave an enormous boost to attainments in art and literature as well as to the growth of industry.

The role of immigrants. Immigration not only provided the cities with a labor force but also made them cosmopolitan rather than narrow in outlook, looking to the future rather than longing for the past. Herman Melville, the New Yorker who wrote the immortal *Moby Dick*, foresaw the importance of the newcomers from abroad. "We are not," he wrote, "a narrow

#See A History of American Dwellings, by James D. Kornwolf, a paperback in the Rand McNally **205** Classroom Library. The influence of technology and mass production are discussed.

tribe of men . . . whose blood has been debased in the attempt to ennoble it, by maintaining an exclusive succession among ourselves. No: our blood is as the flood of the Amazon, made up of a thousand noble currents all pouring into our one. We are not a nation so much as a world."

Sources and quantity. The tide of immigration, which brought somewhat less than 600,000 persons in the 1830's, brought about 2,500,000 people in the 1850's. Principally the newcomers came from areas in western and northern Europe. Between 1850 and 1860 about one and a third million came from the British Isles and slightly less than a million from Germany.

The middle Atlantic states led the rest of the Union in immigrants received, and the population swelled accordingly. To be sure, many thousands of young Irish men and women settled in New England. In fact, in 1854, of 32,000 children born in Massachusetts, only 16,470 were of American parentage. Theodore Parker, a Massachusetts clergyman, declared, "Boston is a young Dublin."

But immigration did not enlarge the population in New England as much as it did that in the middle Atlantic states. These figures tell the story: from 1820 to 1860, of the 5,400,000 immigrants who came to this land, more than two-thirds entered by way of the port of New York. New Orleans, which ranked second as a port of entry, was far down, with 555,000. Boston received only 380,000. In 1854, a peak year for immigration, New York received almost 75 percent of all the new arrivals.

Opposition to the foreign born. The huge immigration created irritations in addition to benefits. Often the immigrants were resented simply because they were foreigners. They were denounced, too, because they sometimes needed financial assistance after they landed. Between 1847 and 1854 alone, 617,000 immigrants were aided in New York City by charity amounting to $2,250,000—then a large sum.

Many Americans insisted that European countries were sending their paupers and criminals here. A former mayor of New York wrote these tart words in his diary: "All Europe is coming across the ocean; all that part at least who cannot make a living at home. . . . They increase our taxes, eat our bread, and encumber our streets, and not one in twenty is competent to keep himself."

Contributions of the newcomers. Many citizens, though, could see that immigrants, especially those with families, became valuable consumers of goods of all kinds as soon as they landed. It was recognized, too, that each newcomer usually brought with him a small sum of money. Even if the average was only $40, the tide of the 1850's meant that $100,000,000 in new capital helped to enrich America.

But most of all, immigrants carried to this country a willingness to join their minds and their physical strength in a common effort with earlier arrivals to fulfill the aspirations of all Americans. As the *New York Tribune* declared in 1851: "Europe pours her surplus millions in armies upon our shore and their first cry is for Work! Work!" Except in periods of economic distress, the middle Atlantic states were able to supply it.

EARNING A LIVING

In 1850 the middle Atlantic states were growing enough food for their own needs. Also, they were able to sell surplus wheat elsewhere in the country. Until 1850 they raised more sheep than any other section. Both New York and Pennsylvania were producing vast quantities of cattle until the eve of the Civil War. The production of dairy products—milk, butter, cheese—in New York in 1850 was double that of Ohio, the second-largest producer in the Union.

Mining and heavy industry. Yet even by 1850 it was clear that mining and heavy industry would soon reshape the section. The steel age had not yet arrived, but the availability of coal and the nearness of iron ore made Pennsylvania ideally suited to show the way to the new era. Already Pennsylvania led all the states in coal extraction. In 1850 it was producing half of the nation's pig iron. Sixty percent of the wrought iron of the country was manufactured in New York, New Jersey, and Pennsylvania.

##The middle Atlantic states had not only better farm land than the New England states, but also valuable mineral resources. Note the position of Pittsburgh, p. 205.

Americans turn out to cheer for the British steamship the *Great Western*—at the left—as it arrives at New York City.

The Great Western flies its own flag and also the flag of the nation whose port it enters.

While New England introduced modern factory machines and methods in the textile industry, the middle Atlantic states created the modern plants and methods for producing iron. The Cambria Iron Works of Johnstown, Pennsylvania, by 1850 covered about 25,000 acres. Its furnaces could produce 800 tons of pig iron a week.

International commerce. The middle Atlantic states dominated the country's foreign commerce by 1850. At the beginning of the 1840's, New York's totals for merchant-marine tonnage and foreign-ship arrivals surpassed Boston's for the first time and were never thereafter challenged. Sailing to every ocean, the ships of that port performed exploits ranking with the most thrilling saga of the sea.

Packet ships. Until 1838 the packet ship, designed for cargo space and comfort, was a familiar sight in the Atlantic ports. In 1818 Isaac Wright and Son established the Black Ball Packet Line, which had regular runs from New York to Liverpool, England, and back, taking about twenty days each way. Competition with other lines was soon lively, and four packets sailed in each direction every month.

Steamers and clippers. In 1836, the Dramatic Line—so called because the ships were named for famous actors—was founded by Edward Knight Collins, with the finest vessels yet. Collins was barely established when steam revolutionized transatlantic shipping. In 1838 the *Sirius* and the *Great Western,* English steam-

ships, raced across the ocean in 17½ and 15 days respectively. Collins rose to the challenge. "I will build steamers," he told a friend in 1840, "that shall make the passage from New York to Europe in ten days or less." Ten years later he fulfilled his pledge.

It was the clipper ship, though, that made the American flag known everywhere on the seven seas. From time immemorial, shipbuilders had said it was possible to have speed or cargo capacity in a vessel, but not both. After considerable experimentation growing out of the keen rivalry among the Atlantic ship designers, the clipper proved that statement wrong. The first of its type was the *Rainbow,* launched at New York in 1845. Sharp-bowed, slender, carrying abundant, billowy sail, the clipper quickly won fame for its beauty and its usefulness.

The clippers brought the eastern cities into closer touch with the western ones, and they were used very successfully in foreign commerce. The lure of the California gold fields and the enticing trade with China especially stimulated the building of the clippers. In 1851 the masterpiece of them all, the *Flying Cloud,* made its maiden voyage from New York to San Francisco, around South America, in eighty-nine days.

The clipper's heyday was short. The coming of the steamship, a temporary slowing of immigrant traffic, and increased competition from Europe brought a marked decline in American

#Trade was expanding not only domestically, but also internationally. Ask the class to turn to page 821. They can see there that in 1840 exports exceeded imports. See later years.

merchant shipping after 1850. Furthermore, Americans were finding it profitable to invest elsewhere—in coal mining, for example.

But between 1830 and 1850 the United States led all other countries in merchant shipping. This supremacy had daily brought to the port cities, and through them to the entire
North, new ideas and new vigor. The bustling activity helped give the North the speedy tempo of life which constantly astonished European visitors. As early as 1857 an observer of Broadway's traffic was in despair: "Look up and down the street . . . ," he said, "and then run for your life." New York, the greatest city

of the middle Atlantic states, had already become a symbol throughout the world of the North's—and America's—driving energy.

Sum and Substance

1. Explain the population growth of the middle Atlantic states between 1830 and 1850. How did it affect the cities? 2. From what places did most immigrants come? 3. Why were immigrants often opposed? What contributions did they make? 4. In what various ways did people of the middle states make a living? Account for the diversity. 5. What kinds of ships were used to carry on our international trade between 1830 and 1850?

Review the meaning of the "old Northwest." "Old" distinguishes it from our new Northwest.

THE OLD NORTHWEST RELIES ON GRAINS AND THE UNION

By 1810 the old Northwest was already receiving the American settlers who had broken into the trans-Appalachian region. The population spread along the Ohio Valley like oil on water.

THE ARRIVAL OF SETTLERS

The National Road from Cumberland, Maryland, to Wheeling, on the Ohio River, was the most important thoroughfare. A migrant on it wrote: "We are seldom out of sight as we travel on this grand track, towards the Ohio, of family groups before and behind us." In 1825 the new Erie Canal turned the line of travel north, and by 1837 Michigan had added its star to the flag.

New cities. From the Ohio to the Great Lakes new cities blossomed: Cincinnati, Cleveland, Toledo, Detroit, and Chicago. The greatest city in the Ohio River Valley was Cincinnati, known as the "Queen City of the West," and sometimes as "Porkopolis" because of the output of its pork-packing plants. One visitor noted in 1828: "The indications of wealth, of business, and refinement, were too striking to pass unobserved by one who reflected how recently the forest frowned upon this spot."

Chicago, on the shore of Lake Michigan, was the largest lake city. It was incorporated only as a village in 1833. But within the next

few years, the surrounding prairie was settled, and Chicago boomed. In 1843 a traveler could write: "There are men here, sensible reflecting men, who affect to believe that in a few years it will be one of the great cities of the Union."

New states. After the Indians of northern Illinois had been subdued in the Black Hawk War of 1832, settlers could take over areas no longer Indian strongholds. In 1836 the town of Milwaukee was boasting of a population of 400, and Wisconsin received a territorial governor and government. It became a state in 1848. Settlers moved across the Mississippi into the Iowa territory, which gained fame as "the land where the tall corn grows." Iowa was admitted to the Union in 1846.

Still the westward migration continued. In 1837 an Indian treaty had opened up Minnesota to settlement. Minneapolis was laid out in 1852 according to a detailed plan. Newcomers poured into the Minnesota River Valley, lavishly proclaiming its beauty. As one of them said, it was "the prettiest country lying wild that the world can boast of, got up with the greatest care and effort by old Dame Nature ten thousand years or more ago, and which she has been improving ever since."

New Americans. The old Northwest beckoned to foreigners, too. By 1850 about one-eighth of the inhabitants were foreign-born. Norwegians

##Important idea: The Erie Canal and the National Road connected the coastal North with the old Northwest. (See the map, p. 210). The road began in the South but veered into the North.

and Irishmen were numerous among them, but the largest number were Germans, many of whom sought homes in Wisconsin. Driven out of their homelands by a potato-crop failure and the political persecutions of 1848 in Europe, the immigrants hoped to find prosperity and freedom in America.

A mixture of traditions. By 1850, 4,500,000 people were making their homes in the old Northwest. The states of the Lakes region—Ohio, Michigan, and Wisconsin—were occupied by emigrants from the older parts of the North, who brought northern patterns of living to the area. In Indiana the early settlers were largely southern in origin, giving the state a southern aspect. In Illinois circumstances and location resulted in an almost even division of northerners and southerners, and consequently a blending of outlooks.

The people of the region were cultivating the mind as well as the soil. A large number of newspapers were published here from an early date—forty-eight in Ohio alone in 1824. It is estimated that by 1840 the presses of the area had turned out 500,000 pamphlets and books —chiefly school texts. Oberlin College was established in Ohio in 1833 and pioneered in co-education, granting degrees to women for the first time in 1837.

DEPENDENCE ON THE SOIL

Using its rich farmland, the old Northwest by 1840 was profitably exporting vast quantities of wheat and flour to other sections. It was also shipping huge quantities of corn and pork. Farmers in the Ohio River Valley, where corn and corn products were the main goods, freighted their produce south to New Orleans. Farmers living farther north, who depended on the Great Lakes for transportation, sent their goods east to cities on the Atlantic coast.

Reaching the market. As the demands of the rapidly industrializing East grew, New Orleans became *comparatively* less important as a mart than New York, Philadelphia, and Baltimore. Nevertheless, the people of the old Northwest needed both the southern *and* the eastern routes for maintaining their trade and prosperity.

Significance of location. Northwesterners liked ## to assert that they were more loyally devoted to the Union than any other people. Their greatest son, Abraham Lincoln, explained in part why they felt this way so strongly:

> The great interior has three outlets; one to Europe by way of New York; to South America and Africa by New Orleans; and one to Asia by San Francisco. Anywhere the line is drawn every man of the interior is cut off from some one or more of these outlets. These outlets east, west and south are indispensable to the well being of the people inhabiting . . . the vast region. Which of the three may be the best is no proper question. All are better than either.

Northwesterners, then, were keenly dependent on the other parts of the Union. When improved transportation finally came, it linked them inseparably to New England and the middle Atlantic states—rather than to the South. It made them a vital part of the expanding North.

Sum and Substance
1. How were the opening of the Erie Canal and the settlement of the old Northwest related? 2. What new areas were settled after 1832? Why? 3. Account for the variety in patterns of living in the old Northwest. 4. What showed the region's interest in education? 5. In what way did the old Northwest ·depend on the rest of the country? 6. What finally linked it to the Northeast?

The ties were good means of transportation and an enthusiasm for reform and progress.

NORTHERNERS BUILD STRONG INTERNAL TIES

If the thumping heart of the North was its bustling port cities, its circulatory system was its interior transportation lines. Through them coursed endless streams of goods and people.

EXPERIMENT AND EXPERIENCE

Even before 1812 the middle and New England states had been joined by a loose sys-

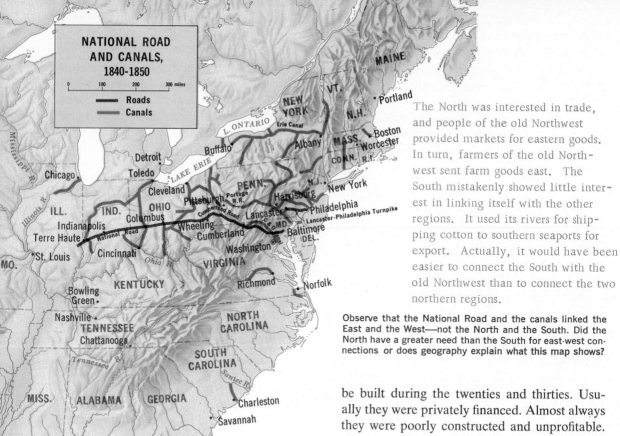

NATIONAL ROAD
AND CANALS,
1840-1850

0   100   200   300 miles

Roads
Canals

The North was interested in trade, and people of the old Northwest provided markets for eastern goods. In turn, farmers of the old Northwest sent farm goods east. The South mistakenly showed little interest in linking itself with the other regions. It used its rivers for shipping cotton to southern seaports for export. Actually, it would have been easier to connect the South with the old Northwest than to connect the two northern regions.

Observe that the National Road and the canals linked the East and the West—not the North and the South. Did the North have a greater need than the South for east-west connections or does geography explain what this map shows?

tem of turnpikes. This included the Lancaster-Philadelphia Turnpike and the National, or Cumberland, Road, which was authorized in Jefferson's presidency.

Turnpikes and plank roads. The British blockade during the War of 1812 forced Americans to resort to land transport instead of coastal shipping. This meant they had to depend on their turnpikes. The results were discouraging. It required, for instance, seventy-five days to move a wagonload of goods from Worcester, Massachusetts, to Charleston, South Carolina.

Turnpikes were usually impassable in the spring, when thaws flooded them and turned them into mud. Nevertheless, they continued to

be built during the twenties and thirties. Usually they were privately financed. Almost always they were poorly constructed and unprofitable. It is estimated that by 1835 half of the turnpikes of the country had been abandoned and were overgrown with weeds.

In the forties plank roads appeared, consisting of heavy boards laid crosswise, side by side. These, too, failed to produce good transportation. The weather rotted the wood, and the constant replacement of planks made the cost of maintenance excessive. Furthermore, when plank roads were not kept in repair, they were positively dangerous.

The canal craze. Canals proved the most satisfactory answer to the problem of how to carry the nation's goods. But since they were expensive to construct, requiring more money than private investment could put up, in 1816 there were only 100 miles of canals. The dramatic success of the Erie Canal, begun in 1817 and completed after eight years of labor, led people to accept canals. Paid for by New York State, it covered 364 miles between Buffalo and Albany, where it was linked to the Hudson River. Connecting the chief cities of New York to the Great Lakes region, the Canal was a remarkable engineering achievement—and a

Travelers on turnpikes paid tolls. Every seven miles a road was blocked by a pole, or pike. When the toll was paid, the pike was swung, or turned, aside--hence "turnpike."

monument to its forceful backer, Governor De-Witt Clinton.

Almost immediately the entire North was in the grip of a canal-building frenzy, giving the period from 1825 to 1840 the name "the canal era." To compete with the Erie Canal, Pennsylvania, between 1826 and 1834, constructed at a cost of $10,000,000 a system of canals linking Philadelphia to Pittsburgh. Canalboats were carried over the Alleghenies on the picturesque Portage Railroad—a system of cable cars on inclined planes. These cars pulled the loaded vessels up one side of the mountains and let them down easily on the other.

This canal system—called the "Main Line" —never threatened the supremacy of the Erie, but it enabled Philadelphia to continue to compete with New York for trade. Extensive canal construction joining the Ohio and the Mississippi ultimately made possible continuous passage by internal waterways from New York to New Orleans.

Yet, even as these canals were being dug, railroads were beginning to make them out of date. On July 4, 1828, President John Quincy Adams turned the first spadeful of earth for the Chesapeake and Ohio Canal. At the same time, not far away, Charles Carroll, the last surviving signer of the Declaration, was turning the first spadeful of earth for the Baltimore and Ohio Railroad. The B & O ultimately put the canal out of business.

The railroad fever. The railroad had been successfully demonstrated in England by George Stephenson in 1825. Earlier experiments by Oliver Evans of Philadelphia and John Stevens of Hoboken, New Jersey, had already shown in this country that it was practical to use steam to move carriages. One of the earliest railroads in the United States, the Mohawk and Hudson Railroad, chartered in 1826 and opened in 1831, proved to be the beginning of the great New York Central Railroad. The Baltimore and Ohio Railroad became the first passenger railway in the United States.

In 1828 the Philadelphia and Columbia was chartered, soon linking the City of Brotherly Love and Columbia, on the Susquehanna River.

This line was the parent of the Pennsylvania Railroad. Massachusetts authorized the Boston and Worcester in 1830, and by 1835 Boston was the railroad hub of the state.

In 1840 there were 3326 miles of canals and 2818 miles of railroad. In the next decade there was little additional canal-building, but the railroad mileage jumped to 9000. By 1860, this figure had risen to 30,626 miles.

The railroad was the most important cause of economic change in the nineteenth century. Its effect was felt everywhere. Worthless land # became valuable, and every town was soon linked directly or indirectly with every other.

The earliest trains were uncomfortable and dangerous. They were cold in winter and hot in summer. A coal stove (there was one in each car) sometimes overturned, burning the car down to the rails. The cars at first were considered unfit for women travelers, who were often urged to arm themselves with long hatpins when trains went through dark tunnels.

Canal companies, of course, kept up an attack on the railroads. One spokesman asserted: "Canals . . . are God's own highway, operating on the soft bosom of the fluid that comes straight from Heaven. The railroad stems direct from Hell. It is the Devil's own invention, compounded of fire, smoke, soot, and dirt, spreading its infernal poison throughout the countryside. . . ."

Soon opposition like this was drowned in a chorus of demands for more roads. A railroad "rage" gripped the country. Independent lines appeared throughout the land, often poorly laid out and equipped, often in unnecessary competition with each other. Many had to be rebuilt later in order to withstand the weight of heavier cars and locomotives.

In the years 1850–1860 a consolidation of the shorter roads into trunk lines took place. The New York and Erie was the first trunk line to join the Atlantic seaboard with the West. In 1851 its trains were running from New York to Dunkirk, on Lake Erie. In 1853 the New York Central was created by the merging of a number of smaller roads between Albany and Buffalo. That same year the Baltimore and Ohio

Students should observe that the earliest railroads were generally built in the Northeast. Look at the network in that area shown on the map on the next page.

211

reached as far as Wheeling, on the Ohio River. In 1854 the Pennsylvania established a connection between Philadelphia and Pittsburgh.

Chicago developed into the railroad center of the West not only because of its choice location but also because of the enterprise of a number of its leading businessmen. By 1860 it had become, as Carl Sandburg, its most famous poet, wrote later, a "player with railroads and the nation's freight handler."

Approximately 8000 miles of rails were laid between the Ohio River Valley and the Gulf of Mexico, but you can see from the map below that the lines joining the Northeast to the Northwest were more numerous than any oth-

ers. These bands of iron and steel followed natural trade channels. The farmers of the Northwest shipped their goods to Atlantic ports, and eastern manufacturers found their best markets in the old Northwest.

THE ZEAL FOR REFORM

Just as remarkable as the railroad in linking northerners was the spirit of reform which found followers in every part of the North. The common characteristic of the reformers was a belief that man by his own efforts could improve his social, religious, and political environment. "What is a man born for," Ralph Waldo Emerson asked, "but to be a Reformer . . .

(There was not enough freight into the interior of the South to make railroads profitable.)

How do you explain the fact that in 1860 the South lagged behind the North in the building of railroads? Into what states beyond the Mississippi had railroads been extended? What cities had become railroad centers?

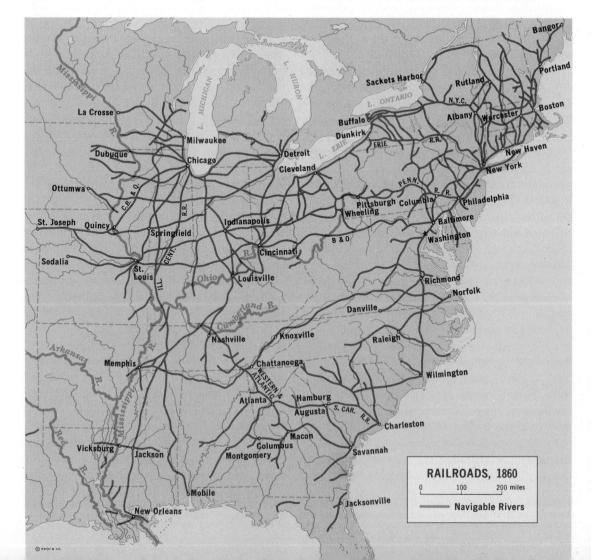

RAILROADS, 1860

0   100   200 miles

—— Navigable Rivers

imitating that great Nature . . . which sleeps no moment on an old past, but every hour repairs herself . . . ?"

Some explanations. The reform movement that marked the years between 1830 and 1850 had comparatively few friends in the South. Its chief supporters were in New England and those parts of the middle Atlantic states and the old Northwest where Yankees had settled. The spirit of reform was a result of a number of elements which seemed to come together in the North.

The first of these elements, undoubtedly, was the leisure time for "doing good" that the rise of industry provided. A second was the outpouring from England of rich ideas about reform—such as equal rights for women and the abolition of slavery—that inspired many sensitive people. A third was the spread of evangelical religion such as Methodism, emphasizing that it is an obligation of the individual to work for righteousness in others.

The variety of reforms the crusaders proposed was remarkable. Robert Rantoul made the 10-hour day his consuming interest; Neal Dow, attacking the manufacture and sale of intoxicating liquor, vowed he would slay "Demon Rum"; Dorothea L. Dix devoted her life to improving the treatment of the insane.

The call for public schools. The movement for free education typified the spirit of this reforming age. Its hero was Horace Mann, who broke his health and impoverished himself in working to establish public schools. The motives that prompted Mann and others like him arose from American democracy itself.

First, education opened the door to opportunity. In this "land of opportunity" it seemed a disgrace to deny to millions the chance for self-advancement that schooling could make possible. Second, now that the suffrage was becoming widespread, good citizenship demanded that voters be literate enough to inform themselves on public questions. Third, the increasing complexity of American life called for education to help people understand and adapt to it.

At first the movement for public schools was handicapped by opposition to paying the necessary taxes. But gradually the idea of supporting schools through taxation took hold, as the benefits became clear. By the mid-1800's most northern states were providing free elementary education for their children. The 1850 census reported that the country had about 80,000 primary schools, attended by almost 3,500,000 young people.

As early as the 1820's, Massachusetts had established the first public high schools. The demand for them spread, and their number grew not only in Massachusetts but also in the other populous states—Ohio and New York. Tax-supported higher education was making an appearance, too. A lengthening list of states, beginning with North Carolina in 1789, had established their own universities. The College of the City of New York, chartered in 1847, was the trailblazer among municipally supported academies.

Woman's rights. One of the most glaring deficiencies in American life was its denial of equal rights to women. A convention of feminists meeting at Seneca Falls, New York, in 1848 drew up a long list of women's grievances against society. Frequently ridiculed by men —by many women, too—the movement for woman's rights bore fruit years later. Its leaders, Elizabeth Cady Stanton and Susan B. Anthony, deserve their places as heroines of democracy.

The antislavery crusade. Of all the reformers, none were more devoted to their purpose than the abolitionists, who were determined to cleanse the country of slavery. The movement for abolition began in the eighteenth century. John Woolman, the inspired Quaker, and practical men like Franklin and Jefferson had condemned slavery in the past.

In the age of reform that opened in the 1830's, abolitionist fervor burned with a new intensity in the North. This was in part because in 1833 England emancipated its slaves and in part because the South now made its prosperity depend upon the *permanence* of slavery.

The vigor of the abolitionist argument was due to the strong and uncompromising convictions of its leaders. William Lloyd Garrison undoubtedly was the most widely known. His fame was based on the publication of his periodical *The Liberator,* which first appeared in 1831. In the opening issue, he advocated the immediate and complete abolition of slavery, saying, "I am in earnest—I will not equivocate—I will not excuse—I will not retreat a single inch—*and I will be heard.*"

The man who may have contributed most to the antislavery movement was Theodore Weld, a Connecticut-born minister whose genius has been forgotten, owing largely to his uncommon modesty. He permitted none of his writings to be published under his name, and he refused to speak where newspapermen were present. At the age of twenty-seven in 1830, he became an antislavery advocate, and in 1831 he moved to Ohio, thereafter making abolition his life's passion. (In 1838 Weld married Angelina Grimké, the most important woman abolitionist.)

Weld converted to the cause of abolition the wealthy Tappan brothers—New York philanthropists who supported his endeavors in Ohio —and Harriet Beecher, famous later as Harriet Beecher Stowe. On a trip to Alabama, Weld converted James G. Birney, who became abolition's outstanding political figure, running for the presidency on the Liberty party ticket in 1840 and 1844. Weld also converted Gamaliel Bailey, who became editor of the *National Era,* the most influential newspaper in the abolitionist cause, and Edwin M. Stanton, who later became Lincoln's Secretary of War. Finally, Weld persuaded John Quincy Adams—then serving in Congress—to open a campaign in the House of Representatives against slavery.

Garrison's and Weld's supporters split in 1840 when Garrison added woman's rights to his reform interests. Garrison argued against participating in politics; his opponents disagreed. The Liberty party, which Weld helped to organize, brought abolition into politics, where it stayed until the Civil War ended slavery.

The plight of the freedman. The concern over Negro slaves was not matched by a comparable concern over free Negroes in the North. Employed in many trades in the cities, some were able to accumulate savings and other property. Yet they felt deeply the discrimination which limited their advancement. Although many communities had given up segregated education by the 1850's, separate schools—if Negro education was provided for at all—continued to be the rule, especially in the old Northwest.

A belief in progress. Of course, not all northerners were reformers, but all of them were influenced by the reformers' belief that men could make tomorrow better than today. Northerners, in short, believed that the free individual could make progress if given the opportunity. The majority were probably indifferent to slavery and did not care either to attack it or to defend it. They sensed, nevertheless, that free labor in their own section helped to stimulate progress —in the arts, in the sciences, in raising the standard of living.

If northerners needed evidence that they were making progress, they had only to look at the remarkable changes in technology that were transforming their lives year by year.* Is it any wonder that they faced the future with supreme self-assurance—and even impatience? Whether they expressed it or not, they were confident that they were traveling in the same direction history itself was moving—toward broadened opportunities for all men, better living, and wider freedom.

Sum and Substance

1. Describe American roads in the first half of the nineteenth century. 2. What years are known as "the canal era"? Account for the name. 3. How did railroad mileage increase between 1840 and 1860? 4. Name effects of the coming of the railroad not mentioned by Thoreau. 5. Why did Chicago become the railroad center of the West? 6. What trait did reformers have in common? Explain why they were so active in the North. 7. Name four reform movements and important names connected with each.

---

* To list only a few: McCormick's reaper in 1834, Colt's revolver in 1836, Deere's steel plow in 1837, Goodyear's vulcanized rubber in 1839, Draper's photograph in 1839, Morse's telegraph in 1839, Morton's use of ether as an anesthetic in 1846, Howe's sewing machine in 1846, Page's electric locomotive in 1851.

What types of discrimination probably limited the advancement of Negroes in the North? (One kind is mentioned--segregated education. How did it limit their advancement?)

THE WORKSHOP

OF LASTING SIGNIFICANCE

Relate each of the following to the development of the North in the period between 1830 and 1860.

Yankee

"Yankee exodus"

Waltham system

company store

yellow-dog
  contract

macadam

packet ship

clipper

Flying Cloud

Black Hawk War

Oberlin College

National Road

Baltimore and Ohio
  Railroad

Erie Canal

DeWitt Clinton

Methodism

Robert Rantoul

Dorothea L. Dix

Neal Dow

Horace Mann

Elizabeth Cady
  Stanton

Susan B. Anthony

William Lloyd
  Garrison

Theodore Weld

The Liberator

PUTTING HISTORY ON THE MAP

1. On two outline maps of the United States, name the principal rivers and the Great Lakes. Show and name the Erie Canal. On one map indicate the ten largest cities in the United States in 1830, and on the other the ten largest in 1860 (see the lists on page 205).

In both years the two largest cities were located in what part of the North? What facts of history have you learned which explain their sizes? In 1790 (see page 165) how many of the ten largest cities were in New England? In 1830? In 1860? By 1860 what cities seem to have replaced the New England cities? Account for the change.

In 1830 how many of the cities were located in the West? How many in 1860? What historical facts can you cite that account for the increase?

2. Examine closely the *relative* locations of the ten largest cities in 1830 and in 1860. That is, in each case see how the location is related to such natural features as waterways, valleys, and mountains (refer to pages 360–361). See also how each location is related to technological development. Refer to maps in this chapter.

HISTORICAL STATISTICS

1. Look at the population table in the Appendix. What was the approximate percent of increase in the population in each decade from 1790 to 1820? From 1820 to 1860? #

2. On the same page compare the figures showing urban and rural populations in the same years. In what decades were the first big ## increases in urban population? How do you account for these increases? About what percent of the population was rural when Jefferson was elected President? The year after Jackson became President? How was this change reflected in Jacksonian democracy? What percent of the population was rural in 1860?

In 1790 the population of the country was predominantly rural. Was this equally true in 1860?

BEING A SOCIAL SCIENTIST

1. What technological advances significantly affected Americans in the first half of the nineteenth century? In what section or sections of the country were most of the advances made? Can you explain why?

2. Describe the changes in the lives of men, women, and children that resulted from the technological advances.

3. How did technological improvements affect farming in New England? In the middle Atlantic states? In the old Northwest?

4. Tell how the development of technology was related to urban growth.

5. How did most of the people make a living in New England? In the middle Atlantic states? In the old Northwest?

6. What outlook on life characterized the northern reformers? How did they influence other northerners?

7. Explain why technological advances and the spirit of reform helped unite the North.

8. Why in your opinion was there a lack of concern about freedmen in the North?

##The first big increases were in the decades from 1830-1860. These were decades of growing industry. About 94 percent of the population was rural in 1800; about 91 percent was rural in 1830.

215

Slavery and cotton cultivation were the two important distinguishing features of southern life in the decades preceding the Civil War. In this chapter the authors desribe the development of both. For inquiry: Sum up the arguments Harper uses in this quotation to make his point. How can students today answer each argument? (See the first three paragraphs, p. 229, under the head, "History and Geography" for some help. See "Documents in History" for other questions on this quotation.)

12

THE SOUTH: THE COTTON KINGDOM

. . . our great staple, cotton . . .

In one thing I concur with the abolitionists; that if emancipation is to be brought about, it is better that it should be immediate and total. But let us suppose it to be brought about in any manner, and then enquire what would be the effects.

The first and most obvious effect, would be to put an end to the cultivation of our great Southern staple. . . . The cultivation of the soil on an extensive scale, can only be carried on where there are slaves, or in countries super-abounding with free labor. No such operations are carried on in any portions of our own country where there are not slaves. . . .

Imagine an extensive rice or cotton plantation cultivated by free laborers, who might perhaps

There are few signs of technological advances here. Hand-picking was slow and tedious.

A cotton plantation at harvesttime in a coastal area of the United States in the mid-nineteenth century. Under the watchful eyes of an overseer (*left*), slaves pick cotton by hand, filling sacks and baskets they drag about.

#Harper was aware that numerous strikes had taken place in northern industries. See p. 403.
##Harper is, of course, referring to Europe. Europeans imported American cotton and manu- factured it into cloth. Factory workers and factory owners are the people he has in mind.

strike for an increase of wages, at a season when the neglect of a few days would insure the destruction of the whole crop. Even if it were possible to procure laborers at all, what planter would venture to carry on his operations under such circumstances? I need hardly say that these staples cannot be produced to any extent where the proprietor of the soil cultivates it with his own hands. He can do little more than produce the necessary food for himself and his family.

And what would be the effect of putting an end to the cultivation of these staples, and thus annihilating, at a blow, two-thirds or three-fourths of our foreign commerce? Can any sane mind contemplate such a result without terror? I speak not of the utter poverty and misery to which we ourselves would be reduced, and the desolation which would overspread our own portion of the country. Our Slavery has not only given existence to millions of slaves within our own territories, it has given the means of subsistence, and therefore existence, to millions of freemen in our confederate States; enabling them to send forth their swarms to overspread the plains and forests of the West, and appear as the harbingers of civilization. . . .

Not only on our own continent, but on the other, it has given existence to hundreds of thousands, and the means of comfortable subsistence to millions. A distinguished citizen of our own State [South Carolina] than whom none can be better qualified to form an opinion, has lately stated that our great staple, cotton, has contributed more than any thing else of later times to the progress of civilization. By enabling the poor to obtain cheap and becoming clothing, it has inspired a taste for comfort, the first stimulus to civilization.

Does not *self-defence,* then, demand of us steadily to resist the abrogation of that which is productive of so much good? It is more than self-defence. It is to defend millions of human beings, who are far removed from us, from the intensest suffering, if not from being struck out of existence. It is the defence of human civilization.

After the Missouri and the nullification controversies (see pages 172 and 189), many southerners became active in explaining and justifying their section's way of life. Actually many of them were distressed by the knowledge that slavery was morally wrong. Yet they believed, in general, that the cotton plantation and the slave system on which it was based were indispensable to their prosperity.

William Harper, a political leader of South Carolina, became one of their chief spokesmen. His Memoir on Slavery *(1837), from which this selection is taken, was among the most influential proslavery arguments ever published.*

SLAVERY TAKES HOLD OF SOUTHERN AGRICULTURE

The South is not separated from the North by high mountain ranges or by impassable rivers. The topography of the section merges easily with that of the North. Yet the economic, political, and social differences between the South and the North were as marked in the years 1830–1860 as if the two sections had been foreign countries. History, more than geographic factors, created these disparities. The most formative event in the history of the South was the establishment of Negro slavery.

ITS BEGINNINGS

Slavery was a system of labor introduced in the seventeenth century to bring under cultivation the seemingly limitless land of America. After its establishment in Virginia (see page 30), it began to spread to other areas as a solution to the persistent shortage of labor for raising tobacco, rice, and indigo.

The slave trade. At first, slave-trading was a monopoly of the Royal African Company, which operated on a British charter. But by the end of the eighteenth century, many New Englanders and others were individually engaged in the business.

Traders bought Negroes on the west coast of Africa from slave dealers, who sold for rum or trinkets Africans of other tribes taken as prisoners of war. Sometimes driven by whiplash to waiting vessels, the victims were stowed like sardines into the holds of ships. It was not unusual for more than half of them to die crossing the ocean. Profits were so great for the sea captains, however, that the high death rate was of little concern to them.

The traffic in Negro slaves added significantly to the profits of northern merchants and supplied laborers needed in the northern as well as the southern parts of English America. At least a million Negroes were imported between 1619 and 1808, when Congress outlawed the foreign slave trade—though many slaves were smuggled into the country after that date.

The coastal "aristocracy." By the 1770's, a small and tightly knit southern planter "aristocracy"

had developed from the labor of the slaves. The bondmen raised tobacco on plantations in Virginia and Maryland and indigo and rice on plantations in South Carolina. The family names of some of the planters—Washington, Lee, Jefferson—are familiar to every school child, for they were the leaders of the South at the time of the American Revolution.

Manumission. Many of the planters felt pangs of conscience when they viewed their owning of slaves in the light of the words of the Declaration of Independence: "all men are created equal." Patrick Henry said of slavery plainly, "I cannot justify it." Jefferson, deeply troubled by it, declared, "I tremble for my country when I reflect that God is just: that his justice cannot sleep forever." George Washington, too, hoped that slavery might be ended. Many seaboard planters upon their deaths manumitted* their slaves. As the Quakers, the Baptists, and the Methodists, in keeping with their religious outlooks, increasingly championed abolition, an interest in freeing the slaves grew.

Plans for liberation. Various plans existed to deal with the Negroes who had been or would be liberated. Slaveowners in Virginia, Maryland, and Kentucky in 1817 organized the American Colonization Society to transport freedmen back to Africa. Five years later it established the Republic of Liberia on the west coast of Africa, naming the capital Monrovia for the president of the United States. Although about a thousand Negroes were transplanted, the scheme as a whole was impractical, and it failed. Most Negroes opposed colonization, feeling that America, the land they helped develop or were born in, was their home.

The declining seaboard. Economic reasons tended to support the humanitarian and religious argument that slavery was evil. The market for tobacco had declined by the time Washington was President, and prices were low. The westward migration to Kentucky, where land was more

---

* "Manumit" means to free from slavery. We rarely see the word today, but before the Civil War it was a part of the ordinary vocabulary of every literate American.

##See also Exercises 2, 3, and 4 under "History and Geography," p. 229. Slavery, not geography, fastened the plantation system and cotton cultivation on the South.

fertile, was already under way. A woman in Virginia wrote to her brother in the Bluegrass country in 1789, "A great many people here are talking of settling in [your] country, for their land is getting so poore here and Money hard to get hold of." In 1831 and 1832 the Virginia legislature seriously debated abolishing slavery in that state, but nothing was done.

Tobacco-raising remained at the same level from 1800 to about 1850, but compared with the total agricultural output of the nation, it was losing its importance. Indigo culture disappeared almost entirely after the Revolution, because the British subsidy which had made it profitable in the first place was no longer available. The raising of rice in the inland swamplands of South Carolina was giving way to the cultivation of the crop on swamplands irrigated by the tidal flow of rivers. But after the end of the eighteenth century, the acreage devoted to rice did not expand much despite this change. By the 1820's it seemed that the time was coming to set the slaves free.

THE COTTON KINGDOM

A remarkable increase and spread in cotton cultivation ended the southern movement to emancipate the slaves. After 1830 every aspect of southern life was dominated by what people called the "Cotton Kingdom." At its height in 1860, the Cotton Kingdom was a veritable white sea extending more than 1000 miles westward from South Carolina to central Texas. It stretched northward from Texas about 200 miles, about the same distance northward from South Carolina, and about 600 miles up the Mississippi Valley.

The crop. Some areas of Virginia and the Carolinas had produced small quantities of cotton during the eighteenth century. Yet as late as 1784 eight bales† of southern cotton were rejected by an English customs officer, who refused to believe they had been produced in the United States! But southern exports of the "white gold," as it was often referred to, grew steadily thereafter—from 79,000 bales in 1800

to 125,000 in 1810 to 484,000 in 1820. By 1860 southern production represented two-thirds of the world's annual supply—the staggering total of 3,841,416 bales. How do we account for this striking development?

Demands and possibilities. The Industrial Revolution in England by the late eighteenth century had resulted in so many technological improvements in the manufacturing of cotton cloth that the demand of English factories for raw cotton far exceeded the supply. The cotton Americans produced for this waiting market was sea-island, or long-staple, cotton, which could be grown in the United States only along the coast. ("Long-staple cotton" means cotton with long fibers.) Short-staple cotton would grow anywhere, but its clinging green seeds had to be removed laboriously by hand. An experienced slave could clean about a pound of short-staple cotton in a day.

If planters could only find a way to produce short-staple cotton profitably, they could feed England's hungry factories. The South would come out of its economic slump and its slaves would be valuable again. The Georgia legislature offered a prize for a machine that could effectively pick seeds from cotton and so remove the barrier to prosperity.

Eli Whitney's gin. A young Yale graduate, Eli Whitney, on his way south to serve as tutor in a southern family, met the widow of the Revolutionary hero General Nathanael Greene. When Whitney arrived at his destination, he found that the position he expected to take had already been filled. Mrs. Greene invited him to spend the winter with her and her family in Savannah.

One evening Whitney listened to some of the General's old friends discussing at dinner the desperate need for a cotton-cleaning device. Whitney had never seen a bale of cotton in his life, but he had rare mechanical ability. Setting to work, in ten days he had built a model machine. By April, 1793, he had produced an ## engine, or gin, capable of cleaning 50 pounds of cotton a day. With a pardonable lack of modesty, Whitney wrote his father: "I had the satisfaction to hear it declared by a number of

† A bale of cotton weighs between 300 and 500 pounds.

##Students should think of the invention as a technological advancement that changed our history. Whitney also devised a system of using interchangeable parts in manufacturing.

219

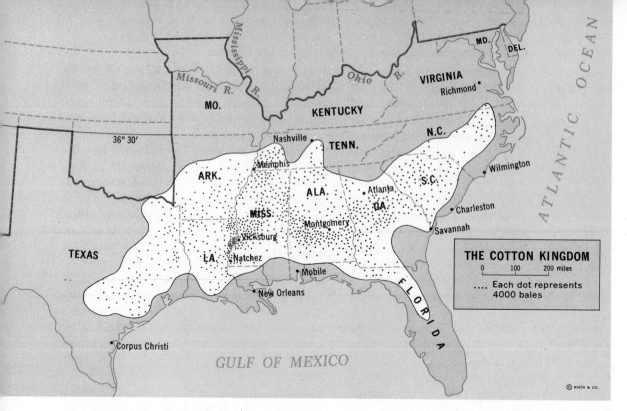

The cotton production shown is that of 1859, the peak year. Which state would you assume had the largest number of slaves? The smallest number? What states would a map of a "cotton kingdom" today include?

It would be made up chiefly of Texas, Mississippi, California, Arkansas, Alabama, and Arizona.

the first men in America that my machine is the most perfect and the most valuable invention that has ever appeared in this country."

The gin revolutionized southern agriculture by making possible large-scale cotton-raising. An immediate effect was to tighten the hold of slavery on the South.

"The flush times." Cotton-growing was admirably suited to unskilled labor because it did not require the complicated cultivation necessary for tobacco and rice. As the market for raw cotton expanded, a steadily increasing demand for new land to be tilled by slaves brought state after state into the Union—Louisiana in 1812, Mississippi in 1817, Alabama in 1819, Missouri in 1821, Arkansas in 1836, Florida in 1845. Texas in 1845 gave up its independence and joined the United States. By the 1840's the Southwest—as this offshoot of the old South was called—was experiencing a wonderful prosperity called "the flush times."

The cotton planters. Cotton-growing produced a new southern class—the cotton planters—

which enjoyed a dominant position, both politically and socially. These "aristocrats" of the Cotton Kingdom built magnificent houses like those in Virginia or South Carolina, which they had only dreamed of owning a few years before. Yet, as one man complained, "it is not so easy to transport to that forest the intellectual society of the mother-land, and to rear there a school or a college in all the perfection of older institutions of the same kind."

To many southerners the planters appeared to be hard-drinking, high-living, and hotheaded. "Affairs of honor" often were settled by duels. A southerner explained the situation this way: "When a man knows that he is to be held accountable for his want of courtesy, he is not so apt to indulge in abuse. In this way duelling produces a greater courtesy in society and a higher refinement."

The number of cotton planters was actually # small. The total population of the South in 1850 was 8,982,612, of which 3,352,198 were Negroes—for the most part, slaves. Among the

#Many people today think of the ante-bellum South as a region where most people lived on
220 plantations. The influence of planters was out of proportion to their number.

remaining southerners, about 1,130,000 families were represented—if we assume an average family had five members.

The number of slaveowners listed, 347,525, tells us that about one family in four owned slaves. A clear majority of these owned fewer than 5 slaves apiece. Only 11 men owned 500 or more apiece. In all the slave states, not over 8000 people each owned 50 or more Negroes, and 300,000 owned between 1 and 10 slaves. Since three-fourths of the southerners owned no slaves, they had only an indirect stake in the slave system and the plantations it served.

Merchants and professional men. Who were these nonslaveholding people? Immediately below the planters on the economic and social ladder were merchants and professional men—doctors, lawyers, and teachers. They ministered to the plantation owner, healing his sick, defending him in court, and teaching his children. Because they depended upon him as much as he did upon them, they were inclined to accept slavery and the plantation system unquestioningly. Although the merchants and professional men owned no slaves, some hoped to own them one day. Believing that their future was tied up with the maintenance of Negro bondage, they voted as the planters did. Authors of books and articles defending slavery came from this group.

Yeoman farmers. Next on the ladder were yeoman farmers, making up the largest single group. They owned small farms and worked them themselves. A yeoman farmer might have a slave or two, but he labored beside them in the fields. These farmers did not defend slavery as a system of labor, and often they were very democratic in their viewpoints. They feared, however, that if slavery was abolished they would be in economic competition with the Negroes. For the yeoman farmers—as for the planters—the continuance of slavery seemed necessary to maintain the social distinction between the races.

Many yeoman farmers, of course, aspired to become planters, although most of them did not expect to have the money to rise that high. Jefferson Davis—later president of the Confederacy—was the son of a farmer from Kentucky who moved to Mississippi. There Jefferson's brother Joseph succeeded in lifting the entire family to a position of wealth and prestige. This case, however, was exceptional.

The people of the pine barrens. Below the yeoman farmers were the poor people who lived for the most part in the less fertile, pine-bearing regions of the Appalachians. They managed a bare existence by raising corn (from which they made mush), pumpkins, and perhaps vegetables. These people were probably the descendants of frontiersmen who had somehow been stranded on the inferior land.

Freedmen. Still lower on the ladder were the freed Negroes and mulattoes, liberated for religious, humanitarian, or economic reasons. In 1790 there were about 30,000 freedmen in the South; by 1860, approximately 260,000. As slaves grew more valuable after 1830, manumission was restricted or forbidden entirely in most states.

The freed Negroes lived uncertain lives. Most of them were located in Delaware, Virginia, North Carolina, Tennessee, Kentucky, and especially Maryland, where they generally huddled together in towns and cities. Other workers scorned them because they feared them as competitors. Planters regarded them as corrupters who probably supplied the slaves with liquor and dangerous ideas about freedom.

Freedmen earned their livelihood as domestic servants or as hired farm workers. Many were skilled craftsmen. For example, there were over 4000 Negro blacksmiths in Virginia on the eve of the Civil War. A few Negroes even owned slaves, although in many cases they had merely bought relatives—a way of getting around the laws against manumission.

A handful of exceptional free Negroes were able to achieve recognition for their attainments in the arts and in business despite their handicaps. John Chavis, for instance, ran a school in North Carolina, with Negro pupils in the evening and white ones during the day. Some of his white pupils became governors and congressmen. John Jones owned one of Charleston's best hotels, and Thomy Lafon left a fortune of $500,000 from his real-estate opera-

##Students should appreciate against what great odds these Negroes achieved their success. Observe that the free Negroes lived in states where there were fewest slaves (see the map).

221

tions in New Orleans. William Johnson owned 1500 acres of land near Natchez. But in general the life of a free Negro was hard, and he lived in fear of being kidnapped and sold into slavery again.

THE SLAVE'S LOT

It is a mistake to believe that the "peculiar institution," as southerners referred to slavery, was a uniform system. A world, for example, separated the experienced house servant, who often bore heavy responsibilities, from the recently arrived field hand, who perhaps was forced to do his job by a whipping.

There was wide variation, too, in the way different masters treated their bondmen. Also, the life of the slave was likely to be harsher in a frontier area than in a more settled, older community. For these reasons, generalizations about how slavery worked in practice are likely to be inaccurate. A few, however, may be made with confidence.

In the field. Plantation slaves worked from sunup to sundown under the watchful eyes of an overseer. He divided the slaves into gangs of about twenty, with a Negro driver in charge of each gang. The driver carried a bull whip and was expected to apply it to laggards.

The overseer apportioned the work and enforced the discipline required to get the tasks done. He recorded expenditures for supplies in an account book and saw to it that slaves received food and medical care.

It was difficult to find good overseers. Moreover, they were cordially disliked by Negroes and planters alike. The best of them might be paid as much as $1500 or $2000 a year each, but the average did not get more than $600. One planter wrote in 1850: "The tribe of men usually known as overseers, the cowhide fraternity, are the most faithless and piratical of our population."

Sometimes overseers received bonuses if production reached a certain high level. Frequently they boosted production by overdriving the slaves. This was a constant concern of slaveholders who looked upon their slaves as investments they did not want to endanger.

Incentive and punishment. Sometimes providing rewards and punishments encouraged slaves in the performance of their labors. A former slave recalled in later years his experiences in North Carolina: "At ten years of age my first task was to pick fifty pounds of cotton. If I failed . . . I would get a lick for every pound I failed to pick. For every pound over fifty pounds I received one cent."

Whippings might also be administered for lying, stealing, attempting to escape, or failing to be clean. Many enlightened slaveowners forbade their overseers to whip their charges. Since discipline was the essence of slavery, however, punishments were considered necessary. Slave agriculture has sometimes been called "military agriculture."

Discipline. Slave codes prescribing the conduct of the Negro were in effect by the 1830's. They grew out of southern fear of slave rebellions. Planters became alarmed when copies of a pamphlet entitled *Walker's Appeal to the Colored Citizens of the World,* published in 1829 by a freed Negro, David Walker, circulated among the slaves. Then an insurrection in Virginia in 1831, led by a slave named Nat Turner, resulted in the slaying of many persons of both races. It opened the way to more rigid restrictions on slaves.

Under the sterner codes Negroes no longer could have their own ministers, since they might preach from the "wrong parts" of the Bible. Slaves could only attend the masters' churches and hear sermons based on the theme of obedience. They were forbidden to be away from their houses without passes; they had to obey a 9 P.M. curfew; they could not own firearms. Roads were patrolled regularly to catch and return Negroes who were out at night without permission. Other parts of the codes carefully prescribed relations between the races. For example, Negroes were barred from testifying in court for or against any persons except other Negroes.

Many slave-code provisions were neglected in practice. It was, for instance, a punishable offense to teach a slave to read. Yet a southern editor remarked that he had never heard of a

New-York Historical Society

Bondmen planting sweet potatoes on a southern planta- —plows the ridges in which the potatoes will grow,
tion in 1862. In the division of labor, one man—far left women cut the "seed," and other slaves plant them.
This picture was taken during the Civil War, when Mathew Brady made photography common.

slave who wanted to read who had been prevented from doing so. Nevertheless, when their
provisions were enforced, the slave codes were
severe.

The underground railroad. From time to time Negroes tried to find freedom by running away to
the North. They were assisted by the underground railroad—a series of way stations established by abolitionists, and operated mainly by
free Negroes, to guide slaves on the dangerous
journey from bondage to liberty. With the help
of the "railroad," many slaves made their way
to Canada. A heroine of "The U.G.R.R." was
\# Harriet Tubman, who is said to have returned

again and again to the South to lead some of
her people to freedom.

Sum and Substance

1. In William Harper's mind, how was civilization
related to cotton and Negro slavery? 2. How and
when was the slave trade formally ended? 3.
Name the early objections southerners made to
slavery. 4. What plans were made for the slave
population? What ended them? 5. How did the
cotton gin affect cotton-growing? 6. Name and
briefly describe the groups that made up the
southern population. 7. How was slave discipline
maintained?

\#A book about her is Harriet Tubman: Conductor on the Underground Railroad, by Ann Petry.

THE "PECULIAR INSTITUTION" IS WEIGHED IN THE BALANCE

The increasing importance of slavery in the
South after 1830 coincided with the growth of
antislavery expression in the North (see pages
213–214). From that period on, many leading
southern minds were constantly presenting
new arguments in favor of the "peculiar institution," in order to refute the abolitionists.

DEFENDERS OF THE SYSTEM

Before 1830 the great majority of abolitionists had been southerners—mostly favoring
\#\# colonization in Africa; by 1837 no antislavery
society existed in all the South. Southerners

were no longer praying hopefully that slavery
might disappear; now they called it a "positive
good."

Thomas Dew. One of the influential advocates
of the slave system was Thomas Dew, a teacher
at the College of William and Mary in Virginia. Since slaves are mentioned in the Bible,
he drew the conclusion that slavery was established by divine authority. He attacked the
"fallacies" of the Declaration of Independence,
the work of Thomas Jefferson, the most distinguished alumnus of William and Mary. Dew
insisted that men are unequal—that some

\#\#Recall that the reform movement in the North began in the 1830's--when cotton cultivation
was expanding in the South. Why did southerners at that time call slavery "a positive good"? 223

are fit only to do manual labor and others are clearly qualified to be the managers of society. "It is," he also wrote, "as much in the order of nature that men should enslave each other as that other animals should prey upon each other." Within a few years the teachings of Dew had become so popular that William and Mary made him its president.

Two South Carolinians. William Harper of South Carolina went beyond Dew in pushing aside Jefferson's philosophy. He asked, "Is it not . . . nearer the truth to say that no man was ever born free and that no two men were ever born equal, than to say that all men are born free and equal?"

John C. Calhoun put the finishing touch to the new point of view when he asserted that *in*equality was necessary for progress. He insisted that the South could model itself on ancient Greece, which practiced "democracy" but based it on slave labor.

George Fitzhugh. The arguments became more militant as the agitation of northern abolitionists became keener. George Fitzhugh, a Virginia lawyer, in the 1850's published two books which became popular: *Sociology for the South* and *Cannibals All! Slaves Without Masters.*

Fitzhugh presented the view that the North increasingly would be forced to deal drastically with strikes and the deteriorating condition of workers. The only solution was for the industrial masters of the North to adopt slavery! "Slavery," he predicted, "will everywhere be abolished or everywhere be reinstated." He was sure it would triumph in the end.

PROTEST BY SOUTHERNERS

Many southerners did not accept these defenses of slavery, believing that they contradicted the principles of liberty on which the nation was founded. But even these thoughtful men were frustrated because they did not see how emancipation might be carried out.

A Tennessee constitutional convention in a report in 1834 granted that slavery was an evil. Yet it lamented: "To prove it to be a great evil is an easy task, but to tell how that evil can be removed is a question that the wisest heads and the most benevolent hearts have not been able to answer in a satisfactory manner."

James G. Birney. With uncommon courage and against fearful opposition, a few southerners arose to argue for abolition. James G. Birney (see page 214) was one of the most prominent lawyers in Kentucky, where he was born and reared. As a result of his antislavery views, he broke with his father and his family. Even when Birney was dying, he refused to see his sister because she owned slaves.

The Grimké sisters. The Grimké sisters, Sarah and Angelina, daughters of a South Carolina slaveholder, dared to leave what they called "the ungentle, uncongenial air" of Charleston for the North. There they played a leading part as abolitionists.

Hinton Rowan Helper. The most influential of the southerners who criticized slavery was Hin-

Senator John C. Calhoun, the foremost southern spokesman, as portrayed by a cartoonist of his own time.

From an 1848 lithograph

#Though there were no antislavery societies in the South by 1837, individual southerners opposed slavery. Point out how difficult it is to take an unpopular stand among neighbors and friends.

ton Rowan Helper. Born in North Carolina, he wrote an antislavery book that made him wealthy. Called *The Impending Crisis of the South, and How to Meet It* (published in 1857), it used none of the moral and humanitarian arguments against Negro slavery. It asserted, instead, that slavery was impoverishing the small farmers and poor people of the South. The planters regarded Helper as particularly dangerous because he pitched his words to the great majority of white southerners—who owned no slaves.

Supporters of slavery scorned these southern opponents of their "peculiar institution." But they resented even more the northerners who criticized slavery and offered them advice on what to do about it. One North Carolina congressman, himself a critic of the slave system, stated in 1841 that wicked as servitude was, the South would not accept northern interference. "I can assure Northern gentlemen," he declared, "that the course of the abolitionists has riveted the chains of slavery with double and triple bolts of steel."

By the 1850's voices attacking slavery were heard less and less *within* the South. Criticism of other social evils also died out. The spirit of reform that was stirring the North (see pages 212–214) was hardly felt in the South.

The reasons are plain. First, all reforming was identified in southern minds with abolition. Second, many of the reform ideas originated in Europe, and immigration to the South, which might have spread them, was sparse. Third, southern postmasters for years censored the incoming mail in order to dam up the flow of abolitionist propaganda into their section. In so doing, they banned much other reform literature, too. In defending slavery, then, southerners were closing the door to useful social improvements and innovations and to new thinking on public problems.

SOCIAL AND ECONOMIC EFFECTS

The southerners most adversely affected by the slave system were, of course, the slaves. Yet one way or another, the whole South was

victimized by the institution. It made the South the scene of much hatred, fearfulness, distrust, and violence. These passions absorbed people's energies, which could have been used more constructively. Nevertheless, any individual southerner's opinion of the system depended largely upon how he himself was affected by its operation.

The planter. For the slaveowner, slavery was, in the main, a profitable arrangement, particularly on the newer lands to the west. Although it did not yield the proceeds which were common in industry, on well-run plantations the returns were substantial.

Many planters believed that slavery was inefficient because under it the bondmen worked grudgingly. Thomas Cooper, president of South Carolina College, wrote in 1826, for example, that a slave produced only two-thirds as much as a free man. Yet the idea of emancipation seemed to raise so many far-reaching problems that few dared to consider it seriously.

Free labor. For free workingmen slavery was also a handicap. As long as slave labor was available, southern states could retain laws forbidding wage earners to bargain as a group. Labor agitation, like abolitionist agitation, was regarded as an attack on slavery itself.

Immigrant laboring people, who, as we have seen, were pouring into the North between 1830 and 1850, shunned the South. Only one immigrant in eight settled in that part of the

The kind of houses slaves had depended on the master.
Slave quarters on a well-run cotton plantation in Louisiana.
Painting by C. Giroux, Museum of Fine Arts, Boston

country. Actually, there were so few southern factories that jobs would have proved scarce. Yet most of the newcomers preferred, anyway, to avoid competing with slave labor.

The slave. To the slave the system was never acceptable. Regarded as a piece of property to be bought and sold, he was denied his dignity as a human being. Not only could he have no ambition for himself or his children, but also he was constantly aware that the full fruits of his toil would never be his.

Slavery, based as it was on tight discipline, was probably keenly resented even by the majority of Negroes who seemed to adjust to it without a murmur—and often with laughter and gaiety. The slaves' running away, their shirking, their destruction of crops and tools, and their stealing from masters have been interpreted as signs of their resistance to slavery.

It is true that there were numberless instances of kindly masters and devoted slaves. Nevertheless, a slave who escaped to Canada

Does the data given here support the assumptions you made upon studying the map on page 220?

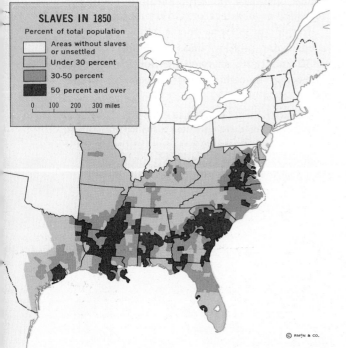

SLAVES IN 1850
Percent of total population

Areas without slaves or unsettled

Under 30 percent

30-50 percent

50 percent and over

0   100   200   300 miles

© RMⅭN & CO.

described the effect on him: "I feel lighter—the dread is gone. It is a great heaviness on a person's mind to be a slave."

The question is sometimes asked, Would slavery have disappeared if it had been left alone? By the time the Cotton Kingdom was at its height, the "peculiar institution" was more than a system of labor that could be discarded when it had lost its usefulness. It had become a deeply ingrained "way of life"—social as well as economic. As such, it could not be easily uprooted. Moreover, the slave population represented an immense investment of money. Governor James H. Hammond, a governor of South Carolina and later a Senator, once put it this way: "Were ever any people, civilized or savage, persuaded by any argument, human or divine, to surrender voluntarily two thousand million dollars?"

THE SOUTH'S PREDICAMENT

Southerners were often aware that the institution of slavery had them caught between the devil and the deep blue sea. By the 1850's the price of a "prime" field hand had risen to around $1600—about a 400 percent increase since 1830. Cotton prices meanwhile had fallen sharply.

The proposal to reopen the slave trade. What was the answer? Some were saying it was time to reopen the African slave trade. This solution, they maintained, would win slavery wider support in the South by making it possible for poorer men to own Negroes. Also, a large influx of new slaves would add to the southern population and thereby increase southern representation in Congress.

But even if the North had been willing to accept this proposal—at best only a remote possibility—the South itself would have been divided on the question. The south Atlantic states, especially Virginia, would have opposed it because now that their farmland was worn out, they obtained income by selling their surplus slaves to the Cotton Kingdom. If this market was lost through a reopening of the slave trade, the only alternative would have been to set their Negroes free.

##The map on p. 220 shows that practically no cotton was grown in Virginia, but this map shows that this state had a remarkably large number of slaves.

Failure to industrialize. Some attempts at manufacturing—of iron in Virginia and cotton cloth in South Carolina—were successful, but the value of the products was small. On the eve of the Civil War, ten times more cotton goods were being turned out in New England than in the entire South.

Wherever industrialization took place in the South, it raised serious problems in labor relations. Free laborers felt keenly the competition of slaves. In 1847, for example, a strike occurred at the Tredegar Iron Works at Richmond, Virginia, the largest iron company in the South. The skilled workers imported from the North refused to teach their specialties to slaves, who were hired from their owners at $100 a year each. In time, perhaps, the problems of manufacturing with slave labor could have been solved. But there was little enthusiasm to work on them; southerners as a rule simply did not invest in industry.

Commercial weakness. In foreign commerce, too, the South lagged far behind the North. It was not for want of good harbors. The section's greatest port was New Orleans, a bustling city of about 150,000 in 1850. Annually thousands of flatboats with produce from the old Northwest descended the Mississippi to this alluring city. To it came also the cotton and sugar of the Gulf area. In the late 1830's and early 1840's

Observe the position of New Orleans on the lists of cities on p. 205.

Steamboats at the port of New Orleans in 1850, when traffic on the Mississippi had reached a peak. As passengers disembark, the unloading of the bales of cotton piled on the lower deck of the *Belle Creole* begins. Emptied of its cargo of cotton, the boat will return upstream with consumer goods for the plantations lining the river.

Gift of the Estate of Mrs. Emily Crane Chadbourne, Corcoran Gallery of Art

The lists on p. 205 show that few southern cities were among the ten largest. What did the commercial weakness have to do with the scarcity of large southern cities?

New Orleans exported more than New York.

The second-ranking southern port was Mobile, Alabama, and after it came Savannah, Georgia. Charleston, South Carolina, a leading port in colonial days, declined swiftly after cotton became the important southern crop. Charleston is not situated on a river that could have received the cotton bales from interior plantations.

Exports were, however, only a part of the story. Imports into southern harbors were far below the outgoing cargoes in their value. New Orleans' imports were usually only about 25 percent of its exports. Ships returning from Europe brought their wares to northern ports, where northerners obtained the middleman's profits in selling manufactured goods to southern customers. Southerners, reinvesting much of their money in slaves, put little into the development of merchandising, insurance, or banking businesses. People in the great port cities in the North almost invariably owned these profitable enterprises.

The planters could get long-term loans from northerners and were usually in debt to them, very much as tobacco planters had been in debt to English middlemen before the Revolution. For this reason many southerners were inclined to consider themselves as being again in the spiteful grip of a "Lord North."

Inadequate rail facilities. A demand for railroads came not from the planters in the interior but from promoters in the seaports, who believed they could enlarge the trade of their home cities. Charleston, thinking it might catch up with its rivals, in 1827 began construction of a line to the Savannah River just opposite Augusta. When its 136 miles were finished in 1833, it was the longest railroad in the world.

Savannah responded by building the Central of Georgia, which enabled it to tap the Macon and Columbus markets. Other projects were soon under way as Norfolk, Richmond, Wilmington, and Baltimore entered the competition for railroads.

All these roads suffered because the "back haul"—that is, from the ports to the interior—of the freight trains was light. This is one reason why there were practically no rail connections between the Gulf states and other parts of the South, as you can see on the map on page 212. Profits promised to be too small to make the construction of such lines attractive to promoters.

The South made a great mistake in failing to complete a line from Charleston to Cincinnati. Former Senator Hayne of South Carolina, whose debate with Webster, you will remember, had made him a national figure, had envisioned such a railroad. Despite enthusiasm for a proposal in the late 1830's to construct it, the $12,000,000 needed was not available. The panic of 1837, followed soon by Hayne's death, ended the project.

Such a line might have created closer economic ties between the farmer of the old Northwest and the planter of the South. Instead, as we saw in the last chapter, the farmers of the old Northwest were growing more and more dependent on their markets in the East.

The South by 1850 was staking everything on the continuation of cotton prosperity. Southerners believed that a need for cotton fiber made the North dependent on the South, although in fact the sections were interdependent.

A few southern writers, like James De Bow, the best-known editor in the South, tried to encourage their section to build railroads, find a means to create direct trade with Europe, and establish industry. But by the 1850's most southerners accepted the boast of James Hammond, who thundered on the floor of the United States Senate, "You dare not make war on cotton—no power on earth dares make war upon it. Cotton is King!"

Sum and Substance

1. What arguments were used by southerners in defense of slavery after 1830? 2. What southerners attacked it? 3. Why was the reform spirit little felt in the South? 4. How did slavery affect immigration to the South? Why? 5. How did it affect free labor? 6. Compare the North and the South just before the Civil War in extent of industrialization, development of railroads, and amount of foreign trade.

##Develop the idea of interdependence of the regions of the country. For what did the South depend on the North? For what did the old Northwest depend on the Northeast, and vice versa?

#This would make an excellent essay question to be used as a test for the chapter or as part of a test. The third paragraph under "History and Geography" contains another good essay question for such a test. One or two could be paired with the test provided on pp. 23-24.

THE WORKSHOP

OF LASTING SIGNIFICANCE

Tell how each of the following was connected with life in the South between 1830 and 1860.

William Harper	yeoman farmer
Royal African	slave code
Company	underground railroad
manumission	Harriet Tubman
American	Thomas Dew
Colonization	George Fitzhugh
Society	James G. Birney
Liberia	Grimké sisters
Cotton Kingdom	Hinton Rowan Helper
long-staple cotton	Tredegar Iron Works
Eli Whitney	James De Bow

HISTORY AND GEOGRAPHY

1. Find in a reference book or obtain from the United States Department of Commerce a map showing current cotton production in this country. Compare the cotton belt shown on that map with the Cotton Kingdom, seen on the map on page 220. What changes are there?

Using a reference book, find out (a) how the United States ranks among cotton-growing countries of the world, (b) what cultivation methods are used by modern cotton-growers.

How do the facts about modern cotton production in the South compare with the predictions made by William Harper in his defense of slavery in 1837?

2. Look at the area included in the South on the map on page 220, and then at the same area on the map on pages 360–361. The largest rivers in the region run in what general direction, north-south or east-west? Would you say that these rivers would tend to tie parts of the South together or to tie the South to the North?

Would you say that geography helps unite or separate the coastal plains making up much of the South? Explain. Which region, the North or the South, has a greater diversity of land surfaces? A greater variety in farming conditions?

3. Explain how each of the following helped unify the South and separate it from the North: (a) the invention of the cotton gin; (b) criticism of slavery by northerners; (c) the failure to build a railroad from Charleston to Cincinnati; (d) the reliance of the South on cotton-growing as its chief source of wealth.

4. Why do historians say that history, not geographic factors, unified the South and separated it from the North?

DOCUMENTS IN HISTORY

1. Identify five arguments against the freeing of the slaves which William Harper presented in the quotation on pages 216–217. Which did he evidently consider his crowning point? By what reasoning did he arrive at it?

2. Which argument showed his awareness of labor problems in industrialized parts of the country? In the light of American farm history since 1837, do you think the argument sound?

3. People from both the North and the South "overspread the plains and forests of the West." How does this fact refute one of his arguments against emancipation?

4. Which arguments were purely *opinion?* Explain. Which doubtless appealed most to the pocketbooks of white southerners? Which probably excited their emotions the most?

BEING A SOCIAL SCIENTIST

In 1807 the British Parliament passed a law which provided that after May 1 of that year no vessel engaged in slave-trading could be cleared from any British-controlled port. After March 1, 1808, no slave could be imported by any British possession. In 1833 Parliament freed all slaves in British lands and appropriated £20,000,000 to compensate the owners.

What were the merits of the British plan for eliminating slavery? Compare America's record in the same period. When was American sentiment for freeing the slaves strongest? Who supported emancipation then? Why? What efforts were made to bring it about? With what results? Account for the failure to free American slaves at that time.

##One merit was the provision for paying the owners for the slaves. The early 1800's--before 1830--was the time when Americans might have freed their slaves. The cotton gin intervened.

229

The concept of "manifest destiny" is an important one to gain from this chapter, which describes how Americans carried out what they believed their destiny was. This quotation from O'Sullivan is especially appropriate, since he coined the phrase "manifest destiny." For inquiry: What shows that the article quoted here was by an English-speaking person? How does he show pride in his culture?

13

THE WEST: MANIFEST DESTINY

. . . beneath the flutter of the stripes and stars . . .

Imbecile and distracted, Mexico never can exert any real governmental authority over such a country [California]. . . . Already the advance guard of the irresistible army of Anglo-Saxon emigration has begun to pour down upon it, armed with the plough and the rifle, and marking its trail with schools and colleges, courts and representative halls, mills and meeting-houses. . . . They will necessarily become independent. . . . Their right to independence will be the natural right of self-government belonging to any community strong enough to maintain it. . . .

Great Salt Lake lies in the right background. Streams may be seen running into it.

Mormons arriving at the valley of Great Salt Lake in what is now Utah. The westward migrations of brave pioneers like these focused Americans' attention on the Far West, fostering a dream of expansion to the Pacific.

What part does technological advancement play in O'Sullivan's predictions? How does he indicate that he believes that the population of Oregon and California will grow fast? What prediction does he make about the population of the United States within one hundred years?

Whether they will then attach themselves to our Union or not, is not to be predicted with any certainty. Unless the projected railroad across the continent to the Pacific be carried into effect, perhaps they may not; though even in that case, the day is not distant when the Empires of the Atlantic and Pacific would again flow together into one, as soon as their inland border should approach each other.

But that great work [the railroad] . . . cannot remain long unbuilt. Its necessity for this very purpose of binding and holding together in its iron clasp our fast settling Pacific region with

To nineteenth-century Americans, the West offered romance, an escape, and better lives.

that of the Mississippi valley . . . the ease with which any amount of labor for the construction can be drawn in from the overcrowded population of Europe . . . and its immense utility to the commerce of the world with the whole eastern coast of Asia . . . —these considerations give assurance that the day cannot be distant which shall witness the conveyance of the representatives from Oregon and California to Washington within less time than a few years ago was devoted to a similar journey by those from Ohio; while the magnetic telegraph will enable the editors of the "San Francisco Union," the "Astoria Evening Post," or the "Nootka Morning News" to set up in type the first half of the President's Inaugural, before the echoes of the latter half shall have died away beneath the lofty porch of the Capitol. . . .

Away, then, with all . . . talk of *balances of power* on the American Continent. . . . Whosoever may hold the balance, though they should cast into the opposite scale all the bayonets and cannon, not only of France and England, but of Europe entire, how would it kick the beam against the simple solid weight of the two hundred and fifty or three hundred millions—and American millions—destined to gather beneath the flutter of the stripes and stars, in the fast hastening year of the Lord, 1945!   #

Americans in the 1840's were supremely confident that nothing could block their path to the Pacific Ocean. They also believed that their country's westward course was predestined and divinely blessed. The outstanding spokesman for these ideas was John L. O'Sullivan. He was editor of a magazine of the Democratic party, the United States Magazine and Democratic Review, *which strongly advocated national expansion to the limits fixed by nature. O'Sullivan coined the phrase "manifest destiny" to describe the policy he pleaded for with such enthusiasm. In this article of 1845, he shows, along with confidence in the country's future, a contempt for Mexico characteristic of believers in "manifest destiny."*

#Students may be surprised to see the date 1945 and may think a mistake has been made.

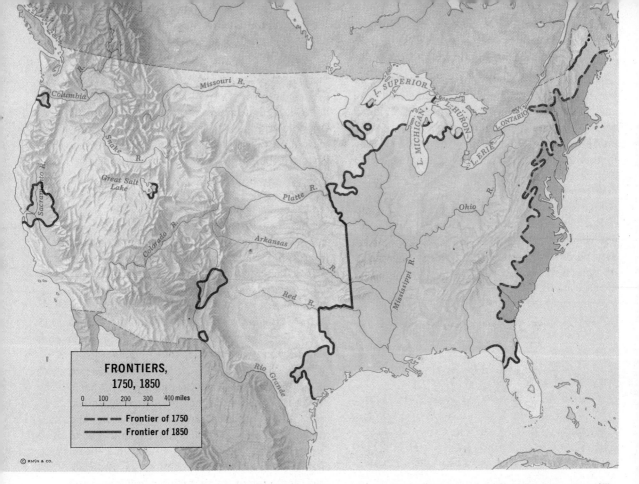

FRONTIERS,
1750, 1850

0   100   200   300   400 miles

--- Frontier of 1750
—— Frontier of 1850

Why had the frontier in 1850 not advanced to the northern border of Maine? Why are there frontier lines *beyond* the continuous frontier of 1850 extending across Wisconsin and southward to the Gulf of Mexico?

(The Maine boundary dispute was not settled until 1842; the Far West was settled first.)

FRONTIERSMEN PUSH RELENTLESSLY TOWARD THE PACIFIC

America's westward movement began when the first settlers landed at Jamestown. Each subsequent generation, in referring to "the West," has had a different region in mind. In the middle of the seventeenth century, it was the west side of the Appalachians. In the mid-1800's, it was the Ohio River Valley. By 1820 the ever-moving "West" had begun to reach the Missouri River. Across its waters lay a new West to conquer, one that would challenge uniquely the resourcefulness and courage of the frontiersmen.

ACROSS THE "GREAT AMERICAN DESERT"

What the pioneers saw beyond the Missouri were great stretches of grassland and bare, sandy areas. They found an almost total absence of trees, a baking sun in summer, terrible blizzards and winds in winter. Most Americans had never encountered a combination of conditions like these.

Major Stephen H. Long, who had explored some of the area in 1820, had made a most discouraging report about it. He described the land between the Missouri River and the Rocky Mountains as "almost wholly unfit for cultivation, and of course uninhabitable by a people depending upon agriculture. . . ." On his map he had called this expanse of land the "Great American Desert."

Long's misleading label to describe the Great Plains was very widely used. Until the Civil War the maps of the United States appearing in school textbooks carried the forbidding

#The concept of the successive Wests should be understood by every student. What do people mean 232 by "the West" today? (The meaning varies in different parts of the country.)

name. Moreover, the lack of water and timber and the hard and stubborn soil did discourage early attempts to settle the Great Plains.

"Manifest destiny." Americans, nevertheless, pushed determinedly westward. Believing that settlement of the "Great American Desert" would be too difficult, they skipped over it for the time being, pressing on to the Pacific coast. Many were inspired by the conviction that the nation must spread out in order to reach the natural geographical limits they maintained Providence had set for it. This expansion, they declared, was America's "manifest destiny."

"Manifest destiny" was not a new idea. Even in the eighteenth century, before much of the continent had been mapped, some people dreamed of making it entirely American. By the 1840's a new pride in the nation's achieve-

ments had produced a freshened faith in the power of the United States to uplift people and make them happy. In their enthusiasm Americans developed a missionary zeal to spread their form of government not only over the entire continent but to peoples elsewhere as well.

Beyond the West. Many Americans were thinking even of bringing the stimulus of the American "way" to the old nations of Asia to make them take on new life. Declared one enthusiast:

> The *untransacted* destiny of the American people is to subdue the continent—to rush over this vast field to the Pacific Ocean—to animate the many hundred millions of its peoples, and to cheer them upward . . . to stir up the sleep of a hundred centuries—to teach old nations a new civilization . . . to unite the world in one social family . . . and to shed blessings round the world!

The fulfillment of these majestic purposes would have to wait until territorial expansion here at home was complete. Meanwhile, it was set down as future business for the nation.

THE MAGNET OF OREGON

The restless spirit of "manifest destiny" was dramatically revealed in the exciting history of the Oregon Country. This territory, shown on the map on page 235, was larger than the combined areas of New England, New York, and

Pennsylvania. At one time or another it was claimed by France, Spain, Russia, and England. ## France gave up its claim when it sold Louisiana to the United States in 1803. Spain gave up its claim when it sold Florida to the United States in 1819. Russia gave up its claim* by a treaty it signed with this country in 1824, recognizing 54° 40' as the southern boundary of Russian America (Alaska).

Only England remained. You will recall that since Americans were unable to agree with the English on a division of the Oregon Country, it had been decided in 1818 to occupy the territory jointly. In 1827, after again failing to make a permanent compromise, the United States had renewed joint occupation for an indefinite period.

A developing attraction. The Oregon Country seemed so remote to Americans that the idea of settling there did not catch on right away. One New York congressman explained the general lack of interest: "Nature has fixed limits for our nation; she has kindly interposed as our western barrier mountains almost inaccessible, whose base she has skirted with irreclaimable deserts of sand."

Floyd's persistence. But such pessimism gradually disappeared. In 1814 Nicholas Biddle,† who could write excellent verse and prose, published a history of the Lewis and Clark expedition that aroused favorable interest. Furthermore, Congressman John Floyd of Virginia, a boyhood friend of William Clark, kept the Oregon question before Congress. Several times, beginning in 1821, Floyd introduced bills to organize the Oregon Country. They were voted down each time because Congress would wait for a clear title to the area and for actual settlement of it.

Astor and the fur trade. America had once had a foothold in the region. Business associates of John Jacob Astor, a German immigrant who became the leading fur merchant in America,

---

* The czar of Russia had expressed a claim to the region when he had decreed in 1821 that the southern boundary of Russian America was at 51°.

† The same Biddle who was later president of the second Bank of the United States and Jackson's archenemy (see page 190).

##Russians coming across Bering Strait claimed the western coast of North America as far south as 51°. Spain had claimed the land as far north as 61° (see the Adams-Onis Treaty, p. 16).

233

New York Public Library

Astoria in 1813. Astor had planned to make it a center for receiving furs and for shipping them to East Asia.

had established on the Columbia River a fur-trading post named Astoria.

Just at the time Astor thought that Astoria was a success, the War of 1812 broke out. Astor's partners, afraid of the British, who were reported to be sending a warship, sold out to a British firm. Only occasionally thereafter did American fur traders venture into the Oregon Country. By the 1830's a handful of missionaries and pioneers—like Father Pierre Jean De Smet and Dr. Marcus Whitman and his bride Narcissa—represented American influence in the region.

Wyeth. Some adventurers were also busy. One, a practical and energetic New Englander named Nathaniel J. Wyeth, had made a fortune in the ice business in Cambridge, Massachusetts. Wyeth made two trips to Oregon, both failures because the supply ships he sent around Cape Horn did not arrive in time. Nevertheless, he proved that the overland treks on which he led his parties were not beyond endurance.

The halting attempts to exploit the Oregon Country attracted attention but did not stimulate migration. In 1840 only 400 settlers were there—mainly missionaries and retired trappers.

Stepped-up migration. But shortly a trickle of prospective settlers, enlarging each year, was flowing across the continent. The panic of 1837 had caused wide distress among farmers in the Mississippi Valley. Oregon's rich Willamette Valley beckoned, offering new opportunity and easy access to the markets of Asia.

Along the Oregon Trail. After 1841 migrants traveled over a road that in time became a glorious national legend: the Oregon Trail. Starting at Independence, Missouri, it took a northwest course to Fort Kearney on the Platte River. It followed the Platte to Fort Laramie and from there entered mountain country. Independence Rock, 838 miles west of the starting point in Missouri, was where travelers proudly inscribed their family names on "the register of the desert."

The Trail crossed the continental divide at South Pass at an elevation of 7500 feet. At Fort Bridger the emigrants usually rested, refitting themselves for the final stages of the journey. Passing Fort Hall, the Trail now bent south and then northwest toward Fort Boise on the Snake River. From there it led into the Columbia River Valley, which led in turn to the Willamette.

The trek required six months of superhuman courage and backbreaking effort. It covered over 2000 miles of grassland, mountains, and desert. It aged young people quickly and often killed off the weak. For twenty-five years, however, the Oregon Trail was the great transcontinental highway. By 1846 the "Oregon fever" had brought more than 10,000 people west, and thousands more were on the way shortly. Each man, woman, and child could have a part in "manifest destiny."

THE MORMON ODYSSEY

A desire to serve God, not land hunger, was the prime motive in the settling of the land that became Utah. Like most of the history of the American West, this story began in the East.

Joseph Smith. The colonizers of Utah, members of the Church of Jesus Christ of Latter-day Saints, were popularly known as Mormons. They originated at Fayette, New York, in 1830.

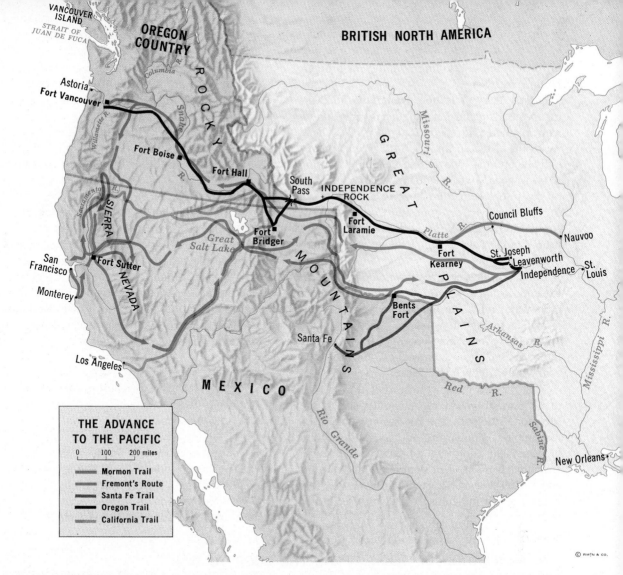

The hazardous routes thousands of Americans took in the 1800's, balancing great risks with hopes of future gains.

What was the starting point for most of the routes? What were the three chief destinations of the travelers?

(Most routes started at Independence; three destinations: Oregon, California, Mormon settlement.)

Their leader was Joseph Smith, who had announced that he had had a divine revelation leading him to a hillside cave. There, he said, he had found a number of thin gold plates, which he transcribed and published as *The Book of Mormon*. This book contains religious teachings binding upon faithful believers.

From pillar to post. Seeking a congenial location, Smith and his Saints moved several times. In 1831 they settled at Kirtland, Ohio, becoming prosperous there. The panic of 1837, however, hurt them badly.

Smith next tried Missouri, where he ran into

severe opposition. This was both because the Mormons hated slavery and regarded themselves as possessing the only true religion and because they expressed themselves freely on both subjects.

Harried out of Missouri, the Mormons fled to western Illinois in 1839, where they established the town of Nauvoo. Then in 1843 a divine revelation, so Smith claimed, authorized the Mormon church to sanction the taking of plural wives. This aroused the Mormons' neighbors. Threatened with violence, Smith was imprisoned for his own protection. But a mob

#Joseph Smith is regarded as the founder of the Reorganized Church of Jesus Christ of Latter Day Saints, which is distinct from the Utah Mormon Church. The former denies that Smith proposed polygamy and states that Brigham Young introduced it in 1852.

235

#Perhaps he was a sufferer from Rocky Mountain spotted fever, caused by the bite of a wood tick.

##Recall that in New England towns early settlers had distributed land on a community basis.

broke into the jail, killing him and his brother, Hyrum, in 1844.

Brigham Young. The new leader of the Mormons was Brigham Young, an inspiring figure, who instructed his people to prepare to head westward in the spring of 1846. Against heavy odds he and his followers succeeded in moving 3700 wagons, 30,000 cattle, and large numbers of sheep, chickens, and hogs to a place along the Missouri River opposite Council Bluffs, Iowa. From there Young set out with a "Pioneer Band" of 146 to find the perfect permanent site.

The State of Deseret. Young was looking for an isolated location where no one again would molest the Saints. He himself was stricken with mountain fever, but when he gazed upon the tablelands overlooking Great Salt Lake, he lifted himself from his sickbed and declared confidently, "This is the Place."

The first two years were hard. The gold rush to California, however, helped to enrich the Mormon settlement, the last stopping-off place for supplies. Young also adopted unique rules of ownership admirably adapted to the sparse environment. The distribution of land, water, and timber became a community matter; the interest of the individual was always second to that of the group.

The Mormon population grew. Between 1840 and 1854 at least 22,000 Europeans who professed Mormonism came to the United States. In 1849 the people formed a local government named the "State of Deseret." But because Mormons advocated taking plural wives, strong opposition to Deseret quickly developed.

When the State of Deseret applied for admission to the Union in 1850, its boundaries included the large area covering what is now Utah and Nevada and extending into present-day California, Arizona, New Mexico, Colorado, Wyoming, Idaho, and Oregon. Congress turned down statehood and organized a greatly reduced Deseret into the Territory of Utah. Not until 1896, after polygamy was declared illegal, was Utah admitted to the Union.

Sum and Substance
1. Trace the changing meaning of "the West."
2. Why did settlers long avoid the Great Plains?
3. What did "manifest destiny" mean? 4. What was the "Oregon Country"? Name the countries that claimed it at various times. 5. What men aroused American interest in it? 6. Describe the route of the Oregon Trail. 7. Tell briefly the history of the Mormons. 8. Under what circumstances was Utah admitted to the Union?

Expansion into the Southwest was accomplished through the Mexican War.

THE ANNEXATION OF TEXAS OPENS THE DOOR TO WAR

Many Americans believed that the United States must one day fight to acquire all of the Oregon Country. Only a few thought that the acquisition of Texas would lead to hostilities. Under the Treaty of 1819, this part of Mexico had remained under Spain's control, but Americans were soon obtaining land there under favorable terms.

AMERICANS AS MEXICANS

An enterprising American, Moses Austin, had received from the Spanish authorities a grant to make settlements in Texas. When he died in 1821, his son Stephen decided to carry out the project. That year Mexico won its independence from Spain, confirmed the grant to Austin, and made similar grants to other Americans.

The present limits of Texas had been marked out roughly by 1830, and 30,000 Americans had settled within its borders. These Texans lived under Mexican law and in theory were Mexicans. Actually they continued to be Americans at heart and were rearing their children as such. Moreover, they were beginning to talk of being separate from Mexico.

Revolt. One Texan, Haden Edwards, in 1826 organized a revolution to establish what he called the "Republic of Fredonia." The revolt was quickly suppressed, but it aroused Mexi-

The promise of good farm land in Texas attracted Americans there. Moses Austin obtained a charter which granted Texas land for the settlement of 200 American families.

#When Mexico won its independence and became a republic in 1824, Texas was part of it.
Mexico encouraged Americans to settle in Texas, selling land for about 12¢ an acre. About
30,000 Americans settled in the part of Texas northeast of the Nueces River.

#
#
co's fears that Texas was becoming too American. Mexico attempted to limit the power of Texas' government; in reply, Texans revolted in 1835.

Under Sam Houston. The leader of this Texan revolt was Sam Houston—a hard-driving, adventurous native of Virginia. As a young man he had fought in Jackson's army. Wise in the ways of the frontier, experienced as governor of Tennessee, he was an ideal spokesman for the Americans living under the Mexican flag. The Mexican leader was General Antonio Santa Anna, who later made himself dictator of his country.

"Remember the Alamo!" When the revolt began, Santa Anna and a large army marched into Texas to crush it. At the Alamo, a mission in San Antonio, a Texan force of less than 200 bravely held off 3000 Mexicans for twelve days. The Alamo fell on March 6, 1836, after its defenders had died to the last man. Houston now turned his little army on its tormentors, screaming: "Remember the Alamo! Death to Santa Anna!" On April 21 the Texans decisively won the Battle of San Jacinto.

Cowering in a hayfield nearby, Santa Anna was taken prisoner. Fearing that he would be put to death by his captors, he signed a treaty of peace. In it he agreed to end hostilities and withdraw all Mexican troops from land north of the Rio Grande. After Santa Anna was freed, he insisted that Mexico was not bound by the treaty because he had been forced to sign it.

THE LONE STAR REPUBLIC

Americans in all sections watched these events closely. Many looked forward to the immediate annexation of Texas to the United States. Others insisted that slavery must not be strengthened by such an addition to the Cotton Kingdom.

President Jackson wanted credit for adding this princely domain to the United States. But he was afraid that because of the slavery issue, he might split the Democratic party and ruin Van Buren's chances for election. The day before Jackson left office—with his successor

safely chosen—he formally recognized the independence of Texas.

To annex or not to annex. Calling itself the Lone Star Republic, Texas now requested the United States to annex it. Van Buren was cool to the proposal, for he, too, wanted to avoid dividing the Democrats. Feelings in the party ran high. Antislavery men, for instance, believed strongly that after annexation Texas might be cut up into five or more slaveholding states.

Tyler's treaty. When John Tyler came to the presidency in 1841, he was more friendly to annexation. Negotiations to bring it about might have been successful if a tragic accident had not occurred. Tyler's Secretary of State, Abel P. Upshur, was killed by the explosion of a gun aboard a new warship he was inspecting. Calhoun, now the chief southern spokesman, succeeded him. The South Carolinian's vigorous support of annexation made northern antislavery men more determined than ever in their opposition to it. Consequently, Tyler's treaty of annexation was defeated in the Senate late in the spring of 1844.

The campaign of 1844. Meanwhile, the preliminaries of the 1844 presidential campaign had begun. It seemed certain that Van Buren would be the candidate for the Democrats and Clay for the Whigs. "The Little Magician" had visited at Clay's home in Kentucky in 1842, and the rivals appear to have agreed to keep the Texas question out of the campaign. Both went on record as opposed to immediate annexation. (This stand cost Van Buren the support of his old friend Jackson, who wanted to see Texas in the Union before he died.)

Clay was nominated by the Whigs. He said that he was for annexation if it could be achieved with the agreement of all sections of the country and without provoking Mexico to war—impossible conditions. The Whig platform ignored the question.

The first dark horse. When the Democrats gathered for their convention at Baltimore, Van Buren did not have the backing of southerners. Northerners would not accept Calhoun. The deadlocked delegates finally nominated a former Speaker of the House of Representatives—

James K. Polk of Tennessee.

People in Washington could hardly believe it when the nominee's name came over the new-strung telegraph line—the first in the nation and at that time only five days old. The Democrats had chosen the first dark-horse candidate in American history. Compared with Clay, Polk was unknown. Throughout the campaign the Whigs chanted the taunt, "Who is James K. Polk?"

Statehood at last. But Clay had miscalculated popular sentiment. Polk received powerful support—including Jackson's. The Democratic platform was frankly expansionist, calling for the "re-annexation of Texas and the re-occupation of Oregon."‡ A number of antislavery Whigs in New York deserted Clay in favor of James G. Birney, the Liberty party nominee. They caused Clay the loss of that pivotal state and, with it, the election.

In the waning days of his term, Tyler seized upon the popular approval of Texas annexation and recommended that Congress admit the Lone Star Republic to the Union by joint resolution. Duly passed, the resolution was signed by the President three days before he retired. At a convention that met on the Fourth of July, 1845, Texas accepted statehood.

MANEUVERING WITH MEXICO

The driving rain that fell during Polk's inauguration could not dampen the enthusiasm of the expansionists. Besides, they heard the President declare boldly that America's title to the Oregon Country was clear and that the annexation of Texas was none of Mexico's concern.

Regarding Texas as still its own possession, Mexico refused to recognize its annexation by the United States. Texans made matters hotter by insisting that the southern boundary line of Texas was not the Nueces River, but the Rio Grande. Furthermore, United States citizens pressed $3,000,000 in claims of various kinds against the Mexican government.

‡ This catchy phrase implied that Texas had been a part of the Louisiana Purchase and that the treaty with Britain providing for joint occupation of Oregon might be annulled.

The California question. As if these unresolved matters were not enough, Americans were already eyeing another part of Mexico—California. Jackson had attempted to purchase the region around San Francisco in 1835, believing it would be an admirable supply port for American whaling vessels. Although the effort had failed, the expectation of eventual success remained lively.

In the 1840's Webster, as Secretary of State, supported the proposal, hoping the United States could in this way make the trade with Asia its own. By 1845 the idea of "manifest destiny" was in full flower. Said the *New York Herald,* "The flight of the eagle is toward the west, and there it is he spreads his wings for freedom." California and the Oregon Country were soon linked in people's minds. Perhaps the country could get both of them, join them together, and dominate the Pacific!

Mexico's hand in California was weakening. Said a westerner, "Once let the tide of emigration flow toward California and the American population will soon be sufficiently numerous to play the Texas game." The birth rate was working for Americans, but would they wait?

Slidell's mission. Polk decided to send a representative to Mexico to settle the outstanding issues between the two countries. Designating John Slidell of Louisiana as a minister to Mexico, he authorized him to deal with three matters: the American claims against Mexico; California; and the Texas boundary. Slidell was to offer to take over the claims in return for the Rio Grande boundary and to offer $5,000,000 for New Mexico and as much as $25,000,000 for California. When Mexican officials refused to see Slidell, Polk was ready to agree that only war could settle the issues.

Orders from the White House. Early in 1846, Polk ordered General Zachary Taylor to move his army from the Nueces River to the Rio Grande—an act certain to arouse the Mexicans. On May 9, 1846, Polk told his Cabinet that he was prepared to ask for war. Only the Secretary of the Navy, George Bancroft, held out, saying the nation should wait until Mexican troops attacked.

##The claims were for the destroying of property and the loss of life Americans had suffered. Mexico had agreed to pay for the damages but had fallen behind in the payments.

Polk's reasons for facing war with Mexico were that Mexico had not paid for damages it had inflicted, it had refused to see Slidell, and it appeared to be unwilling to cooperate in the settlement of difficulties with the United States.

HOSTILITIES BETWEEN NEIGHBORS

Before another meeting of the Cabinet could take place, word arrived from Taylor that on April 25 Mexican soldiers had crossed the Rio Grande and attacked his men. On May 11 Polk sent a war message to Congress. In it he asserted that Mexico had "shed American blood upon the American soil." War, he concluded, "exists by the act of Mexico herself. . . ."

Whig opposition. Although Congress declared war quickly, strong opposition among Whigs and antislavery men developed as the months passed. One of the Whigs was Representative Abraham Lincoln of Illinois, who refused to believe that blood had been shed on *American* soil. Another congressman declared bluntly, "It is our own President who began this war." Among Taylor's soldiers was a young second lieutenant, Ulysses S. Grant, who wrote many years later that this was "the most unjust" war in American history.

The public accepted hostilities. The Richmond *Enquirer* put it this way, "What more

Mexicans at Matamoros ordered Taylor to retreat; he refused; the Mexicans crossed the Rio Grande.

Polk aimed to win the war quickly by seizing northern Mexico, including California, and by capturing Mexico City.

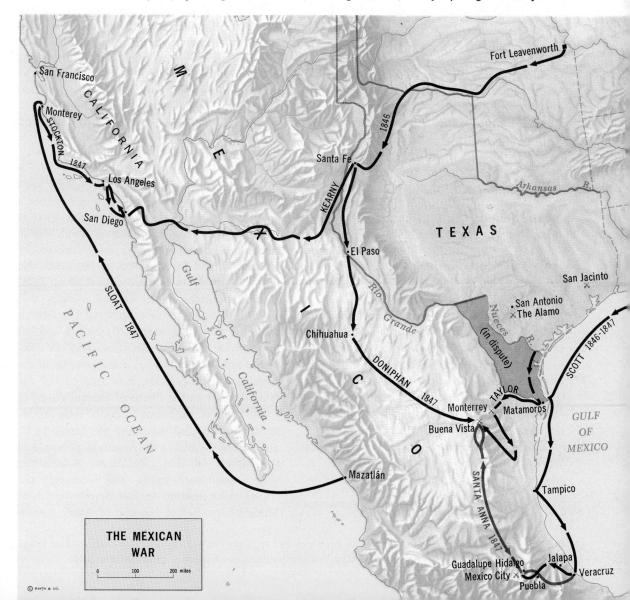

THE MEXICAN WAR

0   100   200 miles

© RMⁿ & CO.

inspiring strain can strike the ears of freemen than the trumpet note which summons our people to the punishment of tyrants?" To carry on the war, Congress authorized an army of 50,000 men and appropriated $10,000,000.

"Old Rough and Ready." The commanding general in the field, Zachary Taylor, was a Whig. Informal in manner, he had in his forty years of army service earned the nickname "Old Rough and Ready."

During the month of May, Taylor pushed the Mexicans back beyond the Rio Grande and followed them across it, occupying the town of Matamoros. In September he captured Monterrey, and by the end of the year three of the more important cities of northern Mexico were in his hands. An American force under Colonel A. W. Doniphan came south from El Paso and occupied the Mexican city of Chihuahua in March, 1847.

California, meanwhile, was passing into American possession. In December, 1845, a youthful army captain and explorer, John C. Frémont—already known as the "Pathfinder of the West"—arrived in California from Missouri with a force of sixty-two men. He was said to be exploring the routes for overland travel. Frightened by the arrival of these Americans in uniform, Mexican authorities ordered them to leave.

The Bear Flag revolt. Frémont and his men went to Oregon. In May, 1846, they returned to California and inspired the Bear Flag revolt,§ an uprising of Americans in the Sacramento Valley against Mexican rule.

Early in July word reached Frémont that war had broken out between the United States and Mexico. He hastened to coöperate with the United States naval forces in California waters, under Commodore John D. Sloat and later Commodore Robert F. Stockton, in the capture of California. Except for resistance in Los Angeles, the conquest of California was practically completed when General Stephen W. Kearny arrived with 100 cavalrymen to take command of American forces late in 1846.

---

§ So called from the design of the flag, which showed a grizzly bear facing a red star.

The General and the President. As the American armies gained their victories, all the territory that Polk wanted from Mexico was conquered. After capturing Monterrey, Mexico, General Taylor had granted an armistice to the Mexicans, hoping they would ask for peace.

Polk disapproved sharply: "In agreeing to this armistice," the President stated in his diary, "General Taylor violated his express orders. . . . He had the enemy in his power and should have taken them prisoners. . . . It will only enable the Mexican army to reorganize and recruit so as to make another stand."

"Old Fuss and Feathers." Polk now decided to send an expedition to capture Veracruz (see the map on page 239) and, if all went well, to move on and seize Mexico City, the capital. To command the undertaking, he chose General Winfield Scott, then sixty years old. Scott was a Virginia gentleman with unsurpassed manners who, like Taylor, had made the army his career. Always jealous of his reputation (one critic called him "too much of an old granny"), he was known as "Old Fuss and Feathers." Like Taylor, Scott was a Whig. Polk had tried vainly to find a suitable general who was also a Democrat.

With an army of 10,000 (including units transferred from Taylor), Scott prepared for a large-scale amphibious landing—the first in American history—at Veracruz. Santa Anna, meanwhile, decided to take advantage of the reduced United States forces to the north. He sent 15,000 of his soldiers against about 4500 Americans under Taylor at Buena Vista.

Even though they outnumbered the Americans, the Mexicans were badly beaten and left 500 men dead before retreating. To Polk's immense annoyance, Taylor, a severe critic of the administration's policies, now had gained national esteem as the "hero of Buena Vista."

The "halls of Montezuma." Scott's men landed at Veracruz at the beginning of March, 1847, and before the end of the month had completed the capture of that city. Santa Anna, who rushed southward again, was stunningly defeated in attempting to halt Scott's march to Mexico City. Before the end of April, Ameri-

Both soldiers and marines landed at Veracruz and took part in taking it. The marines also helped attack Mexico City, and the first line in their hymn commemorates their bravery there.

A young southern soldier interrupts his happy first meal "back home" after the Mexican War to describe to his family some especially stirring experience he has had. His aged grandfather—a Revolution veteran—is visibly moved.

Try to get as many reactions to this picture as possible. ("History repeats itself," etc.)

can soldiers were in Jalapa; from Jalapa they marched to Mexico's second city, Puebla, which they occupied in May.

The road to the "halls of Montezuma"—Mexico City—now lay open. Badly hurt by inadequate supplies, insufficient transport, expiring enlistments, and disease, Scott rebuilt his army and prepared it in the summer months at Puebla for the final fighting.

Trist's negotiations. Hoping that Santa Anna was now ready to talk peace, Polk dispatched a commissioner, Nicholas P. Trist, to Scott's headquarters to negotiate whenever the Mexicans should signify their readiness. Trist was the chief clerk of the Department of State, spoke fluent Spanish, and was supposed to understand the Mexican people. Unfortunately, he had lofty ideas about his ability and importance. Married to Thomas Jefferson's granddaughter, he had once served as private secretary to Andrew Jackson. He hoped that his mission might make him a contender for the Democratic presidential nomination the following year.

When Mexico rejected Trist's offer of peace, Scott immediately marched on Mexico City, which fell to him on September 14, 1847. A New Orleans newspaperman traveling with the American army reported: "An immense crowd . . . congregated in the plaza as the commander-in-chief entered it. They pressed upon our soldiers and eyed them as though they were beings of another world."

The Treaty of Guadalupe Hidalgo. Disappointed in the results of Trist's mission, Polk recalled him early in October. Deciding to ignore the recall, Trist continued his negotiations. The result of his efforts was a treaty signed at Guadalupe Hidalgo, a suburb of Mexico City, on February 2, 1848. By its terms California and the area between Texas and California, known as New Mexico, were ceded to the United States. The

241

boundary of Texas was set at the Rio Grande. In return the United States assumed the claims of its citizens against Mexico (see page 238) # and paid $15,000,000 outright to Mexico.

Polk was put in a difficult position by the arrival of the treaty. In his diary he described Trist as "arrogant, impudent, and very insulting to his government, and even personally offensive." Nevertheless, the treaty, in general, carried out instructions. Polk could not get a better one, and if he chose to resume the war the Whigs might not appropriate the money he would need.

Polk sent the treaty to the Senate, where the Whigs opposed it. One Whig described it as having been "negotiated by an unauthorized agent, with an unacknowledged government, submitted by an accidental President to a dissatisfied Senate. . . ." It was ratified, however, on March 10, 1848.

The Gadsden Purchase. A boundary question that grew out of the treaty was settled in 1853 by the negotiations of James Gadsden of South Carolina, the United States minister to Mexico. The United States agreed to pay Mexico $15,000,000—later reduced to $10,000,000 —for an area of about 29,640 square miles (see the map below). This arrangement, known as the Gadsden Purchase, completed the southern boundary of the United States.

Sum and Substance

1. What led to the Texan revolt in 1835? 2. What events followed the revolt? 3. Give the pros and cons for annexing Texas. When, why, and how was it annexed? 4. How did Polk justify war on Mexico? 5. How did Americans view the war? In what places was it fought? 6. Give the terms of the peace treaty. 7. How and when was the southern boundary fixed?

Have students turn to p. 816. How many years passed between the admissions of Arizona and Alaska?

How the United States expanded between 1783 and 1853 to encompass the land making up the first forty-eight states.

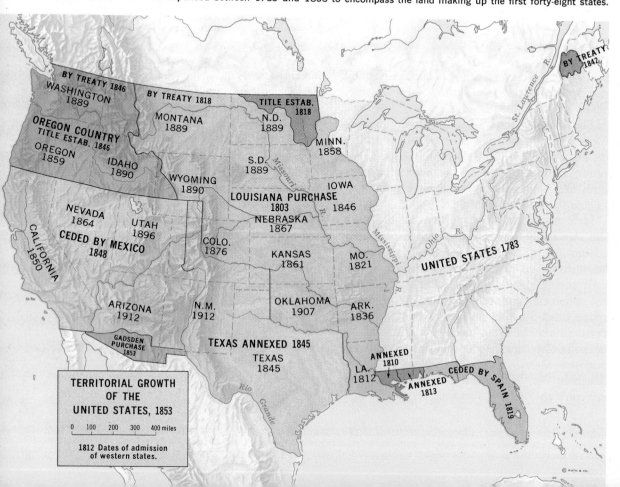

TERRITORIAL GROWTH
OF THE
UNITED STATES, 1853

0   100   200   300   400 miles

1812 Dates of admission
of western states.

DIPLOMACY AND A GOLD RUSH NET AMERICA THE FAR WEST

Polk was able to carry out most of the policies advocated in his party's platform. But though the annexation of Texas had been the chief issue in the 1844 campaign, people in the old Northwest had never ceased looking toward the Oregon Country.

SETTLEMENT WITH ENGLAND

In his first message to Congress in 1845, Polk declared that the United States would assert its rights in the Oregon Country and refuse to compromise again with the British. The joint-occupation arrangement was about to expire. The British, although considerably irritated over Polk's warlike attitude, were ready to give up the Columbia River region because the fur trade there was no longer profitable. Moreover, they very much wanted to retain the friendship of the United States, where the market for English manufactured products was growing bigger all the time.

The treaty. Britain proposed a settlement that provided for extending the northern boundary westward along the 49th parallel of latitude. It provided also for free navigation of the Strait of Juan de Fuca by both countries and of the Columbia River south of the 49th parallel by Britain.

Polk was not happy about this proposed treaty, because it gave the United States considerably less land than Americans had wanted. But the war with Mexico had begun, and he had no choice in 1846 but to accept the terms —or perhaps face war with both Britain *and* Mexico!

Window on the Pacific. The acquisition of California and at least part of the Oregon Country gave the United States a *Pacific* coast. Americans confidently expected that, like the great empires of the past, theirs, too, would build # its prosperity on trade with Asia. For many this was, in fact, the ultimate goal toward which "manifest destiny" was moving the nation.

Already in 1843 John Tyler had sent Caleb Cushing of Massachusetts to negotiate a treaty with China that would open the Chinese ports to American commerce. The following year Cushing concluded arrangements opening five Chinese ports to American vessels and giving Americans extraterritorial privileges—such as the right to try Americans before the United States consul rather than in Chinese courts.

Plans also were being made to send an expedition to Japan, a country long closed to foreigners. In 1852 Commodore Matthew C. ## Perry, under orders from the government, set out for the "Land of the Rising Sun" with a naval expedition.

Received by Japanese officials, he persuaded them in 1854 to sign a treaty favorable to the United States. It ended Japan's seclusion by giving the United States access to Japanese ports, coaling stations for its ships, and a promise of humane treatment for any of its sailors who might be shipwrecked there.

By the beginning of the 1850's, a railroad, American owned, had been built across the Isthmus of Panama, and increasingly men were talking about building a transcontinental railroad. For all these activities, the argument was the same: America's destiny and greatness must ultimately depend on the ability to reach the Asian markets easily.

DISCOVERY IN CALIFORNIA

The majority of those who traveled to the West sought new land on which to farm more profitably. Suddenly thousands also found themselves rushing for gold. Discovery of the precious ore in California in 1848 brought Americans in significant numbers to the edge of the Pacific for the first time. The population of California, which had been about 8000 in 1815, was about 100,000 by 1850.

Sutter's mill. No words can recapture the excitement of those memorable days. James W. Marshall, an eccentric millwright working on Captain John A. Sutter's property, near Sacramento, accidentally found grains of a yellow ore on January 24, 1848. One of his helpers noted in his diary, "This day some kind of mettle was found . . . that looks like goald."

Learning the news, Sutter arrived the next day. He asked his men to say nothing about it for six weeks or so, until several projects on which he was then engaged could be completed. He forgot to silence a cook, whose tongue was soon busy. Sutter himself was indiscreet. Before long, his men were leaving his employ in order to prospect for gold.

The forty-niners. By the beginning of 1849, a rush was on. Some fortune hunters crossed the Great Plains, facing desert hazards and the danger of Indian attacks. Others took to the sea, enduring the discomfort of the six months' voyage around South America. Still others, braving dangers and diseases, crossed the Isthmus of Panama in order to board steamers running north along the Mexican and Californian coasts. Drawn from all parts of the world, these adventurers were fierce in their determination to reach the gold diggings. The Americans among them sang with abandon:

I'll scrape the mountains clean my boys,
I'll drain the rivers dry,
A pocketful of rocks bring home,
So brother don't you cry!

Boom and decline. In spite of the lack of law and order in California and the vicious quarrels among the forty-niners over mining claims, the amount of gold taken from the early diggings rose rapidly. Estimated at $5,000,000 in 1848, the gold yield was reported in 1853 to be $65,000,000.

For a miner who struck it rich, the returns could be anywhere from $500 to $5000 a day. One soldier on a short leave made as much money as he would have been paid in his entire enlistment. But only a few ever hit pay dirt. The people who profited most in the long run were merchants and traders, speculators, restaurant and hotel proprietors, and people who lived off the workingman—professional gamblers, saloonkeepers, and owners of dance halls.

Since the amount of gold that could be easily mined was limited, a decline in production soon set in. The boom period was brief. Although rumors of lucky strikes were still heard in 1853, there were so many brokenhearted and desti-

tute prospectors that the lure of the gold fields steadily dwindled.

A Californian reported as early as 1850: "The appearance of the emigrants had sadly changed since we started. Then they were full of life . . . and the road was enlivened with the song of 'I am going to California with my tin pan on my knee. Oh, California that's the land for me,' but now they crawl along hungry, and spiritless, and if a song is raised at all, it is, 'Oh carry me back to old Virginia, to Old Virginia's shore.' "

The gold strike had in an incredibly short time multiplied California's population to the point that the territory could be admitted to the Union. But the question of its admission opened the whole problem of whether the areas acquired from Mexico were to be free or slave. Everything depended on finding a just solution.

Americans had pushed their way to the Pacific to bring light and improvement to all who should feel the touch of "manifest destiny." But could Americans keep their own house in order? Already the poet James Russell Lowell had raised the curtain on a new scene when he charged:

They just want this Californy
So's to lug new slave states in
To abuse ye, an' to scare ye
An' to plunder ye like sin.

Congressman Alexander Stephens of Georgia expressed the pessimism of thoughtful men when he declared in 1846 that disposing of the new lands would become a national cancer. "I tell you," he said, "the prospect ahead is dark, cloudy, thick, and gloomy."

Sum and Substance

1. What was the status of the Oregon Country from 1818 to 1846? 2. What agreement was made with England in 1846? 3. Why was England willing to agree? 4. How did the United States open trade with China? With Japan? 5. Tell the circumstances of the discovery of gold in California. 6. What were the consequences?

This chapter closes the part describing the three main regions of the United States in the first half of the 1800's. The stage is now set for describing the development of serious sectional trouble.

THE WORKSHOP

OF LASTING SIGNIFICANCE

Explain what role each of the following had in American activities inspired by the spirit of "manifest destiny."

John L. O'Sullivan	Santa Anna
"manifest destiny"	Alamo
Oregon Country	Lone Star Republic
"Great American Desert"	James K. Polk
	dark horse
John Jacob Astor	John Slidell
Nathaniel J. Wyeth	Zachary Taylor
South Pass	John C. Frémont
Oregon Trail	Bear Flag revolt
Mormons	Nicholas P. Trist
Joseph Smith	Guadalupe Hidalgo
Brigham Young	Gadsden Purchase
State of Deseret	Caleb Cushing
Moses Austin	Matthew C. Perry
Sam Houston	John A. Sutter

PUTTING HISTORY ON THE MAP

1. Using a recent road map of the western United States, trace with a colored pencil or crayon and identify the route of each of the western trails. Use a different color for each trail. How are routes of modern highways related to the trails? Can you explain why? Display the map with a descriptive title and provide a key to explain the data shown.

2. On an outline map of the United States, identify the states created out of land making up the nation in 1783. Name the states formed from each of the acquisitions shown on the map on page 242. Using information found on page 816, insert the dates when the various states entered the Union.

Indicate in some way the states that were made from land once belonging to Mexico, to Spain, to France, and to England. How and when was the land making up your own state acquired? How many years elapsed before your state entered the Union? How old is your state? Was its entrance of any special interest to the rest of the country? Explain.

3. In 1950 the population of California was 10,586,223. The populations of Oregon, Washington, Arizona, and New Mexico were, respectively: 1,521,341; 2,378,963; 749,587; 681,187. Use the table on page 816 to find out what their populations are today.

What does a comparison of the figures for the two years indicate about the westward movement of Americans in the intervening years? Which state in the Union is now most populous? Which of the states have had the most spectacular growth since 1950? How do you account for this growth? Find out what states have lost people since 1950. # ##

SIFTING THE SOURCES

Choose an activity that offers an opportunity to use sources giving information on a subject of special interest to you. Look at the Bookshelf on page 248, and use information found in maps and in pictures.

1. Prepare an oral or written report on one of the following: (*a*) Wyeth in the Oregon Country; (*b*) missionaries in the Oregon Country; (*c*) the Texas revolt; (*d*) Frémont's explorations; (*e*) Caleb Cushing in China; (*f*) the California gold rush; (*g*) Matthew Perry's voyage to Japan; (*h*) the Donner expedition to California.

2. Write a short biography of one of these men or of some other person of special significance: (*a*) Stephen Austin; (*b*) Sam Houston; (*c*) James K. Polk; (*d*) Zachary Taylor; (*e*) Alexander Mackenzie; (*f*) Robert Gray.

3. A committee might obtain further information about the Mormons and present its findings to the class. One person should concentrate on Mormon history and religion, another on modern Mormon policies, and another on Mormon buildings and institutions in Salt Lake City today.

4. Organize a class debate on this topic: *Resolved*, That the United States was guilty of starting the Mexican War in order to annex California and New Mexico, to which it had no claim.

##Among the states that have lost population since 1950 are West Virginia, Arkansas, and Alabama. How do students account for the decreases? (Suggestion: lack of adequate economic opportunities.)

245

A LONG VIEW

The Challenge of Sectionalism

IN the twenty-five years after Jackson became President, the American people tried hard to develop a national outlook. As they reached the Pacific they were aware that their country was a veritable "Garden of Eden." They sensed that by emphasizing their similarities and turning aside from their differences they had a chance to fulfill the glowing promise their physical endowment seemed to offer.

The public schools were producing citizens each year with a common set of heroes and a resulting common set of ideals. The leading American hero was George Washington, for whom thirty-two states eventually named counties. Another hero was Benjamin Franklin. Maxims from his *Poor Richard's Almanac*—like "Never leave that till to-morrow which you can do today" and "It is hard for an empty sack to stand upright"—set the moral tone in thousands of "little red schoolhouses."

Furthermore, beginning with the invention of the telegraph, communication became so rapid that no event in one part of the country could long remain unknown in another. By the 1830's the development of modern newspapers made "the news" more than ever a subject of dinner-table conversation. One result was a fuller interest everywhere in the problems of the nation.

Americans as a people were also drawing inspiration from the spectacular beauty of their country. Partly as a result, they were creating a picturesque language of their own. Words were being added to the English tongue at a faster rate than ever in the past. Some were colorful place-names like Crooked Creek, Council Bluffs, and Climax Springs.

Others were shrewdly coined verbs of action that seemed to symbolize American life, like "bulldoze," "yank," and "splurge."

In addition, Americans, always an inventive folk, were showing more and more uses for their technological skill. American gadgets were becoming American calling-cards throughout the world. (In 1860 over 4000 patents were issued, almost eight times as many as in 1830.) The inventions and gadgets deeply affected how people lived, for they simplified such important activities as the preserving of food, the heating of houses, and the making of clothing.

The United States still had much unfinished business to take care of, but its wondrous opportunities had spread the "America fever," especially in Europe. The 3,500,000 Europeans who came to this country between 1847 and 1857 constituted the largest migration of mankind in history up to that time.

The lure of America seems also to have greatly stimulated reform in Europe. Many countries there sought to make life more attractive for their people and to stop the migration to the New World of so many of them. The United States, willy-nilly, was providing an example for these countries. It set the pace in legislating universal manhood suffrage, in establishing free schools for its children, and in organizing voters into political parties. Other peoples were already moving toward these goals; the United States, however, was the first country to establish firmly the pattern of institutions that millions have ever since regarded as essential in a democratic society. ★ ★ ★ ★ ★ ★ ★ ★ ★ ★ #

246 #Three institutions are named in this paragraph. Why are political parties essential in a democratic society? (People in a democracy are free to express differences and act on them.)

PART THREE WORKSHOP

AMERICA IN THE WORLD

In the period of American history discussed in Part Three, Americans were chiefly occupied with their national affairs, but a number of events affected the position of the United States in world affairs.

1. Explain how the Webster-Ashburton Treaty of 1842, the settlement of the trouble caused by the *Caroline* incident, and the Oregon agreement of 1846 reflected the growing prestige of the United States.

2. Two elements of national strength are size and population. Referring to the tables on pages 818 and 819, tell exactly how much the United States increased in area and population between 1830 and 1850. The population increased by what percent? The area by what percent?

Using the table on page 821, compare the figures showing the imports and exports of the United States in 1830 and 1850. What do the figures show?

How did the growth of the United States in area, population, and foreign trade strengthen its position in world affairs in the two decades?

3. How would you describe the foreign policy of John Tyler? James K. Polk? Explain. How did their policies reflect the spirit of most Americans of the time?

4. The Secretary of State is the member of the Cabinet who carries on foreign relations in the President's name. Turn to page 814 and look at the names of the men who served as Secretary of State in the country's first sixty years.

Which man filled the requirements of the office particularly well in the period covered in Part Three? How? Which men later became President? In what special way had the office of Secretary of State prepared them for the presidency? What men distinguished themselves in other branches of the government? How?

In your opinion, what personal characteristics seem most desirable in a Secretary of State? What kind of training do you think he should have? Who holds the office now?

What role does the United States ambassador to the United Nations have in the conduct of American foreign relations?

TIME AND CHANGE

1. Extend the time line you have begun so that it includes the period covered by Part Three. Group events and dates that may be referred to as: (*a*) the Age of Jackson; (*b*) the Development of the Factory System; (*c*) the Canal Craze; (*d*) the Railroad Rage; (*e*) the Zeal for Reform; (*f*) the Growth of Slavery; (*g*) the Completion of Territorial Expansion for the First Forty-eight States.

2. Make a class project out of listing the changes (be sure to include those in technology) that took place. How was each brought about? Explain the effects of each change. Record the list and keep it.

Name some changes that were proposed but not made. Why were they not carried out? How do most people react to change? Why?

OLD PROBLEMS BECOME NEW

Using the list of fundamental problems given on page 179, tell which reappeared in some form in the period covered in Part Three. What was done about each?

One you will name is sectionalism. It was related to the tariff problem. How? Sectionalism also brought to the fore the matter of the relationship between the state and national governments. How? What did Jackson do about settling the trouble sectionalism caused him? Would you say that the problem of sectionalism and the related ones of the tariff and states' rights were solved? Explain.

Add this new problem to your list: How can ## Americans extend and strengthen the practice of democracy in the nation? What solutions were offered in the Age of Jackson? What democratic right did Americans exercise in their open criticism of the involvement of the United States in the Mexican War? How do dictatorships handle such criticism?

##This is a continuing problem that is much with us today. (Suggestions for last two questions: they exercised the right of free speech; dictators do not permit criticism.)

247

THE BOOKSHELF

Eyewitness Accounts

Eaton, Clement. *The Leavening of Democracy.* New York: George Braziller, Inc., 1963.

Meltzer, Milton (ed.). *In Their Own Words: A History of the American Negro, 1607–1865.* Vol. 1 of 2 vols. New York: Thomas Y. Crowell Co., 1964.

Mingay, G. E. *From a Foreign Viewpoint, 1775–1850* [Paperback—Chicago: Rand McNally & Co., 1967].

\# Parkman, Francis. *The Oregon Trail.* Many editions, including paperback.

Giant Men and Women

Coit, Margaret L. *John C. Calhoun.* Boston: Houghton Mifflin Co., 1961 [Paperback—Boston: Houghton Mifflin Co., 1961].

Eaton, Clement. *Henry Clay and the Art of American Politics.* Boston: Little, Brown & Co., 1964 [Paperback—Boston: Little, Brown & Co.].

Holman, Hamilton. *Zachary Taylor.* 2 vols. Hamden, Conn.: The Shoe String Press, Inc.

James, Marquis. *Andrew Jackson: Portrait of a President* [Paperback—New York: Grosset & Dunlap, Inc.].

Seager, Robert, II. *And Tyler, Too: A Biography of John and Julia Gardner Tyler.* New York: McGraw-Hill Book Company, 1963.

Tharp, Louise Hall. *Until Victory: Horace Mann and Mary Peabody.* Boston: Little, Brown & Co., 1953.

————. *The Peabody Sisters of Salem.* Boston: Little, Brown & Co., 1950.

Thomas, John L. *The Liberator: William Lloyd Garrison.* Boston: Little, Brown & Co., 1963.

Living and Making a Living

The American Heritage History of the Great West. Editors of *American Heritage* Magazine. New York: American Heritage Publishing Co., Inc., 1965.

Boorstin, Daniel. *The Americans: The National Experience.* Vol. 2 of 2 vols. New York: Random House, Inc., 1965 [Paperback—2 vols. in 1. New York: Random House, Inc.].

Cash, Wilbur J. *The Mind of the South.* New York: Alfred A. Knopf, Inc., 1960 [Paperback—New York: Alfred A. Knopf, Inc.].

Eaton, Clement. *The Growth of Southern Civilization, 1790–1860.* New York: Harper & Row, Publishers, 1961 [Paperback—New York: Harper & Row, Publishers].

Filler, Louis. *The Crusade Against Slavery, 1830–1860.* New York: Harper & Row, Publishers, 1960 [Paperback—New York: Harper & Row, Publishers].

Franklin, John Hope. *From Slavery to Freedom: A History of American Negroes.* 3rd ed. New York: Alfred A. Knopf, Inc., 1967.

Freehling, William W. *Prelude to Civil War: The Nullification Controversy in South Carolina, 1816–1836.* New York: Harper & Row, Publishers, 1966.

Gates, Paul W. *The Farmers' Age, 1815–1860: Economic History of the United States.* New York: Holt, Rinehart & Winston, Inc., 1960.

Hansen, Marcus L. *The Atlantic Migration, 1607–1860.* Gloucester, Mass.: Peter Smith [Paperback—New York: Harper & Row, Publishers, 1961].

Lavender, David. *Westward Vision: The Story of the Oregon Trail.* New York: McGraw-Hill Book Company, 1963.

McCoy, Charles A. *Polk and the Presidency.* Austin: University of Texas Press, 1960.

Singleton, Otis A. *The Mexican War.* Chicago: University of Chicago Press, 1960 [Paperback—Chicago: University of Chicago Press].

Stampp, Kenneth M. *The Peculiar Institution: Slavery in the Ante-bellum South.* New York: Alfred A. Knopf, Inc., 1956 [Paperback—New York: Alfred A. Knopf, Inc.].

Toppin, Edgar A. *A Mark Well Made: The Negro Contribution to American Culture* [Paperback—Chicago: Rand McNally & Co., 1967].

Tyler, Alice F. *Freedom's Ferment: Phases of American Social History from the Colonial Period to the Outbreak of the Civil War.* Gloucester, Mass.: Peter Smith [Paperback—New York: Harper & Row, Publishers].

Wellman, Paul I. *The House Divides.* New York: Doubleday & Co., Inc., 1966.

Wiltse, Charles M. *The New Nation: 1800–1845.* New York: Hill & Wang, Inc., 1961 [Paperback—New York: Hill & Wang, Inc.].

Confronting the World

Graebner, Norman A. *Empire on the Pacific.* New York: Ronald Press Co., 1955.

Merk, Frederick. *Manifest Destiny and Mission in American History: A Reinterpretation.* New York: Alfred A. Knopf, Inc., 1963.

Art, Science, and the Life of the Mind

Brooks, Van Wyck. *Makers and Finders: The Flowering of New England.* Vol. 2 of 5 vols. New York: E. P. Dutton & Co., Inc. [Paperback—New York: E. P. Dutton & Co., Inc.].

Curti, Merle. *The Growth of American Thought.* New York: Harper & Row, Publishers, 1964.

Reingold, Nathan (ed.). *Science in Nineteenth-Century America: A Documentary History.* New York: Hill & Wang, Inc., 1964 [Paperback—New York: Hill & Wang, Inc.].

Historical Fiction

Guthrie, A. B., Jr. *The Big Sky.* Boston: Houghton Mifflin Co. [Paperback—Boston: Houghton Mifflin Co.]. (Life among the pioneers.)

————. *The Way West.* Boston: Houghton Mifflin Co. [Paperback—New York: Paperback Library, Inc.]. (Life along the Oregon Trail.)

Stone, Irving. *The President's Lady.* New York: Doubleday & Co., Inc., 1959 [Paperback—New York: Avon Books]. (Andrew Jackson's lifetime love affair with his wife.)

Discuss the title of Part Four. (It refers, of course, to the struggle in the Civil War to decide whether or not the Union would be preserved or destroyed by the secession of the states forming the Confederacy.)
#What were these differences? (Students should be able to name the differing views of Americans on protective tariffs, internal improvements, and the extension of slavery into the territories. The differences over the first two had built up antagonisms that had poorly prepared people to deal with the most serious difference of all--over slavery in the territories. Why is it always a serious matter for people to allow their emotions to control or determine their actions?)

TESTING THE FEDERAL UNION

PART FOUR

A civil war—a war between people of the same country—is a terrible human tragedy. This kind of conflict rages more fiercely than any other, and its flames die out more slowly. It leaves ugly scars on the nation—on the victor as well as on the vanquished.

In the early 1850's, few believed that the United States would ever undergo such an ordeal. This land had always seemed divinely blessed. Far-flung continental boundaries had been established, enclosing an enormous expanse for bountiful development. The standard of living for most Americans was rising. The United States had already become the envy of millions of people throughout the world, and a home in America had become the goal of the downtrodden.

Yet, beneath the surface, the corrosion of sectionalism was having its effect. Although the North and the South had been able to reach compromises on their political disagreements, they had failed to settle important differences that remained. Increasingly, they displayed distrust toward each other. As each side attempted in vain to make headway with the other, frustration grew. Emotions instead of reason began to govern.

In the fateful year of 1861, the scourge of war supplanted the political art of give-and-take. The issue was in the hands of soldiers; the decision would be rendered by leveled cannon. Before the nation was whole again, it endured a fearful carnage. When the guns at last fell silent, northerners and southerners were joined together in the firm resolve which Lincoln uttered in behalf of all Americans—"that this nation, under God, shall have a new birth of freedom—and that government of the people, by the people, for the people, shall not perish from the earth."

##To what does "give-and-take" refer? Why do the authors speak of it as a "political art"? (Suggestion: to compromise, or the business of giving something to get something.)

249

George P. A. Healy painted this portrait of Lincoln in Rome, in 1869. Mrs. Robert Todd Lincoln, daughter-in-law of Abraham Lincoln, acquired it and later willed it to the White House. It hangs in the State Dining Room.

Abraham Lincoln, wearing the somber and contemplative expression he habitually had during his years as President. The reserves of strength and determination suggested in this likeness were called upon to sustain him through the agony and discouragement of a ghastly civil war. This painting hangs in the White House.

Ask what Lincoln's nature was. (He was serious and somewhat sad, but he was more so during the war.) Ask how the picture suggests strength and determination.

TESTING THE FEDERAL UNION

CHAPTER 14   THE UNITED STATES DIVIDED   252

The Slavery Issue Takes Center Stage   254

A Vexed Congress "Settles" the Question   255

Senator Douglas Ruptures the Peace of the Nation   260

The South at Last Resorts to Secession   264

CHAPTER 15   THE WAR BETWEEN THE SECTIONS   270

Reconciliation Fails in the Crisis of the Union   272

The Nation Submits to a Decisive Clash of Arms   274

The Home Fronts Shape the Final Outcome   285

CHAPTER 16   REESTABLISHING NATIONAL UNITY   290

Amidst the Ruins of War, Reconstruction Begins   292

The Radical Republicans Land in the Saddle   294

Grant Presides During the Drama of Reconciliation   300

A LONG VIEW   308

The three chapters in this part treat the three phases of the crucial period in American history when the federal union was tested. These are: the period before the Civil War, when one event after another led to violence and battles, the Civil War itself, and the period of reconstruction. The main heads in each chapter--listed here--make up an outline of the content of the part.

The crucial issue that finally led to conflict between the North and the South was: As new western territories are settled, what is to be the status of slavery in each one? Congressional compromises were effective regarding slavery in the territories before the Supreme Court's ruling in the Dred Scott case. After the ruling, further compromises became impossible.

14

THE UNITED STATES DIVIDED

. . . an irrepressible conflict . . .

In states where the slave system prevails, the masters, directly or indirectly, secure all political power, and constitute a ruling aristocracy. In states where the free-labor system prevails, universal suffrage necessarily obtains, and the state inevitably becomes, sooner or later, a republic or democracy. . . .

Hitherto, the two systems have existed in different states, but side by side within the American Union. This has happened because the Union is a confederation of states. But in another aspect the United States constitute only one nation. Increase of population, which is filling the states out to their very borders, together with a new and extended net-work of

Slave traders advertised through newspapers that they would on a certain date buy or sell slaves.

Words to study: consolidation; antagonistic; fanatical; agitator; apprehend; induce; irrepressible.
Why did Seward believe that an "irrepressible conflict" was in the making? What did he think of
the various compromises that had been made?

railroads and other avenues, and an internal commerce which daily becomes more intimate, is rapidly bringing the states into a higher and more perfect social unity or consolidation. Thus, these antagonistic systems are continually coming into closer contact, and collision results.

Shall I tell you what this collision means? They who think that it is accidental, unnecessary, the work of interested or fanatical agitators, and therefore ephemeral [temporary] mistake the case altogether. It is an irrepressible conflict between opposing and enduring forces, and it means that the United States must and will, sooner or later, become either entirely a slaveholding nation, or entirely a free-labor nation.

Either the cotton and rice-fields of South Carolina and the sugar plantations of Louisiana will ultimately be tilled by free labor, and Charleston and New Orleans become marts for legitimate merchandise alone, or else the rye-fields and wheat-fields of Massachusetts and New York must again be surrendered by their farmers to slave culture and to the production of slaves, and Boston and New York become once more markets for trade in the bodies and souls of men.

It is the failure to apprehend this great truth that induces so many unsuccessful attempts at final compromise between the slave and free states, and it is the existence of this great fact that renders all such pretended compromises, when made, vain. . . . Startling as this saying may appear to you, fellow citizens, it is by no means an original or even a moderate one. Our forefathers knew it to be true . . . when they framed the constitution of the United States. . . . They knew that either the one or the other system must exclusively prevail.

In the middle of the nineteenth century, many Americans in both the North and the South still believed that compromise contained the answer to the disturbing slavery question. Yet the middle ground seemed to be vanishing. Important northern leaders were taking a firm moral stand against the further extension of slavery. And important southerners were just as obstinately insisting that the "peculiar institution" must be allowed to spread into the territories set up by Congress. Increasing numbers of people felt that compromise was no longer possible—that the nation now faced an "irrepressible conflict." Senator William H. Seward of New York coined that phrase in a speech—of which this selection is a portion— that he delivered in Rochester, New York, on October 25, 1858.

Kennedy Galleries

A slave market in the deep South. Slaves generally were sold only out of necessity—for example, when an owner died. Most people who sold their bondmen devoutly hoped that families like those seen here would not be separated, but slave traders had no such scruples. The traffic in slaves was distasteful even to the staunchest defenders of the "peculiar institution"; still it was one of the means by which slaves were obtained for extending the domain of the Cotton Kingdom.

#After the morality of slavery became a subject of debate, emotions prevailed.

253

THE SLAVERY ISSUE TAKES CENTER STAGE

The United States was divided rather than united by its easy victory over Mexico: the North and South could not agree on how to handle the new lands they had acquired. Slavery was the cause of the differences.

Slavery had become a forbidden subject in Congress in the years between 1836 and 1844. During that period antislavery petitions had been presented in the Senate, but they had all been rejected. In 1836 the House of Representatives had passed a gag rule—renewed at subsequent sessions—which prevented the discussion of antislavery proposals.

John Quincy Adams, elected a member of the House from Massachusetts after his term as President, won the nickname "Old Man Eloquent" for his brilliant attacks on the gag rule. Partly as a result of them, it was repealed in 1844. Thereafter, the discussion of slavery in Congress could no longer be gagged by the common agreement of both sides.

THE WILMOT PROVISO

One summer evening in 1846 when a bill to buy territory from Mexico was before the House of Representatives, David Wilmot, of Pennsylvania, arose to attach a proviso, or condition, to it. The proviso was that slavery be banned forever from any territory that might be acquired by treaty from Mexico. The wording of the Wilmot Proviso, copied from the Northwest Ordinance, would extend the freedoms of the old Northwest to the new territory.

A hornet's nest. Wilmot was a devoted Jacksonian reformer of the rough frontier type. Few would have looked to him to stir up a hornet's nest. His motives are not clear, but his proposal touched both the North and the South to the quick. Showing how far behind public sentiment he was, President Polk wrote: "What connection slavery had with making peace with Mexico it is difficult to conceive."

Hot tempers. On both sides there were harsh words. The *Cleveland Plain Dealer* declared: "It is time that the lovers of freedom should unite in opposing the common enemy by fixing

bounds to their aggression." Said the *Richmond Enquirer*, "The tocsin, 'the firebell at night,' is now sounding in our ears; the madmen of the North and Northwest have, we fear, cast the die, and numbered the days of this glorious Union." Northern legislatures voted resolutions supporting the Wilmot Proviso, and southern legislatures denounced it as heartily.

The big question. For the time being, the moderates on both sides were able to join together in Congress to defeat the measure. But people now were beginning to face squarely the question, Is slavery to go into the territories or is there to be no further extension of it anywhere?

THE ELECTION OF 1848

In a highly charged atmosphere the election of 1848 took place. Both the Whigs and the Democrats believed that coöperation between North and South was possible. They were aware, though, that their presidential nominees would have to be men with few strong feelings on the main issue of the day.

The Whig ticket. The Whigs passed Henry Clay by again and chose instead Zachary Taylor, the hero of Buena Vista. A slaveowner from Louisiana, Taylor was unacceptable to many northern Whigs. An Indiana newspaper said that his nomination was "an insult to the intelligence and virtue of the American people."

The Whigs had no platform because they had no program. One of their number stated frankly, "General Taylor's military fame is about the best we can make use of at present. . . ." Millard Fillmore, of New York, was chosen to run for the vice-presidency.*

The Democrats' choice. The Democrats picked as their candidate a sixty-five-year-old man, Lewis Cass, of Michigan. A supporter of Jefferson and Jackson, Cass had, during a long career, been a general in the War of 1812, governor of the Michigan Territory, and United States

---

* The Whigs appealed strongly to cotton planters in the South and to cotton manufacturers in New England—men of property sneeringly called "The Lords of the Lash and the Lords of the Loom."

##The Wilmot Proviso was passed in the House of Representatives by a vote of 87 to 64, but the Senate adjourned without taking a vote on it, thus killing the proposal.

Senator. Daniel Webster, who had attended Phillips Exeter Academy with Cass, described him once as a "clever fellow, good-natured, kind-hearted, amiable, and obliging." These qualities now made Cass seem to his party an admirable choice to head its ticket.

The Democratic platform was so timid that it criticized even raising the slavery issue in Congress. Concerning slavery in the territories, the position of Cass was, "Leave it to the settlers who will be affected by this question, to adjust it upon their own responsibility and in their own manner."

Cass was expressing what many westerners believed: the *people* of a territory, not Congress, should decide whether they would or would not have slavery. This principle became known as the doctrine of *squatter sovereignty*.

The Free-Soilers. The Democrats were badly split. The Barnburners†, a radical New York group, withdrew in anger from the nominating convention, naming Martin Van Buren as their candidate. Later in the summer, they and other antislavery Democrats joined with the Liberty party (see page 194) and antislavery Whigs to form the Free-Soil party at Buffalo, New York. The Free-Soil party agreed upon the Wilmot Proviso and the slogan, "Free soil, free speech, free labor, and free men."

Victory for Taylor. In the November election, Taylor won by a narrow margin. The Free-Soilers failed to capture a single state, but they had diverted enough votes from Cass in New York to give that state's electoral votes and the victory to Taylor. Fillmore said of the triumph: "I regard this election as putting an end to all ideas of disunion. It raises up a national party, occupying a middle ground, and leaves the fanatics and disunionists, North and South, without hope of destroying the fair fabric of our Constitution." Fillmore was wrong.

Sum and Substance

1. Why was slavery not discussed in Congress between 1836 and 1844? 2. Give the content of the Wilmot Proviso. What was its effect? 3. What kind of men were sought as presidential nominees in 1848? Why? 4. Who was elected?

This section deals with the last compromise before the Civil War--the Compromise of 1850.

A VEXED CONGRESS "SETTLES" THE QUESTION

Was there a solution to the question of slavery in the territories? There appeared to be at least four alternatives. One was to let slaveowners take their bondmen anywhere they wished. A second was to limit slavery to those areas where it already existed and forbid it to go elsewhere. A third was to allow the territorial settlers themselves to decide—by squatter sovereignty or, as it was also known, popular sovereignty. A fourth was to extend the 36°30′ line of the Missouri Compromise to the Pacific coast (see pages 172–173).

THE COMPROMISE OF 1850

When the new Congress convened in December, 1849, the air fairly crackled with tension and wrath. Polk, who had left office in March,

had recommended that California and what was called New Mexico (see the map on page 256) be organized as territories. (The Oregon

Henry Clay as a young congressman. Destined not to win the presidency, he won fame for his skill at compromise.

Corcoran Gallery of Art

† Originally applied as a name of ridicule, it came from the tale about a Dutch farmer who burned down his barn in order to get rid of the rats.

Territory—with slavery prohibited—had already been created in 1848.)

But what was to be the fate of slavery in these territories—and elsewhere in the country? Even many moderate southerners were prepared to break up the Union if California and New Mexico were closed to slaves and—as was also being suggested—slavery was abolished in the District of Columbia.

In the Senate, meeting together for the last time, was the trio that had controlled it for a # generation: Clay, Calhoun, and Webster. Clay was now seventy-two; Calhoun and Webster were sixty-eight. Calhoun was a dying man, and Clay and Webster would be dead within two years. Presidential ambitions no longer dominated their actions.

New faces, soon to occupy the key places, were also present. One was Stephen A. Doug-

las, the tobacco-chewing "Little Giant" from Illinois, whose self-assured and decisive manner had already made him a favorite of young people. Other recent arrivals included such men as Jefferson Davis, of Mississippi, William H. Seward, of New York, and Salmon P. Chase, of Ohio. These men had reached the conclusion that compromise was impossible.

Clay's proposals. Clay, whose fame already rested upon his role as a compromiser, prepared to make another great effort—his last, it proved—for the unity of the nation. He would try to settle at one stroke all the sectional controversies related to slavery. In spite of a growing feebleness and a hacking cough, he called at Webster's home one day near the end of January, 1850. His purpose was to ask his colleague from Massachusetts to support the resolutions he was about to intro-

Observe the vast extent of the territories in which the future of slavery was still to be determined.

Clay's proposals became the basis for the agreement that held the nation together in 1850. Which proposals were aimed at pleasing the South? The North? How had the Mexican War made an agreement necessary?

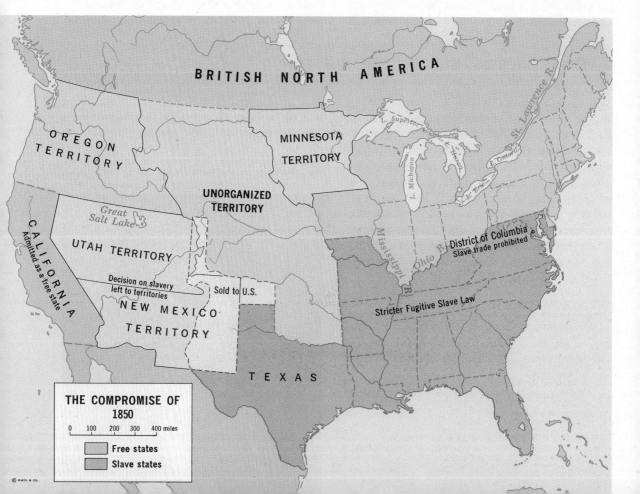

THE COMPROMISE OF 1850

0   100   200   300   400 miles

Free states
Slave states

duce in the Senate. Webster willingly assented.

The resolutions became known as the Compromise of 1850. They called for (1) the admission of California as a free state; (2) the organization of the rest of the territory recently acquired from Mexico without providing for either the introduction of slavery or the banning of it; (3) the assigning to New Mexico of the vacant land in dispute along the Texas border, in return for which the federal government would assume the pre-annexation debts of Texas; (4) the ending of the slave trade in the District of Columbia; and (5) the passage of a more effective fugitive-slave law.

Clay presented these proposals on January 29, 1850, defending them a week later in moving language. California, he pointed out, had already drawn up a free-state constitution. As to the New Mexico Territory: since many people did not believe slavery could be profitable there anyway, it did not seem necessary to arouse the South by taking a stand on the question in that area.

The Texas boundary provision appeared to be just, Clay thought. And concerning the slave trade in Washington, within a stone's throw of the Capitol, he was satisfied that even southerners had always considered this to be disgusting. Finally, a stronger fugitive-slave law would protect the property of southerners as, he said, the Constitution intended.

Clay, who thought his plan was generous to the South, beseeched the North to be high-minded. Concession by the North—the more powerful section—meant, he said, merely a sacrifice of sentiment. For the South, on the other hand, it involved property, "the social fabric, life, and all that makes life desirable and happy." He warned the South, though, that if it tried to dissolve the Union, it would lose more than it could gain.

Calhoun's last speech. In the debate that followed, the rival positions were brilliantly presented. Calhoun was first, although he was so ill that he was unable to read his address himself. As he sat wrapped in blankets, his words were delivered by his friend Senator James M. Mason, of Virginia.

The South, said Calhoun, had yielded ground time after time to the North—in the Northwest Ordinance, in the Missouri question, in Oregon—and now was being asked to yield in the case of the Mexican cession. It was not a question, he said, of whether the South would suddenly secede and wreck the Union; ties that held the Union together were *already* breaking —the Protestant churches had split on North-South lines, and the political parties could not remain national much longer. This would continue, he predicted, until the nation came apart.

Calhoun gave an ultimatum to the North. It must give the South equal rights in the territories; it must faithfully obey the fugitive-slave laws; it must stop its agitation of the slavery question; it must amend the Constitution to restore the balance between free and slave states.

This was the hour for the South to take its stand, Calhoun warned. "We are now," he said, "stronger relatively than we shall be hereafter politically and morally." He sensed that in the struggle for power with the industrial North, the agricultural South would fall further and further behind.

Webster's stand. A few days later Daniel Webster took the floor. His tone was conciliatory. He appealed to the extremists in his own section. If, he said, it came to a choice between abolition and the Union, he would unhesitatingly choose the Union. He emphasized, "I wish to speak today, not as a Massachusetts man, nor as a Northern man, but as an American. . . ." Of course the North must return all runaway slaves, he said, because they are property under the Constitution.

Abolitionists, Webster declared, did not need a Wilmot Proviso with which "to taunt or reproach" the South. Slavery, by its nature, he asserted, would not go into California or New Mexico anyway. He proposed to the South in his conclusion that there not even be talk of secession: "Let us make our generation one of the strongest and brightest links in that golden chain which is destined, I fondly believe, to grapple the people of all the states to this Constitution for ages to come."

Opposition. Antislavery people were outraged by Webster's words. John Greenleaf Whittier, the "Quaker Poet" from Massachusetts, wrote these lines:

> . . . from those great eyes
> The soul has fled;
> When faith is lost, when honor dies,
> The man is dead!

Northern radicals‡ had a new favorite, William H. Seward, of New York. He would have no compromise, because compromise, he believed, meant a surrendering of principles. The majority, he said—by which he meant the North—would decide the issues at stake. He refused to believe that the Constitution was intended to defend slavery. Besides, he asserted, there is a *higher law* than the Constitution which decent men must obey: the law of God.

But the two leading opponents of compromise were Calhoun and President Taylor. Calhoun, it was reported, was preparing to issue a call for the organization of a southern confederacy. Taylor, who had been proslavery before his election, had now been won over by Senator Seward: he announced that he was opposed to the extension of slavery. In the manner of Jackson before him, he warned the South that he would hang any rebels who attempted to disrupt the Union.

The hand of death. Then suddenly the national outlook was transformed: Calhoun and Taylor both died. In March Calhoun gasped his last words: "The South! the poor South! God knows what will become of her!" Taylor, on the following Fourth of July, attended lengthy ceremonies in a broiling sun at the base of the incomplete Washington Monument. Hot and exhausted, he returned to the White House and gulped down large quantities of ice water and milk and a bowl of cherries. Physicians saw a connection between what happened on the Fourth and his death five days later—which was attributed to cholera morbus.

These two deaths had a calming effect on politics. Moderation came to the fore again.

‡ A name sometimes used at that time for people opposed to the spread of slavery.

Millard Fillmore, the new President, proved to be the type of man to save the day. Gentlemanly and dependable, he also favored Clay's proposals.

Passage. The Compromise of 1850 passed the Congress in September. Its enactment owed much to Stephen A. Douglas, who assumed leadership of the undertaking after Clay fell victim to exhaustion and the summer's heat. Nationalism apparently had won a battle over sectionalism. Crowds in Washington paraded in torchlight processions and screamed with one voice, "The Union is saved!"

Despite the rejoicing, some ominous cries were also heard—like that of the southerner who shouted, "Give us slavery, *or* give us death." Nevertheless, quiet settled upon the troubled nation.

UNEASY CALM

The quiet did not last long. The new Fugitive Slave Law aroused many northerners who had been moderates before its passage. It was almost unbearable for some of them to see slaves seized by federal officials, clapped into irons, and sent back to their owners.

Fugitive slaves. After the Fugitive Slave Law was passed, a Boston clergyman led a mob in an unsuccessful effort to rescue Anthony Burns, a fugitive slave who had been caught. Though Burns was finally returned to his legal owner in Virginia, it cost the federal government, according to estimates, almost $100,000. A few months later wealthy Bostonians bought his freedom for $1300. In many places in the North, a "slavecatcher" could expect to meet his death on the streets. With every new example of northern defiance, the anger of the southern extremists, or fire-eaters, as they were called, grew greater.

Literary agitation. Southerners were disturbed also by the widespread influence of *Uncle Tom's Cabin,* a book written by Harriet Beecher Stowe, the daughter of the famous minister Lyman Beecher. Its publication in 1852 was Mrs. Stowe's response to the passage of the Fugitive Slave Law. She had taken seriously the words of her sister-in-law: "Now, Hattie,

##Many moderate northerners thus became abolitionists, whose number continued to grow. Believing that slavery was a moral evil, abolitionists held that there was no compromising with it.

#For a contemporary defense of slavery and a criticism of Harriet Beecher Stowe, see William J. Grayson's poem "The Hireling and the Slave." Hinton Rowan Helper's book (see pp. 224-225) appeared in 1857.

if I could use a pen as you can, I would write something which would make this whole nation feel what an accursed thing slavery is."

The success of Mrs. Stowe's efforts exceeded anyone's wildest expectations. Within a year 300,000 copies of *Uncle Tom's Cabin* had been sold, and the presses ran day and night to keep up with the demand. Although Mrs. Stowe was not personally acquainted with slavery, her attack on it sounded so convincing that it became a powerful force in American politics.

The book was read and reread everywhere, and for years crowds flocked to dramatizations of it. Saintly Uncle Tom, the pathetic little Eva, cruel Simon Legree, were fictional creations, but they became real for millions here and abroad. *Uncle Tom's Cabin* made many Americans look carefully at the problem of slavery for the first time and attempt to square human bondage with their consciences. This book was as important as any political event in making additional extremists on both sides.

Pierce, the "doughface." The moderates in control of the major political parties were desperately trying to appeal to voters in all parts of the nation rather than to those of any one section. The Democratic National Convention that met in Baltimore in 1852 took forty-nine ballots in order to select a presidential nominee. He turned out to be Franklin Pierce, of New Hampshire.

A New Englander with southern principles—a "doughface"—Pierce had been a Senator during the Jacksonian era and a general in the Mexican War. Though well-liked, he was not a forceful leader. Yet some of his friends admired his administrative ability. The author Nathaniel Hawthorne, who had attended Bowdoin College with him, wrote: "There are scores of men in the country that seem brighter than he is, but [he] has the directing mind, and will move them around like pawns on a chessboard."

The Whigs nominated General Winfield Scott, the other Whig hero of the Mexican War—showing how short of leaders they were. Scott's close relationship with Seward made many southern Whigs fear that he had free-soil tendencies and refuse to support him.

On the most baffling issue of the day, neither party contributed anything new. Both party platforms accepted as final the Compromise of

By 1860 approximately 50,000 slaves had escaped throughout the state of Ohio alone.

Runaway slaves were generally young people. They left in groups of two or three, most often in good weather.

Their success depended on obtaining help from other slaves and from former slaves like Harriet Tubman.

Brooklyn Museum

#The bill was passed. Ask why northern congressmen would vote for a bill that opened to slavery
a territory in which it had been forbidden by the Compromise of 1820. (Suggestion: see Douglas'
fourth motive, col. 2; some men argued that the Compromise of 1850 had replaced the earlier one.)

1850; both opposed congressional agitation of the slavery question; both supported states' rights.

Pierce won an overwhelming victory, which looked like a triumph for moderation. In fact, however, the decline of the Free-Soil party vote below that of 1848 suggested that extremists were taking a more restrained position by voting for Pierce.

Sum and Substance

1. Name the three main leaders in Congress in 1850. 2. Give the provisions of the Compromise of 1850. 3. Who proposed it? What two leaders opposed it? How did Webster react? 4. Account for the passage of the Compromise. 5. What effect did the new Fugitive Slave Law have? *Uncle Tom's Cabin*? 6. Who was elected President in 1852? Why?

SENATOR DOUGLAS RUPTURES THE PEACE OF THE NATION

The country was stunned when Stephen Douglas suddenly reopened the slavery question on January 23, 1854. On that day he introduced legislation that generated much extremist talk again—and violence, too.

THE KANSAS-NEBRASKA BILL

\# Douglas' bill was a proposal to organize the Kansas and Nebraska territories on the principle of squatter, or popular, sovereignty. The new territories were to be made from the Indian country just west of Missouri where Indians had been "permanently" located. The Senator's bill also specifically provided for the repeal of the Missouri Compromise. This meant that the line 36°30', agreed upon in 1820, would no

(The southerners were the beneficiaries.)

Compare this map with the one on page 172. What big change did Douglas' bill make? Who benefited most?

longer divide slave states from free states in the Louisiana Purchase. Douglas' bill would give slavery a chance to move north of that line.

Possible motives. One can only guess some of the motives that may have guided Douglas. First, he may have wanted the territory organized in order to get a transcontinental railroad. The South's support for a road over a northern route could only be enlisted by throwing the Kansas and Nebraska territories open to slavery. Second, Douglas very much wanted to be the next president of the United States. Possibly he was simply using this tactic to woo southerners. \#\#

Third, Douglas may genuinely have been implementing the idea of popular sovereignty. Fourth, he may have been responding to the widely held opinion that some new and dramatic move was needed to turn attention from the dull and inactive Pierce administration.

The impact. The Kansas-Nebraska Bill forced innumerable northern people to decide what they wanted their immediate neighbors to be—slaveholding or free. Northern farmers had already cast covetous eyes on Kansas and Nebraska as places where either they or their children might take up homesteads. Douglas' proposal put a damper on their hopes.

In many parts of the North, Douglas was denounced immediately as "the tool of southern slave drivers." To the charge that he was a traitor to his section, Douglas replied that the Missouri Compromise had, in fact, been repealed by the Compromise of 1850. By inter-

KANSAS, NEBRASKA, 1854
0   100   200   300 miles

Fort Benton

MINNESOTA TERRITORY

NEBRASKA TERRITORY

WIS.

IOWA

ILL.

Omaha

Fort Laramie □

Fort Kearney

UTAH TERRITORY

Decision on slavery left to territories

+PIKE'S PEAK

Bents Fort □

Lecompton
Topeka•
KANSAS
Lawrence•
Pottawatomie
Creek

Shawnee
Mission
•Independence

•Osawatomie
JOHN BROWN'S RAID

TERRITORY

Fort □
Scott

MO.

INDIAN TERRITORY
(Unorganized)

ARK.

NEW MEXICO TERRITORY

© RMSN & CO.

\#\#Jefferson Davis had persuaded Pierce to buy land in the South for a transcontinental (Gadsden Purchase).

fering with slavery, he said, Congress had always caused trouble. Leave it to the people to decide, he advised, and there will be peace. Douglas believed also that the western territories were predestined by geography and nature to be free soil. But was nature going to be allowed to take its own sure course?

Enacted. Senator Benjamin Wade, of Ohio, emerging as an ardent northern spokesman, had the Senate floor the day before the vote on the Kansas-Nebraska Bill was taken. "Tomorrow," he said, "I believe there is to be an eclipse of the sun and I think that the sun in the heavens and the glory of this republic should both go into obscurity and darkness together."

Senator Seward hurled a scornful challenge at "the gentlemen of the slave states." Declared this Whig from New York, "We will engage in competition for the virgin soil of Kansas and God give victory to the side that is stronger in numbers, as it is in right." On May 30, 1854, Pierce signed the bill.

"BLEEDING KANSAS"

Most northerners and most southerners had no appetite for moving to the West to engage in the struggle now about to take shape. Those who did, despite the threat of trouble, were quickly caught up in tragic events.

The Emigrant Aid Company. One Eli Thayer, of Massachusetts, decided to make emigrating to Kansas so attractive to New Englanders that the territory would become free soil by colonization. A month before the Kansas-Nebraska Bill passed, Thayer obtained a charter from his state to form the Massachusetts Emigrant Aid Company, with a capital of $2,000,000.

The Company's stated purpose was to make Kansas free, although its interest in land speculation was just as important. The activities of the Company found wide support. Amos A. Lawrence, of Boston, advanced a considerable sum of money for the enterprise, and the first free-soil community in Kansas was named in his honor. It is estimated that by 1857 about 2000 people had been brought into Kansas through Emigrant Aid.

The government at Shawnee Mission. Southerners did not ignore the challenge. The selection, on November 29, 1854, of a delegate to represent the Kansas Territory in Congress gave them the opportunity they wanted. Seventeen hundred armed men streamed over the border from Missouri to elect a proslavery man, then returned home.

The following March, when a territorial legislature was to be chosen, 5000 men—called "Border Ruffians"—poured into Kansas. Notices and posters in Missouri promised, "Free ferry, a dollar a day, and liquor, gentlemen." In this fraudulent election a proslavery legislature was chosen and was soon meeting at Shawnee Mission, Kansas—enacting proslavery laws.

The Topeka government. Refusing to accept the Shawnee Mission legislature, the free-soil settlers decided to ask for admission to the Union as a free state. In October, 1855, they held a convention at the town of Topeka that drew up a free-state constitution. Under the Topeka Constitution they elected a legislature and a governor.

Kansas now had two governments. Each armed itself to stand against the other. A proslavery editor was quoted as saying, "I'd as lief kill a babe in its cradle if I knew it would grow up to be an abolitionist." And a leader among the free-soil settlers stated, "This is the last struggle between freedom and slavery and we must not flatter ourselves that it will be trivial or short."

POLITICAL SHIFTS

Kansas, meanwhile, had become the "Kansas question" to the rest of the country. This question was something on which the whole slavery issue could be focused, and its impact on the shaky political parties was profound.

Throughout the Northwest men who opposed ## the extension of slavery began to drift out of both Whig and Democratic ranks. Having stood behind the Kansas-Nebraska Bill, the Pierce administration had expected loyal Democrats everywhere to do the same. Yet many men still considered themselves to be good Demo-

##At first these men were called "Anti-Nebraska men," but later they took the name Republicans. Review what the authors say is the chief reason for the formation of a new party (p. 192).

crats while opposing the bill. And many others cut their ties with the party over this question.

A similar breakup was going on in the Whig party. Some northern Whigs thought that they could transform their party into an antislavery organization and bring it back to power. Other Whigs, believing that their party was dead and beyond revival, left it.

The Republicans. During 1854 dissatisfied antislavery Democrats and Whigs joined with Free-Soilers at Ripon, Wisconsin, and at Jackson, Michigan, to form a new party based on the *nonextension* of slavery. Still only local organizations, they chose the name "Republican," but they were intent on becoming a national political party.

In the congressional elections in November, dissatisfied former members of both Whig and Democratic parties were so successful that they captured the House of Representatives and elected the Speaker. Now no single party opposed the Democrats; the Whigs had split apart as a national organization.

The Know-Nothings. For a time between 1852 and 1854, it appeared as if the new opposition party might be the Know-Nothing party.§ This was a group that was hostile to immigrants and proposed increasing the period required for their naturalization. Southerners regarded immigrants as an antislavery force, because the new arrivals were helping to swell the populations of the new states that adopted free-soil constitutions.

Northerners, on the other hand, sometimes regarded immigrants as proslavery, because unskilled newcomers frequently tried to break up abolitionist meetings for fear of having to compete for jobs with freed Negroes. But the Know-Nothing party, too, had finally to answer the question of whether or not slavery could enter the territories. Like the Democratic and Whig parties, it came apart at its sectional seams— and disappeared after the election of 1856.

"Beecher's Bibles" and Border Ruffians. In the late spring of 1856, civil war broke out in Kansas.

Free-state supporters were receiving weapons from the East. Hunting rifles called "Sharps' rifles" became known as "Beecher's Bibles," because the congregation of the minister Henry Ward Beecher, brother of Harriet Beecher Stowe, had sent a supply to Kansas.

In May Border Ruffians and Kansas proslavery men pillaged and sacked the free-state town of Lawrence. They had determined to "give distinct notice that all who do not leave immediately for the East, *will leave for eternity!*" Two men lost their lives.

John Brown's attack. At this point, John Brown, a violently antislavery man, led his four sons and three other men in a raid on a proslavery settlement near Pottawatomie Creek, in Kansas. A product of an unhappy family life, Brown was mentally unbalanced and believed that God had selected him to crush wickedness in the world. With cutlasses sharpened like razors, the attackers murdered five people in cold blood. "I have no choice," Brown explained. "It has been ordained by the Almighty God . . . that I should make an example of these men."

The effect of Brown's raid was electric: Missourians vowed that they would rush across the border and wipe out the free-staters. The Kansas civil war had begun.

Sumner's fateful speech. While Congress was trying to find a formula for ending this frightful condition, Senator Charles Sumner, of Massachusetts, delivered in 1856 a fiery antisouthern speech in the Senate—a speech he later called "The Crime Against Kansas." In it he insulted some of his fellow Senators, including Andrew P. Butler, of South Carolina, and Stephen A. Douglas.

Two days after the address, as Sumner sat at his desk in the Senate, a tall stranger approached, who solemnly said, "I have read your speech twice over carefully; it is a libel on South Carolina, and Mr. Butler, who is a relative of mine." Having introduced himself, he beat Sumner into unconsciousness on the floor, clubbing him with a heavy cane until it broke into pieces. The assailant was Preston Brooks, a Representative from South Carolina.

§ Officially called the American party, its members were sworn to secrecy and instructed to reply to questions about it, "I know nothing."

Brooks immediately resigned his seat, but his district reelected him unanimously. Grateful friends presented him with new canes. A Richmond newspaper declared that the abolitionists had got what they deserved: "They have grown saucy, and dare to be impudent to gentlemen!"

Sumner suffered fierce head pains the rest of his life. For over three years he did not occupy his seat in the Senate, and his opponents charged that he was feigning injury. His empty seat was a silent but eloquent reminder that violence had threatened the legislative process in America.

James Buchanan. "Bleeding Kansas," as that unhappy place had come to be known, was in the foreground of the presidential election of 1856. The Democrats made one more attempt to continue as a national party by seeking a candidate not identified with the Kansas question. They therefore would not renominate President Pierce or take Senator Douglas. On the seventeenth ballot they chose James Buchanan, of Pennsylvania.

Buchanan was a party "regular" who had served in many positions. He had recently been out of the country as United States minister to England. While there, he had attended a conference at Ostend, Belgium, with the United States ministers at Madrid and Paris, Pierre Soulé and John Y. Mason.

These men drew up what is known as the Ostend Manifesto. In it they called for seizing Cuba from the Spanish. They expressed concern lest a freeing of slaves take place there leading to race warfare that might spread to American shores. In addition to being a good statement of the "manifest destiny" doctrine, the Ostend Manifesto was also prosouthern.

Buchanan, a sixty-five-year-old bachelor in 1856, suffered from a nervous twitching of the facial muscles. He had helped to rear his niece, Harriet Lane, who served as his social hostess. A Jacksonian in his early days, Buchanan appears to have become afraid of change; he also lacked the instinct of leadership.

Candidate Frémont. Among Republicans, now organized nationally, one person had been mentioned for months as a presidential nominee: John C. Frémont. At forty-three Frémont was a young and adventurous man, one of the best-known Americans of the day, and a perfect representative for a new party. By birth and acquaintance his ties with the South were strong, and although he was a free-soiler, his ideas were not as extreme as those of the abolitionists. He was nominated quickly, and the Republicans' campaign slogan became, "Free speech, free press, free soil, free men, Frémont and victory."

The campaign. The Republican platform supported the right of Congress to make decisions on slavery in the territories. It also expressed approval of a transcontinental railroad and condemned the Ostend Manifesto.

During the campaign, Republicans pitched their appeal not only to farmers of the Northwest but to eastern workers as well. Speakers, harping on Buchanan's statement that ten cents a day ought to be enough for any workingman, dubbed the Democratic candidate "Ten-Cent Jimmy."

The Democrats maintained that the election of a Republican such as Frémont would bring disunion, because he was a candidate of only one section: the North. In general, "cotton" Whigs—both the planters and the manufacturers—men of finance, and industrialists supported Buchanan.

The Democratic party was still a national rather than a sectional party, boasting friends in both North and South. When Buchanan won, his victory was taken as evidence that Americans wanted still to hold the Union together and to have peace.

THE SOUTH AT LAST RESORTS TO SECESSION

In his inaugural address Buchanan made a plea for the principle of popular sovereignty. He admitted that a serious question was, At what point do the people in a territory decide the matter of whether they will accept or reject slavery? But he said that the Supreme Court was about to decide this knotty problem, and he hoped the decision would be accepted cheerfully.

THE DRED SCOTT DECISION

Even before Buchanan's inauguration, rumors were astir that the Court was going to rule that Congress had no power over slavery in the territories. Two days after the ceremony, Chief Justice Roger B. Taney handed down a momentous decision in the Dred Scott case.

The facts. Dred Scott, a Negro slave, was a household servant who had been sold in St. Louis, Missouri, to a Dr. John Emerson, an army surgeon. Emerson between 1834 and 1838 took Scott to Rock Island, Illinois, and Fort Snelling, near the present location of St. Paul, Minnesota. Scott, therefore, spent four years on soil where slavery was prohibited. In 1846 Scott brought a lawsuit for his freedom on the ground that his residence on free soil had made him free. In the Missouri court in which he sued, he won; but in 1852 the state supreme court overruled the lower court.

The case was then taken to the United States Supreme Court. When it was argued there in December, 1856, an imposing lineup of lawyers were on Scott's side, and on the side of his new owner, John F. A. Sanford (Dr. Emerson's brother-in-law). The Court was asked to answer three questions: First, was Scott a citizen of Missouri and therefore entitled to sue in a federal court? Second, had his stay on free soil given him freedom, and if so, did he retain that freedom upon returning to Missouri? Third, was the Missouri Compromise, which had made Minnesota free soil, constitutional?

The Court's ruling. A majority of the justices decided not only that Scott was not a citizen but that no slave or descendant of a slave was a citizen under the Constitution. The Court ruled, therefore, that it had no jurisdiction in the case.

If the Court had stopped at this point, there # might have been no general outcry. However, it gave its incidental opinions‖ on the other questions that the case raised. It held that residence on free soil did not make Scott free in Missouri, because as a resident there he was governed by the laws of that state. The most sensational opinion was that slaves were property protected under the Fifth Amendment and therefore *could be taken into any of the territories.*

The significance. The importance of this assertion was clear to all. The Missouri Compromise, which had limited the area of slavery, was declared unconstitutional even though it had been a law on the books for thirty-four years! Slav- ## ery could go anywhere now, and Congress was powerless to legislate otherwise.

The *Charleston Mercury* maintained that the decision vindicated the views of the "secessionists," who had always contended that the law of the land regarded slaves as property. In the North the decision was widely believed to be the result of a conspiracy on the part of the "slave power" said to control the Court. The *Boston Atlas* denounced the Court's ruling as "the deadliest blow which has been aimed at the liberties of America since the days of Benedict Arnold."

A test in Kansas. The Dred Scott decision severely hurt the Democratic party, which had been able to keep its northern membership largely because it had advocated popular sovereignty. Shortly people had an opportunity to see just how meaningless the doctrine of popular sovereignty could be made.

The Lecompton Constitution. In Lecompton, Kansas, an elected proslavery convention drew up a state constitution that would have been rejected by the antislavery voters if put to a fair vote. Instead, the convention submitted to the

‖ Lawyers call these "obiter dicta."

##The Dred Scott decision was the first such Supreme Court decision after <u>Marbury</u> v. <u>Madison</u>, in which a congressional law was declared unconstitutional by the United States Supreme Court.

people only a special clause authorizing the further introduction of slaves. As a result, if the antislavery men went to the polls and voted no, they merely prohibited the *further* importation of slaves into the territory. Slave property already in the territory would be protected under the general provisions of the United States Constitution.

The Republicans charged that a proslavery minority was trying by this trick to push a constitution through, making Kansas a slave state against the will of the majority. Antislavery voters in Kansas refused to go to the polls.

Douglas called the Lecompton Constitution a mockery of his principle of popular sovereignty. Buchanan, who had supported the admission of Kansas as a slave state, now broke with Douglas, and the Democratic party was torn by dissension. Douglas vowed either to have his way through a fair vote on the whole constitution or "fall in the attempt."# When the constitution as a whole was submitted to the voters in 1858, it was overwhelmingly rejected.

THE LINCOLN-DOUGLAS DEBATES

In his fight with Buchanan, Douglas risked high personal stakes. The "Little Giant," as he was known, had his eyes on the presidency. Only forty-five years old in 1858, he was already widely mentioned as a White House possibility. Ambition burned hotly in him—and in his wife, Adele, a grandniece of Dolley Madison.

The Senate contest in Illinois. Douglas, however, had to run for reelection to his Senate seat in 1858. He would have to walk a tightrope. He wanted to remain acceptable to Illinois voters —who were opposed to the extension of slavery in the territories—and at the same time keep his supporters in the South.

The Illinois Republicans nominated Abraham Lincoln for the Senate. A figure familiar in the state, he was a shrewd and likable lawyer. His keen mind, clear speech, powerful logic, and wizard-like political sense were known only by a few. These attributes would soon be attract-

---

Kansas retained territorial status until 1861, when it was admitted as a free state.

Lincoln believed that slavery was wrong, that a house divided against itself could not stand.

ing the attention of people everywhere in the nation.

In his acceptance speech Lincoln expressed his opinion: "'A house divided against itself cannot stand.' I believe this government cannot endure permanently half *slave* and half *free*. I do not expect the Union to be dissolved —I do not expect the house to *fall*—but I *do* expect it will cease to be divided. It will become *all* one thing, or *all* the other."

The opponents. In July Douglas reluctantly accepted Lincoln's challenge to a series of debates that held the interest not only of Illinois' voters but of the entire nation. The contrast between the two men as they stood side by side on speaking platforms during the next months was remarkable. Lincoln was tall, lanky, and awkward, his clothes ill-fitting, his voice high-pitched at points of dramatic emphasis. Douglas was short and pudgy, his attire faultless, his manner defiant, his voice raspy and deep. Both men scored important points in their public arguments.

The Freeport doctrine. At Freeport, Illinois, Lincoln put a question to Douglas, however, which brought from Douglas what seemed to be a canny reply. Lincoln asked: "Can the people of a United States Territory, in any lawful

Observe the horses and buggies (background).

The largest town in which Lincoln and Douglas debated was Quincy, Illinois, seen here as it looked about that time. The men spoke from a platform before the columned courthouse in the center of the block.

Quincy Herald-Whig

Kean Archives

Neighbors greet Lincoln as he returns home to Springfield, Illinois, after the conclusion of the campaign against Douglas, as represented by a later artist.

way, against the wish of any citizen of the United States, exclude slavery from its limits prior to the formation of a State Constitution?" Douglas' response was that slavery *could* be excluded from a territory if adequate protection for it was not provided by the people locally.

Douglas' Freeport doctrine, as this statement is known, in effect said that *despite* the Dred Scott decision, popular sovereignty continued to be possible. The answer appealed to the voters of Illinois, and they returned Douglas to the Senate. His admission, however, that slavery was not free to go everywhere, despite what the Court had said, brought a storm of abuse upon him from southerners. The Freeport doctrine would cost Douglas southern support for the Democratic nomination in 1860.

Although Lincoln had lost the election to the Senate, he gained prestige from his part in the debates. Having proved himself a match for Douglas, he had become a national figure. He was not radical—he talked only of the "*ultimate* extinction" of slavery. The extension of slavery, which Douglas' Kansas-Nebraska Bill had made possible, Lincoln said, would only make the problem more perplexing, not less. Lincoln pleaded for the *nonextension* of slavery—not for abolition or racial equality.

A leader on his way. Lincoln represented the thinking of the old Northwest, where the Republican party had originated and where it was

#An important point. Abolition of slavery was impossible then; nonextension was not.

strongest. As a former Whig, Lincoln approved of internal improvements and tariffs, which made him acceptable also to the Northeast. Lincoln was only partly right when he wrote after his defeat in the Senate race: ". . . though I now sink out of view and shall be forgotten, I believe I have made some marks which will tell for the cause of civil liberty long after I've gone."

The national scene. Circumstances were already creating a call for a Republican capable of leading nationally. As a result of a depression in 1857, bad times had hit the woolgrowers of Ohio and the iron manufacturers of Pennsylvania. Both pleaded for a higher tariff to protect them from ruinous British competition. In 1858 every Democratic congressman in Pennsylvania was turned out of office.

People in the old Northwest wanted river and harbor legislation in order to improve their marketing facilities. Pierce and Buchanan, however, had repeatedly vetoed such bills. Northwesterners also dreamed of a transcontinental railroad that would enrich one of their own cities, possibly Chicago. Moreover, they were demanding homesteads for themselves or their children.

Southerners watched and listened with growing anxiety. Internal improvements, in general, would not benefit them, yet they had to help pay the cost. Already the burden of the tariff was upon them, they pointed out. Some envisioned the Northwest and the Northeast joining together to milk the South without letup. Furthermore, they knew that free homesteads would only hasten the admission to the Union of more free states to upset further the balance in Congress.

THE ELECTION OF LINCOLN

Americans held their breath as the presidential campaign of 1860 drew near. Was it possible that a Republican triumph would persuade the South to declare its independence of the Union? Reasonable men hoped not. The mutual dependence of the parts of the Union was very great. Said the Nashville newspaper: "No more terrible calamity could befall the

 ##Let the class speculate about the consequences if the North and the South had become two separate countries. In particular, would the economy of either have suffered?

South than the rupture with the North."

The outlook. Moderates on both sides appeared to be in control of events. Attempts by extremists to spread slavery southward to Central America and the Caribbean region had by now failed. An expansionist, William Walker, had had a scheme to take over Nicaragua and bring it into the Union as a slave state, but there had been only limited southern interest. Likewise, some filibustering** attempts to acquire Cuba had been rejected by most southerners as likely to raise more problems for slaveowners that could not be solved. In the North, too, tempers aroused in the 1850's had cooled. Business was improving. The discovery of oil in Pennsylvania (see page 328) was opening new vistas of prosperity.

Raid at Harpers Ferry. Suddenly, like a clap of thunder, came news of violence that once again galvanized the nation. John Brown, with eighteen followers, five of them Negroes, had on October 16, 1859, attempted to seize the federal arsenal at Harpers Ferry, Virginia. His avowed aim had been to distribute the weapons and start a slave insurrection.

After two days of fighting, Brown was captured by a detachment of marines under the command of Colonel Robert E. Lee. The dead included the mayor of Harpers Ferry and two of Brown's sons. Brown was tried for treason, found guilty, and hanged on December 2.

Now the extremists on both sides were heard in a new war of words. Theodore Parker, the Boston minister, asserted that Brown was "not only a martyr . . . but also a saint." The poet Ralph Waldo Emerson said that the hanging of Brown would "make the gallows glorious like the Cross."

A Mobile newspaper described Brown's act as "like a meteor disclosing in its lurid flash the width and depth of that abyss which rends asunder two nations, apparently one." Fearing other attempts to stir the slaves to revolt, the South placed new restrictions on the movements of slaves.

** This use of the word refers to a private citizen's waging unauthorized war against a country with which his own country is at peace.

The time was past when a national leader could appeal successfully to both the North and the South to take the path of moderation. Already the leading Republican candidate for the 1860 nomination, William H. Seward, had called the conflict "irrepressible"—beyond the possibility of being restrained. After Congress convened in December, 1859, the House took weeks even to agree on a Speaker. Senator Hammond said, "The only persons who do not have a revolver and a knife are those who have two revolvers."

The Democratic convention. The Democratic convention of 1860 opened in Charleston, South Carolina, late in April. The southern wing of the party demanded a platform calling clearly for the protection of slavery in the territories. When Douglas' northern supporters, still advocating popular sovereignty, would not agree to this, the southern delegates bolted and the convention broke up.

Later the Douglas Democrats gathered at Baltimore, Maryland, where they quickly nominated their man. The southern bolters, meeting at Baltimore soon afterward, nominated Vice-President John C. Breckinridge, of Kentucky, on a platform that supported slavery in the territories. They also called for the acquisition of Cuba. The rock of slavery had at last split the Democratic party.

The Constitutional Unionists. A handful of former Whigs and Know-Nothings formed the Constitutional Union party. It nominated John Bell, of Tennessee, on a platform denouncing sectional parties—such as the Democratic party had now become—and urging Americans to support the Constitution and the Union.

The Republicans at Chicago. Meanwhile the Republicans were meeting in May in Chicago. A number of hopeful men had their followers there rounding up votes for the nomination. Seward was running first, but he was too closely associated with abolitionists to become the party's choice. The moderates in the Republican ranks did not want to believe that the conflict was "irrepressible," even though they were opposed to the further extension of slavery.

The preceding February Lincoln had gone

east, where he was less well known, and had delivered a speech at Cooper Union, a college in New York City. Although it was a snowy night, 1500 people—the best "of the intellect and culture of our city," according to the *Tribune*'s editor, Horace Greeley—braved the weather to attend.

Lincoln, his new broadcloth suit wrinkled and baggy from the long journey, did not disappoint the audience with his words. He rejected northern extremism as well as popular sovereignty. But he said that slavery was wrong and there must be no extension of it. He also said that the people should not be frightened by threats to destroy the Union. "Let us have faith," he urged, "that right makes might, and in that faith, let us, to the end, dare to do our duty as we understand it."

This was the Lincoln the Chicago convention named on the third ballot. The party platform made a broad appeal. It offered farmers free homesteads; it pledged tariff protection to the iron manufacturers of Pennsylvania and New Jersey; it promised immigrants that there would be no changes in the naturalization laws; and it had generous words for the workingman. It also declared for immediate federal aid to build a railroad to the Pacific.

Triumph for the Rail Splitter. The division in Democratic party ranks made a Republican victory certain. The voting went according to sectional lines, and Lincoln received only 26,400 votes in the slave states. The final results were Lincoln, 1,866,352; Douglas, 1,375,157; Breckinridge, 849,781; Bell, 589,581. Douglas and Bell, the two middle-of-the-road candidates, together polled over 100,000 more votes than Lincoln. In the electoral college, however, the Republican victory was conclusive: Lincoln, 180; Breckinridge, 72; Bell, 39; Douglas, 12.

DISUNION

Lincoln's election aroused deep concern and uncertainty in the South. Southerners had come to believe that a triumph for the Republicans would mean abolition. A Georgian recorded what it was like on election night as he awaited the returns in his home:

I called my wife and little ones together around my family altar, and together we prayed to God to stay the wrath of our oppressors, and preserve the Union of our fathers. . . .

South Carolina's convention. Immediately after the results were known, South Carolina called a convention. On December 20 it passed an ordinance stating "that the union now subsisting between South Carolina and other states under the name of the United States of America is hereby dissolved." In this terrible hour for the Union, President Buchanan, old and sick, did practically nothing. Imagine Jackson at this moment in history!

Buchanan sent a weak message to Congress when it met in December. Seward snorted that in effect the President had said: "It is the duty of the President to execute the laws—unless somebody opposes him; and that no state has a right to go out of the Union—unless it wants to."

Farewell at Springfield. Meanwhile in Springfield, Illinois, the Lincolns prepared to move to the White House. The President-elect bade farewell to his law partner, William Herndon, and climbed aboard the train that would take him to Washington. In the cold rain he said a few words to his Springfield friends and neighbors:

To this place, and the kindness of these people, I owe everything. . . . I now leave, not knowing when, or whether ever, I may return, with a task before me greater than that which rested upon Washington. . . . Trusting in Him who can go with me, and remain with you and be everywhere for good, let us confidently hope that all will yet be well.

Sum and Substance

1. Describe the background of the Dred Scott case and state the decision. 2. How did it affect slavery? The North? The Democratic party in the North? 3. What was the Freeport doctrine? 4. How did the Lincoln-Douglas debates affect the participants? 5. Describe the raid at Harpers Ferry. What was its effect? 6. Who were the presidential nominees in 1860? Who was elected? On what platform?

On the first two ballots at the Republican convention, Seward led. But his views on slavery were too extreme--the party was committed only to preventing its spread.

THE WORKSHOP

OF LASTING SIGNIFICANCE

What part did each of the following have in the dividing of the United States?

William H. Seward	John Brown
gag rule	Charles Sumner
Wilmot Proviso	Preston Brooks
Lewis Cass	James Buchanan
squatter sovereignty	Ostend Manifesto
Barnburners	Dred Scott decision
Free-Soil party	obiter dicta
Compromise of 1850	Lecompton
John Greenleaf	Constitution
Whittier	Abraham Lincoln
Fugitive Slave Law	Lincoln-Douglas
Uncle Tom's Cabin	debates
Franklin Pierce	Freeport doctrine
Stephen A. Douglas	Republicans
Kansas-Nebraska Bill	Know-Nothings
"Bleeding Kansas"	filibustering
Border Ruffians	Harpers Ferry
Topeka Constitution	Cooper Union

DOCUMENTS IN HISTORY

1. In his speech in 1858, what two work systems did Senator William H. Seward discuss? How did he contrast the states in which each prevailed?

2. How did he account for his idea that a conflict between the two systems was "irrepressible"? To what "attempts at final compromise" did he refer?

3. How can you explain that the phrase "irrepressible conflict" caught on in Seward's own time and became well known in American history?

AMERICAN DEMOCRACY

1. State the specific problem connected with slavery which the Mexican War raised in the nation. How was the problem directly related to the war? Was the problem new? Explain.

An early and necessary step in solving any problem is to consider possible solutions. In this case name four. Why was no one of them adopted? Compare the Compromise of 1850 with the four alternatives and tell how Clay combined certain of the ideas from them.

2. How did Douglas bring the same problem before the people in 1854? How was it disposed of then? With what results?

3. In a democracy a new political party is # formed whenever a substantial number of people join efforts in trying by peaceful political means to gain acceptance for their ideas. Why are political parties necessary in democracies?

To break with one party and form another is a democratic privilege. How did Americans exercise it in 1854? Explain how the formation of the Republican party proved that many Americans were dissatisfied with both the Compromise of 1850 and the Kansas-Nebraska Bill.

4. Solving problems is difficult when people's emotions interfere with their ability to think critically about matters of common concern and arrive at workable conclusions through "democratic give-and-take." Cite incidents that occurred between 1846 and 1860 which show that both northerners and southerners allowed their emotions to sway their judgment.

5. Why was the Civil War a particularly ## ugly blot on American democracy?

BEING A SOCIAL SCIENTIST

1. Both the Federalists and the Whigs died out as political parties. How were the Federalist and Whig viewpoints kept alive?

2. Review Calhoun's speech in the House on February 4, 1817 (quoted on pages 162–163), particularly the ending. How had Calhoun's position changed by 1850? What reasons did he give for the change?

3. What are the essential elements of a political compromise? Draw on the compromises in 1820, 1832–1833, and 1850 for details to illustrate your answer.

4. In 1860 a majority of northerners voted for Lincoln, a minority for Douglas. A majority of southerners voted for Breckinridge, a large minority for Bell. Account for this voting.

Lincoln's second inaugural speech was chosen for the beginning of this chapter because it expresses best the President's views on the Civil War near the end of the conflict, and it shows that he was thinking in terms of a united nation in the future, a nation in which sympathy and compassion would be extended to all victims of the war--in both the South and the North. Observe that he says that at the beginning the North was not fighting to end slavery, but to preserve the Union. At stake was federalism, and democracy itself. How had the purpose of fighting changed?

15

THE WAR BETWEEN THE SECTIONS

And the war came.

Fellow-Countrymen: At this second appearing to take the oath of the presidential office [March 4, 1865], there is less occasion for an extended address than there was at the first [March 4, 1861]. Then a statement, somewhat in detail, of a course to be pursued, seemed fitting and proper. . . . The progress of our arms, upon which all else chiefly depends, is as well known to the public as to myself; and it is, I trust, reasonably satisfactory and encouraging to all. With high hope for the future, no prediction in regard to it is ventured.

On the occasion corresponding to this four years ago, all thoughts were anxiously directed to an impending civil war. All dreaded it—all sought to avert it. While the inaugural address

There are 35 stars in the flag seen here. The Confederate flag also had one star for each state--13 stars in all, 11 for the Confederate states and 2 for border states it hoped to win over.

Men and women in Philadelphia hail a parade of volunteers for service in the Union army.

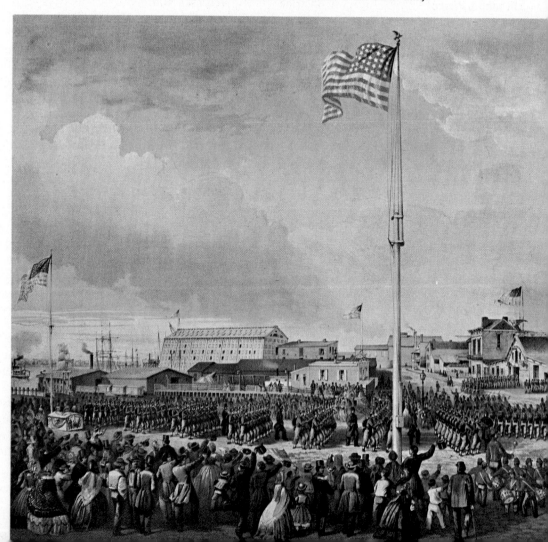

#How true this was. The Confederacy at first relied on victory through swift, decisive successes in battle. Eventually it was thought that the North could be beaten by prolonging the war as long as possible and breaking northern enthusiasm for fighting.

was being delivered from this place, devoted altogether to *saving* the Union without war, insurgent agents were in the city seeking to *destroy* it without war—seeking to dissolve the Union, and divide effects, by negotiation. Both parties deprecated war; but one of them would *make* war rather than let the nation survive; and the other would *accept* war rather than let it perish. And the war came.

One-eighth of the whole population were colored slaves, not distributed generally over the Union, but localized in the Southern part of it. These slaves constituted a peculiar and powerful interest. All knew that this interest was, somehow, the cause of the war. To strengthen, perpetuate, and extend this interest was the object for which the insurgents would rend the Union, even by war; while the government claimed no right to do more than to restrict the territorial enlargement of it.

Neither party expected for the war the magnitude or the duration which it has already attained. Neither anticipated that the *cause* of the conflict might cease with, or even before, the conflict itself should cease. Each looked for an easier triumph, and a result less fundamental and astounding. Both read the same Bible, and pray to the same God; and each invokes His aid against the other. It may seem strange that any men should dare to ask a just God's assistance in wringing their bread from the sweat of other men's faces; but let us judge not that we be not judged. . . .

Fondly do we hope—fervently do we pray—that this mighty scourge of war may speedily pass away. Yet, if God wills that it continue, until all the wealth piled by the bond-man's two hundred and fifty years of unrequited toil shall be sunk, and until every drop of blood drawn with the lash shall be paid by another drawn with the sword, as was said three thousand years ago, so still it must be said "the judgments of the Lord are true and righteous altogether."

With malice toward none; with charity for all; with firmness in the right, as God gives us to see the right, let us strive on to finish the work we are in; to bind up the nation's wounds; to care for him who shall have borne the battle, and for his widow, and his orphan—to do all which may achieve and cherish a just, and a lasting peace, among ourselves, and with all nations.

Kean Archives

Abraham Lincoln came to the White House in 1861, bent on saving the Union above all else. In this, his second inaugural address, in 1865, one sees how the course of the war has changed his viewpoint. Whatever doubts he may have had about abolition before, there is no mistaking his feeling now. His haunting eloquence reveals, too, the intensity of emotion that four years of battle have aroused.

This speech shares a place with the one Lincoln delivered at Gettysburg in 1863 as a superb example of his exquisite gift of language.

##Undoubtedly this would have been the spirit of Lincoln's reconstruction policy, had he lived.

RECONCILIATION FAILS IN THE CRISIS OF THE UNION

The secession of South Carolina sent a wave of shock through the entire Union. Oliver Wendell Holmes, Sr., caught the feeling of the North in a poem he wrote early in 1861 entitled "Brother Jonathan's Lament for Sister Caroline." It contained this verse:

> She has gone,—she has left us in passion and
>   pride,—
> Our stormy-browed sister, so long at our side!
> She has torn her own star from our firma-
>   ment's glow,
> And turned on her brother the face of a foe!

THE CONFEDERACY

South Carolina was not long alone. Although a minority tried to block the step, other states quickly followed it into secession: Mississippi on January 9, Florida on January 10, Alabama on January 11, Georgia on January 19, Louisiana on January 26, and Texas on February 1. Virginia, Arkansas, Tennessee, and North Carolina did not secede at this time, but they served notice that they would oppose any attempt to force a state back into the Union.

On February 4 representatives of the seceded states gathered at Montgomery, Alabama, to arrange for united action. They agreed to establish the Confederate States of America, and they adopted a constitution similar in many ways to the Constitution of the United States.

Constitutional provisions. The new frame of government, as expected, fully protected slavery —although it prohibited the African slave trade. The Confederate congress was specifically forbidden to pass tariff or internal-improvements legislation. The new constitution did not explicitly allow for the secession of states, but the Confederates understood that such specific mention was not required.

In Washington President Buchanan seemed to lack a plan. He hoped to avoid war. "The fact is," he said, "that our Union rests upon public opinion, and can never be cemented by the blood of its citizens shed in civil war."

Crittenden's compromise. For a time optimists believed that compromise might still win out, and a number of proposals were made. A notable set was advanced in December by Senator John J. Crittenden, of Kentucky, who, like his predecessor, Henry Clay, tried to be a peacemaker.

The Crittenden Compromise would have drawn the Missouri Compromise line of 36°30′ to the Pacific. Slavery would have been prohibited north of the line and allowed to expand freely south of it. Owners of slaves would have been compensated for unrecovered runaways.

Lincoln, the President-elect, was willing to accept compromise—but not on extending slavery into the territories. He advised a Republican congressman: "There is no possible compromise upon it [opening the territories to slavery]. . . . Hold firm, as with a chain of steel." Crittenden pressed for a national referendum on his proposals, but Republican support for it was lacking.

The Virginia peace convention. The biggest effort to heal the breach was a peace convention called by Virginia. It brought together in Washington representatives of twenty-one states on the very day the seceding states were meeting in Montgomery. The presiding officer was former President John Tyler. The delegates finally proposed amending the Constitution along the lines of the Crittenden Compromise. When the conclusions were presented to the Senate two days before Buchanan's term ended, practically nobody backed them.

A HARRIED PRESIDENT

The President-elect, meanwhile, was on his way from Springfield. He had been reliably informed that an assassination plot against him was being hatched in Baltimore. Against his wishes he was secretly put aboard a special train that brought him into Washington without fanfare, early on the morning of February 23, 1861.

His inauguration. On March 4 Lincoln rode gravely to the Capitol for his inauguration. Stooped and drawn at eighty-four, Chief Justice Taney—whose court had, in the Dred Scott

##The atmosphere for compromise was hostile. Southerners had already started to withdraw from Congress; Republicans could not retreat from the principle upon which the party was founded.

Harper's Weekly, January 26, 1861

The main battery of guns at Fort Sumter in the early months of 1861, when it was preparing to face an attack from the secessionists. This engraving was made from a drawing by one of Major Anderson's officers.

General Pierre G. T. Beauregard commanded the troops that fired on Fort Sumter, April 12, 1861.

decision, done so much to bring on the crisis—administered the oath of office. Senator Douglas, who had also contributed to the making of the trouble, was among those who sat on the platform. His presence showed that many northern Democrats were lining up with Republicans in this hour of trial.

Lincoln's inaugural address contained words of conciliation, but not of retreat. The new President promised that slavery would be protected wherever it already existed, but he said, "no state, upon its own mere motion, can lawfully get out of the Union. . . ."

Lincoln was appealing, of course, to the slave states that had not seceded to remain loyal to the Union. He hoped, he said in his conclusion, that "the mystic chords of memory, stretching from every battlefield and patriot grave, to every living heart and hearthstone, all over this broad land, will yet swell the chorus of the Union. . . ."

Fort Sumter. No President upon coming to office ever had faced such overpowering problems as Lincoln. The Confederate states had been seizing federal ports and arsenals located within their boundaries. Major Robert Anderson, who commanded United States troops at Fort Moultrie, a fort in Charleston Harbor, South Carolina, had withdrawn his men to the more easily defended Fort Sumter. It was in the same harbor.

Fort Sumter became the symbol of the struggle between the secessionists and the government at Washington. Early in January President Buchanan had attempted to send Anderson provisions and reinforcements; but the unarmed vessel carrying them had been forced by heavy fire from shore to turn back.

The first shot. What to do about Fort Sumter was now Lincoln's problem. He moved slowly lest he make a blunder that could never be undone. Should he make a show of strength by using force to supply Fort Sumter? Or should he avoid this in order to hold the goodwill of moderates—especially those in border states?

Lincoln consulted with his Cabinet and with his friends. But the ultimate decision was his to make and the responsibility his to bear. After searching his mind, he decided on April 6 to send provisions to Fort Sumter. He so in-

#Southerners had seized the United States arsenal at Charleston on December 30, 1860. Buchanan refused to remove United States troops from Charleston Harbor.

formed the state of South Carolina and Major Anderson, whose supplies by now were almost exhausted.

On April 12, before the relief ship arrived, shore batteries opened fire on Fort Sumter.* Two days later its garrison surrendered. The # Civil War had started. Almost immediately Lincoln issued a proclamation calling for 75,000 volunteers to suppress the secessionists.

Sum and Substance

1. In his second inaugural Lincoln gave what as the direct cause of the Civil War? What part did he say slavery had played? 2. Name the first five states of the Confederacy. 3. What was the Crittenden Compromise? Who opposed it? 4. Why did the Virginia peace convention fail? 5. Where and in what circumstances was the first shot in the war fired?

This section describes the course of the Civil War, including international complications.

THE NATION SUBMITS TO A DECISIVE CLASH OF ARMS

All parties in the North were united by the shame and anger that the firing on Sumter evoked. Douglas, who died in June, had said in his last speech: "Whoever is not prepared to sacrifice party organizations and platforms on the altar of his country does not deserve the support . . . of honest people." The administration stopped calling itself "Republican," as Democrats flocked to its support. The Republicans and the Democrats who joined them took the name "Union party."

THE BLUE AND THE GRAY

Throughout the North meetings were called expressing devotion to the Union cause. From the South came sharp words of defiance as both sides girded themselves to fight.

Lincoln's Cabinet. The President's Cabinet represented many shades of opinion. The Secretary of State was William H. Seward of New York— the "red-headed upstart" who had been favored by the more radical Republicans for the presidential nomination in 1860. Seward at first considered Lincoln a country bumpkin whom *he* would have to teach; but shortly the Secretary wrote, "The President is the best of us."

Lincoln had chosen Salmon P. Chase, an Ohio antislavery leader, as head of the Department of the Treasury. Intensely religious, Chase was also intensely ambitious. He often seemed to be under the spell of his attractive daughter, Kate, who wanted to make her father president

of the United States. Gideon Welles, of Connecticut, had been put in charge of the Department of the Navy. This gave representation to New England. Wearing a heavy beard and a light-brown wig, Welles looked like an Old Testament prophet.

The office of Secretary of War had gone to the important Pennsylvania political boss Simon Cameron. The border states were represented by Edward Bates, of Missouri, who became Attorney General, and Montgomery Blair, of Maryland—whose father had been in Jackson's "kitchen cabinet"—who became the Postmaster General. All were strong personalities, but Lincoln was able to get the best out of them.

The border states. The opening of hostilities led Virginia,† Arkansas, North Carolina, and Tennessee to decide to join the seceded states. Only four slave states—the border states—still remained loyal to the federal government: Delaware, Maryland, Kentucky, and Missouri. National feeling prevailed in each, although all contained large numbers of Confederate sympathizers. These people were reassured by Lincoln's statements that he meant to save the Union—not to free the slaves.

Northern confidence. Soon in the North was heard the cry, "On to Richmond!"—where the Confederate capital was located. And why not? The Union had twenty-three states, including those of the border, compared with eleven in

---

* The man said to have fired the first shot was Edmund Ruffin, a Virginian who had recently published a book describing the advantages of a self-governing South.

† The western part of Virginia, which had close ties with the Ohio Valley, was antislavery. Long fiercely hostile to the coastal planters, it refused to secede. In 1863 it was admitted to the Union as West Virginia.

##Lincoln had no personal friends or followers in the Cabinet. The members were political appointees. He was successful, however, in uniting them in the effort to save the Union.

the Confederacy. The North had a population of 22,000,000, opposing one of only 9,500,000, of which over a third was slave.

The North had the advantage of a growing railroad network, expanding industry, and diversified agriculture. The South depended on the raising of agricultural staples: cotton, rice, tobacco, and sugar. It imported much of its food and practically all of its manufactured goods.

The North had banks and plentiful capital; the South was short of both. The South, unlike the North, lacked, as we have seen, an adequate railroad system. In sea power, the North was superior to the South from the start. Many northerners calmly expected that the rebels would be thrashed in three months.

Southern assurance. What, then, accounted for the confidence of the Confederates? First, southerners were strengthened by their belief that they were fighting to preserve their very homes. Second, they had a head start in accumulating war equipment and in recruiting troops. Third, they had superior military leadership, especially in the lower ranks. Southerners had often made the army their careers. Many of their young men had attended not only West Point but also other military schools. Like the Union, the Confederacy relied on West Pointers for its highest-ranking commanders, but it took several years for the Union to find army leaders who matched the southern generals.

Fourth, the Confederates expected that a northern blockade would produce a cotton famine in England and France. This, they thought, would persuade those countries to help the South in order to keep their own factories going. Fifth, southerners refused to conclude that they were going to lose merely because they were outnumbered. A reading of history showed them that superior numbers did not always guarantee an army's victory.

Dixie's leaders. The president of the Confederacy, chosen by the Montgomery convention, was Jefferson Davis, of Mississippi. "A man of throbbing nerves," as his wife described him, he was a West Point graduate who had been Secretary of War in Pierce's Cabinet and a United States Senator. Davis' associates ad-

Harper's Weekly, July 20, 1861 (New York Public Library)

Uncle Sam bars John Bull from the Confederacy—a northern cartoon published in the summer of 1861. The situation depicted is one the southerners expected. Compare the Uncle Sam seen here with the figure used today.

The blockade kept southern cotton in and foreign munitions out of the South.

mired his courage and honesty, but as the war progressed they saw that he was inclined to reject advice and to overestimate the correctness of his own opinions.

Davis' administration consisted in the main of men representing the ideals of the expanding Cotton Kingdom rather than the traditions of the old South. The leading Cabinet figure, often called "the brains of the Confederacy," was Judah P. Benjamin, of Louisiana, who became Secretary of State in 1862, after serving as Attorney General and Secretary of War.

The outstanding military leaders were from the old South—for example, the Virginians Lee, Thomas J. Jackson, J. E. B. Stuart, and Joseph E. Johnston, and the popular Georgian James Longstreet. But whether from the old South or from the newer cotton-raising regions, southerners believed that they were fighting for their independence, as the patriots of 1776 had.

HOSTILITIES: OPENING PHASE

In broad outline, northern strategy was to capture Richmond, Virginia, the southern capital; blockade the ports of the South; and seize control of the Mississippi and Tennessee rivers.

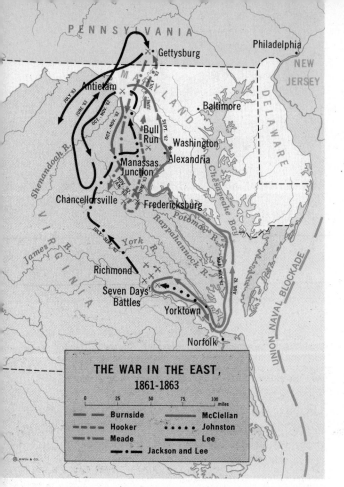

THE WAR IN THE EAST,
1861-1863

| 0 | 25 | 50 | 75 | 100 |
| | | | | miles |

- - - Burnside   —— McClellan
- · - · Hooker   · · · · Johnston
- · — · Meade   —— Lee
- · — · Jackson and Lee

What main objective was the Union army evidently intent
on accomplishing? What were the Confederates seeking
to do? Which plans seemed more promising?
(The Union army was trying to take Richmond.)

The Union army in the West would join the
army in the East to destroy the Confederacy
after first cutting it to pieces. This has sometimes been called the "anaconda policy" after
the snake that crushes its victims to death. The
Confederates intended to race northward, capture Washington, go through Maryland into
central Pennsylvania, and divide the North into
two parts.

First Bull Run. By July there were wild de-
mands in the North for action. General Winfield Scott, general in chief of the army, yielded
to the clamor. On July 16 he sent General Irvin
McDowell, who commanded 30,000 men just
outside Washington, southward on the way to
Richmond.

At Manassas Junction, Virginia, troops under
General Pierre G. T. de Beauregard stopped the

#Lincoln had hoped to avoid battles in the
border states for fear of alienating them.

Union army's advance in the first Battle of
Bull Run (named for a nearby creek). Mc-
Dowell seemed to have victory in his grasp, but
Confederate reinforcements arrived under General Joseph E. Johnston. Moreover, a brigade
under General Thomas J. Jackson held firm as
a rock (and earned Jackson the nickname
"Stonewall"). McDowell's men fled headlong
back to Washington.

A gasp of disbelief went through the North.
Congressmen and their families and some others
had hired carriages, had provided themselves
with box lunches, and had gone to Bull Run
to see the rebels routed. Instead, they had fled
pell-mell back to the capital barely ahead of the
soldiers. Lincoln had grimly watched the confusion from the White House.

The defense of Washington. On the following day
Lincoln called in General George B. McClellan,
placing him in charge of the defense of the
capital. But the war in the East had entered a
period of inaction. McClellan's "Army of the
Potomac," as it was called, would for some
time be laboriously putting itself into shape.

The war in the West. In the West, meanwhile,
major operations were getting under way. A
force under General George H. Thomas, in
January, 1862, decisively defeated the Confederates at Mill Springs, Kentucky. This un-
locked the door to a large-scale invasion of east
Tennessee.

The objectives of the Union forces were the
posts held by the Confederates at Columbus,
Kentucky, on the Mississippi River; Fort Henry
on the Tennessee; and Fort Donelson on the
Cumberland. The seizure of these defended
places was part of the plan to cut the Confederacy in two. In coördination with a gunboat
flotilla, an army under General Ulysses S. Grant
brought about the surrender of Fort Henry on
February 6, 1862.

The evacuation of Nashville. Most of the Confederate garrison had, however, retreated to Fort
Donelson, the strong point from which the
Confederate general Albert Sidney Johnston was
defending the important city of Nashville, Tennessee. Grant moved on Fort Donelson, and
after a short duel between the defenders of the

##The hoped-for advance to capture Richmond, the Confederate capital, resulted in the exposure
to attack of the northern capital, Washington, D.C.

#As a military leader, Grant knew the value of capitalizing on momentum in battle, and he did not hesitate to pursue his enemy in retreat, regardless of his own losses.

fort and the Union gunboats, the Confederate forces prepared to surrender, on February 16. The Confederate general Simon Buckner asked for Grant's terms.

Grant's reply was terse and plain (the Confederates considered it "ungenerous and unchivalrous"): "No terms except unconditional and immediate surrender. . . ." Buckner had no choice but to accept. Not only were 12,000 first-class Confederate troops captured with their equipment; but also Johnston now retreated from Kentucky, where he evacuated Columbus, and from Nashville as well.

\#   **Ulysses S. Grant.** Northerners, rejoicing in their first great triumph, thought victory in the war itself was near. Gloated the *New York Times*, "The monster is already clutched and in his death struggle." Although such optimism was premature, the North had found a general of stature in "Unconditional Surrender" Grant.

Grant was then thirty-nine years old. Rescued from poverty in Ohio by an opportunity to attend West Point, he had been graduated below the middle of his class in 1843. His performance as a lieutenant in the Mexican War had been excellent. After peace came, he was sent to the Pacific coast, where loneliness for his wife, Julia, seems to have led him to drink heavily. Forced to resign from the service

in 1854, he was soon a failure in business, too.

The governor of Illinois had given Grant a fresh chance in the spring of 1861 by appointing him colonel of an unruly regiment. Shortly afterward he was made a brigadier general. Said his father on learning the news, "Be careful, Ulyss, you are a general now—it's a good job, don't lose it!" Lincoln now promoted him to major general. Despite Grant's heavy drinking, Lincoln stood by him, because, the President said, "He fights."

"Bloody Shiloh." Grant shortly moved his army of about 35,000 from Forts Henry and Donelson up the Tennessee River and had pitched camp at Pittsburg Landing. On Sunday, April 6, as the men sat at breakfast, Albert Sidney

(The first, to gain control of the western rivers.)

Which aspects of northern strategy can be identified here? Describe General Bragg's countermove. Notice that there was no significant fighting west of the Mississippi.

Ulysses S. Grant, a son of the old Northwest, who was the successful general President Lincoln had hoped for. Grant was originally named "Hiram Ulysses."

Lincoln's search for an effective general was his greatest frustration in the war.

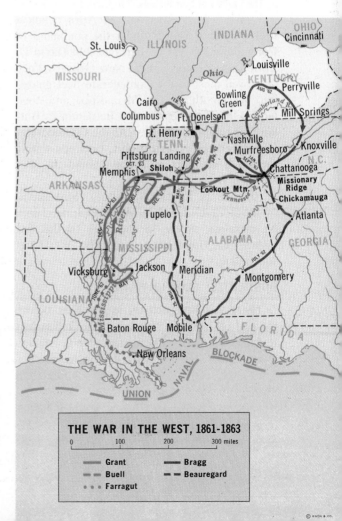

THE WAR IN THE WEST, 1861-1863

| 0 | 100 | 200 | 300 miles |

——— Grant	——— Bragg
— — Buell	— — Beauregard
• • • Farragut	

Johnston attacked them violently. The southern forces drove back Grant's outposts, which had extended toward Shiloh Church, located 2 or 3 miles from Pittsburg Landing.

The ensuing battles raged twelve hours, and in one of them Johnston himself fell mortally wounded. By evening it appeared that the Confederates had won, but during the night General Don Carlos Buell brought Union reinforcements. Their arrival gave Grant 25,000 fresh troops to throw into the battle by daybreak.

When the Confederates, under Beauregard now, finally had been driven into retreat, the Federals—the Blues—counted 13,000 dead, wounded, or missing, and the Grays close to 11,000. On each side one man in four was a casualty. For a generation afterward the mention of "bloody Shiloh" would make veterans of both sides shudder in horror as they recalled the heaviest and costliest fighting of the war.

The capture of New Orleans. The first phase of the war in the West ended late in April, when a fleet of federal vessels under the command of Commodores David G. Farragut and David D. Porter ran past the forts at New Orleans. They destroyed most of the Confederate fleet guarding the mouth of the Mississippi and then landed the troops of General Benjamin F. Butler, who took over the city. As the Confederates abandoned their greatest port, fires consuming thousands of bales of cotton lighted the way for their retreat.

An attempt to take Vicksburg, Mississippi, by naval attack failed in May and June, 1862. Nevertheless, as the second year of the war began, the Union strategy in the West was succeeding.

HOSTILITIES: SECOND PHASE

There was little activity in the East before the end of 1861. In November McClellan had replaced Scott—his old commander in Mexico—as general in chief of the Union forces. Because McClellan was somewhat shorter than average, he was known as "Little Mac" and "The Little Napoleon." As a military leader he was contemptuous of civilian authority. He even had scorn for Lincoln, whom he considered inferior to himself. In fact, he entertained ideas that he might become dictator of the United States if he was successful in battle.

Brilliant in making plans, McClellan was timid in carrying them out. A perfectionist, he was constantly saying that he needed more men and more time to get them ready. His magnificent Army of the Potomac was well drilled, and he held grand reviews of it. But it did not budge. Northern newspapers and politicians were demanding action, and Republicans were even hinting darkly that McClellan, a Democrat in politics, had prosouthern sympathies. In January, 1862, Lincoln issued a special order to McClellan to move his army by February 22.

Edwin M. Stanton. A significant change had occurred in the Department of War. Lincoln, having removed the corrupt and insubordinate secretary Simon Cameron, had replaced him with Edwin M. Stanton, once Buchanan's Attorney General. Stanton at first detested Lincoln. But he came to respect the President and to give needed energy to the directing of the war effort. He decided that McClellan's army must either "fight or run away."

Toward Richmond. Lincoln thought that McClellan should move his army of 130,000 across the Potomac, assault the greatly outnumbered Confederate forces, and advance directly on Richmond. But when McClellan finally pushed off on March 17, he had decided to approach the Confederate capital by way of the lower Chesapeake Bay. This decision meant a peninsular campaign between the James and York rivers.

Laid under siege for a month, Yorktown fell to McClellan on May 4. By the middle of May, the Army of the Potomac stood 20 miles from Richmond waiting for reinforcements—which it did not need—for the drive on the southern capital.

Meanwhile, in the Shenandoah Valley "Stonewall" Jackson, with 10,000 men, was keeping a Union force much larger than his own pinned down. His aim was to harass the Union generals and to threaten the safety of Washington, thus preventing reinforcements

Students should follow McClellan's moves by looking at the map on p. 276. Jackson's and Lee's moves are also shown.

from being sent to McClellan. The strategy worked: 20,000 men had to be detached from McClellan's army and rushed to the valley.

Finally, in slow stages McClellan pressed to within 5 miles of Richmond by the end of May, where the Confederate general Joseph E. Johnston attacked him. An indecisive battle followed, but Johnston was badly wounded.

The defense of Richmond passed to Robert E. Lee, who took command of the Confederate Army of Northern Virginia. At this point began the terrible Seven Days' Battles (June 25 to July 1). In the bloody encounters the Confederates lost twice as many men as the Union army, but McClellan had to retreat 20 miles.

Changes in the Union command. Now arose a cry in the North for McClellan's scalp. The myth developed that with more vigor "Little Mac" could "easily" have captured Richmond. Having removed McClellan as general in chief in March, Lincoln now replaced him with General Henry W. Halleck, who had been in overall command in the West. Certain elements of the Army of the Potomac were placed in the hands of General John Pope.

Neither appointment was a good one, and the experimenting to get a general who would both fight and win continued. Soon McClellan would have command of all the Army of the Potomac again, then A. E. Burnside would have it, then Joseph Hooker, then George G. Meade. Not

until Grant took it did the East have a general who measured up to the needs of the Union.

Robert E. Lee. In 1862 the Confederate army was still immensely strong. Furthermore, no northern generals matched Lee and Jackson. Lee, especially, was already becoming a legend. He was the son of "Light-Horse Harry" Lee, a hero of the American Revolution, and the husband of Mary Custis, the daughter of Martha Washington's grandson. He had had an outstanding record in the Mexican War and as superintendent of West Point.

Second Bull Run. In the closing days of August, 1862, Lee attacked and badly defeated Pope in the second Battle of Bull Run, although the 75,000 Union soldiers faced only 48,000 Confederates. A torrential downpour prevented Lee's army from marching on Washington. Now McClellan resumed his old place, and once again the Union had its cautious general in command of the whole Army of the Potomac. "Little Mac" prepared to meet Lee's army.

Antietam: turning point. At Antietam Creek in Maryland on September 17, McClellan's troops caught Lee's, and they clashed in the most murderous single day of the war. Each side suffered almost 12,000 casualties. Both sides claimed victory: the Confederates because they were allowed to recross the Potomac unmolested, and the Federals because they had stopped the Confederate advance northward.

The place where the Battle of Antietam occurred is marked on the map on p. 276.

Astride his black horse "Daniel Webster," McClellan rides along the northern line in the Battle of Antietam, fought in the hills bordering the creek for which the engagement is named. Lee and Jackson led the Confederates.

Battles and Leaders of the Civil War, The Century Company, 1888

#While England desired southern cotton, cotton could be obtained from other places within the British Empire. However, England could not do without the wheat produced in the North.

The effects of Antietam were profound. The British had already considered calling a meeting to propose mediation in the war when the dispatches about Antietam began to arrive. The French seem to have been prepared to coöperate in such a move.

The news persuaded England and France that the Union was at last strong enough to put down the rebellion. If they had formally offered to mediate, they would, in effect, have been granting official recognition to the Confederacy and opening the way to sending military and financial assistance.

Emancipation. Antietam also gave Lincoln the occasion to resolve the single problem tormenting him most: what to do about slavery. He had continued to seek the goodwill of the war Democrats and the border-state slaveowners by avoiding talk of emancipation. But the antislavery Republicans were pressing him harder and harder to liberate the slaves.

In July Lincoln had told his Cabinet that he had decided to issue an emancipation proclamation. Seward had advised waiting until there should be an important victory in battle. Otherwise, he had said, emancipation would sound like "the last shriek on our retreat."

Five days after Antietam—on September 22—Lincoln announced in a preliminary proclamation his intention to free, on the following New Year's Day, all slaves in states still in rebellion against the United States. Congress, under pressure from the abolitionists, had ended slavery in the District of Columbia and in the territories. On January 1, 1863, the President issued the Emancipation Proclamation.

The Proclamation did not immediately free a single slave. In the Confederate states it could not be enforced, and in the border states it did not apply. Nevertheless, the moral effect was widespread. As Lincoln said, "In giving freedom to the slave, we assure freedom to the free. . . ."

Lincoln did not issue the Proclamation in a spirit of vindictiveness against the South. As commander in chief, he was using it as a military weapon against the enemy—a way of destroying their property. In areas not at war with the United States it had no legal basis. No slave revolt in the Confederacy resulted from the Proclamation, as some southerners had feared; but wherever the Union armies went, slaves flocked to them, seeking refuge.

Negro troops. Like millions of Americans, Lincoln realized as the war went on that the institution of slavery was going to be destroyed. From the start of the struggle, however, Negroes understood the opportunity it could offer them as a people. In many places in the North they tried to enlist in the Union army—only to be rebuffed at first. But, beginning in 1862, they began to be accepted into uniform.

The first Negro soldiers were three regiments of free Negroes of Louisiana and two of former slaves (the First South Carolina and First Kansas Colored regiments). The first unit formed of northern Negroes was the 54th Massachusetts Infantry, under the command of Colonel Robert G. Shaw, of Boston. Frederick Douglass, the leading Negro abolitionist, enthusiastically recruited for the 54th, telling his audiences: "We can get at the throat of treason and slavery through Massachusetts."

Years later Shaw's deputy commander said of the Negro troops: "We called upon them in the day of our trial, when volunteering had ceased, when the draft was a partial failure. . . . Fortunate indeed it is for us, as well as for them, that they were equal to the crisis; that the grand historic moment which comes to a race only once in many centuries came to them, and they recognized it. . . ." Some 38,000 Negro troops died in army service—about a fifth of those enrolled.

Fredericksburg. But only victory over the Confederacy would make emancipation complete. The North was dismayed, therefore, when early in October J. E. B. Stuart's cavalry made a daring raid around the Union army, bringing the colorful "Jeb" temporarily into southern Pennsylvania. Lincoln now removed McClellan again and replaced him with Ambrose E. Burnside.‡

---

‡ Burnside was well known for the style of whiskers he wore on his cheeks, now usually called by his name reversed, "sideburns."

 ##The Proclamation was a military measure issued under the wartime authority granted to the President. It pleased England, the northern states, and the border states.

On the south side of the Rappahannock River at Fredericksburg, Virginia, Lee's men had dug themselves in and were ready when Burnside's army made a frontal assault on them, December 13, 1862. The Union forces had walked into a slaughter. Despite the numerical superiority of the northern troops, the losses they sustained in the two days of the Battle of Fredericksburg were double those of the Confederates.

Chancellorsville. At the end of January, 1863, General Joseph Hooker—affectionately called "Fighting Joe"—took Burnside's place. Late in April Hooker, too, thought the way was clear to march to Richmond, and he was ready to claim everlasting glory. This time, at Chancellorsville, Virginia, Lee drove at Hooker's left and center, as "Stonewall" Jackson jabbed at the right. After three days the northern force withdrew.

The southern victory at Chancellorsville was a costly one for the Confederates. Among their 11,000 casualties was Jackson, wounded accidentally by his own men. Lee said of the fallen general on whom he had depended so heavily, "He has lost his left arm; but I have lost my right arm." A few days later Jackson was dead.

Despite the losses Lee had sustained, he still had not been able to carry the war into the North. This now became his objective.

Gettysburg: beginning of the end. All during the month of June, 1863, Lee maneuvered his great army, under James Longstreet, Richard S. Ewell, and A. P. Hill, northward into Pennsylvania. The climax was at hand. From July 1 to July 3 there raged near the town of Gettysburg the greatest battle of the war, often listed as one of the decisive battles of world history.

On June 28 Lincoln had removed Hooker and turned over the Army of the Potomac to General George G. Meade. During the first day of the battle, the Union forces yielded to Confederate pressure all along their line, and on July 2 they held only a slim footing on a high, curving crest called Cemetery Ridge.

Opposite, about a mile away, on Seminary Ridge, stood the Confederates. Longstreet was planning to outflank Meade's army by attacking at the southern end of Cemetery Ridge on a hill called Little Round Top. But he waited too long: the Union soldiers were dug in well enough to repulse him.

Lee had no choice but to attack head on. On July 3 General George E. Pickett led a daring charge against the Union center. "Up men and to your posts!" he cried. "Don't forget that you are from Old Virginia." Marching with drill-ground precision, the gray-clad figures were mowed down like wheat, and only a handful reached the top of Cemetery Ridge.

The battle was over. On July 4 Lee began his retreat to Virginia. By inexcusably failing to attack, Meade let Lee's army escape. But the high noon of Confederate hopes had now passed, and the shadows began to lengthen.

The fall of Vicksburg. In the West, on the very day Lee's retreat began, the Confederates surrendered Vicksburg to Grant after a six-week siege. The fall of Vicksburg gave the Union complete control of the Mississippi, cutting off Arkansas, Louisiana, and Texas from the rest of the Confederacy.

A Confederate army under General Braxton Bragg had succeeded in occupying strong positions on Lookout Mountain and Missionary Ridge near Chattanooga, Tennessee. Grant, now commanding all Union forces in the West, was joined by General William T. Sherman's Army of the Tennessee, and together they drove Bragg from his position. By December 3 Tennessee, the link between the two parts of the Confederacy, was in Union hands.

HOSTILITIES: FINAL PHASE

Early in 1864 Grant was promoted to lieutenant general and Lincoln called him to the command of all the northern forces. He prepared to go east to conduct the war in Virginia.

Sherman's march. Sherman, who succeeded Grant in the West, began in May, 1864, a drive south from Tennessee. His primary objective was Atlanta, Georgia. After capturing that city, he planned to move toward the Atlantic coast and proceed north to cut off a retreat of Lee's army.

Confederates capture part of the burning Union breastworks in May, 1864, during the battle in the difficult Wilderness area.

The ending of the war in the East, where it began. By 1865 Lee's forces were exhausted and without reserves. The deep South was not only blockaded but was also cut off by Sherman's march to the sea. Lee had no choice but to surrender.

The war ended where it began, in the East.

Diseases claimed as many lives in the war as bullets did.

On September 2 Atlanta fell to Sherman. Leading 60,000 men, he soon set out for the sea, laying waste whatever might have military value in a 50-mile swath across Georgia. Just before Christmas Sherman captured Savannah. Then he turned northward through South Carolina, where his men "lived off the country" in a manner violating his specific orders against pillage and looting.

The Wilderness. Meanwhile, Grant, in Virginia, was moving southward with 100,000 men. At the beginning of May, in his first encounter with Lee—in the fierce Wilderness campaign—he lost 18,000 men; a few days later, at Spotsylvania Court House, he lost another 12,000 men. He left 12,000 more men on the field in a single day's fighting at Cold Harbor on June 3. The battlefields of the Wilderness campaign were among those where the nurse Clara Barton, later the founder of the American Red Cross, gave saintly service to the wounded.

In one month the North had lost more men than were enrolled in Lee's entire army! But the Confederate Army of Northern Virginia was also taking heavy losses, and the outcome

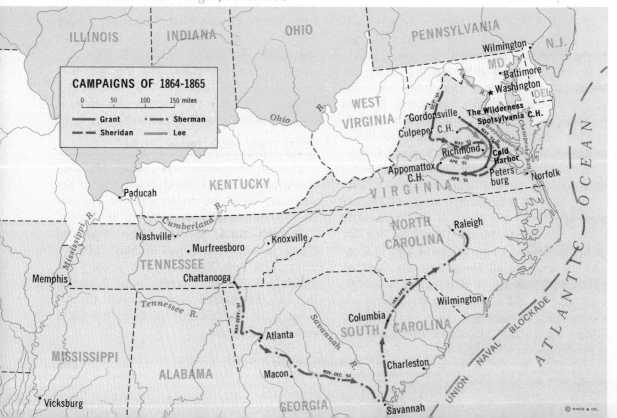

CAMPAIGNS OF 1864-1865

0   50   100   150 miles

—— Grant   •—• Sherman
— — Sheridan   —— Lee

was no longer in doubt. Lee's men were short of food, ammunition, and equipment. They could only delay defeat.

Surrender at Appomattox. By February, 1865, Grant had pushed south of Petersburg, near Richmond. Within six weeks the Confederates were in full and hopeless retreat. Hungry, ill-clad, and exhausted, the magnificent Army of Northern Virginia was no longer a fighting force. On April 7 Lee asked Grant for terms. On April 9 Grant met Lee at Appomattox Court House, a village in Virginia, and the two generals agreed on conditions of surrender. Lee's soldiers were ordered to give up all equipment except side arms and horses and mules which were their own. Grant did not request Lee's sword, and the Virginian did not offer it.

After four nightmarish years, the war was over. The Union had been saved at a fearful cost of about one million battlefield casualties. Peace had come at last. Even today one understands the sense of relief that overwhelmed James Russell Lowell when he wrote in thanksgiving in 1865, "Bow down, dear Land, for Thou hast found release!"

INTERNATIONAL COMPLICATIONS

For more than seventy-five years foreigners had spoken of the United States as the American "experiment." Much evidence seemed to confirm the view that the Union could not last —even the sights a visitor in Washington might see in the late 1850's. Among them were the half-completed dome of the Capitol; the pile of carved stones lying at the base of the monument to Washington, on which work had been abandoned; and the classical Treasury building, still under construction. These looked like the very ruins of an ancient Greek republic. When the Civil War came, it seemed to many people abroad that the American republic, too, was dead and the "experiment" had ended in failure.

Lincoln through foreign eyes. Europeans watched events in America with keen interest. Lincoln, who wore rumpled clothes and whose head was covered with a "thatch of wild republican hair," was unknown abroad. A correspondent for the London *Times* wrote: "A person who

Photo by Mathew Brady, National Archives
The beloved General Lee, after Appomattox. Urging southerners to put aside bitterness, he became president of William College, now Washington and Lee University.

met Mr. Lincoln in the street would not take him to be what—according to the usages of European society—is called a 'gentleman.'" But foreign affairs soon brought Lincoln to prominent public notice in Europe, and his leadership won respect.

England's attitude. When the Civil War began, Lincoln expected foreign governments to maintain officially a hands-off policy. After the North announced its blockade of southern ports, which seemed to recognize the South as a *country* at war with the United States, England announced that it would be neutral. This infuriated northerners because the English were apparently saying that they would treat both sides—as *countries*—equally. The administration argued there was only *one* country and its people were engaged in putting down a rebellion.

Union supporters were especially irritated because, in the main, upper-class Englishmen were openly sympathetic to southerners, whom they considered fellow "aristocrats." But it is doubtful if there would have been popular support in England for English help for the South because English working people were antislavery in sentiment.

Capture on the high seas. Although Britain never recognized the Confederacy, friction developed

#A farmer by the name of McLean had moved from near Manassas, Virginia, to get away from the fighting there. His new farm and house at Appomattox became the scene of the war's end.

in Anglo-American relations. The most serious incident occurred late in 1861, when the Confederacy sent abroad two diplomats, James Mason and John Slidell, in an attempt aimed at obtaining English recognition. They ran the blockade to Havana, Cuba, where they boarded a British mail steamer, the *Trent*, for Europe. Charles Wilkes, § the hotheaded captain of the Union sloop U.S.S. *San Jacinto,* fired across the bow of the *Trent*, stopped the ship, and took off the Confederate commissioners and their secretaries.

The North was delirious with joy at this audacious act. Wilkes was given testimonial dinners as the "hero of the *Trent*." But Lincoln expressed the opinion that the captives might prove to be a heavy burden because the United States would not know what to do with them. In London Wilkes's action was called "a gross outrage and violation of international law"— which it was. Lord John Russell, the British foreign secretary, even hinted at war.

The Union's legal position was weak. In stopping a neutral ship, Wilkes had violated the principle of freedom of the seas, for which the United States had gone to war in 1812. Moreover, if Lincoln yielded the commissioners to the British, as they demanded, northerners would jeer at the weakness of the administration. If he did not yield them, war with England might ensue, which could put an end to the Union.

Happily, the President's patience and tact prevailed: Mason and Slidell were released. In a bold gesture of face-saving, the United States expressed satisfaction over the British recognition at last that the American arguments in 1812 about the rights of neutrals had been correct.

An about-face. But Britons were not always restrained by their government's decision to remain neutral. Despite protests by the American minister Charles Francis Adams, British shipbuilding yards had constructed commerce-

destroying cruisers for the South. Three ships became famous—the *Florida*, the *Shenandoah*, and the *Alabama*. Before ending their raids, they had made over 140 captures.

Although the ships had not been fitted and ## armed—only built—in England, northern feeling against the English ran high. By 1863, when the fortunes of war had turned, the North was thinking of sending privateers against Britain's merchant marine. Almost immediately the British stopped building cruisers for the Confederacy. By the Treaty of Washington in 1871, England expressed regret for its failure earlier to halt the construction of the ships. Ultimately the United States was awarded $15,500,000 for the "*Alabama* claims," that is, for the damages inflicted by Confederate cruisers built in British shipyards.

A French puppet. The Union's relations with France were also tense. The most sensational incident was the French attempt to create a satellite government in Mexico under the Austrian archduke Ferdinand Maximilian. Louis Napoleon aimed to build a Mexican monarchy strong enough to prevent expansion of English-speaking people southward. Maximilian and his lovely and ambitious wife, Carlota, arrived in April, 1864, and went to Mexico City.

At first the United States government seemed indifferent to this obvious violation of the Monroe Doctrine. Then as northern victories began to come after 1862, officials in Washington grew more openly hostile to Maximilian's presence. Fortunately, in April, 1866, the French withdrew, largely because the venture had become too expensive, and guerrilla warfare was taking a heavy toll in lives.‖

Russian goodwill visits. Russia surprised and delighted the Union in 1863 when it sent two fleets to American shores on what was called a goodwill tour. One dropped anchor in New York Harbor, and the other in San Francisco Bay. We now know that fear of war with England and France had led the Russians to send their ships out of European waters, where they

---

§ Wilkes was already known nationally. Between 1838 and 1842 he had commanded the United States Exploring Expedition to the Pacific, the greatest scientific enterprise of its kind in the nineteenth century. Besides charting 280 islands, Wilkes explored 1600 miles of the Antarctica coastline. A part of the continent is today called Wilkes Land.

‖ Maximilian was executed in 1867 after the French had left Mexico. Carlota had gone to Europe to plead—in vain—for aid. She went insane, but lived on tragically in a Belgian château until she died in 1927.

##Confederate ships had also been built in France at the request of the Confederacy. Seeing that the Confederacy could not win, Napoleon III sold the ships to other countries.

could be bottled up easily by the British navy. But at the time, the visiting fleets were looked upon as proof of czarist enthusiasm for the Union cause. Shouted Secretary of the Navy Welles, "God bless the Russians!"

Many people in Europe—maybe more than Americans will ever know—prayed for the success of Union arms. Without exception their governments formally supported the North. This had an important bearing on the war's result, for if the Confederacy had won formal recognition, help might have followed.

Sum and Substance

1. Name the men in Lincoln's Cabinet. 2. What states seceded after April 12, 1861? What ones did not secede? 3. Explain why both the North and the South faced the war confidently. 4. Name the southern leaders. 5. Describe northern war strategy and southern plans. 6. Summarize the hostilities in the first, second, and third phases of the war. 7. When and why did Lincoln issue the Emancipation Proclamation? 8. Give the facts concerning each international difficulty the United States faced during the war.

THE HOME FRONTS SHAPE THE FINAL OUTCOME

As in all modern wars, the men in uniform were dependent on the devotion and productivity of the people at home. The South did not lack devotion, but its economic strength was insufficient for success.

THE SOUTH'S LOST CAUSE

Unquestionably the Union blockade hurt the Confederacy badly,# adding to the economic distress which gradually became more widespread. Food became scarcer as the war progressed. Clothing either was not available or was unevenly distributed. Southern blockade-runners were more concerned with their own private profit than with helping the Confederacy.

Profiteering was a constant source of anger and frustration. Wrote the governor of North Carolina even before the pinch was generally felt, ". . . the demon of speculation and extortion seems to have seized upon nearly all sorts and conditions of men, and all the necessaries of life are fast getting beyond the reach of the poor."

Lack of industrial development. The shortage of southern manufacturing was also a severe handicap from the very start. A few textile mills were started, but a lack of capital, skilled labor, and machinery proved insurmountable barriers to success. Jefferson Davis expressed his annoyance that millions of dollars were being invested in blockade-running, but practically nothing in manufacturing.

Inadequate railway lines. The inadequacy of the ## small southern railroad network also contributed to losing the war. There were 113 companies operating lines with at least eleven different gauges of track. It was often impossible to run through trains from one part of a state to another, let alone from state to state.

Besides, these lines had poor and insufficient cars and engines, which could not be replaced or correctly repaired. Skilled railroad repairmen gradually disappeared into the army or went home as the result of layoffs caused by the Confederacy's embargo on the shipment of cotton. The rails of branch lines sometimes had to be torn up to repair main lines, because, it was said, not a piece of railroad iron was manufactured in the South during the war.

Shortages of supplies. The Confederate effort was handicapped, too, by shortages of certain specific commodities. One was salt, necessary in preserving meat and fish. A sack costing 65¢ in 1861 sold for $20 four years later.

The shortage of quinine, an antimalarial drug, also caused distress among the southern people. Tea and coffee disappeared, and various concoctions tried as substitutes—such as burnt corn and sassafras—were not successful.

A renowned attempt to break the blockade was made in 1862. Reconstructing the steam frigate *Merrimac* as an ironclad, the Confederates sent it against the wooden federal vessels in Hampton Roads, Virginia. The Union's ironclad, the *Monitor*, engaged the *Merrimac* in an indecisive duel, but the South never seriously challenged the blockade thereafter.

Inefficient use of labor. The southern cause was also damaged by the reluctance to use slave labor for the war effort. At first it was feared that the Negroes would rise against their owners. It seemed out of the question to arm the Negroes, though such a policy was proposed as defeat loomed. Slaves could have built fortifications and worked on the railroads. But in spite of the desperate needs of the Confederacy, owners staunchly resisted efforts of the states or central government to hire bondmen for such work. They were afraid the Negroes might be injured or killed or might run away.

Financial policies. Still another weakness in the Confederate states was the handling of public finances. The government tried to pay for the war by borrowing instead of by taxing. Taxes finally imposed in 1863 were inadequate to meet the needs.

The Confederate states floated bond issues here and abroad, but by the time of Gettysburg these securities had declined sharply in value. The treasury relied on printing presses to turn out paper currency for day-to-day transactions. About $1,500,000,000 in Confederate paper money was in circulation when the war ended —three times the amount of the notes, called "greenbacks," issued by the Union side. The effect was an appalling inflation.

States' rights. Finally, the South was weakened by the very principle of states' rights which had led to secession from the Union. Governors maintained the right, for example, to withdraw soldiers from the Confederate army for state military service. Feuds between local and central authorities over arms, supplies, the drafting of soldiers, and the seizing of property for public use sapped the strength of Dixie. Although the South was national in spirit, its principles of government made the day-to-day conduct of public affairs almost impossible.

THE NORTH'S GOLDEN SUCCESS

Industrialization permitted the North to meet the most pressing need of war—a continuous flow of vital supplies. The production of coal, iron, copper, and salt reached new heights between 1861 and 1865. In 1860, 13,000,000 tons of pig iron were produced; in 1864 about 21,000,000 tons were made. Lumbering, wheat farming, and woolgrowing flourished, too.

Tied together by canals and railroads, the East and West prospered without the South. Even at the height of the war in 1864, the *New York Times* expressed the opinion that northerners had never been better housed or clothed or fed. Some observers went so far as to say that prosperity was so great there that some northerners prayed the war would continue.

This great economic spurt not only resulted from the war itself but also was an effect of new laws enacted when the South left the Union. By seceding, the southerners had removed opposition in Congress to tariff, homestead, and national-banking legislation.

Higher tariffs. The tariff had been lowered in 1857, and southerners had no longer considered it a matter for argument. But in 1861, even before Lincoln was inaugurated, the Morrill Tariff** was passed, providing for substantial increases over the low duties of 1857. An act in 1862 sent the rates even higher. At the end of the war, the average duty was about 250 percent more than in 1857. The tariff helped enrich manufacturers by enabling them to raise prices to a point just below what the same product from abroad would cost. In this way manufacturers accumulated funds for expansion and investment.

The Homestead Act. The passage in 1862 of the Homestead Act was very gratifying to farmers. Southerners had been against previous bills to "give every farmer a home," because they feared that such legislation would benefit northern farmers rather than slaveholding planters of the South. The new law provided for a free grant of 160 acres to any American citizen over twenty-one who lived on it for five years. By 1864, 1,261,000 acres had been distributed.

The national-banking system. The war showed up the inadequacies of the banking system inher-

---

** Proposed by Representative Justin S. Morrill, of Vermont. A better-known piece of legislation was his bill to provide land grants to states and territories for the building of state colleges to teach agriculture and mechanical arts. The Morrill, or Land-Grant College, Act was signed by Lincoln in 1862.

##A Homestead Act had been passed by Congress in 1860, but it had been vetoed by President Buchanan. Let the class speculate about his motive.

Angered over the draft law, New Yorkers in 1863 wantonly set fire to the headquarters of the military police chief.

Contrast this scene with the one shown on p. 270.

ited from the time of Jackson. The North lacked a uniform credit system and a standardized currency. In 1863 a national-banking system was created. The law provided that a group of investors might start a bank to be called a "national bank" if they invested at least a third of their capital in United States bonds. Because "national bank notes" could be issued against these bonds, money in circulation could be increased without the irresponsible printing of paper money.

Merchants' gains. Northern businessmen, in short, took advantage of the absence of the southern congressmen to tighten their hold on the nation. They were influencing more and more the policies of the Republican party, which had originally found its chief strength in the farming region of the old Northwest.

Although industrial workers did not lack jobs during the war years, many felt that their economic position was worse than before the conflict. It was reliably stated in 1864 that despite an immense increase in the profits of manufacturers, "wages are only from twelve to twenty percent higher than they were before

the war, and there is absolute want. . . ."

Many industrial workers were unsympathetic to emancipation because they feared competing for jobs with freedmen. And they angrily resented the conscription law under which a man of means might avoid service by hiring a substitute to take his place. In July, 1863, Irish-Americans in New York rioted against the draft and for four days pillaged the city and lynched Negroes. Some of Meade's regiments had to be dispatched to restore order.

UNION POLITICS—AND TRAGEDY

The year 1864 brought the country the high drama of a wartime presidential election. The results were proof of the Union's strength.

Lincoln and Johnson. The war itself, as well as the economic changes it brought, was determining northern politics. The Union party (see page 274) renominated Lincoln at Baltimore in June. Andrew Johnson, a Tennessee Democrat and the only southerner still in the Senate, received the vice-presidential nomination.

The "Copperheads." The Democrats, who met in August, attempted to take advantage of the

#Only a small fraction of all Union soldiers were obtained through the conscription laws of 1863 and 1864. There was a high rate of desertions in both the Union and the Confederate armies.

peace talk that was in the air. Horace Greeley expressed the peace view in a letter to Lincoln: "I venture to remind you that our bleeding, bankrupt, almost dying country . . . longs for peace, [and] shudders at the prospect of fresh conscriptions, of further wholesale devastations, and of new rivers of human blood." Peace, or "Copperhead," Democrats—so called because they were compared to a kind of snake—wanted an immediate end to hostilities.

The nomination of "Little Mac." The Democratic party turned to an army man, General McClellan, as their candidate. He accepted the nomination but promptly rejected the platform. "I could not," he said, "look into the face of my gallant comrades of the army and navy who have survived so many bloody battles and tell them . . . that we have abandoned the Union for which we have so often periled our lives."

\# **The President's reelection.** A group of Republicans attempted in late summer to throw Lincoln over in favor of a more easily dominated candidate, but the movement failed. Lincoln refused to yield to the pressures of the moment. Asked by politicians of his own party to curry popular favor by modifying the draft, he responded: "What is the Presidency to me if I have no country?" In November he won re-election with a majority of only 400,000 out of about 4,000,000 votes cast. In the electoral college, though, he had 212 votes compared with only 21 for McClellan.

When Lincoln was inaugurated again in \#\# 1865, the war was almost over. The Union's salvation was certain. The Rail Splitter from Illinois had guided his country through the cruelest kind of war: one between brothers.

Assassination. On April 14, five days after the war had ended—Good Friday, as it happened—the President and Mrs. Lincoln went to Ford's Theater in Washington to attend a performance of a popular comedy. The gay evening was destined to be filled with horror and tragedy. A famous actor, John Wilkes Booth, deranged by the triumph of the Union, thought he could avenge the South by slaying the President, Vice-President, and key Cabinet members.

Booth's fellow conspirators failed in their missions of murder, but the actor himself shot Lincoln in the head as he sat in a flag-draped box intently watching the play. Booth had committed an act of madness, crying as he made his escape, "Sic semper tyrannis!"†† The President, mortally wounded, died the next morning in the rooming house to which he had been carried, across the street from the theater.

The body lay in state in the White House the following week. Then, as the nation mourned, a crape-covered funeral train bore it back to Springfield by the same route over which Lincoln had come out of the West four years before. "One nation under God, indivisible. . . ." would be his enduring monument.

On Lookout Mountain in Tennessee today, a silent Confederate cannon recalls the struggle for the West in 1863.

David E. Sherman, *Holiday*, © 1953 by Curtis Publishing Company

Sum and Substance

1. Name the reasons for the southern defeat in the war. 2. Account for the wartime economic spurt in the North. 3. Describe the congressional legislation made possible by southern secession. 4. What northerners chiefly benefited from it? 5. Why was Johnson an unusual running mate for Lincoln in the election of 1864? Account for his nomination. 6. When and by whom was Lincoln assassinated?

---

†† The motto of the state of Virginia, meaning "This is always the fate of tyrants."

\#\#Union military successes prior to the election contributed to Lincoln's political victory.

THE WORKSHOP

OF LASTING SIGNIFICANCE

What relationship did each of the following have to the war between the sections?

Confederate States
  of America
Crittenden
  Compromise
Virginia peace
  convention
Fort Sumter
border states
Robert E. Lee
Pierre G. T. de
  Beauregard
A. S. Johnston
Thomas J. Jackson
James Longstreet
Jefferson Davis
J. E. B. Stuart
Irving McDowell
First Bull Run
Ulysses S. Grant
George H. Thomas
"Bloody Shiloh"

David G. Farragut
George B. McClellan
Edwin M. Stanton
Antietam
Emancipation
  Proclamation
Frederick Douglass
Gettysburg
Vicksburg
William T. Sherman
Clara Barton
Appomattox Court
  House
Trent affair
Alabama claims
Maximilian
greenbacks
Morrill Tariff
Homestead Act
Andrew Johnson
"Copperheads"

THE PRESIDENCY

1. Lincoln had three alternatives in the crisis of 1861: (*a*) he could make wide concessions to the South to hold it in the Union; (*b*) he could wait to see if the seceded states would return; (*c*) he could hold federal property and enforce federal law.

Who had already tried the second? With what success? What concessions would Lincoln have had to make to the South in order to keep it in the Union? Why was this impossible?

What was Lincoln's responsibility as president of the United States? (Review the oath of office he had taken.) What earlier President had taken a firm stand in order to carry out the oath? Why was Lincoln's situation much more serious? How did he refer in the second inaugural to his decision (pages 270–271)?

What was the direct result of the decision?

Was Lincoln's main purpose accomplished?

2. The Gettysburg Address contains the finest expression of Lincoln's beliefs about the Civil War. Obtain a copy of it. What did he say the war was testing? What reference did he make to the men being honored in the memorial service? What responsibility did he say must be borne by the living?

3. In the second inaugural (pages 270–271), Lincoln referred to slavery as "somehow, the cause of the war." How did he explain the statement? How had the "cause of the conflict" ceased before the conflict itself ended? What does the last paragraph of the second inaugural reveal about Lincoln's feelings toward the South?

GEOGRAPHY AND HISTORY

1. How was geography involved in the North's military strategy in the Civil War?

2. Using arrows, show on two outline maps the military moves making up northern strategy and those contemplated by the South. Compare these moves with those actually carried out. Which plans were carried out?

3. Why was it necessary and logical for the # North to take the offensive in the war?

INTERNATIONAL POLITICS

1. What policy did Lincoln expect foreign countries would adopt toward the United States during the Civil War? In what respect was he correct so far as Britain was concerned? How was he wrong? How did Lincoln handle the difficulties in Anglo-American relations?

2. Describe the tense situation France created during the Civil War. What principle of American foreign policy was involved? How did the reaction of the United States show clearly the relationship between its foreign policy and its domestic situation?

3. What single fact undoubtedly weighed most heavily in the decision of European governments to support the North in the Civil War? What was the significance in international politics of their failure to recognize the Confederate government?

#(Because its aim was to bring the seceded states back into the Union, it had to attack the Confederacy in order to achieve this aim. Thus the war was fought in the South.)

16

REESTABLISHING NATIONAL UNITY

. . . the new order
of things . . .

As to what is commonly termed "reconstruction," it is not only the political machinery of the States and their constitutional relations to the general government, but the whole organism of southern society that must be reconstructed, or rather constructed anew, so as to bring it in harmony with the rest of American society. The difficulties of this task are not to be considered overcome when the people of the south take the oath of allegiance and elect governors and legislatures and members of Congress, and militia captains. . . .

The true nature of the difficulties of the situa-

Union attacks caused destruction; Confederates often destroyed their property to prevent Union use of it.

A ruined building in Richmond, Virginia, in 1865, part of the devastation the Civil War brought to the Confederacy. Richmond, the capital, suffered fire and bombardment.

tion is this: The general government of the republic has, by proclaiming the emancipation of the slaves, commenced a great social revolution in the south, but has, as yet, not completed it. Only the negative part of it is accomplished. The slaves are emancipated in point of form, but free labor has not yet been put in the place of slavery in point of fact. . . .

It is, indeed, difficult to imagine circumstances more unfavorable for the development of a calm and unprejudiced public opinion [on the subject of free Negro labor] than those under which the southern people are at present laboring. The war

Library of Congress

has not only defeated their political aspirations, but it has broken up their whole social organization. When the rebellion was put down they found themselves not only conquered in a political and military sense, but economically ruined. The planters, who represented the wealth of the southern country, are partly laboring under the severest embarrassments, partly reduced to absolute poverty.

Many who are stripped of all available means, and have nothing but their land, cross their arms in gloomy despondency. . . . Others, who still possess means, are at a loss how to use them, as their old way of doing things is, by the abolition of slavery, rendered impracticable. . . . Others are still trying to go on in the old way, and that old way is in fact the only one they understand, and in which they have any confidence. Only a minority is trying to adopt the new order of things. . . .

The southern soldiers, when returning from the war, did not, like the northern soldiers, find a prosperous community which merely waited for their arrival to give them remunerative employment. They found, many of them, their homesteads destroyed, their farms devastated, their families in distress. . . .

In which direction will these people be most apt to turn their eyes? Leaving the prejudice of race out of the question, from early youth they have been acquainted with but one system of labor, and with that one system they have been in the habit of identifying all their interests. They know of no way to help themselves but the one they are accustomed to. . . .

The practical question presents itself: Is the immediate restoration of the late rebel States to absolute self-control so necessary that it must be done even at the risk of endangering one of the great results of the war, and of bringing on in those States insurrection or anarchy, or would it not be better to postpone that restoration until such dangers are passed?

When hostilities were over, the South's greatest immediate problem was how to adjust to the ending of the slave system. At the same time, in the triumphant North there was grow-

Words to analyze: remunerative; devastated; insurrection; anarchy.

291

ing determination to have the freedmen free in practice as well as in name. This selection is part of a report written by Carl Schurz (pronounced Shirts) following a trip to the southern states in the months after Appomattox. Born in Germany, Schurz—a soldier, diplomat, and *later a Senator from Missouri and a Cabinet officer—had fled to the United States in 1848 as a refugee from political tyranny. He expresses here his understanding appreciation of southern agony as well as his belief that compromise on emancipation was impossible.*

AMIDST THE RUINS OF WAR, RECONSTRUCTION BEGINS

The Civil War, like most wars, failed to solve the problem over which it began. Northerners in 1861 had gone to war to save the union of all the states. By 1865 the North had won the military victory, but the Union of the prewar days was a shambles. Its reconstruction was more complicated than anyone four years before could have dreamed it would be.

DIXIE IN DEFEAT

Even if political and social reconstruction had been unnecessary, the physical rebuilding alone would have been an awesome task. The few southern factories had been ruined; the railroads not actually destroyed were sorely in need of repair; fire had gutted the important cities of Atlanta, Columbia, Mobile, and Richmond and many others. The land between Washington and Richmond, where fighting had been heaviest, was described as "a desert."

An observer wrote of the scene in South Carolina where Sherman had marched: It "looked for many miles like a broad black streak of ruin and desolation—the fences all gone; lonesome smoke stacks, surrounded by dark heaps of ashes and cinders, marking the spots where human habitations had stood; the fields along the road wildly overgrown by weeds. . . ."

Everywhere the sight was desolate. The slaves were gone from the plantations, and no one kept up the buildings, which soon fell into disrepair and decay. The most pathetic victims of the war—as always—were the people, especially women and children, who had been reduced to begging for food and shelter.

Dejection. The effects on individuals varied, of course, with circumstances and place. Many slaves had left their masters as soon as the war had ended; others had remained for a while to make themselves helpful. Incidents of violence were rarer than had been anticipated, but there was considerable bad feeling. Resentful planters who had had princely incomes in 1860 were now trying unaided to grow vegetable crops in order to keep body and soul together. No one could escape the sad fact that, as one veteran put it, "the flower of [our] labors and those of [our] fathers for centuries had been trampled in the dust."

The extremists. Certain southerners, understandably, would never be reconciled to the defeat. Judah Benjamin escaped from the South to London, where he practiced law with his customary brilliance. Some ex-Confederates considered establishing a colony for themselves in Mexico; some moved to Brazil. Edmund Ruffin, who had fired the first shot of the war, committed suicide.

A few civil leaders of the Confederacy were # imprisoned, although only Jefferson Davis spent any significant length of time in jail. Many southerners would never accept the fact that their old way of life was gone. They would live over and over again in their minds the glory of the Confederacy's Lost Cause.

A reviving national loyalty. But Unionist sentiment in the South was reawakening. A war prisoner recently released by Union soldiers observed how uplifting to the spirit it was "for our people to see a Government which was lately fighting us with fire, and sword, and shell, now generously feeding our poor and distressed." This man, along with others, expected that in time a new South would emerge from the ashes of defeat.

Alabamians receive charity rations after the Civil War. Organizations in both the North and the South collected and distributed supplies for southerners in need, who included former rich men as well as former slaves.

Crops in the South were poor in 1865; not until 1867 was there adequate food.

The course of reconstruction, however, helped wipe out the distinction between the unreconciled southerners and the forward-looking ones. The divided South became the solid South: its common bond was hatred for the North.

THE VICTOR'S INTENTIONS

Lincoln had intended to follow a policy of liberality and conciliation toward the South. But a leading group in Congress, called the "Radical Republicans," was vengeful, maintaining that the seceded states should receive no mercy. A problem the country had to face, therefore, was, Who is to be responsible for the reconstruction of the Union, the President or Congress? This was not merely a question of which branch of the government must deal with the matter; it also meant choosing between a generous policy and a harsh one toward the former Confederacy.

Lincoln's 10-percent plan. Lincoln had held that since a state could not secede, the former Confederate states had never been out of the Union. His plan of reconstruction, announced late in 1863, was to give *amnesty*, that is, official pardon, to all ex-Confederates who would take

an oath of loyalty to the United States. When 10 percent of those voting in 1860, in a given state, had taken the oath, and when the state had consented to emancipation, its reconstruction would be considered complete.*

Some congressional views. The Radicals, on the # other hand, insisted that reconstruction was Congress' task, not the President's. They called for a fundamental rearrangement of the relationship between the former Confederate states and the Union. One view was that the defeated areas were nothing other than "conquered provinces." Another was that the rebel states had committed suicide and that even their boundaries had been erased.

The Radicals were saying in effect in 1865 that the Union had been dissolved in 1861. This was precisely the position that the secessionists had taken—one the war had been fought to disprove!

The Radicals had jealously criticized Lincoln's handling of his vast war powers. They had insisted that the war was being mismanaged

---

* Although Arkansas and Louisiana followed this procedure in 1864, Congress refused to allow their Senators and Representatives to be seated.

#There probably would have been no argument if the two branches of the government had seen eye-to-eye on reconstruction policies.

from the military side and that Lincoln was entirely too slow in emancipating the slaves. In 1861 they had created the Joint Committee on the Conduct of the War, which, in addition to ferreting out instances of waste and inefficiency, did not hesitate to harass the President. Lincoln, however, refused to break with the Radicals—or to be dominated by them.

Andrew Johnson at the helm. The assassination of Lincoln gave the Radicals an unexpected opportunity. Even as Lincoln's body lay in the White House, Ben Wade was saying to the new President: "Johnson, we have faith in you. By the gods, there will be no trouble now in running the government!" This sounded ominous because both sympathy and pity were desperately needed to heal the nation's wounds.

Andrew Johnson had been born in poverty in North Carolina. Fatherless at three, he grew up as a tailor's apprentice. Moving to Greeneville, Tennessee, he married a local girl when he was eighteen, who taught him to read and write. To earn a living, he sewed far into the night. His shop turned into a kind of poor man's political club where Jacksonian Democrats gathered.

Johnson became popular, serving in turn as alderman, mayor, state legislator, governor, United States Senator, military governor of Tennessee, and vice-president of the United States. Johnson had two strong prejudices. One was against the "aristocrats" who had scorned him all his life—even after he had won political success. A wealthy Tennessean once declared, "If Johnson were a snake he would lie in the grass and bite the heels of rich men's children."† The second of Johnson's biases was against Negroes. They were the competitors of # the poor people from whom Johnson came, and he was never able to shake off his fear and dislike of them.

Sum and Substance

1. What did Carl Schurz say "reconstruction" meant? 2. How had the war affected the South economically? Socially? Politically? 3. How did Lincoln's plan of reconstruction differ from the Radicals'?

THE RADICAL REPUBLICANS LAND IN THE SADDLE

Burdened by his deep-rooted prejudices, Johnson was not the right man to deal with the Radicals. They spoke for the new industrialists of the North and for those who hoped to uplift as well as to liberate the Negro. The President and the Radicals were soon seriously at odds as they vied with each other for control of the South's reconstruction.

MOTIVES AND MEN

The Radicals may be divided into three main groups. Some were former abolitionists who before the war had demanded an end to slavery. Now they wanted for the Negro fuller social, political, and economic privileges. We may refer to these men as humanitarian-Radicals.

Another group of Radicals, with whom the humanitarians allied themselves, consisted of spokesmen for northern industry, which had gained enormously when the South seceded.

Before the Civil War the South's votes in Congress had been a barrier to high tariffs, internal improvements, a transcontinental railroad in the North, a national-banking system, and free homesteads.

Between 1861 and 1865 all these things had been achieved except the completion of the railroad, which was, however, only two years away. If the southerners should return to Congress—the businessman-Radicals thought—the whole economic program might be thrown out or seriously modified.

A third group of Radicals consisted simply of politicians who recognized that the Repub-

---

† The only significant change Johnson made in Lincoln's 10-percent plan after he succeeded to the presidency was to exempt from the general amnesty any former Confederate who owned taxable property of more than $20,000. Such a person would have to apply to the President personally for pardon, in a situation that would give Johnson a pleasure he had waited for all his life.

lican party was a minority party. The only way it could become a majority party would be by disfranchising southerners, who would vote Democratic, and by enfranchising freedmen, who would vote Republican.

Although the humanitarian-, the business-man-, and the politician-Radicals disagreed about the *ends* to be sought, they were in firm accord on the *means* they would adopt. Those means involved enfranchising the Negro and protecting his political and social rights.

Thaddeus Stevens. It is difficult to fit each Radical leader into the right group: men's motives are complicated. In the House of Representatives, Thaddeus Stevens spoke loudest for the Radicals. "This is not a 'white man's government,'" he declared in explaining his stand, ". . . This is man's government; the government of all men alike." Seventy-three years old when the war ended, Stevens was crippled, ill, and irritable. Some thought that a luxuriant coal-black wig, covering his completely bald head, gave him a sinister appearance.

Hating "aristocracy" passionately, Stevens turned this hatred against the southern slave-holders. As a young man he had been a leader in the movement to establish free public schools in Pennsylvania. Now not only was he demanding complete equality for Negroes, but also he was advocating the confiscation of plantation lands for distribution to ex-slaves.

Charles Sumner. Another leading Radical was Senator Charles Sumner of Massachusetts. Born of an old New England family, a graduate of Harvard College, handsome, and correct, Sumner was a brilliant, polished orator; he was also vain and opinionated. He may have been sincere in his concern for the freedmen, but it appeared to some of his opponents that he was only wreaking vengeance upon the South for the caning Preston Brooks had given him (see page 262).

Benjamin F. Wade. Still another Radical leader was Ben Wade of Ohio. Rough, often vulgar, he fought hard for the punishment of the South. From the beginning of his political career, he had been steadfastly antislavery. But his enemies asserted that his strong stand on

Thaddeus Stevens hated slavery. He also could not forget the destruction of his ironworks and the burning of a settlement in southern Pennsylvania by Lee's men in 1863.

Charles Sumner had opposed the Kansas-Nebraska Bill, and he had helped organize the Republican party. He worked hard to give Negroes equality in civil rights.

reconstruction resulted from his desire to exalt Congress. As chairman of the Joint Committee on the Conduct of the War, he had had great power he did not care to give up.

In both the North and the South people generally believed what they wanted to believe about the purposes of the Radicals. Northerners friendly to the Radicals considered them heroic defenders of the principles in the Declaration of Independence. Many southerners regarded the Radicals as madmen taking pleasure in tormenting their defeated brethren.

THE DEVELOPING POLICIES

The Radicals had already given a preview of their legislative plans. In 1864 they had passed the Wade-Davis Bill, which would have placed reconstruction entirely in the hands of Congress. It had provided that in every seceded state a majority of the voters must swear both past and future loyalty to the United States before the state could be restored to the Union.

Lincoln had killed this bill with a pocket veto. Thereupon, in a vicious attack on Lincoln called the Wade-Davis Manifesto, published in the *New York Tribune,* the Radicals had warned the President to leave political reconstruction to Congress.

Freedmen's Bureau. The Radicals made a successful move in 1865, when Congress created the Freedmen's Bureau. The bureau's purpose was to distribute food and clothing to former slaves, find them jobs, give them shelter when necessary, and establish schools for them. This formidable task was put under the supervision of General Oliver O. Howard, a Radical.

Undoubtedly the Freedmen's Bureau provided much needed relief for Negroes in the difficult days when they moved from bondage to freedom. It also aided tens of thousands of southern whites in need of food and clothing. Many southerners considered the Bureau an instrument of the Republican party, stirring up the freedmen against their former masters. The Radicals maintained that without the Bureau, life would be intolerable for the freedmen.

Presidential plan effected. Before Congress met in December, 1865, every ex-Confederate state except Texas had fulfilled the Lincoln-Johnson terms for reconstruction. (Lincoln had offered his during the war as a means of rallying loyal opinion, but Johnson, disregarding congressional sentiment, hastily pushed through his program when the wartime emergency was over.) In his annual message, President Johnson expressed the opinion that the Union had now

In two years the Bureau gave nearly six million rations to whites, about sixteen million to Negroes.

An official of the Freedmen's Bureau meets with southerners seeking help. Some want to find work, some to settle disputes between members of the two races, and others to ask about abandoned or confiscated land.

New York Public Library

been reconstructed. This seemed to be in accord with the view of General Grant, who had undertaken a tour of inspection of the southern states. Grant had reported: "I was pleased to learn from the leading men whom I met that they not only accepted the decision arrived at as final, but now that the smoke of battle has cleared away and time has been given for reflection, that this decision has been a fortunate one for the whole country. . . ."

Southern codes.

Yet there was more than met Grant's eyes. Former leaders of the Confederacy were being elected to high posts in the "reconstructed" states and were even being sent to Congress. Among them was the Confederate vice-president Alexander Stephens, who was chosen to serve in the United States Senate but was refused a seat. The southern state legislatures were passing a series of laws, or codes, designed to restrict the rights of the recently liberated Negroes and keep them in an inferior position. Southerners generally defended the codes as necessary to meet the new social conditions that emancipation had brought.‡ Many in the South, though, argued that these were bad laws and a mockery of democracy.

According to the codes, Negroes could exercise certain civil rights, like suing or acquiring property, but they could usually appear in court as witnesses only against other Negroes; and in almost every state it was a punishable offense for a freedman to quit his job. A Negro could easily be arrested as a vagrant and then be assigned to labor for the man who paid his fine until he had worked off the money. Homeless Negro youths could be apprenticed to white "masters." Negroes were barred from certain skilled occupations in some states and in one state were denied the right to buy or to rent farmland.

By the time Congress convened in December, the Radicals were incensed. Already the *Chicago Tribune* had pledged: "The men of the North will convert . . . Mississippi into a frog pond before they will allow any such laws to disgrace one foot of soil in which the bones

of our soldiers sleep and over which the flag of freedom waves." Radicals were also alarmed at the mistreatment of Negroes: five thousand were murdered in the first year after the war; Negro schoolhouses were burned down; and white and colored teachers in Negro schools were beaten and driven out by southerners opposed to educating the former slaves.

The Joint Committee of Fifteen. The Radicals used the restrictions in the codes as their excuse to attack presidential reconstruction. Under the leadership of Thaddeus Stevens, the first step was to refuse to seat representatives from states having governments established in accordance with Lincoln-Johnson requirements. A Joint Committee of Fifteen—consisting of members of both houses of Congress—was appointed to be a watchdog on the President's program of reconstruction. Its hearings revealed widespread violence against Negroes and white Unionists in the South.

By 1866 Johnson and Congress were in continual conflict. Congress passed a bill considerably enlarging the power of the Freedmen's Bureau. Johnson vetoed it, because, he said, ## Congress could not pass valid laws while eleven states were out of the Union. Congress enacted the bill over the veto. Congress also passed, over a presidential veto, the Civil Rights Act, which granted citizenship to the Negro. Johnson had contended that citizenship must be defined by the states and not by Congress.

The Fourteenth Amendment. To make sure of the constitutionality of federal action regarding citizenship, Congress in 1866 formulated the Fourteenth Amendment to the Constitution, which defined American citizenship for the first time. It stated in unmistakable language: "All persons born or naturalized in the United States . . . are citizens of the United States and of the State wherein they reside."

These words made the ex-slaves citizens. In another section the amendment invalidated the "three-fifths" clause (see page 120). Another provision established that any state denying the suffrage to any male citizen entitled to vote would have its representation in Congress reduced proportionately.

---

‡ The Thirteenth Amendment, formally abolishing slavery forever, was proclaimed in effect on December 18, 1865.

The Fourteenth Amendment, adopted in 1868, has been used to defend property as well as freedmen, because the word *persons* has been interpreted to include such legal persons as corporations. But most important, it has become an increasingly powerful protective barrier that the individual may invoke against the invasion of his rights by a state government.

CONGRESS AGAINST JOHNSON

Johnson advised the southern states to reject the Fourteenth Amendment, and all the former Confederate states except Tennessee followed the advice. In congressional halls the South's rejection of the Fourteenth Amendment was taken as proof that the former Confederacy had still not learned its lesson. The Radicals now painted Johnson as a man working to undo the results of the war.

The elections of 1866. During the summer of 1866, Johnson's Union party (a new party made up of his followers) held a convention at Philadelphia to prepare for the fall elections to Congress. The Democrats who attended not only outnumbered the Republicans but also included former Confederates. Many businessmen began to fear that a congressional sweep for the Democrats would endanger the economic advantages they had gained. Throughout the summer the Radicals played on the concern of northern industry about its future under Johnson and congressmen allied with him.

The President became the target of incessant personal attacks. To gain the support of temperance advocates, Radicals assailed him as a common drunkard. To woo the Irish-American vote, they pictured him as being pro-British. To frighten holders of northern war bonds, they said he favored repudiating the Union debt and assuming the Confederate.

Late in August, Johnson, goaded to fury, went on an ill-advised speaking tour that carried him into the Midwest. He called it a "swing around the circle." Heckled at every stop, Johnson made many tactless and inept remarks. To many people it seemed undignified for the president of the United States to be making stump speeches.

When white mobs and policemen joined to kill or wound hundreds of Negroes in race riots in New Orleans and Memphis during the spring and summer of 1866, considerable northern sentiment flowed to the Radical side. In the congressional elections that followed, the Radicals won sweeping victories in both House and Senate. Johnson's opponents in Congress would now be able to muster the two-thirds vote they might need to override his vetoes of their bills.

The reasons. The Radicals were obviously finding acceptance in the North for their policies. Reflect for a minute—360,000 Union men had been killed and 275,000 wounded in a war for which northerners blamed the Confederates. Not a town and hardly a family had escaped tragedy. Moreover, responsibility for the high national debt and the taxation to pay it was laid at the door of the South.

Of course southerners had suffered for what they had believed was right, too—258,000 dead, at least 100,000 wounded, and the destruction and loss of their property. But the day had not yet arrived when the victors would offer forgiveness to the vanquished.

Military occupation. The Radicals' plan for reconstruction—sometimes called the congressional plan—passed Congress easily on March 2, 1867, over Johnson's veto. It divided the South into five military districts, each under the jurisdiction of an army general whose troops would enforce his orders.

To be relieved of military occupation and to be represented in Congress once more, a state was required to call a constitutional convention whose delegates were elected by universal manhood suffrage. The convention would have to create a state government acceptable to Congress that would ratify the Fourteenth Amendment and guarantee Negro suffrage.

Trimming the chief executive's powers. Not only did the Radicals take reconstruction out of the hands of the President in this way, but they also reduced his powers generally. On the same day that Congress passed the Reconstruction Acts, it also enacted, over Johnson's veto, two laws severely limiting the powers granted to the President in the Constitution. The first was the Tenure of Office Act, which made necessary the Senate's consent in order to remove any official whose appointment had originally required its consent. The second, the Command of the Army Act, practically stripped the President of his role as commander in chief of the army. This law required that the President issue military orders through only one person, the general in chief of the army—meaning Grant—whom he was forbidden to assign away from Washington.

Deciding to defy Congress, Johnson asked for the resignation of Secretary of War Stanton, a holdover from Lincoln's Cabinet who actually acted as a spy for the Radicals. When Stanton would not resign, the President suspended him and put Grant in his place. The Senate convened in December and immediately refused to approve Stanton's suspension. Grant then stepped aside, and Stanton resumed his office. Johnson at this point, in plain disregard of the Tenure of Office Act, dismissed Stanton.

Impeachment and trial. The Radicals had their opening now. Led by Stevens, the House impeached, that is, accused, Johnson on several grounds, many of them outrageous. It charged that he had violated the new Tenure of Office Act. Stevens, close to death, was a dramatic figure as he leaned hard on his cane, with "the fire of his implacable spirit gleaming from sunken eyes, with a half smile of triumph." "Unfortunate, unhappy man, behold your doom," he warned Johnson.

On March 13, 1868, the impeachment trial began in the Senate with Chief Justice Salmon P. Chase presiding. Among newspaper reporters present was a young man named Georges Clemenceau, destined one day to be premier of France. Charles Dickens, in Washington for a public appearance, wrote his friends that he was following attentively the convulsions of the republic.

At stake was the American form of government itself, now threatened by a congressional dictatorship. If the Radicals could remove Johnson, one of their own number would be president of the United States. Under the presi-

dential succession act then in force, the president pro tempore of the Senate was next in line. He happened to be "Bluff" Ben Wade, already sitting before his fireplace at home planning his Cabinet appointments.

The fateful Senate vote. The trial became a farce, as the prosecution tried to prove Johnson's unfitness to be President. Although Johnson's attorneys ably defended their man, the Radicals were confident of the outcome. They hounded without mercy Senators whose votes were uncertain. Nevertheless, when the balloting came, seven Republicans stood for acquittal. Their stand prevented by one vote a two-thirds majority, which would have removed Johnson from office.

The seven Republicans who braved their party's wrath were committing political suicide—and they knew it. One of them, Edmund G. Ross of Kansas, later described his feelings as he was about to utter his vote of "not guilty": "I almost literally looked down into my open grave. Friendship, position, fortune, everything that makes life desirable to an ambitious man were about to be swept away by the breath of my mouth, perhaps forever."

Today many regard these Republicans as heroes, for by their courage they prevented the development of an imbalance in the American form of government.§ If the Radicals had triumphed, the separation of powers built into the Constitution would have been weakened (see page 124). Congress might have been able to make a President dance to its tune.

Sum and Substance

1. What groups made up the Radicals? 2. How did Congress care for the freedmen? 3. What were the southern codes? 4. Tell briefly what the Thirteenth and Fourteenth amendments provided. 5. Give the provisions of the Radicals' plan of reconstruction. 6. Why was Johnson impeached? What was the outcome?

---

§ The seven included, in addition to Ross, William P. Fessenden of Maine, Joseph S. Fowler of Tennessee, James W. Grimes of Iowa, John B. Henderson of Missouri, Lyman Trumbull of Illinois, and Peter G. Van Winkle of West Virginia. Ironically, none was on the scene when Johnson returned to Washington as Senator from Tennessee.

Johnson had hoped that Grant would not resign, thus forcing Stanton to use the courts to regain his office. In this way, the constitutionality of the Office of Tenure Act would have been tested.

299

GRANT PRESIDES DURING THE DRAMA OF RECONCILIATION

Having failed to remove Johnson from office, the Radicals turned their attention to getting their own man elected President in 1868. They nominated General Grant, who had had no previous party affiliation but who is believed to have voted for Lincoln and Johnson in 1864. Grant had not opposed the attempt to remove Johnson, and he had approved the Republican platform—an outright endorsement of the Radicals' reconstruction policies.

At the Democratic convention Johnson had some support, but the nomination went to former Governor Horatio Seymour of New York. Although Seymour himself was a sound-money man, the Democratic platform called for redeeming the Union bonds in greenbacks rather than gold. The party's theme was: "The same currency for the bondholder and the plough-holder."

The election outcome was a foregone conclusion. Grant, the greatest military hero since Jackson, was strong everywhere. The mere mention of his name brought to mind the bloody fields of Shiloh and the supreme Union triumph at Appomattox. The Grand Army of the Republic, an organization of Civil War veterans that had become practically a branch of the Republican party, backed Grant.

Radical control of the South, as a result of the Reconstruction Acts, assured thumping Republican majorities there. Three states still under military occupation did not participate in the election, while 700,000 newly enfranchised freedmen voted solidly for Grant.

IN THE SOUTH: NEW GOVERNMENTS

Meanwhile, a momentous political upheaval with profound social and economic effects was occurring in the South. Under the congressional plan of reconstruction, many southerners, Negro and white, who had never held public office before were in control of the states. By July, 1868, Arkansas, North Carolina, South Carolina, Louisiana, Georgia, Alabama, and Florida had been readmitted to the Union. When Virginia, Texas, and Mississippi satisfied

the requirements in 1870, Radical, or congressional, reconstruction was complete.

Scalawags and carpetbaggers. In the South, the men who joined with the freedmen in conducting the reconstruction governments in the states were called contemptuously "scalawags" and "carpetbaggers." Scalawags were southerners—often including men of property, Unionists, and certain poor farmers—who found it advantageous to coöperate with the former slaves in establishing a new order in Dixie. Carpetbaggers were northerners who went South to help create Radical governments.

The motives of the scalawags and carpetbaggers were mixed. Possibly a great many were sincere people, eager to complete the work of the war by uplifting the liberated slaves. Many others were adventurers who were fishing in troubled waters for selfish gain.

Negroes in politics. For the first time in southern history, Negroes both voted and held office. Between 1868 and 1877, when the reconstruction governments were ended, seventeen Negroes were elected to Congress—fifteen to the House and two, both from Mississippi, to the Senate. One of these Senators, Blanche K. Bruce, was the most important Negro politician of the era. Born a slave in Virginia, he received an education in the North after the war, becoming a prosperous planter in Mississippi. As a Senator he voted with his fellow Republicans, especially on racial questions. Although Senator Bruce introduced bills involving foreign affairs, aid to education, and railroad-building, he also offered bills affecting his own people and fought the mistreatment of Indians and the movement to exclude Chinese immigrants.

Many Negroes elected to Congress and to state offices were well educated. Among them were Francis Cardozo, of South Carolina, who was educated at the universities of Glasgow and London, and Jonathan Gibbs, of Florida, a graduate of Dartmouth College.

Among the freedmen who served in the reconstruction governments there was undeniably much ignorance—part of the price the South

##Negroes did not win offices in proportion to their population in the southern states. South Carolina was the only state in which there was a Negro majority in the state legislature.

Representative Robert B. Elliott, of South Carolina, delivers a speech on the subject of civil rights in the House of Representatives on January 6, 1874. In 1875 eight Negroes were in the House, from seven southern states. Robert B. Elliott became Speaker of the lower house of the legislature later in the year.

paid for two centuries of slavery. Negroes saw, however, that their social and economic advancement required participation in politics.

High costs. Many lurid stories may be told of the extravagances of the reconstruction legislatures. In South Carolina, for example, under the heading of "state supplies," such things as ladies' finery, horses, carriages, and table delicacies were purchased. The letting of contracts was so careless that in a little over a year more money was spent for public printing than in the entire preceding seventy-eight years. The tax rates increased; state debts rose; and state aid to railroad construction provided a standing invitation to corruption.

An explanation. No one can excuse the Radical governments for their misdeeds. Nevertheless, it may be said in explanation that, first of all, everywhere in the country local governments were taking on new obligations, and all city and state annual budgets were increasing. Second, corruption in high places was a nationwide evil in post-Civil War America. The Grant administration in Washington was shamefully looting the public treasury on a large scale. In New York the Tweed Ring—a group of grafters headed by William Marcy Tweed—was embezzling a sum estimated to have been at least $30,000,000. #

Other corrupt men elsewhere operated on a smaller scale, but with no less thoroughness. There was even bribery of congressmen to conceal a railroad scandal. Also, corruption existed in postwar southern governments before Negroes began voting, and it occurred in southern states after the so-called carpetbag governments were overthrown.

Not all the money spent by the reconstruction legislatures was wasted on debauchery and nonsense. The work of physical rebuilding cried

#Grant personally had nothing to do with the looting. But he was a poor judge of honesty and competence in his choice of subordinates and friends. Tweed was convicted and died in jail.

out for funds in large amounts. Freedmen, often homeless, jobless, and hungry, required a helping and comforting hand. Roads and railroads had to be built or, at least, reconstructed. Schools were needed to provide education for young people who would face new responsibilities and problems. The judicial system and the tax structure required overhauling.

Secret societies. The opposition within the South to the carpetbag governments increased daily. Fundamentally there was resentment that racial equality, at least officially, had been established. Helpless to resist openly as long as federal military power was present, some southerners organized secret clubs.

The most notorious secret society was the Ku Klux Klan, which had been formed at Pulaski, Tennessee, in 1866, two years before Negroes began voting and carpetbaggers began governing. In time it absorbed many of the others. It intimidated Negroes to keep them away from the polls, challenged the idea of equality for Negroes, and pledged itself to make the state governments all white again. Klansmen rode at night, covered with sheets to look like ghosts in order to scare credulous Negroes and to conceal their identities, but they also brazenly resorted to violence, including murder.

The Fifteenth Amendment. Radicals in the North watched with mounting concern this attack on the former slaves. It seemed to mock all the hard-won social and humanitarian results of the war. Besides, disfranchisement of the freedman would surely mean renewed power for the Democrats. In February, 1869, therefore, Congress proposed the Fifteenth Amendment to the Constitution.

This amendment forbade any state to deprive anyone of the right to vote because of his race or color or because he had previously been a slave. Congress required the states that had not already been readmitted to the Union to add approval of this amendment to the list of steps they must take for readmission. Mississippi, Texas, and Virginia were brought back into the Union in 1870, only after they had complied with the new requirement. Georgia—readmitted earlier but expelled for evicting Negroes from

the state legislature—also had to ratify this amendment to gain readmission.

Since the Klan and organizations like it were seeking to prevent the Negro from exercising the ballot, Congress in 1870 and 1871 passed the Ku Klux Klan Acts. These laws provided # severe penalties for violations of the Fourteenth and Fifteenth amendments. The President was authorized to suspend the writ of habeas corpus (the right to speedy trial) and to introduce martial law where the rights of the freedmen were considered endangered. Furthermore, federal rather than state courts were given jurisdiction over cases arising under this legislation.

The Civil Rights Act of 1875. The high-water mark ## of Radical Republicanism was the Civil Rights Act of 1875. This law was an effort to end racial discrimination by the states and by private enterprises serving the public—although it was notably silent about public schools. It guaranteed to all people regardless of race or color the right to serve on juries and "the full and equal enjoyment of the accommodations . . . of inns, public conveyances . . . , theatres, and other places of public amusement."

IN THE NORTH: THE SPOILSMEN

Grant, pictured by many southerners as a sword-wielding conqueror, had no wish to be a tyrant. Weighed down by the burdens of an office too big for him, his presidency suffered not from militarism but from a laxity in public morality that is known as "Grantism."

Grant was the Union's savior, and as such he had been elected. Himself an honest man, he trusted other people and was loyal to them. Since many of the intricate problems of the country did not interest him, his first administration was dominated by the politicians—or spoilsmen‖—who worked their will upon him.

Some names. Who were some of these men? One was Senator Oliver Morton of Indiana,

---

‖ This was a commonly used term of contempt for politicians who believed not that a public office must be conducted in the public interest but that it should be treated as spoils of war, to be taken from the defeated party and bestowed on the victorious one. The word comes from a speech made in 1832 by Senator William Marcy, of New York, in which he said of his opponents, "They see nothing wrong in the rule that to the victors belong the spoils of the enemy."

302   ##This act was declared unconstitutional in 1883 on the ground that the "individual invasion of individual rights is not the subject matter of the Fourteenth amendment."

who often had the President's ear. On one occasion, when Grant was asked the meaning of a phrase in a reconstruction bill, he replied, "I don't know what it means; Morton put that in." Another spoilsman was Senator Roscoe Conkling, who controlled federal jobs in New York.

Still another spoilsman was Zachariah Chandler, of Michigan, fat and heavy-drinking. He pointed out to Grant that it was a mistake to send abroad "literary fellers" like the historian John L. Motley, the United States minister to England, and the poet James Russell Lowell, who served in Spain.

Black Friday. Eastern capitalists also found Grant hospitable to them. In 1869 Jay Gould and James Fisk, two well-known speculating investors, decided to corner, or monopolize, the market for gold. A private gold exchange had grown up, where goldsmiths or merchants engaged in international trade might obtain enough gold to meet their needs. Gould bought up as much gold as he could so that its users would be at his mercy. When Grant learned what had happened, he ordered that government gold be sold in order to break Gould's monopoly. But the sale was not in time to prevent a serious financial panic on September 24, 1869, remembered ever since as Black Friday.

Assorted corruption. Under Grant, politicians not only helped to give unfair advantages to big business, but they also engaged in corruption unprecedented in boldness. The public outcry against this dishonesty in office often was hypocritical. Horatio Seymour expressed well the spirit of the day when he wrote: "Our people want men in office who will not steal, but who will not interfere with those who do."

The Whisky Ring, broken up in 1875, was a conspiracy of internal-revenue collectors and distillers to cheat the government of its just taxes. Among the 238 persons indicted for this crime was the President's private secretary, General Orville E. Babcock. In 1876 Grant's Secretary of War, William W. Belknap, was impeached for accepting bribes connected with the assigning of trading posts in the Indian territory. Further, under the "Salary Grab" Act of 1873, Congress retroactively doubled the pay

of the President and raised that of congressmen by 50 percent.

Crédit Mobilier. One of the most shocking affairs was that of the Crédit Mobilier, exposed in 1872 by the *New York Sun*. The Crédit Mobilier was a corporation organized to manage the construction of the Union Pacific Railroad. Stockholders of this company were also the controlling stockholders of the railroad. Crédit Mobilier charged the railroad line an exorbitant sum for its services and then divided the profits among the stockholders.

Representative Oakes Ames, of Massachusetts, was given shares of Crédit Mobilier stock for distribution among influential congressmen to head off an investigation. Incredible as it is, among those personally involved in this bribery were Vice-President Schuyler Colfax, the Vice-President-elect, Henry Wilson, and eight congressmen. One of them was Representative James A. Garfield, of Ohio, shortly to be president of the United States. The investigating committee issued a report whitewashing the misdeeds of the participants.

Liberal Republicans. By 1872 a reaction against Radical reconstruction policies as well as against "Grantism" became evident in the Republican party. The leaders in this movement, who called themselves Liberal Republicans, included many founders of the Republican party. Important editors, the survivors of Lincoln's Cabinet, and those who had tried to make reconstruction less harsh were the backbone of the new organization.

But when the Liberal Republicans met in Cincinnati to hold a convention, they made the terrible mistake of nominating for the presidency Horace Greeley, editor of the *New York Tribune*. He had signed Jefferson Davis' bail bond! Greeley, so nearsighted that his nose almost touched the paper from which he read, was an erratic man who had taken up many fads, including utopian socialism and vegetarianism. The Democrats took Greeley as their candidate, too, despite the fact that he was a high-tariff advocate.

A second term for the General. Greeley never had a chance. Grant was reelected overwhelmingly,

##Does the class think it possible for a government official to be objective in his responsibilities and still be actively engaged in his personal business activities?

303

the Republicans having engaged in a campaign of "waving the bloody shirt."#

The panic of 1873. Grant had hardly been inaugurated when the panic of 1873 broke on the country. It was brought on by the failure in September of the important Philadelphia banking house of Jay Cooke and Company. The fundamental causes, however, were excessive speculation in railroad construction and a too rapid expansion of industry and agriculture after 1865. The panic had a sobering effect on Americans, who had thought the postwar boom in the North was permanent. In the long depression that followed, many people lost their jobs, with consequent suffering.

THE POLITICS OF REUNION

Despite the fear of many white southerners that Grant would become a military dictator over their section, the reconstruction governments in the states were losing strength. The Democratic voters drove the Republicans out of power in Tennessee in 1869. The next year this happened in Georgia, North Carolina, and Virginia. Alabama and Arkansas went Democratic in 1874, and in 1875 Texas and Mississippi broke away from the Republicans.

The fate of the former slave was becoming less urgent to northerners, now concerned about their own labor problems. Furthermore, many northern businessmen who earlier had vigorously supported Radical Republicanism now looked forward to investing in the South and wanted "safe" state governments to protect their investments. The freedman became the victim of the desire for peace between the sections.

Hayes against Tilden. The election of 1876 finally brought about the withdrawal of the last federal troops from southern soil and the formal end of reconstruction. Tarred by the brush of corruption, the Republicans needed a virtuous candidate with whom to go to the people in 1876. They chose Rutherford B. Hayes, three times the governor of Ohio. He staunchly advocated

Harper's Weekly, March 25, 1876

After the corruption of the Grant regime had been revealed, Thomas Nast, a brilliant cartoonist, showed Uncle Sam wallowing in the shame of corruption.

civil service reform which would make merit—rather than political pull—the chief test in filling public jobs. His wife was a temperance advocate, and although the politicians derided her as "Lemonade Lucy," her views improved her husband's prospects.

The Democrats nominated a millionaire bachelor from New York, Samuel J. Tilden. Having won fame for his success in ousting the Tweed Ring, Tilden became a reform governor. Always morbidly concerned about his health, he nevertheless gave his energy to his party unstintingly. Not a man of sure convictions, Tilden is said to have coined the phrase "See you later," to postpone making decisions. As a candidate, he was called "a Democrat *and* a gentleman."

Disputed returns. The election returns reflected the fact that the Democrats were back in power in the South. Tilden received 4,300,590 popular ballots, and Hayes 4,036,298.

With the returns from South Carolina, Florida, and Louisiana still not in, Tilden had 184 sure electoral votes and required only one vote more for election. Those three states were in the hands of the Republicans, because their

---

"Waving the bloody shirt" was a phrase used in that generation to describe Republican oratory which dinned into American ears the notion that the Democrats were solely responsible for the Civil War.

##Many people who had sought the abolition of slavery were not as enthusiastic about seeking equal civil rights for Negroes. Why do reform movements tend to have ups and downs?

reconstruction was incomplete. They finally certified Hayes's rather than Tilden's electors. # The Democrats immediately were up in arms because, especially in Florida and Louisiana, they had clearly won in the popular vote.

An electoral commission. A long, drawn-out fight ensued over the disputed returns from the three southern states. Since the Senate was Republican and the House Democratic, it took extraordinary backstage diplomacy to break the jam. A bipartisan electoral commission was appointed, consisting of five Senators, five Representatives, and five Supreme Court justices.

It was expected that the lineup would consist of seven Republicans and seven Democrats, and that the deciding vote would be cast by Supreme Court Justice David Davis of Illinois, an independent. At the last minute Davis stepped down from the Court to become a Senator. His replacement, a Republican, voted with the other Republicans, giving Hayes the election by an 8 to 7 vote of the commission. (Hayes's electoral votes were 185 to Tilden's 184.) The dissatisfied Democrats ridiculed Hayes as "His Fraudulency" and "Old 8 to 7."

The Compromise of 1877. Behind the scenes a deal called the Compromise of 1877 had been made between Republican leaders and southern businessmen. In return for supporting Governor Hayes, southern Democrats had been promised that a southerner would be appointed to the Cabinet, that federal troops would be withdrawn from the South, and that money would be made available for internal improvements.

In fulfillment of the agreement, David M. Key, of Tennessee, was named Postmaster General, and a month after Hayes's inauguration the last soldier was removed from the South. But Hayes, through no fault of his own, was unable to make good on the part of the bargain regarding southern internal improvements.

Fundamentally, in accepting the terms of the Compromise of 1877, Hayes was committing himself and the federal government to abandoning the freedmen to their own devices. Although the President deplored the denial of civil rights to Negroes that followed the withdrawal of the troops, he failed to act.

Reconstruction was now formally concluded. On Memorial Day, 1877, for the first time since before the war, a president of the United States was welcomed by cheering crowds in a southern state. Hayes went to Tennessee, where he decorated the graves of Dixie and Union dead. Confederate veterans formed his escort.

Serious barriers to full reconstruction would continue to hinder the progress of both the South and the nation as a whole. Socially, there was the Negro's position as an inferior in a nation that preached equality.** Politically,

---

** In 1883 the Supreme Court declared unconstitutional (except for the part dealing with jury service) the Civil Rights Act of 1875 (see page 302). The Court reasoned that the guarantees of the Fourteenth Amendment did not transfer jurisdiction over social relationships from the states to the federal government.

Practically a full century would pass before Congress again passed a civil rights bill.

"Another such victory, and I am undone," groans this battered Republican elephant, drawn by Thomas Nast after the disputed election of 1876 had been settled.

Harper's Weekly, March 24, 1877

As a result of the course of reconstruction, the white voters of the South became avid Democrats. The Negroes became equally ardent Republicans. Why?

there was the regularity with which the South would vote Democratic and deny itself the advantage of two parties. Economically, there was the gap in the standard of living between the South and the rest of the country.

These disturbing conditions were part of the long-lasting heritage of the Civil War. Eventually—no one could say when—the North and the South would find the right road to eliminating them. Meanwhile, Jefferson Davis had realistic and prophetic words for a group of young men in his last public address: "The past is dead; let it bury its dead, its hopes, and its aspirations; before you lies the future, a future of golden promise, a future of expanding national glory, before which all the world shall stand amazed."

Sum and Substance

1. Who was elected President in 1868? What groups supported him? 2. When was reconstruction completed? 3. What people conducted the reconstruction governments in the southern states? 4. What bad things went on? What helped account for them? 5. Name good things that were accomplished. 6. Give the content of the Fifteenth Amendment. 7. Name and describe several examples of "Grantism." 8. What caused the panic of 1873? 9. Give the facts concerning the election of 1876.

Call attention to the tremendous technological advances indicated here.

Visitors at the Centennial Exposition in Philadelphia in 1876 point to popular displays in Machinery Hall. Exhibits of improved machines as well as of new gadgets for better living saluted American industrial advances.

Frank Leslie's Historical Register of the United States Centennial Exposition, 1876

THE WORKSHOP

OF LASTING SIGNIFICANCE

How was each of the following involved in the reestablishment of national unity?

Carl Schurz
reconstruction
Radicals
10-percent plan
amnesty
Thaddeus Stevens
Benjamin F. Wade
Freedmen's Bureau
southern codes
Thirteenth
   Amendment
Fourteenth
   Amendment
Tenure of Office Act
Command of the
   Army Act
Grand Army of the
   Republic

scalawags
carpetbaggers
Blanche K. Bruce
Tweed Ring
Ku Klux Klan
Fifteenth
   Amendment
Civil Rights Act
   of 1875
"Grantism"
Black Friday
spoilsmen
Crédit Mobilier
Whisky Ring
panic of 1873
Rutherford B. Hayes
Samuel J. Tilden
Compromise of 1877

THE CONSTITUTION TODAY

1. Read Article 5 of the Constitution to find out in what two ways constitutional amendments may be proposed. Which method was used in the case of the Fourteenth Amendment? In the case of the Fifteenth?

How may amendments be approved? What kind of amendment is forbidden? Obviously, amending the Constitution is not easy. Do you approve of this? Why?

2. How many years passed between the addition to the Constitution of the Bill of Rights and the Eleventh Amendment? Between the Eleventh and the Twelfth? Between the Twelfth and the Thirteenth? Why was the Thirteenth Amendment needed after the Emancipation Proclamation had been issued?

3. According to Article 1 of the Constitution, who has the sole power to impeach United States officials? What provisions are made concerning impeachment trials? How may convicted persons be punished?

4. Read in Article 2 the sections describing the powers of the President which were limited by the (a) Tenure of Office Act, (b) Command of the Army Act. Which was invoked in Johnson's impeachment? How?

Cite parts of the Constitution which show that the American government is based on the principle of the separation of powers. How would this principle have been affected if Johnson had been removed?

BEING A SOCIAL SCIENTIST

1. One tragic aspect of war is that the hardships it brings to both sides tend to increase the fears, suspicions, and hatreds with which it begins. From your knowledge of world history, mention instances of bitterness caused by international wars. Can you name any dictator who profited from such feeling?

2. Why is postwar bitterness doubly tragic when it follows war between people of the same country?

3. Both Lincoln and Lee were aware of the dangers of grudges between the sections. When one of his generals planned to write recollections of the war, Lee advised him to tell all necessary facts but to omit all remarks "calculated to excite bitterness . . . between different sections of the country." Quote the part of Lincoln's second inaugural which expresses his feeling of sympathy for all the people of the country. In what way did the 10-percent plan reflect Lincoln's attitude toward southerners?

4. Cite acts or events which show that the nation's postwar leaders lacked the vision and greatness of spirit that would have enabled them to rise above bitterness. To what extent were the American people responsible?

5. Name persons and groups in the reconstruction period that placed their own advantage before the best interests of the nation. What various things did they do? With what effects? Again, to what extent were the American people responsible for what went on during reconstruction?

#The lengthening of the life expectancies of Americans depended upon technological advances, widened educational opportunities, and sanitation requirements (which particularly affected people in the cities). See <u>American Medicine, 1607-1900</u> and also <u>American Medicine since 1900,</u> by Ilza Veith and Leo M. Zimmerman. Both are paperbacks in the Rand McNally Classroom Library.

A LONG VIEW

Testing the Federal Union

AMERICANS have written more about the Civil War than about any other era of their past. One explanation is that they are still dismayed and embarrassed because their proud Union of states came to grief and had to be remade. Realizing how profoundly the war altered the course of the nation's history, they want to know why the disaster happened.

The effect of the Civil War on the people living at the time was incalculable. They felt the emptiness created by their terrible losses of young men, and communities everywhere raised monuments to the fallen. And besides the guilt and the shame and the sadness, the Civil War left a legacy of nasty distrust, in relations both between the sections and between the races.

The nation, nevertheless, began to build a more powerful Union after 1865 on the ruins and the rubble left by the war. Lincoln became a sainted hero, taking his place alongside George Washington among the country's immortal figures.

There were countless other consequences of the war—in every level of life. For instance, many schoolmasters who had marched off to war never returned to their classrooms. The schoolmistress, who had appeared in the 1840's, became an American institution, a result in part of the liberation of women that was gaining momentum.

\# Certain conditions of life, though, were not much different from those of an earlier period. As in the 1850's, the life expectancy of a white male at birth in the 1870's was only about forty years, and that of a nonwhite male several years less. The leading causes of death in 1870 were—as they had long been—tuberculosis of the lungs, typhoid and paratyphoid fever, diphtheria, measles, and smallpox. They respected neither age nor youth.

Preventive medicine was in its infancy. Patent drugs, often palmed off as cure-alls, were in wide use, not controlled by any agency, public or private. Most Americans rarely, if ever, saw a dentist, because there were so few.

One development of the period, the appearance of the first large-scale public amusements, offered sunnier prospects. A leader was P. T. Barnum, whose "colossal museum and menagerie," opened in New York in 1842, becoming a mecca for thousands. Barnum also created a national theatrical idol—the first of its kind in America—in the person of Jenny Lind, the singer whom Barnum billed as the "Swedish Nightingale." She was presented to a worshipful audience of 7000 people in 1850, soon after her arrival from Europe. The success of Barnum and many others like him revealed a market hungry for entertainment. For the first time many Americans were beginning to have the money and the leisure time to enjoy themselves outside their homes.

Understandably, elsewhere in the world America was becoming a stronger and stronger magnet for hopeful men and women seeking personal opportunity. Moreover, the saving of the Union seemed to offer a clue to other nations. The movements which united Germany and Italy drew inspiration from the American Civil War, which had been a "war of unification," too.

The broadening of the suffrage in England from 1867 on, as well as the formation of a republic in France in the 1870's also owed something to the recent struggle in the United States. The United States had furnished fresh evidence that a republic could survive internal divisions and that it need not fear making its people as a whole freer and happier. ★ ★ ★ ★ ★ ★ ★ ★ ★ ★ ★ ★ ★

Able students can read <u>The Strange Career of Jim Crow</u>, by C. Vann Woodward. Some definite progress (later undone) was made in achieving racial equality during and after reconstruction.

PART FOUR WORKSHOP

AMERICA IN THE WORLD

1. Why does the outbreak of a civil war in any country weaken its standing among other nations of the world? Why was the American Civil War of special significance to Europeans?

2. What threat to the Monroe Doctrine developed during the Civil War? How did the United States react? Why?

3. Describe Lincoln's role in making American foreign policy during the *Trent* affair. How did his views compare with those of the British? With those of northerners in general? What risks did the President take in following his course?

4. What effect did the Treaty of Washington have on the international prestige of the United States?

5. How did the ending of slavery affect "the opinion of mankind" regarding America?

6. Would you say that the position of the United States was generally strengthened or weakened by the events discussed in Part Four? Explain.

THE FEDERAL GOVERNMENT

1. Review on page 121 the relationship between federal power and state power established by the Constitution and, on page 124, the federal principle for which the Constitution provided a working formula.

What contrasting views of the federal principle did Lincoln and the leaders of the seceding states hold in 1861? What was the matter with the Confederate constitution?

2. What relation was there between Lincoln's view of the federal principle and his plan for dealing with the seceded states after the Civil War?

3. How did the outcome of the war affect the federal principle?

TIME AND CHANGE

Bring your time line up to date. Name the dates and events that may be grouped and called (*a*) the Civil War, (*b*) the Reconstruction Period. List the major changes in the period discussed in Part Four. What change do you regard as most important? Why? Which seemed hardest to adjust to? Why?

OLD PROBLEMS BECOME NEW

1. The problem of sectionalism became so critical in 1861 that it caused a war between the North and the South. Cite facts proving that southerners had strongly national viewpoints in the early years of the United States. What role had they had in the Constitutional Convention? In launching and establishing the new government in 1787–1789?

2. How did Calhoun speak of sectionalism in 1817? How did he view internal improvements? Chartering the second Bank of the United States? The Tariff of 1816? When did the South Carolinian begin to change his views? Over what issue?

3. What threats of nullification or of secession were made before 1860? What caused each one?

4. At what times was compromise used to settle disputes between the sections? Why, on the other hand, was the Kansas question not settled peacefully?

5. Does the problem of sectionalism exist today? Explain. If so, what should Americans do about it?

6. A new problem appeared after the Thirteenth Amendment was adopted: How can Negroes achieve their civil rights? Explain how the Fourteenth and Fifteenth amendments and the Civil Rights Act of 1875 sought to solve it. What success did they have?

7. How can you account for the fact that almost seventy-five years intervened between the passage of a civil rights bill in 1875 and a second civil rights act?

8. What special handicaps did the freedmen have? Describe the efforts that were made to help the former slaves overcome them.

9. Why is the treatment it gives minorities an excellent test of a democracy? Defend your answer.

##Democratic people respect and value the worth of every individual. Members of minorities do not have the political power of majorities.

309

THE BOOKSHELF

Eyewitness Accounts

Bradford, N. G. (ed.). *Battles and Leaders of the Civil War.* 4 vols. New York: Appleton-Century, 1956.

Chestnut, Mary Boykin. *A Diary from Dixie.* Gloucester, Mass.: Peter Smith.

Eisenschiml, Otto, and Ralph Newman. *Eyewitness: The Civil War as We Lived It* [Paperback—New York: Grosset & Dunlap, Inc., 1960].

Grant, Ulysses S. *Personal Memoirs* [Paperback—New York: Grosset & Dunlap, Inc.].

Wish, Harvey. *Reconstruction in the South, 1865–1877.* New York: Farrar, Straus & Giroux, Inc., 1965 [Paperback—New York: Farrar, Straus & Giroux, Inc.].

Giant Men and Women

Capers, Gerald M. *Stephen A. Douglas, Defender of the Union.* Boston: Little, Brown & Co., 1959.

Current, Richard N. *The Lincoln Nobody Knows* [Paperback—New York: Hill & Wang, Inc., 1963].

Donald, David. *Charles Sumner and the Coming of the Civil War.* New York: Alfred A. Knopf, Inc., 1960.

Freeman, Douglas S. *R. E. Lee.* Abridged ed. New York: Charles Scribner's Sons, 1961.

———. *Lee of Virginia.* New York: Charles Scribner's Sons, 1958.

Klein, Philip S. *President James Buchanan.* University Park: Pennsylvania State University Press, 1962.

McKitrick, Eric L. *Andrew Johnson and Reconstruction.* Chicago: University of Chicago Press, 1960 [Paperback—Chicago: University of Chicago Press].

Nichols, Roy F. *Franklin Pierce.* Philadelphia: University of Pennsylvania Press, 1964.

Randall, Ruth P. *Mary Lincoln: Biography of a Marriage.* Boston: Little, Brown & Co., 1953.

Ross, Ishbel. *Angel of the Battlefield: The Life of Clara Barton.* New York: Harper & Row, Publishers, 1956.

Strode, Hudson. *Jefferson Davis.* 2 vols. New York: Harcourt, Brace & World, Inc., 1955, 1964.

Thomas, Benjamin P., and Harold M. Hyman. *Stanton: The Life and Times of Lincoln's Secretary of War.* New York: Alfred A. Knopf, Inc., 1962.

Living and Making a Living

Catton, Bruce. *Centennial History of the Civil War.* 3 vols. New York: Doubleday & Co., Inc., 1961–1965.

Cornish, Dudley T. *The Sable Arm: Negro Troops in the Union Army, 1861–1865.* New York: W. W. Norton & Co., Inc., 1966 [Paperback—New York: W. W. Norton & Co., Inc.].

Donald, David. *Why the North Won the War.* Baton Rouge: Louisiana State University Press, 1960 [Paperback—New York: P. F. Collier, Inc.].

Eaton, Clement. *A History of the Southern Confederacy.* New York: The Macmillan Co., 1954 [Paperback—New York: P. F. Collier, Inc.].

Foote, Shelby. *The Civil War: A Narrative.* 2 vols.

New York: Random House, Inc., 1958–1963.

Franklin, John Hope. *The Emancipation Proclamation.* New York: Doubleday & Co., Inc., 1963 [Paperback—New York: Archer House].

———. *Reconstruction After the Civil War.* Chicago: University of Chicago Press, 1961 [Paperback—Chicago: University of Chicago Press].

Hendrick, Burton J. *Lincoln's War Cabinet.* Gloucester, Mass.: Peter Smith.

Jones, Virgil C. *The Civil War at Sea.* 3 vols. New York: Holt, Rinehart & Winston, Inc., 1960–1962.

Korn, Bertram W. *American Jewry and the Civil War* [Paperback—New York: Harper & Row, Publishers].

McPherson, James M. *The Struggle for Equality: Abolitionists and the Negro in the Civil War.* Princeton, N.J.: Princeton University Press, 1964.

Patrick, R. W. *Jefferson Davis and His Cabinet.* Baton Rouge: Louisiana State University Press, 1961.

Rose, Willie Lee. *Rehearsal for Reconstruction.* Indianapolis: Bobbs-Merrill Co., Inc., 1964.

Stampp, Kenneth M. *The Era of Reconstruction.* New York: Alfred A. Knopf, Inc., 1965.

Wiley, Bell I. *Life of Billy Yank* [Paperback—Indianapolis: Bobbs-Merrill Co., Inc.].

———. *Life of Johnny Reb* [Paperback—Indianapolis: Bobbs-Merrill Co., Inc.].

Confronting the World

Adams, E. D. *Great Britain and the American Civil War.* 2 vols. in 1. New York: Russell & Russell Publishers, 1958.

Monaghan, Jay. *Diplomat in Carpet Slippers* [Paperback—Indianapolis: Bobbs-Merrill Co., Inc.].

Stern, Philip V. D. *When the Guns Roared: World Aspects of the American Civil War.* New York: Doubleday & Co., Inc., 1965.

Art, Science, and the Life of the Mind

Howard, John T. *Our American Music.* New York: Thomas Y. Crowell Co., 1965.

Larkin, Oliver W. *Art and Life in America.* New York: Holt, Rinehart & Winston, Inc., 1960.

Wilson, Edmund. *Patriotic Gore: Studies in the Literature of the American Civil War.* New York: Oxford University Press, Inc., 1962 [Paperback—New York: Oxford University Press, Inc.].

Historical Fiction

Crane, Stephen. *The Red Badge of Courage.* Many editions, including paperback. (A soldier's pride and fear at the Battle of Chancellorsville.)

Kane, Harnett T. *Lady of Arlington.* New York: Doubleday & Co., Inc., 1953. (Based on the life of Mrs. Robert E. Lee.)

Sinclair, Harold. *The Horse Soldiers.* New York: Harper & Row, Publishers, 1956. (The Union cavalry at war.)

Tourgee, Albion. *Fool's Errand.* Cambridge, Mass.: Harvard University Press, 1961 [Paperback—Cambridge, Mass.: Harvard University Press; New York: Harper & Row, Publishers]. (The failure of reconstruction.)

CREATING INDUSTRIAL STRENGTH

PART FIVE

By the mid-nineteenth century, black smoke pouring from factory chimneys had become a common sight in many American towns and cities. To millions of people it suggested a blight spreading across the landscape.

But to other millions it symbolized fresh and rewarding uses for nature's stored treasures. Coal and iron ore and oil were being put to work on a scale large enough to create undreamed-of wonders. Moreover, steam locomotives—despite the trail of soot they left—were girding the parts of the country together inseparably.

The price for these developments seemed high. The hours of work were inhumanly long; the conditions of labor were grim; and for thousands, there was no relief from the bleakness of urban slums and continual poverty. Besides, in manufacturing plants throughout the land, the individual worker—man, woman, or child—was being regimented # to the tempo of the machine. Its monotonous motion and sound easily depressed the spirit and often made it weak. "What can be expected of a man who has spent twenty years of his life in making heads for pins?" the French visitor Alexis de Tocqueville had asked in the 1830's.

There were many dire predictions, but they proved to be shortsighted. Long hours, woman and child labor, and slums had existed from time immemorial. Now, for the first time in history, the means were at hand to eliminate them. Mass production, new forms of power, and modern technology were capable of ending the drudgery and the misery that had always been the lot of the many.

#The Great Plains were settled by farmers in the latter half of the nineteenth century. North and South Dakota and Nebraska were among the states that entered the Union because of this migration. (See the list of states on p. 816.)

Americans were still pushing westward after the Civil War, battling Indians and enthusiastically opening up gigantic areas of some of the most productive agricultural land in the world. Yet, both on the farms and in the cities, the American people could foresee the shape of things to come: the United States was being made into a mighty nation largely dependent on its industrial vigor.

Compare this picture with the one on pp. 184-185. What contrasts can be seen?

New York in 1870. As the largest city in America, it represented urban opportunities as well as tough problems.

New-York Historical Society

312 (Students should observe the differences in clothing, the increased traffic, the increase in businesses, the electrical lines. Observe the policeman at the right.)

Observe how each of the chapters in this part deals with aspects of the growth in industrial strength. The first treats the growth of business and the development of railroads. The second shows how the settlement of the "last West" depended on industrialization. The third deals with politics in the period of great industrial expansion. The fourth describes the response of workers, and the fifth tells the effects industrialization had on farmers and urban dwellers.

PART FIVE

CREATING INDUSTRIAL STRENGTH

CHAPTER 17	CONSOLIDATING THE FACTORY SYSTEM	314
	Industrialization Remakes the American Scene	316
	Railroad-building Engages the Nation's Energies	322
	Industrial Competition Results in Big Business	328
	Men of Power and Influence Dominate the Scene	332
CHAPTER 18	SUBDUING THE "LAST WEST"	340
	Frontiersmen and Indians Come to a Final Showdown	342
	The Cattle Kingdom Claims the Great Plains	349
	Rushes for Gold and Silver Create a New Frontier	355
	The Pioneer Farmer Finally Tackles the Great Plains	362
CHAPTER 19	PARTISANSHIP AND STATESMANSHIP	370
	Politics Turns Into a Battle of Spoilsmen	372
	America Stretches Uncertainly Beyond Its Borders	388
	The United States Assumes Leadership of the Americas	394
CHAPTER 20	ORGANIZING THE FORCES OF LABOR	398
	Toilers Learn That in Union There Is Strength	400
	Workingmen Take a More Aggressive Stand	407
	A Rising Tide of Foreigners Alarms Labor Leaders	422
CHAPTER 21	THE READJUSTING OF SOCIETY	426
	An Older Way of Life Yields Its Supremacy	428
	Tillers of the Soil Enter the Door of Politics	444
	The Populists Capture the Nation's Attention	447
	A LONG VIEW	457

Discuss the meaning of the title of this chapter. "Consolidation" is the only word that describes the process that factories and industries underwent in the last half of the nineteenth century: unification, or strengthening by rearrangement.

17

CONSOLIDATING THE FACTORY SYSTEM

The sun itself has spots . . .

If there be in human history one truth clearer and more indisputable than another, it is that the cheapening of articles, whether of luxury or necessity or of those classed as artistic, insures their more general distribution, and is one of the most potent factors in refining and lifting a people, and in adding to its happiness. In no period of human activity has this great agency been so potent or so widespread as in our own.

Now, the cheapening of all these good things, whether it be in the metals, in textiles, or in food, or especially in books and prints, is rendered possible only through the operation of the law, which may be stated thus: cheapness is in

What evidence of consolidation in the milling industry is shown here? What is a grain elevator?

314 Ask why Minneapolis became a milling center. (It is located in a region of wheat farming.) Call attention to the method of moving barrels of wheat to the railroad cars (left).

proportion to the scale of production. To make ten tons of steel a day would cost many times as much per ton as to make one hundred tons; to make one hundred tons would cost double as much per ton as a thousand; and to make one thousand tons per day would cost greatly more than to make ten thousand tons.

Thus, the larger the scale of operation the cheaper the product. The huge steamship of twenty thousand burden carries its ton of freight at less cost, it is stated, than the first steamships carried a pound. It is, fortunately, impossible for man to impede, much less to change this great and beneficent law, from which flow most of his comforts and luxuries, and also most of the best and most improving forces in his life. . . .

We conclude that this overpowering, irresistible tendency toward aggregation [massing] of capital and increase of size in every branch of product [ion] cannot be arrested or even greatly impeded, and that, instead of attempting to restrict either, we should hail every increase as something gained, not for the few rich, but for the millions of poor. . . .

Every enlargement is an improvement, step by step, upon what has preceded. It makes for higher civilization, for the enrichment of human life, not for one, but for all classes of men. It tends to bring to the laborer's cottage the luxuries hitherto enjoyed only by the rich, to remove from the most squalid homes much of their squalor, and to foster the growth of human happiness. . . .

It does not tend to make the rich poorer, but it does tend to make the poor richer in the possession of better things, and greatly lessens the wide and deplorable gulf between the rich and the poor. . . .

In all great movements, even of the highest value, there is cause for criticism, and new dangers arising from new conditions, which must be guarded against. There is no nugget free from more or less impurity. . . . The sun itself has spots, but, as has been wisely said, these are rendered visible only by the light it itself sends forth. . . .

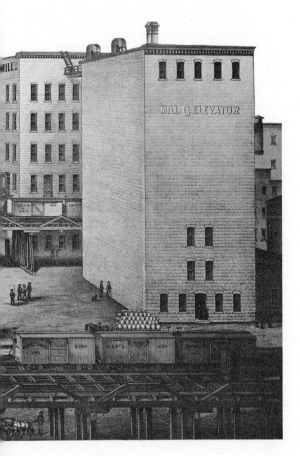

A flourishing flour mill of the late 1800's in Minneapolis, called "Mill City" because of the rapid growth of its milling industry—made possible by the railroads.

Library of Congress

Andrew Carnegie was a self-made man who rose from very humble beginnings to riches beyond dream as a manufacturer of iron and steel. He recognized early in his own industry the advantages of a large-size firm made up of formerly competing rivals it had swallowed up. He perceived, too, how new inventions could help lower prices to consumers. But, above all, he understood that for the first time in man's history a way had been opened to end the curse of widespread poverty. Carnegie took upon himself the task of defending industrialists. This selection is from an article he wrote called "Popular Illusions About Trusts," published in 1900.

Flour was once ground between millstones, but in the late 1800's corrugated steel rollers took the place of the stones. The roller mills shown here housed these rollers.

INDUSTRIALIZATION REMAKES THE AMERICAN SCENE

By the middle of the nineteenth century, manufacturing was providing a noticeable thrust to American life. Agriculture would continue for a long time to be the economic mainstay of the nation, but the growth of the factory already foretold the direction in which the United States was heading.

LOOMS, LASTS, AND LATHES

The stimulus to modern industrialization had been slowly gathering momentum since the days of Hamilton's Report on Manufactures. An unintended combination of help from government, stubborn interest of adventurous and ambitious businessmen, increasing technological skill of workers, and confidence of private investors had been at work.

The government's hand. The assistance of the federal government had taken varied forms. Among them had been tariff and banking laws, land grants for canals and railroads, and the employment of the Army Corps of Engineers to aid in improving rivers and harbors, in making railroad surveys, and in carrying on costly scientific and exploring expeditions. The first telegraph line had been put up with an outright grant of money from Congress.

Sources of capital. Private funds for investment came from European business and banking people and from savings and commercial banks in this country ever watchful for a promising venture. Also, American industrialists were willing to reinvest sizable portions of their earnings in the expansion of their plants. In front of these businessmen was the constant lure—reinforced with each succeeding census report—of the vastness of the potential national market for manufactured goods.

Technical competence. Required technical skills were also gradually developed. No doubt the widespread literacy and free schooling were helping arouse the intellectual curiosity a mechanized society requires. Most inventions were simply practical improvements on existing machines or processes. They were probably thought up when a pressing need to save time or labor or both presented itself. But, beginning in the 1820's, technical schools began to appear, a recognition that inventive tinkering was not alone an answer to the new needs of industry.

The "American method." By the time of the Mexican War, American machine tools were as good as any produced in Europe. Furthermore, American manufacturers had learned how to make separate parts for intricate machines with such accuracy that each part would fit with the others in all machines of the same design. In short, these parts, which could be produced rapidly and in large quantities, were *interchangeable*.

This innovation enabled manufacturers to turn out goods speedily and to cope with the shortage of unskilled labor. European industrialists, better supplied with labor, only gradually adopted the practice of making machine parts interchangeable, but they admiringly called it the "American method."

Made in the factory. Factory-made goods were already commonplace in the 1830's. One of the most important products was cotton cloth. From the time in 1790, when Samuel Slater, an immigrant from England, had spun the first cotton with machinery at Pawtucket, Rhode Island, to 1850, the country had acquired 3,614,000 spindles. In 1850 the industry had almost 100,000 employees and was producing each year about $76,000,000 worth of cotton cloth.

Woolen cloth also commanded an immense market. (The first woolen factory was opened in 1802 by an enterprising man who ran it with only his family as his employees.) In 1830 a single woolen plant built in Lowell, Massachusetts, was worth $100,000 and had 185 operatives—as the early factory workers were called. By 1850, 600,000 tons of iron was being manufactured every year, and the boot-and-shoe industry was annually turning out products worth $53,000,000 with employees numbering 104,000. So it was with the making of paper, steam engines, carpets, and countless other products Americans required.

How well-dressed women looked in 1870. Designers made use of the abundance of cotton and woolen cloth available.

The children are imitations of the adults. What may this say about the way they were reared?

Stylish men of this period also wore clothes made by hand from the products of textile manufacturing.

The man on the left is wearing sideburns (see the footnote, p. 280). The other men wear beards. **317**
Observe the flowing neckties and the stickpins.

"The Lackawanna Valley" by George Inness, Gift of Mrs. Huttleson Rogers, National Gallery of Art

Smoke curls upward from factories and from the locomotive of a train crossing what was once purely agricultural land. How industry was changing nineteenth-century America is obvious in this scene in upper New York State.

The physical changes in the landscape when industry begins to encroach upon it are seen here.

The effect of the war. The immediate effect of the Civil War on industrialization was to slow it down, because the hostilities disrupted the available supplies of labor, raw materials, and even railroad cars. Moreover, business activity was damaged by the breaking of most normal economic ties between the North and the South. In fact, in 1861 there were 12,000 business failures in the free states.

By 1862, however, war contracts and the consequent increased amount of money available for reinvestment somewhat brightened the prospects for industry. Supplying the military needs of the Union encouraged many factory owners to expand their operations. For in-stance, the demand for uniforms led to a tremendous growth of the woolen industry. The use of merchant ships for military purposes paved the way for the construction of new vessels on a large scale in northern shipyards.

Eight hundred miles of railroad track was laid every year of the war to meet the increasing requirements, civilian as well as military, of the Union. The stringing of 13,000 miles of telegraph lines between 1861 and 1865 linked the North more tightly than ever and started the modern communications industry. In 1861 and 1862 the Union had had to import muskets from Europe, but by 1863 Americans had established their own armories, capable of pro-

#Businessmen generally do not want wars for this very reason, although people often express the belief that businessmen profit from war and that for this reason they favor it.

ducing a million small arms a year.

Favorable legislation. In addition, as we have seen, laws favorable to business were passed by Congress: a national-banking system had been created, and the tariff rates had been raised. Also, because the supply of labor was being drained heavily by the military draft, Congress passed the Contract Labor Law in 1864. This allowed employers to engage workers abroad to come here and work for the cost of their ocean passage. These immigrants were made exempt from military service.

The Homestead Act, passed in 1862, played an important part in the growth of prosperity, too. It encouraged western settlement, which, in turn, created a demand for farm—to say nothing of railroad—equipment.

The number of patents increased during the war, and by 1865 Americans were manufacturing such items as passenger elevators, fountain pens, and automatic fans. The war years also gave many men the experience of organizing production on a large scale and finding more efficient ways to run industrial plants.

THE EFFECT ON PEOPLE

Aside from resulting in products that created new ways of living, the development of large-scale industry greatly changed the outlooks and expectations of most Americans. The factories that nourished the growth of the cities helped turn them into centers not only of wealth and elegance but also of discomfort and sometimes despair.

TEN LARGEST CITIES IN THE UNITED STATES*

	1870	1880	1890	1900
1	New York, N.Y. 1,900,000	New York, N.Y. 2,500,000	New York, N.Y. 3,400,000	New York, N.Y. 4,600,000
2	Philadelphia, Pa. 735,000	Philadelphia, Pa. 950,000	Chicago, Ill. 1,200,000	Chicago, Ill. 1,850,000
3	Boston, Mass. 410,000	Chicago, Ill. 590,000	Philadelphia, Pa. 1,175,000	Philadelphia, Pa. 1,575,000
4	St. Louis, Mo. 350,000	Boston, Mass. 550,000	Boston, Mass. 740,000	Boston, Mass. 1,150,000
5	Chicago, Ill. 325,000	St. Louis, Mo. 400,000	St. Louis, Mo. 510,000	Pittsburgh, Pa. 675,000
6	Baltimore, Md. 290,000	Baltimore, Md. 375,000	Baltimore, Md. 475,000	St. Louis, Mo. 650,000
7	Cincinnati, Ohio 275,000	Cincinnati, Ohio 340,000	Pittsburgh, Pa. 450,000	Baltimore, Md. 580,000
8	New Orleans, La. 205,000	San Francisco, Calif. 290,000	Cincinnati, Ohio 425,000	Cincinnati, Ohio 490,000
9	Pittsburgh, Pa. 190,000	Pittsburgh, Pa. 275,000	San Francisco, Calif. 385,000	San Francisco, Calif. 470,000
10	San Francisco, Calif.† 170,000	New Orleans, La. 225,000	Minneapolis–St. Paul, Minn.† 310,000	Cleveland, Ohio† 420,000

* Population figures are approximate and include suburbs.   † New addition to list.   (Continued on page 604)

New millionaires. Fortunes were made not only by those who had invested in the new industrial enterprises but also by the hundreds of men who shared in government contracts for military supplies. A newspaper reported during the war that there were already in New York alone "several hundred men worth $1,000,000 and some worth $20,000,000 while twenty years back there had not been five men in the whole United States worth as much as $5,000,000 and not twenty worth over $1,000,000."

Up the ladder of success. Some of the most humble were enabled in this generation of industrial expansion to acquire great riches. Cornelius Vanderbilt, the railroad man, was the son of a struggling ferryboat worker. Andrew Carnegie, the steel man, an immigrant, began his career as a bobbin boy in a cotton factory, earning $1.20 a week. Jay Gould, the financier, started his business life as a blacksmith's helper.

\# Although spectacular success was limited to relatively few, the standard of living was improving generally, and a diligent man could hope for a better tomorrow. Said the son of an Irish immigrant, who rose to prominence as a lawyer in New York: "In worn-out, king-ridden Europe men must stay where they are born. But in America a man is accounted a failure, and certainly ought to be, who has not risen above his father's station in life."

New hands from Europe. These were encouraging sentiments for people on the other side of the Atlantic to hear. After the Civil War, immigrants came to American shores in a steadily rising wave. The Contract Labor Law was repealed in 1868, for it was no longer necessary. Slightly under 250,000 immigrants came to the United States in 1865; in 1873 an astonishing total of nearly 460,000 was admitted. Seeking opportunity, the newcomers almost without exception settled in the northern cities.

Urbanization. The crowding together of people in the vicinities of factories in the cities inevitably brought slums and other miseries to many.
\#\# Ironically, only further industrialization and technological developments could provide the wealth and the products essential to solving many of the problems of urban society.

Inventors were soon responding to the city's requirements. For communicating faster and oftener, there was Alexander Graham Bell's telephone, which first appeared in 1876. To provide better illumination there was Thomas A. Edison's incandescent electric light, first successfully demonstrated in 1879. The effects of these inventions were felt throughout the world in a few years, but the immediate result was a quickening of American city life. It became gayer and more alluring—and more exhausting.

In the South, industry and consequently urbanization developed more slowly. Nevertheless, in 1880 Alabama produced 347,000 tons of iron, and there were 500,000 cotton spindles in Georgia and the Carolinas. The phrase "the new South" was coined to describe the transformation of the section from its former exclusive reliance on the raising of staple crops.

Conditions in post-Civil War America, then, were ripe for the "take-off" of large-scale industry. What the United States now required was an adequate means of distributing the country's finished goods. The obvious answer was more railroads.

Sum and Substance

1. How did Andrew Carnegie justify large-sized industrial undertakings? 2. Who started the use of machinery in American manufacturing? When? 3. What was meant by the "American method"? What was its advantage? 4. Who supplied funds for American industrialization? 5. How did the Civil War affect industry? What four laws aided it? 6. How was the little businessman affected by expanding industry? 7. What percent of the population in 1880 was foreign-born? 8. Name the good and bad effects of the developing urbanization. 9. What inventions helped to satisfy urban needs? 10. What need developed as industrialization increased after the Civil War?

Right: Page 1 of Edison's application to the United States Patent Office for exclusive rights to his incandescent lamp, including the method of manufacture. During a career spanning more than fifty years, Edison took out more than 1000 patents.

\#\#Ask what this sentence means. (Through technological advancements urban people could be assured healthful water supplies, sanitary plumbing, adequate housing, and transportation.)

Edison was granted over a thousand patents, although most of his inventions or technological improvements were the result of work his associates did.

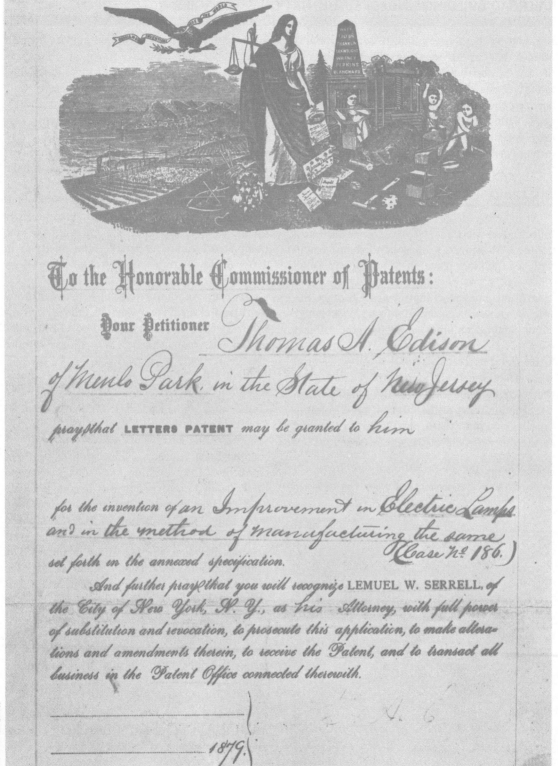

To the Honorable Commissioner of Patents:

Your Petitioner *Thomas A. Edison of Menlo Park, in the State of New Jersey*

prays that LETTERS PATENT may be granted to him

for the invention of *an Improvement in Electric Lamps and in the method of manufacturing the same* *(Case No. 186.)* set forth in the annexed specification.

And further prays that you will recognize LEMUEL W. SERRELL, of the City of New York, N. Y., as his Attorney, with full power of substitution and revocation, to prosecute this application, to make alterations and amendments therein, to receive the Patent, and to transact all business in the Patent Office connected therewith.

1879.

Review what students already know about railroad-building in the country before the Civil War (see pp. 211-212). Note that railroads as well as other industries consolidated. In doing so, they formed trunk lines. Railroads across the West were called transcontinentals.

RAILROAD-BUILDING ENGAGES THE NATION'S ENERGIES

Railroad-builders were quick to see the opportunities that lay before them. The railroads of the South, destroyed in the war, had to be virtually rebuilt. There were few railroad links between the Atlantic seaboard and the Mississippi Valley. Meat-packers in Chicago, petroleum producers in Pennsylvania, and corn farmers in Iowa were complaining about inadequate and crowded railroad lines.

THE TRUNK LINES

At the close of the war the national railroad mileage was 35,085; by 1872 it had almost
\# doubled. Moreover, a consolidation movement had been taking place in which many small and weak roads had been formed into a few great trunk lines reaching toward Chicago. Before, it had not been unusual to have to change trains eight or ten times on a trip to the "Windy City."

The New York Central. The New York Central was one of the leaders in forming trunk lines tying together the East and the Middle West. The guiding hand of the Central was "Commodore" Cornelius Vanderbilt, who had turned to the railroad field at the age of seventy after

a successful career in steamboating. As a result of his efforts to obtain control of competing lines, he enlarged his railroad until it reached to Chicago in 1869—965 miles of track.

The "Pennsy." No less impressive was the establishment of the Pennsylvania system. This road had for a long time handled the important traffic between Philadelphia and Pittsburgh. It reached Chicago about the same time as the New York Central, and it also obtained a route to St. Louis. In addition, a series of farsighted deals gave it connections with the leading cities on the eastern seaboard. Yet not until the line completed a tunnel under the Hudson River in 1910 could its trains finally enter New York City direct.

The Erie. Another trunk line between New York and cities farther west was the Erie Railroad. In 1869 the Erie boasted of "1400 miles under one management; 860 miles without change of cars."

The B & O. A fourth trunk line was the Baltimore and Ohio. It lengthened its line to make connections with Lake Erie, Chicago, and St. Louis. Its main handicap was that it did not itself run trains into New York City.

In the South. Further, the creation of southern trunk lines from existing lines took place, and badly needed construction was begun. Between 1870 and 1873 over 2500 miles of new road were built. The formation of the Chesapeake and Ohio gave Virginia and Ohio direct connections between Norfolk and Cincinnati. The Southern Railway ultimately joined all the large cities on the Mississippi with the important seaboard cities from Washington southward.

The Atlantic Coast Line, the Southern's chief competitor, had connections to important cities from Richmond southward. With 950 miles of track stretching from Chicago to the Gulf, the Illinois Central linked the northern and southern ends of the Mississippi Valley. Later it was extended to Savannah, Georgia, and proved to be an important means of carrying the meats and grains produced in the Midwest into the deep South.

Most railroads ran in an east-west direction.

To see the origins of some of the trunk lines shown on this map, compare it with the one on page 212.

MAIN EASTERN RAILROADS, 1875

0   100   200 miles

Source: *Rand McNally Railroad Guide of July, 1874*

\#Consolidation is still going on. Why?
(Because of decreased use of railroads.)

The Greenwood Iron Works, an eastern plant seen here, and other businesses along the Erie Railroad profited from having a direct connection between the East and the Midwest. Notice the car labeled "New York and Chicago."

Find the Erie Railroad on the map on p. 322. In what sense was it like the Erie Canal?

THE TRANSCONTINENTALS

West of the Mississippi the construction of the transcontinentals gripped the country's attention. Before the Civil War the North and South had contested with each other for the eastern terminus because it was believed that only one such line would ever be built.

The route. When the South left the Union, the problem of selecting a transcontinental route was simplified. Having promised in their platform of 1860 to build a transcontinental railroad, the Republicans hastened to act. Congress in 1862 incorporated the Union Pacific Company to build a road from Omaha, Nebraska, westward. (The construction workers had difficulty with Indians in both Nebraska and Wyoming.) Another line, the Central Pacific, was incorporated to build eastward from Sacramento, California, to join with the U.P.

Federal generosity. The federal government contributed handsomely to these roads in order to attract private investments to them. It provided the rights-of-way; it supplied some of the materials, like timber and stone; it gave generous land grants out of the public domain for every # mile completed. Furthermore, it paid a princely subsidy in the form of a loan for every mile of track laid. It varied, being $16,000 in the level country east of the Rockies, $32,000 in the foothills, and $48,000 across the mountains.

Laying the track. The story of the laying of the Union and Central Pacific railroads endures as part of the great saga of the West. The nation watched to see whether the eastern or the western construction gangs would win for their em-

#In all, some 131,000,000 acres were granted to the railroads by the government. Railroads later profited by selling surplus land to businessmen or to settlers.

323

Library of Congress

Nighttime at a busy railway junction in a large American city. Yardmen hurriedly give signals, and baggagemen load and unload freight. Telephone wires can be seen above the smoke at the far right.

The triangular frame at the front of the train at the right is called a cowcatcher.

ployers the high subsidies for construction through the mountains. Thousands of Chinese were brought in to join Irishmen and Civil War veterans on the labor force, which numbered about 20,000. Besides fighting Indians, these men battled blizzards and sometimes even each other.

Finally, on May 10, 1869, the "impossible" task was completed at Promontory Point near Ogden, Utah. Two locomotives, as the author Bret Harte put it, were at last "facing on a single track, half a world behind each back." The last spike—a gold one—was driven into place to complete the road; every city in the Union heard on the telegraph the clicking of "One, two, three—done!" Chicago celebrated with a parade; church chimes rent the air in New York; and in Philadelphia once again the Liberty Bell pealed.

Further construction. The building of this road encouraged other promoters to undertake similar risks. By the time the panic of 1873 slowed down railroad construction, work had begun on four more transcontinentals: the Northern Pacific, the Atlantic and Pacific, the Texas and Pacific, and the Atchison, Topeka & Santa Fe. The railroads would not have been built without government aid in money and land. In the years immediately after the Civil War, it would have been inconceivable for private investors to undertake the entire task unassisted: the transcontinentals had to be built in advance of the arrival of population.

Once in operation, these railroads sped the growth of the West. James J. Hill, who constructed the Great Northern Railroad, sent agents to Europe in an attempt to encourage settlement of the Northwest. There, in the "Hill country," he built schools, introduced scientific farming, and even gave blooded bulls to the farmers. The Santa Fe Railroad in 1874 brought 15,000 Germans to Kansas. Moreover, railroad

##In other words, towns would be settled in places near the railroads, instead of the reverse. In the

324 East, railroads connected towns or cities that had already become established.

Surveyors in 1864 plan for the first transcontinental over some of the forbidding terrain that had to be mastered.
What factors have to be considered in locating the route of a railroad?
Chinese immigrants leave quarantine at San Francisco and enter the United States, many to find work building the U.P.

Some of these Chinese intended to save their wages and return to China, and some did.

workers appear to have settled throughout the West, hoping to prosper by trying their luck on the soil.

IMPROVEMENT AND IMPACT

In time much of the railroad system, which had been so haphazardly constructed, had to be rebuilt in order to strengthen roadbeds, widen tracks, or eliminate dangerous curves. Steady improvements in technology played a part also in helping the lines to meet heavier demands. The tank car and the refrigerator car, for example, which were well developed by the

1870's, opened up new fields of service for the railroads. Using great quantities of ice, the refrigerator cars carried perishable goods long distances. #

Innovations. Travel became safer especially after the work of George Westinghouse. In 1868 this twenty-two-year-old genius invented an air brake that stopped passenger and freight cars in one-tenth the distance required for older mechanical brakes, which brakemen operated manually, one man for each car.

In 1858 George Pullman ran his first sleeping car. Tradition has it that it did not become

Five were built. Observe that the southernmost railroad ran through the Gadsden Purchase.

This map shows the routes finally chosen for the railroads to the Pacific coast. Before the Civil War Americans had hoped for only one transcontinental line. By 1893 how many had they built?

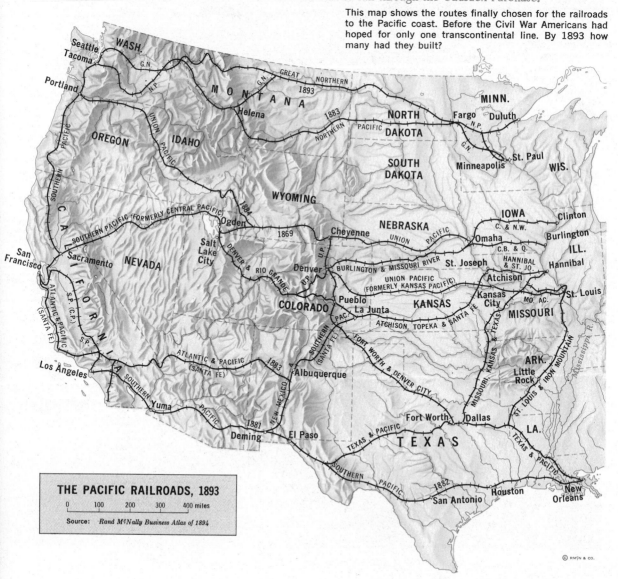

THE PACIFIC RAILROADS, 1893

0   100   200   300   400 miles

Source: *Rand McNally Business Atlas of 1894*

truly popular until Mrs. Lincoln rode in one attached to her husband's funeral train. Train travel was made more comfortable, too, when the danger of accidents from engine sparks and parting rails was reduced. The introduction of timetables and—in 1883—standard time zones helped to make train trips more predictable and convenient.

Binding the nation.

The increase in railroad mileage was a wholesome spur to American industrial development. Manufacturers could reach markets that had previously been inaccessible or unknown. Raw materials in one part of the country now were no more than a week away from any other part. Easier and consequently cheaper transportation of bulky goods like coal and iron and timber increased the number of consumers using them. The farmers of the western states were placed more quickly in touch with the world market in which they sold their produce.

Finally, because every hamlet and town was within reach of every other, manufacturers of a given product competed with one another regardless of where their plants were located. No longer could the Massachusetts boot- and shoe-maker pay no attention to the Missouri boot- and shoe-man. The growth of the railroads had put them into keen rivalry for the market of the entire United States.

Sum and Substance

1. Name four eastern trunk lines formed after the Civil War. 2. What lines operated in the South? 3. Give the important facts concerning the building of the first railroad to the Pacific coast. 4. Name three other transcontinentals. 5. How did the federal government encourage the building of railroads? 6. In what ways was railroad travel improved? 7. What effect did railroads have on American industry? 8. Tell how they affected the nation as a whole.

The Platte Valley is in Nebraska (see pp. 360-361).

Right: A poster appearing in Chicago to advertise the opening of the first transcontinental railroad. What attractions are cited as a way of appealing to prospective users? How long was the trip supposed to take?

Union Pacific Railroad

Today we cannot adequately imagine the novelty of riding across the country on a train.

#Review other influences that had contributed to forming a national culture (see p. 164). What forces are influencing the continuing development of this culture? (Suggestions: radio, television, motion pictures, magazines.) What objections can be made to carrying the development too far?

INDUSTRIAL COMPETITION RESULTS IN BIG BUSINESS

Increasingly dependent on the railroads, the nation became so unified that each geographical part of it quickly responded to the activity of every other part. As the various sections became intertwined, the distinctive sectional ways of life slowly began to blend into a *national* culture. The products of the factories were indispensable in this development. In time aspects of the resulting "American way of life" were transmitted to other places in the world through the exporting of manufactured goods.

RESOURCES AND PROCESSES

America's abundant resources provided a distinct advantage in the battle for the industrial supremacy of the world. In wealth of mineral

Petroleum came into use for lighting.

Edwin L. Drake (*in top hat*) stands before the oil well near Titusville, Pennsylvania, that opened up a new era.

American Petroleum Institute

deposits, especially, the country's chief competitors—England and, a little later, Germany—could not be compared with the United States.

Coal. The most important of the minerals was coal. From it came the energy to turn the nation's machinery. On it rested the ability to produce iron and steel and to move steamboats and locomotives. After processing, it yielded gas for lighting and heating.

By 1870 bituminous coal had overtaken anthracite in annual national consumption. By the end of the First World War in 1918, the quantity of bituminous coal being produced was about six times that of anthracite. The best bituminous coalfields are those that lie beneath the plateau extending from Lake Erie into northern Alabama.

Iron. The second great mineral resource was iron. Iron had been manufactured from iron ore in the colonial period, and this had been one of the points of disagreement with the mother country. By the decade before the Civil War, the iron industry had become established in New Jersey, Pennsylvania, and Virginia.

In 1844 iron ore was discovered near Marquette, Michigan, in the Lake Superior region. Other discoveries in that area followed and by 1854 were being developed. The principal handicap the mineowners saw was the distance from coal and from eastern consumers.

Improvements in transportation soon overcame this flaw in the location of the incredibly rich deposits. The Soo Canal, an improved connection between Lake Superior and Lake Huron after 1855, helped move the ore by steamboat to Lake Michigan and Lake Erie. The coming of the railroad provided another means of transporting it, and shortly iron ore was being shipped cheaply and in large quantity.

Oil. A third great resource was oil. When the Seneca Oil Company, with the help of "Colonel" E. L. Drake, drilled the first commercial well in 1859 near Titusville, Pennsylvania, there was little excitement. The men who promoted what was called "Drake's Folly" had no idea of

##Bituminous (soft) coal was more desirable than anthracite because it burned readily.

The buildings of the Union Iron Company, of Buffalo, New York, about 1860. The business was heavily dependent on coal. Observe how the fuel was delivered and taken to the furnaces. Housing for employees appears at the upper left.

Coal was burned to produce steam power, which surpassed water power as a source of energy.

oil as a source of energy. They were looking for a more plentiful source of kerosine. But Pennsylvania was soon swarming with oil prospectors eager to make a killing. The scene reminded eyewitnesses of the gold-rush frenzy in California only a few years before.

By the time of the depression in 1873, over 40,000,000 barrels of oil had been produced. Then the internal-combustion engine opened within a few years a seemingly unlimited market for gasoline, a by-product which had at first been thrown away as useless.

Coal-mining. Technological improvements in extracting or processing all these raw materials greatly increased the production of them. Coal-mining was least affected. It was not until the twentieth century that power cutters and automatic loaders markedly improved traditional coal-mining techniques. But in the iron-and-steel industry the story was different.

Steel-manufacturing. The fundamental principle of steel-manufacturing, long known, is to remove as much as possible the impurities—chiefly carbon and silicon—from the molten iron. A cheaper and more efficient method of doing this was the result of the work of Henry Bessemer, an English inventor, and William Kelly, an American ironmaster in Kentucky. Conflicting patent claims between Bessemer and Kelly caused difficulties, and neither the English nor the American process could be used without violating the legal rights of one of them. Their patents were combined in 1866, and thereafter the use of the process—called the "Bessemer process"—spread rapidly.

Another method, the open-hearth, or Siemens-Martin, process—named for its German and French inventors—was more expensive than the Bessemer method; it could, however, use all kinds of ores and scrap. First introduced in 1868 by Abram S. Hewitt at his foundry in Trenton, New Jersey, it gradually replaced the Bessemer process.

The expansion of the railroads caused a massive spurt in the demand for steel. When the first steel rails appeared in 1867, their superiority over the brittle iron ones was instantly recognized.

Moreover, steel came into wider and wider # general use. It replaced iron in locomotives and steamships. Its use in building construction made the skyscraper possible. Its use in tin cans revolutionized the food industry and made the distribution of motor oil handy. Its use for

#Peter Cooper, in whose ironworks at Baltimore the first steam locomotive was built, developed wrought-iron structural beams in 1860. Later steel replaced the iron in these beams.

329

COAL PRODUCTION IN THE UNITED STATES   Source: *Statistical Abstract of the United States*

(Thousands of short tons)

1830 1840 1850 1860 1870 1880 1890 1900 1910 1920 1930 1940 1950 1960

The figures are production averages for five-year periods. These totals are expressed in thousands of short tons, a short ton being equivalent to 2000 pounds. (A thousand thousands of anything is, of course, a million.)

Observe the similarity among the curves shown here and on the graphs on p. 333 and p. 335.

barbed wire, as we shall see, made possible the settlement of the Great Plains.

COMPETITION AND COMBINATION

The competition among producers in the same industry for markets as well as raw materials, labor, and prestige became an exciting sport. Businessmen at first liked to believe that competition was "the life of trade," but in time they recognized that it could be "the death of trade," too. A railroad executive in 1851 declared in an address: "We make solemn bargains with each other to be governed by certain principles and rules, and violate them the same day, by a secret bargain with an individual, to obtain a small pittance of freight from another road."

The pool. The cutthroat rivalry led to a type of arrangement known as the gentleman's agreement, or *pool,* one of the earliest attempts by enterprising men to avoid ruinous competition among themselves. Under it, the participating producers agreed to divide their market and to fix prices. They would then place their profits in a joint treasury and later divide them according to the percentage of the market assigned to each.

Pools, widespread in the fifteen years after the panic of 1873, were notable in the railroad, salt, whisky, coal, and tobacco industries. Since pooling agreements were unenforceable and uncertain, they proved inadequate for controlling competition.

The merger. There appeared to be two logical solutions to the problem of reducing self-destructive competition. The first—a *merger*—was for rival businessmen to combine their firms into a single company with the strongest in the field usually buying out the others. The New York Central Railroad was an organization of this kind; Western Union in telegraphy was another.

The trust. A second solution was to create a *trust*. This meant placing control of various competing corporations in the hands of a single group of stockholders. These men were called "trustees," the stockholders of the various corporations receiving "trustee certificates" in exchange for their original stock certificates.

The first such combination was the Standard Oil Trust, formed in 1882. It was shortly followed by others in almost every branch of industry: a cottonseed-oil trust, a lead trust, a whisky trust, a leather trust, a sugar trust.

#The major stockholders in each corporation would sign over their voting rights to the trustees, who in turn would determine policy for it and for all the other corporations in the trust.

"Monopoly" means exclusive or almost exclusive control of an industry. A monopoly need not be bad, but it provides an opportunity for something undesirable to develop. We tend to use the word to designate something bad or undesirable.

Harper's Weekly, September 11, 1869

Anthracite coal comes from mines mixed with slate, which must be removed. Today machines perform the work, but for years boys, supervised by a foreman, bent over slowly moving chutes picking out the pieces of slate by hand.

How old do students think the boys are? In what grade in school would they be today?

"Trust" became a word loosely used to describe *any* monopoly. The tremendous strength a trust could exert explains why this happened. A contemporary described the power of the American Sugar Refining Company, formed under Henry Havemeyer, of New York, in 1887: its directors "can close every refinery at will, close some and open others, limit the purchase of raw material [thus jeopardizing, and in a considerable degree controlling, its production], artificially limit the production of refined sugar, enhance the price to enrich themselves and their associates at the public expense, and depress the price when necessary to crush out and impoverish a foolhardy rival."

The holding company and the interlocking directorate. In 1890 the federal Sherman Antitrust Law made trusts illegal as "combinations in restraint of trade." However, two other kinds of business organizations took the place of the trust. They were the *holding company** and the *interlocking directorate*. Although they differed from the trust in form, they retained the trust's characteristic of seeking to be a monopoly in its field.

These combinations became like gigantic empires, able to resist both economic and political opposition. As men of power who could control whatever assets they needed, the industrialists did not hesitate to influence the state legislatures. Henry Demarest Lloyd, a reformer of the 1880's, said, "The Standard [Oil Company] has done everything with the Pennsylvania legislature except to refine it."

Effects on government. Commodities rather than states seemed to be represented in the national Senate now; there were lumber Senators, coal and iron Senators, banking Senators, cotton Senators, and so on. Hardly an "interest" failed to attempt making its influence felt there.

Sum and Substance

1. Name three mineral resources on which American industrialization depended. Where was each found? 2. How was steel-manufacturing improved? 3. Why did the demand for steel rise? 4. Name three ways by which businessmen sought to control competition. 5. What replaced trusts? Why?

---

*The holding company is a corporation which manufactures nothing and whose sole purpose is to own the stock of a number of corporations in the same or related industries. Interlocking directorates result where a number of firms, again in the same or related industries, are able to operate in concert with one another because men in the same group are serving on the boards of directors of several or all of them.

Holding companies actually sell stocks in themselves to raise money for buying controlling interests in corporations they are interested in.

331

Puck, January 23, 1889

This biting cartoon of 1889, "The Bosses of the Senate," criticizes the links between politics and big business.

Why has it been rather easy in the past for big business to influence politics?

MEN OF POWER AND INFLUENCE DOMINATE THE SCENE

The power of big business appeared to be on the verge of outstripping the power of the government to control it. By 1904 the consolidation movement had proceeded so far that there were more than three hundred huge industrial combinations representing investments, added together, of over $7,000,000,000. About four-fifths of all American industries were organized in this way, and they controlled about two-fifths of the manufacturing capital available in the country.

How these mergers developed, the variety of interests they came to dominate, and the control they wielded are strikingly illustrated in the careers of two men. These were John D. Rockefeller and Andrew Carnegie.

JOHN D. ROCKEFELLER: OIL MAGNATE

Rockefeller, born in 1839, was to live for ninety-eight years—from the day of horsepower to the eve of the atomic age. His mother taught him the value of hard work; his father instilled in him the shrewdness that makes hard work and ambition go far.

Standard Oil. In 1860 Rockefeller invested in petroleum production a part of the $700 that he had saved working as a clerk and book-keeper in Cleveland. The petroleum firm within two years showed a profit of $4000, and the future seemed rosy.

Rockefeller, who dominated the concern from the start, advised his partners to reinvest this money in the business itself. He told them: "Take out what you have [to have] to live on, but leave the rest in. Don't buy new clothes and fast horses . . . let your wife wear her last year's bonnet. You can't find any place where money will earn what it does here." The company grew at a fantastic rate, and in 1870 the Standard Oil Company of Ohio was created with $1,000,000 in cash invested. It now set about to eliminate its competitors.

Some of its methods. As early as 1867 Rockefeller had forced the railroad line over which he shipped to grant him a rebate on the published freight rate. This practice obviously put his competitors at an impossible disadvantage.

Rockefeller, as the largest shipper in the re-

#Recall that this was a Puritan value. Do Americans continue to hold it?

##Rockefeller threatened that if railroads did not give him rebates, he would acquire railroads.

PETROLEUM PRODUCTION IN THE UNITED STATES

Although the largest oil reserves are found in Southwest Asia, the United States produces more petroleum than that area does.

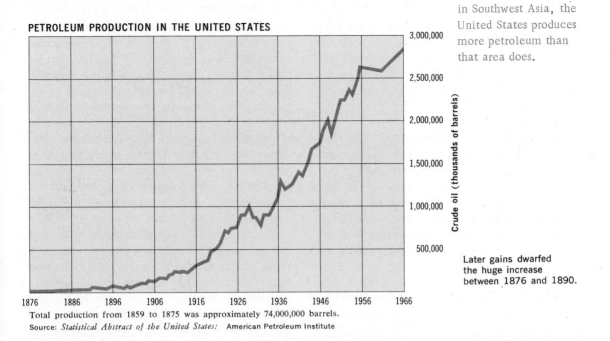

Later gains dwarfed the huge increase between 1876 and 1890.

Total production from 1859 to 1875 was approximately 74,000,000 barrels.

Source: *Statistical Abstract of the United States:* American Petroleum Institute

Why was the octopus perhaps the best characterization of the Standard Oil Company?

The tentacles of the octopus are shown as reaching out to ensnare rivals, other industries, and seats of government.

Puck, September 7, 1904

Students should note the significance of the seizures the octopus has made: the national Capitol, a state legislature, steel and copper industries. He is eyeing the White House.

333

gion, was in a position to force the railroads to do his bidding. By secret agreements with the Pennsylvania, Erie, and New York Central, not only was he obtaining railroad rebates on his own oil shipments, but he was insisting on receiving rebates on every barrel his competitors shipped!

When hard times came in 1873, the rival petroleum firms which had resisted joining their companies to his were more submissive. Their alternatives were now clear: sell out or face bankruptcy. By 1879 Rockefeller ruled about 90 percent of the country's oil-refining business.

By 1882 the Standard Oil Trust was organized as a method of safeguarding legally the

Carnegie set up a foundation to advance teaching.

Andrew Carnegie, a Scotch immigrant who rose from a life of poverty to one of tremendous wealth and influence. His uncommon foresight, skill as an organizer, and shrewdness made his name a synonym for "steel." The books seen here suggest his life-long interest in education and learning.

United States Steel Corporation

far-flung petroleum empire. Its control was given to a board of nine trustees, whose dominant figure was John D. Rockefeller. In his hands were the strings directing practically the entire oil business of the United States.

Explanations of success. The American idea of free enterprise seemed to sanction the activities of industrial monarchs like Rockefeller. Besides, the book on evolution which had been presented to the public in 1859 by Charles Darwin had made a new phrase, "the survival of the fittest," popular. It proved useful in justifying the consolidation of industry.

Businessmen liked to point out that since it appeared to be a divine law for the bigger fish in the oceans to eat the smaller ones, the same high authority surely must sanction business mergers. Rockefeller himself told the Baptist Sunday school class he taught that the Standard Oil Trust was "merely a survival of the fittest. . . . The American beauty rose can be produced in the splendor and fragrance which bring cheer to its beholder only by sacrificing the early buds which grow up around it. This is not an evil tendency in business. It is merely the working-out of a law of nature and of God." The notion was that since this law came from on high, it would be blasphemous to tamper with it by reform legislation.

ANDREW CARNEGIE: STEEL GIANT

Andrew Carnegie came to the United States from Scotland as a twelve-year-old, in 1848. After working briefly in a cotton mill, he got a job as a telegraph clerk in Pittsburgh. Like Rockefeller, Carnegie had a sense of the promise that the future held. Carnegie was writing to his Scottish friends soon after arriving: "The Wolf and the Buffalo are startled by the shrill scream of the Iron Horse where a few years ago they roamed undisturbed. . . . This country is completely cut up with Railroad Tracks, Telegraphs, and Canals. . . . Everything around us is in motion."

At seventeen, Carnegie had much impressed Colonel Thomas A. Scott, the superintendent of the Pittsburgh Division of the Pennsylvania Railroad, who made him his private secretary.

\#Rockefeller retired with a fortune estimated to be one billion dollars, or <u>one thousand millions</u>.

Students will benefit from investigating how Americans have benefited from various gifts Rockefeller and Carnegie made with their wealth. Let them find out how much Rockefeller donated to the University of Chicago, for example.

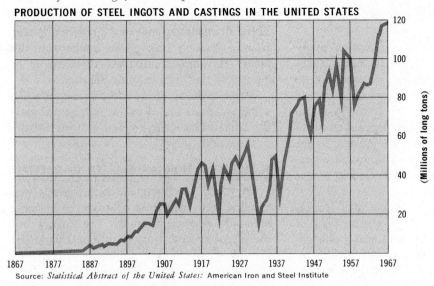

PRODUCTION OF STEEL INGOTS AND CASTINGS IN THE UNITED STATES

Source: *Statistical Abstract of the United States:* American Iron and Steel Institute

Ingots and castings are the forms in which steel is supplied to users. The enormous upswing in production in the late 1800's corresponds to the growth of heavy industry.

Carnegie is said to be chiefly responsible for the expansion between about 1870 and 1900.

At twenty-four Carnegie succeeded Scott as superintendent. But he was determined to have his own business.

His foresight. Recognizing the importance of cheap steel rails, Carnegie in 1864 obtained a one-sixth interest in the Iron City Forge Company. At about the same time he organized the Keystone Bridge Company.

By 1873, when the panic came, Carnegie was already a multimillionaire able easily to buy out weakened rival companies. But new triumphs still lay ahead. Just outside of Pittsburgh he built a plant which he called the Edgar Thomson Works after the president of the Pennsylvania. Undoubtedly flattered, Thomson gave Carnegie the Pennsylvania's tremendously profitable orders for steel rails and bridges.

Henry Clay Frick. Meanwhile, in 1864—just as Carnegie was plunging into the iron-and-steel business—a fifteen-year-old boy at Mount Pleasant, near Pittsburgh, was eyeing shrewdly the manufacture of coke.† He was Henry Clay

Frick, who had saved his money and had purchased a small piece of coal land.

Around this possession he organized Frick and Company in 1871. During the panic of 1873, Frick, like Rockefeller and Carnegie, bought out financially embarrassed competitors, and he became the foremost figure in the coke business. Profits piled up, making Frick a millionaire many times over. He eventually controlled four-fifths of the nation's coke production.

By 1882 the logic of linking coke- and steel-manufacturing under one management appealed to both Carnegie and Frick. Consequently, the Carnegie interests bought the Frick company. Frick, who received stock in the Carnegie works as payment, in this way entered the steel business.

Carnegie and Frick got on brilliantly together. The personality of each man filled some need in the other's. Carnegie was a warm-hearted, inspiring business leader who liked his men to call him "Andy"; Frick was a cold, strong-willed person who made the workers understand that, like the very machinery they

---

†Coke is coal baked into hard gray bricks to remove water and impurities. It is necessary as fuel in the smelting of iron ore.

#Frick gave his home and a fine art collection to be used as an art museum (the Frick Museum in New York City). He also contributed to Princeton University.

#In "The Gospel of Wealth," Carnegie said: "Why should men leave great fortunes to their children? If this is done from affection, is it not misguided affection?... It is not well for the children that they should be so burdened." Let the class discuss his viewpoint.

operated, they were replaceable at a moment's notice.

Expansion. The Carnegie organization established its own steamer lines on the Great Lakes to control the transportation of iron ore to Pittsburgh. It built its own railroad from its ore deposits to the water. In the 1890's the firm acquired the Mesabi iron-ore deposits north of Duluth, Minnesota, among the greatest in the world. When Carnegie retired from active control of the firm in 1892, its stock had a face value of $160,000,000.

"The Gospel of Wealth." Carnegie, like Rockefeller, reflected later in life on the meaning of his enormous success. He developed a philosophy, or point of view, which he described in an essay called "The Gospel of Wealth," published in 1889. His position was that luxury, formerly available only to kings, had now become, through industrialization, available to everybody. The price society had to pay for this great blessing was, he said, that it divided people into two classes: the rich and the poor.

But Carnegie did not expect that the wealthy would gloat over their money. He believed that the rich man must set an example for others by modest living, by caring adequately for his dependents, and by managing his surplus funds carefully. These funds, he said, ought to be regarded as a trust of the community, so that beneficial results would flow to all. He thought a rich man was merely the "agent and trustee for his poorer brethren, bringing to their service his superior wisdom, experience, and ability to administer, doing for them better than they would or could do for themselves."‡

SOME LESSER CAPTAINS OF INDUSTRY

Nearly all industries were headed by men like Rockefeller and Carnegie, who believed that because they were examples of the "survival of the fittest" they must conduct themselves in accordance with the "gospel of wealth." Philip Armour and Gustavus Swift dominated meat-

packing; Charles A. Pillsbury rose to the top of the flour-milling industry; Frederick Weyerhaeuser became king of the lumbermen; and Henry Havemeyer surpassed all others in his control of the sugar-refining industry.

These captains of industry, by means which some regard as foul, some as fair, helped make the United States the greatest industrial nation in the world.

J. PIERPONT MORGAN: MASTER OF CAPITAL

By 1900 the merchant-industrialists were yielding their place to a new type of businessman—the finance capitalist. The finance capitalist could not provide technical industrial know-how or increase productivity. He was a man who exerted his authority over industry through his control of money, credit, and banking. He bought and sold, not steel ingots or barrels of petroleum or tons of coal, but stocks and bonds that American industries had issued in order to obtain cash. J. Pierpont Morgan was the most powerful finance capitalist in America.

Beginnings in England. Born to wealth and also college-educated—unlike most of the industrialists of his day—Morgan in 1856 joined his father's banking firm in London. In 1860 the younger Morgan opened a branch of the family business in New York City. By the 1880's he was helping to finance America's railroads.

The influence of the house of Morgan was ## felt throughout the world of finance; in commercial banking, in insurance companies, in stock-market operations. It was reported in 1912 that the Morgan partners and their satellite banking colleagues held directorates in 112 corporations with assets estimated to be over $22,000,000,000.

The United States Steel Corporation. In 1901 Morgan was responsible for bringing together the Carnegie Steel Corporation and eleven other producers to form the United States Steel Corporation. The new organization had a capitalization of—that is, the face value of its stock was—almost one and a half billion dollars. The Carnegie firm alone cost $447,000,000, perhaps the largest sale in history. Finley Peter Dunne

---

‡Carnegie tried to live by his own advice. His wide-ranging benefactions totaled about $350,000,000. The money was spent for a variety of useful purposes, including the establishment of over 2800 public libraries.

 ##Morgan became so powerful that a President once had to ask for his help. See p. 386. Why was Morgan as important in the development of American industry as industrial leaders?

in his "Mr. Dooley" expressed the public wonder at so much power in one man's grip by having one of his characters, an Irish tavern keeper, say:

> Pierpont Morgan calls in wan iv his office boys, th' prisident iv a national bank, an' says he, "James," he says, "take some change out iv th' damper an' r-run out an' buy Europe f'r me," he says. "I intind to re-organize it an' put it on a paying basis," he says. "Call up the Czar an' th' Pope an' th' Sultan an' th' Impror Willum, an' tell thim we won't need their sarvices afther nex' week," he says. "Give thim a year's salary in advance."

The "money trust." Any large-scale economic power posed a threat, it seemed, to the life of democracy itself. The "money trust" appeared to be the most dangerous monopoly of all. When in 1902 the Northern Securities Company, which Morgan had organized, began to come under attack as being in violation of the Sherman Antitrust Law, Morgan had an interview with Theodore Roosevelt, then president of the United States.

Said Morgan, "If we have done anything wrong, send your man [meaning, of course, the Attorney General] to my man [meaning Morgan's attorney] and they can fix it up." Roosevelt was furious to think, as he expressed it,

Cartoons like this aroused public indignation over the activities of big business.
A cartoonist at the close of the nineteenth century saw "King Monopoly" as growing fat on the tribute of workers.

Puck, May 7, 1890

What various groups were enriching "King Monopoly"? What is "booty"?

that Morgan considered the president of the United States to be "a big rival operator."

INSPIRATION AND CHALLENGE

The big businessmen who controlled America's basic industries became the new American heroes. In the public's estimation they were more to be admired than political leaders. Now—after reconstruction and the Grant era— \# "politician" was a word with a bad odor. Before the Civil War neither a Lincoln nor a Calhoun had been ashamed to call himself a politician. The youth of that day were taught to pattern themselves after the Websters and the Douglases and the Clays, for those men were the public gods.

\#\# One can see why the captains of industry were now the young man's models. It was they

Many people in the early 1900's read Alger's books.

Horatio Alger's *Mark, the Match Boy* opened with this illustration. The author said he planned the "Ragged Dick Series" to call attention to urban poverty as well as to entertain.

Special Collections, Columbia University Libraries

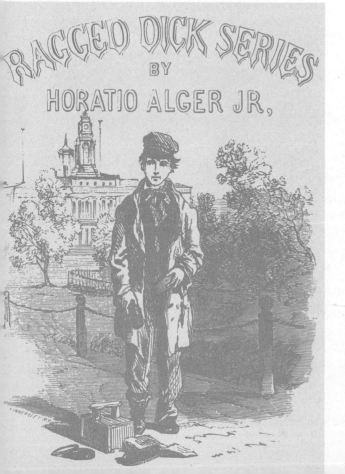

who wielded authority over employees more numerous than the constituents of some congressmen. It was they who negotiated agreements with foreign competitors as if they were monarchs of old. It was they who earned prestige in the community because they were the "big taxpayers," the "big givers" to charities, and the men who could "get things done" because they had "connections."

Between 1870 and the end of the century, American boys were influenced by the dream of rising from rags to riches. The books of Horatio Alger were among the popular books read by young people. Some of their titles tell of their contents: *Strive and Succeed, Brave and Bold, Strong and Steady, Slow and Sure, Fame and Fortune, Try and Trust.*

Many homely sayings became common: "Genius thrives on adversity"; "There's always room at the top"; "Slow but steady wins the race." Big business offered America new goals and new ideals. Voices of protest were barely heard, and protesters were still unorganized.

As a people Americans had solved the problem of how to produce abundantly and efficiently. Could they as quickly and as well answer the question of how to distribute the country's natural bounty to benefit all the people? Could they prevent a small privileged group from rising in their midst whose members, by exercising their economic might, would destroy democracy?

In 1889 Benjamin Harrison became President, and in his inaugural he told his fellow Americans: "God has placed upon our head a diadem and has laid at our feet power and wealth beyond definition. But," he added thoughtfully, "we must not forget that we take these gifts upon the condition that justice and mercy shall hold the reins of power."

Sum and Substance

1. What business methods did Rockefeller use? What did he achieve? 2. What did Frick and Carnegie accomplish? 3. Explain the "gospel of wealth." 4. What is a finance capitalist? What influence did Morgan have? 5. How was industrialization an inspiration and a challenge?

Ask what books are especially popular among young people today. What do they teach?

THE WORKSHOP

OF LASTING SIGNIFICANCE

How was each of the following involved in the expansion of American industry?

Andrew Carnegie
Samuel Slater
"American method"
Contract Labor Law
urbanization
Alexander Graham
  Bell
Thomas A. Edison
Cornelius Vanderbilt
"take-off"
Union Pacific
  Company
Ogden, Utah
James J. Hill
George Westinghouse
George Pullman
E. L. Drake
Henry Bessemer

William Kelly
Siemens-Martin
  process
pool
merger
trust
Sherman Antitrust
  Law
holding company
interlocking
  directorate
John D. Rockefeller
Henry Clay Frick
coke
"The Gospel of
  Wealth"
J. Pierpont Morgan
Horatio Alger

DOCUMENTS IN HISTORY

1. What points did Carnegie make in his defense of trusts in the quotation from his article on pages 314–315? What conclusion did he draw? How did he seek to explain away the public's criticism of trusts?

2. What was Carnegie's strongest point? Do you agree with his idea that "every enlargement is an improvement. . . ."? Explain.

3. What explained Carnegie's viewpoint?

HISTORY IN GRAPHIC MATERIAL

1. On two outline maps of the United States name the Great Lakes, the principal rivers, the Erie Canal, and the Soo Canal. On one of the maps name the states in the Union in 1870, and on the other those included by 1900 (see the chart on page 816). On the map naming the states of 1870, show also the ten largest cities in that year. On the other map show the ten largest cities in 1900 (see page 319).

In 1870 what percent of the cities were in New England? East of the Appalachians? In the South? In the Middle West? In the Far West? Similarly, find these percentages for the ten largest cities in 1820 (see page 165). In the fifty years between 1820 and 1870, how did the percentages change? Can you explain why?

One new city appears on the list for 1870. How can you explain this particular addition? How did Chicago rank in 1860? In 1870? In 1900? Explain its changing position on the list (you may want to refer also to the maps on pages 212 and 322). What city dropped off the list in 1890? Trace its ranking from 1810 to 1880. In what decades did it have its greatest growth? How did its appearance on the lists and its disappearance relate to transportation?

2. Using your outline maps, describe the relative location of each city you showed there. How is the location of each newcomer to the lists of 1870–1900 related to natural features (including mineral resources)? To technological development?

BEING A SOCIAL SCIENTIST

1. Was the federal government justified in helping to finance the Union Pacific–Central Pacific and other transcontinental railroads? Explain. What business undertakings does the # federal government subsidize today? How do you account for these subsidies?

2. Are politicians less respected in the United States today than industrialists and financiers, as in the period after the Civil War? Account for your answer. What aroused respect after the war? What inspires respect today? ##

3. Use reference books to find out more about the inventors and businessmen named in this chapter. Try to find out the reasons for their success. Make reports to the class.

4. How was your own community related to the development of American industry in the nineteenth century?

5. Obtain a copy of a book by Horatio Alger and compare its content with that of popular reading material for young people today. How do you account for the differences?

##This question gives an opportunity to explore the attitudes of students--to find out what qualities they think Americans admire most in public figures, etc.

339

See "Documents in History," p. 369. Bryce gives a promising picture of the "last West" as a land of riches and opportunities. Yet the title of this chapter indicates that this area had to be subdued. How can this seeming contradiction be explained?

18

SUBDUING THE "LAST WEST"

A vast territory, wonderfully rich . . .

Western America is one of the most interesting subjects of study the modern world has seen. There has been nothing in the past resembling its growth, and probably there will be nothing in the future.

A vast territory, wonderfully rich in natural resources of many kinds; a temperate and healthy climate fit for European labour; a soil generally, and in many places marvellously fertile; in some regions mountains full of minerals, in others trackless forests where every tree is over two hundred feet high; and the whole of this virtually unoccupied territory thrown open to a

Observe how the men at the right are trying to break off a tree (see the trees at the left).

#Which of these aims have been accomplished? (Suggestions: mines were opened and ore was extracted; cattle raising was established; wheat cultivation became common in the Pacific Northwest—but there are no prairies there—and grapes and olives became products of California.)

vigorous race with all the appliances and contrivances of modern science at its command—these are phenomena absolutely without precedent in history, and which cannot recur elsewhere, because our planet contains no such favoured tract of country.

The Spaniards and Portuguese settled in tropical countries. . . . They carried with them the poison of slavery; their colonists were separated, some by long land journeys, and all by still longer voyages, from the centres of civilization. But the railway and the telegraph follow the Western American. The Greeks of the sixth and

seventh centuries before Christ, who planted themselves all round the coasts of the Mediterranean, had always enemies . . . to overcome. . . . In Western America the presence of the Indians has done no more than give a touch of romance or a spice of danger to the explorations of some regions. . . .

Nature and Time seem to have conspired to make the development of the Mississippi basin and the Pacific slope the swiftest, easiest, completest achievement in the whole record of the civilizing process of mankind since the founder of the Egyptian monarchy gathered the tribe of the Nile under one government. . . .

All the passionate eagerness, all the strenuous efforts of the Westerners is directed towards the material development of the country. To open the greatest number of mines and extract the greatest quantity of ore, to scatter cattle over a thousand hills, to turn the flower-spangled prairies of the Northwest into wheatfields, to cover the sunny slopes of the Southwest with vines and olives: this is the end and aim of their lives. . . .

The settlement of what still remained of the virgin West by the middle of the nineteenth century is a story composed of a number of incredibly colorful chapters. They include the outbreak of fierce fighting with the Indians, the growth of the cattle industry, the development of the venturesome mining frontier, and the use of novel farming techniques. Taken together, they form a remarkable epoch in America's history, one in which technology was sufficiently advanced to handle the new environment. No one saw this more clearly than James Bryce, a famous, observant English traveler. This selection from his book The American Commonwealth—*first published in 1888—was written after Bryce had made two extensive journeys into the trans-Mississippi region.*

Life Magazine

The first pathbreakers were the Indians and the fur traders and trappers.

Miners at work in a crude camp in the Rocky Mountains. Lured by the hope of sudden wealth, prospectors like these were pathbreakers in the "last West." *Right:* An intent man looks for ore with the help of a "cradle." Left: Another uses a washing pan.

Mining was hard work, but the hope of sudden wealth kept spurring men on.

FRONTIERSMEN AND INDIANS COME TO A FINAL SHOWDOWN

Even as H. C. Frick and J. P. Morgan were filling their luxurious town houses with European art treasures, a vast part of America was still a primitive frontier. Even as the Metropolitan Opera Company began in New York in 1883 and welcomed the best singers in the world, the West was resounding to the "Yippee!" of the cowboy.

THE PRIZE AT STAKE

The "last West" still unoccupied by Americans was the area the settlers of Oregon and the gold seekers of California had passed by during the 1840's. For twenty years beginning in the 1860's it was the scene of constantly stirring drama. It was the bloody battleground of aggressive frontiersmen and desperate Indians. At the same time it irresistibly drew cattlemen, miners, and homesteaders, each group more eager than the other to exploit the natural riches of the mountains and plains.

Terrain. This huge region extended roughly from the 100th meridian to the settled areas on the Pacific coast. The eastern part of it, ending at the foothills of the Rocky Mountains, is called the Great Plains, made up of land that is generally treeless except in river valleys. The farther west one goes, the drier this land is. Once covered with short grass, it is sometimes referred to as grassland.

Immediately west of the Great Plains, and rising abruptly from them, lie the rugged Rockies. Still farther west are the plateaus that are bounded on the east by the Rockies and on the west by the ranges that form the spine of Washington, Oregon, and California. The southern part of this area is very dry and requires irrigation to make it fit for agriculture.

The tribesmen. Before 1860 the Great Plains were inhabited by the Plains Indians. Superb horsemen and warriors, they fought more ferociously than any other Indians the settlers encountered in their westward movement. Previously, settlers had always been able to strike at the Indians by burning their crops and destroying their villages. The Plains Indians, not being dependent upon agriculture, could fight and run away.

Increasing tension. When the forty-niners made their way to California, they sometimes met Indian attacks. In general, however, conflict was on a small scale. As long as the Plains Indians occupied the Great Plains and as long as frontiersmen believed that that region was unsuited for agriculture, there would be no extensive hostilities.

The comparative peace, though, did not last: gold had been discovered in 1859 in the vicinity of Pike's Peak (see the map on page 344), and a hundred thousand miners were shortly in the vicinity, driving the Indians from the land. These Indians—the Cheyenne and Arapaho—at last had no place to go; they must stand and fight.

ON THE WARPATH

The Plains Indians made deadly use of the short bow, which could be fired with uncanny accuracy from horseback. It gave them, for a time, a decided advantage over their enemies. But the Colt six-shooter was introduced into the United States Army in the 1850's. American troops now had a comparable weapon that could be fired easily and rapidly by a mounted person. Indians would no longer be able to draw fire from a soldier and then rush him while he was reloading his old-fashioned rifle.

The Chivington massacre. By the beginning of the 1860's Colorado—made a territory in 1861—was the scene of mean guerrilla warfare with the Indians. Officials of the federal government had aroused the Indians by breaking an agreement with them and treating them harshly. In revenge the tribesmen took to raiding and pillaging. In 1864 Colonel J. M. Chivington, commander of the Colorado militia, leading a thousand volunteers, shamefully butchered 500 sleeping Indians on a reservation at Sand Creek. Men, women, and even children fell victim; only about fifty escaped.

Hardly had peace come in Colorado when the Sioux (pronounced *Soo*) went on the war-

##Among the Plains Indians were the Comanche, the Arapaho, the Hidatsa, the Mandan, the Sioux, and the Cheyenne. The Mandan will be recalled as the Indians whom Lewis and Clark visited.

Observe the rifles that the Indians were carrying--a technological advance provided by the white man.

Montana Historical Society

Plains Indians under cover of rocks watch settlers encroaching on their land. The tribesmen, whose use of horses dated back to the arrival of the Spaniards, enjoyed the freedom of the Great Plains until, at last, farmers began to move there. Their conquest of the Indians was a large part of "subduing the 'last West.'"

Recall that the Indians did not understand the concept of private ownership of property.

path in the Dakota Territory. A number of reports had stirred them up: the news of the Chivington massacre, of miners advancing into the adjoining Montana Territory, and of the federal attempt to build a road connecting Montana with the East. The 16,000 Sioux Indians proved to be a strong enemy, and by 1867 they had killed many settlers and frightened the whole region.

The reservations policy. Congress offered only one solution to the troubles: the Indians must be settled on out-of-the-way compounds, or reservations. There was only one thing the Indians were fighting for: the right to move freely over the Plains. At a peace conference held in St. Louis in 1867, it was decided to set up two reservations—one to contain 54,000 northern Indians in the Black Hills of the Dakota Territory; and the other, 86,000 southern tribesmen in what is now Oklahoma. Situated at a distance from the transcontinental railroad routes and deemed unsuitable for farming, the reservations consisted of land that was not then desirable to new settlers.

#The Indians believed that land had been given for all men to enjoy and use economically. Discuss how hard it would have been if the white men had had to give up their idea about land.

The yellow area shown here is the area of the West that was settled last. Recall that California had become a state in 1850. Oregon had entered the Union in 1859. No other states had been formed in the whole western area.

The solid expanse of the "last West" was marked by only isolated areas of white settlement—containing no more than a handful of inhabitants to the square mile. Nevertheless, the Plains Indians could sense what lay ahead for them: miners were already arriving, and surveyors were marking out railroad routes.

THE "LAST WEST," 1860

0   100   200   300   400 miles

Areas Settled

The Indian reservations that were set up in this area by 1900 are shown on the map on p. 366.

A decade of bloodshed. Many of the young braves vowed to fight to the death against giving up their tribal lands and moving to reservations. By the fall of 1868 and for the next decade, the bloodiest Indian fighting in American history took place in the huge area of the Great Plains. The tribesmen of the southern Plains were not quieted until the Red River War of 1874–1875. This war ended in disaster for the Indians, who encountered the superior strength of troops commanded by Generals William T. Sherman and Philip H. Sheridan.

"Custer's last stand." The northern Plains Indians still believed they could defy the frontiersmen. They soon put their determination to the test. The gold rush to the Black Hills

#The Indians were at a disadvantage in fighting the white man because of their own tribal jealousies which prevented them from presenting a united front.

#See the books about Indian resistance listed on p. 459, especially the first book under "Eyewitness Accounts," the last book under "Historical Fiction," and J. W. Vaugh's book under "Living and Making a Living."

(see the map opposite) in the summer of 1875 brought tens of thousands of miners to the area. They ignored the rights of the Indians, prospecting—at dangerous risk, of course—on the reservation land where the government had placed the Indians and even staking out claims there.

The United States authorities asked the Sioux to sell the mining country. Although the Indians refused, the federal authorities made no attempt to hold back the tide of Americans. The inevitable result was a war, which began in 1876.

The two important Indian chieftains Sitting Bull and Crazy Horse had gathered supplies on the stream called the Little Big Horn River. An ambitious young colonel, George A. Custer, was sent to find the Indian position and then swing his troops around it. This maneuver was expected to prevent the tribesmen from retreating into the mountains when they were attacked by the strong force that would come up the river.

Custer, impatient, did not wait for the main body of troops to arrive. On June 25, 1876, he threw his 264 men at the Indians, who were hiding in ravines. The soldiers were slain to a man in this battle—the Battle of the Little Big Horn—which almost immediately became famous as "Custer's last stand." It symbolized the senseless cruelty and wastefulness of the final conflict between the Indians and their opponents.

The pipe of peace. Indian resistance was doomed to be broken. On October 31, 1876, 3000 Sioux surrendered to Colonel Nelson A. Miles, ending the major Indian wars. Sitting Bull escaped to Canada with a few die-hards; the

The artist drew the horses with more realism than he drew the men.

The approach of Colonel Custer's soldiers before the Battle of the Little Big Horn, drawn in 1881 by Red Horse, an Indian participant. Despite this one overwhelming victory, the Indians were fighting a lost cause. Sitting Bull and his associates bid for peace in 1881, when starvation forced their return from Canada.

Bureau of American Ethnology, Smithsonian Institution

See the first item under "Informed Opinion" on p. 369. The questions there will be useful as the account of the treatment of the Indians is studied. **345**

Brown Brothers

Sitting Bull, the Sioux leader, was born in what is now South Dakota. He encouraged his people to fight to the finish against the steady advance of settlers. Sitting Bull was born in 1834 in what is now South Dakota. He lived until 1890.

#The introduction of the horse had made it possible for the Indians to follow their supply of meat.

conspicuous in the slaughter of the animals was the experienced scout and Indian fighter Colonel William F. Cody. When tracks of the Kansas Pacific were being laid on the Great Plains in 1867, Cody was hired by the railroad to keep its construction crews supplied with buffalo meat. For about a year and a half he killed an average of eight of the beasts daily—about 4280 altogether—earning lasting fame as Buffalo Bill.

The commercial interest in buffalo hides began in 1871, when a Pennsylvania tannery discovered that they could be used for leather. Not long afterward the demand for buffalo leather for harnesses, shoes, belts, and other products became enormous. Bands of hunters roamed the Plains with long-range rifles, each band killing fifty to seventy animals daily.

As a result, almost 4,000,000 animals in the southern herd alone* were slain for their skins between 1872 and 1874, a skin being worth between one and three dollars in the market. A conservative estimate is that between 1870 and 1885 over 10,000,000 buffaloes were killed on the northern and southern plains. In 1886 a Smithsonian Institution expedition looking for specimens of the buffalo for the museum's collection reported difficulty in finding twenty-five preservable animals.

End of the contest. The Indians now had the alternative of either starving or farming. Various suggestions were made about establishing the tribesmen on land of their own. A leading hindrance was the belief that Indians could not make the necessary adjustments and would continue to require supervision.

Few gave thought to the fact that the Indian was being forced to change completely his way of life. Americans as a whole, far from being sympathetic, were numb to the rights of minorities and uninterested in their cultures. Congress reflected this indifference: the Bureau of Indian Affairs had more responsibility than it could handle. Moreover, it was usually mismanaged when it was not downright corrupt.

rest slowly wended their way back to the reservations, never again to go on the warpath. Fighting thereafter was at most only scattered. In the face of the new rapid-fire Hotchkiss guns, the Indians were helpless.

The slaughter of the buffalo. The Indians' will to fight was not broken by superior strategy or arms alone. It was greatly weakened by the destruction of the American bison, or buffalo. It is estimated that once about 15,000,000 buffaloes roamed the West. Sometimes it was possible, so hunters reported, to see 300,000 of them at one time. As long as the Plains Indian could easily find this valuable animal, on which he depended for food and clothing, he could keep his independence. However, he waged a losing fight.

The wanton killing of the buffalo herds commenced in 1867 and was practically completed by 1883. The person whose name was most

---

*The building of the Union Pacific had divided the buffaloes into two herds—one on each side of the tracks.

##Are people in this country numb to the rights of minorities today? Explain. See also item 2, under "Informed Opinion," p. 369.

Plains Indians were careful about killing only the buffalo that they actually needed. Severe penalties faced tribesmen who violated the principle of conserving this natural resource.

Plains Indians hunting buffalo when the beasts were plentiful and when the Great Plains were the tribesmen's domain. The animals were slain with special long lances that were tipped with stone.

What does the picture below tell you about family life among the Plains Indians?

"En route to Winter Camp," by William Cary. Indian families like this one in what is now North Dakota spent their winters in sheltered valleys, where they lived mainly on dried buffalo meat.

Nevertheless, a number of organizations sprang up to defend the rights of the Indians as # "the first Americans." Two books by Helen Hunt Jackson—*A Century of Dishonor* (1881) and a novel, *Ramona* (1884)—called national attention to the plight of the Indian, whose culture the Europeans had finally succeeded in destroying.

Congressional steps. In 1887 the Dawes Act formally dissolved the tribes and divided their lands among the members. To the head of a family, 160 acres was allotted; and to a single man, 80 acres. The land would be held in trust for each Indian, and he would not receive full legal title to it from the government for twenty-

five years. However, from the time the acreage was allotted to him, he would become a citizen of the United States.

This arrangement did not work well: as citizens, Indians could legally obtain liquor, which had a demoralizing effect upon them. Besides, they were often so heavily in debt that they had to sell their land when the trust period was over. The Burke Act of 1906 provided for the postponement of citizenship until the twenty-five-year period was over.

In 1924 all Indians became citizens, but ## their economic condition was saddening. They had never learned to farm profitably, according to the standards of the day, and their

Ask why there was a different attitude among settlers and Indians about the killing of the buffalo.

Passengers and members of the crew manning this train on the Union Pacific Railroad eagerly join in the shooting of buffalo on the Great Plains. In 1870 the number of buffalo on the Plains was estimated to be between five and seven million. By 1883 only 200 such animals could be located throughout the West.

Library of Congress

##Ask when the United States made Negroes citizens (refer them to the Fourteenth Amendment, p. 806). Why was the nation even slower in making the Indians citizens?

#Discuss this sentence in class. In what sense is the memory of the destruction of the buffalo a rebuke? How is the memory of the treatment of the Plains Indians also a rebuke?

lands had usually fallen into the grasping hands of settlers—farmers or traders or lumbermen. Settlers scorned and abused the Indian when they stopped being afraid of him.†

Symbol of America. The "wild and woolly" West became a world-renowned section of the United States, symbolizing the centuries-long struggle of Americans against raw nature. The memory of the Plains Indian and his buffalo, destroyed
so ruthlessly and so abruptly, is a rebuke to Americans even today who delight in their country's resplendent heritage.

Sum and Substance

1. Why did Bryce call western America a "favoured tract of country"? 2. What area did the "last West" include? What physical regions? 3. Explain why trouble with Plains Indians increased after 1859. 4. What was the Chivington massacre? 5. In what two parts of the "last West" were reservations set up? 6. Give the facts about "Custer's last stand." 7. How did the destruction of the buffaloes affect the Plains Indians? 8. What did the Dawes Act of 1887 provide? The Burke Act of 1906?

THE CATTLE KINGDOM CLAIMS THE GREAT PLAINS

The Americans turned the disappearance of the buffaloes to their advantage, for the Great Plains were now freed for other undertakings. Beginning in the late 1860's, the region became the scene of a new era: the fabulous day of the cattleman.

When Confederate veterans from Texas returned home after Appomattox, they found few economic opportunities to brighten their prospects. But the raising of cattle stood out as an alluring possibility.

A man who owned a few thousand head of cattle could optimistically anticipate good profits. Beef was in heavy demand in the markets of the North, where meat consumption had increased notably. A steer that could be sold for only six or seven dollars in the Texas market commanded forty or fifty dollars in northern packing houses. The principal problem was how to get the animals to market.

THE LONG DRIVE

As early as 1856 cattle ready for marketing were driven north as far as St. Louis, Missouri. From there they were transported by rail to the slaughterhouses of Chicago. At the end of

1865, when the Missouri Pacific had reached Sedalia, Missouri, the trail to the railroads became much shorter. The following year more than 250,000 animals were herded over it on the way to market. This was the beginning of the drama that came to be called the "long drive."

On the Chisholm Trail. The most significant event ## in establishing this annual movement of cattle from the southern ranges to the railroad facilities was the opening of the shipping center at Abilene, Kansas, in 1867. The center was the brainchild of an Illinois stockman, Joseph G. McCoy. He had persuaded the railroads to help him create a transportation point that would be convenient to both southern cattle-raisers and northern buyers.

McCoy founded the small community of Abilene, located on the new Kansas Pacific Railroad. He soon made the town a beehive of activity—building yards, pens, chutes, and stables for the cattle and a rooming house for cowhands.

In the first year—1867—3500 animals were led northward on the long drive over the Chisholm Trail from Texas to Abilene. Between 1868 and 1871 it is estimated that not less than 1,500,000 animals made their way to the little Kansas settlement.

Cow towns. As the railroads pushed their lines westward, other cow towns developed the way Abilene had. After 1875 Dodge City, Kansas,

---

†Under the Indian Reorganization Act of 1934, an attempt was made to rehabilitate the remaining Indians by encouraging tribal organization again and by extending the trust period indefinitely. Land was sometimes even purchased for the Indians. However, since 1948 Congress has been moving toward a policy of putting the Indians on their own and withdrawing ultimately all federal supervision.

##See the map on p. 354. The Chisholm Trail ran in an almost straight line to Abilene and Topeka. It was named for Jesse Chisholm, an Indian trader, whose wagon started the trail.

Frightened Texas cattle being driven onto a loading chute at Abilene in 1871, preparatory to their being shipped on the Kansas Pacific Railroad to Kansas City and other points east. Between 1868 and 1871 about 1,500,000 animals, having been driven from Texas, were transported to market from these stockyards.

Observe the absence of trees in this picture of the Kansas shipping center.

was the busiest of them. In all, about 4,000,000 head of cattle went to market during the period 1869–1879, when the long drive was a picturesque feature of the cattleman's life.

Cowboys completing the long drives found the cow towns a relief from the boredom of their work in taking care of the animals. Probably the goings-on there have been exaggerated in films and television shows, but the color and excitement the towns provided were from the beginning exploited by playwrights and other fiction writers.‡ The dime novels dealing with the "West"—the yellowbacks and the blood-and-thunder stories—are a permanent part of the nineteenth-century literary legacy.

‡Generally forgotten were the 5000 Negro cowboys, such as the rodeo star Bill Pickett. The greatest of all bulldoggers, he performed the feat of throwing the steer with his teeth.

The class would enjoy analyzing the lyrics of any authentic cowboy song. What are its themes? What vocabulary does it use? Why was it popular?

Why do Americans think of the cowboy as being quite different from what he actually was?
Why do the myths and the legends about the West hold such a powerful attraction for Americans?

Cowboys engage in a cattle roundup. As ranchers moved into the "last West," they found it hard to keep track of their animals. Twice a year the cowboys rode over the open range, driving the animals to one spot. There the herds were separated on the basis of distinctive brands. Calves, too, could be identified.

Observe the evidence of dryness here. (The area is treeless, and vegetation is sparse.)

The cowboy. The long drive increased the importance of a unique type of American, the cowboy. Guardian of the long drive, he deserves a prominent place in the ranks of frontiersmen, alongside the trapper, the hunter, the miner, and the pioneer farmer.

What the cowboy was actually like has always been embellished beyond recognition by the authors of westerns. He is generally portrayed as an unsmiling, untalkative fellow, quick on the draw (and usually too quick on the trigger). He seems to have spent most of his time catching cattle thieves and other such "varmints."

In reality cowboys were, as one of them said, "merely folks, just plain, every-day bow-legged humans." They carried only one revolver apiece if they carried any at all—not two to

#Listed here are the people who opened up the West, named in the order in which they arrived. The cattlemen came shortly after the miners.

Cowboys took pride in their work, although they often disliked their duties. Many hoped to return to other occupations and localities.

The cowboy, the man who made the Cattle Kingdom possible. Sometimes Negro, he ranked in courage and resourcefulness with other frontiersmen who helped subdue the West.

be fired from the hip simultaneously—and they would never have thought of notching the handles to keep count of the "enemies" they had "gotten."

The cowboy's special garb was not an affectation but an adaptation to the circumstances of his daily life. Cowhide clothes wore better in the saddle than cotton; the bandanna around the neck and the wide-brimmed hat were protection against dust and sun.

The regimen of a cowboy was always hard, often very boring, and at times dangerous. The blizzards in the winter and the hot, dry spells in the summer sometimes created extremely difficult conditions under which the cowboys had to do their work. Horses frequently needed to be shod; the cattle had to be branded; saddles, wagons, lariats, and harnesses had to be inspected and repaired.

Occasionally the cowboys clashed with Indians who had "jumped" the reservations and were rustling, or stealing, cattle. The cattle were, of course, a continual responsibility.

"BOOM AND BUST" IN BEEF

The cattle frontier produced new, sudden wealth which strengthened the faith of Americans that this was indeed a land of opportunity. Colonel Richard King, for example, who started his career as a jeweler's apprentice in upstate New York, established the incredible King ranch near Corpus Christi, Texas.

His quick climb to riches was described this way in 1870: "Before the Civil War, King came to Texas possessing only a horse, a saddle, and ten dollars in cash. Now it is a hundred miles from his front door to his yard gate!" He employed annually 300 hands to manage his 100,000 cattle, his 20,000 sheep, and his 10,000 horses. At his death in 1885, his ranch consisted of half a million acres.

The boom drew to the cattle country many hopeful adventurers like King. As one observer expressed it, "Cotton was once crowned king #
but grass is now. . . ."

Improved animals. On the grassland the American rancher crossbred the scrawny long-horned cattle of the type the Spanish had brought to

#Some of the beef went to the Indians penned up in reservations, and some was destined for army posts, but most of it was shipped east to feed hungry Americans living there.

#Under the Homestead Law, many ranchers filed claims along rivers, but generally only squatter rights were respected. At least for a time, the cowman who first took his cattle into a particular valley would find that his right to be there was not contested. There were no fences.

America with better stock like the Hereford and Aberdeen Angus. The improved animals combined the stamina of the longhorn with the greater weight of the two more recently imported breeds.

Reaching the northern Plains. By 1868 the cattle country had reached the Wyoming Territory, where cattle-raising took hold in the southeastern part; by 1871 the industry was beginning in Montana. As a result of the sharp drop in the price of beef during the panic of 1873, thousands of head of cattle were diverted from early slaughter and sent instead to stock northern grassland. The unfenced Cattle Kingdom now covered the Great Plains.

Decline of the open range. Inevitably, many factors doomed the long drive and open range. First, animals tended to lose weight on the long drive and had to be fattened up again before sale—a costly necessity.§ Second, the trip through Indian territory became expensive. When the tribesmen discovered that trespassing on their reservations was forbidden by law, they charged for each head of cattle passing through.

Third, cattlemen in time found Kansas farmers even more hostile to them than were the Indians. The Kansans were afraid that the dreaded Texas fever which the cattle carried from Texas would infect their own stock, and so they obtained the passage of quarantine laws. These laws prohibited the long drive in the summer months, when the ticks that transmit the disease are most active.

Fourth, protecting the purity of the selectively bred strains of animals was impossible on the open range. The branding of cattle, to distinguish a given owner's steers from his neighbor's, and the famed roundup, which sorted out the steers, were unique features of the Cattle Kingdom. However, fencing the ranches in—particularly after the appearance of barbed wire—made cattle-raising more efficient. The animals could be better protected and shipped if they were held on fenced ranches near the railroads, which by the 1870's had been built deep into cattle country.

Fifth, by 1880 overstocking had become a very troubling problem. By the middle of 1885, prices were beginning to fall sharply.

Disastrous weather. The winter of 1885/1886, moreover, was one of the severest in the history of the range. It brought disaster. Unable to reach food, animals died by the thousands. In the summer of 1886, the weather went to the

---

§Dishonest men sometimes fed their animals salt just as they arrived at the cow towns so that the beasts would drink huge quantities of water before they were weighed. This is how the phrase "watered stock" originated—a phrase that now refers to stock which is issued by a corporation but does not represent actual investment.

Note the barbed wire. Joseph Glidden, who first manufactured it in 1874, did a flourishing business.

Cattle, dead or dying of starvation during one of the disastrous blizzards on the Great Plains in 1886.

Harper's Weekly, February 27, 1886 (Denver Public Library Western Collection)

Compare this map with the one on p. 344. Note how empty the area was in which miners and cowmen operated.

The mining towns in the mountains and the cow towns on the Great Plains mark the temporary domains of the miners and the cattlemen, who paved the way for the farmers. They put the region to a vastly more productive use.

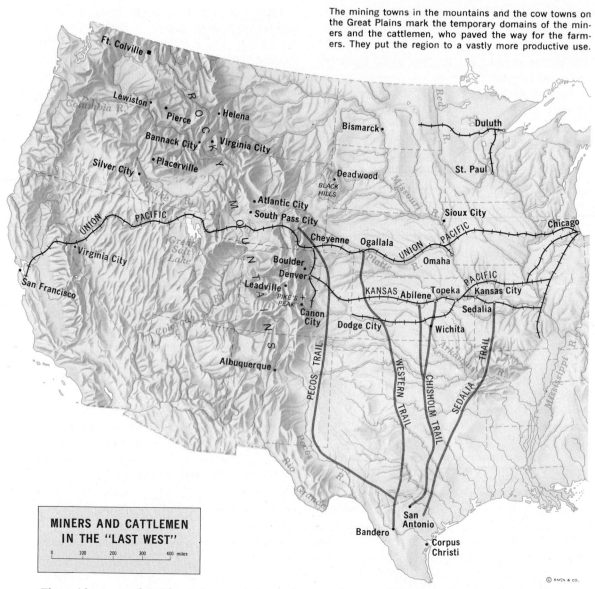

MINERS AND CATTLEMEN IN THE "LAST WEST"

0   100   200   300   400 miles

© RMcN & CO.

The gold miners of California hastened the settlement of that state, and the miners in the "last West" contributed to the settlement of mineral-rich parts of it.

other extreme—withering heat and dryness.

Another devastating winter struck the Plains in 1886/1887, the temperature dropping to as low as 68 degrees below zero. The spring brought an unforgettably tragic sight: thousands of dead animals piled in heaps in the gullies, and thousands of others emaciated and barely able to walk on their frozen legs or to move their frostbitten tails. The public was revolted at the cruelty of allowing the herds to face the elements unprotected. Wrote one rancher: "A business that had been fascinating to me before, suddenly became distasteful. I never wanted to own again an animal that I could not feed and shelter."

The sheepmen. Another severe blow was the arrival from the Ohio Valley of sheepherders seeking cheaper pasturage for their animals.

#Review the kind of climate found in the "last West." (It is classified as dry middle-latitude climate, having extremes of hot and cold. See the second question, col. 1, p. 369.)

The cattlemen complained that sheep cropped the grass close, ruining it for cattle grazing; that cattle would not drink at water holes which sheep had used; that the sharp hoofs of the sheep ruined the turf. The arguments, which raged for twenty years, were often settled by violence, because usually neither cattleman nor sheepman had a case in court; very likely *both* were poaching on the public domain.

The keen hostility practically ceased when fencing came by the end of the 1880's. Hay was then raised on the ranches and fed to the animals during the winter. As one cowboy put it: "I tell you times have changed. You didn't hear the sound of a mowing machine in this country ten years ago." And by the end of the decade, the sound of the threshing machine was also being heard on the Great Plains, for wheat was appearing on fields where buffaloes and then cattle had once roamed.

Sum and Substance

1. When did cattle-raising in Texas begin? 2. What was the long drive? How did cow towns develop? 3. What new cattle breeds were introduced? Why? 4. How did the panic of 1873 affect the Cattle Kingdom? 5. Give five reasons that account for the ending of the long drive. 6. What was the effect on the Cattle Kingdom of bad weather? Of sheepmen? Of fences?

Review "frontier." The miners established a new line dividing settled from unsettled areas.

RUSHES FOR GOLD AND SILVER CREATE A NEW FRONTIER

The miner's frontier which opened on the eve of the Civil War flourished at the same time as the Cattle Kingdom in still another episode in the dramatic history of the West. Possibly only the gold seeker of the sixteenth century would have understood the frenzied quest for precious ores that overtook so many people.

LUCKY STRIKES

Almost simultaneously gold had been found in Colorado and in Nevada in 1859, and word quickly spread in all directions. Especially because it came on the heels of the panic of 1857, it was welcome news.

Pike's Peak. A mining camp established at the mouth of Cherry Creek in Colorado with the name "Denver" became the base of activities. Stories circulated that one could earn between $5 and $20 daily with a pick and pan in the Pike's Peak region.

Thousands set forth in the special type of covered wagon known as the "prairie schooner," determined to reach "Pike's Peak or bust." But luck ran for only a few. "Busted, by God!" was the legend many wrote across their schooners as, penniless and dejected, they took the weary road home.

Central City. Suddenly the scene was transformed. On Clear Creek near Denver on May 6, 1859, a wandering prospector, John H. Gregory, found pay dirt yielding almost $2 a pan. Again the rush was on. Horace Greeley of the *New York Tribune*, who visited the mining camp—Central City—the following month, reported that "the entire population of the valley sleep in tents or under booths of pine boughs, cooking and eating in the air. I doubt that there is as yet a table or chair in these diggings, eating being around a cloth spread on the ground."

As usual, thousands of failures could be contrasted with the few lucky strikes. Some men remained in the leading Colorado towns, like Denver, Boulder, and Canon City, and opened stores to provision and supply the miners. These enterprisers became wealthy with less effort and risk than the hardy men who played for all or nothing—and usually wound up with nothing.

Colorado: the Centennial State. Colorado's development was slow, because the surface gold was soon worked out, and the veins of ore were too deep to be exploited easily. Besides, crops failed, a grasshopper plague fell on the land, and the transcontinental railroad ran through Wyoming, not Colorado.

In 1870 the population of Colorado was less than 40,000, having increased little. But

##A mining camp contained log cabins or huts (see the picture, pp. 340-341) and in time a few stores, sometimes of log construction. Saloons were soon added.

355

Library of Congress

Prospectors make their perilous way to Leadville, in what became Colorado—after silver was discovered there in the 1870's. They are traveling on a "corduroy road."

after 1870 the territory began to grow, entering the Union in 1876 as the Centennial State. Colorado's prosperity, however, was destined to depend upon agriculture rather than upon mining.

The Comstock Lode. In Nevada prospectors were also busy, wisely looking for gold on the eastern slope of the Sierra Nevada because it had already been found on the western slope. One day in 1859 the richest silver deposit in the world was discovered on Mount Davidson. This deposit was named the Comstock Lode for a shiftless braggart named Henry Comstock, who sold his holdings for a pittance. Virginia City‖ # developed as the Comstock Lode town.

Virginia City. Other finds, although less fantastic, were considerable. The history of Nevada, nevertheless, was for a long time the history of Virginia City. A new arrival there described it in 1860: "Frame shanties pitched together as if by accident, tents of canvas, of blankets, of brush, of potato sacks and old skirts, with empty whisky barrels for chimneys; smoking hovels of mud and stone. . . ."

This stark picture was transformed in a few years, for between 1859 and 1880 the Comstock Lode yielded not less than $306,000,000. As a result, some men had seemingly limitless fortunes like the maharajas of India. One mine superintendent filled his water tank with champagne in order to serve his wedding guests conveniently!

Like the sixteenth-century Spaniards who had staked everything on inexhaustible supplies of gold and silver, Nevadans failed even to build a large city like Denver or Sacramento. When the Lode petered out after 1880, the state sank into economic doldrums. (Nevada had been admitted to the Union in 1864. At that time it had been believed that the vote of one more free state might be required to ratify an emancipation amendment to the Constitution.)

On the Columbia. Mining activity was also developing in the Washington, Idaho, and Montana territories. A gold strike at Fort Colville on the Columbia River in 1855 had brought a

‖It is said to have been named by Comstock's partner, whose nickname was "Old Virginia."

Obtain a road map of Nevada or of some other state in which mining was done on a large scale. Observe the names of the towns. How can some of them be accounted for?

rush of prospectors from California. From Fort Colville gold seekers moved into the principal river valleys, where important discoveries of the precious metal were made.

Idaho at that time was part of the Washington Territory, and Idaho miners as early as 1860 were demanding to be separate. In 1863 Congress, at last yielding to the clamor, organized the Territory of Idaho, which included Montana and practically all of Wyoming.

In Montana. Hundreds of miners took part in the great gold rush to Montana in 1863. It attracted the usual enterprising merchants and farmers, populating the region quickly. In 1864

Congress, therefore, organized the Montana Territory, with another Virginia City as its territorial capital.

In the Black Hills. Presently a new rush was on—to the Black Hills of Dakota, where fresh stories and rumors of discovery were arising. Here more names were added to the colorful # record of the mining frontier: Custer City and Deadwood. Characters like Wild Bill Hickok and Calamity Jane entered their exploits in the record of American folklore.

Statehood en masse. In the Omnibus Bill in 1889, North Dakota, South Dakota, Montana, and Washington received statehood at the same

By the end of 1859 about 100,000 people had reached the area where Gregory had struck gold.

Blake Street in Denver, seven years after John Gregory found gold in Clear Creek. Business houses line the street, some evidently catering to people who have driven wagons to town for supplies. Traffic—both human and animal—moves slowly or briskly, as individual needs require, and there is no regard for right or left lanes.

Library of Congress

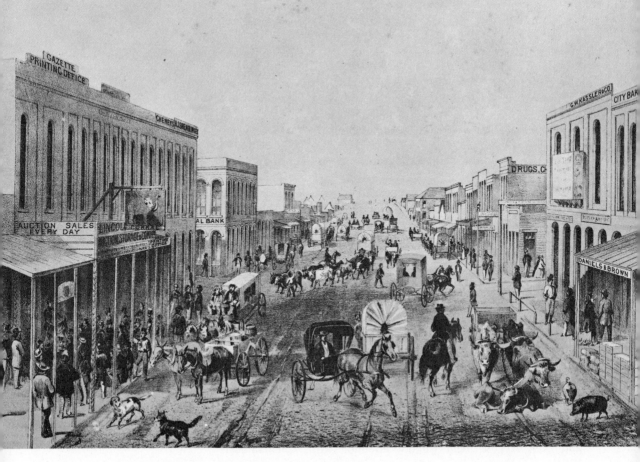

Observe that there were a bank, a printing office, a drugstore, a bakery, a dry-goods store, and evidence of other businesses along the street. Colorado became a territory in 1861.

#Ask how the vigilance committee, or the Vigilantes, got its name. The development of the Vigilantes indicated the necessity of forming some kind of government in a situation in which a group of people is living together.

Library of Congress

Aspects of the mining industry in Virginia City, as an artist represented them in the 1870's. The interior of the mine looked like a beehive: a framework of "square sets" held up the earth.

What evidence of technological advances may be seen here?

time. The following year Wyoming and Idaho were admitted to the Union.

THE MINING DISTRICT

The mining frontier, with its stormy conflicts over claims, cried out for some form of government even before territories could be organized. A *mass meeting* was usually called in a mining district for the purpose of establishing the beginnings of law and order. Almost invariably the self-seeking miners failed to coöperate in community affairs, and soon a *vigilance committee* appeared. Usually made up of the more respectable people in the district, the vigilance committee was a self-disciplined and a resolute group. It did not hesitate to punish lawbreakers and even execute them without attention to

judicial procedure or respect for civil liberties.

The mass meeting and the vigilance committee were institutions that appeared wherever miners settled. Congress did not try to interfere with this special form of government, which was devised in response to the novel demands of mining life.

Sum and Substance

1. In what two areas in the "last West" was gold found in 1859? 2. Which state is called the "Centennial State"? Why? 3. What was the Comstock Lode? 4. What mineral deposits were found along the Columbia River? In present-day Idaho? In the Black Hills? 5. What states entered the Union in 1889? 6. How was order maintained in mining communities?

Walter B. Clark's The Ox-Bow Incident is an excellent short novel dealing with frontier justice (see "Historical Fiction," p. 459).

Eventually, mining operations were mechanized. With the help of eastern money and professional workers, these large-scale mining enterprises squeezed out the small mining operations.

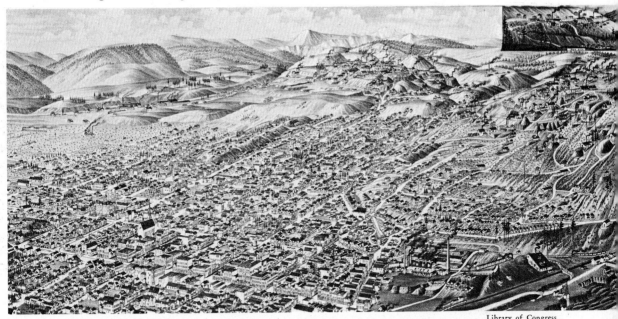

Leadville, Colorado, in 1882, after its beds of rich silver-lead ore had created glowing prosperity. Leadville was incorporated in 1878. Shortly it acquired a railroad, two daily newspapers, eight churches, and several schools.

Some of the ghost towns have become tourist attractions, and some are even resorts.

Leadville has survived to the present, but numerous other towns that sprang up in the short-lived mining era have not. This is Rawhide, a ghost town in Nevada. Observe what is left of the streets.

This is a reference map of the fifty states, combining political and physical features.

Scale 1:15 000 000; one inch to 238 miles. Polyconic Projection
Elevations and depressions are given in feet

0 25 50 75 100   200   300   400   500 Miles

Relief

Meters		Feet
3050		10 000
1525		5000
610		2000
305		1000
152.5		500
0	Sea Level	
152.5		500 Below
1525		5000 Sea Level
3050		10 000
6100		20 000

This section describes the coming of the people who permanently settled the "last West," and it tells how they adjusted to the physical environment they found there.

THE PIONEER FARMER FINALLY TACKLES THE GREAT PLAINS

Just as the cattleman and the miner adapted the Great Plains to their needs, so did the pioneer farmer. The farmer west of the 100th meridian faced the challenge of grappling with an environment to which he was unaccustomed. In fact, America's agricultural frontiersmen had never before faced conditions like those he encountered.

A FORBIDDING ENVIRONMENT

The Great Plains lacked, first of all, the usual building materials for homes or fences or barns. The vast treeless expanse meant a scarcity of lumber and a lack of protection from the fierce summer sun and the rugged blizzards. In the western portion the annual rainfall seldom reached the total of 20 inches that ordinary agriculture requires.

Not until after the Civil War, when American industrial development was well advanced, did settlers conquer the unfamiliar environment of the Great Plains. The result of their mastery, however, was the establishment of one of the richest wheat-producing regions in the world. The tools which the farmers used to meet their needs came from the busy factories of the East.

Homes: the sod house. Dwellings built without timber were a necessary adaptation to the arid conditions of the Great Plains. The earliest settlers built crude dugouts. Later they made their houses out of thick sod, which they cut into bricks.

The sod houses leaked, and sometimes they dissolved in heavy rains. Many a bride newly arrived from the East wept as she gazed for the first time at her new home—made of earth and grass.

But when the sod houses were improved by experience, they were usually warm in winter and cool in summer and could not be blown

Students should read Hamlin Garland's Under the Lion's Paw or Willa Cather's My Antonia.

A farm family poses for a photographer in front of its substantial sod house in the 1880's. The squints on most of the countenances resulted from facing the sun on the treeless plain. The bricklike effect of the sod cover of the roof and sides of the house can be clearly seen. Observe the metal-hooped rain barrel.

Nebraska State Historical Society

down by the wind or burned down during a prairie fire. The railroad later solved the transportation problem, and timber, although expensive, became available. Then the frame house, as elsewhere, took over. By 1890 the sod house had become a thing of the past.

Barbed wire. Another requirement for farming on the Great Plains was an adequate material for constructing fences. This became particularly important as the westward movement of farmers brought them to the edges of the Cattle Kingdom in Kansas and Nebraska. The cattle did not respect unfenced cornfields.

Back east, farmers had built fences out of split rails or of rock or hedges. But on the Great Plains wood was too dear, rock unavailable, and hedges unreliable. Straight wire fences were unsatisfactory because the animals forced their way through them. A farmer in De Kalb, Illinois—Joseph F. Glidden—in 1873 developed a practical way of making a thorny wire like the thorny hedges which the homesteaders had tried earlier. This was, of course, barbed wire.

The manufacture of barbed wire, which began in 1874, supplied a product enabling the plainsmen to protect their land against the animal herders. Before long, barbed wire was being made by machine, and the demand for it seemed unlimited. The price gradually dropped until it was within the means of every homesteader. In 1880 alone, 80,000,000 pounds of it were sold. This invention deserves to rank with the cotton gin in its revolutionary influence on America's agricultural development.

Wells and windmills. A lack of water was another serious handicap to the successful conquest of the Great Plains. The attempt to collect surface water for irrigation in the western part failed because rain was inadequate, and when rain did fall the high winds evaporated it too quickly.

The alternative of tapping the water under the earth's surface presented many difficulties. Open wells could not be dug as easily as back east because the soil was too hard. Furthermore, they had to be so deep—in some places as much as 800 feet—that they could not be drilled without machinery. In addition, there was the problem of how to bring the water to the surface. The "old oaken bucket," raised and lowered by hand, was out of the question.

Again, it was the advancing industrial and technological development of the rest of the country which came to the rescue. Windmills, to be turned by the ever-present Plains wind, would provide the power to raise the water from the earth's depths. By the late 1860's windmills were being manufactured in Illinois and Wisconsin, and windmill salesmen were swarming over the grassland. The cost of drilling wells and of building windmills, however, remained higher than most people could afford. Not until about 1890 were the smaller farms able to stand the expense.

Dry farming. In the meantime, dry farming developed in the western part of the Great Plains —still another adaptation to the unaccustomed environment. Farmers were able to raise crops by using special methods of conserving every drop of moisture in the soil. They learned the value of harrowing their fields after each rainfall before the water could evaporate. For this chore machines were needed, and these also were soon available from factories. The high winds later made dry farming on the Great Plains impractical, but it is still used in limited areas farther west.

New agricultural machinery. Farms had to be larger in the West than in the East because the lower rainfall in large sections of the West made the crop yield smaller. It is estimated that a 360-acre farm on the Great Plains returned about the same profit as one of 80 acres in the East.

The greater size of western holdings had a powerful influence on the development and manufacture of all kinds of machinery. Not only the mechanical harrow, but a number of other time- and labor-savers appeared in the decade after the Civil War. They included a greatly improved plow, a seeding machine, the grain drill, and devices for more efficiently mowing, loading, and baling hay.

Solving the labor shortage. Undoubtedly the reaper, together with such improvements as the twine binder, was indispensable in making possible the tremendous expansion of wheat culti-

Notice how many horses were hitched to each driller. Horses were indispensable on farms in the 1800's and in the early 1900's, but machines gradually displaced them. The care and feeding of his horses were part of a farmer's daily chores.

Kansas State Historical Society

Drilling wheat near Dorrance, Kansas, in the late 1800's. Technological advances caused wheat-growing to spread rapidly on the Great Plains: millers discovered a new way to grind hard spring wheat. Storage places—elevators— were built near railroads to hold wheat for shipping, and mechanical means of loading it were devised.

Observe the flatness of the land, the telephone wires, and the substantial buildings.

vation. The name Cyrus Hall McCormick is inseparably connected with the manufacture of the reaper. Though his experiments had been successful more than twenty years before the Civil War, his machines came into their own during the war and immediately afterward.

The reaper freed farmers from their annual fear that they would not be able to harvest their crops in time. It also gave homesteaders on the Great Plains confidence that they could farm even in places where there was a shortage of agricultural workers. Previously a farmer had limited the amount of wheat he sowed in accordance with the rule that one man could manage only 7½ acres during the limited harvest season. By 1890 a single farmer could handle 135 acres—seated! #

#A writer in 1880 described the reaper's action: "There is a sound of wheels. The grain disappears an instant, then reappears; iron arms clasp it, hold it a moment in their embrace, wind it with wire, then toss it disdainfully at your feet. You hear in the rattling of the wheels the mechanism saying to itself, 'See how easy I can do it.' "

The Great Plains were conquered at last by America's inventiveness and industrial productiveness. If it had once been fashionable, and perhaps even true, to say that the only "producers" in the nation were farmers, it was no longer. The industrialists and agriculturalists discovered they were partners. Together they helped develop America's "breadbasket."

A STEADY STREAM OF SETTLERS

The flow of settlement was replenished by # the army of farmers who poured into the West at the end of the Civil War. Some were demobilized soldiers adjusting to civilian life again; some were homesteaders attracted by the generous law of 1862; some were immigrants looking for opportunity; and some were land speculators and footloose adventurers, whose like had been found on the frontier at every period of American history. The end of the Civil War had released settlers for the West, just as it had released capital for industry.

#In 1860 there were 2,000,000 farms in the United States. By 1900 there were 5,737,000. The farm population almost doubled (see p. 818). But see also how the urban population grew.

Here both oxen and horses are being used. The noise of the threshing machine and the dust accompanying the threshing were part of the day's work. At noon the threshers would stop for a hearty meal, which was prepared in the home of the man whose wheat was threshed.

State Historical Society of Colorado

Harvesting grain on the plains of eastern Colorado about 1880. Wagons drawn by oxen hauled the crop to the threshing machine (*left*). Smaller, horse-drawn wagons carried the sacked grain. The men in the cart (*foreground*) are evidently the bosses. Everybody has stopped work— and some have posed—to have their picture taken.

McCormick, born the same year Lincoln was, began manufacturing reapers in Chicago in 1847.

Cyrus McCormick demonstrating his reaper in 1831. Sliding blades cut the grain, which then fell to one side.

International Harvester Company

Alice Marriott's <u>The Ten Grandmothers</u> is an excellent study of an Indian tribe of the Great Plains (Kiowa) and the changes which took place among the Indians because of the government's policy.

The railroad was the principal magnet for settlers in the "last West." Wherever it ran it seemed to be pulling a stream of people behind it. After the Indian wars and the removal of the Indians from southwestern Kansas, the influx of newcomers followed the line of the Santa Fe Railroad. Other people settled in Nebraska along the route of the Union Pacific. By 1880 the population of Kansas was 850,000, and that of Nebraska about 450,000.

The Dakota Territory. Farther north the Dakota Territory had been created in 1861. Its governor (Lincoln's family physician in Spring-field) lived in a log cabin that served him as the Executive Mansion. Settlement was delayed by the ghastly Sioux massacres in 1862 on the Minnesota frontier. Then a further period of Indian fighting discouraged new arrivals until 1868, when the Sioux were placed on a reservation west of the Missouri River.

In 1870 the Dakota Territory contained almost 15,000 people. Shortly the building of the Northern Pacific Railroad hastened its development; moreover, the Black Hills gold rush in 1875 brought in about 10,000 additional people.

Review Jackson's Indian policy (pp. 188-189), under which the first reservations were set up.

By 1900, when the "last West" had been subdued, Indians west of the Mississippi lived on these reservations.

INDIAN RESERVATIONS, 1900

0   100   200   300   400 miles

© RM̦N & CO.

"Bonanza farms." The Dakota Territory received fresh attention during the depression of 1873. The Northern Pacific, facing bankruptcy, attempted to dramatize the excellent opportunities there. Two of the railroad executives obtained eighteen sections of agricultural land in the Red River Valley and hired a successful wheat farmer, Oliver Dalrymple, to run it for them. They poured substantial amounts of money into the project, employing an army of workers and buying huge quantities of farm machinery for it.

The results were astonishing: the yield of wheat was 25 bushels to the acre at a phenomenally low cost. By 1890 over 300 farms in this fertile river valley averaged more than 1000 acres in size; a few were as large as 100,000 acres. Although some of these huge "bonanza farms" were owned by individuals, many of them were organized and operated as corporations—as large-scale businesses.

Two Dakota states. In 1878 the so-called Dakota boom was on. The settlement of the Dakota Territory was further stimulated by the Great Northern Railroad of James J. Hill. By 1885 the population had reached about 550,000. New arrivals, often from Europe, came in droves and were deposited in the richest wheat country in the world by the new railroad.

The Dakota Territory was divided and organized into two states in 1889. North Dakota's capital, Bismarck—named for Germany's Iron Chancellor—shows clearly that Germans were numerous among the immigrants who settled there. South Dakota's largest city, Sioux Falls, calls attention to the indelible impression the Indian has left on the region.

Wyoming and Montana. Wyoming and Montana—which are semiarid—were not reached by the farmers until the Great Plains were well settled —in the early 1880's. Here the techniques of irrigation had to be learned. By 1890 over 2,000,000 acres were being watered by man-made drainage ditches. But the rewards were slight, and Wyoming's population was less than 65,000 in 1890. In Montana, too, life for farmers on the dry soil was hard; a population of 132,000 in 1890 consisted chiefly of miners, prospectors, and railroad men.

The Indian Territory. During the 1880's the eastern portion of what is now the state of Oklahoma was the last part of the public domain that the western farmers had not claimed. Set aside for the Indians by the United States government, it was the region to which the Cherokee, Creek, Seminole, and Choctaw Indians were removed between 1820 and 1840 (see page 189). This area became known as the "Indian Territory" as more tribes joined those that had arrived earlier, bringing the number of tribesmen to 75,000.

When Texas was being filled up in the 1870's, keeping pace with the peopling of Kansas, farmers and land speculators began to look longingly at the Indians' land. Many frontiersmen boldly poached on the Indian Territory.

Boomers. An "Oklahoma Colony" of settlers nicknamed "boomers" established itself at Wichita, Kansas, in 1883 to agitate for the opening of the Indians' lands to settlement. The "boomers" probably had the active backing of the railroads.

The particular object of the pioneers' attention and of their friends in Congress actually was only the 2,000,000 acres that had been ceded to the government by the Creeks and Seminole. This region was called the Oklahoma District. The influence of the railroads on Congress finally won out. The Creeks and Seminole were paid for their remaining rights in the Oklahoma District.

Run on Oklahoma. On March 23, 1889, President Harrison announced that the Oklahoma District would be thrown open to homesteading "at and after the hour of twelve o'clock noon, on the twenty-second day of April." In the month preceding the event, thousands upon thousands of prospective settlers thronged the roads leading to the area. They built and lived in temporary "shanty towns" while awaiting the hour and day for "the run."

Troops were stationed around the Oklahoma District to hold back the hundred thousand people poised on its borders and to guard against "sooners" who were trying to "jump the

"Boomers," having eagerly awaited the hour when they could cross the border of Oklahoma, rush onto the coveted land. Observe the sunbonnets of the farm wives and the weapons some men were carrying.

gun." At the appointed hour the dam of humanity broke with a mighty roar; by the middle of the afternoon that day 1,920,000 acres had been claimed.

A man who was there described the event:

All men started as enemies. The reward was to the selfish and to the bully; and greed and strength were the winners. The number of homesteaders exceeded the number of claims; and more than one man pitched upon the same quarter section. In some cases as many as four or five insisted on the right of possession. Thus on the very first day began the contests which have ever since been a harvest to the lawyers, and have produced an unhappy condition of society unknown elsewhere.

In the next few years the reservations of one tribe after another were made available for settlement, accompanied each time by another mad scramble. The population in the Oklahoma Territory by 1906 had reached 500,000, not including the scattered tribes of Indians. In the following year, Oklahoma entered the Union as the 46th state.

New Mexico and Arizona. An attempt to bring New Mexico and Arizona into the Union as a single state was attacked and defeated in 1907. New Mexicans were proud of their Spanish inheritance and hoped to prevent its extinction; Arizonans, on the other hand, feared being overshadowed by their more numerous neighbors. In 1912 New Mexico and Arizona were admitted as separate states, giving the flag its 47th and 48th stars.

The geographic base of the American nation had now been brought into the political Union. The conquest of the West, three centuries in the making, was the work not only of countless intrepid and imaginative people but also of America's developing industries. From the factories had come the railroad trains, the special tools for the plains, and the farm machinery out of which old ways of life were transformed and new ones created. Yet even as Americans rejoiced in the unbounded promise of their rich land, they were compelled to cope with the grim side of industrial development. It, too, tested their resourcefulness.

Sum and Substance

1. What handicaps did farmers on the Great Plains have to overcome? 2. How did their houses and fences differ from eastern ones? 3. What steps were taken to solve the water problem in the western part of the Great Plains? 4. Why were farms larger in the West than in the East? 5. In what two ways did machinery aid western farmers? 6. Where and what were the "bonanza farms"? 7. Identify the area known as the "Indian Territory." As the "Oklahoma District." 8. Give the facts about the run on Oklahoma. 9. What were the 46th, 47th, and 48th states?

#Have the people of that state been able to keep elements of Spanish culture? (Suggestions: architecture and certain foods are among the evidence that the people have retained them.)

THE WORKSHOP

OF LASTING SIGNIFICANCE

Explain the relationship of each of the following to the subduing of the "last West."

Great Plains	Central City
Chivington massacre	Comstock Lode
	Virginia City
Sioux	Omnibus Bill
Black Hills	vigilance
"Custer's last stand"	committee
William F. Cody	sod house
Helen Hunt Jackson	Joseph F. Glidden
Dawes Act	dry farming
Indian Reorganization Act of 1934	Cyrus Hall McCormick
long drive	"bonanza farm"
Chisholm Trail	boomer
Abilene, Kansas	sooner
Richard King	Indian Territory
Cattle Kingdom	Oklahoma District

DOCUMENTS IN HISTORY

1. Geographers today do not refer to the climate of the area called the "last West" or to any other climate as "temperate." What name is applied to the climate there? Why is it ill-advised to use the word *temperate* to describe it or any similar climate or climates?

2. What role did Bryce think the western Indians played? What attitude toward the Indians does his idea betray?

3. What feature of American culture did Bryce recognize as decisive in the subduing of the "last West"? How did he characterize the American development of the region?

GEOGRAPHY AND HISTORY

1. On an outline map of the United States, indicate the area known as the "last West." What present-day states are in it?

Find out the sources of the economic wealth of each of these states today and use symbols to show these sources on the map. What relationship can you find between the sources of wealth in the late nineteenth century and today?

2. Certain of the states may be said to form a "Cattle Kingdom" today. What are they? # What kinds of cattle are raised? How?

3. The name of the "last West" seems to indicate an end to the westward movement in American history. Find out which states had the largest increases in population at the time of the last census. What states had decreases? On an outline map of the United States, indicate the percentages of increase or decrease. Has the westward movement stopped? Explain.

4. Find out how the people of the Los Angeles metropolitan area, the Imperial and Central valleys of California, the Rio Grande Valley, the Gila River Valley, the Snake River Valley, and the Columbia River Valley are assured of an adequate water supply. In what sense have the people of the river valleys opened up "new frontiers"?

5. Investigate dry farming in the West today. What techniques does it include and in what ## areas is it carried on?

INFORMED OPINION

1. Review the policy of the United States government toward Indians in the period (*a*) before 1850 (refer to the map on page 189); (*b*) during the settlement of the "last West" and afterward. Use the *Readers' Guide to Periodical Literature* to find out about current Indian policies.

What do you think of the way Americans solved their problems with Indians in the past? How is the situation of Indians today related to those solutions? How are Americans today divided over government policy?

2. Explain the statement: "Americans as a whole, far from being sympathetic, were numb to the rights of minorities and uninterested in their cultures." What minorities are referred to? Support the statement. How did the culture of the settlers of the "last West" differ from that of the Indians they displaced?

How does a culture normally change? Do you think the culture of a minority in a country should be respected by the majority? Explain.

Discuss the meaning of "partisanship." What is statesmanship? What is a statesman? (Suggestions: The best definition of partisanship is a blind and sometimes unreasoning adherence to a single person or group. Statesmanship is leadership characterized by regard for the general welfare rather than by partisan interest. A statesman is a person who exercises such leadership.)

19

PARTISANSHIP AND STATESMANSHIP

. . . face to face with
new problems . . .

The men who controlled Congress [in the Civil War years] . . . were summoned to the public service to deal with tremendous problems, and were lifted up and ennobled by the great cause they were commissioned to serve. It did more for them than it was possible for them to do for it. It took hold on the very foundations of the Government, and electrified all the springs of our national life; . . . it was a great privilege to be permitted to share in the grand battle for the Nation's life. . . .

But I need not . . . linger over the by-gones of a grand epoch. We have entered upon a new

Ordinary Americans went about their daily lives while their leaders played politics in Washington.

dispensation [that is, a new order of things]. The withdrawal of the slavery question from the strife of parties has changed the face of our politics as completely as did its introduction. The transition . . . to the regular and orderly administration of affairs, has been as remarkable as the intervention of the great question which eclipsed every other till it compelled its own solution.

Although this transition has given birth to an era of "slack-water politics" [that is, marked by no strong currents], it has gradually brought the country face to face with new problems. . . .

The tyranny of industrial domination, which borrows its life from the alliance of concentrated capital with labor-saving machinery, must be overthrown. Commercial feudalism, wielding its power through . . . great corporations . . . must be subordinated to the will of the people. The system of agricultural serfdom called Land Monopoly, which is now putting on new forms of danger in the rapid multiplication of great estates and the purchase of vast bodies of lands by foreign capitalists, must be resisted as a still more formidable foe of democratic Government.

The legalized robbery now carried on in the name of Protection to American labor [that is, the protective tariff] must be overthrown. The system of spoils and plunder must also be destroyed, in order that freedom itself may be rescued from the perilous activities quickened into life by its own spirit, and the conduct of public affairs inspired by the great moralities which dignify private life.

National politics in the postwar years showed a distinct letdown after the stirring issues of the previous quarter-century. Politicians were generally unable to come to grips with pressing new questions. Those who saw this most clearly were the men whose careers spanned both periods. This selection is from Political Recollections: 1840–1872, *an autobiographical work by George Washington Julian. Julian, an abolitionist born in Indiana in 1817, had been elected to the House of Representatives as a Republican in 1860. He soon became a Radical and took an important part in the attack on President Johnson. In 1872 he joined the Liberal Republicans, and four years later he supported for President the Democratic nominee, Samuel J. Tilden.*

New York State Historical Association

Do stores today ever provide postal service? (Substations are sometimes found in stores.)

A village store and post office in the late 1800's, when shopping was combined with picking up the mail, neatly inserted in individual boxes. In an era before self-service was common, the proprietor—behind the counter at the right—and an eager clerk (*left*) wait on customers. Local gossip and spirited political views are probably being exchanged around the stove at the rear.

#What modern institutions have replaced the village stores as centers of gossip and discussion?

#A politician is a man who is skilled in government. The name often connotes something bad or undesirable only because politicians have behaved in an unfortunate way. Such politicians gained the name "spoilsmen."

POLITICS TURNS INTO A BATTLE OF SPOILSMEN

\# In the years between 1868 and 1896 politicians seemed to be guided solely by their own self-interest. Important social and economic questions gave them practically no concern.

Election campaigns, to be sure, were waged hotly, because the personal rewards of victory were enormous; but in political principles the major parties were barely distinguishable one from the other. A change of party after an election brought new faces before the public but had little other effect on American life. A famous journalist said that the parties were "like two bottles. Each bore a label denoting the kind of liquor it contained, but each was empty."

Unquestionably "Grantism," with its outrageous corruption, was gradually reduced, but spoilsmen continued to dominate the American political scene. Although many good and sincere men also devoted their lives to politics, in general the tone of public morality remained disgracefully low.

THE ANTAGONISTS

The Republican party—which had nicknamed itself the G.O.P. (the "Grand Old Party")—almost invariably produced the President. Its supporters were the businessmen and industrialists of the East and the grain-growing farmers of the Middle West. In addition, most workingmen in the industrial cities of the country, following the lead of their employers, tended to vote Republican. The Republicans also had the backing of the Union war veterans and of their organization, the GAR (the Grand Army of the Republic) because they credited the party with having saved the Union.

Thousands of Americans from every walk of life voted Republican and would continue to do so as long as they lived, out of respect for the memory of Lincoln. Still others, recalling the idealism with which the Republican organization began in 1854, supported it as the humanitarian party. Understandably, Negroes favored it as the party of emancipation.

The Democratic party relied heavily on the support of voters in the South, which had now become the "solid South,"* although it had strength in many cities throughout the country, too. For a number of years after 1865, the

*This name is used to indicate the fact that after 1876 the former Confederate states almost always voted Democratic.

Ask what organization of former soldiers is active today. (Students have seen American Legion parades.)

Members of the GAR—no longer young—parade in Washington, D.C. The Capitol may be seen in the distance.

Library of Congress

#Review the circumstances in which Hayes became President (see p. 305). What promises did the Republicans make? What do you think should have been done to protect the Negroes' rights? Why was nothing done?

Democrats insisted on keeping Civil War issues alive by continuing to argue for states' rights and against Negro suffrage. They approved of greenbacks for the repayment of government bonds and generally identified themselves with the Confederates' Lost Cause.

But by 1872 the conviction had grown among Democrats that the past was dead and that it was time to stop reliving the war. As we have seen, Horace Greeley, their candidate that year, was swamped by General Grant, who was elected to a second term.

Hayes against the bosses. However great the corruption was in their ranks, the party politicians always looked for a presidential standard-bearer with an untainted record. The Republicans had found such a man in Rutherford B. Hayes, the victor in the disputed election of 1876.

At eighteen Hayes had written: "I am determined from henceforth to use what means I have to acquire a character distinguished for energy, firmness, and perseverance." A former Civil War volunteer, member of Congress, and able governor of Ohio, he was an ideal nominee because he seemed to be looking ahead and to be interested in reform. Hayes's rule of conduct was: "He serves his party best who serves his country best."

Lacking a general program, Hayes did not seek to guide Congress. Although he deplored the denial of civil rights to Negroes in the South after the withdrawal of federal troops, he did nothing to remedy the deterioration of the freedmen's condition.

The new Cabinet. At the very beginning of his administration, the President's choice of Cabinet officers made the party bosses indignant. Hayes named William M. Evarts to be Secretary of State. Evarts, who had been Andrew Johnson's chief counsel during the impeachment trial, aroused deep distrust in the spoilsmen. Chiefly, they feared his burning interest in ending the system of political plunder.

To be Secretary of the Interior, Hayes selected Carl Schurz. A former minister to Spain, Civil War major general, Senator from Missouri, and organizer of the Liberal Republicans in 1872, he too had a passion for honesty

The badge of the GAR—long a northern symbol of honor. Observe the symbols used.

in government. Hayes appointed to be his Postmaster General a former Confederate from Tennessee, thereby outraging many party diehards. This act of conciliation by Hayes was part of the Compromise of 1877.

Stalwarts against Half-Breeds. Being a weak leader, Hayes aroused no enthusiasm among either the politicians or the rank and file of the party. A result was that a split widened between two Republican groups that had emerged: the Stalwarts and the Half-Breeds. Led by Senator Roscoe Conkling, of New York, the Stalwarts sarcastically labeled the President's followers "Half-Breeds" whose policies, they said, were

##Review the belief the first leaders of the United States had concerning personal integrity as a qualification for holding public office (see p. 105). Evarts and Schurz held the same belief.

Puck, May 12, 1880

President Hayes is seen as a peaceful farmer disposing of two of the legacies of the Civil War.
What can be seen in the background?

Advocates of the merit system of appointment hopefully believed that the party jobholders would be replaced by "gentlemen . . . who . . . want nothing from government except the satisfaction of using their talents."

The three most important civil service reformers were Carl Schurz; George W. Curtis, the editor of *Harper's Weekly;* and E. L. Godkin, the editor of *The Nation.* The reformers were, perhaps, too optimistic about the speed with which the changes they desired could be brought about. But they were dedicated men—especially Schurz, who worked to introduce the merit system in his own department.

Conflict with Conkling. The war between reform—represented by the Hayes administration—and "bossism"—represented by Senator Conkling—was fierce. Conkling, who enjoyed wearing white flannel trousers and garish vests, often strutted like a peacock in the Senate. He condemned the reformers with a sharp tongue: "They are wolves in sheep's clothing. Their real object is office and plunder."

For the magazine editors and others who were clamoring for the merit system in the civil service, Conkling had only contempt. Reformers, he insisted, did not understand politics. "They forget," he declared in a remark which became famous, "that parties are not built up by deportment, or by ladies' magazines, or gush!" Parties, he said, would die out if "the faithful" could not be rewarded with jobs. #

Hayes in 1877 ordered that federal employees stop taking part in political activities. When Secretary of the Treasury John Sherman attempted to enforce this order in the customhouse of New York, which was under his jurisdiction, he crossed swords with Conkling. Conkling believed that federal jobs in New York were *his* business. Chester A. Arthur, the collector of the port of New York, and Alonzo Cornell, the naval officer there, both were Conkling's lieutenants, and on his instructions they refused to obey. The New York Senator and his fellow spoilsmen had been challenged.

The outcome. Hayes replied to Conkling's actions in New York by appointing successors to Arthur and Cornell. The Senate, under Conk-

"half-breed" Republicanism. The outstanding leader of the Half-Breeds was James G. Blaine, one of the most influential Senators of his generation.

Civil service reform. The reform of the federal civil service was a high hope of people increasingly disturbed by the close link between the politicians and the new industrialists who openly bought favors. Furthermore, the rotation in office of jobholders had led to inefficient administration of public affairs which was at least as serious as the corruption of the spoils system.

Reformers recognized that as the tasks of government became more complex and varied, the country badly needed people who would make service as bureaucrats their profession.

 ##What similarity is there between Conkling's and Jackson's views (see p. 197)? Why was the Hayes order in 1877 concerning federal employees an admirable act?

ling's influence, refused to confirm the President's selections. Hayes did not have his way until 1879. But the fight within the Republican party even then was far from settled.

The nomination of James A. Garfield. Conkling and the Stalwarts traveled to the Republican convention of 1880 with blood in their eyes. Early in his administration, Hayes had announced his intention of serving for only one term, and the Stalwarts were determined to bring Grant back to Washington for a third term. The Half-Breeds gave their support to Blaine.

Blaine once wrote, "When I want a thing I want it dreadfully." Nothing did he want more "dreadfully" than to be president of the United States. But after more than thirty ballots, with General Grant in the lead, the convention turned to a dark horse, James A. Garfield of Ohio—a Half-Breed. Garfield had once served as the head of Hiram College in Ohio; he had risen to be a major general in the Civil War; and he had been a member of the House and of the Senate. Chester A. Arthur, Blaine's man, was nominated to be Vice-President.

A close vote. The Democrats, meeting at Cincinnati, also selected a Civil War veteran, General Winfield Scott Hancock, of Pennsylvania—a hero of the Battle of Gettysburg. Inexperienced in politics, he waged a lackluster campaign. Hancock was long remembered for a remark he made to a newspaper reporter: "The tariff question is a local question." Manufacturers, who considered the tariff an important national issue, thought the statement foolish.

Although about 9,000,000 ballots were cast in the election, Garfield won by less than 40,000 votes. The voters had obviously found it hard to distinguish between either the candidates or their platforms.

After Garfield's inauguration in 1881, the battle between the Stalwarts and the Half-Breeds was resumed. Garfield tried hard to reach a compromise with Conkling on appointments, but Conkling repeatedly rebuffed him. By putting Blaine in the post of Secretary of State, Garfield provoked the Conkling forces. Then the President antagonized them again when he nominated an anti-Conkling man to be

Harper's Weekly, October 1, 1881

Chester A. Arthur takes the presidential oath of office in his home, becoming the twenty-first chief executive. Review the oath (p. 799).

customs collector for the port of New York.

In protest, Conkling and New York's junior Senator, Tom Platt, resigned their Senate posts. They confidently expected that the state legislature would rebuke the President by reelecting them. To their surprise and chagrin, the legislature refused to reseat them, despite an undignified trip that Vice-President Arthur made to Albany to plead in their behalf.

Assassination. Badgered by political job hunters, Garfield was driven almost to distraction. After only a few months in the White House, Garfield exclaimed, "What is there in this place that a man should ever want to get into it?"

Then tragedy struck suddenly on July 2, 1881. Accompanied at the time by Blaine, Garfield was shot in the back in Union Station at Washington by a disappointed office seeker named Charles Guiteau. Guiteau shouted wildly, "I am a Stalwart and Arthur is President now."

Chester A. Arthur. Garfield lingered through the summer as the nation prayed for his recovery. On September 19 the end came, and Arthur took the presidential oath of office. Thoughtful

#In addition, the Pendleton Act prohibited contributions by federal jobholders to the political-campaign funds of their superiors.
##For example, the President appoints postmasters and postmistresses.

people felt sure that his elevation to the White House would prove to be a national calamity.

THE BEGINNING OF CHANGE

Arthur, however, was equal to the opportunity for high-minded service the presidency offered him. He had no use for the reformers, but he bowed to the public clamor for reforms. It is ironic that Arthur—formerly a spoilsman—signed as President a bill which established the principle of the merit system in the federal civil service. The new law—the Pendleton Act of 1883—also created a Civil Service Commission # to oversee the competitive tests necessary for certain federal jobs.

Arthur had not pressed for this legislation, but to his great credit, he carried it out to the letter. Its operations have been vastly extended by the actions of later Presidents. Today only a relatively small number of jobs may be distrib- ## uted as political plums to party favorites.

The President's independence. President Arthur showed unexpected independence in performing his executive duties. When fraudulent contracts with private companies were discovered in the postal department, he ordered vigorous prosecutions, even though men high in Republican ranks were involved. He also supported tariff reduction despite stiff opposition from his own party.

This convention was held in Chicago, the city in which Lincoln had been nominated in 1860.

Republicans meeting in their national convention in 1884 cheer as they hear that Blaine will be their standard- bearer in the presidential election that year. Twice before he had sought the coveted nomination in vain.

Harper's Weekly, June 14, 1884

376 Blaine, standing on the platform (in front of the eagle), waves to his supporters. Observe the mustaches and beards worn by the men in an era when whiskers were fashionable.

Choosing the Plumed Knight. In 1884 Arthur was eager to obtain the presidential nomination in his own right, but his party rejected him. He had angered too many of its powerful men. At the same time, despite his record of integrity in the presidency, he had not lived down his earlier unsavory reputation so far as the reformers were concerned.

It seemed, surely, that Blaine's hour had now arrived. With Conkling out of the way and Arthur unacceptable, Blaine was quickly nominated by the Republican convention in Chicago.

Blaine had been dubbed the "Plumed Knight" by the orator who had presented his name to the 1876 convention. The name stuck, but it was not appropriate. Blaine, while Speaker of the House in 1869, had done questionable legislative favors for a railroad in Arkansas. The details became a favorite subject of Democratic orators in the 1884 campaign.

Mugwumps. Many Republicans refused to support Blaine on account of his previous record and his efforts to keep alive the bitterness of the Civil War. They made it plain that they would support the Democrats if Grover Cleveland, of New York, should receive the nomination. These independent Republicans were nicknamed "mugwumps."†

The Democrats' man: Grover Cleveland. The Democrats nominated Cleveland, fulfilling the mugwumps' hope. As mayor of Buffalo and governor of New York, Cleveland had aroused admiration for his political courage and honesty. Moreover, he had battled against Tammany Hall, the Democratic organization in New York City that was known for its corruption. As a result, the reformers made Cleveland their darling.

The campaign raised no social or economic questions on which the candidates could express their opinions. Instead, it quickly turned # into a mudslinging affair. The Democrats harped on Blaine's political past, and the Re-

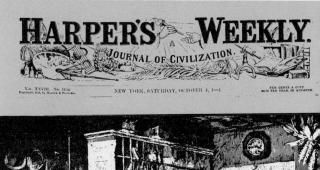

Harper's Weekly, October 4, 1884

Talking it over in 1884: Blaine or Cleveland?

Observe the horseshoe, the spittoon, etc.

publicans revived the memory of a personal scandal that Cleveland had been involved in. ##

Said Henry Adams, John Quincy Adams' grandson and one of the shrewdest observers of his time: "The public is angry and abusive. Every one takes part. We are all doing our best, and swearing at each other like demons. But the amusing thing is that no one talks about real interests [issues]. By common consent they agree to let these alone. We are afraid to discuss them."

---

† The word means a big man, or chief, in the language of the Algonkian Indians. It was used mockingly by the regular Republicans to suggest that the bolters considered themselves superior in intellect and character to the other members of the party. Now the word is generally used to denote one who takes an independent or neutral position.

Puck, February 6, 1884

This cartoon, captioned "The old hose won't work," shows Republican politicians trying to use the worn-out bloody-shirt issue to turn attention from the problems of the day: the tariff and civil service reform.

The dates on the hose indicate that the hose "worked" in 1868 and thereafter until 1884.

In November Cleveland won in a close election, typical of the entire period. His total popular vote was only 29,000 greater than Blaine's, but he captured the electoral college by 219 to 182. The new President was the first Democrat to be elected to the office since the time of James Buchanan, on the eve of the Civil War.

AN UNINSPIRED MAN OF COURAGE

Cleveland had little imagination and no sensitivity to the social injustice around him on every side. He was, though, a purposeful man who subscribed to the motto "A public office is a public trust." Bravely he tried to live up to it.

Pension vetoes. Cleveland's practice of his motto brought him into difficulties with the Union veterans of the Civil War. Increasing numbers of them were seeking pensions based on their war service, by means of individual bills introduced by their congressmen. The former soldiers became hostile to the President when he refused to sign automatically every one of the various private pension bills passed by Congress.

No President had ever vetoed *one* before. But within a short time Cleveland's pension vetoes gave him a record of having vetoed more bills than all his predecessors in the presidency put together. Most of the bills were outrageous: one, for example, was for a man who wanted a pension because he had injured his ankle while *intending* to enlist.

Cleveland earned further condemnation for his veto of the Dependent Pension Bill in 1887. This bill would have given a pension to every former Union soldier who was unable to earn a living, provided only that he had served for ninety days or more. Cleveland's argument was that "though the people support the Government, the Government should not support the people."

Cleveland also irritated Union veterans again

#A student might investigate the history of government military pensions in the United States, beginning with the first pension law, passed in 1792. Any good encyclopedia can be used.

A state dinner at the White House in 1888. Among the guests is a Chinese diplomat, at the far left. Cleveland is at the far right. The elaborate flowers on the table and the palms were characteristic of the period.

Cleveland himself enjoyed good food: he weighed 240 pounds.

when, without very much forethought, he issued an order to return to the southern states the captured Confederate battle flags. These had become a storage nuisance in the basement of the Department of War. The commander of the GAR shouted hysterically to an audience, "May God palsy the hand that wrote that order!"

Cleveland revoked the order, and the flags were kept in Washington until 1905, when President Theodore Roosevelt returned them amid public approval. Cleveland was especially vulnerable to GAR attack because he was not a veteran himself.

Facing the tariff. Convinced that customs duties were too high because they resulted in the accumulation of a large surplus in the federal treasury, Cleveland with his characteristic forthrightness attacked the tariff question. He pleaded for a lowering of the tariff rates, but he was rebuffed. The tariff became an issue in the campaign of 1888.

Although President Cleveland greatly extended civil service, a reformer rebukes him for not doing more. #

#Cleveland practically doubled the number of federal officeholders covered by civil service, but the reformers wanted the number to be larger. What groups of voters did Cleveland alienate?

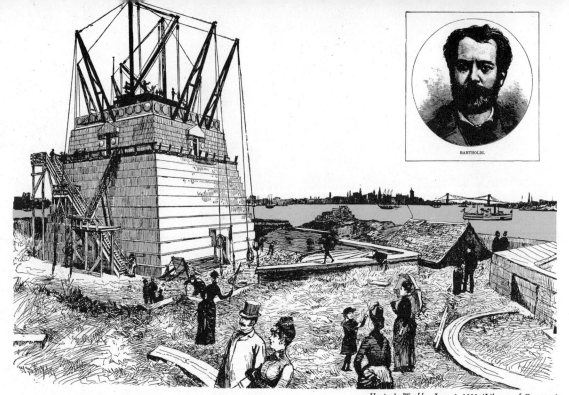

Harper's Weekly, June 6, 1885 (Library of Congress)

A happy event of Cleveland's administration was the dedication of the Statue of Liberty on October 28, 1886.

Designed by Frédéric Bartholdi, it was a gift from the French people. *Above:* The pedestal is being prepared.

Observe the skyline of New York City appearing in the background.

Below: The French ship *Isère* (*foreground*) arrives at New York in 1884, bringing the Statue to America.

Harper's Weekly, June 27, 1885 (Library of Congress)

The Statue of Liberty is 151 feet high, and from thirty to forty people can stand in its head. The cost of the construction was $500,000--not a large sum considering the cost of construction today, but an enormous figure in the late 1800's.

Frank Leslie's Illustrated Newspaper, August 2, 1884 (Library of Congress)

The impressive symbol of French friendship is formally presented to the United States government on July 4, 1884. The Statue was dedicated two years later and opened to the public.

Today the Statue of Liberty is a national monument administered by the National Park Service. Construction of an American Museum of Immigration at the base of the statue is planned.

Judge, September 8, 1888

A protectionist view: a Democrat hands a worker a knife, saying, "Kill the goose that lays the golden eggs."

Running against Benjamin Harrison.
Cleveland was enthusiastically renominated by his party. This time the Republicans assailed him as a free trader—a person opposed to tariffs. They made their chief platform plank a demand for high protection. Their candidate was the Indianan, Benjamin Harrison, a grandson of Old Tippecanoe. Harrison's opponents said he was as "cold as an iceberg"; he was the soul of high-mindedness but not of warmth.

A British mistake.
During the campaign a Republican identifying himself as a naturalized American of English origin wrote to the British minister in Washington, Sir Lionel Sackville-West, asking how he should vote. Innocently, Sir Lionel recommended Cleveland because of the free-trade position the President had taken.

The Republicans seized on this blunder to charge that the President truckled to the British. Almost immediately afterward, the administration demanded the minister's recall, but Cleveland unquestionably lost votes—particularly among Irish-Americans—for having appeared to be "England's candidate." Although

Ask what symbols the cartoonists used. Compare "protection" and "free trade."

An antiprotectionist view: a prosperous-looking factory owner offers to save his employees from a puppet monster labeled "Free Trade" but tells congressmen (*left*),

"Whoop it up boys; make the jaws go—we've got to keep the workingmen frightened." Frightened they are: see how they cling to the proprietor for protection.

Puck, May 5, 1886

Compare the Uncle Sam in the cartoon at the upper left with the one seen on p. 275. What changes can be seen? (Suggestions: the one on this page looks more like Uncle Sam today, etc.)

Cleveland received about 90,000 more popular votes than Harrison, the Republican candidate ＃ won easily in the electoral college.

THE RUMBLE OF BIGGER ISSUES

Harrison was a deeply religious man, personally out of step with the political spoilsmen who had worked for his election. When he was told of his triumph, he said reverently, "Providence has given us the victory." One of the bosses laughed coarsely and asserted that Providence had had nothing to do with it. Harrison would never know, he said, "how close a number of men were compelled to approach the gates of the penitentiary to make him President." But the day of the spoilsmen was drawing to a close.

Businessmen in politics. Many businessmen were finding it agreeable to enter politics themselves. When Harrison was inaugurated on March 4, 1889, as the "Centennial President," his Cabinet—which was sometimes called the "businessman's cabinet"—included John Wanamaker, the dry-goods merchant of Philadelphia, and Redfield Proctor, the marble magnate from Vermont.

The Senate became known as the "millionaires' club," for among its members now were lumbermen, railroad and oil magnates, the owners of silver and gold mines, and bank directors. The Vice-President, Levi P. Morton, of New York, was head of one of the most powerful banking firms in America.

First "billion-dollar Congress." Harrison's administration was from the start subjected to strong pressure from special-interest groups seeking pet legislation. Aided by the Speaker of the House, Thomas B. ("Czar") Reed, the new Republican Congress—elected with Harrison— passed a series of appropriation bills that made it the country's first "billion-dollar Congress." The Civil War veterans cheered an act this Congress put through entitling them all to pensions.

Also, a new law, the Sherman Silver Purchase Act, was passed, requiring the treasury ＃＃ to double the amount of silver bullion it bought each month. The bullion was to be paid for by issuing paper money—silver certificates—

Frank Leslie's Illustrated Newspaper, November 10, 1888

Political excitement in New York City before the election of 1888: Harrison supporters chorus, "Trade, trade, no free trade." Cleveland advocates yell, "Don't, don't, don't be afraid; only low tariff, so don't be afraid."

Are people excited over politics today?

redeemable in silver or gold. Businessmen got the highest tariff rates in history. Farmers especially were placated by the passage of the Sherman Antitrust Act.

The McKinley Tariff. A new tariff, known as the McKinley Tariff because it was the work of Representative William McKinley, of Ohio,

The sack of money into which one "Bill" is dipping represents the treasury surplus which had been accumulated largely because of the tariff. (Observe the label on the sack.) Look at the names of the various "Bills."

Puck, April 16, 1890

The treasury is raided by a parade of special-interest bills, while Harrison (*center*)—dwarfed by his grand-father's big hat—looks on. The man at the President's left is "Czar" Reed, Speaker of the House.

The man standing at Harrison's right is Levi P. Morton, the Vice-President.

raised duties significantly. It removed the levy on raw sugar in order to aid American refineries, but it protected American growers by paying them a bounty of two cents a pound on raw sugar grown in the United States.

With the passage of the McKinley Tariff, # businessmen felt a new sense of power. Who could challenge them? They were unaware that the answer was already in the making.

Cleveland's return. Grumblings of discontent were being heard in the distance. A third party —the People's, or Populist, party—which represented a substantial body of protest, in 1892 put up a presidential candidate, James B. Weaver.

Grover Cleveland, for a third time the candidate of the Democratic party, ran on a low-tariff platform to attract votes among those dissatisfied with the McKinley Tariff. On Election Day, Harrison, who had been renominated,

was defeated. The tariff, labor unrest, and the President's record of yielding easily to pressures were offered in explanation of the Democrat's triumph.

The depression of 1893. In the four years between his two terms as President, Cleveland had practiced law in New York. His attention was centered now on the problems of eastern bankers and businessmen, and he failed to appreciate the plight of unemployed workers and farmers burdened by debt. Shortly after his inauguration, the depression of 1893 began.

A number of conditions were responsible for the hard times. One was the ill effect of the failure of a British banking firm, Baring Brothers. British investors sold their American securities, thereby draining gold out of the United States' reserves. A second cause of the panic was a decline in customs revenues owing to a reduced demand for foreign goods because

384 #The Republican party had become the party of businessmen, largely because it favored a protective tariff. Compare the party of these years with the party of Lincoln in 1860.

It had been expected that the Columbian Exposition would open in 1892, but the buildings and exhibits had not been completed in time. Pullman cars and the Linotype were exhibited.

The "moving sidewalk" at the Columbian Exposition in Chicago in 1893. Exhibits featured new machines and new ideas.

Observe the streetcar tracks in the picture below. Horses were still much in evidence.

Cleveland—at the left in the carriage in the foreground—rides in his inaugural procession from the Capitol.

Grover Cleveland has the distinction of being the only President who served two terms that were not consecutive. In the years between his presidencies, he practiced law in New York.

Since Cleveland had just taken office, he could hardly have been to blame for the depression. What party was responsible for the McKinley Tariff? For reducing the treasury surplus?

Historical Pictures Service

An angry anti-Cleveland cartoon published in 1893 and captioned, "Gone Democratic!" Idle workers gaze at empty factories.

Notice how Cleveland had aged between his first and second administrations (see p. 379).

Cleveland's Cabinet meets in the White House early in 1893. The President sits at the left; the second man from his left is Attorney General Richard Olney, who later served as Secretary of State (see page 395). The number of smooth-shaven faces now equals the number of bearded ones.

Historical Pictures Service

of the McKinley Tariff. The third was the reduction of the treasury surplus as a result of heavy federal expenditures.

Repeal of the Sherman Silver Purchase Act. The measures that Cleveland took to ease the effects of the depression were not generally popular. They did not include direct relief for the least fortunate groups in the country. The President believed his most important task was to halt the flow of gold from the treasury. He knew that if he failed in his effort, the international financial position of the United States would be endangered.

Americans needed to be convinced that there was a sufficient store of gold at the treasury; otherwise they would constantly present silver certificates for redemption in gold and then hoard the valuable yellow coins. An early way was to obtain the repeal of the Sherman Silver Purchase Act of 1890, which had permitted the redemption of silver certificates in gold. This repeal in 1893 angered the silver men, who had been profiting handsomely under the existing law.

The Morgan gold deal. A second method was used in 1895. Through the bank of J. P. Morgan, Cleveland was able to conclude what was labeled the "Morgan bond deal." Morgan, the financier, agreed to sell United States bonds here and abroad in order to build up a supply of gold for the treasury. The arrangement, which paid considerable profit to bankers, irritated "little men" all over the country, who charged that the President was in league with the "money trust."

The attitude toward labor. Two other incidents in Cleveland's second administration particularly angered workingmen. The President in 1894 used military force to break a strike of railway employees which bad times had brought about. During the same year Jacob S. Coxey led an "army" of the unemployed from Massillon, Ohio, to Washington, D.C., to demand help for the jobless. Coxey was arrested and jailed for twenty days because his men walked on the grass of Capitol Hill.

Another tariff. When Cleveland tried again to obtain a revision of the tariff, Congress gave

Pierpont Morgan Library

J. Pierpont Morgan, wealthy art collector and financier, whose banking company helped mold American industry for half a century (see pages 336–338). His vast power was often attacked as excessive.

This photograph was by Edward Steichen.

him the Wilson-Gorman Act of 1894. It called for lower rates than those of the McKinley Tariff, but it was still so strongly protectionist that the President allowed it to become a law without his signature. An income-tax provision in the Act was declared unconstitutional by the Supreme Court in 1895.‡

After the depression of 1893, the signs were that the era of no issues in politics was ending

‡ The Court ruled that an income tax is a direct tax and, since it is not based on population, as such, is expressly forbidden by the Constitution. Subsequently—in 1913—the Sixteenth Amendment was adopted, removing the constitutional barrier to this kind of levy.

Coxey's "army" determinedly makes its way to Washington. Although many groups of unemployed persons set out for the capital, only about 400 men made it. Coxey wanted the federal government to provide direct relief.

The appearance of the men who made the trip to Washington on foot was not prepossessing.

Historical Pictures Service

and giving way to the era of big issues. The nation was growing tired at last of the theatrical political battles revolving around blown-up scandals and make-believe arguments. Deep-seated economic and social questions raised by the growth of big business were about to reach the arena of national politics.

Sum and Substance

1. How can politicians from 1868 to 1896 be characterized? 2. What people supported the Republican party? The Democratic party? 3. Describe the contests between Conkling and first Hayes, then Garfield. 4. How was the merit system established in the federal civil service? 5. Who was elected President in 1884? Account for his election. 6. What was Cleveland's opinion of the Dependent Pension Bill? Of the tariff question? 7. Describe three important laws enacted in the "Centennial President's" administration. 8. Why was Cleveland reelected? Name three groups he antagonized, and tell why.

This section describes events in our history that suggested the coming of an age of imperialism.

AMERICA STRETCHES UNCERTAINLY BEYOND ITS BORDERS

The relations of the United States with foreign countries have always reflected events taking place on the domestic scene. After the Civil War, America was a united nation again. In international affairs it was awkwardly trying to test its strength and measure its place in the world.

TOWARD THE TROPICS

Despite public indifference, interest in the Pacific and the Caribbean—which was older than the republic itself—never completely died out. Moreover, a need for bases in both those waters was brought home to Americans during the Civil War by the acts of marauding Confederate cruisers.

Negotiating with Denmark. Even before Appomattox, Secretary of State Seward had persuaded Denmark to sell the United States two islands in the Danish West Indies, one having an excellent harbor. In 1867 a treaty of transfer was ratified by the Danish king and parliament,

#Review the relationship between foreign affairs in the administrations of Washington, Adams, and Jefferson that proves this statement. Can students think of other examples?

388

and the monarch bade his island subjects farewell. But before the treaty came to a vote in the Senate, the islands were ravaged by an earthquake, a tidal wave, and a severe hurricane, in rapid succession.

Congressmen now regarded the islands to be a wasteful, if not a foolish, investment, and the deal did not go through. (The United States finally purchased all the Danish West Indies for $25,000,000—renaming them the Virgin Islands—in 1917. See the map on page 485.)

The Dominican Republic's offer. Seward, continuing to dabble in the tropics, tried to lease the Bay of Samaná in the Dominican Republic—the eastern part of the West Indian island of Hispaniola. The dictator of the Republic replied to Seward by inviting the United States to annex the whole of it!

The opposition of Congress. President Johnson recommended to Congress in 1868 that it accept this offer, but his advice was rejected. When Grant came into office the following year, he too supported accepting the offer, even though his Secretary of State, Hamilton Fish, was cool to the idea. Late in 1869 a treaty providing for the annexation of the Dominican Republic was submitted to the Senate. There it ran into the unshakable opposition of the august chairman of the Committee on Foreign Relations, Charles Sumner. The treaty failed, making Grant so angry that whenever he passed Sumner's house in Washington he violently shook his fist at it.

Carl Schurz was one of the leaders in the opposition to annexing territory in the tropics.
\# He argued that the task of absorbing an alien population would "demoralize and corrupt our political life . . . and impart to our government a military character most destructive of its republican attributes."

TOWARD THE ICY NORTH

Acquiring land in the frozen North presented no such difficulties. The population there was sparse and docile.

The purchase of Alaska. The United States purchased Alaska in 1867 for $7,200,000, as a

National Carl Schurz Association

Carl Schurz, a German immigrant who became a Senator from Missouri and an outstanding American statesman. A reformer, he worked for the merit system in the civil service. As Secretary of the Interior under Hayes, he undertook sweeping changes in the treatment of the Indians.

The most famous American of German ancestry.

result of Secretary Seward's successful negotiation. Russia, the previous owner, had decided to sell it because of fear that England might seize it in the event of war. The simple treaty of transfer was signed early in the morning of March 30, 1867, word of agreement having recently arrived from Russia on the newly laid Atlantic cable.

\#\#

Public ridicule. Seward bore the brunt of the campaign to gain Congress' support for the treaty. The administration's enemies sarcastically called the acquisition "Seward's Folly," "Johnson's Polar Bear Garden," "Walrussia," and other similar names. But Charles Sumner approved of the purchase, and largely through his efforts the treaty was ratified on April 9, 1867, by a vote of 37 to 2.

Obtaining the necessary funds from the House proved to be much more difficult. The exasperated Russian minister in Washington finally suggested to his home government that Alaska be offered gratis to the Americans in order to embarrass them into paying. The czar refused, however, for fear that this was the kind of opening the United States was waiting for!

Reluctant acceptance. Political pressure was used on some congressmen to win their votes. But other factors prompted the outcome, too. First, Americans felt grateful for the goodwill the

About 100,000 prospectors went to the Klondike from 1897 to 1899. Many remained as farmers.

A camp in Alaska in the late 1890's. The discovery of gold in the Klondike region of the Yukon Territory, across the border of Alaska, attracted prospectors like these, who are traveling through the American possession.

Bancroft Library, University of California

390 Alaska became a territory in 1912 and a state forty-seven years later. Gold discovered in Alaska in the late 1890's helped relieve the depression that had begun in 1893.

Russians had shown during the war by their fleet visits. Second, it was believed that by possessing Alaska, the United States would be closer than ever to the alluring trade with Asia. Third, many, like Sumner, were pleased that this was a way to expel another European country from this continent.

"One by one they have retired," he pointed out, "first France, then Spain, then France again; and now Russia; all giving way to the absorbing Unity which is declared in the na-

tional motto, *E Pluribus Unum*." Many Americans expected that Canada would also fall to the United States shortly, but proposals to acquire it came to nothing.

TOWARD ASIA

The acquisition of Alaska foreshadowed the coming of an age of *imperialism* in which a nation's prestige in international politics would be measured by the number and size of its subject possessions. During the 1870's and

Compare this picture with the one on p. 357.

An Alaskan settlement at the end of the nineteenth century, which is plainly profiting from the Klondike gold rush and from one in Alaska itself. Observe the sign that identifies one store as catering to miners.

Bancroft Library, University of California

##Emphasize this explanation of the age of imperialism. Recall that Britain had long been an imperial power, and that the Atlantic seaboard colonies had been among its possessions.

391

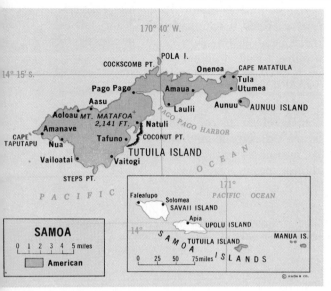

All Samoan Islands east of 171°W. are in American Samoa.

1880's, the principal countries of western Europe were smitten by the desire to own colonies. The contagion spread to the United States rather slowly, but already, as we have seen (pages 233, 243), Americans had marked out the Pacific Ocean as the scene for future undertakings by the nation.

Samoa. The interests of the United States in Pacific waters had been growing steadily since the Civil War. In 1878 the nation acquired a coaling station, Pago Pago, the chief harbor on Tutuila, one of the Samoa Islands. Germans and Englishmen were also active in Samoa, and their rivalry led to squabbling. Finally, in 1899 Germany and England entered into a treaty with the United States by which the United States received several islands, including Tutuila, the remainder of Samoa being given to Germany.

Observe the light colored clothes on the civilians--suggesting the kind of weather they enjoyed.

United States forces on duty in Hawaii in 1893, stationed there to keep order after the bloodless revolution that removed Queen Liliuokalani from her throne. The rebel leaders were nine Americans, two Britons, and two Germans.

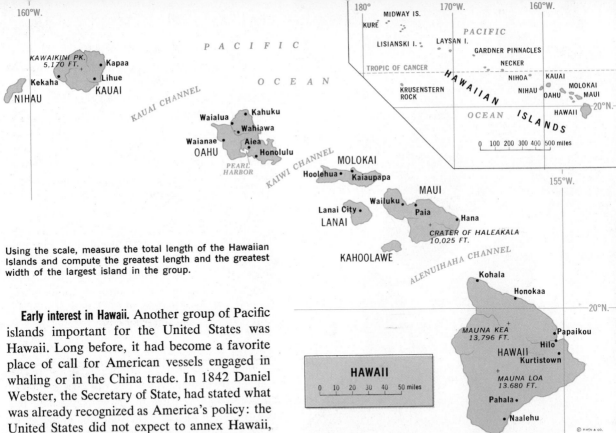

Using the scale, measure the total length of the Hawaiian Islands and compute the greatest length and the greatest width of the largest island in the group.

The total length is about 1700 miles.

Early interest in Hawaii. Another group of Pacific islands important for the United States was Hawaii. Long before, it had become a favorite place of call for American vessels engaged in whaling or in the China trade. In 1842 Daniel Webster, the Secretary of State, had stated what was already recognized as America's policy: the United States did not expect to annex Hawaii, but it did not intend to permit any other power to do so.

In 1875 the United States negotiated with the Hawaiian government a treaty permitting sugar to enter the United States market from Hawaii without duty. This move stimulated the prosperity of the islands, on which many Americans had settled.

"Queen Lil." Hawaii's place in American thinking loomed bigger in the 1880's. In those years the United States Navy was both adding ships and expanding the range of its responsibilities. America acquired Pearl Harbor on the Hawaiian island of Oahu as a coaling and repair station in 1887. This new tie with Hawaii encouraged Americans living there to think that the United States would one day annex the islands.

But no attempt was made to do so until 1891, when Queen Liliuokalani, who was unfriendly to American interests in the islands, came to the throne. The American sugar growers in Hawaii were already in an angry mood over the McKinley Tariff, which allowed all foreign sugar—not only their own—to enter

the United States duty free. Also, they were handicapped by the bounty paid to American producers. Taking matters into their own hands, they revolted against "Queen Lil," forced her to abdicate, and prepared to join the islands to the United States.

To annex or not to annex. Less than a month of Harrison's administration remained when the President sent to the Senate a treaty to annex Hawaii. But Cleveland, in one of his first official acts, recalled the treaty from Capitol Hill. He expressed the hope that the United States would repair "the great wrong done to a feeble but independent state" by restoring the Queen to her throne. The only way to put the Queen back in power, however, was for the United States to use force against the Americans who had helped depose her. Unwilling to do this, Cleveland turned the problem over to Congress, which "sat on" it for the next few years.

After the traders, American missionaries and sugar growers arrived in Hawaii. Students will enjoy reading James A. Michener's Hawaii.

#What value was involved? Recall Americans' pride in winning their own independence.

Uncertainty about the wisdom of having colonies reflected deeply-felt American beliefs. It seemed indecent to deny to others the sacred right of independence that the American people had once so proudly proclaimed to the world. The celebration of the one-hundredth anniversary of American liberty in 1876—including the Centennial Exposition in Philadelphia—had recalled again the devotion of the Founding Fathers to the ideal of self-government.

Furthermore, Americans were so completely absorbed in industrial expansion that they had as yet little interest in engaging in overseas imperialism. Most of them were hesitant, too, about bringing into the national "household" large numbers of people whose languages, races, and cultures were different from their own.

Sum and Substance

1. What places in the Caribbean did Americans talk of acquiring? Which did the United States obtain? When? 2. Give the facts concerning the acquisition of Alaska. 3. In what area in the world were Americans chiefly interested? 4. How did the United States obtain American Samoa? 5. Why was this country particularly interested in Hawaii? 6. Explain why American sugar growers there revolted against the Hawaiian queen. 7. Give two reasons for American opposition to acquiring overseas colonies.

Baker Collection, Bernice P. Bishop Museum

Queen Liliuokalani, who ruled from 1891 to 1893, succeeded to the throne of Hawaii when her brother died.

The queen wrote the song "Aloha Oe." She made two trips to America after losing her throne.

THE UNITED STATES ASSUMES LEADERSHIP OF THE AMERICAS

The defense of the Monroe Doctrine continued to be a fundamental principle of American foreign policy. We have already seen (page 284) how the United States responded during the Civil War to Maximilian's presence in Mexico. When a French company planned to dig a canal across the Isthmus of Panama, President Hayes was quick to point out that such an attempt would infringe on United States interests.

The French company—a private organization—went ahead with its work anyway under Ferdinand de Lesseps, the man who had built the Suez Canal. It spent a large sum of money

to build favorable public opinion in the United States. When the canal-building enterprise failed, Americans became eager to complete the task successfully themselves.

Perhaps if they had been less preoccupied with railroad and factory construction, the people of the United States would not have stood by while the French attempt occurred. Americans had carelessly left the door open to a possible violation of the Monroe Doctrine.

PAN-AMERICANISM

In the post-Civil War years United States relations with its neighbors were largely deter-

##A French syndicate failed to complete a canal between 1880 and 1889, and a second French company failed in 1899. Pp. 532-537 describe the American undertaking.

mined by this country's interpretation of the Monroe Doctrine. Nevertheless, the United States tried also to promote a spirit of Pan-Americanism, that is, willing economic and political coöperation among all the American nations.

Blaine's labors. James G. Blaine deserves much credit for furthering this movement. While serving briefly as Secretary of State under President Garfield in 1881, he had made preliminary arrangements for a conference of representatives from all the New World nations. When he returned to the Department of State in 1889 as Secretary under President Harrison, this first Pan-American Congress was just gathering in Washington.§

Intentions. Blaine's aim was to foster the peaceful settlement of inter-American disputes and to cultivate new markets for United States exports. He planned to set up an inter-American customs union, to improve transportation and communications between North and South America, and to put in use in all the Americas a common silver coin and a uniform system of weights and measures. But it was still too early for such thoroughgoing developments. Moreover, the Latin American countries were somewhat distrustful of their powerful North American neighbor.

First fruit. An important result of the conference was the creation of a Pan-American Union to encourage the exchange of information—on scientific matters, for example—among American countries. The newspapers were inclined to snicker at the generally meager outcome of the gathering; similar meetings, nevertheless, continued to be held from time to time.

A STRENGTHENED MONROE DOCTRINE

Pan-Americanism was, in a sense, an extension of the principles of the Monroe Doctrine. The peace of the Americas was slowly coming to be thought of as a collective responsibility.

§Henry Clay had envisioned a union of American republics. In 1826 as Secretary of State he supported a congress in Panama called by Simón Bolívar. But although the United States appointed representatives, they failed to arrive in time. In the half-century following, other issues held the attention of American countries.

But the United States continued to consider itself the big brother of smaller American nations, and it stoutly upheld the Monroe Doctrine alone.

Venezuela boundary dispute. A notable instance of the kind of role this country played was the Venezuela boundary dispute of 1895. From 1840 on, Venezuela and the British government had been unable to agree on the boundary line between that South American republic and what was then British Guiana.

Anti-British feeling, which had always existed in the United States, was especially high in the early 1890's. At that time many Americans believed that British economic practices had caused the depression of 1893. Early in 1895, Congress by a joint resolution called upon President Cleveland to press the disputing countries to settle their boundary controversy by *arbitration*—that is, by submitting the issue to a neutral umpire for a decision. ##

The Olney doctrine. Secretary of State Richard Olney, a railroad attorney, spoke out boldly against the British government. He declared that if England seized the disputed territory by force, the act would be a violation of the Monroe Doctrine. He pledged that the United States would not sit idly by and watch the violation of a friendly neighbor.

In a strong statement that is sometimes called the Olney doctrine, Olney announced that the United States, because of "its infinite resources combined with its isolated position, is practically sovereign on this continent, and its fiat [that is, its say-so] is law" in any matters on which it considers it proper to interfere.

England's response. The British, of course, rejected this startling assertion of American power. They had never accepted the Monroe Doctrine as a document binding them in any way, and they said now that even if they had accepted it, it did not apply in this case. The dispute, the British foreign secretary said, involved "simply the determination of the frontier of a British possession which belonged to the Throne of England long before the Republic of Venezuela came into existence."

See Questions 9 and 10, col. 2, p. 397, for other queries concerning the Olney doctrine.
##Emphasize the explanation. Arbitration is a common method of settling labor disputes.

Punch, November 21, 1896

A cartoon from a British magazine shows Brother Jonathan and John Bull eating "peace pudding" at last.

"Brother Jonathan" was the name given any patriotic American during and after the Revolution.

Peaceful settlement. Politically, Cleveland could not afford this type of rebuff. Already he was being criticized for his attitude toward Hawaiian annexation. Making clear to England the intention of the United States to defend its "national self-respect and honor," he appointed a commission to arbitrate. The British accepted arbitration because they were having other, more serious difficulties in South Africa. Also, the growth of German power in Europe made them eager to have no new antagonists—least of all in the New World.

Latin American suspicions. Olney's words, which he himself described as "bumptious," had had the effect—shocking to many both at home and abroad—of declaring that the United States was the protector and overlord of the New World. For many Latin Americans the Secretary's statement aroused deep suspicions and fears, for it appeared to be a denial of the lofty principles of Pan-Americanism. The # United States was learning the unwelcome lesson that a display of national strength may sometimes irritate most the very countries that it is intended to protect from harm.

The nation's increasing power in the world for a time found Americans unready for the opportunities that now were theirs. During the period when the United States was becoming rapidly industrialized, politics was often sordid, and the foreign policies produced were often halting and contradictory.

But before the century was out, politics would cease to be a game chiefly for spoilsmen. The country's international relations would then reflect dramatically the new needs and aspirations that economic and political changes were stimulating in the American people.

Sum and Substance

1. What Secretary of State deserves most credit for promoting Pan-Americanism? Why? 2. What did he hope to accomplish? How successful was he? 3. State the facts in the Venezuela boundary dispute. How was it settled? 4. What was the Olney doctrine? How was it received by England? By Latin American countries?

#The relations of the United States with the Latin American countries are haunted today by the memories of our unfortunate interventions in their affairs.

396

THE WORKSHOP

OF LASTING SIGNIFICANCE

How was each of the following involved in the partisanship and statesmanship of the years between 1869 and 1893?

GAR	Jacob S. Coxey
solid South	Wilson-Gorman Act
Stalwart	Virgin Islands
Half-Breed	Dominican Republic
merit system	Alaska
James G. Blaine	imperialism
Chester A. Arthur	Samoa
James A. Garfield	Pago Pago
mugwump	Liliuokalani
Grover Cleveland	Pan-Americanism
Benjamin Harrison	Venezuela
Sherman Silver	arbitration
Purchase Act	Olney doctrine
McKinley Tariff	fiat

INTERNATIONAL POLITICS

1. How did England become involved in the presidential election of 1888? Why did Americans resent the involvement?

2. In what two ways did the purchase of Alaska serve the national self-interest of the United States? In what sense was the purchase a further indication of "manifest destiny"?

3. What years in world history are called the Age of Imperialism? Why? How was the United States affected?

4. How did the acquisition of the islands now called American Samoa involve the national self-interest of the United States? By what method of handling international business were the islands obtained?

5. What principle of American foreign policy was Secretary of State Daniel Webster echoing in 1842 when he said that the United States would not allow another country to annex Hawaii? In what instance did President Hayes invoke the same principle?

6. In what sense was American opposition to owning colonies in the 1880's idealistic? In what sense was it not idealistic? Would Americans today agree with views of most people in those days? Explain.

7. What constructive move in international politics did James G. Blaine make?

8. In what way did events in Germany and Africa affect the settlement of the Venezuela boundary dispute?

9. Would a Secretary of State today be likely to take the position Olney took in the Olney doctrine? Explain.

10. In what sense were the feelings of Latin Americans after the statement of the Olney doctrine similar to the feelings of people of the United States when England appeared to be involved in the election of 1888?

DOCUMENTS IN HISTORY

1. How did George Washington Julian (see pages 370–371) account for the coming of the era of "slack-water politics" after the Civil War?

2. What new problems did he identify?

3. What in your opinion accounts for "slack-water politics" in any period?

BEING A SOCIAL SCIENTIST

1. For many years politicians knew that the electoral votes of the former Confederate states would be cast for Democratic presidential candidates. What effects on candidates for office and on politics in general does the existence of such a large bloc of assured support have? Explain.

2. What similarity was there between the appeals many Democratic politicians made for southern support after the Civil War and those many Republican politicians made for support for their party?

3. Find out why the "solid South" has broken up, judging from recent presidential elections.

4. Name the acts of partisanship and those of statesmanship in the period from 1872 to 1893 and tell why you classify them as you do. What ones can you name in the term in office of the present President?

President Hayes invoked the same principle that Webster did when he said that the attempt of a French company to build a canal across the Isthmus of Panama would infringe on our interests.

397

20

ORGANIZING THE FORCES OF LABOR

. . . only his own labor to sell . . .

In its fundamental principle trade unionism is plain and clear and simple. Trade unionism starts from the recognition of the fact that under normal conditions the individual, unorganized workman cannot bargain advantageously with the employer for the sale of his labor. Since the workingman has no money in reserve and must sell his labor immediately, since, moreover, he has no knowledge of the market and no skill in bargaining, since, finally, he has only his own labor to sell, while the employer engages hundreds or thousands of men and can easily do without the services of any particular individual, the workingman, if bargaining on his own account and for himself alone, is at an enormous disadvantage. . . .

The Statue of Liberty stands on Bedloe's (now Liberty) Island in the distance.

The "individual bargain," or individual contract, between employers and men means that the condition of the worst and lowest man in the industry will be that which the best man must accept. From first to last, from beginning to end, always and everywhere, trade unionism stands unalterably opposed to the individual contract.

There can be no concession or yielding upon this point. No momentary advantage, however great or however ardently desired, no advance in wages, no reduction in hours, no betterment in conditions, will permanently compensate workingmen for even a temporary surrender in any part of this fundamental principle. It is this principle, the absolute and complete prohibition of contracts between employers and individual men, upon which trade unionism is founded.

There can be no permanent prosperity to the working classes, no real and lasting progress, no consecutive improvement in conditions, until the principle is firmly and fully established, that in industrial life, especially in enterprises on a large scale, the settlement of wages, hours of labor, and all conditions of work, must be made between employers and workingmen collectively and not between employers and workingmen individually.

To find a substitute for the individual bargain, which destroys the welfare and the happiness of the whole working class, trade unions were founded. . . . The ideal of trade unionism is to combine in one organization all the men employed, or capable of being employed, at a given trade, and to demand and secure for each and all of them a definite minimum standard of wages, hours, and conditions of work.

Americans who worked in factories long refused to believe their situation was permanent. They looked forward to rising into the ranks of the self-employed. As a result, they often resisted joining with fellow employees in making demands for better wages and conditions. Businessmen, on the other hand, usually considered joint action by the workingmen to be dangerously radical. Successful labor leaders early discovered, therefore, the importance of directing their arguments to capitalists as well as to laboring people. John Mitchell did this in his book Organized Labor, *published in 1903, from which this selection comes. Mitchell, one of the most effective union organizers in American history, became president of the United Mine Workers in 1898, when he was only twenty-eight years old.*

What does the sight of the Statue mean to people?

Immigrants in the early 1900's gaze at the Statue of Liberty after their ship has arrived in New York Harbor. These four people, like thousands and thousands of other foreigners, had left their home, relatives, and friends for the promise of better living in America. Joining the great army of American workers, they contributed their labor and their talents to the development of a powerful, highly industrialized United States. Bringing their diverse traditions, arts, and skills to the new land, they immeasurably enriched an already plural American culture, even though they did not always find ready acceptance.

Brown Brothers

#The craftsman was able to satisfy what kind of demands? (Those of a relatively small group of se-
lective customers.) What kind of demands could machinery satisfy? (Those of a large number of
consumers who found that they could no longer expect the quality that craftsmen provided.)

TOILERS LEARN THAT IN UNION THERE IS STRENGTH

By the middle of the nineteenth century, it was already clear that the industrialization of the United States was changing the American laboring man into a new kind of person. The craftsman, respected and honored in his community, was becoming a factory worker.

CAUGHT BY THE MACHINE

Factory workers tended machines that, like giant robots, made them feel insignificant, if not helpless. These workers might not even know their employers by sight, although they were completely dependent on them for their livelihood and working conditions. Factory workers, moreover, found themselves in keen competition with one another for jobs; years of training as artisans were no longer necessary in order to perform most industrial operations.

A factory hand could not even make himself believe that he was the master of his machine. He could see that he was only a part of it, and a replaceable part at that. The pride in performance, which a skilled craftsman once enjoyed, seemed to have vanished in a factory system that depended on speed and mass production.

Job insecurity. As these changes took place, all workers experienced a sense of insecurity that altered their outlook and frightened them. Periodic depressions and layoffs made their jobs uncertain. Illness or disability—and not least of all, injuries received on the job—often proved disastrous.

Wages for unskilled labor were generally so low that saving money was difficult or impossible. Consequently, few workers could leave their jobs to try their luck elsewhere: they could not afford to move their families and support themselves in the meantime.

Protests to employers were unavailing because owners, who were themselves often in life-and-death competition with each other, felt it necessary to keep labor costs as low as possible. Besides, the steady flow of immigrants made it simple to replace almost any worker at a moment's notice.

Rivalries within the ranks. Fearing the loss of their jobs, laborers became antagonistic toward one another as well as toward the factory owners. Those who had special skills were scornful of the unskilled. Among the unskilled there was often angry rivalry between Americans and immigrants, sometimes between races, and, in some industries, between men and women.

Barriers to group action. The best answer to labor's problems appeared to lie in the work that trade unions could do. Trade unions, as organizations of workers who had joined together voluntarily, could exert pressure to obtain better hours, wages, and other working conditions.

The belief in individual enterprise, however, was so strong that united action was distasteful to many workers, whose ideals had been formed in agricultural America. Employers, moreover, were likely to threaten members of unions with the loss of their jobs. Only the boldest workers, therefore, dared to defy "the boss" by joining a labor organization. Finally, the weight of government often appeared to be on the side of the employer. This had, in fact, been the case since the earliest days of the nation.

EARLY TRADE UNIONS

The first American unions—in the eighteenth century—were really guilds to which master craftsmen of particular trades belonged in the hope of maintaining prices and standards. Conflicts between these masters and the journeymen, or traveling craftsmen who worked for them, were frequent.

Aims. But when journeymen joined together against the masters, it was only to win an argument of the moment and not to create a permanent labor union. For example, the journeymen printers in Philadelphia in 1786 issued this statement: "We will support such of our brethren as shall be thrown out of employment on account of their refusing to work for less than $6 per week." Like journeymen in other trades, they enforced their stand by using the strike, or "turnout," as it was called then.

The men who built the Erie Canal were mainly Irish and German immigrants, many of whom settled in the towns that grew up along the route of this important waterway. The workers lacked the machines that help do heavy construction work today.

Building the Erie Canal, about 1820. Few of the canal workers—or "canawlers," as they were called—had to have special skills to perform their tasks. What they needed were perseverance and strong backs.

The canal here is evidently being built beside a town that had been established years before.

At the beginning of the nineteenth century, the wages of unskilled laborers had generally risen because of the great new demand for hands to construct the canals and turnpikes. Since these workers were supplied with food and shelter in addition to wages, their weekly incomes often exceeded those of skilled artisans.

Consequently, skilled workers—including tailors, carpenters, shipwrights, cabinetmakers, shoemakers, and weavers—began to join together according to their particular skills or crafts in order to protect their standing. Their organizations—called craft unions—became more and more active in demanding economic improvement. Among employers and public officials, however, opposition to them was intense. #

Standing before the law. A strike by the cordwainers—shoemakers—of Philadelphia in 1806 for higher wages, for example, wound up in court. The judge denounced all organization of labor as tending to "public mischief and private injury." This view was in keeping with the old English tradition that a combination of workers was illegal, being deemed a conspiracy. It did no good for the workingmen to point out that associations of merchants or politicians were not similarly regarded as dangerous combinations.

The Mechanics' Union of Trade Associations. But laboring men refused to believe that fighting for their rights could be wrong. Recognizing that their strength lay in uniting, the artisans of Philadelphia in 1827 joined their craft unions in the Mechanics' Union of Trade Associations. For the first time the members of more than one trade had been brought together in a single organization. The forming of this union may be called the beginning of the labor movement in the United States. Some people believed that workingmen had become conscious of themselves as a separate class of people. But this was an exaggeration. Laboring people were merely hopeful that they could halt any decline in their economic position as compared with that of the merchants.

Workingmen's parties. A new phase of labor's history began in 1828 when workingmen's parties appeared in commercial states such as Pennsylvania, New York, and Massachusetts. These parties often were able to use their strength to determine the outcome of local elections. The one in Philadelphia demanded free education for everyone, the abolition of imprisonment for debt, laws to protect workers against bankrupt or dishonest contractors, and the abolition of monopolies—like the Bank of the United States.

In New York the labor party made similar demands. In addition, it complained that working people were not represented in the state legislature. The members of that body, it pointed out, came chiefly from among the wealthier citizens.

The workingmen's parties reflected the spirit of the Jacksonian age, in which they were formed. The members usually were skilled, self-employed craftsmen—hatters or harness makers or wheelwrights—eager to get ahead in the world. They gave Jackson their support

Recall other events of 1860. Note that the sign (far left) is that of a shoe manufacturer.

Eight hundred women shoemakers of Lynn, Massachusetts, went on strike in 1860. Here on a snowy day they march behind the Lynn city band, carrying a sign that declares their firm resolve. Spectators cheer them on.

Culver Pictures

after 1828, because his broad program for democratic improvement—particularly his attack on monopoly—suited their needs.

The *Albany Working Man's Advocate* boasted in 1830 that "throughout the vast Republic the farmers, mechanics, and workingmen are assembling . . . to impart to its laws and administration those principles of liberty and equality unfolded in the Declaration of Independence." In 1832 a workingmen's ditty ran:

> Mechanics, cartmen, laborers
> Must form a close connection,
> And show the rich aristocrats
> Their powers at this election.

Their decline. For a number of important reasons the workingmen's parties disappeared by the mid-1830's. First, their ideas were taken over, in general, by the two major parties, and they were at the same time incorporated into the American tradition as Jacksonian democracy. Second, the workingmen's parties lacked a national organization. Each of them focused its attention on local conditions and needs.

Third, the leaders of the parties often were nonlaboring men—sometimes even employers. These people had more time for political activity than actual workers, but they could hardly be intimately aware of the life of a laboring man. Fourth, the large mass of unskilled laborers had no unions to speak for them in party councils. As the factory system began to prevail, therefore, the workingmen's parties represented workingmen less and less, and consequently they became less effective.

The National Trades' Union. Although working people took a much smaller part in political activity after the early 1830's, labor-organizing itself continued. In 1834 representatives of trade unions and of associations of trade unions from six cities met in New York City and established the National Trades' Union. This was the first national union ever founded in the United States.

The National Trades' Union agreed on a program to improve labor's conditions, but the leaders, nevertheless, were determined to stay out of politics. As one of them stated it, they "belonged to no party; they were neither disciples of Jacksonism nor Clayism, Van Burenism, nor Websterism, nor any other ism but workeyism."

Membership grew rapidly in the unions that this organization represented—from 26,250 in 1834 to 300,000 in 1836. The number of members, however, declined sharply when the panic of 1837 came, as laboring men felt once again the need to depend on the goodwill of their employers.

"From 6 to 6." Between 1833 and 1837 several hundred strikes took place. The leading demand was for a 10-hour day at the same pay as for the prevailing 12-hour day. Workers insisted that they had obligations as family heads and as citizens "which forbid us to dispose of more than Ten Hours for a day's work."

The idea of working only "from 6 to 6"* gradually gained support, and the shortened workday was widely adopted in the nation. In 1840 President Van Buren issued an order establishing the 10-hour day on all work performed for the government. Business leaders followed this example.

A landmark court case. One stumbling block to the growth of organized labor was the attitude of the courts, in which, as we have seen, harassed employers found considerable comfort. Judges continued to rule that labor unions were conspiracies tending to restrain trade—and punishable as such.

But in 1842 a decision handed down in Massachusetts—in the case of *Commonwealth* v. *Hunt*—became a landmark in the history of America's labor movement. The case arose because the bootmakers of Boston had agreed not to work for any person who fired a journeyman for belonging to their union. Chief Justice Lemuel G. Shaw decided that the members' refusal to work under the condition they described did not mean they were engaged in a conspiracy. He declared that the purpose of the organization—to influence other bootmakers to join it—was lawful.

---

*The worker usually spent an hour at breakfast and an hour at lunch.

The enterprises at Brook Farm and New Harmony failed to a large extent because many of the members became disenchanted with farming and with manual labor in general.

Brook Farm, the beautiful New England community created in 1841 with money from the sale of stock to prospective members. It failed as an experiment in communal living, but its literary supporters made it famous. George Ripley was a Unitarian minister. A fire brought an end to Brook Farm in 1846.

Marking time. Even after this important legal opinion, though, the labor movement did not grow markedly before the Civil War. The large body of unskilled workers was not drawn into any organization, and the coming of the Civil War claimed energies that might otherwise have gone into labor reform.

Utopian planning. Besides, there was no unanimous agreement on how to solve the problems of the working people. Some reformers believed that it was possible to avoid the harsh consequences of industrialism by restoring the simpler ways of living of an earlier day. They refused to accept the thought that the individual must become subservient to the machine. They worked devotedly to create ideal—or utopian—communities in which the members raised their own food and filled other needs by their own handicraft.

One of the most famous utopian communities was George and Sophia Ripley's Brook Farm, established on a plot of land near Roxbury, Massachusetts. The leaders of Brook Farm hoped to establish "brotherly coöperation," which, in turn, would create "an attractive, efficient, and productive system of industry." But they never worked out clearly the way in which their community would be governed.

Nathaniel Hawthorne, the writer, was a member of this experiment in "plain living and high thinking." Visitors to it included people like Ralph Waldo Emerson and Margaret Fuller, two other leading literary lights. Brook Farm had become almost unmanageable by the time the experiment was abandoned in 1846.

"Vote yourself a farm." Many thoughtful Americans insisted that the best way for laboring people to overcome their difficulties was for them to return to the land. In the 1840's an organization called the National Reform Association made an appeal to workingmen with the slogan "Vote yourself a farm."

Factory workers were only deceiving them-

#Discuss the origin of the word "utopian" and its use here. Why has the word acquired the secondary meaning "impractical, or visionary"?

Indiana Department of Natural Resources

The Garden House in New Harmony, Indiana, a memorial to George Rapp, founder of a coöperative community— Harmonie. Robert Owen, the British reformer, bought it, renamed it New Harmony, and made it flourish.

Ask a student to find out why it was appropriate for Robert Owen to take over this enterprise.

selves if they believed that without capital they could easily switch to agriculture. Yet pressure from them undoubtedly helped bring about the passage in 1862 of the Homestead Act (see page 286). The laborer tended to think his well-being was linked to that of the farmer. Workingmen, in fact, frequently charged that the eastern industrialized states had opposed passage of the Homestead Bill out of fear that it would drain away the labor supply and make wages rise.

Although few factory workers ever took up farming, many eastern workingmen did seek homes in the newer towns and cities to the west, usually intending only to ply their old trades. In fact, the children of farmers were themselves increasingly deserting the land to find their futures in urban communities and the world of industry.

It was apparent that the easygoing, comparatively simple life of rural America was slowly yielding ground to the more complex, impersonal life brought by the factory. And yet Americans continued to hope that the democratic principle of the dignity of the individual would endure and that the possibility of climbing from poverty to riches could be preserved.

Nationwide craft unions. Laboring people recognized that they could not depend upon the proposals of those who, it seemed, were trying to turn back the clock. By the 1850's a number of trade unions were already national in membership, like the National Typographical Union and the Iron-Moulders International Union. Strikes were frequent: the most dramatic during this period occurred early in 1860 when 20,000 shoemakers in twenty Massachusetts towns walked out in a fight for higher wages.

Effect of the Civil War. When the Civil War came, laboring men responded patriotically, like other northerners, to Lincoln's call for volunteers. Nevertheless, after the wave of enthusiasm ebbed, the workers had many resentments. First, prices rose faster than wages, causing

405

Harper's Weekly, July 23, 1870

Chinese workers in a New England shoe shop, about 1870. Many Chinese entered the United States in the 1860's, some because of the need for laborers on the transcontinentals. Others came because in 1864 the Commissioner of Immigration was empowered to admit workers under contracts, pledging wages against ocean passage. Shortly the American Emigrant Company was formed to bring people into the country under such arrangements.

Look back at the picture on p. 325, bottom of page.

dissatisfaction among workingmen everywhere, from bricklayers in Chicago, to horsecar conductors in New York, to printers in St. Louis. Second, under the draft law working people had no choice but to go into the army if called. Men who had means, however, could legally avoid service—sometimes for good reason, of course—by hiring substitutes for themselves.† Third, the importation of contract labor (see page 319) enabled many employers to become deaf to the demands of their employees, who could be readily replaced.

---
†A good example was Grover Cleveland, later president of the United States, who was excused from service because he had a widowed mother and a family of younger brothers and sisters to support.

Sum and Substance

1. What was the fundamental principle on which John Mitchell said trade unionism was founded? 2. What disadvantages did the factory system bring to workers? 3. Why were workers slow to form unions? 4. What was the nature of the first American unions? 5. What is considered the beginning of the labor movement in this country? 6. When did workingmen's parties appear? When and why did they disappear? 7. Why did union membership decline after 1837? 8. Give the decision in the *Commonwealth* v. *Hunt* case. 9. Give the main facts concerning Brook Farm. 10. What democratic principle seemed threatened by factories? 11. How did the Civil War affect working people?

Contrast the way shoes are being made in the picture on this page with the way a craftsman would make them. Have students seen a factory in which shoes are made today?

WORKINGMEN TAKE A MORE AGGRESSIVE STAND

After the Civil War a new phase of labor history opened. Workingmen were helping to produce the "good things of life," and they yearned for a larger share of them.

NEW CIRCUMSTANCES

A number of developments spurred the working people to organize on a nationwide basis. The first was the tremendous expansion of industry, accompanied by the growth of the railroads. Every producer, it seemed, was selling in a national market. Manufacturers of iron in St. Louis, for example, were competing keenly with those in Pennsylvania. Wages—like prices— were being determined by nationwide competition, not by local conditions. Working people, observing that businessmen were organizing themselves in national associations, could see that the solution to labor's problems might be

found in doing likewise.

A second development was the rising number of immigrants, who, most workingmen believed, helped keep wages down. The newcomers, being mainly unskilled, seemed willing to work for less than the American workers.

A third element was that many manufacturing plants did not operate all year round, laying off their workers periodically, and causing great distress among them. Lastly, the introduction of new high-speed machinery to achieve large-scale production made factory work increasingly monotonous and dangerous, as well as economically insecure.

The National Labor Union and William Sylvis. If laboring men were to be organized successfully in order to meet these conditions in postwar America, they would require a program and the leadership to carry it into effect. In 1866 at

This foundry carried on heavy industry, the kind that developed increasingly in the late 1800's.

A foundry in New York City about 1865, typical of the plants in which new machinery was being introduced

in an effort to speed and improve production. Work became more demanding, as its pace quickened.

Museum of the City of New York

Frank Leslie's Illustrated Newspaper, September 30, 1871 (Library of Congress)

Workingmen in the fall of 1871 ride and march in a demonstration for the 8-hour day, in New York City. Banners identify the various groups that participated. Notice how commonplace beards and moustaches were.

Who was President in 1871? What was going on in the South?

Baltimore, delegates from many local and national trade unions met and organized the National Labor Union. The founders hoped to bring together in "one big family" the farmers and workers of the United States—skilled and unskilled.

The new union's chief aim was to obtain the 8-hour day for all workers. It also advocated the abolition of convict labor, the restriction of immigration, and the establishment of a federal Department of Labor.

The N.L.U. chose a brilliant president in William Sylvis, a former iron-moulder from Pennsylvania, the first national leader of labor in American history. His death within the year proved to be a fatal blow. The N.L.U. became involved in politics and turned itself into a political party. It made a very poor showing in the presidential election of 1872 and collapsed shortly afterward.

The depression of 1873. The onset of the terrible depression of 1873 badly hurt the emerging

#The Department of Labor was not created until 1913. Why would union members oppose convict labor? Recall free workers' opposition to slave labor.

movement to organize laboring people. Between 1873 and 1878 the number of workers belonging to any kind of union at all dropped from 300,000 to about 50,000. Where there had been thirty national craft unions, only seven remained. Labor's outlook was less promising than it had been in Van Buren's time.

As the depression deepened, homeless, hungry, jobless men held mass meetings in the leading industrial cities, greatly frightening the general public. Police did not hesitate to break up their meetings with a severity that today seems intolerable. For the first time, there was a general awareness of the danger to society that distressed working people could become.

The Molly Maguires. In the anthracite coalfields of Pennsylvania in 1874, violence broke out.

Believing that the mineowners were trying to destroy organized labor, many miners formed a secret society, known as the Molly Maguires, which aimed to spread terror among the mineowners.

A private detective hired by the owners worked his way into the inner circle of the organization. Ultimately twenty-four of its members were convicted of crimes, ten being hanged for murder. Union-organizing in the coalfields was set back a quarter of a century.

Strikes on the railroad. Labor unrest reached the railroads in 1877. A strike on the Baltimore & Ohio broke out in July after the road announced a new wage cut—the second since the depression began. The strike quickly spread to other lines, accompanied by riots in a number

A leader is evidently giving his views of the miners' situation and perhaps is suggesting action.

A secret meeting of the Molly Maguires in the coalfields of Pennsylvania, in 1874. The Mollies were one response

to the desperate working conditions from which miners could not escape and to which government was indifferent.

Harper's Weekly, January 31, 1874

of cities, including Baltimore, Pittsburgh, Chicago, and St. Louis.

The rail tie-up that followed almost completely paralyzed the nation. When strikers and the state militia clashed at Martinsburg, West Virginia, President Hayes called out federal troops to protect lives and property.

Even more serious events took place in Pittsburgh, where strikers seized trains and other railroad equipment. The local public appeared to sympathize with the men in their demands for a restoration of the wage cut; the local guardsmen were openly friendly to the strikers. Nevertheless, soldiers of the state militia sent from Philadelphia opened fire on the strikers, killing twenty-five.

A vengeful mob made up not only of striking railroad men but also of friendly miners and factory hands now took the law into its own hands. It burned and pillaged passenger cars, railroad machine shops, roundhouses, locomotives, and the B & O railroad depot itself.

Order was finally restored by federal troops sent by President Hayes, although between five and ten million dollars' worth of damage had been done. The strike ended abruptly, and the trains rolled again. Federal intervention had guaranteed a victory for the railroads.

The public's reaction. American opinion in general had become hostile to the demands of organized workingmen. The common view was that a worker must accept the wages and conditions provided by his employer. As the preacher Henry Ward Beecher said in a remark

One smooth-faced man is seen here, evidence that one of the men's styles was changing.

Uriah S. Stephens—standing, second from left—and the men who helped him organize the Knights of Labor. Its motto was, "That is the most perfect government in which an injury to one is the concern of all."

#What accounted for this feeling (which appeared in places not directly affected by the strikes)? (Undoubtedly the destruction of property by some strikers played a part.)

that became famous: ". . . I do not say that a dollar a day is enough to support a working man. But it is enough to support a man! Not enough to support a man and five children if a man insists on smoking and drinking beer. . . . But the man who cannot live on bread and water is not fit to live."

Although people throughout the country had been shocked by the railroad strikes in 1877, they had been awakened to the serious dissatisfactions stirring beneath the surface of American life. Many states revived their old laws against conspiracy in order to prosecute labor unions; others built new armories to guard against similar occurrences in the future.

THE KNIGHTS OF LABOR

Despite defeat and discouragement—or perhaps because of them—laboring men were beginning to recognize their common interests in the 1870's. This made possible the establishment of the first national labor organization to achieve significant influence—the Noble Order of the Knights of Labor.

Uriah S. Stephens. Led by a very versatile man, Uriah S. Stephens—a tailor and former student for the ministry—the Knights were organized in Philadelphia in 1869. Stephens, who took delight in fraternal clubs, created a secret ritual with a password and grip.

These secret signs were important, because in that day it was usually safer for a man if his employer did not know he belonged to a union. In 1878 the Knights organized themselves nationally, with Stephens as the first Grand Master Workman. The title suggests the sense of fraternity and fellowship he tried to introduce among the laboring people of the country.

Principles. Stephens' unique contribution lay in his idealistic confidence that a single union could embrace all laboring people. The Knights of Labor would admit anyone who worked— or who *had* worked—whether skilled or unskilled, man or woman, and regardless of nationality, race, or creed. (Only doctors, lawyers, bankers, stockholders, professional gamblers, and liquor dealers were excluded.) Despite Stephens' hopes, skilled workers who were already in craft unions shied away from the Knights because there was no special place for them.

Program. The Knights bluntly attacked the "unjust accumulation" of wealth, arguing that it "will invariably lead to the pauperization and hopeless degradation of the toiling masses." They advocated an 8-hour day, the transfer of # public lands to actual settlers only and not to speculators, "equal pay for equal work" for both sexes, and an end to convict and child labor. Later, they called for government ownership of railroads and telegraph lines and a graduated income tax—that is, one in which the levy on larger incomes is at a higher rate than that on smaller ones.

The Knights, like many early labor organizations, believed also that great benefits would result from organizing producers' and consumers' coöperatives. These associations, to be run by the district assemblies, or chapters, of the union, were expected to take care of the laboring man's needs without creating profits for a middleman. Among a variety of undertakings, the Knights operated a coal mine and a shoe-manufacturing plant.

Method and outlook. The Knights relied chiefly on legislation to achieve their program. They frowned on the strike as a method of action, ## supporting arbitration instead as a means of settling differences between employers and employees. They believed that America could somehow return to the days when every man was his own master and every man was his own employer.

Under Terence V. Powderly. In 1879 Stephens retired and was succeeded as president of the Knights by an able young Irishman from Carbondale, Pennsylvania, Terence V. Powderly. Under Powderly the organization grew, particularly after it dropped its veil of secrecy in 1882. That year its membership was 42,000; three years later it was over 100,000.

During the slight depression of 1884–1885, the number of members increased remarkably. Powderly usually refused to approve of strikes, and many strikes by members were, therefore, unauthorized by the Knights. Ironically, a

411

Chicago Historical Society

The scene in a Chicago police station near Haymarket Square after the trouble in 1886, drawn by a contemporary artist. Victims of the violence, for the most part on hastily improvised beds, receive hurried medical aid.

Another example of the contemporary illustrations used in this book.

notable victory in a railroad strike in the West enormously increased the organization's prestige and helped to swell its ranks. In January, 1886, there were 700,000 members, and others were pouring in.

Hard-fought strikes. The year 1886 was filled with labor strife, and there were many strikes in almost every industrial region. The Knights directed only a few, but the public blamed all of them on the Order.

The Haymarket affair. An event in Chicago dealt the Knights a mortal blow. A strike at the ## McCormick reaper plant there early in May had led to a fracas between pickets and strikebreakers. Policemen, attempting to restore order, killed four persons. The following night a protest meeting was held in Haymarket Square. Just as the meeting was dispersing

because of a threatened cloudburst, police arrived to break it up. Suddenly, a bomb was hurled, killing seven policemen and injuring many other people.

Although the identity of the culprit was never established, eight anarchists‡ were arrested and charged with the crime. At the trial, all were found guilty. Four were sent to the gallows, one committed suicide, and the rest were sentenced to life imprisonment. A few years later the surviving three were pardoned by Governor John P. Altgeld of Illinois, who was a friend of labor.

The aftermath. The Knights were outspoken in condemning the criminal act, but because they were the nation's most powerful labor organi-

‡ Anarchists believe that all government is evil and that they should demonstrate against it by violence and terror.

##Relate the identity of the plant to the invention of the reaper and the business enterprise that Cyrus McCormick started in Chicago. Governor Altgeld could be the subject of a report.

zation, they were widely blamed for what had happened. Powderly's response was unhesitating. "Honest labor," he said, "is not to be found in the ranks of those who march under the red flag of anarchy, which is the emblem of blood and destruction." Despite this and other disavowals, the Knights favored pardons for the convicted men, a stand that further blackened the Order in the public's estimation.

Fear of union power. The Haymarket affair was used as an excuse to attack not only the Knights but also the rest of the trade union movement. A period of antagonism to labor organizations set in, and union leaders were represented as wild-eyed radicals who carried bombs as a matter of course and did not hesitate to throw them.

Besides, the strength of the Knights aroused the fears of businessmen. Said the *New York Sun*: "Five men in this country control the chief interests of five hundred thousand workingmen, and can at any moment [by calling a strike] take the means of livelihood from two and a half million souls. These men compose the executive board of the noble order of the Knights of Labor."

Powderly was accused of being a dictator, even though he was ill prepared to cope with the astonishing growth of his organization. "The position I hold," he said frankly, "is too big for any ten men. It is certainly too big for me."

Decline of the Order. The public's generally hostile attitude toward the Knights was only one reason for the Order's sudden decline. There were other no less fundamental reasons. First of all, the Knights' leaders had aims that # seemed extravagant to members in its locals, who were primarily interested in a shorter day and a thicker pay envelope.

Second, skilled workers increasingly resented the presence in the Order of unskilled workers. Skilled men were subject to blacklisting§ by employers after a strike called by the Knights, and they were refusing to take the blame for the walkouts of the unskilled. They found greater protection in their own craft unions.

Third, the methods of the Knights, relying both on political activity and on educating the public, did not please those who believed that economic pressure against employers—the strike—was the only way to success.

Fourth, the idea of the Knights that one big union could serve all of the working people, because all workers had the same interests, did not square with the facts. Fifth, too much of the Order's energy and money was spent on coöperative enterprises which failed.

By 1888, only two years after it had reached its high point in strength, membership in the Order had dropped to 200,000, and by 1893— another year of depression—it had fallen to 75,000. The Knights soon thereafter died out, but they had served the important purpose, as Powderly later said, of "forcing to the front the cause of misunderstood and downtrodden humanity."

THE AMERICAN FEDERATION OF LABOR

In the 1870's—when the Knights of Labor was beginning to grow—several national craft unions were concentrating on immediate practical benefits, like higher wages and shorter hours. One of these was the International Cigar Makers' Union. After a disastrous strike in 1877, it was near extinction.

Two members who had had experience in the European labor movement, Adolph Strasser and Samuel Gompers, put the union back on its feet. They made it so successful that its methods were copied by others. It collected regular dues, limited its membership, and made only what it regarded as reasonable demands on employers. As Gompers explained, "Trade unionism had to be put upon a business basis in order to develop power adequate to secure better working conditions."

A union of craft unions. In 1881 a number of representatives of craft unions met in Pittsburgh, to form the Federation of Organized Trade and Labor Unions of the United States of America and Canada. This name was shortened in 1886—the year the Knights were at the peak of their strength—to the American

---

§ A blacklist contained the names of workers fired for going on strike. Circulated among employers, it made it almost impossible for these "troublemakers" to find new jobs.

AFL-CIO News

The purposeful expression of Samuel Gompers suggests the kind of leadership he gave the cause of labor.

Gompers was an English immigrant.

Federation of Labor, usually known as the AFL.

Samuel Gompers. The guiding hand and mind of the new order was Samuel Gompers, who, until his death in 1924, held the presidency continuously with the exception of one year. Born in a London tenement house, Gompers, whose formal schooling was finished when he

was only ten, spent all his life close to the labor movement.

After he came to the United States, he continued his education on his own by reading widely and attending lectures in whatever spare time he had from his work as a cigar maker. Gompers had no revolutionary intentions—he was interested only in attaining immediate and practical goals that would benefit workers. He therefore had no faith in socialism‖ or in achieving reform through political parties.

A new philosophy. Unlike the Knights of Labor, the AFL did not admit individuals: it was an organization of unions. One became a member only by belonging to a local of a union that had joined the Federation. Moreover, the AFL refused to admit any union to membership if its rolls included unskilled workers.

Not considering itself to be the proper organization to bring about needed civil rights reforms, the AFL also excluded women and Negroes. It avoided politics and preferred to # be wooed by the two major parties rather than to enter politics on its own.

Above all, unlike the Knights, the AFL recognized the conflict in interests between laboring men and employers as one of the inescapable facts of life in the industrial world. It said in effect to employers that the economic pie was big enough to be shared by both capital and labor. Labor, it asserted, wanted only what it felt was a fair portion.

The contract. The practice of drawing up a trade union agreement, or contract, became ## the AFL's principal contribution to the labor movement. Through the contract, labor and capital in a particular business or industry mutually accepted a set of terms for a given period of time. Although contracts existed as early as 1866 in the iron-and-steel industry, not until the 1890's did they become a symbol of the labor movement. In the last decade of

‖ An economic system in which the factories and other means of production are owned by the public rather than by private individuals. Theoretically, under this system each individual contributes his work according to the best of his ability and shares in the products according to his needs. The principles of modern socialism are associated chiefly with the writings of Karl Marx (1818–1883).

##Find out what students know about labor contracts that exist today--a direct tie with the early AFL Do members of the class think that Gompers was right in avoiding politics?

Gompers tried to give labor the same dignity and respect that business enjoyed. A certificate of membership like this emphasizes the unity of the mine workers as well as the individuality of the individual member.

A membership certificate of the United Mine Workers, a union that belonged to the AFL. Episodes in the life of a member are presented pictorially, including his admission to the organization (*upper left and upper right*). Observe the motto under the name of the organization and the statement at the top of the certificate.

the nineteenth century, the cry was often heard among craftsmen in every line, "No contract, no work."

Techniques. The weapon of the AFL was the strike. Although the Federation had no central fund to support workers who walked out, it collected contributions from its members to help win strikes of which it approved.

\# Representing the organized workingmen in legislative matters was an important part of the work of the AFL. Its officers, especially Gompers, became familiar figures before congressional and state legislative committees. Concentrating on raising pay and improving the physical conditions of labor, the AFL never lost touch with the workingman as an individual. This was true even in later years, when Gompers grew accustomed to wearing a top hat and meeting powerful bankers and industrialists on equal terms.

Growing membership. The AFL grew rapidly, boasting 550,000 members in 1890. On the eve of the First World War, it had 2,000,000 members. All the important trade unions in the country belonged to it, excepting the four railroad brotherhoods.\# It had now become the principal spokesman for labor, and Gompers was even recognized as a "gentleman" by many who were quick to sneer at all labor leaders.

When all was said and done, a considerable task still remained. Workers in basic industries, like textile and steel, were unorganized; the new automobile industry was untouched; and no one spoke for the vast army of unskilled men and women who made up a major part of the country's labor force.

Radical opposition. Scorn for the principles and methods of the AFL led to the establishment in 1905 of a radical labor organization, the Industrial Workers of the World. Known usually as the I.W.W., it advocated violent methods —including *sabotage,* that is, the malicious destruction of the employer's property. The I.W.W. for a time had strong appeal among

---

\# The Brotherhoods of Locomotive Engineers, Railway Conductors, Firemen and Enginemen, and Trainmen were founded between 1863 and 1883.

Harper's Weekly, July 28, 1894 (Brown Brothers)

Pinkerton men (*foreground*) in Homestead, Pennsylvania, face the miners during the great strike there.

Observe the weapons.

western miners, lumbering men, migrating farm workers, and others whose conditions of work were bound to make them discontented. Nevertheless, the use of violence was never popular with most American laboring people.

THE RESPONSE OF BUSINESS

Businessmen, meanwhile, were developing methods for dealing with attempts to unionize their employees. For a time, they were successful in their fight.

Spying. A favorite method was to use hired \#\# detectives as spies. One of these was Allan Pinkerton, whose skill as an investigator had brought him favorable attention before the Civil War (he had foiled a plot to assassinate Lincoln in 1861). He had gone into the profitable business of battling labor on behalf of employers.

One of Pinkerton's typical advertisements

 \#\#It had been a Pinkerton spy who had informed on the Molly Maguires (see p. 409).

read: "Corporations or individuals desirous of ascertaining the feelings of their employees, and whether they are likely to engage in strikes or are joining any secret labor organizations with a view of compelling terms from corporations or employers . . . can obtain a detective suitable to associate with their employees and obtain this information." Pinkerton also organized an army of men to be hired out as strikebreakers.

Other devices. A second method of employers was the blacklist. A third was the use of the "yellow-dog contract," in which an employee promised, usually as a condition of being hired, not to join any union. A fourth method was the injunction, or court order. An employer, when he sensed "trouble," could apply to the courts for an order forbidding a strike or a boycott or picketing.** Employees who disobeyed an injunction could be charged with being in contempt of court.

Violence at Homestead. The use of these techniques in the last decade of the nineteenth century in two famous strikes shows the unequal contest that labor was still waging. In July, 1892, the workers at the Carnegie Steel Plant in Homestead, Pennsylvania, refused to accept wage cuts. Henry Clay Frick, Carnegie's lieutenant, thereupon closed the plant. When

---

** A *boycott* is a refusal to deal with an individual—or firm—in order to punish it or to compel it to change its policies. (The word comes from the Captain Boycott who was ostracized by his neighbors in Ireland in 1880.) *Picketing* is the practice of union workers on strike of attempting—usually by carrying signs or shouting protests—to prevent people from entering a struck establishment. In this way they hope to keep out of the place of business both prospective customers and possible strikebreakers.

The river shown is the Monongahela. Homestead is opposite southeast Pittsburgh.

The course of the struggle between the steel workers and the Pinkerton men at Homestead, shown in drawings made at the time. The employees had the advantage of a strategic location from which they could look down upon and attack the "invaders." The soldiers shown were members of the state militia called to preserve peace.

Library of Congress

WORKMEN CANNONADING THE BARGES.

SOLDIERS IN CAMP.

WORKMEN ATTACKING THE BARGES.

GREAT BATTLE OF HOMESTEAD.
Defeat and Capture of the
PINKERTON INVADERS
July 6th 1892.

Eugene V. Debs Foundation

Eugene V. Debs in 1904. He was imprisoned twice in his lifetime and sought the office of President five times.

Debs became a railroad worker when he was 15.

special deputies arrived to surround the plant with barbed wire in order to protect the company property, the watching workers ran them out of town as advance agents of strikebreakers.

On July 6 two barges filled with Pinkerton detectives were towed up the Monongahela River toward Homestead. As these shock troops prepared to come ashore, the barricaded strikers fired on them, and a pitched battle ensued. All day it raged until, unable to escape, the Pinkertons ran up a truce flag, turned over their ammunition, and surrendered.

Scabs. The company's officials turned for aid to the governor of Pennsylvania. He obliged with 8000 militiamen, who encountered no difficulty in establishing peace in the town. Frick now brought in scabs—men hired to take the jobs of strikers in order to break a walkout—and of the original 4000 employees, only 800 were rehired.

The strike leaders were prosecuted for murder because some of the Pinkertons had been killed. The union that had sparked the strike, the Amalgamated Association of Iron, Steel, and Tin Workers, was destroyed.

Opinion in the press was that although union men were entitled to strike for better terms, they had no right to interfere with other employees willing to accept whatever the company offered. But the employers had challenged the very right to strike. Furthermore, the government—in theory a neutral umpire—in fact accepted the position taken by the plant owners.

Trouble at Pullman. Nothing better illustrates the unneutral role of government than the events of the Pullman strike of 1894. George Pullman, whose sleeping car had revolutionized overnight rail travel, had built a "model" town for his employees in Illinois. These workers were forced to buy supplies in the company store, to which they were almost invariably in debt on payday.

Rents ran about 25 percent higher than in other towns nearby, and it was said that Pullman sold Chicago water and gas to his employees at a 10-percent profit. When the depression of 1893 came, the Pullman Company cut wages between 25 and 40 percent without making a comparable reduction in rent. Pullman refused to listen to complaints, even dismissing some of the aggrieved men who protested to him.

A strike and a lockout. The American Railway Union, to which many of the Pullman employees belonged, responded to this action by calling a strike at the Pullman Company. The union's head was Eugene V. Debs, later a socialist, who had made the cause of workingmen the consuming interest of his life. Himself

418 #Debs differed from Gompers in another way: He believed in industrial unionism, not craft unionism. His union took in all railroad workers, regardless of the kind of work they did.

Brown Brothers

Angry strikers line the tracks to protest the use of federal troops in the Pullman strike. The armed soldiers—some of whom are on top of the railroad cars—are seeing to it that the train goes through.

Notice the appearance of the steam locomotive and the contrast between the troops and the strikers.

a gentle person, Debs instructed his members to avoid violence such as had characterized railroad strikes in the past.

When Pullman closed his plant and laid off all his workers—staged a lockout—the American Railway Union instructed its members everywhere to refuse to handle trains with Pullman cars attached. The railroads responded by firing employees who removed Pullmans from trains. By the summer of 1894, railroad traffic in the Middle West was practically halted, and the effects of the tie-up were being felt throughout the country.

The railroads now attached Pullman cars to mail trains. Any attempt to interfere with such trains would be an interference with the mails —a federal crime. Next, the railroads persuaded President Cleveland's Attorney General, Richard Olney, to swear in an army of special deputies—actually in the pay of the railroads—in order to help keep the trains moving. #

Calling federal troops. When violence broke out between these deputies and the strikers, the railroads asked President Cleveland to send federal troops to keep order and to guarantee the safe handling of the mails. Despite the protests of Governor John P. Altgeld of Illinois that troops were not needed, Cleveland dispatched them anyhow. The President is supposed to have said: "If it takes every dollar in the Treasury and every soldier in the United States to deliver a postal card in Chicago, that postal card should be delivered." ##

Breaking the union. When the strike continued to paralyze transportation, the railroads ob-

Puck, March 16, 1904

Observe how unfairly Gompers and Mitchell were lampooned in this cartoon showing the views of enemies of unionism.

Ask a talented student to draw a cartoon illustrating charges unionists made against business.

tained an injunction against the American Railway Union, forbidding it to interfere in any way with their operations. Debs, quickly found in violation of the injunction, was sent # to prison for six months. The strike was broken and the union smashed. The federal government had, it seemed, used its enormous weight solely on the side of capital.

THE OPINIONS OF THE JUDGES

In a number of significant decisions, the courts interpreted important laws in a way that was unfavorable to labor. For a long time the courts prevented any intervention by a state in the unequal relationship between employer and employee.

Disapproval by a state court. In reaching their decisions, judges were not yet ready to accept new legal standards—suited to an industrial age in which workers no longer could cope with their problems unaided. In New York State, for instance, a law enacted in 1882 forbade the manufacture of cigars in tenement houses—a long-needed public health measure. The highest court in the state declared the law unconstitutional, on the ground that it had nothing to do with health.

The decision asserted: "It cannot be perceived how the cigar maker is to be improved in his health or his morals by forcing him from his home and its hallowed associations and beneficial influences, to ply his trade elsewhere." Years afterward, Theodore Roosevelt commented that this decision alone held back tenement-house reform legislation for a whole generation.

Disapproval by the Supreme Court. The same kind of outmoded thinking was shown by the federal Supreme Court in the case of *Lochner* v. *New York* in 1905. The state had enacted a law making a 10-hour day the legal limit in the baking industry. The Court declared the law unconstitutional, stating: "This act is not, within any fair meaning of the term, a health law, but is an illegal interference with the rights of the individual, both employers and employees, to make contracts regarding labor upon such terms as they may think best. . . ."

Wide World

The "Great Dissenter," Justice Oliver Wendell Holmes. Holmes was the son of the author-physician.

Significant dissent. Justice Oliver Wendell Holmes dissented,†† foreshadowing by his words later, more enlightened decisions. He said that New York's law could certainly be considered a health measure, and, in fact, some people might even approve it "as a first installment of a general regulation of the hours of work." Three years later in *Muller* v. *Oregon,* the Supreme Court upheld the right of a state to limit the number of hours a day that women

---

†† When the Supreme Court does not reach a decision unanimously, the justices who are in disagreement with the formal conclusion of the majority of their colleagues usually put their reasons on record, too. These statements are called dissents, or dissenting opinions, thus distinguishing them from the majority opinions. Holmes's dissenting opinions became so famous that he is known to history as "The Great Dissenter." ##

might work. But the view that a state has a duty to protect the health of its citizens did not become generally accepted until many years later.

Interpreting the Sherman Antitrust Act. The courts dealt labor another serious blow by their interpretation of the Sherman Antitrust Act of 1890. You will recall that this law had been aimed at the large corporations having monopolies in their fields or engaging in "conspiracy in restraint of trade."

In practice, the law was used more effectively against labor than against big business. Such a use was in the Danbury Hatters Case of 1908. The members of a hatmakers' union had declared a nationwide boycott of a Danbury, Connecticut, hat firm. The company sued under the Sherman Act, arguing that the union was engaging in a conspiracy to restrain trade. The

\#

Supreme Court upheld the company's view, and the individual members of the union had to pay the heavy damages provided for in the law.

Sum and Substance

1. Why did laboring men form a national organization? Name the first such organization and give its history. 2. Who were the Molly Maguires? 3. Name and describe important labor disputes in 1877. 4. What people joined the Knights of Labor? Describe its program. 5. Name the reasons for the decline of the Knights. 6. How did the AFL differ from the Knights of Labor? What was the main contribution of the AFL? What were its methods? 7. How did employers try to halt the growth of unions? 8. Give the facts about the two strikes in which the federal government sided with the employers. 9. What attitude did the courts show? Name two examples.

This section presents both the positions of the immigrants and those of labor and business.

A RISING TIDE OF FOREIGNERS ALARMS LABOR LEADERS

American businessmen often blamed the immigrants who flocked to the United States after the Civil War for the appearance of anarchistic and socialistic ideas. Labor leaders, on the other hand, complained that immigrants not only worked more cheaply than Americans but served gladly as strikebreakers. These were unfair judgments of people whose strength and numbers were indispensable in the growth of American industry.

SO-CALLED NEW IMMIGRATION

After 1880, as industrialization increased in northern Europe, emigration from that region declined markedly. A wave of newcomers now began to enter the United States from southern and eastern Europe—Italians, Slovaks, Hungarians, Romanians, Serbs, Russians, Greeks, Poles. This so-called new immigration was usually contrasted with the so-called old immigration—from England, Ireland, Scotland, Germany, and Scandinavia.

Opponents of unrestricted immigration considered the eastern Europeans to be clannish, too inclined to remain in the large cities, and

generally undesirable. But if they had read pre-Civil War newspapers and magazines, they would have seen that the same things were being said about the so-called old immigration when it was new!

Numbers. Actually only one thing about the immigration was new, aside, of course, from its source: it was more numerous than ever in the past. Between 1881 and 1901 about nine ## million people came to America, and by 1914 about twelve million more. In one peak year alone—1882—about 800,000 immigrants arrived. In the earlier immigration of the 1840's and 1850's, when thousands left their homes in Europe (particularly in Ireland and Germany, because of crop failures, famine, and political persecution), a total of 400,000 had been reached only once.

Many Americans were frankly alarmed at the size of this mass of humanity. Could so many foreigners become Americanized? Or were they going to undermine the nation?

Understanding the ways of the newcomers. One must remember, first of all, that the immigrants contributed to their adopted country at least as

##Ask the class to turn to p. 818 to see how the population figures reflected this increase in immigration. Also look at the increase in the urban populations in the same years.

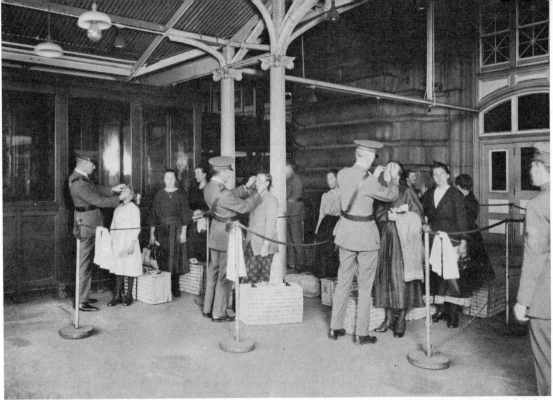

Immigration officials at Ellis Island examine young women for evidence of serious disease before allowing them to proceed to their new homes. Most will pass the tests, but some unfortunates will be detained.

What conditions and what hopes had brought all these people to the United States?

Hopeful immigrants leaving Ellis Island in New York Harbor, then a United States immigration station. Millions of newcomers, carrying all their possessions in their hands or on their backs, disembarked there.

J. Clarence Davies Collection, Museum of the City of New York
The Statue of Liberty, standing on an island in New York Harbor, has greeted an incredible number of immigrants.

"Lifting her lamp beside the golden door."

much as they received. They were consumers as soon as they stepped ashore, and their brawn and talents notably enriched American life.

Second, if they read newspapers written in a foreign language it was a sign of their becoming Americanized, not of their being clannish. In the old country they usually had not read newspapers at all. Third, if they flocked to the cities rather than to farms, Americans in these years were doing the same: opportunity was greater there.

\# Fourth, if they lived more cheaply than the people who had been born here, it usually was because they were under pressure to scrimp and save in order to bring their families over as soon as possible. Fifth, in unskilled jobs, it is true, they may have been willing to work more cheaply than Americans. Yet they quickly discovered that wages have to be determined in

#This paragraph explains why immigrants were subject to charges by labor.

part by the cost of living—which did not discriminate between newcomers and natives.

Sixth, although various brands of socialism and anarchism had been introduced by immigrants from Germany, Italy, and Russia, the large majority of the newly arrived were not aiming to tear society apart. They hoped only that they would be met with sympathy and acceptance. They had come here to adapt \#\# themselves to, not change, American ways.

Restriction. Resentment against the newcomers from eastern Europe was sometimes intense. But attempts to restrict immigration were directed mainly against Asians. A Chinese Exclusion Act was passed in 1882 as the result of demands from the Pacific coast states. A gentleman's agreement with Japan, which kept out Japanese laborers without formal congressional action, was concluded in 1907. Yet, in general, the American policy until the First World War was "Come, all who will."

Despite labor's difficulties and sorrows between 1865 and 1914, its leaders never lost hope that tomorrow would be better. Their optimism was well founded: wages were advancing and the workday was being shortened.

The United States offered a rising standard of living even to those who, in Jefferson's phrase, "worked at a bench." Industrialization, for all the evils it brought, opened promising horizons for factory workers—as well as for factory owners. Europeans and Americans alike knew that the words of Emma Lazarus inscribed on the Statue of Liberty were not empty ones:

. . . Give me your tired, your poor,
Your huddled masses yearning to breathe free,
The wretched refuse of your teeming shore.
Send these, the homeless, tempest-tost to me,
I lift my lamp beside the golden door!

Sum and Substance

1. Why did businessmen and labor leaders often criticize immigrants after the Civil War? 2. How did immigration change after 1880? 3. How were the immigrants misunderstood? 4. What restrictions were made? Chiefly against whom?

\#\#How did the immigrants achieve acceptance? (Suggestions: The main avenue was education, which enabled the newcomers to fit into American life more easily. Night schools taught English.)

THE WORKSHOP

OF LASTING SIGNIFICANCE

Explain the relationship of each of the following to the movement to organize labor.

John Mitchell	Samuel Gompers
craft union	socialism
Commonwealth v.	contract
Hunt	sabotage
Brook Farm	Allan Pinkerton
National Labor Union	injunction
William Sylvis	Pullman strike
Molly Maguires	Eugene V. Debs
Uriah S. Stephens	*Lochner* v. *New York*
Knights of Labor	Danbury Hatters
Terence V. Powderly	Case
anarchist	"new immigration"
Haymarket affair	gentleman's
John P. Altgeld	agreement
blacklist	Chinese Exclusion
AFL	Act

AMERICAN DEMOCRACY

1. How did one of the basic principles of Jeffersonian democracy—that the United States should be a nation of farmers and small shop owners—discourage the organization of trade unions?

2. In what sense was the labor movement an attempt to maintain the democratic principle of the dignity of the individual?

3. How can you account for the fact that labor organizations early met the disapproval of Americans in general? That the courts and even the federal government were on a number of occasions unneutral in cases between employers and employees? Would you say that this disapproval and lack of neutrality were undemocratic? Explain.

4. Reread the statement from the decision in New York State in 1882 about the manufacture of cigars in tenement houses (page 421). Why are Americans appalled by it today?

5. What effect on United States relations with Japan and China would you expect the gentleman's agreement of 1907 and the Chinese Exclusion Act to have? What kind of discrimination was involved?

6. American culture is said to be plural. In what sense is such a culture richer than it would otherwise be? Why should the minorities in any democratic society expect to be permitted to preserve certain aspects of their own cultures? #

HISTORY IN STATISTICS

1. Look at the population table on page 818. In what decade of the nineteenth century did the urban population of the United States increase about 100 percent? What were the percents of increase by decades in the next fifty years?

Note the rate of population increase of the ten largest cities in these decades (see "Cities" in the Index to locate the charts giving this information).

2. In what part of the nineteenth century did large-scale industry begin to develop?

3. When did labor begin to organize on a nationwide scale? In what decades was labor trouble especially difficult?

4. To what extent did increasing urbanization, the growth of large-scale industry, the mounting rate of immigration, and the nationwide organization of labor (with accompanying labor trouble) parallel each other in time? Is there a relationship between them?

BEING A SOCIAL SCIENTIST

1. Make a series of reports on outstanding men and women who were involved directly or indirectly in the labor movement. Aim to explain how these people were drawn to their roles. Make sure that you include both Governor John P. Altgeld and Justice Oliver Wendell Holmes.

2. Part of the difficulty in the case of the Pullman strike was that it affected an industry that was "serving the public interest." Has the problem of what to do about strikes in such industries been satisfactorily solved? Support your answer. ##

The name of this chapter indicates that Americans made some changes that helped them adjust to new conditions. These Americans were the farmers and the people of the cities. This chapter describes the new conditions they faced after the Civil War and what they did about them.

21

THE READJUSTING OF SOCIETY

The money is in the East . . .

The American farmer of to-day is altogether a different sort of a man from his ancestor of fifty or a hundred years ago. A great many men and women now living remember when farmers were largely manufacturers; that is to say, they made a great many implements for their own use. Every farmer had an assortment of tools with which he made wooden implements, as forks and rakes, handles for his hoes and plows, spokes for his wagon, and various other implements made wholly out of wood. . . .

Besides this, mechanics were scattered among the farmers. . . . During winter time the neighborhood carpenter prepared sashes and blinds and doors and molding and cornices for the next

This man is driving a horse-drawn reaper. Recall the horse-drawn drillers, p. 364.

season's building. When the frosts of autumn came the shoemaker repaired to the dwellings of the farmers, and there, in a corner set apart to him, he made up shoes for the family during the winter. . . . When winter approached the butchering season was at hand; meat for family use during the next year was prepared and preserved in the smoke house. . . . Wheat was thrashed, a little at a time, just enough to supply the needs of the family for ready money, and not enough to make it necessary to waste one stalk of straw. Everything was saved and put to use. . . .

Comparatively a very small amount of money was required to conduct the business of farming. A hundred dollars average probably was as much as the largest farmers of that day needed in the way of cash to meet the demands of their farm work. . . .

Coming from that time to the present, we find that everything nearly has been changed. All over the West particularly the farmer thrashes his wheat all at one time, he disposes of it all at one time, and in a great many instances the straw is wasted. He sells his hogs, and buys bacon and pork; he sells his cattle, and buys fresh beef and canned beef or corned beef, as the case may be; he sells his fruit, and buys it back in cans . . . indeed, he buys nearly everything now that he produced at one time himself, and these things all cost money.

Besides all this, and what seems stranger than anything else, whereas in the earlier time the American home was a free home, unincumbered, not one case in a thousand where a home was mortgaged to secure the payment of borrowed money . . . [today] nearly half the farms are mortgaged for as much as they are worth, and interest rates are exorbitant. . . . The farmer now is compelled to go to town for nearly everything that he wants; even a hand rake to clean up the door-yard must be purchased at the city store.

And what is worse than all, if he needs a little more money than he has about him, he is compelled to go to town to borrow it; but he does not find the money there; in place of it he finds an agent who will "negotiate" a loan for him. The money is in the East, a thousand or three thousand or five thousand miles away. . . . The farmers of the country to-day are maintaining an army of middlemen, loan agents, bankers, and others, who . . . by reason of the changed condition of things, have placed themselves between the farmer and the money owner, and in this way absorb a livelihood out of the substance of the people.

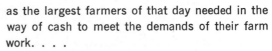

Kean Archives

What was the author of the quotation thinking of as the "good old days"?

An American farmer in the late nineteenth century, when he no longer enjoyed the favored and honored position he had earlier held. Although he was benefiting from advances in technology, particularly in farm machinery, he was smarting over grievances he could not overcome.

What interest do people today pay when they borrow money? What would be considered exorbitant?

The last chapter described the grievances of workers in industry. What methods had they adopted to improve their working and living conditions? What might the farmers do to improve theirs?

The frustration of the farmer in the post-Civil War period was deep. He could observe that his standard of living was rising less rapidly than that of members of other groups in the population. Long accustomed to considering himself practically self-reliant, he now asked for sympathy and help. Among farm editors, one of the most influential was William A. Peffer—later a United States Senator—whose paper was The Kansas Farmer. This selection is from Peffer's book The Farmer's Side, which was published in 1891.

This section describes the difficulties of farmers and tells what problems urban people faced.

AN OLDER WAY OF LIFE YIELDS ITS SUPREMACY

The vast transformation of American society that took place after the Civil War affected profoundly many well-established ideals, standpoints, and even ways of solving public problems. The developments that upset the traditional patterns of living in this fashion could be traced chiefly to industrialization. But they were intertwined also with those caused by increased urbanization and by various remarkable achievements in technology. The new scheme of things, which touched directly the lives of millions in the cities, also had a searing effect on rural America.

A ONCE NOBLE CALLING

The farmer almost from the time the New World was settled had been defending himself against powerful rival forces—first of trade and then of industry. Although he had not always fought a losing battle against these forces, he usually had had to adjust to them.

The Jeffersonian view. Nevertheless, the self-employed farmer had always been a symbol of the American at his best, hard-working and fearless. The Jeffersonians especially had held that farmers bore a special mark of nobility. "Cultivators of the earth," wrote Jefferson in 1785, "are the most valuable citizens. They are the most vigorous, the most independent, the most virtuous, and they are tied to their country, and wedded to its liberty and interests by the most lasting bonds."

Its continued acceptance. Until the period of the Civil War, this notion dominated American thinking. The arguments that were used to support the passage of the Homestead Act, for example, were expressed in language little different from Jefferson's. And even at the end of the nineteenth century, William Jennings Bryan, a candidate for the presidency, declared: "Burn down your cities and leave our farms, and your cities will spring up again as if by magic; but destroy our farms, and the grass will grow in the streets of every city in the country."

The hard facts. The picture of the model American, a self-sufficient, free spirit laboring at his plow from sunup to sundown, in time no longer fitted the facts. After the Civil War the farmer found himself at the mercy of a number of conditions beyond his control. Instead of being the ideal-type citizen, he was ridiculed as a "hayseed" and as a "hick from the sticks." Further, # he watched his children grow up and leave the farm to go to the city—the "wicked" city—because opportunity was more promising there.

This man held a secure place in American society.

Kean Archives

#What attitudes do Americans generally take toward farmers today? Why?

#Recall that many northern farms suffered from a want of workers during the war, when the government was buying large quantities of grain for the army (foreigners also bought grain). The farmers who remained on their farms prospered, failing to see the danger of indebtedness.

THE VIEW FROM THE FARM

The post-Civil War farmer, plainly and simply, had become a pathetic figure. He was beginning to realize that life for him would never again square with his sense of how it ought to be—and maybe even once was.

New circumstances. In the first place, after 1865 both northern and southern farmers were economically crippled. During the war, farmers in the North and West had mortgaged their property to buy more land in order to raise more grain. Wheat was selling at $2.06 a bushel and corn at 78¢. Afterward the mortgages had to be repaid, even though by 1878 wheat prices had fallen to 77¢ a bushel and corn to 31¢.

Not knowing how to make up their heavy losses, the farmers continually complained of the heavy burden of indebtedness from which it was increasingly difficult to escape. Low prices year after year made "meeting the mortgage" a persistent nightmare. When farmers worked to grow larger crops, they succeeded only in driving prices down further by creating an oversupply. Their efforts brought them no nearer to paying off their creditors. A commentator remarked wryly that "increasing the crops per acre serves only to increase the aches per cropper."

In the South, the plantation system had been replaced by a new arrangement known as *sharecropping*. Under it, a planter supplied land, seed, implements, and animals to landless farmers, enabling them to raise cotton. In return,

In 1878, 5,756,000 bales of cotton were produced in the United States.

Bales of cotton on a wharf in the port of Charleston in 1878 await shipment to markets at home and abroad.

Frank Leslie's Illustrated Newspaper, November 16, 1878 (Library of Congress)

##Ask students to account for the origin of sharecropping. (It was a means by which farmers who had no capital could operate. Conditions after the war encouraged its establishment.)

the landowner took a share—varying from a third to a half—of the finished crop. He insisted that his sharecroppers cultivate cotton rather than food crops, since it could more easily be sold for cash.

The system not only kept the South excessively dependent on one crop, but it also was inefficient. Not until 1879 did the South again grow a cotton crop as large as the one of 1859. Moreover, cotton which had sold at $1.01 a pound in 1864 fell to 8¢ in 1878, and after 1880 it did not reach as high as 11¢ again until 1905.

Anger at the railroad. The farmers also felt victimized by the railroad. Agriculture had expanded in the Middle West and West because

of rail transportation. Sometimes, though, the demand for railroads outstripped the money available for their construction. Being by nature speculators, farmers often responded to promoters' appeals for more money by mortgaging their farms in order to buy railroad shares. They hoped to profit not only from the use of a needed railroad but also from the railroad stock they thereby acquired.

The results usually fell far short of expectations. Frequently the railroad went into bankruptcy, making the shares worthless. Yet that was not the end of the disappointment. The mortgage on the farm remained to be paid; and taxes rose because almost invariably the state, county, or town—or all three—had invested in

The farmer's plight, as seen in a cartoon captioned, "Where he has to sell, and where he has to buy."

Puck, August 15, 1894

##Recall the great faith that farmers originally had had in the railroads because through them they had been able to broaden their markets. Now disillusionment was setting in.

the stock. Moreover, freight rates on the completed road looked excessive to most farmers.

To cap it all, the high-handedness of railroad operators was notorious—even if it was sometimes exaggerated. The most important abuse was connected with rates, which in practice appeared to discriminate against the farmers. Rates were fixed not by what seemed to be a reasonable profit but by what the traffic would bear. Sometimes a road charged more for a short haul between two points where it had a monopoly than for a long haul where there was a competing line.

Railroad officials considered the farmers' complaints downright ungrateful. One road president asked: "What would it cost for a man to carry a ton of wheat one mile? What would it cost for a horse to do the same? The railroad does it at a cost of less than a cent."

Another abuse was the free-pass system, under which all state and many federal officials received the right to rail travel without cost to themselves. Because the pass was a form of bribery, the system made practically impossible the adoption of laws to regulate the railroads. Said one observer, "To stand in with the railroads in order to get free transportation seemed to be the main object in life with about one-half of the population."

In the middle. A third reason for the farmers' discontent was their dependence on both the merchants who bought the produce they grew and the retail dealers who sold them supplies. The farmers had only contempt for these middlemen. Everlastingly they groaned that they received too little for their crops and paid too much for their manufactured goods.

One editor wrote of the economic drain on the farmers: "There are three great crops raised in Nebraska. One is a crop of corn, one a crop of freight rates, and one a crop of interest. One is produced by farmers who by sweat and toil farm the land. The other two are produced by men who sit in their offices and behind their bank counters and farm the farmers." Of course, if the farmers' income had been greater they might not have been so hostile to the middlemen who had become indispensable for the marketing and distribution of goods.

Competition in a world market. The world supply of farm products was vastly increased after 1865 by the opening of huge new agricultural areas in Argentina, Australia, Canada, and the American West. Farmers, as a result, had become competitors of other farmers—American and foreign—who produced the same crop. A revolution in transportation and communication had made this so.

Not only were railroads like America's being built in other countries, but also the opening of the Suez Canal in 1869 had reduced international distances. The continents were being linked in a well-spun telegraph and telephone network.* There were no longer local prices for farm goods, with significant variations from place to place. Instead, there was a single price in the great produce markets fixed by world supply and demand. Farmers in the United States shared in the ups and downs of world agriculture. At the same time, the consumer goods they bought were sold to them in a market protected by a tariff.

A period of depression. American farmers after 1865 felt the effects of a stubborn worldwide farm depression. In attempting to maintain their standard of living in the face of falling income, they borrowed money that became, again, harder and harder to repay. The farmers were made all the more frustrated by their knowledge that though the supply of factory goods was expanding continually, they could not readily share in it.

Unstable currency. Still another reason for the farmers' plight was the fluctuation of the currency of the United States. The debtor farmers had borrowed cheapened dollars—greenbacks—during the Civil War and in the six or seven years that followed it. But shortly after Appomattox, the dollar began to rise in value and was more difficult to earn. When the farmers had to pay back their loans, dollars had become much scarcer than they had been when they were borrowed.

---

*The first cable, successfully laid under the Atlantic Ocean by Cyrus W. Field in 1866, linked Europe and North America. Europe and South America were similarly joined in 1874.

Unequal taxation. One more reason for the farmers' distress was the burden of taxes. It fell heavily on farmers, since rates were not adjusted in accordance with ability to pay. Farmers also complained that the way taxes were assessed placed them at a disadvantage because their property—land, buildings, crops, and animals—was always visible.

The businessmen and the corporations, on the other hand, could conceal property—in the form of stocks and bonds—and escape some or all of the tax obligation. And it was evident that more and more the businessmen and the lawyers were in charge of legislation, including tax laws. Farmers could point out that in Congress between 1873 and 1875 only 7 percent of the members were themselves engaged in farming.

Deprived women. Finally, the farmers, aware of the more exciting life that the expanding cities offered, noticed more than ever before the harshness of rural life. Women, especially, considered themselves its victims, even though conveniences like sewing machines were beginning to lift some of the drudgery. Because of their isolation from medical care, thousands of mothers died needlessly in childbirth. Also, the mortality of their infants and children was high.

In books like *A Son of the Middle Border* and *Main-Travelled Roads,* Hamlin Garland, the writer, portrayed the farmer memorably. He once wrote that words failed him when he tried to describe the hard lives of farm women. "Before the tragic futility of their suffering, my pen refused to shed its ink," he said. Women who

The property loss because of the fire has been estimated to be $196,000,000.

Terrified Chicagoans—some lucky enough to take possessions with them—rush across a bridge on the Chicago River to escape the flames of the great fire in 1871. Over 300 persons were killed in the 24 hours it raged.

Chicago Historical Society

##People in what occupations are most likely to be elected to Congress? Why? (Lawyers are elected more often than other people. Teachers are sometimes elected.)

These stockyards, on Chicago's South Side, attracted meat-packers and buyers from slaughterhouses. The animals were herded into pens until they were sold.

Harper's Weekly, October 31, 1868

The Chicago stockyards about the time of the ruinous fire. A bank and a hotel served the businessmen the yards attracted.

Able students should read Upton Sinclair's The Jungle (see p. 504).

made their homes in city slums were also miserable, but no one was yet chronicling their story.

THE VIEW FROM THE CITY

Farm people often expressed their anguish in outspoken attacks on "the East," by which they meant the great urban centers of industry, commerce, and finance. There, they seemed to say, people lived in comfort at the expense of the farmers. Such a view was distorted, for enormous numbers of city people were also having to adjust to the changes that industry and the railroads were causing. Far from gloating over the farmers' perplexities, they were deeply engrossed in their own.

An example: Chicago. Every city had its own growing pains and disarrangements. Chicago's are illustrative. After a disastrous fire in 1871 leaving much of Chicago in ashes, the city revived and began to rebuild. However, struck by the depression of 1873, it faced uncertain days. Almost half the people were foreign-born and

most were unskilled. They depended for jobs upon the stockyards, the grain elevators, the railroads, and McCormick's reaper works.

The city fathers of Chicago—like those of other cities—held ideas of government that had been formed before the Civil War when community problems were comparatively uncomplicated. Such men were practically helpless to deal with big city living conditions. As a result, crime, vice, and human misery flourished, and politicians remained in office by disposing of contracts for public services to private individuals. The idea that essential public services must be run by the public was only beginning to take hold. The idea that the personal welfare of the people ought to be the chief concern of government had not yet been put into practice. #

Tough overnight problems. The rush of people to the urban areas had made the United States a "nation of cities" in an astonishingly short time. In 1860 there had been sixteen cities containing a population of 50,000 or more.

State Street in Chicago about 1890, after the main business district—destroyed in the fire—had been rebuilt.

Deliveries to the stores were made with wagons, now parked at the curbs. Observe the horse-drawn streetcar.

Ask who was these people's President. (Benjamin Harrison.) Observe the lighting.

By 1880 there were thirty-five. Only one city —New York—had a million people in 1870; by 1890 Chicago and Philadelphia each had a comparably large population.

Unlike the farmers' problems, those of the city-dwellers did not appear to lend themselves to political solutions. An immediate requirement was to satisfy the primary physical needs of many people living close together. When these had been met, it was possible to work on a matter of no less importance: the creation of "a sense of community" among peoples of widely varied backgrounds.

Water supplies. The problem of finding a way to provide pure water was particularly troublesome. Only 600 communities had waterworks in 1878, and the rest had to undertake appropriate construction in the next few years. The high rate of typhoid fever in cities lacking a water-supply system dramatized the need.

Sewer lines. Sewage disposal was also a challenge to city people. While New York, Boston, and Chicago had underground sewer mains from the mid-nineteenth century on, many cities relied still on individual cesspools or waste vaults. As late as 1877, when its population was about 900,000, Philadelphia, for example, was still depending on 82,000 such cesspools and tanks. Garbage disposal became harder and harder to manage, especially as the quantity of food being consumed increased. Port cities loaded such refuse on barges and scows and

#Ask how Americans on farms or in villages had obtained their water supplies. (From cisterns or wells, generally. Obtaining water for large numbers of people was a different matter.)

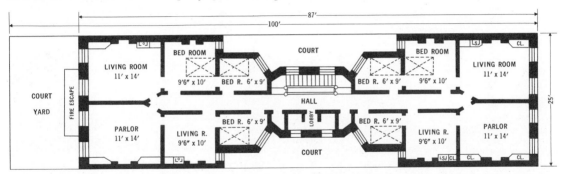

The dumbbell-tenement plan, appropriately named. Observe the small size of the bedrooms.
Try to get students to visualize the size of a bedroom measuring 6 feet by 9 feet.

dumped it a few miles out at sea—helping to make the nearby beaches dangers to health.

Dwellings. Housing was also a besetting question. The rising cost of land led to the building of tenement houses as dwellings for the poor, especially the immigrants. The "dumbbell" tenement—so called after the shape of the floor plan of the building—was first encouraged by New York's Tenement House Law of 1879.

Ideal for New York's standard lot of 25 by 100 feet, a dumbbell tenement provided an air shaft on each side because of the indentations at the middle of the building. These shafts gave a measure of light and ventilation to the interior rooms. Nevertheless, each tenement housed about 400 people. Lined up one next to the other, ten to a block, these structures created frightfully crowded conditions. Hundreds of thousands of people living in slums like these in New York and other cities were constantly exposed to fire, disease, vermin, and a shocking lack of privacy.

New architecture. Business buildings in the cities called for new construction materials as well as new conceptions in design. From the 1840's to 1880, cast iron was in vogue for use in warehouses, department stores, and office buildings. The man most responsible for this imaginative response to a pressing city need was James Bogardus, an accomplished inventor from New York. Bogardus had recognized the usefulness of erecting taller buildings than was customary, with floors unobstructed by the thick masonry walls traditionally required to sustain the tremendous weight.

The use of the elevator, which owed most to Elisha G. Otis, a native of New England, offered a ready answer to the requirements of vertical transportation. Otis' chief contribution was a safety device that worked automatically in case the lifting cable broke. The first Otis elevator, built at Otis' plant in Yonkers, New York, was installed in a New York City department store in 1857.

The achievements of Bogardus, Otis, and others opened the way to the building of a skyscraper. This architectural wonder first appeared in Chicago in 1884, when William Le Baron Jenney put up a ten-story bank building, using a steel skeleton to support its weight. Shortly Louis Sullivan, another Chicagoan, emerged as master architect of the skyscraper.

Mass transport. In solving some city problems, skyscrapers created others, including greater traffic congestion than ever before. Already the need was urgent to provide mass transportation for moving urban people smoothly and quickly. Constant expensive experimentation was carried on by individuals willing to gamble on finding *the* solution. One result was the overhead or elevated railway—first appearing in New York in the 1870's. Unsightly, and dangerous because they scattered hot ashes and oil on the pedestrians below, the "els" also blocked views and polluted the air breathed by people living in the tenements along the rights-of-way. The cable car, operated by an underground cable, was widely popular in the 1880's.

Wires overhead. Beginning in the late 1880's, electric trolleys came upon the scene. They

The "els," or elevated trains, were expensive to construct, prevented light from reaching the streets below them, and dropped soot and hot coals on pedestrians below. But like the skyscrapers, they made economical use of expensive land in the cities.

New Yorkers in 1878 gape at the first "el" in the United States, as horses shy at the noisy apparition.

Compare this picture with the ones on p. 312 and pp. 184-185. What changes are there?

were perfected by Frank J. Sprague, who had once worked for Thomas A. Edison and who completed the first electrified street railway in Richmond, Virginia, in 1888.

"Streetcar suburbs." The development of the trolley car helped hasten in every part of the country the dispersal of city people to outlying towns, or suburbs. Not only did these newer communities contain mainly individual family dwellings, but also they offered pure air and wholesome drinking water. At first only people of means could afford to live in the suburbs, and for a long time real-estate dealers would not sell or rent property to Negroes or some other minorities, including especially Jews.

The telephone. The physical orderliness of suburban towns could be contrasted with the unkempt appearance of many cities. The major streets in any large American city were covered by a "disorderly web of wires," for from 1877 on, telephone wires mingled with trolley and

telegraph lines. The earliest commercial switchboard—making the telephone generally practical—was put into use in 1878 in New Haven, Connecticut. By the end of the century, nearly 800,000 phones were in operation. These instruments were indispensable in tying together the parts of a city and in cementing cities to surrounding areas.

The new bridges. Another way of linking the parts of an urban community was by constructing bridges over the rivers separating them. Railroad bridges of cast iron had already been built in every part of the country. But the completion in 1883 of the steel Brooklyn Bridge connecting the city of Brooklyn and the island of Manhattan was an engineering and architectural feat of world importance. Designed by John A. Roebling, who lost his life in building it, the structure was the longest suspension bridge in the world. Moreover, because it stood 135 feet above the water, the largest

#Obtain a map of any large metropolitan area in the country and count the suburbs surrounding the parent city. Use a map of an area a considerable distance away from the students' homes.

Horse-drawn streetcars at the Third Avenue Depot in New York City in the 1860's.

Electric trolleys on Market Street (*right*) in San Francisco in 1896. At the left is a cable car.

<u>Top picture:</u> The street appears to have been paved with cobblestones (naturally rounded stones); granite blocks were also used in the same way. <u>Bottom picture:</u> Cable cars run in the city.

#See Questions 2 and 3 under "Informed Opinion" on p. 456. Air pollution remains a serious health hazard. What are the special problems of Los Angeles and Chicago? (Suggestion: the location of Los Angeles and the high rate of automobile ownership; the industries in Chicago.)

ships could easily pass under it.

Only a few years earlier, the Eads Bridge, a steel and masonry structure, was built over the Mississippi River at St. Louis, linking that Missouri city to East St. Louis, Illinois. The base of one pier was sunk 90 feet through sand and gravel to bed rock. During the same period Boston bridged the Charles River with a modern structure, Pittsburgh the Allegheny, and St. Paul and Minneapolis the Mississippi. By 1909 the country had 365 bridges exceeding 500 feet in length. Some were made of wrought iron, some of steel, and some of concrete.

An inevitable effect of these developments was to convert the central cities into beehives of activity and to raise land values astronomically in the business and industrial sections. Polluted air as well as other discomforts became a regular part of city living. A Chicago newspaper as early as 1880 declared: "The air stinks. People's clothing, permeated by the foul atmosphere, stinks. . . . No word expresses it so well as stink. . . ."

Some lures. Of course, cities offered exciting advantages, too, that could help balance the drawbacks. The Metropolitan Museum of Art in New York, for instance, was established in 1870, placing on view some of mankind's choicest art treasures. And in time almost every city had a counterpart. Some of the advantages—which included public entertainment—lured thousands of farm boys from their homes.

Music, too, became available for more than a mere few. In 1873, Cincinnati established the May music festival, which became an annual artistic highlight. The major cities also had sym-

By 1870 St. Louis had become the fourth largest city in the United States (see p. 319).

The riverfront at St. Louis—a main port for steamboats on the Mississippi—after the completion of the Eads Bridge (*right*). The span made it easy to bring Illinois coal into the city, benefiting industries there.

Missouri Historical Society

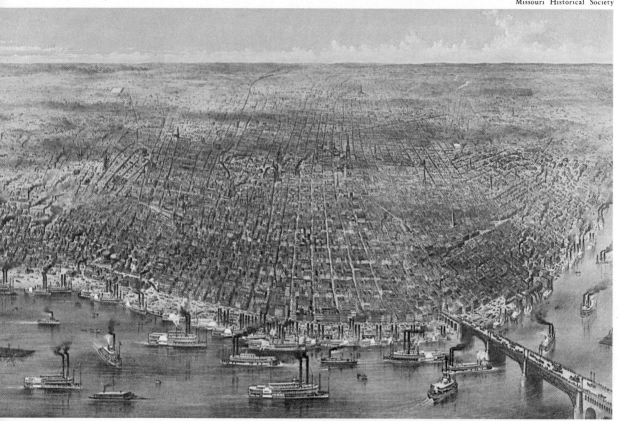

##Raise these questions: Why do almost 75 percent of all Americans live in cities? Do they like urban living better than living in the country? Do the advantages of city living attract them? Do they live where the work is?

Using a corrupt city Board of Audits, Tweed and the "Tweed ring" stole by means of fake leases, padded bills, false vouchers, unnecessary repairs, and kickbacks.

In a cartoon captioned, " 'Who stole the people's money?' 'Twas him," everyone points to the other fellow. "Boss" William Marcy Tweed (*the fat one*) without conscience looted New York City of millions of dollars.

The place where the Tweed organization had its headquarters was named Tammany Hall.

phony orchestras which fostered not only civic pride but musical activity in general. Cities provided libraries, too, opened to the public and supported increasingly by public taxes—a response to the growing sophistication and formal education required of people living in urban communities.

The role of the "boss." The promise of the city, however, was far from being open to everyone equally. Unable to speak English, immigrants struggled to earn a living, often in keen competition with others who had arrived only a few years earlier. The newcomer often had to depend on the assistance—usually limited—of the benevolent associations that his fellow countrymen had formed. In many cases the only helping hand an immigrant had from the larger community in which he lived was that of the local political leader, or "boss." A "boss" was able to build a "machine" out of the loyalty of helpless newcomers he befriended.

The older and well-established city families often decried the city machine, saying it showed how easily immigrants could be gulled and the American electoral process could be poisoned. Before public-welfare agencies existed, however, the neighborhood political club was an informal legal-aid bureau, an employment office, and even a place where one could send an errant son or daughter to seek advice and help. Those who criticized the city machines offered no better solution for the desperate requirements of the people from the slums. The critics, to be sure, often contributed generously to benevolent organizations, but they generally looked down on people who "took charity."

A contrast. Unlike the city man with problems, the farmer did not lack food, and he did not suffer glaring physical discomfort. He spoke English and almost always belonged to a Protestant church. He saw the city-dweller—often

#

#Ask whether such machines exist today and, if so, what makes their existence possible. Are political machines likely to become established in small towns or cities? Explain.

#Recall that these foreign-born people were in the country as a result of the "new immigration" and that they came from the parts of Europe where Roman Catholicism was the predominant religion. Many were Jews. In time they would learn English, as many earlier immigrants had.

Collier's Weekly, November 10, 1906 (Library of Congress)

A city boss manipulates voters, affecting the outcome of elections in which he is interested. Over a period of time a boss built up sufficient influence to assure political offices for candidates he favored.

What were the "strings" the boss had on the "puppets"?

foreign-born and a Catholic or Jew—as his enemy, and he determined to make an effort at having government respond to rural needs. In actual fact, farmers and city people alike were ## caught in the iron grip of new conditions which neither could loosen.

A VIGOROUS EFFORT

By the early 1870's an organization of farmers had been formed. It was called the Patrons of Husbandry or, more commonly, the Grange.

Oliver H. Kelley. The founder of the Grange was a clerk in one of the bureaus of the Department of Agriculture, Oliver H. Kelley.† He was a man of inexhaustible energy—a friend once described him as "an engine with too much steam all the time."

---

†The Department of Agriculture was not created until 1862; its Secretary did not become a Cabinet member until 1889.

440 ##Discuss with the class whether or not the conditions that were causing difficulties could have been foreseen and prevented. What conditions today cause trouble that might have been prevented?

In an extensive trip through the South, Kelley had concluded that farmers sorely needed social and intellectual advancement. A Mason, he was convinced of the usefulness of secret fraternal orders, and he made the Grange a secret national club. At the wise suggestion of his niece, he decided to admit women as members.

Starting from scratch with a treasury "so empty that a five-cent stamp would need an introduction to feel at home," Kelley soon was conducting an incredibly successful membership drive. Said Kelley about the Grange, "It must be advertised as vigorously as if it were a patent medicine." By 1873 there were 20,000 local Granges, and by the spring of 1874—doubtless stimulated by the depression—their number had grown to about 25,000, with at least 1,500,000 members.

A forthright declaration. At first the Grange was chiefly an organization of good fellowship, but soon it assumed another purpose, too. A statement of grievances called the "Declaration of Purpose of the National Grange" was adopted in 1874, heartening Grangers all over the nation. It contained a bold new promise: "We propose meeting together, talking together, working together, buying together, and in general acting together for our mutual protection and advancement as occasion may require."

Enthusiasm in the Midwest. The greatest enthusiasm for the Grange was in the Middle West and South. The eastern farmers, whose agriculture was more diversified than that of the other sections of the country, were less distressed economically. Living near big-city markets, they had little interest in helping their

Group demonstrations to seek public sympathy have always been popular. See pp. 388 and 402.

Grangers mass in a midwestern town to watch a procession conducted by members of their organization. A band and signs bearing spirited slogans attract attention to the farmers' cause. An onlooker calms his frightened horses.

Edward Winslow Martin, *History of the Grange Movement or, The Farmers' War Against Monopolies*, 1873

##In the 1870's large numbers of participants in the Grange movement were wheat farmers in Illinois, Wisconsin, Iowa, and Minnesota.

Frank Leslie's Illustrated Newspaper, August 30, 1873

Grangers in an outdoor meeting in Illinois listen raptly as a speaker advocates measures to ease farm conditions.

Observe the band members.

competitors in the West get lower railroad rates. Besides, they did not require such large amounts of money for expansion and for mechanical equipment, and their property, therefore, was less heavily mortgaged.

Coöperative activities. In the West "Coöperation!" and "Down with Monopoly!" became favorite battle cries. Various coöperative enterprises to buy supplies and even to manufacture goods mushroomed in the agricultural states. The purpose was to eliminate the middleman merchant and thereby bring retail prices down. Coöperative creameries and grain elevators (that is, buildings with machinery for loading, unloading, cleaning, and storing grain) were also established.

Granger laws. But the Grange made its chief contribution in the field of railroad and warehouse regulation. In Illinois, Iowa, Wisconsin, and Minnesota, so-called Granger laws were

passed between 1869 and 1874. This legislation fixed maximum freight and storage charges for grain and in some cases created commissions to regulate rates.

Railroad officials regarded such regulation as contrary to the Fourteenth Amendment of the Constitution (see page 297), and as being in violation of railroad charters, which were unbreakable contracts. In a significant decision, the United States Supreme Court held in the case of *Munn* v. *Illinois* in 1877 that the states have the power to regulate private property when it is "clothed with a public interest." In other words, a state could take steps to control certain private businesses whose operation affected vitally the people's general welfare.

In the Wabash Case of 1886, the Court somewhat modified this decision, holding that a state could regulate railroads only within its own borders. This practically ended state regulation, because most rail lines were interstate. But the way was open for the federal government to take a hand. #

Congress acted in 1887, when it passed the Interstate Commerce Act. This momentous law forbade pooling, rebates, and higher rates for a short haul than for a long haul over the same line. Railroads were now required to post their rates and to make them "reasonable and just."

The Act also created the first regulatory commission in American history—the Interstate Commerce Commission—to supervise enforcement of the law. Pressure from the Grangers had led to this first federal control over large-scale private enterprise in the interest of the public good.

Decline. After the middle 1870's the Granger movement began to lose momentum. Many members became discouraged when their coöperatives failed. Others were disheartened by the inability to find solutions to their numerous and continuing problems.

The Grange became only a social organization after it ceased to be a political force. But ## it had shown that farmers could have great influence when they joined their individual efforts. Like the Knights of Labor, which had also declined after dramatic success, the Grange

##The Grange has not died out. It has national headquarters in Washington, D.C., where it continues to work for legislation to help farmers. It continues to have its own secret ritual.

had learned that to be effective, a protest movement must find the right *kind* of organization.

Many farmers placed great faith in the program of the Greenback party, organized in 1876. The party had adopted a popular notion that the burden of agricultural debts could be # reduced by increasing the amount of paper currency in circulation without backing. Such an increase, it was held, would raise prices and enable farmers to pay off their obligations more easily—as had been the case during the Civil War when the greenbacks were issued.

The Greenback party for a time controlled a substantial number of seats in Congress. It ran candidates for the presidency in 1880 and 1884, but it had lost its appeal after 1879. In 1875 Congress had enacted a law providing for the reduction of the amount of Civil War greenbacks in circulation. Beginning January 1, 1879, the government was to stand ready to issue gold dollars for these greenbacks whenever the greenbacks were presented. The law ## deeply disappointed those who hoped to inflate the currency with *more* greenbacks.

Sum and Substance

1. Contrast the attitudes taken toward the American farmer before and after the Civil War. 2. Name the major difficulties of farmers in the post-Civil War period. 3. What was the Grange? When was it founded? 4. How did the organization change? 5. What did it accomplish? What caused its decline? 6. Why did many farmers want the amount of money in circulation increased? 7. How did the government disappoint these farmers?

By 1887 the figure of Uncle Sam looked very much as he appears today.

This cartoon appeared after the passage of the Interstate Commerce Act. It was captioned, "Uncle Sam's 'Wild West' show—the Interstate Commissioners moving on the animals." Uncle Sam is egging on several timorous officials.

Harper's Weekly, April 9, 1887

##This was the Specie Resumption Act. The amount of greenbacks in circulation was to be reduced **443** to $300,000,000. The law gave people confidence in the soundness of the greenbacks.

TILLERS OF THE SOIL ENTER THE DOOR OF POLITICS

In spite of its meager achievements, the Greenback party was the first national political organization through which farmers had been able to voice their discontent. When it failed, farmers once again lacked both a program and an organization to help advance it.

PRESSURE ORGANIZATIONS

\# In the late 1870's a new group of farmers' pressure organizations, known as alliances, began to appear in farm communities. Farmers banded together in a number of local, then state, and then regional organizations until there were two major sectional alliances: the Southern Alliance and the Northwestern Alliance. By the end of the 1880's, these alliances, together with a second organization in the South, called the Colored Farmers' National Alliance, had become the spokesmen for most farmers in the country.

Courting organized labor. In 1889, when the two large sectional alliances held their conventions in St. Louis, an attempt was made to link them. Representatives of labor were also invited to be present in order to bring about, if possible, a merger of "the organized tillers and the organized toilers" of the nation.

The Knights of Labor, which had begun to decline after 1886, seized the opportunity to participate. But the AFL refused to send representatives because alliance membership included farmers who hired help and who were therefore employers.

Divisions and common ground. Although different aims and interests stood in the way of unity between northern and southern farmers, they agreed on certain demands. One was for an increase in the amount of currency in circulation. A second was for an end to excessive landholding by railroads. A third was for a prohibition against ownership of land by aliens. A fourth was for the ownership and operation by the federal government of all means of transportation and communication.

A kindly Uncle Sam looks on with seeming approval.

The Farmers' Alliances are shown as threats to politicians—mowing down the politicians, even though they lie low.

Judge, August 16, 1890

Creating a party. But how could the farmers put their ideas into practice? How could they make themselves heard in the halls of government? One writer in part explained the difficulty: "If the farmer went to the capital fresh from the plow, among a crowd of lobbyists, he was as clay in the hands of the potter. If his constituents kept him there year after year, until he learned the ways of legislation, then he ceased to be a farmer and became a member of some other class, perhaps a stockholder in a great railroad, or manufacturing corporation, with interests in common with the opponents of agricultural classes."

The old loyalties. The delay of the farmers in organizing a party of their own can only be accounted for by the slowness with which people break their old party ties. It seemed to farmers in the old Northwest that forsaking the Republican party was betrayal of the party that had saved the Union. It appeared to farmers in the South that forsaking the Democratic party—the party that had stood up to the carpetbaggers and the scalawags—was treason.

NEW COMPLAINTS

By the end of the 1880's, the farmers at last were ready to give up old party loyalties in order to achieve their demands. Their woes had become more vexing than ever.

By 1887 the number of mortgages in Kansas was three times what it had been in 1880. In Kansas and North Dakota one person in every two had a mortgage on his property. To be sure, many a man mortgaged his property in response to a quick-talking agent, in order to buy equipment he did not need or could not use profitably. Yet the fall in farm prices was at the root of the trouble.

Bad weather. In addition, terrible weather between 1885 and 1887 produced calamity (see page 353). In going bankrupt, cattlemen on the Great Plains ruined an important market for farm crops. And, in the drought of 1886, grain that was growing in the fields was burned to a crisp under the scorching sun. What did not wither and die was eaten by chinch bugs.

Droves of farmers left the Plains. Many departing covered wagons bore signs reading, "In God We Trusted, in Kansas We Busted." Those who stayed behind could expect only increased debts and misery. For a decade the annual rainfall was inadequate.

As mortgages were foreclosed by the thousands, many farmers borrowed from "loan sharks" in order to keep going—sometimes at rates as high as 40 percent. The prospects were grim. Besides, there seemed to be no explanation of why prices stayed down; and only a rise in them would relieve the farmer of his oppressive troubles.

Scarcity of money. Like most other Americans, the farmer did not understand the technical details of the money supply. But he began to feel that his bad times were in some way linked to its operation. One "explanation" grew in popularity: there was not enough money available to do America's "money work." It was pointed out that the amount of money circulating in 1865—about one billion dollars—had been increased only slightly in twenty-five years. Yet during that time, the population had almost doubled and business had increased tremendously.

Not only was currency scarce, but also it was inelastic. It seemed always to be in short supply when needed most and plentiful when needed least. Was there no way to regulate the supply?

THE CURRENCY QUESTION

The farmers came to believe that if the amount of money in circulation could be increased, farm prices would go up. After the failure of the Greenback party movement, there seemed to be only one way to bring about this development: issue additional silver coins. The discoveries of silver ore in the West and new supplies from abroad made this solution seem convenient as well as good.

The ratio of 16 to 1. During most of the country's history both silver and gold coins had been issued, and both metals had been valued for coinage purposes in 1834 at a ratio of 16 to 1. This means that 16 ounces of silver were equal in value to 1 ounce of gold, or, putting it another way, that there was sixteen times as much silver in a silver dollar as there was gold in a gold dollar. Silver dollars and gold dollars were both legal tender.‡

After the California gold rush of 1849, gold became more plentiful than previously and its value dropped. Yet in striking new coins the United States mint retained the old ratio of 16 to 1. The people began to be aware that the silver in a silver dollar was worth more than the gold in a gold dollar. A silversmith making silver brooches, umbrella handles, snuffboxes, and hundreds of other everyday items would pay more for the metal than did the United States government. Consequently, so little silver was brought to the mint for coinage that in 1873 Congress dropped the silver dollar from the list of coins to be struck. This action is called the *demonetization* of silver. At the time it took place, it attracted almost no attention.

Increased supplies of silver. By the end of the 1870's, however, the effects of the increased silver production, which had begun in the sixties, became evident. The value of silver in relation to gold began to decline. In addition, when the number of greenbacks in circulation was reduced, a lot of silver came out of hiding. There was no longer need to hoard it against the day—which many had feared during the Civil War—when the value of a greenback would fall to zero.

Furthermore, after Germany became a unified country in 1871, it went on the *gold standard*—that is, it made all its currency convertible only into gold. Consequently, it sold its silver in the world market. Other nations with close economic ties to Germany followed suit: Sweden, Norway, Denmark, France, Belgium, Switzerland, Italy, and Greece.

The Crime of '73. Suddenly silver was so abundant that a silversmith would not pay much gold for it. In fact, he would pay less than the mint had formerly paid. After 1875 the silver-mining interests—and the farmers—were angrily describing the demonetization of silver as the "Crime of '73." They demanded that silver dollars be coined again. "Give us back the dollar of our daddies," they urged.

Silver laws. The silver-mine owners wanted the mint to buy their entire production; farmers wanted silver coins to relieve the money shortage. To their joint clamor, Congress responded with the Bland-Allison Act of 1878.

This act authorized the Secretary of the Treasury to purchase monthly not less than two million dollars' worth and not more than four million dollars' worth of silver for coinage into dollars. The resulting coinage hardly satisfied the farmers' plea for more currency.

The increasing pressure for new legislation gradually had its effect. There were now more silverites in Congress because of the admission to the Union in 1889 of a number of silver-producing states. The silverites in 1890 obtained the passage of the Sherman Silver Purchase Act. This law authorized the Secretary of the Treasury to purchase practically all the silver produced in the country at that time.

Despite the Act, which increased the amount of money in circulation, farm prices stayed low. Yet many farmers persisted in their belief that the answer to the money problem was the *unlimited* coinage of silver.

When the alliances met in St. Louis in December, 1889, the members agreed upon a common platform including demands for a graduated income tax, government ownership of railroads, laws against land monopolies, and an end to national banks. The southern farmers added a plank calling for the free and unlimited coinage of silver at a ratio to gold of 16 to 1.§

Sum and Substance

1. How did the alliances differ from the Grange? 2. On what four demands did members of the alliances agree? 3. Through what agencies did they hope to correct farm evils? 4. What new farm difficulties developed in the 1880's? 5. On what did farmers fix the blame? 6. Tell how each of the following dates was related to the currency situation: 1834, 1849, 1871, 1873, 1878, 1879, 1890. 7. Explain "free and unlimited coinage of silver."

---

‡Legal tender is money—that is, currency—which a creditor is required by law to accept in payment of a debt.

§"Free and unlimited coinage of silver" means that no restriction whatever would be placed on the amount of silver bullion that the mint would accept for conversion into coins.

##In other words, they believed that if the current increase in the amount of money in circulation did not succeed, the remedy was to increase the amount indefinitely.

This section describes the farmers' entrance into politics. Recall labor's early attempts to form political parties (see pp. 402-403). What attitude had the Knights of Labor and the AFL taken toward participation in politics? (They favored it but formed no party.)

THE POPULISTS CAPTURE THE NATION'S ATTENTION

Money reform was only one—and a lesser one at that—of a long list of reforms that the farmers advocated. But there was no major political party to serve as a spokesman for the farm demands. And yet farmers were saying openly, "We are mortgaged, all but our votes."

LEADERS AND DIRECTION

By 1890 a remarkable group of colorful leaders began the monumental task of organizing the farm vote. Among them, one of the most fiery was Mary Elizabeth (Ellen) Lease of Kansas (her opponents called her "Mary Yellin'"). Her advice to Kansas farmers became nationally famous: "Raise less corn and more Hell."

A powerful figure also from Kansas was Jerry Simpson, a witty and clever speaker. When he had ridiculed his banker opponent for Congress in 1888 as a man who wore silk socks, a newspaper reporter twisted the statement to mean Simpson wore none! After that he was known as "Sockless Jerry."

Another leader was Ignatius Donnelly, the sage of Nininger, Minnesota, whose talents were diverse. He had written a best seller about a lost continent, Atlantis; also, he believed he had proved that Francis Bacon was actually the author of the plays of Shakespeare.

Still another leader was James B. Weaver, of Iowa, who had been the Greenback nominee for the presidency in 1880. A colonel who was made a brigadier general for "gallantry on the field" in the Civil War, Weaver was a gentle man of strong convictions.

Victories in 1890. In the congressional elections of 1890, candidates favored by the alliances enjoyed a phenomenal success. The Southern Alliance alone captured four governorships, eight state legislatures, forty-four seats in the House of Representatives, and three seats in the Senate.

This brought two leaders from the South to the fore. One was a South Carolinian, Benjamin Tillman, elected governor of his state as a farmers' candidate. When later he ran for the

Senate, he promised, "Send me to Washington and I'll stick my pitchfork into his [President Cleveland's] old ribs." Ever after his friends called him "Pitchfork Ben." The other one, from Georgia, was Thomas Watson. A skinny redhead, Watson became a familiar and outstanding voice of farm protest in the House of Representatives.

The People's Party. Farmer delegates, who gathered at St. Louis early in 1892 to form their

The prop was a robe or blanket.

Mrs. Lease poses for her picture with a prop of the time.

Kansas State Historical Society

#The farm leaders sought to unite farmers nationally, as the Grangers had tried to do. Note that these leaders were mainly from the Middle West and the South--the main farming regions.

447

#Observe the makeup of the Populist party, as shown on the balloon in the cartoon. If you omit the Prohibition party, what do the other groups named have in common? (They all sponsored particular means of improving the lot of the ordinary workingman, farmer, or laborer.)

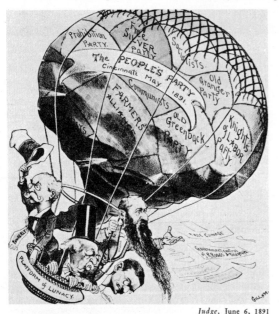

Judge, June 6, 1891

"A Party of Patches," as this cartoon was called, spoofs the components of the People's party.

own party, had high hopes for the coming presidential election. Amid the wildest enthusiasm, they passed resolutions to hold their first national convention at Omaha, Nebraska, on July 4 to select their nominee for the presidency of the United States. A new organization—the People's, or Populist, party—had been born. Reaching out for support, it made an appeal not only to farmers everywhere but to the Knights of Labor as well.

The Omaha platform. The Omaha platform of 1892 was a summary of the demands that had been put forth by farmers for the previous twenty years. It called for antirailroad legislation, free and unlimited silver coinage at a ratio of 16 to 1, economy in government, and the establishment of postal-savings banks. It demanded an end to land monopolies and to landownership by aliens.

The platform advocated also the secret ballot, liberal pensions for Union army veterans,

1872 was before the "Crime of '73," and 1894 was after the repeal of the Sherman Silver Purchase Act.

A defense of bimetallism against the gold standard. What is the significance of the two dates in the cartoon?

Coin's *Financial School,* 1894

448 "Bimetallism" can be easily understood if students remember that "bi" is a prefix meaning "two," or "double," as in "biweekly." "Mono" means "one," as in "monotonous."

the 8-hour day, the direct election of United States Senators, and a one-term limit for both the President and the Vice-President. It endorsed the Knights of Labor and condemned as "a menace to our liberties" the use of Pinkerton detectives to attack strikers in labor disputes. A reporter who was present likened the reception of the platform to the enthusiasm that had greeted the fall of the Bastille in 1789, during the French Revolution.

James B. Weaver. The Populists nominated General James B. Weaver for President. He seemed an ideal choice to head an organization representing not new ideas "but old ones relabeled." When the returns were in, the Populists had carried Kansas, Nevada, Colorado, and Idaho, and had collected 1,000,000 votes—9 percent of the national total.

Free and unlimited coinage. Soon after Grover Cleveland took office for the second time, in 1893, a severe depression fell on the country, and farm prices dropped lower than ever before. Farmers now were being more and more attracted to the possibilities they believed the free and unlimited coinage of silver offered.

Like most eastern political leaders, President Cleveland feared that free silver would lead to uncontrolled inflation. When, on his recommendation, Congress repealed the Sherman Silver Purchase Act in 1893, farmers and mineowners were beside themselves with anger. "The next Congress will be Populist if we do our duty," the Populists promised.

THE ELECTION OF 1896

The Populists looked forward to 1896 with lively anticipation. They assumed that the Democratic and Republican parties would reject free silver at their national conventions. Then *they* would meet and would use free silver as bait to attract the silverites of both major parties to themselves, in this way gaining wider sup-

McKinley was a Civil War veteran. As a congressman he sponsored the McKinley Tariff.

William McKinley, the Republican candidate in 1896, on the front porch of his home in Canton, Ohio.

Buffalo and Erie County Historical Society

Bryan knew what appealed to people in political writing or political speeches. He had been a newspaper editor as well as a professional lecturer in Nebraska. He was popular as a speaker at chautauquas (ask a student to find out what a chautauqua was).

William Jennings Bryan campaigns for the presidency in 1896 as newspaper reporters take notes. At the left hangs a picture of a younger Bryan, but the nominee's strength was in his eloquence, not in his youth.

By now most American men were clean-shaven. The Gillette razor was invented in 1895 (p. 55).

port for their program of broad reform.

The Republicans: Hanna's convention. The Republican convention met in June, in St. Louis. The dominant figure was Marcus A. Hanna, a wealthy industrial magnate from Ohio. He seemed a caricature of the kind of tycoon the Populists habitually condemned.

Hanna pushed the candidacy of his friend from Ohio, William McKinley, whose views on the currency question were not very well known. A high-tariff man, McKinley was considered by most businessmen to be "safe." He was nominated with ease after the silverites walked out of the convention, angered by the gold plank that had been put into the platform. #

Early in his career, McKinley had defended a group of strikers who had been arrested in a riot. This had earned him the lasting respect of workingmen. Workingmen were inclined to vote Republican anyway, believing that the high tariff advocated by the G.O.P. was a way of keeping wages up.

A "silver man's" convention. Three weeks after McKinley's nomination, the Democratic convention opened in Chicago. The silver men were quickly in control. A platform was adopted calling for "the free and unlimited coinage of both gold and silver at the . . . ratio of sixteen to one." Pandemonium broke loose when "Pitchfork Ben" Tillman denounced the Democrats' own Grover Cleveland as a "tool of Wall Street." Now the question was, Who could command the vote of this convention?

"A cross of gold." Suddenly a thirty-six-year-old Nebraskan had the floor. He was William Jennings Bryan, a big, broad-shouldered, and

450

#The platform called for the single gold standard, a high protective tariff, and a firm foreign policy to achieve the control of Hawaii (recall Cleveland's stand on this matter).

#As a member of Congress (he was elected in 1890 and 1892), Bryan was a supporter of the silver interests. Since the delegates who favored free silver were dominant in the Democratic convention, he was in a very favorable position to obtain the nomination.

Puck, September 16, 1896

An anti-Bryan cartoon, "Blowin' Himself Around the Country," shows the Democratic candidate campaigning "windily" while unprepossessing backwoodsmen applaud. Even the reporters are shown in an uncomplimentary light.

What does the label on Bryan's bellows refer to? How does the cartoonist portray farmers?

handsome man whose voice was both vibrant and deep—some said it had the quality of a pipe organ. A spellbinding orator, he had been # awaiting this opportunity to speak for the free-silver cause, and the speech he delivered was well rehearsed. Coming at just the right moment, it thrilled the delegates to the core. Every eye was on Bryan as he concluded: "You shall ## not press down upon the brow of labor this crown of thorns; you shall not crucify mankind upon a cross of gold."

In a mighty roar the convention registered its approval of his words until the hall shook to its foundations. A "silver man" later described how a "gold Democrat" "lost control of himself and literally grabbed hold of me and pulled me up from a sitting to a standing position on my chair. He yelled at me, 'Yell, for God's sake, yell!' as Bryan closed his speech."

Bryan, who had confidently brought his wife to the convention so that she could see him nominated, now outshone all the other candidates. While the delegates chanted deliriously, "Bryan! Bryan! No crown of thorns, no cross of gold!" the Democrats made him the party choice for the presidency.

The Populists: a gloomy convention. The camp of the Populists was filled with gloom. They had been overjoyed at the Republican rejection of free silver, and they had expected that the Democrats would follow suit. In grabbing the free-silver issue, the Democrats had stolen their thunder.

When about 1300 Populists met in St. Louis in July, they were angry and irritable. Unable

##This conclusion became famous and is the single sentence that is always connected with Bryan. Bryan was at the zenith of his political career.

Library of Congress

"Democracy" itself staggers under the load of the pro-silver and pro-gold advocates in 1896, according to this cartoon. Some familiar figures are shown, including Cleveland, who took a "hard-money" stand in 1893.

Observe that Cleveland was a "gold Democrat." Altgeld (the pro-labor governor) was a "silver man."

to afford the high prices being asked for hotel rent and food, many were suffering from exhaustion and hunger. They recognized that it had been a mistake to convene *after* the Republicans and Democrats. They had no choice save to nominate Bryan.‖

The battle of the standards. The struggle was now on in the most vigorous campaign since 1860. It would be known in history as "the battle of the standards"—a bimetallic standard (that is, a two-metal, or gold *and* silver, standard) *versus* the gold standard.

To many, Bryan appeared to be a homespun

‖ But they gagged at taking the Democrats' nominee for vice-president. He was Arthur Sewall of Maine, a shipyard owner who employed labor and who was a bank president and a railroad director! Instead, they named for second place on the ticket Tom Watson of Georgia.

hero, ready to save the country from the grasp of the gold supporters. To well-established people he was a dangerous figure: a New York clergyman called him "a mouthing, slobbering demagogue whose patriotism was all in his jawbone." The free-silver platform, another easterner said, had been "made in hell."

Everywhere Bryan went, huge crowds came out to hear him, partly, perhaps, because he was the first presidential nominee to campaign so extensively. He traveled more than 18,000 miles and made hundreds of speeches. He tried to persuade voters that he represented "the people" in their conflict with "Wall Street."

The Republicans conducted their campaign in a lower key. McKinley, a devoted husband, refused to be away for any length of time from

#Bryan appealed to city workers by defending unions and by promising to appoint Gompers to his Cabinet. Consider that he campaigned strenuously, without the help of airplanes or TV.

Clearly, most westerners and southerners favored bimetallism. (Mining interests influenced the western votes. Southerners were already firmly democratic--the solid South. For this reason, southern farmers voted differently from northern farmers.)

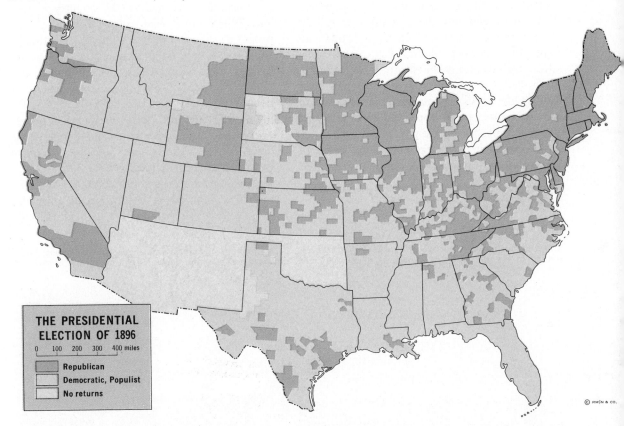

THE PRESIDENTIAL ELECTION OF 1896

0   100   200   300   400 miles

■ Republican
□ Democratic, Populist
□ No returns

© RMSN & CO.

What sections of the country seemed to favor bimetallism? The gold standard? How do you explain this? Why did the agricultural South vote differently from the farm regions of the North? What area was solidly Republican?

New England was solidly Republican. The Northeast and the Midwest were chiefly Republican.

Mrs. McKinley, a chronic invalid. He therefore conducted his campaign from the front porch of his house in Canton, Ohio.

He read carefully prepared statements to innumerable delegations brought from all parts of the country by the Republican National Committee. Although these visitors ruined McKinley's front lawn, they could hear in person their candidate's stand in support of gold.

Victory for McKinley. On Election Day, McKinley won easily. In glee Hanna telegraphed McKinley, "God's in his Heaven, all's right with the world!" McKinley had captured the industrial centers of the East and the important agricultural states of North Dakota, Iowa, Minnesota, Michigan, Illinois, Indiana, Wisconsin, and Ohio.

Some explanations. The Republican triumph can be explained in a number of ways. First, near election time the price of wheat began to rise, reducing considerably the anxiety of the farmers. Second, labor, almost invariably Republican in the past, remained Republican. Wage earners did not have to be told twice that the inflated and unpredictable silver dollar which Bryan was advocating would be against their interest. They knew that inflation would raise the prices of consumer goods long before it raised wages. Third, the Republicans spent huge sums of money in an attempt to convince Americans that a vote for Bryan was a vote for the devil.

Aftereffects. Bryan's defeat was a severe blow to the free silverites, but to the Populists it was a disaster. In the excitement of the campaign, their other—and more far-reaching—proposals were forgotten. Henry Demarest Lloyd, an important reformer of the day, called free silver "the cowbird of the reform movement."# "It waited," he said, "until the nest had been built by the sacrifices and labour of others, and then it laid its eggs in it, pushing out the others which lie smashed on the ground."

The Populist party was now dead. Some of the issues the farmers had raised disappeared

The cowbird, often found near cattle, rudely lays its eggs in other birds' nests.

as prosperity returned to the country by the end of the century. Many of the Populist party's proposals, like the ones for popular election of Senators, a graduated income tax, and postal savings, were adopted later. The Populists also taught city people the value of organizing nationally and in pressure groups. However, for the time being, the large numbers of people who were living in depressed conditions in the cities of the nation were not able to make themselves heard politically.

Though free silver could actually offer little toward a solution of the economic problems

Ask what is ironical or sarcastic about the title of this cartoon. Prosperity for whom?

This cartoon, called "The Age of Prosperity," draws attention to the continuing movement of Americans from the farms to the cities. Says the farmer in overalls, "Nowadays, even the mortgages don't stay on the farms."

Puck

#Founded in 1921, the confederation was composed of state bureaus; that is, it was a union of these. James R. Howard was the president. Similar to the American Federation of Labor, the farm federation catered to the more successful farmers.

State Historical Society of Wisconsin

Bryan campaigning in Columbus, Wisconsin, in 1900. Although the silver issue was dead, he continued to speak on behalf of the downtrodden and fought a second losing battle for the presidency.

Bryan ran on an anti-expansion platform in 1900. Only the South and four western states supported him.

of farmers, the demand for it did not disappear immediately. But exciting discoveries of gold in the Klondike and in Alaska beginning in 1896 increased the supply of money. As a result, Congress enacted a bill in 1900 which put the United States on the gold standard. The silver question ceased thereafter to have any practical meaning.

Lessons learned. The farmer had learned much from his experiences in the post-Civil War decades. Most important, he now recognized that he could not fight big business: he must accept it and make its methods his own. He stayed in local politics, and like the big businessmen, he now pressed continuously—not just in times of depression—for solutions to his problems. He organized lobbies in Congress like the American Farm Bureau Federation to see that his legislative wishes received a respectful hearing.

Not long after 1896, farmers, along with their fellow Americans, were absorbed in watching the United States enter the race for colonies. Domestic matters for a time seemed to be far less urgent than foreign affairs. "The Spanish War finished us," Tom Watson wrote. "The blare of the bugle drowned the voice of the Reformer."

Sum and Substance

1. Name the farm leaders in the 1890's. 2. What political party did farmers organize? What was its platform? Who was its candidate? 3. What states did the farmers' new party carry? 4. Why was the Sherman Silver Purchase Act repealed? 5. How did farmers react? 6. Summarize the main facts about the candidates, their platforms, and their campaigns in the election of 1896. 7. Who was elected? Why? 8. What had farmers learned during the post-Civil War years?

See Question 2 under "Being a Social Scientist," p. 456. Ask what methods farmers have used recently to call attention to their problems. (In 1968 they killed and buried livestock.)

#The facts that many Americans seek homes in the suburbs, where they can have yards and gardens; that many try to grow plants in their homes; that many people spend their vacations on farms which make a practice of offering the use of their homes for vacationers.

THE WORKSHOP

OF LASTING SIGNIFICANCE

What role did each of the following have in the readjustment of American society after the Civil War?

sharecropping
Cyrus W. Field
short haul
long haul
Hamlin Garland
Metropolitan
    Museum of Art
Oliver H. Kelley
Grange
"Granger laws"
Munn v. *Illinois*
Interstate
    Commerce Act
Wabash Case
Greenback party
ratio of 16 to 1

legal tender
demonetization
gold standard
Crime of '73
Sherman Silver
    Purchase Act
Mary Elizabeth
    Lease
Populist party
James B. Weaver
William McKinley
William Jennings
    Bryan
Marcus A. Hanna
battle of the standards

DOCUMENTS IN HISTORY

1. According to William Peffer (see pages 426–427) how were the farmers of his day different from those of a half-century or a century before? In what ways were the farmers of 1891 better off than earlier ones? Worse off?

2. What had given the farmers of the late nineteenth century their advantages? According to Peffer, what accounted for their recently acquired disadvantages?

3. If Peffer were describing farming conditions of today, what picture could he present?

BEING A SOCIAL SCIENTIST

1. From the Decennial Summary of Population given in the Appendix, compare the rate of increase in urban population between 1860 and 1900 with that of the rural population in the same years. Which showed a greater percentage of increase? Why?

2. What percent of Americans today live on farms? What has made it possible for such a relatively small group of people to produce enough food to satisfy the needs of a growing national population and even to provide food products for other countries?

3. How does the present-day attitude of Americans toward farmers compare with the view in Jefferson's day? With the view after the Civil War? What accounts for differences?

4. What aspects of American life today sug- # gest that many people share to some extent Jefferson's love of the soil and its cultivation?

5. What attracts Americans to cities today? ##

6. Find out the functions of the Department of Agriculture and the Department of Housing and Urban Development today; the American Farm Bureau Federation, the National Farmers Union, and the National Grange; farm coöperatives; the Federal Crop Insurance Corporation (FCIC); and the 4-H clubs.

INFORMED OPINION

1. American technology has accounted in large part for the growth of cities in the United States. Explain the statement on page 434 that the solution to urban problems after the Civil War was technological. Give examples from life today proving the truth of the statement.

2. Name the chief problems of American cities after 1865 and compare that list with one of the main problems of these cities today. Which ones remain the same? Which have been solved? How? What new ones have appeared?

3. What do you consider the advantages and the disadvantages of urban living? Of rural living?

4. What similarities can you see between the efforts of farmers and city workingmen to improve their situations in the second half of the nineteenth century? What are the differences? What success did each group achieve?

5. Name the American cities that are included on the list of Largest Metropolitan Centers of the World in the Appendix. How does the number compare with the number included from other leading countries? What does the relatively large number of American cities on the list indicate about the United States?

##Primarily the jobs that are available there. Another important reason is the vast opportunity for education and for amusement.

A LONG VIEW

Creating Industrial Strength

THE United States had come of age before the nineteenth century closed. As a people, Americans now had important involvements throughout the world. For the first time, the great powers were formally taking account of the United States as an equal.

Americans as a whole, however, feeling by turns inferior and superior, were still somewhat unsure of themselves in their relationship with Europeans. Many wealthy Americans insisted upon giving their children a "grand tour" of Europe, as if an education would not be complete without it. On the other hand, millions never doubted that America not only had "caught up" with Europe but was in fact building a far grander civilization.

The art and architecture of America often were gaudy and depressing imitations of what fashionable Europeans—especially Englishmen and Frenchmen—found attractive. Many new buildings of the 1870's and 1880's in America were so ornate that they appeared to symbolize their builders perfectly —newly rich people who wanted to show off.

Underneath this "gingerbread," Americans were forming a society much different from the one in the generation before the Civil War. The hours in factories were still long. Leisure time continued to be available only to the few. The rate of illiteracy was still too high in every section of the country.

Yet the people's lives and outlook were being changed, and there was proof of the changes almost everywhere one turned. The typewriter, # a machine that first appeared in the 1880's, and the telephone revolutionized the business world in a relatively short time. Besides opening careers to young women, they greatly increased the rapidity of commercial transactions.

Photography for the masses was making a mark. Picture-taking and -developing was long and cumbersome until George Eastman invented celluloid film and a simple camera, the Kodak. Now, more accurately than ever, events could be permanently "remembered"—by almost anyone.

The invention of simplified photography and of the phonograph occurred at about the same time. Within a few years the "talking machine," first demonstrated in 1877 by Thomas A. Edison, could bring to anybody not only imperishable voices but also music that previously only the richest and most privileged could enjoy.

In these novelties and in countless others—like the electric light bulb and the telephone—Americans could sample the future. They could see themselves becoming more and more dependent on their inventive genius. They could believe that in time science and technology would help free mankind ## from much of the everlasting burden of work.

At about the same time that dramatic technological changes were raising hopes and spirits, the influence of Charles Darwin's theory of evolution was growing. Because Darwin taught that man had "evolved" from lower forms of life and had not been created outright by God, many began to feel less significant—and even gloomy.

Nevertheless, triumphs of the laboratory and factory, more remarkable each passing year, seemed to offer fresh assurance to man that unlike other animals he was not trapped by his environment. They suggested that he could manipulate the natural world as he saw fit—that he was the captain of his fate.

Such favorable evidence was especially impressive as the 1890's came to an end, because many Americans believed that the nation needed a new lease on life. They observed that the frontier of the small farmer was closing, and they foresaw that the problems of developing industrialization and of the growing cities would have no ready answers. They could balance their fears about the future with the confidence that mechanical wizardry would be a boon to all Americans. ★ ★ ★ ★ ★ ★

PART FIVE WORKSHOP

AMERICA IN THE WORLD

1. What part of the world was involved in the period discussed in Part Five when the United States left the way open for a violation of the Monroe Doctrine? How and why did this happen? At what time and for what reason did Americans vigorously defend the Doctrine? How successful were they? What effect did the Olney doctrine have on the international prestige of the United States?

2. Explain Pan-Americanism and describe the efforts of the United States to foster it.

3. What territory did the United States acquire in the years covered in Part Five? Why? What international relations were involved?

4. On an outline map of the world name and show in color the areas outside the United States on which the attention of the United States was focused in the era treated in Part Five. Identify in some way all the United States possessions.

5. What conditions in the world contributed to the great increase in immigration between 1880 and 1914? What does this say about the reputation the United States had gained among Europeans?

TIME AND CHANGE

1. List the changes in the United States following the Civil War that significantly affected large numbers of Americans. What dates can be associated with each change?

Approximately how long would you say that it took to bring about each change? What and who contributed to each?

2. What large groups of people were chiefly affected by each change? What adjustments did they have to make? Would you say that the adjustments were made easily or not? Explain.

3. Which of the changes you listed is continuing today? Why?

4. What do you regard as the chief advantages American technology and industrialization brought to the people? What were the main disadvantages? Would you say that they have been or are being overcome? Explain.

NATIONAL STRENGTH

1. A nation's strength, like that of an individual, is judged by certain standards. List the elements that make a country strong, not overlooking efficient organization of national life— of official and private institutions.

2. Using Part Five, prove that Americans in the years after the Civil War could be called energetic. What individuals particularly deserve the name? What groups?

3. How was each of the following involved in the growing industrialization: (*a*) human resources, including enterprising spirit; (*b*) natural resources; (*c*) railroads; (*d*) the federal government?

4. How did the settlement of the "last West" add to the national strength of the United States? How did energetic people and the federal government contribute to the settlement?

5. Would you say that in the period covered in Part Five there was too much or too little involvement by the federal government in the lives of the people? Defend your answer.

6. What effect on national strength does political corruption have? Explain.

7. How do you rate the United States today in respect to each element of national strength? What part did good luck play in helping to make this country strong? What role has political freedom had?

OLD PROBLEMS BECOME NEW

1. What problems that Americans of an earlier day faced continued to perplex people between 1865 and about 1900? How was each one handled?

2. To what extent was the lack of a feeling of mutual interest between farmers and city people a new kind of "sectionalism," such as had affected domestic politics before the Civil War?

3. What urban problems appeared? Were these old or new? Explain.

##Students may name large size (area), large population, an educated people with technological skills, an adequate supply of energy resources, and morale--besides organization.

Eyewitness Accounts

Custer, Elizabeth. *Boots and Saddles, or Life in Dakota with General Custer.* Norman: University of Oklahoma Press, 1961.

Garland, Hamlin. *A Son of the Middle Border.* New York: The Macmillan Co. [Paperback—Gloucester, Mass.: Peter Smith, 1960].

Glaab, Charles N. *The American City: A Documentary History.* Homewood, Ill.: Richard D. Irwin, Inc., 1963 [Paperback—Homewood, Ill.: Richard D. Irwin, Inc.].

Litwack, Leon F. (ed.). *The American Labor Movement* [Paperback—Englewood Cliffs, N.J.: Prentice-Hall, Inc., 1962].

Roehm, Marjorie Catlin. *The Letters of George Catlin and His Family: A Chronicle of the American West.* Berkeley: University of California Press, 1966.

Tindall, George B. (ed.). *A Populist Reader* [Paperback—New York: Harper & Row, Publishers, 1966].

Giant Men and Women

Allen, Frederick L. *The Great Pierpont Morgan* [Paperback—New York: Harper & Row, Publishers].

Barnard, Harry. *Eagle Forgotten.* Indianapolis: Bobbs-Merrill Co., Inc. [Paperback—Indianapolis: Bobbs-Merrill Co., Inc.].

Brown, Mark H. *The Flight of the Nez Percé.* New York: G. P. Putnam's Sons, 1967.

Glad, Paul W. *The Trumpet Soundeth: William Jennings Bryan and His Democracy, 1896–1912.* Lincoln: University of Nebraska Press, 1960 [Paperback—Lincoln: University of Nebraska Press].

Johnson, Virginia W. *Unregimented General: A Biography of Nelson A. Miles.* Boston: Houghton Mifflin Co., 1962.

Lutz, Alma. *Susan B. Anthony.* Boston: Beacon Press, 1959.

Mandel, Bernard. *Samuel Gompers: A Biography.* Yellow Springs, Ohio: Antioch Press.

Woodward, C. Vann. *Tom Watson: Agrarian Rebel.* Gloucester, Mass.: Peter Smith [Paperback—New York: Oxford University Press].

Living and Making a Living

Cochran, Thomas C., and William Miller. *The Age of Enterprise* [Paperback—New York: Harper & Row, Publishers].

Dulles, Foster R. *Labor in America: A History.* New York: Crowell Collier & Macmillan, Inc., 1966.

Fite, Gilbert C. *The Farmers' Frontier, 1865–1900.* New York: Holt, Rinehart & Winston, Inc., 1966.

Ginger, Ray. *Altgeld's America.* Chicago: Quadrangle Books, Inc., 1965.

———. *The Age of Excess.* New York: The Macmillan Co., 1965.

Glaab, Charles N., and A. Theodore Brown. *A History of Urban America.* New York: The Macmillan Co., 1967.

Glad, Paul. *McKinley, Bryan, and the People.* Philadelphia: J. B. Lippincott Co., 1964.

Hicks, John D. *The Populist Revolt.* Lincoln: University of Nebraska Press, 1961 [Paperback—Lincoln: University of Nebraska Press].

Jones, Maldwyn. *American Immigration.* Chicago: University of Chicago Press, 1960 [Paperback—Chicago: University of Chicago Press].

Kirkland, Edward C. *Industry Comes of Age: Business, Labor, and Public Policy, 1860–1897.* New York: Holt, Rinehart & Winston, Inc., 1961.

Logan, Rayford W. *The Negro in the United States* [Paperback—Princeton, N.J.: D. Van Nostrand Co., Inc., 1957].

McKelvey, Blake. *The Urbanization of America, 1860–1915.* New Brunswick, N.J.: Rutgers University Press, 1962.

Story, John F. *American Railroads.* Chicago: University of Chicago Press, 1961 [Paperback—Chicago: University of Chicago Press].

Vaughn, J. W. *Indian Fights: New Facts on Seven Encounters.* Norman: University of Oklahoma Press, 1966.

Woodward, C. Vann. *The Strange Career of Jim Crow.* New York: Oxford University Press, 1966 [Paperback—New York: Oxford University Press].

Confronting the World

Dulles, Foster R. *Prelude to World Power.* New York: The Macmillan Co., 1965.

Pletcher, David M. *The Awkward Years: American Foreign Relations Under Garfield and Arthur.* Columbia: University of Missouri Press, 1962.

Art, Science, and the Life of the Mind

Berthoff, Werner. *The Ferment of Realism, 1884–1919.* New York: The Macmillan Co., 1965.

Hylander, C. J. *American Inventors.* New York: The Macmillan Co., 1964.

Josephson, Matthew. *Edison* [Paperback—New York: McGraw-Hill Book Co.].

Mumford, Lewis. *The Brown Decade: A Study of the Arts of America, 1865–1895.* Gloucester, Mass.: Peter Smith [Paperback—New York: Dover Publications, Inc.].

Paulson, Ross E. *American Ideals, 1865–1896* [Paperback—Chicago: Rand McNally & Co., 1967].

Historical Fiction

Adams, Henry. *Democracy* [Paperback—New York: New American Library, Inc.]. (Political corruption in the Gilded Age.)

Clark, Walter V. *The Ox-Bow Incident.* Gloucester, Mass.: Peter Smith [Paperback—New York: New American Library, Inc.]. (Frontier justice.)

Clemens, Samuel L., and C. D. Warner. *The Gilded Age.* New York: Trident Press, 1964. (A hilarious account of the foibles of an era.)

Horgan, Paul. *A Distant Trumpet.* New York: Farrar, Straus & Giroux, Inc., 1960 [Paperback—New York: Fawcett World Library]. (The army in the Southwest tries to make peace with the Apaches.)

Point out that the Linotype and the fountain pen--as well as the typewriter--speeded up communication. Recall that there was a new ability through advertising to excite the public over new inventions.

Remington Rand

The typewriter was opening jobs in business to women.

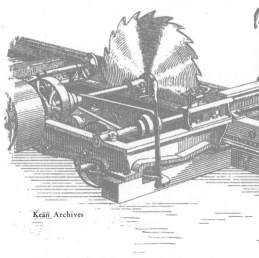

Kean Archives

The circular saw for cutting lumber was usually called the "buzz" saw. The name suggests some characteristics of many of the new machines: they were speedy, noisy, and dangerous to working-men, in a time before compensation laws.

Uniformed policemen and Negroes in positions of authority were still novel.

Special Collections, Columbia University Libraries

Chicago Historical Society

Clean-up time meant more than leaving grime at the plant. It showed a growing concern about cleanliness through bathing and the use of soap.

Why did policemen, firemen, and sanitation workers long resist wearing uniforms? (Uniforms invited closer supervision; in Europe they were the symbols of lackeys--something to avoid.)

The pictures on these three pages show aspects of American life in the late 1800's. There is much evidence of the developing industrialization. Ask if the "standardization of parts" made possible by machines hastened the "standardization of life." (Some existed before.)

THE
QUALITY
OF
LIFE

In the era after Appomattox, most Americans were aware of the vigorous movement of people within the country—from rural regions to urban ones, from South to North, from East to West, from town to town, in all directions. Behind this activity was the tremendous engine of industrialization. Many old styles of living disappeared— some of the losses were not regretted—and the elements of an increasingly dynamic society were already showing.

Discuss the effects of population movement on family life. The youth seen below was one of them.
Young people going from farm to city left saddened homes, just as youthful immigrants leaving the old country did.

A. J. Wyatt for Philadelphia Museum of Art

(Among the effects of population movement on family life are: lack of parental supervision in choosing marriage partners, more frequent abandonment of the elderly to their own resources.)

461

Town pumps were usually displaced by privately owned water systems and then by public works.

THE QUALITY OF LIFE *continued*

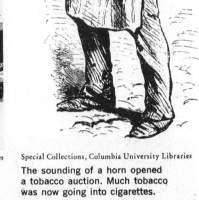

Special Collections, Columbia University Libraries

People still drew water from town pumps, often using child labor.

Most cities built waterworks between 1878 and 1898.

Special Collections, Columbia University Libraries

The sounding of a horn opened a tobacco auction. Much tobacco was now going into cigarettes.

Spectator sports, including horse racing, boxing, and baseball, were helping to fill new-found leisure.

Chicago Historical Society

Discuss effects of public entertainment on leisure activity. Look back at p. 104.

#Discuss the last sentence in this paragraph. Is the statement true of individuals as well as of nations? Give examples to support your answer. Why is much expected of the United States today? Is our country today using its strength for "noble ends"? Explain.
##What are "imperial interests"? Contrast the situation of the colonies in 1770 with the position of the United States in 1898, when the country had "imperial interests."

REACHING INTO THE WORLD

PART SIX

A strong nation has enticing opportunities and occasionally takes
risks which may prove fatal. It can use its strength for noble ends or for
mean ones.

America's hour to make a momentous choice came in 1898. In
the tropics, where Spanish explorers long years before had raised the
banner of absolute monarchy, the United States hitched itself to the rising
star of empire. In a brief struggle against Spain, the nation acquired
colonies in the Caribbean and in the Pacific. America, which had once
been a frontier of the Old World, now had immense imperial interests
of its own across the seas.

The telling questions were: Would the easy triumph on the battlefield only whet the people's appetite for further military conquests? Could
Americans find an acceptable substitute for the excitement and the spoils
of war?

The answers are already part of history. Americans directed their
power toward peace and toward the encouragement of other peoples in
the climb to self-government. They gave their possessions a share in the
nation's riches and the means to develop their own. Within a few years,
the United States voluntarily promised to take no more territory. In
domestic affairs, Americans established new standards of self-criticism
and then of self-improvement—as they engaged in a housecleaning of the
republic.

"There's glory enough for all!" was how Commodore Winfield S.
Schley paid tribute to the heroism of America's sailors at the Battle of
Santiago in the Spanish-American War. Schley's lusty words may well be
applied to the whole generation of Americans who lived at the turn of
the century. They used their country's might not to enlarge the American
empire but to strengthen the domain of democracy.

Discuss the meaning of "domain of democracy." What does it mean to strengthen the domain of democracy? (To make stronger the hold of democracy on the area where it existed.)

In many ways the Panama Canal was a symbol of the United States in the early 1900's: it represented America's technology and wealth, its emphasis on progress, and its increasing role in world affairs.

Steam shovels excavate for the Panama Canal—a waterway that was both a tribute to American technology and an indication of the increasingly large role the United States played in world affairs as the new century opened.

Ask what this painting shows about the terrain the engineers worked with. Without the steam-propelled machines--products of heavy industry--the excavation would have been impossible.

This part describes the new international role of the United States at the close of the nineteenth century and the opening of the twentieth. The chapter on the Spanish-American War is followed by one on the progressive era and another on the international activities of the United States.

REACHING INTO THE WORLD

CHAPTER 22   CARRYING THE FLAG OVERSEAS   466

The United States Draws the Sword Against Spain   468
America Encounters the Obligations of Power   481
The Spoils of War Turn Into the Burdens of Empire   489

CHAPTER 23   THE TIME OF THE PROGRESSIVES   496

A Rough Rider Is Thrust Into the White House   498
Indignant Americans Crusade Against Social Abuses   500
"T. R." Hands the Reins to William Howard Taft   519
Woodrow Wilson Offers America the New Freedom   523

CHAPTER 24   NEW INTERNATIONAL RESPONSIBILITIES   530

The United States Decides to Have a Panama Canal   532
Uncle Sam Makes Himself Policeman of the Americas   537
Troubles to the South Test Patience and Principle   541
America Determines to Prevent the Conquest of China   548
The Peace Movement Aims to Root Out War   551

A LONG VIEW   555

The role of the United States in world affairs enlarged considerably from 1898 on, and for this reason, people tend to think that before that time its role was negligible. Students--who will recall the long-time interest of American merchants, farmers, and industrialists in foreign trade; the war with the Barbary pirates; the War of 1812; our relations with foreign countries during the Civil War; and our relations with Latin American countries--know that the United States was by no means an isolationist country.

The primary source with which this chapter begins represents the thinking of the people who favored the acquisition of new possessions by the United States. They were in the majority. In answering the opposition, what does Beveridge quote? (The Declaration of Independence.)

22

CARRYING THE FLAG OVERSEAS

. . . for liberty and civilization . . .

Hawaii is ours. Porto Rico is to be ours; at the prayer of its people Cuba will finally be ours; in the islands of the East, even to the gates of Asia, coaling stations are to be ours; at the very least the flag of a liberal government is to float over the Philippines, and it will be the stars and stripes of glory. . . .

The opposition tells us that we ought not to govern a people without their consent. I answer, the rule of liberty that all just government derives its authority from the consent of the governed, applies only to those who are capable of self-government. We govern the Indians without their consent; we govern our Territories without their consent.

While foreign policy was being made in Washington, Americans carried on their local politics.

I answer, would not the natives of the Philippines prefer the just, humane, civilizing government of this Republic to the savage, bloody rule of pillage and extortion from which we have rescued them? Do not the blazing fires of joy and the ringing bell of gladness in Porto Rico prove the welcome of our flag?

Today, we are making more than we can use. Therefore, we must find new markets for our produce, new occupation for our capital, new work for our labor. And so, while we did not need the territory taken during the past century at the time it was acquired, we do need what we have taken in 1898, and we need it now. . . . The trade of these islands, developed as we will develop it, will set every reaper in the Republic singing, every furnace spouting the flames of industry. . . .

Fellow-Americans, we are God's chosen people. . . . His power directed Dewey in the east, and He delivered the Spanish fleet into our hands on Liberty's natal day as He delivered the # elder Armada into the hands of our English sires two centuries ago. . . . We cannot retreat from any soil where Providence has unfurled our banner; it is ours to save that soil for liberty and civilization. . . .

The acceptance of the idea in 1898 and 1899 that the United States should own colonies marked a sharp break with the past. Whether or not the idea was right aroused among Americans a penetrating public discussion. Many believed that in acquiring an empire, the United States would be denying to captive peoples the sacred right of self-government. Others were convinced that annexing overseas possessions was an obligation the nation must undertake joyfully. This selection is from a speech entitled "The March of the Flag," delivered by Albert J. Beveridge in 1898, the year before he was elected to the Senate from Indiana. Only thirty-five years old at the time he spoke these words, Beveridge reflects the almost lyrical enthusiasm of the imperialists of his generation.

Compare the quotation from Beveridge with the one from O'Sullivan, pp. 230-231. What similarity can be detected?

#Beveridge is referring to the destruction of the Spanish fleet, which actually took place on July 3, not July 4, 1898. (Students should know that "natal day" means "birthday.")

Kennedy Galleries

Electioneering in an American town about the turn of the century. At the right a candidate—possibly for a federal post—presents the issues as he sees them in an effort to win office. International questions were only very rarely subjects for public dispute—or even discussion. The crowd of absorbed listeners here consists mainly of men because women did not yet have the vote. Observe the hitching posts and note the buggies and wagons that have brought individuals to an occasion of engrossing interest—a political rally.

The large building the people have crowded around may be the town's hotel.

#But recall that before the Civil War they had been interested in obtaining Canada and Cuba.
See p. 90, pp. 157-158, and p. 168. Two attempts to overcome Canada had failed.

THE UNITED STATES DRAWS THE SWORD AGAINST SPAIN

In the years following the Civil War, the American people showed little interest in owning colonies. But by the beginning of the 1890's, there were strong indications that this indifference was vanishing. Before the decade was over, a startling shift in opinion had taken place. Several developments explain this extraordinary about-face.

THE VOICES OF EXPANSION

In the first place, a new era of overseas expansion by the powers of western Europe had been under way since the 1870's. Competing with one another for raw materials and markets, these countries acquired political control of much of Asia and Africa and most of the islands in the Pacific.

Many Americans felt that they owed it to themselves to join in the competition. Said Henry Cabot Lodge, a leader among the expansionists, "As one of the great nations of the world, the United States must not fall out of the line of march."

Second, the campaign of 1896 had aroused in some Americans a deep-seated fear of radicalism. They believed that if national attention could be turned from domestic problems to foreign affairs, "dangerous ideas" would disappear. Third, an extraordinary group of public figures who expressed altered American ideals and purposes had risen to prominence on the national scene.

"Duty and destiny." John Fiske, a historian, and Josiah Strong, a Congregationalist minister, were two of the best known of these new spokesmen. Their writings had an enthusiastic reception.

Both Fiske and Strong had been impressed by the idea that among all living things there is a ceaseless "struggle for existence." Both men had come to the conclusion that the principle of the "survival of the fittest," which biologists claimed to have found in the world of nature, applied also to man's political world.

In the international struggle for existence, Fiske and Strong asserted, the English-speaking peoples had immense intellectual and technological advantages. In consequence, Fiske predicted: ". . . it is 'destined' that every land on the earth's surface that is not already the seat of an old civilization shall become English in its language, in its religion, in its political habits and traditions. . . ."

In 1885, in a widely read book called *Our Country,* Strong wrote of his conviction that the United States was destined to dominate other peoples. The American nation had inherited from the English, he maintained, the energy and perseverance it would require "to spread itself over the earth." Other writers before long added to this idea the notion that America had a divine obligation to hasten the fulfillment of its destiny as a colonizing power.

One of the most influential of the men who accepted this belief was a professor at Columbia University, John W. Burgess. He argued that Americans should seek colonies in order to train people in the art of self-government. A failure to do so, he asserted, "is . . . not only mistaken policy, but disregard of duty."

Naval necessity. Another person who strongly advocated possessing colonies was Navy Captain Alfred Thayer Mahan. As a teacher and writer he declared that overseas imperialism had become necessary for Americans because they had reached the limit of expansion on land.

"In our infancy," Mahan wrote, "we bordered upon the Atlantic only; our youth carried our boundary to the Gulf of Mexico; today maturity sees us upon the Pacific." He insisted, "Whether they will it or no, Americans must now begin to look outward." For this expansion, he said, the United States would require ships and coaling stations and naval bases. Without the bases the vessels would be "like land birds, unable to fly far from their own shores."

This appeal to national pride was especially attractive in the 1890's, when most Americans were already expecting their country to be greater and more powerful than before. Besides, they were ready to heed the warning implied in

##Refer to Darwin's idea about the "survival of the fittest" among the lower forms of life (p. 334) and to the application of his idea to the business world. Discuss Fiske and Strong.

the report of the Bureau of the Census in 1890 that America's land frontier was at last gone.* Many accepted the idea that national suffocation would result if the country's territorial growth could not continue. It was high time, they reasoned, to think of expanding beyond the continental borders.

Theodore Roosevelt and his circle. Among men in politics who spoke out for colonies, the most powerful were Theodore Roosevelt, of New York, and two associates—Senator Henry # Cabot Lodge, of Massachusetts, and John Hay, a career diplomat. Looking upon themselves as gentlemen-politicians, they were disturbed, they said, by both the businessman's single-minded concern with making money and the spoilsman's careless disregard of public honor. They selected themselves to rescue the people of America from both evils. They would, they said constantly, direct attention toward noble national goals. High on the list were war and the acquisition of colonies.

The temper of the times. The generation of Americans for which these expansionists believed they spoke had not seen a war of its own. Furthermore, the Civil War veterans were disappearing from the scene, and with them the vivid recollections of war's horrors. Finally, the writings of Rudyard Kipling, with all their stirring emphasis upon the glories of conquest, were becoming popular. Roosevelt was a friend of Kipling's and helped popularize his writings in this country.

THE JINGO SPIRIT

In the 1890's a fighting spirit was acceptable to many Americans, who were bored by what they considered the dull routine of an industrial society. Ready for some kind of public excitement, they found it in being jingoes†—that is, in being the advocates of an aggressive foreign policy.

---

* The superintendent of the census had declared: "Up to and including 1880 the country had a frontier of settlement, but at present the unsettled area has been so broken into by isolated bodies of settlement that there can hardly be said to be a frontier line."

† "Jingo" is a word that comes from an English music-hall tune of the 1870's—testimony to the fact that overheated patriotism was not found in the United States alone.

Jingoism made it easy to raise love of country to war pitch and to persuade diplomats that points of national honor and pride were in themselves important concerns. Stephen Decatur, the American naval commander, had once said, "Our country, right or wrong." Now the jingo Albert Beveridge was saying in addition, "Fellow-Americans, we are God's chosen people."

Focus on Cuba. American jingoes found an ideal outlet in the United States' interest in Cuba. There on the country's doorstep was a Spanish possession in which Americans had invested between forty and fifty million dollars—chiefly in tobacco and sugar plantations and in manganese and iron mines. American trade with the island amounted to $100,000,000 annually.

Some Cubans are shown as starving.

Newspapers and magazines stirred American interest in Cuba by showing pictures representing Cubans like this.

Harper's Weekly, April 2, 1898

Furthermore, the misery of the Cuban people under the rule of the Spanish enabled Americans to meet other needs. Anxious about urban problems and various significant changes in the country as the nineteenth century neared its end, Americans seemed to require an outlet for their pent-up emotions. One alternative was to show special sympathy to other sufferers, as scared people sometimes do; another was to act tough, as insecure people often do. Toward Cuba Americans could be both warm-hearted do-gooders and cold-eyed bullies.

The movement to acquire Cuba (see page 267) had died down temporarily after the completion of the Union Pacific Railroad in 1869. The existence of this new railroad postponed the building of a canal across the Isthmus of Panama, for which the island of Cuba was to have been an important defense base. But the island continued to fascinate people in the United States. They could see that the government of Spain was weak and apparently incapable of ruling Cuba humanely or well.

Insurrection on the island, which had flared up from time to time for many years, reached a climax in 1873 in the *Virginius* affair. The *Virginius,* a vessel owned by Cubans and illegally flying the Stars and Stripes, was engaged in carrying arms to Cuba. A Spanish naval vessel captured it on October 31, 1873, and the passengers and crew were taken. After a quick court-martial in Cuba, fifty-three people, including Americans and Englishmen, were executed.

Despite the questionable activities of the vessel, in the United States there was bold talk of war to defend the honor of the American flag. But peace held. The depression of 1873 had

The name of Secretary of State Hamilton Fish appears under "U.S. Grant." He influenced Grant.

A cartoon in 1870 shows Cuba as begging to enter the United States, while pitiless Senators look on.

Historical Pictures Service

Uncle Sam is glaring at the "mad Spanish bull" in Cuba, but President Grant restrains him—a cartoon of 1873.

Harper's Weekly, November 29, 1873 (Historical Pictures Service)

just begun, and the United States had no navy to speak of with which to wage war against a power like Spain. Spain later paid indemnities to the families of the Americans who had been executed.

Newspaper sensationalism. By the 1890's conditions had changed. The country now had a large and growing navy. The construction of a modern steel fleet—begun in 1883 under President Arthur and expanded under Cleveland—had made the United States a leading power on the seas.

Finally, the sensational American newspapers, a new development of this period, would surely turn the slightest incident into a national "cause." Aided by the invention of the Linotype machine and the introduction of cheap and quick methods of reproducing pictures, the daily newspaper was now more widely read than ever before.‡ Among New York newspapers, the chief rivals were Joseph Pulitzer's *World* and William Randolph Hearst's *Journal*. Their competition for readers resulted in memorable "circulation wars."

"CUBA LIBRE!"

The outbreak of a new Cuban insurrection in 1895 provided just the right kind of story for the sensational papers, and they made the most of it. Gradually worsening economic conditions had made Cuba ripe for trouble. First, it had been badly affected by the depression of 1893. Then the tariff of 1894 had placed such a high duty on raw sugar that Cuba's market in the United States was greatly reduced.

The Cuban revolutionaries who rose against Spanish rule in 1895 deep down did not believe they could oust the mother country from the island. But they hoped to win concessions by causing so much damage that the island's plantations and trade would be paralyzed.

\# Though the revolutionaries destroyed property recklessly, they aroused genuine sympathy among many Americans, who admired their strong desire for independence, political sta-

‡ Not unimportant was the introduction of the comic section. The *Journal* in New York declared of this feature that its color "makes the rainbow look like a lead pipe."

bility, and self-government. Further, their shout—"Cuba Libre!"—reminded many Americans of their own cry for liberty in 1776.

Some people who had been frightened by the rise in the United States of what they regarded as radicalism hoped that American interest in "a free Cuba" would turn attention from "free silver." Americans, therefore, tended to favor the *insurrectos*—as the Cuban rebels were called—who were supplied with arms that compatriots shipped from United States ports.

Reconcentration. In February, 1896, Spain sent a new commander to the strife-torn island. He was General Valeriano Weyler—quickly nicknamed "the Butcher" by the American press. His policy of *reconcentration* called for herding the whole rural population of large parts of central and western Cuba into cities and towns. The aim was to deprive the *insurrectos* of their source of food—and of recruits.

The *reconcentration* camps, ringed by trenches and barbed wire, were carefully guarded. Inadequate food and sanitation facilities caused a fearful loss of life. It is possible that as many as 200,000 of the 1,600,000 people who had been reconcentrated had died by the beginning of 1898.

The response of Americans. Always strongly attracted to humanitarian causes, Americans were scandalized by these cruelties so close to their own shores. Yet they were not ready to intervene in order to put a stop to them.

Cleveland had said flatly, "I will not mobilize the army," and McKinley had promised Carl Schurz that there would be "no jingo nonsense under my administration." Private organizations, to be sure, raised money for Cuban relief. The prospects for peace brightened noticeably after McKinley came to office in 1897. The Spanish prime minister who had ## sent Weyler to Cuba was assassinated; the new prime minister removed Weyler and began a policy that was confidently expected to bring peace to the troubled island.

Journalistic meddling. If American newspapers had now held their fire, the settlement of difficulties in Cuba might have proceeded in an orderly fashion. But the papers had too large

471

Punch, April 16, 1898

"President McKinley and the Jingo Bird"—a British view of McKinley's struggle to stay out of war. Notice how the cartoonist combined two symbols of the United States--eagle, stars and stripes.

and interested a reading public, and they would not remain quiet about Spanish "atrocities." Hearst had stirred up the women of the country by presenting the touching story of Evangelina Cisneros. This attractive señorita, who had been imprisoned in Havana for *insurrecto* activities, was described in the *Journal* as a girl whose sole crime had been to resist the advances of a # Spanish officer.

The aged Mrs. Jefferson Davis was persuaded to write to the queen regent of Spain for Evangelina's release.§ Also, Mrs. Julia Ward Howe, the honored composer of "The Battle Hymn of the Republic," petitioned Pope Leo XIII to influence the Spanish.

§ A regent rules in behalf of a monarch unable to rule for himself. Since the Spanish king, Alfonso XIII, was only twelve years old, his mother, Maria Christina, was exercising power until he should come of age.

At last one of the *Journal's* adventurous reporters was sent to Cuba to rescue the girl. He snatched her out of the window of her cell by reaching down from a next-door rooftop. The headline of his paper boasted: "An American Newspaper Accomplishes at a Single Stroke What the Best Efforts of Diplomacy Failed Utterly to Bring About in Many Months." Congratulations poured in on the *Journal,* and the governor of Missouri suggested to Hearst that he send 500 reporters to Cuba and liberate the ## whole island!

Rioting in Havana. The new Spanish policy could not quiet this kind of journalism, which was attracting the wide-eyed attention of millions of readers daily. The Cubans, meanwhile, had been granted a considerable amount of self-government, but now the *insurrectos* wanted nothing less than complete independence.

##Hearst later asked permission of the United States government to sail his own yacht to Cuba in order to take part in the war there. The request was turned down.

Early in 1898 riots broke out again in Havana. Americans generally assumed that renewed violence in Cuba would once more endanger American lives and property. The United States sent the second-class battleship *Maine* to Cuban waters.

DeLôme's indiscretion. The newspapers kept the pot boiling briskly. On February 9, 1898, the New York *Journal* printed a letter a Cuban rebel had illegally intercepted in the Havana post office. The letter had been sent to a friend by the Spanish minister at Washington, Dupuy deLôme. Its publication created a sensation; in it the minister had described McKinley as "weak and a bidder for the admiration of the crowd." This was an indiscreet and unfair remark he should not have put to paper—and the Department of State felt obliged to demand his recall. The *Journal* published a cartoon showing an outraged Uncle Sam snarling to the crestfallen Spaniard, "Git!"

A significant explosion. Six days after the publication of the deLôme letter, an even more dramatic event occurred: the *Maine* blew up in Havana Harbor, causing the loss of 260 American lives. The cause of the explosion will probably never be known. After a full investigation, a board of inquiry concluded it had been caused by an underwater mine which touched off the vessel's own powder magazines. Certainly it would have been sheer folly for the Spanish to destroy the *Maine* just at the moment when they believed their policy would succeed in quieting Cuba.

When the disaster occurred, both McKinley and the Secretary of the Navy declared it had resulted from an accidental explosion aboard the ship. Hearst's *Journal,* however, had drawn another conclusion, shouting in headlines: "The warship *Maine* was split in two by an enemy's secret infernal machine." The slogan "Remember the *Maine!*" was quickly heard everywhere.

The active Assistant Secretary. Behind the scenes jingoes were putting pressure on President McKinley to go to war. The most active of them was Theodore Roosevelt, the Assistant Secretary of the Navy. His energy was boundless, and the Secretary of the Navy, John D. Long,

There has been a supposition that Cubans sank it, hoping the Spanish would be blamed.

Uncle Sam says, "It's a good rule, when you're mad, to count twenty before you speak, but by Jingo! I'm up to seventeen now!"

Roosevelt was thirty-nine years of age.

Roosevelt poses for a picture at his desk in Washington in the Department of the Navy. Notice the model ship.

was always afraid that "T. R." would commit some kind of rash act.

On February 25 Long wearily went home for a few hours' rest. With Long away, the Assistant Secretary acted as if he were responsible for the Department of the Navy. The next day Long wrote of Roosevelt in his diary, "He seems to be thoroughly loyal, but the very devil seemed to possess him yesterday afternoon."

What had the Assistant Secretary done? Immediately after Long had departed, Roosevelt had sent for Senator Lodge, and the two of them had taken bold action. They had redistributed the vessels of the fleet, placed orders for ammunition, and sent "messages to Congress for immediate legislation authorizing the enlistment of an unlimited number of seamen."

Long found out later that Roosevelt had also sent a cable to Commodore George Dewey, commander of the Pacific fleet at Hong Kong. Dewey was instructed to begin operations against the Philippines in case war with Spain broke out. Long's note of protest to his Assistant Secretary was pathetic: ". . . my intention was to have you look after the routine of the office while I got a quiet day off."

Sentiment for peace. Expansionists like Roosevelt refused to believe that McKinley had enough courage to go to war. Roosevelt once said the President had "no more back bone than a chocolate eclair." But the President was sincerely devoted to peace because he remembered with horror what he had seen as a soldier in the Civil War. He had told Cleveland just before taking office: "If I can only go out of office . . . with the knowledge that I have done what lay in my power to avert this terrible calamity [war] . . . I shall be the happiest man in the world."

Moreover, businessmen who had supported McKinley earnestly in 1896 were very eager to avoid war. The reasons were apparent: the nation had recently endured the terrible depression of 1893. Scarcely had recovery set in when the silver scare discouraged business improvement. Now the silver issue was ended, and the thought of war was about as welcome to most businessmen as a cloudburst at a picnic.

Pressure on the President. McKinley's peaceful intentions were subjected to an attack from the "yellow press."|| The newspapers insisted that the United States had a humanitarian as well as a patriotic justification for intervening.

The *New York Sun* declared: ". . . the cry of 'hurry' which comes to us alike from the heroism and the misery of Cuba is echoed by every State of the Union." The religious newspapers were also actively supporting war. Said one: "And if it be the will of Almighty God, that by war the last trace of this inhumanity of man to man shall be swept away from this Western hemisphere, let it come!"

Spending many a sleepless night, McKinley ## searched his soul to its depths. Roosevelt was intensely irritated by what he considered the President's unnecessary delay. He told a friend one night, as he pointed scornfully toward the White House, "He has prepared *two* messages, one for war and one for peace, and doesn't know which one to send in!"

The Fifty-Million Bill. Despite the most peaceful intentions, McKinley feared that if he did not ask for war, Congress would proceed to exercise its constitutional power to declare it anyway. He called the chairman of the House Appropriations Committee and said to him: "I must have money to get ready for war. I am doing everything possible to prevent war, but it must come and we are not prepared for war." He requested fifty million dollars "for national defense." The bill providing the funds passed Congress unanimously on March 9, 1898.

News from Madrid. The reaction to the bill in Madrid was reported by the United States minister there: it "has not excited the Spaniards—it has stunned them." Behind the scenes the President's policy had been to attempt to obtain a settlement of the outstanding issues without resorting to force.

The Spanish government was now in a terrible predicament. If it did *not* give Cuba the independence that the United States had declared would be the only satisfactory solution,

---

|| This is a phrase applied to the sensational journalism of this period. It is derived from the popular comic strip "The Yellow Kid," which appeared in the Sunday *New York World.*

##McKinley's desire for peace made him decidedly unpopular in many places. Mention again how difficult it is to face the criticism that follows when a person takes an unpopular stand.

it would have to face a war with the United
States. If it *did* free Cuba, the government
would be embarrassed and the monarchy itself
might possibly fall.

In the face of this awful problem, the Spanish went as far as they could without actually
agreeing to give Cuba its freedom. They were
willing even to submit the question of the
Maine's explosion to arbitration in order to fix
responsibility for the tragedy.

On April 9 Spain announced an armistice in
the Cuban fighting. Thereupon, the United
States minister in Spain reported to the President: "I hope that nothing will now be done to
humiliate Spain, as I am satisfied that the present Government is going, and is loyally ready
to go, as fast and as far as it can." In Washington the ambassadors of six European powers
had called on McKinley to halt the preparations
for war.

The declaration of war. Nothing came of this
move. On April 11 McKinley's message went
to Congress. It contained the information that
Spain had yielded on the major Cuban issues.
Nevertheless, it asked for war—"in the name of
humanity, in the name of civilization, in behalf
of endangered American interests which give
us the right and the duty to speak and to
act. . . ."

Congress quickly passed a war resolution. It
provided for the recognition of Cuba's independence, and it authorized the use of force to
drive the Spanish from the island. In an amendment to the resolution—the Teller Amendment
—Congress denied any intention of keeping
Cuba once the fighting was over. The Teller
Amendment pledged the United States "to leave
the government and control of the Island to its
people."

FIGHTING IN THE TROPICS

The war with Spain proved to be short and—
measured in lives and dollars—comparatively
inexpensive. The modern American navy, which
was by now in a high state of preparedness,
was able to outmatch Spain's. The army of
about 30,000 men and officers, on the other
hand, was ill equipped and untrained for a war

Historical Pictures Service
The Senate hears a presidential message about Cuba.

After war began—Uncle Sam "leads against the foe."
Historical Pictures Service

#Assistant Secretary of the Navy Roosevelt had seen to it that the United States Navy was in fighting readiness. Spain's navy, on the other hand, was totally unprepared for the war. Emphasize that fighting broke out in an Asian location, the first fighting Americans had done in Asia.

WAR IN THE PHILIPPINES, 1898
0 50 100 150 miles
Surrender of Manila Aug. 13, 1898
Manila Bay
Manila
CORREGIDOR
Battle of Manila Bay May 1, 1898
DEWEY
20°N.
120°E.
125°E.
SOUTH CHINA SEA
LUZON
Manila
DEWEY FROM HONG KONG
PHILIPPINE SEA
15°N.
MINDORO
SAMAR
PANAY
LEYTE
PALAWAN
NEGROS
BOHOL
10°N.
SULU SEA
MINDANAO
5°N.

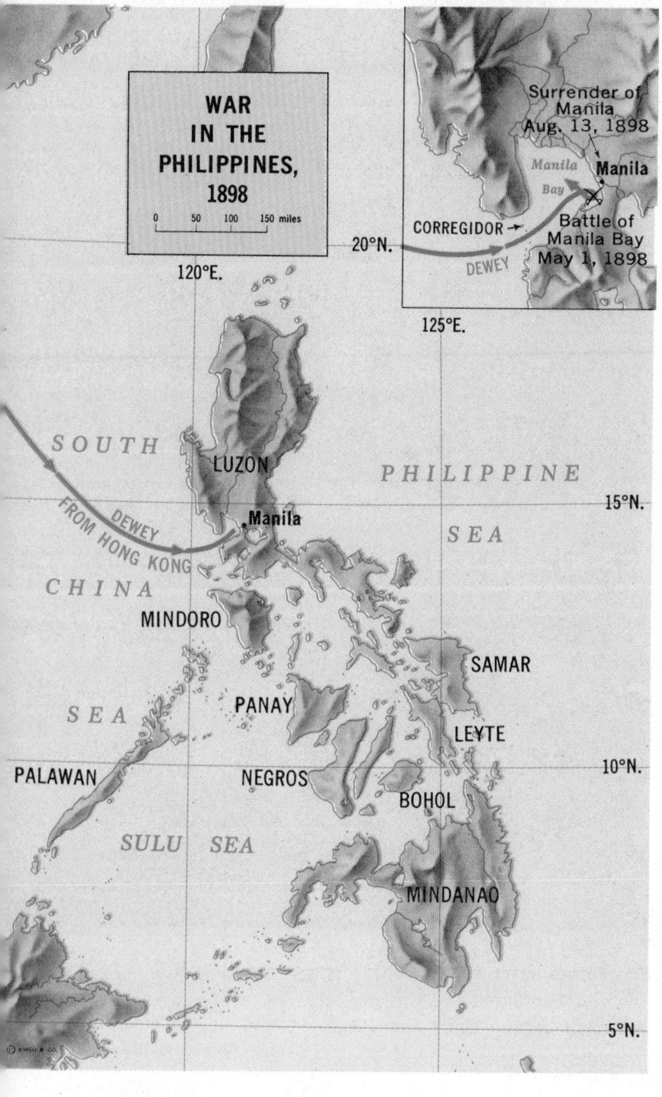

Where do the Philippines lie in relation to the United States? In relation to China? See pages 758–759.

(Southwest of America, southeast of China.)

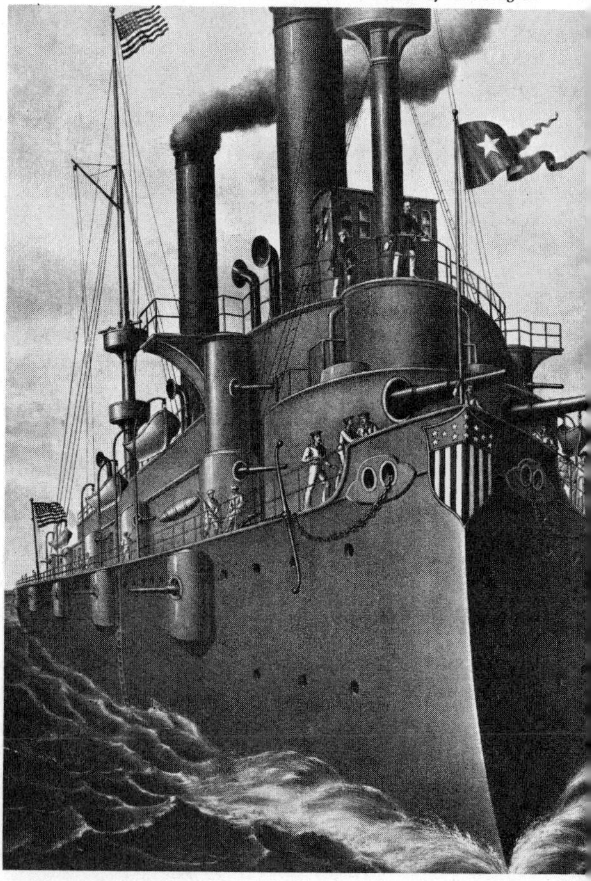

in the tropics. Congress quickly authorized increasing the regular army to 60,000 men and enlisting 200,000 volunteers.

Dewey at Manila. The first military action of the Spanish-American War came in the Pacific. Commodore Dewey, who was in command there, followed the instructions he had received from Roosevelt in February to commence operations against the Philippine Islands. Early on # the morning of May 1, Dewey sailed into Manila Bay and opened fire on the Spanish squadron lined up there. Before noon the entire Spanish naval force of ten ships had been sunk or destroyed, and only eight Americans had been even slightly wounded.

Dewey held Manila Bay while he awaited an army unit to capture the city of Manila itself. Before the end of July, a force of slightly under 11,000 soldiers arrived, led by General Wesley Merritt. By the middle of August, after light resistance, the Spanish troops had surrendered to the Americans and to the Filipino guerrillas ## led by Emilio Aguinaldo.

Sampson and Schley in the Caribbean. Meanwhile, the war against Spain also went forward in the Caribbean. The blockading of Cuba was assigned to Rear Admiral William T. Sampson

Compare this ship with those seen on p. 159.

The *Olympia*, seen here, led the American attack on the Philippines. In instructing the captain, Dewey said simply, "You may fire when you are ready, Gridley."

Library of Congress

 ##Aguinaldo fought for the independence of the Philippines. When he realized that the United States later did not intend to give them their freedom, he led a revolt against it.

A doctor examines a volunteer for service in the Spanish-American War, and other young men await their turns.

In contrast to the United States Navy, the army was poorly equipped to undertake a war.

The Battle of Manila, as depicted by an artist of the time. The *Olympia*, in the forefront, followed by the other American ships—the *Raleigh*, the *Baltimore*, and the *Boston* —fire on the Spanish ships (*left background*).

In the Battle of Manila, the Spanish ships numbered ten. When the battle ended seven hours after it began, the Spanish ships had been destroyed or captured. Americans ships were unhurt. **477**

WAR IN CUBA, 1898

0   50   100   150 miles

What did the army seek to do in the war? The navy?

and Commodore Winfield Scott Schley. A delay in Schley's departure from Key West, Florida, enabled a Spanish fleet under Admiral Pascual Cervera to arrive from African waters and sail into the harbor of Santiago de Cuba on May 19.

Not until May 28 did Schley's unit arrive in Cuban waters. But it had come in time to bottle up the Spanish ships by patrolling the waters outside the harbor. This was the situation when, on June 1, Admiral Sampson took over the command of the blockading squadron.

The Rough Riders. By this time an expeditionary force of 17,000 regulars and volunteers was assembled at Tampa, Florida, under General William Shafter, preparing to invade Cuba. Included among them were the Rough Riders—the 1st United States Volunteer Cavalry Regiment—under the command of Colonel Leonard Wood and the young Lieutenant Colonel Theodore Roosevelt.

On June 14 the troops, including the Rough

Below right: The Rough Riders did not ride in their assault on San Juan Hill. They were afoot.

Roosevelt the Rough Rider in an uncompromising pose.

Theodore Roosevelt Association

The charge up San Juan Hill, a focus of Spanish defense.

Library of Congress

Riders, sailed for Santiago. Arriving just before the end of the month, the men immediately went into action in an assault on the city. After a daylong struggle the fortified village of El Caney fell on July 1, and the Rough Riders, led by Roosevelt, took San Juan Hill.# Having captured the heights dominating the city of Santiago, the American forces were able to bring the city, and, above all, the Spanish fleet, under direct fire from strategic artillery positions.

Cervera's lost gamble. For this reason, Admiral Cervera, under orders not to surrender his fleet, decided on the morning of July 3 to run Sampson's blockade and escape into the open sea. It

---

A friend wrote to Mrs. Roosevelt of this now-famous engagement: "No hunting trip so far has ever equalled it in Theodore's eyes." Roosevelt fought with a bravado that was equal to his warlike behavior before the war. Barely able to see without his eyeglasses, he went into battle with a dozen pairs on his person—several sewed to the lining of his hat—in case a few should get broken or be shot off!

was a dangerous gamble, and Cervera lost it. In a battle that lasted four hours, the technical superiority of the American fleet quickly asserted itself, and the Spanish force was utterly destroyed.

The war was now practically over, and the United States prepared for a thrilling Independence Day celebration. Sampson cabled Washington: "The fleet under my command offers the nation as a Fourth of July present the whole of Cervera's fleet." The same day a small detachment from the Philippines landed on Wake Island (see the map on page 483), which the United States formally occupied in 1899. Before July was over, an American force commanded by General Nelson A. Miles had taken the island of Puerto Rico, meeting only weak Spanish resistance. On July 18, recognizing now that its military and naval situations were hopeless, Spain asked France to help negotiate an armistice.

Some American soldiers found the weather too hot for uniforms. Observe the balloon.

American forces surround and overcome the Spaniards guarding some of the fortifications of Santiago.

Chromolithograph by Kurz and Allison, 1898 (Chicago Historical Society)

Recall the situation of Spain in earlier days. What relations had Americans had with the Spanish? **479**
(After some difficulty, they had bought Florida from Spain.)

Review the events leading to the Spanish-American War and the main military or naval engagements. How long did the war last? (From April 30 to July 18, 1898.)

Sum and Substance

1. What change in American public opinion was apparent in 1890? Give three explanations of the change. 2. Identify four spokesmen for imperialism, and state their views. 3. Account for American interest in Cuba. 4. Give the facts about the *Virginius* affair. 5. What conditions helped cause the Cuban revolt in 1895? How did Spain respond? 6. What events and pressures led the United States to declare war on Spain? 7. Describe the campaigns of the war. 8. What questions arose at the end of the fighting?

Observe the electric lights and the telephones (on desk by window). Why would globes have been useful? News was received by means of the telegraph as well as by the telephone.

President McKinley in his war room in the White House receives news about the course of the struggle. His secretary—standing before the map—uses small flags to pinpoint the locations of the activities.

AMERICA ENCOUNTERS THE OBLIGATIONS OF POWER

The victory over Spain made the United States one of the great world powers. Europeans understood this metamorphosis in the American position even before the makers of United States foreign policy did. A few years after the new century opened, a French politician explained the altered situation in this way: "When a people have . . . interests everywhere, they are called upon to involve themselves in everything. . . . The United States intervenes thus in the affairs of the universe. . . . It is seated at the table where the great game is played, and it cannot leave it."

MAKING PEACE

The first question the "new" United States faced was how to dispose of the conquered territories. The most important of the Spanish island possessions unquestionably were the Philippines. McKinley admitted that when the war began, he could not have said within 2000 miles where they were located. Now he must decide whether to keep them or not.

Businessmen, who early in 1898 had approved the war only hesitantly, were a few months later looking with pleasure upon America's presence in Manila. It seemed to them that Manila, sitting astride the road to China, was necessary to the United States if Americans were to have easy access to the China market. By the middle of 1898, businessmen were becoming as outspoken in demanding colonies as the jingoes were. In the opening days of the war, the United States had eagerly annexed Hawaii. Acquiring colonies seemed cheaper than had been feared and easier than had been expected.

Negotiations. When hostilities ended in August, the outline of peace terms was already clear. Spain would give up Cuba, Puerto Rico, and a Pacific island to be named later (it proved to be Guam), which would be ceded to the United States. Until a decision was reached concerning the Philippine Islands, America would hold "the city, bay, and harbor of Manila." McKinley chose five commissioners to go to Paris to represent the United States in the negotiations, which were to begin on October 1, 1898.

The Philippines question. It was the beginning of November before the peace conference took up the knotty question of what to do with the Philippines. Many Americans believed that the United States could not give the islands independence without leaving them open to seizure by the Japanese and Germans, who were already gazing covetously at them. A New York businessmen's paper dramatically declared that for the United States to give up the islands would be "an act of inconceivable folly in the face of our imperative future necessities for a basis of naval and military force on the western shores of the Pacific."

Refer students to the books on McKinley, p. 557.

McKinley, as he looked in the trying time when he was deciding what to do with the Spanish islands.

Historical Pictures Service

McKinley's decision. What would the nation finally do? McKinley told a religious group which visited him that he had "walked the floor of the White House night after night until midnight," trying to make up his mind. "I went down on my knees and prayed Almighty God for light and guidance more than one night." Finally, "one night late" he decided that the United States must take all of the islands "to educate the Filipinos, and uplift and civilize and Christianize [most were already Christian] them, and by God's grace do the very best we could by them, as our fellow men for whom Christ also died." Said he, "And then I went to bed, and went to sleep and slept soundly."

The treaty terms. The Treaty of Paris that was signed on December 10, 1898, provided that Spain free Cuba and cede the Philippines, Guam, and Puerto Rico to the United States. The United States agreed to pay $20,000,000 to Spain for the Philippines.

The struggle over imperialism. Persuading the Senate to ratify the Treaty of Paris proved difficult.

For, in becoming an imperial country, the United States was straining the cherished principles of the Declaration of Independence. Anti-imperialists maintained that any denial of liberty to others made Americans look like hypocrites in the eyes of the whole world. Not all anti-imperialists were noble in motive: some, out of prejudice, wished to avoid bringing under the flag more people of nonwhite races.

Imperialists, on the other hand, agreed with the sentiment expressed by Theodore Roosevelt: "I have scant patience with those who make a pretense of humanitarianism to hide and cover their timidity, and who talk insincerely about 'liberty' and the 'consent of the governed' in order to excuse . . . their unwillingness to play the part of men." Some imperialists believed that humanitarianism could be served best by occupying the islands. Said one Republican imperialist bluntly, "We come as ministering angels. . . ."

Few questions in American history have divided the nation so deeply. Americans were in

The dignitaries gravely look on as the peace treaty is signed.

The peace treaty officially ending the Spanish-American War is signed in Washington. McKinley stands at the head of the table. Observe the large globe. The inkstands were later made obsolete by the fountain pen.

Chicago Historical Society

Answers to questions in map caption: Alaska was gained in the period of reconstruction directly after the Civil War. The same is true of Midway. The Philippines, Guam, Hawaii, American Samoa, and Puerto Rico were acquired in the age of expansion at the end of the 1800's.

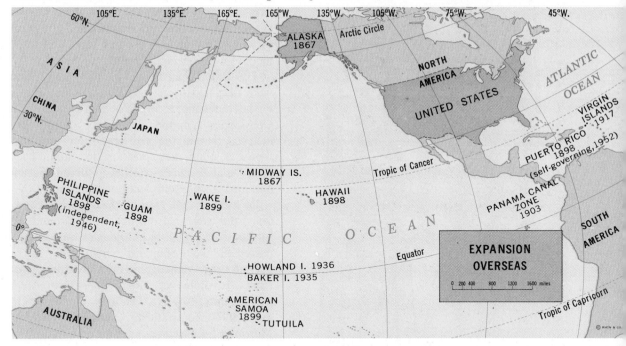

In what period did the United States gain each of the possessions shown here? Which were acquired without war?

In what latitudes do most of them lie? Which are no longer "possessions"? Why?

The Virgin Islands were acquired in the period of the First World War, and Howland and Baker islands during the Great Depression. Most lie in the low latitudes.

The impressive naval parade in honor of Dewey at New York in 1899. The *Olympia* is again in the lead. Admiring fellow Americans contributed money to buy the "hero of Manila" a house in Washington.

After the war, the position of Admiral of the Navy was created by Congress to honor Dewey. Consequently, he is known as "Admiral Dewey," though he was not an admiral during the war.

Harper's Weekly, August 11, 1900

A Republican magazine published this cartoon when the G.O.P. counted on Bryan and his party to abandon free silver and campaign against imperialism.

Bryan fooled the Republicans.

a position to bestow on other peoples what they considered their proudest national heritage: political independence. But they had to decide whether they would serve themselves better by giving freedom to the former Spanish possessions or by keeping them as colonies in defiance of one of the best American traditions.

This important question never became a clear-cut partisan matter. On either side of the argument there was a great variety of people— gold advocates and free-silver men, Republicans and Democrats, labor leaders and university presidents, businessmen and artists. The Senate settled the issue for the time being in February, 1899, ratifying the treaty by a margin of only two votes. The United States had become a power with an empire.

Political consequences. The following year, the Democrats tried to make imperialism the issue in the presidential election. They named Wil-

#In the two years between 1898 and 1900, criticism of imperialism cooled and the issue died.

liam Jennings Bryan to carry their banner again. The Republicans renominated President McKinley and chose Theodore Roosevelt to be their vice-presidential candidate.

The Republican bosses in New York State were delighted to get the Rough Rider out of the governorship, to which he had been elected. Considering him too difficult to control, they believed that in the vice-presidency they had found a blind-alley position for him. They hoped that there any further ambitions he entertained for himself would be squelched.

The issues of 1900. Despite the advance indications, the campaign did not center around the subject of imperialism. Although Congress had passed the Gold Standard Act in 1900, Bryan insisted upon campaigning on a free-silver platform. Advocates of sound money who were anti-imperialists—like Andrew Carnegie, to mention one outstanding example—voted for McKinley because they were afraid of the Democrats' economic ideas.

During the campaign the Republicans tried to paint the Democrats as irresponsible people. Roosevelt said that Bryan's side had attracted "all the lunatics, all the idiots, all the knaves, all the cowards, and all the honest people who are slow-witted." Exclaimed former President Cleveland: "Bryanism and McKinleyism! What a choice for a patriotic American!"

Reelection for the Republicans. McKinley and Roosevelt gained a sweeping victory over Bryan's ticket, capturing the electoral college vote 292 to 155. The postwar prosperity and Bryan's "dangerous ideas" help to explain the Republican victory. It is impossible to say for sure, as the expansionists were now saying, that the Republican victory was an endorsement of imperialism.

THE OPEN-DOOR POLICY

Whether the public in fact approved of owning colonies or not, the United States now had a part to play in world affairs. Especially had the American role in the Pacific grown. By taking the Philippines, the country had obtained easier admission to what Americans had long regarded as the "fabulous China trade." More

##What is the danger of the kind of reasoning the expansionists did--that a Republican President had acquired territories, he was reelected, and therefore the people must favor imperialism?

The tremendous growth of industry that had begun before the war continued after it. The Niagara Falls plant was built in 1894, introducing hydroelectric power. The southern cotton mills steadily produced more cotton cloth, the meat-packing industry grew, and steel production rose.

UNCLE SAM'S BALANCE SHEET.

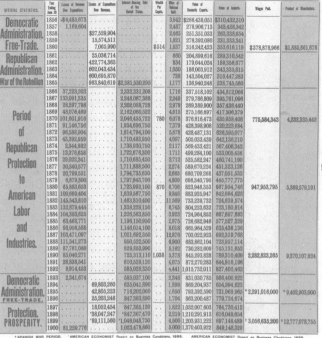

Official Statistics.	Year Ending June 30	Excess of Revenue Over Expenditures.	Excess of Expenditure Over Revenue.	Interest-Bearing Debt of the United States.	Wealth Per Capita.	Miles of Railroad Built.	Value of Domestic Exports.	Value of Imports.	Wages Paid.	Product of Manufactures.
Democratic Administration. Free-Trade.	1856	-$4,485,673				3,642	$266,438,051	$310,432,310		
	1857	1,109,604				2,487	278,906,713	348,428,342		
	1858		$27,529,904			2,465	251,351,033	263,338,654		
	1859		15,574,511			1,821	278,392,080	331,333,541		
	1860		7,065,990		$514	1,837	316,242,423	353,616,119	$378,878,966	$1,885,861,676
Republican Administration. War of the Rebellion.	1861		25,036,714			660	204,899,616	289,310,542		
	1862		422,774,363			834	179,644,024	189,356,677		
	1863		602,043,434			1,050	186,003,912	243,335,815		
	1864		600,695,870			738	143,504,027	316,447,283		
	1865		963,840,619	$2,381,530,295		1,177	136,940,248	238,745,580		
Period of Republican Protection to American Labor and Industries.	1866	37,223,203		2,332,331,208		1,716	337,518,102	434,812,066		
	1867	153,091,335		2,248,067,388		2,249	279,786,809	395,761,096		
	1868	28,297,798		2,202,088,728		2,979	269,389,900	357,436,440		
	1869	48,078,469		2,162,060,522		4,815	275,166,697	417,506,379		
	1870	101,601,916		2,046,455,722	780	6,078	376,616,473	435,958,408	775,584,343	4,232,325,442
	1871	91,146,756		1,934,696,750		7,379	428,398,908	520,223,684		
	1872	96,588,904		1,814,794,100		5,878	428,487,131	626,595,077		
	1873	43,392,959		1,710,483,950		4,097	505,033,439	642,136,210		
	1874	2,344,882		1,738,930,750		2,117	569,433,421	567,406,342		
	1875	13,376,658		1,722,676,300		1,711	499,284,100	533,005,436		
	1876	29,022,241		1,710,685,450		2,712	525,582,247	460,741,190		
	1877	30,340,577		1,711,888,500		2,274	589,670,224	451,323,126		
	1878	20,799,551		1,794,735,650		2,065	680,709,268	437,051,532		
	1879	6,879,300		1,797,643,700		4,809	698,340,790	445,777,775		
	1880	65,883,653		1,723,993,100	870	8,706	823,946,353	667,954,746	947,953,795	5,369,579,191
	1881	100,069,404		1,639,567,750		9,846	883,925,947	642,664,628		
	1882	145,543,810		1,463,810,400		11,569	733,239,732	724,639,574		
	1883	132,879,444		1,338,229,150		8,745	804,223,632	723,180,914		
	1884	104,393,625		1,226,563,850		3,923	724,964,852	667,697,693		
	1885	63,463,771		1,196,150,950		2,975	726,682,946	577,527,329		
	1886	93,956,588		1,146,014,100		8,018	665,964,529	635,436,136		
	1887	103,471,097		1,021,682,350		12,876	703,022,923	692,319,768		
	1888	111,341,273		950,522,500		4,900	683,862,104	723,957,114		
	1889	87,761,080		829,853,990		5,162	730,282,609	745,131,652		
	1890	85,040,271		725,313,110	1,038	5,378	845,293,828	789,310,409	2,282,823,265	9,370,107,624
	1891	26,838,541		610,529,120		4,075	872,270,283	844,916,196		
	1892	9,914,453		585,029,330		4,441	1,015,732,011	827,402,462		
Democratic Administration. FREE-TRADE.	1893	2,341,674		585,037,100		2,346	831,030,785	866,400,922		
	1894		69,803,260	635,041,890		1,899	869,204,937	654,994,622		
	1895		42,805,223	716,202,060		1,850	793,392,590	731,969,965	*2,291,016,000	*9,402,903,000
	1896		25,203,246	847,363,890		1,704	863,200,487	779,724,674		
Protection. PROSPERITY.	1897		18,052,454	847,365,130		1,822	1,032,007,603	764,730,412		
	1898		*38,047,247	*847,367,470		2,219	1,210,291,913	616,049,654		
	1899		*89,111,560	*1,046,048,750		4,500	1,203,931,222	697,148,489	*3,056,635,200	*12,777,078,755
	1900	61,229,776		1,023,478,800		5,000	1,370,403,922	849,148,329		

* SPANISH WAR PERIOD. 'AMERICAN ECONOMIST Report on Business Conditions, 1898. AMERICAN ECONOMIST Report on Business Conditions, 1899.

"Oh, those terrible times of 1857 and 1894! I pray that our people will not again vote for Free-Trade Calamity."

"Behold the splendid results of Protection under the Morrill, McKinley and Dingley Tariffs. Our people will surely continue McKinley Prosperity."

New-York Historical Society

This report—an argument for tariffs—was used in McKinley's campaign for reelection in 1900.

How did the Republicans take advantage of the prosperity as an argument for their tariffs?

A pro-McKinley cartoon published shortly before the election. Notice the labels on the cloth at the right.

Puck, September 9, 1900 (Library of Congress)

Harper's Weekly, November 18, 1899

A cartoon praising the open-door policy: Uncle Sam restrains European powers from warlike designs on China, saying, "I'm out for commerce, not conquest!"

John Bull alone tips his hat to us.

than ever before, the fate of China became an important concern of the United States.

The background. Just at the moment when the United States "arrived" in the western Pacific, changes within China made the outlook dark both for China and for the development of American commerce there. Defeated in a war with Japan in 1894–1895, China stood helpless against the aggression of France, Germany, and Russia—and of the new power in East Asia, Japan.

The British became deeply alarmed when these countries obtained political and economic concessions in the Chinese ports and their environs. Such grants of exclusive rights threatened the chance for the people of all countries to trade freely and equally in China. England advocated, therefore, equal commercial opportunity for all—rather than special privileges for a few. In a word, it wanted an *open-door policy* in China.

Going it alone. Americans had long believed that an open-door policy was the one most likely to bring peace and goodwill to the world. When the British asked Americans in 1898 to go along with them in a statement defending the open door in China, the offer reminded American statesmen somewhat of Canning's offer to Rush in 1823 (see page 168).

Again—as in President Monroe's time—the United States determined to follow a go-it-alone policy, in the belief that England would support the American position anyway. A joint declaration with England might have stirred up traditional anti-British feeling among the American people. This feeling had recently come to the fore again in the Venezuela crisis of 1895. Besides, what the United States was about to ask for conformed with American policy and did not appear to require the assistance of any other country.

John Hay's first note. The Secretary of State in 1899 was John Hay—a man of wide experience. At the age of twenty-two he had been Lincoln's assistant private secretary. Later, he had served in diplomatic posts in the important capitals of Europe—including London. He decided to send almost identical notes to England, Germany, Russia, France, Italy, and Japan, describing what is known as the open-door ## policy. Hay asked them for assurances that all countries would "enjoy perfect equality of treatment for their commerce and navigation" in the portions of China that some nations had carved out for themselves. Although several of the replies could hardly be called straightforward, Hay announced that all the countries had accepted the principle of the open door.

The Boxer Rebellion. On the occasion of the outbreak of the Boxer Rebellion in China in 1900, Hay had another opportunity to define American policy toward that country. The Boxers (so called because their symbol was a clenched fist) made up a secret, anti-Western military organization. With the aid of the dowager empress of China,** they had determined to drive foreigners out of China. In 1900, in a campaign

** A shrewd woman of sixty-six, Tzu Hsi was ruling in place of her nephew, whom she had deposed.

##Ask the students what motives the United States had in advancing the open-door policy. Do they think that the policy showed a certain idealism as well as an interest in protecting trade?

Americans in Peking under siege in the Boxer Rebellion.

United States troops bring help to the beleaguered city.

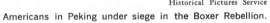

Peking is made up of walled cities, one of which is being scaled at the upper left.

A contemporary cartoonist's view of the rivalry between major powers for the destruction of the Chinese dragon.

Troops from various Western countries join in the drive to rescue their countrymen from the walled city of Peking. Here the outer wall of Peking is approached by troops that arrived from Tientsin.

of violence, they attacked Western missionaries and then seized Peking, the site of the foreign legations.

For a number of weeks there was widespread fear in the West that all foreigners in the Chinese city would be killed. The Boxers believed that they could win even if the Western powers should send a joint military expedition against them. John Hay knew, of course, that the Boxers could be quickly crushed. But he was afraid that European countries might make the sending of such an expedition an occasion for carving up China once and for all.

Hay's second note. The substance of Hay's conclusions on the subject was contained in a new note he sent to the principal powers in July, 1900. In it he declared that it was the policy of the United States to seek to preserve China's territorial unity. Moreover, he urged the other powers to follow a like policy in trying to solve the difficulties growing out of the rebellion.

The nations replied that they accepted Hay's position as a desirable one. Although they sent an expedition—in which about 2500 American

soldiers participated—to free the foreigners, they took only a money indemnity, not territory, for their troubles. The United States afterward gave back to China most of the American portion of the money.   #

The policy of the United States, therefore, had been clearly stated: the United States would preserve both the open door and the territorial integrity of China. However, the Americans made no military arrangements to defend these principles, and later, at great cost, they discovered that the omission had been a very serious mistake.   ##

Sum and Substance

1. What territory did the United States annex in the Spanish-American War? 2. Give the terms of the Treaty of Paris in 1898. 3. Name the issues in the presidential election of 1900. Who was elected? 4. What led to Hay's first note? Name and describe the policy he advocated. 5. What situation caused Hay's second note? What did it contain? 6. Sum up American policy concerning China.

488 #China used part of the American money to educate Chinese students in the United States.
##It can be seen now that the policy was partly idealistic but that it was not guaranteed.

THE SPOILS OF WAR TURN INTO THE BURDENS OF EMPIRE

While Americans were making known their place in the Pacific and establishing their relationship to other world powers, they were also creating ties with their colonies. Long after the dust of battle had settled, this need remained.

GOVERNING THE ISLANDS

Having had no experience in administering the affairs of subject peoples, Americans invented their methods as they went along. They never established coördinated control of colonial matters.

First years. From 1900 on, the government of Hawaii was conducted by a governor and a territorial legislature—the way American territories had always been governed. The Department of the Interior was responsible for Hawaii (and also Alaska).

Being naval stations, Guam, Tutuila in Samoa, and Wake Island were for many years under the jurisdiction of the Department of the Navy. The Philippines—and later the Panama Canal Zone (see page 535)—were put under the control of a bureau in the Department of War. This bureau also took over responsibility for Puerto Rico after 1909.

In accordance with the Teller Amendment, Cuba was granted independence. However, in 1901, under an amendment to an army appropriations bill—the Platt Amendment—limitations were placed upon Cuba's liberty of action. Its treaty-making powers and its right to borrow money were restricted.

Furthermore, Cuba could not refuse to sell or lease lands to the United States for coaling or naval stations. Accordingly, the United States acquired Guantánamo Naval Base by a treaty in 1903. Lastly, the United States retained the right to intervene in Cuba "for the protection of life, property, and individual liberty." The Platt Amendment was a compromise in that it gave Cuba self-government while protecting American interests there. Nevertheless, it was a bone of contention in United States–Cuban relations until it was *abrogated,* that is, canceled, in 1934.

Later years. Also in 1934, a Division of Territories and Island Possessions was organized in the Department of the Interior. This body became principally responsible for all of America's possessions except Guam, Tutuila, Wake Island, and the Canal Zone. The three Pacific islands remained under the Department of the Navy; the Canal Zone remained under the jurisdiction of the Department of War.††

Constitutional problems. An important task was to define the constitutional relationship between the United States and the colonies. This question arose: Does the Constitution follow the flag? This meant, To what extent should the people of the new possessions enjoy the rights and privileges of American citizens?

A number of cases—known as the Insular Cases—raised this question and related ones between 1901 and 1922. The Supreme Court, by what many people regarded as strained reasoning, decided that there were two kinds of colonies to be considered—*incorporated* ones (Alaska and Hawaii) and *unincorporated* ones (Guam, Samoa, and Puerto Rico). The distinction was based on whether or not a given colony had been considered a part of the United States at the time of its annexation.

Having said this, the Court went on to answer the question. In the incorporated colonies, inhabitants would enjoy the fundamental rights guaranteed by the Constitution. In the unincorporated colonies the inhabitants would, of course, enjoy life, liberty, and the right of property, but not necessarily trial by jury or relief from tariff payments on their exports to the United States. As Secretary of State John Hay had once remarked wryly, "The Constitution follows the flag but never catches up with it." ##

---

†† Guam in 1950 and Tutuila in 1951 were transferred from the Department of the Navy to the Department of the Interior. In 1950 Congress granted United States citizenship to the people of Guam, but they do not have an elected representative in Congress and do not vote in national elections. Tutuila is now governed under the first constitution it has ever had, which went into effect in 1960. Since 1951 the Panama Canal has been operated by a federal agency, the Panama Canal Company. The governor of the Zone, chosen by the president of the United States, is always the president of the Company.

##What did Secretary of State Hay's remark mean? In connection with Hay, see Question 7, col. 2, p. 495, under "Inernational Politics."

Puck, June 29, 1904

A cartoon of 1904: "Gee, but this is an awful stretch!"

Harper's Weekly, August 13, 1898

Hawaiians in 1898 receive the news of the annexation.

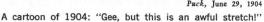

Japanese interest in Hawaii had prompted McKinley to press for annexation.

HAWAII

As in the past, when Americans had dealt with western regions of the continental United States, they encouraged from the first the organization of self-government in the new possessions. Hawaii, by the Organic Act of 1900, became an incorporated territory. Persons who had been citizens of the Republic of Hawaii when the United States acquired the islands in 1898 were declared to be citizens of the United States. All those subsequently born or naturalized there were, of course, also to be citizens of the United States.

Under the act, the governor of Hawaii, who was a citizen of the islands chosen for the governorship by the President, had veto power over the acts of Hawaii's two-house legislature. Hawaii remained a territory until 1959 when, amid celebrations throughout the islands, it proudly joined the Union as the 50th state.

PUERTO RICO

Having suffered badly from poor administration of its affairs by the Spanish, Puerto Rico looked toward the United States with high hopes. General Miles had assured the island's people that this country would provide "the guarantees and blessings of the liberal institutions of our government." But many Puerto Ricans were soon disappointed.

The Foraker Act. Civil government was created in Puerto Rico by the Foraker Act of 1900. It provided for a two-house legislature, the lower one to be popularly elected. Members of the upper one, as well as the governor, were to be appointed by the United States. A resident commissioner representing Puerto Rico in Washing-

Wide World

In 1959 honor guards representing the armed forces join officials in Honolulu to celebrate Hawaii's becoming a state.
Point to the evidence of the tropical climate. Compare this picture with the one on p. 479.

ton would have a seat and a voice—but no vote—in the United States House of Representatives. The act also dealt with the question of citizenship for the Puerto Ricans who were Spanish subjects when hostilities were formally ended in 1899. It was provided that these Puerto Ricans, along with their children born on the island subsequently, were citizens of Puerto Rico—not citizens of the United States.

The Puerto Ricans objected to these arrangements, because under Spanish rule they had been equal in status to citizens residing in Spain. They had also been represented in the Spanish parliament.

United States citizenship. Under a new law, the Jones Act of 1917, United States citizenship was granted to the citizens of Puerto Rico. Furthermore, an elective upper house—a senate—was established. The governor, however, continued to be an appointee of the president of the United States. The Congress of the United States reserved the right to annul or amend any act passed by the island's legislature.

The Jones Act failed to satisfy the Puerto Ricans. Some clamored for independence, others for statehood, and still others for commonwealth status. (As a commonwealth, Puerto Rico would enjoy the political advantages of independence as well as the economic advantages of a continuing connection with the United States.) Independence and statehood both seemed out of the question, but various proposals were seriously considered to enable the Puerto Ricans to elect more of their own officials.

In 1947 Congress passed a law enabling the islanders thereafter to elect their own governor every four years. The governor was authorized

#Because Puerto Ricans are citizens of the United States, they can freely enter this country. Puerto Ricans by the thousands have migrated to large American cities, seeking jobs.

to appoint the heads of the executive departments, with the consent of the island's senate. Judges of the highest court continued to be appointees of the president of the United States.

The Commonwealth. A new constitution was put into effect in 1952 after the Puerto Rican voters and the Congress of the United States had approved it. It created the Commonwealth of Puerto Rico. At present, Puerto Ricans living on the island are not subject to United States taxes—not even the income tax. Male citizens are, however, liable to military draft.

THE PHILIPPINE ISLANDS

The Philippine Islands were the largest and most populous of the new possessions—and farthest from American shores. Years of Spanish misrule had made the islanders suspicious of all government by foreigners. In fact, just as the Spanish-American War was drawing to a close, a group of Filipinos established their own government near the city of Manila.

Before long, fighting broke out between these Filipinos, who wanted the United States to withdraw, and the American soldiers stationed in Manila. The cruel guerrilla war that followed eventually engaged 70,000 American soldiers and was more savagely fought and more costly than the formal one just ending. Hostilities continued until the brave Filipino leader, Emilio Aguinaldo, was captured in 1901 and he and his followers agreed to swear loyalty to the United States.

Under Taft. On July 4, 1901, the rebellion formally ended as William Howard Taft, the first governor of the islands, took over control of affairs from the army. An act for the governing of the Philippines passed Congress on July 1,

Why is the elephant represented as battered? Why is the hay bin labeled "U. S."?

Uncle Sam is the keeper of a battered white elephant in this cartoon, captioned "What will he do with it?"

New York Herald, June 3, 1898

The American flag comes down in 1946 and the flag of the Philippines goes up in Manila to mark independence.

Wide World

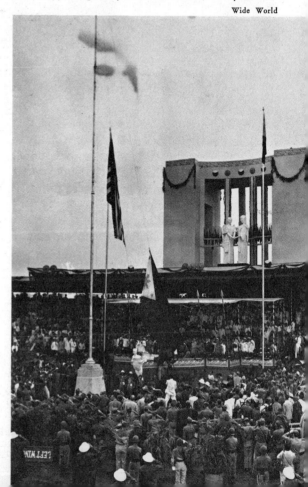

492   In 1967 Puerto Ricans voted to remain a commonwealth.

1902. It made the islands' inhabitants citizens of the Philippines under the protection of the United States. It also provided for a legislative assembly which would be elected every two years and hold annual sessions. The upper house would consist of a commission appointed by the President to conduct Philippine affairs.

A step toward independence. In 1912 the Democratic platform pledged to set the Philippine Islands free as soon as practicable. In fulfillment of this promise, a law called the Jones Act was passed in 1916 (not to be confused with the Jones Act of 1917, regarding Puerto Rico). Under this law an elective senate replaced the commission as the upper house of the Philippine legislature. The purpose was to make independence possible in the foreseeable future.

The Filipinos quickly met their part of the bargain—which was to establish and maintain a stable government. Soon thereafter pressure was building up inside and outside the islands to hasten the redemption of America's pledge to give the Philippines independence eventually. The island's colonial status, to be sure, was an economic advantage to the inhabitants. But dependence upon the United States implied an inferiority intolerable to Filipinos. Consequently, no ambitious politician among them could fail to clamor for independence; and the cries grew louder each year.

Moreover, certain American producers—particularly sugar growers—wanted protection from Filipino competition. They could have it only if the islands were freed and the Filipino sugar—in that event, foreign sugar—was kept out by the protective tariff.

At last. A result of elaborate discussions was the Tydings-McDuffie Act of 1934. Under its

The Philippine flag may be seen in the foreground. It is red, blue, white, and gold.

Military units pass in review along Dewey Boulevard in Manila in ceremonies on July 4, 1946, the day the Philippine Islands became independent. Spectators at the right shield their faces from the bright sun.

Wide World

Wide World

Old Glory is raised at Juneau, Alaska's capital, on July 4, 1959, honoring the entrance of the 49th state.

Alaska is even larger than Texas.

provisions, a new constitution would be drafted by the Filipinos, subject to the approval of the United States. This law, which created the Commonwealth of the Philippines, also provided for a ten-year transition period, at the end of which the Commonwealth would be independent.

A terrible war and devastation were to intervene before independence finally came to the Philippines on July 4, 1946, when the Republic of the Philippines was formed. The United States became thereby the first great power to free an important possession voluntarily. #

The burden of empire, which Americans had so joyfully accepted in 1898, had proved heavier and less satisfying than they had expected. The urge to own colonies declined as Americans discovered that it is more difficult and expensive to administer them properly than to acquire them. Businessmen had failed to realize the big profits anticipated. Military and naval experts had found the Philippine Islands to be especially vulnerable to attacks from which it was impossible to protect them. And ## in addition, the people themselves generally resented America's presence.

In spite of these disappointments, there was ground for mutual congratulations, too. Hawaii and Alaska early ceased to be regarded either by Americans or by themselves as colonies, but rather were viewed as the farthest outposts of the nation. Successive sessions of Congress considered bills to admit these valuable possessions until, in 1959, Alaska and Hawaii were welcomed to full membership in the national community as the newest of the United States.

Today we see that as the parts of the outlying American empire began to move toward self-government from 1900 on, the American venture into political imperialism was being liquidated. The mood of the 1890's, when so many voices had been lifted in argument for colonies, had passed quickly.

Sum and Substance

1. How were American island possessions governed in the early 1900's? In later years? 2. What did the Platt Amendment provide? When was it abrogated? 3. Explain what Supreme Court decisions were made in the Insular Cases. 4. How did the Organic Act of 1900 affect Hawaii? 5. Name the provisions of the Foraker Act and the Jones Act of 1917. 6. What changes were made in Puerto Rico's government in 1947 and 1952? 7. Describe the provisions Congress made for governing the Philippines in 1902 and in 1916. 8. What Americans favored Philippine independence? Why? How and when was it achieved?

494 ##The Japanese did attack and capture the Philippines during the Second World War. This was the war that prevented granting independence to the Philippines before 1946.

THE WORKSHOP

OF LASTING SIGNIFICANCE

How was each of the following related to the era of American imperialism?

John Fiske
Josiah Strong
Alfred Thayer Mahan
Theodore Roosevelt
jingoism
Virginius affair
Joseph Pulitzer
William Randolph
   Hearst
insurrecto
Valeriano Weyler
Maine
Dupuy deLôme
George Dewey
William T. Sampson
Winfield S. Schley
Pascual Cervera
Rough Rider

William Shafter
imperialist
open-door policy
John Hay
Boxer Rebellion
Platt Amendment
abrogate
Insular Cases
Organic Act of 1900
Foraker Act
Jones Act, 1917
Jones Act, 1916
Commonwealth of
   Puerto Rico
Emilio Aguinaldo
Tydings-McDuffie
   Act

AMERICAN DEMOCRACY

1. The issue of the freedom of the American press was involved in the trial of Peter Zenger, a colonial newspaper publisher. Find out what significance the verdict had for the people of the United States. What does the First Amendment say about freedom of the press? Why does conflict over the meaning of "freedom of the press" occur often in the United States?

2. What charges can be made against newspapers of the period just before the Spanish-American War? How did their activities relate to freedom of the press? What responsibility accompanies freedom of the press?

\# 3. On what democratic basis did many Americans oppose United States imperialism? What was undemocratic about the views of other anti-imperialists?

INTERNATIONAL POLITICS

1. With what foreign countries did the United States have dealings in the 1890's? In each case, what determined or helped determine American policy? To what extent did domestic politics influence international politics?

2. Describe the status of United States–China relations today. How would you describe American foreign policy toward China between 1894 and 1900? Today? Explain the change.

3. Account for the interest of the United States in the Pacific (*a*) in the early years of the republic, (*b*) in 1898–1900, and (*c*) today.

4. Investigate the history of the Philippines since their independence. Would you say that the United States was successful or reasonably successful in its relations with the Philippines? Defend your answer. What stand does the Philippine government take in world affairs today?

5. Similarly, find out what the current status of Puerto Rico is and how its people have fared since 1898.

6. Use reference books and current literature to learn the history of Cuba since its independence. Report on it to the class.

7. Compare the role of John Hay in American relations with England in 1899 with that of John Quincy Adams in a similar situation in 1823. What motivated each man? What responsibility does an American Secretary of \#\# State have?

DOCUMENTS IN HISTORY

1. Name the various arguments Beveridge (see pages 466–467) used in support of American imperialism. How did he answer people who opposed governing others without their consent?

2. In what respects does the quotation from Beveridge's speech remind you of the one from John L. O'Sullivan, pages 230–231? What techniques did each use to influence his audience?

3. What did technological change and industrialization have to do with the attitudes of Beveridge and of other American imperialists?

4. What public question did Beveridge and people like him raise? How did the majority of Americans stand on the issue? What answer did Americans ultimately give to the question?

##If the duties of the American Secretary of State have not been discussed in class, take this opportunity to make students aware of his responsibilities regarding foreign policy.

495

This chapter title refers to the years between about 1900 and 1914, when the group of people known as progressives had succeeded in bringing about much social legislation. The progressives were the people who attacked the social abuses that had been created by industrialization.

23

THE TIME OF THE PROGRESSIVES

... there is clearly need of supervision ...

One of the features of the tremendous industrial development of the last generation has been the very great increase in private, and especially in corporate, fortunes. We may like this or not, just as we choose, but it is a fact nevertheless; and as far as we can see it is an inevitable result of the workings of . . . various causes, prominent among them steam and electricity.

Urban population has grown in this country, as in all civilized countries, much faster than the population as a whole during the last century. . . . Many of us prefer the old conditions of life, under which the average man lived more to

La Follette was one of the leading progressives. Observe the clothing of these people.

What point is La Follette making in this quotation from one of his speeches? What credit does he give to industry? How do you compare what he says with what Andrew Carnegie said about industry, pp. 314-315?

himself and by himself, where the average community was more self-dependent, and where even though the standard of comfort was lower on the average, yet there was less of the glaring inequality in worldly conditions which we now see about us in our great cities.

It is not true that the poor have grown poorer; but some of the rich have grown so very much richer that, where multitudes of men are herded together in a limited space, the contrast strikes the onlooker as more violent than formerly. On the whole, our people earn more and live better than ever before, and the progress of which we

are so proud could not have taken place had it not been for the upbuilding of industrial centres. . . .

But . . . there is clearly need of supervision—need to possess the power of regulation of these great corporations through the representatives of the public—wherever, as in our own country at the present time, business corporations become so very powerful alike for beneficent work and for work that is not always beneficent. . . .

The immediate necessity in dealing with trusts is to place them under some sovereign to which, as its creatures, the trusts shall owe allegiance. . . . In my judgment this sovereign must be the national government. When it has been given full power, then this full power can be used to control any evil influence. . . .

At the beginning of the twentieth century, Americans frequently expressed fears that they were entering a period which would be less sunny than the past had been. They were inclined to blame big business primarily for the social ills they observed—like urban slums, child labor, political corruption, and many others. They believed that the first step in removing these evils lay in bringing the large corporations under government control in order to prevent them from growing even larger. President Theodore Roosevelt enthusiastically seized upon this idea and tried to put it into effect. He made "trust-busting" a symbol of his "progressive" outlook. These words are from a speech he delivered in Providence, Rhode Island, on August 23, 1902.

The progressives saw the evils that had developed in American cities. Why was it that inequality in worldly conditions of people could be seen so well there?

Robert La Follette makes a lively political speech to a curious crowd in his home state of Wisconsin. A leading member of the Progressive party, "Battling Bob" fought for reforms in government as a member of the House of Representatives, as governor, and as a United States Senator. In a career spanning more than forty years, he brought new life and inspiration to the politics of the "Badger State" and of the nation.

As governor, La Follette sponsored the "Wisconsin idea" (see p. 504).

497

This section describes Theodore Roosevelt's two terms as President. Review his role in the Spanish-American War (see pp. 469, 473-474, 476, 478-479). Like Johnson and Arthur, he became President because a President had been assassinated.

A ROUGH RIDER IS THRUST INTO THE WHITE HOUSE

On September 5, 1901, President William McKinley spoke before 40,000 people at the Pan-American Exposition in Buffalo, New York. The next day, as he shook hands with admirers, an intelligent-looking young man offered the President his left hand because his right one—apparently injured—was covered by a handkerchief. Suddenly from beneath the handkerchief a shot rang out and the President fell mortally wounded. The assassin was an anarchist named Leon Czolgosz, who was immediately seized by persons standing nearby.

On September 14 McKinley died, and for the third time in thirty-six years the United States was plunged into mourning for a martyred President. In each of the two previous instances, there had been grave doubts about the quality of the Vice-President who was suddenly thrust into the White House. Andrew Johnson had been considered by many to be an uncouth man and even a common drunkard; Chester A. Arthur had been thought to be little better than a cunning spoilsman. Now Theodore Roosevelt came into office, and though his personal integrity had never been questioned, he was believed to be dangerously unpredictable.

A sickly boy, Roosevelt grew to be a robust man, attributing the change to outdoor life.

McKinley at the Pan-American Exposition the day before he was shot. At his right is the Mexican ambassador.

Buffalo and Erie County Historical Society

Theodore Roosevelt, McKinley's successor, loved the West. Here he poses in Yosemite National Park.

Theodore Roosevelt Association

#Roosevelt wrote <u>The Naval History of the War of 1812</u> and <u>The Winning of the West.</u>

HIS STRENUOUS LIFE

When the Republican convention had nominated Roosevelt for the vice-presidency in 1900, Mark Hanna had gasped in horror, "Don't you realize that there's only one life between this madman and the White House?" Scarcely more than a year later "the worst" had happened, and "that damned cowboy"—which was Hanna's phrase—had become the president of the United States.

Early career. Theodore Roosevelt was born in 1858 of well-to-do parents in New York City. Sickly and weak, he had bad eyes; in time he lost the sight of his left eye completely. A boyhood encounter led him to take up boxing, and he began to lead "the strenuous life" that he later urged others to take up. Even in the White House as President, he still took boxing lessons.

A graduate of Harvard in the class of 1880, Roosevelt served as a member of the New York state legislature for three years. After two years as a rancher in what is now North Dakota, he returned to politics in 1886, when he ran unsuccessfully for mayor of New York.

President Harrison made Roosevelt a member of the federal Civil Service Commission, on which he served until he left to become head of New York City's board of police commissioners. In 1897 President McKinley appointed him Assistant Secretary of the Navy. We have seen the course of his career from that time on. First, there was a military adventure with the Rough Riders, then a hero's election to the governorship of the state of New York, and then a kick upstairs as vice-president of the United States.*

Varied interests. A brief description of the varied activities of Roosevelt cannot do him
justice. He wrote some distinguished history books and some excellent essays. He had a legion of friends—monarchs and prizefighters, politicians and naturalists, ranchers and art experts—in almost every walk of life.

Abundant energy. He followed his own advice to "hit the line and hit it hard." A famous English historian who visited the United States

---

* "To kick upstairs" is an expression in American political vocabulary meaning "to get rid of" by promotion.

Brown Brothers

When Roosevelt was nominated for the vice-presidency, he said, "I do not expect to go any further in politics."

"Big stick" refers to his foreign policy.

"McKinley filled it—will Roosevelt empty it?" Would Roosevelt's bold policies destroy prosperity?

Harper's Weekly, April 3, 1907 (Culver Pictures)

The name for the child's toy the "teddy bear" is derived from the name "Teddy" Roosevelt. A cartoonist drew a cartoon showing Roosevelt shooting bears that were dubbed "teddy bears."

declared: "Do you know the two most wonderful things I have seen in your country? Niagara Falls and the President of the United States, both great wonders of nature!"

In the opening years of the twentieth century, "T. R.," as he was known affectionately, commanded more attention than any other President since Lincoln. The Englishman Rudyard Kipling described his reactions when "T. R." spoke: "I curled up on the seat opposite and listened and wondered until the universe seemed to be spinning around and Theodore was the spinner."

A TALENT FOR LEADERSHIP

President at forty-two, Roosevelt was the youngest chief executive in American history. To old-guard Republicans and businessmen who were worried about his impulsiveness, Roosevelt gave immediate reassurances. He promised "to continue, absolutely unbroken, the policy of President McKinley for the peace,

the prosperity, and the honor of our beloved country."

It was quickly clear that Roosevelt had changed his viewpoint in the few years since the Battle of San Juan Hill. He had come to recognize that national affairs could be just as exciting as acquiring colonies had been.

In fact, Roosevelt's claim to lasting fame lies in the ability he showed to make government # serve as the friend of the people in improving life in America. His huge success as a domestic leader was the result not only of his uncommon political talent but also of a new movement in which he became the leading figure— the progressive movement.

Sum and Substance

1. What reasons did Theodore Roosevelt give to explain why he thought supervision of large corporations was necessary? 2. Under what circumstances did Roosevelt become President? 3. Describe Roosevelt's life before 1901.

This section deals with the efforts to correct abuses affecting the lives of the people.

INDIGNANT AMERICANS CRUSADE AGAINST SOCIAL ABUSES

The progressive movement was a large-scale attack—by people called "progressives"—on glaring abuses that industrialization had brought about or helped make worse in the generation after the Civil War. The range of these evils was broad: child labor, discriminatory railroad rates, monopolistic trusts, urban slums, adulterated food and drugs, corruption in public office, tariff excesses, drunkenness, occupational diseases, and organized crime.

STRIKING AT THE EVILS

Out of the general problems arose a host of specific ones that touched the heart and conscience of Americans and cried aloud for solution. What could be done, for instance, for the many children who each day manufactured artificial flowers until midnight in New York tenement houses? For slaughterers who risked life and limb in the meat-packing plants of Chicago? For women who worked 60 hours a week in the textile plants of New England?

The plight of child workers aroused the progressives.
Lewis W. Hine Collection, National Committee on Employment of Youth

Recall the pictures on p. 203 and p. 331. This child worked in a textile mill.

A baseball game on a tenement "playground" in the early 1900's: spectators at the right have "grandstand" seats.

The conditions seen in these pictures were among the ones the progressives wanted to correct.

A tenement home: chairs (*left*) pushed together form improvised beds in a room too crowded for its dwellers.

To strengthen democracy. Progressives believed that if properly enlightened, the people would bring an end to these and other blots on the nation. Simply and hopefully, progressives diagnosed the public ills. They concluded that, above all, the country needed improved management of the affairs of government: better men in office who would make better laws. Progressives were certain that when the United States government had been strengthened, it would be able to find ways to provide *social justice* for all the people.

To restore equal opportunity. Progressives maintained firmly that government itself must take an active part in achieving reforms. They held that a major task of the federal government was to play the role of referee in business competition. This, they thought, would make it possible once more for the small man to enjoy economic opportunity. It would also end the danger, they were sure, that the wealth of the country would be concentrated in fewer and fewer hands.

To satisfy the middle class. The progressive movement was especially appealing to small-business people and white-collar workers—two groups sometimes said to make up the *middle class.* These men and women, who felt victimized by big business on the one hand and big labor on the other, could hide their insecurity by vigorously attacking the problems both were creating. Furthermore, as the country became more urbanized and more dynamic, many people in the older, established classes, the old gentry, sensed a loss of status or standing in the community. They, too, could show their resentment at being displaced by decrying the public disgraces that were increasingly developing around them.

The progressives were not radicals. Actually through reforms they hoped to prevent the socialists from making headway among dissatisfied people. The progressives did indeed seek to enlarge the power of government. It was only to get rid of the evils they saw, however; it was never because they believed that a stronger government was in itself either desirable or necessary.

POWERFUL PENS

After the Civil War there had been a number of reform groups: the Greenbackers, the Grangers, the Liberal Republicans, and the Populists. The progressives, however, were the first to win the support of a great mass of the public. This success was no doubt due to the efforts of numerous talented authors and newspaper editors who happened to be at work at about the same time in the beginning of the present century. These journalists, called muckrakers,† drew much of their inspiration from the writings of two men of twenty-five years before: Henry George and Henry Demarest Lloyd.

Henry George's teachings. While living in California in the 1860's, Henry George had watched land speculators reap huge profits—which he considered to be unearned—from the rise in real-estate values. These profits, George said, had resulted simply because of the pressure of the growing population.

George commenced to gather material for a book on the subject, which he published in 1879 as *Progress and Poverty*. The work quickly achieved unexpected popularity. Its author argued that the inequalities in wealth in the nation were due to the "unfair" increase in the value of land, resulting in profits for only a few. He proposed a *single tax,* to replace the existing variety of levies. This tax would be on the unearned increases in the value of the land.

George's book became an all-time best seller. Many of its readers did not accept the proposal for a single tax. Nevertheless, the idea made a deep impression because it suggested that a solution was possible to the terrible problem of how to eliminate the poverty that existed amid America's plenty.

The work of Henry Demarest Lloyd. What deeply distressed Henry Demarest Lloyd was the growth of monopoly he saw wherever he turned. In 1881 he wrote an article for the *Atlantic*

---

† Theodore Roosevelt gave them this name. He said they were like the character in John Bunyan's *The Pilgrim's Progress* "who could look no way but downward with the muckrake in his hands." Roosevelt always disapproved of sensational muckraking.

##Ask what various kinds of people today make up the middle class. (Besides small-business people and white-collar workers, one could include teachers and social workers, among others.)

#Recall the influence the press had had previously in American history. (Students should recall Common Sense and the newspaper stories before the Spanish-American War. They should think of the effect Uncle Tom's Cabin had. "Press" refers to printed publications generally.)

Monthly called "The Story of a Great Monopoly" in which he discussed the methods of operation of the Standard Oil Company. This magazine piece was the forerunner of Lloyd's book, *Wealth Against Commonwealth* (1894), which assured him fame. Lloyd offered no solution for the conditions that he described, but he created a sense of their magnitude by piling fact upon fact—even though he may have exaggerated somewhat.

Muckraking. The muckrakers, writing in an accusing but analytical style like George's and Lloyd's, boldly set about exposing the dark corners of America in order to light and cleanse them. And, in rousing the public to demand reform laws, the muckrakers through their books and especially their articles played a very important part in fostering the progressive movement.

Although articles revealing political corruption had been written in the past, the muckraking magazines and newspapers soon gained unusually large circulations, running into the hundreds of thousands. These publications could pay high prices for the pieces they wanted to print. Moreover, they could afford the expensive research required to examine the practices of politicians and businessmen or the deeds and the misdeeds of local police officials and district attorneys. Examinations of political graft or infant mortality or Wall Street deals # became the regular diet of millions of readers every month.

Especially to lure women into the growing audience, newspapers and magazines invented the human-interest story. This new kind of feature called attention to touching problems that never before had fallen into the domain of proper journalism. These could include, for example, the difficulties of the unemployed father or the maltreated foundling or the abused sweatshop worker.

These were doubtless women who lived in a city. They had more leisure time than rural women.

Members of a women's organization hold a meeting in 1889, when women were becoming active outside their homes. Their serious looks suggest that the business at hand is related to the problems of the time.

Historical Pictures Service

Muckrakers, however, were not fault-finding men and women who criticized for the sake merely of criticizing. Said one of them later: "We 'muckraked' not because we hated our world but because we loved it. We were not hopeless, we were not cynical, we were not bitter."

Outstanding figures. S. S. McClure, a farsighted publisher, deserves considerable credit for popularizing the technique of muckraking. Beginning in 1902, *McClure's Magazine* published a series of articles by Ida M. Tarbell on the Standard Oil Corporation. They were an immediate success. In a series running in the magazine at the same time and later collected in a book called *The Shame of the Cities* (1904), Lincoln Steffens discussed municipal corruption. Ray Stannard Baker wrote about railroad abuses in a widely read series called "The Railroads on Trial."

Many writers and magazines also entered the muckraking field. Thomas W. Lawson's "Frenzied Finance," an attack on the "money kings," appeared in *Everybody's* in 1905 and 1906. David Graham Phillips' account of political bribery, "The Treason of the Senate," was published in *Cosmopolitan* in 1906. *Collier's* ran pieces on such subjects as food adulteration, fraud in patent-medicine advertisements, and professionalism in college football.

Novels were also written by muckrakers. One of the most successful was Frank Norris' *The Octopus* (1901), a story of the rivalry between California's wheatgrowers and the railroads. Norris' *The Pit* (1903) exposed the speculation in the operation of the wheat exchange in Chicago. The book that probably attracted the most attention was Upton Sinclair's *The Jungle* (1906), which revealed shockingly unhealthful conditions in meat-packing plants.

Decline. By 1914 muckraking had lost its effectiveness as a force for bringing about change. Unquestionably the pressure of advertisers and big business on the muckraking magazines forced some of them to back down or close up shop. But the most important reason was that after a decade of muckraking, some large corporations began to pay more attention to their public relations. By explaining their policies to the public, they were able to blunt many an exposure. Furthermore, most of the political reforms muckrakers advocated had been achieved.

POLITICAL RESULTS

The beneficial results of the progressive movement on America's political institutions were considerable. Many long-sought reforms were realized as a result of campaigns in the press conducted by the muckrakers.

Cleaning up municipal government. The progressives had taken to heart the assertion of the British visitor James Bryce that municipal government was the greatest single failure in American democracy. Practically every city produced reformers who won some notable victories at the polls by promising to "clean house." ##

In Toledo, Ohio, in 1897, Samuel "Golden Rule" Jones became mayor, and he determined to make the golden rule the main principle in his administration. His successor, Brand Whitlock, also won a national reputation for urban reform. In Cleveland, Tom L. Johnson served with distinction as a reform mayor in the years from 1901 to 1910. Hazen S. Pingree brought much needed reform to the city of Detroit. In New York City, Seth Low was elected mayor as a reformer in 1901.

Rescuing the states from the "interests." On the state level the progressives tried to break the control that vested business interests had over political affairs. The outstanding reforming figure in this venture was Robert "Bob" La Follette of Wisconsin.

La Follette served as governor of his state from 1901 to 1906 and then represented it for the next nineteen years in the United States Senate. His efforts to obtain reform legislation in order to loosen the hold of railroad and lumber interests on state affairs became nationally famous as the "Wisconsin idea." It included also reorganizing the state's tax system, enacting a variety of laws affecting labor, and pioneering in the conservation of natural resources.

La Follette dramatized the numerous possibilities of the progressive movement, but other

##Ask students what reasons they could give that would explain, or help explain, this statement. (Suggestion: The cities grew without planning; bosses built up political machines.)

reform governors also labored against the "special interests." Among them were men like Hiram W. Johnson of California, Albert Cummins of Iowa, Charles Evans Hughes of New York, Charles B. Aycock of North Carolina, and Joseph Folk of Missouri.

Remodeling the electoral process. Another political effect of the progressive movement was to give the voters themselves greater power over the choice of officeholders. This was the logical alternative to "boss rule," which the progressives despised. In 1903 Wisconsin adopted the *direct primary* as a method of making nominations for all statewide offices. Its novelty lay in providing a special election in advance of the regular election, at which time the voters could select their party candidates—rather than leave this function to nominating conventions. By the time the First World War began in 1914, a great majority of the states had accepted the direct primary in one form or another.

By 1912, in more than half of the states the legislatures were regularly confronted with "nominations" for the Senate made in direct primaries. They usually felt morally, though not legally, bound to follow them. This practice paved the way for the popular election of United States Senators, which was accomplished with the ratification in 1913 of the Seventeenth Amendment to the Constitution.

Enlarging the people's role in lawmaking. In still other ways the progressives increased popular control over state legislation and legislators. One method adopted was the *initiative,* which enabled voters to petition for the consideration of a proposed law or even to gain its enactment. Another was the *referendum,* which made it possible to solicit the approval of the voters for bills contemplated by the legislature. The initiative and referendum were adopted in many states after South Dakota accepted both in 1898. Legislation permitting the *recall* of public officials by special election was also widespread.

Extending woman suffrage. The progressive movement, moreover, helped make woman suffrage acceptable to the nation. The woman's club movement grew strong after the beginning of the century as the "weaker sex" attempted to

Gilloon Photo Agency

La Follette early in his career has a confident expression and stride that bespeak his hopes for success.

put its increasing leisure time to good works. Many woman's clubs made woman suffrage a special concern. Opposition was great at first, but the old arguments that voting was not lady-like and that suffragettes were just trying to become "self-made men" generally collapsed.

Before 1900 Wyoming, Colorado, Utah, and Idaho provided in their constitutions for female suffrage—a recognition of the important role women had played in the conquest of the West. By 1912 a number of states had amended their constitutions to give the vote to women, but the progress of the movement was very slow and uneven. The work of Carrie Chapman Catt and many other dedicated woman's rights advocates led finally in 1920 to approval of the Nineteenth Amendment. This hard-earned addition to the Constitution prohibited the denial of the vote to anyone "on account of sex."

THE SOCIAL HARVEST

The progressives' attempts to build a better world succeeded in reawakening the humanitarian spirit of pre-Civil War days. The idea became widely accepted that government must help those unfortunates unable to help themselves. The progressives struck a hard blow at #

Historical Pictures Service

Women of Wyoming exercise the right to vote in 1888.

The Capital may be seen at the far right.

A parade in Washington, D.C., dramatized in the early 1900's the demand of American women to be allowed to vote.

Brown Brothers

506 Observe the picture at the upper left: What shows that the women were not enjoying the secret ballot? How were they voting? The lunch basket shows that some voters came from a distance.

What indicates that the weather is quite hot? (Someone has opened a fire hydrant--a dangerous practice and now forbidden. Some of the bedding on the balconies may have been used by people seeking cool air. Why are there so many vendors?)

Slum housing in New York City: unscreened windows, fire-escapes filled with the overflow of crowded rooms, and stench and flies from the debris in the street below characterized the human habitations seen here.

Brown Brothers

Observe the debris piled in the street at the far left and the unpaved street. Food displayed on the stands and in the carts is uncovered and unprotected from flies.

#Riis states that about 1,200,000 men, women, and children lived in dumbbell tenements (see p. 435) in New York City. Look up the population of New York City in 1890 (p. 319). What percentage of the people were living in these tenements? (About 33 percent.)

the long-standing belief that the reason people fail in life is because they are naturally lazy or wicked.

Slum clearance. One of the most important crusades was carried on in behalf of better housing. The American conscience had been pricked by Jacob Riis, a Dane who became a carpenter in this country. In his days as a young immigrant, Riis learned of slum housing conditions in New York City at first hand.

Later, as a writer and police reporter, Riis became an advocate of slum clearance. His book, *How the Other Half Lives* (1890), shocked the reading public. Like other reformers, he thought that solutions were obvious.

"The battle with the slum," he said, "began the day civilization recognized in it her enemy. . . . When common sense and the golden rule obtain among men as a rule of practice, it will be over."

Settlement houses. A handmaiden of slum clearance was the settlement-house movement. The place best known was Hull House in Chicago, founded in 1889 by Jane Addams, the daughter of a Quaker businessman in Illinois. Other cities learned from Miss Addams, and by 1900 hardly a large urban community lacked a settlement house. Here slum-dwelling children and grownups might find recreation and, above all, encouragement in life's battles.

Observe the signs of age in the building at the right. The backyards of slum buildings provided neither room nor healthful surroundings for children's play. Filled

Notice the curtain at the window. with trash that made walking perilous for the unwary, they offended the eye and constantly invited fire.

Library of Congress

##Settlement houses were places where social workers lived to learn by personal experiences what kind of lives the slum dwellers lived and what kinds of problems they had.

A gas-lit classroom in a public school on a slum block in New York City—photographed by Jacob Riis.

Compare this schoolroom with your own classroom. There are no window shades here.

A settlement worker instructs a group of youngsters in a tenement area on the East Side of New York City.

Playgrounds and the scout movement. The playground movement that began in the big cities in 1885 and grew rapidly thereafter was another of the responses of the progressives to the problems created by urbanization. How strange public playgrounds would have seemed to agricultural America fifty years before. Yet the crowded cities were squeezing out not only trees and grass but also the fun of being a child amid unspoiled fields and streams.

In 1910 the Boy Scouts of America, and two years later the Girl Scouts and the Camp Fire Girls, were organized. In part these associations represented attempts to take children to the country and give them some experience in

Compare her with a model girl today.

The Gibson girl, who set the style for women: tiny-waisted, full-skirted, high-collared, and well-hatted.

Gift of Mrs. David Brewer Eddy, Corcoran Gallery of Art

open-air living. On the other hand, progressives also thought that scouting would help produce stronger citizens—physically and morally. Theodore Roosevelt was especially interested in this movement.

Temperance. Many progressives wrestled also with the threat to the nation's life which they believed was resulting from the excessive use of alcoholic beverages. The cities' saloons were blamed for an apparent increase in drunkenness, and the reformers began to talk about a "saloonless nation." Although the movement to prohibit the manufacture and sale of liquor had a long history, it became a strong force only in the second half of the nineteenth century. By 1900 five states had gone dry—Kansas, Maine, North Dakota, New Hampshire, and Vermont.

The progressives' emphasis on public and private morality gave new encouragement to the temperance movement. Its leading advocates were the Woman's Christian Temperance Union and the Anti-Saloon League. The evils of drunkenness among industrial workers were especially shocking, and the attempt to root out "Demon Rum" revealed again the deeply felt humanitarianism of the period. Most progressives considered the enactment of temperance laws to be not an interference with individual liberty but a step toward removing a crying social shame.

The triumph of the temperance movement came at last in 1919, when the Eighteenth Amendment was added to the Constitution. It forbade the "manufacture, sale, or transportation of intoxicating liquors." A national law to enforce prohibition—the Volstead Act—went into effect in 1920.

New models to imitate. Although the progressives looked ahead to the future, they also were sorry that the "good old days" were apparently gone forever. Particularly were the progressives afraid that the wide variety of people now coming from abroad might prevent the development of dominant types of American—like those existing in the past. Consequently, they popularized in their writings a picture of the ideal young man. He was personally upstanding, well tailored, athletic, and clean-cut—as well as

##Discuss how Americans' ideal girls and boys or young men and women have changed over the years. What causes the changes? Describe the model young man of today.

clean-shaven.§ He was in sharp contrast to the European immigrant—often bearded or moustached—who was sometimes suspected of being unwilling to lose his foreign accent.

The model American young lady was the Gibson girl—a creation of the artist Charles Dana Gibson. She represented the country's ideal of female beauty. A lover of sports and the outdoors, she was slender, graceful, and a trifle arrogant and aloof.

The majority of Americans, therefore, adopted model types to pattern themselves after. These might be said to have embodied some of the fundamental ideals the progressives hoped to promote: physical health and strength, cleanliness and high personal morality, and a sense of national superiority.

The unfavored. For Americans who were not white, Protestant, and Anglo-Saxon in origin, the way was no less difficult in the progressive # era than it had previously been. Immigrants—particularly those from eastern and southern Europe—found themselves scorned as "the foreign element." In vaudeville acts everywhere jokes frequently spoken in dialect about Italians, Jews, Germans, Poles, Irishmen, and others were sometimes offensive. Nevertheless, offensive or not, they underscored the fact that newcomers had to wait—sometimes a long time —in order to be "accepted."

Even Irish Catholics, who ran many a city hall and sometimes a state house, frequently were excluded from business and professional opportunities because they were of the "wrong" religion and national background. Although Oscar S. Straus, who served under Theodore Roosevelt as Secretary of Commerce and Labor, was a Jew—the first to hold a Cabinet post—Jews had to endure widespread social prejudice.

Negroes did not benefit as a race from the humanitarian spirit of the progressive period. From the 1890's on, discriminatory legislation established Jim Crow regulations in all the southern states. That is, laws were passed providing that separate facilities must be created for Negroes in almost every activity of life. Until then, the races had not been stringently separated. However, northern reform sentiment had become weaker after 1877. The southern moderates had meanwhile become less influential, and many rural southerners took out their frustrations and misery in aggression against the Negro.

The Negroes' choices. Negroes themselves were ## divided as to how they ought to plan for the future. Booker T. Washington, who had been born a slave, had become famous in pressing for vocational education for his people and in establishing Tuskegee Institute in Alabama. Advising Negroes to make the best of their situation, he told them in a speech in Atlanta in 1895 to "cast down your bucket where you are." And he accepted the separation of the races, declaring as he held up his hand with the fingers spread wide, "In all things that are purely social we can be separate as the fingers, yet one as the hand in all things essential to mutual progress."

A northern-born Negro, William E. B. Du Bois—the first of his race to win a Ph.D. degree from Harvard—took a different position. He accused Washington of wanting Negroes to do only the heavy and menial work of society. Du Bois advocated a policy of ceaseless agitation for full equality, and he lived to witness the beginning of the civil rights revolution of the 1960's.||

Even as the Negroes debated their course, other Americans were generally unconcerned about the hard lot of people of color. To be sure, Moorfield Storey, a New England descendant of Puritans, played a leading role in organizing in 1910 the National Association for the Advancement of Colored People. Nevertheless, the work to be done, not only to improve their lot but also to protect these people, was enormous: in the previous year at least sixty-nine Negroes had been lynched, that is, slain for alleged wrongdoing without due process of law.

---

§ The beard went out of style during the progressive era, the result in part of the invention, by King Camp Gillette in 1895, of the safety razor with throwaway blades. Since Benjamin Harrison none of the Presidents—who often reflect their times better than people realize—has worn whiskers.

|| In his nineties Du Bois became a Communist and moved to Ghana.

ROOSEVELT'S SQUARE DEAL

Theodore Roosevelt stimulated a public awareness of many problems requiring attention, and progressives enthusiastically considered him their leader. "I have never sought trouble," he once wrote, "but I have never feared to take the initiative." The public at large sensed his sincerity in wanting to make wrong things right even if some people would disagree with his order of priorities. He vigorously conveyed to his fellow Americans his feeling that they deserved a *square deal* from their government.

The coal strike of 1902. Roosevelt's handling of the anthracite-coal strike of 1902 was his first great success in office. It won "T. R." great popularity as a friend of "the plain people" rather than as the special pleader for either businessmen or workingmen.

The strike had been blamed on the stubbornness of the mineowners, who had refused to negotiate a dispute over wages and conditions. One of them had declared that the interests of the workingmen would be cared for not by the labor leaders but by the employers. These he described as "the Christian men to whom God in his infinite wisdom has given the control of the property interests of this country."

The dispute dragged on as the autumn chills became more noticeable. Roosevelt at last took a step which had never been taken by a President and which was regarded at the time as radical. He called a conference of the coal operators and union officials to meet with him in Washington. At the meeting, the mineowners refused to budge an inch. Roosevelt thereupon announced his intention to appoint a commission and to use the army, if necessary, in order to get coal.

These were the people who lived in the kind of homes seen on p. 501 and p. 507.

Tenement dwellers line up to buy sacks of coal during the coal famine brought about by the strike of 1902.

Culver Pictures

##Compare the way Roosevelt proposed to use the army with the way Cleveland did use it in 1894 (see pp. 418-419). Roosevelt had the results of the meeting published.

Finally yielding, the operators agreed to sub-mit the issues to an arbitration commission. In the settlement that was finally reached, the miners got the wage increase they wanted. But more important in the long run, Theodore Roosevelt earned national esteem as the man who was determined to get coal for the public—no matter who won the strike.

"Trust-busting." The acclaim that the President earned stood him in good stead when he em-barked on the campaign that was to win him a reputation as "the trustbuster." Like others of this period, Roosevelt was alarmed by the in-creasing power of monopoly. He knew that the trusts could not be eliminated from American life, but he believed that they ought to be brought under the control and regulation of government.

Mr. Dooley, the Irish character created by the humorist Finley Peter Dunne, summed up Roosevelt's attitude toward trusts: "On wan hand I wud stamp thim undher fut; on th' other hand not so fast." Roosevelt himself believed that trusts must remain responsive to the public interest. Nevertheless, he later observed, "We drew the line against misconduct, not against wealth. . . ."

The Northern Securities Case. The most widely publicized "trust-busting" effort was the North-ern Securities Case which "T. R." took to the courts and which the Supreme Court decided in 1904. The Northern Securities Company, or-ganized by James J. Hill, J. P. Morgan, and others, had created a railroad monopoly in the Pacific Northwest. The company had brought together under one management the Northern Pacific, the Great Northern, and the Chicago, Burlington, and Quincy lines.

The government prosecuted the company for violating the Sherman Antitrust Act, and the

Left: Roosevelt is scrubbing a chagrined-looking American eagle.

President Roosevelt vigorously tackles a cleaning job.
Theodore Roosevelt Association

"Jack and the Wall Street giants," published in 1904.
Puck, January 13, 1904

Right: Students can identify some of these men--Hill, Rockefeller, Morgan.

Theodore Roosevelt Association

The President speaks to the people of Hannibal, Missouri—Mark Twain's hometown—in the late fall of 1903.
Some daring individuals climbed a telephone pole for a better look.

Supreme Court in its decision ordered that the firm be dissolved. Roosevelt's reaction to the news was to call it "one of the great achievements of my administration. . . . The most powerful men in this country were held to accountability before the law." The nation cheered the President.

The election of 1904. Roosevelt, who had actually damaged none of the vital interests of big business, continued to retain its support. By the time of the Republican convention of 1904, there was no serious rival candidate to "T. R." and he was nominated with unanimous approval.#

He became, thereby, the first "accidental" President to be nominated for the number one place in his own right. Tyler in 1844, Fillmore in 1852, Johnson in 1868, and Arthur in 1884 for one reason or another did not win the nomination for the presidency.

Lyndon B. Johnson was another "accidental" President who was nominated and elected in his own right (in 1964). Can students recall why any of the men named in the footnote was not nominated?

#On that election night, Roosevelt said, "Under no circumstances will I be a candidate for or accept another nomination." He later regretted that promise, and he became a candidate again.

Roosevelt—seen directly above the right wing of the eagle—before a huge crowd is happily inaugurated as President. He was inaugurated on March 4, 1905. Ask when Presidents are inaugurated today. (On January 20.)

Roosevelt's Democratic opponent was a lackluster New York judge, Alton B. Parker, who, unlike Bryan in 1896 and 1900, was strong in his support of the gold standard. But Parker was swamped in the election, as the immensely popular "Teddy" won with no difficulty.

A second term. Roosevelt is said to have declared the night before his inauguration in 1905: "Tomorrow I shall come into my office in my own right. Then watch out for me!"

Roosevelt's second administration opened with new attacks on the trusts—the beef trust, the tobacco trust, the oil trust, the sugar trust. But it was easier to talk of breaking up the trusts than to do so in practice. A trust, after being "busted," might be reorganized and become a monopoly again.

Roosevelt was well aware of the obstacles to

Discuss the inauguration of the President. What does the word inaugurate mean? (To induct into office with formal ceremony.) Look again at the picture on p. 128.

rooting out monopoly, which had become one of the nation's most persistent problems. The Supreme Court itself had difficulty deciding when a trust had gone too far. It devised what it called "the rule of reason," which would allow courts to judge each case on its own merits.

The panic of 1907. Roosevelt himself talked of a distinction between "good trusts" and "bad trusts," but he could not define either. Midway in his term came the panic of 1907—sometimes called the "businessman's panic" because its effects were not especially widespread. It put Roosevelt into the embarrassing position of actually increasing the power of the largest corporation in the country, United States Steel—organized by J. P. Morgan in 1901.

The President was told that he could prevent a stock-market collapse by allowing United States Steel to purchase a controlling interest in another large steel firm, the Tennessee Coal and Iron Company. Roosevelt gave Henry Clay Frick and Elbert H. Gary, who represented J. P. Morgan, advance assurance that United States Steel would not be prosecuted as a trust if it completed the deal.

He spoke from a carriage with the top down.

Roosevelt in 1907 defends his policies on a speaking tour.
Library of Congress

Roosevelt afterward said, "While I could not advise them to take the action proposed, I felt it no public duty of mine to interpose any objections." He had had to face the difficulty of modern Presidents—to use his own words—"in working out methods of controlling the big corporations *without* paralyzing the energies of the business community." Like most progressives, he was trying to deal with the evils that private enterprise had produced without destroying private enterprise itself.   #

Conception of his office. Roosevelt put into practice his belief that the president of the United States should *use* the enormous powers at his command. "I believe," he said, "in a strong executive." He insisted that he was "a steward of the people bound actively and affirmatively to do all he could for the people. . . ." As a result, he wrote to a friend, "the people who believed in me and trusted me and followed me . . . [felt that] I was the man of all others whom they wished to see President."   ##

LEGISLATIVE ACHIEVEMENTS

Out of Roosevelt's conception of his place in the nation came a series of actions intended to serve the interest of all the people. Considering the variety of the public problems and the extent of the public discussion of them, the laws passed amounted to only a modest legislative accomplishment.

Harnessing interstate shipping. In response to Roosevelt's call for an end to various kinds of railroad-rate abuses, Congress in 1903 passed the Elkins Act. This law, which expanded the powers of the Interstate Commerce Commission, provided for the punishment of railroad officials and shippers guilty of giving or receiving rebates. It also made illegal any unauthorized departure from the published schedule of railroad rates.

Because the Elkins Act was not strong enough to satisfy the President, three years later Congress passed another law—the Hepburn Act. It empowered the Interstate Commerce Commission to set maximum railroad rates, which would be subject to court approval. It also broadened the powers of the Commis-

##What other Presidents had used their powers? (Jefferson, Jackson, Lincoln.)

sion in order to include the supervision of express and sleeping-car companies, oil pipelines, ferries, terminal facilities, and bridges.

The Pure Food and Drug Act. Nothing attracted more favorable attention than Roosevelt's attempts to guard the purity of foods and drugs. The work of arousing the public to act on this subject had been begun by Dr. Harvey W. Wiley, who for many years was chief chemist in the Department of Agriculture. In addition, the publication of Upton Sinclair's novel *The Jungle* helped to interest Roosevelt himself in the matter.

Congress in 1906 passed the Pure Food and Drug Act. It provided for the elimination of some shocking abuses in the processing of food and the manufacturing of patent medicines. A companion law, the Meat Inspection Act, was passed the same year, making compulsory the federal inspection of all meats sold in interstate commerce.

Conservation program. In the field of the conservation of natural resources, Roosevelt made his most original and lasting contribution to American life. In part, the President's work here was a by-product of his campaign against the misbehaving trusts. In part, it grew out of an appreciation of the wonderful riches of the West, which "T. R." had become acquainted with as a youth. In part, it reflected his buoyant optimism for the United States' future and his concern with posterity's needs. In part, it developed from his belief that national material resources were the property of *all* the people.

Roosevelt helped to bring about the passage of the Newlands Act in 1902. This law set aside for the irrigation of arid tracts the money received from the sale of public lands in sixteen

What does this picture indicate that would ruin one's appetite for chocolates?

A federal official in the early 1900's inspects a candy factory in order to be sure that the manufacturing is in keeping with the regulations laid down in the Pure Food and Drug Act. The girls are boxing chocolates.

Food and Drug Administration, National Archives

While Roosevelt was President, five national parks, two national game preserves, and fifty-one bird refuges were created. He also started twenty-five irrigation or reclamation projects, the largest being the Theodore Roosevelt Dam in Arizona.

Food and Drug Administration, National Archives

Inspecting the processing of oysters: although the appearance of this factory and of the workers seems less than desirable, conditions are better than those that existed before the Pure Food and Drug Act was passed.

The federal inspector (with the light hat on) stands beside two workers at the right.

western states and territories. The President also acted to preserve the national forest and mineral lands by withdrawing millions of acres # from public sale. He was instrumental in creating the Division of Forestry—now the United States Forest Service. As its head he appointed his friend and untiring fellow conservationist, Gifford Pinchot.

Roosevelt ceaselessly publicized the need for conservation—for "saving for the human race the things . . . on which alone a peaceful, progressive and happy life can be founded." ## The Conservation Conference which he summoned to the White House in 1908 was one of the high points of his administration. Attended by Cabinet officers, the members of the Supreme Court, congressmen, and governors of thirty-four states, it drew nationwide attention to the urgency of the subject.

Sum and Substance

1. Explain "progressive movement." 2. What evils did the progressives attack? 3. What new role did progressives think the federal government should assume? 4. To what Americans did the progressive movement particularly appeal? 5. What influence did Henry George have? Henry Demarest Lloyd? 6. Name important muckrakers and tell what abuses they uncovered. 7. Name five political effects of the progressive movement. 8. What social changes did the progressives help bring about? What new models of Americans were created? 9. Give the main facts about the coal strike of 1902. How was Roosevelt regarded afterward? 10. Describe the Northern Securities Case. 11. Explain how and why the President was embarrassed during the panic of 1907. 12. Summarize the legislative accomplishments of Roosevelt's administration.

518 ## The National Conservation Commission was formed after the conference, with Pinchot as its chairman. It made a report in 1909 that provided the first inventory of our natural resources.

"T. R." HANDS THE REINS TO WILLIAM HOWARD TAFT

A measure of a President's political success is his ability to dictate to his party the name of his successor. After Jackson picked Van Buren in 1836, no one until Roosevelt had been in such a powerful position.

When the Republicans convened at Chicago in June, 1908, they nominated Roosevelt's choice, William Howard Taft, on the first ballot. Their platform endorsed the policies of the Roosevelt administration and contained a promise to revise the tariff—a delicate and explosive issue that the President had hesitated to touch.

The Democrats for the third time nominated William Jennings Bryan, this time on a platform calling for an income tax and an end to the use of the injunction in labor disputes. The overwhelming victory for Taft in November showed in reality the esteem in which Roosevelt was held by the people.

MOUNTING TROUBLES

As Taft began the term of office which his good friend had made possible, Roosevelt retired from the scene temporarily, in order to go lion-hunting in Africa. "Health to the lions!" was a toast supposedly offered by his enemies as he departed. But the nation would hear from him again.**

Taft, an Ohioan, was an experienced administrator and lawyer. He had been solicitor general of the United States, a federal judge of the Circuit Court, governor of the Philippines, and Secretary of War in the Roosevelt Cabinet. Though a well-meaning man, he lacked the aggressive drive of his tireless predecessor. Weighing over 300 pounds, he was the heaviest President in American history. Before he was in office many months, it was apparent to many observant Americans that he lacked the political skill needed to manage his party's affairs effectively.

** Roosevelt's love of big-game hunting had long been a subject of public fascination and amusement. It was as a joke that the cartoonist of the *Washington Evening Star*, Clifford K. Berryman, in 1902 had drawn the first Teddy bear—a creation that became a permanent enrichment of American childhood.

Senator Robert Taft was the Senator whose name is used in "Taft-Hartley Law."

Tinkering with the tariff. Taft's first step was to call Congress into special session in March, 1909, in order to deal with the tariff question. The western farmers in the Republican party had long been clamoring for a lowering of duties on manufactured goods. The House quickly passed the Payne Bill, which contained some important reductions in rates.

In the Senate, however, the old-guard Republicans, led by Senator Nelson W. Aldrich of Rhode Island, restored many of the cuts and raised some others in the Payne-Aldrich Tariff. This defeated the efforts of many congressmen to cut the tariff significantly. What had started out to be a farmer's bill proved to be an industrialist's delight.

The insurgents. A number of western Republicans exhausted themselves fighting for a downward revision of the tariff. They became known

About the dress: Look back at p. 510.

Taft, his wife, and his younger son Charles, in 1908. Robert Taft, the elder son, who later became a Senator from Ohio, is not in the picture.

Library of Congress

Harper's Weekly, April 2, 1910

A cartoon on Cannon's fall: "Once clothed with power, now almost bare, he's lost his pull, but saved his chair." The letters on the barrel spell "speakership."

as *insurgents*—that is, politicians who opposed the policies of their own party. The insurgents included Senators like La Follette of Wisconsin, Joseph L. Bristow of Kansas, Beveridge of Indiana, and A. B. Cummins and Jonathan P. Dolliver of Iowa. From Taft they received little encouragement in their battle.

The Winona speech. Unlike the vigorous Roosevelt, Taft was not a leader of opinion who could direct public attention to an urgent issue and demand action on it. As he put it once, "There's no use trying to be William Howard Taft with Roosevelt's ways . . . our ways are different."

The high-tariff act infuriated the farmers, and Taft made a terrible mistake which antagonized them further. In Winona, Minnesota, before a gathering of grain growers, he called the new law "the best [tariff] bill that the Republican party ever passed." The President, who often put off urgent duties, was notoriously careless about preparing his speeches. He later

said, "I dictated the speech to a stenographer on the cars between two stations and glanced through it only enough to straighten out the grammar."

But the damage had been done. Taft had seriously offended the farmers—the historic backbone of his party. The generally unpopular tariff was indelibly associated in the public mind with the President, who was actually a low-tariff man himself.

Just as Roosevelt was about to return from Africa, he received an ominous letter from Taft which said in part: "I have had a hard time. . . . I have been conscientiously trying to carry out your policies but my method of doing so has not worked smoothly." And Taft's troubles were only beginning.

The Ballinger-Pinchot controversy. Taft seemed to stub his toe at every step. He replaced Roosevelt's Secretary of the Interior, James R. Garfield, son of the martyred President, with his own man, Richard A. Ballinger. This aroused both the insurgents and Roosevelt's fellow conservationists, who charged, unfairly, that it was the beginning of an attempt to restore the public domain to the "interests."

When Gifford Pinchot, the dedicated chief of the Division of Forestry and a close friend of Roosevelt's, was dismissed by Taft for criticizing Ballinger, a veritable storm raged around Taft's head. Taft had made a new and powerful enemy. When "T. R." came back from his hunting trip, Pinchot was waiting impatiently—in Egypt—to appeal to him.

The fall of Speaker Cannon. Another of Taft's mistakes lay in identifying himself with Joseph Cannon, the tyrannical standpat Speaker of the House of Representatives. Under the House rules then in force, the Speaker had the power to select all committees. In his appointments, Cannon in 1909 had ignored the House insurgents—including George W. Norris, of Nebraska—who were entitled to important posts by seniority, that is, by length of service.

The insurgents bided their time until one day in March, 1910, Norris caught Cannon without warning, got the floor, and pushed through a resolution that the Democrats also supported.

##In this way Taft was made to look unsympathetic to conservation, though he was a staunch friend of it. Taft not surprisingly said, "Politics makes me sick."

#In fighting the trusts, Taft was following Roosevelt's policy. But whereas Roosevelt had won acclaim for his policy without really hurting big business (see p. 514), Taft prosecuted the United States Steel Corporation, antagonizing big business.

It stripped the Speaker of his absolute powers and made it the duty of the House to elect the important Committee on Rules, which would then appoint the other House committees.

Taft intensely disliked Cannon and even hated being photographed with him. The President was linked with him in the public mind, though, because Cannon was one of the important Republican leaders in Congress, and Taft felt he had to defend him against the insurgents. Now, as a result of this House "Revolution of 1910," Taft could not help being identified with the most stinging reprimand ever administered by the House to its Speaker.

THE RETURN OF THE LION HUNTER

When Roosevelt returned to the United States in June, 1910, all eyes turned toward him. Taft seemed doomed to travel in the shadow of his illustrious predecessor. Besides, political fortune was continuing to frown on the President.

The parting of friends. The midterm elections of 1910 brought into office a Congress controlled by Democrats. The Democrats had made the high cost of living their chief issue and had benefited from the discontent the Payne-Aldrich Tariff had produced. So it happened that after only twenty months in office, Taft had brought disaster to the Republican party. Roosevelt considered himself to have been let down by Taft. A rift between the two men opened and steadily widened.

Canadian reciprocity. In the meantime, Taft attempted to hold the party together. But he seemed able to please no one. He called another special session of Congress to obtain a lower tariff. This time he advocated a reciprocity agreement with Canada.††

But the result proved to be even more weighted against the farmers than the Payne-Aldrich Tariff had been. Manufacturers would now be able to sell freely in Canada, and Canadian wheat would flow freely into the United States. Republicans in rural communities denounced the President. As if Taft had not suffered enough reverses, the Canadian Parliament rejected the treaty. The members feared that it might be a first step to the annexation of Canada by the United States.

Attacking the trusts. Taft believed now that his only hope for recapturing public esteem lay in a campaign against the trusts. Actually, Taft was far more successful in this field than was Roosevelt. During Taft's four years in the presidency, the Department of Justice prosecuted twice as many cases as it had during Roosevelt's seven years in the White House. But by his actions Taft merely succeeded in upsetting the very businessmen who had been, up to this time, the only group in his party that he had failed to irritate.

The years in the presidency were the unhappiest of Taft's life. If it had not been for his brothers and Mrs. Taft, who had wanted him to be President, he would never have run for the office the first time.‡‡ He correctly judged early in his term that he could not be reelected, and furthermore he lacked the urge to make the fight.

He wrote to a brother in 1911: "I am not very happy in this renomination and re-election business. I have to set my teeth and go through with it. . . . But I shall be willing to retire and let another take the burden." Roosevelt was soon helping Taft realize his wish.

The "new nationalism." Roosevelt's return to politics began late in the summer of 1910 when he openly sided with the insurgents. In a speech at Osawatomie, Kansas, he asserted that "property shall be the servant and not the master" of the people.

Roosevelt had been reading an important new book, published in 1909: Herbert Croly's *The Promise of American Life*. In this work Croly maintained that the general good could only be achieved through social planning by the national government. In this way the humane social goals of prosperity and happiness for all would be realized through a strong government

---

†† Under a reciprocal-tariff treaty, a country makes concessions on duty rates in return for comparable concessions by the other country or countries involved.

‡‡ He fulfilled his true heart's desire when in 1921 he was appointed Chief Justice of the United States and became thereby the only man to have held these two high offices.

of the kind Hamilton had admired.

These ideas appealed strongly to Theodore Roosevelt, who made them his own, calling them the "new nationalism." Said he, "The New Nationalism regards the executive power as the steward of the public welfare." For him big business was here to stay; it was a function of government to regulate it.

La Follette and the progressives. Meanwhile many progressives in and out of Congress were pushing Senator Robert M. La Follette of Wisconsin as their candidate for the presidency. They were hoping to persuade the Republican party to take him in 1912. In January, 1911, these insurgents organized the National Progressive Republican League in Washington, D.C.

The program the progressives advocated included the direct election of Senators, the direct primary for nominating all elective officers, and the direct election of the delegates to national conventions. Other demands were for the adoption in all states of the initiative, referendum, and recall, and a corrupt-practices act to guard against the possibility of election fraud.

Roosevelt, to whom many turned for guidance, would not push the nomination of the popular Wisconsin Senator. Instead, he allowed seven Republican governors to appeal to him to run. Early in 1912 he stated that his "hat was in the ring." Shortly afterward he announced that he accepted the progressives' program.

The President's determination. Compared with Roosevelt, Taft appeared even less vigorous than he was. But the President did not have to feel ashamed to stand on his record. During his term, the Postal Savings Bank and the parcelpost systems had been introduced; New Mexico and Arizona had been admitted to the Union, making forty-eight states; the trusts had been prosecuted; and steps had been taken to achieve more economy and efficiency in government.

To his military aide, Archibald Butt, Taft said: "It is very hard to take all the slaps Roosevelt is handing me, Archie. . . . I don't understand Roosevelt. I don't know what he is driving at except to make my way more difficult . . . it is hard, very hard, Archie, to see a devoted friendship going to pieces like a rope

of sand." In May Taft said: "I am a man of peace. I don't want to fight. But when I do fight, I want to hit hard."

The divided Republicans. The Republican convention refused to seat many of the Roosevelt # delegates when it met in Chicago in June. It was controlled by Taft's supporters, who quickly renominated the President. Roosevelt's friends shouted fraud and urged Roosevelt—who by now needed very little urging—to bolt the party and run for the presidency as an independent. With religious fervor Roosevelt told his followers: "We fight in honorable fashion for the good of mankind; fearless of the future; unheeding of our individual fates; with unflinching hearts and undimmed eyes; we stand at Armageddon, and we battle for the Lord."

The Progressive party met in national convention on August 5 and with near-hysterical enthusiasm chose its nominee—the beloved "Teddy." The platform that he stood on included not only the original program of the National Progressive Republican League but also a call for woman suffrage, federal aid to agriculture, laws to protect women in industry, an end to child labor, and minimum-wage and maximum-hour legislation.

Roosevelt must have known that his Bull Moose party,§§ as the Progressives came to be called, would only split the Republican vote ## and insure a Democratic victory. But he was determined to make the run.

Sum and Substance

1. Who was elected President in 1908? 2. Characterize the Payne-Aldrich Tariff and tell how it originated. 3. Who were the insurgents? 4. Describe three episodes that hurt Taft's popularity. 5. Why did Roosevelt become unfriendly to Taft? 6. What did Roosevelt's "new nationalism" mean? 7. Name the steps the insurgents took in 1911. 8. What new party was formed in 1912? Describe its platform and name its candidate in the election of 1912.

---

§§ It was so named from Roosevelt's statement in 1900, when, as vice-presidential nominee, he told the Republican National Chairman, who was planning the campaign, "I am as strong as a bull moose and you can use me to the limit."

##Review the effect a split in the ticket of one of the major parties has on the outcome of presidential elections. Students should recall the election of 1860.

WOODROW WILSON OFFERS AMERICA THE NEW FREEDOM

The Democrats, sensing victory at last after a long drought, approached their convention in Baltimore with high hopes. Bryan seemed once again to be able to dominate the proceedings.

But the deliberations soon developed into a struggle between Woodrow Wilson, the reform governor of New Jersey, and Speaker "Champ" Clark, of Missouri. By the time Bryan threw his support to Wilson on the fourteenth ballot, Clark's defeat was assured. Thereafter Wilson's strength mounted until, on the forty-sixth ballot, he was nominated.

A THREE-CORNERED RACE

As the campaign got under way, it was apparent that Taft did not have much of a chance because most voters were going to choose between Roosevelt and Wilson. A number of powerful businessmen who had supported Taft in 1908 now were backing "T. R."

The man from New Jersey. Wilson hammered away on his theme, the need for the "new freedom." By this he meant that America must try to establish the Jeffersonian ideal of limited government, restore free economic competition, and put an end to trusts. Wilson believed it should be the task of government to help the small businessman in his struggle against big business.

The Bull Moose party. In the campaign Roosevelt tried to revive the feeling of affection for him so many people had displayed in the past. On one occasion a bullet fired by a would-be assassin lodged in his breast, but he refused to seek medical attention until he had fulfilled a speaking engagement.

He told his audience: "I am going to ask you to be very quiet and please excuse me from making a long speech. I'll do the best I can, but there is a bullet in my body . . . I have a message to deliver and will deliver it as long as there is life in my body."

The result. Roosevelt's Democratic opponent relied on rare oratorical eloquence in winning his audiences. Wilson received only 42 percent of the popular vote in November, but the split in the Republican party gave him a majority in the electoral college. Under Democratic party guidance this time, the progressive era was now entering a new stage.

A SCHOLAR IN THE PRESIDENCY

Woodrow Wilson was the most learned man to come to the presidency since John Quincy Adams. Born in 1856 in Staunton, Virginia, he was a student of politics all his life. He received his higher education at Davidson College in Georgia, Princeton and Johns Hopkins universities, and the University of Virginia. After trying his hand briefly at the law, he made college teaching his life's work, developing into one of the master teachers of his time.

Notice the name of the train.

A British look at the election of 1912: Conductor Taft tries to halt a passenger, who in turn stops *him*.

Punch, June 26, 1912

#Wilson received 435 electoral votes; Roosevelt, 88; and Taft, 8 (Wilson got less than half of the popular votes). Debs, the Socialist party's candidate, got nearly 1,000,000 popular votes.

523

Culver Pictures

Wilson and Taft on the day Wilson became President. Taft confided, "This is the lonesomest place in the world."
Wilson was fifty-six years old when he entered the White House.

Entering public life. In 1902 Wilson became president of Princeton. In this office, he reinforced his economic views, which were very conventional, and he also denounced Roosevelt as a "radical." In 1908 Wilson said he hoped that Bryan's ideas about the money question would be "knocked once and for all into a cocked hat."

As early as 1906 George Harvey, an associate of J. P. Morgan's, had begun to talk of Wilson for the presidency. Who would have thought that "Dr. Wilson" would turn out to be a reforming progressive!

Wilson was reared in a stern Presbyterian home, where there was bred in him a certainty that he knew what was right and what was wrong. He early felt that he must use his talents to serve his fellow men. He often seemed cold and withdrawn, but as a young man in 1884 he wrote: "I have a sense of power in dealing with men collectively which I do not feel always in dealing with them singly."

Even as Wilson was distinguishing himself as a scholar and teacher of political science, he was writing: "I do feel a very real regret that I have been shut out from my heart's *first*—primary—ambition and purpose, which was to take an active, if possible, a leading part in public life, and strike out for myself, if I had the ability, a statesman's career."

When in 1910 he entered politics and ran for the governorship of New Jersey, he said that actually all his training had prepared him for service in government. He wrote in a letter: "I shall make mistakes, but I do not think I shall sin against my knowledge of duty."

Taking office. Wilson's presidential inaugural address was a stirring call to "service"—a theme the progressives found attractive. Said Wilson: "This is not a day of triumph; it is a

#The dissertation he had written to fulfill the requirements for a Ph. D. had called for stronger executive leadership in the federal government and had criticized congressional ineptness.

Seen here are (standing) Margaret, Eleanor, and Jessie Wilson, the three daughters of the Wilsons. Wilson met his wife Ellen (seated) on a trip to Georgia. Three years after her death Mr. Wilson married Edith Galt in Washington.

A summertime picture of Woodrow Wilson and his family in 1912. Mrs. Wilson tragically died two years later. Observe the influence of the Gibson girl on the clothes of the Wilson girls.

day of dedication. Here muster, not the forces of party, but the forces of humanity. . . . I summon all honest men, all patriotic, all forward-looking men to my side. God helping me, I will not fail them, if they will but counsel and sustain me!" The administration started out with such seriousness that, for the first time in memory, the traditional inaugural ball was eliminated.

Some methods. Wilson believed that a President must exercise firm leadership over Congress and not allow himself to be led around by the legislators. He had written of "T. R." some years before: "Whatever else we may think or say of Theodore Roosevelt he is an aggressive leader. . . . We may not approve his methods but we must concede that he made Congress follow him."

Wilson's first moves were to call Congress into special session to deal with the tariff and currency questions and then to appear personally at the Capitol to deliver the tariff message. Wilson was reviving a tradition that had been broken by Jefferson, who had been a poor public speaker. Instead of presenting his messages, Jefferson had sent them to Congress to be read by a clerk. Wilson said that he was glad to verify that the President was "not a mere department of the Government hailing Congress from some isolated island of jealous power . . . that he is a human being trying to coöperate with other human beings in a common service."

THE DEMOCRATS' PROGRAM

The Wilson program aimed to legislate the "new freedom" into being. The "old freedom," said the President during his campaign, had led to monopoly and a narrowing of economic opportunity. Now, he said, there would be positive governmental action in order "to make men in

#Wilson attempted to carry out the ideas he had presented in his dissertation. Ask what kind of person would be most likely to succeed in leading Congress.

New York Sun, November 17, 1914

"Move on!" the Federal Reserve Bank orders "Panic."

"Panic": another word for "depression."

#House worked with Democratic-party leaders, congressional leaders, and foreign dignitaries.

Philip Dru, Administrator, that appeared anonymously the following year. It tells the imaginary story of a social revolution in America led by a new national hero who, with his council of wise men, brought much needed reform to the country. This reform included a federal income tax, a federal incorporation act, the 8-hour day, and other labor gains. There were also public relief for the unemployed, easy loans to farmers, and simplified means of amending the Constitution. House's book reflected many of the progressive ideas which were filling the air as Wilson set about planning his legislative program.

A "scientific" tariff. In his special message to Congress, Wilson had asked for a lowered tariff to "open once more the free channels of prosperity to a great people. . . ." In response, Congress passed the Underwood-Simmons Act of 1913. ##

The new measure was hailed as "the most intelligent" tariff bill ever enacted. It lowered the rates on most items and placed on the free list wool, paper, wood pulp, steel rails, lumber, and—after three years—sugar. The act was hardly on the books when the First World War broke out, making it impossible to judge fairly the effects of this "scientific" tariff.||||

The Federal Reserve Act. Assured of the tariff he wanted, Wilson again went before Congress in person. This time he pressed for a new banking and currency law. He asked for a government-controlled and decentralized banking system able to provide a currency that could be increased or decreased in volume according to the changing needs of business.

In response, Congress in 1913 passed a law called the Federal Reserve Act. The act provided for between eight and twelve Federal Reserve districts, or regions, in the country (twelve were actually created), each to be controlled by a central Federal Reserve Board. A Federal Reserve bank was established in each district. All national banks were required to #

a small way of business as free to succeed as men in a big way . . . to destroy monopoly and maintain competition as the only effectual instrument of business liberty." Much of his thinking about the trust problem and monopoly came from his study of the writings of Louis D. Brandeis, a Massachusetts lawyer whom he later appointed to the Supreme Court.

Colonel House's influence. Another strong influence on Wilson was a shrewd Texan, Colonel Edward M. House, who had become the President's principal adviser. Wilson said of House, "His thoughts and mine are one." A man identified with reform movements, the Colonel believed that government must be responsive to the needs of the people.

In 1911 House was working on a novel,

|||| The Sixteenth Amendment to the Constitution was finally ratified in February, 1913. It made it possible for Congress to tax income directly and in this way make up for the reduced revenue resulting from the operation of the Underwood-Simmons Act.

##Earlier leaders had argued that a high tariff made the country prosperous (see p. 485). What people opposed a high tariff? (Farmers. See p. 520.) Why did they take this position?

#Ask the class what banks in the community belong to the Federal Reserve system. Are they nation-
al or state banks? What backing do Federal Reserve notes have? In what way did the system make
the currency elastic? Observe that the elasticity can be controlled.

join the Federal Reserve System, and other banks might join.

The member banks would be able to obtain loans from the Federal Reserve banks by putting up acceptable promissory notes—commercial paper—they had received from their customers in exchange for loans. The Federal Reserve banks would, of course, charge a commission for cashing the promissory notes. By raising or lowering this commission—called the *rediscount rate*—the Federal Reserve banks could control the flow of currency and credit in the nation.

The loans to member banks would be paid to them in currency called Federal Reserve notes. These would be issued by the Federal Reserve banks against the value of the commercial paper they accepted for deposit from their member banks. This act was acceptable to bankers because it provided them with sound money and with facilities they had long needed.

Besides, it was greeted by farmers with some enthusiasm because it made possible an elastic currency far superior even to Bryan's "fifty-cent" silver dollars.

Dealing with the trusts. In 1914, at Wilson's request, the Federal Trade Commission Act was passed to deal with the trust problem. It outlawed certain unfair methods of competition in interstate commerce. The Commission it created was empowered to issue "cease and desist" orders—subject to court review—in such cases as the mislabeling and adulteration of products, the formation of combinations for raising resale prices, and others.

Wilson strengthened the Sherman Act by obtaining the passage of the Clayton Antitrust Act in 1914. This law forbade a number of corporation practices that had not before been definitely labeled as illegal. It gained wide notice, for it seemed to exempt labor and farm organizations from the operation of the antitrust act.

The spindles seen here show that these young people were working in a textile factory.
A badly needed social reform when Wilson became President was the elimination of child labor like that seen here.

National Archives

Later interpretations of the law by the courts weakened this apparent victory for labor; nevertheless it served to bring union men to Wilson's side. In fact, in 1917 Wilson became the first President to address a convention of the American Federation of Labor.

Federal Farm Loan Act. Farmers, too, appeared to benefit from the coöperation Congress was giving the President. In 1916 the Federal Farm Loan Act was passed, providing long-term credit to farmers similar to that extended through the Federal Reserve System to business and industry. Twelve Farm Loan districts were created, in each of which there was established a Farm Loan Bank. Through these banks farmers might borrow more cheaply than through existing commercial banks.

New social-reform laws. A step toward social justice taken in the Wilson administration was the passage of the La Follette Seamen's Act in 1915. This law gave the men who sailed the merchant fleet improved working conditions, a 9-hour day while in port, and protection from cruel and despotic captains. Another measure which also benefited a special group of workers was the Adamson Act of 1916, which provided for an 8-hour day for railroad employees.

The urgent problem of child labor was attacked by the Keating-Owen Act, also passed in 1916. It forbade the shipment in interstate commerce of the products of factories employing children under fourteen years of age and of mines employing children under sixteen. This law was declared unconstitutional by the Supreme Court in 1918.

Despite the lofty interest in social justice displayed by Wilson and many of his progressive contemporaries, a failure to see the depressed situation of the American Negro was one of their serious blind spots. Although Wilson was idealistic in his outlook, he did not prevent the establishment of Jim Crow laws in the capital during his years in the presidency.

A SLOWING DOWN

As Wilson approached the end of his first administration, the drive behind the progressives' program was beginning to slow down.

The war in Europe, which had broken out in 1914, had turned public attention and activity from social evils to war production. But most important of all, the principal progressive proposals had been enacted. The enthusiasm for reform had run down, and like an exhausted storage battery it would not work again until it was recharged. Circumstances would discourage this for a number of years.

Not all of the progressives were satisfied with the results of the era that came to an end in 1916. Nevertheless, the progressive movement had altered the character of American life. It had enlarged the programs of democratic reform. It had enlisted the leaders of the urban middle class in attacking modern social and economic problems. It had criticized privilege and monopoly. It had established the principle that it is up to big business to exercise public responsibility.

Wilson himself thought that only a beginning had been made. He had told a group of Princeton students who serenaded him on election night in 1912 that the reshaping of American life would take "a generation or two." But sooner than Wilson had expected, the task was interrupted.

Like Jefferson, whose principles he so much admired, Wilson saw his energies drained in wrestling with international problems. He had long feared this might be the case. He wrote to a friend just before departing for Washington in 1913: "It would be the irony of fate if my administration had to deal chiefly with foreign affairs."

Sum and Substance

1. Why can the campaign of 1912 be called a "three-cornered" race? Who was elected and why? 2. Describe Woodrow Wilson's career before 1912. 3. What tradition did Wilson revive? 4. State the provisions of the Underwood-Simmons Act; the Federal Reserve Act; the Federal Trade Commission Act; the La Follette Seamen's Act; the Adamson Act; the Keating-Owen Act; the Federal Farm Loan Act. 5. When did the progressive movement begin to slow down? Why? What had it been able to accomplish?

##Like other progressives, Wilson did not see the injustice being done to the Negroes. Be sure that students know what Jim Crow laws were. Why were they an affront to American Negroes?

THE WORKSHOP

OF LASTING SIGNIFICANCE

What was the role of each of the following in the time of the progressives?

social justice
middle class
muckraker
Henry George
single tax
Henry Demarest
    Lloyd
Lincoln Steffens
The Jungle
Robert M.
    La Follette
Wisconsin idea
direct primary
Seventeenth
    Amendment
initiative
referendum
recall
Nineteenth
    Amendment
Jacob Riis
Carrie Chapman
    Catt
"new nationalism"
Bull Moose party
Woodrow Wilson
Underwood-Simmons
    Act
Federal Reserve
    Act
Sixteenth
    Amendment
rediscount rate

Jane Addams
Eighteenth
    Amendment
Booker T.
    Washington
William E. B.
    Du Bois
square deal
Northern
    Securities Case
Elkins Act
Hepburn Act
Pure Food and
    Drug Act
Newlands Act
William Howard
    Taft
Payne-Aldrich
    Tariff
insurgent
Ballinger-Pinchot
    controversy
Canadian
    reciprocity
Federal Trade
    Commission Act
Clayton Antitrust
    Act
Adamson Act
La Follette
    Seamen's Act
Federal Farm
    Loan Act

THE PRESIDENCY

1. Review Theodore Roosevelt's conception of the office of president of the United States (see page 516). What earlier Presidents can you name whose administrations showed that they had a similar idea? Account for your answer.

2. What accomplishments in Roosevelt's years in the White House can be attributed to his conception of his office? Explain.

3. Would you say that Taft's idea of the presidency agreed with Roosevelt's? Explain.

4. In what respect did Woodrow Wilson resemble John Quincy Adams? How was he unlike the second Adams? What steps did Wilson take and what methods did he use which justify calling him a "strong President"? #

5. What incidents in the progressive era can you cite which show the necessity for political know-how in a President? Why is a President expected to be the leader of his party? ##

INFORMED OPINION

1. With what previous periods of reform in American history can the time of the progressives be compared? Why? Compare the accomplishments in each period.

2. To what extent were the evils the progressives fought results of increasing industrialization and technological change? Account for your answer.

3. Describe the model American girl and the ideal young American man today. What do their characteristics reveal about American life today? Are your ideas of the ideal types similar to the progressives'? Explain.

BEING A SOCIAL SCIENTIST

1. Which of the evils the progressives wrestled with still exist? What is being done about them?

2. What new evils are being attacked today? How? With what success? Would you say that muckraking has survived? Explain.

3. Investigate your state's use of the initiative, the recall, the referendum, and the direct primary.

4. What special conservation problems does the United States have today? Your own state and community? What is being done about the problems?

5. What humanitarian movements are current in the United States? How many had their origin in ideas promoted by the progressives?

##Taft's unfortunate experiences during his term as President show that a President needs political know-how. A President is the elected leader of his party--his party chose him.

529

This chapter deals with foreign relations during the administrations of Roosevelt, Taft, and Wilson in the years preceding the First World War. In the last chapter, the domestic aspects of their administrations were treated together.

24

NEW INTERNATIONAL RESPONSIBILITIES

. . . dollars for bullets . . .

The foreign relations of the United States actually and potentially affect the state of the Union to a degree not widely realized. . . . The position of the United States in the moral, intellectual, and material relations of the family of nations should be a matter of vital interest to every patriotic citizen. . . .

The diplomacy of the present administration [William Howard Taft's] . . . has been characterized as substituting dollars for bullets. It is one that appeals alike to idealistic humanitarian sentiments, to the dictates of sound policy and

Roosevelt sent the fleet around the world to demonstrate the nation's strength (see p. 549).

Ask students to compare these ships with the one that Dewey commanded in 1898 (see pp. 476-477).
Sending the fleet on the trip was an example of showing the Americans' "big stick."

strategy, and to legitimate commercial aims. . . .

In China the policy of encouraging financial investment to enable that country to help itself has had the result of giving new life and practical application to the open-door policy. The consistent purpose of the present administration has been to encourage the use of American capital in the development of China by the promotion of those essential reforms to which China is pledged by treaties with the United States and other powers. . . .

In Central America the aim has been to help such countries as Nicaragua and Honduras to help themselves. . . . The national benefit to the United States is twofold. First, it is obvious that the Monroe doctrine is more vital in the neighborhood of the Panama Canal and the zone of the Caribbean than anywhere else. There, too, the maintenance of that doctrine falls most heavily upon the United States. It is therefore essential that the countries within that sphere shall be removed from the jeopardy involved by heavy foreign debt and chaotic national finances and from the ever-present danger of international complications due to disorder at home. Hence the United States has been glad to encourage and support American bankers who were willing to lend a helping hand to the financial rehabilitation of such countries. . . .

The second advantage of the United States is one affecting chiefly all the southern and Gulf ports and the business and industry of the South. The Republics of Central America and the Caribbean possess great natural wealth. They need only a measure of stability and the means of financial regeneration to enter upon an era of peace and prosperity, bringing profit and happiness to themselves and . . . creating conditions sure to lead to a flourishing interchange of trade with this country.

The "Great White Fleet" as it steamed out on its sensational trip around the world in 1907. Its orders from Roosevelt were simple: "Proceed to duty assigned."
#What natural wealth do they possess?

Authenticated News International

In the early days of the twentieth century, Americans were becoming aware for the first time of the problems of being a leading world power. The maintaining of an open door in China (see page 484) and the defense of the Panama Canal quickly turned into key concerns in American international relations. Within a few years the Department of State had made it a practice to encourage American investors to put money into troubled areas like China and the Caribbean countries in order to help stabilize them. This policy of using the influence of government to promote the business activities of private citizens was often criticized as "dollar diplomacy." President Taft's explanation of the policy is provided in this selection from his annual message to Congress in 1912.

Words to analyze: jeopardy, chaotic, rehabilitation, regeneration, consistent, capital.

THE UNITED STATES DECIDES TO HAVE A PANAMA CANAL

During the time of the progressives, the United States pursued a foreign policy which, in general, was as gratifying to Americans as the program of social reform at home. Jacob Riis, the muckraker, declared: "I am not a jingo; but when some things happen I just have to get up and cheer. The way our modern American diplomacy goes about things is one of them."

Riis found much to cheer about. The most dramatic episode of all was the building of the Panama Canal. As an engineering feat, it ranked with the construction of the first transcontinental railroad; as a diplomatic undertaking, it was far less admirable.

THE BACKGROUND

The United States astonished the world when it kept its promise and withdrew from Cuba after the Spanish-American War. But it had no intention of withdrawing entirely from the Caribbean area. From early colonial days Americans had carried on an important trade with this region, and they had long planned to build a canal across the Isthmus of Panama. After Puerto Rico became a United States possession, the nation had a strategic interest in the canal project. Furthermore, a canal would bring the country's East and West coasts so close together by sea travel that the power of the American navy would in effect be doubled.

A dramatic voyage. An event in 1898 had seemed to place beyond question the need for a canal. When the United States mobilized the fleet in the Gulf of Mexico after the *Maine* was destroyed, the *Oregon,* an indispensable battleship, was at San Francisco. The nation waited breathlessly while the ship took seventy-one days laboriously making its way south along the Pacific coast, around Cape Horn, and north along the Atlantic coast. Nothing brought home better to Americans the need for a canal than that nerve-tingling "race of the *Oregon*" in the spring of 1898.

Overcoming diplomatic obstacles. When Theodore Roosevelt became President, he courted popular approval by getting busy on the construction of a canal and, as he said, "making the dirt fly." The chief diplomatic obstacle to commencing work immediately was a treaty that England and the United States had completed in 1850—the Clayton-Bulwer Treaty. Under it the two countries had agreed that neither would ever exercise exclusive control over or fortify an isthmian canal.

By the beginning of the twentieth century, England was willing to abrogate this treaty. The English had become alarmed by Germany's growing power, and they recognized the value of a friendly United States—particularly one whose navy would be strengthened by an isthmian canal. Negotiations were started.

In November, 1901, the Secretary of State and the British ambassador concluded a treaty giving the United States the exclusive right to build, own, and fortify a canal. The canal was to be open on equal terms to ships of all nations. England agreed also to reduce its fleet in the West Indies and allow the United States to become the primary power in the Caribbean Sea. Britain and the United States were at the beginning of a long period of friendship resulting from the fact that throughout the world their chief interests were in harmony.

A choice of routes. Now that the United States had a green light to build a canal and control it exclusively, the perplexing question of whether to construct it through Nicaragua or through Panama remained. In 1879 a French company had undertaken to dig a waterway across Panama—at that time a part of Colombia—but finally had abandoned the project.

The financial backers of the French canal company were now offering to sell the United States for the sum of $109,000,000 their right-of-way, their rusting equipment, and their agreement with Colombia. To avoid paying this huge amount of money, Congress turned friendly eyes toward the rival Nicaraguan route.

The chief spokesman of the French canal company was an astute lobbyist, Philippe Bunau-Varilla. He began publicly to discredit the Nicaraguan route. His purpose was to per-

##This was the Hay-Pauncefote Treaty, arranged for by Secretary of State Hay (see p. 486). England sought American friendship, since it was having difficulties with Germany and Russia.

suade the United States government to purchase the French holdings—the price of which was suddenly reduced to $40,000,000. Bunau-Varilla insisted that volcanoes in Nicaragua would always threaten the safety of a canal built through that country. No one paid him much heed.

But a natural disaster played into Bunau-Varilla's hands. In May, 1902, a volcano erupted without warning on the West Indian island of Martinique. About 40,000 people in and near the city of St. Pierre lost their lives. A few days later, a volcano in Nicaragua began to rumble ominously. Obtaining copies of a Nicaraguan postage stamp depicting the volcano, Bunau-Varilla sent one to every United States Senator with the telling note: "An official witness of the volcanic activity of Nicaragua." The bill before Congress approving a *Panama* route was hurriedly passed in June, 1902.

AN INSISTENT PRESIDENT

Now only the consent of the government of Colombia was lacking. Accordingly, Secretary of State Hay induced the Colombian representative in Washington, Tomás Herrán, to sign a treaty in 1903. By the Hay-Herrán Treaty the United States would lease a canal zone 6 miles wide for $10,000,000 in cash and an annual rent of $250,000.

Colombia's resistance. When this document reached the dictator of Colombia, he was incensed. He wanted a portion of the $40,000,000 that the United States was prepared to pay the French company. This demand was actually not unreasonable. The French rights in the Panama area were due to expire in September, 1904. The French properties would go to Colombia, which could, if it wished, then claim the entire $40,000,000 from the United States.

"Bogota" (Bogota) is the capital of Colombia. Observe the waiting ships.

"The news reaches Bogotá—a cartoon published shortly after the Hay–Bunau-Varilla Treaty went into effect.

Roosevelt, wearing the bandanna and jeans of a cowboy, is shown approvingly as a man of action.

New York Herald, November 15, 1903

This uncomplimentary cartoon lampoons the diplomatic maneuvers that led to the creation of the Panama Canal Zone. "T. R." is dressed as an overstuffed Rough Rider who benefits from the work of Bunau-Varilla, the villain.

President Roosevelt was beside himself with rage: "Those contemptible little creatures in Bogotá [Colombia's capital]," he said, "ought to understand how they are jeopardizing things and imperiling their own future." If they delayed in accepting the treaty, he declared, it might be necessary to take action "which every friend of Colombia would regret." Several newspapers urged that the United States build a canal through Nicaragua in order to avoid unpleasantness. Roosevelt, however, was determined that Colombia must not be permitted "permanently to bar one of the future highways of civilization."

A handmade revolution. Leading Panamanians, who were afraid that the Americans would switch to the Nicaraguan route, decided to revolt against Colombia. They soon had the coöperation and assistance of the United States. In fact, the details of the revolution were planned in Room 1162 of the old Hotel Waldorf-Astoria in New York City. The principal planner was the Frenchman Bunau-Varilla! The "revolutionists" in Panama numbered about 500 local firemen and about an equal number of Colombian soldiers bribed $50 apiece.

Discreetly Roosevelt let it be known that the warship U.S.S. *Nashville* would arrive at Colón in Panama on November 2, 1903. The American vessel was ordered to maintain "free and uninterrupted transit" across the isthmus in accordance with a treaty of 1846 between the United States and Colombia. This order had the effect, of course, of preventing Colombian troops ## from landing in Panama and crushing the revolt.

The success of the "revolution," then, which broke out on November 3, was a foregone conclusion. Within three days the United States recognized the independent Republic of Panama.* Its new president shouted happily as the "bought" soldiers were paid off: "Free sons of Panama, I salute you! Long live the Republic of Panama! Long live President Roosevelt! Long live the American Government!"

Under way at last. Panama's first minister to the United States was, of all people, Bunau-Varilla,

---

* Panama's first flag was designed and fashioned by Madame Bunau-Varilla.

#The treaty also gave the United States the right to fortify the canal zone. The zone was to be neutral in accordance with the Hay-Pauncefote Treaty (see p. 532).

and on November 18 the Hay–Bunau-Varilla Treaty was signed. By its terms the United States leased a zone 10 miles wide—the Panama Canal Zone—for the projected canal. The United States agreed to pay Panama $10,000,000 outright and $250,000 annually, beginning nine years after the ratification of the treaty. The Senate approved the treaty early in 1904.

At last the construction of the canal could begin. The work was carried on in the face of obstacles that sometimes seemed insuperable, and there were many heroes. Two of the most important were William C. Gorgas and George W. Goethals. Gorgas rid the Canal Zone of dreaded yellow fever by wiping out the breeding places of the mosquitoes that carried the disease. Goethals became the chief engineer of the canal project in 1907, providing brilliant leadership for the undertaking. Involving a cost of more than $365,000,000 and the removal of about 240,000,000 cubic yards of earth, the 50-mile waterway was opened on August 15, 1914—

Aileen Gorgas Wrightson

William C. Gorgas as a general. Using experience gained in Cuba, he conquered yellow fever in the Canal Zone.

Without railroad cars, the construction work would have been impossible. Notice the umbrella.

The cutting of the canal called for the leveling of mountains. Because the work required heavy equipment, only a well-industrialized nation could conduct such an enterprise so far from home.

Historical Pictures Service

Why were Americans especially susceptible to the diseases that were common in Panama? (Suggestion: They had developed no immunity to them. Recall the deaths among the Indians from diseases brought to America by the first Europeans.)

Historical Pictures Service

Fumigation brigades like this one, shown with its ladders, were organized by the canal authorities to clean up Panama's cities. Shortly Panama City and Colón were turned into models of urban sanitation.

The train and tracks were those of the railroad the Americans had built across the isthmus.

"T. R." (*in white at the rear of the train*) reviews American troops during a visit to the Canal Zone in 1906.

Wide World

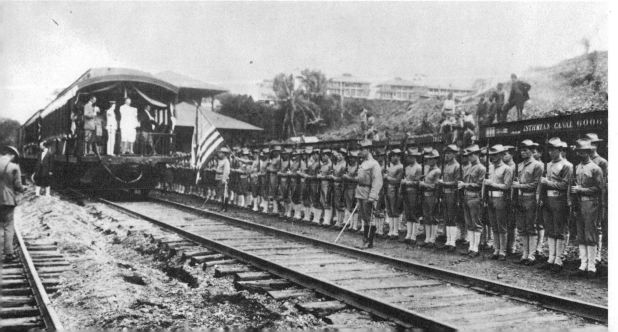

ahead of schedule, as a matter of fact.

\# Many Americans were shocked at the high-handed methods "T. R." had employed. In 1911 he declared in a public address: "I am interested in the Panama Canal because I started it. If I had followed traditional, conservative methods, I would have submitted a dignified state paper of approximately 200 pages to the Congress and the debates on it would have been going on yet; but I took the Canal Zone and let Congress debate; and while the debate goes on the Canal does also."

Repercussions. This speech revealed Roosevelt's characteristic reliance in foreign affairs on acting first and discussing afterward—a policy often irritating even to America's friends in the world. The attitude shown in the words "I took the Canal Zone" cost this country much goodwill, particularly in Latin America.

Roosevelt insisted he had acted "in accordance with the highest principles of national, international, and private morality." As long as he lived, it was impossible to make amends to Colombia for its loss of Panama. But in 1921, two years after Roosevelt's death, the United States paid to its aggrieved southern neighbor $25,000,000 in a gesture of goodwill. Even Senator Henry Cabot Lodge, Roosevelt's close friend, voted for the treaty that made this payment possible.† The discovery of oil in Colombia helped to stimulate the anxious concern.

Sum and Substance

1. Name two benefits which Taft said the United States obtained from dollar diplomacy. 2. What two events strengthened American interest in a Panama canal? 3. How did the United States win the right to build such a canal? What concession did it make? 4. What canal route was chosen? Why? 5. How was Colombia involved? 6. Explain how difficulties were overcome (a) in obtaining land for the canal, (b) in building the canal.

This section deals with situations in which the United States disciplined Latin America.

UNCLE SAM MAKES HIMSELF POLICEMAN OF THE AMERICAS

Roosevelt's diplomacy was explained best by his own statement in 1900: "I have always been fond of the West African proverb, 'Speak softly and carry a big stick, you will go far.'" As the President, Roosevelt could take bold steps because his large and devoted following forgave him his mistakes. William Allen White, a famous Kansas newspaper editor, described his first meeting with "T. R." in Washington:

"He overcame me. And in the hour or two we spent that day . . . he poured into my heart such visions, such ideals, such hopes, such a new attitude toward life and patriotism and the meaning of things, as I had never dreamed men had."

UNDER ROOSEVELT

As soon as the construction of the Panama Canal was started, it became necessary to maintain the security of the region immediately around it. This need provided the President with excellent new opportunities to wield the big stick.

The matter of political instability. The invariable occasions for the strong steps Roosevelt took were the political upheavals that have long been characteristic of most Latin American republics. An important reason for this persistent instability has been that everywhere a wide gulf has separated rich people—usually European in background—from poor people—Indian or African in background. Moreover, the difficulty of establishing easy contact between people along the coast and those in the interior in many of these countries has helped prevent the growth of national feeling.

In addition, the majority of people in Latin American nations have never had any experience in self-government or education for it. Instead of representing the people, government has remained the plaything of a handful of insiders—to be seized now by one political group, now by another.

---

† Despite the belated gesture, the diplomacy surrounding the building of the Panama Canal has remained heavy on the conscience of the United States (see page 769).

537

Difficulties in Cuba. Cuba was the scene of trouble even before the canal was half-finished. In accordance with the Platt Amendment the United States had withdrawn from Cuba in 1902. But a provision in the amendment giving the United States the right to intervene, if necessary, to maintain law and order on the island caused problems and misunderstanding.

Suspicion of American motives was aroused in 1906, when the United States felt obliged to send troops to Cuba, at the request of the Cuban president, to help put an end to unrest there. Roosevelt registered his feelings in a private communication: "Just at the moment I am so angry with that infernal little Cuban republic that I would like to wipe its people off the face of the earth. All that we wanted from them was that they would behave themselves and be prosperous and happy so that we would not have to interfere."

In 1909, upon becoming assured that the Cuban government was strong enough to maintain its authority, the United States withdrew its forces from the island. A doubting world could see that the United States was concerned with preserving order in the Americas, not in acquiring new colonies.

The Venezuela debt crisis. Roosevelt recognized that the failure of any American republic to fulfill its obligations to some European power might be the excuse for foreign intervention in the New World. Such intervention, he believed, would be a violation of the Monroe Doctrine; therefore he unhesitatingly assumed for the United States a vigorous role in warding off this possibility.

During his first year as President, Roosevelt had insisted that American countries were responsible for their own good conduct. If any misbehaved—for example, by contracting debt obligations they could not meet—injured Europeans might properly take steps to have their countries punish the offenders.

But Roosevelt changed his mind significantly when Germany, Britain, and Italy in 1902–1903 sent threatening warships to Venezuela in order to collect debts from dictator Cipriano Castro. The Department of State set its diplomatic ma-

chinery into gear to persuade Venezuela to accept arbitration and bring about a peaceful settlement of the dispute.

The European powers finally restrained themselves in the use of force, relying instead on the United States to end the conditions that would have led to serious difficulties. The Monroe Doctrine therefore had acquired new and enlarged authority now that the United States had become a world power.

The Roosevelt corollary. Yet what would happen if creditors could not collect their debts from American nations? This possibility arose in 1904 after the Dominican Republic had experienced many revolutions and had become practically bankrupt.‡ That little Caribbean country was in danger of being occupied by foreign powers seeking to recover on their claims. Roosevelt acted to have the United States step in, in order to head off intervention by any other country.

In effect, the United States was saying to the rest of the world, and to Europe in particular, "*You* may not spank countries in the New World, but if spanking becomes necessary, *we* will do it for you." This principle, announced in 1904, is known as the "Roosevelt corollary" to the Monroe Doctrine. In words now famous the President explained it to Congress:

> If a nation shows that it knows how to act with reasonable efficiency and decency in social and political matters, if it keeps order and pays its obligations, it need fear no interference from the United States. Chronic wrongdoing, or an impotence which results in a general loosening of the ties of civilized society, may in America, as elsewhere, ultimately require intervention by some civilized nation, and in the Western Hemisphere the adherence of the United States to the Monroe Doctrine may force the United States, however reluctantly . . . to the exercise of an international police power.

The United States, in short, took upon itself the unpopular but what it regarded as necessary task of being a policeman. Especially because

---

‡ It has been estimated that in the seventy years between 1844 and 1914, the Dominican Republic had had nineteen constitutions and fifty-three presidents, of whom only three were lucky enough to complete their terms.

##Ask what Latin Americans probably said when they read his explanation of the Roosevelt corollary. What parts of the explanation would make them angriest?

#The United States repudiated the Roosevelt corollary in 1930 (see p. 677). In cases in which it had been invoked, after American troops left an involved country, a dictatorship was established or a revolution followed.

New York Herald, December 16, 1902

A resolute Uncle Sam reminds England and Germany during the Venezuela crisis in 1902, "That's a live wire, gentlemen!" The notion of the United States as a world power was still as novel as the use of electricity.

Germany is represented by the figure of the kaiser, the German ruler (see p. 486).

it was self-appointed in this role, the United States aroused grave suspicions among Latin American nations. Americans showed no desire to annex any more territory. Some felt hostility toward Latin Americans that was based on prejudice. Others had concluded that Latin Americans would never be able to govern themselves effectively.

Occupying the Dominican Republic. Although the United States guaranteed the independence of the Dominican Republic, it placed the custom-house under United States supervision in 1905 and collected all duties on imports. In large part the revenues taken in were used to help meet the country's debts. But a few years later a larger-scale intervention by the United States seemed necessary. Plunged into turmoil by rival political groups, the Dominican Republic again

contracted a debt larger than it could manage. The Dominicans refused during Wilson's administration to permit a renewal of customs supervision by the United States.

When conditions grew worse and a revolution broke out in the spring of 1916, United States marines were landed to restore order. In the face of continued Dominican refusal to yield to American wishes, a military government was established over the island, administered by the United States Department of the Navy. Despite differing views on domestic political matters, then, "T. R." and Wilson agreed on the subject of this country's responsibility in the Caribbean region. Both looked after the security of the United States by exercising an "international police power" over lands in the vicinity of the Panama Canal.

##On the map on the next page, locate the Dominican Republic. It occupies a large part of what island? (Hispaniola.) What occupies the rest of the island? (Haiti.)

Observe the location of the Panama Canal.   Name Panama's closest neighbors.

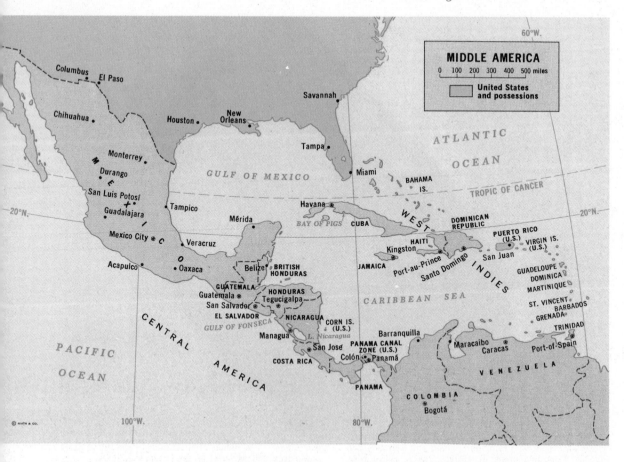

The United States had long been keenly interested in this varied region, where Columbus first landed in the New World. From 1898 on, the interest became political and strategic, as well as commercial.

Middle America is an important part of Latin America.   What culture is predominant here?

UNDER TAFT

The policy of protecting the canal is shown also in the case of Nicaragua. Conditions in that country became chaotic during Taft's administration. Again it was the case of a Latin American nation acquiring a debt too large to handle.

Intervention in Nicaragua. The first step the United States took was to oust the Nicaraguan dictator, José Zelaya, in 1909. He had irritated American businessmen by announcing his intention to cancel some of the concessions he had made to them. Also, rumors were flying that he was dickering with England and Japan to allow one or the other of them to build a canal through his country. The interest of the United States in these Nicaraguan matters

seemed as clear as it had been in the case of the Dominican Republic. Said the Secretary of State, Philander C. Knox, in 1912:

The logic of political geography and of strategy, and now our tremendous national interest created by the Panama Canal [which was about to be completed], make the safety, the peace, and the prosperity of Central America and the zone of the Caribbean of paramount interest to the Government of the United States. Thus the malady of revolutions and financial collapse is most acute precisely in the region where it is most dangerous to us.

Dollar diplomacy. Under Taft the cure for "the malady" came to be known as "dollar diplomacy." This meant that the United States would make loans abroad to create favorable condi-

#Ask what possible reasons would account for the fact that some Latin American countries could not handle their debts. (Taxes were not paid by large numbers of people, for one thing.)

tions for investments in foreign countries by its own businessmen.§ In a word, Roosevelt's big-stick policy was being replaced by one less colorful, although just as positive.

In an important instance, loans were made to Nicaragua to help that country straighten out its financial difficulties. It was hoped that domestic peace would be reestablished as a result and an occasion for European intervention avoided.

One of Zelaya's successors, Adolfo Diaz, had a desire to establish law and order. To achieve his goal, he was prepared to grant the United States extensive power to intervene in Nicaragua. When some of his countrymen objected, starting a revolt against him in 1912, 2000 United States marines were sent to put down the insurrection. For thirteen years marines remained in Nicaragua, until at last the country was deemed once again to have a stable government. The marines returned in 1926, when new trouble arose, and remained until 1933.

A Nicaraguan canal route. Negotiations to give the United States a long-term option to construct a Nicaraguan canal were begun by Secretary of State Knox. These diplomatic discussions finally led to the Bryan-Chamorro Treaty of 1914, named for the then Secretary of State and the Nicaraguan minister to the United States.

By the terms of this treaty, the United States obtained a perpetual right to build a Nicaraguan canal and a 99-year lease on the Corn Islands, off Nicaragua's Caribbean coast. The United States was also granted a 99-year right to construct a naval base in Nicaragua on the Gulf of Fonseca. For these two handsome concessions, the United States paid Nicaragua $3,000,000. The United States acquired not only the exclusive right to construct another canal, when and if it should be needed, but also the right to establish naval bases at either end of the route the waterway would take.

This country's intention in the Caribbean was unchanged: to strengthen the national security. On this Republicans and Democrats continued to agree.

Sum and Substance

1. With whom is the big stick associated? Why?
2. What are some reasons for political instability in Latin American countries? 3. What was the American motive in sending troops to Cuba in 1906? 4. How did Roosevelt justify such intervention? 5. Give the facts concerning the Venezuela crisis and its settlement. What was the Roosevelt corollary to the Monroe Doctrine? 6. How and why did Americans become involved in the Dominican Republic? In Nicaragua? 7. Give the provisions of the Bryan-Chamorro Treaty. 8. What was the "malady" Secretary of State Knox referred to in 1912? How did Taft wish to remedy it?

This section discusses the experiences Wilson had with Latin Americans.

TROUBLES TO THE SOUTH TEST PATIENCE AND PRINCIPLE

Woodrow Wilson was heart and soul opposed to the use of force in settling international disputes. But he did not shrink from it in defending the Panama Canal region. He felt obliged to carry on more armed interventions in Latin America than Roosevelt or Taft had.

WILSON'S LATIN AMERICAN POLICY

Wilson had begun his administration hoping that the frequent revolutions in Latin American

§ In Latin American nations the term often meant the exploiting of their natural resources for the benefit of financiers in the United States.

countries might be replaced by just and orderly processes. Optimistically he had declared, "I am going to teach the South American republics to elect good men!" When he failed, he, too, turned to "the exercise of an international police power."

The case of Haiti. Haiti, like its neighbor the Dominican Republic, had fallen into a condition of political and economic confusion. Its presidents had been driven from office in one revolution after another. In a shocking instance in 1915, President Vilbrun Guillaume Sam, who had been forced to seek refuge in the French

Wide World

Woodrow Wilson, who held deep convictions, believed that all nations, especially those in Latin America, ought to create sound republics in order to establish "constitutional liberty." Despite his unusual sensitivity, however, he never appreciated the extent to which the Latin American peoples resented the interference of the United States in their affairs.

legation, was hunted down and seized by a mob and killed in the street.

The United States once again feared intervention from abroad, particularly from Germany. Acting quickly, the United States forced a treaty upon Haiti which put the United States in control of the country's finances. Most Haitians objected, but they appreciated that the alternative to accepting it was American military occupation.

Haiti came now under the firm rule of United States advisers and officers of the navy and of the marine corps. These men worked diligently to place Haitian finances on a more secure basis in order to prevent periodic political upheavals. Self-government would come again # only when it seemed reasonably likely to succeed. The Panama Canal and its surroundings were too essential to American interests to permit a premature withdrawal from Haiti—however painful the violation of Haitian independence was to Wilson personally.

Acquiring the Virgin Islands. It was the same strategic interest that persuaded the United States in 1917 to purchase what are now the Virgin Islands (see page 389). The islands, a tourist and resort attraction today, are valuable because they lie near Puerto Rico, in the passage leading to the Panama Canal.

The canal-tolls controversy. Despite the importance of the Panama Canal to the United States, this country did not deny its use to others. But in 1912 Congress passed the Canal Tolls Act, which exempted from the paying of tolls vessels engaged in the American coastwise trade. Foreign governments objected. The British were especially distressed. They considered that the United States had shown bad faith in breaking the equal-terms provision of the treaty they had signed with this country in 1901.

Although there was much support for the act, ## Wilson personally went before Congress and asked for its repeal. He said with all the power of his eloquence: "We ought to reverse our action without raising the question whether we were right or wrong, and so once more deserve our reputation for generosity. . . . I ask this of you in support of the foreign policy of this administration. I shall not know how to deal with other matters of even greater delicacy and nearer consequence if you do not grant it to me in ungrudging measure."

Congress obliged him, unaware how soon things of "even greater delicacy and nearer consequence" would arise. These would involve the neighbor immediately to the south: Mexico.

Uprising in Mexico. Military force or the threat of it—the obvious weapons of an "international policeman"—would not suffice in Mexico, where the gravest events were occurring. In 1911 its dictator president, Porfirio Díaz, who had ruled with an iron hand for almost all of the preceding thirty-four years, was overthrown in a sudden revolution.

"The unspeakable Huerta." Díaz' successor, Francisco Madero, attempted to establish some long-overdue democratic reforms which appealed especially to the landless poor throughout the country. Although he was very popular with his own downtrodden people, Madero was savagely opposed by foreign and domestic interests. Individuals holding profitable mining and oil concessions were likely to lose them if his program succeeded.

Politically inexperienced, Madero was overthrown in a plot engineered by one of his own trusted generals, Victoriano Huerta. Forcing Madero to resign, Huerta then had him arrested. Shortly afterward Madero was shot in cold blood; suspicion pointed immediately at the new president, Huerta.

Because these events occurred as Taft's term was nearing its end, the President wanted to do nothing that would tie the hands of the incoming administration. When Wilson moved into the White House, he inherited the knotty problem of whether or not to recognize "the unspeakable Huerta," as he called the general.

A strong-armed man like Huerta could produce orderly government, but this would be an undemocratic arrangement. "My ideal," Wilson declared, "is a tranquil and righteous government in Mexico; but my passion is for the submerged eighty-five per cent of the people of that Republic who are now struggling toward liberty."

Nonrecognition. Wilson's determined refusal to recognize Huerta aroused the ire of American businessmen. They thought they saw in Huerta another Porfirio Díaz who would welcome foreign exploitation of Mexico even at the expense of his own people. A well-known editor asked: "What legal or moral right has a President of the United States to say who shall or shall not be President of Mexico?"

Wilson would not be turned from his course of nonrecognition. His position had no precedent in United States history. Since the time of Thomas Jefferson, it had been this country's policy to recognize governments established in foreign nations without inquiring how they had come into existence. Taking the novel stand that a government must be democratically elected in order to merit recognition, Wilson was defending a new rule of diplomacy. #

The Mobile speech. In a speech at Mobile, Alabama, in October, 1913, Wilson explained his Mexican policy: "We dare not turn from the principle that morality and not expediency [convenience] is the thing that must guide us. . . ." Then he added an important promise in order to reassure Latin Americans. He declared that although the United States would not recognize a government not chosen democratically, it would not use the Monroe Doctrine as a cloak for imperialistic land-grabbing.

Wilson pledged that "the United States will never again seek one additional foot of territory ## by conquest. She will devote herself to showing that she knows how to make honorable and fruitful use of the territory she has. . . ."

With these words of self-denial, the United States heartened many Latin Americans. For after the announcement of the Roosevelt corollary in 1904, they had grown deeply distrustful of the powerful "Yanquis."

"Watchful waiting." Wilson's policy of "watchful waiting" and his refusal to recognize a "government of butchers" did not, of course, relieve his country of responsibility. Without sending troops, the United States in effect intervened in Mexican affairs by calling for Huerta's resignation and by allowing arms to flow to Huerta's opponents. But Wilson refused to go

Historical Pictures Service

American sailors setting out to occupy Veracruz. Their avowed aim was to force a salute from Huerta, but an unspoken purpose was to prevent arms from reaching him and producing more havoc and bloodshed. The Americans had found out that a German ship was approaching Veracruz with arms.

any further, maintaining that "we can afford to exercise the self-restraint of a really great nation which realizes its own strength and scorns to misuse it."

The Tampico incident. On April 9, 1914, the crew of an American naval vessel loading supplies at the port of Tampico, Mexico, was arrested without warning. The men were hu- miliatingly paraded through the streets and ac- cused of violating martial law. A Mexican official apologized for the episode and the men were released. But Admiral Henry T. Mayo, in command of the fleet, was not satisfied.

The Admiral sent a 24-hour ultimatum to General Huerta in Tampico. In it Mayo de- manded an official apology and the punishment

##The Americans had trespassed on a restricted area. They were released promptly, and an officer apologized for what had happened.

of the officer responsible for the arrests. Mayo # insisted that the General "publicly hoist the American flag in a prominent position on shore and salute it with twenty-one guns, which salute will be duly returned by this ship." The Mexicans met every demand except the one for the flag salute.

This refusal, taken as an insult, immediately aroused war sentiment in the United States. President Wilson went before Congress on April 20, 1914, and asked for, and quickly received, authority to use force.

Occupying Veracruz. Operations were commenced against Mexico, although Wilson considered the action to be taken only against the followers of Huerta. American naval units pounded Veracruz with their artillery and occupied the city. Wilson did not want full-scale war, but he would not withdraw before he had driven Huerta from office.

Mediation. Late in April the United States accepted an offer of the ABC powers (Argentina, Brazil, and Chile) to mediate the dispute. The ABC conference met at Niagara Falls, Ontario, and soon showed itself opposed to Huerta. ##

The bandit Pancho Villa. Huerta, now under pressure, finally resigned on July 15, 1914. But it was a hollow victory for the United States. A civil war broke out in the scramble to succeed him. Many believed that Huerta's chief opponent, Venustiano Carranza, would be able to maintain himself as president. Although

A breastwork is any defense work built to be breast high. These sailors don't appear worried.

Here the bluejackets have established themselves behind improvised breastworks to guard a warehouse in Veracruz.

Eventually the navy left the city without forcing Huerta out or receiving the salute from him.

Historical Pictures Service

##The ABC powers were acting as arbitrators. Find out if students know where the ABC powers are. On the map on pp. 758-759, let them locate these powers in relation to Venezuela.

545

#Pershing, a graduate of the United States Military Academy, had served in the Spanish-American War. He had served in the Philippines, also. His greatest fame resulted from his role as commander of American Expeditionary Forces in the First World War (see p. 580).

Carranza assumed the office, he was beset by his own rivals, one of them an illiterate farmer and bandit named Pancho Villa.

It looked for a time as if Villa was going to be the next president and would prove to be more responsive to American influence than Carranza. When Villa suffered a stinging defeat at the hands of Carranza's troops, this "solution" to the problem vanished. Hoping to end the struggle, the United States recognized Carranza in October, 1915.

The Columbus raid. Still, peace did not come to Mexico. Villa continued to be active against Carranza, apparently planning to force Mexico into war with the United States. Villa's guerrillas came close to bringing this about in January, 1916, when they shot all but one of a party of American mining engineers that Carranza had invited to Mexico. Again in March they caused trouble when they crossed the United States border and raided the town of Columbus, New Mexico. The response of the American public was instantaneous, and there was much talk of a full-scale invasion of Mexico.

Pershing on the march. Bowing to the aroused public sentiment, Wilson immediately acted. He sent troops under the handsome and popular brigadier general John J. Pershing to seek out Villa and punish him. The expedition proved to be a wild-goose chase. Furthermore, not only did Pershing fail to find Villa, but also he clashed with the forces of Carranza, who resented the presence of the American soldiers on Mexican soil.

Wilson steadfastly refused to be drawn into hostilities. The United States finally accepted Carranza's suggestion that the perplexing difficulties be settled by a joint United States–Mexican commission. This body arrived at no solution, but with war looming between the United States and Germany in January, 1917, Wilson wanted at any cost to be free of the quarrel to the south. Wilson withdrew the troops, finally bringing the dispute to an end.

Pancho Villa was guilty of stopping trains in Mexico and shooting Americans present.

Pancho Villa and some of his followers. Wilson's misguided support of Villa upset Carranza's program of reform. Later the effort to capture Villa was a failure and increased anti-United States sentiment in Mexico.

##Pershing was forbidden to use Mexican railroads, which might have been helpful in finding Villa. After the Americans withdrew, Carranza was elected President.

#Wilson's Mobile speech had won favorable attention. The President also won Latin American friends by exposing the need for farm and political reforms in Mexico.

General Pershing, before his tent and with troops. He first won fame fighting in the Philippines. He was known as "Black Jack" because he commanded Negro soldiers before the army was desegregated.

Pershing belonged to an era when horses were important elements in a soldier's life.

PRELUDE TO A NEW ERA

Wilson's troubles with Mexico marked the end of an old era in American diplomacy and the beginning of a new one. First, Wilson had earned respect throughout the world by basing his policies on justice and morality.

Second, Wilson had made the fostering of democracy in Latin American countries one of the main principles of United States foreign policy. Third, Wilson had encouraged Latin Americans to understand that it was not "Yankee imperialism" but the security of the entire New World that the United States had hopes of serving.

Fourth, by turning to the ABC powers for mediation, the President had taken a significant step toward sharing responsibility for the sta-bility and greater solidarity of the New World. Moreover, in accepting mediation Wilson had improved the possibility of substituting the machinery of peace for the engines of war everywhere in the world.

Sum and Substance

1. What did Wilson hope to accomplish in the Latin American countries? 2. What action did he take in the case of Haiti? Why? 3. What was the Canal Tolls Act? Why did Wilson seek and secure its repeal? 4. What caused American difficulties with Mexico? 5. What new principle did Wilson adopt? 6. What new promise did his Mobile speech contain? 7. Describe the Tampico incident. What was its result? 8. How did the United States try to end its trouble with Mexico? Why and when did it end?

##The United States had taken the responsibility for carrying out the Monroe Doctrine and for making nations of the New World more stable. Why was sharing the responsibility a good thing?

The United States had already proposed the open-door policy for China (see pp. 486-487). This section covers further efforts the United States made to keep China from falling into the hands of other Asian countries.

AMERICA DETERMINES TO PREVENT THE CONQUEST OF CHINA

The United States' interest in the Pacific was less clear than its interest in the region of the Panama Canal. Nevertheless, in the early 1900's America also became involved in the international politics of Asia, even though its actions were sometimes inconsistent.

DEALING WITH JAPAN

Committed to the policy of the open door in China, the United States directed its efforts toward preventing any nation—European or Asian—from slamming the door shut. The United States also said it would be vitally concerned over any threat to the territorial integrity of China.

Russia's attempt to take over Manchuria, a large region of China on the southeastern border of Russia, at the beginning of this century, was, in effect, a move to violate Chinese territory. The United States was alarmed by this development. Consequently, when Japan made a surprise attack on Russia in 1904, President Roosevelt quickly assured the Japanese that the United States would not stand in their way. A victory for Japan, he felt, would help offset the power of Russia. Besides, this appeared to be a struggle between David and Goliath, and American public sentiment was on the side of the little fellow, Japan.

Mediation at Portsmouth, N.H. But during the course of the war, the Japanese astonished the world with their sterling military performance. It resulted in seemingly effortless victories. Many Americans now began to fear that if the war continued to its logical end, the Japanese would wind up in possession of eastern Russia. In that case, Japan might be a threat to China.

Partly because of this fear, Roosevelt agreed to help bring hostilities to an end. He called a peace conference, to meet at Portsmouth, New Hampshire, in August, 1905.

Although the conference almost broke up over Japan's insistence that Russia must pay a huge indemnity, Roosevelt succeeded in persuading the Japanese delegates to cut their demands. The Treaty of Portsmouth, how-

ever, signed in September, 1905, considerably strengthened Japan's position on the Asian continent. Under the treaty's terms, the Japanese took over a Russian leasehold in China and also obtained control of the South Manchurian Railroad.

But by helping Japan against Russia and then keeping Japan from crushing Russia, Roosevelt had succeeded in preventing either power from dominating Asia. In this way he had kept both from closing the open door in China completely. Moreover, the United States itself was able to avoid being drawn further into Asian troubles. For his efforts in bringing the war to an end, Roosevelt in 1906 became the first American to be awarded a Nobel Prize for Peace.

The Taft-Katsura Agreement. Roosevelt's Secretary of War, William Howard Taft, in 1905 arrived at an important understanding with Count Taro Katsura, the Japanese prime minister. By the Taft-Katsura Agreement, Japan promised to respect this country's possession of the Philippines, while the United States, in turn, promised to approve of Japanese domination of Korea. #

When, later in the year, Japan took over control of Korea's foreign relations and in 1910 made the peninsula its protectorate, the United States raised no objections. Since China at that time claimed sovereignty over Korea, the Taft-Katsura Agreement weakened America's stated policy of protecting China's territorial integrity.

Anti-Japanese feeling. Because of unwillingness to back up the open-door policy with anything stronger than words, the United States was helpless to prevent what shortly came to pass. This was Japan's disregard of the open door, particularly in Manchuria.

Meanwhile, on the West Coast of the United States, growing anti-Japanese feeling was antagonizing Japan and making United States–Japanese relations more strained. Although Japan ceased issuing passports to Japanese laborers after 1900, Japanese in considerable numbers continued to arrive in the United States from Hawaii, Canada, and Mexico. Will-

#Roosevelt realized that there was nothing the United States could do about Korea. Further, if Japan was not appeased, it might attempt to seize the Philippines.

ing to work for lower wages than their neighbors, the Japanese were unwelcome to many Americans because they were considered to be unfair competitors.

The school question. A serious development in 1906, just as Japan entered the ranks of the leading world powers by defeating Russia, understandably aroused Japanese resentment. The San Francisco public schools banned Japanese children from attending classes, insisting that they attend a school previously created for Chinese and Korean youngsters. Angry words were heard from Tokyo, and the protest of the Japanese ambassador was heeded seriously in Washington.

President Roosevelt held a conference with the mayor of San Francisco and representatives of the city's educational system which resulted in abolishing the school order. Nevertheless, "T. R." promised the Californians that he would seek to restrict Japanese immigration further.

In 1907 Roosevelt concluded a gentleman's agreement with Japan by which that country would continue to refuse passports to laborers intending to come to these shores. America, in turn, promised not to ban the Japanese officially. Moreover, Japan consented to raise no objections to the United States' decision to bar all Japanese immigrants coming via Hawaii, Canada, and Mexico. This agreement remained in force until 1924.

Sending the fleet around the world. Roosevelt had originally hoped to use Japan as a counterweight to Russia in East Asia. By 1907 he began to be alarmed at Japan's growing strength. He hit upon the dramatic move of sending the entire United States fleet around the world—specifically to demonstrate its power to the Japanese.

Said the President: "I am exceedingly anxious to impress upon the Japanese that I have nothing but the friendliest possible intentions toward them, but that I am nonetheless anxious that they should realize that I am not afraid of them and that the United States will no more submit to bullying than it will bully."

Some members of Congress objected to the

voyage, being afraid to strip the Atlantic coast of its guardian vessels. But Roosevelt responded that as commander in chief he could order the fleet anywhere he wanted to. He had sufficient funds, he said, to dispatch it to the Pacific coast, and if Congress did not appropriate money for its return, it would remain there. Congress had no choice but to oblige him. The ships departed from Hampton Roads, Virginia, just before Christmas, 1907. In a festive mood, the bands played "The Girl I Left Behind Me."

The voyage proved successful beyond the most optimistic hopes in promoting goodwill. The American sailors were cordially greeted everywhere and in no place with greater warmth and enthusiasm than in Japan. There, among other friendly gestures, thousands of Japanese school children were turned out to sing "The Star-Spangled Banner."

Roosevelt had skillfully brandished the big stick. Even his critics cheered him as the fleet finally returned to American waters on Washington's birthday, 1909—a few days before "T. R." turned the presidency over to Taft. It was Roosevelt's firm belief that sending the fleet around the world was "the most important service that I rendered to peace. . . ."

The Root-Takahira Agreement. One of the results of the voyage was a clearing of the diplomatic atmosphere between the United States and Japan. This led, late in 1908, to the Root-Takahira Agreement between Secretary of State Elihu Root and the Japanese ambassador in Washington. The two countries agreed to maintain conditions in the Pacific as they were, respect each other's possessions there, and support the open door in China and China's independence.

Because the United States had no imperialistic designs on Asia—as Japan apparently did—this agreement seems to have tied the hands of the Japanese. Actually, by accepting the existing conditions in the Pacific area, the United States in effect recognized the favored position of Japan in Manchuria—another weakening of the open-door policy.

The consortium. Taft's coming to the presidency in 1909 opened a new phase in this country's

##Ask students to look at Article 2, Section 2, Clause 1, of the Constitution, p. 799, and to read there the words that gave Roosevelt his power.

549

The sending of the fleet around the world was part of our foreign policy toward Japan. What showed that Roosevelt was displaying shrewdness?(The Root-Takahira Agreement.) What advantages did Japan receive from the agreement? (American acceptance of the status quo.)

Theodore Roosevelt Association

Roosevelt with "Fighting Bob" Evans, the admiral in command of the fleet sent around the world—just before it departed. Evans, wounded as a marine in the Civil War, was a flamboyant navy man whom "T. R." admired.

550 The American fleet, led by sixteen new battleships, had to stop in foreign ports for fuel and supplies. These stops indicated a need for smaller auxiliary ships in case of an emergency.

relations with Asia. Taft and his Secretary of State, Knox, were prepared to use dollar diplomacy to maintain the territorial integrity of China. In July, 1909, Taft wrote direct to the prince regent of China asking that American bankers be allowed to participate along with those of England, France, and Germany in the financing of China's railroad construction. After Russia and Japan were included in 1912, this arrangement—which proved to be short lived—came to be known as the six-power consortium, or partnership.

Knox planned also to have American and European banking interests help China purchase the railroads of Manchuria in order to "neutralize" them. Because Japan controlled the South Manchuria line and Russia the Chinese Eastern Railway, the effect expected was to free Manchuria from the grasp of both the Japanese and the Russians. But this proposal of Knox's failed because Japan and Russia were determined to stay in Manchuria. To this country's concern and displeasure, the open door was slowly being closed.

The overthrow of the Manchus. In 1912, shortly before Taft's term ended, the Manchu Dynasty—which had ruled since 1644—was overthrown in China, and a republic was established in its place. The new government, desperately needing money, sought a $125,000,000 loan from the consortium. American bankers were not attracted by the prospects for profit from this loan. But they agreed to participate in it in order to strengthen the policy of the Department of State. This policy continued to be one of preventing China from falling into a chaos that could lead to its being carved up by other countries.

A new attitude. Immediately after Wilson took office in 1913, the American bankers made it clear that they would seek a share of the loan only should it prove to be the President's wish. Wilson did not press them, because, he said, "the conditions of the loan seem to us to touch very nearly the administrative independence of China itself, and this Administration does not feel that it ought . . . to be a party to those conditions." American involvement in the consortium therefore ended.

But in trying to protect China's independence in this fashion, the United States actually weakened China greatly. For in withdrawing from the consortium, the field was left clear for Japanese aggression. Soon the First World War came, and fully engaged elsewhere, the United States was powerless to interfere with Japanese imperialism on the continent of Asia. By 1916 the open door not only had become the closed door but also had acquired a doorman—in Japanese uniform.

Sum and Substance

1. Why did Roosevelt support Japan in its war with Russia? What accounted in part for his acting as peacemaker? 2. Name the peace treaty and give its provisions. 3. What had Roosevelt accomplished? 4. Give the terms of the Taft-Katsura Agreement. 5. How did it affect American policy in respect to China? 6. What was the gentleman's agreement? What was its background? 7. Explain how Roosevelt brandished the big stick in 1907. 8. What was accomplished by the Root-Takahira Agreement? 9. Explain what the six-power consortium was, and describe the United States' part in it. What events followed American withdrawal from it?

This section describes the first cooperative efforts to bring about international peace.

THE PEACE MOVEMENT AIMS TO ROOT OUT WAR

The reforming spirit of the progressive era was reflected in American attempts to play a part in seeking a substitute for war. Private peace organizations grew in size, and their members were no longer only starry-eyed idealists. At the beginning of the twentieth century, the American Peace Society, almost a hundred years old, was attracting for the first time a membership of men of affairs, especially businessmen.

In 1910 the World Peace Foundation was established in Boston with the substantial assistance of Edwin Ginn, the textbook publisher.

At practically the same time Andrew Carnegie was founding the Carnegie Endowment for International Peace, a similar research and study group. Other organizations also were formed to find ways of ending the use of force in resolving international disputes.

INTERNATIONAL GATHERINGS

In its diplomacy the United States relied on a go-it-alone policy, seeking no allies and accepting no commitments for concerted action with other nations. Nevertheless, in the fifteen years before 1914 it began officially to support movements for international coöperation.

The first Hague Conference. The United States participated in one of the first notable attempts to achieve disarmament: the Hague Peace Conference, called by the czar of Russia in 1899, at The Hague, in the Netherlands. The twenty-six nations attending agreed to outlaw poison gas, the dropping of missiles from the air, and explosive bullets. But the countries were inclined to deal only with the effects of war, not its causes. One of the American delegates was Alfred Thayer Mahan, not in sympathy with the idea of disarmament, the very purpose for which the conference had been convened.

Look back at the map on p. 196.
The recent discovery of gold in Alaska had made this part of the Americas seem more important than before.

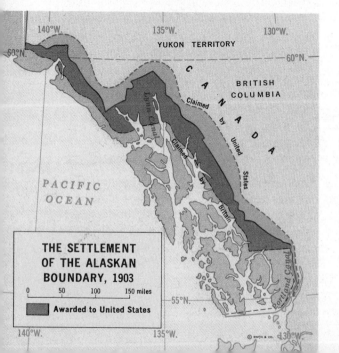

**THE SETTLEMENT
OF THE ALASKAN
BOUNDARY, 1903**

0   50   100   150 miles

Awarded to United States

The Permanent Court of Arbitration. The only noteworthy result of the conference was the creation of the Permanent Court of International Arbitration. The Court would provide judges to arbitrate such disputes as might voluntarily be brought to it by the member nations. Although no machinery was provided to make nations use its facilities or to enforce its decisions, its establishment greatly encouraged the world peace movement.

Another Hague Conference. A second Hague Peace Conference gathered in 1907, again as a result of the czar's call. President Roosevelt, who had proposed such a meeting himself in 1904, was now outspokenly cool to proposals for disarmament. His belief was: "Unjust war is dreadful; a just war may be the highest duty. To have the best nations, the free and civilized nations, disarm and leave the despots and barbarians with great military force, would be a calamity compared to which the calamities caused by all the wars of the Nineteenth Century would be trivial."

The second Hague Conference, attended by forty-six countries, extended the agreements made eight years before. There were practically no other tangible results. The conference adjourned after agreeing to meet again in eight years. Seven years later the First World War broke out.

ARBITRATION OF DISPUTES

In the progressive era the United States' reliance on the big stick often seemed to contradict American interest in promoting coöperation among nations. A notable instance arose in connection with the Alaskan-boundary dispute in 1903.

The Alaskan boundary. This dispute concerned the line between British Columbia and the Alaskan panhandle, the narrow arm of land bordering the Canadian province. Roosevelt, who considered the Canadian claims to be "dangerously near blackmail," refused to submit the case to the Hague Court. The claims of the United States were very strong, but the British seemed to want arbitration in order to protect Canadian pride.

The map shows the Alaskan panhandle. Gold seekers used water routes (seen here) to Alaska.

By an agreement with Britain, the issue was to be put into the hands of "six impartial jurists of repute"—three to be British and three American. The British named two Canadians and one Englishman. Roosevelt promptly chose Henry Cabot Lodge, Secretary of State Elihu Root, and a former Senator of the state of Washington, which had an important interest in the decision. The British—and the Canadians—were angered by this violation of the spirit of the agreement.

Then when it appeared that the commission might be deadlocked, three against three, Roosevelt took steps. He privately let it be known to the British that if the line did not satisfy him, he would take matters into his own hands and "run the boundary on my own hook." Thereafter, the English delegate voted with the three Americans to give this country the boundary it desired.

The Algeciras Conference. Despite this unhappy incident, arbitration as a means of avoiding war gained popularity during the progressive era. Roosevelt was instrumental in calling the Algeciras Conference in Algeciras, Spain, in 1906 to settle differences that had arisen between France and Germany over the North African state of Morocco. "T. R." believed that if a war had begun, it "would probably have extended through a considerable part of the world."

The Senate condemned the President's departure from the pledge in the Monroe Doctrine to stay out of European affairs. Nevertheless, Secretary of State Root believed that by Roosevelt's action the United States had protected the peace of the world. For the first time an American President had taken an active hand in averting an international catastrophe.

Special treaties. During Taft's administration, arbitration treaties were signed with Britain and France—and, it was hoped, more would be negotiated with other countries. These new treaties provided for the judicial settlement of those questions which did not affect either the signers' "vital interests" or their "national honor." Fearing the limiting of its treaty-making power, the Senate modified the arbitration treaties so drastically that Taft did not press for their ratification.

William Jennings Bryan's service for three years as Wilson's Secretary of State produced another kind of peace-keeping mechanism—the conciliation treaty. Sometimes known as the "cooling-off" treaty, it provided that if diplomacy should fail in an international dispute, both parties before resorting to arms would submit their problems to a five-man commission. Both parties would agree to delay the start of hostilities at least until the commission had handed down its decision.

These "cooling-off" treaties were negotiated with twenty-one countries and duly ratified. Many Americans looked upon them with derision, but Bryan believed that they were his outstanding service to the country.

In the progressive era, the United States had attained standing as a world power. Unhesitatingly American leaders had staked out a dominant role on this continent and geared foreign policy to maintaining it. On the other side of the Pacific, the United States argued for the open door in China—even though in practice it sometimes retreated from its position.

In relations with European countries, the United States tried to be guided by the principles of decency and justice. Americans were fairly sure, though, that Europe's affairs were too far away to trouble this country seriously.

A high national purpose was to make democracy work at home in order to keep the "lamp burning brightly on this western shore as a light to all nations." And Wilson had once declared, "The idea of America is to serve humanity." Few stopped to think that the day might be near when the United States would have to test its devotion to these ideals—even by going to war.

Sum and Substance

1. Name two private organizations formed to promote peace in the early twentieth century. 2. Describe international efforts before 1914 to bring about world peace. What results did they have? 3. Name and describe two instances where arbitration was used to settle a dispute. 4. What idea for promoting peace did Bryan offer?

THE WORKSHOP

OF LASTING SIGNIFICANCE

What role did each of the following have in the years when the United States assumed new international responsibilities?

dollar diplomacy
Clayton-Bulwer
  Treaty
Nicaragua
Philippe
  Bunau-Varilla
Colombia
Hay-Herrán Treaty
Hay–Bunau-Varilla
  Treaty
Panama Canal Zone
William C. Gorgas
George W. Goethals
big stick
Venezuela crisis
  of 1902–1903
Roosevelt corollary
Bryan-Chamorro
  Treaty
Victoriano Huerta
Haiti
Virgin Islands
canal-tolls
  controversy
Mobile speech

Tampico incident
Pancho Villa
ABC powers
John J. Pershing
Treaty of
  Portsmouth
Taft-Katsura
  Agreement
gentleman's
  agreement
Root-Takahira
  Agreement
consortium
first Hague
  Conference
second Hague
  Conference
Permanent Court
  of Arbitration
Alaskan-boundary
  dispute
Algeciras
  Conference
conciliation treaty

HISTORY IN MAPS

1. Turn to the map on page 540. What two possible sites of isthmian canals did the United States consider? What is the special advantage of the Panama site? Ships entering from the Pacific Ocean travel in what direction?

2. Locate the Panama Canal in relation to (a) Cuba, (b) Puerto Rico, (c) Mexico, (d) New York, (e) Miami. Why is the security of the canal of permanent interest to the United States?

3. The map on page 552 shows that the dispute over the Alaskan boundary was ended in a compromise. The conflicting claims extended over about how many miles of the coastline? # Compare the handling of the Alaskan-boundary and the Maine-boundary disputes (see page 196). Who played the major role in each?

INTERNATIONAL POLITICS

1. Characterize the foreign policy of each of these Presidents: Roosevelt, Taft, and Wilson. What do you think motivated each man? Describe an example of the use of Roosevelt's and Taft's foreign policies in Latin America; in Asia.

2. What policy did Wilson hope to follow in Latin America? What one did he actually carry out? Explain the shift.

3. How and under what circumstances did Wilson depart from Taft's policy in Asia?

4. Contrast the situation the United States wished to create or maintain for China with the one it actually set up. Account for the difference and tell how it came about.

5. Explain this statement: "By 1916 the open door [in China] not only had become the closed door but also had acquired a doorman— in Japanese uniform."

6. How did each of the following affect the position of the United States in international politics: (a) the Roosevelt corollary, (b) the manner in which the United States obtained the right to build the Panama Canal, (c) the Canal Tolls Act, (d) the Hague conferences, (e) the settlement of the Alaskan-boundary dispute?

7. What actions did the United States take in the progressive era which showed that it was a world power?

8. How does the United States seek to encourage democracy in Latin American countries? ##

INFORMED OPINION

1. Do you agree with Wilson that the national interest of the United States is served best by uncompromising integrity in international dealings? Explain.

2. State and explain Wilson's idea of the national purpose of the United States. Do you think it is the purpose of the United States today? If not, should it be? Explain.

##The United States encourages democracy in Latin America today by providing aid through the Alliance for Progress. Opportunities for democracy increase as the people are educated.

A LONG VIEW

Reaching Into the World

DESPITE glaring imperfections remaining in American life, the public came out of the progressive era proud of many conquests that were, in a favorite word of Theodore Roosevelt's, "bully." Some were technological—like the development of the automobile and the building of the Panama Canal. One of the most remarkable was the flight of the Wright brothers at Kitty Hawk, North Carolina, in 1903. Another was *the* triumph of 1909—when Robert E. Peary, accompanied by four Eskimos and his Negro assistant, Matthew H. Henson, "discovered" the North Pole.

Other conquests, less dramatic but no less consequential, were in the realm of the mind. For example, under the gentle but positive inspiration of Oliver Wendell Holmes, Jr.—whom Roosevelt appointed to the Supreme Court—the courts reinterpreted American law. Through brilliant and often unpopular decisions, Holmes showed that laws can never be established once and for all. They must be modified constantly, he insisted, in order to satisfy society's changing needs.

Another thinker who made an indelible mark on the period was John Dewey, a professor at Columbia University. Dewey taught that the schoolroom is the chief training ground for democracy. He argued that classroom instruction ought to be organized around student interests and needs. Dewey's magnetism resulted in a revolutionary recasting of American educational ideals and methods that was called "progressive education."

Although the work of Holmes and Dewey and many other social thinkers has endured, in their time it drew less public attention than the activities of the muckrakers. Yet, despite the excitement caused by the muckrakers, most Americans in the progressive era were uninformed about, or insensitive to, sweeping alterations occurring in the country. These changes included the growth in power of the national government, the paying of closer attention on state and local levels to the everyday needs of people, and an increase in the prestige and power of the President.

The reasons for the public blindness varied. In part it was accounted for by the gradualness of the shifts. In part it was because many Americans —including large numbers of newcomers scarcely able to make headway with the English language— were exhausting themselves in sweatshops or mines or factories. At least as numb to the emerging trends were some Americans who were rich, literate, and native-born. Many of them lived lavishly, their chief concern seeming to be how they could best display their wealth.

Americans in all walks of life probably showed less interest in public issues as a result of the rise of spectator sports. In 1902, the first Rose Bowl football game took place at Pasadena, California. (The University of Michigan beat Stanford University, 49–0.) In 1903 big league baseball held its first World Series (which the Boston Red Sox won over the Pittsburgh Pirates).

Most people traveled very little, and vacations # were still a luxury only few could afford. The small number of Americans who traveled abroad could see how accurate was the point made in a widely read book published in England in 1901. Called *The Americanization of the World*, the book maintained that Europeans were slowly but inevitably taking on American economic, political, religious, and technological ideas. The truth was undeniable: the United States, not a powerful country militarily, had become more influential than any other great power. ★ ★ ★ ★ ★ ★ ★ ★ ★ ★ ★ ★

PART SIX WORKSHOP

AMERICA IN THE WORLD

1. On an outline map identify by name the places in which the United States was involved or became interested in the era of imperialism. Write a separate account of American relations in the period with (a) East Asian countries, (b) islands of the Pacific, (c) islands of the Caribbean, (d) Mexico, (e) Canada, (f) South American countries, (g) countries of Europe. Include your opinion of how well the diplomacy was handled in each of the cases you describe.

#
What does your account show about the difficulties of making American foreign policy?

2. Compare the foreign policy of George Washington and John Adams with the policies of Roosevelt and Wilson. Account for the differences.

3. How was the influence of the progressives shown in American foreign policy in the days of imperialism? Describe the practical results of this influence.

4. In what part of the world was the United States chiefly interested in its early years? Why? How did the country's focus of interest change in the late 1800's? Why?

5. Would you say that, on the whole, the United States used its strength "for noble ends or mean ones" in the period of imperialism? Defend your answer.

6. Does jingoism exist today? If so, where? Account for your answer.

7. What is the present status of most colonies acquired by the United States or by European countries?

OLD PROBLEMS BECOME NEW

1. Review the list of evils the progressives saw in American society. Which of them had probably existed from the beginning of United States history? Which were new or fairly new? What accounted for them?

2. How did the progressives expect to solve the problems created by the evils? In what way was it a purely democratic solution?

3. What role did the progressives believe that government had to play in achieving reforms? Would you say that their idea is shared by most people today? Explain.

TIME AND CHANGE

1. What years make up the progressive era? The Age of Imperialism? List the activities or events which, taken together, make up each.

2. Characterize politics in the United States in the years immediately following the Civil War and in the progressive era. What accounted for the change?

3. What social changes were brought about in the period covered in Part Six? What political changes? How was each accomplished?

4. Name at least two economic changes that occurred in the years of imperialism. What accounted for them? ##

THE FEDERAL GOVERNMENT

1. What question involving the Constitution arose after the United States acquired colonies at the end of the nineteenth century? What answer did the Supreme Court give? What did Secretary of State John Hay mean when he said, "The Constitution follows the flag but never catches up with it"?

2. Name three laws passed in Roosevelt's years in the presidency and three in Wilson's that helped strengthen the power of the federal government. In each case tell how the greater strength was achieved.

3. What amendments were added to the Constitution in the progressive era? What effect would you say each has had on the federal government?

4. Describe the role Roosevelt and Wilson played in increasing the prestige of the American presidency. What role did each have in enlarging the power and influence of the national government?

5. Would you say that American democracy became more firmly established as the power of the national government was strengthened? Explain your viewpoint.

##Two economic changes: The United States (1) went on the gold standard (Gold Standard Act of 1900) and (2) acquired easier access to trade with China (by taking the Philippines).

Eyewitness Accounts

Addams, Jane. *Twenty Years at Hull House*. New York: The Macmillan Co. [Paperback—New York: New American Library, Inc.].

Dunne, Finley P. *The World of Mr. Dooley* [Paperback—New York: P. F. Collier, Inc.].

Hofstadter, Richard (ed.). *The Progressive Movement, 1900–1915* [Paperback—Englewood Cliffs, N.J.: Prentice-Hall, Inc., 1964].

Post, Charles J. *Little World of Private Post*. Boston: Little, Brown & Co., 1960.

Resek, Carl (ed.). *The Progressives* [Paperback—Indianapolis: Bobbs-Merrill Co., Inc., 1967].

Weinberg, Arthur, and Lila Weinberg (eds.). *The Muckrakers, 1902–1912*. New York: Simon & Schuster, Inc., 1961 [Paperback—New York: G. P. Putnam's Sons].

Giant Men and Women

Blum, John M. *Woodrow Wilson and the Politics of Morality*. Boston: Little, Brown & Co., 1964 [Paperback—Boston: Little, Brown & Co.].

Farrell, John C. *Beloved Lady: A History of Jane Addams' Ideas on Reform and Peace*. Baltimore: Johns Hopkins Press, 1967.

Garraty, John A. *Woodrow Wilson*. New York: Alfred A. Knopf, Inc., 1956.

Harbaugh, William H. *The Life and Times of Roosevelt* [Paperback—New York: P. F. Collier, Inc.].

Leech, Margaret K. *In the Days of McKinley*. New York: Harper & Row, Publishers, 1959.

Morgan, H. Wayne. *William McKinley and His America*. Syracuse, N.Y.: Syracuse University Press, 1963.

Pringle, Henry F. *Theodore Roosevelt* [Paperback—New York: Harcourt, Brace & World, Inc.].

Swanberg, W. A. *Citizen Hearst*. New York: Charles Scribner's Sons, 1961.

Walworth, Arthur C. *Woodrow Wilson*. Boston: Houghton Mifflin Co., 1965.

Living and Making a Living

Faulkner, Harold U. *Politics, Reform, and Expansion*. New York: Harper & Row, Publishers, 1959 [Paperback—New York: Harper & Row, Publishers].

Hollingsworth, J. R. *The Whirligig of Politics: The Democracy of Cleveland and Bryan*. Chicago: University of Chicago Press, 1963.

Millis, Walter. *The Martial Spirit*. Boston: Houghton Mifflin Co. [Paperback—New York: Viking Press, Inc.].

Mowry, George E. *Theodore Roosevelt and the Progressive Movement*. New York: Hill & Wang, Inc., 1960 [Paperback—New York: Hill & Wang, Inc.].

Nye, Russell B. *Midwestern Progressive Politics, 1870–1958*. East Lansing: Michigan State University Press, 1959.

Pratt, Julius W. *Expansionists of 1898*. Chicago: Quadrangle Books, Inc., 1964 [Paperback—Chicago: Quadrangle Books, Inc.]

Regier, C. C. *The Era of the Muckrakers*. Gloucester, Mass.: Peter Smith.

Rischin, Moses. *The Promised City: New York's Jews, 1870–1914*. Cambridge, Mass.: Harvard University Press, 1964 [Paperback—New York: Citadel Press].

Wiebe, Robert H. *The Search for Order, 1877–1920*. New York: Hill & Wang, Inc., 1967.

Confronting the World

Beale, Howard K. *Theodore Roosevelt and the Rise of America to World Power*. Baltimore: Johns Hopkins Press, 1956 [Paperback—New York: P. F. Collier, Inc.].

Clandenen, Clarence C. *The United States and Pancho Villa*. Ithaca, N.Y.: Cornell University Press, 1961.

Grenville, J. A. S., and G. B. Young. *Politics, Strategy, and American Diplomacy: Studies in Foreign Policy, 1873–1917*. New Haven, Conn.: Yale University Press, 1966.

Healy, David F. *The United States in Cuba, 1898–1902*. Madison: University of Wisconsin Press, 1963.

May, Ernest R. *Imperial Democracy*. New York: Harcourt, Brace & World, Inc., 1961.

Quirk, Robert E. *An Affair of Honor: Woodrow Wilson and the Occupation of Veracruz*. Lexington: University of Kentucky Press, 1962.

Art, Science, and the Life of the Mind

The American Heritage History of Flight. Editors of American Heritage. New York: American Heritage Publishing Co., Inc., 1962.

Geismar, Maxwell. *Last of the Provincials*. Boston: Houghton Mifflin Co. [Paperback—New York: Hill & Wang, Inc.].

Kazin, Alfred. *On Native Grounds*. Boston: Houghton Mifflin Co. [Paperback—New York: Doubleday & Co., Inc.].

Oliver, J. W. *History of American Technology*. New York: Ronald Press Co., 1956.

Paulson, Ross E. *American Ideals, 1865–1896* [Paperback—Chicago: Rand McNally & Co., 1967].

Historical Fiction

Dreiser, Theodore. *The Titan*. Cleveland: World Publishing Co., 1914 [Paperback—New York: New American Library, Inc.]. (Financial skulduggery in the progressive era.)

London, Jack. *The Sea Wolf*. Many editions, including paperback. (The Darwinian theory wrapped in a rousing tale of adventure.)

McKenna, Richard. *The Sand Pebbles*. New York: Harper & Row, Publishers, 1963 [Paperback—New York: Fawcett World Library]. (A brilliant story of a navy gunboat on the China Station.)

Tarkington, Booth. *The Magnificent Ambersons*. Many editions, including paperback. (Middle-class life in the Midwest.)

Why are abstract art and computers particularly alluring and useful to Americans today? (Suggestion: The computer is one means of dealing with the "knowledge revolution"; abstract art is another way of "seeing reality"--the chief way is through photography.)

This math teacher explains how a computer—able to store and retrieve millions of items of information—can be used for learning.

Pablo Picasso's untitled steel sculpture installed in 1967 in Chicago's Civic Center Plaza, like other examples of abstract art, produces fascination and controversy.

Why is "equality of the sexes" a peculiarly American idea? (Industrialization, standard of living.)

Coeducation, at one time unthinkable, is now commonplace, as at Michigan State University.

Rockets, once used chiefly for fireworks, have been developed into military threats with intercontinental range.

Convair Division, General Dynamics

Analyze the possible advantages of the space program, weighing them against various other national requirements.

THE
QUALITY
OF
LIFE

In the first two-thirds of the twentieth century, the public's attention was often directed toward international crises that obscured a revolution in daily living. As electronics helped create machines more obedient than ever, life appeared to become more impersonal. Some of the old discontents, such as poverty, were still present. Yet most Americans were lifting their aspirations, with lively hopes of fulfilling them in a way that would make their lives longer and richer.

Below: How is technological advancement involved?

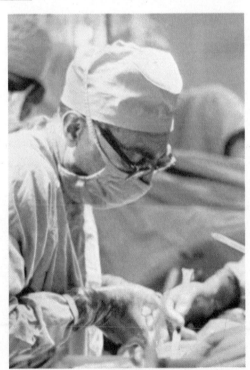

Baylor University College of Medicine

Improvements in medical technology, like open-heart surgery, offer hope to many.

559

Point out that the life expectancy of women exceeds that of men. Ask for reasons why.

Examine ethnic discrimination (based on nationality). (A particular difficulty the Puerto Ricans have is that they are

THE QUALITY OF LIFE *continued*

American citizens but have language and educational hurdles to overcome.)

Wide World

Many Puerto Ricans have come here in search of fuller opportunity. Finding that they must overcome cultural hurdles and sometimes prejudice, they are often greatly disappointed.

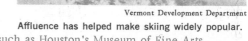

Vermont Development Department

Affluence has helped make skiing widely popular.

Wealth and the development of the arts go hand in hand. Mention some American artistic showpieces, such as Houston's Museum of Fine Arts.

Gulf coast oil production has stimulated the development of Houston—and of other cities in the South and Southwest.

Texas Highway Department

Part Seven emphasizes that--largely because of technological advances--the people of the world have become increasingly interdependent. The difficulties of one group of people have become the difficulties of others, and the aggressive policy of one country can menace all the others. Thus it has become all the more significant to find ways of avoiding war and to live in harmony and security with other peoples. This part describes the world's quest for security in a threatening world.

THE
QUEST
FOR
SECURITY

PART SEVEN

The vision of a secure America living in a world at peace was shattered by a cycle of wars that began in 1914. Although the United States was spared most of their cruel destructiveness on its own soil, it could not escape involvement in them. Americans were forced, year after year, to use valuable strength in arming themselves and their friends against real and potential enemies. The oceans had ceased to be protective #
barriers for the New World, and the day of happy separation from affairs on other continents was done.

The destiny of Americans was now tied to the destiny of the whole human race. Together all mankind stood poised at the gateway to a vaster unknown than it had ever confronted before. Even while wrestling with tormenting national and international problems, humanity was unchaining itself from the earth. Scientists, who could create energy out of the nucleus of the atom, were now putting the heavens themselves within reach.

But would this control over nature serve human beings well or badly? Were they in the twilight of life on this planet, or were they gazing upon a new dawn? Could they muster the wisdom and the perseverance to dispel the nightmare of annihilation? On the answers rested the fate of the "second chance" given to mankind five centuries ago.

Despite the chaos produced in recent times by new political and scientific forces, the torch of liberty still shed its light on America in the second half of the twentieth century. Though people everywhere in the world were in the grip of uncertainty, those who loved freedom could continue to say as the poet once sang:

"But, westward, look, the land is bright."

#Ask why the oceans were no longer barriers. When had the United States become interested in and concerned about happenings on other continents?

There are six remaining chapters in this book. Covered are the First World War (Chapter 25), the postwar years (Chapter 26), the New Deal (Chapter 27), events before the outbreak of the Second World War (Chapter 28), the Second World War (Chapter 29), and the period since the end of the war (Chapter 30).

PART SEVEN

THE QUEST FOR SECURITY

CHAPTER 25	**INVOLVEMENT IN EUROPE**	564
	Europe's Armed Camps Plunge the World Into War	566
	America Bends Its Efforts to Stay Neutral	570
	The United States Joins the Fight Against Germany	577
	Wilson Pleads to Establish a League of Nations	588
CHAPTER 26	**PROSPERITY'S PROMISE**	598
	Harding of Ohio Ushers In a "Return to Normalcy"	600
	New Movements and Diversions Take Hold of America	603
	The Nation Looks Forward to a Permanent Boom Time	622
CHAPTER 27	**CRASH, CRISIS, AND THE NEW DEAL**	628
	A Disastrous Depression Lays America Low	630
	Franklin D. Roosevelt Experiments to Bring Recovery	638
	The President Battles in Defense of His Policies	657
CHAPTER 28	**THE END TO ISOLATION**	666
	America Finds Itself the World's Economic Leader	668
	The United States Tries New Roads to Security	671
	Diplomacy Repairs Relations with Latin America	674
	Grave Dangers Menace International Peace	680
	Aggressive Dictators Set Off a Second World War	686
CHAPTER 29	**THE GLOBAL WAR**	696
	The United States Aids the Enemies of the Axis	698
	America Leads the Allied Powers to Full Victory	706
	The Big Three Lay Plans for a World at Peace	731

CHAPTER 30   IN AN UNEASY WORLD   738

        The Postwar Era Opens Under Harry S Truman   740

        The United States Fights a Cold War and a Hot One   744

        The Pendulum Swings from Eisenhower to Kennedy   752

        As a Superpower, America Defends Global Interests   757

        The Americans and the Soviets Compete in Outer Space   772

        The Nation Moves to Remodel Society   774

        A LONG VIEW   786

The picture of the Peace Corpsman seen here represents the efforts of the United States to help other peoples and other countries of the world, efforts that became herculean in the years after the Second World War.

A Peace Corpsman works in the field side by side with farmers of the arid country of Niger, in tropical Africa.

Peace Corps

This quotation from the war message Wilson delivered to Congress in 1917 was chosen to be used here because it sums up the American motives for entering the First World War. The United States had traditionally remained neutral in the face of the war in Europe.

25

INVOLVEMENT IN EUROPE

The world must be made safe for democracy . . .

The present German submarine warfare against commerce is a warfare against mankind. It is a war against all nations. American ships have been sunk, American lives taken, in ways which it has stirred us very deeply to learn of, but the ships and people of other neutral and friendly nations have been sunk and overwhelmed in the waters in the same way. There has been no discrimination. The challenge is to all mankind. Each nation must decide for itself how it will meet it. . . .

There is one choice we cannot make, we are incapable of making: we will not choose the path

Submarine warfare was a feature of the war. It led the United States to declare war.

A German submarine shells an American merchantman into flames in the perilous North Atlantic Ocean in 1917.

of submission and suffer the most sacred rights of our Nation and our people to be ignored or violated. . . .

With a profound sense of the solemn and even tragical character of the step I am taking and of the grave responsibilities which it involves, but in unhesitating obedience to what I deem my constitutional duty, I advise that the Congress declare the recent course of the Imperial German Government to be . . . war against the Government and people of the United States; that it formally accept the status of belligerent [that is, of a nation at war] which has thus been thrust

upon it. . . .

We are accepting this challenge of hostile purpose because we know that in such a Government, following such methods, we can never have a friend. . . . We are now about to accept the gage of battle with this natural foe to liberty and shall, if necessary, spend the whole force of the nation to check and nullify its pretensions and its power. . . . The world must be made # safe for democracy. . . .

It is a fearful thing to lead this great peaceful people into war, into the most terrible and disastrous of all wars, civilization itself seeming to be in the balance.

But the right is more precious than peace, and we shall fight for the things which we have always carried nearest our hearts—for democracy, for the right of those who submit to authority to have a voice in their own Governments, for the rights and liberties of small nations, for a universal dominion of right by such a concert of free peoples as shall bring peace and safety to all nations and make the world itself at last free.

To such a task we can dedicate our lives and our fortunes, everything that we are and everything that we have, with the pride of those who know that the day has come when America is privileged to spend her blood and her might for the principles that gave her birth and happiness and the peace which she has treasured.

God helping her, she can do no other.

The outbreak of the First World War in 1914 brought to an end what have been called America's years of innocence. The tradition, long standing, of remaining aloof from Europe's quarrels was promptly tested—and soon broken. President Wilson, a keen student of United States history, found it torturing to decide to lead the country into active fighting across the seas. But he finally overcame his great reluctance. This is a portion of the war message Wilson delivered before Congress on April 2, 1917. It is not only a statement of his lofty idealism but also an example of his superb eloquence.

Smithsonian Institution (Henry Beville)

#"Balkan countries" means those occupying the Balkan Peninsula, the peninsula in southern Europe lying south of the Danube River and bordered by the Black, Aegean, and Adriatic seas. Ask the class to look at the peninsula on the map on p. 567 and name the countries there.

EUROPE'S ARMED CAMPS PLUNGE THE WORLD INTO WAR

After the close of the nineteenth century, Europeans talked loudly about international peace while they busily prepared for a world war which they feared they could not avoid. Peace for them had become a delicate balance between armed camps. On the one side was the Triple Alliance—consisting of Germany, Italy, and Austria-Hungary—and on the other, the Triple Entente—France, Russia, and England.

THE CHAIN OF EVENTS

On several occasions the skillful work of diplomats had prevented a general war from breaking out. In 1906, the United States had helped to settle the Moroccan question (see page 553). In 1911 trouble had broken out between Italy and Turkey. In 1912–1913 two short but fierce wars among the Balkan countries* had been restricted by the action of the great powers. But beneath the surface of international politics, a wide range of economic rivalries, boundary disputes, and nationalistic tensions were constantly wearing thin the probability of lasting peace.

Assassination at Sarajevo. On June 28, 1914, the Austrian archduke Franz Ferdinand and his wife were assassinated by a Serbian patriot while visiting in the Bosnian town of Sarajevo (see the map opposite). This double murder proved to be a fateful event.

At first not many Americans were impressed with the seriousness of the tragedy. But they soon learned the startling accuracy of the *New York Times'* grim comment: "A couple of revolver shots probably never before formed a connection between such a line of complicated causes and such an infinite variety of possibly still more complicated effects." Within a month the continent of Europe was ablaze with war.

Austria's ultimatum. The assassin of the Austrian couple belonged to a revolutionary group in Serbia which hoped to destroy the Austrian

monarchy. For that reason, Austria presented to Serbia—on July 23—an ultimatum demanding satisfaction within 48 hours. Serbia refused to comply but offered instead to submit the issue to the Hague Tribunal. The offer was not accepted, and Austria declared war on Serbia on July 28.

The alliances in action. Two days later, Russia, considering itself to be a Slavic country with interests in the Balkans, befriended Serbia by mobilizing. On August 1 Germany, in fulfillment of its treaty pledges to Austria, declared war on Russia and on August 3 on France—Russia's ally. On August 4 German troops began to march into Belgium in order to reach French soil. Britain thereupon declared war on Germany in accordance with a seventy-five-year-old agreement to defend Belgium's neutrality.

THE BATTLE FRONTS

Germany confidently expected to win the war by what was called the Schlieffen plan (in honor of the general who had devised it). It called for a quick blow at Paris in a great wheeling movement by way of Belgium and then—after the defeat of the western enemies—a concentrated attack on Russia.

Unexpected resistance. But Germany miscalculated. The small Belgian army, fighting against hopeless odds, delayed the Germans for two weeks. Then, early in September, French and British troops—reinforced by the Paris garrison transported to the front in taxicabs—halted the German march against Paris in the first Battle of the Marne. Turning now, the Germans attempted to reach the English Channel in order to seize French ports. British and French troops joined forces to stop the German army short of its goal.

Russian successes. Meanwhile, the Russians, mobilizing with greater speed than had been anticipated, drove hard across Germany's eastern frontier, with Berlin itself as their objective. Frightened, the Germans abandoned the Schlieffen plan. They quickly sent troops to

---

* In the first of these wars, Serbia, Bulgaria, Greece, and Montenegro had defeated Turkey. In the second, Serbia joined by Romania, Greece, and Turkey went to war against Bulgaria and defeated it.

##Bosnia had recently been made part of Austria-Hungary. Its people spoke the Serb language. The plot to kill the archduke had been made without official Serbian approval.

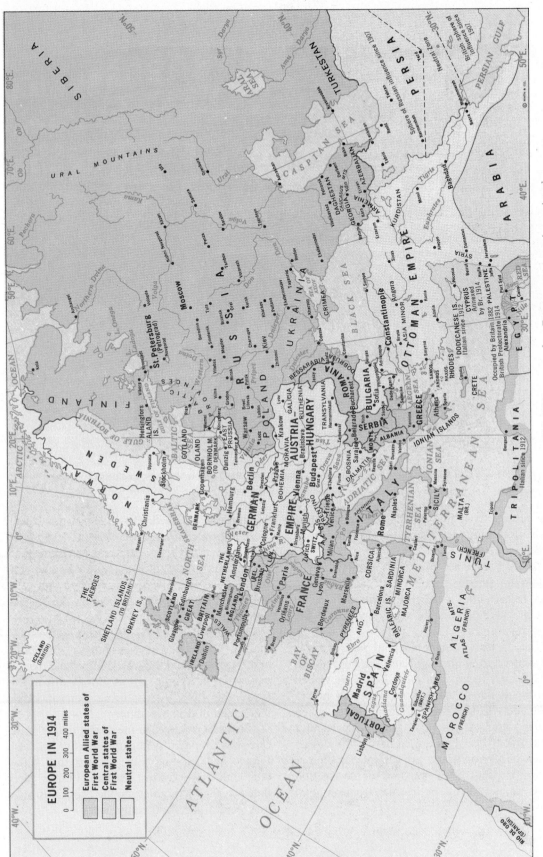

Students should compare this map with the one on pp. 758–759 to see what European countries existed in 1914 which do not exist today. For example, Bosnia is part of Yugoslavia.

UPI

the eastern front to stop the Russians before their chief aim, destroying the French army, had been accomplished.

New techniques and weapons. The hope for a quick and decisive triumph had vanished. The war turned into a war of attrition—one in which each side tries to wear down the other by slow degrees.

The opposing armies adopted new patterns of combat. They burrowed into the ground like ants as they faced each other in savage trench warfare in which gains were measured not in miles but in yards and often in feet. When artillery fire had cleared the way in a particular area, troops literally crawled across the devastation of no-man's-land to penetrate the line of enemy trenches. New weapons of destruction were employed by both sides—poison gas, tanks, and machine guns.

Struggle of the fleets. On the seas the British were in firm control. Their fleet in 1916 forced the German navy to retire and to remain bottled up until the end of the war. German submarines, however, were not affected and were able to inflict crippling damage on the English merchant fleet.

By the end of 1915, the Central Powers—that is, Germany, Austria-Hungary, Bulgaria, and Turkey—held central Europe and Southwest Asia in a tight grip. A British attempt to break this hold by capturing Constantinople had ended in dismal failure.

Stalemate in France. In the spring of 1916, the Germans prepared a mighty offensive to crush France and end the war. Though they threw their full force against eastern France, they failed to win victory despite the enormous price they paid in men and equipment.

 ##Ask what the Central Powers' geographical position had to do with their success in obtaining the grip (see p. 567). Why would the capture of Constantinople have broken it?

1917: a decisive year. By the beginning of 1917, Germany had not broken the resistance of the Entente powers—the Allies—nor had the Central Powers been badly injured. But signs showed that a climax was at hand. One indication was that, because of revolution at home, Russia was threatening to withdraw from the war. A second was that, after three years of disappointment, the British were on the verge of defeating the Turks and capturing Baghdad.

A third was that war exhaustion was developing on both sides. Finally, it was observed that the Allies were increasingly dependent on the economic and industrial strength of the United States.

Sum and Substance

1. Name the rights that Wilson said Americans would be fighting for in entering the war. 2. What was the Triple Alliance? The Triple Entente? 3. Describe the course of events which led to the outbreak of the First World War. 4. What countries came into the war? Why? 5. Name and describe Germany's war plan. 6. How did it turn out? Why? 7. What was the status of the war in 1915? In 1916? In 1917?

State Historical Society of Wisconsin

Barbed wire stretched over a trench and sharp stakes at its edge were expected to slow the enemy.

Upper right: The area between the trenches of the two opposing sides was called "no-man's-land."

The Germans use elephants to accomplish the heavy work of removing barricades and clearing streets in Belgium.

State Historical Society of Wisconsin

This section describes the period directly preceding the entrance of the United States into the war. The feelings of Americans were mixed.
#Ask what the present relationship between the two countries is.

AMERICA BENDS ITS EFFORTS TO STAY NEUTRAL

The periodic crises in Europe's international politics that had absorbed the best energies of its diplomats for a generation were unfamiliar to most Americans. The war seemed to them just one more episode in the age-old struggle for power.

NATURAL SYMPATHIES

Few on this side of the Atlantic stopped to think of any possible effect the war's outcome might have upon the United States. Yet it is safe to guess that a majority of Americans hoped for a victory by the Allies, led by England and France, over the Central Powers, led by Germany and Austria.

Feelings toward England. This partiality did not only result from the profound shock and anger that Americans felt over Germany's wanton invasion of Belgium. It was also accounted for in part by the fact that because of training and tradition most Americans were partial to England and France, especially to England.

Think of the countless millions of Americans who had read Shakespeare, Dickens, Thackeray, Scott, Wordsworth—and other English authors. Consider how familiar were the names "Big Ben," "Westminster Abbey," and "the Tower of London." England's history to 1776 was also America's history; its language and its political institutions, including the traditional freedoms, were America's precious inheritance.

Despite the conflicts of the past, the period since 1897 had witnessed a gradual growth of Anglo-American friendship. Almost all the historic sources of friction between the United States and Britain had been removed. This development was enthusiastically accepted by Englishmen and Americans. As early as 1898 Joseph Chamberlain, a British Cabinet member, had said, ". . . I even go so far as to say that, terrible as war may be, even war itself would be cheaply purchased if in a great and noble cause the Stars and Stripes and the Union Jack should wave together over an Anglo-Saxon alliance."

Those who had always distrusted England were still active. But England's cordiality to the United States during the Spanish-American War and afterward seemed to provide convincing evidence to many Americans that "blood is thicker than water."

Friendship with France. Friendly feelings of long ago were evoked toward France as many Americans recalled the assistance the French had given this country during its struggle for independence. Almost from the beginning of the war in 1914, many Americans waxed sentimental over the French. Franklin K. Lane, Wilson's Secretary of the Interior, spoke of "glorious golden France, the preserver of the arts, the land of noble spirit, the first land to follow our lead into republican liberty."

Response of Americans. To be sure, some Americans who had been born in Europe took up the arguments of their native lands. Many Americans of German descent, for instance, were outspoken in their support of the fatherland. Most Americans of Irish extraction were pro-German because they were anti-British.

Nevertheless, everywhere—and along the Atlantic seaboard, especially—opinion seemed to favor the Allies. The sturdy Belgians, standing like a brick wall against the onrushing Germans, aroused the warmest feelings of sympathy. The brave stand of the French was admired generally. Moreover, stories about atrocities allegedly committed by German soldiers made a deep impression on many Americans.

Desire for peace. The outburst of hurrahs and goodwill for the Allies, however, did not lead to an overwhelming desire to enter the war. The United States was separated by 3000 miles of ocean from the blood feuds of Europe. The issues that had brought on hostilities were not clear to most Americans. Besides, to a generation bombarded with the propaganda of the peace movement in the previous fifteen years, a resort to force in settling international disputes seemed both futile and wrong.

Finally, public attention had not been con-

##Many young Americans joined the English army and the French army and air force. Others formed ambulance corps to assist the Allies in Europe.

#Would a presidential candidate today be likely to fail to mention foreign affairs in his campaign for election? Why? Would he omit mention of foreign affairs or foreign policy in his inaugural? How has the position of Americans changed since 1917?

centrated on foreign policy. In fact, the Democratic platform on which Wilson had been elected in 1912 had hardly mentioned the subject, and Wilson had not referred to foreign affairs at all in his inaugural address.

A prophecy and a hope. Only farsighted and perceptive people sensed what Theodore Roosevelt understood. Said the former Rough Rider: "We have no choice, we people of the United States, as to whether we shall play a great part in the affairs of the world. That has been decided for us by fate, by the march of events." In time, Americans would come to accept the meaning of these prophetic words. Meanwhile, priding themselves on the nation's might, they did not intend to sap it by foreign ventures.

WILSON'S POLICY

Wilson did not at first differentiate—at least not publicly—between the stated war aims of the two opposing sides. He wanted, he said, to "reserve judgment until the end of the war, when all its events and circumstances can be seen in their entirety and in their true relations." The President warned the nation not to be thrown off its balance by a war with which it had nothing to do.

Impartiality. Wilson fully appreciated that his countrymen were already forming their sympathies. Yet he urged in a memorable speech of August 19, 1914, "We must be impartial in thought as well as in action, must put a curb upon our sentiments." Actually Wilson, whose words sometimes seemed high-flown, must have known that it was impossible for the American people to keep their emotions neutral. Nevertheless, passionately wanting the United States to stay out of the war, Wilson had expressed this wish, trusting that it might somehow come true.

At first, American naval pilots serving in France had to use planes manufactured abroad.

American naval planes at a navy station in Pensacola, Florida, in 1914; military aviation was in its infancy.

State Historical Society of Wisconsin

##Discuss the national leaders today who have the power to influence people through their writing or speeches. What kind of language do they use?

571

#Recall that Roosevelt had helped settle the Russo-Japanese War in 1905 (see p. 548) and that the Germans had sought his further mediation in the Moroccan crisis (see p. 553).

His private view. Wilson himself was hardly "impartial in thought." Colonel Edward M. House, Wilson's personal adviser, wrote when the war was barely a month old: "I was interested to hear him [the President] express as his opinion . . . that if Germany won, it would change the course of our civilization and make the United States a military nation." In private the President once blurted out, "England is fighting our fight."

Possible mediation. Wilson hoped that the United States could remain out of the conflict in order, at the appropriate time, to play the role of mediator—that is, be the conciliator between the warring sides. Walter Hines Page, the United States ambassador at London, wrote the President in the first month of the war: "Be ready, for you will be called upon to compose this huge quarrel."

Wilson was certain that the world would accept the United States as the peacemaker, because, he said, America has "nothing to covet." The United States, he declared, must keep itself peaceful and impartial so that it "may be fit to be Europe's friend when the day of tested friendship comes."

Stubborn realities. The difficulty was, of course, that the United States would not be able to exercise its moral influence if the Central Powers won the war. In such an event this country would have to prepare a war machine with which to face them. Theodore Roosevelt expressed the thought that it would be "quite in the cards to see Germany and Japan . . . join together against the United States and any other power that stood in their way."

Secretary of State William Jennings Bryan saw little distinction between the aims of the Allies and those of the Central Powers. He believed the United States must avoid taking a position against Germany so strong that the country might be drawn into the fray.

Other American diplomats disagreed with Bryan. They carefully analyzed the possible effects of a German triumph, pointing out how dangerous it was to America to be indifferent concerning who might win. They argued that a German victory would, for the first time in history, confront the United States with a hostile country supreme on land *and* sea. Such an outcome, they asserted, would seriously alter life in America by forcing the nation to become militaristic. Therefore, they concluded, Americans had to recognize that the collapse of the British would be equivalent to a defeat for themselves. The United States must exert every effort, they believed, to prevent such a disaster.

Publicly Wilson never dwelt on the relationship between the war in Europe and the national security. To have done so would have disqualified him to serve as mediator in the event—which many expected—that neither side was able to achieve a clear-cut victory on the fields of battle.

TROUBLES ON THE HIGH SEAS

Wilson's hope of being a mediator was never fulfilled. The defense of American rights as a neutral nation, able to trade everywhere, unavoidably brought the country into conflict with both sides.

Defending neutral rights against Britain. From the start of the war, the British seemed as careless of American rights on the seas as they had been in the years before the War of 1812. The British insisted that granting the United States' demand to be permitted to trade anywhere—even with the enemy—would aid the Germans. They labeled such trading *un*-neutral behavior, declaring that it would nullify the efforts of England's fleet to keep food, supplies, and munitions from reaching Germany.

The British, naturally, would not give up the principal weapon at their command. In consequence, the abuses of United States rights as a neutral came close to rupturing relations between the two English-speaking nations.

Ship seizures. It became British practice to stop neutral merchantmen at sea to find out if they were carrying contraband goods.† But instead

---

† Goods essential to warfare, like guns and ammunition, are called contraband of war. According to international law, these goods may be seized by a nation at war if they are on the way to the enemy—even though they are being transported by a neutral nation. Because almost any item in commerce can be important in modern war, the British interpreted the word *contraband* broadly.

 ##Review the situation before the War of 1812. Which countries were at war then? How did the neutral United States get into trouble as a result of the war between them?

of examining the ships and permitting those that could be cleared to sail on, the English took the vessels into port for a closer inspection. British captains argued reasonably that, although they regretted this practice, any naval vessel stopping to conduct a search on the high seas was a "sitting duck" for torpedoes fired from a submarine.

American shippers—particularly the ones who traded in perishables—frequently suffered severe losses at the hands of the British. Their resentment seemed justified. Many Americans, angry at England for its policies, shared the view of Wilson's Secretary of the Interior, who asked, "Can it be that she is trying to take advantage of the war to hamper our trade . . . ?"

The blockade. The blockade the British established also incensed Americans. It was applied not only to German ports but also to neutral ones. Germany's neutral neighbors had to provide guarantees that certain goods they were importing were intended for their own use and not for reshipment to Germany. American exporters were angry because they had to endure such humiliating and costly interference with their legitimate trade.

Other irritations. Still other British practices added to the woes of Americans engaged in ocean trade. For example, the British intercepted the mails and blacklisted American firms carrying on trade with Germany. Also, the British used the American flag to disguise their own vessels.

American protests against such activities were frequent. But the inescapable fact was that, in spite of difficulties, the profits from American trade with the Allies were so great that it would have been foolish to risk losing them. Besides, the British methods, though extremely irritating, were only damaging to American *property;* after the war the monetary cost could be adjusted by the courts and paid.

The German submarines. Far more serious than the British violations of American rights were German submarine activities that threatened American *lives.* The submarine, said Wilson, violates the "fundamental rights of humanity."

One Hundred Cartoons by Cesare, 1916

The Kaiser and John Bull judge the neutral nations. They agree on the verdict: "Guilty!"

Compare the two John Bulls.

A German cartoon has John Bull dictating to Wilson.

Historical Pictures Service

Early in February, 1915, the Germans announced that the waters around Great Britain constituted a war zone in which submarines would sink enemy vessels on sight. Germany, knowing that the British were sometimes using neutral flags for protection, could not guarantee that no neutral vessel would be sunk.

A warning from the Department of State. The American response was immediate. The Department of State warned Germany that it would be held to "a strict accountability" for the loss of American vessels or lives. Furthermore, the Department served notice that the United States would take every measure "to secure to American citizens the full enjoyment of their acknowledged rights on the high seas." The country shortly had to fulfill this promise.

An iceberg sank the Titanic in 1912.

"Cold as the iceberg"—comparing the Kaiser, responsible for torpedoing the *Lusitania*, with the foe of the *Titanic*.

One Hundred Cartoons by Cesare, 1916

Basically, the submarine rather than Germany had created new conditions in sea warfare. Traditional practice had been to stop a vessel suspected of being the enemy's, visit and search it, and if justifiable, take it into port as a prize. International law also recognized the right to sink a vessel after its passengers and crew had been removed. A submarine, however, was not large enough to hold more than its own men. Furthermore, being vulnerable to attack, it dared not even approach an armed merchant vessel, which was able to sink or mortally damage a submarine with one shot.

The easiest way to avoid difficulties would have been for the United States government to warn Americans that they must not travel in the war zone on the ships of belligerents. This was the policy proposed by Secretary of State Bryan. But Wilson refused to accept such a solution. "I cannot," he said, "consent to any # abridgment of the rights of American citizens in any respect."

Tragedy off the Irish coast. The stand of the President was put to the test when the British liner *Lusitania* was torpedoed and sunk off the Irish coast by a German submarine on May 7, 1915. Of the nearly 1200 people who drowned, 128 were Americans—including children.

Before the *Lusitania* had sailed from New ## York, the German embassy in Washington had taken space in New York newspapers to warn Americans to stay off the ship. But the destruction of the vessel was the result of chance rather than of deliberate planning. The commander of the German U-boat‡ responsible, discouraged by slim pickings on the ocean, had decided to head homeward. Suddenly he caught a glimpse of the *Lusitania* in his periscope, took aim, and fired.

When the news of the disaster reached the United States, there was a national gasp of shock and horror. The war had suddenly taken a new turn: the distinction between combatants and noncombatants had disappeared. Even children appeared to be in the front lines.

---

‡ "U-boat"—derived from the German word for submarine, *Unterseeboot*—was a widely used name for this kind of craft.

##The sinking of the Lusitania cost 1198 lives. Among them were the lives of 128 Americans. Americans had lost their lives in earlier sinkings, but never in such numbers.

But against the clamor for immediate war with Germany, Wilson stood firm. Three days after the sinking he told an audience in Philadelphia: "There is such a thing as a man being too proud to fight. There is such a thing as a nation being so right that it does not need to convince others by force that it is right."

Exchanging notes. The Germans rejected an American note of protest that demanded reparation. They insisted that the sinking was an act of self-defense because, they declared, the ship carried a cargo of munitions. They steadfastly refused to assume responsibility for the loss of American lives. A second note of protest sent by Wilson was so strong that Bryan, fearing it would lead to war, refused to sign it. Bryan at this point resigned as Secretary of State and was succeeded by Robert Lansing, who could agree with the President.

The German government dragged out the ensuing discussion for months. In the end, although refusing to yield publicly to the Americans, it secretly instructed its submarine captains to refrain from attacking passenger vessels without warning. In effect, unrestricted submarine warfare was suspended. Germany believed it could win the war without it.

A pledge. Yet in March, 1916, almost a year after the sinking of the *Lusitania,* the French steamer *Sussex* was torpedoed in the English Channel. Although it was not sunk, the loss of life was heavy. Some Americans were injured.

A new crisis in German-American affairs was at hand. Lansing wanted to break off relations with the government of Germany immediately. Wilson, preoccupied with Mexico and not convinced that the public would follow him in drastic action against Germany, decided to negotiate again. He sent a stern ultimatum:

> Unless the Imperial Government should now immediately declare and effect an abandonment of its present methods of submarine warfare against passenger and freight-carrying vessels, the government of the United States can have no choice but to sever diplomatic relations with the German Empire altogether.

Once more the Germans yielded to America, giving a promise that has come to be called

One Hundred Cartoons by Cesare, 1916

A cartoon about the Sussex torpedoing: "I cannot tell a lie—He did it with his little submarine."

What is the point of the caption?

the "*Sussex* pledge." Merchant ships would henceforth "not be sunk without warning and without saving human lives." But the Germans attached a string to the pledge: the United States, for its part, must seek to persuade the British to give up their "starvation blockade" of Germany. Obviously, the United States could not compel England to change its strategy.

PROPOSING MEDIATION

Even though Wilson had not obtained a truly binding pledge from Germany, his insistence seemed again to force that country ## to back down. But the United States had put itself into a dangerous position. In the event of the sinking of another ship, it must either go to war or retreat with a serious loss of national prestige. Wilson hoped against hope that Germany would honor its pledge. In addition, be-

##Americans were pleased, thinking that Wilson had saved the day and that peace would now be maintained. Ask why people who make threats should consider them carefully beforehand.

575

deviled by British abuses of neutral rights, he was almost at the end of his patience with England.

The missions of Colonel House. By 1916 the conviction grew in Wilson's mind that he must work to end the war. He sent Colonel House abroad early in the year to sound out the leaders of the warring nations. In 1915 a similar mission by House had been fruitless because each side still optimistically expected to be the victor. The outcome of House's new round of talks was just as disappointing.

Germany was still in too strong a military position to accept a peace settlement that did not reflect the success of the German armies. Triumphant against Russia in the east and exerting tremendous pressure on France all along the western front, Germany was eager for Wilson to call a peace conference, where it could state its demands. The military position of England, on the other hand, was too unfavorable for the British to submit to such a conference at this time.

A last effort. In December, 1916, Wilson asked both sides to state their terms for peace. The replies were so extravagant that there was no possibility of using them as a basis for ending hostilities. Wilson was profoundly disappointed. He knew that the collapse of this attempt to make peace could only lead to the resumption by Germany of unrestricted submarine warfare in order to end the war quickly. Such a step would greatly increase the possibility that the United States would be drawn into the fighting.

A "peace without victory." At this point Wilson decided to make a statement of his own idea of suitable peace terms. The President had been developing a concept of a league of nations able to prevent wars in the future.

Before the Senate on January 22, 1917, Wilson stated his belief that the United States would willingly join a "League for Peace." Furthermore, he said, "No covenant of coöperative peace that does not include the peoples of the New World can suffice to keep the future safe against war; and yet there is only one sort of peace that the peoples of America could join in guaranteeing."

What kind was that? The answer Wilson supplied was new in the history of modern warfare. ". . . It must be," he said, "a peace without victory. . . . Victory would mean peace forced upon the loser, a victor's terms imposed upon the vanquished. . . . Only a peace between equals can last."

Response abroad. To the warring nations Wilson's "peace-without-victory" address seemed impertinent and indecent. Their youth had been dying in the trenches for two and a half years, and to talk of anything less than victory seemed a breach of faith with the dead. Nevertheless, Wilson found that he was beginning to acquire international standing as a spokesman for the conscience of mankind.

PEACE OR HONOR

Meanwhile, Wilson displayed skill in presenting to the people at home the complex problems the United States now faced. These are the moving words he used to express his— and America's—fundamental problem:

I know that you are depending upon me to keep the nation out of war. So far I have done so, and I pledge you my word that, God helping me, I will—if it is possible. You have laid another duty upon me. You have bidden me see that nothing stains or impairs the honor of the United States. And that is a matter not within my control. That depends upon what others do, not upon what the government of the United States does, and therefore there may at any moment come a time when I cannot preserve both the honor and the peace of the United States.

Preparedness. Wilson's strong hope for peace was a barrier to his making full military and naval preparations for the possibility of going to war. But his slowness stood him in good stead—particularly among pacifists—in the presidential campaign of 1916.

"He kept us out of war." The slogan "He kept ## us out of war" made a deep and favorable impression upon peace-loving Americans everywhere. Hailed by his party as the greatest Democratic leader since Jackson, Wilson was recognized as a friend of labor in the big industrial cities. Election posters showing a

##To what did the slogan refer? (To Wilson's handling of the sinking of the Lusitania and to the torpedoing of the Sussex.)

worker's family bore the caption, "He has protected me and mine." The Republicans made an issue of the alleged lack of military preparedness. They distributed placards showing the widow of a drowned American and her children and the words, "He has neglected me and mine."

Charles Evans Hughes. The Republicans might have been able to win if they had nominated Theodore Roosevelt. "T. R." would have been willing to make the race,§ but the regulars would not take a man who had run out on the party four years before and campaigned independently (see page 522). Besides, they wanted a more predictable candidate. They found him in Charles Evans Hughes, of New York.

Tall, stately, and handsome, Hughes wore a full beard—he was one of the last major politicians to do so. Hughes was a distinguished lawyer who had made an outstanding record as a progressive governor of New York. Now after six years as a member of the Supreme Court of the United States, he was submitting his resignation to Wilson in order to run against him.

The hyphenate vote. Hughes lacked Wilson's fire. Besides, he was hampered by the instructions of his party to curry favor with the so-called hyphenate vote, Irish- and German-Americans. Wilson's strong stand against Germany, it was assumed by the Democrats,

had already lost him the support of these people anyhow. He was, therefore, less interested in going out of his way to court them.

Reelection of the President. On election night it appeared that Hughes had won. It was said of the Democratic gathering which received the returns at the Hotel Biltmore in New York that never had there been "such a morgue-like entertainment in the annals of time." Shortly after midnight, when newspapermen sought interviews with Hughes, they were informed that the president-elect of the United States was asleep and could not be disturbed.

The following day the returns from California came in, showing Wilson to be the victor after all. For the first time since Jackson, a Democratic President had been elected to a second successive term.

Sum and Substance

1. Which of the warring sides did most Americans favor? Give their reasons. 2. Why did they not wish to enter the war? 3. What role did Wilson hope the United States might play? 4. What varying points of view were expressed by Americans concerning a German victory? 5. Describe this country's difficulties with Britain; with Germany. 6. What crises developed in the United States' relations with Germany in 1915? In 1916? How was each handled? 7. What peace efforts were made by Wilson? 8. Give the main facts concerning the presidential election of 1916.

This section describes American participation in the First World War.

THE UNITED STATES JOINS THE FIGHT AGAINST GERMANY

Although Wilson's reelection was by a narrow margin, the President interpreted it as a command from the people. He proposed to use his new lease on power.

THE IMMEDIATE CAUSE

The German government presently provided the opportunity. Six days before the President's

"peace-without-victory" speech, the German ambassador to the United States had received word from home that starting on February 1, 1917, the Imperial Navy would resume unrestricted submarine warfare.

The fateful note. The ambassador, Count J. H. von Bernstorff, tried in the short time at his disposal to influence his government to change its decision. He knew that war with the United States was hanging in the balance, but he was unable to alter his country's resolve. On January 31 he carried out instructions to deliver

§ The Progressives nominated him again, but he declined to accept. Shortly afterward, the Progressive party, unable to find effective leadership, disbanded. Most of its supporters followed Roosevelt sheepishly back to the Republican fold, but many others, refusing to do this, voted for Wilson.

to the Department of State a note announcing that unrestricted submarine warfare would begin again.

Not only would vessels of known or presumed Allied ownership be sunk on sight and without regard to life, but also *all* neutral merchantmen would be subject to attack. The United States would be permitted to send one ship weekly to Europe if it was clearly painted red and white, traveled a specified route, and carried no contraband.

As one American newspaper put it, "Freedom of the seas would now be enjoyed by icebergs and fish." Plainly, Germany had decided that even though the United States might be provoked into entering the war, England would be crushed before the effect of America's power could be felt.

Breaking relations. On February 3 the United States severed diplomatic relations with Germany. Wilson, however, was still bent on avoiding war. Colonel House wrote in his diary of a conversation he had with the President on February 1, 1917. It reveals Wilson's agony in deciding between peace and honor:

> He [Wilson] reiterated his belief that it would be a crime for this Government to involve itself in a war to such an extent as to make it impossible to save Europe afterward. He spoke of Germany as 'a madman that should be curbed.' I asked him if he thought it fair to the Allies to ask them to do the curbing without doing our share. He noticeably winced at this, but still held to his determination.

Arming the merchant ships. Eager to discourage submarine attacks on American ships—and thereby possibly prevent war with Germany—Wilson asked Congress for authority to arm United States merchant vessels. A determined band of Senators—called by Wilson "a little group of willful men"—blocked the approval the President wanted. But he went ahead anyhow to install guns and gun crews on the ships.

The Zimmermann note. At this moment Germany made an important blunder. The German foreign minister, Arthur Zimmermann, proposed to Mexico that if the United States went to war, Mexico should join Germany and, in re-

turn, recover "the lost territory in New Mexico, Texas, and Arizona." Mexico was urged # also to invite Japan to ally itself with Germany. The Zimmermann note—sent in secret code— was intercepted and "broken" by British naval intelligence. It was passed on to American authorities in full expectation of the stunning effect it would have on American opinion.

The publication of the note in the United States on March 1 created a sensation, as anticipated. Particularly in the Southwest, where the issues of the war had so far aroused little interest or concern, there was unfeigned outrage. Also, Germany's wooing of Japan had angered people on the Pacific coast. The United States was now on the knife's edge of war. A series of sinkings—a result of the unrestricted submarine warfare—showed that Germany would continue its disregard of America's rights as a neutral unless *forced* to stop.

The decision. Despite many provocations, Wilson doggedly tried to avoid the necessity of entering the fight. He had concluded, though, that a German victory would end whatever hope men had for a better world and a secure future. Wilson was aware of the high cost in blood and money of waging war. Still, he hoped that the results for mankind would justify the sacrifices.

The war message. Wilson's public announcement of his decision, when it came, was clear. On April 2, having called a special session of Congress, the President asked for a declaration of war against Germany (see pages 564–565).

As for the future, Wilson asserted that peace could be made secure only through "a partnership of democratic nations." And in a phrase which was to become a rallying cry, he declared, "The world must be made safe for ## democracy." Suddenly Wilson had been transformed from a man "too proud to fight" into a war leader.

Congressional approval. Even Wilson's political opponents congratulated him on his war message. Henry Cabot Lodge, soon to become a stubborn foe of the President's, shook his hand and said, "Mr. President, you have expressed in the loftiest manner possible the sentiments of the American people."

When Wilson left the Capitol, the crowds cheered him lustily. Later that day, after he had returned to the White House and as he thought of the cheers that had greeted him earlier, he said to his secretary: "My message today was a message of death for our young men. How strange it seems to applaud that." And the President is reported to have put his head on the table and wept. Congress passed a # war resolution on April 6, 1917.

ENGAGING THE ENEMY

Wilson no longer talked of a "peace without victory." He now was saying, "Force, Force to the utmost, Force without stint or limit, the righteous and triumphant Force which shall make Right the law of the world." But most Americans were not prepared for heavy military participation. Nevertheless, Allied representatives without any delay began to arrive in the United States, pleading for full and quick assistance to save their countries from defeat.

Raising an army. Since the congressional Defense Act of 1916 had provided for a regular army of only 175,000, Wilson's administration turned to the draft in order to build up the armed forces. The Selective Service Act, which went into effect in May, 1917, aroused considerable opposition because it represented a ## break with the time-honored tradition of relying first on volunteers.

The Speaker of the House, "Champ" Clark, said he saw "precious little difference between a conscript and a convict." But the public, in general, accepted the draft as a necessity. Ultimately the age range affected by the Selective Service Act was extended to include all men between the ages of eighteen and forty-five. The Act raised 2,800,000 of the 4,791,172 men who made up the United States armed forces during the war.

The role of the navy. The United States Navy in Europe was under the command of Admiral William S. Sims, one of the world's leading experts on naval marksmanship. The fleet safely

convoyed to Europe not only the American troops but also about 5,000,000 tons of supplies.

Despite the best that the German submarines could do, the navy did not lose a single troopship on the eastward voyage. The navy also aided considerably in helping the British fleet keep the Baltic Sea clear of German vessels.

The uniform was of khaki, a dull brown.

An American soldier says good-by to his family.

National Archives

A sketch of a doughboy by a soldier-artist.

This soldier wears a helmet, which provided better protection than a hat.

The A.E.F. In response to the urgent pleas of the Allies, an American Expeditionary Force—the A.E.F.—was speedily organized. The first units arrived in Paris in June, 1917. Its commander was the good-looking, fifty-six-year-old major general John J. Pershing, who had made headlines in 1906 when President Roosevelt "jumped" him in rank from captain to brigadier general. Pershing had again attracted attention by his pursuit of Pancho Villa in 1916.

In the Allied lines. The American soldiers, green but enthusiastic, represented the vast manpower available in the New World. Their appearance in the battle line unquestionably heartened the Allies and seriously shook the morale of the Germans.

Marshal Ferdinand Foch, the supreme commander of the Allied forces, was deeply im-

About 2,000,000 Americans saw service on this front, over 1,000,000 in the Meuse-Argonne offensive alone. Observe how dangerously close the Germans came to Paris, the French capital.

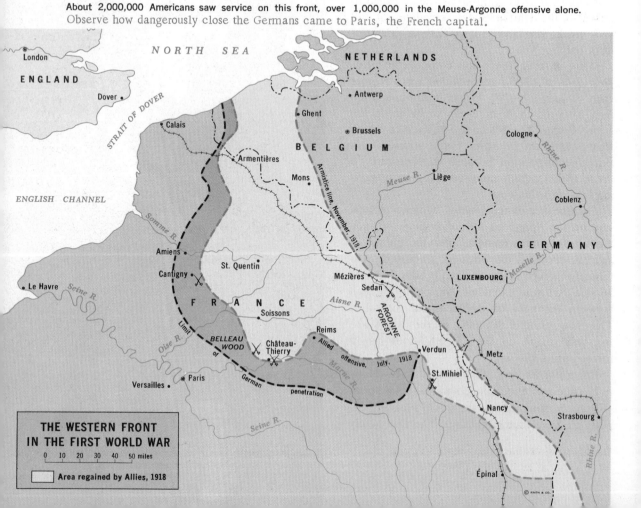

THE WESTERN FRONT IN THE FIRST WORLD WAR

0 10 20 30 40 50 miles

Area regained by Allies, 1918

#Ask what Pershing's motive was in making this request. (He doubtless thought that the Americans' morale would be better if they were a distinct unit, that he could have greater control over them in such a circumstance, and that their contribution could be seen better.)

pressed by the quality of the American soldiers. (His judgment contrasted sharply with that of the Germans before the war, who had scornfully ranked American military prowess somewhere between that of the Belgians and the Portuguese.) Foch honored Pershing's instructions that the United States forces were to be a distinct unit, "the identity of which must be preserved."

But the Allied military situation was desperate in the spring of 1918. In March the Germans had launched an offensive to end the war before the strength of the United States could be fully felt. At Pershing's discretion, United States units were thrown into battle where needed.

Château-Thierry. By the beginning of June, the Germans had fought to within 50 miles of Paris. In this desperate moment for the Allies, American troops were pressed into action in the Battle of Château-Thierry (pronounced sha*tow*-tee-eh*ree*), where they helped the French stop the enemy advance.

Cantigny. The war was now reaching a decisive stage. The Germans were attempting to deliver a massive assault on Paris. But they were discovering the formidable fighting ability of the "Yanks." In the first offensive in which Americans were engaged, they bravely captured from the Germans and held the key town of Cantigny (pronounced can-teen*yee*)—on the road to Paris.

Belleau Wood. Substantial numbers of Americans participated also in the recapture from the Germans of Belleau (pronounced *bel*low) Wood—west of Château-Thierry and also on the path to Paris. In this battle, elements of the United States marines played an especially

This picture shows the difficulty of regaining the area in yellow on the map on p. 580.

Yanks fire 37-millimeter guns in a crucial and precarious advance along the battered western front.

U.S. Signal Corps, National Archives

##The battles named here and on the next page are marked with battle symbols on the map on the opposite page. The Americans took part in stopping the Germans and in beginning to push them back.

State Historical Society of Wisconsin

United States troops battle in the streets of a French town in 1918 to take it from its German captors. Much of the area regained by the Allies (shown on the map on page 580) was won by just such fighting.

Compare this picture with the one on p. 291. These buildings had once been French homes.

distinguished part. The German offensive was finally slowed in the weeks from July 18 to August 6. Then, in the second Battle of the Marne, Allied troops, reinforced with 85,000 Americans, halted the German army.

Now it was Marshal Foch's turn. In a powerful counteroffensive against the enemy on a line from the Aisne (pronounced *enn*) to the Marne, the Allies began to force the Germans back. About 270,000 United States troops participated in this mighty effort. In August, the First American Army was organized, and a portion of the Allied front was assigned to it. Before the war's end in November, the Yanks would hold about a quarter of the entire battle line.

St. Mihiel. The first distinctively United States offensive took place in September, 1918, as part of the final stages of the war. The Americans were assigned the mission of driving the Germans out of the St. Mihiel (pronounced san-me*yel*) area (see the map on page 580), which they had held since 1914. The action ultimately engaged about 550,000 Americans. The four days of bloody fighting straightened the line but cost 7000 American casualties. The Yanks, though, had exacted a heavy price that included taking 16,000 prisoners and capturing 443 guns.

The Meuse-Argonne offensive. Having been tested under fire, the American troops were now sent to the area between the Meuse River and the

A major difficulty American soldiers in France had was trying to adjust themselves to life in a foreign country--where English was not the language. These men had had about six months of drill, then had gone overseas for two months of instruction, and finally had gone into battle.

Soldiers of the A.E.F. are massed in a French village awaiting orders to advance in the United States offensive against St. Mihiel. Its success proved that Americans could conduct a major operation.

Each of these soldiers carried an identification disk at all times so that he could be identified in case he was injured or killed. His daily life was full of hardships and dangers.

#If possible, students should talk to older people in the community who can remember the celebration of the armistice in the United States. The wild joy and excitement shown on that day were unlike the reactions shown by Americans when the Second World War ended.

Argonne Forest. The goal was the Sedan-Mézières Railroad, the principal supply line of the German forces on the western front. The attack, which began near the end of September, in 1918, was part of a general offensive launched by Foch to compel the Germans to retreat.

A gigantic American force of 1,200,000 was engaged in the battle—the greatest action in which Americans had ever participated—and before it was done, the troops had sustained 120,000 casualties. Although the doughboys did not succeed in taking Sedan before hostilities ended, they nevertheless severed the railroad and greatly weakened the German military position. This engagement without any question hastened Germany's call for an armistice—a truce—which came at last on November 11, 1918.

The price of victory. America's total casualties in the war—49,000 killed in action and 230,000 wounded—were small compared with the losses sustained by the countries that had been fighting since 1914. But in proportion to the number of Americans engaged and the length of time the United States was in the war, the losses were heavy. They aroused new determination in this country to help bring about an enduring peace.

MOBILIZING THE HOME FRONT

The home front demonstrated to a remarkable extent that, as Wilson stated it, "beyond all question the highest and best form of efficiency is the spontaneous coöperation of a free people." Understanding from the beginning that the fighting front depended on a well-organized and responsive people at home,

By the end of the war, there were about 860 American planes in service at the front.
An American pilot flies a mission over Europe in a plane borrowed from the Netherlands air unit.

Painting by Henry Farré, Air Force Art Collection

584 The Rand McNally paperback (in the Classroom Library Series) entitled A History of the American Air Force, by W. H. Ruenheck and P. M. Flammer, describes the growth of our air force.

When Germany asked for an armistice, Turkey, Bulgaria, and Austria-Hungary had already asked for peace. The German ruler--the kaiser--was about to flee to the Netherlands. Germany asked for an armistice on November 6 and agreed to the Allies' terms on November 11.

U.S. Navy

Americans on the U.S.S. *Texas* view with satisfaction the surrender of the German fleet in November, 1918.

Below: Again, additional evidence of the destruction brought by war. Bombs had fallen here.

Men of the signal corps, confident of victory, advance past the former headquarters of the German crown prince.

U.S. Signal Corps, National Archives

JOIN THE ARMY AIR SERVICE BE AN AMERICAN EAGLE!

Smithsonian Institution

The Army Air Service in time became the Air Force.

#The board provided centralized control of the industrial strength of the country.

Wilson dedicated his best efforts to bringing this about.

The War Industries Board. One of the most important steps Wilson took was the creation of the Council of National Defense in 1916, which set up the War Industries Board after # the United States entered the conflict. Under the chairmanship of Bernard M. Baruch, a successful financier, this board was a kind of general staff for production.

The board procured supplies for the government and for the Allies. It controlled the distribution of raw materials, keeping an eye on both military and civilian needs. Baruch persuaded many business executives to give up their highly paid positions in private enterprise and contribute their talents and labors to the war effort at a "salary" of a dollar a year.

Administering the food supply. To be food administrator, the President in 1917 chose Herbert C. Hoover, a California mining engineer who had earlier demonstrated outstanding ability in distributing Belgian relief. Hoover encouraged

Notice the attention given to cottage cheese as a source of protein (besides meat).

An exhibit prepared for consumers shows them how they can help the fighting forces win the war.

State Historical Society of Wisconsin

the planting of "war gardens" in order to increase the vegetable supply. His efforts resulted in greatly increased production of almost every kind of agricultural commodity.

The public was urged to conserve food and to find substitutes. Wheatless and meatless days were proclaimed. "To Hooverize" became a commonly used verb meaning "to save food." Hoover and his program deserve much credit for the fact that after the war ended, America could ship enough food to Europe to prevent general starvation there.

Conserving fuel. A fuel administrator was also appointed by the President. The task of this officer was to see that coal, especially, was conserved for the war effort. "Save a shovelful of coal a day" became a well-known slogan. Also, daylight saving time was introduced to make the sun available longer in the workday. "Gasless" Sundays saved gasoline and oil, and "heatless" Mondays saved fuel.

Railroads and shipping. The government temporarily took over the management and operation of railroads of the country. The railroad administrator, William Gibbs McAdoo—one # of Wilson's sons-in-law—operated them as if they were one line. The United States Shipping Board took charge of a program of shipbuilding. In a single day—July 4, 1918—ninety-five vessels were launched, totaling 475,000 tons. A familiar sign in shipyards read: "Three ships a week or bust."

National War Labor Board. The active support for the war effort provided by the labor movement was in no small way responsible for the nation's military success. The National War Labor Board, which was created in April, 1918, and remained in existence until the end of the fighting, sat as final judge in labor disputes. One of those who served as its chairman was former President Taft.

The Liberty loans. Nothing dramatized better the importance of civilian participation in the war effort than the sale of the enormously popular Liberty bonds, which raised over sixteen billion dollars. The first Liberty Loan, in June, 1917, ##

Observe the young civilian's stiff collar and high-topped shoes--typical of that time.
Civilians as well as men in uniform buy Liberty bonds from a saleswoman on a street in Washington.

Library of Congress

was oversubscribed by a billion dollars.

The three loans that followed were equally well received. The fourth and last, in October, 1918, was oversubscribed by a billion dollars three weeks after it went on sale. A fifth, or Victory loan—in 1919—raised an additional four and a half billion dollars. In all, 20,000,000 people—more than half the adult population—had purchased bonds.

The Creel committee. The aims and policies of the government were widely advertised through the Committee on Public Information. Dominated by its chairman, George Creel, it came to be known popularly as the Creel committee.

This new agency enlisted poster artists, college professors, and novelists. An army of 75,000 volunteers explained everywhere—between movie reels in theaters, at church gatherings, at labor-union meetings, and on Indian reservations—things like "Why We Are Fighting" and "The Meaning of America." In this way the Creel committee was able to "sell the war to America." Soon Creel went further: he was selling America *to the world*—especially America's war aims as President Wilson expressed them in his public addresses.

Sum and Substance

1. What was the direct cause of the United States' entrance into the First World War? 2. Describe the episode concerning the Zimmermann note. 3. What was the effect on Americans? 4. When did the United States enter the war? 5. How was an American army raised? Who was its commander? 6. What part in the war was played by the navy? 7. Name the military engagements in which American soldiers took part. 8. Describe the war effort at home.

This section describes how Wilson vainly tried to implement his war aims (see p. 565).

WILSON PLEADS TO ESTABLISH A LEAGUE OF NATIONS

The war transformed the United States. A mere world power before the war, it was a world leader after it. The fall of Germany, the collapse of Austria-Hungary and of Russia, and the weakening of Britain and France helped bring this country to the fore.

But the relative decline of other countries was not alone responsible for the development. The United States emerged from the war as a powerful military nation in its own right (even though it disbanded its armed strength immediately after the armistice). The country had demonstrated an unexampled capacity to muster and merge its technological, financial, and human resources. The President's voice was now listened to—if not always heeded—everywhere in the world.

THE FOURTEEN POINTS

Wilson's wartime addresses had international circulation. A volume of them became a best seller in China. A leaflet containing some of his ideas was adopted—in a Spanish translation—as a textbook in a Madrid school.

None of Wilson's speeches became more famous than his statement of war aims known as the "Fourteen Points." The President had presented it to Congress on January 8, 1918.

An appeal for justice. Frankly propaganda designed to elevate the war purposes of America, the statement made an appeal to thinking people everywhere. The first five points were general:

1. The ending of secret diplomacy

2. The establishment of freedom of the seas for all nations

3. The removal of economic barriers to international trade

4. The reduction of armaments

5. The "impartial adjustment of all colonial claims, based upon . . . the interests of the populations concerned"

The eight points that followed called for a number of territorial adjustments in Europe that would conform with the wishes of the various nationalities living under foreign domination. Wilson was advocating what he called "national self-determination."

The fourteenth. The fourteenth point expressed what had now become Wilson's chief goal. This

American soldiers in France rejoice at the news of the armistice. November 11, proclaimed Armistice Day by Wilson in 1919, is now observed as Veterans Day, honoring veterans of all the nation's wars.

Americans in France, homesick and tired of war, rejoiced in the thought of going home.

goal was to establish a league of nations "for the purpose of affording mutual guarantees of political independence and territorial integrity to great and small states alike."

As war aims. Presented as "the only possible program" for peace, the Fourteen Points soon were viewed as the war aims of all the Allied powers. Actually, they were the aims of the president of the United States only. The Fourteen Points were appealed to by the Germans in the fall of 1918, when the Imperial Government stared defeat in the face.

Basis for armistice. In asking for peace in October, the enemy's spokesman said, "The German Government believes that the governments associated with the United States also accept the position taken by President Wilson. . . ."

This was far from being the case. But war weariness and the horrifying thought of another winter of fighting made the Allies willing to accept an armistice based upon the Fourteen Points. They refused, however, to accept the principle of freedom of the seas, and they insisted on demanding reparations from Germany.

The firing ceased on November 11, 1918, and plans were soon under way for a peace conference. One of Wilson's Cabinet members described the President's mood: "He is certainly in splendid humor. . . . And why shouldn't he be, for the world is at his feet, eating out of his hand! No Caesar ever had such a triumph!"

Soon fortune ceased to smile.

AT PARIS

Wilson appears to have decided by October that he would attend the peace conference—a step without precedent. First, however, his party faced the midterm congressional elections in November.

The elections of 1918. The President called for a vote of confidence in himself and his policies—that is, he asked for the election of Democratic

#Observe that the League of Nations would carry out another of Wilson's war objectives--to protect the rights and liberties of small nations.

Library of Congress
In 1919: a parade of returned soldiers in Buffalo.
Observe the automobiles.

majorities to the Senate and the House. With some justice, the Republicans were infuriated. As Theodore Roosevelt said, Republicans had been "good enough to spill their blood like water overseas under the flag." Having shared in the trials of the war, they did not intend to be excluded from the peacemaking.

For a number of reasons, Republican prospects in the elections of 1918 were good. First, because of the anticipated armistice, the Democrats could not use the valuable argument that it would be wrong to swap horses in midstream.‖ Second, the Republican party, divided in 1916, was at last reunited. Third, local is-

‖ This phrase, apparently originated by Lincoln in 1864, means to vote a man out of office during a crisis.

sues had aroused serious opposition to Democratic congressmen.

The returns gave the Republicans twenty-five new seats in the House, and they now outnumbered the Democrats substantially. They controlled the Senate by two votes.

Partisan resentment. Despite this defeat for his party, Wilson was determined, against all arguments, to leave for Europe. Many regarded his going abroad with deep resentment. Others believed that because of the attention the Fourteen Points had received, the people of the world wanted and expected him to be at the peace table. Republican leaders were angry that not one of their number was in the official United States delegation, which departed for Paris aboard the *George Washington* on December 4. Wilson would shortly have cause to regret ignoring the opposition party in this way.

Enthusiastic reception. But for the moment no disappointments seemed to loom ahead. People in Paris welcomed the President with a frenzy that in the past they had reserved only for the heroes of war. Above the historic avenue Champs Élysées, along which Wilson's motorcade proceeded, were hung banners reading: "Honour to Wilson the Just." In other countries Wilson visited—in England and especially in Italy—he was also greeted with wild enthusiasm.

These trips were a personal triumph for Wilson. But they annoyed many of the leaders of Europe, who considered Wilson an impractical man unwilling to understand the realities of international politics.

The Big Four. The representatives of the Allies were experienced in the delicate art of diplomacy. Georges Clemenceau, the French premier, was known as "the Tiger." Seventy-seven years of age, he had waited a large part of his life to avenge the German defeat of his country in the Franco-Prussian War of 1871. Now he meant to impose a severe peace on Germany. David Lloyd George, England's prime minister, was a gifted politician from Wales. He had once said, "If you want to succeed in politics, you must keep your conscience well under control." Lloyd George was determined to

These were the men who controlled the peace conference by acting together as a board.

The Big Four in an informal moment in Paris: Orlando (*second from left*) shares a joke with Lloyd George (*far left*); a relaxed Wilson listens, and only Clemenceau (*next to the President*) looks at the photographer.

defend his country's interests against the plans of the visionary American President.

Clemenceau and Lloyd George were often impatient with Wilson's idealism. Clemenceau once sarcastically referred to the Fourteen Points as the "Fourteen Commandments," adding that "even the Almighty had only Ten."

A less important figure at Paris was Vittorio Orlando, the Italian premier. His country's minor contribution to the Allied victory gave him a lesser role at the peace conference, but he was a member of the Big Four—in company with Wilson, Lloyd George, and Clemenceau.

THE TREATY OF VERSAILLES

The possibility of a lasting peace depended upon the successful outcome of the conference over which the men presided. Wilson stated his expectations in a speech he made on arriving in France: "Friends, men, humble women, little children, we are here; we are here as your friends, as your champions, as your representatives. We have come to work out for you a world in which all countries can enjoy the heritage of liberty. . . ."

The League Covenant. The peace conference, dominated by the Big Four, produced the Treaty of Versailles. It was named for the palace where it was signed in June, 1919. Even though Wilson's idealism was not generally shared by his colleagues at Paris, he was able to see some of his ideas incorporated into the # treaty. To the President, the most important contribution he had made was the Covenant of the League of Nations.

#Wilson was also able to stop some of the moves made by some of the participants, and he was successful in winning British, Italian, and French support for the League.

Historical Pictures Service

President Wilson arrives at the hotel of the Trianon Palace at Versailles, as sketched at the time. Built by King Louis XIV of France, the sumptuous palace had long been one of the homes of the French monarchs.

Wilson was received in France as the American "man of peace."

The Covenant's provisions. The Covenant provided for a League of Nations, with a permanent Secretariat (the administrative and secretarial staff), an Assembly, and a Council, and for a Permanent Court of International Justice and an international labor office. The Assembly, consisting of representatives of the member nations of the League, would advise on international questions brought before it. The Council, composed of delegates from the United States, England, France, Italy, Japan, and four other nations to be chosen by the Assembly, would mediate disputes between members. It would also seek ways to end aggression and devise plans for bringing about disarmament.

The Court would hear disputes and advise the Assembly and Council on how to settle them justly. The ILO—the International Labor Organization—would work "to secure and maintain fair and humane conditions of labor for men, women, and children. . . ."

The most important and, as events showed, the most disputed part of the Covenant was Article 10. This Article established that "Members of the League [would] undertake to respect and preserve as against external aggression the territorial integrity and existing political independence of all Members of the League." #

The mandate system. The League was Wilson's ## proudest effort in behalf of world peace, but he gave his attention to other matters, too. Believing that imperialism had been a powerful cause of the war, he succeeded in preventing

592 ##A mandate is a commission given one nation by an associated group of nations to administer the government and affairs of a people. It also can mean the mandated territory.

U.S. Signal Corps, National Archives

Making the peace in the Hall of Mirrors, at Versailles. The Big Four are seated at the table, their backs to the ornate wall. Journalists and representatives of interested countries, are among the spectators.

The palace at Versailles contains hundreds of rooms. This is one of them.

the former colonies of Germany and of Turkey # from being handed over to the Allies. Instead, on his suggestion they were made *mandated territories*# of the League.

New nations. To carry out still another of Wilson's principles, the peacemakers redrew the boundary lines of eastern Europe to create new, independent countries for national groups living there. These countries were formed from parts of the Austrian, German, Russian, and Turkish empires. Among the new nations were Austria, Poland, Czechoslovakia, Hungary, and Yugoslavia (compare eastern Europe before

Under the *mandate system* the colonies of the defeated countries were placed under the jurisdiction of the League. The League assigned them to various Allied powers, which would administer them under the supervision of the League and presumably prepare them for independence.

and after the war on the maps on pages 567 and 682).

A victor's settlement. Despite Wilson's earlier wish that there might be a "peace without victory," the treaty in the end was a victor's treaty. The full blame for having started the war was laid on Germany. Its navy was taken away and scuttled; it lost territory in the east and in the west; it was deprived of its colonies; and, finally, it was forced to assume a reparations bill that ultimately was fixed at $56,000,000,000. Wilson's dream, the League ## of Nations, was tied to this treaty.

A HOSTILE SENATE

By the time the Treaty of Versailles reached the United States Senate in July, 1919, the opposition was already brisk. In March a number of Republican Senators and Senators-elect had signed a round robin** stating that the treaty was not acceptable in the form then proposed.

Opposing arguments. The chief bone of contention was the Covenant of the League of Nations, which Wilson said was the very heart of the document. Opponents of the League concentrated their attack on Article 10 particularly. They argued that if the United States joined the new organization, it would be giving up its identity as a nation. Moreover, they said, it would be destroying the Monroe Doctrine and yielding to others the power to declare war and make peace. The critics also added the assertion that Americans would be doing England's fighting to protect the British Empire.

One angry Senator condemned Wilson's administration for "the infamous, criminal insanity of the attempt to barter [Americans] and their posterity to the Old World." Wilson's reply was that Americans must "follow the vision" of world leadership. Senator Frank B. Brandegee of Connecticut, an arch opponent, said that the President's words were mere "soap bubbles of oratory." As the battle over ratification progressed, Wilson cried out in anguish, "They have poisoned the wells of public sentiment."

During most of the summer of 1919, the Senate Foreign Relations Committee held hearings supposed to explore the meaning of the treaty. The committee served the intended purpose of seriously damaging the chances of ratification.

Among the treaty's opponents were many Americans of German background who had not forgiven Wilson for having entered the war against the fatherland. They denounced him also for having promised Germany justice and having helped impose a harsh treaty instead.

Some others who attacked the treaty were Americans of Italian extraction. They disapproved of the territorial arrangements made at Paris affecting Italy. Still other critics were

among Democrats who regarded Wilson as having betrayed his own generous principles in fastening the sole blame for the war on Germany.

The irreconcilables. In the Senate, the opponents of the treaty were dividing into two groups. The first, known as the "irreconcilables," included such men as Hiram Johnson of California, William E. Borah of Idaho, and Robert M. La Follette. They were determined to fight tooth and nail against acceptance of the document *under any conditions.*

The reservationists. A second and larger group, called "reservationists"—no less unwavering— was led by Henry Cabot Lodge of Massachusetts. It favored participation in the League provided certain *reservations* were agreed to which would protect American interests. Lodge, whose hostility to the President was largely personal, drew up a list of fourteen such reservations. (Wilson's friends said this was a petty attempt to match the President's Fourteen Points.)

Stumping the country. In the face of unyielding senatorial opposition, Wilson grew more stubborn and uncompromising himself. His dislike for Lodge, like himself a scholar in politics, was intense. He once said: "Accept the Treaty with the *Lodge* reservations? Never! Never!" In September—against better advice, both political and medical—Wilson decided to stump the country, speaking directly to the people.

Inspired oratory. Huge crowds greeted him everywhere in the Middle West; on the Pacific coast the throngs seemed to be particularly large. With his usual eloquence and fierce conviction, Wilson appeared to be making progress among his hearers.

Nevertheless, even if he had been able to bring about the defeat of every opposing Senator standing for reelection in 1920, he still would have lacked the two-thirds vote needed for ratification of the treaty. But the fire burned deep within him. He told an audience in Spokane, Washington, "I am ready to fight from now until all the fight has been taken out of me by death to redeem the faith and promises of the United States."

** This is a document on which the signatures are written in a circle so that the order of signing is concealed.

##Senators Johnson and Borah followed Wilson, speaking against the treaty wherever he spoke in favor of it. In each case, they tried to counteract the arguments Wilson had offered.

Library of Congress

President Wilson waves to a crowd in Los Angeles, where he is carrying his fight for an unamended peace treaty.

The second Mrs. Wilson—nearly hidden by the masses of flowers—rides in the limousine.

Wilson's reception in Los Angeles and Seattle was especially warm.

Tragedy. Then tragedy struck. The President suffered a physical collapse shortly after addressing an audience at Pueblo, Colorado, on September 25, 1919. In the town high school at that time he had talked of his "clients in this case . . . the children . . . the next generation."

The tour was abruptly ended, and the President returned to Washington, where on October 2 he suffered a stroke that paralyzed his left side. Said a friend bluntly: "He has had his say. He has shot his bolt . . . now let the Senate act."

An ailing chief. The attempt made to hide from the public the severity of the President's ailment was a grave mistake. Congressmen were angered by their inability to confer with Wilson, and his opponents became more averse to his proposals than ever. Mrs. Wilson carefully screened beforehand the names of visitors her

##How are illnesses of the President handled today? (The utmost attempt is made to give the public complete details.) Why is frankness better than secrecy?

595

husband might see, in order to avoid upsetting him.

Wilson remained as stubborn as before in his insistence upon the treaty without reservations. When the French ambassador at Washington brought him word that the Allies were willing to accept reservations on United States membership in the League if the President was also, he snapped: "Mr. Ambassador, I shall consent to nothing. The Senate must take its medicine."

Competing interests. Meanwhile, other issues were demanding public attention: labor disputes in the coal mines and the steel mills, a fear of radicalism, and the question of how to dispose of the railroads, which were still in government hands. Moreover, a young heavyweight boxer named Jack Dempsey was making sports news with his fists, and a Boston Red Sox pitcher and outfielder named Babe Ruth was attracting crowds with his long-ball hitting. As the public's attention was drawn elsewhere, the original favorable sentiment toward the League began to wane.

Rejecting ratification. When the Senate vote on the Treaty of Versailles was taken in November, 1919, it fell short of ratification—there being 38 yeas and 53 nays. Upon hearing the news, Wilson said quietly, "They have shamed us in the eyes of the world."

A vote on the treaty *with* the Lodge reservations also failed. Wilson had urged his supporters to reject them because, he had continued to maintain, their passage would # "nullify" the treaty. If he had not asked this of his Democratic friends, evidence indicates that the treaty with reservations would have been ratified 81–13.

As his second term drew to a close, Wilson, ailing and embittered, waited hopefully for the election of 1920. He was sure that he would be vindicated. "Personally," he said, "I do not accept the action of the Senate of the United States as the decision of the nation."

Actually the issue had already been settled. Said Lodge: "The situation . . . is simple. It has come down to Wilson's taking our reservations . . . or losing the Treaty altogether."

The President held his ground: "Better a thousand times to go down fighting than to dip your colors to dishonorable compromise."

Formal end to hostilities. When the treaty was brought up for reconsideration in 1920, the Senate once more defeated it, both *with* and *without* reservations. In 1921, after Wilson had left office, Congress ended the state of war with Germany and Austria-Hungary by a joint resolution. Later in the year treaties of peace were signed separately with Germany, Austria, and Hungary.

On Inauguration Day, March 4, in 1921, Wilson rode to the Capitol with his successor, Warren G. Harding of Ohio. The retiring President was only a shadow of the vibrant figure who had taken the oath of office for the first time eight years before. Limping pitifully, his eyesight weak, he prepared to perform his last official act: signing the final bills of the congressional session then ending.

By an ironic twist of fate, it was Henry Cabot Lodge, as Senate majority leader, who had the formal duty to say to the President, ". . . the two Houses have completed their work and are prepared to receive any further communications from you." Wilson, tight-lipped and agitated, replied tartly: "Senator, I have no further communication to make. . . . *Good morning, sir.*"

A few minutes later, the new President was sworn in. The American people bade farewell to an age of reforming at home and of crusading abroad.

Sum and Substance

1. Describe Wilson's Fourteen Points. 2. Upon what basis was an armistice accepted? When? 3. What were the results of the congressional elections of 1918? How can they be explained? 4. Who were the Big Four? 5. Describe three proposals of Wilson's which were included in the Treaty of Versailles. 6. What was Article 10? 7. Name and describe the two groups in the Senate that fought the treaty. 8. How did Wilson attempt to win support for the treaty? With what result? 9. What action did the Senate take on the Treaty of Versailles? How did Congress formally end the war?

About 158, 000 students and professors in 311 colleges voted on questions relating to the treaty. In this straw vote, 30 percent approved the treaty; 38 percent favored compromise.

#Students should read the provisions of the Twenty-fifth Amendment to the Constitution (see p. 809) and be able to tell what is provided. Notice the date of the amendment (1967).

THE WORKSHOP

OF LASTING SIGNIFICANCE

Tell how each of the following was related to American involvement in Europe in the early twentieth century.

First World War	A.E.F.
Triple Alliance	Château-Thierry
Triple Entente	Cantigny
Balkan countries	Belleau Wood
Sarajevo	second Battle of
Schlieffen plan	the Marne
first Battle of	St. Mihiel
the Marne	Meuse-Argonne
war of attrition	offensive
Central Powers	Bernard M. Baruch
Allies	Herbert C. Hoover
contraband	Liberty loans
Lusitania	Fourteen Points
U-boat	Ferdinand Foch
Sussex pledge	Big Four
Edward M. House	Treaty of Versailles
Charles Evans	League of Nations
Hughes	Article 10
hyphenate vote	mandate
J. H. von Bernstorff	"irreconcilable"
Zimmermann note	Henry Cabot Lodge
Selective Service Act	Warren G. Harding

DOCUMENTS IN HISTORY

1. Wilson's war message to Congress (pages 564–565) is a very important American document. (*a*) Describe fully the events he referred to in the first paragraph; (*b*) what action of his later that day showed the sincerity of the first five lines of the second paragraph?

2. What did Wilson mean when he said that "the right is more precious than peace"? Compare the rights for which he said Americans would fight with the war aims he expressed in the Fourteen Points and explain how they are specifically related.

3. What principle or right was Wilson asking America to fight for which "gave her birth"? Explain the meaning of "The world must be made safe for democracy. . . ."

THE CONSTITUTION TODAY

1. Read the part of the Constitution (see the Appendix) which grants the power to declare war. Who has sole power? What powers of the President are particularly significant in time of war?

2. Read the constitutional provision explaining why the Senate was the scene of the fight over ratification of the Treaty of Versailles. How many votes were required for its acceptance?

3. How does the Constitution now provide for the situation the United States found itself in after Wilson became disabled.

INTERNATIONAL POLITICS

1. Compare the conditions the United States faced before it entered the War of 1812 and the First World War. In each case, what led to the declaration of war?

2. Why did the Zimmermann note have an especially stunning effect on American public opinion?

3. Where was the First World War chiefly fought? What countries were primarily affected?

4. Name the new countries that were created after the First World War. Explain why each was formed.

BEING A SOCIAL SCIENTIST

1. Analyze the causes of the failure of the Senate to ratify the Treaty of Versailles. What role did Wilson have in it?

2. Investigate the present status of the areas made mandated territories after the First World War. Would you say that the mandate system was generally a success? Explain.

3. Find out what part aviators and airplanes—especially American ones—played in waging the First World War and bring the information to class.

4. Make a report on the activities of the League of Nations in the years between 1920 and 1946. What did it accomplish?

##Mandated territories: Iraq, Palestine, Tanganyika, Syria, Ruanda-Urundi, Western Samoa, South West Africa. Islands and parts of the Cameroons and Togoland were included.

After the First World War, there was a period of prosperity in which Americans turned to self-indulgence as much as possible. Americans were sick of war and of war regulations. They were not inclined to be interested in the responsibilities Wilson had said the war brought.

26

PROSPERITY'S PROMISE

. . . the full garage . . .

During one hundred and fifty years we have built up a form of self-government and a social system which is peculiarly our own. It differs essentially from all others in the world. It is the American system. It is just as definite and positive a political and social system as has ever been developed on earth. It is founded upon a particular conception of self-government in which decentralized local responsibility is the very base. . . .

The Gibson-girl influence is still strong. Compare modern dress with that seen here.

We have demonstrated that our system is responsive enough to meet any new and intricate development in our economic and business life. We have demonstrated that we can meet any economic problem and still maintain our democracy as master in its own house and that we can at the same time preserve equality of opportunity and individual freedom. . . .

By adherence to the principles of decentralized self-government, ordered liberty, equal opportunity and freedom to the individual, our American experiment in human welfare has yielded a degree of well-being unparalleled in all the world. It has come nearer to the abolition of poverty, to the abolition of fear of want, than humanity has ever reached before. . . .

. . . our people are steadily increasing their spending for higher standards of living. Today there are almost nine automobiles for each ten families, where seven and one-half years ago only enough automobiles were running to average less than four for each ten families. The slogan of progress is changing from the full dinner pail to the full garage. Our people have more to eat, better things to wear and better homes. We have even gained in elbow room, for the increase of residential floor space is over twenty-five percent, with less than ten percent increase in our number of people. Wages have increased, the cost of living has decreased. The job of every man and woman has been made more secure. We have in this short period decreased the fear of poverty, the fear of unemployment, the fear of old age; and these are fears that are the greatest calamities of human kind. . . .

I have endeavored to present to you that the greatness of America has grown out of a political and social system and a method of control of economic forces distinctly its own—our American system—which has carried this great experiment in human welfare further than ever before in all history. We are nearer today to the ideal of the abolition of poverty and fear from the lives of men and women than ever before in any land. . . .

Brown Brothers

Americans in the 1920's wanted to believe that hard times would soon be a thing of the past. Herbert Hoover was an outstanding spokesman for this viewpoint. Abroad, his relief work in the First World War had earned him an international reputation. At home, his inventive programs as Secretary of Commerce

The family is on the New Jersey side.

A family spends a holiday shortly after the First World War picnicking on the scenic Palisades, the cliffs that form the western bank of the lower Hudson River. Opposite is a part of upper Manhattan.

from 1921 to 1928 gave him standing as a possible candidate for the presidency. In 1928 he became the Republican nominee. This selection comes from a campaign speech Hoover delivered in Madison Square Garden in New York City on October 22 of that year. After his election in November, the address was published—along with others he had made during the summer and fall—in a book entitled The New Day.

HARDING OF OHIO USHERS IN A "RETURN TO NORMALCY"

The defeat of the League of Nations brought forth no public outcry. Americans wanted a rest from the driving leadership of energetic and brilliant Presidents. Said one Senator as the Republican National Convention of 1920 began, "The times do not require a first-rater."

THE FIRST POSTWAR CAMPAIGN

The outcome of the Republican convention, held in Chicago, had been forecast by Harry M. Daugherty, a party leader from Ohio. The convention would be deadlocked, he said, and

What is the point here?
A 1920 cartoon: "Say, where d'ya want to put it?"

Life, October 28, 1920

a decision would be made in a "smoke-filled" hotel room during the early morning hours to nominate Senator Warren G. Harding, of Ohio. This offhand prophecy was startlingly correct.

The Republican ticket. On the tenth ballot Senator Harding was chosen to be his party's nominee. Harding was the opposite of Woodrow Wilson in intellect and firmness. A handsome, ingratiating man, the Senator knew he would not make the best President the country had ever had, but he hoped to be the best loved.

The running mate selected for Harding was Governor Calvin Coolidge, of Massachusetts. Flinty and habitually silent, Coolidge was in stark contrast to the genial and talkative Harding.

In his acceptance speech Harding talked of his opposition to Wilson's plans for international peace. He urged his countrymen, "Stabilize America first, prosper America first, think of America first, exalt America first!" #

Cox and Roosevelt. The Democrats named as their candidate Governor James M. Cox, of Ohio, who, like Harding, was a newspaper publisher. Their vice-presidential nominee was the youthful, energetic Franklin D. Roosevelt, of New York, Assistant Secretary of the Navy.

The League issue. Although he tried to straddle the League question in order to appear to be on both sides of it, Harding was actually opposed to the League. Cox upheld the Wilson viewpoint, saying of the League, "I am in favor ## of going in." But as the campaign wore on, he wavered somewhat in his determination.

The majority of voters seem not to have been aroused sufficiently by the issue of the League to want to take a strong stand either for it or against it. On Election Day it appeared that the forecast of one of Wilson's Cabinet

##But the Democratic party in its platform did not take a stand against reservations, as Wilson had. Thus it tried to appeal to the moderates who had favored the League.

#What steps should Harding have taken? How can the class account for the fact that time often
lay heavy on Harding's hands? (They may say that he was not bright enough for the position,
that he did not have able assistants, that he had insufficient education, etc.)

members had been fulfilled: "Cox will be defeated not by those who dislike him, but by those who dislike Wilson."

The outcome. The Republicans won an overwhelming victory: in popular votes, Harding received 16,143,000 to Cox's 9,130,000; in the electoral college the vote was 404 to 127. Declared one leading Democrat, "It was not a landslide, it was an earthquake."

A HARRIED PRESIDENT

During the campaign, Harding had talked of a "return to normalcy." By the word *normalcy,* which he coined, he seems to have meant the simpler, bygone days before the war. After his inauguration, the nation, waiting for "normalcy" to return, watched Harding occupying a position that was too big for him. Those who knew him best looked on with dismay. Even Mrs. Harding had said at the time of the nomination, "I can see but one word written

over his head if they make him President, and that word is Tragedy."

Pressing problems. Harding vastly underestimated the tasks he would face in the presidency. A newspaper in Philadelphia observed: "Never has any President come to the tremendous office with so much unfinished business and so many fresh problems of moment."

The peace treaty was still to be disposed of; unemployment was growing; agriculture demanded help; relations with Mexico, China, Japan, and Russia had to be restudied. Germany needed close attention, as did the reparations question and the problem of what to do about the war debts. Yet even in the midst of these perplexing subjects, Harding found that time lay heavy on his hands. He once told a newspaper reporter, "Oftentimes, as I sit here, I don't seem to grasp that I am President."

The official family. The Cabinet contained some of the ablest men in his party—as Harding had

Observe the high-topped shoes, customary at the time. Note the picture of Lincoln.
Harding and his Cabinet: Charles Evans Hughes is at the front right; Herbert Hoover is before the fireplace.

Gilloon Photo Agency

The Vice-President, Calvin Coolidge, sits at the far end of the table in front of a door. Hughes still is wearing a full beard, but most of the men are clean-shaven.

promised it would. Charles Evans Hughes, the Republican presidential candidate in 1916, was appointed Secretary of State; Andrew Mellon, the aluminum magnate, became Secretary of the Treasury; Henry C. Wallace, an influential farm editor from Iowa, was named Secretary of Agriculture; and Herbert Hoover, the famous war-relief administrator, was made Secretary of Commerce.

But there were also some in the official family who handled their responsibilities so carelessly that Harding's administration became the most corrupt since Grant's. Though they were cronies of the President, they proved to be his undoing. Harding confessed frankly to a newspaperman: "I have no trouble with my enemies. I can take care of my enemies all right. But my . . . friends . . . they're the ones that keep me walking the floor nights!"

Last journey. By 1923 Harding appeared to close observers to be a tired and worried man. Few were then aware that he was deeply distressed by knowledge of wrongdoing within his administration. Early in the summer, thinking ahead to the 1924 election, he journeyed westward on a fact-finding trip. He visited in the Pacific Northwest and then in Alaska—the farthest north any President had ever traveled.

On his return to the mainland, Harding was visibly ill. First reports referred only to a digestive upset, and he was expected to recover quickly. Suddenly, on August 2 in San Francisco, he died of a blood clot.

CALVIN COOLIDGE OF MASSACHUSETTS

Calvin Coolidge became president of the United States in the early hours of August 3 in Plymouth, Vermont. His father, a justice of the peace, administered the oath of office to him by the light of a kerosine lamp.

Disclosure of scandals. The nation mourned the passing of its President, who was praised as "one of the knightliest, gentlest, truest men who ever lived in the White House." Disclosures soon showed how wrong that glowing judgment was. The Harding administration was revealed to be contaminated with the misconduct of important public officials. Harding, who was morally weak himself, must bear the blame in history for having permitted dishonest men #

Most of the women wore long hair. Observe the look of pride on the father's face.

John Coolidge and his neighbors use earphones to listen to his son, the President, speak over the radio in 1924.

UPI

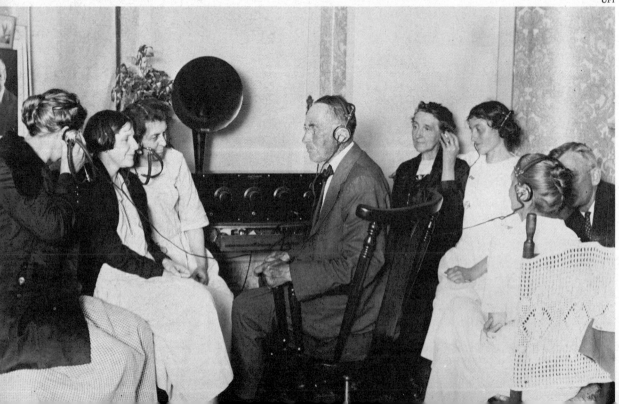

to occupy places of trust in the national government.

The most shocking case concerned the Secretary of the Interior, Albert B. Fall. Fall had persuaded Harding to transfer to the Department of the Interior two oil fields held as reserves by the Department of the Navy. One —at Elk Hills in California—Fall promptly leased to a wealthy oilman, Edward L. Doheny; the other—the Teapot Dome reserve in Wyoming—he leased to Harry F. Sinclair, another oil magnate.

In both cases Fall had been heavily bribed. He stood trial and was sentenced to a term in jail. The Secretary of the Navy, Edwin Denby, who appears to have been foolish rather than dishonest, resigned.

Other revelations followed. The custodian of the Office of Alien Property and the director of the Veterans Bureau had both brazenly accepted bribes; both were tried and jailed. The Attorney General, Harry M. Daugherty, who more than anyone else was responsible for Harding's nomination, was forced to resign his office because he was personally involved in the scandals. Twice Daugherty was tried; each time the jury was divided and he went free.

A man of character. Coolidge's coming to the White House may well have saved the Republicans from political disaster. The new President possessed undisputed personal integrity. A man of such character was badly needed to restore the nation's respect for holders of high office.

Coolidge was not a strong and resourceful leader. But Congress was not looking to the presidency for direction. In fact, practically without executive guidance, Congress had been enacting significant legislation dealing with a number of subjects. One of the most important subjects was the tariff.

Adjusting tariff rates upward. In 1921 an "emergency" tariff was passed placing duties on wool, sugar, meat, wheat, and corn. This was an attempt to satisfy farmers, who were complaining that the importation of foreign foodstuffs had forced down the price of the crops they sold.

The following year this act was replaced by the Fordney-McCumber Act, which raised rates generally to the level at which they had stood in the Taft administration. Although the act created a tariff commission that was empowered to raise *or* lower rates by as much as 50 percent, in practice the rates were almost invariably raised.

In response to a growing demand from industry for more protection, Congress in 1928 began work on a further increase in tariff rates. The result was the Hawley-Smoot Act of 1930. Because these tariff laws kept domestic prices for manufactured products higher than they might otherwise have been, American consumers were being compelled to help businessmen meet foreign competition. A truly golden age for businessmen seemed about to begin.

Sum and Substance
1. Describe the presidential campaign of 1920. Who was elected? Characterize his administration. Who succeeded him? 2. Name and describe tariff changes begun in the 1920's.

This section describes some of the most important events and characteristics of the 1920's.

NEW MOVEMENTS AND DIVERSIONS TAKE HOLD OF AMERICA

In the 1920's Americans had, on the whole, little interest in criticizing big business. The nation's powerful energies were thrown enthusiastically in other directions.

THE MEANING OF THE TWENTIES

The period of the 1920's has been variously described: "the roaring decade," "the golden daze," "the jazz age." Its distinctiveness was the result of many forces at work in American life.

Postwar letdown. First of all, the seemingly incessant excitement of the twenties was a reaction against the progressive era. Americans had experienced years of moral preaching—beginning in the last decade of the nineteenth

For inquiry: What does the list of cities in 1920 tell you about the population pattern of the United States in that year? How can you account for the inclusion of two new entries?

TEN LARGEST CITIES IN THE UNITED STATES*

	1910	1920	1930	1940
1	New York, N.Y. 6,500,000	New York, N.Y. 8,000,000	New York, N.Y. 10,925,000	New York, N.Y. 11,750,000
2	Chicago, Ill. 2,475,000	Chicago, Ill. 3,200,000	Chicago, Ill. 4,400,000	Chicago, Ill. 4,550,000
3	Philadelphia, Pa. 1,950,000	Philadelphia, Pa. 2,400,000	Philadelphia, Pa. 2,800,000	Philadelphia, Pa. 2,850,000
4	Boston, Mass. 1,450,000	Boston, Mass. 1,750,000	Los Angeles, Calif. 2,150,000	Los Angeles, Calif. 2,725,000
5	Pittsburgh, Pa. 930,000	Detroit, Mich.† 1,175,000	Boston, Mass. 2,150,000	Detroit, Mich. 2,325,000
6	St. Louis, Mo. 840,000	Pittsburgh, Pa. 1,100,000	Detroit, Mich. 2,125,000	Boston, Mass. 2,250,000
7	San Francisco– Oakland, Calif. 690,000	St. Louis, Mo. 975,000	Pittsburgh, Pa. 1,300,000	San Francisco– Oakland, Calif. 1,350,000
8	Baltimore, Md. 675,000	Cleveland, Ohio 950,000	San Francisco– Oakland, Calif. 1,250,000	Pittsburgh, Pa. 1,350,000
9	Cleveland, Ohio 625,000	San Francisco– Oakland, Calif. 900,000	St. Louis, Mo. 1,225,000	St. Louis, Mo. 1,300,000
10	Cincinnati, Ohio 575,000	Los Angeles, Calif.† 880,000	Cleveland, Ohio 1,225,000	Cleveland, Ohio 1,250,000

* Population figures are approximate and include suburbs. † New addition to list. (Continued on page 776)

Which city had dropped off the list by 1920?

century. They had been urged to reform this or that, to uphold their country's destiny in the world, and to exert the responsibilities of world leadership. Now they wanted to have a fling.

Disillusionment and rebellion. Second, among the younger generation especially, many were disillusioned with the failure of the war to bring either peace or economic stability to the world. Consequently, they became critical of numerous things their elders believed were right and necessary.

Wrote one young man in a national maga-# zine: "The older generation had certainly pretty well ruined this world before passing it on to us. . . . They give us this thing knocked to

pieces, leaky, red-hot, threatening to blow up; and then they are surprised that we don't accept it with the same attitude of pretty, decorous enthusiasm with which they received it, way back in the 'eighties.' " To a greater degree than youth in previous generations, it seemed, young people took pride in being rebellious. Often callously disregarding traditional moral behavior, they took pride in being labeled "flaming youth."

Emphasis on recreation. Third, leisure—the sweetest fruit of the Industrial Revolution— was changing the national outlook. Hard work had once been one of the great American virtues; in the twenties leisure time was also be-

#This provides a good opportunity to discuss the criticism of the older generation by the younger one. These young critics were in turn criticized by their children and other young people.

coming a goal of life for millions of people.

Vacations were playing a more important part in the lives of an ever increasing number of people. The working day was growing significantly shorter, with the 8-hour day becoming the aim of the labor movement. "Take it easy," were words friends now commonly used when they said good-by to one another.

In this kind of atmosphere, recreation loomed larger and larger. It was no longer incidental to a hard day in office or factory; for many workers, it had become the most important part of the day.

A stepped-up pace. Fourth, the development of tabloid newspapers* and of the radio made it possible to arouse keen public excitement over a particular aspect of life and then abruptly switch it to something else. This no doubt helped to create the impression that the pace of American life was speeding up and that every year it was faster than the previous year.

Jazz music, which captured the fancy of Americans in the 1920's, was an excellent symbol of this new spirit. Jazz developed mainly among Negro musicians, including Louis Armstrong, in New Orleans and Memphis. It is usually played in a more excited tempo than other music, and its beat is unconventional.

A mask for problems. Fifth, there seemed to be a sense that darker times lay ahead. The world war had provided a glimpse into what the future might hold. People felt that they must enjoy themselves before it was "too late." Americans also sounded as if they were afraid to carry the world responsibility that had fallen to them. The behavior of many seemed like that of Peter Pan, "the boy who would not grow up." Beneath the revelry and joyfulness there lurked problems that Americans were trying to avoid.

CLOSING THE GATES TO IMMIGRANTS

A notable development of the twenties was the movement to restrict immigration. Actually, the interest in closing the door had long been

---

* The tabloids were generally smaller in size and shape than ordinary newspapers. They specialized in carrying photographs—often of a sensational kind.

present. For a number of reasons, restriction now became popular.

Some explanations. First of all, large-scale unemployment occurred after the war. Immigrants who had come from eastern Europe in a steady torrent before 1914 appeared to be displacing from their jobs native Americans or earlier arrivals. Second, when the reaction against the war set in, it was convenient to blame foreigners for the miscarried crusade to make the world "safe for democracy"—and to attack them.

Third, it was easy to look upon foreigners as dangerous radicals in the period after 1918, when eastern Europe was threatened by the tide of Russian communism. These changes in Europe brought suspicion of spies, which in turn produced fears—as one man put it—of "bewhiskered, ranting, howling, mentally-warped, law-defying aliens."

Fourth, because many of the immigrants were Jewish or Catholic, people could turn hidden anti-Semitism and anti-Catholicism into antiforeignism, which was not so embarrassing to express. Fifth, because the immigrants usually became urban dwellers and strengthened the cities, rural communities were often resentful. Their people sometimes took the lead in the growing movement to end unrestricted immigration.

The hatreds caused by the war and the falling birth rate among the older American families also aroused strong determination to keep new immigrants out. Furthermore, there was a widespread belief that the "whole world" was preparing to move to the United States and that this migration must be prevented at all costs.

A literacy test. The proposal that a literacy test —testing the ability to read and write—be demanded of everybody seeking to enter the country was a crafty move against immigration. Such a bill had been vetoed by Cleveland in 1897, by Taft in 1913, and by Wilson in 1915 and again in 1917. But Congress passed the measure over Wilson's second veto.

Quota acts. The enactment of additional anti-immigrant legislation was only a matter of

time. In 1921 Congress passed the Emergency Quota Act, which restricted the admission of foreigners to 3 percent of the number of each nationality living in the United States in 1910.

Many Americans considered this law to be unsatisfactory because the year chosen for determining the size of the quotas was one that came *after* the arrival of millions of eastern Europeans. Continuing to believe that the immigrants from northern and western Europe were more desirable (see page 422), Americans of older stock brought about a change through a new law. By the Immigration Quota Act of 1924, 1890 was made the base year. The ratio was reduced from 3 percent to 2 percent. In 1927 all immigration was reduced to 150,000 annually.

Many people, former President Charles W. Eliot of Harvard, for example, defended unrestricted immigration wholeheartedly. Eliot inquired bravely, "Is this generation to be frightened out of this noble policy by any industrial, racial, political, or religious bogies?" But for the time being, the tide was running hard against his way of thinking.

FEAR OF RADICALS

By the end of 1919, events abroad were convincing many Americans that the world as they knew it was fast disappearing and that they were in deadly danger. German Communists for a few days were able to hold the city of Berlin; Communists ruled Hungary for five months; there was serious unrest in Italy; and in India, nationalists were making new problems for the British.

At home it did not relax American nerves to learn that a well-known anticommunist had received in the mail a bomb that exploded and crippled the housemaid who opened the package. Or that another bomb had destroyed the home of Attorney General A. Mitchell Palmer, who, fortunately, was away at the time.

Red scare. The government's law-enforcement agencies were carrying on a vigorous campaign against left-wing organizations. In January, 1920, some 2500 radicals of various kinds were arrested in a series of federal raids. De-

portation proceedings were begun against 5000 aliens whose views were considered to be leftist. The wave of fear spread to the state governments, too. In New York in 1920, for instance, five Socialist members were expelled from the legislature at Albany.

Tension mounted seriously after a bomb exploded in Wall Street at noontime on September 16, 1920, killing over thirty people and injuring hundreds of others. In every part of the country hysteria developed as Attorney General Palmer's view gained acceptance: the Reds, he charged, were preparing "to rise up and destroy the Government at one fell swoop."

Boston police strike. Fear was widespread that property rights were being seriously endangered. Restive labor contributed to this fear. The most startling outbreak took place in Boston. On September 9, 1919, the city policemen, who had formed a union, walked out on strike at the time of their evening roll call. Hoodlums had a field day, smashing windows and looting stores practically at will.

The mayor called for Massachusetts state troops, and Governor Calvin Coolidge sent the ## National Guard. Meantime a volunteer corps consisting largely of Harvard students and recently demobilized veterans patrolled the streets. Coolidge overnight became a public hero as he told Samuel Gompers that there is "no right to strike against the public safety by anybody, anywhere, any time." Boston, frightened by the events, lost its original sympathy for the strikers and began gradually to recruit a new police force.

Steel and coal disputes. The Boston police strike was hardly over when two paralyzing industrial strikes occurred. The first of them—against the United States Steel Corporation—broke out in Gary, Indiana. The second—under the leadership of John L. Lewis, head of the United Mine Workers—was against the operators of the bituminous coal mines.

The steel strike, which represented an attempt to unionize the steel industry, was a failure. The coal strike was ended when the federal government intervened by obtaining a court injunction ordering the miners to return

##Coolidge's action made him favorably known among Americans. Let the class discuss whether or not Coolidge was right. Should public employees have a right to strike?

to work. Ultimately they received a wage increase as the result of arbitration.

What had happened was that labor, having taken a "no-strike" pledge during the war, considered itself no longer bound at the end of hostilities. Laboring men were especially aggrieved because, though the cost of living had risen sharply during the war, wages had remained practically stationary. Further, industrial workers no longer considered acceptable certain conditions of work—like the 69 hours in a seven-day week in the steel plants. Unions were ready to fight for improvements. Businessmen struck back vigorously: the Russian Revolution of 1917 had made many of them excessively afraid of labor.

The Sacco-Vanzetti case. A notable legal battle drew not only national but also world attention to America's fear of radicals. In 1921 Nicola Sacco and Bartolomeo Vanzetti were tried for murder and robbery in Braintree, Massachusetts, and found guilty. In the view of many people the conviction of the men resulted from their reputations as anarchists rather than from evidence of their guilt. Although there was widespread public protest over the manner in which the trial and appeal had been conducted, Sacco and Vanzetti were executed in 1927.

No subject aroused deeper emotions in the twenties than did the Sacco-Vanzetti case. Grave doubts persisted in the minds of a large number of Americans that these men had been guilty as charged. Possibly for this reason, the Red scare seemed to die down after the trial.

The decline of reform. An important effect of the wave of fear was to still the voices of many reformers. Some "do-gooders," for example, unwilling to be thought radical, contented themselves with being silent.

Even the muckrakers of the progressive period often appeared to be content at last with things as they were. Ida M. Tarbell, whose *History of the Standard Oil Company* in 1904 had aroused the anger of businessmen, published in 1925 an admiring account of the life of Elbert H. Gary, the steel magnate. Finley Peter Dunne ("Mr. Dooley"), the popular Irish wit of the turn of the century, was writing

UPI

Sacco (*left*) and Vanzetti are taken from a Boston court. Both men were Italians.

warmly about President Harding.

Along with contentment came an ugly outbreak of intolerance that mocked this country's claim of being one of the leading democracies of the world. Although discrimination had always existed in one form or another in the United States, a number of organizations declaring themselves guardians of "Americanism" now appeared on the scene.

The Ku Klux Klan. The most powerful of these organizations was the Ku Klux Klan. Taking

##Another opportunity to discuss the meaning and results of discrimination. Why did it "mock this country's claim to being one of the leading democracies of the world"?

607

the name and the methods of the Klan that had flourished in reconstruction days but that was now dead, it was formed on Thanksgiving night in 1915. It did not begin to grow, however, until 1920, when its promotional program was placed in professional hands.

Feeding on hatred and stirring up distrust among Americans, the Klan developed an elaborate, secret ritual revolving around the officers, who were called "wizards," "goblins," and "kleagles." Well supplied with funds that came from its four or five million members, it # aimed its sharp thrusts at Negroes, Jews, and Catholics.

The Klan sometimes used brutal methods in combating its enemies—floggings, tar-and-feather parties, and even murder. But for the most part it relied on boycotts, spying on schoolteachers and public officials, and other forms of pressure. By 1926 the peak of Klan activity had passed; yet in five years it had spread poison and terror that were contrary to

the good Americanism it professed to be protecting.

Modern religion and traditional religion. The distressing fear of change that overtook the United States in the 1920's was reflected also in an attack on new viewpoints in religion. A tendency had grown among many younger clergymen to question the idea that every word in the Bible is to be taken as literally true. They doubted, for example, in the light of modern science, whether the earth had actually been created in seven days and whether hell or the devil really existed.

Other people sprang to the defense of traditional religion. Their greatest spokesman was William Jennings Bryan, whose speeches in its ## behalf helped to draw popular attention to the controversy.

The Scopes trial. Partly as a result of Bryan's tireless efforts, bills to prohibit the teaching of the theory of evolution became law in Tennessee, Mississippi, and Arkansas. In Tennes-

Ask if the theory of evolution is taught in all states today.

The Scopes trial being held outdoors in late July, 1925. So many curious people crowded into the courtroom of the old court building that the judge, fearing the floor would cave in, ordered everybody outside.

UPI

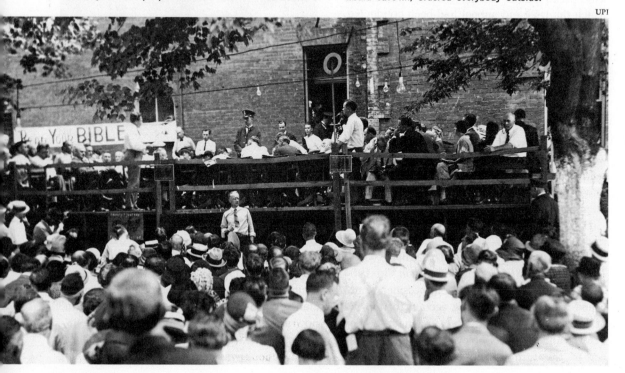

##Review the part Bryan had already played in history, including his "cross of gold" speech.

see the enactment was challenged by a young high school biology teacher, John Thomas Scopes, who was arrested because he taught that man had evolved from lower forms of animal life. To Scopes's defense came Clarence Darrow, the most famous criminal lawyer of the day; counsel for the state of Tennessee was William Jennings Bryan.

The Scopes trial in 1925 attracted worldwide attention. Its high point came when Bryan himself took the witness stand. From there he stated his belief that Jonah had literally been swallowed by a whale, that Joshua had made the sun stand still, and that the world had come into existence in the year 4004 B.C. Darrow maintained these were "fool ideas that no intelligent Christian on earth believes."

But the legal issue in the case was not whether Bryan or Darrow was right; it was whether or not Scopes had violated the law by his teaching. The court decided that he had.

The exertions in the blistering summer heat were too much for Bryan, and five days after the trial he was dead. The ideals he so valiantly represented were also vanishing from the scene.

"THE NOBLE EXPERIMENT"

The change from the old to the new in the twentieth century was illustrated also by the new turn in the prohibition movement. This was "the noble experiment" to eliminate the sale and consumption of alcoholic beverages throughout the nation.

How it began. The prohibition movement had begun in the middle decades of the nineteenth century, a part of the reforming impulse of the 1830's and '40's (see page 213). The first dry law was passed by Maine in 1851. Prohibitionists, often working with clergymen, believed that if democracy in this country was to flourish, the individual needed to be protected against forces that would undermine his self-control.

Its justification. Further, the economic waste resulting from drunkenness was clearly unnecessary. Factory owners, particularly, grew interested in prohibition because the absenteeism and illness among employees resulting from

drink reduced plant efficiency and, consequently, profits.

Although chronic intoxication was deplorable when it appeared in rural communities, its effects were greatest in the cities, where abandoned families easily became public charges. Citizens who were aware that public almshouses and asylums increased their tax burdens often supported the movement to end the sale of alcoholic beverages.

Crusading organizations. For a long time prohibitionists believed they could rely on persuasion alone. In 1874 the Woman's Christian Temperance Union was formed in an effort to bring the Protestant churches into the struggle. But an effective organization of the churches was not created until 1893, when the Anti-Saloon League was formed in Oberlin, Ohio. Baptist, Methodist, Presbyterian, and Congregational churches were now joined in the temperance movement. They were so successful that by 1917 they had been able to bring about passage in two-thirds of the states of local-option laws, allowing individual counties to adopt prohibition.

The Eighteenth Amendment. By this time the Anti-Saloon League was lobbying in Washington for a constitutional amendment to bring about prohibition everywhere in the country. The Webb-Kenyon Interstate Liquor Act of 1913 made illegal the transportation of alcoholic beverages into dry states. On December 18, 1917, amid the moral uplift provided by the progressives and the war, Congress passed and sent to the states the Eighteenth Amendment to the Constitution. On January 16, 1919— two months after the war ended—the amendment was declared ratified. Prohibiting the manufacture, sale, or transportation of intoxicating liquors, it went into effect on January 16, 1920.†

Enforcement. If those who inaugurated the nation's dry era believed that crime and vice would end with the closing of the saloon, they

---

† The Volstead Act of 1919, designed to carry out the intent of the Eighteenth Amendment, defined an intoxicating liquor as one containing more than one-half of 1 percent alcohol.

were soon rudely surprised. Many Americans considered the Volstead Act an unwarranted interference with their personal freedom. Moreover, many who themselves refrained from taking alcoholic drinks saw little reason to interfere with those who did partake of them.

Enforcement of the law became, therefore, a stupendous and ultimately a losing battle. Many people, who in other respects were law abiding, violated the law in this matter without scruple or failed to report others they knew were violating it. Against a generally indifferent, if not hostile, public opinion, the enforcement of prohibition was impossible.

"Bootlegging." By the middle of the twenties, "bootlegging" had become big business. Liquor was smuggled into the country across the international borders or from rum-running vessels carrying foreign-made whisky. In place of saloons, there were now "speakeasies" or "booze joints," where, by whispering the name of somebody who vouched for him or her, a person could buy "something to drink."

Illegal stills—which in the past had always posed a problem for revenue agents—grew in number and size. Moreover, it was sometimes said that physicians had assumed new duties— in writing approximately 11,000,000 prescrip-

These ships were just outside the territorial waters of the United States.

"The Volstead Market Day"—liquor-laden ships sell supplies outside the limit of government jurisdiction.

Cartoon by Rollin Kirby, *New York World*, January 18, 1923

##In large cities stores sold copper stills with all the material needed to make beer and whisky. Students should read the Eighteenth Amendment to see why this was illegal.

tions each year for alcohol to be taken "for medicinal purposes."

Probably the great majority of city dwellers were opposed to prohibition. Among people of German heritage beer-drinking was common, and among those of French and Italian origin the wine-drinking habit was strong. Had the manufacture and sale of wine and beer been permitted, the attempts at enforcement might have been more successful. As it was, many people considered it a mark of cleverness or social success to be able to boast possession of "a bottle."

An evaluation. The effect of prohibition was much disputed, but certainly it did not accomplish what its advocates had predicted. Admittedly, there was probably a good deal less drinking than before.

The "drys," as the prohibitionists were called, boasted that the nation's remarkable prosperity was the result of the closing of the saloon. As evidence, they pointed to the rise in savings-bank deposits. They also declared that the mounting sales of automobiles, radios, and houses showed that money formerly squandered on alcohol was now being spent more wisely. On the other hand, the "wets," as the antiprohibitionists were labeled, insisted that "the noble experiment" had promoted crime, encouraged immorality, and greatly increased disrespect for law and order.

Although there was widespread dissatisfaction with prohibition, few believed that the sale of liquor would ever be legalized again. Declared a Senator in 1930, "There is as much chance of repealing the Eighteenth Amendment as there is for a humming-bird to fly to the planet Mars with the Washington Monument tied to its tail." Nevertheless, the law-enforcement agencies hoped for the day when they would no longer have to deal with prohibition—which was producing insurmountable obstacles for them.

Organized crime. Violating the liquor laws could be profitable, and petty hoodlums who turned to rum-running sometimes made fortunes. What to do about crime, now organized on a large scale, became a problem of terrifying proportions. Linked from one state to another, the underworld became the charge particularly of the Federal Bureau of Investigation—a newly formed division of the United States Department of Justice.

The Capone gang. The most spectacular criminal in the prohibition era was Al Capone, of Chicago. He controlled the flow of "bootleg" liquor into the city's 10,000 "speakeasies." In his gang were hundreds of strong-arm men skilled in the use of machine guns and sawed-off shotguns. By about 1925 Capone had gained political control of the city government of Cicero, Illinois, a suburb of Chicago. His reign was marked by gang warfare without precedent in this country. Between 1920 and 1929 more than 500 gangland-style murders were committed in Chicago. In other great cities of the land, a similar story was being written. The murders were carried out in a variety of ways, but to "bump off" a victim after first "taking him for a ride" was a rather common practice.

Essentially, "bootlegging" appears to have been chiefly responsible for the increase in violence. This was large-scale enterprise engaging men who could not take their disputes into courts of law. They settled their differences on roadways and in alleys—by force.

Automobiles, which drys said were being driven more safely because there was less drinking, were also responsible for giving crime a wide range. They made crime detection not only a state function but also a federal one.

THE AUTOMOBILE

The advent of the automobile was of revolutionary importance to Americans. The effects were at first so overwhelming that motor cars became, for a time, synonymous with "the American way of life."

Foreign origins. The automobile originated in Europe, not in the United States. Almost all the important inventions used in the making of cars—including the engine and the steering gear—were created abroad. This fact shows in the large number of French words associated with the automobile, like "chauffeur," "garage,"

#Production on a mass scale was encouraged in a number of ways: Americans liked to handle machinery, they were eager for new products, they had money in the postwar years, they often had great distances to cover, and they bought so many cars that prices were lowered.

General Motors Corporation

The Oldsmobile runabout, built between 1900 and 1904. A two-passenger car, it held 5 gallons of gas.

How did passengers enter this model?

"chassis"—and even the word *automobile* itself. The American contribution included thousands of inventions, but principally it was the # system for producing cars on a mass scale.

The horseless carriage. The first automobiles built abroad were custom-made for a limited market consisting of men of wealth. These were usually sportsmen who used the new devices for showing off, since they could afford the servants necessary to keep the machines polished and in working order.

In this country the automobile at the beginning of the 1890's still looked like a buggy without a horse—truly a "horseless carriage." In France and Germany it was already beginning to look like a modern car. The European makes, for example, had tires inflated with air, while those manufactured in America still had wheels of iron that were braked on the rim. Moreover, the Europeans had demonstrated the advantages of gasoline-driven automobiles over the steam-driven—which for some time persisted as the favorites among Americans.

Henry Ford. Although American automobile makers lagged somewhat in technical matters, the immediate future for the automobile industry lay in the United States. With more open space than Europe had and a faster-rising standard of living, this country offered an enormous potential market for cars. The American businessman who could devise an efficient, easily maintained, easily repaired, and *cheap* car able to travel over bad country roads would open the door to success.

Such a man was Henry Ford. His "Model T" is considered the most revolutionary machine of this century—comparable in American history to the cotton gin and barbed wire. ##

The "Model T." A superb craftsman and a mechanical genius, Ford believed devoutly that the automobile could be made so cheaply that everybody could own one. After a long period of experimenting with various models, Ford in 1908 produced the first "Model T." Lacking in grace, sitting high above the ground, it had a 20-horsepower engine and gave the appearance

##Review the effects of the invention of the cotton gin and of barbed wire. How can the three inventions be compared? (In their long-reaching economic and social effects.)

—soon confirmed by performance—of being sturdy and durable. Shortly the vast waiting market found the new car. By 1913 Ford was producing over 500 a day, and two years later the one-millionth was on the road.

The assembly line. This amazing production was made possible by the assembly-line system of manufacturing—Henry Ford's most important contribution. Its main feature was fully developed by 1913: a continuous conveyor belt to bring materials to the workingmen for assembly. Ford later recalled, "The idea came in a general way from the overhead trolley that the Chicago packers use in dressing beef."‡

In his autobiography Ford described the way the parts of his automobiles were put together:

---

‡ In the meat-packing plants conveyor belts attached to the ceiling had long been in use. Each butcher would remove a certain cut from the carcass as it passed him and then return what was left to the moving belt, which would carry it to the next butcher, and so on.

In the chassis assembling are forty-five separate operations or stations. The first men fasten four mud-guard brackets to the chassis frame; the motor arrives on the tenth operation and so on in detail. Some men do only one or two small operations, others do more.

The man who places a part does not fasten it—the part may not be fully in place until after several operations later. The man who puts in a bolt does not put on the nut; the man who puts on the nut does not tighten it. On operation number thirty-four the budding motor gets its gasoline; it has previously received lubrication; on operation number forty-four the radiator is filled with water, and on operation number forty-five the car drives out. . . .

Competition. Ford was able by efficient production to turn out his "tin Lizzies" cheaper almost every year, until by 1924 the price was $290. Within a few years, however, the Chevrolet, familiarly called the "Chevy," made by a powerful rival, General Motors, was attract-

As sales boomed, Ford raised wages and cut prices. He permitted no unions.

The first assembly line in the Ford plant at Highland Park, Michigan. The cars—not the workers—moved.

State Historical Society of Wisconsin

ing customers. An inexpensive car, it copied the features of higher-priced ones like the Oldsmobile and the Cadillac. Consequently, in 1928 Ford put a competing "Model A" on the market, and the day of the "Model T" was over.

Economic importance. By 1929 the automotive industry had become the country's biggest business. Over 23,000,000 cars were on the roads, and the annual production of new ones was valued at about $3,500,000,000. Yearly passenger-car production had reached almost 4,800,000; a different, improved model became an accepted fact for millions of Americans, and "two cars in every garage" the long-range goal of many.

Worldwide impact. Americans were on wheels to stay. But more than that, all over the world the Ford became a tangible symbol of the nation's productive capacity. Priced low enough "for the multitude," this car was, in addition, a token of the material possibilities that democracy offered mankind.

Fords seemed to appear everywhere in the world. Wrote Ford's advertising manager: "Naked little urchins on the narrow streets of Bombay dodge the rapidly moving cars. Scantily clad Ethiopian giants pilot tourist-laden cars through the mining districts of South Africa. The Sphinx, if he were to speak, would comment on the horseless steed of vanadium steel that so frequently is seen before it. . . . natives of old China view with interest or alarm the noiseless vehicles that so quickly pass by. . . ."

A PLEASURE-SEEKING PEOPLE

If the 1920's had become the age of the automobile, they just as surely had become the age of electricity. Electricity was everyone's slave, freeing people from countless duties that now could be done automatically.

By 1917, the nation was producing yearly 43,429,000,000 kilowatt-hours of electricity. The total was just below 117,000,000,000 by 1929 and was soon to reach that huge figure. What did the country do with the electrical energy it was creating and the human energy the electricity was helping to save?

Electrical appliances. The rising figure for electrical production reflected the great increase in the number of industrial uses of electricity. But it measured also a change in consumers' habits. Millions of radios, vacuum cleaners, electric lamps, toasters, refrigerators, and washing machines by the mid-1920's were remaking American life. Because of everyday conveniences, the home was becoming a more agreeable place than before.

The uses of advertising. Since the public was always on the lookout for novelty and greater comfort, the advertising industry was constantly busy. In the process of creating new tastes and needs, it grew to be big business. The use of slogans in advertising—an old technique—took a new form. Now they could be dinned into the consumers' ears on the radio, whereas formerly they had appeared only in print.

The success of flaked breakfast food, which appeared at the turn of the century, for example, was a triumph of the power of advertising. One of the best-known brands of corn flakes bore a statement that became nationally familiar: "The Genuine bears this signature—W. K. Kellogg." One of Kellogg's competitors, Charles W. Post, meanwhile was telling the public: "Remember, you can recover from any ordinary disease by . . . using Postum Food Coffee and Grape-Nuts."

In 1899 the National Biscuit Company also pioneered in the field of advertising when it started to push Uneeda biscuits. By 1903 Cadillac was proclaiming its product as "the smartest of runabouts" (able to travel up to 30 miles an hour, too).

Even before the First World War, enticing advertisements had become commonplace for almost every consumer product. The great national magazines were making familiar such trademarks as the Victor dog, listening to "his master's voice," and the Campbell Soup kids. By the mid-twenties the market for goods had been extended incredibly by advertising. Also, new customers were being created by the encouragement of credit, or installment, buying. A person could obtain almost any type of commodity he might want by buying it "on time."

##Advertising created an active demand for goods which earlier had been considered luxuries. Advertisements, chiefly in magazines and papers, represented these goods as being necessities.

Liberated women. Laborsaving and timesaving devices poured in a flood from the factories. These were particularly important in freeing women finally from much of the ceaseless drudgery that had been the lot of housewives since time immemorial. Outside the house women also had more freedom.

The Nineteenth Amendment to the Constitution had given women the vote at last. The long-standing demand of the suffragettes for political equality between the sexes had been fulfilled. The effects were not immediately apparent. But, meanwhile, in addition to political freedom, the so-called gentle sex was finding social freedom in postwar America that was startling even to the suffragettes.

Many a grandmother, born perhaps in the 1860's, was confident that her granddaughter's generation in the 1920's was on a one-way trip to disaster. Chaperones no longer were inevitable attendants at young people's parties. A fashion editor wrote of another cause for alarm in reporting in 1920 that "the American woman . . . has lifted her skirt far beyond any modest limitation." The hemline was now 9 inches from the ground! It soon had reached the knee.

The wearing of lipstick and rouge became commonplace, and women were smoking in public for the first time. Not so many years earlier, Theodore Roosevelt's daughter Alice had felt forced to puff secretly into the White House fireplaces in order to avoid her parents' disapproval of her smoking. Women cut their hair short—and differently, it seemed, every year. When Irene Castle, a famous dancer, bobbed her hair in 1922, millions, including many movie actresses, imitated her.

Motion pictures. Movies had, in fact, become the style setters for many Americans in manners as well as in morals and dress. The infant motion-picture industry produced its first screen story, *The Great Train Robbery*, in 1903. Shortly afterward an enterprising promoter in Pittsburgh set up in a warehouse crude facilities for projecting one-reel shows, to which the admission charge was five cents. The interest in nickelodeons—where the films

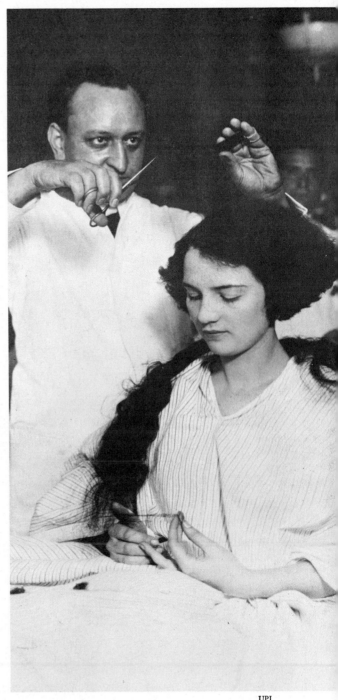

UPI

A big step in the early 1920's: getting her hair bobbed. Young women all over the country invaded men's barber shops to be shorn of their customary long hair and to have it cut close to their heads in back—or, in other words, shingled. Fascinated spectators witness the end of the masculine monopoly of this shop.

##Beauty shops in time took the business of styling hair away from barbers. After their hair was cut, women no longer wore large hats, and hatpins became a thing of the past.

615

#The new motion-picture industry was centered in a suburb of Los Angeles, Hollywood, chiefly because of the climate there. (Look back at the chart on p. 604 to see how Los Angeles grew between 1920 and 1930. The climate attracted fruit growers and tourists, among others.)

were shown—spread like wildfire to other cities, and out of them the movie theater was born. By 1907 nearly every large city could boast of having at least one, and more were being built each year.

The nation's new heroes and heroines were the actors and actresses of the screen: the Gish sisters, Charlie Chaplin, Mary Pickford, Douglas Fairbanks, and others. When Rudolph Valentino, one of Hollywood's romantic leading men, died in 1926 at the age of thirty-one, a line eleven blocks long was formed in New York City by movie fans who had come to pay their last respects. Talking pictures, which ## appeared in 1927, made the movies the nation's leading form of entertainment.

Commercial radio. The beginning of commercial radio broadcasting was another major milestone not only of the 1920's but also of the twentieth century. It owed much of its success to the wizardry in electronics of Lee De Forest, who was trained at Yale, and Edwin H. Armstrong, a graduate of Columbia University. De Forest laid the groundwork for the radio tube, and Armstrong designed the basic circuit used in nearly all receivers.

A popular song was entitled "The Sheik of Araby."

Agnes Ayres, the heroine, faces "the sheik" in a spellbinding movie of 1921. Valentino and his associates display the exaggerated expressions and gestures that were characteristic of early motion pictures.

Brown Brothers

616 ##The first successful talking picture was <u>The Jazz Singer</u>, in which Al Jolson starred. Actors and actresses without good speaking voices were soon doomed.

#Industries responsible for making radio supplies were the first to begin to broadcast programs on a definite schedule. The Westinghouse Electrical and Manufacturing Company began such a schedule. Most of the music was provided by records.

#

The first commercial station was KDKA in Pittsburgh. Its first broadcast—on November 2, 1920—consisted of the Harding-Cox election returns. Within a few years radio sets had become ordinary in American homes: by 1929 about ten million sets had been bought, an indication of radio's great popularity.

This miraculous new means of transmitting news, general information, and entertainment quickly helped to regulate the lives of millions. People everywhere seemed to arrange affairs to conform with the schedules of their favorite programs. Furthermore, for the first time,

the attention of tens of millions of people could simultaneously be focused on a single subject. This was a powerful source of benefit to the country—and in the wrong hands, a potential source of evil.

##

Two great coast-to-coast chains of radio stations were created—the National Broadcasting Company in 1926 and the Columbia Broadcasting System the following year. In 1927 the federal government established the Federal Radio Commission—an independent agency—to regulate the 700 stations then in operation.

Griffith's most famous picture was The Birth of a Nation, which embittered race relations.

The fragile Lillian Gish (right) and Dorothy, her sister, in a film directed by D. W. Griffith, called Orphans of the

Storm. This typical scene was obviously calculated to pull at the heartstrings of moviegoers in the 1920's.

Movie Star News

##The Birth of a Nation was adapted from a reconstruction novel in which the Ku Klux Klan was shown as the defender of white supremacy. The movie had a powerful, unfortunate influence.

Fueling an American plane in the International Aviation Meet at Grant Park in Chicago in 1911. Only a few years after the Wrights' epic flight, airplane buffs were promoting the machine and advertising its possibilities.

Compare these planes with modern airliners.

A plane carrying 64 pounds of mail lifts off the field at Pasco, Washington, in April, 1926, bound for Elko, Nevada. This was the first flight by a private airline under contract to the federal government to carry mail.

618 Airmail postage was first set at twenty-four cents for a one-ounce letter, but it was reduced in 1928 to five cents. What is it now?

An early passenger plane—which also carried mail—used on transcontinental flights. The passengers had to fly from San Francisco to Chicago and then transfer to another plane for New York City, and vice versa.

The government's subsidizing of airmail carriers stimulated design and manufacture of planes.

Varied fads. Radio had a major part in standardizing American tastes in the performing arts. It probably also stimulated a growing tendency of the public to go from one fad to another in an incessant quest for novelty and excitement. The crossword puzzle§ and then the game of Mah-Jongg were the rage. The opening of the tomb of the ancient Egyptian ruler Tutankhamen in 1922 led to a craze for clothes with a "King Tut" motif that manufacturers aroused in the feminine public.

Sports heroes and heroines. An astounding interest in spectator sports grew, and in every branch of athletics there was a hero who excelled his contemporaries. Bobby Jones led in golf, Bill Tilden in tennis, Jack Dempsey in boxing, Babe Ruth in baseball, and Red Grange in football. Crowds turned out to greet these heroes wherever they went.

And there were heroines, too. In 1926 when Gertrude Ederle became the first woman to swim across the English Channel, New York City gave her a homecoming rivaling that of a returning conqueror in ancient Rome.

§ The Baltimore and Ohio Railroad went so far as to put dictionaries aboard all its main-line trains for the convenience of passengers.

ENTERING THE AIR AGE

The greatest hero of the twenties was Charles A. Lindbergh, the first man to fly solo # across the Atlantic. He dramatized the progress the airplane industry had made since its start in 1903. In that year the Wright brothers —Orville and Wilbur—had demonstrated in trial flights at Kitty Hawk, North Carolina, that a heavier-than-air machine could remain aloft. In the first trial their machine stayed up for 12 seconds and traveled 120 feet.

Airmail. From this modest start aviation improved gradually, and in the First World War it was already playing a military role. The government placed factory orders for thousands of planes, but it had to cancel many of them when the armistice came. The new industry suffered a severe setback, but fresh opportunities beckoned.

The first daily airmail route was opened in 1918 between Washington and New York, with planes owned by the Post Office Department. It extended the service within a few years to the carrying of mail between New York, Chicago, and San Francisco. Not until 1925 did Congress begin to follow the practice,

#Flying men, mechanics, and many military airmen disapproved of Lindbergh's flight because the weather reports were not good. About three hundred of these men saw Lindbergh take off.

long before established in European countries, of providing government subsidies to regular airlines for carrying the mail.

The Air Commerce Act. In 1926 the Air Commerce Act placed control over commercial aviation in the hands of the Department of Commerce. As a result of this law, commercial air service began. In one year eighteen lines had carried over 5000 passengers, and the air routes covered over 3000 miles.

Lindbergh's miracle. The United States Navy seaplane NC–4 in 1919 had become the first to cross the Atlantic by air. But its flight was not as sensational as a nonstop flight from New York to Paris would be—for which a New York hotel owner in 1919 offered a prize of $25,000. In the rain on Long Island, on the morning of May 20, 1927, Charles A. Lindbergh, of Minnesota, took off in his plane, *The Spirit of St. Louis*. Handsome, young (he was twenty-five), alone, he set out on one of the most memorable flights in history.

A symbolic figure. Lindbergh irresistibly attracted the eyes and interest of Americans as he soared into the sky. Forty thousand fans at a boxing bout in Yankee Stadium in New

The Distinguished Flying Cross is awarded for heroism or extraordinary achievement in flight.

The tall, good-looking Lindbergh is presented the Distinguished Flying Cross by President Coolidge after his return from the flight to Paris. In only a few days Lindbergh had become an international hero.

Gilloon Photo Agency

620   In this group, only two of the men wear mustaches, and they are older persons.   The day of the soft-collared shirt had not yet come.

#Lindbergh married Anne Morrow, daughter of Dwight Morrow (see p. 675). Their small son was kidnapped and killed in 1932, possibly because his father was famous. A federal law providing the death penalty for kidnappers who take victims across state lines was enacted in 1934.

New York, June 17th, 1927

Bryant Park Bank

Pay to the Order of Charles A. Lindbergh

Twenty-five Thousand No/100 Dollars

Payable in funds current at New York Clearing House

$25,000. No/100

Raymond Orteig

Raymond Orteig

Margaret Romer

A photograph of the check Lindbergh received for his flight. The prize offered—a handsome sum—had been donated by Raymond Orteig in 1919 and had remained unclaimed for eight years. Observe the motifs.

How promptly did Mr. Orteig make good his offer? (He paid in less than a month.)

York that night bowed their heads in silent prayer for his success.

Then word came that Lindbergh had been sighted flying over the Irish coast, then over the English Channel. Not long afterward, on May 21, he brought his plane down at Le Bourget Airfield near Paris, after a flight of 33½ hours. Crowds broke down a steel fence to mob him. Modestly he presented to United States Ambassador Myron T. Herrick credentials which he had brought along as a means of identification.

The United States took "Lucky Lindy" to its heart at once. Hundreds of thousands of extra editions of newspapers were sold; the army commissioned Lindbergh a colonel in the air corps. New York City gave Lindbergh such a wildly enthusiastic reception when he returned that it cost the city $16,000 just to clean up the confetti dropped on him from # windows and rooftops!

When Lindbergh refused to cash in on his magnificent achievement through signing testimonials and accepting movie contracts, he was idolized even more. Americans, who are fundamentally idealistic, had found in Lind-

bergh many of the personal qualities they re- ## garded as most worthy even if, in the 1920's, they did not always display them.

Sum and Substance

1. Name five reasons for the letdown in American life in the 1920's. 2. What new immigration policy developed? Why? 3. Describe the legislation enacted to carry out this policy. 4. What events led to a Red scare? 5. Give the facts concerning the Boston police strike. 6. What industrial strikes occurred? With what outcomes? 7. Give an account of the Sacco-Vanzetti case. 8. Characterize the Ku Klux Klan. What methods did it use? 9. Describe the Scopes trial. 10. What crusading movements helped accomplish prohibition? Name the difficulties of enforcing it. 11. Explain the increase in organized crime. 12. Where did the automobile originate? 13. What improvement in automobile production can be credited to Ford? Explain. 14. Name the new amusements and the new means of communication people of the twenties enjoyed. 15. What did the Air Commerce Act provide? Explain the result it had. 16. Give the main facts about Lindbergh's achievement.

##Ask the students to identify these personal qualities. (Suggestion: bravery, perseverance, personal integrity.) Do students regard Americans as fundamentally idealistic?

THE NATION LOOKS FORWARD TO A PERMANENT BOOM TIME

In the 1920's millions of Americans wore the air of prosperity. Wages did not increase much, but prices remained steady. Moreover, in industry, especially, the future looked rosy. Even though unemployment was a persistent problem, the number of people employed was increasing. Businessmen's profits were good, and the gross national product, measured by the total of goods and services produced, was rising steadily.

SPECULATION IN STOCKS

By the middle of the 1920's, however, a stock-speculation mania was absorbing American interest. It was based on several developments in American business.

There had been a vast expansion and consolidation of business after the war. From 1919 to 1928 mergers of one kind or another had absorbed about 6000 mining and manufacturing firms, about 4000 public-utilities companies, and about 1800 banks. The small retail businessmen throughout the country felt also the pressures of the great retail chain stores, like those of F. W. Woolworth and the Great Atlantic and Pacific Tea Company. These chain-store enterprises had already become established American institutions.

But most of the time business *as a whole* was expanding from 1919 to 1927. And then, in 1927 something serious happened: business started to slacken, and commodity prices began to slip.

Up, up, up. Despite this drop, the market prices of shares of stock in the great corporations generally continued to rise. At first these prices had reflected solid business expansion. But as they zoomed higher and higher, they represented chiefly the upward spiral of speculation.

Vicious cycle. Since stock prices were high, many corporations sold new shares to acquire capital, instead of borrowing from banks the money they needed. This practice insured that there would be no interest payments to make to a bank.

With the additional funds in hand, corpora-

tions expanded their plants and produced more goods. When profits went up, so did stock prices; and the spiral began again. The grave danger was that the annually expanding production of goods would not be consumed by the available market—in other words, that there would not be enough buyers.

SOME DISCOURAGING SIGNS

The largest body of consumers in the country consisted of farmers and working people. But in the 1920's they were not prosperous enough to absorb the production of industry.

Falling farm income. Agriculture had slipped into # an economic depression in the summer and fall of 1920, from which it did not emerge until 1935. In order to raise cash crops of wheat, farmers had overextended their operations during the world war—just as they had during the Civil War.

Statistics can give no idea of individual suffering, but one can imagine the anguish that engulfed thousands as total farm income dropped from $17,825,000,000 in 1919 to $10,521,000,000 by 1921. This occurred at the very time when young men, released by the army, were returning to American farms. It was also a period when farmers wanted just as badly as their city brothers the wonderful consumer products the factories were turning out with so much advance advertising.

The farm bloc. In 1921 a group of congressmen from the farm states organized themselves, without regard to party, into what was called the "farm bloc." These men aimed to create and seek the enactment of a legislative program for agriculture. They were instrumental in obtaining the passage of several laws.‖

One was the Grain Futures Trading Act, which gave the Secretary of Agriculture broad control over the grain exchanges.# A second

---

‖ For a number of years—almost until it broke up in 1928—the farm bloc held a commanding position in the House and in the Senate.

\# Grain exchanges are farm-commodity markets in which speculators arrange sales based on estimated future prices of crops still to be harvested.

#Recall the situation of the farmers during the Civil War and afterward (see p. 429). The same thing had occurred.

was a law exempting farm coöperatives from the operation of the antitrust laws against them. A third was the very impressive Agricultural Credits Act of 1923. This act, the most significant that the farm bloc could obtain, helped make loans available to organized groups of farmers for periods of from six months to three years.

Crop surpluses. These measures, nevertheless, still did not solve the biggest of the farm problems: the huge annual crop surpluses. The farmer was forced to sell his crops in a competitive world market even though he bought his manufactured goods in a tariff-protected home market. The farm bloc attempted in the McNary-Haugen Farm Relief Bill of 1924 to provide a fair exchange value to farmers. This bill aimed to make it possible for them to receive for the wheat they sold in the United States a higher price than they were able to obtain for wheat sold abroad.

Despite great enthusiasm in farm communities for the McNary-Haugen Bill, President Coolidge, who looked upon it as governmental price-fixing, vetoed it twice. Coolidge summed up a widespread public feeling on one occasion when he remarked casually: "Farmers have never made money. I don't believe we can do much about it."

Wages and hours. Among urban producers there were economic problems, too. In the six years between 1923 and 1929, for instance, the output—measured in man-hours—of American manufacturing plants went up about 32 percent. But hourly wages rose only 8 percent in the same period. The average wage of workers never went above $1500 a year in the 1920's, and the average work week was 50 hours.

Labor's weakness. Industrial labor had not been able to establish unions in the great mass-production industries, those turning out automobiles and steel, for example. Unions were woefully feeble in the textile industry, too. Organized labor was strong only in the older skilled trades, such as building, printing, and railroading.

The American Federation of Labor had over 4,000,000 members in 1919, in contrast to only 2,716,900 in 1914 when the war boom began, but it lost members in the decade after 1919. Its membership represented less than one-eighth of the whole wage-earning population. Besides, many of the gains of the AFL were in the munitions and metalworking industries, both rapidly demobilized after the armistice.

The status of the Negro. The 11,000,000 Negroes in the United States during the 1920's felt too little the boom times other Americans were experiencing. Negroes had fought in the A.E.F.—although in segregated units—to make the world "safe for democracy." Yet at home in both the North and the South their situation mocked these bold words: they lived, for the most part, in conditions of poverty and deprivation. The anguish of the Negroes showed itself in the summer of 1919—called "The Red Summer" by the Negro poet James Weldon Johnson—when twenty-five riots shook northern cities.

One cause of the outbreaks was the unrelieved cramping of Negroes into "ghettos" in the major urban centers. During the First World War many Negroes "went north" to fill jobs in defense industries. After the war, the steady introduction of machines drove still more Negroes out of cotton agriculture, and they left the South in large numbers. Settling in segregated areas in New York's Harlem and on Chicago's South Side and in other cities, they were quickly disillusioned about finding the better opportunities they sought. Moreover, they faced the hostility of white competitors for jobs—with almost no protection against discrimination in hiring and firing.

The travails of the Negro produced the first large-scale black nationalist movement in the United States. The leader was Marcus Garvey, who had come to New York from the West Indies in 1917. Garvey, who preached a "back to Africa" philosophy, used the slogan "Africa for the Africans at home and abroad." The height of his influence—in the early 1920's—coincided with the so-called Harlem Renaissance, a period of extraordinary creativity for Negro artists and musicians.

THE POLITICS OF PROSPERITY

Coolidge, known as a man of few words, was called "Silent Cal," but he managed to gain the respect of his countrymen. His quiet integrity was a great relief in a noisy, often hypocritical age when the older virtues no longer seemed to be so acceptable. It is for this reason that a friend of the President called him "a Puritan in Babylon." In 1924 unhesitatingly the Republicans nominated Coolidge for President.

The Democratic convention of 1924. The Democrats battled fiercely among themselves at their convention in New York's old Madison Square Garden. Contending for the nomination were William Gibbs McAdoo, of California, and Governor Alfred E. Smith, of New York. Beneath this rivalry lay the deep antagonism of many delegates to the hopes and aspirations of urban America. In their minds Smith represented all of these. He had been born in an

East Side slum area of New York City; he was a Roman Catholic; and he had assailed both the Ku Klux Klan** and prohibition. In the

---

** Meeting in convention, the Democrats refused to denounce the Klan by name, the proposal failing by one vote.

end, neither Smith nor McAdoo could carry the convention.

On the 103rd ballot the tired and sweltering delegates gave the nomination to John W. Davis, originally from West Virginia. A former congressman and ambassador to England, he was a distinguished lawyer. Yet he proved to have little vote-getting ability. Moreover, the Democratic platform—aside from endorsing the League of Nations—was indistinguishable from that of the Republicans. The Republicans and Democrats alike, under the spell of the prosperity and the ballyhoo of the twenties, had put aside the progressive ideals of their recent past.

La Follette's Progressive party. But Robert M. La Follette had remained true to his reforming principles. Now, in 1924, "Fighting Bob" organized, out of the reformers and the discontented, a third party that called itself "Progressive." La Follette had support from the Scripps-Howard newspapers, the American Federation of Labor, and a number of earlier reformers—including "General" Jacob S. Coxey (see page 387).

"Keeping cool with Coolidge." Although the Progressive party polled nearly five million votes, Americans were not in a mood for crusading

Observe the smiling, expectant looks on the faces of the Hoover supporters.
Candidates used the radio extensively in the presidential election of 1928: here Hoover makes the most of it.

Brown Brothers

against monopoly or seeking government intervention in business. The campaign lacked spirit, and only about half the qualified voters took the trouble to go to the polls on Election Day. The President was elected to the White House, this time in his own right. He had carried thirty-five of the forty-eight states, using the slogan "Keep cool with Coolidge."

Herbert Hoover's candidacy. In an uneventful term as President, Coolidge's name became synonymous with the prosperity that many Americans were enjoying. Coolidge left policy-making to Congress, believing this was not a proper function of the President. Moreover, although he could see that serious economic problems were in the making, he lacked the imagination—as well as the will and energy—to tackle them.

The nation generally believed Coolidge would run for reelection. But in the summer of 1927, he calmly announced, "I do not choose to run for President in 1928." Republican eyes turned to Herbert Hoover, the Secretary of Commerce.

Born in Iowa in 1874, Hoover was orphaned at eight and went to live with an uncle in Oregon. In time he became independently wealthy as a mining engineer and business promoter. As postwar food-relief administrator in Belgium, Hoover showed talents that were recognized in Washington. Among those who admired him was the Assistant Secretary of the Navy, Franklin D. Roosevelt, who once remarked: "I wish we could make him President of the United States. There could not be a better one." By the late 1920's, even if Roosevelt, a Democrat, no longer said this, many had come to agree with such a sentiment. At the Republican convention in 1928, Herbert Hoover was nominated on the first ballot.

Al Smith, the "happy warrior." In the Democratic camp, Alfred E. Smith of New York drew support from two groups—those who called for stricter government control of big business and those who sympathized with labor's needs. Himself a sincere reformer, Smith seemed a strong choice for the Democrats, now reemerging as a genuine opposition party. Smith, labeled the "happy warrior" by Roosevelt when

Cartoon by Rollin Kirby, *New York World*, October 28, 1928
Politics, 1928. "Nobody but me can make you rich."

Look back at the cartoons on p. 485.

he placed the name in nomination, easily won on the first ballot.

A nasty campaign. The campaign proved to be one of the nastiest in American history. As a Roman Catholic, a wet, and a big-city man who smoked a cigar and wore a brown derby, Smith was a new kind of presidential candidate, and wherever he went, brass bands struck up "The Sidewalks of New York."

In the campaign and in the way people voted, bigotry showed itself. Many thought Smith's religion rendered him unfit for the White House. Often, ashamed to say this directly, they put it indirectly. This is how a famous Republican journalist expressed it to a Kansas audience: "It is not that Governor Smith is a Catholic and a wet which makes him an offense to the villagers and town dwellers, but because his record shows the kind of Presi-

##Ask the class if religious bigotry plays a role today in presidential elections. Do people today vote or refuse to vote for a candidate because he follows a certain religion?

625

Wide World

Already well traveled, the President-elect *(at left in the car)* early in 1929 visits Montevideo, Uruguay. American Presidents had become aware of the need for good Latin American relations.

dent he would make—a Tammany president."

Smashing the solid South. Yet it is wrong to think that intolerance was alone responsible for Smith's defeat. Hoover's name was a household word everywhere. Furthermore, it seemed to many that prosperity would soon be general throughout the country. Only rarely has a party been turned out of power when economic prospects have been good. Herbert Hoover won an overwhelming victory, receiving 444 electoral votes to Smith's 87.

For the first time since reconstruction days, the Republicans had smashed the solid South. On the other hand, the twelve largest cities in the country, carried by the Republicans in 1924, were now in the Democratic column. The Democrats had broken into the Republican North. In short, the Democratic party was beginning to be the favorite of urban Americans, who felt shortchanged in the amount of attention their problems received.

A rosy future. Meanwhile, as always, the future was hidden. In his speech of acceptance, Hoover had stated: "We in America today are

nearer to the final triumph over poverty than ever before in the history of any land. The poorhouse is vanishing from among us . . . we shall soon, with the help of God, be in sight of the day when poverty will be banished from this nation."

As Hoover took the oath of office on March 4, 1929, the outlook was bright. Americans could be confident: their new President, an experienced executive, was the first successful businessman ever elected to the White House. ##

Sum and Substance

1. Give the facts concerning stock speculation in the twenties. 2. What was the effect on the production of manufactured goods? 3. Describe the farmer's situation. 4. Who made up the farm bloc? Tell what it accomplished. 5. What problem did the McNary-Haugen Bill seek to solve? What happened to it? 6. Describe the condition of industrial workers. 7. Describe the situation of Negroes during and after the First World War. 8. Who were the candidates in the election of 1924? In 1928? Who was elected?

##Discuss the kinds of experience our Presidents have brought to the White House. Many have been lawyers, some have been military men, and others have been political leaders.

THE WORKSHOP

OF LASTING SIGNIFICANCE

What did each of the following have to do with prosperity's promise in the 1920's?

Calvin Coolidge	"Model T"
Teapot Dome reserve	assembly line
	Lee De Forest
Fordney-McCumber Act	Edwin H. Armstrong
	KDKA
Hawley-Smoot Act	Charles A. Lindbergh
anti-Semitism	Wright brothers
literacy test	Air Commerce Act
Emergency Quota Act	farm bloc
Boston police strike	Grain Futures
Sacco-Vanzetti case	Trading Act
Ku Klux Klan	Agricultural
Scopes trial	Credits Act
Clarence Darrow	McNary-Haugen
"bootlegging"	Farm Relief Bill
Henry Ford	Alfred E. Smith

THE PRESIDENCY

1. Compare Calvin Coolidge's conception of the presidency with that of Woodrow Wilson.

2. In what ways was the Democratic candidate for the presidency in 1928 handicapped? Why?

3. Describe the qualities Hoover possessed which seemed to many Americans to make him a good choice for the presidency.

4. Under what circumstances were these words spoken, "The times do not require a first-rater"? What were the direct political results of the adoption by the country of the attitude thus expressed?

INFORMED OPINION

1. What relationship do you see among (a) the increases in tariff rates between 1921 and 1930, (b) the rapid development of business and industry, and (c) Republican administrations in the period? Explain.

2. Reread and sum up the quotation from the article written by a young man, page 604. If one assumes that he was twenty-four in 1924, how old would he be today if he were still living? What viewpoint do young people today have of his generation?

3. How did young people of the 1920's show rebellion? Would you say that young people today have the same attitude? If so, how do they indicate their feelings?

4. Are Americans today "afraid to carry world responsibility"? Explain.

5. Why was the poison and terror spread # by the Ku Klux Klan contrary to the good Americanism the organization professed to be protecting?

6. In your opinion, is there a similarity ## between the 1920's and today in respect to national interest in amusements? Explain.

7. Why were urban Negroes in a particularly disadvantageous situation in the twenties? Compare their condition then and today.

STATISTICS IN HISTORY

1. Compare the table on page 319 with the one on page 604. What changes occurred in the list of the ten largest cities between 1900 and 1910? How do you explain the appearance of Detroit on the list in 1920?

When was Los Angeles first counted as one of the ten? What connection can you see between the growth of that city and the opening of the Panama Canal?

2. In 1930 how many of the ten largest cities were located on the East Coast? In the Middle West? In the South? On the West Coast? Now turn back to page 205 and answer the same questions for the year 1830.

What cities on the list in 1930 were not on it a century before? What conclusions can you draw about the movement of population in the intervening years? What did technological change have to do with it?

3. Turn to the table on page 821. In what years did America's imports continuously exceed its exports. How do you account for that situation? When did the United States have an occasional excess of exports? When did this occasional excess become continuous?

##There is a great interest in spectator sports in the United States today, as well as in other amusements. What does the development of urbanization have to do with this interest?

627

This chapter deals with the Great Depression. The quotation is from Franklin D. Roosevelt's first inaugural speech, in 1933. Observe that Roosevelt was deliberately reassuring the American people. How did he do it? What indicated that he would be a strong President?

27

CRASH, CRISIS, AND THE NEW DEAL

. . . the only thing
we have to fear is fear itself . . .

. . . I am certain that my fellow Americans expect that on my induction into the Presidency I will address them with a candor and a decision which the present situation of our Nation impels. This is pre-eminently the time to speak the truth, the whole truth, frankly and boldly. Nor need we shrink from honestly facing conditions in our country today. This great Nation will endure as it has endured, will revive and will prosper.

So, first of all, let me assert my firm belief that the only thing we have to fear is fear itself —nameless, unreasoning, unjustified terror which paralyzes needed efforts to convert retreat

Ask what the closing of a bank generally means. (It cannot meet the demands of its patrons.)

into advance. In every dark hour of our national life a leadership of frankness and vigor has met with that understanding and support of the people themselves which is essential to victory. I am convinced that you will again give that support to leadership in these critical days. . . .

I am prepared under my constitutional duty to recommend the measures that a stricken Nation in the midst of a stricken world may require. These measures, or such other measures as the Congress may build out of its experience and wisdom, I shall seek, within my constitutional authority, to bring to speedy adoption.

But in the event that the Congress shall fail to take one of these two courses, and in the event that the national emergency is still critical, I shall not evade the clear course of duty that will then confront me. I shall ask the Congress for the one remaining instrument to meet the crisis—broad Executive power to wage a war against the emergency, as great as the power that would be given to me if we were in fact invaded by a foreign foe.

For the trust reposed in me I will return the courage and the devotion that befit the time. I can do no less. . . .

We do not distrust the future of essential   #
democracy. The people of the United States have not failed. In their need they have registered a mandate that they want direct, vigorous action.   ##
They have asked for discipline and direction under leadership. They have made me the present instrument of their wishes. In the spirit of the gift I take it.

In this dedication of a Nation we humbly ask the blessing of God. May He protect each and every one of us. May He guide me in the days to come.

When the bubble of prosperity burst in the autumn of 1929, the United States was unprepared to cope with the bad times that quickly followed. In the next few years, the growing economic distress turned the eyes of the public more and more toward the presidency for leadership. This is a selection from the first inaugural of Franklin D. Roosevelt— delivered on March 4, 1933. One of his most memorable addresses, it helped revive the sagging spirits of millions of Americans.

Franklin D. Roosevelt Library

An excited crowd of New Yorkers in early 1933 gathers in front of a bank that has closed its doors. Between 1930 and 1933 over 5500 others shut down, and on the day he became President, Franklin D. Roosevelt faced an unprecedented situation: in all but one state the banks were completely or partly closed.

A DISASTROUS DEPRESSION LAYS AMERICA LOW

The year 1929 has become a year to remember. Like 1776 or 1861, it marks a significant turning point in the country's history. When 1929 began, very few prophesied that it would witness the start of the worst economic depression in American history. In fact, President Hoover said in his inaugural address in March, "I have no fears for the future of our country."

THE STOCK-MARKET "BUST"

One measuring stick of prosperity in 1929 was the stock market, which was attracting widespread public attention. By September, stock prices had soared to the highest point on record. General Electric stock, for example, which had sold for $128 per share on March 3, 1928, stood at $396 eighteen months later.

Optimism. Hearing optimistic predictions on every side, investors saw no reason to believe prices would not go even higher. Americans were in a mood to speculate with their money. They were encouraged by the words of Secretary of the Treasury Andrew W. Mellon: "There is no cause to worry. The high tide of prosperity will continue."

Advance signs. Yet by the summer of 1929 important signals of trouble afoot were appearing. Spending by consumers was slackening, and a noticeable decline in the amount of new building construction had set in. It was disturbing, too, that loans by brokers to their stock-buying clients in September totaled about $8,000,000,000. These clients were buying stocks on margin—that is, they were putting up only part of the purchase price and borrowing the rest through their brokers. If stock prices should start to fall, disaster for these people was sure.

Through the Federal Reserve Board, the national government had warned banks about the dangers of lending money for speculative purposes. But for a long time the government hesitated to go beyond a warning. A rise in interest rates, making the borrowing of money more expensive, might reduce speculation somewhat, but it might also slow down investment in industrial expansion. The result could be widespread unemployment. Devising correct policies was, therefore, like walking a tightrope.

Trouble in England. The continuance of any boom depends upon maintaining public confidence. Anything that seriously undermines this confidence can cause a business downswing. In October, 1929, a loss of confidence in this country seems to have resulted from the unmasking and consequent failure in September of an English stock manipulator named Clarence Hatry. The effects severely jolted the English stock exchange and were immediately felt here, too.

But it is idle and probably wrong to blame the disastrous collapse of the American stock market, which was shortly to occur, on a single event or even on a series of events. The simple fact is that thousands of investors throughout the country were independently beginning to fear that the boom could not go on much longer. They were ready to sell their shares of stock at the first good opportunity.

October, 1929. Although stock prices were at record highs in September, the *trend* of the market appeared to be downward. Brokers expected that this tendency would soon reverse itself, but on Wednesday, October 23, the prices of stock suddenly dropped, and a wave of stock-selling began which continued the following day. Because this kind of feverish "stock-dumping" is contagious, the New York Stock Exchange closed the visitors' gallery on Thursday afternoon. (That morning one of the onlookers had been England's former Chancellor of the Exchequer, Winston Churchill.)

Crowds of curious spectators jammed Wall Street in New York City, where the Exchange is located. Special police details were sent. "Black Thursday," as the day is called, saw the bottom drop out of the stock market, as stock-owners all over the country tried to unload shares at once.

At noon that day a group of bankers met in the offices of J. P. Morgan. Shortly afterward they announced that they were going to sup-

#As spending by consumers slackened, factories cut production and laid off workers, thereby reducing spending further.

#Better students may be interested in reading John K. Galbraith's The Great Crash for an analysis of the stock-market disaster.

Hoover Institution

President Hoover, a Quaker, seeks respite from the tensions of Washington in a deepening depression by attending services at the new Friends' Meeting House. His wife, Lou Henry, and a Secret Service man are along.

Observe the small hats the women are wearing--after the advent of bobbed hair.

port the market by buying stocks—each of them with millions of dollars supplied by his bank. For four days confidence seemed to be restored. Optimistic statements came from high places. Said President Hoover, "The fundamental business of the country—that is, the production and distribution of goods and services—is on a sound and prosperous basis."

But by Tuesday, October 29, the stock-selling impulse had seized hold again, and the Stock Exchange once more was swamped as people rushed to retrieve what they could of their money. Before that day was done, over # 16,000,000 shares had been sold. In the weeks that followed, the prices of stock sank stead-

ily—despite continued assurances from political and financial leaders that all was well. By the middle of November, it was apparent that stock prices were not going to "bounce back" quickly.

BAD TIMES

The collapse of the stock market was the initial stage of the long and bleak "Great Depression." Unemployment, which had been ## growing since the previous July, continued to increase at an alarming rate following the crash on Wall Street. Spending by consumers, which had been declining since July, continued to slacken. As businessmen stopped build-

##Business companies curtailed operations and in many cases shut down. As increasing numbers of workers became unemployed, demand for goods and services dropped even more.

ing new plants, the number of jobs available decreased. Income was not distributed well enough to keep people employed through an increase in spending by consumers.

Farmers found prices lower than ever; millions of working people could neither buy factory goods nor find employment. Middle-class people everywhere—storekeepers, stock-and-bond salesmen, and craftsmen—could not meet the time payments on their cars, refrigerators, or houses.

The "prosperity decade" had ended with a sickening thud. Said the humorist Will Rogers, "There has been more 'optimism' talked and less practiced than at any time during our history."

Fear of the future. Just as confidence breeds further confidence in people's minds during prosperous periods, so too, in depressions fear of the future breeds further fear of the future. Gloom and disillusionment spread to millions of homes in the next few years as factories put out signs saying "No work" or "Closed." Credit companies frequently reclaimed furniture, automobiles, radios, refrigerators—even clothing —that had been purchased on the installment plan.

Mortgages were foreclosed on the houses of millions of people, who then faced eviction by the sheriff. In the cities, forlorn families unable to pay their rent sat on the sidewalks beside their earthly possessions, hoping that friends and neighbors could give them shelter and meals.

The effects of the economic collapse were at first considered only temporary. But optimism vanished as clothes wore out without replacement, as more and more people found food scarce, and as young people finishing their schooling faced discouraging idleness.

Unemployment. Some businessmen continued to insist, up to the end of 1931, that the depression was only an illusion. But before that year was over, about 10,000,000 people were unemployed, and in the following twelve months the ranks grew steadily larger. Despair increased as the disaster widened. If there was a kind of cheerfulness in the popular song of

1931, "Life Is Just a Bowl of Cherries," it gave way to grimness in the 1932 song, "Brother, Can You Spare a Dime?"

A new symbol: the apple. One symbol of the depression came to be the humble apple. Late in 1930 the International Apple Shippers' Association offered to sell the fruit to the unemployed for resale at five cents apiece. Before many weeks had passed, 6000 jobless people were selling apples on the streets of New York, and the idea rapidly spread to other parts of the country.

The selling of the fruit was a tribute in a way to the determination of stricken Americans not to depend upon charity but to try to pull themselves up by their own bootstraps. Moreover, it was in harmony with the traditional view that the surest way out of a depression was to rely on individual initiative—certainly not on the national government.

Hoover's role. President Hoover hoped that private charity and self-help would tide the nation over. This view did not reflect indifference or callousness to the frightful suffering of so many Americans. Nevertheless, Hoover, who during the war had planned relief for the French and Belgian peoples, was accused of being indifferent to the anguish of his own countrymen.

Some of the criticism was justified. Having claimed for his party the credit for prosperity, Hoover could not now escape responsibility for the depression. And because he gave many the impression of shirking his obligations, he was jeered and denounced in public as no other President had been. The homeless unemployed slept at night under old newspapers called "Hoover blankets," and the shanties these unfortunate men hastily erected at the edge of towns were nicknamed "Hoovervilles."

Hoover was convinced that he was using the best policy for the nation—the best even for people who had lost their jobs. He was sticking to the traditional principle that the federal ## government had no direct responsibility for curing the evils of economic depression and that things ought to be allowed to "take their course."

 ##Relate Hoover's policy to the view he expressed in the campaign speech quoted on pp. 598-599. How had Americans developed a reliance on individual initiative?

Wide World

Selling apples on a street corner in St. Louis: the nickels received were the seller's only income.

The young apple salesman was to be admired, but he made little money.

Government policies. The administration resorted to insufficient remedies for the disastrous conditions. Through the Agricultural Marketing Act of June, 1929, it had created a Federal Farm Board. The Board tried to shore up farm prices and discourage the raising of surplus crops. Second, through the Federal Reserve Board interest rates were lowered in order to encourage businessmen to borrow for the expansion of their industrial plants. Third, through the Reconstruction Finance Corporation (the RFC), established in 1932, loans were made to banks, railroads, and other institutions in financial trouble.

Farm distress. The condition of the farmers—already bad—grew worse after the depression set in. As in the past when economic difficulties had arisen, the farmers tried to increase their income by raising more crops. They then found that this increase in supply lowered prices for farm products even more than before. Besides, unemployment in the cities reduced further the domestic market for the food the farmers raised.

To make matters worse, in 1931 the farm population increased by more than 300,000. Clearly many anxious city people were turning to agriculture—at least by farming they could expect to eat regularly. When crop prices remained low, the Secretary of Agriculture in 1932 justified them on the ground that "sustained farm production, though it depresses farm commodity prices, makes life easier for wage earners with reduced incomes. . . ."

This country, then, was facing a baffling situation in which there was a scarcity of food in

633

One of the unemployed leans dejectedly against the window of a restaurant that closed for want of customers.

Observe the signs in the window back of the man.

the cities and an excess of produce on the farms. Kansas editor William Allen White lamented: "Every farmer, whether his farm is under mortgage or not, knows that with farm products priced as they are today, sooner or later he must go down."

Suffering in the cities. The prospects for city people appeared no brighter. The federal public construction program on which President Hoover had counted heavily failed to accomplish its aim because the administration was determined also to balance the national budget. Hoover believed that nothing would more quickly restore confidence in the government than the maintenance of a sound financial position. Consequently, funds for public-works projects were limited.

The President was strongly opposed to borrowing money to meet the extraordinary costs of dealing with the emergency. In the main, Americans agreed with him—even the governor of New York, Franklin D. Roosevelt.

Social effects. But the suffering in the city was extensive and growing daily. The effects of the hard times were easily visible everywhere. Even in established middle-class homes, families began to scrimp: preserving foods, making soap and clothes, and perhaps even baking bread— activities they had not engaged in since grandmother's day. The purchase of electrical appliances, jewelry, and new cars declined sharply. Many people canceled telephone service. Between 1930 and 1931 alone New York lost the use of about 40,000 instruments.

#Hoover was opposed to recommending direct relief for unemployed people, and Congress would not have approved it. Local agencies had always provided such help to families.

Men grew old before their time as, almost panic-stricken, they sometimes tramped the streets by day in search of work and lay awake at night beset by worry and fear. The skills of workingmen began to rust and then vanish because of disuse, making readjustment to employment—when it became available—difficult.

The long-held beliefs of Americans were being seriously challenged. Elderly people were concluding, as bank failures wiped out their hard-earned nest eggs, that thrift was a dubious virtue. Younger people were saying that one could advance in the world only through "pull" —not by hard work. A note of pessimism crept into American thinking about the future. Although business and government spokesmen were predicting by 1931 that "prosperity is just around the corner," it somehow stubbornly failed to make its appearance.

Attempts at relief. As early as 1931 Governor Roosevelt in New York had appointed an emergency relief administrator, and other states had followed Roosevelt's example. But the task was much too vast to be accomplished on the local level alone. Furthermore, President Hoover's "Give-a-job" campaign in 1931 was inadequate for the large number of unemployed. Hoover had tried to persuade people to offer a day's work to a jobless neighbor—cleaning a cellar or whitewashing a fence, for example. The scheme at best would have led to further humiliations, and it failed in practice.

The administration's attitude was that the crisis Americans found themselves in differed only in kind from other critical emergencies of the past, like the Chicago fire in 1871 or the San Francisco earthquake in 1906. Chief reliance, therefore, should be on American neighborliness and coöperation and on local resources.

Yet many municipalities were bankrupt or close to that condition. In 1932 more than a hundred towns and cities could not afford to give people any public aid, or relief. In places where local money was appropriated, it had to be divided among too many people. In Toledo only 2¢ a meal could be paid each person for

Franklin D. Roosevelt Library

A "hunger line" grows long on a cold winter day in New York City, in February, 1932. The signs calling attention to a generous restaurant are designed to appeal to passers-by fortunate enough to carry spare coins.

Many people who had been employed steadily all their working lives had to accept charity during the Great Depression. The line seen in the picture contained some of these people.

Discuss the effects the necessity for living off charity would have on men who had long been proud of being able to provide for themselves and their families. Observe the policeman, one of the public employees fortunate enough to have jobs.

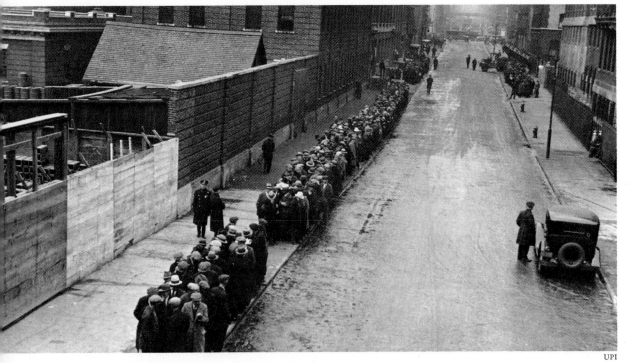

Hungry men waiting for a meal on the opening day of a new municipal lodging house in New York City.

Below: Study the expressions on the faces of the men receiving soup.

Receiving food at a "soup kitchen" in an urban area. The expenses may have been met by a private charity.

#Use the opportunity provided here
to review "free enterprise."

relief, and in New York City whole families were receiving only $2.39 a week.

Many businessmen were afraid that federal unemployment relief would destroy the country by destroying free enterprise. On the other hand, there was no use telling millions of decent, unemployed men the obvious untruth that "anybody can find work if he wants it." Many community leaders—often businessmen —who at first had opposed federal help changed their minds as they saw private charity overwhelmed by the demands on it.

The Red Cross was called upon to play its part—and it did, aiding almost a million people in the winter of 1931/1932. In March, 1932, 40,000,000 bushels of wheat, bought by the government through the Federal Farm Board, were distributed to feed the unemployed. Under Red Cross direction, 500,000 bales of cotton were manufactured into clothing. However, federal relief in the form of money to be paid directly to the unemployed seemed out of the question.

Federal aid. Nevertheless, pressure for federal unemployment relief remained strong. In response, the President in July, 1932, agreed to a bill permitting the Reconstruction Finance Corporation to lend $1,800,000,000 to states and municipalities for both relief and public construction.

The same month Congress also passed a law establishing twelve Federal Home Loan Banks to lend money to credit institutions whose resources had been severely drained by loans on farms and private dwellings. The benefits, therefore, were to be distributed at the "top," and officials hoped that they would seep downward to the level of the unemployed. The arrangement proved inadequate because of the size of the problems.

The "Bonus Army." As suffering and discontent grew, a "Bonus Army" began a march on Washington. In 1924 Congress had passed a bill providing for the issuing of service certificates to veterans of the world war. These certificates were to be redeemable in money in twenty years, and against them the holders could borrow up to about 25 percent of the

UPI

The "Bonus Army" tries to enter the Capitol in 1932. Policemen and iron gates kept them out.

<u>Below:</u> How was the man victimized?

"A wise economist asks a question." This cartoon won a Pulitzer prize in 1932.

McCutcheon in the *Chicago Tribune*

##Review the episode involving Coxey's "army" (see p. 387). How did the "Bonus Army" compare with Coxey's "army"? What result did each accomplish?

matured value. The certificates were popularly referred to as "bonuses." By 1931—fourteen years before the certificates were payable— around 272,000 soldiers of the former A.E.F. were on relief. Over the President's veto, Congress authorized the payment of an additional loan on the certificates. But a clamor went up to pay the balance of the sum immediately. In the early summer of 1932, between twelve and fifteen thousand unemployed war veterans began to move on the capital from various parts
of the country in order to lobby for such a bill. They encamped in empty government buildings or pitched tents on the shores of the Potomac.

In July Congress passed a bill to pay the fare home for the impoverished marchers, and all but about 2000 departed. President Hoover then instructed his Chief of Staff, General Douglas MacArthur, to disperse the rest. Fixed bayonets and tear gas sent the veterans on their way.

Although the clamor for a new bonus bill had failed, and although radical political influence among the discontented generally was very slight, the "Bonus March" was a frightening spectacle. The marches were denounced in many quarters as unpatriotic, but the action of the administration was severely criticized as a cruel reward for men who had once fought under the flag. Many Americans—including businessmen—were asking one another whether or not the administration's hands-off attitude in regard to unemployment and the hardships of individuals was a sufficient response to the desperate crisis.

Economic planning, which to many suggested the Communist Soviet Union, was now being discussed in several quarters. Said a thoughtful eastern Republican, "Gentlemen, if we wait too long, somebody will come forward with a solution we may not like." Leaders of the American Federation of Labor and of the railroad brotherhoods were reminding other Americans that sometimes out of widespread starvation revolutions are born.

Sum and Substance

1. Give the main facts about the stock-market crash in 1929. What was its significance? 2. What policy concerning the depression did President Hoover follow? Describe early measures his administration took. 3. What effect did the depression have on farmers? On city people? 4. Describe the social effects of the depression. 5. What efforts were made to give aid to the unemployed? 6. Describe the "Bonus March."

This section describes the new viewpoints and policies used by Franklin D. Roosevelt.

FRANKLIN D. ROOSEVELT EXPERIMENTS TO BRING RECOVERY

In the midst of these appalling conditions, the country faced a presidential election. Hoover would certainly be renominated by the Republican party, but few people believed that he could be reelected. The Democrats, on the other hand, were certain in 1932 that they
could elect any man they nominated.

THE CAMPAIGN OF 1932

When 1932 opened, a number of men seemed to stand a reasonably good chance of winning the Democratic nomination. But none appeared to be an outstanding choice.

The governor of New York. Franklin D. Roosevelt, who had been elected a second time to the governorship of New York in 1930, was an eager contender. He possessed a winning smile and an attractive public-platform manner, but he had no clearly conceived program for handling the problems the depression had brought. At the time, many Americans agreed with the lukewarm estimate of Roosevelt's qualities made in January, 1932, by the newspaper columnist Walter Lippmann. He had described the New York governor as "a pleasant man who, without any important qualification for the office, would very much like to be President."

Hyde Park "aristocrat." Born at Hyde Park, New York, on the banks of the Hudson River, "home" to Roosevelt was the ancestral estate on which he first saw the light of day in 1882.

##Ask why the Democrats had such an idea. Consider Hoover's position and the position of all Republican leaders. They had been elected in 1928 expressing what expectation?

His father, James Roosevelt, fifty-three at the time of Franklin's birth, had known Sam Houston. To Franklin the elder Roosevelt conveyed a deep love of history. Franklin's mother, Sara Delano Roosevelt, twenty-six years younger than her husband, had traveled extensively in Europe and East Asia. She inspired in her son—her only child—a keen interest in the world beyond the Hudson.

A family of wealth and leisure, the Roosevelts were Democrats who were intensely interested in politics. At the age of five, young Franklin was taken by his father to the White House for the first time. Grover Cleveland, deeply troubled by the problems of his day, patted the boy's head and said: "My little man, I am making a strange wish for you. It is that you may never be president of the United States."

Personal history. After his graduation from Harvard in 1904, young Roosevelt entered the Columbia University Law School. In the same year he wed a distant cousin, the gifted and energetic Eleanor Roosevelt. (She was given in marriage by her Uncle Theodore, the president of the United States, who had come from Washington for the occasion.) Leaving law school, young Roosevelt began a career in politics, serving as a member of the New York state senate and then as Wilson's Assistant Secretary of the Navy. In 1920 he became well known nationally for the first time when he ran unsuccessfully for the vice-presidency on the Democratic ticket.

His ordeal. Shortly afterward, while vacationing with his family in Canada, Roosevelt was stricken with poliomyelitis. Persuaded by friends and by his wife that his paralysis had by no means finished his career, Roosevelt kept up an active correspondence with political leaders. His election to the governorship in 1928 was ample proof that he had been rehabilitated, but he never again was able to walk unaided. To the people of the country, struck by national disaster as he had been struck by a personal one, Roosevelt was magnetic. To
millions he was a living example of how hard work and dogged determination could bring triumph over tragedy.

##In 1960 a New Yorker (Kennedy) again was paired with a Texan (Johnson).

Nomination in Chicago. When the Democratic National Convention met in Chicago in 1932, the delegates on the fourth ballot nominated Roosevelt for President. They chose John ## Nance Garner of Texas, the Speaker of the House, as their candidate for the vice-presidency.

It was usual for a presidential nominee to await formal notification that he was to be the

Roosevelt shows his winning smile.

The zestful Roosevelt in 1920—before polio struck.

Franklin D. Roosevelt Library

#In this way Roosevelt named his program--the New Deal. Recall that Theodore Roosevelt had used the term "square deal" (see p. 512). "New Deal" was especially effective, since it suggested a change from Hoover's policies.

Franklin D. Roosevelt Library

Roosevelt, accompanied by his only daughter, Anna, and by Mrs. Roosevelt, waves to a crowd during the cam-paign for the presidency in 1932. Here he displays the contagious confidence so many Americans admired.

Notice the smiles on the faces of people in the crowd.

party's standard-bearer, before accepting. Roosevelt, wishing to demonstrate his vigor, flew to the convention and delivered a rousing acceptance speech. He told the cheering Demo-crats, "I pledge you, I pledge myself, to a

new deal for the American people."

The campaign and the returns. Roosevelt's words during his campaigns for the nomination and for election offered hope to the nation but not a blueprint for recovery. Roosevelt struck responsive chords in American hearts. When he spoke with sympathy about "the forgotten man at the bottom of the economic pyramid," millions felt he was speaking to them. When he talked about a "new deal" for the nation, he was reminding his hearers of "T. R.," whose

"square deal" had aroused enthusiasm a gener-ation earlier. Roosevelt's attractive smile and buoyant manner contrasted sharply with the picture of defeat and anguish that Hoover seemed to present.

Americans looked forward to the election, thinking that any political change would be for the better: it was estimated that more than 15,000,000 people were out of work. For the first time in the twentieth century, the price of corn had fallen close to thirty cents a bushel. Roosevelt said that as he gazed upon the faces of people who came to hear him during the campaign, they seemed to be saying: "We're caught in something we don't understand; perhaps this fellow can help us out."

 ##Compare the expressions on Roosevelt's face, seen on this page and on p. 639, with the one Hoover wears in the picture on p. 631.

#The idea of having a "brain trust" had been used originally by Governor La Follette in Wisconsin, in the early 1900's. At times members of Roosevelt's "brain trust" were more important than members of his Cabinet.

Franklin D. Roosevelt Library

The President, who had closer contact with the press than any previous President, holds his first press conference just four days after his inauguration. The reporters and the President are obviously posing here.

Roosevelt flashes his smile. Observe the Phi Beta Kappa key and the type of telephone.

In November, by a landslide vote, the people made Roosevelt their President. He had received almost 23,000,000 votes; Hoover, fewer than 16,000,000. Roosevelt's margin in the electoral college was even more overwhelming: 472 votes to 59.

The brain trust. While awaiting his inauguration, "F. D. R."—as Roosevelt came to be familiarly known—relied on a group of intimate advisers nicknamed the "brain trust." He drew on its collective wisdom and experiences. In the group were several college professors, such as Rexford G. Tugwell and Adolf A. Berle, Jr. Roosevelt also consulted with labor leaders, such as William Green of the AFL, and with the financier Bernard M. Baruch.

INAUGURATING THE NEW DEAL

In the agonizing months between November and March, when Roosevelt took office, economic conditions went from bad to worse. The closing of banks throughout the country brought tragedy to millions—and to elderly people especially, hopelessness. The magnitude of the calamity reckoned in human suffering is impossible to calculate. Thousands upon thousands of people in every part of the country had had their gas and electricity shut off because they could not pay the bills. Midwestern farmers, organized into the National Farmers' Holiday Association, were in rebellion, refusing to ship food into the cities until the prices

##The closing of some banks brought "runs" on others, causing them to close, also. Banks did not have the ready cash to satisfy all the demands of depositors.

641

they were receiving went up. As Hoover prepared to attend the swearing-in ceremony of his successor, he lamented, "We are at the end of our string."

It was a chilly day on March 4, 1933, when Roosevelt was inaugurated. Coatless and hatless, standing in the wind, he delivered to the country an address filled with uplifting reassurance (see pages 628–629). He promised to ask for emergency powers, if necessary, that would enable him to deal with the problems of the country as if it had been invaded.

The Cabinet. Roosevelt chose the "good gray judge," Senator Cordell Hull, of Tennessee, to be Secretary of State. Roosevelt put in charge of the Department of Agriculture Henry

A. Wallace, the son of Harding's Secretary of Agriculture. Harold Ickes, who in 1912 had been a Progressive supporter of "T. R.," became Secretary of the Interior. In the office of Secretary of Labor Roosevelt placed Frances Perkins, who had been his associate when he had been governor of New York. She became the first woman to sit in a President's Cabinet.

Experimentation. Roosevelt brought to his great office a new spirit of experimentation. As he told the nation in a radio talk, "I have no expectation of making a hit every time I come to bat."* He soaked up new ideas enthusiastically but dropped those that did not work.

---

* "Fireside chat" was the name he liked to use for this kind of report to the people, which he frequently made.

Postmaster General John A. Farley sits in the second chair behind Hull.

Roosevelt and his Cabinet: Hull is at his right; Ickes sits before the mantel; Wallace is beside Miss Perkins.

Harris and Ewing

##Roosevelt made a practice of giving radio talks to the people. His voice was reassuring as he began with, "My fellow Americans...." The radio brought him into people's homes.

He revealed a marked ability to draw on the inspiration of others.

Roosevelt recognized that the economic crisis through which the nation was passing was a test of democracy's ability to solve its problems successfully and harmoniously. Moreover, the test had come at a moment when free men everywhere were turning to the United States for light and leadership as the dark night of Adolf Hitler's Nazi dictatorship descended upon Germany. In the very month that Roosevelt launched his New Deal, triumphant Nazi troops marched and sang in the streets of Berlin.

Roosevelt believed that the vast power of government should be enlisted in the service of the "little" man as well as in that of the "big" man. In Roosevelt the respect for a strong national government that his cousin Theodore had always had was combined with a warm sympathy for the small man.

A bank holiday. Many banks throughout the country were in dire difficulties. The failure of some and "runs" on others had undermined public confidence—and wiped out thousands of depositors. Roosevelt's first important step was to declare a short bank holiday, during which *all* banks were closed. Only the sound ones were allowed to reopen. This move ended an alarming series of bank failures. Soon the President took even bolder steps.

THE "HUNDRED DAYS": RECOVERY LAWS

On March 9, 1933, Congress, summoned by the President, met in special session. In rapid-fire succession in the next three months it passed a series of bills that made that session one of the most memorable—and exhausting —in history. In fact, the time in which it met is now recalled as the "Hundred Days." The legislation the President proposed falls into # three classifications: *relief measures* to provide emergency assistance, *recovery measures* to help end the depression, and *reform measures* to provide solutions for long-standing problems.

Conserving resources. A very dramatic relief measure was one providing for the Civilian Conservation Corps—the CCC. It aimed to

put at least 250,000 young men to work by the summer, clearing marshlands, planting trees, extinguishing forest fires, and constructing dams. Through this law the new administration would not only help conserve the nation's land and forests but also help save the most valuable national asset—the human resources. In addition, the measure would take the sting out of unemployment by giving temporary work to youths who might otherwise be in bread lines.

Helping the jobless. Another relief law created the Federal Emergency Relief Administration (the FERA). It represented a new experiment in relieving the anguish of the unemployed: providing grants of money to the states for the direct relief of the jobless.

Postponing mortgage payments. Another item of ## relief legislation created the Home Owners Loan Corporation, which aimed to save the small homeowner from foreclosure of the mortgage on his house. Since foreclosures were being made at the rate of a thousand a day, prompt action was desperately needed. The new law provided for postponing the payment of both interest and principal if the applicant could prove his need.

For industry: the NRA. For a time the most talked-about recovery law was the National Industrial Recovery Act. It provided for the NRA: the National Recovery Administration. The NRA asked employers in industries to coöperate with one another in preparing "codes of fair competition" which would establish standard prices, wages, and hours in their businesses.

An important purpose of the NRA was to raise the level of wages. Employers, therefore, were exempted from the provisions of the Sherman Antitrust Act forbidding agreements among producers on prices and wages. In a widely discussed part of the law, employees were given the right to bargain collectively with their employers through agents of their own choosing. A picture of a blue eagle with the accompanying slogan "We Do Our Part" was made the symbol of the NRA. The blue eagle was displayed in stores and factories

##Three relief measures and three reform measures are described in this section. The CCC camps were established by the army, and enlistments were handled by the Department of Labor.

643

Bachelder in the *New York Daily News* (Brown Brothers)

A cartoon published after the establishment of the NRA. Its caption read: "Watchful waiting."

throughout the country to signify that those establishments were complying with the "codes" of their respective industries.

The National Industrial Recovery Act also gave the President power to commence a vast program of public works through the Public Works Administration (the PWA). The federal government, for the first time, could grant large-scale direct relief to the unemployed # by giving employment in construction work.

For farmers: the AAA. Another recovery step was the passage of a bill designed to aid the farmers —the Agricultural Adjustment Act (the AAA). This act provided for direct payments to farmers in return for their withholding portions ## of land from cultivation and their reducing the production of hogs. Funds to reimburse the farmers would come from a *processing* tax to be paid by the processors of farm goods— such as the flour millers and meat-packers. The tax would be passed on to the consumers.

About 23,000,000 workers were employed in industries covered by codes.

A tailor places a sign bearing the NRA emblem in his shop window in Jersey City, New Jersey. In return for his observance of the code for his industry, he was expecting customers to bring him work.

UPI

##The law provided direct relief for farmers, as the act creating the PWA had provided it for other Americans. Discuss the meaning of "processing" of farm goods.

THE "HUNDRED DAYS": REFORM LAWS

The reform bills that were enacted were # meant to be a *permanent* part of American life. They dealt with serious, persistent conditions in America that cried out for improvement and that were not necessarily related to the depression.

The TVA. The first of these laws was the Tennessee Valley Authority Act, passed in May—building on policies followed by Roosevelt while he was governor of New York. The act, which created the Tennessee Valley Authority (the TVA), provided a model for government sponsorship and ownership of hydroelectric plants on the great rivers of the country. Its passage was a triumph for Senator George W. Norris, of Nebraska, who had long sought to place the power resources of the Tennessee River at the disposal of the people.

The TVA planned to build dams in the Tennessee River Valley (see the map on pages 360–361). The dams were to furnish electric power, control floods, and aid navigation. Some of the electricity produced was to be used in making nitrogen fertilizers. The TVA was also authorized to compete directly with private electric-power companies. Electricity would be provided at "reasonable rates" for farms and villages not otherwise supplied with electricity.

The TVA was to be an independent public corporation conducted by a board of three directors whose broad mission was to develop the economic and social well-being of the Tennessee Valley region. This included areas in the states of Kentucky, Tennessee, North Carolina, Virginia, Mississippi, Alabama, and Georgia. By 1944 nine main river dams and many others on tributary waters had been constructed. In the Second World War munitions and aluminum production drew on the TVA's power facilities. Because of these facilities,

Between 1933 and 1944 four main dams and many lesser ones were built in the valley.

Norris Dam in eastern Tennessee, named after the man who first envisioned TVA, was begun in 1933 and completed three years later. Between 1934 and 1942, the use of electricity in the TVA region nearly doubled.

Tennessee Valley Authority

atomic-bomb production could go forward at Oak Ridge, Tennessee.

Supervising the stock market. A second much-needed reform was embodied in the Federal Securities Act, also passed in May. It was popular with the many small investors embittered still by the collapse of the stock market in 1929. They felt, rightly or wrongly, that they had been defrauded by stock-and-bond salesmen. Under the act's provisions, new issues of stock—before being put up for sale—would have to be registered with the Federal Trade Commission. The purpose of the law—sometimes known also as the "Truth-in-Securities Act"—was to guard against misrepresentation and fraud in the sale of stocks and bonds. Violators of the provisions were subject to prosecution.

The following year a new law established the Securities and Exchange Commission (the SEC) to take over the enforcement of the Federal Securities Act. The SEC—an independent regulatory commission—was also given broad powers to license and regulate stock exchanges. Wall Street firms quickly recognized the usefulness of this government regulation in weeding out unscrupulous operators.

Preventing bank panics. A third great reform law was the Glass-Steagall Banking Act, passed in June. It aimed to eliminate the practices that had led in turn from unhealthy inflation to depression and then to the severe banking crisis which had followed. It provided that commercial banking be separated from investment banking. This was done to prevent a bank of deposit from speculatively investing its customers' funds.

The act also created a Federal Deposit Insurance Corporation (the FDIC) for protecting, up to a fixed amount, the account of every depositor in subscriber banks. This law would, in the future, prevent bank panics and runs on banks like those that had led to financial sorrow in hundreds of communities.

Observe the collection on Roosevelt's desk, especially the donkey.

Roosevelt prepares to sign the Glass-Steagall Banking Act. Henry Morgenthau, Jr., stands behind him.

Wide World

Taken off the relief rolls, these Chicagoans clean an alley as part of a Civil Works Administration project.
These men were receiving direct relief under the Civil Works Administration (see p. 648).

OTHER ECONOMIC MATTERS

For millions the sudden dramatic effect of these unprecedented laws was heightened by the repealing of prohibition, as promised in the Democratic platform of 1932. To them it justified at last "F. D. R." 's campaign song, "Happy Days Are Here Again."

Revenue from liquor. Repeal was the result of the growing knowledge that "the noble experiment" was not working as its framers had intended. On December 5, 1933, the Twenty-first Amendment became effective, and intoxicating liquors became available for sale.

Eight states remained dry, staunchly refusing to accept "the return of the saloon." Within a few years, as revenue from liquor taxes helped pay the large federal expenditures caused by the hard times, prohibition was forgotten.

Going off the gold standard. President Roosevelt inspired confidence that the legislation so rapidly enacted would "cure" the depression. He was reluctant to admit that the slump in the United States was related to the depression in Europe. He did not share the belief of many that only through international monetary reform could recovery be brought about.

In fact, in July, 1933, an international gathering, the London Economic Conference, was held with a view to exploring such remedies. But Roosevelt himself broke up the gathering by sending his famous "bombshell" message.

In it he stated his conviction that the United States must remain free to tinker with its own currency independently of other nations.

Already the value of the dollar was falling, for prices were rising. The President believed that the rise was a sign of economic recovery. Under an amendment to the AAA, the President had been authorized to reduce the gold content of the dollar and to coin silver at a ratio he himself could establish. Roosevelt had quickly used this authority to take the country off the gold standard, that is, to stop using gold as the backing for the dollar. #

Critics were horrified by this daring policy and, gloomily shaking their heads, predicted catastrophe. The administration, on the other hand, believed that the rise in prices resulting from the inflation that would follow would be a tonic to business and that wage raises and reemployment would follow naturally.

Actually, during the summer of 1933 there were signs that recovery had in fact at last begun. Both prices and production rose, and the stock market started to climb again, too. But wages lagged behind. The public was unable, consequently, to purchase the goods resulting from the increased production of the factories. As a result, by late summer and early fall, business activity again was declining.

Direct relief to the unemployed. Another step the President took was to arrange for unemployment relief, which long remained a necessity.

#Meaning that its currency would no longer be convertible only to gold (see p. 446). Recall
that the Populists had wanted a bimetallic standard (see p. 452).

The Civil Works Administration (the CWA) was organized under Harry Hopkins, Roosevelt's relief administrator in New York State, a former social worker. Since spring Hopkins had been directing the FERA. Taking charge of the CWA in November, 1933, Hopkins had 4,000,000 previously unemployed men at work on federal projects by mid-January, 1934.

The CWA differed in a significant respect from the FERA: it was not administered through the states but provided direct aid for the unemployed from the federal government. A very important feature was that it helped preserve the self-respect of the jobless person by giving him again a feeling of usefulness. Only a temporary measure, it was intended to "prime the pump"† of industry by increasing

† The phrase originates in the practice of pouring a fluid into a pump until suction has been established and the pump's operation begins.

the purchasing power of the people. Such a move would inevitably prove to be a stimulus to private enterprise.

THE SECOND NEW DEAL

By the beginning of 1934 signs again indicated that conditions were improving. In November there was a notable victory for the New Deal at the polls. The Democrats made significant gains in both houses of Congress—an unusual occurrence in a midterm election, when the trend usually runs against the President's party.

Criticism and hopefulness. Roosevelt's policies were now coming under increasing attack from many businessmen, who believed that some of them were too extreme. Nevertheless, hope and confidence were gradually being restored in millions of hearts. Where people had been singing "Brother, Can You Spare a Dime?"

Ask the point of the label on the luggage ("The Modern Rip Van Winkle").
This cartoon of 1934 portrays the bewilderment of an American who has just returned home after long years abroad.

Drawing by Clifford Berryman, July 27, 1934 (Library of Congress)

#Ask how big business had been "saved." (Suggestion: The relief measures had improved the purchasing power of individuals, as had some of the recovery measures. The CWA also played an important part, as did the NRA. The nation had not turned to socialism or to revolution.)

they were now singing "Who's Afraid of the Big Bad Wolf?"

But by the end of 1934, it was apparent that recovery had still not taken place. Furthermore, the AAA and the NRA did little to help the very people who needed help most. For instance, the small farmer was less concerned with cutting down the size of his crop than he was with preventing his farm from being foreclosed by the bank. The small businessman, for his part, found that he was unable to pay the wages established in the NRA codes, which were almost invariably written by his larger competitors.

In a word, the first New Deal, as the early part of Roosevelt's administration has now come to be known, seemed to favor the big farmer and the big businessman and to slight their smaller colleagues. Moreover, it was # clear that big business, having been saved, wanted a swift end to experimentation‡ and would no longer support the President. By late 1934 it seemed certain that the poorer people in the nation, intensely faithful to the President—as the fall election showed—were going to receive his fuller attention.

Aiding the underprivileged. The President's annual message to Congress on January 4, 1935, began what is now called the second New Deal. Roosevelt pledged his administration to broad new goals: security of livelihood, better housing, and financial protection from the effects of old age, unemployment, and disablement. Roosevelt's dominant advisers now were more inclined to want to regulate business than to coax and nurse it. They were more will-

‡ A number of big businessmen together with dissatisfied Democratic leaders—including Al Smith—in the summer of 1934 organized the Liberty League. This organization had pledged itself to work for the election of an anti-New Deal Congress in November. ##

Compare the cars and trucks seen here with those made today.

Seeking federal relief jobs, an army of unemployed New Yorkers forms a queue at the state labor bureau building.

Wide World

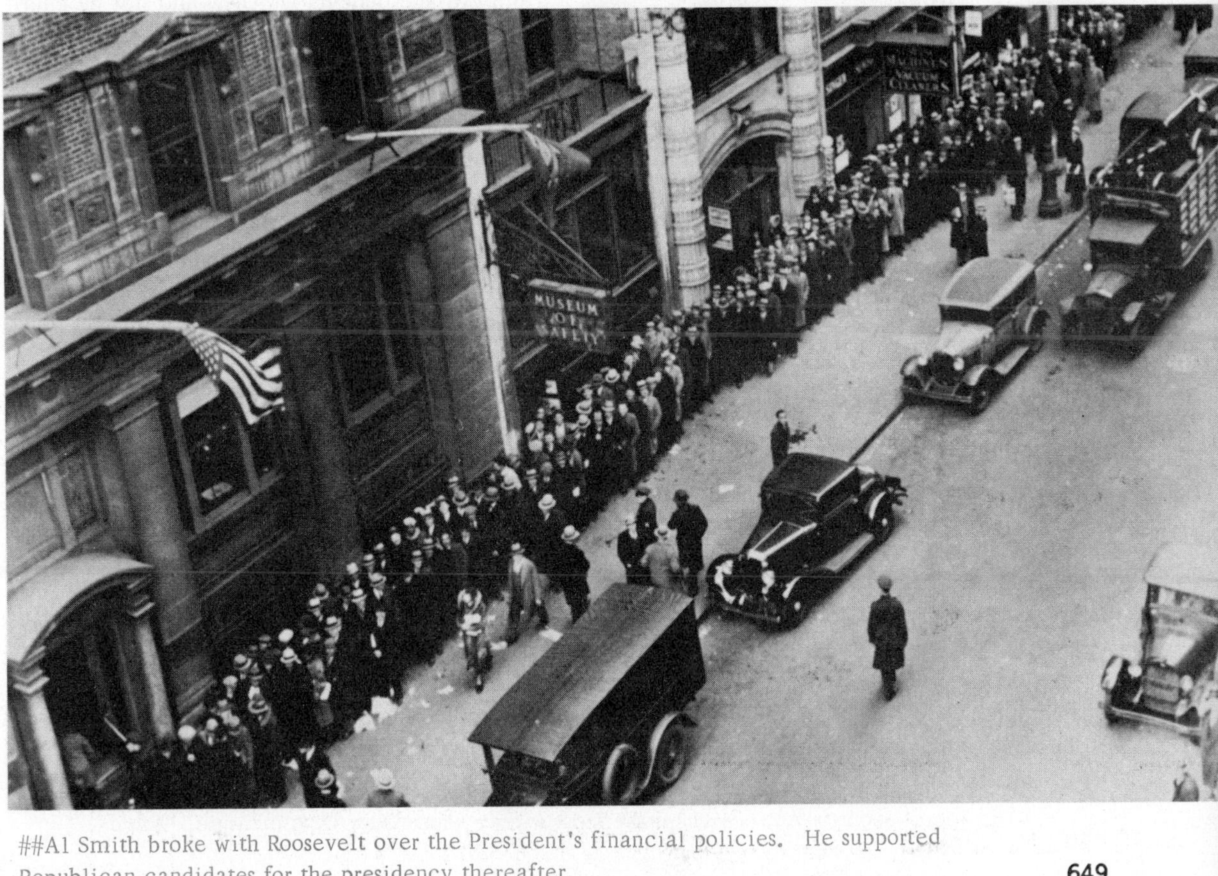

##Al Smith broke with Roosevelt over the President's financial policies. He supported Republican candidates for the presidency thereafter.

Wide World

Senator Long—the "Kingfish"—is interviewed in 1935.

creases for enough workingmen to bring about economic recovery in the nation. The President was now going to regard American enterprise as a tree to be watered at the roots. He seemed to want to focus attention on the workingman.

Extremist proposals. Roosevelt undoubtedly was # influenced in his decision to change his course drastically by a number of very bold proposals which were making an appeal to many discontented Americans. One such proposal was Senator Huey P. Long's "share-our-wealth" movement in Louisiana. Another was the program of the Californian Dr. Francis E. Townsend, who was calling for a pension of $200 a month for every person over sixty years of age. A third was a plea for radical inflation of the currency being made over the radio by a Roman Catholic priest, Father Charles E. Coughlin.

Social Security. A major feature of the second New Deal was the Social Security Act of 1935. This many-sided law created unemployment assistance, a health and child-welfare program, and old-age benefits which would not be charitable "handouts." The handling of the unemployment insurance was left to the states, which were generously encouraged by the federal government to establish acceptable plans. The financial inducements proved to be sufficient to bring every state into line by July 31, 1937.

Federal grants-in-aid were authorized for old people in need of financial help. Similar provisions were made for the blind and for dependent children. Arrangements were also made for certain health and welfare work, including vocational rehabilitation.

The most important provision for the long run, however, was the one establishing benefits for retired people. Except in some exempted fields, employers and employees were to pay payroll taxes which would go into a federal old-age insurance trust fund. The tax rate would start at 1 percent and be increased gradually. After January 1, 1942, retired workers over sixty-five years of age would receive pensions ranging from $10 to $85 a month. (The tax rate and the benefits have since been greatly increased.) ##

ing, also, to rely upon heavy spending—even though it meant increasing the national debt— than upon the hope of balancing the budget.

Roosevelt himself used stronger language than previously. He declared: "In spite of our efforts and in spite of our talk, we have not weeded out the overprivileged and we have not effectively lifted up the underprivileged. Both of these manifestations of injustice have retarded happiness." But, he was insistent, "No wise man has any intention of destroying what is known as the profit motive; because by the profit motive we mean the right by work to earn a decent livelihood for ourselves and for our families."

Roosevelt had decided that increased profits for businessmen had not resulted in wage in-

##The Social Security Act is perhaps the most widely known New Deal measure. Ask a student to find out what the present tax rate and benefits are.

650

UPI

Men and women learn to read in the Adult Education Division of the WPA, in 1938. The man receiving help is the millionth grown-up, who, lacking a grade-school education, at last had a chance to overcome illiteracy.

In 1930 illiterates made up 4.3 percent of the nation's population.

When the Social Security bill was before Congress, many critics throughout the country declared that it would spell the end to the American system by substituting government control of life for free enterprise. When the President signed the bill in August, 1935, after extended debate in Congress, he described it as modern, not radical. He pointed out that it remedied the insecurity of workers that industrialization had been responsible for creating.

The WPA. To deal with the persistently nagging question of unemployment, "F. D. R." now employed Herculean methods. Halfway steps had failed. Drawing on the experience gained under the CWA, on May 6, 1935, the President established by executive order the Works Progress Administration (the WPA), with Harry Hopkins as administrator. The appropriation for it—almost $5,000,000,000— was by far the largest in peacetime in American history. The purpose of the law was to give men work that would restore their self-respect. Roosevelt was determined to end relief once and for all, despite the cries of some businessmen that it was preferable to pay relief because it was cheaper.

Projects had to be found that could meet the needs of this great experiment in government job-making. These projects had to have local sponsors and general public usefulness, and they had to be carried out on public property. Furthermore, they would not be permitted to interfere with private employment or make such excessive demands for materials that funds would go for supplies rather than for wages. Finally, each project had to be completed within one year, because Congress made only annual appropriations.

Many carping remarks were offered about the WPA; cartoons lampooned it; and work

##The WPA was explicitly prohibited from competing with private industry. It could not become involved in work normally assigned to other government agencies.

651

on the projects was assailed as "boondoggling." Nevertheless, by December, 1935, 2,667,000 unemployed were receiving work through the WPA. Within two years the agency had erected 11,000 buildings and repaired 30,000 others. It had laid or repaired 200,000 miles of roads. Hardly a town failed to show some improvement resulting from the WPA: a new airport or playground, a new sewer or culvert, a swimming pool or highway, a dam or bridge. The WPA planted millions of trees; it organized orchestra and theater projects; it restored historical shrines.

The pay scale on the projects was lower than that prevailing in private enterprise. Nevertheless, the salaries paid the workers—ranging from $15 a month for the unskilled man to $90 a month for the professional man—considerably increased the nation's purchasing power. By the time the WPA was ended in 1943, over 8,500,000 persons had been on its payrolls at one time or another, and it had spent about $11,000,000,000.

The Wagner Act. Unquestionably, the capstone of the second New Deal was the National Labor Relations Act (the Wagner Act), passed in July, 1935. It raised workers to a new position of eminence in American life. Under this bold law a National Labor Relations Board was created to enforce the right of employees to bargain collectively with their employers. The new board could also take testimony about unfair employer practices and issue orders to offending companies to cease and desist.

Opponents of the law declared that it would open an era of warfare between employers and employees hitherto unknown in America. The New Dealers answered that because collective bargaining had been made compulsory, this grave possibility had been prevented.

The NYA. As the second New Deal progressed, direct relief by the federal government increased, despite Roosevelt's desire to end it. Roosevelt was particularly concerned about the large number of unemployed young people. Many of these, having been forced to leave school prematurely, had joined the army of job hunters. For these youthful victims of the depression, the National Youth Administration (the NYA) was organized. This agency made payments to thousands of needy high school and college students for part-time work in schools in which they were enrolled.

The variety of experiments the New Deal undertook was truly remarkable. As a whole they aimed to correct the specific problems of a wide range of people. One of the most imaginative experiments was in the field of urban living—where slums could make poverty a curse. The so-called green-belt project, which built brand-new towns—towns near places of employment but surrounded by green countryside—drew international attention.

Another program was conducted under the Federal Housing Administration. This one assisted people of moderate income in obtaining needed loans—from private lending institutions insured by the federal government—to modernize, repair, or buy houses. For the small farmer, tenant, sharecropper, or migrant worker, there was the Resettlement Administration (the RA). Although limited in its possibilities, it sought to transplant agricultural people from unproductive and unyielding soil to more fertile acres elsewhere.

A Rural Electrification Administration (the REA) was created in May, 1935, to string power lines and build power stations in various parts of the United States in order to bring electric current to farms. This new agency was to provide electricity in places private companies bypassed because prospects for profits were slight.

Taxes on concentrated wealth. Entirely in keeping with the spirit of the second New Deal was Roosevelt's tax measure of August, 1935. The measure's opponents labeled it a "soak-the-rich" scheme. Roosevelt explained his intention, "Social unrest and a deepening sense of unfairness are dangers to our national life which we must minimize by vigorous methods."

What did the President propose to do? Levy taxes designed to help eliminate "an unjust concentration of wealth and economic power." Accordingly, Congress enacted a law providing sharp increases in taxes on large incomes, both

##When the REA was established, fewer than 11 out of 100 farms had electricity. Today about 98 out of 100 enjoy it. The REA functions today as part of the Department of Agriculture.

Unemployed veterans of the First World War share kindling in a colony of huts along the shore of the Hudson River in the winter of 1934. The poor housing of many Americans deeply troubled Roosevelt.

Below: The "dust bowl" is a dry area in the southern Great Plains.

The Resettlement Administration is moving this family from a "dust bowl" farm to irrigated land farther west. During the RA's two years of existence, about 4000 families were relocated.

UNIONIZATION IN THE UNITED STATES

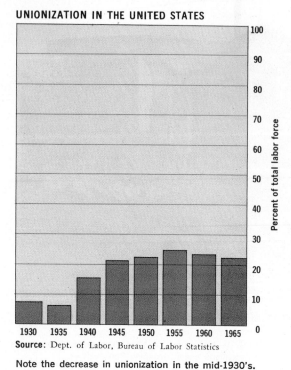

Percent of total labor force

1930 1935 1940 1945 1950 1955 1960 1965

Source: Dept. of Labor, Bureau of Labor Statistics

Note the decrease in unionization in the mid-1930's.

Above: Jobs were scarce in the mid-1930's.

A cartoon of the time: "What about labor?"

Lewis in the *Milwaukee Journal*

individual and corporate. Estate and gift tax rates were increased, too. Although the pained outcry of wealthy people was loud, the law actually did little to redistribute income.

The influence of the labor movement. Changes occurring inside the labor movement also had a momentous influence on the administration's policies. The AFL—led by William Green—still refused to consider organizing all the workers for each industry into one big union. It held to its traditional reliance on organization by separate crafts, ignoring the fact that most factory workers, being unskilled, were not in such unions. The laboring people in the new mass-production industries—automobile, rubber, cement, radio, aluminum—were, in general, "unorganized." #

John L. Lewis. The leader of an insurgent group in the AFL that sought to bring about the organization of industrial unions was John L. Lewis. Lewis, whose father had been a member of the Knights of Labor, had been sent into the coal pits to work at the age of twelve. By keen effort and a constant demonstration of his superior talents, he rose in the ranks of the United Mine Workers to the position of president, in which he served with great success.

The CIO. Dissension among the members of the AFL over the issue of craft unions *versus* industrial unions led to the formation within the federation of the Committee for Industrial Organization. This committee was organized in November, 1935, and Lewis became its chairman. When its members were suspended from the AFL as rebellious, the committee in 1938 became a separate organization. It retained the same initials—CIO—but it called itself the Congress of Industrial Organizations. At once it began to organize industrial unions that included both skilled and unskilled workers.

Stimulated by these changes and by the favorable attitude of the administration, unions ## commenced vast organizing campaigns. The years 1937 and 1938 witnessed some of the angriest labor struggles in American history. Marked by violence and bloodshed, strikes in the automobile and steel industries drew the

##The CIO attracted members away from the AFL. Why? (Some craft unions in the AFL could become part of an industrial union and benefit from the strength such a union had.)

whole nation's attention. In the steel industry a frightful Memorial Day "massacre" took place in 1937 in which ten men were killed as a result of a flare-up at a Chicago plant of the Republic Steel Company.

In the automobile industry the "sit-down" strike made its appearance as workers refused to leave the factories where work stoppages had been called. They chanted:

> When the boss won't talk, don't take a walk,
> Sit down! Sit down!

When the fierce battles had subsided, the effects were clear: the major American industries had been unionized despite the opposition.

Labor's rights came generally to be recognized by businessmen as the 1930's drew to a close. This recognition was as important in American history as the extension of the suffrage or the emancipation of the slaves. And despite the deplorable violence, even more noteworthy is the fact that such a profound change was effected in labor-management relations with so *little* bloodshed. The change was hastened by the attitude of President Roosevelt, who had determined to make the increasingly powerful laboring man his ally.

THE SUPREME COURT'S DECISIONS

As Roosevelt faced 1936—a presidential-election year—he had vast popular support, but he had made many enemies. (Some of them liked to call the New Deal the Raw Deal.) The only effective barrier to his proposals, however, turned out to be the Supreme Court. In some cases that had come before it in 1935, the Court had shown hostility to the kind of social rehabilitation in which the New Deal was engaged.

The "sick-chicken case." "Black Monday" for the New Deal came on May 27, 1935. The Court declared the NRA unconstitutional by a 9–0 vote. In this interesting case, a Brooklyn, New York, poultry company had violated its industry's "code of fair competition" by paying wages below the minimum and by selling unfit chicken. The company declared that it was not engaged in interstate commerce and that

consequently the code did not apply to it.§

The Court agreed with the company, saying that if the national government were able to regulate *everything* affecting interstate commerce, then "there would be virtually no limit to the federal power and for all practical purposes we should have a completely centralized government." The President angrily told his press conference, "We have been relegated to the horse-and-buggy definition of interstate commerce."

Interpreting "general welfare." Soon a new blow fell upon the administration. In January, 1936, the Agricultural Adjustment Act was also declared unconstitutional. In this decision the Supreme Court declared that the processing tax established by that act was unconstitutional because taxes could be levied only to promote the general welfare of the people.

The tax, the justices said, was passed solely for the regulation of agricultural production. They held that to interpret "general welfare" as broadly as this act did would be to take away the last barriers between the responsibilities of the states and those of the federal government. The effect, the Court declared, would be to create a central government with unlimited power.

With direction from the White House, Congress quickly tried to repair the damage this decision did by passing the Soil Conservation and Domestic Allotment Act. Under its terms, farmers were to plant portions of their land to grasses and legumes instead of to cotton, tobacco, corn, and wheat—crops which decreased the fertility of the soil. The farmers were to be paid for their efforts on the principle that they were helping in the government's program of soil conservation. In this way, the farmers were cutting down on their crops, as under the AAA, and they also were serving another useful purpose for the nation—reducing the dust storms that were harassing the people of the Great Plains.

---

§ Congress—which had created the NRA—has jurisdiction over interstate commerce but none over commerce conducted entirely within a state's borders. Yet Congress took the position that anything *affecting* interstate commerce was subject to national legislative control.

##The difference between this act and the AAA was that now the government paid benefits to farmers who practiced soil conservation, thus restricting crop production.

655

#Compare this case with the case of Lochner v. New York. Observe that in each case the Supreme Court cited the Fourteenth Amendment. Review Justice Holmes' dissenting opinion, and compare it with Justice Stone's dissent.

The dust storms, which caused untold discomfort and loss of life and property, were the result of careless farming methods employed between 1919 and 1929. A relentless expansion of agriculture in those years had resulted in tearing from the land's surface the protective cover of trees, shrubs, and grasses that served to anchor the topsoil.

Swept up by the wind, this loosened earth would suddenly seem to fill the air when a storm arose. A vast area from the Texas panhandle to the Canadian border became known as the "dust bowl." The scope of the disastrous dust storms is suggested by the grim joke of a Nebraska farmer, spoken during such a storm, "I'm counting the Kansas farms as they go by."

In his response to the decision of the Supreme Court declaring the AAA unconstitutional, the President seemed to be ahead in a daring game of leapfrog with the Court. He appeared to be assuring the New Deal a new lease on life.

On the regulation of wages and hours. In May, 1936, however, the Supreme Court declared unconstitutional the Bituminous Coal Conservation Act (the Guffey-Snyder Act). This law, enacted in 1935, had been designed to establish fair wages and fair working conditions in the soft-coal industry. The Court's argument this time was that the tax levied under its provisions was not a true tax—that is, its purpose was not to raise money. Instead, it had been designed to regulate hours and wages in the bituminous fields.

The regulation of wages and of hours, clearly a central feature of the second New Deal, was now imperiled. Any hope that there might soon be a federal law regulating both was shattered. Roosevelt's supporters believed, nevertheless, that this important task of regulation could continue to be performed by the states. The belief was soon rudely shaken.

The Court, continuing to interpret the Constitution narrowly, on June 1, 1936, declared unconstitutional a minimum-wage law for women and children passed by the New York State legislature in 1933. In its majority decision, the Court maintained that by establishing a minimum wage for women, New York was denying to them the freedom to make contracts guaranteed by the Fourteenth Amendment.

Two powerful dissents. Presenting a dissenting opinion, Chief Justice Charles Evans Hughes maintained, using the powerful words of John Marshall in the case of *McCulloch* v. *Maryland*: "The end is legitimate and the means appropriate. I think that the Act should be upheld."

Justice Harlan F. Stone expressed in his dissenting opinion the conclusions that millions of Americans were beginning to accept concerning the rightful tasks of government. Said Stone:

> We have had sufficient opportunity to perceive more clearly that a wage insufficient to support the worker does not visit its consequence upon him alone; that it may affect profoundly the entire economic structure of society and, in any case, that it casts on every taxpayer, and on government itself, the burden of solving the problems of poverty, subsistence, health, and morals of large numbers. . . . these are public problems. A generation ago they were for the individual to solve; today they are the burden of the nation.

But the view of Hughes and Stone, however popular among the people, was not the majority opinion of the Court. The majority had said the nation was without power to act on these problems. This interpretation was, for the time, final. Roosevelt said to a press conference that there obviously was a no-man's-land where neither the state *nor* the federal government could act. The New Deal depended upon finding a solution to the knotty problem within the framework of the Constitution.

Sum and Substance

1. Briefly summarize the life of Franklin D. Roosevelt before his presidency. 2. Name the members of Roosevelt's first Cabinet. 3. What was the purpose of the bank holiday? 4. Name and describe the recovery measures of the "Hundred Days"; the reform measures. 5. Explain how and why Roosevelt changed the value

##Perhaps even a generation back there had been problems the individual could not solve. Emphasize that Stone was saying that the people of the country were interdependent.

of the dollar and what the effect was. 6. How did the administration give direct relief? 7. In what respect did the President change his policy in the second New Deal? Why? 8. What proposals were made by extremists? 9. How did the second New Deal provide for old people? For the unemployed? For the small farmer? 10. Describe the formation of the CIO. 11. What did the Wagner Act provide? 12. What three New Deal laws were declared unconstitutional? On what grounds? 13. What state law was declared unconstitutional? Why?

This section completes the treatment of the New Deal and summarizes Roosevelt's contributions.

THE PRESIDENT BATTLES IN DEFENSE OF HIS POLICIES

It was now June of 1936. Within a few weeks a presidential campaign would be under way. The voters would have an opportunity to show at the polls whether or not they wanted a continuation of the New Deal.

THE JUDGMENT OF THE PEOPLE

The fears that had assailed millions in 1932 had begun to vanish by 1936. But many Americans were sure that the philosophy of the New Deal was a worse evil than the depression itself.

Renomination. The renomination of the President to serve a second term was taken for granted. Meeting at Philadelphia, the Democrats ecstatically named their man again after approving an unusually outspoken platform. It contained a plank promising to seek a constitutional amendment if those national problems that demanded national solution "cannot be effectively solved by legislation within the Constitution. . . ."‖

In a rousing acceptance speech the President stood on the record of his first administration. "Governments can err, Presidents do make mistakes, but," he said, "better the occasional faults of a Government that lives in a spirit of charity than the consistent omissions of a Government frozen in the ice of its own indifference."

In the Republican camp. The Republicans had gathered in Cleveland in a tense and angry mood. Though speaking for himself, Senator Arthur Vandenberg, of Michigan, expressed well the feeling of every delegate: "I belong to but one bloc and it has but one slogan—stop Roosevelt." #

But the party platform reflected the extent to which Republicans had already been converted in only four years to the New Deal principle that the government has a responsibility for the individual citizen's welfare. It favored unemployment insurance and old-age pensions, benefit payments to farmers for

Roosevelt, the President and a candidate for reelection in 1936, flashing his ready smile.

Franklin D. Roosevelt Library

‖ The convention also abrogated an ancient rule of the Democratic party requiring the votes of a two-thirds majority of the delegates to nominate a candidate. Subsequently a simple majority would be sufficient to nominate. An effect of the change was to make it impossible for delegates from the South to exercise a veto on the nomination of a person acceptable to delegates from other sections.

Roosevelt had become vastly popular with the majority of people and tremendously unpopular with others. There were no people with lukewarm opinions, seemingly.

657

soil conservation, collective bargaining for labor, and state legislation to protect working conditions of women and children.

The Republican candidate was Governor Alfred M. Landon of Kansas, a colorless man whose drabness seemed more pronounced when he was compared with Roosevelt. A difficulty he faced in the campaign was in having to condemn the New Deal and at the same time practically promise to abolish none of it if elected.

Roosevelt made his personal platform the record of his administration. He told a friend: "There's one issue in this campaign. It's myself, and people must be either for me or against me." In a campaign speech in Madison Square Garden in New York, he hurled down the gauntlet to his enemies: "They are unanimous in their hate for me—and I welcome their hatred."

Roosevelt listed his intentions if reelected: to increase prosperity in factories and on farms; to extend rural electrification; to assist young men and women, the crippled and the blind, the unemployed and the aged; and finally, to keep consumers' purchasing power high. Then he concluded, as his supporters made the Garden vibrate with cheers: "For these things, too, and for a multitude of things like them, we have only just begun to fight."

A landslide. On Election Day, Roosevelt swamped Landon in a victory so overwhelming that one had to turn back to James Monroe's election in 1820 to find its equal. The President had captured every state in the Union except Maine and Vermont.# He had received almost 61 percent of the popular vote. Roosevelt's strength was shown everywhere, but it was greatest among the people of the northern cities. These people included especially ethnic

---

James A. Farley, the chairman of the Democratic National Committee—the party's ruling body—had forecast this stunning victory exactly, but few except the Roosevelt faithful took him seriously. The *Literary Digest*, a national magazine whose straw ballots had accurately forecast elections before, had predicted that Landon would win decisively. It ceased publication shortly after Election Day.

The passenger car in the caravan was, at that time, a recent model.

Supporters of Roosevelt and his running mate, John Nance Garner, campaign before the Capitol.

minorities—the descendants of immigrants—and Negroes.

Negroes were not successful in obtaining civil rights legislation under Roosevelt. But he appointed Negroes to some major positions for the first time in American history, and he and Mrs. Roosevelt showed warm sympathy for people of this minority. Moreover, relief money given without discrimination lured many Negroes to the Democratic banner. The depression had persuaded them to leave at last the party of Lincoln and emancipation.

Commencing a second term. Although Roosevelt had not revealed during the campaign his plans for reforming the Supreme Court, he now believed that he had the popular support to press forward the New Deal. He could proceed without delay, for he became the first President to be inaugurated in the month of January, in accordance with the Twentieth Amendment, ratified early in 1933.

The members of the Constitutional Convention, who had had to allow for the slowness of travel in 1787, had specified that the President be inaugurated in the month of March. They had also provided that Congress meet the following December—over a year after election. Practice had shown that often public sentiment had changed by the time the Congress it had chosen finally convened. Besides, the Congress still in session when a new President came to office voted upon his legislative proposals even though some or perhaps many of its members were serving as *lame ducks.***

A President is now inaugurated on January 20, and Congress convenes normally on January 3. A new President can now present his program to a Congress which, having convened two weeks earlier, is organized and ready to receive it.

In his inaugural address, Roosevelt spoke of the work ahead: "I see one-third of a nation ill-housed, ill-clad, ill-nourished. It is not in

---

** A lame duck is a congressman who serves the last part of his term of office in a short session of Congress meeting after he has been defeated at the polls or has not run again.

An "ill-clad, ill-nourished" family travels from one town to another in hopes of a job and decent housing.

UPI

##Emphasize the term "lame duck." A lame-duck President is one who cannot be reelected because of the Twenty-second Amendment or because he has withdrawn from the race.

659

A family sits outside its home near a city in California in the summer of 1937. Communities formed in many parts of the country of improvised "houses" like these did not disappear immediately under the New Deal.

Wide World

The conditions inside this "house" can only be imagined.

despair that I paint you that picture. I paint it for you in hope—because the nation, seeing and understanding the injustice in it, proposes to paint it out. . . ."

ASSAULT ON THE COURT

For the gigantic task which he set as the goal of his second term, the President would need favorable Supreme Court decisions. He made up his mind to launch an attack on the Court.

A retirement scheme. Six of the Supreme Court judges who were hostile to the New Deal were over seventy (of the older men, only Louis D. Brandeis was fully sympathetic). Therefore, the President determined to strike at their ages rather than their political opinions. In a com-

plicated scheme, he proposed to add a justice to the Court for each one who did not retire # within six months after reaching his seventieth birthday. The number of justices who served on the Supreme Court could be increased from nine to as many as fifteen. Justices who retired from the Court were to receive liberal pensions.

There were other provisions in the plan, affecting the whole judicial structure of the country, but the intent was clear. It was to add to the Court enough justices who favored New Deal legislation to counterbalance the votes of the six justices who did not. But Roosevelt's indirect attack upon the Court was too artful, and it cost him some of the good- ## will of the voters who had given him his recent triumph at the polls.

##In the minds of Americans the Court was not something to be tampered with. An attempt to influence its decisions was not like trying to influence members of Congress.

660

#Roosevelt, an astute politician, had erred in underestimating the people's respect for the Court and their feeling that it was above politics. In what sense was the reaction a tribute to John Marshall? .

Angering the public. The President had overreached himself. Congress was reluctant to pass the bill he wanted. What had started out to be a war between the Court and the President became instead a struggle between Congress and Roosevelt. By July Vice-President Garner told Roosevelt bluntly: *"You are beat. You haven't got the votes."*

The Court's response. The Court, meanwhile, was shifting its views. A number of New Deal laws were upheld, including the National Labor Relations Act and the vital unemployment-insurance tax provision of the Social Security Act. Furthermore, in upholding the constitutionality of a minimum-wage law of the state of Washington, the Court reversed its own earlier decision in the New York case. Some people explained the Court's new outlook with the quip, "A switch in time saves nine."

Shortly, the retirement of some of the justices gave the President his first opportunities to make new appointments to the Court. It then was no longer a barrier to New Deal legislation. Roosevelt, looking back upon the fight the following year, called it "a lost battle which won a war."

Political effects. When the President turned again to the completion of his second New Deal, he found that his support had weakened. Many Democrats from the South now expressed suspicion of Roosevelt's intentions. And because these members of the President's own party were tending to join with Republicans in Congress, it became more difficult than before to put through New Deal legislation.

A cartoonist indicates the furor the President's Court plan caused. Note the donkey.

An unperturbed Roosevelt, mildly surprised at the furor aroused by his plan for the Supreme Court, in a cartoon published in March, 1937. The caption: "Thus ended the Era of Good Feeling."

Clifford Berryman, March 9, 1937 (Library of Congress)

##Roosevelt appointed eight justices altogether. Among them were Hugo L. Black, Felix Frankfurter, and William O. Douglas.

#Recall why the first AAA had been declared unconstitutional (see p. 655) and ask how the second AAA avoided the difficulty. The new act empowered the Secretary of Agriculture to fix a marketing quota whenever surpluses of such crops as corn, cotton, and wheat threatened price levels.

Recovery and setback. Early in 1937 recovery appeared to be well on its way—production and employment were both rising. Some businessmen even talked of a boom period again. The administration decided to cut its spending program in order to reduce the possibility of a runaway inflation. The reduction could be accomplished in part by a sharp cut in the number of people on the rolls of the WPA.

There had been a miscalculation. Government expenditures were reduced too quickly, and a serious recession had set in by the time summer arrived. Republicans were quick to blame "that man in the White House" and to denounce the Roosevelt administration for what they considered to be its "prolabor" and its "antibusiness" policies. Although recovery seemed to have come by the end of November, 1938,‡ the New Deal had lost much prestige. The setback to recovery had encouraged Roosevelt's critics both inside and outside the Democratic party.

LOSING MOMENTUM

The second New Deal had almost run its course. But before it had lost its momentum entirely, there were a few more legislative accomplishments to its credit.

Four legislative achievements. For the benefit of the small farmer who had not been aided by the AAA, the Bankhead-Jones Farm Tenant Act was approved in July, 1937. It created the Farm Security Administration (the FSA) to oversee lending a total of $10,000,000 at a low interest rate to tenant farmers who wanted to purchase the land they worked.

\# Because of huge harvests in 1937, a second AAA was passed in 1938. Like the first, it aimed to maintain farm-price levels by reducing the production of crops. Instead of the processing tax, which was unconstitutional (see page 655), the federal treasury was to be the source of benefit payments. Through a

system of storing surplus cotton, rice, wheat, corn, and tobacco, the government hoped to have an "ever-normal granary" for the nation in fat years and in lean.

To benefit the city man at the bottom of the economic heap, the National Housing Act (the Wagner-Steagall Act) was designed to make a start on slum clearance. This act of 1937 created the United States Housing Authority (the USHA) to lend money, also at low interest rates, to local agencies that would provide at least 10 percent of the cost of a housing project. Only those people whose incomes did not exceed a fixed level were eligible to become tenants in the completed dwellings.

Congress in 1938 was finally persuaded to pass the Fair Labor Standards Act providing eventually for a minimum wage of forty cents an hour and a maximum of 40 hours of work a week. Its provisions were to apply to industries engaged in interstate commerce. This act represented the first attempt in American history to place a national ceiling on hours and a floor under wages. Three-quarters of a million workers received wage increases as a result of the act. The weekly hours of work for more than a million and a half people were \#\# reduced.

Politics. By the beginning of 1938, the President was shifting his attention from his domestic reforms to the mounting crises in Europe and Asia. Adolf Hitler in Germany and Benito Mussolini in Italy, on one side of the world, and the Japanese war lords, on the other, were engaged in a joint enterprise aiming at nothing less than world mastery. Roosevelt's New Deal had not yet been completed when ominous rumblings from abroad were heard. But certain important facts were being brought home to the President, time and time again.

First, he could count on eastern Democrats to support both his domestic reform program *and* his desire to take a strong stand against the dictators of Europe. Second, he could usually count upon midwestern Republicans to support his New Deal reforms *but not* an involvement in Europe's quarrels. Third, he could usually count upon southern Democrats to vote for

‡ The depression did not end until the Second World War (1939–1945), when the need for war goods here and abroad produced full employment. Consequently, it is difficult to judge the effectiveness of the New Deal measures alone in bringing the bad times to a close.

\#\#The law also forbade children under the age of sixteen to work and provided that young people under the age of eighteen could not work in hazardous occupations.

#Discuss "aggression." What examples of aggressive acts on the part of individuals can students name? What aggression among countries can students think of? An example is the Japanese invasion of Manchuria (see p. 551).

measures supporting a vigorous foreign policy *but not* for the domestic social and economic reform bills.

The passage of legislation required the backing of at least two sections of the country. To win sure support for both his domestic *and* his foreign-policy measures, he would have to have in Congress either midwesterners willing to back his foreign policy or southerners willing to accept the New Deal.

Unsuccessful "purge." Roosevelt decided to campaign in the Democratic primaries in some southern states in 1938 against the men who had consistently voted in Congress against his domestic program. But his efforts to defeat them failed. His opponents, already comparing him with dictators in Europe, referred to his efforts to remove the Senators and Representatives who had thwarted him as "the Roosevelt purge."

Threat from abroad. The President continued to believe that further reform was needed to strengthen democracy at home. Yet both Hitler and Mussolini were immediate, dire threats to democracy itself. Dealing with the problems that their aggression created gradually took more and more of the administration's interest and energy.

In his annual message to Congress at the beginning of 1939, the President proposed no new major legislation but talked instead of the need to "preserve our reforms." Before the year was out, Europe was engulfed in the Second World War, and the task of improving democracy at home had been changed into the task of defending it from foreign attack. Or, as "F. D. R." himself stated a few years later, democracy's physician, "Dr. New Deal," had been replaced by "Dr. Win-the-War."

"F. D. R." IN HISTORY

Roosevelt's place in the history of the United States is secure. Roosevelt provided the longest and one of the most controversial presidencies. He had devoted supporters who sincerely believed he could do no wrong and others who, with equal sincerity, believed the republic would never recover from his acts. Neither

Fitzpatrick in the *St. Louis Post-Dispatch*

An eminent cartoonist's view of one of Roosevelt's legislative monuments: "A prop against human erosion."

opinion has proved to be wholly correct. Now that Roosevelt's era has receded into the past, it must no longer be judged in a partisan way. Instead, it must be evaluated as a permanent part of the nation's past.

In keeping with the past. The Roosevelt program was in many ways a resumption of the work of reform left undone when the progressive era came to an end at the conclusion of the First World War. "F. D. R.," far from being a radical, tried to conserve American freedom and opportunity by making plans in keeping with those already laid out by his predecessors.

If he kept an eye on business, the Interstate Commerce Act of 1887 and the Sherman Act of 1890 provided ample precedent. If his

##Discuss the meaning of judging "in a partisan way." Are there people today who still judge the Roosevelt era through Republican eyes, or with the viewpoint of a party?

farm-relief program was far-reaching, it had been foreshadowed by both the Populist program and the laws enacted during the Wilson administration.

If he took giant steps to save the country's natural resources, the example of his illustrious cousin, Theodore, was always before him. If his control over the securities exchanges seemed bold, Congress in the 1920's had provided for the supervision of grain and commodity exchanges. If his attack on big business seemed sharp, it was much less intense than the war against the "money power" promised by William Jennings Bryan at the beginning of the century.

If his firm belief in the value of Social Security seemed novel, the idea was already accepted in a number of states and in several countries in western Europe. If his friendship with labor seemed out of place, Theodore Roosevelt thirty years before had entertained both John Mitchell and Samuel Gompers in his own home.

New horizons. On the other hand, Roosevelt broke new ground that none of his predecessors had even looked at. For this reason some historians describe the era of the New Deal as the Roosevelt Revolution.

Roosevelt was the first President to give the economic life of the country centralized direction. For the first time the federal government turned its prodigious power on a depression with a determination to make the wheels of business turn smoothly again.

Under Roosevelt the recognition of labor's right to organize and the readiness of government to support the right created a new balance in American society. The workingman no longer stood cap-in-hand before his employer but had acquired new respect as a vital producer. Moreover, in establishing the principles contained in the Social Security Act, Roosevelt made it easier for large numbers of Americans to maintain their human dignity.

A tonic to America. But aside from the permanent legacy of laws and their effects, Roosevelt's contribution to American history is difficult to measure because so much of it is in the realm of the spirit. His sweeping influence may be felt and seen everywhere. First of all, he renewed the faith of Americans in the power of democracy to solve its own problems boldly and decisively. These problems were greatest just at the moment when dictatorship was coming to the fore in Europe. The nation's ability to manage its difficult affairs without damage to its political institutions was a tonic to democracy when it was needed desperately.

Second, Roosevelt enormously rehabilitated the physical condition of the country. The face of the land was changed and improved marvelously by the TVA and the reforestation program. These substantial changes will long be visible legacies of the New Deal era.

Third, and perhaps most impressive of all, Roosevelt added to the people's conception of democracy the conviction that the conservation of human resources is as important as the conservation of physical resources. The whole array of new laws placed on the statute books with such astonishing rapidity represented a new role of the federal government in the life of the ordinary citizen. The government, far from being a tyrannical force, was the welcome friend of its masters—the people.

It is an irony of history that like Woodrow Wilson, from whom he had learned so much, Roosevelt was interrupted in his work at home by war abroad. Strengthened and chastened by the trials of the depression and refreshed in its faith in democracy, the nation now turned, somewhat unwillingly, to confront a world in which tyranny threatened to overwhelm freedom.

Sum and Substance

1. Who were the candidates in the campaign of 1936? Who was elected? 2. What was unique about the inauguration? 3. Give the main facts about the attack on the Supreme Court. What were the effects? 4. Name and describe four major laws passed during the second New Deal. 5. What foreign threats were claiming the President's complete attention by 1938? 6. What were the contributions to democracy made by Franklin Roosevelt?

##Ask in what ways Roosevelt had shown that he believed in conserving human resources. (Suggestion: through Social Security, minimum-wage legislation, curtailing child labor, etc.)

THE WORKSHOP

OF LASTING SIGNIFICANCE

Explain how each of the following was involved in the Great Depression and the New Deal.

"Black Thursday"	CWA
RFC	Huey P. Long
"Bonus Army"	Francis E. Townsend
brain trust	Charles E. Coughlin
Cordell Hull	Social Security Act
Henry Morgenthau, Jr.	WPA
	Harry Hopkins
Henry A. Wallace	Wagner Act
Harold Ickes	NYA
Frances Perkins	REA
fireside chat	William Green
Adolf Hitler	John L. Lewis
bank holiday	CIO
"Hundred Days"	"sick-chicken case"
CCC	Guffey-Snyder Act
FERA	Alfred M. Landon
NRA	James A. Farley
PWA	Twentieth Amendment
AAA	
TVA	lame duck
Federal Securities Act	FSA
SEC	National Housing Act
FDIC	"the Roosevelt purge"
gold standard	Benito Mussolini

THE DEVELOPMENT OF DEMOCRACY

1. Quote Roosevelt's expression of his view on the basic premise of democracy—a strong faith in people's ability to solve their own problems—which all our great democratic leaders have accepted. For what reason was Roosevelt's view a "tonic" in the 1930's?

2. How did Roosevelt's idea concerning the proper role of government compare with Jefferson's? With Jackson's? Explain. How did his idea about the nation's physical resources compare with that of Theodore Roosevelt?

3. On what basis can it be said that Franklin D. Roosevelt added to Americans' idea of democracy the belief that conserving human resources is as important as conserving physical resources? Explain in detail. How did Roosevelt's concern for people go beyond Jefferson's and Jackson's?

4. In spite of their great popularity, both Jackson and Roosevelt were the targets of angry criticism during their presidencies. What acts of each President aroused criticism? In what way did this criticism itself show the strength of American democracy? #

DOCUMENTS IN HISTORY

1. To what episodes in American history was Roosevelt probably referring in lines 16–17 of his first inaugural (pages 628–629)?

2. How does the speech reflect Roosevelt's earnest desire to carry out the oath of office every President takes at his inauguration?

3. What pledges did Roosevelt make to the American people?

4. Which portion of the address had a Jeffersonian ring? Explain. ##

5. Identify Roosevelt's central aim in his first inaugural. How did he achieve it?

UNRAVELING PUBLIC PROBLEMS

1. State the national problem Roosevelt faced when he became President. How did his attitude toward it differ from Hoover's?

2. Distinguish between the relief, recovery, and reform measures the President proposed. What specific purpose did each have? Which seem most likely to prevent the recurrence of some of the acute distress of the 1930's?

3. How did the second New Deal differ from the first? Account for the differences.

4. What changes have been made in the Social Security Act since 1935? Why?

5. What steps were taken to improve the position of labor?

6. What causes extremist proposals such as those of Senator Long?

7. What useful purpose does the Twentieth Amendment serve?

8. Explain why the New Deal has been called the "Roosevelt Revolution."

A good essay question for a test on the chapter: Roosevelt considered Hamilton one of the greatest Americans. Explain why he would hold such an opinion.

665

The chapter title indicates that the United States abandoned a policy that it had maintained after the First World War--that of remaining aloof from European troubles. Review the feelings of Americans after the First World War. This quotation from a speech by Hull is from a time when Americans were trying hard to be aloof.

28

THE
END
TO
ISOLATION

. . . civilized
international relations . . .

. . . the interest and concern of the United States—whether in the Far East . . . in Europe, or anywhere else in the world—are not measured alone by the number of American citizens residing in a particular country, or by the volume of investment and trade, or by exceptional conditions peculiar to the particular area. There is a much broader and more fundamental interest—which is, that orderly processes in international relationships . . . be maintained. . . .

The momentous question . . . is whether the doctrine of force shall become enthroned once more and bring in its wake . . . international anarchy and a relapse into barbarism; or whether

The Nazis were threatening "orderly processes in international relationships."

Ask what course Hull was advocating for the United States in the face of aggression in the world. What arguments did he use to support his position? What kind of world did he say the United States wanted?

this and other peaceful nations . . . shall work unceasingly . . . to promote and preserve law, order, morality, and justice as the unshakeable bases of civilized international relations.

We might, if we could reconcile ourselves to such an attitude, turn our backs on the whole problem and decline the responsibility and labor of contributing to its solution. But let us have no illusions as to what such a course of action would involve for us as a nation.

It would mean a break with our past, both internationally and domestically. It would mean a voluntary abandonment of some of the most important things that have made us a great nation. It would mean an abject retreat before

those forces which we have, throughout our whole national history, consistently opposed.

It would mean that our security would be menaced in proportion as other nations came to believe that, either through fear or through unwillingness, we did not intend to afford protection to our legitimate national interests abroad, but, on the contrary, intended to abandon them at the first sign of danger. Under such conditions the sphere of our international relationships—economic, cultural, intellectual, and other—would necessarily shrink and shrivel, until we would stand practically alone among the nations, a . . . hermit state. . . .

We want to live in a world which is at peace; in which the forces of militarism, of territorial aggression, and of international anarchy in general will become utterly odious, revolting, and intolerable to the conscience of mankind; in which the doctrine of order under law will be firmly established; in which there will no longer be one code of morality, honor, justice, and fair play for the individual in his relations with other individuals, and an entirely different code for governments and nations in their relations with each other.

Cordell Hull served as Secretary of State longer than any of his predecessors in the office. A Senator from Tennessee when President Franklin D. Roosevelt appointed him in 1933, he was head of the Department of State until near the end of 1944. In those crowded years Hull time and again called upon the nations of the world to be guided by the principles of morality in dealing with one another. Furthermore, he argued consistently that the free nations, including the United States, must join their efforts in a common defense against the aggressor nations of that time: Germany, Italy, and Japan. This selection is a portion of a speech entitled "Fundamentals of American Foreign Policy" that Hull delivered in Washington on March 17, 1938.

Look back at the picture of Hull, p. 642.

U.S. Army

Members of the Nazi party mass in an evening ceremony in Germany: on the arm of each man is a band bearing the swastika, the official emblem of the organization.

The swastika has ever since represented the evils of Nazism.

This section describes the favorable economic position in which the United States had found itself after the First World War. In treating the events leading up to the Second World War, the authors had to go back to the 1920's.

AMERICA FINDS ITSELF THE WORLD'S ECONOMIC LEADER

In urging the United States to join the League of Nations, Woodrow Wilson had spoken optimistically of the postwar future of the nation: "The financial leadership will be ours. The industrial primacy will be ours. The commercial advantage will be ours. The other countries of the world are looking to us for leadership and direction." Wilson's prediction was fulfilled magnificently, but the United States wavered in meeting the challenge.

THE PICTURE OF STRENGTH

The First World War itself had pushed the nation toward economic expansion. The unusual demand for goods had greatly speeded up the growth of industry; new markets had been opened to Americans as hostilities caused an interruption in the trade of the warring countries. The center of world finance shifted from London to New York.

Natural resources. Furthermore, the rapid development of the country's natural resources helped create at the end of the fighting an awe-inspiring picture of American strength. The United States produced 40 percent of the world's coal—twice the amount produced by Britain, the nearest competitor. This country produced a somewhat larger percentage of pig iron, and just less than 70 percent of the world's petroleum, products that are vital to a modern industrial country. America lacked some strategic resources, like rubber and tin, but on the whole, it was more nearly independent of the rest of the world than any other country.

Other evidence. In the 1920's the United States was second only to Britain in total exports and # imports. The value of its manufactured products amounted to 46 percent of the world's total. The income of Americans as a whole was equal to the combined incomes of the peoples of Britain, Germany, France, Canada, Japan, and seventeen other nations.

From debtor to creditor. Before the First World War Americans never invested as much money in Europe as Europeans invested in the United

Observe the expressions on the faces of the two characters.

Uncle Sam is generous about giving out unsolicited advice to Europe after the First World War.

Carmack in the *Christian Science Monitor*

WHAT YOU NEED IS TO BE MORE EFFICIENT, WORK HARDER, AND PRODUCE MORE—

U.S.

EUROPE

#The information given here about the thriving industries of the United States helps account for the optimism that Hoover and other Republicans felt about the future.

States. Americans had built their factories and railroads with borrowed money—obtained mainly from Europeans. Americans paid it back with what they earned from exporting more goods than they imported (see the table on page 821).

Americans shipped to foreign markets principally agricultural goods and raw materials. Manufacturers, for the most part, did not sell abroad; they were mainly concerned with keeping out of this country the products of their foreign competitors. They could do this with the aid of a protective tariff. America was a *debtor* nation—that is, its people owed more money to foreigners than foreigners owed to them. Lending countries like England and France were America's *creditor* nations—that is, they were the nations from whom Americans had borrowed.

The war changed significantly this state of affairs. Immediately after the outbreak of hostilities, the European demand not only for American agricultural goods but also for a wide variety of manufactured products began to increase. The purchases included materials of war and ordinary goods as well. The total value of American exports each year now exceeded the total value of American imports by a figure greater than any before (again refer to the table on page 821).

In order to obtain the money to pay for the products they so badly needed, Europeans sold their American stocks and bonds—which represented what Americans owed them. (Investors in the United States were happy to buy these profitable securities.) As the war progressed and the requirements of Europeans became even greater, they and their governments were forced to borrow money—from America.

By the time of the armistice, the United States had ceased being a debtor nation and had become instead a creditor nation. In 1914 Americans had owed about $3,700,000,000; but five years later this debt had been wiped out, and $12,500,000,000 was now owed to Americans. Of that amount, foreign governments owed the United States *government* ## about $10,000,000,000.

Direct investments. American financial power had become enormous. The rebuilding of war-

Uncle Sam had made much of <u>his</u> money by selling goods to Europeans.
"How about it, Sam?"—the embarrassing situation the high tariffs of the United States could create.

Carmack in the *Christian Science Monitor*

##Besides the war loans the United States had made to the Allied countries, it had loaned money after the Armistice for relief or as advances on the payment for surplus war materials.

669

torn areas of the world depended on loans from the United States. An important source of employment for thousands of Europeans was the direct investing of United States corporations—like Ford, American Telephone and Telegraph, General Electric—in branch factories overseas. By 1929 American private loans and investments abroad amounted to over $8,000,000,000.

A DARKER SIDE

A time would come when American lending and investing in Europe would slow down or stop altogether. Then it would become necessary for Europeans to sell their own goods and services in the United States. This would provide the income with which to pay both the principal sum they had borrowed and the interest on it. Nevertheless, fearing the competition of European products, American manufacturers were able by means of tariffs to prevent the sale of large quantities of competing foreign goods in this country.

Tariff walls. The American policy of maintaining a high tariff aroused deep hostility in Europe. Soon after the war, Congress passed a high emergency tariff. In 1922 the rates were raised again in the Fordney-McCumber Act. They went even higher eight years later under the provisions of the Hawley-Smoot Tariff of 1930.

The aim of the Hawley-Smoot Tariff, as stated by Senator Reed Smoot of Utah, was to provide for the United States "a high degree of self-sufficiency." After first protesting the passage of this law, nation after nation passed self-protecting tariffs aimed at the United States.

Economic nationalism. The belief that a country can be self-sustaining is called "economic nationalism." An attempt to put it into practical operation raises many difficulties, as Americans quickly discovered. Obviously, as long as Americans continued to lend money to the Europeans so that they could pay for the goods they needed, all would be well.

But it was evident that unless Europeans could sell their products to Americans, they would stagger a little more each year under a growing burden of debt they could not repay. In addition to the economic problems these facts raised, many Europeans envied and resented the United States.

War debts. The problem of paying off the intergovernmental debts—that is, the loans the United States had extended to the Allied countries during and immediately after the war— also plagued international relations. The twenty debtor nations began as early as 1919 to urge the United States to cancel the so-called war debts. Amounting to about $10,000,000,000 at the war's end, these increased by 1929 to about $11,700,000,000.

The arguments for cancellation were insistent. First, it was said, the money had been spent primarily in the United States, and Americans ought to regard the profits of their businessmen as ample repayment. Second, it was asserted, heavy European casualties in the joint war effort were surely the equivalent of the borrowed American dollars. The debtors believed that payment of their obligations should be made dependent upon their collecting the reparations due them from the Central Powers under the Treaty of Versailles.

The French made the point that America's huge obligation for their military assistance during the War for Independence had never been fully repaid. The United States, they said, should now be as generous as France had been.

The problem of repayment. The United States would hear no arguments. Calvin Coolidge probably expressed the sentiment of most Americans when he said, "They hired the money, didn't they?" Americans refused to accept the European assertion that there was a direct relationship between the ability to repay war debts and the ability to collect reparations. Certainly no such conditions had been set when the money was borrowed.

The European view that American loans had made up the United States' share of the war effort and ought to have been canceled is unacceptable. First, the sum involved postwar loans, also—not war loans only—and second,

Americans had made a very large sacrifice in lives, too. Besides, under the Treaty of Versailles, the other victorious countries had acquired territory and promises of reparations. The United States had—by choice, to be sure —come from the peace table empty-handed.

Reparations. Despite its inflexible position on the relation between war debts and reparations, the United States gave considerable assistance in devising plans to speed up Germany's payment of its obligations. A widely-publicized # effort—in 1924—was the Dawes Plan, the work of Charles G. Dawes, a Chicago banker. Under it, Germany's annual payments were reduced. Germany was to pay a substantial amount of gold to the Allies in 1925, and in succeeding years an annual amount to be increased gradually.

Germany's complaint that no date had been set for completing its payments led in 1929 to the adoption of the Young Plan—the work of Owen D. Young, an American industrialist. Under it the annual payments by Germany were cut down and limited to fifty-nine years. Although the United States wanted as little as possible to do with European affairs, it was being forced to recognize that a role in them was unavoidable.

Sum and Substance

1. What did Cordell Hull consider America's most important goal in its relations with the rest of the world? How did he think it could be achieved? 2. Give the main facts concerning the economic development of the United States after the First World War. 3. How did American tariffs affect European trade with the United States? 4. What arguments did European nations use for not paying their war debts? 5. What was the viewpoint of this country concerning the debts? 6. What help did Americans give in speeding up the payment of reparations by Germany?

This section describes American efforts to bring about world peace in the postwar years.

THE UNITED STATES TRIES NEW ROADS TO SECURITY

America's voice was missing—at least formally —when in the postwar years joint efforts were undertaken by Europeans to seek solutions to recurring world problems. The silence was sometimes embarrassing and, worse, potentially dangerous.

Republicans were keenly aware that in having been largely responsible for defeating Wilson's League of Nations, they were duty-bound to find a substitute. The Harding administration had scarcely settled into office when this work got under way. The United States made separate treaties with Germany, Austria, and Hungary. In them America reserved to itself "all rights, privileges, and indemnities" to which it was entitled as one of the victorious nations. The country also reserved to itself any rights it might have obtained as a result of the Treaty of Versailles.

At first the United States officially shunned the League of Nations. But in time Americans began to participate in its nonpolitical activities, such as those dealing with international opium control and with health and labor questions. By 1931 the United States had five permanent representatives at Geneva, Switzerland (where the work of the League was conducted), to look after American interests that might be involved.

NAVAL DISARMAMENT

Almost from the day the United States refused to join the League of Nations, thoughtful Americans recognized that the nation might not be able to stand alone in the world. It was ## historical justice that Senator William E. Borah, who had helped prevent his country from becoming a member, took the lead in making other arrangements for the country's security.

Senator Borah's part. Disturbed by Japan's growing navy, as a great many other Americans were, Borah worked to bring about naval disarmament. The British, also watching with dismay the naval race developing among the world powers, were seeking a chance to discuss disarmament. The Senator proposed an in-

##In what sense was the United States embarked on a "go-it-alone" policy? (Suggestion: It was not a member of the League, and its high tariff indicated economic nationalism.)

671

ternational conference to deal with the subject.

When Borah's resolution to hold such a meeting was finally passed by the Senate and the House in 1921, Charles Evans Hughes had taken office as Secretary of State. Hughes saw clearly that it would be idle to talk about disarmament unless other problems—especially those relating to Asia—were discussed, too. Japan's aggressive acts in China were menacing the open door. Also, the military activities of Japan in the territories it had received as mandates from the League of Nations (see the map on page 681) raised doubts about the good faith of the Japanese in accepting them.

Britain's interest. The British—like the Americans—hoped that a conference could be held to deal with affairs in the Pacific. They were eager to avoid having to renew an alliance they had made with Japan in 1902—the Anglo-

Japanese Alliance—which was now expiring. Under its terms, Britain had agreed to aid Japan in case of war. The thought that Britain might be obliged to join Japan in a possible future war between Japan and the United States was especially disturbing to Canadians and Australians. They feared that their countries might become battlegrounds.

The Washington Conference. The British were already trying to arrange a conference to discuss Pacific questions when invitations to meet in Washington arrived from Secretary Hughes. Not only were the leading naval powers—England and Japan—invited, but also all the other countries having direct interests in Asia: France, Italy, the Netherlands, Portugal, Belgium, and China.

The conference, held in Washington's Memorial Continental Hall, demonstrated that the

Observe that a number of women attended the conference.

The Washington Conference. Hughes faces the camera, the third from the right at the main table. Lodge is the fourth.

UPI

Review the open-door policy established at the end of the nineteenth century (see pp. 484-488). Emphasize that in calling the conference the United States was seeking to protect China.

settling of world problems had become—despite what most Americans might have wished—a major concern of the United States.

Hughes's bombshell. The meeting opened on November 12, 1921. On the previous day, the Unknown Soldier of the First World War had been buried with impressive ceremony in Arlington National Cemetery in Virginia. Consequently, the thoughts of world leaders were on the futility and high price of war. But only a few Americans—Henry Cabot Lodge, Chairman of the Senate Committee on Foreign Relations, was one—knew about the bombshell that Secretary Hughes was about to drop.

The Secretary declared in the opening speech that the time was at hand "not for general resolutions or mutual advice, but for *action*." He proposed a ten-year holiday in the construction of all capital ships, that is, ships of the battleship class. This meant a scrapping of many ships afloat and even a halt to the completion of vessels whose keels had already been laid. An English military commentator said, "Secretary Hughes sank in thirty-five minutes more ships than all the admirals of the world have sunk in a cycle of centuries."

The audience was stunned by this bold proposal for naval disarmament. Adjourning over the weekend, the delegates had ample time to discuss among themselves the astounding speech of the American Secretary of State. H. G. Wells, the English literary man, who was present, wrote: "After Secretary Hughes had finished, there was a feeling that we wanted to go away and think." By the time the delegates reassembled the next week, public reaction throughout the world was recognized as favorable.

Three treaties. Subsequent deliberations produced a number of agreements. The first was a naval-armaments treaty—called the Five-Power Treaty—signed by the United States, Britain, Japan, France, and Italy. It provided for a ten-year naval holiday in the construction of capital ships. It also set a ratio in tonnage of capital ships at 5 : 5 : 3 : 1.75 : 1.75 for the United States, Britain, Japan, France, and Italy, respectively.

Another agreement was the Four-Power Treaty, in which the United States, Britain, France, and Japan agreed to respect one another's island possessions in the Pacific. A Nine-Power Treaty was also concluded, in which all the members of the conference agreed to respect the independence and territorial unity of China.

A "parchment peace." The results of the conference, apparently substantial, were hailed by the great majority of Americans. When the Senate ratified the treaties, the *Literary Digest*, recalling the defeat of the Treaty of Versailles, expressed its satisfaction at the change in sentiment. The magazine said it applauded the fact "that the highest legislative body of the nation is actually capable of coöperating with executive policy and of serving civilization."

But what had been achieved was only a "parchment peace." There was no method of enforcing it. It depended solely on the good faith of the nations that signed it.

The Geneva Conference. The United States in the next few years enjoyed its growing domestic prosperity. The country did not even construct as many capital ships as it was entitled to under the Five-Power Treaty. Other countries were busier than the United States in building armaments. In fact, a serious race was now developing in the construction of smaller vessels.

Concerned over the new naval competition, President Coolidge in 1927 invited all the nations that had signed the Five-Power Treaty to meet at Geneva, Switzerland. Only Britain and Japan accepted the invitations. An agreement to limit small craft proved impossible, and the Geneva Conference had to be considered a failure.

OUTLAWING WAR

While the efforts to bring about peace by naval limitation were under way, a hopeful movement was also afoot to banish war altogether. It had friends in high places.

Briand's proposal. On April 6, 1927, the tenth anniversary of the United States' entrance into the First World War, the French foreign minister, Aristide Briand, made a proposal. He

##In effect, this agreement was a guarantee of the open door. Observe that Japan was one of the signatories.

673

publicly called for the immediate negotiation of an agreement between the United States and France that would outlaw war between the two countries.

The Pact of Paris. After a delay, Frank B. Kellogg, the United States Secretary of State, cabled Briand, suggesting that the proposed agreement be broadened to include other countries as well. At first the French hesitated to accept this offer, knowing that under their obligations to the League of Nations they # might be called upon to fight a defensive war. But in the end, they consented.

The result was a simple treaty called the Pact of Paris (sometimes, also, the Kellogg-Briand Pact) outlawing war "as an instrument of national policy." This treaty allowed a nation to fight, but only in self-defense. Entered into by the United States and fourteen other countries on August 27, 1928, it was in time signed by most nations.

Public reaction. The treaty aroused considerable popular enthusiasm and optimism. A Boston newspaper declared, "It is a thing to rejoice over, it is superb, it is magnificent." Careful analysts, though, saw quickly that it was only a gesture toward solving the problem of how to bring about world peace. Again, there was no machinery for enforcement. It was merely, as one Senator called it, "an international kiss." Its value was that, if a war came, for the first time the world might make a distinction between the aggressor and his victim.

Sum and Substance

1. To what extent did the United States participate in the work of the League of Nations? 2. Tell the main facts concerning the Washington Conference of 1921. What did it accomplish? 3. Describe the Geneva Conference and tell what it achieved. 4. Give the provisions of the Pact of Paris. 5. What was its weakness? Its chief value?

In this section the authors tell how we sought to regain the good will of Latin America.

DIPLOMACY REPAIRS RELATIONS WITH LATIN AMERICA

Some of the most dramatic efforts in the 1920's to achieve international goodwill occurred in the New World. They concerned attempts by the United States to cement friendships with neighbors to the south.

CONCILIATORY STEPS

After the First World War, United States relations with a number of Latin American nations were strained. Financial difficulties in many of these countries had brought them partially under the control of United States banks. Sometimes, to preserve order, it had been deemed necessary to land United States marines. This was in keeping with the "international police power" the United States had ## assumed for itself in the Roosevelt corollary to the Monroe Doctrine (see page 538).

Withdrawal from Nicaragua. In Nicaragua the United States had intervened with marines in 1912. Because that country's financial situation had improved, the troops were withdrawn in 1925.

No sooner were the marines out of Nicaragua than a revolt occurred there, overthrowing a newly elected government. The United States refused to recognize the rebels. As civil war developed in the little country, the United States again landed marine units, until almost 6000 men were on the scene. Throughout Latin America a hue and cry was raised against the "Yanquis."

Inside the United States, too, people severely condemned the President's action. In 1927 Coolidge forthrightly defended the steps he had taken. He asserted—as other Presidents before him had—that the United States was especially concerned over the stability of countries in the vicinity of the Panama Canal. The President was aware of the rumor that Communists were trying to influence Nicaraguan affairs from Mexico. He was determined, he said, to protect American interests, "especially if such state of affairs is contributed to or brought about by outside influence or by any foreign power."

##Review Theodore Roosevelt's Latin American policy and particularly the Roosevelt corollary to the Monroe Doctrine (see pp. 532-541).

Settlement with Mexico. Among Latin Americans the reason for United States intervention in Nicaragua was never so clear, and hostility between the "Norte Americanos" and their Spanish-speaking neighbors was considerable. The charge that the United States was imperialistic was heard throughout Latin America in the 1920's. Relations with Mexico helped, especially, to keep the antagonism alive. They were no doubt damaged by the troubles with Nicaragua, but even without them a variety of outstanding issues stood between the United States and its southern neighbor.

Mexico's constitution of 1917 contained an article stating that the rights to all mineral resources—including oil—belonged to the Mexican government. Alarmed American investors feared that the constitutional provision would be made retroactive, canceling the rights that had been previously granted them.

These fears were increased in 1920, when Alvaro Obregón became president of Mexico as the result of an armed revolt. When Obregón's administration refused to sign a treaty guaranteeing the holdings of United States citizens, the United States refused to recognize his government.

Already unable to pay its debts, Mexico found it difficult to float a loan without United States recognition. Investors would not support a government that might fall at any moment. Under these circumstances, Mexico in 1923 agreed not to interfere with United States mineral and oil rights granted before 1917. At this point the United States recognized Obregón, and other nations quickly followed suit.

Kellogg's warning. Shortly after coming to office in 1924, Obregón's successor, President Plutarco Calles, plunged Mexico and the United States into new difficulties. He made it clear that he was eager to abandon the agreement made in 1923 in favor of a new arrangement. In a stern warning, Secretary Kellogg announced, "The government of Mexico is now on trial before the world." Kellogg also stated his belief that Mexico was a center of communistic activity that was stirring up Nicaragua against the United States.

The work of Dwight Morrow. Amid dark hints of war—which neither country wanted—United States–Mexican relations were strained to the limit. American oil producers in Mexico were asking their government for protection, and many of them refused to comply with Mexican

What are the qualities of a gifted diplomat?
Ambassador Morrow, an uncommonly gifted diplomat, in a plane piloted by Charles A. Lindbergh.

UPI

restrictions. At this point Calvin Coolidge appointed as United States ambassador to Mexico Dwight W. Morrow, who had been his classmate at Amherst College.

Morrow's efforts, combined with Calles' need for money, led to the working out of a peaceful compromise on the American rights to Mexican oil and minerals. Other questions were also put on the road to settlement. The success of the negotiations was furthered by the visit of Charles A. Lindbergh, fresh from his conquest of the Atlantic and soon to become Morrow's son-in-law.

A CHANGE IN ATMOSPHERE

The diplomatic tension between Latin American countries and the United States seemed at last to be lessening. In 1928, shortly after his election as President, Herbert Hoover went on a goodwill tour of Latin America.

Even though the reception for Hoover was not overwhelming, it indicated a possible beginning of better understanding between the Latin republics and the United States. Moreover, a number of significant events were occurring during the twenties which—despite the Nicaraguan and Mexican affairs—were paving the way for a new relationship.

Treaty with Colombia. First of all, in 1921 the United States settled its dispute with Colombia over the seizure of the Panama Canal site in 1903 (see page 537). The discovery of oil in Colombia had brought pressure from petroleum interests in the United States to settle the disagreement once and for all. Colombia received $25,000,000 and equal rights with other nations to the use of the canal.

Recalling the marines from the Dominican Republic. Second, in 1924 the United States withdrew the marines from the Dominican Republic, where they had been stationed since 1916. Chaotic financial conditions were ending there, and the Dominican government would now have present only an American supervisor of finances to oversee the repayment of loans made by Americans.

Ending the Tacna-Arica dispute. Third, the United States, after seven years of difficult negotiations, brought about in 1929 an acceptable settlement of a boundary dispute between Chile and Peru. This quarrel—the Tacna-Arica dispute—had for many decades kept Chile and Peru on the knife's edge of war. The settlement, based on a proposal made by Hoover during his goodwill tour of Latin America, brought praise for the United States from many Latin Americans.

Creating the machinery for Pan-American peace. A fourth event was the organizing of a commission to arbitrate disputes among American nations, the work of a Pan-American conference. These conferences seemed to be assuming increasing significance in the affairs of the American nations. One may trace in their results a growing "retreat from imperialism" in United States policy. At Santiago, Chile, in 1923 a Pan-American conference accepted the principle that in a dispute between any American republics, a commission of inquiry be appointed to recommend a peaceful settlement.

Coolidge's visit to Havana. President Coolidge revealed the importance he attached to United States relations with the Latin American nations when he personally attended the second Pan-American conference of the 1920's, held in Havana, Cuba, in 1928. In the opening address he boldly asserted, "All nations here represented stand on an exact footing of equality."

This conference only barely beat down a resolution, which could have been very embarrassing to the United States, denying the right of any country to intervene in the affairs of another. Secretary Hughes persuaded the delegates to hold a special meeting in Washington, D.C., to strengthen the machinery for settling disagreements among American nations.

The treaties of conciliation and arbitration resulting from the conference in Washington brought the American republics nearer the day when all disputes would be settled without resort to force. The willingness of the United States to sign these treaties foreshadowed a change in the policy of intervening in Latin American affairs.

The Clark Memorandum. The Undersecretary of State, J. Reuben Clark, in 1928 produced a

#Observe that both the Republican and the Democratic administrations after the First World War made it their policy to improve Latin American relations. The Clark Memorandum was issued in Coolidge's last year in the White House.

UPI

President Roosevelt confers with Secretary Hull at Hyde Park, New York, in the late autumn of 1933. Observe the serious looks on the faces of the two men. What may they be talking about?

memorandum which, after its publication two years later, helped clear the air between the United States and Latin America. To the evident satisfaction of the United States' neighbors, # it changed the interpretation of the Monroe Doctrine. Specifically, it rejected the Roosevelt corollary, which had earned the United States so much ill will. It gave reassurances that the Monroe Doctrine states the case of the United States *versus* Europe, not of the United States *versus* Latin America.

The Good Neighbor policy. When Franklin Roosevelt became President in 1933, the way had been paved for a formal statement of new policy. It was not long delayed. In his inaugural address Roosevelt declared, "In the field of foreign relations I would dedicate this nation

to the policy of the good neighbor. . . ."

Late in 1933 at the International Conference of American States held at Montevideo, Uruguay, Cordell Hull asserted on behalf of the United States, "No state has the right to intervene in the internal or external affairs of another." Just before the year was out, the President announced that it would be United States policy henceforth to oppose armed intervention in other countries. The Good Neighbor policy had been launched. ##

The abrogation of the Platt Amendment. In the next few years the United States showed its apparent sincerity in a number of ways. Not least important was that it refrained from sending marines into Cuba in 1934 to help establish order there—despite grave provocation. In fact

##Roosevelt had said in his first inaugural speech that he would dedicate the nation to the policy of the "good neighbor," who "respects the rights of others."

677

Franklin D. Roosevelt Library

In an informal moment in Buenos Aires, the President appears to delight his companions with a joke.

Roosevelt exhibits his ingratiating personality.

the United States abrogated the Platt Amendment (see page 489), which had soured relations with Cuba almost from the time it had been passed. Later in the same year this country withdrew the last of the marines from Haiti (see pages 541–542). In 1936 the United States signed a treaty with Panama that met some of the objections—now long-standing—to the Hay–Bunau-Varilla Treaty (see page 535).

The reciprocal-trade program. Latin American countries found an advantage also in the Trade Agreements Act of 1934, sometimes called the Hull Reciprocal Trade Program. It had been passed after much debate, in response to President Roosevelt's appeal to Congress to aid business and agriculture by reducing tariff barriers to international trade.

Under the act the President was authorized to negotiate trade agreements with other countries in order to obtain new markets for products of the United States. He was empowered to raise or lower the Hawley-Smoot rates by as much as 50 percent, in return for concessions from other nations.*

This act was credited by Secretary Hull with having considerably stimulated United States and world trade. Originally created for

*The effect of the reciprocal-trade program has been to lower the whole schedule of duty rates. This is because the United States had previously negotiated with many foreign countries commercial agreements containing a "most-favored nation" clause. This clause provides that each party grants tariff rates to the other as low as those laid on the goods of any third nation. Reduced rates negotiated with a single country under the Trade Agreements Act, therefore, went into effect with many other countries as well—automatically.

##Under the act it was not necessary to obtain congressional approval to lower specific duties by as much as 50 percent.

＃ How would Roosevelt's proposal have changed the original intent of the Monroe Doctrine? Why, in the opinion of the students, did the Latin American countries not act upon Roosevelt's idea? (Doubtless they did not want to involve themselves in defensive wars.)

a three-year period, it was renewed in 1937 and extended again subsequently. Since the nations of Latin America were among the first beneficiaries of the law, it won the United States much goodwill among them. Today, of course, many other nations of the world also have reciprocal-trade treaties with this country.

Extending the Monroe Doctrine. The strengthened political and economic ties with the Latin neighbors became increasingly important when the United States had to take steps to make the Americas more secure from attack. In December, 1936, President Roosevelt traveled to Buenos Aires, Argentina, where still another inter-American conference was being held. There he stated hopefully that an aggressor nation would find the American peoples fully prepared to act together for their common good.

This grand attempt to make the defense of the Monroe Doctrine the serious purpose of *all* of the nations of the Americas, not just one,

failed. Nevertheless, the effort showed how much progress the United States had made in turning aside from the policy of the big stick. ＃＃

Sum and Substance

1. What two events marked United States relations with Nicaragua in the 1920's? 2. Give the main facts concerning American difficulties with Mexico. 3. How were they finally settled? 4. How did Latin Americans regard this country's conduct toward Nicaragua and Mexico? 5. Name and describe four events in the 1920's which helped improve the relations of the United States with Latin America. 6. Describe the achievements of the Pan-American meeting in Washington in 1928. 7. How did the Clark Memorandum affect the Monroe Doctrine? The Roosevelt corollary? 8. What moves did Franklin D. Roosevelt make to improve this nation's relations with Latin America? 9. How did Hull's reciprocal-trade program work? What was its effect?

James Roosevelt frequently was on hand to assist his physically handicapped father.

President Roosevelt is in a serious mood as his limousine approaches the United States embassy in Buenos Aires, Argentina. His oldest son James, in uniform, rides in the front seat. In attending the Buenos Aires Conference, the President showed how important he considered Latin American affairs to be.

Franklin D. Roosevelt Library

＃＃Who had been responsible for the policy of the big stick? How had it affected United States relations with Latin America?

GRAVE DANGERS MENACE INTERNATIONAL PEACE

In spite of important diplomatic achievements after the First World War, many Americans saw that the United States, not having joined the League of Nations, was playing with fate. If hostilities should break out in the world, the nation might have to face alone an enemy menacing American interests.

IN ASIA

As the 1930's dawned, the situation in Asia plainly pointed to serious danger. Conditions developing there clearly threatened the independence of China.

China against the Soviet Union. An undeclared war broke out between China and the Soviet Union at the end of 1929 when China attempted to oust the Soviets from Manchuria (see page 548). These hostilities provided the first test of the Kellogg-Briand Pact. The United States took the lead in trying to end the fighting. But peace came only after a Soviet army had wiped out Chinese resistance in Manchuria. The affair seemed to show that the efforts of # one country alone were not enough to cause nations in conflict to lay down their arms.

Japan in Manchuria. In 1931 trouble again arose—this time because of Japan. Japan had shown expansionist tendencies shortly after it had begun to become westernized in the 1860's. It had seized the Kuril Islands in 1875 and Taiwan (Formosa) in 1895. After the Russo-Japanese War of 1904–1905, it had taken the southern part of the island of Sakhalin.

In 1931 China became the prime Japanese target. In a short time Japan swallowed up the rich province of Manchuria, renamed it Manchukuo, and installed a puppet government there.

The Japanese declared that their action was carried out only in order to protect the South Manchurian Railroad, which they controlled. But the United States Department of State understood well the meaning of Japan's movements. The Japanese were planning to dominate the whole of Asia. This meant they would have to conquer China.

League efforts. The Council of the League of Nations appointed a neutral commission to study the Manchurian question in detail. Its report, accepted by the Assembly of the League, condemned Japanese action in Manchuria as unjustified aggression. Japan thereupon promptly withdrew from membership in the League.

The Stimson doctrine. In notes sent to China and Japan in 1932, Secretary of State Henry L. Stimson set forth the American policy, which has come to be called the Stimson doctrine. It ## held that the United States would refuse to recognize any territorial change brought about in violation of the Pact of Paris, that is, a change that was the result of aggression.

Americans as a whole were pleased with this declaration. But behind it lurked an inescapable fact: no force existed to stand in the path of a determined peacebreaker. Both the Pact of Paris and the League of Nations had already been shamefully scorned by a determined aggressor: Japan.

Recognizing the Soviet Union. Japan's aggressiveness was one of the reasons behind a startling diplomatic step the United States took in 1933. Late that year, in response to an invitation from President Roosevelt, the Soviet Union opened negotiations to bring about recognition by the United States.

For years the United States had maintained no official relations with the Soviets. When the Bolsheviks had seized power in November, 1917, they had quickly repudiated the debt obligations that the previous Russian regimes had entered into. The Soviets had refused to repay a loan made by the United States and the interest and principal on a Russian bond issue that had been sold here. The revolutionists had also confiscated $443,000,000 worth of American property.

The activity of Soviet diplomatic representatives abroad had been another important reason for the refusal of the United States to establish official connections. Said the Secretary of State, "We cannot recognize, hold relations with, or

##Stimson was Hoover's Secretary of State. The Stimson doctrine was adopted by the League of Nations. Some Americans wanted to boycott Japanese goods, but Hoover said no.

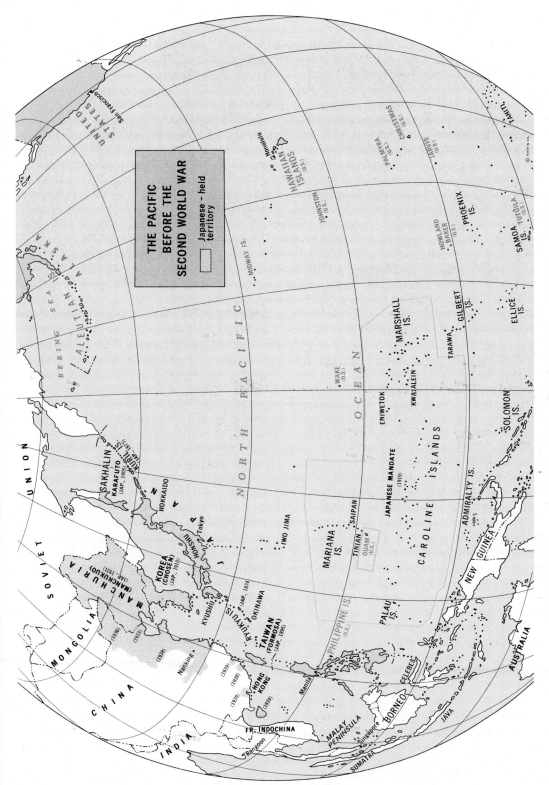

THE PACIFIC
BEFORE THE
SECOND WORLD WAR

Japanese – held
territory

The expansion of Japan, long an immediate threat to China, had become a serious threat to world peace.

Recall that some Pacific islands were mandated to countries after the First World War.
Inside the yellow bar the islands that became a mandate of Japan are shown and named.

681

give friendly reception to the agents of a government which is determined and bound to conspire against our institutions, whose diplomats will be the agitators of dangerous revolt." Throughout the twenties the United States stoutly held to this policy.

In an agreement signed in November, 1933, this country at last recognized the Soviet Union and agreed to exchange ambassadors. The Soviets made no promise to pay their long-standing debt, but they pledged that they would refrain from carrying on subversive propaganda in the United States.

Many Americans, disturbed over the decline in United States foreign trade in the 1930's, hoped that commerce with the Soviet Union would be beneficial. A major reason, though, for the change of policy was a belief that the United States must build up the Soviet Union in Asia in order to have a counterweight to Japan.

IN EUROPE

Throughout the twenties and early thirties, it became increasingly apparent to Americans that peace in Europe and in Asia could no longer be kept solely by Britain and France. In entering the First World War, the United States had prevented the scales from being tipped against the Allies. By withdrawing from the scene after the armistice, the United States had left Europe prey once more to aggression that England and France alone could not stop.

American concern. Events in Europe helped conceal these facts. Weakened by war and revolution, the Soviet Union for a long time after 1918 was concerned with domestic affairs. Germany, defeated and disarmed, faced a large task of reconstruction. Austria-Hungary had been chopped into separate countries, which remained weak.

But if ever again a European nation became powerful enough to threaten the entire continent, the United States could not play turtle and hide inside its shell. Even Henry Cabot Lodge had once said that, League or no League, the United States could always be counted upon to spring to the defense of western Europe. Why was this so?

The explanation was clear. Any hostile nation capable of overrunning western Europe and occupying the Atlantic ports could do so only by first defeating Britain. Britain would never willingly tolerate a hostile force on the opposite side of the English Channel.

The conquest of Britain would almost surely mean the shifting of the English fleet to the New World, making America's home waters a naval battleground. Moreover, the fall of England would leave the British West Indies— at the gateway of the Panama Canal—exposed to enemy occupation. If the United States for its own protection seized these islands, it would immediately be involved in war. It was obviously the business of the United States to act before such grim events occurred in the New World.

Peace sentiments. But in devising a suitable plan to guarantee the country's security, American leaders had to consider a number of significant facts. First, disillusionment with the results of the "war to end war" had strengthened the national determination to stay out of any future war at all costs. This attitude seriously limited the extent to which a President could make international commitments that, in guaranteeing peace, might unavoidably lead to war.

Second, the failure of European countries to pay their war debts had aroused a deep conviction that the United States must never again provide an occasion for such "ingratitude." Third, because "Wall Street" was often blamed in the 1930's for the nation's economic distress, it was easy to make the charge—which became popular—that bankers also helped cause wars. The argument was that men in the world of finance made loans to warring nations and then tried to influence the United States to join in the hostilities in order to guarantee repayment.

Fourth, the growing horror of modern war, that now included such dreaded weapons as poisonous gas and aerial bombs, had created a widespread sentiment for peace throughout the country. One organization called "World Peaceways" received free advertising space in the pages of national magazines. In 1933 it as-

##The traditional tendency of Americans to avoid foreign involvements--except trade--also played a part in limiting the President in making these commitments.

sembled what it called the "biggest book in the world." Weighing over 2330 pounds and containing messages from Mrs. Franklin D. Roosevelt and Secretary of State Hull, the book petitioned for the establishment of a Department of Peace in the Cabinet.

Fifth, the high cost of a large military establishment appeared out of the question at a moment when much national income was being allocated to rescuing the country from the depression at home. Expenditures for a big army and navy seemed to many people not only wasteful but also sinful.

The Nazis. Still, no thoughtful American could truthfully deny that on the opposite side of the Atlantic there were serious threats to world peace. The most important was the revival of Germany.

Taking advantage of the antiwar sentiment in America and Europe, the Germans returned to first rank among the powers by the mid-1930's. Under the driving guidance of Adolf Hitler and his Nazi party supporters, Germany made bold plans for the future.

The new German leader appealed to the consciences of the English and French when he complained of the harshness of what he called the "dictated peace of Versailles." He callously exploited people's fear of war by building up a huge military machine, with which he hoped to frighten other countries into giving him what he wanted. He took advantage of the weakness of the League of Nations and the lack of solidarity among Britain, France, and the United States. Defiantly he developed his aggressive design to build a greater Germany in the very heart of Europe.

The Italian Fascists. In Italy plans were also being made to carry out military adventures. Benito Mussolini had become Italy's dictator in 1922. In the next few years, with the help of faithful followers, the Fascists, he wiped out democratic institutions in Italy and made his country a police state.

From the time they began their schooling, Italian youngsters were taught to follow Mussolini as their leader—*Il Duce* (pronounced eel *doo*cheh)—blindly. Taught that war was the

UPI

Hitler—bare-headed—proudly reviews his troops. Observe the swastikas.

noblest human expression, they were ready for hostilities whenever they should come. In foreign affairs, Mussolini's primary aim was to convert the Mediterranean Sea into an Italian lake and in this way revive some of the glories of the ancient Roman Empire.

Attack on Ethiopia. Mussolini was the first European dictator to strike a blow. The time was October, 1935; the victim, Ethiopia (see the map on pages 758–759). The capture of this East African country would make it possible

##Like other dictators, Mussolini stopped free speech, the free press, and free elections. Discuss "police state." (The power of a dictator is maintained by secret police.)

683

Wide World

The Italian army looses screaming shells as it advances in northern Ethiopia during the unprovoked attack.
Ethiopia (see pp. 758-759) was a weak, defenseless country.

for Italy to threaten Egypt and challenge British control of the Red Sea. The war was fought fiercely on both sides, but it was an unequal struggle. The Ethiopians were defeated in seven months and then were forced to submit to # Italian domination.

NEUTRALITY LEGISLATION

In the face of this flagrant aggression, the United States passed the first of what would prove to be a series of neutrality laws. This was the Neutrality Act of 1935.

Restrictions on trade and travel. Under the law's provisions, when the President proclaimed that a war existed, he could embargo—that is, prohibit—the sale or transportation of munitions to the belligerents. Also, the President could, at his discretion, forbid United States citizens to travel on ships of countries at war, ## except at their own risk. Congress, it was apparent, was hoping to prevent a repetition of the *Lusitania* incident (see page 574).

Restrictions on loans. Keeping up with constantly changing international conditions led in 1936 to a second Neutrality Act. It added to the previous law a provision that no loans could be made to belligerents. This provision answered people who maintained against all arguments that bankers' loans to England and France had been responsible for the United States' entry into war in 1917.†

"Cash and carry." These attempts to guard the national security by legislation not only were temporary but also were undertaken to meet specific international questions after they arose. Permanent neutrality legislation was enacted on May 1, 1937.

The new measure summarized previous laws in providing for an embargo on loans and on the sale of munitions and for an absolute prohibition on travel aboard belligerent vessels. But a new feature was added—the "cash-and-carry" plan. Commodities other than arms could be sold to belligerents who sent non-American ships for them and who paid for them in cash. Senator Borah later described the nation's policy, "We seek to avoid all risks,

---

† Under the Johnson Act of 1934, further loans to those nations which had defaulted on their war-debt payments had already been forbidden.

##Recall Wilson's position on the matter of travel by American citizens (see p. 574).

Recall Jefferson's efforts to preserve neutrality before the War of 1812.

all dangers, but we make certain we get all profits."

An estimate. The neutrality laws were based on the view that trade in arms and private loans to the Allies had involved the United States in war in 1917. Advocates of the legislation were convinced that if this country was drawn into war again, it would be because the pattern followed between 1914 and 1917 had been repeated.

Actually, the laws were *un*neutral. First, the embargo on arms greatly aided Germany, which already had in its stockpiles the largest supply of weapons in Europe. Second, the cash-and-carry principle was an advantage to those countries that had both money and vessels. Further, in making no distinction between an aggressor nation and nations that were victims of aggression, the laws violated a dearly-held American tradition.

Put to the test. No sooner had the law of 1937 gone into effect than a new outbreak of hostilities occurred. In 1937 the Japanese resumed large-scale fighting against their giant neighbor, China. It started with a clash between Japanese and Chinese troops stationed in Peking, China. This gave Japan a pretext for a major attack on the northern Chinese provinces. Under the leadership of Chiang Kai-shek (Jee-*yang* kuy-*shek*), China fought back courageously. Nevertheless, its leading coastal ports fell to Japan, whose troops began to overrun the interior.

If the new neutrality law had been invoked by President Roosevelt, he plainly would have been
playing into the hands of the Japanese. The Chinese had no navy, little money, and a supply of munitions decidedly smaller than that of the Japanese.

Sensitive to the charge of being an aggressor nation, the Japanese referred to these hostilities not as a war but as an "incident." The administration took this name as its cue not to consider a state of war to exist and therefore not to invoke the neutrality legislation. The Department of State allowed supplies to be delivered to China, plainly a victim of aggression. The "China incident" offers another illustration of

how it had become impossible for the United States to remain truly neutral. Any step the country either took or failed to take helped to determine what the outcome of hostilities would be.

Roosevelt's "quarantine speech." This cruel fact was beginning to dawn on a great many Americans, but were they yet ready to act upon it? Roosevelt decided to test public sentiment in a speech he delivered in Chicago—the center of much isolationist sentiment—on October 5, 1937.

The President declared frankly that the state ## of international affairs was "growing progressively worse." Countries that loved peace, he said, would have to join in "a concerted effort to uphold laws and principles on which alone peace can rest secure." They must do this, he also declared, the way a community which

Observe the Japanese flags.

The Japanese seizure of China: "Piece by piece."

Fitzpatrick in the *St. Louis Post-Dispatch*

##The speech was probably intended to sound out public opinion. Although the American people were not ready to accept his idea, feeling against Japan grew afterward.

685

is faced by an epidemic disease "joins in a quarantine of the patients in order to protect the health of the community against the spread of the disease."

The "quarantine speech," as it was hailed by some, proved to be a "dud." Public opinion in the United States would not accept a policy of standing together with other peaceseeking nations in order to achieve "collective security."

Rearming: a two-ocean navy. The President well knew that words alone could not protect the country. Other Americans were also alive to the dangers confronting the country. Congress had passed a bill in 1934 allowing the navy to be built up to full strength.

Although the hope persisted that there might be general naval disarmament, the Japanese now were unwilling to hear of any arrangement which did not put them on a par with the United States and Britain. A second London naval-disarmament conference, which met in 1935, was, therefore, a failure. Only the United States, Britain, and France accepted even the slight limitations finally agreed upon.

Deeply concerned, the President in his annual message of January, 1938, called for a naval appropriation of $1,000,000,000. This would give the United States a two-ocean navy capable of defeating the combined forces of Germany, Italy, and Japan.

During the spring that followed, as Japan made progress in defeating China and as Germany swallowed up Austria, Congress moved toward passage of the legislation Roosevelt had asked for. A bill providing the appropriation became law in May. The American voice for peace would now have behind it the force of a country equipped to defend itself.   #

Sum and Substance

1. Describe the difficulty China had with the Soviet Union in 1929. What was the outcome? 2. What new move did Japan make? 3. What action did the League of Nations take? This country? With what results? 4. When did the United States recognize the Soviet Union? 5. What five considerations prevented Americans from making a plan to guarantee their own national security? 6. What activities in Europe alarmed Americans in the late 1920's and mid-1930's? 7. Describe the Neutrality Act of 1935; of 1936; of 1937. 8. What new Japanese aggression began in 1937? 9. Describe the purpose and content of Roosevelt's "quarantine speech." 10. What steps toward rearmament did Americans take in the 1930's?

In this section the course of the Second World War is described.

AGGRESSIVE DICTATORS SET OFF A SECOND WORLD WAR

As the United States attempted to strengthen itself, the world moved recklessly from one crisis to another. And before long, it seemed, the crises were coming faster—one upon the heels of another.

THE SURGE OF THE NAZIS

In March, 1938, Adolf Hitler's war machine had rumbled into Austria. By September Hitler was menacing Czechoslovakia in an attempt to make it yield a part of its territory. Shaken from the inertia that had allowed them to tolerate the occupation of the Rhineland (see the map, page 688) and the conquest of Austria, both England and France seemed ready to prevent further German aggression.

The Munich agreement. While the leaders of the European democracies trembled with mingled fear and anger, Hitler consented to a conference to be held at Munich, Germany, in September, 1938. Present would be the spokesmen of Germany, Britain, France, and Italy.

The result of the meeting was a new agreement called by the British prime minister, Neville Chamberlain, "peace in our time." Shamefully deserting Czechoslovakia—the most successful democracy that arose out of the First World War—the Western democracies tried appeasement: they gave Hitler the area in Czechoslovakia he wanted. In return, he pledged that he had no more territorial de- ## mands to make upon Europe.

##Recall that Czechoslovakia had been created after the First World War. Discuss "appeasement." Why was it foolish to believe the word of a dictator?

#Hitler had said that he wanted only Sudetenland, the part of Czechoslovakia in which a large number of German people lived. This was doubtless a pretext for taking the whole country. Recall that Poland had also been created after the First World War (see p. 593).

At a reception following the Munich Conference, Musso- premier, Edouard Daladier, is seen between them. Her-
lini shakes hands with Chamberlain (*right*). The French mann Goering (*left*), a leading Nazi, almost hides Hitler.
Observe the expressions on Mussolini's and Goering's faces.

The disappearance of Czechoslovakia. The following March the German dictator, callously # breaking his promise, seized the remainder of Czechoslovakia. He then began to make demands on Poland. Encouraged by Hitler's success, Benito Mussolini overpowered Italy's eastern neighbor, Albania, and occupied it. Even without war, the peace of Europe was being shattered. The policy of appeasing the aggressors in the hope that they would finally become satisfied had failed.

Anxiety in the democracies. A few voices in the Western democracies were raised against ap-

peasing the dictators. In England, even as the multitude cheered Chamberlain upon his return from Munich, the words of Winston S. Churchill—a member of the House of Commons—rebuked him, "We have sustained a total and unmitigated defeat."

Here in the United States Roosevelt also expressed his distress. But opposition to joint action with other countries, that is, collective security, was still dominant in the United States.

Hitler's outrageous acts produced outspoken condemnation everywhere. His barbaric per- ## secution of the Jews within his own country

##A common practice of dictators is to find scapegoats that can be used as outlets for frustrations among people they control. In Germany the Jews were made the scapegoats and became the objects of the most ruthless and savage persecutions.

687

The course of three aggressors in Europe: Fascist, Nazi, and Germany ruthlessly invaded the borders of countries of central and western Europe; the U.S.S.R. seized three neighbors and parts of others.

Observe that Poland was the victim of both German and Soviet aggression.

was an affront to all civilized people. His aggressive policies outside Germany's borders were a menace to all nations.

Fear of "entanglements." By the beginning of 1939, Roosevelt was sure that neutrality laws could not protect the United States from international dangers. "But," he told Congress, "there are many methods short of war" with which the United States might stand against aggression. He did not specify further.

Isolationism—opposition to "entanglements" —was still very strong, and the President, attuned to public sentiment, wanted to avoid a battle at this time over foreign policy. But many newspaper editorials and public-opinion polls reflected a change in the nation's attitude. Americans were beginning to be aware at last that the defeat of the democracies in western Europe would seriously endanger the United States. The time seemed ripe to ask Congress to permit the purchase of arms—and other goods—on a cash-and-carry basis, at least.

HOSTILITIES: SEPTEMBER 1, 1939

On September 1, 1939, after Poland refused to give in to Hitler's demands, the German dictator sent his troops streaming into that country, with dive bombers wailing overhead. True to a promise to come to the aid of the Poles, Britain, almost exactly twenty-five years after the outbreak of the First World War, went to war against Germany.

Within a day the French also entered the conflict—to fulfill a treaty obligation to defend Poland against attack. At once, Roosevelt promised the American people that he would exercise every power at his command to keep the United States out of the struggle. He said, however, that he would not shrink from taking measures necessary for the national defense.

Repeal of the arms embargo. Shortly the President called Congress into special session in order to bring about a repeal of the arms embargo. Though Roosevelt hoped to aid the

#The Germans and the Soviets had signed a nonaggression pact on August 23. Each party had pledged not to attack the other. Both were intent on expansion.

In a fireside chat on September 3, President Roosevelt said, "This nation will remain neutral, but I cannot ask that every American remain neutral in thought as well."

People of German descent in a city made part of Poland in 1919 hail the arrival of Nazi troops in September, 1939.

The Soviets invaded Poland also, and on September 28 they took part of it.

German tanks and trucks pause during the German thrust into western Poland. The Soviets were also on the march.

European democracies, he had to present his plea to Congress on the ground that the repeal would strengthen American neutrality.

Angry controversy. The administration believed that if England and France won the war this country could remain at peace, and that if Germany won it could not. The Nazi propaganda minister had already declared, "The German idea must conquer the world, including the United States."

Isolationists reasserted their contention that the repeal of the embargo was only the first step the United States would take. Said Senator Borah, "In the end we would be sending armies as well as arms. . . ." Neither the administration's nor the isolationists' argument was new.

The climax came when Roosevelt declared in a radio address late in October, "The simple truth is that no person in any responsible place in the national administration in Washington . . . has ever suggested . . . the remotest possibility of sending the boys of American mothers to fight on the battlefields of Europe."

Congress finally voted to follow the President's wish. In November, in the Neutrality Act of 1939, it lifted the arms embargo and placed the sale of arms and ammunition on a cash-and-carry basis.

The fighting in Poland. Within the first month of the fighting in Europe, Poland fell. The Soviet Union had treacherously invaded it from the east while the Nazis' mechanized columns were pouring in from the west. Germany and the Soviet Union, having made a compact as allies, divided their victim between them. The effort had cost Hitler little in time, men, or matériel. It had been, in fact, practically a field maneuver in which the German commanders had tested their equipment and tactics. Europe was terror-stricken by the power and precision of the mighty Nazi army.

Inactivity at the front. As winter approached, the war in western Europe settled into a period of inactivity, and in derision newspapermen were calling it a "phony war." Hitler's blitzkrieg, or lightning war, seemed to them to have become a "sitzkrieg," or "sitting-down" war, but the Nazis were merely biding their time.

Welles's mission. To Roosevelt it appeared that this interval might provide an opportunity to mediate a peace. Accordingly, he sent Undersecretary of State Sumner Welles to Europe to

Borah's serious face shows his misgivings. He remained an isolationist to the end.

Senator William E. Borah (*center*) talks to newsmen about the embargo repeal.

Wide World

Using every available ship and boat, the British retrieve their men from the flaming beaches at Dunkerque.
The British maintained control of the air and were able to protect the evacuation.

see if terms were possible. The effort failed.

In his State of the Union message at the beginning of 1940, Roosevelt warned Americans against believing they could live serenely in isolation while European civilization was being destroyed. "I hope," he said, "that we will have fewer American ostriches in our midst. It is not good for the ultimate health of ostriches to bury their heads in the sand." But the President did not go beyond expressing his hope that the United States might take the lead in restoring peace when the appropriate moment should arrive.

THE TERRIBLE YEAR: 1940

Then came the springtime of 1940. It brought to western Europe invasion, death, and destruction that stamped the year 1940 a tragic one.

Western Europe at bay. One by one the brave but defenseless democracies of western Europe fell before the fury of the Nazis. Without warning they invaded and defeated Norway and Denmark in April, 1940, and Luxembourg, Belgium, and the Netherlands in May.

The Battle of Dunkerque. Before the month was out, France, too, was at bay. Its army was no match for that of the Germans, who were powerfully supported from the air. The French fought a hopeless battle side by side with a British force of 350,000 men. Pressed into a little pocket on the beaches at Dunkerque, a French port, the English withdrew their troops across the English Channel but could not save their guns or tanks.

The fall of France. In the middle of June, in an old railway car in France—the very place where the Germans had surrendered in 1918—

#Recall that the Germans had also overrun Belgium in the First World War.

the French laid down their arms. They were forced to sign a humiliating armistice. Hitler, who had hurried to be present, strutted like a peacock. Moreover, the Nazis were soon directing their full attention to England—only 20 miles across the water from the coast of France at the nearest point.

A change in American sentiment. A wave of shock spread through the United States as accounts of these momentous events arrived. No one, not even President Roosevelt, had been prepared for the quick German victories, and the outlook was for more bad news to come. Said William Allen White, a well-known Kansas newspaper editor: "The old British lion looks mangy, sore-eyed. . . . He can't even roar. Unless a new government takes the helm in Britain, the British Empire is done."

Then news came that Winston Churchill, who, like the conscience of mankind, had warned that Hitler could not be appeased, had become the prime minister of England. A courageous and imaginative man, he nevertheless did not underestimate the danger. Promising his people only "blood, tears, toil, and sweat," he prepared for the Nazi onslaught that was certain to come.

Even the strongly isolationist *Daily News* in New York City was declaring now: "Hitler may win. After that he may feel the United States should be given the blessings of Nazism, too." The paper urged the raising of an adequately prepared army. Although public sentiment for avoiding American involvement was still strong, there was overwhelming conviction that the time had come to provide every possible assistance to the Allies, short of war.

An election amid crisis. The year 1940 brought a presidential election. In the midst of the mighty events in the world, the country would choose a chief executive. For Roosevelt to serve for a third term would mean breaking a tradition that had been held sacred since Washington had retired in 1797 after two terms. But as the crisis abroad grew, the support for retaining Roosevelt also grew.

"We want Roosevelt." Roosevelt played coyly with Democratic party leaders until convention time. He gave no clear word that he would run, because he wanted a call to come to him from his party. Privately he told James A. Farley, his Postmaster General, who was opposed to the # third term, "Jim, if nominated and elected, I could not in these times refuse to take the inaugural oath, even if I knew I would be dead within thirty days."

With the incessant cry of "We want Roosevelt" ringing from the galleries, the Democratic convention, meeting in Chicago, nominated Roosevelt on the first ballot. Henry A. Wallace, the Secretary of Agriculture, was named the vice-presidential candidate.

"We want Willkie." The President in this, his third run for the presidency, encountered his first formidable Republican opponent: Wendell L. Willkie, of Indiana. A powerfully built ## man, with tousled hair, baggy pants, and socks that would not stay up, he appealed to Americans as a person without pretense or pose.

Willkie was a former Democrat whose nomination as a Republican made him a political phenomenon. Carefully built up by his business associates and friends, he was made to appear a knight in armor. His rivals for the Republican nomination—Robert A. Taft, of Ohio, and Thomas E. Dewey, of New York—had been easily overwhelmed.

On the issue of international politics, there was no disagreement between Willkie and Roosevelt. Willkie had said before his nomination, "A man who thinks that the results in Europe will be of no consequence to him is a blind, foolish and silly man."

The Battle of Britain. The only issue, then, was that of the third term. Yet as the summer dragged on, it lost its importance. The Battle of France was over, and the Battle of Britain was commencing. England began to undergo a furious "softening up" from the German air force in preparation for an invasion. As the Nazi attack became more intense, the public-opinion polls in this country showed that Roosevelt's popularity was rising. This was an indication of the growing confidence the public felt in the President's leadership against the Nazi threat.

##Willkie had been president of a southern utilities company and was an opponent of the TVA. The Republican candidate for the vice-presidency was an isolationist.

Willkie's candidacy was significant, even if he was defeated. His support of the New Deal program and spirit showed that both major political parties had accepted the changes of the past eight years—meaning that the people in general had accepted them.

In a pouring rain, the Republican candidate Wendell Willkie determinedly campaigns from an open car. The movie being advertised at the right was Gone with the Wind.

The destroyer deal. The English desperately needed aid, especially destroyers with which to help repel the expected German invasion fleet. What would Roosevelt do—in an election year—when any step he took could be interpreted as one taking the country closer to war?

After extensive negotiations, the United States concluded an agreement with Britain, announced in September, 1940, giving the British what they asked for: fifty overage American destroyers—small, fast warships. In return, the President gained enough to make the transfer a shrewd bargain. First, he received a gift of air and naval bases in Newfoundland and Bermuda. Second, he obtained 99-year leases on additional bases in the British West Indies and in British Guiana (now Guyana).

Roosevelt called the destroyer deal the most important contribution to the national defense since the Louisiana Purchase. Wendell Willkie, who agreed with the need for the deal, condemned the President as dictatorial because he had not consulted Congress.

The campaign. With the transfer of the warships, America's neutrality was ended. Declared the *New York Daily News:* "The United States has one foot in the war and the other on a banana peel." At last the nation had tied its fate to that of other democracies standing against aggression.

But how far would the United States have to go? As the contest drew to its close, the President, forced by the pressure of the powerful Republican campaign, solemnly declared,

#Why did Roosevelt want the bases named here? (As means of protecting access to the New World and of defending possible attacks on the Americas, including the Panama Canal.)

"I have said this before, but I shall say it again and again and again: Your boys are not going to be sent into any foreign wars." Roosevelt, who often had said this previously, had always followed it with "except in case of attack." Now he dropped that phrase, considering it unnecessary. "If we're attacked," he explained, "it's no longer a foreign war."

A third term. Although the election was the closest in popular votes of any since 1916, it nevertheless brought a substantial victory to the Democrats. Roosevelt won 27,307,819 votes to Willkie's 22,321,018. In the electoral college the vote was 449 to 82. Roosevelt captured every city in the country with a population over 400,000 except Cincinnati (the home city of Robert A. Taft). An explanation was that the crisis abroad had taken the sting out of the third-term issue and that the returning prosperity had nullified the attacks on the New Deal.

In the aggressor countries—Germany, Italy, and Japan—where Roosevelt's defeat had been ardently hoped for, there was deep gloom. Roosevelt, who had warned against the aggressors since his "quarantine speech" in 1937, had been judged right by the American voters. The President interpreted his victory as an order to go forward in sending aid to the beleaguered victims of aggression.

The Lend-Lease Act. In January, 1941, a bill that became a landmark in American history was introduced into the House of Representatives. It would authorize the President to sell, transfer, lease, or rent, under terms he might # fix, munitions, food, weapons, or other articles to any nation whose defense he considered vital to the defense of the United States itself.

For two months a debate over this proposal raged in Congress. Some believed that its effect would be to drag the United States closer to war, while others argued it would guarantee that the nation would not be involved. The "Lend-Lease" bill, as it was called, passed, and Roosevelt signed it on March 11, 1941. The sum of $7,000,000,000 was appropriated to begin the new program of aiding embattled friends abroad. Roosevelt told the public in a fireside chat, "Our nation is going to be what our people have proclaimed it must be—the arsenal of democracy." Now the United States stood on the brink of involvement.

In 1940 a new novel by Ernest Hemingway was achieving wide popularity. Called *For Whom the Bell Tolls,* its setting was Spain during the recent civil war there; its theme was that freedom is more than a local matter— it is international. Hemingway's title came from a sermon written by an Elizabethan cleric and poet, John Donne. In it Donne had said: "No ## man is an island, entire of itself; . . . any man's death diminishes me, because I am involved in mankind; and therefore never send to know for whom the bell tolls; *it tolls for thee."‡*

When had the bell begun to toll for the United States? When Ethiopia fell in 1936? Or was it at Munich in 1938, when the fate of Czechoslovakia was sealed? Or perhaps it was when the Low Countries and France were conquered in 1940? Or maybe in 1919, when the United States refused to join the League of Nations?

No one could say for sure. But many Americans had become convinced that national survival itself was at stake. How symbolic of their fears and hopes for the country that the Lend-Lease Bill had been introduced into Congress as House Bill No. 1776!

Sum and Substance

1. Describe the purpose, content, and result of the Munich agreement. 2. How and when did the Second World War begin? 3. Describe the Neutrality Act of 1939. 4. How was the fall of Poland brought about? 5. What was Welles's mission? 6. Give the main facts concerning the war in Europe in 1940. 7. How were Americans affected? 8. Who were the candidates in the presidential election of 1940? What was the main issue in the election? Which candidate was elected? 9. Describe the destroyer deal; the Lend-Lease Act.

---

‡ This phrase refers to the custom of churches to toll a "passing bell" upon the death of a parishioner.

##The quotation from John Donne is frequently quoted today, and students should be familiar with its meaning. The statement that no man is free while another is unfree says the same thing.

THE WORKSHOP

OF LASTING SIGNIFICANCE

Tell what part each of the following had in the period that brought an end to American isolation.

strategic products	Good Neighbor
debtor nation	policy
creditor nation	Trade-Agreements
economic nationalism	Act
reparations	Manchuria
Dawes Plan	Stimson doctrine
Young Plan	Nazi
William E. Borah	Ethiopia
Washington	Fascist
Conference	Chiang Kai-shek
Five-Power Treaty	"quarantine speech"
Four-Power Treaty	Munich agreement
Nine-Power Treaty	Battle of Dunkerque
Geneva Conference	Winston S. Churchill
Pact of Paris	Wendell L. Willkie
Dwight Morrow	Battle of Britain
Tacna-Arica dispute	destroyer deal
Clark Memorandum	Lend-Lease Act

INTERNATIONAL POLITICS

1. Explain how the First World War changed the economic and financial status of the United States. How did the changes affect the position of the United States in international politics?

2. Name the issues that disturbed world affairs after the First World War ended. What position did this country take on them? For what reasons?

3. In what areas of the world did existing tensions threaten world peace in the period between 1918 and 1931? What steps did the United States take to reduce the tensions? What were the results?

4. Explain how events in international politics influenced America to recognize the Soviet Union.

5. Describe the situation in international affairs President Roosevelt faced in 1935, 1937, 1939, and 1940. How did he react to each one and what objective did he keep uppermost in each case?

DOCUMENTS IN HISTORY

1. On what occasion did Cordell Hull deliver the speech that is quoted on pages 666–667? What was his chief point? How did he make it?

2. What insights into the character of the Secretary of State does the address give?

3. Would you say that morality is at a higher level in international affairs today than in 1938? Defend your answer.

MAPS IN HISTORY

1. On an outline map of Asia, name and call attention in some way to the areas directly affected by Japanese expansion in 1931 and 1937. What countries were directly threatened by Japanese aggression? How was the United States involved?

2. On an outline map of Europe, name and indicate (a) the countries overrun by Germany in 1938 and 1939, (b) those it conquered in 1940, (c) those controlled by Italy. Identify the countries that remained unconquered in 1940. How did the situation you have indicated affect the United States?

INFORMED OPINION

1. Why is economic nationalism no longer such a live issue in the United States?

2. In the years when the German armies were overrunning Europe, Hitler was openly contemptuous of the Western democracies. # Why?

3. What lessons about avoiding war did the ## Western nations learn from the events that preceded the Second World War? How is international politics affected today by what they learned?

4. Roosevelt filled the presidency longer than any other person. How do you explain his reelection three times? What grounds for objecting to his long tenure did many people see? Who originated the two-term tradition? Why?

##They learned that an aggressor cannot be satisfied with appeasement and that appeasement is not the road to true peace.

695

This chapter describes the Second World War. The quotation is from General Eisenhower's address to the troops who invaded France in 1944. The picture below shows Americans fighting in the Pacific, where American forces played the major role in the war.

29

THE GLOBAL WAR

. . . security for ourselves
in a free world. . . .

Soldiers, Sailors, and Airmen of the Allied Expeditionary Force:

You are about to embark on a great crusade toward which we have striven these many months. The eyes of the world are upon you. The hopes and prayers of liberty-loving people everywhere go with you.

In company with our brave Allies and brothers in arms on other fronts, you will bring about the destruction of the German war machine, elimination of Nazi tyranny over the oppressed peoples of Europe, and security for ourselves in a free world.

The marines had learned how to fight in the tropics during their stays in Latin America.

During the war, the countries fighting the Nazis and Fascists were not officially called Allies, as in the First World War. They were spoken of as the United Nations, a name later taken by the world organization formed in San Francisco.

Your task will not be an easy one. Your enemy is well-trained, well-equipped, and battle-hardened. He will fight, fight savagely.

But in this year 1944, much has happened since the Nazi triumphs of 1940 and 1941. The United Nations have inflicted upon the Germans great defeats in battle, man to man. Our air offensive has seriously reduced their strength in the air and their capacity to wage war on the ground.

Our home fronts have given us an overwhelming superiority in weapons and munitions of war, and placed at our disposal great reserves of trained fighting men.

The tide has turned. The free men of the world are marching together to victory. I have full confidence in your courage, devotion to duty and skill in battle. We will accept nothing less than full victory. Good luck and let us all beseech the blessing of the Almighty God upon this great and noble undertaking.

After France fell in June, 1940, Britain faced alone the onslaught of the enemy in the Second World War. The British people were resolutely determined—as Prime Minister Winston Churchill put it—to "carry on the struggle, until, in God's good time, the New World, with all its power and might, steps forth to the rescue and the liberation of the Old." Under the supreme command of General Dwight D. Eisenhower—a West Point graduate of the class of 1915—deliverance for Europe came in the spring of 1945. This selection is General Eisenhower's "Order of the Day" to his troops on June 6, 1944, delivered just before they left England on their historic mission to free the continent from tyranny.

Navy Combat Art Section (Henry Beville)

For the role of the marines in the Second World War, see A History of the U. S. Marines, a paperback in the Rand McNally Classroom Library, by Lt. Col. Bernard E. Trainor.

American forces in a hiding place on the island of New Britain in the Southwest Pacific grimly watch for signs of the enemy. These marines are some of the troops that re-captured New Britain in 1943–1944. Having gained a toehold on the shore, they mean to stay. The Japanese seizure of this and other islands in the Pacific made it necessary for United States troops to retake them in deadly offensive-defensive fighting.

Americans in the Pacific engaged in large-scale naval operations and hand-to-hand fighting.

THE UNITED STATES AIDS THE ENEMIES OF THE AXIS

Just as earnestly as the United States hoped to avoid involvement in the new world war that had broken out in 1939, Germany wished to avoid provoking the United States to join the fight. After the outbreak of hostilities in Europe, Adolf Hitler's official aim was to make this wish a fact.

Both were at the height of their power.

Mussolini and Hitler fraternize in a wartime meeting.

Library of Congress

HITLER'S SCHEME

Hitler believed that if he could keep America out of the conflict, he could conquer England and then attack the United States when it was left alone, without allies. His plan was to defeat the nations that opposed him "one at a time," to use Churchill's words.

Soft speaking. So softly did the Nazis speak to the United States that even when Congress repealed the arms embargo, the Germans did not publicly denounce this unneutral step. Moreover, Hitler—to the intense annoyance of his naval commanders—steadfastly refused to allow submarines to operate off Halifax, Nova Scotia. This was a place from which the flow of American supplies to England could have been checked. Hitler was determined not to arouse American anger.

In June, 1940, while the conquest of France was being completed, Hitler gave soothing reassurance that he had no territorial interest in America. "Whoever asserts the contrary," he said, "is lying for some purpose."

Two jolts. Hitler's calm confidence in his plans was shaken by two major turns. The first was his inability to crush the British in the summer of 1940; the second was the destroyer deal between England and the United States.

Courting the Japanese. Germany's response to these two facts was to woo the Japanese more actively. In September, 1940, Japan joined # the Axis powers—Germany and Italy—in the Tripartite Pact.* The Germans hoped to frighten Americans into remaining out of the war by keeping before them the threat that the United States would have to fight Japan in the Pacific.

More triumphs. In the early part of 1941, Romania, Bulgaria, Hungary, Yugoslavia, and Greece—one after another—came under Nazi domination. Swollen with victory, Germany

---

* The alliance between Fascist Italy and Nazi Germany, formed in 1936, was known as the Axis, or the Rome-Berlin Axis. Japan's adherence to it made it the Rome-Berlin-Tokyo Axis.

#Why would Japan join the Axis powers? What was Japan's ambition?

had increased in size under Hitler from an area of 180,976 square miles to one of 323,360. Within the German domain were 106,000,000 people, compared with 66,000,000 before the rise of Hitler.

ROOSEVELT'S POLICIES: TOWARD GERMANY

Sometimes success can be so great that it defeats itself. United against Hitler in 1941 were the powerful force of world opinion, England's increasing armed might, and—most important—the immense resources of the United States.

American coöperation with England had grown closer after 1940, as the British war effort became more and more dependent upon supplies from the United States. President Roosevelt explained simply: "Suppose my neighbor's home catches fire, and I have a length of garden hose. . . . if he can take my garden hose and connect it up with his hydrant, I may help him to put out his fire." Nevertheless, it remained Roosevelt's desire to stay out of the war.

\# **The occupation of Greenland.** The President repeatedly emphasized also the importance of strong national defenses in discouraging aggression against this country. On April 9, 1941, aware of German activities in the vicinity of Greenland, the United States took over the defense of that Danish island for the duration of the emergency. Denmark itself had fallen under Nazi occupation.

"Unlimited national emergency." Toward the end of May, the Nazis' power was reaching new heights. German troops brought by gliders were taking the important British-held island of Crete in the Mediterranean. In the Battle of the Atlantic, ships were being sunk by Nazi submarines at a rate that greatly exceeded the capacity of the British and American shipyards to replace them.

The President cautioned his countrymen that if England fell, the Germans would "close in relentlessly on this hemisphere." He proclaimed a state of "unlimited national emergency." But, fearing to arouse the isolationists, he did not take new steps—like asking Congress to repeal

the Neutrality Act of 1939 (see page 690) or authorizing the convoying of American supplies to England. The President may have known of the coming Nazi attack on the Soviet Union and looked forward to such a war because it would lessen German pressure on the Allies in the Atlantic.

The Nazi attack on the Soviet Union. Despite continued warnings from his principal military advisers that he was making a grave mistake, Hitler on June 22, 1941, sent his mechanized columns pouring into the Soviet Union. The Nazi-Soviet pact of friendship entered into in 1939 had been an arrangement of convenience from the beginning, and few had believed it would last. Yet many had expected that Hitler would wait until he had finished with western Europe before turning toward the east.

A two-front war—one in the east, the other in the west—had always been the nightmare of German military planners. Hitler's seemingly insane act of invading the Soviet Union was based on the expectation that victory over the Russians would come quickly. Hitler hoped that with new resources—particularly of food and oil—a massive attack on the west could be undertaken. He expected also that England would be discouraged from offering any further resistance.

An immediate problem that confronted the United States was whether to extend its aid to the Soviet Union, even though Americans were unsympathetic to the principles for which the Communists stood. The United States finally accepted the position—taken also by Britain— \#\# that *any* aid in the death struggle with Hitler would be welcomed. As Churchill stated it: "I have only one purpose, the destruction of Hitler. . . . If Hitler invaded Hell, I would make at least a favourable reference to the Devil in the House of Commons."

Hitler's hands were soon full. Instead of collapsing quickly, the Soviet Union put up remarkable resistance. This provided the breathing spell the United States required in which to aid the British to the utmost. "Give us the tools, and we will finish the job," was the word America had had from Churchill.

#Compare the principles named here with Wilson's Fourteen Points (see pp. 588-589). What similarities can you find? Do the principles named here contain any ideas which were not included in the Fourteen Points?

Anglo-American coöperation. The President and the prime minister in August, 1941, dramatized their personal friendship—as well as the friendship of their countries—by meeting at sea off the coast of Newfoundland. The two leaders, accompanied by high-ranking military and naval chiefs, discussed urgent matters that included measures to make American aid more effective.

The Atlantic Charter. In a joint declaration, called the Atlantic Charter, which they issued to the press, Roosevelt and Churchill stated the principles on which they were basing their hopes for peace in the postwar world. These # principles included the right of all people to self-government; full economic coöperation among all nations in order to raise their standards of living; equal access for all nations to necessary raw materials; freedom of the seas; and an abandonment of the use of armed force in settling international disputes. Once again there were cheers for the President from interventionists and jeers from isolationists at this sensational statement linking the United States—still not at war—and Britain.

"Shoot on sight." In the beginning of September, Roosevelt announced that henceforth naval escorts would be provided for American merchant vessels traveling in the North Atlantic. The President's decision was made after a Nazi attack had occurred on a United States destroyer en route to Iceland. Roosevelt warned, "From now on, if German or Italian vessels of war enter the waters the protection of which is necessary for American defense, they do so at their own peril."

The message, which amounted to an order to "shoot on sight," was indeed a serious step.

The publication of the principles proposed by these men raised people's hopes everywhere.

Prime Minister Churchill bids President Roosevelt good-by after their meeting on a cruiser in August, 1941. Roosevelt's son Franklin, Jr., may be seen at his right, his son Elliott in the center background.

UPI

#Ask students how they can account for the difference in Americans' attitudes toward Europe and Asia. (Suggestion: They had a history of being suspicious of European activities and of being involved in them. Perhaps they thought that Asians would be more easily cowed.)

Wide World

A poster issued by the Chinese government in 1932 denouncing to its people the flagrant Japanese aggressions. Notice that the poster shows military aggression against unarmed civilians.

Yet after Congress approved the Lend-Lease Bill, it was inevitable that the United States would act to insure the delivery of aid to its friends.

Revision of the Neutrality Act. At the President's request, Congress changed the Neutrality Act of 1939 to make possible the arming of merchant vessels and to permit them to carry cargoes direct to belligerent ports. The revision went into effect on November 17, 1941. Roosevelt declared at that time, "We Americans have cleared our decks and taken our battle stations."

The American people, as public-opinion polls clearly showed, had come to realize that defeating the Axis was more important than maintaining neutrality. But few would have predicted that the *immediate* cause of America's formal entrance into the struggle would grow out of events taking place not in the Atlantic but in the Pacific.

ROOSEVELT'S POLICIES: IN ASIA

Since the time Commodore Perry "opened" Japan (see page 243), Americans have been more willing to accept a firm policy—even one that might lead to war—toward Asia than toward Europe. One of the leading isolationist Senators, Burton K. Wheeler of Montana, for example, was urging with respect to the Japanese that the United States "call their bluff so they will not start anything."

Help to China. Japan's continual aggressions against China since 1932 and its union with the Axis in 1940 had combined to mark it as a threat to world peace. In addition, in the late summer of 1940 its troops occupied northern Indochina. Although absorbed in the business of halting the Axis in Europe, the United States found equally dangerous the Greater East Asia Co-prosperity Sphere that Japan claimed to be establishing.

##Laos, Cambodia, and North and South Vietnam made up the area at the time called Indochina. It was under the control of France.

From 1940 on, the United States gradually shut off the flow to Japan of iron and steel scrap, so important to the Japanese war machine.† After the beginning of 1941, America made Lend-Lease supplies available to China. Moreover, the government's leaders staunchly refused to recognize Japan's conquests; they insisted upon arguing for the open door in China; they condemned Japan's wanton bombing of civilians; they demanded damages for the destruction of American property. But beyond this they would not ask the country to go.

---

† Despite heavy pressure, Roosevelt refused to put an embargo on the shipment of oil. He was concerned lest the Japanese in desperation plunge into full-scale war against the Western powers in order to win supplies.

The nation's military leaders were convinced that if the United States must join the war, it would have to fight first in Europe.

The march on Indochina. Relations with the Japanese came to a terrible pass in July of 1941. Japan seized the remainder of Indochina and already looked longingly toward the Netherlands East Indies, Thailand, the Malay Peninsula, and the Philippines. But the United States did not break with the Japanese because it wanted to avoid a two-ocean war against the Axis partners.

Instead, the United States resorted to the serious steps of freezing Japanese assets in the United States and, finally, of putting an embargo on the shipment of oil to Japan. All the

Students should locate Shanghai in relation to Japan (see pp. 758-759).
Japanese troops parade in the streets of Shanghai after their invasion of that Chinese city in 1937.

Wide World

702 ##Ask what an embargo is and what particular hardship an embargo on the shipment of oil placed on the Japanese. (Oil was the fuel that made their war machine operate.)

#Discuss these terms. What did the Japanese have in mind in making each of the demands? (They would have been left with more or less a free hand in East Asia.) Observe that the United States continued to follow a policy of protecting China.

time the United States was trying to find out what the Japanese would do if Americans became involved in open war with Germany.

Discouraging as American-Japanese relations looked, all was not yet lost. Negotiations to settle the outstanding differences were still in progress. A proposal was even seriously considered to have Roosevelt meet Japan's prime minister, Fumimaro Konoye, in Alaska or Honolulu to try bringing about a settlement of Pacific questions. Secretary Hull opposed such a meeting unless an agreement could be made in advance that Japan would become a law-abiding nation. Yet the door to a solution of mutual problems remained open.

Japanese plans. Meanwhile, the Japanese military leaders were becoming more and more concerned at the increase of American, Dutch, and British military and naval strength in the western Pacific. The Japanese high command reached a decision in the first week of September. It was that Japan must prepare for war against the United States, Britain, and the Netherlands unless Japanese demands upon the United States were met by the beginning of

October. The demands were that the United States and England cease aid to China, that the United States and England reestablish their trade relations with Japan, and that the United States and England help Japan to obtain raw materials—including oil—in the southwest Pacific. The Anglo-Americans were to agree also not to establish new bases in East Asia and not to reinforce their old ones.

In a word, the United States was to grant Japan everything it had been fighting for for a generation. Japan reserved to itself the right to be sole judge of what its obligations to the Axis would be if the United States and Germany went to war against each other.

Japan's situation was not difficult to understand. Its supplies of raw materials—especially of oil—were dwindling. In order to obtain enough oil, bauxite, rubber, rice, and iron ore to carry on war, it would have to seize Java, Sumatra, Borneo, and Malaya. To protect the supply lines from these lands to Japan, the Japanese would have to drive the United States

out of the Philippines, Guam, and Wake Island and the British out of Singapore (see pages 710–711).

General Tojo to power. By the beginning of October, the military group that clamored for war was gaining the upper hand in the Japanese government. Members of the group grew impatient to throw their plans into high gear, especially as daily there appeared to be less hope of negotiating a settlement with the United States. On October 17 General Hideki Tojo, the war minister, forced the overthrow of the Japanese Cabinet, and he himself became the prime minister. The die had now been cast against peace. Nevertheless, the emperor of Japan asked the new prime minister to cancel the earlier decision to make war and to examine one more time the entire international situation.

The Kurusu mission. Tojo and the army and navy leaders early in November arrived at a new decision to embark on war. Orders went out to the Japanese military services to prepare for hostilities against the United States, Britain, and the Netherlands. Tojo announced, however, that Japan was sending a special ambassador, Saburo Kurusu, to Washington to assist the Japanese ambassador, Kichisaburo Nomura, in his talks with Hull.

In the United States, American officials were reading the radio messages that passed between Nomura in Washington and the Japanese foreign office in Tokyo. (The army had been able to "break" the secret cipher that Japan was using.) The nation's leaders knew, therefore, that the Japanese were becoming daily more impatient with the fruitless talking going on in Washington.

The conditions for peace. The United States repeated time after time that agreement was possible only if the Japanese would withdraw from China and Indochina and recognize Chiang Kai-shek's Nationalist government as ## the only government of China. The Japanese position was that they would withdraw from Indochina if America would supply them with oil, but that they wanted a free hand in forcing their will on China.

##The Communists had proclaimed a Chinese Soviet Republic in the southeast. When the Japanese attack on northern China was progressing, Chiang Kai-shek had to join the Communists.

Nomura (*left*) and Kurusu arrive to talk with Hull.

The breakdown of talks. On November 26 nego- #
tiations broke down. Both sides had made
their final proposals. Secretary Hull later said
that in conducting the talks, he and the Japanese had always seemed "to come to a certain
point and then start going around and around
the same circle." "Hull," said Kurusu later,
"remained solid as a rock."

The government knew by now from reading
the secret Japanese messages that Japan was
planning grave mischief, but it did not know
where the blow would fall. Instructions to be
on the alert had been sent to the United States'
commanders in the Pacific. Nevertheless, the
guess was that the expected attack would come
on the Malay Peninsula or Thailand, not on
American soil. The nation was unprepared for
it where it came. Unknown to America, on
November 25 a Japanese naval task force had
sailed eastward in the Pacific. Its destination ##
was Hawaii.

The Japanese had planned the attack on Pearl Harbor ten months before it occurred.

An American battleship struck during the Japanese attack on Pearl Harbor is engulfed in flames.

##The Japanese had planned to cripple the American Pacific fleet and then quickly seize Thailand,
Burma, the Malay Peninsula, the Philippines, and the Netherlands East Indies.

#The news of the attack reached Americans in their homes Sunday afternoon. Few Americans who heard it have forgotten what they were doing or where they were when they learned of the bombing of Pearl Harbor, and "Remember Pearl Harbor!" became a rallying cry during the war.

A day of infamy. On Sunday, December 7— # called by Roosevelt "a date which will live in infamy"—bombs and death rained out of the skies on the American naval base at Pearl Harbor. The military and naval leaders there were taken completely by surprise. The dastardly attack came while Hull was still holding conversations with Nomura and Kurusu.

Before the assault was over, three American battleships and a number of smaller vessels had been sunk, one battleship had been grounded, and another capsized. Severe damage was inflicted on three other battleships and three destroyers. One hundred seventy-seven planes had been destroyed. Furthermore, the United States had sustained heavy casualties—2343 dead, 960 missing, and 1272 wounded. Within one hour the navy had suffered greater injury than it had endured in the entire First World War. The nation gasped in anger and sorrow. The war it had hoped to avoid had come at last.

Sum and Substance

1. What facts did General Eisenhower cite in his "Order of the Day," June 6, 1944, to encourage his forces? 2. What policy did Hitler carry out toward the United States after the outbreak of the Second World War? Why? What two events disturbed him? 3. What nations made up the Axis powers? 4. Explain the American occupation of Greenland. 5. What pact of friendship did Hitler break in June, 1941? How? 6. What were the principles of the Atlantic Charter? Who formulated it? Where? 7. What step did Roosevelt take in 1941 to protect American merchant vessels? 8. How did Congress change the Neutrality Act of 1939? 9. What new act of aggression did Japan commit in July, 1941? How did the United States respond? 10. What demands did Japan make of England and the United States? 11. Describe the events that immediately preceded the bombing of Pearl Harbor. What damage was inflicted by the attack?

This damage was part of the destruction caused by about 360 Japanese planes in the attack.

A launch picks up a man who has jumped overboard from the torpedoed *West Virginia*, which is sinking out of sight.

AMERICA LEADS THE ALLIED POWERS TO FULL VICTORY

The Germans seemed to be as completely surprised by the bold step their ally had taken as the Americans were. In fact, even after the bombs had fallen, the German foreign minister refused to believe the news was true, preferring to believe it was a propaganda trick of the enemy! Germany's carefully nurtured plan to keep the United States neutral had been ruined. Now, urged by Japan, Hitler declared war upon the United States—as Mussolini did— in fulfillment of his obligations as an Axis partner.

Because of the war in the Pacific, therefore, the United States entered the war in the Atlantic. For the beleaguered British, the attack on Pearl Harbor was a distressing but welcome event. Churchill later wrote that after hearing the news and pondering its significance, he "went to bed and slept the sleep of the saved and thankful."

Roosevelt was mourning his mother's death.
The President gravely signs the war resolution.
Franklin D. Roosevelt Library

RETREAT AND RECOVERY

The Japanese newspapers reported boastfully that the United States had been reduced to a third-rate power overnight. This, of course, was ridiculous, but the Japanese victory was substantial. In addition to knocking out temporarily the United States Pacific fleet at Hawaii, Japan had been able to destroy most of the American heavy bombers based on the Philippine Islands before they could get into the air. It had also wrecked the British battle squadron at Singapore. With these paralyzing blows it had achieved mastery of the western Pacific.

The declaration of war. On December 8 Roosevelt asked Congress to recognize a state of war to exist with Japan. Approval came with no dissenting vote in the Senate and with only one dissent in the House. Three days later the country formally went to war against Germany and Italy, too.

Americans closed ranks in rallying to the defense of the nation. Charles A. Lindbergh, for instance, who had been an important critic of the President's views on foreign affairs, ceased his opposition. Now that war is upon the country, Lindbergh stated, "we must meet it as united Americans regardless of our attitude in the past toward the policy our government has followed." The determination to have revenge on the Japanese was heightened when the public learned of the alleged taunt of the Japanese admiral who had led the raid on Pearl Harbor: "I am looking forward to dic- # tating peace to the United States in the White House at Washington."

The "Europe-first" decision. The plans for conducting the war had been laid even while it was still hoped it would not be necessary to use them. American strategy was based on the belief, first, that Germany would be a more ## stubborn opponent than Japan and, second, that the enemy in Europe would have to be defeated before the one in Asia.

The "Europe-first" decision was irritating to the many Americans who were more eager to

#Review pp. 492-494 to recall the effect the war had on American plans for the independence of the Philippines. What earlier reference has there been to Douglas MacArthur? (Look back at p. 638.) Be sure that students know where Corregidor is.

come to grips with the Japanese than with the Germans. The sneaky character of the Japanese attack had touched the nation to the quick. Moreover, it was galling to watch the rapid, almost unhindered advance the Japanese were making. In quick succession they occupied the possessions of the Americans, Dutch, and British in the western Pacific.

The fall of the Philippines. The greatest Japanese triumph was the conquest of the Philippine # Islands, completed on May 6, 1942. There 15,000 American and 40,000 Filipino soldiers had fought gallantly until they could resist no longer. Their commanding general, Douglas MacArthur, was evacuated from the island

fortress of Corregidor (see the map on page 476). He declared solemnly on arriving in Australia, "I came through and I shall return."

The American marine garrison on Wake Island had surrendered in December, 1941, only after making a brave fight. Overpowered by an invading force, the last message from the commander was a valiant understatement: "Urgent! Enemy on island. The issue is in doubt." The Japanese took Guam in the same ## month.

Victories at sea. The furious aggression was halted by two gigantic American naval-air triumphs that left Japan's fleet crippled. The first, in May, was the Battle of the Coral Sea,

The defense proved in vain, for the Japanese were better equipped and had more men.

Men of the Fourth Marine Regiment transport equipment along a rocky road of Bataan, a peninsula on the island of Luzon. They had moved in to bolster the defense of the Philippines when Japanese-American relations grew worse.

Wide World

##See the map on p. 483. What was Japan's object in taking these islands? (Doubtless to prevent American use of the strategically located bases there.)

707

While Doolittle's mission had little strategic effect, it boosted the morale of the Americans, who badly needed an opportunity to initiate an attack of their own.

Bombers under Colonel "Jimmy" Doolittle's direction, poised to launch an attack on Tokyo in April, 1942.

The Marianas can be located on the map on pp. 758-759.

Army reinforcements arrive on Saipan, one of the Japanese-held Mariana Islands the Americans liberated in 1944.

708   The recapturing of the Japanese-held islands was deadly work, since the Japanese could fire on the Americans from a vantage point on land.

which stopped the advance on Australia; the second, in June, was the Battle of Midway, which ended the threat to Hawaii. Despite these reverses for Japan, Japanese ships proceeded to the Aleutian Islands, where the enemy began to set up bases.

Capturing the Solomons. The first great American offensive in the Pacific was launched in August, 1942, when a powerful force of United States marines landed on Guadalcanal, one of the Solomon Islands. This island group had been taken by the Japanese earlier in the year. Savage, often hand-to-hand fighting was conducted on jungle terrain—the most difficult conditions under which Americans had ever waged war. But by fall, a victorious outcome for them was assured. Moreover, before the Solomons had been completely liberated, Australian and American soldiers under the command of General MacArthur had invaded the island of New Guinea and forced the Japanese into retreat there.

"Island hopping." By the beginning of the next year—1943—the forlorn sense of defeat had left Americans. Well-trained forces retook the islands previously lost in the Aleutians; they also gained control of the Gilbert Islands. Through a series of "island hops," the Allies went forward from there to Kwajalein in the Marshalls. Next came the islands of Saipan, Guam, and Tinian in the Marianas.

American forces were bringing themselves into a position to pound the Japanese home islands with land-based bombers (see pages 681 and 710–711). Up to then the reliance had been on carrier-based planes, which were unable to deliver the sustained air attacks needed to destroy Japan's industrial power, on which its military capacity rested. The Allied war planners were not then aware of how seriously Japan had been weakened by the heavy toll the submarine patrols were taking of Japanese shipping. Japan was losing the ability to supply and defend its overseas garrisons.

Find Attu on the small insert at the lower left on the map on pp. 360-361.

The Stars and Stripes flies over Attu, the westernmost island of the Aleutians. The United States Army's 7th Division invaded it in May, 1943, and took it after twenty days of fighting. The American dead numbered 700.

U.S. Army

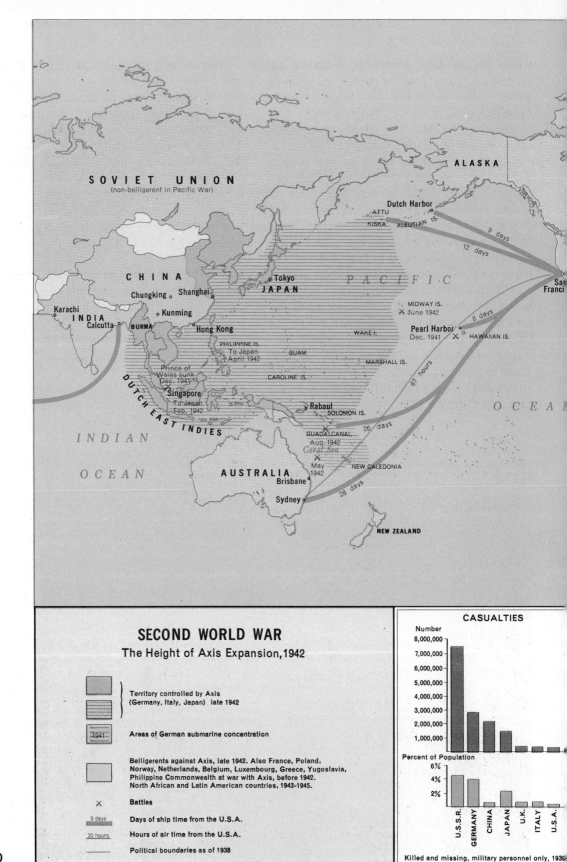

ALASKA

SOVIET UNION
(non-belligerent in Pacific War)

Dutch Harbor
ATTU
KISKA   ALEUTIAN IS.   9 days
                                    12 days

CHINA   PACIFIC   San
Chungking Shanghai   Tokyo   Franci
                    JAPAN
Karachi   MIDWAY IS.
INDIA   Kunming   × June 1942   8 days
Calcutta BURMA   Pearl Harbor
          Hong Kong   WAKE I.   Dec. 1941 × HAWAIIAN IS.
          PHILIPPINE IS.   61 hours
          To Japan   GUAM   MARSHALL IS.
Prince of April 1942
Wales sunk   CAROLINE IS.
Dec. 1941   OCEAN
Singapore
To Japan   Rabaul
Feb. 1942   SOLOMON IS.   26 days
INDIAN   GUADALCANAL
          Aug. 1942
OCEAN   Coral Sea
          May   NEW CALEDONIA
AUSTRALIA 1942
          Brisbane   28 days
Sydney

NEW ZEALAND

SECOND WORLD WAR
The Height of Axis Expansion, 1942

Territory controlled by Axis
(Germany, Italy, Japan) late 1942

1941   Areas of German submarine concentration

Belligerents against Axis, late 1942. Also France, Poland,
Norway, Netherlands, Belgium, Luxembourg, Greece, Yugoslavia,
Philippine Commonwealth at war with Axis, before 1942.
North African and Latin American countries, 1943-1945.

×   Battles

9 days   Days of ship time from the U.S.A.

20 hours Hours of air time from the U.S.A.

————   Political boundaries as of 1938

CASUALTIES
Number
8,000,000
7,000,000
6,000,000
5,000,000
4,000,000
3,000,000
2,000,000
1,000,000

Percent of Population
6%
4%
2%

U.S.S.R. | GERMANY | CHINA | JAPAN | U.K. | ITALY | U.S.A.

Killed and missing, military personnel only, 193

710

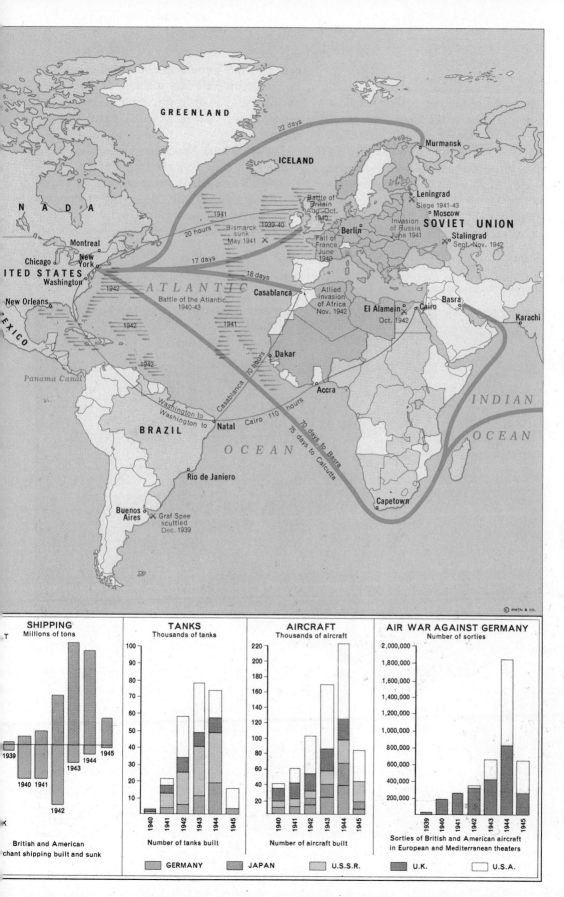

GREENLAND

ICELAND

22 days

Murmansk

Leningrad
Siege 1941-43

Moscow

Invasion
of Russia
June 1941

SOVIET UNION

Battle of
Britain
Aug.-Oct.
1940

Berlin

Stalingrad
Sept.-Nov. 1942

N A D A

1941

Bismarck
sunk
May 1941

1939-40

20 hours

Montreal

Chicago

New
York

ITED STATES

Washington

17 days

Fall of
France
June
1940

18 days

Casablanca

Allied
Invasion
of Africa
Nov. 1942

El Alamein
Oct. 1942

Cairo

Basra

Karachi

1942

A T L A N T I C

Battle of the Atlantic
1940-43

New Orleans

MEXICO

1942

1941

Panama Canal

1942

Dakar

Washington to

Washington to

Accra

INDIAN

BRAZIL

Natal

Casablanca 70 hours

Cairo 110 hours

70 days to Basra

75 days to Calcutta

O C E A N

OCEAN

Rio de Janiero

Buenos
Aires

Graf Spee
scuttled
Dec. 1939

Capetown

© RM®N & CO.

SHIPPING
Millions of tons

1939
1940 1941
1942
1943
1944
1945

British and American
chant shipping built and sunk

TANKS
Thousands of tanks

100
90
80
70
60
50
40
30
20
10

1940 1941 1942 1943 1944 1945

Number of tanks built

AIRCRAFT
Thousands of aircraft

220
200
180
160
140
120
100
80
60
40
20

1940 1941 1942 1943 1944 1945

Number of aircraft built

AIR WAR AGAINST GERMANY
Number of sorties

2,000,000
1,800,000
1,600,000
1,400,000
1,200,000
1,000,000
800,000
600,000
400,000
200,000

1939 1940 1941 1942 1943 1944 1945

Sorties of British and American aircraft
in European and Mediterranean theaters

| GERMANY | JAPAN | U.S.S.R. | U.K. | U.S.A. |

711

THE ASSAULT ON "FORTRESS EUROPE"

The completion of the war against the Japanese was slowed because the United States and # its friends had to fight in Europe, too. From the beginning of the American war effort, the European side of the global war was better supplied with men and equipment than the Pacific side.

This seemed right to American strategists because it would enable the United States to carry on the war there while Britain and the Soviet Union were still standing. It would also answer the clamor in this country and abroad for a second front to divide German forces in Europe.

Landing in North Africa. The United States Air Force soon after Pearl Harbor was flying with Britain's Royal Air Force in massive strikes on "Fortress Europe"—as Hitler called the part of the continent under his control. American ground forces went into action on November 8,

In what connection have the students heard of Harry Hopkins? (See p. 648, p. 651.)

During an inspection of United States troops in Morocco, in 1943, President Roosevelt eats food from the regular army mess with General Mark W. Clark (*seated at left*) and Harry Hopkins (*back to camera*).

UPI

#Recall that Hitler's strategy was to defeat the Western countries one by one. Britain had blocked his program by failing to surrender, and the Soviet Union had also failed to fall.

1942. On that day a combined American and British team under General Dwight D. Eisenhower made a landing in North Africa (see the map on pages 710–711). "Ike" had been named commander of all United States forces in Europe that year.

In North Africa Germans and Italians had been engaging with the British in a seesaw struggle for control. The Axis aim was to capture Egypt, seize the Suez Canal, and cut this indispensable supply line of the British Empire.

After the landing, Allied progress was slow, not only because of stubborn resistance but also because the enemy forces had mud and rain on their side. At last, however, in May of 1943, North Africa had been cleared of Axis troops, and—in the words of Churchill—the "soft underbelly" of Europe lay open to an Allied attack launched from the southern shore of the Mediterranean.

The end of Mussolini. It was not long in coming. In July of that year American forces led by

Where is Sicily? (It is the large island near the southern end of Italy.)

Despite antiaircraft bursts, a Flying Fortress from a North African base drops bombs on Axis installations located on Sicily, in a "softening-up" operation prior to the invasion of that Italian island and stronghold.

Wide World

##Be sure students know where the Suez Canal is and that it links the Mediterranean and the Arabian seas. Students should know how it enables ships to bypass the route around Africa.

713

the colorful and brilliant field commander General George S. Patton, Jr., joined with British troops in invading the island of Sicily. The fighting was hardly ended there when the Allies invaded the Italian mainland.

With this blow, the Italians forced Benito Mussolini to resign and flee to the Nazis for refuge. He was the first of the Axis dictators to fall. People everywhere who loved freedom could congratulate one another with: "One down, and two to go!"

The capture of Rome. The Nazis had recognized that there would be grave danger to Germany if Italy were to fall to the Allies. Consequently, Hitler sent many of his best soldiers to help stiffen Italian resistance. The result was that Italy witnessed some of the most costly and bloody battles of the war. Even though Italy formally surrendered in September of 1943, the Nazis continued to wage terrible war there.

It was June of 1944 before American soldiers led by General Mark W. Clark entered Rome to hasten the conquest of Italy.

Earlier, in December of 1943, the President, who was visiting in North Africa, had said to Eisenhower, "Well, Ike, you are going to command OVERLORD." "OVERLORD" was the code name for the invasion of western Europe. This meant that Eisenhower was to be the supreme commander of the Allied Expeditionary Force.

Operation OVERLORD. Eisenhower went to England immediately to begin laying plans for a gigantic invasion designed to liberate Europe. The planning was conducted for many months, on the most extensive scale in the annals of warfare. Over 2,000,000 American and British ## troops were mobilized and trained in the British Isles. In the late spring of 1944, they were finally ready.

Observe the four stars worn by Eisenhower and the three stars worn by Bradley.

General Eisenhower (*right*) with General Omar N. Bradley, the "GI's General," in North Africa in 1943. Bradley, a West Point classmate of Ike's, commanded the American ground forces in the assault on western Europe.

U.S. Army

##Try to give students some conception of what 2,000,000 troops would need to eat and wear while they were waiting. Planes, tanks, and other equipment were made ready.

On February 14, 1944, Eisenhower was ordered to "enter the continent of Europe and, in conjunction with the other United Nations, undertake operations aimed at the heart of Germany and the destruction of her armed forces."

Dwight David Eisenhower, the career soldier who led the combined Allied forces in Europe in the war with the Axis.

Eisenhower wears the famous "Eisenhower jacket." Note the expressions on the faces. "Ike" has some final words for paratroopers in England just before the invasion of France on D day.

#In addition to the preparations described here, the troops who went aground in the first thrusts of the invasion were aided by paratroopers, who landed in waves on French soil.

D day. On D day, June 6, the Allies landed in northern France, marking the beginning of the end for the Nazis. Beforehand a vast armada of 4000 vessels and 11,000 planes had pounded Hitler's coastal fortifications and the beaches to be invaded in northern France. Then thousands of tense-lipped soldiers set forth across the English Channel under an enormous "air umbrella" to defy Hitler's boast, made four years earlier when he had started to build these defenses. He had said, "No power on earth can drive us out of this region against our will."

On the night of D day, millions prayed with President Roosevelt as he spoke on the radio, "Almighty God: Our sons, pride of our nation, this day have set upon a mighty endeavor, a struggle to preserve our Republic, our religion and our civilization, and to set free a suffering humanity. . . ." By July 2 a million men were ashore with great quantities of supplies. A successful invasion had been started.

Try to imagine the feelings of these Americans.

Aboard a destroyer in the English Channel, men wait to be ferried ashore during the D day invasion.

National Archives

The invasion started at 5:30 A.M. By nightfall about 155,000 troops had landed. The Germans were taken by surprise--the German commander was in Germany for his wife's birthday, and Hitler was asleep. His subordinates were afraid to awaken him.

American troops leave the ramp of a landing barge to make their way toward the French coast on D day.

Below: Some 22,000 vehicles--trucks, etc.--were landed, as well as about 1500 tanks. Men and equipment accumulate on the beaches to back up the troops already in combat.

The invasion was launched on a 60-mile line along the coast of Normandy. General Montgomery commanded the ground forces. General Bradley commanded the U.S. First Army.

717

DEFEAT FOR GERMANY

The advance of the Allied troops was at first halting, because the German defense was well-prepared. But American soldiers under the immediate command of General Omar N. Bradley broke through the enemy's resistance and pressed on toward the city of Paris.

The liberation of Paris. On August 15 a combined force of American, British, and French troops invaded the southern coast of France and raced rapidly northward. On August 25 Paris was liberated by a French army amid scenes of delirious joy. Millions of delighted Parisians cheered Eisenhower as he reviewed French, American, and British troops marching in victory under the historic Arc de Triomphe. By September Allied armies were poised facing Germany along a line stretching from the Netherlands to Switzerland.

The Battle of the Bulge. Although it was weakening, Germany was still far from beaten. In December Hitler's forces succeeded in mounting a tremendous offensive. Feeling that everything was at stake, they fought ferociously, creating a gigantic bulge in the Allied line where they succeeded in pushing back Allied troops in Belgium and Luxembourg. Allied headquarters immediately rushed reinforcements to the region.

After first falling back, the Allied troops stood their ground. At one critical point, when the Germans demanded surrender, a young American general, Anthony C. McAuliffe, gave a simple, memorable reply: "Nuts!"

The terrible Battle of the Bulge—which cost the United States alone 77,000 casualties, including 8000 dead—was the Germans' last powerful effort to defend the fatherland. By the end of January, 1945, they had lost all their

The winter of 1944-1945 added to the discomforts that accompanied the retaking of western Europe.

GI's of the 82nd Airborne Division slog behind a tank moving through Belgium in early 1945.

U.S. Army

#Churchill was urging Roosevelt to move the Allied troops as fast as possible through Germany, since the Soviets were rapidly advancing westward and already controlled eastern Europe. Churchill was mindful of the Soviet Union's past aggressions.

U.S. Army

An American tank rolls through a town in Germany as the Allied forces pursue the Nazis into the fatherland.

On March 7 American forces captured the Remagen bridge and then moved into Germany.

gains of the previous month.

Soviet and British successes. Germany, moreover, was beginning to reel under blows from every direction. In the east, Soviet forces with iron courage had driven out the Nazis and were pushing forward. In the south, British forces had pressed northward into Italy's Po Valley. During a single week in February, more than twice as many bombs were dropped over Germany as had been dropped by the German air force during the entire Battle of Britain!

The bridge at Remagen. While this relentless bombing was reducing the industrial plants and railroad system of Germany to rubble, the

Americans had smashed through to the Rhine. The Germans had planned to blow up all the bridges across the river, but they had missed one, at Remagen—southeast of Cologne. The discovery of this bridge opened the way to the interior of Germany. #

The "death factories." As the armies swarmed over Germany, the extent of the Nazis' barbarity was brought to light—Allied soldiers came upon the infamous German concentration camps. These "death factories" housed not only political "enemies" of Hitler and his Nazi party but also many Jews—the unfortunate people ## whom the Nazis had especially singled out for

##The Jews were a minority in Germany. Recall that Hitler had made them scapegoats for German frustrations.

#Germans living near the camps maintained that they did not know what was going on. Is this possible? What conditions could exist in a country that would lead to mass murder? This subject deserves discussion, since students should be impressed with the horror of genocide.

horrible persecution. The invading forces found that over *six million* Jews had been murdered in these concentration camps in accordance with a diabolically planned system for dealing death.

A new word was coined to name this incredible slaughter of whole peoples: genocide. Eisenhower personally inspected one of these murder camps so that he could always bear witness that the accounts of Nazi brutality were not mere Allied propaganda. Amid pitiable scenes, survivors in these camps welcomed as soldiers of humanity itself the troops who liberated them.

V-E Day. The doom of the European Axis was sealed. On May 2, 1945, hostilities ended in Italy, only a few days after Mussolini had been seized, killed, and hanged by his own people. Hitler, to avoid capture, committed suicide in his air-raid shelter in Berlin just as Soviet forces entered the city. Admiral Karl Doenitz, his successor, quickly asked for peace, and on May 7 the Allied representatives agreed to accept Germany's unconditional surrender. The announcement of their decision was made on May 8—now celebrated as Victory-in-Europe, or V-E, Day.

The taking of the city by the Soviets had been something Churchill had wanted to avoid.

Berlin in July, 1945. The city fell to the Soviets on May 2, after a frantic German defense. Air raids caused much of the damage seen here. In the background at the left is the famous landmark, Brandenburg Gate.

U.S. Army

 ##Mussolini was captured as he tried to take refuge in neutral Switzerland. He was hanged--an ignominious end for the once-jubilant dictator (see p. 687).

Let the class speculate on the possible or probable results of a German victory in the war. Do students think that the terrific sacrifice the Allies made was worthwhile?

Wide World

German prisoners gave themselves up to the United States Third Army as Nazi resistance crumbled. When the end neared, thousands of Hitler's troops surrendered meekly and handed over their weapons.

Recall that this was the second time within a generation that the Germans had lost a war. (Only twenty-seven years intervened between 1918 and 1945.)

Having given a continuous account of the defeat of Italy and Germany, the authors now describe the course of the war in the Pacific. Review the reason for pursuing the war in Europe before giving full attention to Japan.

THE COLLAPSE OF JAPAN

Japan braced itself now to withstand alone the full fury of Allied might. Forces under General MacArthur had been fighting their way northward in the Pacific. The navy, under the command of Admiral Chester W. Nimitz, was the spearhead of amphibious operations.

MacArthur's return to the Philippines. In October, 1944, Allied troops had landed in the Philippines—redeeming MacArthur's pledge to return—and commenced the long, hard fight to reach Manila, which fell at last on March 3, 1945. The home islands of Japan were now within easy reach, although some of the hardest fighting still lay ahead. As the war drew closer to Japan, the Japanese soldiers fought with increasing doggedness.

Taking Iwo Jima and Okinawa. The capture of Iwo Jima, a tiny island 750 miles south of Tokyo, cost the United States 20,000 marine casualties—including over 4000 dead. The taking of Okinawa, a somewhat larger island lying to the west of Iwo Jima, cost America 49,000

In 1942 MacArthur was made Supreme Allied Commander of forces in the Southwest Pacific.

Paratroopers land on Corregidor in February, 1945, to retake the tiny island guarding Manila Harbor.

U.S. Army

General MacArthur—"Big Mac"—who directed the Allied military campaigns against the Japanese in the Pacific.

U.S. Army

722 #Invading Leyte, an island in the Philippines (see the map on p. 476), MacArthur began his drive. The Battle of Leyte Gulf was the greatest naval battle of the war.

The Battle of Leyte Gulf destroyed most of Japan's sea power. Having lost two battleships, four carriers, nine cruisers, and nine destroyers, the Japanese fleet withdrew. On December 15 Americans landed on Mindoro Island (again, see p. 476).

American troops pour ashore on Leyte Island in the Philippines, as the invasion of that island begins.

American forces invaded Luzon on January 9 and took Manila in February.

Freed by Americans, Filipino women and children return to their homes carrying their possessions.

Again a scene showing the destruction of war. The husbands and fathers and brothers of some of these people had harassed Japanese occupation troops through guerrilla warfare.

723

casualties, including 11,000 dead. Severe damage was also done to the fleet by Japanese suicide planes, the *kamikazes*.‡ The pilots sacrificed their own lives by crashing their planes on the decks of American ships in order to deliver their bomb loads.

Pounding the enemy's homeland. Day and night Japan was hammered from the air. Its industrial regions lay in ruins; its merchant fleet had been largely sunk; its cities had been gutted by fire. American ships under Admiral William F.

‡ The Japanese, counting now on supernatural intervention, had named these special units after the typhoon—or "divine wind"—that had destroyed the fleet of Kublai Khan in 1281, saving Japan from invasion.

("Bull") Halsey roamed at will in Japanese waters. But still the Japanese would not surrender, doggedly hanging on. #

The call for surrender. On July 26 the Big Three —the United States, Britain, and the Soviet Union—called upon Japan to surrender unconditionally or face total destruction. After deliberating the question the Japanese government announced that it would "ignore" the summons. Actually, Japan, still at peace with the Soviet Union, was trying to obtain its help in making a more favorable settlement.

Atomic bombs. Behind the Allies' threat of ## total destruction lay a new and frightful secret weapon that had lately been perfected in the

What inspired the pilots of the suicide planes? (Often a threat of physical harm to their families.)

The smoke and fire from two kamikazes that have fallen on the U.S.S. *Bunker Hill* less than 30 seconds apart, in May, 1945. Altogether, the kamikazes sank 34 American warships and damaged 288 others.

National Archives

##Refer students to the book The Atomic Bomb and the End of World War II, listed under "Confronting the World," p. 788.

#An excellent description of the effects of the atomic bombs on Japan may be found in John Hershey's <u>Hiroshima.</u> The United States took the position that the use of the atomic bombs would save hundreds of thousands of American lives.

United States: the atomic bomb. After years of experimentation it had been proved successful in a test in July. On the morning of August 6, a giant Superfortress B-29 plane dropped one on Hiroshima, a Japanese city with a population of about 343,000. Exploding with the force of 20,000 tons of TNT, it destroyed half the city and killed 100,000 persons.

Three days later an atomic bomb was dropped on Nagasaki. It created an explosion described by a *New York Times* reporter in the plane as "a thousand Old Faithful geysers rolled into one blast."

Surrender in Tokyo Bay. The Soviet Union now declared war on Japan, and Red soldiers marched southward into Manchuria and Korea. Before the week was over, Japan had surrendered unconditionally. On September 2 in Tokyo Bay, almost exactly where Commodore Perry had "opened" Japan in 1854, the surrender documents were signed aboard the United States battleship *Missouri*.

The flag that had been atop the Capitol in Washington on Pearl Harbor Day and that later had been flown in triumph over Rome and Berlin, was now brought to Tokyo. MacArthur commanded that it be "unfurled and in Tokyo's sun let it wave in its full glory as a symbol of hope for the oppressed and as a harbinger of victory for the right."

Harry S Truman, who had become President on the death of Roosevelt, was a Missourian.

General MacArthur, after signing the surrender documents, hands one of the pens to General Jonathan M. Wainwright, for whom the event had special significance. In 1942 he had been captured at Corregidor.

Wide World

THE CIVILIAN FRONT

At home, spared the death and destruction visited upon homelands of the other combatants, American civilians had supported their fighting men with energy and enthusiasm. They could in good conscience claim the victory as theirs, too.

Mustering the armed forces. The coming of the war tested, as war often does, the citizens' love for their country. It was not found wanting. The army, mustered from civilian ranks, became the finest and best-equipped force in the world. By the end of the war, 8,300,000 men —and women, too—had served in the Army; 3,500,000 in the Navy; 486,000 in the Marine Corps; and 180,000 in the Coast Guard. The great majority of men had been drafted into the service.

The draft, administered through about 6500 local boards under the supervision of Major General Lewis B. Hershey, was, all in all, justly and efficiently conducted. Deferment of service often had to be made for reasons of the national interest, and this was sometimes mis-

understood by the families and friends of those who already had been drafted.

For the first time, Americans were fighting total war. A well-trained toolmaker, a learned linguist, or an electronics expert had indispensable talents to contribute to the nation's war effort. People with special skills might serve their country better as civilians than as soldiers. This fact had to be accepted.

Finances. To pay for the enormous military undertaking, the United States government borrowed to meet its financial needs. From 1941 to 1945, the national debt increased nearly fivefold. The government sold bonds to rich and poor everywhere in the country, using the motion pictures, the radio, the press, and public rallies to advertise them.

Millions of workingmen at home and soldiers in the field purchased bonds regularly through a payroll-deduction plan. The sales totaled over $61,000,000,000 from 1941 to 1946. Income taxes were increased, and for the first time, employee tax payments were withheld by employers to assure the government of immediate collection. #

Women learned new skills to relieve the labor shortage and to "do their bit."
Women took the place of men in factories: this worker in a Milwaukee plant is welding a gasoline tank for a trailer.

State Historical Society of Wisconsin

In a tour of a war-production factory, President and Mrs. Roosevelt hear how tanks are constructed. Production of many nonessential goods was halted to save materials for the war effort.

Military production. The money collected by the government was poured into industry for the millions of items needed to run the mighty military machine. To administer this side of the war, the President had created an Office of Production Management; as time passed, it was replaced by the War Production Board.

By the middle of 1945, the total of industrial goods produced had reached a staggering sum —including almost 300,000 airplanes; 71,000 naval vessels of all types; 86,000 tanks; approximately 6,000,000 short tons of aircraft bombs; and nearly 42,000,000,000 rounds of small-arms ammunition. The income of American business firms rose accordingly.

Labor legislation. The achievement of such unprecedented totals of production required labor's wholehearted coöperation. When the war began, John L. Lewis spoke words accepted on all sides: "When the nation is attacked, every American must rally to its support. . . . all other considerations become insignificant." Nevertheless, laboring men sometimes felt forced to strike in order to keep wages in balance with the rise in prices that gradually lifted the cost of living.

Congress in 1943 passed the War Labor Disputes Act, or Smith-Connally Anti-Strike Act, # enabling the President to seize a business for the national defense in case it was threatened by a strike. The establishing of wage rates absorbed much energy and attention. As shortages of labor grew and living costs rose, the National Labor Relations Board found it increasingly difficult to keep wages fixed.

Attempting to control prices. Holding prices in check was no less difficult, but the effort was notable and without it they might have gone sky-high. The large amount of money in circulation produced a great demand for consumer goods and created a mounting pressure on prices. The attempt to draw off the excess money in bond purchases and taxes was only partly helpful.

A great burden fell on the Office of Price Administration—the OPA—created early in the war. Its purpose was to keep the lid on prices by setting price ceilings on a large list

#The law was passed over Roosevelt's veto. Because a strike was threatened among railway workers, the United States took control of all railroads in the country for a period.

Americans at home did not suffer during the war, as many other peoples did, but they made sacrifices. Among the foods that were rationed were sugar, meat, butter, coffee, and canned and frozen foods. Gasoline was also rationed.

A clerk in a store tears stamps from the customer's war-ration book to cover rationed articles being purchased.

Stamps were collected from each consumer as a way of controlling the distribution of certain scarce goods.

By the end of November, 1945, all rationing was ended except that of sugar and rubber.

of commodities that were especially in demand. Although not always successful in achieving its aims, the OPA did an admirable job. A ceiling placed on rents held them within bounds during the war.

The rights of citizens. There was little hysteria at home. The Department of Justice performed unobtrusively and with its usual effectiveness. Although several thousand aliens were interned when war came, they were not mistreated. Considering the tremendous scope of the conflict, the record of the federal government in upholding democratic rights in the course of a terrible war was excellent.

A permanent blot on the country's record, however, was the forcible evacuation of about 110,000 Americans of Japanese ancestry who lived on the West Coast. The removal of these

Recall the theory of economic nationalism (see p. 670). The war demonstrated that Americans were dependent on tin and rubber, both produced by Southeast Asia, controlled by Japan.

people to relocation centers, which took place in a wave of fear immediately after the attack on Pearl Harbor, violated their civil liberties —their enjoyment of freedom of movement and their use of their property. It should be observed that no Japanese-American was convicted of espionage during the war. In fact, many naturalized citizens as well as *nisei* (pronounced nee-say and meaning native American citizens of Japanese ancestry) served with distinction in the armed forces.

A fourth-term candidate. By 1944, a presidential year, victory over the Axis was already certain. But the drama of a democratic election held during wartime—the first such American election since 1864—was a stimulant to the Free World.

Roosevelt, noticeably tired, became the first fourth-term candidate for President. He stated, "All that is within me cries out to go back to my home on the Hudson River." Nevertheless, he was willing to serve again, he said, if "the Commander in Chief of us all"—as he described the American people—should call him. His fourth renomination was a certainty.

For the first time in the country's recent history, the selection of a vice-presidential candidate attracted much attention. The renomination of Vice-President Henry A. Wallace became impossible because of opposition from southern Democrats and leaders of northern city machines. Combining their strength, they named Harry S Truman, of Independence, Missouri, whose senatorial watchdog committee on war production had attracted national attention and approval.

Thomas E. Dewey, of New York. The Republicans nominated as their presidential candidate Thomas E. Dewey, an able governor of New York, who earlier had made a reputation as a "rackets buster." It soon became evident that the Republicans would support all the major policies, both domestic and foreign, of the Democrats. Dewey, as a result, was dubbed the "me, too" candidate. His careful campaign could not dislodge the most successful vote getter in American history.

Dewey, the unsuccessful presidential candidate in 1944, had been elected governor of New York State in 1942—the first Republican to hold that office in twenty years. During the campaign he criticized Roosevelt for failing to prosecute the war in the Pacific with sufficient vigor—just before the powerful invasion of the Philippines.

Dewey was born in Owosso, Michigan.

A close election. In popular votes, though, Roosevelt's margin of victory was less than that in any of his three previous campaigns. In the electoral college the results were decisive. There Roosevelt had 432 votes (thirty-six states), and Dewey 99 (twelve states).

##See the haggard look on Roosevelt's face in the picture on p. 730. Charges of ill health were denied, and he rode in the rain in an open car, apparently to show his vigor.

UPI

The exultant President and the Vice-President-elect greet a radio audience on their return to the capital after their victory in the election. Vice-President Wallace, the incumbent, appears to enjoy the occasion, too.

Truman was Roosevelt's choice as his running mate in 1944.

Sum and Substance

1. When and on what countries did the United States declare war? What was its strategy? 2. Relate the main facts concerning American reverses and victories in the Pacific in 1942. 3. Describe the "island hopping" in 1943. 4. Where and when did United States forces begin fighting in the European war? What was their next move? With what results? 5. Give the main facts concerning the invasion of Europe on D day. 6. Describe the Battle of the Bulge. 7. What evidence of German atrocities did the armies find? 8. Give the facts concerning the surrender of Germany. 9. Describe the events in the Pacific which preceded the surrender of Japan. 10. How did the government of the United States seek to pay the expenses of the Second World War? To increase the production of industries? 11. How did labor coöperate? 12. Give the provisions of the War Labor Disputes Act. 13. What efforts were made to keep prices down? 14. How were Japanese-Americans affected by the war? 15. Name the candidates in the presidential election of 1944. Who won?

Ask students to sum up Roosevelt's contributions during the Second World War--in alerting Americans to the threat of Germany and Italy, etc.

The Big Four after the First World War (see p. 591) were replaced by the Big Three in the Second World War. France was no longer in a major role, having been defeated by Germany in 1940. Discuss the two views of the Soviet Union described. Who was right?

THE BIG THREE LAY PLANS FOR A WORLD AT PEACE

When the Second World War—the most destructive war in history—ended, the world was at peace for the first time in a generation. People in every country asked themselves whether this time mankind had truly fought its final war. The answer would depend on the kind of statesmanship the nations could muster.

THE GRAND ALLIANCE

From the beginning of the war, President Roosevelt had given thought to avoiding the mistakes made by President Wilson as a peacemaker. One of the most important had been Wilson's failure to keep the leaders of Congress in both parties informed of his major plans and decisions. Moreover, Roosevelt had learned from Wilson's experience the necessity of maintaining an effective working relationship with the leaders of the countries associated with the United States.

Transatlantic relations. The President kept in almost constant touch with Churchill. Before the war was over, hundreds of letters had passed between the two men who had become fast personal friends, speaking to each other on the transatlantic telephone almost daily.

Working with the Soviets. Relations with the Soviet leaders were far less close. The language difference, to be sure, was a very important reason, but the fundamental one was the difference in political system and social outlook. Yet Roosevelt, especially, believed that the Soviets would coöperate after the war as well as during it if they could be convinced the West had friendly intentions toward them.

The Declaration of the United Nations. Laying the groundwork for a just and lasting peace was arduous work. The first step was taken when Churchill came to the United States shortly after Pearl Harbor. Among the results of his talks with the President was the Declaration of the United Nations, signed early in 1942.

Each of the twenty-six countries at war against the Axis accepted this agreement, pledging to make no separate peace with the enemy and to fight on with the others until all were victorious. One representative of the smaller nations commented that they had been invited as "poor relations whom rich and powerful uncles have to see from time to time." There was no doubt that the Big Three leaders —Roosevelt, Churchill, and Stalin—would play the largest part in making peace.

The switch of isolationists. American policy aimed to make sure that this "Grand Alliance" held together. The United States was determined not to try again to sidestep its responsibilities as a world power. Many Americans were thinking along the lines of Senator Arthur H. Vandenberg of Michigan, who in 1940 had been the leading isolationist candidate for the Republican presidential nomination. Declared Vandenberg: "In my own mind, my convictions regarding international coöperation and collective security for peace took firm form on the afternoon of the Pearl Harbor attack. That day ended isolation for any realist."

Vandenberg played a large role in converting others to his new outlook. The President could count now on the help of both Republicans # and Democrats. Americans for the most part shared Roosevelt's view that "it is useless to win a war unless it stays won."

THE WARTIME MEETINGS

The major problem was how to keep the Big Three working together in harness. The Soviet leader, Joseph Stalin, was personally a stranger to Roosevelt and Churchill when the war began. What they knew of his political philosophy they did not like. But both war and politics make strange bedfellows, and here was no exception. That being so, the Americans and the English wanted to be able to get along with the Soviets.

Stalin was interested at first, almost to the exclusion of everything else, in getting a second front opened up in western Europe. This would help relieve Soviet forces then battling the Germans in eastern Europe. In fact, when Churchill went to Moscow in August, 1942, and raised his fingers in the V-for-Victory sign

#How did the situation described here differ from the one in 1918? What had caused the change in the view of the traditional isolationists?

731

Copyright by Karsh

Prime Minister Churchill, "half-American and all British." Churchill's mother was an American.

The Casablanca Conference. The next in the series # of meetings of the Allied leaders was the Casablanca Conference of Churchill and Roosevelt, held on the Atlantic coast of North Africa in January, 1943. There the two statesmen announced that the terms to be offered to the enemy would be "unconditional surrender." Roosevelt, who was chiefly responsible for this stand, was trying to prevent the negotiation of peace terms by the enemy nations before they had laid down their arms. The announcement was widely hailed as a foretaste of the punishment that was going to be meted out to the Axis countries.

The Moscow Declaration. In October, 1943, Secretary of State Hull journeyed to Moscow for a meeting with the Soviet and British foreign ministers. The outstanding result of the gathering was the Declaration on General Security— sometimes called the Moscow Declaration. In it, public assurances were given that a new world organization for maintaining international peace, which the United States and the U.S.S.R. would join, would be created after the war.

The Cairo Conference. Attempts to get Stalin to travel to the west to meet with Roosevelt and Churchill failed. They, therefore, agreed to journey to Southwest Asia to see him at Tehran, capital of Iran, in November, 1943. On their way they stopped off in Cairo, Egypt, and met for the first time with the defender of China, Generalissimo Chiang Kai-shek. Madame Chiang, who had been educated in the United States, served as interpreter. The result of these talks was a new promise to push the Japanese back into their home islands and strip them of all the gains they had made since the First World War.

The Tehran Conference. Roosevelt and Churchill met face to face with Stalin in the Tehran Conference, the first of the historic meetings at which all three wartime leaders were present. Stalin was assured that a second front would be opened shortly, a pledge that greatly pleased him. This conference may be said to mark the high point of Big Three coöperation. When it ## ended, the men announced in a joint declara-

that he made famous,§ people in the streets mistakenly cheered. They thought he had signaled that a second front had been created. But once the Nazis were on the run, the Soviets, like their allies, looked ahead to the postwar period.

---

§ The letter "V" scrawled on the walls of buildings in Axis-occupied countries awaiting liberation was a constant source of inspiration to the oppressed during the war. Short-wave broadcasts to these nations from the Free World often began with the opening bar of Beethoven's *Fifth Symphony*, which goes "da-da-da-daa"—comparable to the Morse code for "V," which is dot-dot-dot-dash.

##Roosevelt and Churchill were negotiating with the hope that the Soviet Union would declare war on Japan, thus diverting the Japanese armed forces from the Americans.

De Gaulle pledged in London, on June 18, 1940, that he would continue French resistance to Germany. His stand, so different from that of Henri-Philippe Pétain, who became the new head of the German-supported French government, won widespread admiration.

The French generals Henri Giraud (*left*) and Charles de Gaulle pose at Casablanca with Roosevelt and Churchill. At this meeting the men made Eisenhower supreme commander of the North African fighting.

tion, "We leave here friends in fact, in spirit and in purpose."

The military plans made by the three countries brought rich results in the next fourteen months. When the three leaders met the next time, in February, 1945, victory all over the world seemed to be only a matter of time. Germany was caving in, and Japan was being torn and broken. The postwar period was about to begin.

\# Since Stalin refused to leave the Soviet Union, after much discussion concerning the choice of a site, Roosevelt and Churchill obligingly set forth once more. The President and the prime minister met first on the British island of Malta in the Mediterranean. Then they went on to the little Russian town of Yalta, located on the Crimean Peninsula in the Black Sea, where Stalin joined them. Churchill had rhymed in jest for Roosevelt:

No more let us falter!
From Malta to Yalta!
Let nobody alter!

The Yalta Conference. The Yalta Conference itself, the only meeting attended by the Big Three heads *and* their foreign ministers, was the most momentous of the entire war. There important decisions were arrived at for the days of peace ahead.

At this meeting final plans were made for defeating, dismembering, and occupying Germany. Poland, it was pledged, would have a representative government selected in a free election. It was promised that other liberated countries of eastern Europe—like Hungary, Romania, and Bulgaria—would have help in establishing governments "broadly representative of all democratic elements." The voting procedure for the big powers in a new world organization was agreed upon, and it was an-

\#Why is the location of a site for negotiations important for antagonists--which the Big Three had become? (Certain locations may seem like concessions, implying loss of strength.)

nounced that a conference to establish this organization would be held in San Francisco the coming April.

Secret provisions. A number of secret agreements were also made at Yalta. As events would soon reveal, these provided, first, for the entry of the Soviet Union into the war against Japan within two or three months after the surrender of Germany. Second, they called for the recognition of the independence of Mongolia (see pages 758–759). This land, also called Outer Mongolia, had been claimed by the Chinese, but it had come under Soviet influence.

Third, it was also provided that the Soviet Union would receive the Kuril Islands and the southern half of the island of Sakhalin. The latter had been surrendered by Russia to Japan after the Russo-Japanese War in 1905 (see page 680). Fourth, the Soviet Union would recover the rights and privileges it had enjoyed # in Manchuria before 1905.

Criticism. The Yalta agreements have been much criticized. It has been said that Roosevelt needlessly strengthened the U.S.S.R. in the postwar world, and that Soviet assistance obviously was not necessary in order to win the war. But this could be seen only after events had unfolded.

At the time of the conference, neither Germany nor Japan had yet surrendered; no one— not even the scientists who designed it—could guarantee that the atomic bomb would actually work. Soviet soldiers might have proved necessary to help defeat Japan. Furthermore, Roosevelt—and to a lesser extent Churchill— believed that concessions made to the U.S.S.R. would end long-standing Soviet suspicions of the West and pave the way for postwar coöperation.

Disappointment. No one was yet aware that Stalin would coldly demand that Poland and the neighboring countries submit to Communist rule. The failure of Yalta as a postwar settlement, then, was the failure of the Soviets to live up to their agreements with respect to eastern Europe. The United States and Britain were scarcely in a position to prevent them from taking by force what they were granted at the conference table. The Soviet armies were ## already in eastern Europe and they were poised on the Manchurian border of China.

Roosevelt believed he was serving the United States well in obtaining a pledge from the Soviet Union to join the war against Japan. Some military people estimated at the time that the lives of a million American soldiers had been spared. It was only when the war ended six days after the Soviets entered it that people realized how big a bribe had been paid for their participation.

Roosevelt's passing. The President addressed Congress after he had returned to Washington in March. Visibly weary and under strain, he nevertheless spoke with confidence of the future, of a "people's peace," and of the triumph of international morality over the irresponsible use of force.

In April Roosevelt traveled to Warm Springs, Georgia, for a much-needed rest. There, while sitting for a portrait on April 12, 1945, he was stricken with a cerebral hemorrhage. He put his hand to his head, moaned, "I have a terrific headache," and lapsed into unconsciousness. In a few hours he was dead.

Though at that very time the armies of the Grand Alliance were dashing for Berlin, the Free World's rejoicing suddenly was muffled. One of its most persuasive leaders had not lived to see the victory over barbarism and aggression. His passing was felt everywhere.

In a gallant gesture, across the fires of war, the Japanese prime minister expressed his sympathies to the American people. The Nazis, however, publicly boasted that Roosevelt's death was divine justice, and Hitler was overjoyed, not knowing that he himself would be dead within the month. To a hushed House of Commons in London, Churchill delivered a eulogy in which he called Roosevelt "the greatest champion of human freedom who has ever brought help and comfort from the New World to the Old."

Americans mourned, regardless of political affiliation. Many a man then fighting for his country had grown up without knowing any other President than Franklin D. Roosevelt,

##The Soviets' position in eastern Europe and in Germany was something the canny Churchill had feared all along.

#Recall the circumstances in which the Soviet Union had become allied with Britain and the United States. What had the Soviet Union accomplished for itself prior to its invasion by Germany? (See the map on p. 688.)

who had served for twelve years. The new President, Harry S Truman of Missouri, gave immediate assurance that the prosecution of the war would continue as planned.

Breakup of the Allies. Within a few months after Roosevelt's death, the world scene was significantly altered as mighty events crowded one upon another. In May Germany collapsed; in June the Japanese were sending out peace feelers; in July Churchill was voted out of office and replaced by the Labour Party leader Clement Attlee. In New Mexico in July, the explosion of the first atomic bomb demonstrated its practicality. The possibility of defeat that had brought the nations of the Grand Alliance together vanished, and now there was no bond of union.

Moreover, the ties of mutual respect the Big Three leaders had forged during the war no longer served. Even before the fight against Japan was ended, only Stalin remained in a position of leadership. The increasingly stubborn diplomatic positions taken by the Soviet Union quickly shook Americans out of their naive belief that the common victory would lead to durable understanding and goodwill.

PROSPECTS FOR PEACE

Yet if the outcome had its disappointing side, the defeat of the Nazi and Fascist dictators in Europe and Asia removed a scourge of humanity. If these dictators had won, democracy might have perished and a black night would have descended on mankind.

Looming over the whole world was the atomic bomb—casting a very dark shadow. It probably had caused the greatest revolution in international politics since the invention of gunpowder. Although it was a weapon of annihilation, no one was prepared to deal with its implications for mankind. Almost immediately a nuclear-arms race was on.

On April 25, 1945, in the War Memorial Opera House in San Francisco, 200 representatives of the world's peoples met in accordance with plans laid at Yalta. Their mission was to attempt for the second time in the century to create a workable international organization.

The UNO. Although many vexing problems aroused angry discussion, the United Nations Organization was formed after the conference had spent two months in session. The plan that

Why is the UN depicted as an infant, in contrast to his adversaries?

An infant—a David with slingshot—*versus* two well-known causes of many wars, including the Second World War.

Justus in the *Minneapolis Star*

the representatives brought forth was in some respects like that for the League of Nations. There was to be a Security Council, whose membership would include the Big Five—the United States, Britain, the Soviet Union, France, and China. Each member of the Big Five was to have a veto over matters brought before the Security Council. There would be a General Assembly, where each member nation, small or large, would have one vote. There would be a new International Court of Justice.

The UNO started its career hopefully, and this country was a member. Isolationism for the United States had ended. Senator Vandenberg wrote his wife when the Senate ratified the UN Charter: "I am very proud to have been at least one of its fathers."

While the debate on the Charter was in progress, Truman, Attlee, and Stalin were meeting in Potsdam, Germany, to prepare the final steps in bringing Japan to the ground. The atmosphere was cordial. A few weeks later Japan, hit by atomic bombs, toppled as Germany and Italy had. The United States now turned to the task of dismantling its military might and returning to the pursuits of peace.

The outcome of the war was far different from what had been anticipated, for it did not bring real peace and security for the democratic peoples. Many Americans had accepted "total victory" and "unconditional surrender" as magic formulas that would produce a sunny postwar world.

Germany. It seemed perfectly obvious that a wealthy Germany would be indispensable to Europe's ability to recover economically. Yet Germany, broken up into artificial zones, would pay for its heinous crimes, and divided Germany would become a new theater of international conflict.

In Asia. Japan lay in ruins, no longer a threat to China. Yet the end of the fighting would leave the Nationalist supporters of Chiang Kai-shek beleaguered by the Communists led by Mao Tse-tung (*Mow* Dzoo-*doong*). A civil war was in the making with the control of China as the prize. The hope that Nationalist China could stabilize peace in Asia was dying.

The decline of colonialism. Throughout the world colonial empires were being dismantled—a process Roosevelt had supported. Yet no significant preparation was being made to maintain peace in those areas where the independence of colonial peoples would raise new problems.

In Latin America there were also dangers. The Communist World recognized it as a place where seeds of revolution could be cultivated.

During the war years the nation had faced its responsibilities on the home front with remarkable calm. It had not brooded over battles lost nor grown ecstatic over battles won. The war had produced no patriotic songs like "We'll Rally 'round the Flag, Boys," "A Hot Time in the Old Town," or "Over There"—remembrances of earlier wars.

This had been a hard war—fought by a generation that remembered the First World War either directly or through its parents. Ten million men of the Allied forces had been killed, over 300,000 of them American.

Americans sensed that they had paid the price for having turned their backs on Europe at the end of the First World War. They knew they had an opportunity to avoid making the same costly mistake again. Such is the meaning of this inscription, found by a newspaper reporter on a wall of the fortress of Verdun:

> Austin White—Chicago, Ill. 1918
> Austin White—Chicago, Ill. 1945
> This is the last time I want
> to write my name here.

Sum and Substance

1. Describe the purpose of the Declaration of the United Nations. 2. What was accomplished at the Casablanca Conference? At the Cairo Conference? At the Tehran Conference? 3. Name the agreements concluded at Yalta concerning eastern Europe; concerning a new world organization. What four secret agreements were made? 4. How have the Yalta agreements been criticized and defended? 5. When and how did Truman become President?. 6. Give the main facts about the establishment of the United Nations Organization.

##Be sure students know the meaning of "colonialism." (Suggestion: the relationship involved in being a colony.) What were the chief colonial powers?

THE WORKSHOP

OF LASTING SIGNIFICANCE

How was each of the following involved in the global war?

Rome-Berlin Axis
Tripartite Pact
Battle of the Atlantic
Atlantic Charter
Indochina
Greater East Asia Co-
    prosperity Sphere
Kichisaburo Nomura
Hideki Tojo
Saburo Kurusu
Pearl Harbor
Singapore
Corregidor
Douglas MacArthur
Battle of the Coral Sea
Guadalcanal
Dwight D. Eisenhower
"Fortress Europe"
George S. Patton, Jr.
Mark Clark
OVERLORD
D day
Omar N. Bradley
Remagen

genocide
Battle of the Bulge
V-E Day
Iwo Jima
Okinawa
kamikaze
William F. Halsey
Hiroshima
Lewis B. Hershey
War Production Board
War Labor
    Disputes Act
OPA
nisei
Harry S Truman
Joseph Stalin
Casablanca
    Conference
Moscow Declaration
Cairo Conference
Tehran Conference
Yalta agreements
United Nations

GEOGRAPHY AND HISTORY

1. What natural resources encouraged Hitler to plan an invasion of the Soviet Union? How did geography aid the Soviets during the German onslaught?

2. The British sought to keep control of the Mediterranean out of Axis hands. Why? How was such control prevented?

3. Describe Allied strategy in the European war from 1942 to 1945. How did geography aid Britain during the war? Which were the neutral nations of Europe? In what way or ways may geography have played a part in making them neutral?

4. At what places did the Axis powers come closest to the New World?

5. What made it especially difficult to aid the forces of Chiang Kai-shek? Account for the American strategy of "island hopping" in the Pacific war and tell how it was carried out.

INTERNATIONAL POLITICS

1. Sum up the events which drew the United States closer to the Soviet Union in the period between mid-1941 and February, 1945. Specifically, what led to American disillusionment with the Soviets?

2. One of Woodrow Wilson's Fourteen Points had called for an end to secret agreements in international politics. Did his case against them seem strengthened after the Second World War? Explain.

3. Trace the steps beginning in 1894 by which Japan reached the position it had attained by 1942. At what times did the United States become involved in the path Japan took? How and why?

4. Two individuals, Franklin D. Roosevelt and Winston Churchill, were not only national but also international leaders during the Second World War. Find out what qualities of leadership each man possessed and how he exercised them.

5. Find out the cost of the Second World War in men and money to the United States and the other Allied powers. What costs of any war cannot be measured?

6. What postwar conditions in Europe, Asia, and Latin America dimmed the dreams of people who had hoped for a peaceful world?

BEING A SOCIAL SCIENTIST

Use reference books to prepare oral reports on (a) individuals active in the war, (b) any of the following subjects: the Battle of Britain; the fighting in North Africa; the siege of Stalingrad; the Normandy invasion; the Battle of the Bulge; the Burma and Stilwell roads; James Doolittle's raid on Tokyo; the Battle of Midway; the use of atomic bombs; the contributions of the various branches of the United States armed forces.

The costs of war that cannot be measured in money or in statistics are the griefs and human suffering caused, which continue for years after any conflict.

737

Chapter 30 covers the years after the Second World War. The title indicates that no adequate organization for maintaining peace was set up and that postwar problems afflicted the people of the world. The picture suggests one of our reactions to these problems.

30

IN
AN
UNEASY
WORLD

. . . above the confines
of nationalism . . .

This year marks the twenty-fifth anniversary of the discovery of plutonium and the coming year will mark the twenty-fifth anniversary of [Enrico] Fermi's great experiment in controlled nuclear fission. . . . both events had much to do with ushering in the nuclear age.

In science, the recognition of certain past events serves a worthwhile purpose. . . . [M]ost of us have little time to pause and reflect on our overall direction and progress and we need occasions when we can take the larger view and assess trends toward their broad implications.

I would like to spend some time on the "larger view": namely, the growing internationality of science.

The United States B-58 Hustler prepares to refuel in practice over Lake Michigan.
A supersonic bomber of the Strategic Air Command prepares to refuel in flight from a jet stratotanker.

Students interested in science can enlighten other members of the class about the contributions of the scientists named in this quotation. How did the Second World War affect scientists of the world? How was science after the war different from science before it?

The internationality of science is far from being a new phenomenon; there is a long history of early exchanges of ideas and information among scientists of different nations. Within this history there are even stories involving such exchanges between nations at war with one another: for example, during the eighteenth and early nineteenth centuries French and English men of science were allowed to cross each other's national borders safely though they were politically and militarily "enemy lines." It was also during this era that Sir Humphrey Davy received an award from the French government while his country was at war with France, and that Benjamin Franklin, during the American Revolution, requested American naval ships and privateers to grant the British vessels of Captain Cook safe passage because of the scientific nature of Cook's expedition to the South Seas and the Antarctic.

But all this was true in part because of the nature of science in those days—because it had yet to be strongly allied with technology and thus had very little to do with people, political activity, or the power and prestige of nations. All that, of course, has changed—but, relatively speaking, only very recently.

Prior to the twentieth century the body of knowledge in physics grew from theories and experiments of men of many countries—among them Galileo, Gilbert, Descartes, Huygens, Newton, Faraday, and Roentgen. The close of the nineteenth century found many scientists—physicists in particular—feeling, like Alexander the Great, that they had no more worlds to conquer. After all, what could come after the discovery of the electron, x-ray, and radioactivity?

Seldom has resignation been so quickly shattered. Einstein's theory of relativity and Planck's equations of quantum action revealed how much still remained unexplored in the scientific world and gave rise to important future discoveries. . . .

But exciting as these advances were to the scientific community, they did little to capture the imagination of the public or change the rather isolated position of science. The events of World War II ended that isolation and lifted the scientist to a new position among his fellow men. With the development of nuclear fission, # radar, the rocket, and the computer, science became an important instrument for national survival. By the end of the war governments were convinced of the importance of science, at first primarily for defense, but soon for its applications to health, welfare, economic growth, and even national prestige. By 1950 our new scientific revolution had begun in earnest. . . . It literally took the awesome explosion of a nuclear weapon to awaken the world to the power of scientific knowledge.

An immediate result of this rude awakening was to emphasize nationalism in some areas of

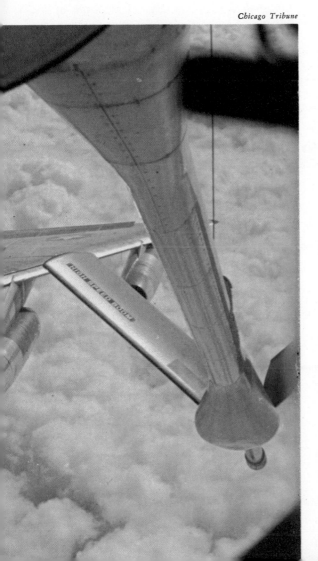

Chicago Tribune

#What does each of these inventions have to do with national survival?

739

science by making them a matter of national concern related heavily to defense and security. But at the same time it gave the scientists around the world the greater prestige and resources they needed, and science, springing from a universal heritage and being international in nature, was bound to rise above the confines of nationalism. The result has been remarkably favorable to international cooperation in nearly all areas of science, and I believe this may ultimately be mankind's greatest blessing. I base # this belief on two ideas.

The first, and more obvious, is that international cooperation in science will accelerate those advances of mankind which, if applied wisely and equally around the world, will help to eliminate the causes of political and economic strife.

The second idea is that internationality in science extends the rational processes of science to other human activities in all countries, and that the ascendancy of scientists within their respective countries will influence national leaders and their people to deal with problems in a more rational and hence more peaceful and productive way. I certainly do not think that

science or scientists hold the answers to all human problems, but if we view science in its broadest terms, that is, as a highly organized and penetrating pursuit of knowledge and truth, some good is going to come by having the attitudes and approaches of science applied to other areas.

Scientists have become a new force and interest group in all advanced countries in the last quarter of a century. Holding a significant key to the strength of nations and the destiny of human beings as individuals, they are national heroes who speak an international language. Scientists themselves are increasingly conscious of their power and their relationship to society at large. This selection is from a speech given by Glenn T. Seaborg in 1966 and published in the January, 1967, issue of the Bulletin of the Atomic Scientists. Seaborg, one of America's most distinguished nuclear chemists, shared a Nobel Prize in 1951 for the discovery of the element plutonium. He was appointed chairman of the Atomic Energy Commission in 1961.

President Truman's domestic program is discussed in this section.

THE POSTWAR ERA OPENS UNDER HARRY S TRUMAN

At Roosevelt's death even his severest critics acknowledged that a towering, imaginative leader had left the scene. It was the lot of Vice-President Harry S Truman to take over the reins from such a President just as the country was passing into the critical postwar period.

Truman himself, like millions of other Americans, continued for some time to refer to Roosevelt unconsciously as "the President." He said to newspapermen on the first day he spent in office, "Boys, if you ever pray, pray for me now. . . ."

DEMOBILIZATION

Stubborn problems sprang at the new President from every side. Confronted by what he himself called a "year of decisions," Truman had to lay the groundwork for the demobiliza-

tion of the country's military might.* He had to solve problems of labor-management relations. He had to face a Congress beginning to ## assert its own power again after years of being directed by the White House.

Soaring prices. The President quickly removed wartime controls on prices, and prices increased sharply. Labor, after a long period of fulfilling a wartime "no-strike" pledge, now demanded higher wages. Businessmen were granting these increases and raising the prices of their goods.

Another explanation of the rise in prices was that the American market was a hungry one.

---

* The returning veterans themselves were aided under the Servicemen's Readjustment Act, the so-called GI Bill of Rights, which—in part because of the efforts of the American Legion —Congress had passed in June, 1944. The law provided generous educational opportunities and financial assistance to all honorably discharged servicemen and servicewomen.

##For how many years had Congress been directed from the White House? (For twelve years; Roosevelt died early in 1945.)

After four years of war, the demand for consumer goods—new cars, new homes, new everything—seemed unlimited. This demand helped push prices upward. Because all controls on prices were removed—although not those on rent—there was danger of runaway inflation. By the end of 1945, prices were about one-third higher than in 1941.

Major strikes. After 1945 workers continued to feel the squeeze of rising prices. The end of the war put a stop to Sunday, holiday, and overtime work in most branches of industry. For many industrial employees this meant a reduction in take-home pay. Everywhere in the country labor sought 30-percent increases in wages in order to catch up with current prices. A number of prolonged and embittering strikes in the basic industries followed.

BATTLING WITH CONGRESS

Truman considered himself to be in the New Deal tradition of friendliness toward labor. He soon found out that in order to achieve his legislative program, he—like Roosevelt—would have to battle a coalition of southern Democrats and northern Republicans.

The President's program. President Truman's legislative program was ambitious. It called for an increase in the number of Americans covered by Social Security, for a program of national health insurance, for federal aid to education, and for an enlarged public-housing and slum-clearance effort.

Full employment. Truman did not flinch from the battle that achieving this program required. In the autumn of 1945, he proposed to Congress the Full Employment Bill, designed to assure jobs for all who were employable. The goal was 60,000,000 jobs—a figure that seemed visionary. The bill, which failed to pass, was much disputed because it would have required federal outlays in order to guarantee jobs.

A compromise proposal, which led to the Employment Act of 1946, did not contain a provision for federal expenditures but only a promise that the federal government would use all its resources to bring about full employment. Some people dismissed the act as a

Fitzpatrick in the *St. Louis Post-Dispatch*

Rising higher and higher in a tidal wave of inflation.

What is meant by "tidal wave"?

meaningless resolution. Others saw the law for what it was: acceptance by the government—in advance of economic depression—of the responsibility for heading off widespread unemployment.

Republican triumph. But national sentiment as a whole was turning against New Deal measures. By the middle of 1946, the country was in an anti-Democrat mood. In the fall elections, the Republican party captured both houses of Congress for the first time since 1928. Republican leaders, taking their victory as a sign of public anger over the strikes in basic industries, prepared now to regulate labor unions more closely.

The Taft-Hartley Act. The result was the Taft-Hartley, or Labor-Management Relations, Act of 1947. It affirmed the rights of labor guaranteed in the Wagner Act. But it extended the list of unfair labor practices to include the coercing of nonunion employees into a union shop, the refusal to bargain collectively, and the establishment of a secondary boycott—one against a firm other than the one being struck.

Unions were made liable for losses sustained as a result of illegal activity. They—as well as companies—were denied the right to make contributions to political parties; furthermore, they were now required to publish financial statements. Their officers had to sign affidavits stating that they were not Communists and did not advocate the overthrow of the government.

An unusual feature was the provision for a "cooling-off period": union or management had to give sixty days' notice of a decision to terminate a labor contract. Provision was also made for the government to obtain an injunction prohibiting for seventy-five or more days any threatened strike or shutdown that might endanger the national health or safety.

Truman vetoed the bill, to the delight of labor leaders. But Congress overrode the veto, as southern Democrats and northern Republicans found themselves on the same side in opposing the President. Despite dire predictions, the tension between labor and management greatly lessened in the years after the Taft-Hartley Act was passed.

A landmark in postwar labor history was the contract signed in 1948 between General Motors and the United Automobile Workers (the UAW), renewed in 1950. It provided for automatic wage increases for employees, based on increases in productivity. It also provided for the raising or lowering of wages in accordance with fluctuations in the cost of living as determined by government statistics.

Throughout the union movement there was a growing tendency for labor to seek and receive "fringe benefits," such as health and pension plans.† In pressing its demands, organized labor after December, 1955, spoke with a single voice for the first time in a generation. This was the result of the merger of the AFL ## and the CIO.

A POLITICAL CINDERELLA

In the struggle between the President and Congress, Truman's program was thoroughly beaten. Moreover, within the Democratic party itself, serious opposition to Truman was growing. Under attack from people within his own party, the President's chances for the nomination in 1948—let alone the election—seemed bleak.

The Democratic convention at Philadelphia. With little hope for victory and far from unanimous agreement, the Democrats nominated Truman. As his running mate they chose the popular Senate minority leader, Alben W. Barkley, of Kentucky. The platform included a strong civil rights plank. The President made a fighting speech that woke up the delegates—and was seen by millions in the first televised convention in history.‡

Dewey again. Confident of winning, the Republicans prepared for their convention, also to be held in Philadelphia. On the third ballot Governor Thomas E. Dewey, of New York, was nominated—the first time any defeated standard-bearer of the Republican party had been given another chance. His running mate was the dynamic governor of California, Earl Warren.

The Dixiecrats. The Republican chances seemed to be increased by two developments that had split the Democrats. The first was the bolt of a group of southerners—the Dixiecrats—from the Democratic party. They named J. Strom Thurmond, the governor of South Carolina, as their candidate. The principal argument of the Dixiecrats was that in pressing for civil rights legislation, the Democrats were violating state sovereignty.

---

† A new development was the so-called guaranteed annual wage, inaugurated in 1955 in agreements between the UAW and certain automobile manufacturers. It was an attempt to stabilize wages by providing a fund—to be maintained by the employers—from which workers temporarily laid off might supplement their benefits from unemployment insurance.

‡ Television, developed in the 1920's and 1930's, revolutionized communications after the Second World War, when sets became widely available. The first transcontinental telecast took place on September 4, 1951, allowing the nation to watch ceremonies in San Francisco connected with the signing of the peace treaty with Japan.

##Review the history of the CIO (see p. 654). What kind of unions did the AFL include? The CIO? (When the AFL and the CIO merged, craft and industrial unions were given equal rank.)

The day after the electoral upset, the newly elected President rejoices in Kansas City with fellow Missourians. Even members of his own party had predicted Truman's defeat.

The Progressives. The second development was the appearance of still another new "splinter" party, the Progressive party.§ It consisted of Communists and left-wing Democrats who disagreed with the strong stand Truman had been taking against the Soviet Union. The Progressives chose as their candidate Henry A. Wallace, formerly Vice-President.

An electoral surprise. In the campaign Truman traveled the length and breadth of the land on what he called a "whistle-stop" tour, pausing to deliver hundreds of extemporaneous talks in towns and villages everywhere. Even so, by fall the major public-opinion sampling services were predicting that Dewey would win easily.

On election night the nation listened in wonderment to the returns. By morning it was clear that an astounding political upset had occurred: Truman had won. He had polled slightly over 24,000,000 votes, and Dewey had a little under 22,000,000. Four of the southern states—South Carolina, Mississippi, Alabama, and Louisiana—had gone into the Dixiecrat column. Truman had carried the

§ This party should not be confused with the party of the same name that nominated Theodore Roosevelt for President in 1912 or the one that named Robert M. La Follette in 1924.

large industrial centers and the seven largest agricultural states. He had confounded his critics.

Inaugurating the Fair Deal. As Truman took office in January, 1949, he dedicated himself and his administration to obtaining a "fair deal" for the American people. In his inaugural address he listed the goals he would seek to achieve.

Point Four. Among these goals, the fourth—later called "Point Four"—was strikingly novel. The President said: ". . . we must embark on a bold new program for making the benefits of our scientific advances and industrial progress available for the improvement and # growth of underdeveloped areas." Truman had seen a need to confront the growth of communism in various parts of the world with imaginative uses of American capital—private and public.

Sum and Substance
1. What did the Employment Act of 1946 provide? The Taft-Hartley Act? 2. What new advantages did labor gain in the postwar years? 3. Who were the candidates for President in 1948? Who was elected? 4. What was "Point Four"?

#This signaled the beginning of the vast foreign-aid program of the United States. Why did Truman believe that such aid would help prevent the spread of communism?

This section covers foreign affairs from 1945 to the election of Eisenhower in 1952. The central theme is the spread of communism and the efforts made to combat it.

THE UNITED STATES FIGHTS A COLD WAR AND A HOT ONE

In the years after the Second World War, American diplomats and political leaders were more and more concerned with devising a foreign policy to combat the spread of Soviet power and influence. Other Western peoples shared in these efforts to defend the democratic way of life. Americans recognized as precious the privileges they enjoyed and that Communists were denied. These include the freedom of the individual citizen to think, speak, write, and worship as he pleases and to differ with his leaders.

Soviet spokesmen had long boasted that communism would one day dominate the entire world. They were determined to spread their system by any or all means—by persuasion, by force, by subversion. Americans were determined that this should not be.

OCCUPATION POLICIES

Overshadowing the differences between the Soviet Union, on the one hand, and the Western democracies led by the United States, on the other, was the fear of an all-out war. Both sides knew that such a clash could bring no victory for either of them and would probably bring doom to both. Germany became the first scene of the struggle for power between the two sides.

The four zones. At the Potsdam Conference in 1945, it had been agreed that Germany was to be divided into four occupation zones, one each under the United States, the Soviet Union, Britain, and France. The city of Berlin itself was to be jointly occupied by all four.

Disagreements on policy among the Big Four

Truman believed that Stalin would be amiable because he would want aid for war repairs.

At Potsdam, with their advisers, President Truman (*right, face turned to the camera*), Premier Stalin (*in white uniform*), and Prime Minister Attlee (*left foreground, chair pulled out*) sit down to talk.

Harry S Truman Library

#Stalin was a dictator, as Mussolini and Hitler were. All three established totalitarian governments. In dealing with communism, Americans faced another kind of totalitarianism.

were commonplace from the very start. The Soviets wanted to prevent Germany from rebuilding its industrial plants; the British wanted it to rebuild its industries in order to provide a healthy market for English goods once again. The position of the United States was somewhere in between: it was eager to avoid a revival of German military power and at the same time was hopeful that a new Germany would arise capable of withstanding aggression from outside its borders.

The Nürnberg trial. On one subject there *was* agreement: the desire to punish the Nazi leaders for having committed monstrous crimes against humanity and for having waged aggressive war. The trial of the "war criminals" began in the city of Nürnberg, Germany— where Hitler only a few years before had boasted that Germany's troops were invincible. The cases were tried before the International Military Tribunal, on which all the Big Four powers were represented. After sensational sessions that lasted ten months, the chief defendants were sentenced to death by hanging; others received prison terms.

Two Germanys. In 1948, after it was clear that the Soviet Union would not permit Germany to be unified, the Western countries permitted western Germans to draw up and adopt a new republican constitution. In 1949 Germany, meanwhile, became two distinct countries. One was Communist East Germany, a political satellite of the Soviet Union. The other was West # Germany—its capital at the city of Bonn— made by merging the three western zones. It had the strong moral and financial backing of the Western powers.

MacArthur in Japan. In Japan the problems connected with the occupation were simpler. Japan, unlike Germany, had not been divided into zones. The Supreme Allied Commander in the Pacific, General Douglas MacArthur, ruled Japan with a full authority in which the emperor himself concurred. MacArthur found the defeated enemy coöperative.

The execution of Tojo. A war-crimes trial in Japan, held, as in Germany, before the International Military Tribunal, punished several Jap-

anese war leaders. The most important was former Premier Hideki Tojo, who was sentenced to death and hanged.

THE MARCH OF COMMUNISM: CHINA

In Asia—as in Europe—the scene was already opening upon new aggression. Japan, now uneasily situated in the democratic camp, watched across the China Sea the gradual loss of China to Communist domination.

The end of the civil war. The fate of China was particularly upsetting to many Americans. After years of believing China might have an open door, they realized that the door had at last been slammed completely shut. What had happened?

When the Second World War ended, a civil war in China that had been suspended for years was resumed between the Nationalist Chinese, under Chiang Kai-shek, and the Chinese Communists, led by Mao Tse-tung. The United States openly supported the Nationalist forces. The Soviet Union was, on the other hand, obviously sympathetic to the Chinese ## Communists.

Marshall's mission. President Truman sent General George C. Marshall to China in 1945 to attempt to bring about a settlement between the Chinese Nationalists and the Chinese Communists. After a year of intense and frustrating effort, Marshall returned to admit failure. When he became Secretary of State in 1947, one of the administration's first actions was to withdraw the remaining American military and naval forces stationed in China.

Chiang Kai-shek on Taiwan. Late in 1948 news came that, after they had taken over Manchuria, the Chinese Communists were pressing southwest to overrun the remainder of China. In the latter part of 1949, Chiang Kai-shek himself fled the mainland of China and set up the Nationalist government on the island of Taiwan.

China proper now belonged to the Communists. To have prevented the triumph of the Communists in China would have required more men and materials than the United States was prepared to provide.

##Recall that during the war with Japan, the Communists had at least in part joined Chiang Kai-shek's forces to defeat Japan. Discuss the shift in the allegiances of China and Japan.

745

THE MARCH OF COMMUNISM: EUROPE

For the Western powers the most pressing question in international politics after 1945 was how to stop or contain Soviet expansion. By the spring of 1947, pro-Communist governments had been set up in Yugoslavia, Finland, Poland, Hungary, Romania, and Bulgaria, and the Communist pressure on Czechoslovakia was strong. The "Iron Curtain," a phrase coined by Winston Churchill, had descended on eastern Europe. Other countries were in danger of being whisked behind it.

The Truman doctrine. In February, 1947, Britain informed the United States that it no longer could afford to sustain the anti-Communist government in Greece it had created. Greek Communist guerrillas fighting the forces of the established government appeared to be receiving aid from Greece's Communist neighbors. If Greece fell under Communist—that is, So-viet—influence, Turkey, situated next door, would be seriously menaced. If Turkey then also fell under Soviet domination, a major disaster for the Western powers would have occurred in the strategically important eastern Mediterranean region.

In March Truman went before Congress to ask for an appropriation of $400,000,000 in economic and military aid for Greece and Turkey. His principles, immediately called the "Truman doctrine," were clearly stated, "I ## believe that it must be the policy of the United States to support free peoples who are resisting attempted subjugation by armed minorities or by outside pressures."

After long debate, the measure was passed. A threat to freedom anywhere in the world was now to be considered a threat to America's own freedom—and the nation was prepared to act accordingly. The United States would be fighting a new kind of war—a "cold war." This

Truman--unlike Wilson--sought advice and help from members of both leading parties.

President Truman makes a personal appeal to a joint session of Congress for aid for Greece and Turkey.

##Point out that Truman was proposing a major step in foreign policy and that his action illustrates the President's role of creating foreign policy.

#The money poured into West Germany enabled the Germans there to rebuild war-damaged areas and factories and in time to restore their country to prosperity. Meanwhile, East Germany remained ravaged and underdeveloped.

phrase was a way of describing hostilities that existed without open fighting.

Economic warfare. It was quickly apparent that aid would be required for countries other than Greece and Turkey. The United States decided it would have to fight with economic rather than with military weapons. It would concentrate on raising the living standards of people who might otherwise be tempted to accept communism.

The Marshall Plan. On June 5, 1947, Secretary of State George C. Marshall announced the remarkable proposal since labeled the "Marshall Plan." Under its terms, the United States offered to help the countries of Europe restore their "normal economic health." "Our policy," Marshall said, "is directed not against any country or doctrine, but against hunger, poverty, desperation and chaos."

The Soviet Union and its satellites rejected the offer. But by the fall of 1947 a conference

of other European countries formulated a plan requiring from the United States over four years about $22,000,000,000 in loans and outright assistance.

In December, 1947, President Truman asked Congress to approve granting $17,000,000,000 in aid during the next four years. The request was hotly debated. Already, from the end of the war in Europe to the spring of 1947, the country had spent about $11,000,000,000 in various forms of foreign aid. However, full recovery had not come to Europe. The Marshall Plan would cost billions more.

The fall of Czechoslovakia. When in February, 1948, a Communist government was established in Czechoslovakia, the arguments against Truman's bill were softened to a whisper. An act was passed creating the Economic Coöperation Administration to manage and distribute the funds for the European Recovery Program—the official name of the Marshall Plan. The

Vandenberg (third from left at left table) supported the Marshall Plan and the Truman doctrine.

Members of the House and Senate hear of Europe's needs from Marshall (*at end of small table, profile to camera*).

Wide World

Above: Back of Truman are Vandenberg (left), president pro tem of the Senate in 1947, and Joseph E. Martin, Jr., Speaker of the House. Both were Republicans.

AMERICAN AID TO EUROPE

COMMUNISM

Justus in the *Minneapolis Star*

One way of heating up the cold war.

Observe the dropping of one glove.

first appropriation was to be $5,300,000,000; more soon followed. (Altogether the United States gave about $12,000,000,000 in aid to western Europe between 1948 and 1951.)

Stemming the tide. Almost from the moment of its passage, the Marshall Plan was a success. By the end of 1949, western Europe's production of goods and services had been increased by 25 percent and of grains by 57 percent. These effects of the Marshall Plan undoubtedly helped to ward off Communist control of Italy —possibly even of France.

PRESSURE FROM THE SOVIETS

Another measure of the Marshall Plan's success was the growing tension between the Soviet Union and the Western powers. Unable to win the struggle for Europe by merely awaiting the lowering of the Europeans' standard of living, the Soviet Union now tried a new tack: it would try to force the Western powers to leave Germany.

The Berlin blockade. The Soviets in 1948 declared that when the four-nation rule of Germany had ended, the Western powers no longer had business in Berlin, situated in the center of # the Soviet zone of Germany. In June of that year, the Soviets shut off all rail, highway, and river traffic in and out of Berlin. Berliners living in the sectors assigned in 1945 to the Western countries were denied essential goods.

If the United States and the other Western powers had departed from the famous old German capital, they would have handed to the Soviets a uniquely important prize. Truman expressed United States policy: "We are going to stay, period."

The airlift. Immediately a gigantic airlift was organized by the United States to defeat the "Berlin blockade." At the height of its operation, between four and five thousand tons of supplies were being flown daily into the beleaguered city. In the spring of 1949, the Soviet Union, recognizing that the Western powers would not be driven out of Berlin, lifted the blockade.

The North Atlantic Treaty Organization. By the beginning of 1948, the Marshall Plan nations were aware that coöperative military measures might be as necessary as coöperative economic measures in discouraging the westward march of Soviet power. In March five nations—Britain, France, Belgium, the Netherlands, and Luxembourg—were linked in the Brussels Pact, each pledging itself to aid the others in case of military aggression.

The Senate welcomed this treaty by approving a resolution sponsored by Senator Arthur Vandenberg. The Vandenberg Resolution called for the United States to join such regional groupings of Western countries as might strengthen its own national security.

A result of the Vandenberg Resolution was a series of discussions that led to the signing of the North Atlantic Treaty at Washington on ## April 4, 1949. The nations that signed were the members of the Brussels Pact, together with Italy, Portugal, Denmark, Iceland, Norway,

##Point out that American foreign policy was bipartisan--representing two parties. Compare the situation Wilson faced in 1918 with the one Truman enjoyed in 1947-1949.

Canada, and the United States.||

Under the terms of the treaty, an armed attack against one country would be considered an armed attack against all. Moreover, joint military forces were to be organized. The institution formed for collective defense was called the North Atlantic Treaty Organization (NATO).

Never before in peacetime had the United States agreed in advance to go to the aid of a country outside the Americas in the event of # aggression. The break with the past policy of "no permanent alliances" was now complete. The United States made itself chiefly responsible for NATO's expenses. Americans had learned, as Secretary of State Dean Acheson said, that "if the free nations do not stand together they will fall one by one."

Eisenhower's return to Europe. Late in 1950 President Truman appointed General Dwight D. Eisenhower to be supreme commander of the military forces of NÁTO. By April, 1951, the Supreme Headquarters of the Allied Powers in Europe (SHAPE) was operating at top speed to create an effective defense force.

An atomic-arms race. Europeans had justifiable confidence in the strength of the United States because the United States was in exclusive possession of the atomic bomb. But that confidence was undermined in September, 1949, when President Truman announced that an atomic explosion had occurred inside the Soviet Union—a bomb had apparently been tested. An atomic-arms race was now on.

Making a hydrogen bomb. In the beginning of 1950, President Truman, after a period of painful decision-making, made another significant announcement. It was that he had directed the Atomic Energy Commission—which was responsible for nuclear developments in this country—"to continue its work on all forms of atomic weapons, including the so-called hydrogen or super-bomb." Late in 1952 the United States successfully exploded the first ## H-bomb. Shortly afterward, the Soviets duplicated this technological accomplishment.

|| In 1951 Greece and Turkey joined, and in 1954 the recently formed West Germany became a member.

UPI
Flour flown to Berlin by an American plane is unloaded. These men helped break the blockade.

THE KOREA TANGLE

A war with a Soviet puppet state—North Korea—confronted the United States in June, 1950. The consequences were far-reaching: not only was peace in Asia ruptured once again, but also the American domestic scene was seriously shaken.

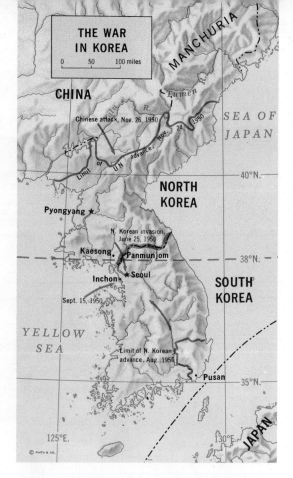

THE WAR
IN KOREA
0   50   100 miles

CHINA

Tumen R.

Chinese attack, Nov. 26, 1950

SEA OF
JAPAN

Limit of UN advance, Nov. 24, 1950

40°N.

NORTH
KOREA

Pyongyang ★

N. Korean invasion,
June 25, 1950

Kaesong ★ Panmunjom

38°N.

Inchon ★ Seoul

SOUTH
KOREA

Sept. 15, 1950

YELLOW
SEA

Limit of N. Korean
advance, Aug., 1950

Pusan

35°N.

125°E.

130°E.

JAPAN

© RAND & CO.

Having occupied North Korea since 1945, the U.S.S.R. had planned to extend communism into South Korea as well and dominate the whole peninsula.

Observe the Chinese-Korean border.

The 38th parallel. Long under Japanese rule, Korea had emerged from the Second World War a country divided into two parts—North Korea and South Korea—with the 38th parallel as the boundary line between them. This line lay just north of the city of Seoul (see the map above).

\# Free elections in South Korea, sponsored by the United Nations, had established the Republic of Korea. Its leaders hoped one day to incorporate North Korea into the Republic of Korea. Similarly, the Communist government in North Korea looked forward to attaching South Korea.

Hostilities. The thoughts of Americans were far from Korea when, early in the morning of
\#\# June 25, the Communist armies of North Korea marched across the 38th parallel, bent on unifying the country. This assault was more than

\#Recall that at Yalta the Soviet Union had been given an occupation zone in Korea.

an attack on the authority of the United Nations; it was, as Secretary of State Acheson said, "a challenge to the whole system of collective security . . . everywhere in the world."

United States forces in battle. On June 27 this country authorized the Supreme Allied Commander in the Pacific, General MacArthur, to use his air and naval forces to clear South Korea of its invaders. The Security Council of the United Nations passed a resolution urging the member countries to extend all aid necessary to repel the assault on the independence of South Korea.\#

The onrushing North Koreans before long overwhelmed the Republic of Korea's army. In response, President Truman on June 30 authorized MacArthur to send into action the ground units under his command and to blockade North Korea. In a few months, an American army of 210,000 men was fighting in Korea.

A police action under the United Nations. Early in July, MacArthur, at the request of the Security Council of the United Nations, was designated the commander of the unified fighting forces that might be provided by member nations. For the first time in history military force was being applied by an international organization to bring a halt to military aggression.

Outnumbered three, five—sometimes ten or twenty—to one, the combined American and R.O.K. (Republic of Korea) forces gradually retreated south on the Korean peninsula. (The brunt of the battle was being borne chiefly by American soldiers and those of South Korea.)

The race northward. By December, the retreat was over. A strong UN force (mainly American) struck northward, driving the North Koreans back. The UN empowered MacArthur to proceed across the 38th parallel in pursuit. With North Korean resistance collapsing fast, UN troops were able to race to the northern border of Korea, facing Manchuria.

Enter the Chinese Communists. The United States had assumed that a threat by the Chinese Com-

_____

\# The Soviet Union would unquestionably have vetoed this resolution, but at the moment its representative was absent from the Security Council.

\#\#By early 1949 both the Soviet Union and the United States had withdrawn their troops from Korea; but before leaving, the Soviets had trained a large Korean army.

Heavily clothed because of the weather, American troops return the fire of North Korean troops hidden in the mountains surrounding this town. The climate and terrain sharply challenged the military planners.

For the third time since 1917 Americans were fighting aggression abroad.

munists to intervene in the war if the UN forces crossed into North Korea was only a bluff. Between 200,000 and 300,000 Chinese Communist troops had massed in the mountain fastnesses of North Korea. These Chinese "volunteers," as they were called, struck the allied forces with devastating power.

Retreat again. The troops thus attacked now began a long, winding retreat. The weather was bitter cold; there were fierce snowstorms; and there was unknown treacherous mountain country for which American soldiers were ill trained. The radio in Peking, the Chinese Communist capital, sent word that the Communists intended to drive the UN troops into the sea.

The rearming of America. December, 1950, was one of the grimmest holiday seasons this country has ever known. Commanders of American troops stationed all over the world were in-structed to keep their units in a state of readiness. Within a very short time, America was arming itself and its allies with startling speed.

Heavy casualties. The Chinese Communists and the North Koreans failed to conquer South Korea, and their attempt was costing them dearly in men and supplies. Early in the summer of 1951, they announced that they were prepared to commence armistice negotiations. Meanwhile, the terrible bloodshed continued. Before hostilities finally ceased, American casualties alone totaled about 140,000, including 34,000 dead.

Truce talks. The truce talks that ensued seemed interminable. And, as casualties mounted, the war became increasingly unpopular at home. Americans felt they had a tiger by the tail. The conflict became a major issue in the elections of 1952.

#The Chinese troops were aided by Soviet-made jet planes. Americans saw the wisdom of restricting the war to Korea, and MacArthur was removed for advocating the bombing of China.

THE COMMUNIST ISSUE AT HOME

Americans were acutely aware that great changes in world affairs had been in the making for a long time. The industrialization of the Soviet Union, the decline of British influence, the growth of national feeling among colonial peoples, the shrinking of the world through advancing transportation and communication—all helped to account for these changes.

The case of Alger Hiss. New developments at home further upset Americans. An astonishing court case strengthened the growing suspicions that sinister forces were working to undermine the government—not to say engineer a "sell-out" to the Soviets. In 1948 Alger Hiss, a career man in the Department of State, was accused of having perjured himself in denying that he had engaged in Soviet espionage.

His accuser, Whittaker Chambers—whose own activities as a former Communist were most disturbing—remained unshaken in his amazing story of Hiss's subversive activities. Despite vigorous denials by Hiss and expressions of disbelief by his friends, Hiss was convicted after two sensational trials.

An atmosphere of distrust. Americans were profoundly shocked by the revelations in Hiss's trials in 1949 and 1950. Furthermore, there were occasionally other disclosures of Communist infiltration or attempted infiltration in high places. An atmosphere of distrust—for the most part unwarranted—developed.

The junior Senator from Wisconsin. Into this picture stepped an ambitious, self-assured young politician, the junior Senator from Wisconsin, Joseph R. McCarthy. He boldly claimed that he had a list of 205—later reduced to 57—names of people he asserted were Communists who were shaping policy in the Department of State. A Senate committee was not able to verify the charge, but McCarthy, undeterred, went from one accusation to another, inflaming the public.

"McCarthyism." McCarthy was cleverly exploiting a public inclination to believe that wicked conspirators here at home had brought the United States into troubles in international affairs. His accusations of disloyalty intimidated many Americans in public and private life in the years 1950 to 1954. Among the Senator's critics, the expression "McCarthyism" became familiar as a synonym for reckless name-calling.

Sum and Substance

1. Why do democracies oppose communism? 2. Describe the occupation of Germany. 3. What was the Nürnberg trial? 4. The Communists gained what victory in Asia? What action did the United States take as a result? 5. Name the parts of Europe that became Communist in the spring of 1947. 6. Describe the Marshall Plan. 7. Give the main facts about the Berlin blockade. 8. What caused the formation of NATO? 9. Give the background of the outbreak of hostilities in Korea. 10. What was "McCarthyism"?

Domestic history during Eisenhower's and Kennedy's presidencies is discussed in this section.

THE PENDULUM SWINGS FROM EISENHOWER TO KENNEDY

As 1952 began, the Republicans waited expectantly. Early in the year, President Truman took himself out of the running for the election, saying: "I shall not accept a renomination. I do not feel that it is my duty to spend another four years in the White House."**

** In 1951 the Twenty-second Amendment to the Constitution had been ratified. It limited any President to two terms in office (see page 808). Truman was exempted from the operation of this amendment because it had been made a part of the Constitution during his term of office.

A WIDE-OPEN RACE

By the time the Democrats met in Chicago in July, there were several favorite sons. Many of the delegates favored Adlai E. Stevenson, the governor of Illinois.

The nomination of Stevenson. On the third ballot Adlai E. Stevenson received one of the few genuine political draft calls in American history. A gifted man, Stevenson spoke with singular eloquence and grace.

"We like Ike." The Republicans, who also gathered in Chicago, were torn by a struggle between the delegates who supported Senator Robert A. Taft, of Ohio, and those who favored General Eisenhower. After exceedingly angry proceedings, Eisenhower was nominated on the first ballot to the chant "We like Ike."

Eisenhower's running mate was Richard M. Nixon, the California Senator who had brought the Hiss case to public attention. Eisenhower had not engaged in party politics before, but he turned this inexperience to his advantage. A "new man" in the national political arena, he was able through radio and television to display the simple sincerity that had made him an extraordinarily engaging war hero.

A landslide. The Republicans hammered away at instances of corruption in the Truman administration. They insisted that after twenty years of Democratic domination of the presidency, it was "time for a change."

But the most telling stroke in the Republican campaign was Eisenhower's dramatic promise near its end: "I will go to Korea." Widely interpreted as a promise to end the fighting—which it was not—the pledge made an irresistible appeal to Americans. The country's most successful general would bring to an end a costly, frustrating war.

\#   Eisenhower won by a landslide. He also became the first Republican to break into the solid South since 1928.

Truce in Korea. Eisenhower quickly made good his promise to go to Korea. Although his visit to the battlefront had no effect on the truce negotiations, it dramatized the intention of the President-elect to bring the exhausting war to a halt.

After Eisenhower discreetly threatened to use nuclear weapons, the Communist negotiators softened, and on July 27, 1953, a truce was signed. It provided for a line of demarcation between the opposing forces, near the 38th parallel. A commission consisting of members from neutral countries was created to supervise the armistice terms.

The Americans and their UN allies had prevented the success of aggression by a strong

Columbia University

President-elect Eisenhower flashes his famous grin. The letters spell "Alma Mater" (Columbia).

nation upon a weak one. Yet it was hard to rejoice—the thousands of casualties and the billions in expenditures sickened Americans. \#\#

A MODERATE ADMINISTRATION

With the ending of the struggle in Korea, the Eisenhower administration commenced on a

753

high note. The President hoped to elevate the tone of American politics. He had an instinctive faith in his countrymen's ability to discover and do what was right.

The Cabinet. The Eisenhower Cabinet contained a number of former supporters of Senator Taft, as the new President attempted to satisfy the friends of his recent rival. John Foster Dulles, a New York lawyer, became Secretary of State.

Accepting the reforms of the past. It was soon obvious that the Eisenhower administration did not intend to tamper with the main body of social reforms enacted in the previous generation. In fact, in 1954, 10,000,000 persons were added to the ranks of those entitled to receive Social Security benefits. Social Security was no longer an experiment; it had become a permanent part of the American system.

A political calm. Moderation became the theme of both major political parties by the middle of Eisenhower's first administration. A large number of Americans who had stood in bread lines in the 1930's were now homeowners, seeking to keep taxes down by reducing government expenditures. Significant disputes over domestic questions were fewer than at any time in recent years, although many farmers were distressed by the policies of Secretary of Agriculture Ezra Taft Benson, who sought to reduce farm surpluses by reducing benefits to farmers.

A new law for labor. Congress in 1959 enacted the first major labor law since the Taft-Hartley Act. It barred former convicts from holding union office and sought by a "bill of rights" to protect rank-and-file union members from abuses in leadership. It closed loopholes that had permitted certain kinds of secondary boycotts.

A SECOND TERM FOR "IKE"

Early in Eisenhower's administration it had become clear that Republicans in general were far less popular than the President himself. His renomination in 1956 became a certainty, and Vice-President Nixon was once more named to be his running mate.

On the first ballot, the Democrats again nominated Adlai E. Stevenson. Their nominee for the vice-presidency was Senator Estes Kefauver, of Tennessee.

The election returns. Eisenhower triumphed easily in November, polling about 35,500,000 votes. Stevenson received slightly more than 26,000,000. In the electoral college the results were even more decisive: 457 votes to 73. It was the most overwhelming presidential victory since Roosevelt crushed Landon in 1936. Crises in Southwest Asia, Poland, and Hungary, which had arisen shortly before the election, had brought fresh support to the President. Americans had felt the need to rely upon his prestige abroad and his intimate knowledge of military affairs.

A balance of facts. Two satisfying events of Eisenhower's second administration were the admission of Alaska and Hawaii to the Union. There were now fifty stars in the flag. But regrettably, Eisenhower's second term was characterized by an intensification of the cold war between the United States and the Soviet Union. United States foreign policy continued to be one of containing the Soviet Communists.

A YOUTHFUL CHIEF

Conscious of the increasingly heavy burden the man they chose would have to bear, Americans held the presidential election of 1960. Eisenhower was out of the race, being debarred by the Twenty-second Amendment from seeking a third term.

The party choices. Meeting in Los Angeles in July, the Democrats chose as their candidate Senator John Fitzgerald Kennedy, of Massachusetts. His rival for the nomination, the majority leader of the Senate, Lyndon B. Johnson, of Texas, became the party's choice for the vice-presidency. The Republicans, gathering in Chicago, nominated Vice-President Richard M. Nixon to carry their standard, the first Vice-President since Martin Van Buren designated by his party to succeed his chief. Nixon's running mate was Henry Cabot Lodge, Jr., of Massachusetts, the United States Ambassador to the United Nations.

#It should not be difficult for students to talk with someone who heard and saw the "debates."
What earlier debates had made at least one American political figure nationally known?
(The Lincoln-Douglas debates.)

New York Times

Candidate Kennedy speaks from an improvised platform at a hotel in New York City during his campaign for the presidency. Evident here are the youthfulness and handsomeness that strongly appealed to Americans.

Kennedy was forty-three years old in 1960.

The TV "debates" and the issues.

The stirring campaign was enlivened by a series of four "debates" on television, which, for the first time, enabled Americans everywhere to gauge their candidates in close comparison. There was considerable agreement that Kennedy took the measure of Vice-President Nixon and performed more impressively.

A vital issue that lay beneath the surface of public discussion was Kennedy's religion. Everywhere people were asking, Would the first Roman Catholic to run for the presidency since Alfred E. Smith in 1928 be defeated because of his faith?

##Recall the prejudice against Roman Catholics as presidential candidates (see pp. 625-626).
Discuss the fact that descendants of the "old immigration" were generally Protestant.

755

Wide World

The President, his wife Jacqueline, and their children.

The Kennedys had just left church.

A narrow triumph. The returns showed Kennedy to be the victor in the closest election since 1884 (see page 378). He had won by a margin of only about 120,000 out of nearly 69,000,000 ballots cast.

Because of his religion and people's attitudes toward it in the past, Kennedy had attracted the sympathies and the votes of many minority groups—particularly in states having some of the largest blocs of electoral votes. Further, Johnson's presence on the ticket had held southern states in the Democratic column. Finally, the excellence of Kennedy's performance on TV had gained him many admirers.

The Cabinet. Kennedy set about selecting his Cabinet with great deliberateness. His choices included for Secretary of State, Dean Rusk, president of the Rockefeller Foundation; for Secretary of Defense, the Republican Robert S. McNamara, president of the Ford Motor

#Large cities, such as Chicago, helped elect Kennedy. Large cities are traditionally Democratic.

Company; for Secretary of Labor, Arthur J. Goldberg, special counsel for the AFL-CIO; for Attorney General, the President's own younger brother, Robert ("Bob") Kennedy. Adlai Stevenson was appointed Ambassador to the United Nations.

A new emphasis. Kennedy, the first President born in the twentieth century, was a man of striking good looks, who presented a picture of vigor contrasting with the impressions made by other world leaders. Almost without exception, they belonged to his father's era. Said Kennedy in a moving inaugural address, delivered in front of the Capitol on January 20, 1961, "Let the word go forth from this time and place to friend and foe alike that the torch has been passed to a new generation of Americans. . . ."

Kennedy kept uppermost his awareness that the leadership of free humanity rested on his shoulders. To succeed in that delicate role was more than a matter of solving immediate pressing problems or even of making impregnable the physical defenses of the country. It meant inspiring people everywhere with the idea that America's democratic society ministers to the spirit as well as to the stomach.

The Peace Corps. No activity of the Kennedy administration better symbolized its imaginativeness and its affection for youth than did the establishment of the Peace Corps. Open to volunteers of both sexes and of all ages willing to work in the developing countries as teachers or "technician helpers," it generated widespread enthusiasm among American young people. The Peace Corps concentrated on the fields of education—particularly English-language teaching—agriculture, and urban renewal; it assigned its members only on the invitation of the nations seeking assistance.

The general success of the Corps' projects in many countries led to the expansion of its ranks. By mid-1967 almost 12,000 volunteers were at work on programs in forty-six countries of Asia, Africa, and South America.

The assassination of the President. The hopes and ambitions of the Kennedy administration were abruptly ended in the fall of 1963. On November 22, while riding at Mrs. Kennedy's side

##If possible, invite a returned member of the Peace Corps to speak to the class about his experiences. How does the Peace Corps carry out American foreign policy?

in an open automobile in Dallas, Texas, President Kennedy was mortally wounded in the head by gunfire and died a few minutes later in a local hospital. The man charged with the slaying, Lee Harvey Oswald, was himself killed in a bizarre shooting before he could be brought to trial.

For the fourth time in American history, a chief executive had been martyred during his term in office. As the stunned nation responded in anguish and outrage, Vice-President Johnson, in Dallas with the Kennedy entourage, took the presidential oath of office, becoming the thirty-

sixth president of the United States. The public's outpouring of grief reached its climax as uncountable millions watched John F. Kennedy's funeral on television and saw him laid to a hero's rest in Arlington National Cemetery.

Sum and Substance
1. Name the candidates, the issues, and the victors in the presidential elections of 1952, 1956, and 1960. 2. What characterized the first of the administrations? 3. What does the Twenty-second Amendment provide? 4. What event made Lyndon B. Johnson President?

AS A SUPERPOWER, AMERICA DEFENDS GLOBAL INTERESTS

In the foreign field—as well as at home—shattering changes and trends have been in the making since the Second World War. They have raised many issues that in duration have run beyond the four-year term of a President, extending from one administration to the next. To a greater degree than ever before, since 1945 a change in Presidents has involved the transfer to new hands of a vast backlog of unfinished business.

IN SOUTHEAST ASIA

In the titanic rivalry between the Free and the Communist worlds, moreover, international questions everywhere became America's immediate concern. Even when the interest of the United States was not strategically vital, the country put itself on the alert. This was because the Soviet and the Chinese Communists were working to persuade people, especially in the newly emerging nations, that the future would witness the triumph of communism over democracy. The United States strove to demonstrate that the *continuing* American Revolution —not the Russian Revolution—offers mankind the best blueprint for social progress and for the happiness of the individual.

In such an intense struggle, events almost daily seemed to endanger the general peace. The former colonial peoples watched intently the gigantic contest between the United States

and "the other side." Unhappily, some of them in Southeast Asia did not long remain mere spectators.

Indochina. After the Communists' seizure of control in China, the local Communist parties grew more active in almost every Asian country. Indochina, dominated by France since the nineteenth century, had been restored to the French after the Second World War. At that time, the people of Indochina had been granted self-rule but not independence, which they wanted.

In 1954, a long war against the French was continuing in Vietnam—the eastern part of Indochina—and Communist forces there inflicted serious defeats on the French colonial army. As the French withdrew from the country, widespread fear that the whole of Southeast Asia might fall to the Communists developed among the Western countries.

Geneva agreement. An important international conference was called to meet at Geneva beginning in April. The chief participating nations —the United States, the Soviet Union, Communist China, France, Britain—and Indochina agreed to a division of Vietnam at the 17th parallel. Northern Vietnam, with its capital at Hanoi, was surrendered to Communist domination, and the fate of southern Vietnam, with its capital at Saigon, was to be determined in a free election in 1956. In 1955 southern Vietnam became the Republic of Vietnam.

THE WORLD

A R C T I C   O C E A N

FRANZ JOSEF LAND (SOV. UN.)
SEVERNAYA ZEMLYA
NEW SIBERIAN ISLANDS
KOTELNY FADDEYEV
NOVAYA ZEMLYA
C. ZHELANIYA
KARA SEA
C. CHELYUSKIN
LAPTEV SEA
NOVAYA SIBIR
EAST SIBERIAN SEA
WRANGEL I.
PT. BARROW
BROOKS RA.
BEAUFORT SEA
C. BATHURST Inuvik
PRINCE PA. I.
LANDS END

TAYMYR PENINSULA
Nordvik
Tiksi
Vorkuta
Dudinka
Igarka
Arctic Circle
Verkhoyansk
Ambarchik
ANADYR RANGE
ALASKA
Nome Fairbanks Dawson
St. Michael MT. MC KINLEY 20,320 FT. Simps
Anchorage

Salekhard
Nizhnyaya Tunguska
VERKHOYANSK MTS.
Seymchan
GYDAN MTS.
Anadyr
ST. LAWRENCE
ST. MATTHEW I.
NUNIVAK I.
GULF OF ALASKA

S O V I E T   U N I O N
Olekminsk
Yakutsk
Magadan
Okhotsk
KAMCHATKA PEN.
KOMANDORSKIYE IS.
BERING SEA
PRIBILOF IS.
Sitka
Juneau
A L A S K A PEN.
KODIAK I. ALEXANDER ARCH.
Ketchikan Prir
QUEEN CHARLOTTE Rup
VANCOUVER I.

Yeniseysk
Tomsk
Krasnoyarsk
Kirensk
Aldan
Nikolayevsk
Komsomolsk
SAKHALIN
Petropavlovsk
C. LOPATKA
KISKA
ATTU Dutch Harbor
ALEUTIAN IS.

Sverdlovsk
Omsk Novosibirsk
Chelyabinsk Novokuznetsk
Barnaul SAYAN MTS.
Lake Baykal
Khabarovsk
SEA OF OKHOTSK
KURIL IS. (SOV. UN)

Karaganda
Balkhash Semi-palatinsk
Kyzyl
ALTAI MTS.
L. Balkhash
Ulan Bator
M O N G O L I A
GOBI DESERT
Vladivostok
MANCHURIA
Hakodate
HOKKAIDO
HONSHU
San Francis
Oakl

Alma-Ata
Tashkent
Samarkand
Yarkand
Urumchi
Lanchow
KUNLUN MTS.
Peking Mukden
Tientsin Tsingtao
KOREA Seoul
Pyongyang
Kyoto TOKYO
Nagoya JAPAN
Osaka Kitakyushu
Portla

Kabul AFGHANISTAN
Islamabad PAK.
Lahore
Delhi
MT. EVEREST 29,028
NEPAL
Chengtu
Chungking Wuhan
Changsha Foochow
Nanking
Shanghai
TAIWAN (FORMOSA)
BONIN IS.
MIDWAY IS.
HAWAIIAN ISLANDS (U.S.A.)
Honolulu
OAHU HAWAII

New Delhi
Hyderabad
Karachi
I N D I A
Bombay
Calcutta Dacca
Mandalay
Hanoi Canton
HAINAN
Rangoon
BURMA
KUNMING
Tropic of Cancer
WAKE (U.S.A.)
GUADA

Bangalore
Madras
Kozhikode
Hyderabad
Bangkok THAILAND
VIET-NAM
Saigon
LUZON
Manila
Quezon City
MARIANA ISLANDS (U.S.A. TRUST)
CAROLINE
GUAM (U.S.A.)
MARSHALL
BIKINI
PALMYRA
CHRISTMAS (BR. & U.S.A.)

Colombo CEYLON
DONDRA HEAD
NICOBAR IS. (INDIA)
ANDAMAN IS. (INDIA)
BAY OF BENGAL
CAMB.
GULF OF SIAM
SOUTH CHINA SEA
PHILIPPINES
MINDANAO
PALAU IS.
HALMAHERA
PONAPE ISLANDS (U.S.A. TRUST)
TARAWA
GILBERT ISLANDS (BR.)
Equato

MALDIVE ISLANDS
CHAGOS ARCHIPELAGO (B.I.O.T.)
Equator
Singapore
Padang MALAYSIA
SUMATRA
BORNEO
CELEBES
EAST INDIES
WEST IRIAN (INDON ADMIN)
NEW GUINEA (AUSTL. TRUST.)
NAURU
ELLICE IS. (BR.)
WESTERN SAMOA
STARBUCK (BR. & U.S.A.)
MALDEN (BR. & U.S.A.)
TONGAREVA
MANIHIKI IS. (N.Z.)
MARQUESAS IS. (FR.)

Djakarta
JAVA
CHRISTMAS (AUSTL.)
COCOS IS. (KEELING) (AUSTL.)
SUMBA TIMOR
TIMOR SEA
BANDA SEA
ARAFURA SEA
PAPUA (AUSTL.)
Port Moresby
NEW BRITAIN
SOLOMON
BISMARCK ARCH. (AUSTL.)
NEW HEBRIDES (BR. & FR.)
FIJI IS. (BR.)
TOKELAU (N.Z.)
TONGAREVA

I N D I A N   O C E A N
Tropic of Capricorn
Darwin
Cairns
Townsville
GREAT BARRIER REEF
CORAL SEA
NEW CALEDONIA (FR.)
LOYALTY IS. (FR.)
Suva
TONGA IS. (BR.)
Apia
SOCIETY IS. (FR.) TAHITI (FR.) Papeete
COOK IS. (N.Z.)
TUAMOTU OR LOW ARCHIPELAGO (FR.)

AMSTERDAM (FR.)
ST. PAUL (FR.)
NORTH WEST CAPE
Broome
Alice Springs
Carnarvon
Geraldton
A U S T R A L I A
GREAT VICTORIA DESERT
Brisbane
Darling
S O U T H   P A C
Tropic of Capricorn
PITCAIRN (BR.)

KERGUELEN (FR.)
Fremantle Perth
C. LEEUWIN
Albany
GREAT AUSTRALIAN BIGHT
Adelaide
Melbourne
Newcastle
Sydney
Canberra
TASMAN SEA
KERMADEC IS. (N.Z.)
O C E A N

HEARD (AUSTL.)
MC DONALD (AUSTL.)
BASS STRAIT
TASMANIA
Hobart
Invercargill
Auckland NORTH ISLAND
NEW ZEALAND
SOUTH ISLAND
Gisborne
Wellington
Christchurch
Dunedin
CHATHAM IS. (N.Z.)
BOUNTY IS. (N.Z.)
O C E

AUCKLAND IS. (N.Z.)
ANTIPODES (N.Z.)
CAMPBELL (N.Z.)
MACQUARIE IS. (AUSTL.)

SHACKLETON ICE SHELF
WEST ICE SHELF
Antarctic Circle
C. DARNLEY
MAC-ROBERTSON COAST
AMERY ICE SHELF
AMERICAN HIGHLAND
C. PENCK
C. HOADLEY
C. GOODENOUGH
W I L K E S   L A N D
BALLENY IS.
C. WILLIAMS
C. ADARE
Antar
WRIGLEY DA.
MT. SI 10,17

VICTORIA LAND
ROSS SEA
MT. EREBUS 12,280 FT.
ROSS I.
Little America
ROOSEVELT I.
C. WILSON
R O S S   I C E   S H E L F
BYRD
MT. MARKHAM 15,272 FT.

A N T A R C T I C A

Longitude East of Greenwich   Longitude West of Greenwich

A-510000-22 -4°5-17ᴺ
COSMO SERIES WORLD
Copyright by
RAND MCNALLY & COMPANY
Made in U.S.A.

759

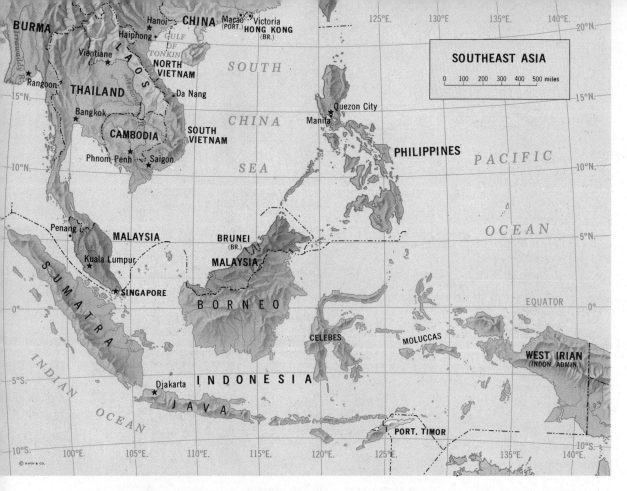

East Asia and the region shown here have been centers for Communist activity and of consequent American con-cern for years. What countries make up Southeast Asia? Observe how near each is to Red China.

Southeast Asia includes all of Burma, its neighbors, and the Philippines and Indonesia.

Laos. In 1960 a Communist upsurge in neighboring Laos, carrying with it the possibility of Chinese intervention, became a stark challenge to peace in that part of the world. It seemed incredible that American interest should be involved in a tiny landlocked Asian country, but a glance at the map on this page shows why. Laos has common borders with Red China, Vietnam, Burma, Thailand, and Cambodia. If # Laos were to fall into the Communist camp, it could become a gateway for a drive into the rest of Southeast Asia.

A "neutralist" settlement. The danger to both East and West was obvious, but both sides seemed convinced, too, that Laos was not worth a war. Consequently, at a meeting in Vienna in 1961, Kennedy and Khrushchev agreed to establish "a neutral and independent Laos." Prince Souvanna Phouma, a so-called neutralist, was installed in the summer of 1962 as premier and head of a coalition government representing rival factions.

In the jungles of South Vietnam. But peace was broken by events in Vietnam. The North Vietnamese leader, Ho Chi Minh (*Hoh chee min*), expected to take over South Vietnam in the elections promised for 1956, but they were never held. The South Vietnamese regime refused to be bound by the Geneva agreement, declaring that it had been made by a foreign military command—the French. Saigon also charged that Hanoi had built up its military strength in violation of the Geneva agreement. Soon after the date for the elections passed, Communists (called Vietcong) began guerrilla warfare in South Vietnam against the government there, which was supported by the United States.

#The map shows how the countries of Southeast Asia are situated in relation to China. Recall the entrance of the Chinese Communists into the Korean War.

A major buildup. During the Eisenhower administration, the United States sent military "advisers" in order to help South Vietnam, but in 1961 it began a major buildup of troops there. By the spring of 1967, almost 450,000 American men under the command of General William C. Westmoreland were engaged in a cruel war in the jungles of South Vietnam.

In their effort American military forces had to learn the tactics and strategy required by guerrilla warfare. In this kind of skirmishing, men fight in small units on a hit-and-run basis, live off the land, and melt into the general population when surrounded. Because North Vietnam has been used as a base and because people in Laos and Cambodia have helped the guerrillas, the drive on South Vietnam has been hard to resist. Further, the Vietcong have had the direct assistance of North Vietnamese regulars, a considerable part of the population of South Vietnam, and equipment from Red China and the Soviet Union.

In the late winter of 1965 the United States, holding Hanoi responsible for the aggression against South Vietnam, started to bomb North Vietnam. This step was intended to raise the price of North Vietnamese aggression, to lift the morale of the South Vietnamese, and to slow the supplying of the Vietcong. Hanoi responded by infiltrating South Vietnam at an increased rate with both guerrilla fighters and North Vietnamese regulars.

A struggle against aggression. Many Americans have insisted that the United States has no business being in Vietnam and that its activity there may lead to a war with China or even with the Soviet Union. The administration's position has been that the aggression of the Vietcong must be halted in order to discourage other such wars of "national liberation."

Westmoreland said he felt that the Negro soldiers understood best what the war was about.
General Westmoreland with troops in South Vietnam. Negroes made up over 20 percent of the American forces.

Rentmeester from *Life* Magazine, © Time, Inc.

Although about 70 percent of all Negroes were rejected by the draft, the proportion of Negro combat troops is nearly double the ratio of Negroes to whites in the nation.

The United States has tried—but has failed—to bring the North Vietnamese to peace talks. Meanwhile, the waging of the war against the enemy has been severely hampered by the inability of successive Saigon governments to make themselves generally popular with their own people.

Red China. In the background of the struggle over Vietnam looms Communist China. Although torn by internal dissension, its potential strength and enormous population give it an impressive position. It shows signs of operating under at least two powerful pressures. One is its competition with the Soviet Union for leadership of the Communist World. Developing differences between the two countries have sharpened this struggle.

A second pressure is the catastrophic long-term food shortage that has produced widespread suffering within China. A combination of national calamities and misguided agricultural and industrial programs has served ill a population of over 700,000,000 human beings. The Chinese, at the present rate of growth, will number 1,000,000,000 within the present generation.

The pressures, different in kind but tightly intertwined, could dictate expansionist policies—for prestige and power and for new and possibly more productive land. Important signals were the severity of the Chinese in crushing rebellion in Tibet in 1959 and their invasion of northern India in 1962.

IN SOUTHWEST ASIA AND NORTH AFRICA

At one time, the political and economic stability of the vast predominantly Arab region of Southwest Asia and North Africa was maintained by Britain and France, Western countries long influential there. British interest and control had been felt at various times in Jordan, Iraq, Palestine, and Egypt. But the decline in British power after the Second World War persuaded the United States to take over many of Britain's international obligations.

Intense Arab nationalism, especially, presented many difficulties. The Arab peoples had long desired a larger share in the oil resources of their own lands. Their recent history made them anti-British—and anti-French—in their points of view, and correspondingly subject to Soviet allurements.

The state of Israel. Complicating relationships with the Arabs was the new state of Israel, created in 1948 as a homeland for the Jewish people. Israel's neighbors, organized into the Arab League,‡ pledged themselves to destroy the infant country, one of the few successful democracies to appear in recent times.

Arab armies invaded Israel but were defeated in the war that followed in 1948–1949. (Ralph Bunche, the UN mediator who arranged the armistice halting the fighting, received the Nobel Prize for Peace in 1950, the first Negro so honored.)

Sympathetic to the Israelis, but also interested in the friendship—and oil—of the Arabs, the United States has wavered from apparent support of one side to apparent support of the other. The Arabs often seem interested only in playing Americans off against the Soviets for their own advantage. For example, the Egyptians overthrew their king in 1952 and soon established a republic. In 1954 Gamal Abdel Nasser became Egypt's prime minister. Not long afterwards, he was elected president and assumed dictatorial powers.

In the fall of 1955, Egypt began to receive arms in large quantities from the Soviet Union and Czechoslovakia—a Soviet satellite. This strongly suggested that Egypt might soon fall into the Soviet orbit. To outbid the Soviets for Egyptian support, Secretary of State Dulles offered financial aid to Egypt for the construction of the new, long-projected Aswân Dam. Like the first Aswân Dam, it would harness the power of the Nile River for the production of electricity. After repeated anti-West actions by Egypt, however, Dulles withdrew the offer.

Seizure of the Suez Canal. Dulles' action brought swift retaliation by Egypt. Needing money, Nasser in July, 1956, seized the Suez Canal, taking over its operation from the British and

---

‡ The charter members were Syria, Lebanon, Jordan, Iraq, Saudi Arabia, Yemen, and Egypt. Libya later became a member.

##"Southwest Asia" correctly names the part of Asia long known as the Middle East, a term meaningful only to Europeans. (Egypt is not in Asia; it lies in North Africa.)

Another group of students might conduct a discussion of relations between the United States and Southwest Asia and North Africa. After doing research, the students should present the views of the Israeli and the Arabs, which led to the Arab-Israeli War.

French. This was a breach of the agreement under which the canal had been constructed. Attempts to make the Egyptian prime minister accept international operation of the waterway proved unavailing.

The outbreak of war. Meanwhile, Israel, angered by repeated attacks on its citizens from Egyptian bases, began an attack on Egypt in November, in order to destroy those bases. While Israel's armies plunged into Egypt from the east, the British and French—possibly in coordination with the Israelis—struck Egypt from the Mediterranean island of Cyprus.

When the British and French announced that they would stay in the canal zone and operate the waterway, the Soviet Union hinted darkly of a plan to send "volunteers" to Egypt.

Eisenhower made it clear that the United States, through the UN, would oppose Soviet intervention. England and France both yielded to United States and Soviet pressure to withdraw from the canal zone. As part of the settlement, a United Nations Emergency Force (UNEF) was stationed on Egyptian soil to serve as a buffer between Egypt and Israel along the armistice line.

The Eisenhower doctrine. In addition to having to # mend relations with its allies, the United States was faced with the necessity of maintaining Western prestige in Southwest Asia and North Africa to avoid seeing countries there fall under Soviet influence. The President acted quickly. He called upon Congress to enact what is called the "Eisenhower doctrine" for nations

This meeting was held at the time of the Suez crisis.
Dulles (*at Eisenhower's right*) reports to the President and other members of the Cabinet.

Abbie Rowe for National Park Service

#Secretary of State Dulles, whom Eisenhower greatly respected, was responsible for the Eisenhower doctrine. He forced Britain and France to stop the attack on the Suez Canal.

763

Wide World

Nasser, looking pleased (*third from right, at the table*), and the deputy premier of Iraq (*wearing glasses*) sign a new military alliance in Cairo on June 4, 1967. The third Arab-Israeli war began the next day.

Nasser, an army colonel, became dictator after the army overthrew the Egyptian king.

of the region, similar in purpose to the Truman doctrine for Greece and Turkey.

The Eisenhower doctrine, incorporated into law in March, 1957, authorized the expenditure of up to $200,000,000 annually for economic and military assistance. It also provided that military aid might even involve the use of United States armed forces. These would protect the countries in that area of the world from armed aggression on the part of any # nation controlled by international communism.

The underlying conditions. Plainly, several influences were operating in the region. The first was Arab nationalism. After years of foreign domi- ## nation, many Arabs wished to create a single powerful Arab nation. A second influence was the interest of the West. The region is the chief source of oil to turn the wheels and machines of western Europe. A third was that after the shame and tragedy of the destruction of the Jews by Hitler, the West had committed itself to supporting Israel as a Jewish homeland. A fourth influence was the interest of the Soviet Union. The Soviets were exerting themselves to win a foothold in this valuable region by posing as the "friend of the Arabs."

##Recall that after the First World War Britain and France had acquired mandates in Southwest Asia and North Africa. Britain had held Palestine.

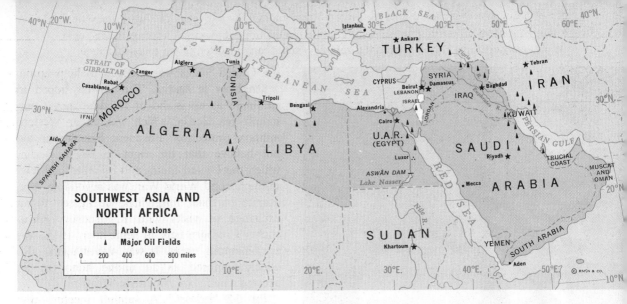

SOUTHWEST ASIA AND
NORTH AFRICA

Arab Nations
▲ Major Oil Fields

0 200 400 600 800 miles

Israel, a nation of 2,000,000 people, is surrounded—except on the northwest—by hostile Arab, Moslem countries. Which countries of Southwest Asia and North Africa are not Arab countries?

The Arab-Israeli war of 1967. President Nasser in the late spring of 1967 aimed to turn circumstances to his advantage, possibly in order to shore up his own tottering regime and to reassert his leadership in the Arab world. He decided to insist that UNEF be withdrawn; UN Secretary-General U Thant obliged him almost immediately. Nasser's own troops, now unrestrained, imposed a blockade on Israeli shipping through the Gulf of Aqaba, placing Israel in a desperate position because the Gulf is a lifeline for trade.

The United Arab Republic (as Egypt is known officially) and its allies, Syria, Jordan, Iraq, and Kuwait, confident of their strength and their Soviet military equipment, were laying plans to destroy Israel—as they had often said they would. Israel, encircled by enemies, and militarily outnumbered by at least two to one, made plans, also.

Despite international peace efforts, war broke out on June 5. Within a few days Israeli forces won a smashing victory over their Arab enemies—to the astonishment of the world and to the satisfaction of the West (for the victory was, in effect, a defeat for the Soviet Union). Because the Arab countries broke diplomatic relations with the United States and shut off supplies of oil, the United States faced the necessity once more of rebuilding its relations with the countries of the region.

Identify the areas claimed by Israel as a result of the war.

ISRAEL

Area gained in
Arab-Israeli War

0 20 40 60 80 miles

#What was the United States giving its major attention to at the time? (The Vietnam War.) The Soviet Union was able to rearm the Arab countries and entrench itself in the region.

765

New York Times

Eisenhower and Khrushchev during the latter's visit.

A star represents the Communist party.

IN EUROPE

In Europe a major crisis of steady duration began in late 1958. At that time Soviet Premier Nikita S. Khrushchev demanded that the Western Big Three withdraw their troops from Berlin and sign peace treaties with West and East Germany. The Western powers announced flatly that they would not abandon Berlin. Moreover, they knew that separate treaties with the two Germanys would end the hope of ever reunifying Germany in freedom—a goal the United States was pledged to help attain.

Khrushchev in America. The Soviets hoped to eliminate as an island of freedom in a Communist sea Berlin, which was under Western military protection. President Eisenhower did not believe that the right to be in Berlin, which the United States and its allies had won in the Second World War, was negotiable. Yet, despite personal misgivings, he agreed to an exchange of visits with Khrushchev. Khrushchev's sojourn here in September, 1959, was a momentous event. It was, nevertheless, also widely opposed as an undue honor to an avowed enemy of American ideals.

The U-2 "incident." A summit meeting was # planned for the end of May, 1960, in the city of Paris, to be attended by Eisenhower, Khrushchev, the British prime minister Harold Macmillan, and President Charles de Gaulle of France. But a dramatic event intervened. On May 1 a United States high-altitude reconnaissance plane, a U–2, flying well inside the air space over the Soviet Union, was brought down, apparently by Soviet rocket fire.

The pilot admitted that his mission had been to map military targets in the Soviet Union for the use of the Central Intelligence Agency in Washington. Khrushchev expressed himself as horrified that the President approved such "aggressive acts."

Wrecking the Paris "summit." Eisenhower and his colleagues from western Europe journeyed to Paris, but the summit parley was never held. In an incredible display of temper, Khrushchev insisted, as an impossible condition for sitting down to negotiate, that Eisenhower apologize for the U–2 "incident."

The question of separate treaties. Finding the United States firmly standing its ground concerning Berlin, Khrushchev awaited the choice of a new American President. In the late spring of 1961, when he met Kennedy for the first time, he talked of a six-month deadline for settling the question, warning that the Soviets would sign their oft-threatened separate ## peace treaty.

The Soviets' trump card was that the signing of a separate treaty with East Germany—

##Emphasize the position of the Western countries, which wanted a united, free Germany. Recognizing East and West Germany (by signing separate treaties) would have been bad.

#See p. 720 (the picture and caption). In what sense was the building of the Berlin Wall a confession that communism in East Berlin and in East Germany was a failure? Why does a totalitarian government deny free travel and communication to the people it controls?

a Soviet satellite—would allow them to turn over to it control of the routes of access to Berlin. This strategy, they hoped, would bring about virtual Western recognition of East Germany by forcing the West to deal with it in order to maintain traffic into the city. But the Western powers held to their position of refusing to recognize East Germany as a sovereign state, reaffirming their right to move freely in and out of Berlin.

Kennedy—like Eisenhower before him—restated the right of the Western powers to be in Berlin. He called for and obtained a buildup of United States armed strength, and he asked for an increase in the expenditures for civil defense.

The Soviet countermove was quick, partly because of the steady traffic of people fleeing East Germany via West Berlin. Khrushchev described the existence of this prospering oasis within his empire as a "bone in my throat."

The Berlin Wall. The measures the Communists took to end the movement of people were
stern. The first was to close the famous Brandenburg Gate at the line between East and West Berlin. The second was to seal off any movement of people between the two parts of the city by building between them a high wall of concrete and barbed wire. The effect on the world was startling: on *both* sides of the Iron Curtain, it looked like the wall of a prison, designed to prevent escape.

The Common Market. Not all the issues the United States faced concerned hostile governments. One of the most serious and interesting has involved American relations with the European Economic Community, sometimes called the EEC and more familiarly the Common Market. This organization brought together in 1958 the six nations of France, West Germany, Italy, Belgium, the Netherlands, and Luxembourg in order to tear down the old economic barriers that historically separated them. They
established a common market for buying and selling agricultural and manufactured goods. The members aim ultimately to unify the economic systems of their countries.

The Common Market is already a powerful

Wide World

Adding to the Berlin Wall—the German "wall of shame."
Why is it a wall of shame?

economic factor in world affairs. As the member nations become more closely knit, it may well prove to be a new superpower, joining the ranks of the United States and the Soviet Union at the head of the parade of nations. Maintaining good relations with the Common Market is politically and economically important to the United States. Many people regard as inevitable the establishment of an Atlantic union of nations, with which the United States would have to be friendly.

##The Common Market has helped maintain and increase European prosperity. Stress that it is an economic union--not a political union--of the countries.

IN LATIN AMERICA

Before and during the Second World War the emergencies of war and diplomacy made it necessary for the United States to give Latin America much more attention than previously. The Rio Pact of 1947, committing the nations of the Americas to a realistic awareness of the need for collective security and mutual defense, seemed to indicate a perpetuation of this trend.

Shortchange of foreign aid. The cold war, however, forced the United States to shift its emphasis to containment of communism in Europe and Asia and to neglect the special problems of Latin America. Between 1946 and 1961 Latin America received only about 6 percent of United States foreign aid. Even this aid did not seep down to the level of the great mass of people. (The population of Latin America, now more than 200,000,000, has been increasing at a yearly rate in excess of that of any other area in the world.)

Guatemalan upheaval. As a result of poverty and frustration among the people, communism has made an effective appeal in many countries. Communist ministers entered the cabinets of Cuba, Chile, and Ecuador (see pages 758–759), and the Communist party of Guatemala gained great strength between 1946 and 1952. Under President Jacobo Arbenz the Communists held the upper hand in the government. To achieve complete power Arbenz in 1954 began to import arms from Communist nations in Europe.

In response, the United States sent arms and military aid to the adjoining state of Honduras. There an exiled colonel, Carlos Castillo Armas organized an army, presumably with United States assistance, and used it to return to Guatemala and overthrow Arbenz. Armas was assassinated in 1957. His successor was shortly overthrown by a military clique.

In Latin America generally—as in Guatemala —the lack of an established middle class has stood in the way of the development of democracy. A result has been public impatience or reliance on extremely conservative or even reactionary governments.

Anti-Americanism. Americans generally became acquainted in 1958 with the virulence of anti-United States sentiment in Latin America as a result of Vice-President Nixon's difficulties on a South American tour. In Lima, Peru, he was mobbed; and in Caracas, Venezuela, where his automobile was hit by stones and eggs, he was forced to abandon the remainder of his trip.

Castro of Cuba. Further, developments only 90 miles from the coast of Florida on the island of Cuba gave the United States a sobering shock. Premier Fidel Castro, who had led a successful revolution against the Cuban dictator General Fulgencio Batista (Fool*hen*syo Ba*tee*sta), brought about sweeping economic and political changes. These included not only long-overdue reforms but also the seizure of foreign holdings of property.

Having postponed the elections he had promised, Castro made savage anti-Americanism a # weapon of his dictatorship. Moreover, he accepted economic and technical aid from the Soviet and Chinese Communists, as well as arms from Moscow. If the Castro movement should spread to other Latin American countries, Soviet influence would increase, and the Monroe Doctrine would be seriously challenged. The repercussions would be worldwide.

One answer of the United States was to stop the importation of Cuban sugar and to halt all American exports to the island except food and medicines. Just before Kennedy's inauguration, Cuba ordered the United States to cut the size of its embassy staff. Angrily the United States met this new affront by breaking diplomatic relations.

Disaster at the Bay of Pigs. What to do about Cuba was one of the first issues facing President Kennedy. In April, 1961, an invasion of the island at the Bay of Pigs (see page 540) ## by anti-Castro exiles failed. The United States had sanctioned the undertaking but had failed to give it the necessary military and naval support. The fiasco dealt a stunning blow to the prestige of the United States.

The Alliance for Progress. By the late summer a new program had restored in many Latin Americans confidence in United States meth-

768 ##An able student could provide the class with details about the Bay of Pigs disaster. Emphasize the word _fiasco_. The Bay of Pigs may be located on the map on p. 540.

ods. At the resort town of Punta del Este in Uruguay, the Alliance for Progress—a ten-year aid program—was ratified by the United States and, after considerable State Department pressure, by all the Latin American countries except Cuba.

According to the terms of the Alliance, the United States promised, over a period of a decade, at least $20,000,000,000 in aid. (In 1965 President Johnson pledged that the Alliance would be extended beyond 1971. Its aims would take longer to achieve than originally planned.)

The Alliance set ambitious goals that included a bold attack on illiteracy, malaria, and slums. It proposed to promote, also, tax and agricultural reforms and to redistribute for the benefit of the needy both the national income and the large landholdings long in the hands of a minority of Latin Americans.

The missile crisis. Cuba, however, remained a particular source of difficulties. In the summer of 1962, the Soviets began an arms buildup of Cuba, which the United States accepted as "defensive." Suddenly in late October, aerial reconnaissance photographs showed that the Soviet Union was constructing offensive missile bases able to bring into firing range most of the major cities of the New World.

\# Kennedy immediately ordered a naval "quarantine" of Cuba as the first step toward the "prompt dismantling and withdrawal" of the Soviet installations. As soon as Khrushchev saw that the United States meant business, he yielded. He promised that the Soviet missiles and jet bombers would be dismantled and returned to the Soviet Union under UN supervision. Aerial photographs indicated that Khrushchev was living up to his pledge, although Castro refused to accept on-the-spot inspection of the missile sites.

Landings in the Dominican Republic. In April, 1965, a new source of anxiety developed in the

\#\# Caribbean. A political coup in the Dominican Republic turned into a civil war threatening the lives of Americans there. President Johnson, mentioning also a possibility of a Communist take-over, sent in United States marines. By the time of the peaceful inauguration of President Joaquín Balaguer on July 1, 1966, most of the 30,000 troops had been withdrawn. The remainder left soon afterward.

The Panama crisis. Another very delicate situation arose in 1964 when anti-American riots occurred in the Panama Canal Zone. President Johnson responded by announcing that the United States would "press forward with Panama and other interested governments, in plans and preparations for a sea level canal. . . ." Furthermore, the United States and Panama would negotiate an entirely new treaty regarding the existing Panama Canal (see page 540). Johnson also promised that the new treaty would recognize Panama's control over the present canal zone. The treaty agreed upon in June, 1967, provided for the surrender of absolute United States control of the Panama Canal Zone. Panama would share in the operation of the canal and would receive more of the financial returns.

Toward an American common market. Joint undertakings were also in the minds of the presidents of the American republics who met in Punta del Este in the spring of 1967. In the Declaration of the Presidents of the Americas the signers inaugurated a movement to found a Latin American common market by 1970 and put it into "substantial operation" by 1985. A chief aim was the lowering of tariffs among members.

Two other important steps were contemplated: an arrangement permitting capital and labor to flow freely from one country to another and the establishment of a common currency. The guarded optimism of the conference was summed up by President Fernando Belaúnde Terry of Peru: "The documents of this conference are like the score of a symphony. It all depends on how it is played."

IN AFRICA SOUTH OF THE SAHARA

In Africa there were troubles, too, no less threatening to the United States because it was only indirectly involved. One of the most baffling was the struggle for power in The Congo, following the end on June 30, 1960, of seventy-

##Discuss the meaning of "coup." (An unexpected stroke, or blow; pronounced ko͞o.)
Opinions of the landing in the Dominican Republic were mixed. Why?

769

five years of Belgian rule. This area, which produced one-half of the Free World's uranium, was notably unprepared for self-rule when independence came.

In July the United Nations sent a military force to help establish order there. It was soon caught in a fierce, many-sided contest.

Pinning its hopes on the success of the UN effort, the United States was aware that on the outcome might well depend the course of America's future relations with other newly freed African and Asian countries. Although they were in rivalry with each other, the Soviets and the Chinese employed the tragic situation for propaganda ends. They sought to persuade the Congolese that the UN troops really represented, in a new form, the old imperialism they had cast off.

SECURITY FOR THE FREE WORLD

In addition to joining NATO, the United States has entered into a number of other defense agreements. Their effect has been to give the United States military and moral commitments to defend almost fifty countries.

The OAS. The Organization of American States —the OAS—was established at Bogotá, Colombia, in 1948 by agreement of twenty-one American republics. It is committed to protect the mutual security of the signatories.

ANZUS and SEATO. In 1951, the ANZUS Treaty was concluded, joining Australia, New Zealand, and the United States in a guarantee of close coördination in meeting mutual needs of military defense.

Considering this arrangement inadequate in the light of the Indochina crisis, in September, 1954, Britain and the United States took steps to establish the Southeast Asia Treaty Organization—SEATO. Comparable to NATO, this alliance has as members the United States, Australia, France, New Zealand, Pakistan, the Philippines, Thailand, and the United Kingdom.

SEATO is not as firm an alliance as NATO. The signers did not, as members of NATO did, agree in advance to an immediate resort to arms in the event of aggression against any member.

CENTO. In Southwest Asia the United States worked closely with members of the Baghdad Pact from 1958 on—even though the United States was not formally a member. The original members in 1955 were Iraq, Iran, Pakistan, Turkey, and Britain. In 1959 its name was changed to the Central Treaty Organization— CENTO.

NATO today. The alliances have not been unchanging. Even NATO, the most important and powerful of the alliances, has been altered significantly and may require further revisions. In 1966 President de Gaulle informed the United States and its NATO allies that all NATO forces and bases on French territory would have to be under French control. Early in 1967 NATO moved these forces and bases to Belgium.

Foreign aid. In their quest for security, Americans have also relied on their ability to win the respect and friendship of the so-called neutral or uncommitted nations, which have not openly taken sides in the cold war. To them the United States sent in the years from 1946 to 1965 over $116,000,000,000, of which two-thirds was economic aid and one-third military.

Intercontinental bombers. The defense of the United States in the final analysis rests heavily on the power of the bombers of the United States Strategic Air Command (SAC). This organization is the portion of the Air Force responsible for conducting air attacks—in case of war—against any designated target anywhere in the world. It has the resources to deliver "massive retaliation" against any nation ## attacking the United States.

Intercontinental missiles. The defense system of the United States includes also intercontinental ballistics missiles (ICBM's). The success of the powerful Atlas missile has given the United States, and, therefore, the Free World, an operational ICBM. Moreover, in 1960 the Polaris missile, which can be fired 1200 miles from a submerged submarine, was added to the American arsenal. In 1961, the huge Minuteman missile—60 feet long, weighing 70,000 pounds, and capable ultimately of reaching a target 6300 miles away at a speed of more than

The explosion of this atomic bomb at the Nevada test site was the last before the nuclear-test ban treaty.
Every nuclear explosion produces a fireball of intensely hot gases.

15,000 miles an hour—was fired from an underground "silo."

The designing of a missile that can destroy an enemy's missile in flight—a "bullet to hit a bullet"—became a necessity as the international arms race gained momentum. In 1967 the Defense Department announced that the United States would build as a shield against # Chinese nuclear attack an anti-ballistic missile system costing $5,000,000,000.

A nuclear-test ban treaty. From 1958 on a promising truce on the testing of atomic weapons had been in effect. But in 1961 the Soviet Union resumed testing in the atmosphere, high over Asia. Before their series of shots was

completed, the Soviet scientists had detonated an H-bomb of incredible explosive force— 3000 times more powerful than the A-bomb that destroyed the city of Hiroshima in 1945. One effect was to increase the pressure on President Kennedy to order a resumption of United States testing, which he reluctantly authorized.

From the time of the cessation of testing in 1958, talks were held at Geneva, Switzerland, aimed at achieving a ban on nuclear testing. Repeatedly they foundered on the divergent positions of the United States and the Soviet Union, especially about inspection to insure compliance. But in 1963 the Soviet Union, in

#What does such a system consist of? (Of powerful radar posts capable of warning of a surface attack by an ICBM or other ballistic missile.)

a sudden about-face, decided to accept a Western offer of long standing: a ban on nuclear testing in the atmosphere, in space, and under water.

Shortly, in Moscow, representatives of the United States, Britain, and the Soviet Union signed a treaty embodying this agreement. Other nations also accepted its terms. France, aspiring to be a nuclear power, and Red China, looking forward to detonating a bomb, too, refused to be bound by it. The Senate ratified the treaty, having received President Kennedy's pledge that the United States would keep its guard high.

The Glassboro meeting. Late in June, 1967, Premier Alexei N. Kosygin of the Soviet Union came to the United Nations to discuss the situation growing out of the Arab-Israeli war. Recognizing their responsibilities for maintaining peace, Kosygin and President Johnson took advantage of the visit to hold lengthy and apparently cordial talks. Meeting at a mansion called Holly Bush on a college campus in Glassboro, New Jersey, they discussed a wide range of issues. Particularly, they talked about the need to control "nuclear proliferation," that is, the spread of nuclear "capability" among the countries of the world.

Sum and Substance

1. Summarize the important facts in the background of the war in Vietnam. 2. Identify two pressures on Red China. 3. Name four forces operating in Southwest Asia and North Africa. Describe the course of events there. 4. What steps did the Soviet Union take in Europe between 1958 and 1962? 5. Give the facts about difficulties in Latin America between 1946 and 1967. 7. What is the Common Market? 8. Describe the Alliance for Progress. 9. Sum up the plans the United States has made for its own defense and that of its allies.

This short section describes the race in space between the two superpowers.

THE AMERICANS AND THE SOVIETS COMPETE IN OUTER SPACE

A remarkable scientific achievement by the Soviet Union in 1957 temporarily shook the confidence of many people in American technological leadership. On October 4 the Soviet Union successfully launched a man-made earth satellite called a *sputnik*. Weighing 184 pounds, it whirred around the earth at a speed of 18,000 miles an hour. The exploration of outer space had begun, sharpening the rivalry between the East and the West and intoxicating the human imagination.

After a number of disappointing and widely publicized failures, the United States on January 31, 1958, successfully launched a small satellite, too. Several other dramatic space shots followed in the next few months. The way was being paved for manned flights to the moon, and a race was on between the United States and the Soviet Union.

THE FIRST MEN IN SPACE

On April 12, 1961, a Soviet air force officer, Major Yuri Gagarin, joined his name to those of the great explorers of the past when he orbited the earth and returned to it, apparently without ill effects. The acclaim for this fantastic technological achievement was worldwide. While it was still reverberating, an American naval commander, Alan B. Shepard, Jr., was rocketed to an altitude of 115 miles on a suborbital flight from Cape Canaveral (now Cape Kennedy). The United States, too, was almost ready to send a man into full orbit, a culmination of Project Mercury, the man-in-space program.

The momentous event took place on February 20, 1962. Lieutenant Colonel John H. Glenn, Jr., of the Marine Corps and New Concord, Ohio, was lifted into space before the eyes of the prayerful and tremulous thousands who watched at Cape Canaveral and the millions who saw him on television. Aloft a little under 5 hours in his craft, *Friendship 7,* Glenn orbited the earth three times before returning to it in a hair-raising descent. He was immediately the hero of the hour.

##The launching of Sputnik impressed Americans with the fact that they were behind the Soviets in space technology. What changes have been made in our schools as a result?

An astronaut, who is practicing work tasks during under-water training, steps into a foot plate designed to hold him securely in the spacecraft. The underwater environ-ment simulates the condition of zero gravity in space.
What position in American society have astronauts achieved? Why?

THE ACHIEVEMENTS OF NASA

Year by year the United States space program under the direction of the National Aeronautics and Space Administration (NASA) achieved fantastic aims. A two-man Gemini was sent aloft in 1965 and an astronaut performed the feat of "walking in space." Early in 1966 a Gemini capsule was linked, while in orbit, to a rocket that had been launched separately.

This achievement of "docking" was regarded as a necessary preliminary step in reaching the moon. The three-man Apollo program was being developed to land two men on the moon by 1970. A tragic fire aboard the *Apollo 1*, on the launching pad at Cape Kennedy in January, 1967, took the lives of three astronauts, causing a brief suspension of the project. Nevertheless, the desire to reach the # moon was undiminished, even though the early target date appeared less realistic.

Sum and Substance

1. Describe the Soviet and American achievements that led to a race to the moon. 2. Who were the first men in space? 3. Summarize the achievements of NASA.

#Critics of space programs have said that money spent on space efforts might better be spent on more worthwhile projects. What benefits come from space exploration?

773

The authors have discussed separately in this chapter the domestic affairs of Presidents Truman, Kennedy, and Eisenhower. Now, after treating the foreign affairs in the administrations of these men and Johnson, they discuss Johnson's domestic program for the nation.

THE NATION MOVES TO REMODEL SOCIETY

Lyndon B. Johnson's entrance into the White House in late 1963 marked the beginning of an energetic movement to create what the President named the Great Society. He described it: "It is a society where no child will go unfed, and no youngster will go unschooled. Where no man who wants work will fail to find it. Where no citizen will be barred from any door because of his birthplace or his color or his church. Where peace and security is common among neighbors and possible among nations."

The overwhelming election of Johnson to the presidency in his own right in 1964 could be viewed as a thumping endorsement of the goals of the Great Society. Johnson's running mate was Senator Hubert H. Humphrey, of Minnesota, for years an honored member of the liberal wing of the Democratic party. Johnson's opponent was Senator Barry M. Goldwater, of Arizona, long an outspoken, sharp critic of heavy government spending for social programs.

Compare this picture with pictures of tenements seen in Chapter 23.

A tenement backyard in Washington. The majority of the people living in the capital are Negroes, many of them badly housed, poorly fed, and inadequately schooled. They are often unable to find jobs.

Wide World

#What kinds of discrimination was Johnson speaking of? (Ethnic, racial, and religious.)
How have Americans shown such discrimination in the past? Has it disappeared? Explain.

AN ATTACK ON POVERTY

The President saw poverty as one of the chief obstacles to achieving the lofty goals he set. As 1964 began he opened a "war on the sources of poverty" based on an awareness that the lack of opportunity, including access to skilled jobs, good schooling, decent housing, and proper medical care, played a key part in creating hard-core poverty.

An omnibus bill. Drawing on blueprints from the Kennedy administration, an antipoverty program unfolded in the Economic Opportunity Act of 1964. It provided a wide-ranging series of enterprises. One was the establishment of the Job Corps, offering vocational and remedial education to young people. Another was the Work-Training Plan to keep about 200,000 teen-agers from dropping out of school because of financial difficulties. Still another was the Work-Study Plan to help needy college students by financing part-time projects for employing them.

Further, the program authorized assistance for urban and rural community action programs. This arrangement permitted giving aid to public and private nonprofit agencies for undertaking at the local level such activities as slum clearance, remedial education, and counseling of the poor. Some money was also allocated to aid through retraining the heads of families on relief and persons who had been chronic unemployables.

Another feature provided by the law was the VISTA (Volunteers in Service to America) program, in which youthful volunteers serving for the nominal wages of $50 a month would form a kind of domestic peace corps. They would be assigned to work in slum areas, in mental hospitals, on Indian reservations, and in other places requiring deeply sincere public service. The supervision of the antipoverty program was lodged in the newly created Office of Economic Opportunity. President Johnson asserted, "Its Director will be my personal Chief of Staff for the War against poverty."

In 1967 the antipoverty program was spending about $2,000,000,000, but it was not quickly achieving the results desired. In most major cities the relief rolls were growing. The job-training programs were teaching only basic skills—not ones that help a person qualify for a well-paying position. There was concern also that too much pressure was being exerted to distribute money as quickly as possible, while too little energy was being directed toward long-range objectives.

Riots in the cities. The miseries of urban poverty were dramatized afresh in the summer of 1967, when riots of incredible destructiveness broke out in Negro ghettos in dozens of cities. Unemployment and deeply-felt frustration, especially among young people, were generally regarded as the root causes. In Detroit, where the violence was fiercest, it was necessary to obtain federal troops to help quell the uprising in the streets.

MEDICAL AND EDUCATIONAL BENEFITS

The changing age distribution of the population was also reflected in new legislation. Almost a tenth of the American people are sixty-five or over and almost half are under twenty-eight.

Medicare. Congress in 1965 provided—with limitations—hospital and nursing care for the elderly by means of an increase in the Social Security taxes. It was a recognition that Americans sixty-five years of age or older are hospitalized more often and for longer periods of time than younger people and are less able as a group to pay the costs. Long awaited, Medicare opened a new era for millions of elderly people.

Beefing up education. The federal government undertook a vigorous program of aid to education for young people. In 1967 the government spent almost $3,000,000,000 for school services of all kinds. Educational facilities were expanded at every level. Moreover, education was being interpreted in its broadest sense. Substantial sums were being expended also by the National Science Foundation and the National Foundation on the Arts and Humanities to encourage and stimulate research at the frontiers of knowledge.

URBAN ISSUES

The concentration of over 70 percent of the population in urban areas had created problems that required solution before the Great Society could be achieved. President Johnson once explained the situation: "In the remainder of this century, urban populations will double, city land will double, and we will have to build homes, highways and facilities equal to all those built since this country was settled. In the next 40 years we must rebuild the entire urban United States."

The movement to the suburbs. The nation spends almost $2,000,000,000 each year for slum clearance, but the sickness of the central cities is not curable in this way alone. The reason is that in increasing numbers people are moving to the suburbs in quest of more open space, better schools, and serene streets. Taking their places are relatively unskilled newcomers, usually Negroes, often requiring many social services, including welfare payments.

If the cities seek to increase the taxes on those people remaining, it speeds even more the flight to the suburbs. If the cities try to increase taxes on businesses and corporations, they too move out. One effect is to reduce further the jobs available for unskilled men and women, who often cannot afford to travel to outlying areas for work. Many of them are high school "dropouts."

Water and air pollution. The possibility of living comfortably in American urban areas depends

Notice the amazing jump in the population of Los Angeles between 1950 and 1960.

TEN LARGEST CITIES IN THE UNITED STATES*

	1950	1960	1970 (projected)
1	New York, N.Y. 13,115,200	New York, N.Y. 15,250,000	New York, N.Y. 17,500,000
2	Chicago, Ill. 5,495,400	Los Angeles, Calif. 6,550,000	Los Angeles, Calif. 9,300,000
3	Los Angeles, Calif. 4,134,000	Chicago, Ill. 6,425,000	Chicago, Ill. 7,750,000
4	Philadelphia, Pa. 3,302,100	Philadelphia, Pa. 3,885,000	Philadelphia, Pa.–Trenton, N.J.–Wilmington, Del. 5,400,000
5	Detroit, Mich. 3,043,200	Detroit, Mich. 3,825,000	San Francisco–Oakland–San Jose, Calif. 4,375,000
6	Boston, Mass. 2,478,000	San Francisco–Oakland–San Jose, Calif. 3,250,000	Detroit, Mich. 4,375,000
7	San Francisco–Oakland, Calif. 2,041,400	Boston, Mass. 2,820,000	Boston, Mass. 3,675,000
8	St. Louis, Mo. 1,538,100	Cleveland, Ohio 2,035,000	Washington, D.C. 2,725,000
9	Cleveland, Ohio 1,490,500	Washington, D.C. 2,000,000	Cleveland, Ohio 2,375,000
10	Washington, D.C. 1,477,200	St. Louis, Mo. 1,960,000	St. Louis, Mo. 2,350,000

* Population figures are approximate and include suburbs.

to no small extent on being able to reduce water and air pollution. The Hudson River, for instance, has been termed "an open, running sewer," because hundreds of millions of gallons of raw sewage are dumped into it each day. A condition like this one near New York City and its environs exists for urban communities throughout the country.

Air pollution often shows itself as smog in the atmosphere over major cities. It is conservatively estimated that each day 350,000 tons of pollutants are lofted in the air above the United States. The Clean Air Act of 1963 authorizes federal action to help halt the trend toward greater and greater contamination of the atmosphere. It was estimated that 6000 communities would find in the law the help they require through research and greater coöperation among federal, state, and local governments and also between government and industry.

Inadequate transportation. From the time the first post roads were built, Congress has supported improved transportation—as technological advances permitted—including canals, railroads, highways, and airlines. In 1964 Congress passed the Urban Mass Transportation Act, placing federal support behind plans to ease the burdens and discomforts involved in moving people in the great metropolitan centers by bus and rapid transit systems.

In 1966 legislation created at last the Department of Transportation, whose chief officer, Alan S. Boyd, is a member of the President's Cabinet. He has as a major goal the completion by 1972 of a 41,000-mile network of controlled-access superhighways forming a national system of roads. His problems are immense. In addition to dealing with urban transportation problems, he must face the condition, physical as well as financial, of many of the railroads, which require far-reaching attention and help. The airlines also need assistance—in providing adequate airport and air-safety facilities.

Housing in the cities. In recognition of the gravity of urban questions in general, Congress in 1965 created the Department of Housing and Urban Development. To head it, President Johnson chose Robert C. Weaver, of New York, who thereby became the first Negro Cabinet member.

A powerful instrument for the new Department was the Housing and Urban Development Act of 1965. It extended and enlarged existing programs. It also broke new paths in providing grants for the beautification of urban areas through the acquisition of open spaces to be used for parks and other kinds of recreational areas.

But no law aroused more enthusiasm than the Demonstration Cities Act of 1966. It provided for large grants to sixty or seventy cities willing to offer blueprints for renewing whole neighborhoods. The "model cities" thus created would dare to reorganize the total environment in which some city people live.

The inadequacy of housing in the cities was felt especially keenly not only by Negroes but also by recent arrivals from Puerto Rico. Puerto Ricans had begun to come to the United States in large numbers after the Second World War. Hoping to find better living conditions than those on their native island, they often found themselves mired in new despair.

THE WARREN COURT

Helping to usher in a society with new ideals and practices has also been a role of the Supreme Court, especially under Chief Justice Earl Warren, who was appointed by President Eisenhower in 1953. The Court in general has handed down decisions that make the Constitution more responsive to the needs of individuals than before. Specifically, the Supreme Court has been gradually seeing to it that the provisions of the Bill of Rights—once commands applying only to the federal government —apply also to the governments of the states.

The protection of the accused. Some of the most momentous decisions have been in the field of race relations. But the Court has looked into other aspects of American life, too, offering equally bold opinions. In two notable cases, *Escobedo* v. *Illinois* (1964) and *Miranda* v. *Arizona* (1966), the Court extended the pro-

##Why was it especially fitting that Mr. Weaver became the Secretary of Housing and Urban Development? (Suggestion: Negroes have suffered particularly from bad or inadequate housing in large cities. Urban development must take their situation into account.)

777

Justice Black has said that there is a "tendency now to look to the judiciary to make all the major policy decisions of our society under the guise of determining constitutionality." What did he mean? He said he preferred to leave policy to elected officials. Meaning?

The Warren Court in 1965. The Court has aimed to bring the Constitution into line with changed society. Chief Justice Warren sits in the center; at his right is Associate Justice Hugo L. Black, the oldest member.

Justice William O. Douglas, like Black, an "F. D. R." appointee, sits at Warren's left.

vision of the Fifth Amendment prohibiting self-incrimination. The Court decreed that before policemen question a suspect in a crime, he must be warned that he has a right to remain silent. He must also be told that any statement he makes may be used against him and that he has a right to the presence of a lawyer.

It seems clear that as a result of these decisions it may become more difficult than in the past to achieve convictions in certain types of cases. But all people must be protected from situations in which they may give testimony under duress.

Keeping church and state separate. The Court has been sensitive, too, to the delicate relationship between church and state. In *Engel* v. *Vitale* in 1962, the Court declared unconstitutional the recitation of a nondenominational prayer in New York schools. The Court held that while no compulsion was involved in the so-called Regents' prayer, which was at issue, the First Amendment's provisions about the establishment of religion were nevertheless violated.

In *School District of Abington Township* v. *Schempp,* the following year, the Court ruled that daily Bible readings and the recitation of the Lord's Prayer constituted "a religious ceremony." Such "a ceremony," the Court held, was unconstitutional. The reasoning was that the First Amendment, dictating separation of church and state, applied to state governments as well as to the federal government because of the wording of the Fourteenth Amendment.

Defending the right of political dissent. The Court has also opened new vistas in the control of subversive activity and the guarding of loyalty to the government. In the case of *Dennis et al.* v. *United States* (1951) the Court had upheld the constitutionality of the Smith Act—a law

#Be sure students know the meaning of "duress." Ask the class to read the Fifth Amendment (p. 804) and the commentary. How were the two decisions extensions of this amendment?

passed in 1940 making it a crime to advocate the violent overthrow of the government.

But the *Dennis* decision was modified in 1957 in *Yates* v. *United States*. The Court decided that the mere advocacy of the violent overthrow of the government, without any overt action toward that end, was not in itself a crime. In his decision Justice Hugo Black said, "I believe that the First Amendment forbids Congress to punish people for talking about public affairs, whether or not such discussion incites to action, legal or illegal."

In *Albertson* v. *Subversive Activities Control Board* (1965) and also in later cases the Court removed the requirement that members of the Communist party register themselves with governmental authorities. In 1966, in *Elfbrandt* v. *Russell* the Court declared unconstitutional Arizona's requirement of a loyalty oath from state employees. These decisions along with others indicate that the Court has grown increasingly vigilant and precise in its definition of civil liberties.

Guaranteeing the equality of the vote. The Court has also been attentive to the meaning and value of the vote itself. Of particular concern has been the disproportionate representation of rural areas as compared with urban areas in state legislatures. In 1962 in the case of *Baker* v. *Carr* the Supreme Court held that the federal courts can play a part in reapportioning state legislative districts. This case and others subsequently decided put the Court on record as favoring the principle that no citizen's vote should yield him any more or less representation than another citizen's. The idea is summed up in the telling phrase, "one man, one vote."

The Warren Court has widened the horizons of democratic practice in a fashion that will very greatly alter American life. Already the decisions of the Court, taken as a whole, appear to have been more influential than any since the days of John Marshall. The Court's work gives the era that began in the 1950's a unique, though controversial, place in the history of democracy.

Johnson thus appointed the first Negro to a Cabinet position and the first one to the Court.

Johnson and Thurgood Marshall, the President's choice to succeed Tom C. Clark (*at the far left in the picture on* page 778) as Associate Justice of the Supreme Court. Marshall became the first Negro to hold this position.

Wide World

ECONOMIC PERFORMANCE

Successive administrations since the Second World War have used the teachings of modern economics to "manage" the nation's economic life and prevent a serious depression. Despite the continuing need to maintain a high level of expenditures for defense, Americans experienced continuing prosperity.

Hard facts. Because of the inflationary pressure produced by the Korean War, the Eisenhower administration was concerned about both balancing the federal budget and preventing further price increases. The military needs and the recessions of 1953, 1958, and 1961 prevented the reduction of the mounting budget. Although prices remained stable, the rate of growth of the nation's productivity was not impressive.

Moreover, huge agricultural surpluses piled up—in 1956, $8,500,000,000 worth was held in government storage. In establishing a "soil bank," the administration felt forced to revert to the old New Deal idea of paying farmers to reduce their productive acreage by giving the land over to conservation practices.

The tendency toward large-scale, highly-

mechanized commercial agriculture and the flight of the small farmers to the city have not been halted by the farm policy of any administration since 1945. The number of farmers of all kinds decreased sharply from approximately 7,000,000 in 1950 to something over 3,000,000 in 1966.

Sluggish economic growth. President Kennedy pressed for more social legislation than did President Eisenhower, but he too tried to meet the threat of inflation and to balance the budget. Persistent unemployment and a halting economic growth appeared as significant barriers to overcome.

A tax cut. Eventually Kennedy proposed a cut in income taxes, based on the assumption that the public would then have more money to purchase consumer goods and would thus make more funds available for companies to reinvest. Particularly he hoped that businessmen would construct more modern plants.

President Johnson actually achieved a tax cut of $11,500,000,000 early in 1964. By the end of the year the gross national product—the total of goods and services produced—had risen by $38,000,000,000 and unemployment was somewhat reduced.

Like Eisenhower and Kennedy, Johnson worked hard to prevent inflation, employing even his own considerable personal persuasiveness to keep wages and prices within federally-approved guide lines. Nevertheless, the commitment to Great Society programs as well as the expenditures for defense, the war in Vietnam, and foreign aid made it inevitable that # inflation would gain new momentum.

Automation. A prevailing characteristic of ## American industry since 1945 has been increased automation.‡‡ One result was a stunning increase in the gross national product. The figure, which was spectacularly high in 1950 when it stood at $284,800,000,000, soared to $713,900,000,000 in 1966.

‡‡ Automation is a method of manufacturing in which all or almost all the processes are performed by self-operating machinery. It was made possible in large measure by the remarkable advances in the field of electronics after the Second World War. A major invention was the *transistor*. Able to do some of the work of the radio tube, it can also be "miniaturized" to occupy very little space.

Inquire about the meaning of "doldrums."
Observe the huge increases since the postwar doldrums.

RISING WORLD TRADE

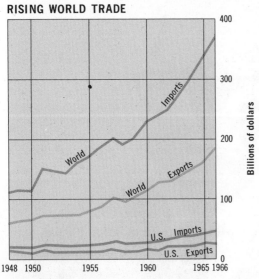

Billions of dollars

1948 1950   1955   1960   1965 1966

Source: Adapted from the *New York Times*

##The most significant examples of automation are systems of machines that follow the orders given by computers. There are automated banks, automated steel mills, etc.

Automation unfortunately blighted the employment opportunities of many. At the same time, new industries—especially in electronics and in fields related to space exploration—were creating more and more jobs.

Unhappily, the people whose jobs have been eliminated by automation have not been those who have obtained the jobs—often requiring sophisticated skills and training—in the burgeoning new industries. The relatively unskilled members of the population have become chronic unemployables. These make up the bulk of the unemployed in the country, who in the late spring of 1967 amounted to less than 4 percent of the employable population.

Since the end of the 1950's, there have been serious labor disputes revolving around the technological changes in the steel, newspaper, and airplane industries and in railroading. In each case, management was trying to adjust working conditions to new developments in the industry, thereby producing fear of lay-offs among employees.

Threatened revolt in the ranks. No single powerful figure dominated the labor movement as in earlier years. In 1967 Walter P. Reuther, the president of the United Automobile Workers, threatened to withdraw his organization from the AFL-CIO. He charged that the AFL-CIO under the presidency of George Meany was "undemocratic" and lacking in dynamism.

The Kennedy Round. Both capital and labor stood to gain from the remarkable achievement in 1967 of agreement on tariff reductions after a long series of talks held at Geneva. Named the Kennedy Round in honor of the late President, the negotiations among the United States and the Common Market nations of Europe produced tariff cuts affecting 70 percent of these countries' dutiable imports. Of the forty-six nations signing the agreement, thirty-eight made tariff concessions. The predicted increase in world trade was bound to benefit American industry and agriculture.

CIVIL RIGHTS

A long-smoldering issue crossing both party and sectional lines began to emerge in the 1950's. In time it became the spearhead of American democracy's unfinished business. Involving civil rights for Negroes, it revived a movement of reconstruction days to end legal and *de facto* discrimination—the latter being that established not by law but by custom and practice. Before the 1950's, efforts to eliminate discrimination had mainly involved obtaining state fair-employment laws.

A historic decision. In May, 1954, the Supreme Court handed down a momentous decision in the case of *Brown* v. *Board of Education of Topeka*. In this decision the Supreme Court held unconstitutional the practice of providing "separate but equal" school facilities for Negroes—in effect in seventeen states of the Union and in the District of Columbia. The Court asserted that the practice violated the Fourteenth Amendment, which guarantees to every citizen "the equal protection of the laws."

Said Chief Justice Warren in the unanimous opinion: ". . . in the field of public education the doctrine of 'separate but equal' has no place. Separate educational facilities are inherently unequal."

The Court later called for the exercise of "all deliberate speed" in complying with the decision. Despite some zealous opposition, desegregation at an uneven pace proceeded voluntarily and under pressure of court orders. In the South, the percentage of Negro students going to school with white students rose from 6.4 percent in 1960 to almost 16 percent by the beginning of 1966. But in some states the figure was almost zero.

First steps in Congress. The school decision marked the beginning of a movement to change by law the pattern of segregation that had become fastened on the country. In 1957 Congress passed the first civil rights act in eighty-two years. The law created a bipartisan Civil Rights Commission to investigate abuses and recommend legislation. It also authorized the appointment of an Assistant Attorney General to head the new Civil Rights Division in the Department of Justice. A 1960 act prescribed ways of proceeding when voting rights were denied on account of race.

Wide World

The Reverend Martin Luther King, Jr., a winner of a Nobel Prize for Peace, speaks on Long Island of civil rights. The late Dr. King won the respect of Americans at home and of people abroad.

The continued fight over civil rights. As the 1950's ended, the Negroes' struggle to end their condition of "second-class citizenship" became more insistent. In 1955–1956 Negroes used a new weapon, passive resistance, in a boycott of buses in Montgomery, Alabama. Aimed at ending segregation on these conveyances, the effort attracted wide attention. The leader of this protest was Martin Luther King, Jr., a minister originally from Atlanta.

Again employing nonviolence, Negro students in February, 1960, began to occupy stools at lunch counters in Greensboro, North Carolina, in order to desegregate the restaurants. Quickly these sit-ins spread to many other southern communities. As the new tech-

nique commenced to win its objectives, other similar campaigns in the South were planned.

In the spring of 1961, segregated bus and terminal facilities came under attack. The so-called Freedom Riders—Negroes and sympathizers—rode buses into various southern cities, entering segregated waiting rooms and restaurants. In several places, violence flared as policemen sought to enforce local laws.

The Kennedy administration at first attempted to guarantee civil rights through executive action, rather than by seeking new legislation. For example, the President issued one order providing equality of job opportunity on all work done under contracts with the federal government, and another eliminating dis-

##The nonviolent sit-ins were probably adopted because of the examples set by union members years before. Union members engaged in sit-ins within industrial plants.

crimination in any housing that was federally subsidized. Moreover, through the Civil Rights Division of the Department of Justice, a legal assault was launched against barriers to voting by Negroes in some parts of the South. The Twenty-fourth Amendment outlawing poll taxes in national elections was approved by Congress. It was added to the Constitution in 1964.

The administration also pressed hard to further the desegregation of schools throughout the country. Behind these various activities was the strong support of the federal judiciary, which consistently held that racial discrimination offends the United States Constitution.

The walls of segregation thus began to crumble in the border states, in parts of the deep South, and in the North. In some places, however, Negro communities became increasingly restive over the slow rate of change. The Negroes' demands were plain: an end to segregated schools, stores, theaters, restaurants, and other public facilities.

Negotiations, brought about by federal assistance, between Negroes and those resisting their demands seemed to reduce tensions. But demonstrations occurred in various cities of the South and in major cities of the North in protest against discrimination by employers ## and unions and against *de facto* segregation in schools. In many northern communities, although legal segregation did not exist in school systems, Negroes protested against so-called racial imbalance in classes.

In the lap of Congress. President Kennedy decided he must try to move the Negro "revolt" out of the streets and into the courts. In June, 1963, he asked Congress for legislation to make illegal a range of discriminatory practices and to strengthen the hand of the Department of Justice in attacking them.

Attention was increasingly focused on the economic position of Negroes. Not only did they suffer heavy unemployment but they also were generally found in the lower-paid occupations, a situation that made the difference in income between Negroes and other Americans considerable.

The march on Washington. Negro and other civil rights leaders organized a mammoth march on Washington, D.C., which was held on August 28, 1963, to help dramatize the urgency of Kennedy's proposed civil rights legislation. The Reverend Martin Luther King, Jr., spoke to the cheering throng of his dream that his four little children would one day live in a nation where they would be judged not by the color of their skin but by their character.

The Civil Rights Act of 1964. When Lyndon Johnson succeeded to the presidency, he pledged himself to continue the fight for the Kennedy program, of which civil rights had become a symbol. Congress responded, after a long filibuster by southerners in the Senate had been broken, by passing the Civil Rights Act of 1964, in time for the Fourth of July.

The heart of the law lay in its prohibition of racial discrimination in most public accommodations—hotels, restaurants, theaters, and the like. It outlawed also discriminatory racial practices by employers and unions. It authorized the Attorney General to initiate suits in school-desegregation cases. It permitted the cutting of funds to federally assisted programs in which racial discrimination persisted. It required registrars to apply the same standards to Negro voting applicants that were applied to everyone else.

The Voting Rights Act. The following year Johnson led Congress to pass the Voting Rights Act of 1965, which closed the last loopholes by which Negroes could be prevented from voting. Vast changes in southern politics were predicted when a million new voters emerged. Progress was halting even though by the beginning of 1967 there had been an increase of 72 percent in the registration of Negro voters in five states.

The advance in civil rights owed much to the efforts of the National Association for the Advancement of Colored People (NAACP), the Congress on Racial Equality (CORE), the Student Non-Violent Coordinating Committee (SNCC) and to many individuals of both races. The evidence was mounting, though, that the desire for economic improvement was

##Be sure students know the meaning of "de facto," a widely used expression. (A Latin phrase, it means "in fact," "in reality.")

783

#The word ghetto originally meant a part of a city in which Jews were required to live. It is now used to mean the crowded part of a city where Negroes have had to live largely because of segregated housing, another form of racial discrimination.

Burck in the *Chicago Sun-Times*

Liberty undergoes a new kind of lynching.

What is the cartoonist saying?

at the center of Negro discontent, often showing itself in violence or threats of violence and sometimes appearing in the form of a call for "black power."

Open housing. By 1967, many civil rights leaders were concentrating on obtaining open-housing laws. Such legislation would make it illegal to refuse to rent or sell housing to another person on account of his race or religion. It had become apparent that open housing # might lead to an end to "ghettos," which result in *de facto* school segregation and contribute to the endless cycle of poverty.

A new civil rights law. In 1967 Congress enacted another civil rights measure. Interfering with, injuring, or intimidating anyone because of his race, religion, national origin, or political affiliation or because of his engagement in certain protected activities was made a federal offense. Among such activities are voting, attending public schools, using public facilities, or taking part in federally assisted programs.

THE PRESIDENT'S DILEMMA

President Johnson was troubled by his awareness that the needs of foreign policy were a stumbling block to the attainment of his goals at home. Yet he faced the fact with resignation. He spoke these words in May, 1967, at the christening of the aircraft carrier U.S.S. *John F. Kennedy*:

> Today, as throughout our history, we bear fateful responsibilities in the world. From the moment of our national creation, American ideals have served as a beacon to the oppressed and to the enslaved.
>
> In times past, it has often been our strength and our resolve which have tipped the scales of conflict against aggression or would-be aggressors. That role has never been an easy one. It has always required not only strength but patience . . . and sacrifice—the tragic price we pay for our commitment to our ideals. ##

It was clear in 1967 that the war in Vietnam was taking more and more public attention and money—to say nothing of American lives. Widespread opposition to the war, which took many forms, became a thorn in the side of the administration. Some argued that solving the problems of poverty and of race relations would depend ultimately on the willingness to appropriate much larger sums of money than Congress had yet provided—or could, in the face of the war costs.

Sum and Substance

1. Summarize President Johnson's attack on poverty. 2. How did his administration assist the elderly? How did it stimulate education? 3. Name the chief urban problems. 4. How did the Supreme Court provide greater protection to the accused? Help keep church and state separate? Defend the right of political dissent? Guarantee the equality of the vote? Bring about the desegregation of schools? 5. Describe the Civil Rights Act of 1964 and the Voting Rights Act.

##What American ideal was Johnson evidently referring to? (Suggestion: Probably to liberty, since Americans had undertaken to free an Asian people from aggression.)

THE WORKSHOP

OF LASTING SIGNIFICANCE

Explain the relationship of each of the following to the period between 1945 and the present.

GI Bill of Rights	U-2 incident
Employment Act of 1946	Berlin Wall
	Fidel Castro
Taft-Hartley Act	OAS
Earl Warren	nuclear-test ban
Mao Tse-tung	treaty
George C. Marshall	John H. Glenn, Jr.
Truman doctrine	NASA
Marshall Plan	antipoverty program
Berlin blockade	VISTA
NATO	Medicare
Alger Hiss	*Escobedo* v. *Illinois*
"McCarthyism"	*Engel* v. *Vitale*
Adlai E. Stevenson	political dissent
John Foster Dulles	*School District of*
Dean Rusk	*Abington Township*
Peace Corps	v. *Schempp*
Vietnam	*Baker* v. *Carr*
Laos	Kennedy Round
Ho Chi Minh	*Brown* v. *Board of*
Vietcong	*Education of*
Arab League	*Topeka*
Suez Canal	Civil Rights Act
Eisenhower doctrine	of 1964
SAC	Voting Rights Act

INTERNATIONAL POLITICS

1. Since 1945, the countries of the world have acted generally in accordance with the position they have taken in the struggle between the Western and Communist nations. Identify (*a*) the Western countries, (*b*) the Communist nations, (*c*) the neutrals, or nonaligned, and (*d*) those that have played off Western countries against Communist ones.

2. What motives does each of the groups have? Name the areas of the world that have been centers of international difficulties. In each case, tell (*a*) what nations have been involved, (*b*) what role the United States has played, (*c*) how the difficulty arose, and (*d*) what the outcome has been.

3. Name the international alliances the United States has joined or supported since the end of the Second World War. What other countries are members? What is the purpose of these organizations? Find out how each has performed in carrying out its purpose.

INFORMED OPINION

1. Every country plans its foreign policy in order to accomplish certain objectives. What are the purposes of United States foreign policy? Of these, which is *fundamental?* In the light of American history, would you say that the purposes have changed over the years? #

2. How does the United States seek to carry out its foreign policy? Give specific examples of its efforts to achieve each of the purposes you named.

3. Who is chiefly responsible for American foreign policy? What part does public opinion have in its formulation? How is public opinion formed? How can it be mobilized by makers of foreign policy?

4. A former President once said: "Although the nation has always united against any external peril, blind obedience to authority has never been characteristic of Americans. Rather, they have been questioners, doubters, experimenters, and very often articulate . . . dissenters. This attitude has been our most valuable national asset. . . ."

Does American history bear out the first ## statement? Defend your answer. How have Americans shown dissent? Do you agree with the last idea expressed? Explain.

AMERICAN DEMOCRACY

1. Explain by giving concrete examples the statement that the decisions of the United States Supreme Court gave the era beginning in the 1950's a unique and honored place in the story of the growth of democracy.

2. What principle of democracy does "McCarthyism" violate?

785

#Discuss the meaning of this last sentence in the paragraph. How can a country lead through the "force of its ideals"? What ideals does the United States have that can exert force? (Its various democratic ideals, its sympathy and charity for the "underdog" or the oppressed, etc.) What is the "richness" of a culture? (The quality that is measured by a culture's achievements in education, in the arts, and in the quality of life the people enjoy.)

A LONG VIEW

The Quest for Security

FOR more than half a century the United States has been one of the foremost countries in the world. A measure of its might has been its awesome industrial prowess. Some additional yardsticks have been the strength of its military and naval establishment and the size of its atomic arsenal. Nevertheless, any country's power is best demonstrated in its ability to lead other nations through persuasion—by the force of its ideals and the richness of its culture.

Americans rediscovered only a generation ago that they have a role in international politics which they cannot avoid even if they would. They have learned it is alluring to exercise leadership in the world—but sometimes frustrating, in part because in the past they have known so little about other peoples.

Moreover, Americans have had to find out how to balance their characteristic humaneness and charitableness against the knowledge that life in the international arena unhappily rests on force. Since the close of the Second World War, the United States has had to create "hardware" capable of inflicting incalculable destruction on mankind. In the same period, however, it has distributed $100,000,000,000 in foreign aid to countries everywhere.

Americans have also shown their openhandedness toward fellow human beings in countless humanitarian efforts unrelated to the vital interests of the country. They have aided victims of earthquakes, rescued sufferers from starvation, safeguarded others with medical assistance, and made sincere efforts to raise the living standards of people throughout the world. The United States does not ask if its benevolence is appreciated; it acts out of deeply bred instincts and traditions.

It is hard to say where an America that respects both realism and idealism is heading—toward permanent and ever deepening engagement in the world's problems or toward disillusionment and a reduction of its sense of obligation. Whatever the answer, Americans must be sure they continue to encourage the world by their example—by the way they live at home as well as abroad.

America's affluence, based on fantastic national productivity, is both an aid and a hindrance to its leadership. Most Americans have become lovers of luxury and of material things. After centuries of what sometimes must have seemed to be unending labor, the people are harvesting and enjoying the crop of "good living" and leisure their forebears sowed—and no doubt prayed for.

A central question is whether the free time now available and the speedup of life accompanying it will prove to be a boon to creativeness or an intolerable burden. How Americans respond may decide the future standing of the United States among the other nations of the world. One effect of the increased facilities for playing and the increased pace of living, so far, has been to leave fewer moments for uninterrupted contemplation. No society can afford the price that such a large-scale interference with intellectual effort can entail.

As old institutions decay, young people particularly must develop their imagination and insight so that they can establish new and better institutions when they assume the governing of the country. Young people must use their best energies to cultivate their ingenuity in order to improve upon the unprecedented accomplishments of their parents and grandparents at home and abroad. ★ ★ ★

##Discuss the "generation gap." Is such a gap unique in American history? What causes it? How does it show itself? Is it productive? How can it be overcome?

786

PART SEVEN WORKSHOP

AMERICA IN THE WORLD

1. Briefly summarize the role the United States has played in international politics since 1917. For your purpose, divide the years into three periods: (*a*) from 1917 to 1941; (*b*) from 1941 to 1960; (*c*) from 1960 on.

What aims was the country seeking to carry out in each period? What methods did it use? What success was achieved? If there were failures, how do you account for them? How was American life at home affected by events abroad in each period?

2. Identify the major problems that confront the United States in international politics today. Why are solutions dependent on understanding the historical backgrounds of the problems? Illustrate your answer by using an example. What are Americans doing to help solve the problems?

3. How does the history of the last sixty years support the statement that life in the international area "rests on force"? How has this fact altered life in America?

4. Foreign critics have frequently said that Americans are too immature, too hasty, and even too "trigger-happy" to exercise the wise leadership expected of a people in their position in the world. In your opinion, what accounts for such a judgment? How would you answer a person making it? Support your reply with details.

TIME AND CHANGE

1. Why would it have seemed foolish to try to enact legislation like the Economic Opportunity Act of 1964 before the Great Depression? What arguments are used to oppose such legislation today?

2. How does the changing status of Negroes and the greater acceptance of religious differences among Americans reflect a widening and a maturing of democracy? In what other ways can the extent of democracy be measured?

3. Contrast the situation of labor in the last years of the nineteenth century and in the years after the New Deal. How would you describe its situation today?

4. How does the Kennedy Round show a changed American conception of world trade? How do you account for the altered thinking?

5. Significant changes have taken place in American family life since the Second World War especially: the number of women working outside the home has steadily increased, and young people have assumed a more important position than ever before. How do you explain these changes? What are the effects? In what other ways have families changed?

6. The urbanization of the United States and the overall increase in the population have caused American life to become more and more impersonal. What does this mean? How are human beings affected? What can be done to help overcome these effects?

7. What aspects of American life do you think are in need of changing? Why? How can the change or changes be achieved?

AMERICAN HISTORY IN REVIEW

1. What crisis or crises did Americans meet in 1861; in the 1930's; in 1941; in 1950; in the 1960's? In each case, describe the outcome.

2. The United States was once an "emerging" or "developing" country. How did it become the strongest and richest in the world?

3. What do you regard as the most admirable of the traits Americans have displayed in the course of the history of their country? On what occasions did they display them best?

4. Compare the ratios of rural and urban population in the United States in 1790 and today. How has the federal government reacted to the change?

5. In what periods of American history has democracy showed outstanding growth? Defend your answer.

6. Americans have opposed acts of totalitarianism—centralized control by an autocratic leader—on a number of occasions. What were they? What threat or threats to the United States existed in each case?

THE BOOKSHELF

Eyewitness Accounts

Congdon, Don (ed.). *The Thirties: A Time to Remember.* New York: Simon and Schuster, Inc., 1962.

Eisenhower, Dwight D. *Mandate for Change, 1953–1956,* and *Waging Peace, 1956–1961* ("The White House Years," 2 vols.). New York: Doubleday & Co., Inc., 1963, 1965 [Paperback—New York: New American Library, Inc.].

Flower, Desmond, and James Reeves (eds.). *The Taste of Courage: The War, 1939–1945.* New York: Harper & Row, Publishers, 1960.

Shannon, David A. (ed.). *The Great Depression.* Englewood Cliffs, N.J.: Prentice-Hall, Inc., 1960 [Paperback—Englewood Cliffs: Prentice-Hall, Inc.].

Sorensen, Theodore C. *Kennedy.* New York: Harper & Row, Publishers, 1965.

Giant Men and Women

Burns, James M. *John Kennedy: A Political Profile.* New York: Harcourt, Brace & World, Inc., 1960 [Paperback—New York: Avon Books].

Farago, Ladislas. *Patton: Ordeal and Triumph.* New York: Ivan Obolensky, Inc., 1964.

Means, Marianne. *The Woman in the White House: The Lives, Times and Influence of 12 Notable First Ladies.* New York: Random House, Inc., 1963 [Paperback—New York: New American Library, Inc.].

Sinclair, Andrew. *The Available Man: The Life Behind the Masks of Warren Gamaliel Harding.* New York: The Macmillan Co., 1965.

Steinberg, Alfred. *Man from Missouri: The Life and Times of Harry S Truman.* New York: G. P. Putnam's Sons, 1962.

White, William S. *The Professional: Lyndon B. Johnson.* Boston: Houghton Mifflin Co., 1964 [Paperback—New York: Fawcett World Library].

Living and Making a Living

Bird, Caroline. *The Invisible Scar.* New York: David McKay Co., Inc., 1966 [Paperback—New York: Pocket Books, Inc.].

Buchanan, A. Russell. *The United States and World War II.* 2 vols. New York: Harper & Row, Publishers, 1964 [Paperback—New York: Harper & Row, Publishers].

Fehrenbach, T. R. *This Kind of War: A Study in Unpreparedness.* New York: The Macmillan Co., 1963 [Paperback—New York: Pocket Books, Inc.].

Fredericks, Pierce. *The Great Adventure: America in the First World War.* New York: E. P. Dutton & Co., Inc., 1960.

Goldman, Eric F. *The Crucial Decade, and After; America, 1945–1960* [Paperback—New York: Vintage Books, Inc.].

Morison, Samuel E. *The Two-Ocean War: A Short History of the U.S. Navy in the Second World War.* Boston: Little, Brown & Co., 1963.

Schlesinger, Arthur M., Jr. *A Thousand Days: John F. Kennedy in the White House.* Boston: Houghton Mifflin Co., 1965.

———. *The Crisis of the Old Order, The Coming of the New Deal,* and *The Politics of Upheaval* ("The Age of Roosevelt," 3 vols.). Boston: Houghton Mifflin Co., 1957–1961.

Stallings, Laurence. *The Doughboys: The Story of the AEF.* New York: Harper & Row, Publishers, 1963.

Trainor, Bernard E. *A History of the U.S. Marines.* Chicago: Rand McNally & Co., 1967.

White, Theodore H. *The Making of the President, 1964.* New York: Atheneum Publishers, 1965 [Paperback—New York: Pocket Books, Inc.].

———. *The Making of the President, 1960.* New York: Atheneum Publishers, 1961 [Paperback—New York: Pocket Books, Inc.].

Confronting the World

Divine, Robert A. *The Reluctant Belligerent: American Entry Into the Second World War.* New York: John Wiley & Sons, Inc., 1965 [Paperback—New York: John Wiley & Sons, Inc.].

Feis, Herbert. *The Atomic Bomb and the End of World War II.* Rev. ed. Princeton, N.J.: Princeton University Press, 1966.

Graebner, Norman (ed.). *An Uncertain Tradition: American Secretaries of State in the Twentieth Century.* New York: McGraw-Hill Book Co., Inc., 1961.

Smith, Daniel M. *The Great Departure: The U.S. and World War I, 1914–1920.* New York: John Wiley & Sons, Inc., 1965 [Paperback—New York: John Wiley & Sons, Inc.].

Spanier, John. *American Foreign Policy Since World War II.* 2nd ed. New York: Frederick A. Praeger, Inc., 1965 [Paperback—New York: Frederick A. Praeger, Inc.].

Art, Science, and the Life of the Mind

Caidin, Martin. *Wings Into Space.* New York: Holt, Rinehart & Winston, Inc., 1965 [Paperback—New York: Holt, Rinehart & Winston, Inc.].

Hunter, M. W. *Thrust Into Space.* New York: Holt, Rinehart & Winston, Inc., 1966 [Paperback—New York: Holt, Rinehart & Winston, Inc.].

Kazin, Alfred. *Contemporaries.* Boston: Little, Brown & Co., 1962 [Paperback—Boston: Little, Brown & Co.].

Historical Fiction

Brown, Harry. *A Walk in the Sun* [Paperback—New York: New American Library, Inc.]. (The U.S. Infantry in the Second World War.)

Michener, James. *The Bridges at Toko-ri.* New York: Random House, Inc., 1953 [Paperback—New York: Bantam Books, Inc.]. (The grimness of Korea.)

Warren, Robert Penn. *All the King's Men.* New York: Harcourt, Brace & Co., Inc., 1946 [Paperback—New York: Bantam Books, Inc.]. (The life and times of a demagogue.)

THE DECLARATION OF INDEPENDENCE

In Congress, July 4, 1776.

A Declaration by the Representatives of The United States of America, in Congress Assembled.

When, in the course of human events, it becomes necessary for one people to dissolve the political bands which have connected them with another, and to assume, among the powers of the earth, the separate and equal station to which the laws of nature and of nature's God entitle them, a decent respect to the opinions of mankind requires that they should declare the causes which impel them to the separation.

We hold these truths to be self-evident:—That all men are created equal; that they are endowed by their Creator with certain unalienable rights; that among these are life, liberty, and the pursuit of happiness. That, to secure these rights, governments are instituted among men, deriving their just powers from the consent of the governed; that, whenever any form of government becomes destructive of these ends, it is the right of the people to alter or to abolish it, and to institute a new government, laying its foundation on such principles, and organising its powers in such form, as to them shall seem most likely to effect their safety and happiness. Prudence, indeed, will dictate that governments long established should not be changed for light and transient causes; and, accordingly, all experience hath shown that mankind are more disposed to suffer, while evils are sufferable, than to right themselves by abolishing the forms to which they are accustomed. But, when a long train of abuses and usurpations, pursuing invariably the same object, evinces a design to reduce them under absolute despotism, it is their right, it is their duty, to throw off such government, and to provide new guards for their future security. Such has been the patient sufferance of these colonies; and such is now the necessity that constrains them to alter their former systems of government. The history of the present King of Great Britain is a history of repeated injuries and usurpations, all having, in direct object, the establishment of an absolute tyranny over these States. To prove this, let facts be submitted to a candid world.

He has refused his assent to laws the most wholesome and necessary for the public good.

He has forbidden his Governors to pass laws of immediate and pressing importance, unless suspended in their operation till his assent should be obtained; and, when so suspended, he has utterly neglected to attend to them.

He has refused to pass other laws for the accommodation of large districts of people, unless those people would relinquish the right of representation in the legislature—a right inestimable to them, and formidable to tyrants only.

He has called together legislative bodies at places unusual, uncomfortable, and distant from the depository of their public records, for the sole purpose of fatiguing them into compliance with his measure.

He has dissolved representative houses repeatedly, for opposing, with manly firmness, his invasions on the rights of the people.

He has refused, for a long time after such dissolutions, to cause others to be elected; whereby the legislative powers, incapable of annihilation, have returned to the people at large for their exercise; the State remaining, in the meantime, exposed to all dangers of invasion from without, and convulsions within.

He has endeavored to prevent the population of these States; for that purpose obstructing the laws for the naturalization of foreigners; refusing to pass others to encourage their migration hither, and raising the conditions of new appropriations of lands.

He has obstructed the administration of justice, by refusing his assent to laws for establishing judiciary powers.

He has made judges dependent on his will alone for the tenure of their offices, and the amount and payment of their salaries.

He has erected a multitude of new offices, and sent hither swarms of officers to harass our people and eat out their substance.

He has kept among us in times of peace, standing armies, without the consent of our legislatures.

He has affected to render the military independent of, and superior to, the civil power.

He has combined with others to subject us to a jurisdiction foreign to our constitutions, and unacknowledged by our laws; giving his assent to their acts of pretended legislation:

For quartering large bodies of armed troops among us;

For protecting them, by a mock trial, from punishment for any murders which they should commit on the inhabitants of these States;

For cutting off our trade with all parts of the world;

For imposing taxes on us without our consent;

For depriving us, in many cases, of the benefits of trial by jury;

For transporting us beyond the seas, to be tried for pretended offences;

For abolishing the free system of English laws in a neighboring province, establishing there an arbitrary government, and enlarging its boundaries, so as to render it at once an example and fit instrument for introducing the same absolute rule into these colonies;

For taking away our charters, abolishing our most valuable laws, and altering, fundamentally, the forms of our governments;

For suspending our own legislatures, and declaring themselves invested with power to legislate for us in all cases whatsoever.

He has abdicated government here, by declaring us out of his protection, and waging war against us.

He has plundered our seas, ravaged our coasts, burnt our towns, and destroyed the lives of our people.

He is at this time transporting large armies of foreign mercenaries to complete the works of death, desolation, and tyranny, already begun with circumstances of cruelty and perfidy scarcely paralleled in the most barbarous ages, and totally unworthy the head of a civilized nation.

He has constrained our fellow-citizens, taken captive on the high seas, to bear arms against their country, to become the executioners of their friends and brethren, or to fall themselves by their hands.

He has excited domestic insurrection amongst us, and has endeavored to bring on the inhabitants of our frontiers the merciless Indian savages, whose known rule of warfare is an undistinguished destruction of all ages, sexes, and conditions.

In every state of these oppressions we have petitioned for redress, in the most humble terms; our repeated petitions have been answered only by repeated injury. A prince whose character is thus marked by every act which may define a tyrant is unfit to be the ruler of a free people.

Nor have we been wanting in our attentions to our British brethren. We have warned them, from time to time, of attempts by their legislature to extend an unwarrantable jurisdiction over us. We have reminded them of the circumstances of our emigration and settlement here. We have appealed to their native justice and magnanimity; and we have conjured them, by the ties of our common kindred, to disavow these usurpations, which would inevitably interrupt our connections and correspondence. They, too, have been deaf to the voice of justice and of consanguinity. We must, therefore, acquiesce in the necessity which denounces our separation; and hold them, as we hold the rest of mankind, enemies in war, in peace friends.

We, therefore, the Representatives of the United States of America, in General Congress assembled, appealing to the Supreme Judge of the world for the rectitude of our intentions, do, in the name and by the authority of the good people of these colonies, solemnly publish and declare, That these united Colonies are, and of right ought to be, free and independent states; that they are absolved from all allegiance to the British crown, and that all political connection between them and the state of Great Britain is, and ought to be, totally dissolved; and that, as free and independent states, they have full power to levy war, conclude peace, contract alliances, establish commerce, and to do all other acts and things which independent states may of right do. And, for the support of this declaration, with a firm reliance on the protection of Divine Providence, we mutually pledge to each other our lives, our fortunes, and our sacred honor.

The foregoing Declaration was, by order of Congress, engrossed and signed by the following members:—

JOHN HANCOCK.

NEW HAMPSHIRE.
JOSIAH BARTLETT,
WILLIAM WHIPPLE,
MATTHEW THORNTON.

DELAWARE.
CAESAR RODNEY,
GEORGE READ,
THOMAS M'KEAN.

PENNSYLVANIA.
ROBERT MORRIS,
BENJAMIN RUSH,
BENJAMIN FRANKLIN,
JOHN MORTON,
GEORGE CLYMER,
JAMES SMITH,
GEORGE TAYLOR,
JAMES WILSON,
GEORGE ROSS.

CONNECTICUT.
ROGER SHERMAN,
SAMUEL HUNTINGTON,
WILLIAM WILLIAMS,
OLIVER WOLCOTT.

NEW JERSEY.
RICHARD STOCKTON,
JOHN WITHERSPOON,
FRANCIS HOPKINSON,
JOHN HART,
ABRAHAM CLARK.

MARYLAND.
SAMUEL CHASE,
WILLIAM PACA,
THOMAS STONE,
CHARLES CARROLL
     OF CARROLLTON.

RHODE ISLAND.
STEPHEN HOPKINS,
WILLIAM ELLERY.

NEW YORK.
WILLIAM FLOYD,
PHILIP LIVINGSTON,
FRANCIS LEWIS,
LEWIS MORRIS.

NORTH CAROLINA.
WILLIAM HOOPER,
JOSEPH HEWES,
JOHN PENN.

GEORGIA.
BUTTON GWINNETT,
LYMAN HALL,
GEORGE WALTON.

MASSACHUSETTS BAY.
SAMUEL ADAMS,
JOHN ADAMS,
ROBERT TREAT PAINE,
ELBRIDGE GERRY.

SOUTH CAROLINA.
EDWARD RUTLEDGE,
THOMAS HEYWARD, JR.,
THOMAS LYNCH, JR.,
ARTHUR MIDDLETON.

VIRGINIA.
GEORGE WYTHE,
RICHARD HENRY LEE,
THOMAS JEFFERSON,
BENJAMIN HARRISON,
THOMAS NELSON, JR.,
FRANCIS LIGHTFOOT LEE,
CARTER BRAXTON.

Resolved that copies of the Declaration be sent to the several assemblies, conventions, and committees, or councils of safety, and to the several commanding officers of the continental troops; that it be proclaimed in each of the United States, at the head of the army.

THE CONSTITUTION OF THE UNITED STATES and What It Means Today

The Constitution, the set of basic laws on which the federal government is founded, appears below in full. It is printed in black, part by part. After each part comes a section printed in color. This section will help you to understand the Constitution or the way it has worked in practice.

The word "clause" and the explanatory titles have been added for convenience. The spelling and punctuation of the original document have been modernized for easier reading.

Many changes have taken place in the United States and in the government since 1787, when the Constitutional Convention met in Philadelphia and wrote the Constitution. It has been in continuous use longer than any other written constitution in the world. As time passed and conditions changed, some parts of the Constitution went out of date. Some other parts have been set aside by amendments—additions or changes made after the original Constitution was adopted. These parts are in black like the rest of the Constitution but are in smaller type.

PREAMBLE:

The Purposes of the Constitution

We, the people of the United States, in order to form a more perfect Union, establish justice, insure domestic tranquillity, provide for the common defense, promote the general welfare, and secure the blessings of liberty to ourselves and our posterity, do ordain and establish this Constitution for the United States of America.

The people of the United States want to join the states more closely than they were under the Articles of Confederation. They want to set up fair laws. They want peace and order within their nation. They want to make their nation strong against foreign enemies. They want all their people to be prosperous and happy. And they want to make sure that this nation's people can be free not only now but forever. These are the purposes in making this Constitution for the United States of America.

ARTICLE 1

Congress, the Legislative Branch

The Power to Make Laws

SECTION 1. All legislative powers herein granted shall be vested in a Congress of the United States, which shall consist of a Senate and House of Representatives.

All national laws must be made by Congress, not by any other part of the government. Even Congress cannot make any laws except those kinds that the Constitution gives it permission to make. Neither Congress nor anybody else can make certain kinds of laws that might harm the citizens. Congress is made up of two separate parts, or "houses." These are the Senate, or "upper house," and the House of Representatives, or "lower house."

How Representatives Are Elected

SECTION 2, CLAUSE 1. The House of Representatives shall be composed of members chosen every second year by the people of the several states, and the electors in each state shall have the qualifications requisite for electors of the most numerous branch of the state legislature.

Members of the House of Representatives are elected in each state every two years. Any citizen whose state government permits him to vote for representatives in the state legislature must also be allowed to vote for members of the national House of Representatives. (Notice that this last rule really gives a state government the right, except if an amendment stipulates otherwise, to decide which of its citizens may vote for national Representatives.)

Who May Be a Representative

SECTION 2, CLAUSE 2. No person shall be a Representative who shall not have attained to the age of twenty-five years, and been seven years a citizen of the United States, and who shall not, when elected, be an inhabitant of that state in which he shall be chosen.

A person must be at least twenty-five years old before he can become a Representative. He must have been a United States citizen for seven years or more and must live in the state that elects him. These rules help to make sure that the laws are passed by mature persons.

791

Representatives and State Populations

SECTION 2, CLAUSE 3. Representatives and direct taxes shall be apportioned among the several states which may be included within this Union according to their respective numbers, which shall be determined by adding to the whole number of free persons, including those bound to service for a term of years, and excluding Indians not taxed, three-fifths of all other persons.

The number of Representatives that each state is entitled to send to Congress depends on the size of the state's population. (If State A, for instance, has twice as many people as State B, it may have, roughly, twice as many Representatives.) The amount of direct taxes— taxes handed over directly to the government by the taxpayer—which the federal government collects from any state must also depend on the number of people in the state. But the Sixteenth Amendment has changed this last rule as far as income taxes are concerned. Also, the long clause beginning "which shall be determined" is out of date, for there are no slaves or persons "bound to service" in this country any longer. Because of the Fourteenth Amendment, all the people of a state are now counted in full to decide how many Representatives that state may have.

Taking the Census

The actual enumeration shall be made within three years after the first meeting of the Congress of the United States, and within every subsequent term of ten years, in such a manner as they shall by law direct. The number of Representatives shall not exceed one for every thirty thousand, but each state shall have at least one Representative; and until such enumeration shall be made, the state of New Hampshire shall be entitled to choose 3; Massachusetts, 8; Rhode Island and Providence Plantations, 1; Connecticut, 5; New York, 6; New Jersey, 4; Pennsylvania, 8; Delaware, 1; Maryland, 6; Virginia, 10; North Carolina, 5; South Carolina, 5; and Georgia, 3.

Congress may decide how the populations of the states are to be counted. But such a count, or census, must be made every ten years. Besides finding out how many Representatives each state is entitled to, the census gathers many other valuable facts about the people.

The Constitution rules that (1) the House of Representatives must have not more than one member for every 30,000 people in the nation, but that (2) every state is entitled to at least one member no matter how small its population. If there were still one Representative for every 30,000 people, the House would contain more than 6000 members. To keep this from happening, Congress decided in 1929 that the House of Representatives should contain not more than 435 members. There is now one Representative for about every 400,000 people. (You can find out how many Representatives your state is entitled to by dividing its population by 400,000.) In 1960 a number of states had fewer than 400,000 persons each, yet each of these states had one Representative in the House.

Filling Vacancies in the House

SECTION 2, CLAUSE 4. When vacancies happen in the representation from any state, the executive authority thereof shall issue writs of election to fill such vacancies.

When a state does not have all the Representatives in the House that it is entitled to—as for instance, when a Representative dies or resigns—the state governor must call for a special election to fill the vacancy.

Officers of the House • Impeachment

SECTION 2, CLAUSE 5. The House of Representatives shall choose their Speaker and other officers; and shall have the sole power of impeachment.

The House of Representatives elects its own officers, including the Speaker—that is, the chairman—the majority and minority leaders, the sergeant-at-arms, and the chaplain. Only the House has the right to impeach an official of the United States, that is, to accuse him of wrongdoing for which he may be tried (see page 299).

The Senate

SECTION 3, CLAUSE 1. The Senate of the United States shall be composed of two Senators from each state, chosen by the legislature thereof for six years; and each Senator shall have one vote.

Each state has the right to send two Senators to Congress. (With fifty states, the Senate now contains 100 members.) Each Senator serves for a six-year term and has one vote. In the Senate even the smallest state has as much power as the largest state. Without this guarantee of equal power, the small states among the original thirteen might not have been willing to adopt the Constitution. They were afraid that the strong states would have too much power over them in the House, where the states with the most people had the most votes. Compare this section with Section 2, Clause 3.

Senators are no longer chosen by the legislatures of their states. Under the Seventeenth Amendment, adopted in 1913, United States Senators are now elected by the voters of their states, just as members of the national House of Representatives are.

When the Senators' Terms Expire

SECTION 3, CLAUSE 2. Immediately after they shall be assembled in consequence of the first election, they shall be divided as equally as may be into three classes. The seats of the Senators of the first class shall be vacated at the expiration of the second year, of the second class at the expiration of the fourth year, and of the third class at the expiration of the sixth year, so that one-third may be chosen every second year; and if vacancies happen by resignation or otherwise during the recess of the legislature of any state, the executive thereof may make temporary appointments until the next meeting of the legislature, which shall then fill such vacancies.

The three different classes of Senators ordered by this clause were intended only to get the Senate started. After the first four years of the Constitution, Senators were no longer divided into classes; all Senators now have six-year terms. But because of this "staggering system," there is never more than one-third of the Senators who have just been elected—or reelected; one-third have served for two years, and one-third have served for four years. For this reason the Senate carries on its work without ever having a complete turnover in its membership.

The last part of this clause, describing how vacancies in the Senate were to be filled, has been changed by the Seventeenth Amendment.

Who May Be a Senator

SECTION 3, CLAUSE 3. No person shall be a Senator who shall not have attained to the age of thirty years and been nine years a citizen of the United States, and who shall not when elected be an inhabitant of that state for which he shall be chosen.

This clause names the requirements for becoming a Senator. Notice that the requirements for a Senator are more demanding than those for a Representative.

The Vice-President

SECTION 3, CLAUSE 4. The Vice-President of the United States shall be President of the Senate, but shall have no vote unless they be equally divided.

The vice-president of the United States serves as president of the Senate. That is, he serves as its chairman, in the same way that the Speaker serves as the chairman of the House of Representatives. The Vice-President is not a regular, elected member of the Senate. For this reason, he is not allowed to vote in the Senate unless his vote is needed to break a tie.

Other Officers of the Senate

SECTION 3, CLAUSE 5. The Senate shall choose their other officers, and also a President pro tempore, in the absence of the Vice-President, or when he shall exercise the office of the President of the United States.

The Senate chooses its other officers, for instance, its sergeant-at-arms and its chaplain. Sometimes the vice-president of the United States is unable to serve as chairman of the Senate. Then the Senate chooses a Senator to be president pro tempore—president for the time being—who serves as the chairman.

Impeachment Trials

SECTION 3, CLAUSE 6. The Senate shall have the sole power to try all impeachments. When sitting for that purpose, they shall be on oath or affirmation. When the President of the United States is tried, the Chief Justice shall preside; and no person shall be convicted without the concurrence of two-thirds of the members present.

Persons who are believed to have done serious wrongs as officials of the United States may be removed from office by the process called impeachment. Only the House of Representatives has the right to begin an impeachment, that is, make charges against a suspected official (Section 2, Clause 5). Only the Senate has the right to try the official after the House of Representatives has impeached him. In an impeachment, the official on trial is declared not guilty unless at least two-thirds of the total number of Senators who are present vote that he is guilty.

Ordinarily the president of the Senate presides at impeachment trials. But the Chief Justice of the United States must preside over the Senate when the president of the United States is being tried. It would not be fair to let the Vice-President preside then, for he would be the one to succeed to the presidency if the President were found guilty.

Punishment in Impeachment Trials

SECTION 3, CLAUSE 7. Judgment in cases of impeachment shall not extend further than to removal from office and disqualification to hold and enjoy any office of honor, trust, or profit under the United States; but the party convicted shall nevertheless be liable and subject to indictment, trial, judgment, and punishment, according to law.

If the Senate declares an impeached official guilty, it can punish him in only one way, and that is by putting him out of office and forbidding him ever to hold another office in the federal government. But this does not mean that a federal official can commit crimes without severe punishment. After being put out of office, he can then be tried by a jury in a regular court. If the court finds him guilty, he can be punished like anyone else.

Members of Congress are never impeached. But they may be expelled by action of the house to which they have been elected. (See Section 5, Clause 2.)

Elections to Congress

SECTION 4, CLAUSE 1. The times, places, and manner of holding elections for Senators and Representatives shall be prescribed in each state by the legislature thereof; but the Congress may at any time by law make or alter such regulations except as to the places of choosing Senators.

The legislature of each state has the right to pass laws deciding when, where, and how Senators and Representatives are to be elected. But Congress has the right to pass laws that change a state's election laws. One federal law requires that secret ballots be used.

In every state, the day for congressional elections is the first Tuesday following the first Monday in November of even-numbered years (1968, 1970, and so on).

The last phrase of Clause 1 is not in effect. As a result of the Seventeenth Amendment, both Senators and Representatives are chosen by the same methods and in the same places.

Meetings of Congress

SECTION 4, CLAUSE 2. The Congress shall assemble at least once in every year, and such meeting shall be on the first Monday in December, unless they shall by law appoint a different day.

Congress must hold at least one meeting, or session, each year. This helps to guarantee that no executive can ever gain control of the government by putting an end to the work of the elected members of Congress. In 1933 the day for beginning each session of Congress was changed to January 3, by the Twentieth Amendment.

Rules of Congress

SECTION 5, CLAUSE 1. Each house shall be the judge of the elections, returns, and qualifications of its own members, and a majority of each shall constitute a quorum to do business; but a smaller number may adjourn from day to day and may be authorized to compel the attendance of absent members in such manner and under such penalties as each house may provide.

Each house of Congress has the right to decide whether its members were elected fairly and meet the requirements for members of Congress. A Senator or Representative who is newly elected can be kept from taking office if a majority in the house to which he was elected voted to keep him out.

A quorum is the number of members of a group that must be present before the group can conduct its official business. The Constitution says that a majority—half the members plus one—is the number needed to make a quorum in either house of Congress. But in practice, work may often be carried on without a quorum—provided that no member demands that those present be counted. When less than half the members of either house are present, that house may adjourn until the next day and may use penalties to force the absent members to attend.

More Rules of Congress

SECTION 5, CLAUSE 2. Each house may determine the rules of its proceedings, punish its members for disorderly behavior, and, with the concurrence of two-thirds, expel a member.

Each house has the right to make rules about the work it carries on and the actions of its members and may punish its members for misbehaving. Each house has the right to expel any of its members by a two-thirds vote. This provides a way of getting rid of wrongdoers in Congress, much as impeachment gets rid of officials who do wrong in other branches of the federal government. (See Section 3, Clauses 6 and 7.)

Records of the Actions of Congress

SECTION 5, CLAUSE 3. Each house shall keep a journal of its proceedings, and from time to time publish the same, excepting such parts as may in their judgment require secrecy; and the yeas and nays of the members of either house on any question shall, at the desire of one-fifth of those present, be entered on the journal.

Each house of Congress must keep a separate record of what goes on at its meetings and must publish the record periodically. But the members may vote not to publish everything—that is, to keep some things secret. How each member votes on a particular question—whether yea (for) or nay (against)—is put into the record if one-fifth of the members who are present wish this to be done.

The Congressional Record, published for every day that Congress is in session, records the actions of both houses of Congress. At longer intervals, the House publishes The House Journal, and the Senate, The Senate Journal.

Adjournments

SECTION 5, CLAUSE 4. Neither house, during the session of Congress, shall without the consent of the other adjourn, for more than three days, nor to any other place than that in which the two houses shall be sitting.

During the period when Congress is meeting, neither house may suspend its meetings for more than three days unless the other house gives permission. Since the work of the two houses is closely related, neither house is allowed to move to another city unless the other house agrees.

Pay and Privileges of Members of Congress

SECTION 6, CLAUSE 1. The Senators and Representatives shall receive a compensation for their services, to be ascertained by law, and paid out of the Treasury of the United States. They shall in all cases, except treason, felony, and breach of the peace, be privileged from arrest during their attendance at the session of their respective houses, and in going to and returning from the same; and for any speech or debate in either house they shall not be questioned in any other place.

Members of Congress are paid out of the United States treasury. The size of the salaries they receive is determined by Congress.

Members of Congress may not be arrested at meetings of Congress or on their way to or from those meetings—unless they are suspected of committing serious crimes or disturbing the peace. They may not be arrested or be punished for anything they may say in Congress except by the house of which they are members. These privileges, called "congressional immunity," allow members of Congress to say without fear of punishment what they believe is for the good of the country.

What the Members of Congress May Not Do

SECTION 6, CLAUSE 2. No Senator or Representative shall, during the time for which he was elected, be appointed to any civil office under the authority of the United States which shall have been created or the emoluments whereof shall have been increased during such time; and no person holding any office under the United States shall be a member of either house during his continuance in office.

Until his term has ended, no member of Congress may take any other job in the federal government if that job was set up or the pay for that job was increased during the member's term. This rule helps to keep congressmen from creating good jobs for themselves. Furthermore, no person is allowed to become a member of Congress without first giving up any other federal job that he may hold.

Bills for Raising Money

SECTION 7, CLAUSE 1. All bills for raising revenue shall originate in the House of Representatives; but the Senate may propose or concur with amendments as on other bills.

Either the Senate or the House of Representatives has the right to start most kinds of bills, but only the House may start a bill for raising money by taxes. But the Senate has the right to make amendments, or changes, in the tax bills begun in the House.

How a Bill Becomes a Law

SECTION 7, CLAUSE 2. Every bill which shall have passed the House of Representatives and the Senate shall before it becomes a law be presented to the

President of the United States. If he approve, he shall sign it; but if not, he shall return it with his objections to that house in which it shall have originated, who shall enter the objections at large on their journal and proceed to reconsider it. If after such reconsideration two-thirds of that house shall agree to pass the bill, it shall be sent, together with the objections, to the other house, by which it shall likewise be reconsidered; and if approved by two-thirds of that house, it shall become a law. But in all such cases the votes of both houses shall be determined by yeas and nays, and the names of the persons voting for and against the bill shall be entered on the journal of each house respectively.

This clause of the Constitution gives most of the method by which the nation's laws are made. Except for any tax bills (see Section 7, Clause 1), either the Senate or the House may write a bill proposing a new law. Suppose, for instance, that a bill is introduced in the Senate. If a majority of the Senators who are present vote against the bill, it dies in the Senate and does not become a law. But if a majority vote for it, it is then sent to the House of Representatives. Here, too, it either dies or is passed, depending on the vote of the majority. But very likely the House passes the bill only after having made amendments to it. If this is the case, it must be sent back to the Senate, to be voted on there in its amended form.

When both the Senate and the House have voted in favor of the bill, with its amendments if any, it is sent to the president of the United States. He studies it and usually gets advice from some of his assistants. If he favors the bill, he signs it, and it then becomes an official law of the country—often called an Act of Congress. But if the President is against a proposed law, he vetoes the bill—refuses to sign it. He then sends the bill, usually with a written statement of his objections, back to the house in which it originated (in this example, to the Senate).

Next, the Senate votes on the bill again, but this time the bill dies if less than two-thirds of the Senators present vote for it. When this occurs, the veto is "sustained." If two-thirds or more vote for the bill, it is passed in spite of the President's objection to it. This is called overriding the veto. When a veto is overridden, the name of each member of each house and the way he voted must be entered on the official record.

A bill repassed by the Senate over the President's veto is sent on to the House, still accompanied by the President's objections. Here the bill goes through the same process, and the President's veto either is sustained or is overridden by a two-thirds vote. If both houses override the veto, the bill becomes a law that is just as binding as if it had been signed by the President.

The rules for turning a bill into a law work the same way whether the bill begins in the Senate or in the House.

The "Pocket Veto"

If any bill shall not be returned by the President within ten days (Sundays excepted) after it shall have been presented to him, the same shall be a law in like manner as if he had signed it, unless the Congress by their adjournment prevent its return, in which case it shall not be a law.

If the President receives a bill passed by both houses and keeps it for ten days or more (not counting Sundays) without either signing it or vetoing it, it becomes a law without the need for Congress to do anything more about it. (The President sometimes does this when he does not want to take a stand either for the bill or against it.) But if Congress adjourns before the ten days are up and before the President has either signed or vetoed the bill, the bill dies. This is called the pocket veto.

By using his veto power, the President exercises one of the checks and balances intended by the framers of the Constitution (see page 124). So does Congress when it overrides a veto.

Other Actions of Congress

SECTION 7, CLAUSE 3. Every order, resolution, or vote to which the concurrence of the Senate and House of Representatives may be necessary (except on a question of adjournment) shall be presented to the President of the United States; and before the same shall take effect, shall be approved by him, or being disapproved by him, shall be repassed by two-thirds of the Senate and House of Representatives, according to the rules and limitations prescribed in the case of a bill.

Besides bills, there are other actions of Congress that take effect only after they have been approved by the President, or, if vetoed by him, have been repassed by two-thirds of both houses. These actions include "every order, resolution, or vote"—except a vote to adjourn Congress, which need only be passed by both houses.

The Laying of Taxes

SECTION 8, CLAUSE 1. The Congress shall have power to lay and collect taxes, duties, imposts, and excises, to pay the debts and provide for the common defense and general welfare of the United States; but all duties, imposts, and excises shall be uniform throughout the United States.

Congress may pass laws for collecting taxes of various kinds. It may do this for three purposes: (1) to pay the nation's debts, (2) to defend the nation against its enemies, and (3) to do whatever is necessary for the good of the people. If the federal government had no power to tax, the nation could not meet its obligations and would soon fall to pieces.

All federal taxes must be the same in all parts of the country. This rule keeps Congress from unfairly favoring or discriminating against any state or district.

The Borrowing of Money

SECTION 8, CLAUSE 2. To borrow money on the credit of the United States.

Congress has the power to borrow money for the use of the federal government and promises to repay this money when it is due.

Foreign and Interstate Commerce

SECTION 8, CLAUSE 3. To regulate commerce with foreign nations, and among the several states, and with the Indian tribes.

Because of this clause, known as the "commerce clause," Congress has passed laws to control trade (1) between this country and foreign countries (foreign commerce) and (2) between one state and another state (interstate commerce). These laws control the movements across national or state boundaries of persons, goods, and messages. These laws also control the facilities for international and interstate transportation and communication: ships, harbors, canals and navigable rivers, highways, railroads, bus lines, airlines, and telegraph, telephone, radio, and television systems.

Under the commerce clause, Congress encourages the commerce that means prosperity for the country and keeps the states from taxing goods sent in from other states. Congress can impose tariffs, or import taxes, on goods brought into this country, or can keep out goods— or undesirable persons—altogether. Throughout United States history Congress has passed many laws based upon powers granted in this section.

Naturalization • Bankruptcy

SECTION 8, CLAUSE 4. To establish a uniform rule of naturalization, and uniform laws on the subject of bankruptcies throughout the United States.

Congress is empowered to decide which citizens of foreign countries may be naturalized—that is, which may become United States citizens—and how this may be done. A federal bankruptcy law, which is the same for all parts of the country, helps to make sure of fair treatment for everybody to whom a person owes debts that he cannot pay.

Coinage • Weights and Measures

SECTION 8, CLAUSE 5. To coin money, regulate the value thereof and foreign coin, and fix the standard of weights and measures.

Congress controls the minting of money from metals, and decides how much the coins shall be worth. It can set the value of foreign money in this country. By using its power to borrow money (Section 8, Clause 2), Congress orders that paper money be printed. Congress has set up the standards for measuring weights and distances. Much confusion is saved by having a pound, for instance, or a yard, exactly the same in all parts of the United States.

Counterfeiting

SECTION 8, CLAUSE 6. To provide for the punishment of counterfeiting the securities and current coin of the United States.

Congress passes laws ordering severe punishments for persons who make false money or false government bonds and notes. Secret Service men in the Department of the Treasury protect people against counterfeiters.

Postal Service

SECTION 8, CLAUSE 7. To establish post offices and post roads.

Congress controls the postal system and the post offices for handling the mail and can have the roads over which the mail is carried built and maintained. Over the years, the Post Office Department has taken on additional functions besides delivering letters. It carries parcels, handles postal-savings accounts, and sells postal money orders.

Rights of Authors and Inventors

SECTION 8, CLAUSE 8. To promote the progress of science and useful arts, by securing for limited times to authors and inventors the exclusive right to their respective writings and discoveries.

Congress encourages this country's art, science, and industry by means of laws helping artists and inventors of various kinds. Copyright laws protect authors, composers, and artists from having their writings, music, paintings, and other creative works copied by others without payment. Patent laws protect in the same way those who invent or discover new and useful manufactured articles or valuable new methods in science and industry.

Federal Courts

SECTION 8, CLAUSE 9. To constitute tribunals inferior to the Supreme Court.

Congress sets up federal courts that have less authority than the United States Supreme Court. Courts of appeals, district courts, and courts of claims are some of the different kinds of federal courts.

Crimes at Sea • Crimes Against International Law

SECTION 8, CLAUSE 10. To define and punish piracies and felonies committed on the high seas, and offenses against the law of nations.

Congress rules what acts committed at sea are crimes and how they are to be punished. It may also make laws about crimes in which foreign countries or foreign citizens are involved.

Declarations of War

SECTION 8, CLAUSE 11. To declare war, grant letters of marque and reprisal, and make rules concerning captures on land and water.

Congress, and only Congress, is authorized to declare war. But in the face of an attack by a foreign country, this country may need to use its armed forces even before Congress can act. Letters of marque and reprisal were licenses given to privateers to seize the ships of an enemy. This kind of activity is illegal today.

The Army

SECTION 8, CLAUSE 12. To raise and support armies, but no appropriation of money to that use shall be for a longer term than two years.

Congress may create an army for the United States and vote the money to pay for it. But Congress must not give the army at any one time more than enough for two years' expenses.

The Navy

SECTION 8, CLAUSE 13. To provide and maintain a navy.

Congress may create a navy for the United States and vote the money to pay for it.

796

Rules for the Armed Forces

SECTION 8, CLAUSE 14. To make rules for the government and regulation of the land and naval forces.

Congress may make the rules for the armed forces, which now include the Air Force.

Use of the Militia

SECTION 8, CLAUSE 15. To provide for calling forth the militia to execute the laws of the Union, suppress insurrections, and repel invasions.

Congress may rule how and when the militia—that is, the citizen-soldiers in the various states, now called the National Guard—are to be called to help the federal government. The militia may be called on to enforce federal laws, end rebellions, and drive out foreign enemies.

Control of the Militia

SECTION 8, CLAUSE 16. To provide for organizing, arming, and disciplining the militia, and for governing such part of them as may be employed in the service of the United States, reserving to the states, respectively, the appointment of the officers and the authority of training the militia according to the discipline prescribed by Congress.

Congress may organize the militia, furnish weapons to them, and make rules for those members of the militia who are in the service of the United States. But although the government of each state has the right to appoint the officers of its militia, it must train the militia as Congress directs.

The National Capital   •   Other Federal Property

SECTION 8, CLAUSE 17. To exercise exclusive legislation in all cases whatsoever over such district (not exceeding ten miles square) as may, by cession of particular states and the acceptance of Congress, become the seat of government of the United States, and to exercise like authority over all places purchased by the consent of the legislature of the state in which the same shall be, for the erection of forts, magazines, arsenals, dockyards, and other needful buildings.

Congress makes all the laws for governing the District of Columbia (containing the national capital—established in Washington). The capital is not under the control of any state or county government.

Congress also governs all other property belonging to the federal government—post offices, national forests, etc.

Other Necessary Laws

SECTION 8, CLAUSE 18. And to make all laws which shall be necessary and proper for carrying into execution the foregoing powers and all other powers vested by this Constitution in the government of the United States, or in any department or officer thereof.

Besides the lawmaking powers specifically granted to Congress by the Constitution, Congress may make any other laws that are needed in order to carry out the orders in the Constitution. This clause is called the elastic clause because it can be stretched to fit the changing needs of the nation. But the elastic clause does not permit Congress to legislate without any restrictions. The Supreme

Court and the other federal courts have the power to rule out, as unconstitutional, any law of Congress which they consider to be not "necessary and proper" (Article 3, Section 1).

The Slave Trade

SECTION 9, CLAUSE 1. The migration or importation of such persons as any of the states now existing shall think proper to admit shall not be prohibited by the Congress prior to the year one thousand eight hundred and eight, but a tax or duty may be imposed on such importation, not exceeding ten dollars for each person.

This clause made it possible to outlaw the bringing of slaves into the United States, beginning in 1808.

Habeas Corpus

SECTION 9, CLAUSE 2. The privilege of the writ of habeas corpus shall not be suspended, unless when in cases of rebellion or invasion the public safety may require it.

The federal government is not allowed to take away the right of habeas corpus except in time of great danger to the country. Habeas corpus gives a person accused of a crime a means by which he may obtain a prompt hearing on the charges. It protects a person from arbitrary arrest or long imprisonment without a hearing.

Bills of Attainder   •   Ex Post Facto Laws

SECTION 9, CLAUSE 3. No bill of attainder or ex post facto law shall be passed.

Congress must not pass any bill intending to punish one particular person—a bill of attainder. Congress must not pass any law that would punish a person for doing something that was not against the law at the time he did it.

Direct Taxes in Proportion to Population

SECTION 9, CLAUSE 4. No capitation or other direct tax shall be laid, unless in proportion to the census or enumeration hereinbefore directed to be taken.

Congress must not order any direct tax except in proportion to the populations of the various states as determined from the census count. An income tax is one kind of direct tax, but the Constitution has been amended to make it permissible. See the Sixteenth Amendment.

Export Taxes Forbidden

SECTION 9, CLAUSE 5. No tax or duty shall be laid on articles exported from any state.

Congress must not tax goods sent from one state to another or goods sent to other countries.

Ports and Port Duties

SECTION 9, CLAUSE 6. No preference shall be given by any regulation of commerce or revenue to the ports of one state over those of another; nor shall vessels bound to or from one state be obliged to enter, clear, or pay duties to another.

Congress must not give the ports of one state any advantage over the ports of another state. Congress must not allow ports in one state to collect duties on the cargoes of vessels traveling from another state.

Accounting for Public Money

SECTION 9, CLAUSE 7. No money shall be drawn from the Treasury but in consequence of appropriations made by law; and a regular statement and account of the receipts and expenditures of all public money shall be published from time to time.

Money can be paid out of the treasury only if an act of Congress gives permission. Statements showing how much money was received in the treasury and how much was paid out must be published from time to time.

Titles of Nobility • Gifts

SECTION 9, CLAUSE 8. No title of nobility shall be granted by the United States; and no person holding any office of profit or trust under them shall without the consent of the Congress accept of any present, emolument, office, or title of any kind whatever from any king, prince, or foreign state.

The federal government must not create noble rank for anybody. No federal official may accept any gift, position, or title from any foreign government unless Congress gives its permission. This rule helps to keep United States officials from accepting bribes from foreign countries.

Actions Forbidden to the States

SECTION 10, CLAUSE 1. No state shall enter into any treaty, alliance, or confederation; grant letters of marque and reprisal; coin money; emit bills of credit; make anything but gold and silver coin a tender in payment of debts; pass any bill of attainder, ex post facto law, or law impairing the obligation of contracts, or grant any title of nobility.

State governments must not make treaties or pacts of union with foreign countries. State governments may not grant their citizens permission to fight against foreign countries, make coins or paper money for themselves, or allow anything but gold and silver coins to be used as legal money. These powers belong exclusively to the national government.

The state governments, like the national government, are forbidden to pass acts that punish people without giving them trials, to pass laws that would punish people for things they did that were not against the law when they did them, or to grant titles of nobility. State governments must not pass any laws that would destroy the contracts by which people make legal agreements with one another.

Taxation by the States

SECTION 10, CLAUSE 2. No state shall, without the consent of the Congress, lay any imposts or duties on imports or exports, except what may be absolutely necessary for executing its inspection laws; and the net produce of all duties and imposts, laid by any state on imports or exports, shall be for the use of the Treasury of the United States; and all such laws shall be subject to the revision and control of the Congress.

States must not interfere with commerce by taxing goods entering or leaving their territory—except that they may charge fees for inspecting such goods. But any money the states collect as inspection fees must be paid into the treasury of the United States. Congress has the power to change the inspection laws of any of the states.

Other State Actions Forbidden

SECTION 10, CLAUSE 3. No state shall, without the consent of Congress, lay any duty of tonnage, keep troops or ships of war in time of peace, enter into any agreement or compact with another state, or with a foreign power, or engage in war, unless actually invaded, or in such imminent danger as will not admit of delay.

Unless Congress gives permission, no state may do these things: (1) charge a tax on ships that enter its ports, (2) have its own army—except the militia—or navy in peacetime, (3) make treaties with other states or with foreign countries, (4) make war except when it has been invaded or is threatened with invasion. All these are powers that should be exercised only by the national government for the good of the whole country.

ARTICLE 2

The Presidency and the Executive Branch

Terms of the President and the Vice-President

SECTION 1, CLAUSE 1. The executive power shall be vested in a President of the United States of America. He shall hold his office during the term of four years and, together with the Vice-President, chosen for the same term, be elected as follows.

The nation's laws are enforced, or executed, by the president of the United States. His term of office is four years. The Vice-President also has a four-year term.

The Presidential Electors

SECTION 1, CLAUSE 2. Each state shall appoint, in such manner as the legislature thereof may direct, a number of electors, equal to the whole number of Senators and Representatives to which the state may be entitled in the Congress; but no Senator or Representative, or person holding an office of trust or profit under the United States, shall be appointed an elector.

According to the Constitution, but not in actual practice nowadays, the President and the Vice-President are to be chosen by electors in each state. These electors are selected according to rules set up by the state legislatures. The electors from all the states form what is known as the electoral college, though they never meet as a single group. The number of electors in each state is equal to the number of that state's Senators and Representatives in Congress. Nobody who has any federal-government position may be an elector.

The election of the President and the Vice-President, both as it now is and as the writers of the Constitution intended it to be, is explained following the Twelfth Amendment.

Duties of the Electors

SECTION 1, CLAUSE 3. The electors shall meet in their respective states and vote by ballot for two persons, of whom one at least shall not be an inhabitant of the same state with themselves. And they shall make a list of all the persons voted for, and of the number of votes for each, which list they shall sign and certify and transmit, sealed, to the seat of the government of the United States, directed to the president of the Senate. The president of the Senate shall, in the presence of the Senate and the House of Representatives, open all the certificates, and the votes shall then be counted. The person having the greatest number of votes shall be the President, if such number be a majority of the whole number of electors appointed; and if there be more than one who have such majority, and have an equal number of votes, then the House of Representatives shall immediately choose by ballot one of them for President; and if no person have a majority, then from the five highest on the list the said House shall in like manner choose the President. But in choosing the President, the vote shall be taken by states, the representation from each state having one vote. A quorum for this purpose shall consist of a member or members from two-thirds of the states, and a majority of all the states shall be necessary to a choice. In every case, after the choice of President, the person having the greatest number of votes of the electors shall be the Vice-President. But if there should remain two or more who have equal votes, the Senate shall choose from them by ballot the Vice-President.

This clause did not work well in practice and was changed in 1804 by the Twelfth Amendment.

Election Day

SECTION 1, CLAUSE 4. The Congress may determine the time of choosing the electors and the day on which they shall give their votes, which day shall be the same throughout the United States.

Congress may decide on what day the electors are to be elected and the day when they are to cast their ballots for President and Vice-President. This day is the same in all parts of the United States. See the explanation of presidential elections following the Twelfth Amendment.

Who May Become President

SECTION 1, CLAUSE 5. No person except a natural-born citizen or a citizen of the United States at the time of the adoption of this Constitution shall be eligible to the office of President; neither shall any person be eligible to that office who shall not have attained the age of thirty-five years and been fourteen years a resident within the United States.

Nobody may become President unless he is a citizen of the United States by birth, is at least thirty-five years old, and has lived in the United States for fourteen years or more.

Succession to the Presidency

SECTION 1, CLAUSE 6. In case of the removal of the President from office, or of his death, resignation, or inability to discharge the powers and duties of the said office, the same shall devolve on the Vice-President, and the Congress may by law provide for the case of removal, death, resignation, or inability, both of the President and Vice-President, declaring what officer shall then act as President, and such officer shall act accordingly until the disability be removed or a President shall be elected.

If the presidency becomes vacant, the Vice-President assumes the office. (See the Twenty-fifth Amendment, which tells exactly how he may assume it and also how the office of Vice-President is filled when a vacancy in it exists.)

The President's Salary

SECTION 1, CLAUSE 7. The President shall at stated times receive for his services a compensation, which shall neither be increased nor diminished during the period for which he shall have been elected, and he shall not receive within that period any other emolument from the United States, or any of them.

The President receives a salary, which must not be made either larger or smaller during his term of office. This rule keeps Congress from getting too much control over the President by threatening his income or by trying to bribe him. His salary is now $100,000 a year, besides other sums for his expenses. He must not receive any other kind of salary from either the federal government or any state government.

President's Oath of Office

SECTION 1, CLAUSE 8. Before he enter on the execution of his office he shall take the following oath or affirmation: "I do solemnly swear (or affirm) that I will faithfully execute the office of President of the United States, and will to the best of my ability preserve, protect, and defend the Constitution of the United States."

Before the President starts his term, he must make a solemn promise to perform his duties faithfully and to protect this country's form of government.

Military Powers • Pardons

SECTION 2, CLAUSE 1. The President shall be commander in chief of the Army and Navy of the United States, and of the militias of the several states when called into the actual service of the United States; he may require the opinion, in writing, of the principal officer in each of the executive departments, upon any subject relating to the duties of their respective offices, and he shall have power to grant reprieves and pardons for offenses against the United States, except in cases of impeachment.

The President is the commander in chief of the armed forces of the United States and of the militia when it is called into national service. He may order written reports from Cabinet officers about the work of their departments. He may pardon persons convicted of crimes against the federal government or order their punishments to be delayed—but he may not do this for impeached government officials.

Treaties and Appointments

SECTION 2, CLAUSE 2. He shall have power, by and with the advice and consent of the Senate, to make treaties, provided two-thirds of the Senators present concur; and he shall nominate and, by and with the advice and consent of the Senate, shall appoint ambassadors, other public ministers and consuls, judges of the Supreme Court, and all other officers of the United States whose appointments are not herein provided for and which shall be established by law; but the Congress may by law vest the appointment of such inferior officers as they think proper in the President alone, in the courts of law, or in the heads of departments.

The President may make treaties with foreign countries, but at least two-thirds of the Senators present must approve a treaty before it becomes a law. He may appoint certain important officials only if the Senate approves his choices. But Congress may transfer, to the President, to his department chiefs, or to the courts, exclusive control over the appointment of less important officials.

Filling Vacant Positions

SECTION 2, CLAUSE 3. The President shall have power to fill up all vacancies that may happen during the recess of the Senate by granting commissions which shall expire at the end of their next session.

If positions become vacant when the Senate is not meeting, the President may appoint persons to fill them. These are temporary appointments which end at the conclusion of the next session of the Senate.

In practice, the great majority of those who work for the federal government are now appointed through the United States Civil Service Commission.

Other Duties of the President

SECTION 3. He shall from time to time give to the Congress information of the state of the Union, and recommend to their consideration such measures as he shall judge necessary and expedient; he may, on extraordinary occasions, convene both houses, or either of them, and in case of disagreement between them, with respect to the time of adjournment, he may adjourn them to such time as he shall think proper; he shall receive ambassadors and other public ministers; he shall take care that the laws be faithfully executed, and shall commission all the officers of the United States.

The President must give Congress information about the condition of the country and suggest to Congress what he thinks Congress ought to legislate on. This information is presented in the State of the Union message. By custom, the President delivers such a message in a speech to Congress every January. He may call a special session of either house or both houses of Congress if there is an urgent need. He may end a session of Congress if the two houses cannot agree on a time for ending. He receives representatives of foreign governments. It is his duty to make sure that the nation's laws are properly carried out. He signs official papers appointing persons to jobs in the federal government.

Impeachments

SECTION 4. The President, Vice-President, and all civil officers of the United States shall be removed from office on impeachment for, and conviction of, treason, bribery, or other high crimes and misdemeanors.

The President, the Vice-President, or any civilian official of the federal government must be put out of office if he has been impeached and found guilty of disloyalty to his country, of bribery, or of other crimes.

ARTICLE 3

The Supreme Court and the Judicial Branch

Federal Courts • Federal Judges

SECTION 1. The judicial power of the United States shall be vested in one Supreme Court, and in such inferior courts as the Congress may from time to time ordain and establish. The judges, both of the Supreme and inferior courts, shall hold their offices during good behavior, and shall at stated times receive for their services a compensation, which shall not be diminished during their continuance in office.

This, the third great branch of the federal government, is the judicial branch, which has the task of judging cases and of explaining what the laws mean. The United States Supreme Court is at the head of the judicial branch. In addition there are other federal courts set up by Congress, including courts of appeals, district courts, and courts of claims. The federal judges, including the Supreme Court justices, are appointed by the President, with Senate approval. These judges may hold their jobs as long as they live, unless they are impeached and found guilty. Their salaries cannot be lowered while they are in office.

One of the most important powers of the federal courts, and especially of the Supreme Court, is not mentioned in the Constitution. This is their power to decide that certain federal, state, and local laws are unconstitutional—that they are in violation of the Constitution. In this way, the federal courts exercise one of the important checks and balances in the American system of government.

Kinds of Cases Tried in Federal Courts

SECTION 2, CLAUSE 1. The judicial power shall extend to all cases in law and equity arising under this Constitution, the laws of the United States, and treaties made or which shall be made under their authority; to all cases affecting ambassadors, other public ministers, and consuls; to all cases of admiralty and maritime jurisdiction; to controversies to which the United States shall be a party; to controversies between two or more states; between a state and citizens of another state; between citizens of different states; between citizens of the same state claiming lands under grants of different states, and between a state, or the citizens thereof, and foreign states, citizens, or subjects.

The cases tried by the federal courts are those concerning (1) the Constitution and the nation's laws and treaties, (2) the representatives of foreign governments, (3) the laws controlling ships and sailors, (4) disagreements between the government and other governments or persons, (5) disagreements between states, (6) disagreements between citizens of different states, (7) disagreements in which citizens of the same state claim lands granted by different states, (8) disagreements between a state or its citizens and a foreign country or foreign citizens.

The jurisdiction over disagreements between a state and citizens of another state was changed by the Eleventh Amendment.

Jurisdiction of the Supreme Court

SECTION 2, CLAUSE 2. In all cases affecting ambassadors, other public ministers and consuls, and those in which a state shall be party, the Supreme Court shall have original jurisdiction. In all the other cases before mentioned, the Supreme Court shall have appellate jurisdiction, both as to law and fact, with such exceptions and under such regulations as the Congress shall make.

The Supreme Court has two kinds of jurisdiction—that is, authority to try cases. First, it can try new cases being brought to court for the first time, if those cases concern one of the states or a representative of a foreign government. This is the original jurisdiction. Second, it can try cases again that have already been tried in the lower federal courts—but only if one of the parties in the case objects to the decision of the lower courts and appeals the case. This is the appellate jurisdiction. After a case has been tried in the Supreme Court, there is no higher court to which the case can be appealed.

Trial by Jury for Criminal Cases

SECTION 2, CLAUSE 3. The trial of all crimes except in cases of impeachment shall be by jury; and such trial shall be held in the state where the said crimes shall have been committed; but when not committed within any state, the trial shall be at such place or places as the Congress may by law have directed.

Except for impeachment trials, all trials for crimes against federal laws must be held before juries in the states where the crimes occurred. But if they took place outside of any state—at sea, for instance—then Congress can decide where the trials should be held.

Every citizen's right to a jury trial when he is accused of a crime keeps him from being punished unless a jury of his fellow citizens finds him guilty.

The Definition of Treason

SECTION 3, CLAUSE 1. Treason against the United States shall consist only in levying war against them, or in adhering to their enemies, giving them aid and comfort. No person shall be convicted of treason unless on the testimony of two witnesses to the same overt act, or on confession in open court.

Only these acts by a United States citizen may be considered treason: (1) making war against this country, and (2) helping this country's enemies. Nobody can be punished for treason unless two or more citizens both swear they saw him commit the same act of treason or unless he confesses in court.

The Punishment for Treason

SECTION 3, CLAUSE 2. The Congress shall have power to declare the punishment of treason, but no attainder of treason shall work corruption of blood or forfeiture except during the life of the person attainted.

Congress can pass laws ordering how treason is to be punished. But the families of descendants of a person found guilty of treason cannot be punished for his crime.

ARTICLE 4

The States and the Nation

Official Acts of the States

SECTION 1. Full faith and credit shall be given in each state to the public acts, records, and judicial proceedings of every other state. And the Congress may by general laws prescribe the manner in which such acts, records, and proceedings shall be proved, and the effect thereof.

Congress can force each state to respect the laws, records, and court decisions of all the other states. If the states did not respect each other's laws, the confusion would be intolerable.

Privileges of Citizens

SECTION 2, CLAUSE 1. The citizens of each state shall be entitled to all privileges and immunities of citizens in the several states.

Citizens of one state who move into or do business in another state have the same rights as the citizens who live in that state. (But a citizen who moves to another state must wait for a specified length of time before he may vote there.)

Fugitives from Justice

SECTION 2, CLAUSE 2. A person charged in any state with treason, felony, or other crime, who shall flee from justice, and be found in another state, shall, on demand of the executive authority of the state from which he fled, be delivered up, to be removed to the state having jurisdiction of the crime.

A person accused of a crime sometimes flees to another state to escape trial and punishment. If the governor of the state where the crime was committed requests it, the person sought may be returned. Sending fugitives from justice back for trial or punishment is called extradition. In practice, there is no way to force a state to extradite a criminal.

Runaway Slaves

SECTION 2, CLAUSE 3. No person held to service or labor in one state, under the laws thereof, escaping into another, shall, in consequence of any law or regulation therein, be discharged from such service or labor, but shall be delivered up on claim of the party to whom such service or labor may be due.

This clause has not been applied since the addition of the Thirteenth Amendment.

The Forming of New States

SECTION 3, CLAUSE 1. New states may be admitted by the Congress into this Union; but no new state shall be formed or erected within the jurisdiction of any other state, nor any state be formed by the junction of two or more states, or parts of states, without the consent of the legislatures of the states concerned as well as of the Congress.

New states may be added to the nation if Congress approves. But no new state may be made inside the boundaries of another state unless both Congress and the legislature of the state that would lose territory approve. No new state may be made out of the lands of two states without the consent of Congress and of the legislatures of both those states.

Federal Territory

SECTION 3, CLAUSE 2. The Congress shall have power to dispose of and make all needful rules and regulations respecting the territory or other property belonging to the United States; and nothing in this Constitution shall be so construed as to prejudice any claims of the United States, or of any particular state.

Congress can govern and decide what to do with federal territories and other property. Here the word territories means lands that have not yet come under the government of any state.

Federal Guarantees to the States

SECTION 4. The United States shall guarantee to every state in this Union a republican form of government, and shall protect each of them against invasion; and, on application of the legislature, or of the executive (when the legislature cannot be convened), against domestic violence.

It is the duty of the federal government to make sure that every state has and keeps a representative form of government—a government conducted by the people under a state constitution. It also has the duty to protect every state from being invaded by enemies. If the state asks the federal government for help in stopping riots, the federal government must give it.

ARTICLE 5

Amending the Constitution

The Congress, whenever two-thirds of both houses shall deem it necessary, shall propose amendments to this Constitution, or, on the application of the legislatures of two-thirds of the several states, shall call a convention for proposing amendments, which, in either case, shall be valid to all intents and purposes, as part of this Constitution, when ratified by the legislatures of three-fourths of the several states, or by conventions in three-fourths thereof, as the one or the other mode of ratification may be proposed by the Congress, provided that no amendment which may be made prior to the year one thousand eight hundred and eight shall in any manner affect the first and fourth clauses in the Ninth Section of the First Article, and that no state, without its consent, shall be deprived of its equal suffrage in the Senate.

The Constitution can be changed by amendments. An amendment can be proposed in either of two ways: (1)

by the vote of two-thirds of the Senate and two-thirds of the House of Representatives, (2) by a special convention called by Congress at the request of two-thirds of the state legislatures. After an amendment has been proposed, it is adopted as part of the Constitution if it is approved (1) by the legislatures of at least three-fourths of the states, or (2) by special conventions in at least three-fourths of the states. But no amendment can be adopted that would take away any state's right to have two Senators in Congress—unless the state gives its permission.

The clause beginning "that no amendment which may be made" was set aside by the passage of time and by laws passed in 1808.

It is possible but not easy to make changes in the Constitution—and in the form of the federal government —when such changes are necessary. It is probably advantageous that the Constitution is hard to amend.

ARTICLE 6

The Supreme Law of the Land

The National Debt

CLAUSE 1. All debts contracted and engagements entered into before the adoption of this Constitution shall be as valid against the United States under this Constitution as under the Confederation.

In this clause the men who wrote the Constitution promised that the new United States government would pay the debts and carry out the agreements made by the Congress that acted under the Articles of Confederation.

Federal Laws Are Above State Laws

CLAUSE 2. This Constitution and the laws of the United States which shall be made in pursuance thereof, and all treaties made or which shall be made under the authority of the United States, shall be the supreme law of the land, and the judges in every state shall be bound thereby, anything in the constitution or laws of any state to the contrary notwithstanding.

Sometimes the Constitution, laws, and treaties of the United States provide for one thing and the constitutions and laws of the states provide for something else. When this happens, the Constitution, laws, and treaties of the United States must be obeyed.

Oaths of Allegiance • Religious Tests

CLAUSE 3. The Senators and Representatives before mentioned, and the members of the several state legislatures, and all executive and judicial officers, both of the United States and of the several states, shall be bound by oath or affirmation to support this Constitution; but no religious test shall ever be required as a qualification to any office or public trust under the United States.

Members of Congress and of the state legislatures and all other officials of the federal and state governments must promise solemnly to uphold the Constitution and the form of government provided for by the Constitution.

Nobody who can meet the other requirements for holding a position in the United States government may be kept out of this position because of his religion.

ARTICLE 7

Adoption of the Constitution

The ratification of the conventions of nine states shall be sufficient for the establishment of this Constitution between the states so ratifying the same.

Done in convention by the unanimous consent of the states present the seventeenth day of September, in the year of our Lord one thousand seven hundred and eighty-seven and of the independence of the United States of America the twelfth. In witness whereof, we have hereunto subscribed our names.

GEORGE WASHINGTON—PRESIDENT AND DEPUTY FROM VIRGINIA

NEW HAMPSHIRE
JOHN LANGDON
NICHOLAS GILMAN

MASSACHUSETTS
NATHANIEL GORHAM
RUFUS KING

CONNECTICUT
WILLIAM SAMUEL JOHNSON
ROGER SHERMAN

NEW JERSEY
WILLIAM LIVINGSTON
DAVID BREARLEY
WILLIAM PATERSON
JONATHAN DAYTON

NEW YORK
ALEXANDER HAMILTON

PENNSYLVANIA
BENJAMIN FRANKLIN
THOMAS MIFFLIN
ROBERT MORRIS
GEORGE CLYMER
THOMAS FITZSIMONS
JARED INGERSOLL
JAMES WILSON
GOUVERNEUR MORRIS

DELAWARE
GEORGE READ
GUNNING BEDFORD, JR.
JOHN DICKINSON
RICHARD BASSETT
JACOB BROOM

GEORGIA
WILLIAM FEW
ABRAHAM BALDWIN

VIRGINIA
JOHN BLAIR
JAMES MADISON, JR.

NORTH CAROLINA
WILLIAM BLOUNT
RICHARD DOBBS SPAIGHT
HUGH WILLIAMSON

SOUTH CAROLINA
JOHN RUTLEDGE
CHARLES COTESWORTH PINCKNEY
CHARLES PINCKNEY
PIERCE BUTLER

MARYLAND
JAMES MCHENRY
DAN OF ST. THOMAS JENIFER
DANIEL CARROLL

The Constitution was signed on September 17, 1787, by thirty-nine men sent to the Constitutional Convention from all the states except Rhode Island. As soon as special conventions in nine of the states had met and voted in favor of the Constitution, it was to go into effect in those states. Each state called a convention to vote on the plan for a new national government. Within about nine months the conventions in nine states had voted to adopt the Constitution. By the middle of 1790, all the thirteen original states had voted in favor of it.

AMENDMENTS TO THE CONSTITUTION

The Bill of Rights: Amendments 1 to 10

The First Congress began its meetings in 1789. Because many Americans felt that the Constitution did not guarantee enough liberties to the people and the states, twelve amendments were proposed in this First Congress. Ten of them were approved by the state legislatures and in 1791 became an official part of the Constitution. These first ten amendments have come to be known as the American Bill of Rights.

AMENDMENT 1. Freedom of Religion, Speech, Press, Assembly, and Petition

Congress shall make no law respecting an establishment of religion, or prohibiting the free exercise thereof; or abridging the freedom of speech, or of the press; or the right of the people peaceably to assemble, and to petition the government for a redress of grievances.

Congress must not pass any laws that (1) make any religion the official religion of the country or keep people from following the religion they prefer, (2) forbid the people to say and print whatever they may choose, (3) keep the people from meeting together in a peaceable manner to talk about their government or keep them from making any rightful complaints to their government.

AMENDMENT 2. The Right to Bear Arms

A well-regulated militia being necessary to the security of a free state, the right of the people to keep and bear arms shall not be infringed.

The federal government must not interfere with the right of the states to drill their citizens in state militias. The Supreme Court has held that the guarantee of the right to bear arms applies only to arms that have "some reasonable relationship to the preservation or efficiency of a well-regulated militia."

AMENDMENT 3. Quartering Soldiers

No soldier shall in time of peace be quartered in any house without the consent of the owner; nor in time of war but in a manner to be prescribed by law.

In peacetime, people must not be forced to take soldiers into their houses and give them room and board. Even in wartime, people must not be forced to do this except according to laws passed by Congress.

AMENDMENT 4. Searches and Seizures

The right of the people to be secure in their persons, houses, papers, and effects, against unreasonable searches and seizures, shall not be violated; and no warrants shall issue, but upon probable cause, supported by oath or affirmation, and particularly describing the place to be searched and the persons or things to be seized.

No federal official may arrest or search a person, or search his home, or seize his belongings, unless a warrant —an official order from a judge—gives him permission to do so. No judge may give out such warrants unless he is convinced that they are necessary to prevent crimes.

AMENDMENT 5. Rights of Those Accused of Crimes

No person shall be held to answer for a capital or otherwise infamous crime unless on a presentment or indictment of a grand jury, except in cases arising in the land or naval forces, or in the militia, when in actual service in time of war or public danger; nor shall any person be subject for the same offense to be twice put in jeopardy of life or limb, nor shall be compelled in any criminal case to be a witness against himself, nor be deprived of life, liberty, or property without due process of law; nor shall private property be taken for public use without just compensation.

No person may be tried in a federal court for a serious crime unless a grand jury has examined the evidence and decided that the person ought to be tried. The only persons not covered by this rule are those serving in the armed forces in time of war or other grave emergency for the nation. If a person has been tried for a crime and judged not guilty, he can never be tried again for the same offense. No person may be forced to give evidence that will help to prove his guilt, for then torture might be used to make him confess. No person may be executed, imprisoned, or fined except as a punishment after a fair trial. Private property must not be taken for public use unless the owner is paid a fair price for it.

AMENDMENT 6. Jury Trial in Criminal Cases

In all criminal prosecutions, the accused shall enjoy the right to a speedy and public trial, by an impartial jury of the state and district wherein the crime shall have been committed, which district shall have been previously ascertained by law, and to be informed of the nature and cause of the accusation; to be confronted with the witnesses against him; to have compulsory process for obtaining witnesses in his favor and to have the assistance of counsel for his defense.

A person being tried for a crime in a federal court must be tried promptly—and in public. It is his right to have a jury of fair-minded citizens hear the evidence and decide whether he is guilty or not guilty. These citizens must live in the district where the crime took place. The accused person must be told why he is being tried and must have a chance to see and hear those who give evidence against him. Witnesses who might prove that he is innocent can be forced to come to court and give their evidence. If the accused cannot pay for a lawyer, he has the right to one appointed by the court.

AMENDMENT 7. Civil Suits

In suits at common law where the value in controversy shall exceed twenty dollars, the right of trial by jury shall be preserved, and no fact tried by a jury shall be otherwise re-examined in any court of the United States than according to the rules of the common law.

If a sum of money larger than $20 is involved in a lawsuit, the persons in the case may insist on a jury trial.

AMENDMENT 8. Unreasonable Bail • Cruel Punishments

Excessive bail shall not be required, nor excessive fines imposed, or cruel and unusual punishments inflicted.

A person accused of a crime can get out of jail until his trial by handing over a sum of money to the court. This money, called bail, is returned to him if he comes to court to be tried when he is ordered to; if not, he loses his bail. Federal courts must not force accused persons to give unreasonably large amounts of bail.

A person tried in a federal court and found guilty of a crime must not be punished by an unreasonably heavy fine or an unreasonably long prison sentence. He must not be punished in cruel or unusual ways—by being tortured or branded, for instance.

AMENDMENT 9. Other Rights of the People

The enumeration in the Constitution of certain rights shall not be construed to deny or disparage others retained by the people.

It was not possible to list in the Constitution all the rights that United States citizens should have. There are other important rights that are to belong to the people even though the Constitution does not mention them.

AMENDMENT 10. Powers Kept by the States or by the People

The powers not delegated to the United States by the Constitution, nor prohibited by it to the states, are reserved to the states respectively, or to the people.

The Constitution authorizes the federal government to use certain powers and forbids the state governments to use certain powers. All other powers are to be kept by the states or by the people.

Amendments 11 to 25

AMENDMENT 11. Suits Against a State (1798)

The judicial power of the United States shall not be construed to extend to any suit in law or equity commenced or prosecuted against one of the United States by citizens of another state, or by citizens or subjects of any foreign state.

No federal court is allowed to try any case in which a state government is being sued by a citizen of another state or of a foreign country. Such a case must be tried in a court of the state that is being sued. This amendment changed a part of Article 3, Section 2, Clause 1.

804

AMENDMENT 12. Presidential Elections (1804)

The electors shall meet in their respective states, and vote by ballot for President and Vice-President, one of whom, at least, shall not be an inhabitant of the same state with themselves; they shall name in their ballots the person voted for as President, and in distinct ballots the person voted for as Vice-President, and they shall make distinct lists of all persons voted for as President and of all persons voted for as Vice-President, and of the number of votes for each, which lists they shall sign and certify, and transmit, sealed, to the seat of the government of the United States, directed to the President of the Senate; the President of the Senate shall, in the presence of the Senate and House of Representatives, open all the certificates, and the votes shall then be counted. The person having the greatest number of votes for President shall be the President, if such number be a majority of the whole number of electors appointed; and if no person have such majority, then from the persons having the highest numbers, not exceeding three, on the list of those voted for as President, the House of Representatives shall choose immediately, by ballot, the President. But in choosing the President, the votes shall be taken by states, the representation from each state having one vote; a quorum for this purpose shall consist of a member or members from two-thirds of the states, and a majority of all the states shall be necessary to a choice. And if the House of Representatives shall not choose a President, whenever the right of choice shall devolve upon them, before the fourth day of March next following, then the Vice-President shall act as President, as in case of the death or other constitutional disability of the President. The person having the greatest number of votes as Vice-President shall be the Vice-President, if such number be a majority of the whole number of electors appointed, and if no person have a majority, then, from the two highest numbers on the list, the Senate shall choose the Vice-President; a quorum for the purpose shall consist of two-thirds of the whole number of Senators and a majority of the whole number shall be necessary to a choice. But no person constitutionally ineligible to the office of President shall be eligible to that of Vice-President of the United States.

This amendment replaced Article 2, Section 1, Clause 3, which ordered the electors in each state to vote for President and Vice-President on one ballot, without showing which person they wanted for each of the two positions. The person with the highest total of electoral votes was to be President, and the person with the next highest total was to be Vice-President. But serious problems arose because of a tie in the presidential election of 1800. The Twelfth Amendment was adopted to prevent such confusion later.

Although the Twelfth Amendment does not tell how the President and the Vice-President are actually elected today, this is its meaning: the electors of each state meet in that state and vote for President and Vice-President. (Their votes are little more than a formality now.) Either the presidential or the vice-presidential candidate they vote for must live outside of the electors' own state. The electors must cast two separate ballots, one for President and one for Vice-President, and must record their votes on two separate lists. The lists from each state are sent to the United States Senate, where the votes are counted in the presence of the Senators and the Representatives. The presidential candidate with the most electoral votes becomes President if he has a majority of all the electoral votes for that office. If he does not have a majority, the House of Representatives chooses a President from among the three presidential candidates with the most electoral votes. But if the House of Representatives fails to choose a President by the time the new presidential term is to begin—now January 20 following the election, instead of March 4—then the man who was elected Vice-President acts as President.

The vice-presidential candidate with the most electoral votes becomes Vice-President if he has a majority of all the electoral votes for that office. If he does not, the Senate chooses a Vice-President from among the two vice-presidential candidates with the most electoral votes.

The Vice-President must meet the same requirements of age, citizenship, and residence as must the President.

The writers both of the original Constitution and of the Twelfth Amendment intended to have the President and the Vice-President chosen by small groups of men—the presidential electors—with greater wisdom and experience than the ordinary voters of the country had. However, the real power to choose the President and Vice-President has been taken away from the presidential electors and given to the ordinary voters. This change resulted from new customs.

The voters in each state and in the District of Columbia vote for presidential electors who are known to belong to a particular political party. These electors still follow the rules in this amendment, but they usually cast their ballots for the candidates belonging to their own political party. The result is that when a voter fills in his ballot on Election Day, he seems to be voting for President and Vice-President but is actually voting for an elector.

The day when presidential electors are to be elected by the voters is the first Tuesday after the first Monday in November of every fourth year—1968, 1972, 1976, and so on. Within a day or so everyone knows who the next President and Vice-President are to be, but the electors do not go through the ceremony of casting their ballots until about one month later.

AMENDMENT 13. Slavery Forbidden (1865)

SECTION 1. Neither slavery nor involuntary servitude, except as a punishment for crime whereof the party shall have been duly convicted, shall exist within the United States or any place subject to their jurisdiction.

SECTION 2. Congress shall have power to enforce this article by appropriate legislation.

Nobody in the United States or its territories may be held in slavery. Nobody may be forced to work against his will except as a punishment for a crime after he has been tried in the courts and found guilty. Several amendments have enabling acts like Section 2. Compare their wording.

President Lincoln's Emancipation Proclamation of 1863 had ordered the freeing of the slaves only in the Confederate states. The Thirteenth Amendment freed all slaves in all states and territories.

AMENDMENT 14. Restrictions on the States (1868)

SECTION 1. All persons born or naturalized in the United States, and subject to the jurisdiction thereof, are citizens of the United States and of the state wherein they reside. No state shall make or enforce any law which shall abridge the privileges or immunities of citizens of the United States, nor shall any state deprive any person of life, liberty, or property without due process of law, nor deny to any person within its jurisdiction the equal protection of the laws.

All persons born or naturalized in the United States and ruled by this nation's laws are citizens—citizens both of the United States and of the state they live in. (This amendment superseded the Supreme Court's Dred Scott decision of 1857, which had held that Negro slaves were not citizens.)

No state may take away the rights of United States citizens or take any person's life, freedom, or property except according to law. All the laws of a state must apply in the same way to everybody.

SECTION 2. Representatives shall be apportioned among the several states according to their respective numbers, counting the whole number of persons in each state, excluding Indians not taxed. But when the right to vote at any election for the choice of electors for President and Vice-President of the United States, Representatives in Congress, the executive and judicial officers of a state, or the members of the legislature thereof, is denied to any of the male inhabitants of such state, being twenty-one years of age, and citizens of the United States, or in any way abridged, except for participation in rebellion, or other crime, the basis of representation therein shall be reduced in the proportion which the number of such male citizens shall bear to the whole number of male citizens twenty-one years of age in such state.

A part of Article 1, Section 2, Clause 3, had ruled that only three-fifths of the Negro slaves in each state were to be counted when the number of Representatives which that state was entitled to send to Congress was being determined. But because of this section of the Fourteenth Amendment, Negroes were henceforth to be counted in full, like other citizens, in determining the number of Representatives. If a state kept any of its citizens who were entitled to vote from voting in national or state elections, that state's right to send members to the House of Representatives was to be cut down accordingly, as a penalty. This section was an attempt to force the southern states to let Negro citizens vote. No state has ever been penalized in this way for failing to do so.

SECTION 3. No person shall be a Senator or Representative in Congress, or elector of President and Vice-President, or hold any office, civil or military, under the United States or under any state, who, having previously taken an oath as a member of Congress, or as an officer of the United States, or as a member of any state legislature, or as an executive or judicial officer of any state, to support the Constitution of the United States, shall have engaged in insurrection or rebellion against the same or given aid or comfort to the enemies thereof. But Congress may by a vote of two-thirds of each house remove such disability.

According to this section, no person could ever become an official of the federal government or a state government if he had ever held such an office in the past and then had rebelled against the federal government. But Congress could end this rule when two-thirds of the Senators and two-thirds of the Representatives voted to end it.

The effect of this section was to weaken the political power of the southern states and punish the leaders of the Confederacy. But the section was soon out of date. Congress gave back full political rights to most of the Confederate leaders in 1872, and to the rest of them in 1898.

SECTION 4. The validity of the public debt of the United States, authorized by law, including debts incurred for payment of pensions and bounties for services in suppressing insurrection and rebellion, shall not be questioned. But neither the United States nor any state shall assume or pay any debt or obligation incurred in aid of insurrection or rebellion against the United States, or any claim for the loss or emancipation of any slave; but all such debts, obligations, and claims shall be held illegal and void.

SECTION 5. The Congress shall have power to enforce by appropriate legislation the provisions of this article.

Under Section 4 the federal government was ordered to pay back the money it had borrowed for the expenses of the Civil War. But neither the federal government nor any state government was to be allowed to repay money that was borrowed by the Confederacy for fighting against the Union, or to pay slaveowners for slaves who had been set free.

AMENDMENT 15. Negroes' Right to Vote (1870)

SECTION 1. The right of the citizens of the United States to vote shall not be denied or abridged by the United States or by any state on account of race, color, or previous condition of servitude.

SECTION 2. The Congress shall have power to enforce this article by appropriate legislation.

Neither the United States nor any state may keep a citizen from voting because of his race or color or because he was once a slave.

AMENDMENT 16. The Federal Income Tax (1913)

The Congress shall have power to lay and collect taxes on incomes, from whatever source derived, without apportionment among the several states, and without regard to any census or enumeration.

Congress has the right to tax all kinds of incomes. The amount of money which the citizens of a state pay to the federal government as income tax does not have to be in proportion to the population of that state.

In 1895 the Supreme Court ruled that the federal government had no right to collect income taxes from the peo-ple of the states because such a tax was a direct tax and did not obey Article 1, Section 9, Clause 4. Eighteen years later, the Sixteenth Amendment overruled the Supreme Court's decision.

AMENDMENT 17. Election of Senators by the People (1913)

CLAUSE 1. The Senate of the United States shall be composed of two Senators from each state, elected by the people thereof, for six years; and each Senator shall have one vote. The electors in each state shall have the qualifications requisite for electors of the most numerous branch of the state legislatures.

This clause changes Article 1, Section 3, Clause 1. See the explanation of that clause.

tation of any state in the Senate, the executive au-thority of such state shall issue writs of election to fill such vacancies: Provided that the legislature of any state may empower the executive thereof to make temporary appointments until the people fill the va-cancies by election as the legislature may direct.

CLAUSE 3. This amendment shall not be so construed as to affect the election or term of any Senator chosen before it be-comes valid as part of the Constitution.

Clause 2 changes the last part of Article 1, Section 3, Clause 2, which gave the governor of a state the right to appoint a Senator temporarily if one of that state's seats in the Senate became vacant while the legislature was not meeting. Under the present law, a vacancy in the Senate may be filled by the state's voters, who vote at a special election. Or, as more often happens, the governor has the legislature's permission to fill the vacancy by appointing a temporary Senator and does so.

AMENDMENT 18. Prohibition (1919)

SECTION 1. After one year from the ratification of this article the manufacture, sale, or transportation of intoxicating liquors within, the importation thereof into, or the exportation thereof from the United States and all territory subject to the jurisdic-tion thereof for beverage purposes is hereby prohibited.

SECTION 2. The Congress and the several states shall have concurrent power to enforce this article by appropriate legisla-tion.

SECTION 3. This article shall be inoperative unless it shall have been ratified as an amendment to the Constitution by the legislatures of the several states, as provided in the Constitution, within seven years from the date of the submission hereof to the states by the Congress.

This amendment forbade the manufacture, sale, or ship-ment of intoxicating drinks, and it gave to both Congress and the states the right to pass laws that would enforce it. In 1933 this amendment was repealed by the Twenty-first Amendment.

AMENDMENT 19. Women's Voting Rights (1920)

CLAUSE 1. The right of citizens of the United States to vote shall not be denied or abridged by the United States or by any state on account of sex.

CLAUSE 2. Congress shall have power to enforce this article by appropriate legislation.

Neither the federal government nor any state govern-ment may keep a woman citizen from voting merely be-cause she is a woman. Congress may pass laws necessary to carry out this amendment.

AMENDMENT 20. Terms of Office (1933)

SECTION 1. The terms of the President and Vice-President shall end at noon on the twentieth day of January, and the terms of Senators and Representa-tives at noon on the third day of January, of the years in which such terms would have ended if this article had not been ratified; and the terms of their successors shall then begin.

The President's and the Vice-President's terms in office end at noon on January 20 in the years following presi-dential elections—1969, 1973, 1977, and so on. Before this amendment was adopted, the President and the Vice-President did not take office until March 4. The terms of one-third of the Senators and all the Representatives end at noon on January 3 in the years with odd numbers—1969, 1971, 1973, and so on. The new terms for all these offices begin as soon as the old terms end.

This section of the amendment cut down the long delay that had previously occurred between the time of election of the President, the Vice-President, and the members of Congress and the time that they began doing the work for which the voters had elected them.

SECTION 2. The Congress shall assemble at least once in every year, and such meeting shall begin at noon on the third day of January unless they shall by law appoint a different day.

This section changes Article 1, Section 4, Clause 2, which ordered Congress to begin its meetings on the first Monday of December each year. Formerly the new Sena-tors and Representatives that were elected to Congress in November did not actually begin their work until more than one year later. But under the Twentieth Amendment, Congress must meet at least once a year, beginning its meetings at noon on January 3 unless a law passed by Congress orders a different day.

SECTION 3. If, at the time fixed for the beginning of the term of the President, the President-elect shall have died, the Vice-President-elect shall become President. If a President shall not have been chosen before the time fixed for the beginning of his term, or if the President-elect shall have failed to qualify, then the Vice-President-elect shall act as President until a President shall have qualified; and the Con-gress may by law provide for the case wherein neither a President-elect nor a Vice-President-elect shall have qualified, declaring who shall then act as President, or the manner in which one who is to act shall be selected, and such person shall act accordingly until a President or Vice-President shall have qualified.

If the person elected President dies before January 20, when his term was to begin, then the person elected Vice-President becomes President. If no President has been chosen by January 20, or if the person chosen does not meet the Constitution's requirements for the presidency, then the newly elected Vice-President acts as President until a President who meets the requirements can be chosen. Congress may pass a law deciding what is to be done if neither the newly elected President nor the newly elected Vice-President can meet the requirements for the presidency that have been set up in the Constitution.

Section 4. The Congress may by law provide for the case of the death of any of the persons from whom the House of Representatives may choose a President whenever the right of choice shall have devolved upon them, and for the case of the death of any of the persons from whom the Senate may choose a Vice-President whenever the right of choice shall have devolved upon them.

Section 4 of the Twentieth Amendment permits Congress to pass laws deciding what should be done if any of the candidates whom one or the other house of Congress might have chosen to be the President or the Vice-President should die. (See the Twelfth Amendment.)

Section 5. Sections 1 and 2 shall take effect on the fifteenth day of October following the ratification of this article.

Section 5 set the date at which the first two sections of this amendment were to go into effect after the amendment had been adopted by the states.

Section 6. This article shall be inoperative unless it shall have been ratified as an amendment to the Constitution by the legislatures of three-fourths of the several states within seven years from the date of its submission.

Section 6 of the Twentieth Amendment ruled how and when it was to be adopted as a part of the Constitution. This amendment has of course already been ratified by the several states.

AMENDMENT 21. Repeal of Prohibition (1933)

Section 1. The eighteenth article of amendment to the Constitution of the United States is hereby repealed.

The Eighteenth Amendment, the Prohibition Amendment, is repealed by this amendment.

Section 2. The transportation or importation into any state, territory, or possession of the United States for delivery or use therein of intoxicating liquors, in violation of the laws thereof, is hereby prohibited.

Any states, territories, or possessions of the United States that want to prohibit intoxicating liquors have the right to do so by laws of their own.

Section 3. This article shall be inoperative unless it shall have been ratified as an amendment to the Constitution by convention in the several states, as provided in the Constitution, within seven years from the date of the submission hereof to the states by the Congress.

This section ruled how and when the Twenty-first Amendment was to be adopted.

AMENDMENT 22. Number of Terms for a President (1951)

Section 1. No person shall be elected to the office of the President more than twice, and no person who has held the office of President, or acted as President, for more than two years of a term to which some other person was elected President shall be elected to the office of President more than once. But this Article shall not apply to any person holding the office of President when this Article was proposed by the Congress, and shall not prevent any person who may be holding the office of President, or acting as President, during the term within which this Article becomes operative from holding the office of President, or acting as President during the remainder of such term.

Nobody may be elected to the presidency more than twice. If any person serves for more than two years in place of an elected President, that person may himself be elected to the presidency only once.

This amendment was worded so that it did not apply to Harry S Truman, who was President when the amendment was proposed and adopted.

Because of the Twenty-second Amendment, the longest time that any person can serve as President is ten years— that is, not more than two years in completion of a predecessor's term plus two four-year terms as elected President.

Section 2. This Article shall be inoperative unless it shall have been ratified as an amendment to the Constitution by the legislatures of three-fourths of the several states within seven years from the date of its submission to the states by Congress.

This section ruled how and when the Twenty-second Amendment was to be adopted.

AMENDMENT 23. Presidential Voting in the District of Columbia (1961)

Section 1. The District constituting the seat of Government of the United States shall appoint in such manner as the Congress may direct:

A number of electors of President and Vice-President equal to the whole number of Senators and Representatives in Congress to which the District would be entitled if it were a state, but in no event more than the least populous state; they shall be in addition to those appointed by the states, but they shall be considered, for the purposes of the election of President and Vice-President, to be electors appointed by a state; and they shall meet in the District and perform such duties as provided by the twelfth article of amendment.

The vote in presidential elections previously denied to residents of the District of Columbia because it is not a state is made possible by this amendment. It creates and assigns to the District as many votes in the electoral college as are assigned to the state with the smallest population. At the present time this means three votes, because that is the number that Alaska has. The members of the electoral college from the District of Columbia, meeting in the District, now cast their votes at the same time as members of the electoral college from the states, in accordance with the Twelfth Amendment to the Constitution.

Section 2. The Congress shall have power to enforce this article by appropriate legislation.

Congress has the power to pass such laws as may be required to put this amendment into force.

This amendment is the first amendment ever passed that applies only to one particular part of the country.

AMENDMENT 24. Poll Taxes Forbidden (1964)

SECTION 1. The right of citizens of the United States to vote in any primary or other election for President or Vice-President, for electors for President or Vice-President, or for Senator or Representative in Congress, shall not be denied or abridged by the United States or any state by reason of failure to pay any poll or other tax.

SECTION 2. The Congress shall have power to enforce this article by appropriate legislation.

Neither the federal government nor any state or local government may prevent any citizen from voting in national elections on grounds of his failure to pay a tax of any kind. The Congress is empowered to enact laws necessary for the enforcing of this amendment.

AMENDMENT 25. Presidential Continuity and Disability (1967)

SECTION 1. In case of the removal of the President from office or his death or resignation, the Vice-President shall become President.

SECTION 2. Whenever there is a vacancy in the office of the Vice-President, the President shall nominate a Vice-President who shall take the office upon confirmation by a majority vote of both houses of Congress.

SECTION 3. Whenever the President transmits to the President pro tempore of the Senate and the Speaker of the House of Representatives his written declaration that he is unable to discharge the powers and duties of his office, and until he transmits to them a written declaration to the contrary, such powers and duties shall be discharged by the Vice-President as Acting President.

SECTION 4. Whenever the Vice-President and a majority of either the principal officers of the executive departments, or of such other body as Congress may by law provide, transmit to the President pro tempore of the Senate and the Speaker of the House of Representatives their written declaration that the President is unable to discharge the powers and duties of his office, the Vice-President shall immediately assume the powers and duties of the office as Acting President.

Thereafter, when the President transmits to the President pro tempore of the Senate and the Speaker of the House of Representatives his written declaration that no inability exists, he shall resume the powers and duties of his office unless the Vice-President and a majority of either the principal officers of the executive department, or of such other body as Congress may by law provide, transmit within four days to the President pro tempore of the Senate and the Speaker of the House of Representatives their written declaration that the President is unable to discharge the powers and duties of his office. Thereupon Congress shall decide the issue, assembling within 48 hours for that purpose if not in session. If the Congress, within 21 days after receipt of the latter written declaration, or if Congress is not in session, within 21 days after Congress is required to assemble, determines by two-thirds vote of both houses that the President is unable to discharge the powers and duties of his office, the Vice-President shall continue to discharge the same as Acting President; otherwise, the President shall resume the powers and duties of his office.

Should a vacancy occur, the President has the power to nominate a Vice-President, who must be approved by both houses of Congress before he can take office. In case the President is or expects to be disabled, he is to inform Congress of this in writing. If the President refuses to or is unable to surrender his powers, the Vice-President may become Acting President with the approval of a majority of the Cabinet or other body provided by Congress. The conditions are presented under which the President may and may not resume his office.

1095	Pope Urban II called for first Crusade, begun in 1096
1271–95	Marco Polo visited the Orient
1416	Henry the Navigator established observatory
1492	Oct. 12—Columbus landed in West Indies; claimed land for Spain
1494	Treaty of Tordesillas
1497	Cabot explored east coast of North America; claimed land for England
1498	Vasco da Gama reached India
1513	Balboa and his men first to see Pacific Ocean
	Ponce de León discovered Florida
1519	Cortés began conquest of Mexico
	Magellan began round-the-world voyage
1524	Verrazano explored east coast of North America
1531–33	Pizarro conquered Peru
1535	Cartier explored St. Lawrence River
1539–43	De Soto explored what is now the southern United States
1540–42	Coronado explored what is now the southwestern United States
1541	De Soto discovered Mississippi River
1585	Raleigh sent first colony to Roanoke Island (abandoned in 1586)
1587	Raleigh sent second colony to Roanoke Island (colony had disappeared by 1590)
1588	English defeated Spanish Armada
1607	First permanent English settlement founded at Jamestown
1608	Champlain founded Quebec
1609	Hudson discovered Hudson River
1612	Rolfe began cultivation of tobacco at Jamestown
1619	Virginia House of Burgesses met—first representative legislative body in America
	First Negro slaves brought to Virginia
1620	Nov. 11—Mayflower Compact signed
	Dec. 16—Pilgrims landed in Plymouth
1624	First permanent Dutch settlers began living in New Netherland
1630	Winthrop and settlers arrived in Massachusetts Bay Colony
1634	First Maryland settlement at St. Mary's, under Calvert
1636	Williams founded Providence, first settlement in Rhode Island
	Harvard College founded
1638	Swedish settlers founded Fort Christina at present site of Wilmington, Delaware
1639	Fundamental Orders of Connecticut—first written constitution in America
1647	Massachusetts started public education
1649	Maryland gave religious freedom to Christians
1651	Navigation Act of 1651
1655	New Sweden in Delaware conquered by Dutch and made part of New Netherland
1660	Navigation Act of 1660
1663	Charter granted for colony in Carolinas
1664	Charter granted for colony in New Jersey
	English captured New Netherland and renamed it New York
1673	Joliet and Marquette explored Mississippi River
1681	First colonists arrived in Pennsylvania
1682	La Salle reached mouth of Mississippi River and claimed region for France
1693	College of William and Mary founded
1701	Yale College founded
1733	First settlement in Georgia, at Savannah
	Molasses Act

1735	Zenger Case confirmed freedom of press
1745–48	King George's War
1749	Ohio Company granted land in Ohio Valley
1754–63	French and Indian War
1763	Treaty of Paris ended French and Indian War
	Proclamation Line of 1763
1764	Sugar Act
1765	Stamp Act
	Stamp Act Congress met
1766	Stamp Act repealed
1767	Townshend Revenue Act
1770	Boston Massacre
1772	Committees of Correspondence organized
1773	Tea Act
	Boston Tea Party
1774	"Intolerable Acts"
	Quebec Act
	First Continental Congress, at Philadelphia
1775	April 19—Battles of Lexington and Concord
	May 10—Second Continental Congress met in Philadelphia
	June 15—Washington made commander in chief
	June 17—Battle of Bunker Hill
1776	Jan. 15—*Common Sense,* by Paine, published
	July 4—Continental Congress adopted Declaration of Independence
	Dec. 26—English defeated at Trenton
1777	Jan. 3—English defeated at Princeton
	June 14—Congress adopted Stars and Stripes as United States flag
	Oct. 17—Burgoyne surrendered at Saratoga
	Nov. 15—Congress adopted Articles of Confederation
1778	France joined in war against England
1781	Oct. 19—Cornwallis surrendered at Yorktown
1783	Sept. 3—Treaty of Paris ended War for Independence
1784	Trade with China began
1785	Mount Vernon Conference
	Land Ordinance of 1785
1786	Shays' Rebellion
	Annapolis Convention
1787	May 25—Constitutional Convention met in Independence Hall, Philadelphia
	July 13—Congress approved adoption of the Northwest Ordinance
	Sept. 17—Constitution signed by members of Constitutional Convention
	Oct. 27—Publication of *The Federalist* begun
1788	Ninth state, New Hampshire, ratified Constitution, making it law
1789	March 4—First Congress met at New York
	April 30—Washington inaugurated
	July 14—French Revolution began
1790	First United States census
1791	Feb. 25—First Bank of the United States
	Dec. 15—Bill of Rights adopted
1792	First political parties in United States
	Gray explored mouth of Columbia River
1793	Washington issued Neutrality Proclamation
	Whitney invented cotton gin
	Slater built first cotton mill
1794	Whisky Rebellion
	Jay's treaty
1796	Pinckney's treaty
1797–98	X Y Z affair
1798	Naturalization Act

1798	Alien and Sedition Acts	1842	*Commonwealth* v. *Hunt*
	Virginia and Kentucky resolutions	1844	Morse sent first telegraph message
1800	Washington, D.C., became new capital	1845	Texas entered Union
1801	John Marshall appointed Chief Justice	1846	Oregon Treaty signed with England
	Judiciary Act of 1801		Wilmot Proviso
1801–5	Tripolitan War		Howe patented sewing machine
1802	Judiciary Act of 1802		Morton first used ether as anesthetic
1803	*Marbury* v. *Madison*	1846–48	Mexican War
	Louisiana Purchase	1847	First Mormon settlers reached Great Salt Lake
1804–6	Lewis and Clark expedition	1848	Gold discovered in California
1805–6	Pike's explorations		Treaty of Guadalupe Hidalgo
1806	Nonimportation Act		First woman's rights convention met
	Webster's dictionary published		Free-Soil party formed
1807	Orders in Council	1849	Great gold rush to California
	Chesapeake-Leopard affair	1850	Compromise of 1850
	The *Clermont* made first successful trip		Clayton-Bulwer Treaty
	Embargo Act		Fugitive Slave Law
1808	Jan. 1—Importation of slaves forbidden	1851	Maine prohibition law
1809	Nonintercourse Act	1852	*Uncle Tom's Cabin* published
1810	*Fletcher* v. *Peck*	1853	Gadsden Purchase
	Macon's Bill No. 2	1854	Perry's treaty with Japan
1811	National Road begun		Kansas-Nebraska Bill
1812–14	War of 1812		Republican party organized
1813	Perry won Battle of Lake Erie		Ostend Manifesto
1814	Aug. 24—British invaded Washington	1855	The Soo Canal completed
	Sept. 14—Francis Scott Key wrote words of "The Star-Spangled Banner"		Pro- and anti-slavery governments in Kansas
	Dec. 15—Hartford Convention	1856	Civil strife in Kansas
	Dec. 24—Treaty of Ghent ended War of 1812	1857	Dred Scott decision
1815	Jan. 8—Jackson won Battle of New Orleans		Depression of 1857
1816	Second Bank of the United States	1858	Trade treaties with China and Japan
	Tariff of 1816		Lincoln-Douglas debates
1817	Madison vetoed "Bonus Bill"	1859	Gold discovered near Pike's Peak
1818	Agreement with England fixed 49th parallel as northern boundary of United States		Comstock Lode discovered in Nevada
			First oil well drilled, near Titusville, Pa.
1819	Adams-Onís Treaty		John Brown's raid at Harpers Ferry
	McCulloch v. *Maryland*	1860	Pony Express began operations
1820	Missouri Compromise		South Carolina seceded from Union
1823	Monroe Doctrine announced	1861	Telegraph line to California completed
1824	*Gibbons* v. *Ogden*		Confederate States of America established
1825	Erie Canal opened		Morrill Tariff
1827	Mechanics' Union of Trade Associations formed		Confederate forces fired on Fort Sumter
1828	Workingmen's parties organized		*Trent* affair
	"Tariff of Abominations"	1861–65	Civil War
	Baltimore and Ohio Railroad begun	1862	Homestead Act
1830	Webster-Hayne debate		Battle of Antietam
	Jackson vetoed Maysville Road bill		Morrill Land-Grant College Act
	Indian Removal Act	1863	Emancipation Proclamation
1831	First issue of Garrison's *The Liberator*		National-banking system established
	National nominating convention first held		Battle of Gettysburg
1832	Black Hawk War		*Alabama* claims
	Jackson vetoed Bank Bill		Lincoln's Gettysburg Address
	Tariff Act of 1832		Proclamation of Amnesty and Reconstruction
	Ordinance of Nullification	1864	First Bessemer steel made in United States
1833	Compromise Tariff of 1833		Contract Labor Law
1834	McCormick's reaper patented		Wade-Davis Bill
	National Trades' Union established	1865	Freedmen's Bureau
1836	Colt revolver patented		Lee surrendered at Appomattox Court House
	Texas won independence		President Lincoln assassinated
	Specie Circular issued		Maximilian affair
1837	Depression of 1837		Thirteenth Amendment abolished slavery
	Deere's steel plow introduced	1866	Civil Rights Act
	Caroline affair		First successful Atlantic cable
1838	Underground railroad organized		National Labor Union organized
1839	Draper introduced photography in America	1867	Reconstruction Act
	Goodyear invented method of vulcanizing rubber		Tenure of Office Act
			Command of the Army Act
1840	Ten-hour day established for federal employees		Alaska purchased from Russia
	Independent Treasury Act became law		Patrons of Husbandry—the Grange—organized
1841	First wagon train over Oregon Trail	1868	President Johnson impeached and acquitted
1842	Webster-Ashburton Treaty	1869	First railroad to Pacific completed
	Whig Tariff of 1842		Knights of Labor organized in Philadelphia
		1869–74	Granger laws passed

1871	Treaty of Washington
1872	Crédit Mobilier affair exposed
1873	"Salary Grab" Act
	Demonetization of silver—"Crime of '73"
	Panic of 1873
	Virginius affair
1874	Manufacture of barbed wire begun
1875	Resumption Act
	Commercial treaty with Hawaii
	Whisky Ring broken up
1876	Bell invented telephone
	Centennial Exposition in Philadelphia
	Disputed presidential election
1877	*Munn* v. *Illinois*
	Railroad strikes
1878	Treaty with Samoa gave United States coaling station at Pago Pago
	Bland-Allison Act
1879	Resumption of specie payment
	Edison's electric light successful
1881	American Red Cross organized
	President Garfield assassinated
	Gompers founded labor organization (in 1886 became American Federation of Labor)
1882	Standard Oil Trust organized
	Chinese Exclusion Act
1883	Pendleton Act
1886	Haymarket affair
	Statue of Liberty dedicated
1887	United States acquired use of Pearl Harbor in Hawaiian Islands
	Interstate Commerce Act
	Dawes Act
1888	Mills Bill
1889	Omnibus Bill
	First Pan-American Congress
	Farmers' alliances held national convention
	Hull House in Chicago founded by Jane Addams
1890	Dependent Pension Bill
	Sherman Antitrust Act
	Sherman Silver Purchase Act
	McKinley Tariff
1892	Homestead strike
	First national convention of Populist party
1893	Ford tested his first automobile
	Depression of 1893
	Anti-Saloon League organized
	Sherman Silver Purchase Act repealed
1894	Pullman strike
	Wilson-Gorman Act
1895	Insurrection against Spanish rule in Cuba
	Venezuelan boundary dispute
	Olney doctrine announced
1897	Dingley Tariff
1898	*Maine* blew up in Havana Harbor
	Formal declaration of war against Spain
	Battle of Manila Bay
	Rough Riders captured San Juan Hill
	Naval battle of Santiago
	Annexation of Hawaii
	Treaty of Paris ended Spanish-American War
1899	First Hague Peace Conference
	Hay stated open-door policy for China
	Germany, England, and United States signed Samoan treaty
1900	Gold Standard Act
	Foraker Act
	Organic Act of 1900
	Boxer Rebellion
1901	Platt Amendment
	President McKinley assassinated
	Hay-Pauncefote Treaty

1901–20	Insular Cases
1902	Coal strike
	United States withdrew from Cuba
	Newlands Act
	Philippine Government Act
1902–3	Venezuela crisis
1903	Hay-Herrán Treaty
	Elkins Act
	Alaskan boundary dispute settled
	Panama revolted against Colombia
	Hay–Bunau-Varilla Treaty
	First successful airplane flights
1904	Russo-Japanese War began
	Northern Securities Case
	Roosevelt corollary
1905	*Lochner* v. *New York*
	Industrial Workers of the World organized
	Taft-Katsura agreement
	Treaty of Portsmouth ended Russo-Japanese War
1906	Algeciras Conference
	Burke Act
	Hepburn Act
	Pure Food and Drug Act
	Meat Inspection Act
1907	Gentleman's agreement with Japan
	Second Hague Peace Conference
	United States fleet began trip around world
1908	Danbury Hatters Case
	Muller v. *Oregon*
	Root-Takahira Agreement
1909	Payne-Aldrich Tariff
1910	World Peace Foundation established
1911	National Progressive Republican League formed
1912	Eight-hour day for federal employees
	Progressive party organized
	Canal Tolls Act
1913	Webb-Kenyon Interstate Liquor Act
	Underwood-Simmons Tariff
	Federal Reserve Act
1914	Tampico incident
	United States marines landed at Veracruz
	First World War began
	Panama Canal opened
	Federal Trade Commission Act
	Clayton Antitrust Act
1914–18	First World War
1915	La Follette Seamen's Act
	Lusitania sunk
1916	Bryan-Chamorro Treaty
	Sussex pledge by Germany
	Council of National Defense created
	Federal Farm Loan Act
	Jones Act for Philippines
	Adamson Act
1917	United States acquired Virgin Islands
	President Wilson's "peace-without-victory" speech
	Literacy test for immigrants
	Jones Act for Puerto Rico
	United States declared war on Germany
	First Liberty Loan
	Selective Service Act
	First A.E.F. troops landed in France
1918	President Wilson announced Fourteen Points
	Battle of St. Mihiel and Meuse-Argonne offensive
	Armistice ended First World War
1919	President Wilson attended peace conference at Versailles
	Treaty of Versailles signed
	Steel and coal strikes

1920	Prohibition went into effect
	United States Senate rejected Treaty of Versailles for second and final time
	Nineteenth Amendment gave women the vote
	First commercial radio broadcast
1921	Emergency Quota Act
	Emergency tariff legislation
	United States signed peace treaties with Germany, Austria, and Hungary
	Washington Conference
1922	Fordney-McCumber Act
	Teapot Dome scandal
1923	Agricultural Credits Act
	Death of President Harding
1924	Soldiers' bonus bill
	Immigration Quota Act
	Indians granted citizenship
	Dawes Plan
1926	Air Commerce Act
1927	Federal Communications Commission
	Television first successfully demonstrated
	Lindbergh flew nonstop to Paris
	Geneva Conference on naval disarmament
1928	Pact of Paris
	Clark Memorandum
1929	Young Plan
	Agricultural Marketing Act
	Stock-market crash began Great Depression
1930	Hawley-Smoot Tariff
1931	Japan seized Manchuria
1932	Stimson doctrine
	Reconstruction Finance Corporation
	"Bonus Army" in Washington
1933	New Deal inaugurated
	Bank holiday proclaimed
	Civilian Conservation Corps
	Gold standard abandoned
	Agricultural Adjustment Act
	Tennessee Valley Authority
	Federal Emergency Relief Administration
	National Industrial Recovery Act
	United States recognized Soviet Union
	Good Neighbor policy announced
1934	Gold Reserve Act
	Civil Works Administration
	Tydings-McDuffie Act
	Platt Amendment abrogated
	Securities and Exchange Commission
	First Trade Agreements Act
	Wheeler-Howard Law
	Federal Communications Commission
1935	Second New Deal begun
	Works Progress Administration
	Rural Electrification Administration
	NRA declared unconstitutional
	National Labor Relations Act
	Social Security Act
	Neutrality Act of 1935
	Italy invaded Ethiopia
	Committee for Industrial Organization formed
1936	AAA declared unconstitutional
	Rome-Berlin Axis formed
1937	Neutrality Act of 1937
	Japan renewed aggression in China
	Farm Security Administration
	National Housing Act
1938	Second Agricultural Adjustment Act
	United States naval rearmament
	Fair Labor Standards Act
	Munich agreement
1939	Hitler invaded Czechoslovakia
	Nazi-Soviet pact of friendship

1939	German invasion of Poland began Second World War
	Neutrality Act of 1939
1939-45	Second World War
1940	Nazis overran Norway, Denmark, Luxembourg, Belgium, and the Netherlands
	Fall of France
	Battle of Britain
	Destroyer deal with Britain
	Japan joined Germany and Italy in Tripartite Pact
1941	Lend-Lease Act
	Nazis invaded and occupied Balkans
	United States occupied Greenland
	Nazis invaded Soviet Union
	Atlantic Charter
	Kurusu mission
	Neutrality Act revised
	Pearl Harbor attacked
	United States declared war against Axis
1942	Declaration of United Nations signed
	Office of Price Administration
	Battle of the Coral Sea
	Fall of the Philippines
	United States landing on Guadalcanal
	Allied invasion of North Africa
1943	Casablanca Conference
	War Labor Disputes Act
	Allied invasion of Sicily and Italy
	Italy surrendered
	Moscow Declaration
	Cairo and Tehran conferences
1944	D day—Allied invasion of France
	Servicemen's Readjustment Act
	Liberation of Paris
	Battle of the Bulge
1945	Yalta Conference
	San Francisco Conference began
	V-E Day—end of the war in Europe
	United Nations Charter signed in San Francisco
	Potsdam Conference
	Atomic bombs dropped on Japan
	Soviet Union declared war on Japan
	V-J Day—end of the war in the Pacific
1946	Postwar labor strikes
	Employment Act of 1946
	Republic of the Philippines established
1947	Truman doctrine announced
	Aid sent to Greece and Turkey
	Marshall Plan proposed
	Taft-Hartley Act
	Conference on European Economic Coöperation
1948	Communist government in Czechoslovakia
	Brussels Pact
	Economic Coöperation Administration
	Organization of American States formed
	State of Israel created
	Berlin blockade
	United States–British airlift to Berlin
	Chinese Communists took Manchuria
1949	Fair Deal inaugurated
	Point Four program announced
	North Atlantic Treaty Organization
	West Germany adopted constitution
	Atomic-arms race began
	Chinese Nationalists fled to Taiwan
1950	Korean War began
	UN forces aided South Korea
	Chinese Communist "volunteers" in Korea
1950-53	Korean War
1951	Supreme Headquarters of Allied Powers in Europe established

1951	ANZUS Treaty	1957	Civil Rights Bill
	First transcontinental telecast		Soviet Union launched first *sputnik*
	Japanese peace treaty	1958	United States launched first satellite
1952	Commonwealth of Puerto Rico created		Pro-Nasser government established in Iraq
	United States tested hydrogen bomb		United States demonstrated successful ICBM
1953	Truce ended Korean War		Common Market formed
1954	*Brown* v. *Board of Education of Topeka*	1959	Alaska became the 49th state, Hawaii the 50th
	Geneva Conference on Indochina	1960	Castro embraced communism
	Communists overran northern Vietnam	1961	Invasion of Cuba failed
	Southeast Asia Treaty Organization		Alliance for Progress formed
	Investigation of McCarthy by Senate	1962	John Glenn orbited the earth
1955	Summit conference		Cuban missile crisis
	Baghdad Pact	1963	President Kennedy assassinated
	AFL and CIO merged	1964	Civil Rights Act
	Salk vaccine developed		Economic Opportunity Act
1956	Egypt seized Suez Canal	1965	Voting Rights Act
	Castro became premier of Cuba	1966	War in Vietnam escalated
	Montgomery bus boycott	1967	Arab-Israeli War erupted
	Violence at Little Rock		Riots occurred in cities
1957	Eisenhower doctrine announced		Kennedy Round agreed upon
	International Geophysical Year		Panama Canal Treaty agreed upon

As a review of significant foreign affairs, choose representative Secretaries of State and ask the class to describe briefly the foreign affairs each was concerned with. Or you might ask for the special contributions of men like John Quincy Adams, Daniel Webster, William H. Seward, John Hay, etc.

PRESIDENTS, VICE-PRESIDENTS, AND SECRETARIES OF STATE

NO.	NAME	BORN	DIED	YEARS IN OFFICE	POLITICAL PARTY	STATE	VICE-PRESIDENT	SECRETARY OF STATE
1	George Washington	1732	1799	1789–97	None	Va.	John Adams	Thomas Jefferson Edmund Randolph Timothy Pickering
2	John Adams	1735	1826	1797–1801	Federalist	Mass.	Thomas Jefferson	Timothy Pickering John Marshall
3	Thomas Jefferson	1743	1826	1801–9	Republican	Va.	Aaron Burr George Clinton	James Madison
4	James Madison	1751	1836	1809–17	Republican	Va.	George Clinton Elbridge Gerry	Robert Smith James Monroe
5	James Monroe	1758	1831	1817–25	Republican	Va.	Daniel D. Tompkins	John Quincy Adams
6	John Quincy Adams	1767	1848	1825–29	Republican	Mass.	John C. Calhoun	Henry Clay
7	Andrew Jackson	1767	1845	1829–37	Democratic	Tenn.	John C. Calhoun Martin Van Buren	Martin Van Buren Edward Livingston Louis McLane John Forsyth
8	Martin Van Buren	1782	1862	1837–41	Democratic	N.Y.	Richard M. Johnson	John Forsyth
9	William Henry Harrison	1773	1841	1841	Whig	Ohio	John Tyler	Daniel Webster
10	John Tyler	1790	1862	1841–45	Whig	Va.		Daniel Webster Hugh S. Legaré Abel P. Upshur John C. Calhoun
11	James K. Polk	1795	1849	1845–49	Democratic	Tenn.	George M. Dallas	James Buchanan
12	Zachary Taylor	1784	1850	1849–50	Whig	La.	Millard Fillmore	John M. Clayton
13	Millard Fillmore	1800	1874	1850–53	Whig	N.Y.		Daniel Webster Edward Everett
14	Franklin Pierce	1804	1869	1853–57	Democratic	N.H.	William R. King	William L. Marcy
15	James Buchanan	1791	1868	1857–61	Democratic	Pa.	John C. Breckinridge	Lewis Cass Jeremiah S. Black

NO.	NAME	BORN	DIED	YEARS IN OFFICE	POLITICAL PARTY	STATE	VICE-PRESIDENT	SECRETARY OF STATE
16	Abraham Lincoln	1809	1865	1861–65	Republican	Ill.	Hannibal Hamlin Andrew Johnson	William H. Seward
17	Andrew Johnson	1808	1875	1865–69	Republican	Tenn.		William H. Seward
18	Ulysses S. Grant	1822	1885	1869–77	Republican	Ill.	Schuyler Colfax Henry Wilson	Elihu B. Washburne Hamilton Fish
19	Rutherford B. Hayes	1822	1893	1877–81	Republican	Ohio	William A. Wheeler	William M. Evarts
20	James A. Garfield	1831	1881	1881	Republican	Ohio	Chester A. Arthur	James G. Blaine
21	Chester A. Arthur	1830	1886	1881–85	Republican	N.Y.		F. T. Frelinghuysen
22	Grover Cleveland	1837	1908	1885–89	Democratic	N.Y.	Thomas A. Hendricks	Thomas F. Bayard
23	Benjamin Harrison	1833	1901	1889–93	Republican	Ind.	Levi P. Morton	James G. Blaine John W. Foster
24	Grover Cleveland	1837	1908	1893–97	Democratic	N.Y.	Adlai E. Stevenson	Walter Q. Gresham Richard Olney
25	William McKinley	1843	1901	1897–1901	Republican	Ohio	Garret A. Hobart Theodore Roosevelt	John Sherman William R. Day John Hay
26	Theodore Roosevelt	1858	1919	1901–9	Republican	N.Y.	Charles W. Fairbanks	John Hay Elihu Root Robert Bacon
27	William Howard Taft	1857	1930	1909–13	Republican	Ohio	James S. Sherman	Philander C. Knox
28	Woodrow Wilson	1856	1924	1913–21	Democratic	N.J.	Thomas R. Marshall	William J. Bryan Robert Lansing Bainbridge Colby
29	Warren G. Harding	1865	1923	1921–23	Republican	Ohio	Calvin Coolidge	Charles E. Hughes
30	Calvin Coolidge	1872	1933	1923–29	Republican	Mass.	Charles G. Dawes	Charles E. Hughes Frank B. Kellogg
31	Herbert Hoover	1874	1964	1929–33	Republican	Calif.	Charles Curtis	Henry L. Stimson
32	Franklin D. Roosevelt	1882	1945	1933–45	Democratic	N.Y.	John N. Garner Henry A. Wallace Harry S Truman	Cordell Hull Cordell Hull Edward R. Stettinius, Jr.
33	Harry S Truman	1884	——	1945–53	Democratic	Mo.	Alben W. Barkley	James F. Byrnes George C. Marshall Dean G. Acheson
34	Dwight D. Eisenhower	1890	——	1953–61	Republican	N.Y.	Richard M. Nixon	John Foster Dulles Christian A. Herter
35	John F. Kennedy	1917	1963	1961–63	Democratic	Mass.	Lyndon B. Johnson	Dean Rusk
36	Lyndon B. Johnson	1908	——	1963——	Democratic	Texas	Hubert H. Humphrey	Dean Rusk

Which six states does a presidential candidate regard as most important to carry? (California, New York, Pennsylvania, Ohio, Illinois, and Texas.) The combined electoral vote (177) of these states is equal to that of how many other states?

FACTS ABOUT THE STATES

The number in front of each state name shows the order in which that state was admitted to the Union (or the order in which it adopted the Constitution, if one of the thirteen original states). The population figures for the states are those of the 1960 census, and the numbers of representatives in Congress are based on the 1960 census.

NUMBER IN ORDER	NAME	YEAR OF ENTRANCE	AREA IN SQUARE MILES	POPULATION	REPRESENTATIVES IN CONGRESS
22	Alabama	1819	51,609	3,266,740	8
49	Alaska	1959	586,400	226,167	1
48	Arizona	1912	113,909	1,302,161	3
25	Arkansas	1836	53,104	1,786,272	4
31	California	1850	158,693	15,717,204	38
38	Colorado	1876	104,247	1,753,947	4
5	Connecticut	1788	5,009	2,535,234	6
1	Delaware	1787	2,057	446,292	1
27	Florida	1845	58,560	4,951,560	12
4	Georgia	1788	58,876	3,943,116	10
50	Hawaii	1959	6,421	632,772	2
43	Idaho	1890	83,557	667,191	2
21	Illinois	1818	56,400	10,081,158	24
19	Indiana	1816	36,291	4,662,498	11
29	Iowa	1846	56,290	2,757,537	7
34	Kansas	1861	82,276	2,178,611	5
15	Kentucky	1792	40,395	3,038,156	7
18	Louisiana	1812	48,523	3,257,022	8
23	Maine	1820	33,215	969,265	2
7	Maryland	1788	10,577	3,100,689	8
6	Massachusetts	1788	8,257	5,148,578	12
26	Michigan	1837	58,216	7,823,194	19
32	Minnesota	1858	84,068	3,413,864	8
20	Mississippi	1817	47,716	2,178,141	5
24	Missouri	1821	69,674	4,319,813	10
41	Montana	1889	147,138	674,767	2
37	Nebraska	1867	77,227	1,411,330	3
36	Nevada	1864	110.540	285,278	1
9	New Hampshire	1788	9,304	606,921	2
3	New Jersey	1787	7.836	6,066,782	15
47	New Mexico	1912	121,666	951,023	2
11	New York	1788	49,576	16,782,304	41
12	North Carolina	1789	52,712	4,556,155	11
39	North Dakota	1889	70,665	632,466	2
17	Ohio	1803	41,222	9,706,397	24
46	Oklahoma	1907	69,919	2,328,284	6
33	Oregon	1859	96,981	1,768,687	4
2	Pennsylvania	1787	45,333	11,319,366	27
13	Rhode Island	1790	1,214	859,488	2
8	South Carolina	1788	31.055	2,382,591	6
40	South Dakota	1889	77,047	680,514	2
16	Tennessee	1796	42,244	3,567,089	9
28	Texas	1845	267,339	9,579,677	23
45	Utah	1896	84,916	890,627	2
14	Vermont	1791	9,609	389,881	1
10	Virginia	1788	40,815	3,966,949	10
42	Washington	1889	68,192	2,853,214	7
35	West Virginia	1863	24,181	1,860,421	5
30	Wisconsin	1848	56,154	3,951,777	10
44	Wyoming	1890	97,914	330,066	1
..	District of Columbia	1791	69	763,956	..
TOTALS			3,615,210	179,323,175	435

Name the eight oldest states. (Connecticut, Georgia, Maryland, Massachusetts, New Hampshire, New York, South Carolina, Virginia.) Name the two newest. (Alaska, Hawaii.)

AREA—TERRITORIAL EXPANSION: 1790 TO 1960

YEAR	NUMBER	YEAR	NUMBER	YEAR	NUMBER
1780	2,781,000	1720	474,388	1660	84,800
1770	2,205,000	1710	357,500	1650	51,700
1760	1,610,000	1700	275,000	1640	27,947
1750	1,207,000	1690	213,500	1630	5,700
1740	889,000	1680	155,600	1620	2,499
1730	654,950	1670	114,500	1610	210

AREA—TERRITORIAL EXPANSION: 1790 TO 1960

ACCESSION	DATE	GROSS AREA (LAND AND WATER) SQ. MI.
Total, 1960 (excluding P.I.)[1]	—	3,680,073
United States	—	3,675,633
Gadsden Purchase	1853	29,640
Mexican Cession	1848	529,017
Oregon	1846	285,580
Texas	1845	390,144
By treaty with Spain:		
Florida	1819	58,560
Other areas	1819	13,443
Louisiana Purchase	1803	827,192
Territory in 1790[2]	—	888,811
Alaska	1867	586,400
Hawaii	1898	6,424
Territories and possessions	—	4,440
Virgin Islands of the United States	1917	133
Panama Canal Zone	1904	553
American Samoa	1900	76
Guam	1899	212
Puerto Rico	1899	3,435
Miscellaneous Pacific Islands[3]	—	31

[1] The Philippine Islands (area 115,000 square miles), ceded by Spain in 1898, constituted a territorial possession of the United States from 1898 to 1946; they were granted independence as of July 4, 1946, becoming the Republic of the Philippines.

[2] Includes that part of the drainage basin of the Red River of the North, south of the 49th parallel, sometimes considered part of the Louisiana Purchase.

[3] Includes Howland, Baker, Midway, Wake, and certain other small islands.

POPULATION, DECENNIAL SUMMARY

SEX, URBAN RESIDENCE, AND RURAL RESIDENCE: 1790 TO 1970

YEAR	UNITED STATES	SEX		URBAN AND RURAL	
		MALE	FEMALE	URBAN	RURAL
1970‡	204,500,000	100,000,000	104,500,000	150,000,000	54,500,000
1960*	179,323,175	88,331,494	90,991,681	125,268,750	54,054,425
1950	150,697,361	74,833,239	75,864,122	96,467,686	54,229,675
1940	131,669,275	66,061,592	65,607,683	77,669,275†	54,000,000†
1930	122,775,046	62,137,080	60,637,966	70,775,046†	52,000,000†
1920	105,710,620	53,900,431	51,810,189	54,710,620†	51,000,000†
1910	91,972,266	47,332,277	44,639,989	41,998,932	49,973,334
1900	75,994,575	38,816,448	37,178,127	30,159,921	45,834,654
1890	62,947,714	32,237,101	30,710,613	22,106,265	40,841,449
1880	50,155,783	25,518,820	24,636,963	14,129,735	36,026,048
1870	38,558,371	19,493,565	19,064,806	9,902,361	28,656,010
1860	31,443,321	16,085,204	15,358,117	6,216,518	25,226,803
1850	23,191,876	11,837,660	11,354,216	3,543,716	19,648,160
1840	17,069,453	8,688,532	8,380,921	1,845,055	15,224,398
1830	12,866,020	6,532,489	6,333,531	1,127,247	11,738,773
1820	9,638,453	4,896,605	4,741,848	693,255	8,945,198
1810	7,239,881	——	——	525,459	6,714,422
1800	5,308,483	——	——	322,371	4,986,112
1790	3,929,214	——	——	201,655	3,727,559

* Includes Alaska & Hawaii. † Revised from official figures to reflect new definitions of "urban" and "rural" introduced in 1950.
‡ Projected. Figures exclude armed forces overseas.

AREA AND POPULATION

UNITED STATES: 1790 TO 1970

YEAR	AREA (SQUARE MILES)			POPULATION	
	GROSS AREA*	LAND	WATER*	NUMBER	PER SQ. MI. OF LAND AREA
1970 (projected)†	3,675,630	3,548,913	66,295	204,500,000	55.6
1960†	3,675,630	3,548,913	66,295	179,323,175	49.6
1950 (Apr. 1)	3,022,387	2,974,726‡	47,661‡	150,697,361	50.7
1940 (Apr. 1)	3,022,387	2,977,128	45,259	131,669,275	44.2
1930 (Apr. 1)	3,022,387§	2,977,128	45,259	122,775,046	41.2
1920 (Jan. 1)	3,026,789	2,973,776	53,013	105,710,620	35.5
1910 (Apr. 15)	3,026,789	2,973,890	52,899	91,972,266	30.9
1900 (June 1)	3,026,789	2,974,159	52,630	75,994,575	25.6
1890 (June 1)	3,026,789	2,973,965	52,824	62,947,714	21.2
1880 (June 1)	3,026,789	2,973,965	52,824	50,155,783	16.9
1870 (June 1)	3,026,789	2,973,965	52,824	39,818,449	13.4
1860 (June 1)	3,026,789	2,973,965	52,824	31,443,321	10.6
1850 (June 1)	2,997,119	2,944,337	52,782	23,191,876	7.9
1840 (June 1)	1,792,223	1,753,588	38,635	17,069,453	9.7
1830 (June 1)	1,792,223	1,753,588	38,635	12,866,020	7.3
1820 (Aug. 7)	1,792,223	1,753,588	38,635	9,638,453	5.5
1810 (Aug. 6)	1,720,122	1,685,865	34,257	7,239,881	4.3
1800 (Aug. 4)	892,135	867,980	24,155	5,308,483	6.1
1790 (Aug. 2)	892,135	867,980	24,155	3,929,214	4.5

* These figures do not include the Great Lakes (60,422 sq. mi.).
† Includes Alaska and Hawaii.

‡ Change in area due to remeasurement for census of 1950.
§ Change in area due to remeasurement for census of 1940.

CONTINENTS AND METROPOLITAN CENTERS

The Continents

	AREA (sq mi.)	POPULATION
World	57,280,000	3,237,000,000
Africa	11,685,000	290,200,000
Antarctica	5,100,000	Uninhabited
Asia	17,085,000	1,877,000,000
Oceania, including Australia	3,295,000	17,400,000
Europe	3,825,000	601,900,000
North America	9,420,000	289,700,000
South America	6,870,000	160,800,000

Largest Metropolitan Centers of the World

RANK		POPULATION (metropolitan area)	(city proper)
1	New York, U.S.	16,325,000	8,085,000
2	Tokyo, Japan	15,400,000	8,850,000
3	London, U.K.	11,025,000	3,175,000
4	Osaka, Japan	8,700,000	3,250,000
5	Moscow, Soviet Union	8,450,000	6,475,000
6	Paris, France	8,000,000	2,800,000
7	Buenos Aires, Argentina	7,700,000	2,950,000
8	Shanghai, China	7,600,000	10,400,000
9	Los Angeles, U.S.	7,475,000	2,660,000
10	Chicago, U.S.	7,090,000	3,575,000
11	Calcutta, India	6,700,000	3,000,000
12	Mexico City, Mexico	6,100,000	3,050,000
13	São Paulo, Brazil	5,450,000	4,425,000
14	Rio de Janeiro, Brazil	5,250,000	3,600,000
15	Essen, Germany	5,200,000	729,000
16	Bombay, India	4,700,000	4,500,000
17	Cairo, United Arab Republic	4,600,000	3,800,000
18	Peking (Peiping), China	4,200,000	7,000,000
19	Detroit, U.S.	4,170,000	1,610,000
20	Philadelphia, U.S.	4,150,000	2,040,000
21	Berlin, Germany	4,025,000	2,180,000
22	Leningrad, Soviet Union	4,000,000	3,100,000
23	San Francisco, U.S.	3,730,000	750,000
24	Boston, U.S.	3,480,000	665,000
25	Tientsin, China	3,400,000	3,800,000
26	Hong Kong, Hong Kong	3,275,000	725,000
27	Seoul, Korea	3,200,000	3,125,000
28	Djakarta, Indonesia	3,150,000	3,150,000

Some Important Cities in the United States

	ESTIMATED POPULATION (metropolitan area)	(city proper)
Akron, Ohio	615,000	295,000
Atlanta, Ga.	1,115,000	515,000
Baltimore, Md.	1,700,000	930,000
Birmingham, Ala.	650,000	346,000
Boston, Mass.	3,480,000	665,000
Buffalo, N.Y.	1,285,000	515,000
Chicago, Ill.	7,090,000	3,575,000
Cincinnati, Ohio	1,315,000	495,000
Cleveland, Ohio	2,260,000	865,000
Columbus, Ohio	790,000	495,000
Dallas, Tex.	1,180,000	750,000
Dayton, Ohio	715,000	262,000
Denver, Colo.	1,020,000	520,000
Detroit, Mich.	3,970,000	1,610,000
Fort Worth, Tex.	530,000	360,000
Hartford, Conn.	858,000	158,000
Houston, Tex.	1,420,000	1,045,000
Indianapolis, Ind.	840,000	510,000
Kansas City, Mo.	1,110,000	525,000
Los Angeles, Calif.	7,475,000	2,660,000
Louisville, Ky.	780,000	395,000
Memphis, Tenn.	680,000	515,000
Miami, Fla.	1,500,000	335,000
Milwaukee, Wis.	1,315,000	760,000
Minneapolis, Minn.	} 1,540,000	{ 470,000
St. Paul, Minn.		{ 310,000
New Orleans, La.	950,000	645,000
New York, N.Y.	16,325,000	8,085,000
Norfolk, Va.	636,000	315,000
Philadelphia, Pa.	4,150,000	2,040,000
Pittsburgh, Pa.	1,975,000	575,000
Portland, Ore.	770,000	368,000
Providence, R.I.	833,000	194,000
Rochester, N.Y.	630,000	314,000
St. Louis, Mo.	2,155,000	720,000
San Antonio, Tex.	765,000	627,000
San Diego, Calif.	1,015,000	640,000
San Francisco, Calif.	} 3,730,000	{ 750,000
Oakland, Calif.		{ 372,000
San Jose, Calif.		{ 305,000
Seattle, Wash.	1,035,000	565,000
Toledo, Ohio	545,000	334,000
Washington, D.C.	2,265,000	785,000

How can the sharp increase in the excess of imports in the years 1915-1921 and 1940-1944 be accounted for? How can the long period of excess of imports in the eighteenth and nineteenth centuries be explained?

EXPORTS AND IMPORTS OF MERCHANDISE BY THE UNITED STATES, WITH TRADE BALANCES: 1790–1966

[In thousands of dollars. Fiscal years ending Sept. 30, 1790 to 1842, June 30, 1843 to 1915; calendar years thereafter.]

YEAR	EXPORTS[1]	IMPORTS[1]	EXCESS OF EXPORTS (+) OR IMPORTS (−)
1790	20,205	23,000	−2,795
1792	20,753	31,500	−10,747
1794	33,044	34,600	−1,556
1796	58,575	81,436	−22,861
1798	61,327	68,552	−7,225
1800	70,972	91,253	−20,281
1802	71,957	76,333	−4,376
1804	77,699	85,000	−7,301
1806	101,537	129,410	−27,873
1808	22,431	56,990	−34,559
1810	66,758	85,400	−18,642
1812	38,527	77,030	−38,503
1814	6,927	12,965	−6,038
1816	81,920	147,103	−65,183
1818	93,281	121,750	−28,469
1820	69,692	74,450	−4,758
1822	61,350	79,872	−18,522
1824	68,972	72,169	−3,197
1826	72,891	78,094	−5,203
1828	64,021	81,020	−16,999
1830	71,671	62,721	+8,950
1832	81,521	95,122	−13,601
1834	102,260	108,610	−6,350
1836	124,339	176,579	−52,240
1838	104,979	95,970	+9,009
1840	123,669	98,259	+25,410
1841	111,817	122,958	−11,141
1842	99,878	96,075	+3,803
1843[2]	82,826	42,433	+40,393
1844	105,746	102,605	+3,141
1845	106,040	113,184	−7,144
1846	109,583	117,914	−8,331
1847	156,742	122,424	+34,318
1848	138,191	148,639	−10,448
1849	140,351	141,206	−855
1850	144,376	173,510	−29,134
1851	188,915	210,771	−21,856
1852	166,984	207,440	−40,456
1853	203,489	263,777	−60,288
1854	237,044	297,804	−60,760
1855	218,910	257,809	−38,899
1856	281,219	310,432	−29,213
1857	293,824	348,428	−54,604
1858	272,011	263,339	+8,672
1859	292,902	331,333	−38,431
1860	333,576	353,616	−20,040
1861	219,554	289,311	−69,757
1862	190,671	189,357	+1,314
1863	203,964	243,336	−39,372
1864	158,838	316,447	−157,609
1865	166,029	238,746	−72,717
1866	348,860	434,812	−85,952
1867	294,506	395,761	−101,255
1868	281,953	357,436	−75,483
1869	286,118	417,506	−131,388
1870	392,772	435,958	−43,186

YEAR	EXPORTS	IMPORTS	EXCESS OF EXPORTS (+) OR IMPORTS (−)
1871	442,820	520,224	−77,404
1872	444,178	626,595	−182,417
1873	522,480	642,136	−119,656
1874	586,283	567,406	+18,877
1875	513,443	533,005	−19,562
1876	540,385	460,741	+79,644
1877	602,475	451,323	+151,152
1878	694,866	437,052	+257,814
1879	710,439	445,778	+264,661
1880	835,639	667,955	+167,684
1881	902,377	642,665	+259,712
1882	750,542	724,640	+25,902
1883	823,839	723,181	+100,658
1884	740,514	667,698	+72,816
1885	742,190	577,527	+164,663
1886	679,525	635,436	+44,089
1887	716,183	692,320	+23,863
1888	695,955	723,957	−28,002
1889	742,401	745,132	−2,731
1890	857,829	789,310	+68,519
1891	884,481	844,916	+39,565
1892	1,030,278	827,402	+202,876
1893	847,665	866,401	−18,736
1894	892,141	654,995	+237,146
1895	807,538	731,970	+75,568
1896	882,607	779,725	+102,882
1897	1,050,994	764,730	+286,264
1898	1,231,482	616,050	+615,432
1899	1,227,023	697,148	+529,875
1900	1,394,483	849,941	+544,542
1901	1,487,765	823,172	+664,592
1902	1,381,719	903,321	+478,398
1903	1,420,142	1,025,719	+394,423
1904	1,460,827	991,087	+469,740
1905	1,518,562	1,117,513	+401,049
1906	1,743,865	1,226,562	+517,303
1907	1,880,851	1,434,421	+446,430
1908	1,860,773	1,194,342	+666,431
1909	1,663,011	1,311,920	+351,091
1910	1,744,985	1,556,947	+188,038
1911	2,049,320	1,527,226	+522,094
1912	2,204,322	1,653,265	+551,057
1913	2,465,884	1,813,008	+652,876
1914	2,364,579	1,893,926	+470,653
1915	2,768,589	1,674,170	+1,094,419
1915 (6 mos.)	1,852,863	912,787	+940,076
1916	5,482,641	2,391,635	+3,091,006
1917	6,233,513	2,952,468	+3,281,045
1918	6,149,088	3,031,213	+3,117,875
1919	7,920,426	3,904,365	+4,016,761
1920	8,228,016	5,278,481	+2,949,535
1921	4,485,031	2,509,148	+1,975,883
1922	3,831,777	3,112,747	+719,030
1923	4,167,493	3,792,066	+375,427
1924	4,590,984	3,609,963	+981,021

YEAR	EXPORTS	IMPORTS	EXCESS OF EXPORTS (+) OR IMPORTS (−)
1925	4,909,848	4,226,589	+683,258
1926	4,808,660	4,430,888	+377,772
1927	4,865,375	4,184,742	+680,633
1928	5,128,356	4,091,444	+1,036,912
1929	5,240,995	4,399,361	+841,634
1930	3,843,181	3,060,908	+782,273
1931	2,424,289	2,090,635	+333,654
1932	1,611,016	1,322,774	+288,242
1933	1,674,994	1,449,559	+225,435
1934	2,132,800	1,655,055	+477,745
1935	2,282,874	2,047,485	+235,389
1936	2,455,978	2,422,592	+33,386
1937	3,349,167	3,083,668	+265,499
1938	3,094,440	1,960,428	+1,134,012
1939	3,177,176	2,318,081	+859,095
1940	4,021,146	2,625,379	+1,395,767
1941	5,147,154	3,345,005	+1,802,149
1942	8,078.988	2,755,893	+5,323,095
1943	12,964,906	3,381,498	+9,583,408
1944	14,258,702	3,928,866	+10,329,837
1945	9,805,625	4,159,138	+5,646,487
1946	9,738,321	4,942,054	+4,796,267
1947	14,429,747	5,756,333	+8,673,413
1948	12,653,058	7,123,877	+5,529,181
1949	12,051,108	6,622,390	+5,428,718
1950	10,275,102	8,852,161	+1,422,941
1951	15,020,409	10,961,550	+4,058,858
1952	15,201,000[3]	10,717,000[3]	+4,483,000
1953	15,774,000[3]	10,873,000[3]	+4,900,000
1954	15,110,000[3]	10,215,000[3]	+4,894,000
1955	15,547,000[3]	11,384,000[3]	+4,163,000
1956	19,090,000[3]	12,615,000[3]	+6,475,000
1957	20,850,000[3]	12,982,000[3]	+7,868,000
1958	17,892,700	12,792,500	+5,100,200
1959	17,621,400	15,207,200	+2,414,200
1960	20,549,700	14,653,900	+5,895,800
1961	20.874,100	14,449,200	+6,424,900
1962	22,096,000	16,605,000	+5,491,000
1963	23,593,000	17,253,000	+6,340,000
1964	27,056,000	18,791,000	+8,264,000
1965	28,685,000	21,533,000	+7,152,000
1966	30,336,000	25,550,300	+4,785,700

[1] Includes gold and silver prior to 1821. [2] Period beginning Oct. 1, 1842, and ending June 30, 1843. [3] Approximate.
Source: Department of Commerce, Bureau of Census; annual report, *Foreign Commerce and Navigation of the United States,* and records.

Why did the federal government urge that our exports be increased in the 1960's? (To help reduce our balance-of-payments deficit, created by foreign aid and the Vietnam War.)

An asterisk (*) indicates a picture.

Key to pronunciation: ā, as in āte; â, as in senâte; â, as in câre; ă, as in ăm; ᾰ, as in finᾰl; ä, as in ärm; ȧ, as in ȧsk; ȧ, as in sofȧ; ē, as in ēve; ê, as in crēate; ĕ, as in ĕnd; ĕ, as in novĕl; ē, as in cindēr; ī, as in īce; ĭ, as in ĭll; ῐ, as in charῐty; ō, as in ōld; ô, as in ôbey; ô, as in lôrd; ŏ, as in ŏdd; ǒ, as in cǒnnect; ōō, as in fōōd; ŏŏ, as in fŏŏt; oi, as in oil; ou, as in thou; ū, as in pūre; ù, as in ùnite; û, as in ûrn; ŭ, as in stŭdy; ᴜ, as in circᴜs; N indicates the nasal tone, as in French, of the preceding vowel; g, as in go; t̶h̶, as in t̶h̶at; κ, as in German ich.

AAA. *See* Agricultural Adjustment Act

ABC powers, 545, 547

Aberdeen Angus cattle, 353

Abilene, Kansas, 349, 350*

Abolitionists: early, 213–214; in South, 223, 224–225; Webster on, 257

Abolition of slavery: Compromise of 1850, 256, 257; William Harper on, 216–217; Lincoln on, 271; southern views on, 223–224

Abrogation of Platt Amendment, 489

Acheson, Dean, 749, 750

Adams, Abigail, 139, 146

Adams, Charles Francis, 284

Adams, Henry, quoted, 377

Adams, John: character, 139; in Continental Congress, 82; and Declaration of Independence, 77*, 78; and federal courts, 148; minister to England, 113; at peace negotiations, 95–97; as President, 139–142; quoted, 75, 82; and truce talks, 90; as Vice-President, 128, 135, 139; in War for Independence, 90; in White House, 146; and X Y Z affair, 140–141

Adams, John Quincy, 167, 169; character, 175; and Chesapeake and Ohio Canal, 211; in Congress, 214, 254; elected President, 174, 175; and Monroe Doctrine, 168; as peace commissioner, 160; quoted, 176, 194–195; as Secretary of State, 168

Adams, Samuel, 72, 72*, 73, 74, 76, 77, 122; in Continental Congress, 82; quoted, 76–77; and religion, 84

Adamson Act, 528

Adams-Onís Treaty, 167

Addams, Jane, 508

Advertising, 614

A.E.F. *See* American Expeditionary Force

AFL. *See* American Federation of Labor

Africa: Barbary coast, 147; crops from, 16; Dutch trade with, 44; exploration, 8, 12; problems in, 769; settlers from, 40, 99; slave trade, 67, 218

Africans, 40. *See also* Negroes

Aggressions: of China, 750–751; of Communists, 745, 746–747, 750–751, 757, 760–762; in Europe, 682, 688 (map); of European powers in China, 486; of Germany, 663, 667, 686–688, 688 (map), 689*, 702, 702*; of Italy, 663, 667, 683–684, 684*, 688 (map); of Japan, 630, 667, 683–684, 685, 685*, 701, 704*, 705, 707; of North Vietnam, 760–762; of the Soviet Union, 688 (map), 746–747, 750

Agricultural Adjustment Act, 644, 649, 655, 662

Agricultural Credits Act, 623

Agricultural Marketing Act, 633

Agriculture: American, 128; in Colorado, 356; in 1820's, 178; in English colonies, 27–28, 55–56; mechanized, 780; nineteenth-century, 316; at Plymouth, 34; in South, 218–219, 220; in Spanish colonies, 15; surpluses, 780. *See also* Farming

Agriculture, Department of, 440, 440n, 517

Agriculture, Secretary of, 622, 633

Aguinaldo (ä′gē-näl′dō), **Emilio,** 476, 492

Air age, 619–621

Air attacks, on Europe in Second World War, 712

Air Commerce Act, 620

Airlift, 748

Airmail, 618*, 619

Airplanes: in First World War, 584*, 619; passenger, 619*, 620

Air pollution, 438, 777

Aisne River, 582

Alabama: admitted to Union, 166n, 220; Dixiecrats in, 743; food distribution, 293*; iron production, 320; politics, 304; readmitted to Union, 300; secession, 272; and TVA, 645

Alabama claims, 284

Alabama River, 62

Alamo, 237

Alaska: admitted to Union, 494, 754; boundary settlement, 552–553, 552 (map); flag-raising ceremony, 494*; gold in, 455; gold seekers, 390*; government, 489;

Harding in, 602; purchase of, 389–391; Russian, 233

Albania, 687

Albany, New York, 44, 45, 62, 64, 65, 210; in War for Independence, 91, 92

Albany Plan of Union, 64

Albemarle Sound, 25

Albertson v. *Subversive Activities Control Board,* 779

Aldrich, Nelson W., 519

Aleutian Islands, 709

Algeciras (ăl′jē-sēr′ȧs) **Conference,** 553

Alger, Horatio, 338, 338*

Algeria, 147

Alien and Sedition Acts, 141, 142, 146

Alien Property, Office of, 603

Aliens, 728

Allegheny River, 64, 438

Allen, Ethan, 90

Alliance for Progress, 768–769

Alliances: European, 566; Farmers', 444, 446

Allied Expeditionary Force, 714

Allies: in First World War, 569, 580–584, 590–591; in Second World War, 706–709, 713

Altamaha River, 53, 54

Altgeld, John P., 412, 419

Amendments, to Constitution, 120, 123. *See also* Constitution

America: crops brought by Spanish, 16; as debtor nation, 669; divisions, 100; extent of, 17–18; origin of name, 10; as refuge, 23; resources, 328–330; settlers, 40; in the world, 100

American Colonization Society, 218

American Expeditionary Force, 580, 583*

American Farm Bureau Federation, 455

American Federation of Labor, 413–416, 444, 623, 638, 641; addressed by Wilson, 528; in 1930's, 654; in 1924, 624

American Federation of Labor–Congress of Industrial Organizations, 781

American ideals, 181, 510–511

American life: in cities, 433–436, 438–439, 507*, 508*, 634; after Civil War, 308; before the Civil

War, 246; colonial period, 99, 102*, 103*, 104*; early national years, 178; effects of industry, 319–320; in Great Depression, 632, 633–635, 636*; on Great Plains, 362–364; late 1800's, 457, 460*, 461*, 462*; late 1900's, 558*, 559*, 560*; on midwestern farms, 430–433; in 1920's, 603–605, 614–617; in North, 202–209; in progressive era, 500, 501*, 507*, 508*; and the railroad, 200–201; in South, 220–222, 428–429

"American method," 316

American party. See Know-Nothing party

American Peace Society, 551

American Railway Union, 418, 419, 421

American Red Cross, 282

American Revolution, 80–95; background, 67–77; continuing, 757; results, 97, 99. See also War for Independence

Americans: in battle, 581–582, 581*, 583*, 584; in Battle of the Bulge, 718*; become a nation, 105; colonial ties with England, 82; as described by Crèvecoeur, 80–81; after French and Indian War, 68; in Hawaii, 399; at Louisbourg, 66; in Paris, 718; in North Africa, 713. See also American life

American Samoa, 392, 392 (map)

American Sugar Refining Company, 331

"American system," 174, 175, 192, 598–599

American Telephone and Telegraph, 670

Amherst, Jeffrey, 65–66

Amnesty, meaning, 292

"Anaconda policy," 276

Anarchists, 412, 412n

Anderson, Robert, 273–274

Anglicans, 31, 35, 84

Anglo-America, 100

Anglo-Japanese Alliance, 672

Annapolis, Maryland, 31, 118

Annapolis Convention, 118

Anthony, Susan B., 213

Anti-Americanism, 768

Anti-ballistics missile system, 771

Antietam, Battle of, 279, 279*

Antifederalists, 122

Antimasonic party, 192, 192n, 198n

Antipoverty program, 775

Anti-Saloon League, 510

ANZUS Treaty, 770

Apollo 1, 773

Appalachian Mountains, 60, 68, 74, 93, 111, 202, 221, 232

Apples, 632, 633*

Appomattox Court House, 283

Aqaba, Gulf of, 765

Arab-Israeli war, 765

Arab League, 762, 762n

Arabs, 762, 764

Arapaho Indians, 342

Arbenz, Jacobo, 768

Arbitration: Alaskan boundary dispute, 552–553; in coal strike of 1902, 513; of international disputes, 552; of Venezuela–British Guiana boundary, 395–396

Architecture, 457; of cities, 435, 435 (diagram)

Argentina, 15, 431, 545

Argonne Forest, Battle of, 584

Arizona, 368, 522

Arkansas: admitted to Union, 220; in Civil War, 281; politics in 1874, 304; readmitted to Union, 300; in reconstruction, 293; secession, 274; teaching of evolution prohibited, 608

Arkansas River, 14, 60

Arlington National Cemetery, 673, 757

Armas, Carlos Castillo, 768

Armistice, after First World War, 584, 589*

Arms embargo, 684, 688, 698

Armstrong, Edwin H., 616

Armstrong, Louis, 605

Army, American. See Army, United States; Continental Army

Army, British, 89, 91

Army, United States: and Colt six-shooter, 342; in First World War, 579; in Mexican War, 238, 240–241; in Second World War, 708*, 717*, 718–720, 718*, 722, 722*, 723*; in Spanish-American War, 475–476

Army Corps of Engineers, 316

Army of Northern Virginia, 279–283

Army of the Potomac, 276, 278, 279, 281

Arnold, Benedict, 90, 93

Aroostook War, 197

Arthur, Chester A., 374, 375–376, 498; in election of 1884, 377, 514n; sworn into office, 375*

Articles of Confederation, 110, 111, 117, 118, 119

Arts, 6, 7

Ashburton, Lord Alexander, 196–197

Ashley, William H., 152

Asia: aggressions in, 701–704, 707, 749–751, 757, 760–761; attraction for West, 6; in colonial trade, 53, 55; crops from, 16; early routes, 6 (map), 11, 17; hope for trade with, 391; Japanese in, 701–704; and "manifest destiny," 233; opened to trade, 243; Portuguese in, 8; relations with, 680–682; search for route to, 24; after Second World War, 736; in Seven Years' War, 65

Assembly line, 613, 613*

Association, The, 75

Astor, John Jacob, 233–234

Astronauts, 772–773, 773*

Aswân Dam, 762

Atahualpa (ăt'ȧ-wäl'pȧ), 13, 13*

Atchison, Topeka, and Santa Fe Railroad, 324

Atlanta, Georgia, 281–282, 292, 699

Atlantic, Battle of the, 699–700

Atlantic and Pacific Railroad, 324

Atlantic Charter, 700, 700*

Atlantic Ocean, 1, 3, 9, 11, 16, 699–700

Atlas missile, 770

Atom, 561

Atomic bombs, 646, 734; dropped on Japan, 724–725; exploded in Nevada, 771*; in Soviet Union, 749; tested in New Mexico, 735

Atomic Energy Commission, 740, 749

Attlee, Clement, 735, 736

Attu, 709

Attucks, Crispus, 72

Augusta, Georgia, 228

Austin, Moses, 236

Austin, Stephen, 236

Australia, 431, 709, 770

Austria: after First World War, 593; peace treaty with, 596, 671; in Seven Years' War, 65; at war with Serbia, 566

Austria-Hungary, 566, 568, 682

Austrian Empire, 593

Automation, 780–781, 780n

Automobiles: and American life, 611–614; in Europe, 611–612; mass production, 612. See also names of makes

Axis powers: defined, 698, 698n; joined by Japan, 701; in Second World War, 710–711 (map)

Azores, 5, 8

Aztecs, 13

Babcock, Orville E., 303

Baghdad Pact, 770

Baker, Ray Stannard, 504

Baker v. Carr, 779

Balboa, Vasco Nuñez de, 12

Balkan Wars of 1912–1913, 566, 566n

Baltimore, Maryland, 113; Democratic convention, 267; growth, 204; as market for farm products, 209; and railroads, 228; railroad strike, 410; in War of 1812, 160

Baltimore, Lord. See Calvert, Cecilius; Calvert, Sir George

Baltimore and Ohio Railroad, 211–212, 322, 409

Bancroft, George, 238

Bankhead-Jones Farm Tenant Act, 662

Banking, commercial, 336–338

Banking system, 184–185

Bank of Massachusetts, 115

Bank of North America, 115
Bank of the United States, 133, 148
Bank of the United States, second, 170; chartered, 171; destroyed by Jackson, 191; issue in election of 1832, 190, 191; opposition to, 172
Banks: during Civil War, 286–287; closed, 628–629, 629*; failure in Great Depression, 641–643; Federal Reserve, 526–527, 526 (cartoon); state (wildcat), 191
Banneker, Benjamin, 161
Baptists, 218
Barbados (bär-bā'dōz), 43
"Barbara Frietchie," 202
Barbary coast, 147, 147 (map)
Barbed wire, 353, 363, 569
Bargaining, collective, 398–399
Barkley, Alben W., 742
Barnburners, 255, 255n
Barry, John, 93
Barton, Clara, 282
Baruch, Bernard M., 586, 641
Bases, military, 468, 693, 705; attack on Pearl Harbor, 704*, 705*
Bataan, 707*
Batista, Fulgencio, 768
"Battle Hymn of the Republic," 202
Bay of Pigs, 768
Bear Flag revolt, 240
Beauregard, Pierre G. T. de, 276, 278
Beavers, 18, 49
Beckwourth, James P., 152
Beecher, Henry Ward, 262, 410–411
Beecher, Lyman, 258
"Beecher's Bibles," 262
Belgium: and Battle of the Bulge, 718, 718*; in Common Market, 767; in First World War, 586; on gold standard, 446; invaded by Germans, 566, 691; in NATO, 748; relief to, 586; at Washington Conference, 672
Belknap, William W., 303
Bell, Alexander Graham, 320
Bell, John, 267, 268
Belleau Wood, Battle of, 581–582
Bemis Heights, 92
Benjamin, Judah P., 275, 292
Bennington, Vermont, 92
Benson, Ezra Taft, 754
Berkeley, John Lord, 50
Berle, Adolf A., Jr., 641
Berlin, Germany: airlift to, 748, 749*; blockade of, 748; in First World War, 566; in 1945, 720, 720*; occupation, 744, 766
Berlin Wall, 767, 767*
Bermuda, 693
Bermuda Company, 28
Bernstorff, Count J. H. von, 577
Bessemer, Henry, 329
Bessemer process, 329
Beveridge, Albert J., 469, 520; quoted, 466–467
Biddle, Nicholas, 190, 233, 233n

Big business, 328–331, 332–338
Big Four, 590–591, 591*, 745
Big stick, 499*, 537
Big Three, 731
"Billion-dollar Congress," 383
Bill of Rights, 121–122, 123, 777
Biloxi, Mississippi, 60
Birney, James G., 194, 214, 224, 238
Bismarck, North Dakota, 367
Bituminous Coal Conservation Act (Guffey-Snyder Act), 656
Black, Hugo L., 778*; quoted, 779
"Black Friday," 303
Black Hawk War, 188, 208
Black Hills, 343, 344–345, 357, 366
Blacklisting, 413, 413*, 417
"Black power," 784
Blaine, James G., 374, 375, 395
Bland-Allison Act, 446
"Bleeding Kansas," 261, 263
Blockade: of Berlin, 748; British, 573; in Civil War, 285; in Napoleonic wars, 154–155
Bogardus, James, 435
Bogotá, Colombia, 534, 770
Bombers: attack on Tokyo, 708*; intercontinental, 770; over Sicily, 713*; of Strategic Air Command, 738–739*
Bon Homme Richard, 93
Bonn, West Germany, 745
"Bonus Army," 637–638, 637*
Book of Mormon, 235
"Boomers," 367–368, 368*
Booth, John Wilkes, 288
"Bootlegging," 610, 610 (cartoon), 611
Borah, William E., 594, 671–672, 684–685, 690, 690*
"Border Ruffians," 261
Bosses, political, 439, 439 (cartoon), 440 (cartoon), 505
Boston, Massachusetts, 70*, 434, 438; British troops in, 72; colonial, 38, 55, 55*, 103*; evacuated by British, 90; financial speculators in, 132; growth, 165; and immigrants, 206; police strike, 606; riots against customs duties, 71; sewage disposal, 434; after "Tea Party," 73–74; in War for Independence, 76
Boston and Worcester Railroad, 211
"Boston Massacre," 72, 72*
Boston Tea Party, 73
Boulder, Colorado, 355
Bowdoin College, 259
Boxer Rebellion, 486, 488
Boycott, 417, 417n; of English goods, 70, 71. See also Nonimportation Act
Boyd, Alan S., 777
Boy Scouts, 510
Braddock, Edward, 64–65
Bradford, William, 33
Bradley, Omar N., 714*, 718
Bragg, Braxton, 281

Braintree, Massachusetts, 607
"Brain trust," 641
Brandegee, Frank B., 594
Brandeis, Louis D., 526, 660
Brandenburg Gate, 720*, 767
Brandywine, Battle of, 91, 92–93
Brazil, 545; Cabral in, 10; colony from South, 292; Jews from, 46
"Bread colonies," 55
Breckinridge, John C., 267, 268
Breed's Hill, 76
Brewster, William, 33
Briand, Aristide, 673
Bridger, James, 152
Bristow, Joseph L., 520
Britain, 196–197, 486, 671, 699, 736, 770; defense of colonists, 65 (map), 68; in First World War, 566; in NATO, 748; and Panama Canal Treaty, 532; problems after French and Indian War, 69; relations with in Civil War, 283–284; and rights of neutrals, 153, 572–573; in Second World War, 682, 688, 691–692, 712–713; and test-ban treaty, 772; and Venezuela, 538. See also England
Britain, Battle of, 692–693
British: in Battle of the Marne, 566; in Italy, 719; and Japan, 672; at Munich, 686; in North Africa, 713; in Oregon Country, 167; in Paris, 718; plans for Germany, 745; in Southwest Asia and North Africa, 762. See also English
British Empire, 100; early, 49; relation to colonies, 97; after 1763, 67–68; slaves freed, 229
British Guiana, 395–396
Brock, Isaac, 159
Brook Farm, 404, 404*
Brooklyn Bridge, 436, 438
Brooklyn Heights, Battle of, 90
Brooks, Preston, 262–263, 295
Brown, John, 262
Brown v. Board of Education of Topeka, 781
Bruce, Blanche K., 300
Brussels Pact, 748–749
Bryan, William Jennings: death, 609; in election of 1896, 450–451, 450*, 451 (cartoon), 452; in election of 1900, 455*, 484; in election of 1908, 519; on farms (quoted) 428; on First World War, 572; and the "money power," 664; in 1912, 523; in Scopes trial, 608, 609; as Secretary of State, 553, 575
Bryan-Chamorro Treaty, 541
Bryce, James, 504; on the West (quoted), 340–341
Buchanan, James, 263, 268, 273
Buell, Don Carlos, 278
Buena Vista, Battle of, 240
Buffalo, New York, 210, 255, 329*, 377, 398
Buffaloes: end of herds, 346; hunt-

ing, 346, 348*; seen by Spaniards, 14

Bulgaria, 566n, 698, 733, 746

Bulge, Battle of the, 718–719

Bull Moose party, 522, 523. See also Progressives

Bull Run: first Battle of, 276; second Battle of, 279

Bunau-Varilla, Philippe, 532, 534

Bunche, Ralph, 762

Bunker Hill, Battle of, 76

Bureau of Indian Affairs, 346

Burgess, John W., 468

Burgoyne, John, 91, 92

Burke Act, 348

Burma, 760

Burnside, Ambrose E., 279, 280

Burr, Aaron, 142, 152–153

Business: consolidations, 330–331, 332, 334–337; expansion after First World War, 662; during War for Independence, 87. See also Big business

Businessmen: attitude toward immigrants, 422; in depression of 1893, 384; national associations of, 407; in politics, 383, 432, 450; power and influence, 332–338, 382; response to unionizing, 416–419; role in industrialization, 316; views on competition, 330; wealth, 320

Cabeza de Vaca, Alvar, 14

Cabinet, 129; of John Adams, 140; of Cleveland, 386*; of Eisenhower, 754, 763*; of Grant, 303; of Harding, 601–602, 601*; of Hayes, 373, 374; of Jackson, 186; of Jefferson, 146–147; of Kennedy, 656; of Lincoln, 129, 129n; of Franklin D. Roosevelt, 642, 642*; of Washington, 129, 129n

Cable, Atlantic, 431n

Cable cars, 435, 437*

Cabot, Andrew, 87

Cabot, John, 24

Cabot, John (of Massachusetts), 87

Cabral, Pedro, 10

Cadillac (automobile), 614

Cahokia, Illinois, 93

Cairo, Egypt, 732

Cairo Conference, 732

Calhoun, John C., 156, 224 (cartoon); and Compromise of 1850, 257, 258; death, 258; in election of 1824, 174; member of Cabinet, 188, 237; proposed transportation network, 172; and protective tariffs, 171; quoted, 162–163; resigned as Vice-President, 188n; in Senate, 256; on slavery, 224; support of nullification, 188–189; Vice-President, 175, 187; as Whig, 192

Calhoun, Mrs. John, 186–187

California, 342; admitted as free state, 257; Americans in, 240; ceded to United States, 241; gold in, 236, 243–244, 342; and "manifest destiny," 238; in Mexican War, 238, 240; routes to, 244; and slavery question, 257; Jedediah Smith in, 152; Spanish, 148

Calles, Plutarco, 675

Calvert, Cecilius, 31

Calvert, Sir George, 31

Cambodia, 760

Cambridge, Massachusetts, 55

Camden, Battle of, 93

Cameron, Simon, 274, 278

Camp Fire Girls, 510

Canada: and Alaska boundary, 552–553, 552 (map); in American Revolution, 89–90, 91, 92; border with, 114, 135, 202; British conquest, 67; under British rule, 196; closed to American shipping, 113; farming, 431; French in, 60–67; fur trade, 60, 114; and Maine boundary, 196–197, 197 (map); in NATO, 749; reciprocity agreement with, 521; refuge for slaves, 223, 226; in War of 1812, 157–158. See also New France

Canals: Chesapeake and Ohio Canal, 211; to 1850, 210 (map); Erie Canal, 182*, 210–211, 401*; need for, 162–163; in Nicaragua, 532, 541; in North, 210–211, 286; Panama Canal, 464*, 532–537, 534*, 536*

Canal Tolls Act, 542–543

Canning, George, 156, 168

Cannon, Joseph, 520, 520 (cartoon)

Canon City, Colorado, 355

Cantigny, Battle of, 581

Canton, Ohio, 453

Cape Breton Island, 24, 63, 63*

Cape Canaveral, 772

Cape Cod, 34

Cape Kennedy, 772, 773

Cape Verde Islands, 8, 9, 10

Capital, for industries, 316, 336–338, 743

Capital, national, location, 132. See also Washington, D.C.

Capitol, 372*; in 1826, 176*

Capone, Al, 611

Caracas, Venezuela, 768

Cardozo, Francis, 300

Caribbean islands, 267, 388, 476. See also West Indies

Carnegie, Andrew, 320, 484; gifts of, 336n; and peace movement, 552; and Pennsylvania Railroad, 335; quoted, 314–315; and steel, 334–336

Carnegie Steel Corporation, 336–337, 336*; in Homestead, Pennsylvania, strike, 417–418

Carolinas, 51 (map); colonial, 55–56; cotton in, 219, 320; government, 51; Loyalists in, 82; name, 50; paper money in, 86; rice in,

55; slavery in, 50; in War for Independence, 94. See also North Carolina; South Carolina

Carpetbaggers, 300

Carranza, Venustiano (kä-rän′zá, bä′nōōs-tyä′nò), 545–546

Carroll, Charles, 82, 164, 211

Carteret, Sir George, 50

Cartier, Jacques, 16–17; routes, 18 (map)

Cartoons, political: "Age of Prosperity," 454; aid to Europe, 748; American-European relations, 668, 669; anti-Bryan, 451; anti-Cleveland, 386; antiunion, 420; big stick and dinner pail, 499; bimetalism and monometalism, 448; bootlegging, 610; boss control of voters, 440; bosses of the Senate, 332; Calhoun, 224; campaign issues, 378; China, 486; China and European powers, 487; civil service, 379; Cleveland campaign, 377; corruption, 304, 439; Cuba, 470, 473; demand for war with Spain, 472; "democracy" overloaded with gold and silver advocates, 452; depression of 1837, 193; disorder in cities, 784; the economy, 637; election of 1876, 305; fall of Cannon, 520; farmer mowing down politicians, 444; favoring free trade, 382; favoring protective tariffs, 382; Federal Reserve Bank, 526; fighting in Cuba, 475; Harrison and money bills, 384; Hayes as farmer, 374; imperialism, 484; inflation, 741; Interstate Commerce Act, 443; Jackson, 191; Japanese aggression in China, 685; jingoism, 472; labor organizations, 654; League of Nations, 600; monopoly, 337; neutrality, 573; 1928 campaign, 625; NRA, 644; overseas possessions, 490; Philippines, 492; Populist party, 448; pro-McKinley, 485; returning Americans, 648; Roosevelt and Panama Canal, 533, 534; Roosevelt and Taft, 523; Roosevelt reforms, 573; Standard Oil, 333; trust-busting, 513; United Nations, 735; Venezuela crisis, 539; wage and hour bills, 663; War for Independence, 92

Casablanca Conference, 732, 733*

Casa de Contratación (käs′á dē kōn-trá-tá-syōn′), 14–15

"Cash-and-carry" policy, 684–685, 688, 690

Cass, Lewis, 188, 254–255

Castle, Irene, 615

Castro, Cipriano, 538

Castro, Fidel, 768

Casualties, American: Civil War, 283; First World War, 584; Korean War, 751; Second World War, 736

Catholics: and Ku Klux Klan, 608; in Maryland, 31; in New France, 20; in politics, 625, 755; in Quebec, 74; Queen Mary as, 24; restrictions on, 85; in Spain, 44; in Virginia, 31
Catt, Carrie Chapman, 506
Cattle: breeds in West, 352–353; on Great Plains, 349–355, 350*, 351*, 353*; introduced by Spanish, 16; long drives, 349–352; markets for, 349–350
Cattle Kingdom, 349–354, 363
Cattlemen, 342
CCC. See Civilian Conservation Corps
Cemetery Ridge, 281
Centennial Exposition, 306*, 385*, 394
CENTO. See Central Treaty Organization
Central America, 267; American policy in, 531; raided by English, 24; Spanish control, 15
Central City, Colorado, 355
Central Intelligence Agency, 766
Central of Georgia Railroad, 228
Central Pacific Railroad, 323
Central Powers: American treaties with, 596; in First World War, 568, 569
Central Treaty Organization, 770
Century of Dishonor, A, 348
Cervera (thĕr-vä′rä), Pascual, 478, 479
Chain stores, 622
Chamberlain, Joseph, 570
Chamberlain, Neville, 686, 687*
Chambers, Whittaker, 752
Champlain, Lake, 19, 62, 90, 114
Champlain, Samuel de, 18–19
Chancellorsville, Battle of, 281
Chandler, Zachariah, 303
Chaplin, Charlie, 616
Charles I, of England, 31, 47, 50
Charles II, of England, 39, 48, 49, 50, 51, 52
Charleston, South Carolina, 113, 136, 174*, 429*; in Civil War, 273, 273*; colonial, 50, 51, 53, 56*; Democratic convention in, 267; Genêt in, 136; as port, 228; railroads to, 228
Charles Town. See Charleston
Charters, colonial, 26; of Carolina, 50; of Connecticut, 39; of Georgia, 53; of Maryland, 31; of Massachusetts, 34; of Massachusetts Bay Company, 35; of New Hampshire, 39; of Pennsylvania, 52; of Rhode Island, 37; and western lands, 69
Chase, Kate, 274
Chase, Salmon P., 256, 274, 299
Château-Thierry, Battle of, 581
Chatham, Earl of, 70–71. See also Pitt, William
Chattanooga, Tennessee, 281

Chavis, John, 221
Checks and balances, 84; in Constitution, 124
Cherokee Indians, 64, 198, 367
Chesapeake and Ohio Canal, 211
Chesapeake and Ohio Railroad, 322
Chesapeake Bay, 27; in American Revolution, 94; in Civil War, 278
Chesapeake-Leopard affair, 154
Chevrolet automobiles, 613–614
Cheyenne Indians, 342
Chiang Kai-shek, 685, 732, 736, 745
Chicago, Illinois, 208, 385*, 558*, 618*, 647*; air pollution, 438; Democratic convention, 450; fire, 432*, 433; first skyscraper, 435; gangs in, 611; Haymarket Square, 412; Hull House, 508; immigrants in, 433; meat industry, 322, 349, 500, 613, 613n; in mid-nineteenth century, 433; as railroad center, 212, 322; railroad strike, 410; Republican convention, 267; sewage disposal, 434; stockyards, 433, 433*
Chicago, Burlington, and Quincy Railroad, 513
Chickasaw Indians, 63, 114
Chief Justices: Charles Evans Hughes, 656; John Jay, 138; John Marshall as, 148, 169*; Roger B. Taney, 264; Earl Warren, 777–779, 778*
Chihuahua, Mexico, 240
Child, Sir Josiah, quoted, 42–43
Child labor, 500, 500*, 527*, 528; after Civil War, 311; in textile mills, 204
Chile, 545, 676, 768
China, 701*; American policy in, 484, 486, 488, 531, 548; civil war in, 745; Communists in, 736, 745; and The Congo, 770; and European powers, 487 (cartoon); and Japan, 672, 680, 685, 701–702; Lend-Lease to, 702; Marco Polo in, 6; Nationalist, 736; new government, 551; open-door policy, 484, 486, 486*; ports opened to American ships, 243; search for route to, 16; and Soviet Union, 680; trade with, 7, 393, 481; on UN Security Council, 736; war with Japan, 486; at Washington Conference, 672
Chinese: Communists, 745, 750–751; immigrants, 324, 325*, 406*; Nationalists, 745
Chinese-Eastern Railway, 551
Chinese Exclusion Act, 424
Chisholm Trail, 349
Chivington massacre, 342, 343
Choctaw Indians, 114, 367
Christianity, 1
Church and state: separation of, 84; Supreme Court on, 778–779
Churches: established, 84; in War for Independence, 84–85

Churchill, Winston S., 630, 633*, 697, 732*, 744*; and Atlantic Charter, 700, 700*; at Cairo, 732; as peacemaker, 731; on Pearl Harbor (quoted), 706; as prime minister, 692; quoted, 687, 697, 699, 734; voted out of office, 735; at Yalta, 733–734
Church of England, 33, 37
Church of Jesus Christ of Latter-day Saints, 234–236
Cibola, Seven Cities of, 14
Cicero, Illinois, 611
Cincinnati, Ohio, 165, 208; music festival, 438; railroads, 322
Cisneros, Evangelina, 472
Cities: air pollution, 438; architecture, 435; attractions, 438–439; colonial, 56; in election of 1940, 694; farmers move to, 428, 461*; as financial centers, 115; garbage disposal, 435; growth of, 165, 165 (table), 204, 205 (table), 319 (table), 433–434, 604 (table), 776 (table); housing in, 435; and immigrants, 423–424; Italian, 6, 7; living conditions, 433–435; nineteenth century, 320, 433–439; population, 433–434; problems, 454; reformers in, 504; riots in, 775; water supply, 434
Citizenship: defined in Fourteenth Amendment, 297; of Filipinos, 493; for freedmen, 297; for Hawaiians, 490; for Indians, 348, 349
Civilian Conservation Corps, 643
Civil liberties: in Bill of Rights, 123; protection by Supreme Court, 777–778; violation of Japanese-American, 729
Civil rights, and Constitution, 123; of Negroes, 309, 781, 782–784, 782*; of women, 505–506, 506*
Civil Rights Act: of 1866, 297; of 1875, 302, 303; of 1957, 781; of 1964, 783; of 1967, 784
Civil Rights Division, 781
Civil service, 379 (cartoon); reform, 304, 374
Civil Service Commission, 376
Civil War: background, 226–228, 249, 264–268; beginnings, 249, 273–274; definition, 241; in East, 275–276, 276 (map), 278–283, 279*, 282*; effects, 308; and foreign relations, 283, 309; and industrialization, 318–319; and labor movement, 405–406; lasting results, 306; legislation during, 286–287; northern advantages, 275; northern strategy, 275–276; railroads in, 285; riots in, 287; southern advantages, 275; veterans, 300, 373, 373*; in West, 276–278, 277 (map)
Civil War, Chinese, 745
Civil War, English, 47–48

Civil Works Administration, 648, 651

Clark, Bennett "Champ," 523; quoted, 579

Clark, George Rogers, 93, 151; route, 93 (map)

Clark, Mark W., 712*, 714

Clark, William, 151–152

Clark Memorandum, 676–677

Clay, Henry, 156–157, 255*; and "American system," 174; and Compromise of 1850, 256–258; in election of 1824, 174; in election of 1832, 191; on election of 1840 (quoted), 194; in election of 1844, 237; in election of 1848, 254; enemy of Jackson, 188; and Latin America, 395n; leader of Republican faction (quoted), 171–172; peace commissioner, 160; proposed tariff compromise, 189–190; as Secretary of State, 175; in Senate, 196, 256; and United States Bank, 190; as a Whig, 192

Clayton Antitrust Act, 527–528

Clayton-Bulwer Treaty, 532

Clean Air Act, 777

Clemenceau, Georges, 299, 590

Clermont, 165

Cleveland, Ohio, 208, 332, 504

Cleveland, Grover, 379*, 385*, 639, 686*; on Cuban insurrectos, 471; in election of 1884, 377–378; in election of 1888, 382–383; in election of 1892, 449; and Hawaii, 393; in New York, 384; opposition to, 386 (cartoon); as President, 378–379, 419; quoted, 484; reelected, 384; second administration, 449; vetoed literacy bill, 605

Climate: of Carolina, 51; of cattle country, 353–354; of Georgia, 54; of Great Plains, 362; of New World, 40; of West, 232

Clinton, De Witt, 157, 211

Clinton, George, 122, 136

Clinton, Sir Henry, 93, 94

Clipper ship, 207

Clothing: colonial, 102*; of cowboys, 351–352, 352*; in 1870's, 317*; Gibson girl, 510; in 1920's, 615

Coal, 328, 331*; in Pennsylvania, 409, 409*; production, 330 (graph); strikes, 512–513, 512*, 606–607

"Codes of fair competition," 643

Cod fishing, 16

Cody, William F., 346

Coeducation, 558, 558*

Coins, 164, 445–446

Coke, 335, 335n

Cold Harbor, Virginia, 282

Cold war, 746–747, 754; and uncommitted nations, 770

Colfax, Schuyler, 303

College of New Jersey, 55. *See also* Princeton University

College of the City of New York, 213

College of William and Mary, 56

Colleton, Sir John, 50

Colombia: and Panama Canal, 533–534; payment to, 537; treaty with, 676

Colón, Panama, 534

Colonialism, 736

Colonies, British, 20, 22–41, 35 (map), 38 (map), 50–57; agriculture, 27–28, 34, 55–56; British troops in, 69; Carolina, 50–51, 51 (map); charters, 26; education, 55–56; expansion, 60; fishing in, 26; after French and Indian War, 68; fur trade, 62; life in, 99, 102*, 103*, 104*; Maryland, 31–32, 31 (map); Massachusetts Bay Colony, 35 (map), 38 (map); in mid-eighteenth century, 54 (map), 55–56; New England, 32, 55; plan for union, 64; population, 60; proposed by Hakluyt, 24–25; proprietary, 31; self-government in, 29; Swedish, 45 (map), 46; taxation of, 70; thirteen original, 54 (map); trade with, 42–43, 49; Virginia, 26–30, 27 (map)

Colonies, Dutch, 38, 42–43, 43*, 44–49, 45 (map), 60

Colonies, French, 19–20, 44, 56, 60–67, 61 (map)

Colonies, Spanish, 14–16, 17 (map), 44, 53, 56, 60, 62, 67, 97

Colonies of United States, 481–482, 484; American attitude toward, 394; and public opinion, 468

Colonists: Dutch, 45, 46–47; English, 25–30, 32, 33–34, 35–36, 35*, 40, 56, 63*, 67–70, 71–73, 74–76; French, 19–20, 19*, 20*; Spanish, 14–16; Swedish, 46

Colorado, 356*, 365*; admitted to Union, 356; carried by Populists, 449; gold in, 355–356; Indians of, 342; made a territory, 342; and woman suffrage, 506

Colored Farmers' National Alliance, 444

Colt six-shooter, 342

Columbia, South Carolina, 292

Columbia Broadcasting System, 617

Columbia River, 234, 243

Columbia University, 55, 555, 616, 639

Columbus, Kentucky, 276, 277

Columbus, New Mexico, 546

Columbus, Christopher, 8–9, 21; departure from Palos, 9*; report on first voyage, 4–5

Combinations, business, 330–331

Command of the Army Act, 299

Commerce: of colonial New England, 55; foreign, 207–208; of New England, 202; of old South, 227–228; regulating power of Congress, 117–118, 120; of Spain with Americas, 14; during War for Independence, 87. *See also* Trade

Commerce, Department of, 620

Committee for Industrial Organization, 654

Committee on Public Information, 588

Committee on Rules, in Senate, 521

Committees of Correspondence, 72, 73, 74, 76

Common man, rise of, 197

Common Market, 767

Common Sense, 77; quoted, 58–59

Commonwealth v. Hunt, 403

Communication: in 1817, 163; improvements in, 436, 602*, 616–617, 616*

Communism: in China, 745; in Cuba, 768–769; in Europe, 746–749; means of spreading, 744; in North Korea, 749–752; in Southeast Asia, 757, 760–762; in Soviet Union, 605, 745; spread of, 745–752, 757, 760–762; threat to democracy, 744, 757; in United States, 752

Communist China, 762

Communists: aggressions, 750, 757, 760–762; aims, 744; American attitude toward, 699; Chinese, 736, 745, 750–751, 768; in Czechoslovakia, 747; in Europe, 734, 746–748; in Germany, 606, 748, 766–767; in Hungary, 606, 746; in Latin America, 736, 768–769; in Poland, 746; in Second World War, 719, 731–734; in Southeast Asia, 757, 760–762; in South Vietnam, 760; Soviet, 768; in United States, 752

Community action programs, 775

Company of One Hundred Associates, 19–20, 60

Competition, in business, 330

Compromise of 1850, 256–258, 256 (map), 259–260

Compromise of 1877, 305, 373

Compromises: in Constitution, 120; between North and South, 253

Compromise Tariff of 1833, 189–190

Computer, 560*, 739

Comstock Lode, 356

Concentration camps, 719–720

Concord, Massachusetts, 76

Concord, Battle of, 75*, 76

Conestoga wagon, 162–163*

Confederacy, 272; at beginning of Civil War, 275; established at Montgomery, 272; financial policy, 286; hopes for British recognition, 283–284; military leaders, 275; not recognized by Europeans, 285; political leaders, 275; shortages in, 285; weaknesses, 285–286

Confederate army: at Antietam, 279; and federal ports and arsenals, 273; of Northern Virginia, 282–283; opening campaigns, 276

Confederation, 77, 117

Congo, The, 769–770

Congregational church, 84

Congregationalists, 33. *See also* Separatists

Congress: admission of Texas to Union, 238; under Articles of Confederation, 110–113; "billion-dollar," 383–384; and colonial possessions, 389–391, 393; declared war against Britain, 157; and embargo repeal, 688, 690; first meeting, 128; in First World War, 578–579, 593–594; in Great Depression, 637–638, 643–646, 650–655, 678–679, 684–685; and Greenback congressmen, 443; after independence, 96; Indian policy, 343, 348–349; and internal improvements, 172; and Andrew Johnson, 297, 298; legislation, 141, 195, 286–287, 319, 383–384, 387, 446, 455, 474, 491, 510, 516, 517, 605–606, 670, 754, 755, 777, 784; Missouri Compromise, 172–173; and Northwest Territory, 113; powers of, 120–121, 124, 169–170; during reconstruction, 293, 294–299; after Second World War, 740–742, 754, 784; in Second World War, 694, 701, 706, 727; and slavery issue, 173, 255–258; and Spanish-American War, 475; and transportation, 323, 777; Twelfth, 156–157; and United States Bank, 133, 172, 190–191; War Hawks in, 156–157; Webster-Hayne debate, 187–188; and Wilson, 526–528, 542, 578, 593–594, 605

Congress of Industrial Organizations, 654–655

Congress on Racial Equality, 783

Conkling, Roscoe, 303, 373–374, 374–375, 377

Connecticut, 120; colonial, 32, 39, 55; debts, 132; established church, 84; land claims, 111; manufacturing, 115; ratified Constitution, 122; settlement, 38–39

Connecticut Compromise, 120

Connecticut Valley, 38, 62

Conquistadors, 12, 16, 20

Conscription, 287, 288

Conservation, 517–518, 655–656; human resources, 643

Conservation Conference, 518

Conservatives, 83–84

Consolidations, in business, 332

Consortium, 549, 551

Constantinople, Turkey, 568

Constitution: adopted, 123–124; amendments, 307; and bank bill, 133; Bill of Rights, 123; compromises in, 120; decided upon, 119–120; and Dred Scott case, 264; Eighteenth Amendment, 609; Fifteenth Amendment, 302; Fifth Amendment, 264, 778; First Amendment, 778, 779; Fourteenth Amendment, 297–298, 442, 778, 781; as interpreted by Marshall, 170; laws in conflict with, 148; "loose construction," 133; Nineteenth Amendment, 615; opposition to, 121–122; ratification, 122–123; and runaway slaves, 257; signing, 119*, 121; Sixteenth Amendment, 387n; and slavery, 258; and state laws, 169, 187–188; and states' rights, 142; "strict construction," 133; as supreme law of the land, 121; text, 791–809; Thirteenth Amendment, 297n; Twelfth Amendment, 142n; Twentieth Amendment, 659; Twenty-first Amendment, 647; Twenty-fourth Amendment, 783; Twenty-second Amendment, 752n, 754; writing of, 120–121

Constitutional Convention, 118–122; members, 118–119, 119*; organization, 118

Constitutional Union party, 267

Constitutions: of Confederacy, 272; of states, 83–84; of West Germany, 745

Continental Army, 83*, 87–88, 88*; officers, 88–89

Continental Congress: and Articles of Confederation, 110; debts incurred, 131; First, 74–76; Second, 76–78, 77*, 82–83, 86, 87, 90, 96, 97

Contraband, 572, 572n

Contract labor, 319, 406

Contract Labor Law, 319, 320

Cook, James, 739

Coolidge, Calvin, 600, 620*; became President, 602; elected President, 624–625; in election of 1928, 625; on farmers (quoted), 623; as governor of Massachusetts, 606; in Havana (quoted), 676; and Mexican problems, 675; and Nicaragua, 674; as President, 602–603; on war debts, 670

Coöperatives, 413; farm, 623; sponsored by Grange, 442; supported by Knights of Labor, 411

Cooper Union, 268

Copperheads, 287–288

Coral Sea, Battle of the, 707

CORE. *See* Congress on Racial Equality

Corn: Indian, 27, 35*; in South, 221

Cornell, Alonzo, 374

Corn Islands, 541

Cornwallis, Charles, 93–95

Coronado, Francisco, 14, 17

Corporations: combinations, 330–331, 336–337; need for regulating, 337–338; privileges of, 185

Corpus Christi, Texas, 352

Corregidor, 707, 722*

Cortés, Hernando, 13

Cotton: as cash crop, 429; and the cotton gin, 219, 221; exports, 219; manufacture, 219, 316; plantation, 216–217, 216–217*; planters, 220–221; sea island (long staple), 219; short staple, 219; trade in, 47

Cotton, John, quoted, 35–36

Cotton gin: effects, 220; invention, 219–220

Cotton Kingdom, 219–222, 220 (map)

Coughlin, Charles E., 650

Council Bluffs, Iowa, 236

Council for New England, 32–33, 34, 39

Council of National Defense, 586

Courts: circuit, 146; federal, 129, 146, 147–148, 777–779; and labor, 403; state, 52, 169–170, 421; and unions, 421–422. *See also* Supreme Court

Courts, international: Permanent Court of International Arbitration, 532; Permanent Court of International Justice, 592

Cowboys, 351–352, 351*, 352*

Cowpens, Battle of, 93–94

Cow towns, 349–350

Cox, James M., 600

Coxey, Jacob S., 387, 388*, 524

Craftsmen: and factory workers, 400; self-employed, 402–403

Craft unions, 413–416, 654; AFL, 413–414; early nineteenth century, 401; nationwide, 405

Crawford, William H., 174–175

Crédit Mobilier, 303

Creek Indians, 63, 64, 114, 167, 367

Creel Committee, 588

Crèvecoeur, Michel Guillaume Jean de, quoted, 80–81

Crime: in cities, 433; organized, 611; during prohibition, 609–610

"Crime of '73," 446

Crittenden Compromise, 272

Crockett, Davy, quoted, 192

Croly, Herbert, 521

Cromwell, Oliver, 47–48

Crop surpluses, 623

Crown Point, New York, 62, 90

Crusades, 6, 7

Cuba, 168, 469*, 470 (cartoon), 473 (cartoon); American intervention, 538; American investments in, 469; as American possession, 466; American withdrawal from, 532; attempts to acquire, 267; captured by British, 67; Columbus in, 8; Communists in, 768–769; freed from

Spain, 481, 482; insurrection in, 470, 471; limited independence, 489; and newspapers, 471; and Ostend Manifesto, 263; relations with, 677–678; Soviet missiles in, 769; in Spanish-American War, 469–475, 476, 478–479, 478 (map)

Culture: in Civil War period, 308; colonial, 99, 102–104; in early national period, 178; French, 18; Indian, 18, 348; in late nineteenth century, 460–462, 555; Moslem, 7; in 1960's, 558–560, 786; plurality of, 425; Spanish, 15–16. See also American life

Cumberland, Maryland, 208

Cumberland River, 114, 276

Cumberland Road. See National Road

Cummins, A. B., 520

Currency: after American Revolution, 116; after Civil War, 431; in Confederacy, 286; crime of '73, 446; demand for increased amount, 444, 445; and Federal Reserve Banks, 527; Greenback party, 443; ratio of 16 to 1, 445–446, 448; silverites in 1896, 449–453; silver laws, 446. See also Money

Curtis, George W., 374

Cushing, Caleb, 243

Custer, George A., 345, 345*

Custis, Mary, 279

Cutler, Manasseh, 112, 113

CWA. See Civil Works Administration

Czechoslovakia: Communists in, 746–747; and Egypt, 762; after Second World War, 593; taken by Nazis, 686–687

Czolgosz, Leon, 498

Dakota Territory: "bonanza farms," 367; created, 366; divided, 367; Indians of, 343. See also North Dakota; South Dakota

Dallas, Texas, 757

Dalrymple, Oliver, 367

Danbury Hatters case, 422

Danish West Indies, 388–389. See also Virgin Islands

Dare, Virginia, 26

Darrow, Clarence, 609

Darwin, Charles, 334, 457

Daugherty, Harry M., 600, 603

Davidson, Mount, 356

Davidson College, 523

Davis, David, 305

Davis, Jefferson, 221, 285; on the future (quoted), 306; imprisoned, 292; president of Confederacy, 275; in Senate, 256

Davis, Mrs. Jefferson, 472

Davis, John W., 624

Davis, Joseph, 221

Davy, Sir Humphrey, 739

Dawes, Charles G., 671

Dawes, William, 76

Dawes Act, 348

Dawes Plan, 671

Daylight-saving time, 587

Dayton, Jonathan, 119

D day, 716, 716*, 717*

Deadwood, South Dakota, 357

Dearborn, Henry, 158, 159

De Bow, James, 228

Debs, Eugene V., 418–419, 418*, 421

Debtors: imprisonment of, 197; nations as, 668–669; after Revolution, 116

Debts: after American Revolution, 97, 114; domestic, 131; of farmers, 116–117; foreign, 131, 669, 670–671; national, 127, 131–132; state, 131–132

Decatur, Stephen, 469

Declaration of Independence, 77–78, 78*, 82, 85, 90, 119, 124; and slavery, 218; text, 789–790

Declaration of Purpose of the National Grange, 441

Declaration of the Presidents of the Americas, 769

Declaration of the United Nations, 737

Declaration on General Security. See Moscow Declaration

Declaratory Act, 70

Defense: Pact of Paris, 674; SAC, 738*–739*, 770–771; treaties, 748–749, 770. See also names of defense alliances

De Forest, Lee, 616

De Gaulle, Charles, 733*, 766, 770

De Kalb, Illinois, 363

De Kalb, Johann, 93

Delaware: and Annapolis Convention, 118; in colonial times, 55; and Constitution, 120, 122; freedmen in, 221; remained in Union, 274; separated from Pennsylvania, 52

Delaware, Lord, 28

Delaware Bay, 44, 52; Swedes on, 46

Delaware River, 44, 50, 52, 91

De Lesseps, Ferdinand, 394

DeLôme, Dupuy, 473

Demarcation, Line of, 9, 10

Demobilization, after Second World War, 740, 740n

Democracies: European, 690; reaction to Munich agreement, 687–688

Democracy, 452 (cartoon); and Alien and Sedition Acts, 141–142; development, 84–85, 463, 665, 779; and education, 555; early meaning, 117; feared by Federalists, 141; foundations, 40, 84; government under, 181; institutions of democratic society, 246;

Jacksonian, 197, 198, 403; Jefferson's beliefs about, 130, 145, 425; nature of, 269; and Franklin D. Roosevelt (quoted), 628–629, 664, 665; and social justice, 502; threats to, 339, 744; and Wilson, 565, 578. See also Civil liberties; Civil rights; Freedom

Democratic party: and annexation of Texas, 237; after Civil War, 372–373; and Dred Scott case, 264; in election of 1836, 192; in election of 1840, 194; in election of 1844, 237–238; in election of 1848, 254–255; in election of 1856, 263; in election of 1860, 267; in election of 1864, 287–288; in elections of 1866, 298; in election of 1868, 300; in 1870's, 304; in 1876, 304–305; in election of 1884, 377; in election of 1900, 484; in election of 1904, 515; in election of 1908, 515; in elections of 1910, 521; in election of 1912, 523; in election of 1918, 589–590; in election of 1920, 600; in election of 1924, 624; in election of 1928, 625–626; in election of 1932, 638, 639–641; in election of 1936, 657, 657n; in election of 1940, 692; in election of 1948, 742; in election of 1952, 752–753; in election of 1960, 754; and farmers, 445; gain in 1934 elections, 648; after Jackson, 192; joined Union party, 274; after Kansas-Nebraska Act, 261–262; origin, 175; and slavery, 259–260, 261–262, 263, 267; and subtreasury policy, 193; and Tyler, 196

Democratic-Republicans, 135, 175. See also Democratic party

Demonetization of silver, 446

Demonstration Cities Act, 777

Dempsey, Jack, 596, 619

Dennis et al. v. United States, 778–779

Denmark, 446, 691, 699, 749

Denver, Colorado, 355, 357*

Dependent Pension Bill, 378

Depression, 630–657; of 1819, 172; of 1837, 192–194; of 1857, 266; of 1873, 329, 367, 408–409, 433, 470–471; of 1893, 384, 387, 418, 449, 471. See also Great Depression

Derby, Elias Hasket, 87

Deseret, State of, 236

De Smet, Pierre Jean, 234

De Soto, Hernando, 13–14, 14*, 17

Destroyers, 693, 698

Detroit, Michigan, 68, 114*, 208; founded, 60; held by British, 137; reforms in, 504; riots in, 775; in War of 1812, 159

Dew, Thomas, 223-224

Dewey, George, 467, 474, 476

Dewey, John, 555
Dewey, Thomas E., 692; in election of 1944, 729, 729*, 730; in election of 1948, 742, 743
Dias, Bartholomeu, 8
Diaz, Adolfo, 541
Díaz, Porfirio, 543
Dickens, Charles, 299
Dickinson, John, 71, 76, 77–78
Dinwiddie, Robert, 64
Diplomacy: after American Revolution, 95–97; role in relations with Latin America, 674–679; secret, 588; Wilson's, 547. See also Foreign policy
Discrimination: against Negroes, 781–782; by unions and employers, 783
Discovery, 27
Discovery, Age of, 11
Dissenting opinions, Supreme Court, 421n
District of Columbia, 148; slavery ended, 280; slave trade ended, 257
Dix, Dorothea L., 213
Dixiecrats, 742
Documents in American history, 5, 129; Declaration of Independence, 78, 78*; Mayflower Compact, 34; use, 167, 177, 229, 269, 339, 369, 397, 456, 495, 597, 665
Dodge City, Kansas, 349–350
Doenitz, Karl, 720
Doheny, Edward L., 603
Dollar, in New Deal, 647
Dollar diplomacy, 531, 540–541
Dominican Republic, 538, 538n; debts to Europeans, 538; Civil War in, 769; occupied by American troops, 539; marines withdrawn, 676; question of annexation, 389
Doniphan, A. W., 240
Donnelly, Ignatius, 447
Douglas, Stephen A.: candidate for Senate in Illinois, 265–266, 268; and Compromise of 1850, 258; at inauguration of Lincoln, 273; insulted by Sumner, 262; and Kansas-Nebraska Bill, 260–261; in Senate, 256
Douglass, Frederick, 280
Dow, Neal, 213
Draft: in Civil War, 287, 287*; in First World War, 579; in Second World War, 726
Drake, Edwin L., 328–329, 328*
Drake, Sir Francis, 24, 26
Dred Scott decision, 264, 272–273
Dry farming, 363
Du Bois, William E. B., 511, 511n
Dulles, John Foster: and Egypt, 762; as Secretary of State, 754, 763*
Dumbbell tenements, 435, 435 (diagram)
Dunkerque, Battle of, 691, 691*

Dunkirk, Ohio, 211
Dunne, Finley Peter, 607; quoted, 336–337, 513
Du Pont de Nemours, E. I., 141
Duquesne, Marquis, 64
Dust storms, 655–656
Dutch, 47*; in America, 44–49; conflicts with English, 46–47; colonies, 42; at New Amsterdam, 38; in New Netherland, 53; religion, 44; settlements, 45 (map)
Dutch East India Company, 44
Dutch Reformed Church, 45
Dutch West India Company, 44, 45
Dyewoods, 43, 49

Eads Bridge, 438, 438*
Eagle, bald, 164, 164*
East: capitalists in, 303; Civil War in, 276, 276 (map), 278–283, 282 (map); favored protective tariff, 174. See also East Asia; Southwest Asia
East Asia: Anglo-American bases in, 703; Boxer Rebellion, 486–488, 487*; English search for routes to, 24; Japanese power in, 486, 680, 685, 701; open-door policy, 486; routes to, 16
East Florida, 97, 114, 157, 166–167
East Germany: Communist, 745; refugees from, 767; and Western powers, 766–767
East India Company, 28, 43, 72–73
East Indies, 7, 9, 42, 44
Eastman, George, 457
East St. Louis, Illinois, 438
East River, 90
Eaton, John H., 186–187
Eaton, Peggy, 186, 187
Eaton affair, 186–187, 188
Economic Coöperation Administration, 747
Economic growth, 668–670
Economic nationalism, 670
Economic Opportunity Act, 775
Economic warfare, 747
Ecuador, 768
Ederle, Gertrude, 619
Edgar Thomson Works, 335
Edison, Thomas A., 436, 457; and incandescent lamp, 320, 321*
Education: after Civil War, 302; colonial, 55, 56; in 1820's, 178; federal aid to, 741, 775; of freedmen, 214; in New England, 202; progressive, 555; provision for in Northwest Territory, 113; in the reform movement, 213. See also Schools
EEC. See Common Market
Egypt, 1, 762n
Einstein, Albert, 739
Eisenhower, Dwight D., 715*, 753*, 777; and Berlin, 766; and Cabinet, 754, 763*; in Germany, 720; in North Africa, 714, 714*;

in Paris, 718; as President, 753–754, 763; quoted, 696–697; supreme commander in Europe, 713; supreme commander of NATO, 729
Eisenhower doctrine, 763–764
El Caney, Cuba, 479
Elections, 144–145*, 181; of 1788, 128; of 1796, 139; of 1800, 142; of 1808, 155; of 1816, 170; of 1824, 174–175; of 1828, 175; of 1832, 190–191; of 1840, 194; of 1844, 237–238; of 1848, 254–255; of 1852, 259–260; of 1856, 263; of 1860, 266–268; of 1864, 287–288; of 1866, 298; of 1868, 300; of 1872, 303–304, 373; of 1876, 304–305; of 1880, 375; of 1884, 377–378; of 1888, 382–383; of 1892, 384; of 1896, 449–455, 453 (map); of 1900, 484; of 1904, 514–515; of 1908, 519; of 1912, 523, 523 (cartoon); of 1916, 577; of 1920, 600–601; of 1924, 624–625, 624*; of 1928, 625–626, 626 (cartoon); of 1932, 638, 640, 640*; of 1936, 656–657; of 1940, 692; of 1944, 729–730; of 1946, 741; of 1948, 742–743; of 1952, 752; of 1956, 754; of 1960, 754–756, 755*; of 1964, 774
Electoral college, 121, 198
Electoral commission, 305
Electricity: electrical appliances, 614; in 1920's, 614
Electric light, 320, 321*
Electric trolleys, 435–436, 437*
Electronics, 559, 616, 780n, 781
Elevators, 435
Eliot, Charles W., 606
Elizabeth I, of England, 22, 24
Elkins Act, 516
El Paso, Texas, 240
Emancipation: problems of, 225; results in South, 291–292
Emancipation Proclamation, 280
Embargo Act, 154
Emergency Quota Act, 606
Emerson, John, 264
Emerson, Ralph Waldo, 404; quoted, 76, 212–213, 267
Employment, 400–401, 401*; in depression of 1893; in Great Depression, 632, 647, 651–652, 685; of Negroes, 623; in New England, 203; in Second World War, 726, 726*, 727
Employment Act of 1946, 741
Encomiendas, 15
England, 135, 136, 137–138; and American Civil War, 280; American heritage from, 570; Buchanan minister to, 263; civil war in, 47–48; colonial trade with, 55; colonies of, 20, 22–41, 43, 48–49, 55, 60–67, 74–78; Columbus in, 8; and the Confederacy, 275;

as creditor nation, 669; under Cromwell, 47–48; earliest railroads, 211; enclosures, 29; Elizabethan, 23; expansion, 7, 24–25; explorations, 24–26; and France, 60–67, 63*; as guardian of European peace, 682–685; and Henry Hudson, 44; immigrants from, 422; and Industrial Revolution, 219; influences on America, 59; Jay's treaty with, 138; in joint occupancy of Oregon Country, 233; and Netherlands, 46–48, 49; reaction to Munich agreement, 687; relations during Confederation, 113; Separatists in, 33; in Seven Years' War, 65–67; slavery abolished, 213; and Spain, 48, 53, 54, 56; trade with, 115; in Triple Entente, 566; unemployment problem, 29; during War for Independence, 82–107; in War of 1812, 157–160; at war with France, 135, 148, 158; at war with Spain, 22–23*, 24–25, 26; at Washington Conference, 672; Woodrow Wilson in, 590. *See also* Britain; United Kingdom

English: in America, 20, 40; conflicts with Dutch, 46–47; conflicts with French, 60, 61 (map), 62; fur trade, 26, 38; in Newfoundland, 25, 28, 31; in slave trade, 30; in West Indies, 26, 35, 62; west of Appalachians, 60

English Channel, 566, 682; on D day, 716, 716*, 717*

English Colonies in America. *See* Colonies, British

English language, 105

Entail, meaning, 84

Entertainment: in cities, 391, 438–439; in 1920's, 604–605, 615–617, 616*, 617*; spectator sports, 462, 462*, 619

"Era of Good Feelings," 170–177

Erie, Lake, 62, 64

Erie Canal, 182*, 208, 210–211, 401*

Erie Railroad, 322, 323*, 334

Escobedo v. *Illinois,* 777–778

Established churches, 34–35, 84. *See also* Church of England

Estevanico, 14

Ethiopia, 683–684, 683*

Europe: aggressions in, 688 (map), 745, 746–747, 748; aid to, 746–749, 746*, 747*, 750*; and America, 59; American attitudes toward, 168, 169, 457; and American tariff, 668*, 669*, 670; communism in, 746–748; conflicts, 44, 46–48; crises in, 766–769; depression in, 647; expansion overseas, 468; after First World War, 593, 682–685; during First World War, 568; growth of nation-states, 7–11; heritage from, 81,

105; immigrants from, 115, 206, 226, 246; and invention of automobile, 611; and Louisiana, 148; in 1914, 567 (map); reforms in, 246; relations with during Confederation, 113–115; during Renaissance, 7; in Second World War, 712; settlers from, 40; in Seven Years' War, 65, 67; trade routes, 6 (map), 44; trade with East, 6–7

European Economic Community. *See* Common Market

Europeans: adaptation to New World, 40; in America, 20; at discovery of New World, 1–2; in English colonies, 80–81; in Latin America, 537; in Spanish colonies, 15

Evans, Oliver, 211

Evarts, William M., 373

Excise tax, 133

Expansionism, 156–157, 340–341, 389–394, 466–467, 468–471

Exploration: of the Americas, 12; Dutch, 44; English, 24–26; French, 18–19; by La Salle, 60; Negro, 14; of northern North America, 18–19; routes, 10 (map); of South America, 10

Exploration, Age of, 12–21

Exports: colonial, 43, 49, 69; of cotton, 219; before First World War, 669; and imports, 668; through New Orleans, 227–228; from South, 228

Exposition and Protest, 188–189

Extraterritoriality, 243

Factories: growth of, 316, 318–319; in Massachusetts, 204; in New England, 115, 201, 203–204, 203*; in South, 226; workers in, 400–402, 405, 460*

Factory system, 314–315

Fads, 619

Fair Labor Standards Act, 662

Fall, Albert B., 603

Fallen Timbers, Battle of, 136–137

Farley, James A., 658n, 692

Farm bloc, 622–623

Farmers: assistance to, 644–645, 662, 663–664; attitude toward city people, 439–440; after Civil War, 429–433; colonial, 99, 106; under Confederation, 115; and crop surpluses, 623; discontent, 431–433; in early national period, 115–117, 130, 429*; equipment, 319, 363–364, 365*; and factory workers, 405; in Great Depression, 633, 641–642; on the Great Plains, 362–364, 362*; income, 622; Jeffersonian view, 130, 130*, 198, 428; in Kansas, 353; in late nineteenth century, 426–427, 426–

427*, 439–445; loans to, 528; and markets for crops, 430, 430 (cartoon); and middlemen, 431; move to cities, 454*, 780; in New England, 202; in old South, 221; oppose excise taxes, 133; organization of, 440–442, 444–446, 447–452, 455; political leaders, 447; in politics, 444–449; and railroads, 430–431, 442; and Shays' Rebellion, 116–117, 116*; southern, 429–430; and tariff acts, 519, 520; tenant, 32; in Union territory, 286; United States, 428–432; during War for Independence, 86–87, 90; western, 174; women, 432. *See also* Agriculture; Farming

Farmers' Alliances, 444, 444 (cartoon)

Farming: in colonial New England, 55; on Great Plains, 363–364; in Maryland, 31–32; in middle Atlantic states, 206; in New England, 202–203; in old Northwest, 209

Farm Loan Bank, 528

Farm Security Administration, 662

Farragut, David G., 278

Fayette, New York, 234

FDIC. *See* Federal Deposit Insurance Corporation

Federal Bureau of Investigation, 611

Federal Deposit Insurance Corporation, 646

Federal Emergency Relief Administration, 643, 648

Federal Farm Board, 633

Federal Farm Loan Act, 528

Federal government: abandonment of freedmen, 305; aid to education, 775; and air pollution, 777; assistance to industry, 316; and banking, 526–527, 647; and Bill of Rights, 777; and civil rights, 782–783; and coal strike, 606; under Constitution, 129–130; direct aid to unemployed, 649; duties of, 117; established, 124; and Federalists, 141–142; generosity to railroads, 323–324; in Great Depression, 633, 637, 646, 649, 650–652, 664; growth in power, 555; help to industries, 316; Jackson's view of, 189; Jefferson's economy in, 146–147; and national debt, 131–132; outlined in Constitution, 120–121; in railroad strike, 410; reforms, 502; regulation and control of railroads, 442, 444, 513–514; regulation of communications, 617; during War for Independence, 77, 82–83, 84–87; and western lands, 111

Federal Hall, New York City, 128*, 129

Federal Home Loan Banks, 637

Federal Housing Administration, 652

Federalist, The, 122

Federalists, 135, 139, 154; in John Adams' administration, 139–140, 141; and Constitution, 122, 124; after 1816, 171; in election of 1800, 142; and England, 136, 137–138; and Hamilton, 127, 129, 131, 135; and Hartford Convention, 160; in Jefferson's administration, 147–148, 150; and Louisiana Purchase, 150; in Washington's administration, 131–134

Federal Radio Commission, 617

Federal Reserve Act, 526

Federal Reserve Board, 526, 630, 633

Federal Reserve System, 528

Federal Securities Act, 646

Federal Trade Commission, 646

Federal Trade Commission Act, 527

FERA. *See* Federal Emergency Relief Administration

Fermi, Enrico, 738

Feudal system: in Carolina, 51; in Maryland, 31–32

Fiat, defined, 395

Field, Cyrus W., 431n

Filibustering, defined, 367n

Fillmore, Millard: in election of 1848, 254–255; on election of 1848 (quoted), 255; in election of 1852, 514n; as President, 258

Finance capitalists, 336

Finances: of Confederacy, 286; Hamilton on, 126–127; in Second World War, 726; of Van Buren, 193–194; in War of 1812, 158–159

Finland, 746

Fireside chats, 642n

Fish, 55

Fish, Hamilton, 389

Fishing: in colonies, 26; French, 16; New England, 43; off Newfoundland, 16, 67

Fisk, James, 303

Fiske, John, 468

Fitzhugh, George, 224

Five-Power Treaty, 673

Flag, American, 164

"Flaming youth," 604

Flatboats, 227

Fletcher v. *Peck,* 169

Florida: admitted to Union, 220; boundary of Spanish, 139; discovery, 12–13; Indians of, 14*, 166–167; name, 13; readmitted to Union, 300; secession, 272; in 1783, 97; Spanish in, 14*, 148, 167. *See also* East Florida; West Florida

Floyd, John, 233

Foch (fôsh), **Ferdinand,** 580–581, 582, 584

Fonseca, Gulf of, 541

Food: of colonists, 40, 99; of Continental Army, 89; during First World War, 587

Food administrator, 586

Foraker Act of 1900, 490, 491

Forbes, John, 66

Force Bill, 189–190

Ford, Henry, 612–613

Ford automobiles, 612–613, 613*, 614, 670

Ford Motor Company, 756

Fordney-McCumber Act, 603, 670

Ford's Theater, 288

Foreign affairs: under John Adams, 140–141; in Civil War, 283–285; at end of nineteenth century, 455; and Eisenhower, 757, 761, 763–764, 766; and expansion, 388–394; and Jefferson, 153–155; and Lyndon B. Johnson, 769; and Kennedy, 760, 767, 768; and Latin America, 394–396, 541–546, 674–679; and McKinley, 471, 472*, 474, 475–479, 481–482, 486–488; and Madison, 155–158; and Polk, 238–239, 240–242, 243; and Franklin D. Roosevelt, 662–663, 677–679, 684–686, 688, 690–691, 693–694, 699–705, 706–708, 712–720, 722–725, 731–734; and Theodore Roosevelt, 464*, 473–474, 532–539; and Taft, 540–541; and Truman, 744–751; and Washington, 135–139; and Wilson, 541–546, 564–565 (quoted), 566, 569, 570–584, 588–594

Foreign aid, 768, 770, 780, 786

Foreign policy, 168–169, 179, 532; toward China, 484–488, 701–702, 762; and colonies, 481, 482, 484; toward Communist countries, 757, 762; and domestic policy, 784; and Eisenhower doctrine, 763–764; toward Germany, 744–745, 748, 766–767; and isolationism, 688; jingoism, 469, 472*; toward Latin America, 674–679, 768–769; and Marshall Plan, 747; and Monroe Doctrine, 168, 394, 679; and neutrality, 136, 139, 684–686, 693; in progressive era, 553; after Second World War, 744; toward Soviet Union, 680–681, 731–734, 744, 746, 766–767; Truman doctrine, 746–747; and Washington, 135; and world peace, 673–674, 680, 731

Foreign relations, 388–396, 530–531. *See also* Foreign affairs

Foreign trade, 682

Forests, 518, 643

Forest Service, United States, 518

Formosa. *See* Taiwan

Forts, 54, 64–65; Boise, 234; Bridger, 234; Christina, 46; Clatsop, 151; Colville, 356; Dearborn, 159; Donelson, 276–277; Duquesne, 64, 66; Frontenac, 60, 66; Greenville, 137n; Hall, 234; Henry, 276, 277; Kearney, 234; Laramie, 234; Lawrence, 63; Le Boeuf, 64; Mandan, 151; Miami, 137; Michilimackinac, 60, 159; Moultrie, 273–274; Nassau, 44; Necessity, 64; Niagara, 60, 62, 68; Orange, 44; Oswego, 62, 65, 66; Pitt, 66, 68; Prince George, 64; St. George, 54; Scott, 167; Snelling, 264; Sumter, 273–274, 273*; Ticonderoga, 90, 92; Toulouse, 62; Venango, 64; Washington, 90

Forty-niners, 244, 342

"Founding Fathers," 119, 119*, 394

Four-Power Treaty, 673

Fourteen Points, Wilson's, 588–589

Fourth of July, 164

Fox, George, 51–52

France, 47; and Algeciras Conference, 553; Allied invasion, 715*, 716, 716*, 717*; American friendship with, 570; in American Revolution, 77, 92, 96–97; and China, 486; and Civil War, 275, 284; claims in America, 16–20, 18 (map), 60; colonial forts and posts, 61 (map), 62, 63, 64; colonies, 44, 56, 60–67; in Common Market, 767; as creditor nation, 669; decree of 1810, 150; diplomatic relations with, 140, 141; expansion, 7; explorations by, 60; in First World War, 566, 568, 581–582, 582*, 583*, 584; fur trade, 18, 60, 62; on gold standard, 446; as guardian of European peace, 682–685; member of SEATO, 770; under Napoleon, 148; in NATO, 748; and Oregon Country, 233; and Panama Canal, 532–533; rivalry with England, 60–62, 77; in Second World War, 688, 691–692, 716, 717*, 718; after Seven Years' War, 67; trade with Asia, 7; in Triple Entente, 566; on UN Security Council, 736; wars with English, 62–63, 64–67, 135, 157; at Washington Conference, 672

Franco-Prussian War, 590

Franklin, Benjamin, 69, 76, 77*, 97*, 105; Albany Plan, 64; and alliance with France, 92; American hero, 246; at Constitutional Convention, 119; at peace negotiations, 95–97; quoted, 95, 96, 121; and slavery, 85, 213; and War for Independence, 90

Franklin, William, 82

Franz Ferdinand, 566

Frederick II, of Prussia, 65, 67

Fredericksburg, Battle of, 281

Freedmen: in 1870's, 304; help to, 302; in old South, 214, 221–222; southern treatment of, 297

Freedmen's Bureau, 296, 296*

Freedom, 32. *See also* Democracy; Religious toleration

Freedom Riders, 781

Free enterprise: in colonies, 73; growth of, 197; profit motive under, 650

Freeman's Farm, Battle of, 92

Freemen, 36, 39, 52

Freeport doctrine, 265–266

Free silver, 449, 450–451, 484

Free-Soil party, 255, 260

Free World, 757, 770

Frémont, John C., 240, 263

French: in America, 60–67, 74; in Battle of the Marne, 566; conflicts with English, 60, 61 (map), 62; conversion of Indians, 20*; fishermen, 16, 18; fur traders, 18; in India, 67; and Indians, 62; in King George's War, 63; in Louisiana, 148–149; at Munich, 686; in Newfoundland, 67; in Ohio Valley, 64, 68; in Southwest Asia and North Africa, 762; in War for Independence, 89, 94; in West Indies, 42, 62

French and Indian War, 64–65, 68, 89; British strategy, 65 (map); results, 66 (map). See also Seven Years' War

French Canadians, 74

French Revolution, 129, 135, 135*, 136, 136n, 141

Frick, Henry Clay, 335–336, 342, 418, 516

Friendship 7, 772

Fringe benefits, 742

Frontier: advance to 1850, 232 (map); closed, 469, 469n; in early colonies, 32; in Georgia, 54; miners', 355–359; in West, 342

Frontiersmen, 173*; and Indians, 136–137; as Loyalists, 82; in Ohio Valley, 64; supporters of Jefferson, 133; in War for Independence, 93; in West, 342; and western lands, 69

FSA. See Farm Security Administration

Fuel, 328, 587

Fugitive Slave Law, 258

Full Employment Bill, 741

Fuller, Margaret, 404

Fulton, Robert, 165, 170

Fundamental Constitutions, 51

Fundamental Orders of Connecticut, 39

Fur trade: in Canada, 60, 114; in colonies, 26; Dutch, 44; French and English rivalry, 62–63; after French and Indian War, 68; in Oregon Country, 233–244; Pennsylvania, 52

Fur traders: English, 62, 68; French, 18, 62*, 68; and proclamation line, 68–69; in West, 152

Gadsden, Christopher, 74

Gadsden Purchase, 242

Gagarin, Yuri, 772

Gage, Thomas, 76

Gag rule, 254

Gallatin, Albert, 141, 146, 160

Galloway, Joseph, 74

Gama, Vasco da, 8

Garbage disposal, in cities, 434–435

Garfield, James A., 303, 375–376

Garner, John Nance, 661

Garrison, William Lloyd, 213–214

Garvey, Marcus, 623

Gary, Indiana, 606

Gary, Elbert H., 516, 607

Gasoline, 329

Gaspee incident, 72

Gaspé Peninsula, 17

Gates, Horatio, 92, 93

Gemini, in space, 773

General Assembly. See United Nations

General Motors, 613, 742

Genêt, Edmond, 136

Geneva, Switzerland, 771–772, 781

Geneva agreement, 757, 760

Geneva Conference of 1927, 673

Genoa, Italy, 7, 8, 24

Genocide, 720

George II, of England, 67–68

George III, of England, 68, 76, 77, 82, 85, 113; quoted, 75

George, Henry, 502, 503

Georgia: colonial, 54, 55–56; cotton industry, 219, 320; founding, 53, 54; Indians of, 53, 114, 166–167, 198; land claims, 111; politics, 304; railroads, 228; ratified Constitution, 122; readmitted to Union, 300; sale of western lands, 169; secession, 272; and TVA, 645; in War for Independence, 93

German-Americans, 594

Germans, 511; after Battle of the Marne, 566; in Brussels, 568; in English colonies, 68; at Munich, 686; in North Africa, 713; in North Dakota, 367; offensive of 1918, 581; in old Northwest, 209; in Pacific, 48; in Poland, 689*, 690; in Russia, 576; settled in Kansas, 324; surrender, 585*, 721*; as war criminals, 745

Germantown, Battle of, 91, 92

Germany, 446; and Algeciras Conference, 553; ally of Soviet Union, 690; and Austria, 686; as Axis power, 698; break with United States, 578; and China, 486; communists in, 606; divided, 736, 745; fall of, 584, 588; after First World War, 593, 596, 682; and France, 568; growth of power, 396; under Hitler, 643, 662, 683, 698–699; immigrants from, 206, 422, 546; reaction to Pearl Harbor, 706; and reparations, 589, 671; in Samoa, 392; after Second World War, 744–745; submarine warfare, 564–565, 573–575, 574

(cartoons), 577–578; surrender terms, 720; in Triple Alliance, 566; and Venezuela, 538; war with Russia and France, 566; and Yalta Conference, 733

Gerry, Elbridge, 140; quoted, 118

Gettysburg, Battle of, 281

Gettysburg Address, 289

Ghettos, 623, 784

Gibbons v. Ogden, 170

Gibson girl, 510*, 511

Gilbert, Sir Humphrey, 25, 32

Gilbert, Raleigh, 32

Gilbert Islands, 709

Ginn, Edwin, 551–552

Girl Scouts, 410

Gish, Lillian, 616, 617*

Glassboro meeting, 772

Glass-Steagall Banking Act, 646

Glenn, John H., Jr., 772

Glidden, Joseph F., 363

Goethals (gō'thălz), George W., 535

Gold: in Alaska, 455; and Black Friday, 303; in California, 236, 243–244; coins, 445–446; European need for, 7; at Fort Colville, 356–357; from Mexico, 13; in Montana, 357; near Pike's Peak, 342; shortage in 1890's, 387; sought in colonies, 26–27; from Spanish colonies, 12, 15, 16; supply after California gold rush, 446; in trade, 7

Goldberg, Arthur J., 756

Gold standard, 446, 455, 647

Gold Standard Act, 484

Goldwater, Barry M., 774

Gompers, Samuel, 413, 414, 414*, 416, 606, 664

Good Hope, Cape of, 8, 11, 24

Good Neighbor policy, 677

G.O.P. See Republicans

Gorgas, William C., 535, 535*

Gorges, Ferdinando, 32, 34

Gould, Jay, 303, 320

Government: under Articles of Confederation, 110–113; church and, 84–85; colonial, 35–36, 51, 52, 53; German, 565; of Hawaii, 489; in mining districts, 358; municipal, 504; need for stronger, 115–118; of Philippines, 492–494; and public opinion, 145; of Puerto Rico, 490–492; reforms in, 504–506; regulation of business, 331, 513; relation between nation and states, 121, 142, 169, 187–188; during Renaissance, 7; self-government, 28–29, 124; in South during reconstruction, 300–302; Spanish colonial, 14–15; state, 121, 504–505; territorial, 208. See also Federal government

Graft, 503

Grain elevators, 433, 442

Grand Alliance, 731

Grand Army of the Republic, 300, 372, 372*, 373*

Grand Banks, 16
Grand Canyon, 14
Grange, 440–443, 441°, 442°
Grant, Julia, 277
Grant, Ulysses S., 276, 277–278, 277°; accepts Lee's surrender, 283; commander in chief of northern forces, 281; and Dominican Republic, 389; in election of 1880, 375; and Johnson, 299; in Mexican War, 239; as President, 300, 302–304; reelected in 1872, 303–304, 373; on South (quoted), 297
Grantism, 302, 372
Grasse, Francois de, 94
"Great American Desert," 232–233
Great Britain, 58–59. See also Britain; England
Great Depression, 631–638, 641–642
Greater East Asia Co-prosperity Sphere, 701
Great Falls of the Missouri, 151
Great Lakes, 60, 62, 208, 209, 210, 336
"Great migration," 35
Great Northern Railroad, 367, 513
Great Plains, 152, 342, 362–363, 362°; as cattle country, 349–354; climate, 362, 445, 655–656; farmers, 362–368, 445; Indians of, 342–348; settlement, 233, 330
Great Salt Lake, 236
Great Society, 774, 776, 780
"Great White Fleet," 530–531°
Greece, 466; aid to, 746–747; in Balkan Wars, 566; and communism, 746; heritage from, 1; and Nazis, 698
Greeley, Horace, 268, 303, 373; quoted, 288, 355
Green, William F., 641, 654
Greenback party, 443, 444, 445, 502
Greenbacks, 386, 431, 443
Green Bay, 19, 60
Green-belt project, 652
Greene, Nathanael, 93
Greene, Mrs. Nathanael, 219
Greenland, 697
Green Mountain boys, 90
Greensboro, North Carolina, 782
Gregory, John H., 355
Grenville, George, 69, 70
Grimké sisters, 214, 224
Grundy, Felix, 156
Guadalcanal, 709
Guadaloupe, 67
Guadalupe Hidalgo (gwä'-dá-loōp' hǐ-dǎl'-gō), Treaty of, 241
Guam, 481, 482, 489, 489n, 707, 709
Guantánamo Naval Base, 489
Guatemala, 768
Guerrillas, 476, 760, 761
Guffey-Snyder Act. See Bituminous Coal Conservation Act
Guinea coast, 8
Guiteau, Charles, 375

Habeas corpus, 302
Hague Peace Conferences, 552
Hague Tribunal, 566
Haiti, 67, 541–542
Hakluyt, Richard, 24–25; quoted, 22–23
Hale, Nathan, 90–91
Half-Breeds, 373–375
Halifax, Nova Scotia, 63, 82, 698
Halleck, Henry W., 279
Hamilton, Alexander: and John Adams, 139–140; and Constitution, 119, 119°, 121, 122–123; financial program, 148; in first administration, 129, 130–134; and Jay's treaty, 138; lasting value of programs, 134; letter to Robert Morris, 126–127; opinion on United States Bank, 170; plan for encouraging industry, 133–134; policies, 171; political ideas, 131; in quarrel with Britain, 138; Report on Manufactures, 316; as Secretary of the Treasury, 129, 130–131; shot by Aaron Burr, 152
Hammond, James, quoted, 226, 228
Hampton Roads, Virginia, 285n, 549
Hancock, John, 71, 71°, 73, 74–76, 77°, 82, 122
Hancock, Winfield Scott, 375
Hanna, Marcus A., 450, 499
Hanoi, North Vietnam, 757
Harding, Warren G.: Cabinet, 601°; as President, 596, 600, 601
Harlem, New York City, 623
Harlem Heights, 90
Harlem Renaissance, 623
Harper, William, quoted, 216–217
Harpers Ferry, West Virginia, 262
Harrison, Benjamin: Cabinet of, 383; in election of 1888, 382; in election of 1892, 384; as President, 338, 367, 383–384
Harrison, William Henry, 156, 159, 192, 194
Hartford, Connecticut, 160
Hartford Convention, 160
Harvard College, 55, 176
Harvard University, 639
Havana, Cuba, 115, 284, 472–473, 676
Havemeyer, Henry, 331, 336
Hawaii, 392°, 393–394, 393 (map), 490°, 709; admitted to Union, 490, 494, 754; as American possession, 466, 481; Japanese attack, 704–705; as territory, 489, 490
Hawley-Smoot Tariff, 603, 670
Hawthorne, Nathaniel, 404; quoted, 259
Hay, John: and imperialism, 469; and Panama Canal, 533; as Secretary of State, 486–488
Hay–Bunau-Varilla Treaty, 535, 678
Hayes, Rutherford B.: in election of 1876, 304, 305, 373; as President, 394, 410

Hay-Herrán Treaty, 533
Haymarket affair, 412–413, 412°
Hayne, Robert Y., 187, 228
H-bomb. See Hydrogen bomb
Headrights, 30
Health: in American Revolution, 88; in cities, 432, 434, 435; after Civil War, 308; public, 434, 536, 536°; and Social Security, 650, 741
Hearst, William Randolph, 471, 472
Helper, Hinton Rowan, 224–225
Hemingway, Ernest, 694
Henry, Patrick, 72, 74, 122; quoted, 70, 75, 218
Henry the Navigator, 7–8
Henry VII, of England, 24
Henson, Matthew H., 555
Hepburn Act, 516–517
Herndon, William, 268
Herrán, Tomás, 533
Herrick, Myron T., 621
Hershey, Lewis B., 726
Hessians, 91
Higginson, Stephen, quoted, 115
Hill, A. P., 281
Hill, James J., 324, 367, 513
Hiroshima, Japan, 725, 771
Hispaniola, 12, 67, 389
Hiss, Alger, 752
Hitler, Adolf, 643, 662, 683, 683°, 687°, 698°; and "Fortress Europe," 712; at French surrender, 692; at Munich, 686; and Poland, 687, 688; policy toward United States, 698; quoted, 716; suicide, 720; at war with United States, 706
Ho Chi Minh, 760
Holding company, 331, 331n
Holmes, Oliver Wendell, 202; quoted, 272
Holmes, Oliver Wendell, Jr., 421, 421n, 555
Holy Alliance, 168
Holy Land, 6
Holyoke, Massachusetts, 204
Home Owners Loan Corporation, 643
Homestead, Pennsylvania, 416°, 417–418, 417°
Homestead Act, 286, 319, 405, 428
Homesteaders, 342, 364
Honduras, 8, 531, 768
Hooker, Joseph, 279, 281
Hooker, Thomas, 38, 39°
Hoover, Herbert, 601°, 624°, 631°; on American system (quoted), 598–600; and business, 631; in election of 1928, 624°, 625, 626; as food administrator, 586–587; in Great Depression, 631, 632, 634, 638; inaugural address (quoted), 630; in Latin America, 626°, 676; on poverty (quoted), 626; as President, 632–633, 634, 635, 637, 638; as Secretary of Commerce, 602
"Hoovervilles," 632

Hopkins, Harry, 648, 651, 712*
Hopkinson, Francis, 82, 123
Horses, 16, 104*
Hotchkiss guns, 346
House, Edward M., 526, 572, 576; quoted, 578
House of Burgesses, 29, 70, 74
House of Representatives, 254, 295, 301*; in election of 1800, 142; in election of 1824, 175; gag rule, 254; impeachment of Andrew Johnson, 299; powers of, 121; representation in, 120; Speaker, 520–521
Houses, 15*, 37*, 102*, 140
Housing: in Great Depression, 653*, 659, 660*; for low-income tenants, 662; urban, 777
Housing and Urban Development, Department of, 777
Houston, Texas, 560, 560*
Houston, Sam, 237
Howard, Oliver O., 296
Howe, Julia Ward, 202, 472
Howe, Richard, 90
Howe, William, 90, 91–92
Hudson, Henry, 44
Hudson River, 42–43, 43*, 44, 45, 50, 220; pollution, 777; tunnel under, 322; valley, 62, 91
Hudson's Bay Company, 63
Huerta, Victoriano (wĕr'-tä, bĕk'-tō-ryä'-nô), 543
Hughes, Charles Evans, 601*; as Chief Justice, 656; in election of 1916, 577; as Secretary of State, 602, 672; at Washington Conference, 673
Hull, Cordell, 677*, 683; in Moscow, 732; quoted, 666–667, 677, 704; as Secretary of State, 642, 642*, 667; talks with Japanese, 703, 705
Hull House, 508
Human resources, 664
Human rights, 99
Humphrey, Hubert H., 774
"Hundred Days," 643–644, 645–646
Hungary: Communists in, 606, 746; after First World War, 593; occupied by Nazis, 698; United States treaties with, 596; and Yalta, 733
Huron, Lake, 19, 62
Hutchinson, Anne, 38
Hydroelectric plants, 645–646
Hydrogen bomb, 749, 771

ICBM. See Intercontinental ballistics missile
Iceland, 42, 749
Ickes, Harold, 642, 642*
Idaho: admitted to Union, 358; and Populists, 449; as territory, 350, 357; and woman suffrage, 506
Illinois, 209; admitted to Union, 166n; in election of 1896, 453; Granger laws, 442; and Lincoln-

Douglas debates, 265; manufacturing, 363; and slavery, 256, 264
Illinois Central Railroad, 322
Immigrants, 510–511; Catholic, 605; after Civil War, 407; contributions to American life, 206; from Europe, 246; Jewish, 605; as laborers, 400; in middle Atlantic states, 205–206; in New England, 204, 206; in New York, 398–399*, 423*; numbers, 320, 422; in old Northwest, 208; and political bosses, 439; resented, 206; Romanians as, 422; in slave-free controversy, 262; in South, 225–226; in West, 364
Immigration: in John Adams' administration, 141; and Chinese Exclusion Act, 424; after Civil War, 330; during Civil War, 319; colonial, 60, 80–81; and Emergency Quota Act, 606; from Japan, 548–549; and labor, 422; restrictions, 424, 549, 605–606
Immigration Quota Act, 606
Impeachment, of Andrew Johnson, 299
Imperialism, Age of, 391–392
Imperialism, American, 466–467; advocates of, 468–469; as political issue, 482, 484, 484 (cartoon)
Imperialism, Japanese, 551
Imports: colonial, 48, 69, 70, 73; duties on, 134, 138, 174, 379; to South, 228
Impressment, 153–154
Incas, 13, 13*
Income tax: cut under Lyndon Johnson, 780; declared unconstitutional, 387; payroll deductions, 726; and Sixteenth Amendment, 526n
Indentured servants, 29–30, 31
Independence, Missouri, 234
Independence, Declaration of. See Declaration of Independence; War for Independence
Independence, U.S., 77–78, 92 (cartoon); recognized, 95–97
Independence Hall, 108–109*, 118
Independent Treasury Act, 193–194, 195
India: Chinese invasions, 762; English in, 67; after First World War, 606; Marco Polo in, 6; Portuguese in, 11; trade, 7; Vasco da Gama in, 8
Indiana, 209, 254; admitted to Union, 166n; in election of 1896, 453
Indian Reorganization Act, 349n
Indians, 63, 64, 114, 167, 367; Arapaho, 342; of Canada, 60, 157; Caribbean tribes, 16; Cherokee, 198, 367; Cheyenne, 342; Chickasaw, 63, 114; Choctaw, 114, 367; as citizens, 348–349; in colonial Virginia, 30; in Colorado, 342; Creeks, 63–64, 167, 367; of Dakota Territory, 343; defense of,

348; and De Soto, 14; and Dutch colonists, 46; of Florida, 14*, 157, 166–167; French trade with, 18; and fur trade, 60, 62; in Georgia, 53, 114, 166–167, 198; on Great Plains, 342–349, 343*, 345*, 347*; handicrafts, 40; houses, 15*; Incas, 13, 13*; Iroquois, 62; and Jackson, 186; and Jamestown, 27; in King George's War, 63; land purchased from, 45; in Latin America, 537; Mandan, 151; of Massachusetts, 37; Narraganset, 37; at New Amsterdam, 46, 47*; in New England, 62; in New York, 44; of northern North America, 18, 20, 20*; in Northwest Territory, 112, 136–137; of old Northwest, 208; Ottawa, 68; at Plymouth, 34; and Ponce de León, 13; in Pontiac's war, 68; problems about, 97, 100; and Raleigh's colonies, 25–26; removal to reservations, 189 (map), 343–345, 366; Seminole, 166–167; Shoshone, 151; in South, 114, 139; in Spanish colonies, 12–15; under Tecumseh, 156; in War for Independence, 93; of West Indies, 9
Indian Territory, 303, 367
Indigo, 49, 218, 219
Indochina, 757, 770
Industrialization: and Civil War, 311–312, 318–319; development of, 316, 317*, 318–319, 328–329, 407, 457, 668; in early national period, 171; effects, 314–315, 317*, 319–320, 328, 329–330, 336, 363–364, 368, 400, 407, 428, 457, 461, 500; Hamilton's views on, 133–134; in New England, 200–201, 203–204; in North, 286, 287; resources for, 328–330, 668; and social change, 319–320, 336, 400, 407, 428, 457, 461, 500; in South, 227, 285; in Union territory, 286
Industrial Revolution, 219
Industrial Workers of the World, 416
Industry: automobile, 611–614; capital for, 316; colonial, 87; defense of by Carnegie, 314–315; in early national period, 171, 178; expansion after Civil War, 312, 318, 363, 407; expansion after First World War, 668; and federal government, 316, 319, 419; in First World War, 586; improvements in technology, 316, 329–330, 363–364, 428; and labor, 400–404, 742; in New England, 202, 203–204; in North, 286, 287; regulation of, 512–514, 515–517, 527–528, 643–644; in Second World War, 727, 741; social features, 496–497, 500, 599; in South, 227–228, 285; "take-off," 320

Inflation, 86–87, 727–728, 740–741, 741 (cartoon)
Initiative, 505
Injunction, 417
Installment buying, 614
Insular Cases, 489
Insurance, 336; health, 650, 741; old-age, 650; unemployment, 650
Insurgents, 519–520
Insurrectos, 471
Intellectual life, 55, 209
Interchangeable parts, 316
Intercontinental ballistics missile, 770–771
Interior, Department of, 489, 603
Interlocking directorate, 331
Internal improvements: and John Q. Adams, 175; favored by Calhoun, 162–163, 172; and Henry Clay, 174; federal support, 172, 175, 323; in North, 210–212, 322; promise of in Compromise of 1877, 305; in South, 228, 285, 322; west of Mississippi, 323–324
International Conference of American States, 677
International Cigar Makers Union, 413
International Court of Justice, 592, 736
International Labor Organization, 592
International law, 284, 574
International Military Tribunal, 745
International politics. *See* Foreign affairs
International relations: American policies in, 168; Cordell Hull on, 666–667; in Tyler's administration, 196–197. *See also* Foreign affairs
Interstate commerce: regulation of, 170; Supreme Court decision, 170
Interstate Commerce Act, 446, 663
Interstate Commerce Commission, 443 (cartoon), 516, 517
"Intolerable Acts," 73
Inventions: American, 246; of early 1800's, 205; of nineteenth century, 320, 457. *See also* names of inventions
Investments, United States, 668–670
Iowa: admitted to Union, 208; in 1896 election, 453; farmers of, 322; Granger laws, 442
Iran, 770
Iraq, 765, 770
Ireland, 48, 204, 206, 422
Irish, 209, 324, 511
Irish-Americans, 382
Iron, 329*; colonial trade in, 49; natural resource, 206, 328; in Pennsylvania, 206–207; production by 1850, 316
Iron City Forge Company, 335
"Iron Curtain," 746, 767
Iron industry, 206–207, 316
Iroquois Indians, 62
Irrigation, 342

Isabella, of Spain, 5, 8
Isolationists, 692, 699, 700, 731
Israel, 763, 764, 765 (map)
Italians: as immigrants, 422, 511; at Munich, 686; in North Africa, 713
Italy, 446; as Axis power, 698; British in, 719; in Common Market, 767; early trade routes, 6 (map); under Fascists, 683, 684; invaded by Allied troops, 714; leadership in Europe, 7; under Mussolini, 662; in NATO, 749; and trade with East, 7; in Triple Alliance, 566; and Turkey, 566; unrest after First World War, 606; and Venezuelan debt crisis, 538; and Washington Conference, 672; Wilson in, 590
Iwo Jima, 722

Jackson, Andrew, 186, 187*; Age of, 184–192; in antislavery party, 262; attacks United States Bank, 190–191; at Battle of New Orleans, 160; break with Calhoun, 188; Cabinet of, 186; in election of 1824, 174–175; in Florida, 167; and frontiersmen, 175; Indian policy, 188; and nullification, 189; as President, 175–176, 186–192; recognized independence of Texas, 237; quoted, 157, 184–185, 186; spokesman for laboring people, 185; and workingmen's parties, 402; and the West, 188–189
Jackson, Helen Hunt, 348
Jackson, Thomas J., 275, 276, 279, 281
Jacksonian democracy, 197–198
Jacksonians, 189–190, 191, 194
Jalapa, Mexico, 240–241
James River, 27, 28, 30, 278
Jamestown, Virginia, 26*, 27–28, 29
Japan: aggressions, 672, 701–704; breakdown of talks with, 243; expansion in 1930's, 680, 681 (map); and Germany, 578; invasion of China, 685; naval growth, 671; occupied, 745; opened to American trade, 243; in Second World War, 698, 701, 703, 707–709, 724–725; trade with, 7; war lords, 662; war with China, 486; war with Russia, 548; Washington Conference, 672; in Yalta plans, 734
Japanese: advance in western Pacific, 707; aggression in Asia, 551, 685 (cartoon), 701*; excluded as immigrants, 424; as immigrants, 548–549; military code broken, 703, 704; in Pacific, 481; in Second World War, 722, 723–725
Japanese-Americans, 728–729
Jay, John, 74, 85, 95, 122, 129, 138, 138*

Jazz, 605
Jefferson, Thomas, 76, 77*, 85*, 118; attitude toward industry, 2, 78, 85; Cabinet of, 146–147; and courts, 146; and Declaration of Independence, 78, 85; and embargo, 154–155; and Federalists, 141–142; land policy, 111; and Louisiana Purchase, 150; as minister to France, 129; and national debt, 146; and navy, 146; opinion of Washington, 138, 138n; political ideas, 131; as President, 142, 146–155; quoted, 2, 78, 85, 115, 142, 145, 151, 218, 428; and religious freedom, 84–85; as Secretary of State, 129–130; on slavery, 85, 213, 218, 223; support of Hamilton's plan, 132; and United States Bank, 133; as Vice-President, 139
Jeffersonian democracy, 198
Jeffersonians. *See* Democratic-Republicans
Jesuits, 18, 31, 60
Jews: in colonies, 46; as immigrants, 605; in Israel, 762; and Ku Klux Klan, 608; persecuted by Hitler, 687–688, 719–720; prejudice against, 511; restrictions on, 85
Jim Crow laws, 511
Jingoism, 469, 472 (cartoon)
Job Corps, 775
Johns Hopkins University, 523
Johnson, Andrew, 498; and Congress, 297, 298–299; and Dominican Republic, 387; in election of 1864, 287; in election of 1868, 300, 514n; impeachment and trial, 299, 373; as President, 294, 298–299; and reconstruction, 296–297
Johnson, Hiram, 594
Johnson, James Weldon, 623
Johnson, Lyndon B., 779*; and civil rights program, 783; and Dominican Republic, 769; in election of 1960, 756; on foreign policy (quoted), 784; as President, 757, 774–775, 777; as Vice-President, 754
Johnson, Tom L., 504
Johnson, William, 222
Johnston, Albert Sidney, 276–278
Johnston, Joseph E., 275, 276, 279
Joint Committee of Fifteen, 297
Joint Committee on the Conduct of the War, 294, 296
Joliet, Louis, 60
Jones, John, 221
Jones, John Paul, 93
Jones, Samuel, 504
Jones Act of 1916, 493
Jones Act of 1917, 491
Jordan, 762n, 765
Judaism. *See* Jews
Judicial review, 148
Judiciary, federal, 121, 147–148
Judiciary Act: of 1789, 148; of 1801, 146; of 1802, 146, 148

Julian, George Washington, 371
Justice, Department of, 611, 728

Kamikazes, 724, 724n, 724*
Kansas: admitted to Union, 265n; civil war in, 262; effects of Kansas-Nebraska Bill, 261–263; in 1854, 260 (map); and election of 1856, 263; emigration to, 261; farmers, 353, 363; farm mortgages, 444; prohibition in, 510; settlement, 324, 366
Kansas Pacific Railroad, 349
Kaskaskia, Illinois, 60, 93
Katsura (kä'tsoo-rä), Taro, 548
Kearney, Stephen W., 240
Keating-Owen Act, 528
Kefauver, Estes, 754
Kelley, Oliver H., 440–441
Kellogg, Frank B., 674, 675
Kellogg-Briand Pact, 680
Kelly, William, 329
Kennedy, John Fitzgerald, 755*, 756*; assassination, 756–757; Cabinet, 756; and Cuba, 768–769; and Germany, 767; inaugural address (quoted), 756; and Khrushchev, 760, 766–767; and Peace Corps, 756; as President, 754, 756–757, 780; religion, 755, 756; and Southeast Asia, 760
Kennedy Round, 781
Kentucky, 157, 224; in Civil War, 274, 277; freedmen in, 221; and Maysville Road, 188; and TVA, 645
Key, Francis Scott, 160
Khrushchev, Nikita (kroosh-chôf', nyĭ-kĕ'tá), 760, 766, 766*, 769
King, Martin Luther, Jr., 782, 782*, 783
King, Rufus, 171
King's College, 55, 119. See also Columbia University
Kings Mountain, Battle of, 93, 94 (map)
Kitty Hawk, North Carolina, 555, 619
Knights of Labor, 411–413, 442, 444, 654
Know-Nothing party, 262
Knox, Philander C., 540, 541, 551
Konoye, Fumimaro (kô-nô-yĕ, fōō-mĕ-mä-rô), 703
Korea, 725, 748, 750, 751*. See also North Korea; South Korea
Korean War, 749–751, 750 (map), 753, 780
Kosciusko (kŏs'ĭ-ŭs'kō), Thaddeus, 93
Kosygin, Alexei N., 772
Ku Klux Klan, 302, 607–608, 624
Kuril (koo'rĕl) Islands, 680, 734
Kurusu, Saburo (koo-roo-soo, sä-bōō-rô), 703, 704, 704*, 705
Kuwait, 765
Kwajalein (kwŏj'á-lĭn), 709

Labor: and boycotts, 742, 754; child, 204, 311, 500, 500*, 527*, 528; during Civil War, 319, 405–406; and Cleveland, 387; in colonies, 28–30, 31; conditions for workers, 204, 311, 400, 403, 405, 407, 418, 460, 460*, 517*, 518*, 555, 623, 656; in Confederacy, 286; and courts, 403–404, 421–422, 656, 661; disputes since 1950, 781; and Eisenhower, 754; factory, 203–204, 203*, 400, 407, 555; farm, 203, 221, 363–364, 430, 432–433; and federal government, 410, 419, 637, 649*; freedmen, 221–222; fringe benefits, 742; immigrant, 206, 207–208, 320, 422, 424, 605; indenture system, 29–30, 31; and Jackson, 185, 402–403; leaders, 411, 414, 416, 418, 418*, 654, 727; legislation, 652, 656, 662, 727, 741–742, 754; minimum-wage law, 656, 661, 662; Molly Maguires, 409, 409*; need for organization, 398–399, 400, 407–409; Negro, 414, 511, 623; opposition to unionizing, 416*, 417–421, 420 (cartoon); organization, 400–401, 402–403, 405, 407, 411, 412–414, 623, 654–655, 654 (cartoon), 742; in politics, 402–403; rights recognized, 655, 656, 741; and Franklin D. Roosevelt, 643, 647–649, 647*, 648*, 651–652, 654–656, 662, 664; and Theodore Roosevelt, 512–513; skilled, 401, 413; slave system, 30, 213–214, 216–217, 221, 222, 225–226; strikes, 401, 402*, 409–411, 412, 417–418, 419, 419*, 512–513, 606–607, 742; supply of, 316, 318, 363–364; and Truman, 741–742; unemployment, 384, 409, 631–632, 635*, 636*, 637, 637*, 643, 647–649, 649*, 651–652, 653*, 741; unskilled, 401, 413, 424; use of violence, 410, 412, 416, 417–418, 654–655; weakness of, 623; woman, 311, 414, 432; workday, 403, 408, 408*, 411, 421, 528, 623, 656, 662. See also Industry
Labor, Department of, 408
Labor-Management Relations Act. See Taft-Hartley Act
Lafayette, Marquis de, 93, 95, 164, 168
La Follette, Robert M., 496–497*, 504, 505*, 520, 522, 594, 624
La Follette Seaman's Act, 528
Lafon, Thomy, 221
Lame ducks, 659, 659n
Land: claims to western, 111, 111 (map); colonial grants, 27, 27 (map), 30, 31; grants to companies, 112, 192; grants to railroads, 323; Homestead Act, 286; and Indians, 189, 343, 348–349,

367–368; national domain, 69, 111–112, 342; of old Northwest, 209; Ordinance of 1785, 111–112, 112 (map); Ordinance of 1787, 113; of Oregon Country, 243; ownership of, 31–32, 45, 84, 221; policy, 111; speculators, 112; struggle for trans-Appalachian, 60–62, 61 (map)
Land companies, 64, 112, 192
Land-Grant College Act, 286n
Landon, Alfred M., 658
Lane, Franklin K., 570
Lansing, Robert, 575
Laos, 760
Large-state plan, 120
La Salle, Robert Cavelier, Sieur de, 58–59*, 60
"Last West," 342–343, 344 (map), 367
Latin America, 100, 768–769; Alliance for Progress, 768–769; attitude toward United States, 543, 674, 676, 678; and communism, 674, 768–769; and dollar diplomacy, 540–541; Good Neighbor policy, 677; governments in, 537, 768, 769; and Panama Canal, 532–537, 538, 769; plans for common market, 769; Roosevelt corollary, 537–538, 674; after Second World War, 736; trade with, 678–679; United States relations with, 396, 537–541, 547, 674–679
Laurens, Henry, quoted, 85, 86, 96
Lawrence, Kansas, 261, 262
Lawrence, Amos A., 261
Lawson, Thomas W., 504
Lazarus, Emma, 424
Leadville, Colorado, 359*
League of Nations, 600 (cartoon); Covenant of, 591–593; and election of 1920, 600–601; Japanese withdrawal from, 680; mandate system, 592–593, 593n; opposition to, 594–595; United States participation, 671; Wilson's fourteen points, 588–589
Lease, Mary E., 447, 447*
Lebanon, 762n
Le Bourget (lĕ boor'zhä') Airfield, 621
Lecompton Constitution, 264–265
Lee, Richard Henry, 72, 74, 77, 78, 122
Lee, Robert E., 275, 283*; in Civil War, 279, 280–281; at Harpers Ferry, 267; in Mexican War, 279; at West Point, 279
Legal tender, 446, 446n
Leisure, 604–605
Lend-Lease Act, 694, 701, 702
L'Enfant (län' fän'), Pierre, 161
Leo XIII, Pope, 472
Letters from a Farmer in Pennsylvania, 71
Letters from an American Farmer, quoted, 80–81

Lewis, John L., 606, 654; quoted, 727
Lewis, Meriwether, 151–152
Lewis and Clark Expedition, 151–152, 233
Lexington, Kentucky, 157
Lexington, Massachusetts, 76
Liberal Republicans, 303, 373, 502
Liberia, Republic of, 218
Liberty, 106, 784 (cartoon); and Declaration of Independence, 78; limitations on, 36–37; political, 46, 181; religious, 32, 37–38, 51–52, 84; and slavery, 218, 280; Noah Webster on, 108–109
Liberty Bell, 164
Liberty League, 649n
Liberty loans, 587–588, 587*
Liberty party, 194, 214, 238
Libya, 762n
Liliuokalani (lē-lē'wô-kä-lä'nê), 393, 394*
Lima, Peru, 768
Lincoln, Abraham, 250*, 266*; assassination, 288, 294; in Black Hawk War, 188; Cabinet of, 273, 274; and Civil War, 278, 281; in Congress, 239; criticism of, 293; on Crittenden Compromise, 272; in election of 1858, 265–266; in election of 1860, 267; in election of 1864, 287–288; and emancipation, 280; first inauguration, 272–273; and foreign affairs, 283–285; and Mexican War, 239; as national hero, 308; policy toward South, 293, 296; as President, 268, 272, 273–274; quoted, 209, 249, 265, 268, 270–271; reconstruction plan, 293–294, 296; as seen by Europeans, 283; and slavery, 265–266, 268, 273, 280
Lincoln, Mrs. Abraham, 327
Lincoln-Douglas debates, 265–266
Lindbergh, Charles A., 619, 620–621, 620*, 675*, 676, 706
Linotype machine, 471
Lippmann, Walter, 638
Liquor, 609–611, 609 (cartoon), 647
Lisbon, Portugal, 8
Literacy test, 605
Little Big Horn, Battle of the, 345
Little Round Top, 281
Liverpool, England, 207
Livingston, Robert R., 128, 149, 170
Lloyd, Henry Demarest, 331, 454, 502–503
Lloyd George, David, 590–591, 591*
Loans: to belligerents, 684; to Dominican Republic, 676; to European countries, 669–671; to United States, 668–669
Local-option laws, 609
Lochner v. New York, 421
Locke, John, 51
Lockout, 419

Lodge, Henry Cabot, 468, 469, 474, 537, 553, 578–579, 594, 596, 673, 682
Lodge, Henry Cabot, Jr., 754
Log cabin, 46n, 113*
London, England, 336
London Company, 26–27
London Economic Conference, 647
Lone Star Republic, 237
Long, Huey P., 650, 650*
Long, John D., 473–474
Long, Stephen H., 232
Long drive, 349, 351
Long-horn cattle, 352–353
Long Island, 90
Longstreet, James, 275, 281
Lookout Mountain, Battle of, 281; Confederate cannon on, 288*
Los Angeles, California, 240, 595*
Louisiana: admitted to Union, 166n, 220; in Civil War, 281; in election of 1948, 743; plantation, 225*; readmitted to Union, 300; in reconstruction period, 293; secession, 272
Louisiana Purchase, 149–151, 260; exploration, 150 (map), 151–152; French in, 60, 62, 67; history, 148–149; limits defined, 167; opposition to, 150; slavery barred north of 36° 30', 172–173; under Spain, 148
Louisville, Kentucky, 165
L'Ouverture, Pierre Toussaint, 149
Lowell, Massachusetts, 203*, 316
Lowell, James Russell, 244, 283, 303
Lower Canada, 159, 159n
Loyalists, 82, 84, 93, 97
Lusitania, 574, 684
Lutherans, 54
Luxembourg, 691, 718, 748, 767

McAdoo, William Gibbs, 587, 624
MacArthur, Douglas, 638, 707, 722, 725, 725*, 745, 750
McAuliffe, Anthony C., 718
McCarthy, Joseph R., 752
McCarthyism, 752
McClellan, George B., 276, 278, 288
McClure, S. S., 504
McCormick, Cyrus Hall, 364
McCoy, Joseph G., 349
McCulloch v. Maryland, 170, 190, 656
McDowell, Irvin, 276
Machine guns, 568
Machinery, 400, 407; agricultural, 219–220, 362, 363–364, 365*, 426–427*, 433, 780; factory, 207, 780–781, 780n
Mackinac, Straits of, 19
McKinley, William, 449*, 480*, 481*, 498*; assassinated, 498; in Congress, 383–384; and Cuba, 471, 473; in election of 1896, 450;

in election of 1900, 484; peace efforts, 474; and the Philippines, 481–482; prosperity under, 485 (cartoon); and Spanish-American War, 471, 474–475, 480–481
McKinley Tariff, 383–384, 393
McLeod, Alexander, 196
Macmillan, Harold, 766
McNamara, Robert S., 756
McNary-Haugen Farm Relief Bill, 627
Macon, Georgia, 228
Macon's Bill No. 2, 156
Mactan Island, 11
Madagascar, 51
Madeiras, 8
Madero, Francisco, 543
Madison, Dolley, 146, 156, 265
Madison, James, 156*, 168; and Bill of Rights, 123; at Constitutional Convention, 119, 119*; "Father of the Constitution," 124; opposed to Hamilton, 132; as President, 155, 157; as Secretary of State, 146, 149, 155; and Supreme Court, 148; and War of 1812, 157
Madrid, Spain, 474–475
Magellan, Ferdinand, 11, 12, 13
Magellan, Strait of, 24
Mahan, Alfred Thayer, 468, 552
Maine, 16; boundary settlement, 196–197, 196 (map); in election of 1936, 658; first dry law, 609; and Missouri Compromise, 173; prohibition in, 510; settlement, 32, 39; in War for Independence, 90
Maine, 473, 475, 532
Malaria, 27, 51
Malaya, 6
Malta, 733
Manassas Junction, Virginia, 276
Manchu Dynasty, 551
Manchukuo, 680
Manchuria: and Communists, 745; Japanese in, 680; and Russia, 548; and Soviet Union, 680, 725; and Yalta, 734
Mandamus, writ of, 148, 148n
Mandan Indians, 151, 152*
Mandates, Japanese, 672, 681 (map)
Mandate system, 593
Manhattan Island, 44, 46, 90
Manifest destiny, 211, 231, 233–234, 238, 243, 244
Manila, Philippines, 476, 481, 722
Manila Bay, Battle of, 476, 477*
Manufacturers: competition among, 203, 204; demand for high tariffs, 174; in Federalist party, 171; increase in profits, 286, 287; markets, 209, 327, 431
Manufacturing: and automation, 780; after Civil War, 311; during Civil War, 319; colonial, 75; in Confederacy, 285; in 1820's, 178; Hamilton's report on, 133–134; in

Illinois, 363; middle Atlantic states, 206–207; New England, 202–204; nineteenth century, 316; in 1920's, 668; products, 316, 327, 668; and protective tariffs, 171, 174; report on, 133–134; after Revolution, 115; textile, 316, 317*; in Union territory, 286, 287; in Washington's administration, 133–134

Manumission, 218, 221

Maps. *See* Contents, pages xi–xii

Mao Tse-tung, 736, 745

Marbury v. *Madison*, 148

Marines, United States, 696–697*, 707*; in Dominican Republic, 676, 769; in First World War, 581–582; in Nicaragua, 674; in Second World War, 707*, 709, 722; use of technological advances, 316; view of Jefferson on, 171

Marion, Francis, 98

Marne: First Battle of the, 566; Second Battle of the, 582

Marquette, Michigan, 328

Marquette, Jacques, 60

Marshall, George C., 745, 747 (quoted), 747*

Marshall, James W., 243–244

Marshall, John, 122, 164, 169*, 656, 779; as Chief Justice, 148, 169–170; and Constitution, 170–171; at trial of Burr, 152–153; and X Y Z affair, 140

Marshall, Thurgood, 779*

Marshall Islands, 709

Marshall Plan, 747–748

Martinique, 67, 553

Marx, Karl, 414n

Maryland: colonial, 50, 51, 55–56; and Confederacy, 276; freedmen in, 221; land claims, 111; name, 31; and Potomac River, 117; ratified Constitution, 122; religious toleration, 32; remained in Union, 274; settlement, 31–32, 31 (map), 35; tobacco plantations, 218

Mason, George, 122

Mason, James M., 257, 284

Mason, John Y., 263

Massachusetts, 32, 34–37, 55; child labor in, 204; debts, 132; education, 202, 213; established church in, 84; government, 35; home of Adams family, 105; Indians, 37; land claims, 111; and Ohio Company, 112; population, 206; ratified Constitution, 122; Shays' Rebellion in, 116–117; shoemakers' strikes, 405; slavery abolished, 85; in War for Independence, 73–76, 87; workingmen's parties, 402

Massachusetts Bay Colony, 34–37, 38 (map)

Massachusetts Emigrant Aid Company, 261

Massachusetts General Court, 36, 38

"Massive retaliation," 770

Mass production, 311, 612

Matamoros, Mexico, 240

Mather, Cotton, quoted, 40

Maumee River, 137

Maximilian, in Mexico, 284, 394

Mayflower, 33*, 34

Mayflower Compact, 34

Mays, Henry T., 544–545

Maysville Road, 188

Meade, George G., 279, 281

Meany, George, 781

Meat: government inspection, 517; packing, 322, 613, 613n

Meat Inspection Act, 517

Mechanics Union of Trade Associations, 402

Mediation, 575–576

Medicare, 775

Mediterranean Sea, 7, 8, 147 (map)

Mellon, Andrew, 602, 630

Melville, Herman, quoted, 205

Memorial Day "massacre," 654

Memphis, Tennessee, 298, 605

Mendoza, Antonio de, 14

Merchant Marine, 153, 700, 701

Merchants: British, 26–27, 33, 77; colonial, 71, 75; and Embargo Act, 154; Italian, 7; members of trading companies, 28; in old South, 221; in War against Napoleon, 153

Mergers, 330, 622, 742

Merit system, 374

Merrimac, 285n

Merritt, Wesley, 476

Mesabi Range, iron ore in, 336

Methodists, 218

Metropolitan centers, 820 (table)

Metropolitan Museum of Art, 438

Metropolitan Opera Company, 342

Meuse River, 582

Mexican War, 239–242, 239 (map), 241*, 259, 277

Mexico: an American opinion of, 231; and annexation of Texas, 238; and California, 230–231, 238, 240; Cortés in, 13; Indian culture, 15; intervention in, 543–546; invaded, 240–241; and Maximilian, 284, 394; Spanish, 148; uprising in 1911, 543; and Wilson, 543–547; and Zimmermann note, 578. *See also* New Spain

Mexico, Gulf of, 60

Mexico City, 13*, 14, 241

Michigan, 209; admitted to Union, 208; in election of 1896, 453

Michigan, Lake, 62, 208

Middle America, 540 (map)

Middle Atlantic states, 202; cities, 204; immigrants in, 205–206; industry, 206–208

Middle class, 502

Middle East. *See* Southwest Asia; North Africa

Middlemen, 431

Middle West, 298; agriculture, 430; cities, 433, 438, 438*; Grange in, 441–442, 441*; railroads, 322, 323, 430

Midway, Battle of, 709

Miles, Nelson A., 345, 479

Militia, state, 417*, 418

Mill Springs, Kentucky, 276

Milwaukee, Wisconsin, 208

Minerals, 206, 243–244, 328–329, 356–357

Miners, 340–341*, 342, 344, 345, 354, 354 (map), 355–359

Mining, 206, 340–341, 356, 358*

Minneapolis, Minnesota, 208, 314–315*, 438

Minnesota, 442, 453

Minuit, Peter, 46

Minuteman missile, 770–771

Minutemen, 76

Miquelon, 67

Miranda v. *Arizona*, 777–778

Missiles: anti-ballistic, 771; intercontinental ballistic, 770–771

Missionaries, 12, 15, 18, 60, 234

Missionary Ridge, 281

Mississippi: admitted to Union, 166n, 172–173, 220; in election of 1948, 743; Negroes in politics, 300; politics, 304; readmitted to Union, 300; secession, 272; teaching of evolution forbidden, 608; and TVA, 645

Mississippi River: boundary of western lands, 111; bridges, 438, 438*; in Civil War, 275, 276, 278, 281; discovery, 14; exploration, 59, 60; French forts on, 60; in Louisiana Purchase, 149; in Pinckney's Treaty, 138; settlement beyond, 208; and Spain, 114; as transportation route, 227–228, 227*; United States boundary, 97

Mississippi Valley, 59, 61 (map), 322

Missouri: admitted to Union, 220; Mormons in, 235; remained in Union, 274

Missouri Compromise, 172–173, 172 (map), 255, 260, 264

Missouri Pacific Railroad, 349

Missouri River, 151, 236

Mitchell, John, 398–399, 664

Mobile, Alabama, 228, 292, 543

Moderates, 74, 267

Mohawk and Hudson Railroad, 211

Mohawk Valley, 66, 91

Molasses, 55, 62, 69

Molasses Act of 1733, 69

Molly Maguires, 409, 409*

Moluccas, 11

Money: demonetization of silver, 446; and farmers, 116, 427, 428; gold standard, 446, 452, 647; and the Greenback party, 443; as legal tender, 446; paper, 190, 191, 286; ratio of 16 to 1, 445–446, 450–451; scarcity, 431, 445, 447; silver coinage, 445–446, 449, 450, 454–455; specie, 191–192; and United States Bank, 190–192; during War for Independence, 86, 86°, 88; from western lands, 112

Mongolia, 734

Monmouth, Battle of, 93

Monongahela River, 418

Monopoly, 331, 337, 337 (cartoon); and Bank of the United States, 190; colonial, 73; and Theodore Roosevelt, 513–514; threat to democracy, 338, 526; and trusts, 331, 513–514

Monroe, James, 169; character, 173; and Louisiana Purchase, 149; minister to France, 140; as President, 167, 170–177; Senator from Virginia, 135

Monroe Doctrine, 168–169, 394–395, 543, 553; changed interpretation, 677; and Communists, 768; extension of, 395–396, 679; and foreign policy, 168–169, 394, 395–396; and France, 284; and League of Nations, 594; and Panama Canal, 531; Roosevelt corollary to, 538

Monrovia, Liberia, 218

Montana: admitted to Union, 357; cattle industry, 353; irrigation in, 367; mining in, 343, 356, 357; organized, 357

Montcalm, Louis, 66–67

Monterrey, Mexico, 240

Montevideo, Uruguay, 626°, 677

Montezuma, 13

Montgomery, Alabama, 272, 782

Montgomery, Richard, 90

Monticello, Virginia, 155

Montreal, Canada, 17, 18, 60, 62, 67, 90

Moon, exploration, 773

Morgan, Daniel, 93–94

Morgan, J. Pierpont, 336–338, 342, 387, 387°, 513, 524, 630

Morgenthau, Henry, Jr., 646°

Mormons, 230°, 234, 235, 236

Moroccan question, 566

Morocco, 11, 147, 553

Morrill Tariff, 286

Morris, Gouverneur, 119, 121

Morris, Robert, 87, 128, 129

Morristown, New Jersey, 91

Morrow, Dwight W., 675–676, 675°

Mortgages, 429, 430, 445, 632

Morton, Levi P., 383

Morton, Oliver, 302–303

Moscow, Soviet Union, 24, 731–732, 772

Moscow Declaration, 732

Moslems, 6, 7, 8

Motion pictures, 615–616, 616°, 617°

Motley, John L., 303

Mount Vernon, 117°, 128

Mount Vernon Conference, 117–118

Muckrakers, 502, 502n, 503–504, 555

Mugwumps, 377, 377n

Munich, Germany, 686

Munich Conference, 686, 687°

Munn v. Illinois, 442

Music, 438, 605

Mussolini, Benito, 662, 663, 683, 687, 687°, 698°, 706, 714, 720

NAACP. See National Association for the Advancement of Colored People

Nagasaki, Japan, 725

Napoleon Bonaparte, 148, 153, 156, 168

Narraganset Indians, 37

Narragansett Bay, 37

NASA. See National Aeronautics and Space Administration

Nashville, Tennessee, 276–277

Nasser, Gamal Abdel, 762, 763, 764°

Nast, Thomas, cartoons, 304°, 305°

Natchez, Mississippi, 60, 115

National Aeronautics and Space Administration, 773

National Association for the Advancement of Colored People, 511, 783

National-banking system, 286–287, 319. See also Bank of the United States; Federal Reserve System

National Broadcasting Company, 617

National debt, 127; Hamilton and, 131–132; Jefferson and, 146; in Second World War, 726

National Farmers' Holiday Association, 641

National Foundation on the Arts and Humanities, 775

National government. See Federal government

National Housing Act, 662

National Industrial Recovery Act, 643

Nationalism, 246; Arab, 762, 764; Calhoun on, 162–163; economic, 668–669 (cartoons), 670; before First World War, 566; "new," 521–522; in New England, 202; and sectionalism, 258; and Supreme Court, 169–170; after War of 1812, 164

Nationality, 164–165

National Labor Relations Act, 652, 661

National Labor Relations Board, 652, 727

National Labor Union, 407–408

National Progressive Republican League, 522

National Recovery Administration, 643, 644, 649, 655

National Reform Association, 404–405

National Republicans, 175

National Road, 208, 210, 210 (map)

National Science Foundation, 775

National Trades' Union, 403

National Typographical Union, 405

National War Labor Board, 587

National Youth Administration, 652

Nations: growth, 7–11; new, 593, 770

NATO. See North Atlantic Treaty Organization

Naturalization Act, 141, 146

Natural resources: conservation, 517–518, 643, 655; development, 328–329, 668

Nauvoo, Illinois, 235–236

Naval stores, 49, 50

Navies: British, 49, 67, 89, 153, 159, 568, 579, 671–673, 703; Dutch, 703; French, 93, 94, 154, 673; German, 568, 585°; Italian, 673; Japanese, 671, 672, 704, 705, 707; reduction in, 671–673; Russian, 284; Spanish, 154, 479. See also Navy, United States

Navigation Acts, 48–49, 62

Navy, Department of the, 489, 539, 603

Navy, United States, 393, 471, 483°, 530–531°, 532, 571°, 686; in Civil War, 278, 284; in First World War, 579; fleet sent around the world, 549, 550°; and Jefferson, 146–147, 148; Alfred Thayer Mahan on, 468–469; in Mexico, 544–545, 544°, 545°; at Pearl Harbor, 706; in Second World War, 709, 722; in Spanish-American War, 474, 475, 476, 476°, 477°, 478; in War of 1812, 154–155, 159, 159°; in War for Independence, 93

Nazis, 683; expansion, 699; invasion of Soviet Union, 699; in Italy, 714; massed in ceremony, 666–667°; pact with Soviet Union, 699; as war criminals, 745

Nebraska, 260 (map), 450; farmers of, 363; Indians in, 323; settlement, 366

Negroes, 99, 460°, 461°, 558°, 776, 779°; in cities, 775; citizenship 297–298; Civil Rights acts, 302, 781–782, 784; after Civil War, 292, 293; in Civil War, 280; and desegregation, 781–783; discrimination against, 436, 511, 528, 623, 783; emancipation, 280; in exploration, 12, 14, 555; free, before Civil War, 214, 221–222; on frontier, 152, 350n; as indentured servants, 30; and Andrew Johnson, 294; leaders, 149, 511, 782°; movement north, 623, 775; as musicians, 605, 623; in 1920's, 623; organizations, 444, 511, 783; in politics, 300–302, 301, 301°, 372; in progressive period, 511;

and Radical Republicans, 294, 295, 297; during reconstruction, 295, 300–301; riots in cities, 775; runaway, 223, 258, 259*; as slaves, 8, 30, 72, 99, 198, 218, 220–221, 222–223, 223*, 226, 226 (map), 286; and southern codes, 297; struggle for civil rights, 782–783, 782*; and Supreme Court, 264, 781; violence against, 297, 302, 511, 608; and voting, 198, 302, 372, 383; in Vietnam, 761*; in War for Independence, 70, 72, 85. *See also* names of Negroes

Netherlands: colonies in America, 42–49, 42–43*, 45 (map), 60; in Common Market, 767; expansion, 7; independence, 44; and Maine boundary, 197; in NATO, 748; invaded by Nazis, 691; recognized American independence, 95; Separatists in, 33; trade, 44, 46–47, 49; at Washington Conference, 672

Netherlands East Indies, 702

Neutrality: in First World War, 570–571; under Jefferson, 154; F. D. Roosevelt on, 688; in Second World War, 684–685, 690; violations of, 137–138, 153–154, 572–573; Washington's Proclamation of, 136

Neutrality Act: of 1935, 684; of 1936, 684; of 1937, 684–685; of 1939, 690

Neutrals, rights of, 284

Nevada: admitted to Union, 356; atomic testing in, 771; gold in, 355; mining, 356; Populists in, 449

New Amsterdam, 38, 44, 46, 46*, 47*, 49

New Britain, marines on, 696–697*

New Brunswick, 17

New Concord, Ohio, 772

New Deal, 640, 641–643, 649–656; recovery laws, 643–644; reform laws, 645–646; relief measures, 647–650; second, 650–655; and Supreme Court, 655–657

New England, 202–204; colonial towns, 36, 36 (plan); colonists, 35*; commerce, 202; cotton industry, 227; expanding settlements, 62; explored by Champlain, 19; exports, 43; farming, 115, 202–203; fishing, 43; immigrants, 204, 206; industrialization, 200–201; manufacturing, 115; opposed War of 1812, 157, 158; patriots, 84; population, 60; products, 43; and reform movement, 213; settlement, 32–40, 35 (map), 38 (map); slave traders, 218; smuggling, 62; textile industry, 207, 500; trade, 43, 69, 75–76; in War for Independence, 87, 89, 89 (map)

New Englanders, 202

Newfoundland: and Atlantic Charter, 700; bases in, 693; fishing, 16, 67; Gilbert in, 25; settlement, 31; trade, 43

New France, 20*; expansion, 60; lost by France, 67; resources, 19; settlement, 19–20

New Guinea, 709

New Hampshire, 120, 259; colonial, 55–70; manufacturing, 115; prohibition in, 510; ratified Constitution, 122; settlement, 32–39

New Haven, Connecticut, 55, 436

New Inverness, Georgia, 54

New Jersey: and Annapolis Convention, 118; colonial, 53 (map), 55; founding, 50; iron industry, 206, 328; Loyalists in, 82; a middle Atlantic state, 204; name, 50; ratified Constitution, 122; Washington in, 91, 94

New Jersey plan, 120

Newlands Act, 517–518

New Mexico, 238, 735; admitted to Union, 368, 522; ceded, 241; and the Compromise of 1850, 257; and the slavery question, 257

New nationalism, 522

New Netherland, 45–46, 49, 51

New Orleans, Louisiana, 67; Battle of, 160; captured by Union forces, 278; closed to American shipping, 149; cotton prices in, 193; in early 1800's, 149*; founded, 60; growth, 165; immigrants to, 206; musicians in, 605; in Pinckney's treaty, 138; as port, 227–228, 227*; race riots, 298; shipping point, 114, 209

"New South," 320

New Spain, 14–15. *See also* Mexico

Newspapers: and abolition, 214; comic sections, 471n; and Cuba, 471; development of, 246; human-interest stories, 503; importance of, 145; and muckrakers, 503; in old Northwest, 209; quoted, 168, 206, 238, 239, 254, 264, 266, 267, 277, 472, 473, 474, 566, 692, 693; sensationalism in, 471; tabloid, 605, 605n

New Sweden, 46

Newtown, Massachusetts, 38

New World, 11, 12; discovery, 1, 4–5; English claims, 24; Europeans in, 40, 62, 81; exploration, 4–5*; explored by Columbus, 8–9; fishing in, 16; Portuguese claims, 24; Spanish in, 12–14, 17 (map), 24, 168; Spanish culture, 16; in world affairs, 561

New York, New York, 129*, 207*, 407*, 437*, 635*, 636*; bridges, 436, 438; British in, 93; celebration of adoption of Constitution, 123, 123*, 124; Clinton's headquarters, 94; colonial, 55; demon-

stration for 8-hour day, 408*; in 1836, 184–185*; in 1870, 312–313*; in election of 1888, 383; federal jobs, 373–375; as financial center, 132; first elevateds, 435, 436*; growth, 165, 204; help to Boston, 74; housing, 435; immigrants in, 206, 398–399*; Lincoln in, 267–268; market for farm products, 209; Metropolitan Museum of Art, 438; as national capital, 128; railroads, 322; relief payments, 637; riots, 193, 287, 287*; sewage disposal, 434; shipping, 207, 207*; slums, 508, 509*; Stamp Act Congress in, 70; welcome for Lindbergh, 621; world financial center, 668

New York (state), 318*; and Annapolis Convention, 118; child labor in, 500; Erie Canal in, 182*, 210–211; farming, 206; fur trade, 62; iron industry, 206; labor party, 402; land claims, 111; Loyalists in, 82; a middle Atlantic state, 204; name, 49; ratified Constitution, 122; relief in, 648; schools, 213; and steamboat monopoly, 170; in War for Independence, 89–91, 90 (map), 92; in War of 1812, 159; workingmen's parties, 402

New York and Erie Railroad, 211

New York Bay, Verrazano in, 16

New York Central Railroad, 211, 322, 330, 334

New York Stock Exchange, 630–631

New Zealand, 748, 770; member of SEATO, 770

Niagara River, 159, 196

Nicaragua, 267, 531; intervention in, 540; as possible canal route, 532–533, 541; relations with, 674; volcanoes, 533

Nickelodeons, 615–616

Nicolet, Jean (nĕ-kô-lā', zhän), 19

Niger, 563*

Nile River, 762

Nimitz, Chester W., 722

Nine-Power Treaty, 673

Nisei, 729

Nixon, Richard M., 753–754, 768

Nobel Prize for Peace, 548, 740, 782

Nominating convention, national, 198

Nomura, Kichisaburo (nô-mōō-rä, kĕ-chĕ-sä-bōō-rō), 703, 704, 704*, 705

Nonimportation Act, 154

Nonintercourse Act, 155

Norfolk, Virginia, 228, 322

"Normalcy," 601

Norris, Frank, 504

Norris, George W., 520–521, 645

North, 81, 200, 215; abolitionists in, 223; agriculture in, 202–203, 204, 209; canals in, 182*, 210–211;

cities, 204–205, 208; and Civil War, 274–275, 276–278, 286–287; free states of, 256 (map); immigrants in, 205–206, 208; industry in, 203, 203*, 204, 206–207, 263; opposes slavery, 253; railroads, 200–201, 211–212; reform movements, 212–214; and sectionalism, 255–258

North Africa, 712, 762–763, 765 (map)

North America, 100; Dutch settlement in, 44; exploration, 16; in 1763, 66 (map); in 1783, 96 (map)

North Atlantic Treaty, 748–749

North Atlantic Treaty Organization, 748–749, 770

North Carolina, 123, 294, 304; colonial, 16, 25*, 51, 54; freedmen in, 281; land claims, 111; prohibition in, 510; readmitted to Union, 300; secession, 274; and TVA, 645; University of, 213; in War for Independence, 86, 93

North Dakota: admitted to Union, 357; in election of 1896, 453; farm mortgages, 445; Lewis and Clark in, 151; Theodore Roosevelt in, 499

Northern Pacific Railroad, 324, 366, 367, 513

Northern Securities Company, 337, 513–514

North Korea, 749–751, 750 (map)

North Vietnam, 760, 761

Northwest, old, 112 (map), 202, 208–209, 227, 266

Northwestern Alliance, 444

Northwest Ordinance, 113, 254

Northwest Passage, 19, 44

Northwest Territory, 113*; Indians in, 156; organized, 111–112, 112 (map), 113; settlers, 156; slavery issue, 261–262

Norway, 446, 691, 749

Norwegians, in old Northwest, 208–209

Nova Scotia, 63, 90

NRA. See National Recovery Administration

Nuclear fission, 738, 739

Nuclear weapons, 724–725, 739, 769, 770–772, 771*

Nueces River, 238

Nullification: doctrine of, 189; Jackson on, 189; in South Carolina, 189–190

Nürnberg (nürn'bĕrk) trial, 745

NYA. See National Youth Administration

Oahu Island, 393

Oak Ridge, Tennessee, 646

OAS. See Organization of American States

Oberlin, Ohio, 609

Oberlin College, 209

Obregón (ō'brä-gōn'), Alvaro, 675

Occupation zones, in Germany, 744–745

Office of Economic Opportunity, 775

Office of Price Administration, 727–728

Office of Production Management, 727

Ogden, Aaron, 170

Oglethorpe, James, 53

Ohio, 209, 266; admitted to Union, 166n; in election of 1896, 453; farming, 206; newspapers, 209; railroads, 322; schools, 213

Ohio Company, 64, 112

Ohio River: boundary of Northwest Territory, 111; cities on, 208; forts on, 64; in Quebec Act, 74

Ohio Valley: English and French rivalry, 64; farmers, 209; French in, 68; as old West, 232; sheepmen from, 354

Oil, 328*; in Colombia, 676; in Mexico, 676; in Pennsylvania, 267, 328–329; production, 333 (graph); and John D. Rockefeller, 332–334; in Southwest Asia and North Africa, 762, 765 (map)

Okinawa, 722, 724

Oklahoma, 367; admitted to Union, 368; De Soto in, 14; Indian reservations, 343; run on, 367, 368, 368*

"Old Ironsides," 202

Oldsmobiles, 614

Olive Branch Petition, 76

Olney, Richard, 386*, 419

Olney doctrine, 395

Omaha, Nebraska, 323, 448

Omnibus Bill, 357–358

O'Neal, Peggy. See Eaton, Peggy

Onís, Luis de, 167

Ontario, Canada, 159

Ontario, Lake, 19, 60, 62, 66

OPA. See Office of Price Administration

Open-door policy, 484, 486, 488, 548

Open housing, 784

Orchestras, 438–439

Orders in Council, 154, 157

Oregon, 342

Oregon Country, 234, 235 (map); claims to, 167; claims settled, 243; migration to, 233–234; Polk's demands, 238

Oregon Trail, 234, 235 (map)

Organic Act of 1900, 490

Organization of American States, 770

Oriskany, New York, 92

Orlando, Vittorio, 591

Ostend Manifesto, 263

O'Sullivan, John L., 231

Oswald, Lee Harvey, 757

Otis, James, 70

Ottawa River, 60

Outer Mongolia, See Mongolia

Outer space, 772

OVERLORD, 714

Overseers, 222

Owen, Robert, 405

Pacific islands: 391–394, 466–467, 476, 476 (map), 477*, 481–482, 483 (map), 489–490, 492–494, 704–705, 707, 709, 722, 723*; naval bases on, 393, 468

Pacific Northwest, 513–514, 602

Pacific Ocean, 53; American interests in, 152, 388, 392, 484; in American policy, 548–551; discovery, 12; Drake on, 24; Magellan on, 11; reached by Lewis and Clark, 151; before Second World War, 681 (map); in Second World War, 696–697*, 705, 705*, 707*, 708*, 709, 722–725, 722*, 723*, 724; in world affairs, 672–673

Packet ship, 207

Pact of Paris, 674, 680

Page, Walter Hines, 572

Pago Pago, (päng'ō päng'ō), 392

Paine, Thomas, 77; quoted, 58–59, 91

Pakistan, 770

Palmer, A. Mitchell, 606

Palos, Spain, 8, 9*

Panama: canal route, 532–533; explored by Columbus, 8; Republic of, 534; revolt and independence, 534; treaties with, 535, 678, 769

Panama, Isthmus of, 12, 15, 394, 470, 532

Panama Canal, 532–537, 548, 682; choice of routes, 532–533; construction, 535, 535*, 537; control of, 769; excavation for, 464*; French efforts, 394; and Monroe Doctrine, 531; protection of, 539–540, 542; and relations with Colombia, 676

Panama Canal Company, 489n

Panama Canal Zone, 489, 489n, 535, 536, 769

Pan-American conferences, 676

Pan-American Congress, 395

Pan-American Exposition, 498, 498*

Pan-Americanism, 394–395

Pan-American Union, 395

Panic: of 1837, 234, 235, 403; of 1857, 355; of 1869, 303; of 1873, 304, 353; of 1893, 384, 387; of 1907, 516. See also Great Depression

Paper money. See Money

Paratroopers, 715*

Paris, France, 92, 129, 590; liberation of, 718; and peace conference after First World War, 590; saved from German attack, 566; threatened by Germans, 581

Paris, Treaty of: of 1763, 66 (map),

67; of 1783, 96–97, 96 (map); of 1898, 482

Parker, Alton B., 515

Parker, Theodore, 267; quoted, 206

Parliament, English: and colonies, 69–71, 73, 74–76; granted Rhode Island charter, 38; and Pennsylvania, 52, 53

Pasadena, California, 555

Patents, 319; application for, 321*

Patriotism: of expansionists, 157, 468; spirit of, 88, 164, 168; symbols of, 164–165; taught through books, 164

Patriots, 70, 72, 73, 74, 82, 84

Patrons of Husbandry. See Grange

Patroon system, 45

Patton, George S., Jr., 714

Pawtucket, Rhode Island, 316

Payne-Aldrich Tariff, 519–521

Payne Bill, 519

Peace conferences: after First World War, 590–593; after Second World War, 733, 744–745, 744*; after Spanish-American War, 481; at Versailles, 593*. See also Hague Peace Conferences

Peace Corps, 563*, 756

Peace movement, 551–552, 566

Pearl Harbor, Hawaii, 393, 704–706, 704*, 705*

Peary, Robert E., 555

"Peculiar institution," 222, 223–224, 253

Peffer, William A., quoted, 426–427

Peking, China, 6, 487*, 488*, 685

Pendleton Act, 376

Penn, William, 51–52

Pennsylvania, 51–53, 53 (map), 55, 105; and Annapolis Convention, 118; canals, 211; Confederate plans for, 276; farming, 206; iron industry, 206, 207, 266, 328; Loyalists in, 82; manufacturing, 115; a middle Atlantic state, 204; oil in, 267, 322, 328–329; ratified Constitution, 122; state constitution, 83; Stuart's raid, 280; University of, 55; in War for Independence, 91–92, 94; Whisky Rebellion in, 133; workingmen's parties in, 402

Pennsylvania Railroad, 211–212, 322, 334, 335

Pensacola, Florida, 167, 571*

Pension bills, 378

Pensions, 383

People's party. See Populists

Perkins, Frances, 642, 642*

Permanent Court of International Arbitration, 552

Perry, Matthew C., 243, 701

Perry, Oliver Hazard, 159

Pershing, John J., 545, 547*, 580, 581

Persia, 7

Peru, 13, 13*, 676; viceroyalty, 15

Petersburg, Virginia, 283

Petroleum. See Oil

Philadelphia, Pennsylvania, 144–145*; Bank of North America in, 115; celebrating adoption of Constitution, 124; Centennial Exposition in, 306, 394; colonial, 44, 52, 55, 64; Continental Congress in, 74, 76; as financial center, 132; growth, 204; and Knights of Labor, 411; as market for farm products, 209; as national capital, 136; parade of volunteers for Union army, 270–271*; in 1787, 118; railroads, 322; sewage disposal, 434; strikes in, 400, 401; in War for Independence, 91–92, 93, 94

Philadelphia Academy, 55

Philadelphia and Columbia Railroad, 211

Philip II, of Spain, 24

Philippine Islands, 7, 492*, 548, 723*; Allied landing, 722; as American possession, 466, 467, 482; British capture, 67; captured by Japanese, 707; Drake in, 24; government of, 489, 492–493; independence, 494; member of SEATO, 770; rebellion in, 492; after Spanish-American War, 481–482; war in, 476 (map)

Phillips, David Graham, 504

Phonograph, 457

Photography, 457

Picketing, 417, 417n

Pickett, Bill, 350

Pickett, George E., 281

Pickford, Mary, 616

Pierce, Franklin, 259–260, 261

Pike, Zebulon Montgomery, 151

Pike's Peak, 342, 355

Pilgrims, 33–34. See also Separatists

Pillsbury, Charles A., 336

Pinchot, Gifford, 520

Pinckney, Charles C., 140, 142

Pinckney, Thomas, 138–139

Pingree, Hazen S., 504

Pinkerton, Allan, 416–418; detectives, 416*, 417*

Pioneers. See Westward movement

Pitt, William, 65, 67, 70–71, 92; quoted, 89. See also Chatham, Earl of

Pittsburgh, Pennsylvania, 165; American Federation of Labor organized, 413; bridge, 438; Carnegie in, 334; first radio station, 617; name, 66; railroads, 322; riots in railroad strike, 410

Pittsburg Landing, Tennessee, 277–278

Pizarro, Francisco, 13

Plains Indians, 342–348, 343*, 347*

Plains of Abraham, Battle of, 67

Plantations: colonial, 32, 50–51, 216; cotton, 216–217, 216–217*; disappearance of, 429; slaves on, 216–217*, 220–222

Platt Amendment, 489, 538, 678

Platte River, 234

Plymouth, Massachusetts, 32–34

Plymouth Company, 26–27, 32, 34

Pocahontas, 28

Point Four, 743

Poison gas, 568

Poland, 688 (map); Communists in, 734, 746; defeated and occupied, 690; after First World War, 593; Germans in, 688, 689*; and Yalta Conference, 733

Political dissent, right of, 778–779

Political parties: beginnings, 135; after Civil War, 372; need for, 269. See also names of parties

Politicians: after Civil War, 370–371, 372–375, 376*, 377–378, 383–384; Clay as type of, 157; corruption and, 302–304, 304 (cartoon), 372, 500, 503; "gentlemen," 469; insurgents, 520; Lincoln and, 293–294; viewed by public, 338, 502–503

Politics: abolition and, 214; and John Adams, 139–141; and business, 294, 303, 331, 332, 333*, 334–338, 372, 504; and Civil War, 286–287, 370–371, 372; and farmers, 442–443, 444–446, 447–455; and foreign policy, 396, 589–590; "Grantism," 302–303, 372–373; influence of foreign affairs on, 135; international, 397, 785; and labor, 402–403, 414; Negroes in, 300–302, 301*, 372; party bosses in, 439, 439*; political liberty, 181; power of voters in, 198, 502; and progressive movement, 497, 504–506, 506*; public interest in, 197–198; and reconstruction, 293–299, 300–304; relation between domestic and foreign affairs, 399; Franklin D. Roosevelt in, 638–641, 649–650, 657, 662–663; sectional parties in, 267–268; "slack-water," 371; and slavery issue, 172–173, 173 (map), 254–258, 259–263, 264–268; slogans in, 194, 238, 263, 576; in South, 300–302; spoils system in, 197, 198, 506; and states' rights issue, 189–190; techniques of, 194–195, 195*, 198, 506; "waving the bloody shirt," 304, 304n. See also names of parties

Polk, James K., 238–243; quoted, 254

Polygamy, 236

Ponce de León, Juan, 12–13

Pontiac, 68, 68*

Pools, business, 330

Popular sovereignty, 260, 261, 264, 266

Population: and admission of states, 113; of American cities, 165 (table), 205 (table), 319 (table), 433n, 434, 496, 604 (table), 776 (table); of California, 244; of colonies, 60; in 1820's, 178; growth, 165, 204–206, 245, 818 (table); of North, 274–275; of old Northwest, 209; proportion of slaves, 226 (map), 271; rural, 428, 633–634; of South, 274–275; of West, 364, 366–367

Populists, 384, 447–448, 448*, 449–450, 451, 454, 502, 664

Portage Railroad, 211

Porter, David D., 278

Portsmouth, New Hampshire, 548

Portsmouth, Treaty of, 548

Portugal, 7–8, 9–10, 24, 46, 48, 672, 749

Postal savings banks, 522

Post Office Department, 619

Post offices, 165–166

Potomac River, 28, 31, 117, 117*, 279

Potsdam Conference, 736, 744–745, 744*

Pottawatomie Creek, Kansas, 262

Poverty, war on, 775

Powderly, Terence V., 411, 413

Presidency, 128–129, 198, 663

President: powers of, 121, 198; term of office, 121, 754. See also names of Presidents

Prices, 86, 87, 429, 430, 445, 727–728, 740

Primary, direct, 505

Primogeniture, 84

Princeton, New Jersey, 91

Princeton University, 55, 119, 523, 524, 528

Privateers, 87

Proclamation Line of 1763, 66 (map), 68–69

Products: during Civil War, 286, 287, 318–319; colonial, 28, 40, 49, 50, 55, 69, 70; dairy, 202; farm, 40, 202, 209, 219–221, 349, 431, 633–634; after First World War, 612–614, 623, 688; manufactured, 174, 316, 319, 329–330, 335–336, 346, 363–364, 612–615, 612*, 613*; markets for, 209, 212, 228, 327, 334; of middle Atlantic states, 204–206; mineral, 206, 244, 335–337, 366; of Pennsylvania, 407; of postwar Europe, 668–669, 668*, 669*, 670; of Southwest Asia and North Africa, 762; strategic, 727

Profit motive, 650

Progressive movement: and American life, 510–511, 528; and foreign policy, 528, 555; and muckrakers, 503–504; nature of, 500, 502; and politics, 504–506, 516–518; reaction to, 603–604; reforms, 504–506, 508, 528; Theodore Roosevelt and, 512–518, 513*; and social betterment, 506, 508; and Wilson, 525–528

Progressives (party), 496–497*, 497,

522, 624; of 1948, 742

Prohibition, 609, 610, 611, 647

Project Mercury, 772

Promontory Point, Utah, 324

Proprietary colony, 31, 32, 50

Protestants, 24, 31, 44, 257

Providence, Rhode Island, 37–38, 72, 497

Public credit, 131–132

Public domain, 111–112, 355

Public housing, 741

Public land, 187–188, 191–192

Public libraries, 439

Public schools, 213, 246. See also Education

Public Works Administration, 644

Pueblo, Colorado, 595

Puerto Ricans, 491, 560*, 777

Puerto Rico, 12, 466, 467, 479, 481, 482; as Commonwealth, 492; government, 489, 490–492; and Panama Canal, 532

Pulaski, Casimir, 93

Pullman, George, 326–327, 418, 419

Pullman Company, strike at, 418–419, 421

Punta del Este, Uruguay, 769

Pure Food and Drug Act, 517

Puritans, 34–37, 35 (map), 37*, 38, 48

Put in Bay, Battle of, 159

PWA. See Public Works Administration

Quakers, 51–52, 218

Quebec, Canada, 19, 66–67, 90; province, 17, 20, 66, 66 (map), 74

Quebec Act, 74

Quota acts, 605–606

RA. See Resettlement Administration

Race relations: after Civil War, 302; and Supreme Court, 777; today, 784

Radar, 739

Radical Republicans, 293–299, 300, 303

Radicals: in Continental Congress, 74; fear of, 606, 607; and slavery, 258; before War for Independence, 75, 76; in War for Independence, 83

Radio, 605, 616, 617, 624*

Railroads, 318*, 322–328, 323*, 324*; benefits of, 327, 328, 349–350, 366; building of, 211–212, 212 (map), 228, 318, 322, 322 (map), 323–324, 326 (map), 349–350; and cattle, 349–350, 350*; charters, 442; in Chicago, 433; in Confederacy, 285; consolidation, 211; about 1850, 200–201, 200–201*; in 1860, 212 (map); employees, 324, 528; ex-

pansion, 327; and farmers, 430–431, 442; federal aid, 323–324; government management, 587; improvements, 326–327; main eastern in 1875, 322 (map); in Manchuria, 551; and national markets, 407; need for after Civil War, 322; in North, 211–212, 286; oil shipments, 333, 334; rates, 516–517; strikes, 409–411, 419, 421; transcontinental, 294, 323–326, 325*, 326 (map); trunk lines, 322, 322 (map). See also names of railroads

Raleigh, Sir Walter, 23, 25–26, 25 (map)

Randolph, Edmund, 120, 133

Rappahannock River, 28, 281

Reaper, 364, 365*

Rebates, 332, 334

Recall, 505

Reciprocal-trade program, 678, 678n

Reciprocity agreement, with Canada, 521, 521n

Reconstruction, 290–302, 304; end of, 304–306

Reconstruction Finance Corporation, 633, 637

Red Cross, 637

Rediscount rate, 527

Referendum, 505

Reform movement, 212–214, 225

Religion: changes during War for Independence, 84–85; in colonies, 31, 40, 84–85, 99; in election of 1928, 624; in election of 1960, 755–756; freedom of, 37–38, 52; in Maryland, 32; in New England, 32, 33, 34–37; in Pennsylvania, 51–52; of Quakers, 52; and reform movement, 213; Washington on, 139; and westward movement, 234–236

Religious toleration: in Connecticut, 39; in Maryland, 32; in Massachusetts, 36; in Northwest Territory, 113; in Pennsylvania, 51–52; during Revolution, 84–85; in Rhode Island, 37–38

Remagen, bridge at, 719

Rent ceilings, 728

Reparations, 589, 593

Report on Manufactures, 133–134

Republican National Committee, 453

Republicans: after Civil War, 293–300, 301–306; during Civil War, 280; in election of 1856, 263; in election of 1860, 267–268; in election of 1864, 287–288; in election of 1868, 300; in election of 1872, 303–304; in election of 1876, 304–305, 373; in election of 1880, 375; in election of 1884, 377–378; in election of 1888, 382–383; in election of 1892, 384; in election of 1896, 449–453; in election of 1900, 484; in election of 1904,

515; in election of 1908, 519; in election of 1912, 523; in election of 1916, 576–577; in election of 1920, 600–601; in election of 1924, 624–625; in election of 1928, 625; in election of 1932, 639–641; in election of 1936, 657–659; in election of 1940, 692; in election of 1944, 729–730; in election of 1948, 742–743; in election of 1952, 752–753; in election of 1956, 754; in election of 1960, 754–756; in election of 1964, 774; old guard, 519; organized in 1854, 262; and slave issue, 262, 263, 265–268; supporters, 372; and Washington Conference, 672–673. *See also* Radical Republicans

Republicans, (of early 1800's), 135; in Adams' administration, 139–140, 141; divided in Monroe's administration, 171–172; in 1834, 192; and Federalist policies, 171; under Monroe, 171; opposition to Jay's treaty, 138; policies of, 146–147; in power, 146–161; problems, 155. *See also* Democratic-Republicans

Resettlement Administration, 652, 653*

Reuther, Walter P., 781

Revere, Paul, 76

RFC. *See* Reconstruction Finance Corporation

Rhine River, 44, 719

Rhode Island, 37–38, 52, 55, 85, 115, 116, 120n, 123

Rice, 49, 50–51, 55–56, 217, 218, 219

Richmond, Virginia, 227, 228, 274, 275, 278–279, 290–291*, 322, 436

Riis, Jacob, 508; quoted, 532

Rio Grande, 238, 240, 242

Rio Pact, 768

Ripon, Wisconsin, 262

Roads: early 1800's, 162–163*; macadamized, 205; need for, 162–163; in North, 209–210; Roman, 6. *See also* National Road

Roanoke Island, 25

Rochambeau, Jean Baptiste, 94

Rockefeller, John D., 332–334

Rockets, 739

Rockingham, Marquis of, 70, 95

Rock Island, Illinois, 264

Rocky Mountains, 151–152, 342

Roebling, John A., 436, 438

R.O.K. *See* Korea

Rolfe, John, 28

Romania, 566, 733, 746

Rome, Italy, 714

Rome-Berlin Axis, 698n

Rome-Berlin-Tokyo Axis, 698n

Roosevelt, Eleanor, 639, 640*, 659, 683, 727*

Roosevelt, Franklin D., 625, 639*, 641*, 657*, 677, 706*, 712*, 714*, 727*, 730*, 744*; and the arms embargo, 688, 690; and Atlantic Charter, 700, 700*; in Buenos Aires, 678, 678*, 679, 679*; Cabinet, 642, 642*; candidate for vice-presidency, 600; death of, 734–735; elected to second term, 657, 658; elected to third term, 692, 693–694; elected to fourth term, 729–730; in election of 1932, 639–640, 640*; as governor of New York, 634, 635, 638; in history, 663; New Deal, 641–660, 662–663; plans for peace, 731; policies in Asia, 701–702; and poliomyelitis, 639; "quarantine speech," 685–686; quoted, 628–629, 650, 694, 716; reaction to aggression in Europe, 688; reaction to Munich agreement, 687; second term, 659–663; State of the Union Message, 691

Roosevelt, Theodore, 146n, 421, 478*, 498*, 514*, 515*, 516*, 550*, 639; in Africa, 519; as Assistant Secretary of the Navy, 473, 473*, 474; in Canal Zone, 536; and conservation, 517–518; early career, 499; in election of 1900, 484; in election of 1904, 514–515; in election of 1912, 521–523; in election of 1916, 577, 577n; and First World War, 572; and imperialism, 469, 482; and Japanese-Russian War, 548; as leader of Progressives, 521–523; and Panama Canal, 532; and panic of 1907, 516; preparations for war, 474; as President, 337–338, 500; quoted, 338, 484, 496–497, 516, 537, 538, 552, 590; return to politics, 521–522; second term, 515–518; in Spanish-American War, 478–479

Roosevelt corollary, 538, 543, 664, 674, 677

Root, Elihu, 549, 553

Root-Takahira Agreement, 549

Ross, Edmund G., quoted, 299, 299n

Rough Riders, 478–479, 478*

Royal Air Force, 712

Ruffin, Edmund, 274n, 292

Rule of 1756, 153

Rum, 55, 69

Rural Electrification Administration, 652

Rush, Benjamin, 88; quoted, 124

Rusk, Dean, 756

Russia: and China, 486; claims to Oregon country, 233; collapse of, 588; communism in, 605; Czar of, 552; relations with in Civil War, 284–285; in Seven Years' War, 65. *See also* Soviet Union

Russian Revolution, 569, 593, 607

Russo-Japanese War, 680, 734

Rutledge, Edward, 74, 90

Sabotage, 416

SAC. *See* Strategic Air Command

Sacajawea (sä-kä′jä-wä′à), 151

Sacco-Vanzetti case, 607, 607*

Sacramento, California, 243, 323

St. Augustine, Florida, 13, 20, 54

St. Lawrence River, 16, 17, 18, 18 (map), 19, 20, 60, 62, 90

St. Leger, Barry, 91, 92

St. Louis, Missouri, 151, 322, 343, 349, 410, 438, 438*, 444, 450

St. Marys, Maryland, 31

St. Mihiel, France, 582

St. Paul, Minnesota, 438

St. Pierre Island, 67

Saipan, 708*, 709

Sakhalin, 630, 734

"Salary Grab" Act, 303

Salem, Massachusetts, 37, 37*

Salem, Peter, 76

Salomon, Haym, 85

Sam, Villbrun Guillaume, 541–542

Samoan Islands, 392, 392 (map)

Sampson, William T., 476, 477, 478, 479

San Antonio, Texas, 323

Sanford, John F. A., 264

San Francisco, California, 238, 325*, 437*; and founding of UN, 735; schools and Japanese children, 549

San Jacinto, Battle of, 237

San Salvador, 5

Santa Anna, Antonio, 237, 240

Santa Fe Railroad, 324, 366

Santiago, Chile, 676

Santiago, Battle of, 463, 479*

Santiago de Cuba, Cuba, 115, 478, 479

Santo Domingo, 149. *See also* Dominican Republic

Sarajevo, Bosnia, 566

Saratoga, New York, 92, 95

Satellites, 772

Saudi Arabia, 762n

Savannah, Georgia, 53, 228, 219–220, 322

Savannah River, 53, 54, 228

Scabs, 418

Scalawags, 300

Schley, Winfield, 463, 478

Schlieffen plan, 566

School District of Abington Township v. *Schempp*, 778

Schools, 509*; colonial, 36; and Negroes, 781–782; technical, 316. *See also* Education

Schurz, Carl, quoted, 290–291; 373, 374, 389, 389*

Schuylkill River, 52

Science, 738–740, 772–773

Scioto Company, 112

Scopes trial, 608–609

Scotch-Irish, 68, 82

Scott, Dred, 264

Scott, Thomas A., 334–335

Scott, Winfield, 197, 240–241, 259, 276, 278

Seaborg, Glenn T., quoted, 738–740
Seas, freedom of, 153–155, 156, 160, 572–575
SEATO. See Southeast Asia Treaty Organization
Secession, 189, 257, 271
Sectionalism, 173–175, 187, 247, 249
Securities and Exchange Commission, 646
Securities Exchange Act, 646
Security, national: collective, 673–674, 682, 688, 694, 748–749, 750, 757; and foreign policy, 743, 746–748, 757, 763–764, 767; and world problems, 686, 743
Security Council, 736
Sedan-Mézières Railroad, 584
Sedition Act, 141
Selective Service Act, 579
Self-government: colonial, 1, 28–29, 32, 34, 36, 37, 39, 40, 52, 69–73, 78, 99; and Constitution, 115, 117–118, 119–122, 123, 124; and Latin America, 537–538, 541–542, 543; in overseas possessions, 489–494; in South, 286, 300–302; state, 83–84. See also Government
Seminary Ridge, 281
Seminole Indians, 166–167, 367
Senate, 475*; business interests in, 383, 384*; of 1849, 256; election of Senators, 120, 505; foreign relations committee, 594; opposition to Treaty of Versailles, 594–595; and Paris Treaty of 1898, 482; powers of, 121; seniority in, 520; and slave-free balance, 172 (map), 173; and slavery issue, 255–258, 261, 262–263; and trial of Andrew Johnson, 299. See also names of Senators
Seneca Falls, New York, 213
Seneca Oil Company, 328
Separation of powers, 124
Separatists, 32–33, 52
Serbia, 566n
Servicemen's Readjustment Act, 740n
Settlement houses, 508, 509*
Seven Years' War, 65–67. See also French and Indian War
Sewage disposal, 434–435
Seward, William H., 256, 267, 274, 280; and Alaska, 389–390; and Compromise of 1850, 258; and foreign affairs, 389; quoted, 252–253, 261–262
Seymour, Horatio, 300–303
Shafter, William, 478
SHAPE. See Supreme Headquarters of the Allied Powers in Europe
Sharecropping, 429–430
Shawnee Mission, Kansas, 261
Shays' Rebellion, 116–117, 116*, 122, 144, 145
Sheepmen, 354–355

Shelburne, Lord, 95
Shenandoah Valley, 278–279
Shepard, Alan B., Jr., 770
Sheridan, Philip H., 344
Sherman, Roger, 82, 128
Sherman, William T., 281, 282, 292, 344
Sherman Antitrust Act, 331, 337, 383, 422, 513, 527, 643, 663
Sherman Silver Purchase Act, 383, 387, 445, 449
Shiloh, Battle of, 278
Shipbuilding, 587
Shipping: and blockades, 153–155, 275, 573–575; and embargo, 154–155; middle Atlantic states, 207–208; in Second World War, 700–701; southern, 228, 275
Shoemakers, 401, 402*, 405, 406*
Shoshone Indians, 151
Sicily, 713*, 714
"Sick-chicken" case, 655
Siemens-Martin process, 329
Silk, 53–54
Silver, 7, 12, 13, 15, 16, 26–27; in California and Nevada, 356; and campaign of 1896, 449–455; coinage, 445–446, 448, 449–450; demonetization of, 446; in depression of 1893, 387; politics and, 387, 445–446, 449–455; Sherman Silver Purchase Act, 387, 450; Specie Circular and, 191–192
Simpson, Jerry, 447
Sinclair, Harry F., 603
Sinclair, Upton, 504, 517
Single tax, 502
Sioux Falls, South Dakota, 367
Sioux Indians, 343, 345, 366
"Sit-ins," 782
Sitting Bull, 345, 346*
Skyscrapers, 435
Slater, Samuel, 316
Slavery, 100, 252–253; abolished in British Empire, 197; and abolition movement, 213–214, 223, 225, 271; and annexation of Texas, 237; beginnings in America, 30, 218; and the cotton gin, 219–221; forbidden in Northwest Territory, 113; in Carolina, 50; codes, 222–223; defenders of, 216–217, 223–224, 225; and Democrats, 254–255, 267; in District of Columbia, 280; effect of Revolution on, 85; in 1860, 267; extension, 254, 255–256, 260–262, 265–266, 267; as issue in Congress, 254, 255–261, 262–263, 265; Jefferson and, 111; Lincoln on, 266, 268, 273; in Massachusetts, 85; in Missouri, 172–173; and plantation system, 225–226, 429; and politics, 172–173, 254–255, 257, 258, 260–261, 263; Republicans and, 262, 263, 265–268; social and economic results of, 189; and states'

rights, 189; system, 222–226; Supreme Court decision on, 264; Thirteenth Amendment, 297; and George Washington, 128; in West, 244; in West Indies, 50. See also Abolitionists
Slaves, 29*, 30*, 216–217*, 223*, 225*; in Age of Jackson, 198; attitude toward slavery, 226; during Civil War, 286; in colonies, 30, 50, 218; and cotton production, 216–217, 219–221, 227–228; counted for representation and taxing, 120; in 1850, 221, 226 (map); emancipation, 280; freed in British Empire, 229; life of, 223–224; manumission, 218; on plantations, 222; in population, 271; as property, 226, 264; runaway, 223, 259*; sale of, 50*, 226, 252–253*
Slave trade, 120, 197, 218, 257, 271; English, 30, 62, 114; French, 67; Portuguese, 8; Spanish, 15, 30, 55, 62; triangular, 55
Slidell John W., 238
Sloat, John D., 240
Slums, 435, 507*, 508, 508*, 652, 741
Small-state plan, 120
Smith, Adam, quoted, 49
Smith, Alfred E., 624, 625–626, 649n, 670, 755
Smith, Hyrum, 236
Smith, Jedediah, 152
Smith, John, 27, 28, 32–33; map of Virginia by, 2
Smith, Joseph, 234–236
Smith, Robert, 155
Smith Act, 778–779
Smith-Connally Anti-Strike Act. See War Labor Disputes Act
Smog, 777
Smuggling, 62, 154
SNCC. See Student Non-Violent Coordinating Committee
Socialism, 414, 414n, 424, 606
Social justice, 502, 506, 508, 528
Social reform, 457; government help in, 506, 508; and the Great Society, 774–775; and the middle class, 502; and Negroes, 511, 528; and the progressives, 500–502, 506–510; and the Supreme Court, 777–782; and Wilson, 528
Social Security Act, 650–651, 741, 754, 775
Sod house, 362–363, 362*
Soil Conservation and Domestic Allotment Act, 655
Solid South, 292, 372–373, 626
Solomon Islands, 709
Sons of Liberty, 70
Soo Canal, 328
Soulé, Pierre, 263
South, 216–229; after Civil War, 292–293, 320; in Civil War, 272, 275, 283, 285–286; colonial, 28,

30, 32, 50–51, 53–54, 55–56, 60, 84; commerce of, 227–228; Confederacy, 272, 285–286; and the cotton gin, 219–221; differences with North, 187–190, 249, 252–253, 254–260, 262–263, 264, 268; farming, 115, 219, 429–430, 441–442; industry, 222, 227; opposed protective tariffs, 174, 175; population in 1850, 220–221; railroads, 228, 285, 322; and reconstruction, 290–302; and slavery, 213, 216–219, 224–225; social organization in, 220–223, 290–291; and states' rights, 187–188, 286; in War for Independence, 93–94, 94 (maps); and War of 1812, 157

South Carolina, 51, 54; in Civil War, 300; cotton industry, 227; in election of 1948, 742; indigo and rice plantations, 218; land claims, 111; Loyalists in, 82; ratified Constitution, 122; readmitted to Union, 300; reconstruction government, 301; secession, 272; slavery in, 217, 224; state constitution, 83–84; and states' rights, 189–190; in war with French, 64; in War for Independence, 93–94

South Carolina College, 225

South Dakota, 357, 367, 505

Southeast Asia, 757, 760–762, 760 (map); Communists in, 757, 760–762

Southeast Asia Treaty Organization, 770

Southern Alliance, 444, 447

Southern Railway, 322

South Korea, 750, 750 (map)

South Manchurian Railroad, 548, 551, 680

South Pass, 152, 234

South Vietnam, 757, 760–762, 760 (map)

Southwest, 14, 15

Southwest Asia, 762, 763, 765 (map); activity of Soviet Union in, 764, 765; Arab-Israeli war, 762–763, 765, 765 (map); in First World War, 568

Souvanna Phouma, 760

Soviet Union, 731; activities in Southwest Asia and North Africa, 762; and Africa south of the Sahara, 770; aggressions, 688 (map), 690; and China, 680, 745; and cold war, 735, 746; communism in, 744; and Cuban crisis, 769; in East Asia, 749–750, 761; expansion, 688 (map), 746; after First World War, 682; and Germany, 745, 766–767; industrialization, 752; and Korea, 749–750; and Marshall Plan, 748; and nuclear weapons, 749, 771; relations with United States, 680, 682, 771; in Second World War, 690, 699, 719; space explorations, 772; in

United Nations, 736; in world affairs, 757, 771; at Yalta Conference, 734

Space, outer, 772–773

Spain, 5, 7, 15, 47; as ally of France, 92, 114; bid for western lands, 114; civil war in, 694; claims in New World, 9–10, 24, 233; colonies of, 14–16, 17 (map), 44, 56, 60, 62, 168; and England, 24, 26, 48, 53, 54; expansion, 7, 8–9; explorations of, 11, 12–14; and Florida, 54, 97, 167; John Jay in, 95; loss of Mexico, 236; in Louisiana, 148; and the Netherlands, 44; Pinckney's treaty with, 138–139; relations during Confederation, 114; in Seven Years' War, 67; and *Virginius* affair, 470–471

Spanish: in America, 12–16, 23, 25–26, 54; culture in New World, 16; in West Indies, 42

Spanish-American War, 463, 468–480, 477*, 532; peace terms, 481

Specie Circular, 191–192

Speculation, 622, 630

Spice Islands. See Moluccas

Spirit of St. Louis, 620

Spoilsmen, 302–303

Spoils system, 374

Spokane, Washington, 594

Sports, 462*, 555, 619

Spotsylvania Court House, 282

Springfield, Illinois, 267*, 268

Sputnik, 772

Square deal, 512, 640

Squatter sovereignty, 255. See also Popular sovereignty

Stalin, Joseph, 731–732, 736, 744*

Stalwarts, 373–374, 375

Stamp Act, 69–70

Stamp Act Congress, 70

Standard of living, 249, 599–600, 622

Standard Oil Company, 330–331, 333*, 334, 503, 504

Stanton, Edwin M., 278, 299

Stanton, Elizabeth Cady, 213

"The Star-Spangled Banner," 160

State, Department of, 455, 531, 574, 578, 752

State, Secretary of: John Quincy Adams as, 167, 168, 174; Bryan as, 572, 575; Clay as, 175; Dulles, 762, 763*; Evarts as, 373; Fish as, 389; Hughes as, 601*, 602, 672, 672*, 673; Hull as, 642, 642*, 666–667; Jefferson as, 129, 130, 131; Lansing as, 575; Madison as, 146, 149, 155; Marshall as, 745, 747, 747*; Rusk as, 756; Seward as, 388, 389, 390; Smith as, 155; Stimson as, 680; Van Buren as, 186; Webster as, 195, 196

Staten Island, 90

States: admitted to Union, 166,

166n; under Articles of Confederation, 110; constitutions, 83; creation of new, 111; debts of, 131, 132; and federal government, 121, 169–170; governments, 84; powers of, 170; and reconstruction, 298, 300–302; relations among, 115; and Supreme Court, 169–170; during War for Independence, 83; and western lands, 111. See also names of states; States' rights

States' rights, 142; in Confederacy, 286; conflict over, 141–142, 187–189; and public land, 187–188; supported by Democrats, 373; and Supreme Court, 169–170

Statue of Liberty, 380*, 381*, 398–399*, 424, 424*

Statute of Religious Freedom, 84–85

Stay laws, 116

Steamboats, 165, 227*

Steamships, 207, 336

Steel industry, 318, 329–330, 330 (graph)

Steffens, Lincoln, 504

Stephens, Alexander, 244, 297

Stephens, Uriah S., 410*, 411

Stephenson, George, 211

Steuben, Friedrich Von, 93

Stevens, John, 211

Stevens, Thaddeus, 295, 295*, 297, 299

Stevenson, Adlai, 752–753, 754, 756

Stimson doctrine, 680

Stock market, 336, 630–631, 646, 647

Stock-market exchanges, 630, 636

Stockton, Robert F., 240

Stockyards, 433, 433*

Stone, Harlan F., quoted, 656

Stowe, Harriet Beecher, 214, 258–259, 262

Strasser, Adolph, 413

Strategic Air Command, 738–739*, 770

Strict construction, of Constitution, 133, 150

Strikes: and AFL, 416; in automobile industry, 654; early nineteenth century, 403; Homestead, 416*, 417–418, 417*; and Knights of Labor, 411; McCormick reaper works, 412; Pullman, 418; railroad, 387, 409–410; after Second World War, 741; shoemakers', 401. See also Labor

Strong, Josiah, 468

Stuart, J. E. B., 275–280

Student Non-Violent Coordinating Committee, 783

Stuyvesant, Peter, 46, 47*, 49

Submarines: in First World War, 564n, 565*, 568, 573–575; and international law, 574; in Second World War, 699, 709

Suburbs, 436, 776

Suez Canal, 431, 762–763
Suffrage: in Age of Jackson, 197; for freedmen, 297; for women, 505–506, 506*
Suffragettes, 506, 506*
Sugar, 16, 43, 49, 55, 62, 69, 384, 393, 515
Sugar Act, 69, 70
Sumner, Charles, 295, 295*, 389, 390; quoted, 262–263
Superior, Lake, 62, 114, 328
Supreme Court: attacked by F. D. Roosevelt, 660–661; and Dred Scott case, 264; and Marbury case, 148; and John Marshall, 169–170; and New Deal, 655; powers of, 121, 169–170; and school desegregation, 781; and slavery, 264; and states' rights, 194–195; and trusts, 513–514, 516; Warren Court, 777–779, 778*. See also Chief Justices
Supreme Headquarters of the Allied Powers in Europe, 749
Sussex pledge, 575
Sutter, John A., 243–244
Sweden, 46, 53, 65, 446
Swift, Gustavus, 336
Switzerland, 446
Sylvis, William, 408
Symbols, national, 164–165
Syria, 762n, 765

Tacna-Arica (tak'-ná-á-rē'ká) dispute, 676
Taft, Robert A., 692, 753, 754
Taft, William Howard, 519*, 522, 524*; as Chief Justice, 521n; in election of 1908, 519; in election of 1912, 522; and foreign affairs, 540–541, 543, 549; as governor of Philippines, 492–493; as President, 519–521, 605; quoted, 530–531; as Secretary of War, 548; and tariff, 519
Taft-Hartley Act, 741, 742
Taft-Katsura Agreement, 548
Taiwan (Formosa), 680, 745
Talleyrand, 140, 149, 186n
Tallmadge, James, 172–173
Tammany Hall, 377, 626
Tampa, Florida, 478
Tampico (tăm-pē'kō), Mexico, 544–545
Taney, Roger B., 191, 264, 272–273
Tanks, 568, 718*, 719*
Tarbell, Ida M., 504, 607
Tariff, 316; of Abominations, 175; American system, 174, 175; during Civil War, 272, 286, 294, 319; under Cleveland, 379, 382, 384; commission, 603; and Common Market, 767, 781; compromise of 1833, 189–190; of 1816, 171; of 1828, 189; of 1832, 188, 189; of 1842, 195; in 1850's, 266; election of 1888, 379, 382–383, 382

(cartoon), 383 (cartoon); and farmers, 174, 519, 520, 603; Fordney-McCumber, 603, 670; Hamilton and, 133–134; Hawley-Smoot, 603, 670; McKinley, 383–384, 387, 393; and manufacturers, 171, 174, 382 (cartoon), 670; Morrill, 286; Payne-Aldrich, 519–521; protective, 134, 171, 174, 189–190, 371, 382 (cartoons), 387, 669; reciprocal, 521, 678, 781; under Trade Agreements Act, 678; Underwood-Simmons, 526; and war debts, 670; Wilson-Gorman, 387, 471. See also Trade; tariffs by name
Taxes: after Civil War, 301, 432; during Civil War, 286; colonial, 15, 45, 52, 69, 70–71, 73; on concentrations of wealth, 652–653, 654; by Congress, 120, 124, 158–159; and Constitution, 120, 124; for education, 213; excise, 133; and farmers, 116–117, 116*, 133, 432; for general welfare, 655; Hamilton on, 133; on income, 411, 446, 454, 492, 526, 780; Jefferson and, 146; and L. B. Johnson, 780; for Korean War, 753; on liquor, 647; national, 110, 129, 132; payroll, 650; processing, 644, 655; for regulation of wages and hours, 656; after Second World War, 646, 754, 777, 780; in Second World War, 726; single, 502; and Stamp Act, 69–70, 71; and states, 132, 170; and Sugar Act, 69; for unemployment insurance, 650
Taylor, Zachary, 239, 240, 254, 255, 258
Tea, 71, 72, 285
Tea Act, 73
Teachers, 221, 308, 509*, 558*
Teapot Dome, 603
Technology, 99; advances in, 99, 178, 205, 219, 316, 326, 428, 780–781; effects of, 205, 311, 457, 781; in exploration of space, 772–773; influence on cities, 205; technical skills, 316. See also Electronics; Machinery
Tecumseh, 156
Tehran Conference, 732–733
Telegraph, 238, 246, 318, 431
Telephone, 320, 432, 436, 634, 731
Television, 742n, 755, 756
Teller Amendment, 475, 489
Temperance, 304, 510, 609. See also Prohibition
Tenant farming. See Farmers
Tenements, 435, 435 (diagram), 501*, 780*
Tennessee: in Civil War, 276; constitutional convention, 224; freedmen in, 221; Hayes in, 305; and Jackson, 167, 186; politics, 304; secession of, 274; teaching of evo-

lution prohibited, 608–609; and TVA, 645
Tennessee River, 114, 275, 276, 277, 645–646
Tennessee Valley Authority, 645–646, 664
Tenure of Office Act, 299
Territories and Island Possessions, Division of, 489
Texas, 14, 162, 236–237, 304; admitted to Union, 220, 238; annexation of, 243; boundary, 257; cattle-raising, 349, 352, 353; in Civil War, 281; and Compromise of 1850, 257; readmitted to Union, 300; secession of, 272
Texas and Pacific Railroad, 324
Textile industry, 49, 203–204, 207, 623
Textile mills, 204, 500, 500*, 527*
Thailand, 702, 760, 760 (map), 770
Thant, U, 765
Thayer, Eli, 261
Thomas, George H., 276
Thomas, Jesse B., 173
Thoreau, Henry David, quoted, 200–201
"Three-fifths" clause, 120, 297, 792, 806
Thurmond, J. Strom, 742
Tibet, 762
Tilden, Samuel J., 304
Tillman, Benjamin, 445, 447
Tippecanoe, Battle of, 156, 192
Titusville, Pennsylvania, 328–329
Tobacco, 26, 28, 29*, 31–32, 43, 46–47, 48, 49, 55, 115, 218, 219, 462*, 515*
Tocqueville, Alexis de, quoted, 311–312
Tojo, Hideki (tō-jō, hĕ-dĕ-kĕ), 703, 745
Tokyo, Japan, 549, 703, 708, 725, 820 (table)
Toledo, Ohio, 137, 208, 504, 635, 637
Toleration, Act of, 32
Topeka Constitution, 261
Tordesillas, Treaty of, 9–10, 11
Tories. See Loyalists
Town meeting, 36–37, 38
Townsend, Francis E., 650
Townshend Act, 70, 71
Township, 36–37, 111, 112 (map)
Town system, in New England, 36, 36 (plan), 38
Trade: boycotts, 70, 71, 75, 154–155, 160; with Britain, 135, 136, 154, 155, 157, 219, 572–573; British, 22–23, 28, 42–43, 47–49, 53–54, 62, 69, 73, 75, 275; with Canada, 113, 521; with China, 207, 238, 243, 484, 485, 531, 549, 551; during Civil War, 275, 284, 285, 286; colonial, 28, 42–43, 47–49, 50–51, 52, 55–56, 62, 69, 71, 73, 74, 75–76; and Common Market, 767, 781; under Confedera-

tion, 110, 113–114, 115; Congress and, 154–155, 156, 171; and Embargo Act, 154–155, 160; Europe and East Asia, 7, 8, 11, 24; Europe and New World, 14, 16, 18, 22–23, 24–25, 26, 28, 42–43, 62; Europe and Southwest Asia, 6–7, 6 (map), 28; during First World War, 572–575, 578; foreign, 136, 153–155, 155–156, 157, 207–208, 219, 572–574, 578, 668–671, 767; and foreign affairs, 135, 136, 137–139, 149, 153–155, 155–156, 157, 227–228, 275, 285, 530–531, 540–541, 549, 551, 572–575, 578, 668–671; with France, 153, 154, 155; free, 382–383, 382 (cartoon); 383 (cartoon); international, 207–208, 431, 588, 623; interstate, 170, 182*, 202–203, 206, 209, 322, 327; with Japan, 243, 702; with Latin America, 395, 531, 675–676, 769; Macon's Bill No. 2, 156; Navigation Acts, 48–49, 62; of Netherlands, 44, 46–48; and neutrality acts, 684–685, 688, 691, 699, 701–702; and Nonimportation Act, 154; and Nonintercourse Act, 155, 156; and reciprocal trade program, 521, 678–679; regulation of, 48–49, 69, 75–76, 110, 120, 134, 170; during Revolutionary War, 86–87, 89; Rule of 1756, 153; during Second World War, 688, 691, 694, 699, 701–702; trading companies, 19–20, 26, 28, 32, 35–36, 44–45; trading posts, 19, 44, 114, 114*, 135, 136–138, 137 (map); with West Indies, 55, 69, 75, 113; world, 780 (graph). See also Commerce; Tariff

Trade Agreements Act, 678–679

Trade routes: to East, 6–8, 6 (map), 10 (map), 11, 16, 17, 24, 481; in Latin America, 532, 541, 542

Trade unions. See Unions

Transistor, 780n

Transportation: canal, 210–211, 210 (map); in cities, 435–436, 436*; colonial, 28; and farmers, 114, 116–117, 133, 442; improvements in, 777; of iron ore, 328; ocean, 207; to old Northwest, 208; railroad, 211–212, 285, 322 (map); 323–327, 323 (map); and state monopoly, 169–170; steamboats, 202; after War of 1812, 204

Treason: Burr trial, 152–153; John Brown, 267

Treasury, Secretary of the, 127, 146, 191; Hamilton as, 129–134

Treasury Department: gold in, 387; and national bank, 133, 191; surplus, 379

Treaties: Adams-Onís, 166 (map), 167; of Alliance of 1778, 92; Bryan-Chamorro, 541; of concilia-

tion and arbitration, 676; after First World War, 591–594, 596; Five-Power, 673; Four-Power, 673; of Ghent, 160; of Greenville, 137n; of Guadalupe-Hidalgo, 241–242; Hay–Bunau-Varilla, 535, 678; Hay-Herrán, 533; Hay-Pauncefote, 532; with Indians, 188, 208; Jay, 138; with Latin American countries, 676, 678; Nine-Power, 673; North Atlantic, 748; Pact of Paris, 674; of Paris (1763), 66 (map), 67; of Paris (1783) 96–97, 96 (map), 135; of Paris (1898), 480–482; Pinckney's, 138–139; Portsmouth, 548; test-ban, 771–772; Tripartite Pact, 698; Tripoli, 147; Versailles, 591–594, 596, 670; Webster-Ashburton, 196–197, 196 (map)

Tredegar Iron Works, 227

Trench warfare, 568, 581*

Trent **affair,** 283–284

Trenton, New Jersey, 91, 126–127*, 329

Triangular trade, 55

Tripartite Pact, 698

Triple Alliance, 566

Triple Entente, 566

Tripoli, 147

Trist, Nicholas, 241

Truman, Harry S: and Berlin blockade, 748; and China, 745; and Congress 740–742, 746*; elected Vice-President, 729–730, 730*; in election of 1948, 742, 743*; in election of 1952, 752; and foreign aid, 743, 746–748; and Korean War, 750–751; and nuclear weapons, 725, 749; at Potsdam, 736, 744*; as President, 735, 740–751

Truman doctrine, 746–747, 764

Trusts: Clayton Antitrust Act, 527; development of, 330–331; Theodore Roosevelt and, 497, 513, 513 (cartoon), 515–516; Sherman Antitrust Act, 331, 422, 513, 527; Taft and, 521; Wilson and, 527–528

"Truth-in-Securities" Act, 646

Tubman, Harriet, 223

Tugwell, Rexford G., 641

Tunis, 147

Turkey, 566, 566n, 746, 770

Turner, Nat, 222

Turnpikes, 210

Tuskegee Institute, 517

Tutuila (tōō'tōō-ē'-lä) **Island,** 392, 392 (map), 489, 489n

TVA. See Tennessee Valley Authority

Tweed, William Marcy, 301, 439 (cartoon)

Tweed Ring, 301, 304

Tydings-McDuffie Act, 493–494

Tyler, John, 194, 195–197, 237, 243, 272, 514n

Typewriter, 457, 460*

U–2 "incident," 766

U-boats, 574, 574n. See also Submarines

UN. See United Nations

Uncle Sam, 164–165, 164n, 275 (cartoon), 443 (cartoon)

Uncle Tom's Cabin, 258–259

Underground railroad, 223

Underprivileged, 649–650

Underwood-Simmons Act, 526

Unemployment, 781; in depression of 1873, 304; in 1837, 194; in Great Depression, 631–632, 633*, 634*, 635*, 636*, 643, 647–648, 651, 652, 653*; in Harding's administration, 601; insurance, 650; after Revolution, 116; after Second World War. See also Labor

Union: Albany Plan of, 64; under Articles of Confederation, 110, 117–118; conflict over nature of, 187–190, 252–253, 254, 257–258, 265–267; and Constitution, 124; and Continental Congresses, 74–78, 82–83, 86; after 1865, 308; in 1865, 292; and Hartford Convention, 160; Lincoln's attitude toward, 273; New England supporters of, 202; reconstruction, 292–306; secession crisis, 267–268, 272–273; and sectional differences, 187–190, 254–268; and Stamp Act Congress, 70; territorial growth, 242 (map)

Union Pacific Railroad, 274, 303, 327*, 346n, 366, 470; construction, 323–324

Union party, 298

Unions, 400, 402, 405, 415*; AFL, 413–416, 654; AFL-CIO, 655, 781; in automobile industry, 654, 742, 781; CIO, 654–655; in coal industry, 409; contracts, 414–415; and courts, 403, 421–422; early, 400–403; federal government and, 419, 742; growth, 403, 416, 623, 654 (graph); industrial, 654; Knights of Labor, 411–413; leaders, 407, 414*, 418*, 464; national, 405, 407–408; National Labor Union, 407–408; need for, 399; power of, 413; in railroad industry, 418–421; restrictions on, 742; after Second World War, 781. See also Labor; Strikes

United Arab Republic, 742. See also Egypt

United Automobile Workers, 742, 781

United Kingdom, 770. See also Britain

United Mine Workers, 399, 415*, 606, 654

United Nations, 763, 765, 770; in Korea, 750; organized, 735–736, 735 (cartoon)

United States, 360–361 (map); and Atlantic Charter, 700, 700*; and

Baghdad Pact, 770; beginnings, 106, 110, 111; boundaries, 96 (map), 166 (map), 167, 241–242, 241 (map), 249, 552–553, 552 (map); and China, 484, 486, 488, 680, 701–702, 745, 750–751, 762; and communism, 744, 745, 747, 752, 757–762, 767, 768–769; as creditor nation, 669; defense, 673–674, 686, 749, 767, 770–772; democracy of, 197–198, 780; and disarmament, 671–674; explorations of space, 772–773, 773*; as federal union, 121, 124, 129, 188–189, 272, 304; in First World War, 577–588; foreign aid, 746–747; government, 97, 108–125, 504–506, 542; growth, 148–150, 167, 241–242 (map), 389–391, 481–482; human resources, 664; immigration to, 320, 422–424; industrialization, 311, 316–319, 500; in NATO, 748–749, 770; natural resources, 206, 209, 312, 328–329, 355–357, 664; and neutrality laws, 684–685, 688, 701; in 1920's, 600–626; and nuclear weapons, 724–725, 749, 770–772; occupation of Germany, 744–745; possessions, 389–391, 481–482, 483 (map), 489–494; productivity, 623, 727, 780, 786; relations with Britain, 135–136, 153–155, 160, 468, 572–573, 699; relations with Europe, 135, 570–572, 573–576, 682–684, 686–688, 692, 699, 745, 748–749; relations with France, 135; relations with Japan, 548–549, 680, 685, 702–704; relations with Latin America, 394–396, 674–679, 768–769; after Second World War, 740–745; in Second World War, 705–730; and Southeast Asia, 757, 760–762; and Southwest Asia and North Africa, 762, 765; and Soviet Union, 680, 731–734, 748–749, 769, 771–772; standard of living, 394; in United Nations, 735–736, 735 (cartoon); urbanization, 198, 204–205, 433–439, 776, 777; as world power, 481–488, 666–667, 786. *See also* Foreign policy; Foreign affairs

United States Housing Authority, 662

United States Steel Corporation, 336–337, 516, 606

Upshur, Abel P., 237

Urbanization, 496–497; nineteenth-century, 320; problems of, 510, 776; and social change, 428

Urban Mass Transportation Act, 777

USHA. *See* United States Housing Authority

U.S.S.R. *See* Soviet Union

Utah, 234–236, 506

U Thant. *See* Thant

Valentino, Rudolph, 616, 616*

Valley Forge, Pennsylvania, 92–93

Van Buren, Martin, 403; and Democratic party, 196; and depression of 1837, 193–194; and Eaton affair, 187; in election of 1832, 191; in election of 1836, 192; in election of 1840, 194; in election of 1844, 237–238; in election of 1848, 255; as President, 192–194; quoted, 181, 271; as Secretary of State, 186; and the 10-hour day, 403; and Texas annexation, 237

Vandenberg, Arthur H., 657, 731 (quoted), 736, 748

Vandenberg Resolution, 748–749

Vanderbilt, Cornelius, 322

Van Rensselaer, Stephen, 159

V-E Day, 720

Venezuela, 395–396, 396 (cartoon), 486, 538, 539 (cartoon)

Veracruz, Mexico, 240, 545, 545*

Vergennes, Count de, quoted, 96

Vermont, 92, 510, 560*, 658

Verrazano, Giovanni da (vär-rä-tsä′nô, jô-vän′nê dä), 16

Versailles (vĕr-sī′y), France; peace conference, 592*, 593*; Treaty of, 591–593, 596, 599, 670, 671, 673

Vespucci, Amerigo (vĕs-pōō′chê, ä′-mä-rē′gô), 10, 11

Veterans Bureau, 603

Viceroyalties, in Spanish colonies, 15

Vicksburg, Mississippi, 278, 281

Vienna, Austria, meeting on Laos, 760

Vietcong, 761

Vietnam, 757; war in, 760–762, 780, 784. *See also* North Vietnam; South Vietnam

Vigilance committees, 358

Vikings, 9

Villa, Pancho, 546, 546*

Vincennes, Indiana, 93

Vinci, (dä vēn′chê), Leonardo da, 8

Virginia: and Annapolis Convention, 118; in Civil War, 282; colonial, 23, 26–31, 31 (map), 35, 40, 51, 55–56, 64, 95; cotton in, 219; debts, 132; divided, 274n; freedmen in, 221; House of Burgesses in, 70; iron-working, 227, 328; land claims, 111; and Ohio Company, 64; opposition to Quebec Act, 75; paper money in, 86; peace convention, 272; and Potomac River, 117; public leaders from, 105, 170; reconstruction, 300; religious freedom in, 84–85; secession, 274; slavery in, 218–219; John Smith's map, 2; "starving time," 27–28; and tobacco, 47, 55, 218; trade, 43, 47; Nat Turner rebellion, 222; and TVA, 645; University of, 523

Virginia and Kentucky Resolutions, 142

Virginia City, Montana, 357

Virginia City, Nevada, 356

Virginia Company, 26, 27, 27 (map), 28, 32, 33, 34, 47

Virginia Plan, 120

Virginia Statute of Religious Freedom, 84

Virgin Islands, 389, 542. *See also* Danish West Indies

Virginius affair, 470–471

VISTA. *See* Volunteers in Service to America

Volstead Act, 510, 609n, 610

Volunteers in Service to America, 775

Voting: and Articles of Confederation, 110; in colonies, 83–84; Fifteenth Amendment on, 302; increase in, 197; of Negroes, 297, 300, 783, 784; power of the people, 505; for President, 128, 141, 142; in seceded states, 293, 295, 297, 298, 299; secret ballot, 448; in Senate, 120; Twelfth Amendment on, 142n; Voting Rights Act of 1965, 783–784; woman suffrage extended, 505–506, 506*

Voyageurs, 18. *See also* Fur traders; French

Vulcanizing, of rubber, 214n

Wabash Case, 442

Wabash River, 156

Wade, Benjamin F., 261, 294, 295–296, 299

Wade-Davis Manifesto, 296

Wages, 407; adjustment, 742; during Civil War, 287, 405–406; of coal miners, 512–513, 606–607; in early nineteenth century, 401; factory, 203, 400; government regulation, 656, 662, 727; in Great Depression, 643, 647, 650, 652, 656, 662; of immigrants, 422; increases in, 424, 742; and inflation, 87, 453, 727, 742; minimum, 522, 656, 661, 662; in 1920's, 623; on railroads, 409–410, 418; after Second World War, 740–741; during Second World War, 727; during War for Independence, 87. *See also* Labor; Unions

Wagner Act, 741. *See also* National Labor Relations Act

Wagner-Steagall Act. *See* National Housing Act

Wainwright, Jonathan, 725

Wake Island, 479, 489, 703, 707

Walden, 200–201

Waldseemüller (vält′zä-mül′ẽr), Martin, 10

Walker, David, 222

Walker, William, 267

Wallace, Henry A., 642, 642*, 692, 729, 730*, 743

Wallace, Henry C., 602
Wall Street, 129, 450, 452, 503, 606, 630, 631
Walpole, Horace, quoted, 67
Waltham, Massachusetts, 203
Wanamaker, John, 383
War, Department of, 489
War, Secretary of, 158, 186–187, 188
War debts, after First World War, 601, 670–671, 682
War for Independence: changes resulting from, 84–87; finances, 86–87; foreign officers in, 93; French in, 94, 670; Loyalists in, 82; military equipment, 89; in New England, 76, 89 (map); 90; in New Jersey, 91, 94; in New York, 90–91, 90 (map); northern campaigns, 91–93, 91 (map); peace negotiations, 95–97; recruiting poster, 83*; in South, 93–94, 94 (map); in West, 93, 93 (map). See also American Revolution; Continental Army
War Hawks, 157
War Industries Board, 586
War Labor Disputes Act, 727
Warm Springs, Georgia, 734
War of 1812, 152, 157–160, 158 (map), 234
War Production Board, 727
Warren, Earl, 742, 777–779, 778*, 781 (quoted)
Warren, Joseph, 72
Washington (state), 342, 356; joins Union, 357; minimum-wage law, 661
Washington, D.C.: in John Adams' administration, 140*; and airmail, 619; "Bonus Army" in, 637–638; burning of, 159–160; as capital, 146; civil rights march, 783; in Civil War, 276, 278; in 1850's, 283; G.A.R. parade, 372*; ghetto, 774*; inauguration of Cleveland, 385*; Kurusu mission to, 703; and North Atlantic Treaty, 748–749; Pan-American conference in, 676; planning of, 161; railroads, 322; and slavery, 256; Virginia Peace Convention in, 272; woman suffrage parade, 506*
Washington, Booker T., 511
Washington, George, 95*, 106*, 122; as American hero, 246; with Braddock, 65; character, 87, 128; as commander in chief, 87, 88–89; in conflict with French, 64; conspiracy against, 93; at Constitutional Convention, 118, 119; in Continental Congress, 76, 82; Farewell Address, 139; as Federalist, 122; inauguration, 128, 128*, 129; and Jay's Treaty, 138; in New York campaign, 90–91; as President, 128, 129–139; quoted, 106, 108–109, 117, reelected,

135; retirement, 139, 692; on slavery, 218; in the South, 94; and western lands, 69
Washington, Treaty of, 284
Washington Conference: on Latin America, 676; on Pacific questions, 672, 672*, 673
Water, 363, 434, 776–777
"Watered stock," 353n
Watling Island, 8. See also San Salvador
Watson, Thomas, 452n, 455 (quoted)
Wayne, Anthony, quoted, 89
Wealth Against Commonwealth, 503
Weaver, James B., 384, 447, 449
Weaver, Robert C., 777
Webb-Kenyon Interstate Liquor Act, 609
Webster, Daniel, 46, 202; on abolitionists, 257; on annexation of Hawaii, 393; and Bank, 190; and Compromise of 1850, 256–258; debate with Hayne, 187–188; on public credit, 134; quoted, 134, 187–188, 255, 257; as Secretary of State, 195, 196–197, 238, 393; and Whigs, 192, 194
Webster, Noah, 108–109, 196; and language, 164, 165
Webster-Ashburton Treaty, 196–197, 196 (map)
Webster-Hayne debate, 187–188
Weed, Thurlow, 192
Weld, Theodore, 214
Welles, Gideon, 274, 285
Welles, Sumner, 690–691
West. See Western democracies; Western nations; Western powers
West, American, 344 (map), 367 (map); in American Revolution, 93, 93 (map); cattle kingdom of, 349–354, 354 (map); change in meaning of term, 232; Civil War in, 276–278, 277 (map); exploration, 14, 151–152, 235*; farmers in, 367–368; farming in, 362–364, 362*, 364*, 367–368, 430, 431; frontiers, 68, 232 (map), 469; Indians of, 342–349, 343*, 346*, 347*; in literature, 350; and "manifest destiny," 230–231, 233–234; minerals in, 243–244, 340–341*, 354 (map), 355–358, 356*, 357*, 358*, 445; national domain in, 110–111; physical features, 232–233, 325*; in politics, 188, 260–263; railroads in, 323–326, 349–350, 366, 430–431; settlement, 233–236, 244, 261, 349–350, 357*, 358*, 364, 366–368; sheepmen in, 354–355; territorial expansion in, 149–150, 150 (map), 238, 241–242, 242 (map)
Western democracies, against communism, 744
Western lands, disposal of, 110–113, 111 (map)

Western nations, 731, 734, 760, 762, 764, 766–767, 770–772
Western powers, 746, 763; in Germany, 748
Western Union, 330
West Florida, 97, 114, 157, 167
West Germany, 745, 748, 766–767
West Indies, 4–5, 12, 16, 26, 35, 42, 43, 50, 388–389, 532; British in, 26, 35, 62, 69, 75, 76, 115; Dutch in, 115; European rivalries for, 63, 67; French in, 69, 115, 142, 149; slavery in, 50; Spanish in, 42, 69, 115; trade with, 55, 114, 115, 135
Westinghouse, George, 326
Westmoreland, William C., 761, 761*
Weston, Thomas, 33, 34
West Point, New York, 93, 275, 277, 279, 697
West Virginia, 274
Westward movement: after the Civil War, 312, 349, 364; colonial, 32, 37, 60; continuing, 232–236; in 1820's, 178; of farmers, 362–364, 362*, 364*, 367–368; and Jeffersonian policy, 151; of miners, 355–358, 356*; into old Northwest, 208–209; toward the Pacific, 232–236; of sheepherders, 354–355; and slavery, 218–219
Weyerhaeuser, Frederick, 336
Weyler, Valeriano, 471
Whaling, 238, 393
Wheat, 16, 27, 40, 55, 355, 362, 363–364, 364*, 367, 427, 429, 453, 603, 623, 637
Wheeler, Burton K., 701
Wheeler, William A., 815 (table)
Wheeling, West Virginia, 208, 212
Whigs, 193 (cartoon); attack Van Buren, 194; beginning of party, 192; and depression of 1837, 193; in 1840 election, 194–195, 195 (cartoon); in 1844 election, 237–238; in 1848 election, 234, 255; in 1852 election, 259; end of party, 262; after Kansas-Nebraska Act, 261, 262; and Mexican War, 239; and subtreasury policy, 193; and treaty with Mexico, 242; and Tyler, 195–196
Whisky Rebellion, 133
Whisky Ring, 303
White, Austin, 736
White, Hugh, 192
White, John, 25–26
White, William Allen, 537, 634, 692
White-collar worker, 502
White House, 146, 146n, 195, 250, 258, 268, 276, 288, 379*
White Plains, Battle of, 91
Whitlock, Brand, 504
Whitman, Dr. Marcus, 234
Whitman, Narcissa, 234
Whitman, Walt, 198
Whitney, Eli, 219–220

Whittier, John Greenleaf, 202; quoted, 258
Wichita, Kansas, 367
"Wildcat" banks, 191
Wilderness Campaign, 282–283, 282*
Wilkes, Charles, 284, 284n
Wilkes Land, Antarctica, 284n
Wilkinson, James, 152
Willamette Valley, 234
William and Mary, College of, 56, 223
Williams, Roger, 37–38
Williamsburg, Virginia, 28
Willkie, Wendell, 692, 693*, 694
Willoughby, Sir Hugh, 24
Wilmington, Delaware, 46, 228
Wilmington, North Carolina, 94
Wilmot Proviso, 254, 257
Wilson, Henry, 303
Wilson, James, 118, 129
Wilson, Samuel, 164n
Wilson, Woodrow, 523, 524*, 525*, 542*, 600; and Congress, 525, 526, 593–596; in election of 1912, 523; in election of 1916, 576–577; after First World War, 589–596, 591*, 592*, 595*, 731; before First World War, 571, 572; in First World War, 575–576, 578–579, 584, 586, 588–589; foreign policy of, 539, 541–546, 551, 571–572, 574–577; and Latin America, 539, 541–547; and League of Nations, 588–589, 591–593; on Monroe Doctrine, 543; as President, 523–528, 524*, 605; quoted, 524, 524–525, 525–526, 541, 542–543, 564–565, 571, 575, 576, 578, 584, 591, 594, 596, 668; on submarines, 573, 575; war message, 564–565, 578–579
Wilson, Mrs. Woodrow: first, 525*; second, 595–596, 595*
Wilson-Gorman Act, 387, 471
Wine, 48, 53–54, 611
Winnebago Indians, 19
Winona, Minnesota, 550
Winthrop, John, 35
Wisconsin, 209, 363, 442, 453; admitted to Union, 208; reforms in, 505
Wisconsin River, 60
Wolfe, James, 66–67
Woman's Christian Temperance Union, 510, 609

Women: excluded from AFL, 414; in labor force, 416, 517*, 726*, 776; role in society, 447*, 457, 503*, 615; struggle for rights, 213, 505–506, 506*, 615
Wood, Leonard, 478
Wool, 43, 316, 603
Woolman, John, 85, 213
Woolworth, F. W., 622
Work, hours of, 203, 213, 403, 411, 413, 421, 500, 522, 526, 528, 605, 607, 623, 662
Works Progress Administration, 651–652, 662
Work-Study Plan, 775
Work-Training Plan, 775
World: changing concept of, 10–11; political, 758–759 (map)
World affairs, 464, 481–488, 571
World Peace Foundation, 551
World War, First, 505, 526, 528, 551, 564–597, 573 (cartoons), 668, 682, 685, 736; airplanes in, 571*, 584*, 586*, 619; background of, 566, 567 (map); battlefronts, 566–569, 569*, 580 (map), 581–584, 581*, 582*, 583*, 585*, 589*; casualties, 582, 584; economic effects, 569, 573, 668–670; effect on trade, 572–574; and farmers, 622–623; Germany in, 566, 568–569, 569*, 572, 573–575, 576, 577–578, 580–584, 589, 593; home front, 584, 586–588, 586*, 587*; and Negroes, 623; outbreak of, 564–565, 566; peace conference, 589–593, 591*, 592*, 593*; soldiers in, 579, 579*, 580*, 581*, 582*, 583*, 585*; submarines in, 568, 573–575, 574 (cartoon), 575 (cartoon), 577–578, 579; United States in, 577–588; United States neutrality, 570–577
World War, Second, 662n, 686–694, 696–736, 744–745, 757, 764; airplanes in, 705, 706, 707, 708*, 709, 712, 713*, 715*, 716, 719, 720*, 722, 724*, 727, 728; Allied invasion of Europe, 714–720; casualties, 705, 718, 719–720, 736; civilians in, 726–730, 726*, 727*, 728*; demobilization, 740–741; and Egypt, 713, 732; English in, 637, 698, 700; in Europe, 712–721; fall of France, 697;

financing, 726; geography of, 710–711 (map), 712; Germany in, 706, 718–721, 721*, 733, 736; as global war, 696–697, 710–711 (map), 712; height of Nazi aggression, 710–711 (map); Italy in, 713–714; Japan in, 703–705, 707–709, 708*, 722–725; and Korea, 750; in North Africa, 712–713; outbreak, 663, 680–684, 686–694, 689*, 704*, 705, 705*; in Pacific, 697*, 707–709, 707*, 708*, 722–724, 722*, 723*, 724*; peace plans, 731–736; Russians in, 699, 724, 734, 735; and science, 739; United States in, 696–736, 709*, 712*, 721*
WPA. See Works Progress Administration
Wright, Isaac, 207
Wright, Orville and Wilbur, 555, 619
Wyeth, Nathaniel, 234
Wyoming, 323, 353, 355, 357, 367; admitted to Union, 358; and woman suffrage, 506

X Y Z affair, 140

Yale University, 55, 616
Yalta Conference, 733–734
Yankees, 202
"Yanks" (Americans), in First World War, 581
Yates v. United States, 779
"Yellow-dog contract," 203, 417
Yellow fever, 149, 535
"Yellow press," 474, 474n
Yemen, 762n
Yonkers, New York, 435
York, Canada, 158
York, Duke of, 49, 50, 51–52
York River, 94, 278
Yorktown, Virginia, 94, 97, 278
Yorktown, Battle of, 94–95
Yosemite National Park, 498*
Young, Brigham, 236
Young Plan, 671
Yugoslavia, 593, 698, 746

Zelaya, José, 540
Zenger, Peter, 143, 495
Zimmermann note, 578